MANAGEMENT
ACCOUNTING

Third Edition

Wayne J. Morse
Clarkson University

James R. Davis
Clemson University

Al L. Hartgraves
Emory University

▲▼▼ ADDISON-WESLEY PUBLISHING COMPANY

Reading, Massachusetts ▪ Menlo Park, California ▪ New York
Don Mills, Ontario ▪ Wokingham, England ▪ Amsterdam ▪ Bonn
Sydney ▪ Singapore ▪ Tokyo ▪ Madrid ▪ San Juan

Sponsoring Editor: ■ *Mac Mendelsohn*
Production Supervisor: ■ *Kazia Navas*
Production Coordinator: ■ *Jason Jordan*
Text Designers: ■ *Marie E. McAdam & Vanessa Piñeiro*
Cover Designer: ■ *Marshall Henrichs*
Art Consultant: ■ *Loretta M. Bailey*
Illustrator: ■ *George Nichols*
Copyeditor: ■ *Lorraine Ferrier*
Permissions Editor: ■ *Mary Dyer*
Manufacturing Supervisor: ■ *Trish Gordon*

Material from the *Certified Management Accounting Examinations,* copyright © 1972 through 1985 by the National Association of Accountants, is reprinted (or adapted) with permission.

Material from *Uniform CPA Examination Questions and Unofficial Answers,* copyright © 1969 through 1985 by the American Institute of Certified Public Accountants, Inc., is reprinted (or adapted) with permission.

Material from the *1978 Certified Internal Auditor Examination,* by the Institute of Internal Auditors, Inc., Altamonte Springs, Florida, is reprinted with permission.

Library of Congress Cataloging-in-Publication Data

Morse, Wayne J.
    Management accounting / Wayne J. Morse, James R. Davis, Al L.
  Hartgraves. — 3rd ed.
       p.   cm.
    ISBN 0-201-52827-4
    1. Managerial accounting.   I. Davis, James Richard, 1947–
  II. Hartgraves, Al L.   III. Title.
  HF5635.M864   1991
  658.15′11—dc20   90-35213
                                                                            CIP

IBM and IBM PC are registered trademarks of International Business Machines Corporation.

Lotus and 1-2-3 are registered trademarks of Lotus Development Corporation.

3 4 5 6 7 8 9 10 HA 9594939291

Preface

anagement Accounting is addressed to aspiring managers who must know how to use accounting information effectively to achieve their career goals. The third edition of *Management Accounting* is concerned with the development and use of accounting information within specific organizations for the purposes of planning, control, and analysis of special decisions. We had four primary goals in revising *Management Accounting:*

- to improve the usefulness of the text as a tool for student learning;
- to incorporate important new manufacturing environment topics such as just-in-time inventory management and activity-based costing;
- to further strengthen the coverage of nonmanufacturing organizations;
- to respond to requests for separate chapters on job costing, process costing, financial statement analysis, and the statement of cash flows.

As in the previous editions we continue to emphasize the "big picture" before discussing the details of a particular topic. (Examples of this focus on the big picture are found on pages 27–31, 222–230, 474–485, and 705–707.) We believe a solid conceptual understanding of management accounting is necessary before students can truly understand and apply the many technical details of the subject.

PROVEN, CLEAR, FLEXIBLE

As a third edition, *Management Accounting* is a well tested and proven pedagogical tool. Materials retained from previous editions have met the most rigorous test possible—the successful use by thousands of students and their instructors. New material has been thoroughly reviewed and class-tested, and all problems and solutions have been carefully checked and rechecked for accuracy.

A number of steps have been taken to help clarify materials for students. Learning objectives, presented at the start of each chapter, inform students of expectations. New terms are highlighted when first introduced, listed again at the back of each chapter, and defined again in the glossary, thus focusing the student's attention and providing for easy review. Review problems at the end of all but Chapter 1 allow students to receive immediate feedback on their mastery of technical material. The solutions to review problems are also contained in the book.

Alternative sequencing of material can provide a product costing emphasis, a planning and control emphasis, or a broad survey. Advanced topics are placed in appendices and optional chapters. Redundant assignment material makes it possible to vary assignments between sections and subsequent course offerings. Instructors desiring to introduce spreadsheets may use the optional software supplement (developed using Lotus® 1-2-3®). Details on course sequences are included in the *Solutions Manual*.

NEW MOTIVATIONAL MATERIALS

One of the most significant changes in the third edition is the inclusion of new motivational materials designed to show students the relevance of management accounting to real world situations.

- Part openers describe how key concepts within that part are utilized by MCI Communications Corporation, thus giving students a sense of real world application.

- A series of Managerial Practices is included in each chapter. These inserts provide additional insights into text material and describe the importance of the material to a specific company or real world situation.

- An appendix written to the student provides an overview of careers in management accounting as described by the Financial Vice President of a medium sized manufacturing company.

MANUFACTURING ENVIRONMENT TOPICS

A major goal of the third edition is to incorporate important new manufacturing environment topics. As we go to press, this book is unique in the number of manufacturing environment topics covered. It is even more unique in *presenting them within the context of management accounting topics and issues*. This helps students understand the relevance of management accounting and how it relates to other areas.

New manufacturing environment topics are as follows:

- Job costing issues are *introduced within the context* of the manufacturing environment. Contextual topics include world class manufacturing, production planning and control procedures, the impact of computers on manufacturing (AIS, CAD, CAM, FMS, and CIM), and just-in-time inventory management. (See pages 474 and 482–484.)

■ Just-in-time inventory management is given thorough coverage and integrated into the discussion of relevant accounting issues rather than being completely relegated to a separate chapter. (See pages 483–485, 539–541, 546–549, 657–665, 724, and 812.)

■ New cases, based on plant layouts and intended to encourage students to think about the design of product costing systems without having to perform numerical analysis, are included. (See pages 530–535, and 583.)

■ Backflush costing is introduced as an appropriate techique when JIT results in major reductions of inventory. (See pages 546–549, 556, and 665.)

■ Activity-based costing is given thorough coverage and integrated into the discussion of the reassignment of indirect costs. (See pages 605–612.)

■ The problem of cross-subsidization is discussed within the context of job costing in Chapter 11 and examined further in Chapter 13. (See pages 499–501 and 606–612.)

■ "Cost drivers" are defined in Chapter 11 and examined further in Chapter 13. (See pages 499–501, 590, and 606–612.)

Other important new topics included in an appendix to Chapter 14 are "quality costs," "life cycle costs," "productivity," and "design for manufacture." All have received significant attention in recent professional literature.

MANAGEMENT ACCOUNTING IN SERVICE AND NOT-FOR-PROFIT ORGANIZATIONS

As in previous editions, *Management Accounting* includes extensive coverage of service organizations. Every chapter that discusses product costing issues also discusses service costing. (See pages 31, 502–504, 558–561, and 612–615.)

Other major illustrations or discussions of nonmanufacturing situations are included throughout the book. Chapter 1 uses a department store to introduce basic concepts. (See pages 6–12.) A section in Chapter 4 deals with "Not-for-Profit Applications" of cost-volume-profit analysis (see pages 135–136), and a major appendix to Chapter 6 considers budgeting in not-for-profit organizations. (See pages 245–253.) Care is taken in Chapter 7 to provide examples of cost centers for nonmanufacturing activities. (See pages 287–288.) Assignment materials dealing with the use of management accounting in merchandising, service, manufacturing, not-for-profit, and government organizations are presented throughout. (See pages 62–63, 204–206, 309–312, 513–514, 581–582, and 753–754.)

IMPORTANT ORGANIZATIONAL CHANGES AND NEW FEATURES

A number of organizational changes were made in response to suggestions received from accounting instructors. For example, old Chapter 11, *Product Costing,* was split into two chapters: Chapter 11, *Job Costing and the Manufacturing Environment,* and Chapter 12, *Process Costing.* The material on FIFO process costing was moved from an appendix to the body of Chapter 12. Old Chapter 16, *Financial Statement Analysis and the Statement of Resource Flows,* was split into two chapters: Chapter 17, *Financial Statement Analysis,* and Chapter 18, *Statement of Cash Flows.* Care was taken to present the material in these chapters in a manner that emphasized their relevance to managers. The emphasis is on concepts and interpretation rather than procedures. Finally, a discussion of vertical and horizontal financial statement analysis was added to Chapter 17.

Chapter 16 provides an overview of different types of taxes and considers the impact of taxes on a wide variety of management decisions. This material is of particular value to nonaccounting majors, most of whom will not enroll in a tax course.

Other important changes include the development of additional assignment materials, the further classification of assignment materials into review questions, exercises, problems, and cases, and the addition of suggested readings to the end of most chapters.

SUPPLEMENTS

A variety of supplementary materials accompany the text:

- The *Solutions Manual* contains alternative course outlines, solutions to all review questions, exercises, problems, cases, and check figures.

- *Transparency Acetates* for the solutions to all exercises, problems, and cases are available to adoptors.

- An *Instructor's Resource Guide,* prepared by Professor Barry Nab of the University of Minnesota-Duluth, contains useful information for instructors new to teaching Management Accounting.

- A *Test Bank,* prepared by Professor Marvin Bouillon of Iowa State University, is available in hardcopy or disk for use on the IBM® personal computer or compatibles.

- A *Student Study Guide,* prepared by Professor Al Hartgraves, reemphasizes and reinforces basic concepts and techniques. For each chapter it contains: a list of learning objectives; a chapter review outline; a self test with multiple choice questions, completion questions, and up to four exercises, as well as solutions to the self test.

■ A *Data Disk* for use with Lotus 1-2-3 software, if not included in the back of this book, is available separately. This data disk was prepared by Professor Linda Dening of Jefferson Community College, and contains additional assignment material designed for solution with Lotus 1-2-3 student or professional versions on the IBM personal computer or compatibles.

ACKNOWLEDGMENTS

Management Accounting could not have been completed without the generous cooperation, assistance, and support of numerous individuals and organizations. We are indebted to the following professors who offered helpful comments on the second edition of this textbook or reviewed the manuscript for the third: Mark Alford (University of Texas at San Antonio); Garth Blanchard (University of Puget Sound); Phillip Jones (University of Richmond); Robert Koeler (Pennsylvania State University); William Lawler (Babson College); Susan Milstein (Western Maryland College); Ronald Moore (Idaho State University); Daniel J. O'Mara (Villanova University); Ron Pawliczek (Boston College); Ray Powell (University of Notre Dame); Denis Raihall (Drexel University); Khalid A. Razaki (Illinois State University); Edward B. Schwan (Susquehanna University); Stephen V. Senge (Western Washington University); G. A. Swanson (Tennessee Technological University); Jack Truitt (Washington State University); William C. Tuthill (Emory University); Richard Veazey (Grand Valley State College); Ara Volkan (West Georgia College).

A special note of thanks goes to our students at Clarkson University, Clemson University, and Emory University. We appreciate both their comments on earlier editions and their feedback on material new to the third.

Appreciation is extended to the Institute of Certified Management Accountants of the National Association of Accountants for permission to use adaptations of problem materials from past Certified Management Accounting examinations; these materials are identified as "CMA Adapted." We are also indebted to the American Institute of Certified Public Accountants and the Institute for Internal Auditors for permission to use adaptations of materials from their professional examinations; these materials are identified as "CPA Adapted" or "IIA Adapted."

Comments or suggestions from users are most welcome.

Potsdam, NY   W.J.M.
Clemson, SC   J.R.D.
Atlanta, GA   A.L.H.

About Our Profile Company

Bob Perkins likes to think of himself as a businessman on the cutting edge of communications technology. Whenever he travels, he carries a cellular phone to keep in touch with the home office and a notebook-size Sinclair Z88 mini-laptop to write and store letters or memos on the plane. Back at the New York offices of his Perkins, Butler ad agency, where his secretary downloads the letters from his Sinclair onto her Apple® Macintosh® to polish them up, Perkins uses his own Apple to comb through the memos that have piled up on the company's Wang E-mail system. Those memos might come from colleagues in any of the fast-growing agency's six North American offices or its recently opened London outpost.*

For this edition of *Management Accounting,* we are profiling the type of company responsible for Bob Perkins's becoming a manager of the nineties. You will thus find examples from MCI Communications Corporation (MCI) acting as real-world counterpoints to our previews of each major part of the text.

A world leader in fiber optics and global telecommunications, MCI provides a full range of the type of telecommunications services Perkins uses—integrating telephone, television, and computer media—around the world. It is one of the largest companies in the telecommunications industry, with 1989 revenues exceeding $6 billion. It also boasts some of the industry's most advanced technologies. One integrated network control and data center alone can conduct over 1 million telephone or computer transactions per hour, with as many as 300,000 transactions going on simultaneously. MCI's focus for the 1990s will be on its network capabilities, because it believes that instant access to real-time information will be one of the most important goals in the competitive global business environment of this decade. This goal will allow customers to concentrate on business opportunities rather than on worries about how the technology works.

We selected telecommunications as our profile industry for several reasons. First, like management accounting, the field of telecommunications is in the business of *communication*. Whereas management accounting focuses on communicating the organization's financial information to its users (management), telecommunications focuses on communicating all types of information from every corner of the world for its users. As a future business professional, you

---

* Jeffrey Ferry, "The Wired World," *Continental Profiles,* May 1990, 19–22.

will be on either the sending or the receiving end of accounting information, and you and your organization will also be players in the worldwide communications scheme of the next century.

Additionally, telecommunications is one of the most technologically advanced industries in the world—and one that plays a key role in the increasingly important service sector of the global economy. Spurred on by customer demand, the industry's competition is generating more and better solutions to customer needs. As solutions create even more advanced technologies, they give rise to new possibilities, driving still greater customer demands in an ongoing cycle of progress. Innovative diversity of customer choice and value—as defined by a combination of price and service—are the new standards for having a service market advantage. These are also MCI's standards of performance evaluation, defining the way the company operates across all its markets.

MCI is at the forefront of its industry and thus provides us with a fine model of management accounting at the cutting edge, adapting and growing to meet the challenges of the nineties: succeeding amid global competition, anticipating and meeting customers' service demands, and pushing out the frontier of value.

Brief Contents

Contents

C   H   A   P   T   E   R   3

COST BEHAVIOR ANALYSIS   69

C   H   A   P   T   E   R   4

COST-VOLUME-PROFIT ANALYSIS   115

C H A P T E R   5

RELEVANT COSTS FOR MANAGEMENT DECISIONS   163

 **PART 2   PLANNING AND CONTROL 219**

C H A P T E R   8

PERFORMANCE EVALUATION OF STANDARD COST CENTERS   328

C H A P T E R   9

C H A P T E R   1 0

PART 3   PRODUCT COSTING AND COST REASSIGNMENT   471

C H A P T E R   1 1

JOB COSTING AND THE MANUFACTURING ENVIRONMENT   473

MANAGERIAL PRACTICE

C H A P T E R   1 2

PROCESS COSTING   537

C H A P T E R   1   3

THE REASSIGNMENT OF INDIRECT COSTS AND ACTIVITY-BASED COSTING   586

 **P A R T   4**   SELECTED TOPICS FOR FURTHER STUDY   645

C H A P T E R   1   4

RELEVANT COSTS FOR QUANTITATIVE MODELS AND INVENTORY MANAGEMENT   647

MANAGERIAL PRACTICE

C H A P T E R   1 5

CAPITAL BUDGETING   704

P A R T 1

Essential Elements of Management Accounting

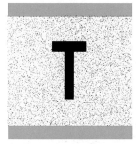 o provide a sound background for accounting-related decision making—that is the goal both of this part of the text *and* of one of MCI Communications Corporation's management training programs. MCI offers two in-house courses for its managers. These courses, Money Matters and More Money Matters, provide MCI's managers with the basics necessary for sound accounting decisions. Topics studied include cash control and budgeting, forecasting, general cost accounting concepts, the company's financial reporting needs, and capital budgeting. This section of the text also provides the basic cost concepts you will need before studying more specific decision-making concepts related to management accounting.

Chapter 1 discusses the relationships between accounting and management and provides an overview of what distinguishes management accounting from financial accounting.

Chapter 2 introduces basic cost concepts, with their many related terms and measurements. Different types of inventories are discussed, along with basic ways of analyzing the activity in inventory accounts. One of the most important cost concepts introduced in the chapter is that of establishing, monitoring, and controlling cost objectives. Although you may not think of service companies like MCI as having inventory, products, and production departments, MCI does have large inventory investments. For example, MCI has over $50 million a year in sales literature expenses—promotional and advertising mailings—with an average sales literature inventory of approximately $4 million. Thus, sales literature is obviously a cost objective—an activity to which costs are assigned—at MCI. These costs are then charged each month to the territories using them.

Chapter 3 introduces cost behavior with detailed discussions of variable, fixed, and mixed costs. Chapter 4 extends that cost behavior discussion with the introduction of cost-volume-profit (break-even) analysis. It is important for every organization to know how its costs behave so that they can be planned for and controlled. However, MCI has a unique problem with its variable costs: originating and receiving calls are billed at different rates. The time charged by the local telephone companies with which MCI contracts to provide connecting service between customers and MCI's long-distance system differs from the time MCI can charge its customers for a call. For example, MCI customer A calls MCI customer B in another state. MCI is charged at one rate by the local company serving customer A and at another rate by the local company serving customer B. In addition, both companies charge MCI total connect time rather than simply the time during which customer A actually has a direct connect with customer B. Because MCI cannot control which customers call which other customers, or even noncustomers, it must estimate the likely combination of calls to and from each local telephone company in its service area—which is almost the entire world. Whereas a manufacturing company generally has good control over its variable costs, MCI is more at the mercy of its customers' need to call different areas, which have different charge rates. Although the line costs are variable, MCI's ability to predict and control them is limited. MCI uses break-even analysis to evaluate such costs. MCI does this to make sure that the local telephone companies charge amounts that are reasonable given each one's size and the types of services it offers.

Chapter 5 deals with the identification of relevant costs, analyzing which costs change for which decisions and how to predict relevant costs using Chapter 3's cost behavior techniques. With so many different costs possible for the same services and with an ever-expanding portfolio of services, relevant costs are very important decision tools for MCI's management. It must constantly evaluate capital investment decisions, for instance, many of which have buying, leasing, and even building alternatives. Buy-versus-lease alternatives (which are a variation on the make or buy decisions discussed in Chapter 5) are of particular interest to MCI. Almost all of its building investment decisions are evaluated with both buying and leasing decision models.

Chapter 5 concludes with a discussion of pricing decisions and how relevant costs influence such decisions. MCI must constantly evaluate its pricing techniques because of the competition, changing customer demands, and the needs and various combinations of local telephone companies that are involved with its customers.

C H A P T E R 1

Accounting and Management

Learning Objectives

Upon completion of this chapter you should:

- **Be familiar with the primary functions of managers.**

- **Understand the role of management accounting information in managing profit and not-for-profit organizations.**

- **Be able to identify the duties of the controller and the treasurer.**

- **Understand the relationship of the various accounting functions to the controller's department.**

- **Know the differences and similarities between management accounting and financial accounting.**

An **organization** is a group of people united to achieve a common goal. As students, instructors, employees, citizens, relatives, sports players, and, perhaps, volunteers, we are members of a variety of organizations. The members who direct the affairs of an organization are identified as **managers.** In the process of performing their duties, managers use many kinds of information, including that provided by management accounting.

The purpose of this chapter is to provide an overview of **management accounting,** which is concerned with providing information to managers and other persons inside specific organizations. Because management accounting is concerned with providing information to managers, we begin by discussing some important characteristics of organizations and the functions of management. We then describe how managers use accounting terms, relationships, and information in performing their duties. We also consider the duties of accountants and the relationships that exist among managers, accountants, and other information specialists.

Accounting is broadly classified into financial accounting and management accounting. This classification is based on differences in the relationship between the organization and the person or persons to whom information is supplied. To provide an orientation to the study of management accounting, we carefully distinguish between these two types of accounting. We conclude this chapter by summarizing why managers and management accountants must thoroughly understand management accounting.

ORGANIZATIONS AND THEIR GOALS

Organizations vary widely in their goals. Whereas the goal of a college or university is to provide educational services, the goal of a department store or a steel company is to earn a profit by providing customers with goods, and the goal of the Red Cross is to provide humanitarian service. An organization is likely to have several goals. The local department store, for example, which has profit and providing customers with consumer goods as goals, may also support cultural activities and local charities with the goal of being regarded as a good community citizen.

We frequently distinguish between organizations on the basis of profit motive. **For-profit organizations** have profit as a primary goal, and **not-for-profit organizations** do not have profit as a goal. Clearly, the General Electric Company is a for-profit organization, whereas the City of New York and the Red Cross are not-for-profit organizations.[1] Regardless of the presence or absence of a profit motive, an organization should use resources efficiently in accom-

---

[1] The term *nonprofit* is frequently used to refer to what we have identified as *not-for-profit* organizations. We avoid this term because it can be confused with a *non-profit* (i.e., zero or negative profit) situation.

plishing its goals. Every dollar the Salvation Army spends for fuel is a dollar that cannot be used to feed the indigent. Private not-for-profit organizations (such as colleges) and government units (such as cities) can go bankrupt if they are unable to meet their financial obligations. The common need to use resources efficiently indicates the existence of a common need for a good accounting system that will help management plan, organize, and control the use of the organization's limited resources.

FUNCTIONS OF MANAGEMENT

Smooth functioning organizations do not just happen. They are a result of the actions of the managers who are responsible for their operation. Management entails planning, organizing, and controlling. In all but the smallest organizations, the manager's job is to get things done through people. The manager of the local department store does not order goods, stock shelves, place advertising, operate the cash register, drive the delivery truck, or record accounting transactions. The manager has to decide what tasks are needed and how they should be accomplished (planning). The manager then assigns these tasks to other people (organizing) and ensures that they are properly completed (controlling).

Planning

Planning, which is the formulation of a scheme or program for the accomplishment of a specific purpose or goal, consists of two basic activities: (1) setting goals and (2) selecting a way to accomplish these goals. A distinction is often made between long-range planning and short-range planning. Long-range planning emphasizes the selection of goals that the organization hopes to achieve over several years and the selection of programs that will enable the organization to achieve these goals. Short-range planning is based on the organization's long-range plan as well as its current situation and focuses on specific activities to be taken in the near term to move the organization from its current situation toward its long-range goals. Short-range planning involves both the interpretation of long-range goals into performance objectives for the coming year and the selection of specific actions to achieve these objectives. The following example illustrates the difference between long-range and short-range plans.

Good Department Stores currently operates three stores in the suburbs of a large metropolitan area. Professional people such as engineers, scientists, doctors, lawyers, and managers live in this market area. Good's long-range plans are to achieve the highest annual dollar sales volume of all suburban department stores in the market area and to provide their investors with an acceptable level of earnings. Important elements of this plan include: the opening of one new store during each of the next five years, a reorientation of merchandise lines toward goods likely to be purchased by professional people, and increased support of cultural activities. Good's short-range plans for the coming year call for the hiring of personnel and the acquisition of merchandise for one new store currently under construction. Discontinuing the sale of hardware, expanding the offerings of furniture and women's business apparel, adding an art department, and starting a Good Summer Concert Series are also among management's plans. Management believes these activities will produce a 40 percent increase in sales revenue and a 35 percent increase in after-tax profits during the coming year.

Good's short-range plans are made in the light of its long-range plans. Care is taken to ensure that the short-range plans support the long-range goals. Short-range goals are more specific than long-range goals; they have to be because they are statements of what management hopes to accomplish next year.

Organizing

Through **organizing,** the process of making the organization into a well-ordered whole, management attempts to structure and divide the tasks that need to be done. Specific people are assigned specific tasks. Within a formal structure established to show the relationships between organization members, authority is delegated to managers and other employees who are subsequently held accountable for the activities they control.

An **organization chart** illustrates the formal set of relationships that exist among the elements of an organization. An organization chart for Good Department Stores is shown in Exhibit 1–1. The blocks represent organizational units, and the lines represent the relationships between organizational units. Top management delegates authority, which flows down the organization, to use resources for limited purposes to subordinate managers who, in turn, delegate more limited authority to accomplish more structured tasks to their subordinates. Responsibility increases as one moves up the organization. People at the bottom of the chart are responsible for specific tasks, but the president (chairman, agency head) is responsible for the operation of the entire organization.

Following the formal sequence of authority and responsibility (sometimes referred to as the chain of command), a problem in the Appliance Department of the Eastside Store is first brought to the attention of the Store Manager and then to the Vice President of Operations by the Store Manager. Normally, the head of the Appliance Department does not take the problem directly to the attention of a manager two or more levels above him or her because this action violates the chain of command.

A distinction is made between line and staff managers. Line managers are directly responsible for the activities that create and distribute the goods and services of the organization. They exercise authority over all other managers and employees below them on the organization chart. Staff managers, on the other hand, exercise authority over only the employees in their own departments. Staff departments exist to help facilitate line activities. Although staff members often advise line managers, they do not exercise authority over them. In Exhibit 1–1 we see that Good Department Stores has two levels of staff organizations, corporate and store. The corporate staff units are Purchasing, Advertising, Treasurer, and Controller. Staff departments at the store level are Personnel, Accounting, and Maintenance. All other units are line departments.

EXHIBIT 1–1   Good Department Stores Organization Chart

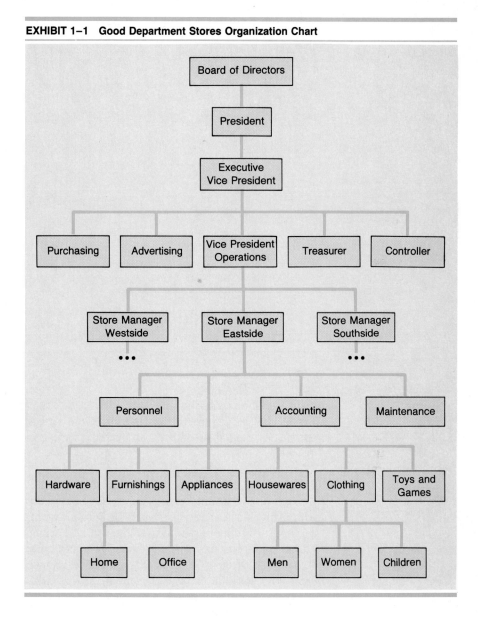

Note that a change in plans can necessitate a change in the organization. For example, Good's plan to discontinue the sale of hardware and add an art department during the coming year will necessitate an organizational change.

In addition to the formal relationships specified in the organization chart, many informal relationships develop between individuals and organizational units. Such relationships can become so important that the organization cannot function without them. Many times knowledgeable and persuasive individuals

EXHIBIT 1–2   Planning, Organizing, and Controlling Are a Continuous Cycle

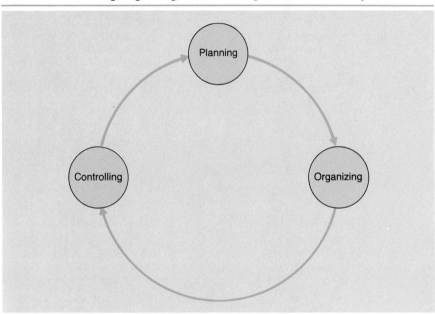

exert an influence on the organization far in excess of what their formal position would suggest; this is especially true in the case of staff members who are experts in a specialized area and offer advice concerning that area to line managers.

Controlling

Controlling is the process of ensuring that results agree with plans. In the process of controlling operations, management compares actual performance with plans. If actual results deviate significantly from plans, management either attempts to bring operations into line with the original plan or adjusts the plan. The original plan is adjusted if management determines that it is no longer appropriate because of changed circumstances. Hence, the process of controlling feeds back into the process of planning to form a continuous cycle. This cycle is illustrated in Exhibit 1–2.

ACCOUNTING AS A MANAGEMENT TOOL

Managers make extensive use of accounting in the performance of their functions. This is true regardless of the nature of their business. Accounting information is important in managing a volunteer fire department, a religious organization, the city of Chicago, and General Motors. There are two basic reasons for this: (1) accounting terms are the language of business, and (2) accounting relationships serve as a model of the organization.

Accounting Terms Are the Language of Business

Accounting terms are an important part of every manager's vocabulary. Because financial data provide a common denominator for measuring and summarizing widely diverse activities, accounting terms are a basic means of communication within and between organizations. The need to summarize widely diverse activities becomes increasingly important as we move up the organization chart. Good's President would be overwhelmed by detailed information on the unit sales of specific items in individual stores, but could easily understand a summary of sales in terms of dollars of sales revenue. Note, however, that the manager of the Home Furnishing Department in a particular store would want detailed unit sales information. Dollars also provide a convenient measure of effectiveness in for-profit organizations. By looking at the bottom line of the income statement, a manager can immediately determine if the organization met its profit goal for the period.

Accounting Relationships Model the Organization

A model is a simplified representation of some real-world phenomenon. Managers study models to obtain an understanding of the related real-world phenomenon, and they use models to predict the impact of a proposed action. A proper understanding and use of models leads to better decisions. Because the accounting system used to classify and summarize data reported in general purpose financial statements touches every area of activity within an organization, accounting relationships serve as a model of the organization.

An understanding of the organization's accounting system helps the manager understand the organization and the interrelationships that exist within it. The statement of cash flows summarize the economic activity of the organization during a period of time. An understanding of these and other accounting reports also helps the manager understand the organization. These statements are particularly valuable in planning; for example, a manager who is familiar with the income statement can use it to quickly predict the probable impact of a proposed action on net income.

Accounting Information Assists in Planning, Organizing, and Controlling

Accounting relationships are used extensively in planning, organizing, and controlling activities. These relationships provide the framework used to develop the budget for the coming year. A budget is a formal plan of action expressed in monetary terms. An organization's budget for the coming year includes projected financial statements and detailed schedules indicating the financial consequences of all expected activities. In budgeting, the same accounting relationships that are used to report the financial implications of transactions after they have occurred are also used to predict the financial consequences of transactions before they occur. By analyzing the financial consequences of alternative actions, management is better able to select those transactions that lead to the most desirable outcome(s).

The budgeting process also assists management in its organizing function. Detailed supporting schedules for revenues, expenditures, costs, and activities are drawn up for all units of the organization. Because all these pieces must fit together in the overall budget, flaws in organizational design become apparent as the budgeting process is nearing completion.

Accounting information also assists management in controlling operations subsequent to the adoption of a budget. During and after the budget period, management is provided with **performance reports** that compare actual results with plans. Performance reports may be prepared for the organization as a whole or for any area of responsibility within the organization. They may report

MANAGERIAL PRACTICE 1.1

Management Accounting Matters

William G. Holbrook, Vice President of Administration for Stanadyne Automotive Products Group, is emphatic about what the managers reporting to him need to know. He states, "If you have an accounting student who understands the industrial, manufacturing environment, he ought to be taught how industrial engineering, manufacturing engineering, product design, all come together. Teach them manufacturing, teach them cost accounting, all these things rolled together. Then you've got one very valuable employee."

Robert Kelder, manager of IBM's Cost Accounting Competency Center, is in charge of an extremely elaborate organizational structure for cost management. According to Kelder, "We have cost engineers who are in the industrial engineering organization. We have financial planners who are in the financial planning organization which is entirely separate from the accounting organization. Then we have the accounting organization where you will find cost accounting, and another department called overhead accounting. With the need to communicate, talk and develop plans, develop cost estimates, and do some sort of actual comparison and measurement, these people have to talk to one another and understand one another's operations."

Sources: William G. Holbrook, "Accounting Experiences in a JIT Environment," and Robert H. Kelder, "Era of Cost Accounting Changes," in *Cost Accounting, Robotics, and the New Manufacturing Environment*, ed. Robert Capettini and Donald K. Clancy (Sarasota, Fla.: American Accounting Association, 1987), 4.16, 3.25.

on revenues, or costs, or both. A report measuring the effectiveness of the Maintenance Department of the Eastside Good Department Store in controlling costs is presented in Exhibit 1–3. The differences between actual and allowed costs are identified as variances. Expenditures of less than the allowed amounts are favorable variances (F), and expenditures of more than the allowed amounts are unfavorable variances (U).

Copies of this performance report are provided to the Maintenance Department supervisor and to the store manager. The maintenance supervisor, who uses the report as a *scorecard*, can determine from it how well he or she is doing. The store manager, who uses the report as an *attention director*, can determine from it whether or not he or she should inquire further or take some action regarding the performance of the Maintenance Department. This is consistent with the concept of management by exception, whereby managers focus their attention on those aspects of operations that are not operating as planned, rather than constantly inquiring about all aspects of performance. If the store manager deemed any of the variances in Exhibit 1–3 to be significant, the manager would inquire further about their cause. If the unfavorable variance for salaries and wages was caused by an increase in wage rates, management might revise the budget (change its plans) for this item. If the variance was caused by excessive labor hours due to poor supervision, management would attempt to bring operations into conformity with the original plans.

Performance reports are developed for all units and subunits in the organization, and all revenues and costs incurred by the organization during a period should appear in at least one of these performance reports. Furthermore, some manager, or group of managers, should be held responsible for the generation of revenues or incurrence of each cost. The process of developing a system to assign revenues and costs to responsible managers assists management in its

EXHIBIT 1–3   Typical Performance Report

Good Departmental Stores: Eastside
Maintenance Department Performance Report
For the month of September, 19×2

	Actual Costs	Allowed Costs	Variance*
Salaries and wages	$14,000	$12,000	$2,000 U
Utilities	800	850	50 F
Supplies	300	210	90 U
Equipment rentals	1,000	1,000	—
Totals	$16,100	$14,060	$2,040 U

* F = Favorable
  U = Unfavorable

organizing and controlling functions. If problems are encountered in assigning responsibility for revenues and costs, the most likely cause is either a weakness in organization structure or a failure to communicate areas of authority and responsibility to organization members. The resolution of responsibility problems is accompanied by the development of a clearer organizational structure and a better understanding of the delegation of authority and responsibility within the organization.

Though we are particularly concerned with the role of monetary data, nonmonetary data are an important part of planning and control systems. Nonmonetary data increase in importance as we move down the organization chart. Performance reports stated in terms of units of production, pounds of materials, and hours of labor are more useful to clerks, factory workers, and first level production supervisors who work with physical units rather than with monetary symbols. First level managers must be able to speak to their subordinates in terms of units of activity and to their supervisors in accounting terms.

Nonmonetary measures of performance are also important in organizations where units of output cannot be related to revenue generation and profit. This

MANAGERIAL PRACTICE 1.2

Reshaping Pitney Bowes for the Long Run

An established mail-metering company with a virtual monopoly on its markets, Pitney Bowes was known as a profit machine. Nevertheless, top management initiated an expensive ($400 million since 1986) and risky research and development campaign to transform the firm into a producer of high-tech systems for mailing. Reflecting this new strategy, Pitney Bowes recently introduced Post Edge, a system for high-volume users, which stuffs envelopes; reads addresses on outgoing mail; bar-codes the envelopes (the U.S. Postal Service has reduced rates for bar-coded mail); and adds the extra four digits for the new nine-digit ZIP code. Although the new plan may prove profitable in the long run, investment in it has depressed both corporate earnings and the market price of Pitney Bowes' stock. This is a clear example of long-run corporate R&D objectives being accepted as more important than short-run profits.

Source: Todd Vogel, with Mark Lewyn, "Search for Tomorrow at Pitney Bowes," *Business Week*, 5 March 1990, 50–51.

is likely to be the case in the research and development department of a for-profit organization as well as for many activities of not-for-profit organizations, especially government agencies. It is difficult, for example, to determine the bottom-line impact of a good fire department. A budgeting and performance evaluation technique known as management by objectives is widely used in organizations where activities cannot be related to profit.

Under a program of **management by objectives** the head of an agency or department and the head's immediate superior agree to a set of short-run nonmonetary objectives. Care is taken to ensure that the short-run objectives are in agreement with the overall objectives of the organization. The short-run objectives are subsequently used as a performance measure for the agency or department head. One possible objective for a fire department might be to reduce the average response time to a fire alarm from five to four minutes.

Accounting Information Assists in Problem Solving

Accounting information is useful in evaluating unusual problems or opportunities. For example, a supplier might offer to provide a major component that goes into a manufactured product. The manufacturer must determine whether it is better to continue to manufacture the component or to purchase it from the supplier. A detailed analysis of cost data helps determine the costs to manufacture the component, which are then compared to the costs to buy the component. Another example might involve a government agency contracting with a university to provide educational services on the basis of the costs of those services. In this case it must be clearly understood by both the government agency and the university how costs are to be determined. As a final example, consider the case of a bank that is trying to determine whether to continue or discontinue operating a particular branch. Before deciding, the bank should carefully analyze how the bank's total revenues and expenses will change if the branch is closed. In these and many other examples discussed in later chapters, the proper accounting information focuses on how revenues or costs, or both, differ under each alternative.

External Forces Increase the Importance of Accounting

A number of forces outside business organizations have increased the importance of accounting information as a basis for management decisions. Large insurance companies often require hospitals to justify their rates by using prescribed accounting procedures for cost assignments. Several government agencies award contracts on the basis of cost plus a specified allowance for profit. The U.S. Government has occasionally imposed controls limiting price increases to amounts that can be justified by documented increases in costs. Numerous lawsuits are initiated in an attempt to recover damages caused by the alleged failure of persons or organizations to complete their contractual obligations. The damage claims are based on cost data, and the success of the suit, or the defense, often centers on how well the parties demonstrate an understanding of cost concepts and develop and explain cost data supporting their position. In this type of environment, all managers should have a basic understanding of cost concepts.

ACCOUNTANTS IN THE ORGANIZATION

Accounting activities within an organization are usually under the overall supervision of the **controller,** who is the organization's chief accountant.[2] Many people erroneously equate "controller" with "control" and assume that the controller regulates, directs, or dominates the organization. In fact, as shown in the organization chart illustrated in Exhibit 1–1, the controller is a top management staff member. As a staff member, the controller does not have any formal authority to direct the activities of anyone outside the controller's department but does, however, exert a strong influence on other members of the organization. This influence comes about because of the controller's role in coordinating the development of the budget and because the position provides the controller with an in-depth understanding and detailed knowledge of the organization, making him or her a valuable advisor.

Duties of the Controller

As the organization's chief accountant, the controller is responsible for a widely diverse set of activities. Although they vary from organization to organization, the duties most frequently assigned to the controller's office include:

- Designing, installing, and maintaining the accounting system.
- Preparing financial statements for external users.
- Coordinating the development of the budget.
- Accumulating and analyzing cost data.
- Preparing and analyzing performance reports.
- Providing information for problem solving and special decisions.
- Consulting with management about the meaning of accounting information.
- Planning and administrating taxes.
- Designing, installing, and maintaining computer-based information systems.

Somewhat related to the controller's function is that of the treasurer. The **treasurer** is the officer responsible for money management and serves chiefly as the custodian of the organization's funds. Typical duties of the treasurer include:

- Receiving, maintaining custody of, and disbursing monies and securities.
- Investing the organization's funds.
- Directing the granting of credit.
- Maintaining sources of short-term borrowing.
- Establishing and maintaining a market for the organization's debt and equity securities.

---

[2] The word controller is occasionally spelled "comptroller." The pronunciation remains the same as the first spelling, and both refer to the same position.

MANAGERIAL PRACTICE 1.3

Wanted: Controller

Financial Vice-President

A large retail organization seeks a financial vice-president who will be its chief financial officer. Person reports to the president and board of directors. The person will have general oversight of all financial matters, including investments, financial planning, financial controls, accounting, payroll and purchasing functions, and benefit programs.

Vice-President of Operations

Assembly equipment manufacturer seeks vice-president of operations. Reporting directly to the president, position's responsibilities include management of engineering, purchasing, and production. The position requires good organization skills, strong leadership skills, hands-on engineering management, and an ability to maintain budgetary control.

Division Controller

Health care industry firm seeks division controller who will be responsible for the financial health of the division. Vision and the ability to creatively solve problems are needed to counsel management in the different options facing the division. The ability to work effectively in a team atmosphere is critical.

Plant Controller

Local plant seeks to fill position of controller. Requirements include familiarity with financial spreadsheet software, an understanding of MRP and JIT, knowledge of taxes, accounting experience in a manufacturing environment, a background with computerized systems, and strong knowledge of PCs. Person must be a good communicator with strong leadership skills and a team player.

Product Cost Accountant

Division of large manufacturer needs product cost accountant to develop and modify cost data to meet the information needs of management with timely and accurate reports on labor, material, and overhead charges. Job entails providing vital information for management decision making and planning by contributing analyses and suggestions on capital budgeting, product mixes, inventory planning, and make-or-buy decisions. Person must have comprehensive knowledge of product costing and willingness to learn our production and manufacturing processes.

Sources: Synthesized from advertisements in the *Wall Street Journal* and position descriptions from various organizations.

The positions of the controller and the treasurer are sometimes combined into the single position of **chief financial executive.** Other titles of this combined position include chief financial officer and vice president of finance.

As a member of top management, the controller personally performs few of the above duties. Rather, the actual execution of these tasks is delegated to members of the controller's department. The organization chart for a typical controller's department is illustrated in Exhibit 1–4. By studying this exhibit from left to right, you should be able to determine where each of the duties listed above would be performed in the controller's department. The first two duties (designing, installing, and maintaining the accounting system; preparing financial statements for external users) are part of General Accounting, and the next three are part of Cost Planning and Analysis.

The actual structure of a controller's department varies between organizations. The duties assigned Special Studies, Electronic Data Processing, and Internal Auditing in Exhibit 1–4 are likely to be performed elsewhere. The Special Studies section is assigned the task of providing information for problem solving and special decisions. This unit also spends considerable time consulting with management about the meaning of accounting information.[3] Establishing a separate accounting unit for special studies was one of the major recommendations of a research effort conducted by Herbert A. Simon and others more than thirty years ago. They believed that the unstructured, analytic tasks of providing information for problem solving and special studies could not be performed effectively by the persons who were responsible for record keeping.[4] The required, day-to-day record keeping activities that have near-term due dates would always be done first, and frequently to the exclusion of unstructured tasks. Although our experiences support this conclusion, many organizations request accountants, who are performing more structured tasks, to complete special studies as staff time is available.

Electronic data processing (EDP) involves the storage, manipulation, retrieval, and communication of data by electronic means. Electronic data processing systems almost always involve the use of computers. Because the first large-scale applications of EDP systems were in accounting (payroll, receivables, payables), the responsibility for EDP operations has traditionally been placed under the overall direction of the controller. Today, however, an ever-increasing amount of computer time in large organizations is devoted to nonaccounting applications: engineering, scientific, personnel management, word processing, and so forth. To recognize and encourage applications of electronic data processing across functional areas, many firms have now established EDP as an independent staff department reporting directly to top management. In many

---

[3] Many other persons within the controller's department would also provide such consultations in conjunction with their other duties.

[4] Herbert A. Simon et al., *Centralization vs. Decentralization in Organizing the Controller's Department* (New York: Controllership Foundation, 1954).

EXHIBIT 1–4   Organization Chart of a Controller's Department

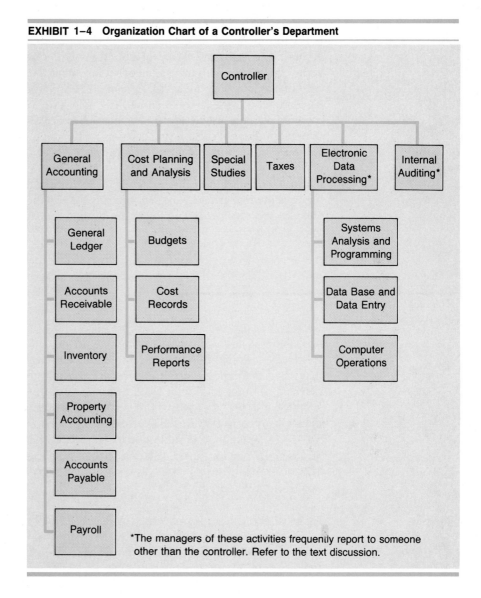

*The managers of these activities frequently report to someone other than the controller. Refer to the text discussion.

organizations electronic data processing activities are placed within a department that has the more inclusive title of management information systems (MIS). The title of management information systems is broad enough to include all aspects of management accounting, but MIS activities are usually related to electronic data storage and processing. Regardless of where EDP activities are placed in the organization, the controller has a vital interest in the availability, accuracy, timeliness, and security of financial information.

Internal auditing is intended to safeguard an organization's assets from fraud and theft, and to ensure that the organization's accounting records are accurate and adequate. Many organizations also rely on internal auditing to verify compliance with management's policies and procedures and to promote operational efficiency. Since 1977, when the Foreign Corrupt Practices Act was passed by the U.S. Congress, all publicly held American companies have been *required* to maintain an adequate system of internal control. Even though the Internal Auditing section is presented as part of the Controller's Department in Exhibit 1–4, the internal auditors most often report to the president or board of directors. Many persons believe that reporting to the board strengthens the internal auditor's independence. The U.S. Securities and Exchange Commission requires the internal auditing staff of many public corporations to report to the outside directors[5] regardless of where the internal audit staff is placed in the organization chart.

FINANCIAL ACCOUNTING AND MANAGEMENT ACCOUNTING

Accounting is an information system.[6] We previously indicated that accounting is broadly classified into financial accounting and management accounting and that this classification is based on the difference in the relationship that exists between the organization and the person or persons to whom information is supplied. **Financial accounting** is concerned with providing financial information to persons outside the firm, especially investors, creditors, labor unions, and the general public. **Management accounting** is concerned with providing financial information to persons inside the organization, especially managers. This difference in orientation results in significant differences between these two types of accounting.

Financial Accounting Has an External Orientation

Financial accounting is concerned with the development of *general purpose* financial statements (such as the statement of financial position and the income statement) that are intended for the primary use of persons *external* to the organization. These statements, which are *highly aggregated* and, therefore, provide little detail, are summaries of the financial affairs of all the organization's subunits and activities and are typically issued quarterly and annually. Compared

---

[5] Outside directors are members of the organization's board of directors who are independent of management. That is, they are neither officers nor employees of the organization.

[6] *Information* is something that contributes to knowledge. Data taken alone do not contribute to knowledge. The number 500 is a datum, but, taken by itself, it is not knowledge. An advertisement stating that a local discount store is selling color television sets for $500 is information. It contributes to our knowledge.

to the frequency with which management accounting reports are issued (daily, weekly, monthly), financial accounting reports cover *relatively long time periods.*

Financial accounting statements report on management's handling of the affairs of the organization in the *past.* The U.S. Securities and Exchange Commission *requires* publicly held corporations to issue financial statements. To ensure conformity, understandability, and fairness, general purpose financial statements are prepared in accordance with *external standards* imposed by the public accounting profession (in the form of generally accepted accounting principles) and by regulatory agencies (such as the U.S. Securities and Exchange Commission). A significant feature of these external standards is their emphasis on *objectivity.* General purpose financial statements should not be influenced by emotion, surmise, or personal prejudice. They should be based on observable phenomena, such as the historical cost actually paid for a product or service.

You should not interpret the preceding comments on external reporting as implying that management has little interest in financial accounting. Managers can benefit greatly from financial accounting information. Management often uses financial statements as a starting point in evaluating and planning the overall affairs of the firm. Because financial accounting data are widely available, managers can learn a great deal about their firm's operations by a comparative financial analysis of their own and competing firms. Financial accounting numbers, such as net income, or ratios, such as earnings per share of common stock, are often used as goals. Furthermore, financial accounting statements are a major means of communication with persons outside the firm. Obviously, management is most interested in the content of this message. Finally, employees, who have a personal interest in the economic health of the organization for which they work, can gain an understanding of this economic health by studying their firm's financial statements.

Management Accounting Has an Internal Orientation

Management accounting is concerned with providing information to managers and other persons *inside* the organization. Management accounting reports are *special purpose.* Designed to fit the specific needs of individual or group decision makers, they emphasize factors under the decision makers' control. In this regard management accounting might be called a decision support system. At lower levels of management, planning and control decisions must be made quite frequently. To serve the needs of these desicion makers, management accounting provides information for *relatively short periods of time*—a month, a week, a day, or even some portion of a day. Because managers are primarily concerned with the impact of their decisions on the future performance of the organization, management accounting reports are *future oriented.* Past and current activities are reported to the extent that this information helps management plan for the future or ensure future conformance with current plans. Management accounting reports exist to serve the needs of management. Because they are *not required* by law, the development and use of these reports are subject to a cost-benefit analysis. Management accounting reports should only be provided if the perceived benefits of their development and use exceed the related costs.

EXHIBIT 1–5   Differences Between Financial and Management Accounting

Financial Accounting	Management Accounting
Provides information to external users	Provides information to internal users
Generates general purpose financial statements	Generates special purpose financial statements and reports
Statements highly aggregated; provide little detail	Statements and reports may be disaggregated; provide much detail
Relatively long time period	May be relatively short time period
Reports on past	Reports on past or outlines future plans
Required by law	Not required by law
Must conform to externally imposed standards	Has no externally imposed standards
Emphasizes objective data	Allows subjective data

No external standards are imposed on information provided to internal users. Consequently, management accounting reports may be quite *subjective*. In developing a budget, management is more interested in a subjective estimate of next year's sales volume than in an objective report on last year's sales. The significant differences between management accounting and financial accounting are summarized in Exhibit 1–5.

Professional Accountants

Public corporations are required by law to have outside auditors independently evaluate their general purpose financial statements. This audit is performed to determine whether or not the statements are prepared in accordance with generally accepted accounting principles. In the United States the persons who perform these independent evaluations are designated as **Certified Public Accountants (CPAs).** In Canada and several other countries they are designated as **Chartered Accountants (CAs).** All CPAs have passed an examination and met the education and experience requirements of the state in which they are certified. The CPA is widely recognized as a professional designation. Indeed, until recent years, U.S. business executives often cited the CPA as the only available guide to the professional competence of American accountants. This situation has changed since the National Association of Accountants (NAA) established the Institute of Certified Management Accountants and a program to recognize professional competence and educational attainment in the field of management accounting. The program leads to designation as a **Certified Management Accountant (CMA).** According to a booklet distributed by the Institute:

> *A Certified Management Accountant is well prepared to be an active participant in management. The CMA program is founded upon the dynamic role the management accountant plays in the management process. The program recognizes all aspects*

of business, with the focus on the development and analysis of information used in decision making. A CMA has demonstrated the knowledge and professional skills to become an influential member of the management team.[7]

The CMA examination is a comprehensive four-part examination that covers all aspects of accounting as well as related disciplines. Questions on ethical issues may appear on any part of the exam. Its interdisciplinary nature is reflected in the names given the four parts of the exam:

1. Economics, finance, and management.
2. Financial accounting and reporting.
3. Management reporting, analysis and behavioral issues.
4. Decision analysis and information systems.

The interdisciplinary nature of the CMA examination is intended to reflect the dual role of the management accountant as both an accountant and a member of the management team. Robert Shultis, former Executive Director of the National Association of Accountants, has even expressed the view that "the management accountant needs to be a businessman *first* and an accountant *second.*"[8]

MANAGERIAL PRACTICE 1.4

When to Take the CMA Exam

The best time to take any professional credentialing exam is as soon as possible after mastering the required subjects. The advantage of taking the exam when test-taking skills are sharpest far outweighs the advantage of professional experience. Students can now take the CMA exam as soon as they reach senior standing, but a completed college degree is still required before a candidate is eligible to receive the CMA certificate. In addition, students enrolled in six or more semester hours (or the equivalent) qualify for a special student examination fee. To qualify for this reduced rate, students must apply while they are still in school. Additional information about the CMA program is available from the Institute for Certified Management Accountants, 10 Paragon Drive, Montvalle, NJ 07645-1759.

---

[7] *Certified Management Accountant*, Institute of Certified Management Accountants, 1986–1987 announcement, p. 1.

[8] Robert Shultis, "Management and Management Accountants," *Survey of Business*, Fall, 1981, p. 6.

Statements on
Management
Accounting

The National Association of Accountants established a Management Accounting Practices (MAP) Committee in 1969 to express the official position of the NAA on accounting and financial reporting issues raised by standard setting groups and to develop guidelines on management accounting concepts, policies, and practices. The MAP Committee has promulgated these guidelines in a continuing series of Statements on Management Accounting. These statements have dealt with a wide variety of topics, ranging from the definition of important terms and issues in cost and performance measurement to standards of ethical conduct for management accountants. References are made to several of these statements in this text.

The MAP Committee takes a very broad view of management accounting and the functions performed by management accountants. According to Statement on Management Accounting Number 1B, persons involved in such functions as controllership, treasury, financial analysis, planning and budgeting, cost accounting, internal audit, systems, and general accounting are management accountants. Based on this list of functions, all professional personnel in the controller's department, and many within the treasury department would be management accountants.

The MAP Committee also defines management accounting very broadly. In Statement on Management Accounting Number 1A, management accounting is defined as

the process of identification, measurement, accumulation, analysis, preparation, interpretation, and communication of financial information used by management to plan, evaluate, and control within an organization and to assure appropriate use of and accountability for its resources. Management accounting also comprises the preparation of financial reports for nonmanagement groups such as shareholders, creditors, regulatory agencies, and tax authorities.

This broad definition of management accounting is somewhat troublesome when attempting to delineate the scope of this text or the content of management accounting courses. Accordingly, for the purpose of defining the subject matter included in this text, a more traditional view is taken. Thus, this text restricts management accounting to that segment of accounting concerned with providing financial information to managers and other persons within specific organizations.

SUMMARY

Accounting is an information system that is classified into financial accounting and management accounting. Financial accounting is concerned primarily with providing information to persons outside the organization. Management accounting is concerned primarily with providing information to persons inside the organization.

A manager is someone who directs the affairs of an organization. In planning, organizing, and controlling the activities of an organization, managers use many types of information, including that provided by management accounting. To perform their jobs, managers need to have a thorough understanding of accounting in general and management accounting in particular. Managers use accounting terms to communicate with employees, other managers, and persons in other organizations. They use accounting information as a basis for decision making and are very much involved in budgeting. Accounting reports are used to evaluate their performance and the performance of others. Accountants must also have a thorough understanding of management accounting concepts to ensure that the accounting information system supplies the information management needs for planning and controlling ongoing operations and for solving special problems.

SUGGESTED READINGS

Sources of additional information about each chapter's subject are presented at the end of most chapters. Suggested readings are carefully selected on the basis of their interest to students taking their first management accounting course.

Brown, Victor H., "The Tension Between Management Accounting and Financial Reporting," *Management Accounting* (May 1987): 39–41.

Fern, Richard H., "Controllers as Business Strategists: A Progress Report," *Management Accountant* (March 1988): 55–58.

Jayson, Susan, and Kathy Williams, "Women in Management Accounting: Moving Up . . . Slowly," *Management Accounting* (June 1986): 21–24, 63–64.

Lander, Gerald H., James R. Holmes, Manual A. Tipgos, and Marc J. Wallace, Jr., *Profile of the Management Accountant*, Montvalle, N.J.: National Association of Accountants, 1983.

Management Accounting Practices Committee, *Statements Number 1A through 1E:*

　　1A: Definition of Management Accounting, 1981.
　　1B: Objectives of Management Accounting, 1982,
　　1C: Standards of Ethical Conduct for Management Accountants, 1983,
　　1D: The Common Body of Knowledge for Management Accountants, 1986,
　　1E: Education for Careers in Management Accounting, 1988.

Montvalle, N.J.: National Association of Accountants.

Martin, James R., "Integrating the Major Concepts and Techniques of Cost and Managerial Accounting: A Recommendation," *Issues in Accounting Education* (Spring 1987): 72–84.

Worthy, Ford S., "Accounting Bores You? Wake Up," *Fortune* (October 12, 1987): 43–50.

Rich, Anne J., "Certificate in Management Accounting—Its Development and Acceptance," *Corporate Accounting* (Summer 1984): 55–60.

Runk, Randall C., and Ralph G. Loretta, "Controllers on the Firing Line," *Management Accounting* (November 1989): 38–42.

Smith, Roger B., "Competitiveness in the '90s," *Management Accounting* (September 1989): 24–29.

Additional Readings   The following readings contain material relevant to a number of chapters. They may be referred to throughout the course or used near the end of the course to provide an overview.

Anthony, Robert N., "Reminiscences About Management Accounting," *Journal of Management Accounting Research* (Fall 1989): 1–19.

Berliner, Callie, and James A. Brimson, ed., *Cost Management for Today's Advanced Manufacturing*, Boston, Mass.: Harvard Business School Press, 1988.

Cost Accounting for the 90s, Montvalle, N.J.: National Association of Accountants, 1986.

Haydon, Roger L., and Richard M. Peters, "How to Ensure Spreadsheet Integrity," *Management Accounting* (April 1989): 30–33.

Horngren, Charles T., "Cost and Management Accounting: Yesterday and Today," *Journal of Management Accounting Research* (Fall 1989): 21–32.

Johnson, H. Thomas, and Robert S. Kaplan, *Relevance Lost: The Rise and Fall of Management Accounting*, Boston, Mass.: Harvard Business School Press, 1987.

Howell, Robert A., James D. Brown, Stephen R. Soucy, and Allen H. Sneed, III, *Management Accounting in the New Manufacturing Environment,* Montvalle, N.J.: National Association of Accountants, 1987.

Lee, John Y., *Managerial Accounting Changes for the 1990s*, Reading, Mass.: Addison-Wesley, 1987.

Mecimore, Charles D., and William G. Sullivan, *Cost Management Systems: A Digest of Relevant Literature*, Montvalle, N.J.: National Association of Accountants, 1987.

Shillinglaw, Gordon, "Managerial Cost Accounting: Present and Future," *Journal of Management Accounting Research* (Fall 1989): 33–46.

KEY TERMS

Budget	Management by exception
Certified Management Accountant (CMA)	Management by objectives
	Managers
Certified Public Accountant (CPA)	Model
Chartered Accountant (CA)	Not-for-profit organization
Chief financial executive	Organization
Controller	Organization chart
Controlling	Organizing
Electronic data processing	Performance report
Favorable variance	Planning
Financial accounting	Treasurer
For-profit organization	Unfavorable variance
Internal auditing	Variance
Management accounting	

REVIEW QUESTIONS

The review questions at the end of each chapter are intended to assist in reviewing conceptual material. These questions are arranged in the same order that material is covered in the chapter.

1–1 Why do not-for-profit organizations need a good accounting system?

1–2 Identify and briefly describe the three functions of management.

1–3 What is the proper relationship between short-range and long-range planning?

1–4 Distinguish between the authority of staff and line managers. Why do staff departments exist?

1–5 What characteristic of accounting data is largely responsible for top management's wide use of accounting?

1–6 Why is a model useful to management?

1–7 How does the accounting model of the firm assist in planning?

1–8 How does accounting assist in controlling?

1–9 How does budgeting and the development of a system of responsibility accounting assist in organizing?

1–10 The controller frequently exerts a stronger influence on the affairs of line managers than one would expect from a staff officer. Why?

1–11 Identify several duties frequently assigned the controller.

1–12 Identify several duties frequently assigned the treasurer.

1–13 Why should the responsibility for special studies be assigned to a separate unit within the controller's department?

1–14 Why is electronic data processing frequently under the overall direction of the controller? Why are many large organizations establishing separate departments for electronic data processing?

1–15 Distinguish between financial and management accounting on the basis of the following: specificity of reports, users who receive reports, level of aggregation in reports, relative time period between reports, time orientation of reports (past, future), legal requirements for reporting, external pressures specifying content and form of reports, and emphasis on objective data.

Basic Cost Concepts

Learning Objectives

Upon completion of this chapter you should:

- Be familiar with the basic components of cost measurement systems.

- Be able to identify the various types of inventories in service, merchandising, and manufacturing organizations.

- Know the difference between product costs and period costs.

- Be familiar with the three elements of product costs for manufactured inventories.

- Be able to prepare a statement of cost of goods manufactured and sold.

- Understand generally how predetermined rates are established for applying factory overhead costs to manufactured inventory.

- Be familiar with several basic cost concepts for management decision making, including sunk costs, relevant costs, and opportunity costs.

Cost is generally defined as a monetary measure of the economic sacrifice made to obtain some product or service. The economic sacrifice can be a cash expenditure, the giving up of another valuable asset, the forgoing of an economically desirable opportunity, or the incurrence of an obligation to pay cash in the future. Cost measurement is a significant aspect of financial and management accounting. However, although the general definition of cost is adequate for most external purposes, a variety of cost concepts and related measurements are needed for internal planning and control.

The purpose of this chapter is to introduce cost concepts and measurements that are widely used in management accounting. In the course of our study, we will determine how costs are best measured for different purposes. Much of the material presented here is an overview with in-depth coverage contained in subsequent chapters.

Managers, in order to communicate with one another and with accountants, must be familiar with cost concepts. Accountants must be equally familiar with cost concepts to ensure that the accounting information system provides management with the information it needs. Both managers and accountants should understand the basic cost measurements that comprise a significant part of the accounting model of the organization, which is used to plan and control organizational activities.

DIFFERENT COSTS FOR DIFFERENT PURPOSES

Accountants and managers employ many different cost concepts, such as historical costs, budgeted costs, future costs, allowed costs, relevant costs, opportunity costs, and sunk costs, to name just a few. These cost concepts are not used randomly; instead, *different costs are used for different purposes.* Consider, for example, some of the alternative inventory costs that might be used in a department store. For the purpose of external reporting, the cost of goods sold is based on the historical cost actually paid for inventory. In developing a budget for next year, the store's management predicts the future cost of inventory purchases. The performance of the store's purchasing agent is evaluated by comparing the actual cost of purchases to the planned or allowed cost of purchases.

Cost Measurement Systems

Though purpose is the primary consideration in selecting a cost concept, a system of cost measurement also needs one or more cost objectives, a determination of the cost elements assignable to each objective, and one or more techniques for assigning cost elements to cost objectives. The costing purpose is the basic reason a cost concept is used and a cost measurement is made, the cost objectives are the objects or activities to which costs are assigned, the cost elements are the detailed categories of costs assignable to a cost objective, and the costing techniques are the procedures used to assign cost elements to cost objectives.

One purpose of a public corporation's accounting system is to provide general purpose financial statements to persons outside the organization. For this purpose each major type of asset, such as buildings, is a cost objective. The cost elements assignable to buildings include the amount paid to purchase them and the cost of major improvements. Alternative costing techniques for measuring the adjusted cost of buildings include straight-line, sum-of-the-years'-digits, and double-declining-balance depreciation.

Costs and Benefits of Cost Measurement

Cost measurement is intended to provide useful information. In general, information should not be developed unless the benefits derived from its use exceed its acquisition cost. Exceptions to this generalization occur when forces outside the organization (such as government agencies) require the disclosure of certain information.

Many corporations are legally required to maintain an accounting system capable of providing cost data for inclusion in general purpose financial statements. It is possible to estimate the cost of installing and operating this system, but the related benefits are difficult to quantify. To a large extent the benefits accrue to shareholders, creditors, and other persons outside the organization.

Even with a system primarily designed for external reporting, many cost reducing measures are taken that do not significantly reduce the accuracy of cost measurement. One example is the treatment of transportation-in on goods purchased for resale. Theoretically, these costs should be assigned to inventory

MANAGERIAL PRACTICE 2.1

Basic Cost Concepts Go Company-Wide At Coca-Cola

The Coca-Cola Company has found that a comprehensive, easy-to-reference accounting manual is one of the most important tools in maintaining strong financial controls in a multinational corporation. Part I of the Coca-Cola manual begins with a chart of accounts and account definitions. Part II describes all accounting concepts and procedures. A special section is devoted to cost accounting, including specifics of the company's inventory valuation. Many management accounting practices are defined, and uniform costing techniques for all areas are outlined.

Source: Andrew L. Nodar, "Coca-Cola Writes an Accounting Procedures Manual," *Management Accounting* (October 1986): 52–53.

items at the time of purchase and included in the valuation of ending inventory and cost of sales. In practice, however, the less costly and slightly less accurate treatment of immediately assigning transportation-in to a separate expense account is widely used.

Because management accounting information is not required by law, it should be provided only if the benefits obtained from the information exceed the costs of its measurement and processing. To reduce costs, wherever the information needs of management can be satisfied with data accumulated for external reporting, the data used for external reporting may be rearranged in a format suitable for management. Consider, for example, the cost of merchandise in a department store. For external reporting purposes, the financial accounting system must account for the actual cost of merchandise purchased either as merchandise inventory or as cost of goods sold. For the purpose of evaluating the performance of the purchasing department, the management accounting system compares the actual cost of purchases to the allowed cost of purchases. Although actual cost data are contained in both the external financial statements and the internal reports, they are configured differently.

Because much management accounting information is derived from the financial accounting information system, much of this chapter is devoted to costing objectives, elements, and techniques developed for external reporting. Study of this chapter will provide an understanding of the accounting data base used in both financial and management accounting.

INVENTORY COSTS IN DIFFERENT ORGANIZATIONS

The importance and complexity of inventory cost measurement varies widely among organizations. The importance of inventory costing is a function of the dollar size of inventories, whereas the complexity of inventory costing is a function of the number of major inventory categories and the number of cost elements assigned to each category. Using inventory as a basis, we can distinguish between service, merchandising, and manufacturing organizations. **Service organizations** perform work for others. Included in this category are banks, barbershops, hospitals, restaurants, movie theaters, electric utilities, schools, most government agencies, railroads, bus companies, and accounting firms. **Merchandising organizations** buy and sell goods. Included in this category are department stores, grocery stores, wholesale distributors, shoe stores, and discount stores. **Manufacturing organizations** process raw materials into finished products. Included in this category are automobile manufacturers, steel mills, computer manufacturers, and furniture makers.

In general, service organizations have a low percentage of their total assets invested in inventory, which usually consists only of the supplies needed to facilitate their operations. Merchandising organizations usually have a high percentage of their total assets invested in inventory. Their most significant inventory is merchandise purchased for resale, but they also have supplies inventories.

EXHIBIT 2–1   Inventory Costs in Various Organizations

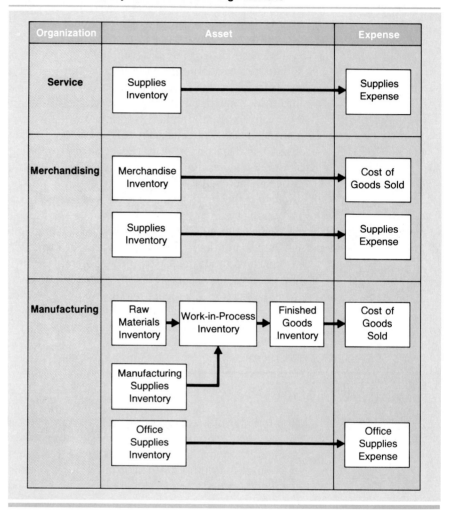

Manufacturing organizations convert raw materials into finished products that are sold to other organizations and, like merchandisers, usually have a high percentage of their total assets invested in inventories. However, rather than just one inventory category, manufacturing organizations have three major categories: raw materials, work-in-process, and finished goods. Raw materials inventories contain the physically existing items that are to be converted into a finished product. Work-in-process inventories contain materials that are in the process of being converted into a finished product. Finished goods inventories contain the manufactured products that are intended for sale to others.

Manufacturing organizations also have investments in supplies inventories. Some of these supplies are used to facilitate production. Others are used in selling and administrative activities. The cost of supplies that are used in production, such as lubricating oils and small tools, are a cost element of the finished product.

Exhibit 2–1 illustrates the flow of inventory costs in service, merchandising, and manufacturing organizations. Note that in all three types of organizations all inventories are eventually consumed or sold and become expenses.[1]

PRODUCT COSTING AND SERVICE COSTING

The process of assigning costs to inventories as they are converted from raw materials to finished goods is called product costing. Product costs must be determined for the purposes of inventory valuation and expense measurement in required general purpose financial statements. Product cost information is also used by management to plan and control firm activities.

The process of assigning costs to services is called service costing. Examples of service costing include measuring the cost of check processing (for a bank), instructional hours (for a college), operating room minutes (for a hospital), and passenger miles (for an airline). Though costs are seldom accumulated by service categories in external financial statements, service cost information is used internally to plan and control firm activities. The management of a bank, for example, might like to know the cost of processing a check drawn on a customer's account or the cost of processing an application for a personal loan. This information would assist in budgeting, pricing, and performance evaluation.

This chapter is presented in the context of product costing, rather than service costing, because product costing concepts are more fully developed and easier to generalize and understand. Note, however, that most product costing concepts are applicable to service costing.

PRODUCT COSTS FOR
EXTERNAL REPORTING

In financial accounting it is important to differentiate between unexpired costs and expired costs. Unexpired costs are recorded as assets on the statement of financial position, and expired costs are deducted from revenues on the income statement. A cost is classified as an asset, or an unexpired cost, to the extent that the cost objective it is related to has a potential to generate future

---

[1] For the purposes of this classification, agriculture might be included in the category of manufacturing organizations. A cattle ranch, for example, has a high percentage of its total assets invested in cattle (work-in-process). The cattle are raised from calves (raw material) and sold to slaughterhouses or feed lots when they obtain sufficient size (finished goods).

revenues from the sale or use of the asset or to avoid future costs. For instance, the cost of merchandise inventory is an asset to a retail store because future revenues can be generated from the sale of merchandise; the cost of an apartment building is an asset to its owners because future revenues can be generated from apartment rentals; and the cost of prepaid insurance is an asset because the purchaser can avoid the cost of buying additional insurance for the coverage period.

As a cost objective loses its revenue producing or cost avoidance potential, the costs assigned to that objective are reclassified as expired costs. The loss may be sudden or gradual. Thus, the cost of merchandise inventory is reclassified as the costs of goods sold when the merchandise is sold, the cost of an apartment building is depreciated over the building's life, and the cost of prepaid insurance is reclassified as insurance expense with the passage of the coverage period.

The difference between expired and unexpired costs is often difficult to discern. Consider the case of a newly constructed office building. Because the building presumably has a future service potential, the cost of the building is initially recorded as an asset. As this service potential is realized, the cost of the building is systematically reclassified as an expense. The accounting problem is how and when to properly record the expiration of the cost of the building.

MANAGERIAL PRACTICE 2.2

Pinching Postage as a Service Costing Objective at Vanguard

Every day the Vanguard Group, a large investment service, processes as much mail as a small city post office. By centralizing and carefully monitoring the cost of mail operations (a service costing objective), Vanguard has developed methods of serving its clients more cost-effectively. Introducing a combined statement containing information on all of a client's accounts resulted in 1989 cost savings of $118,000. Running a computer program to eliminate duplicate mailings of newsletters produced postage savings of $63,000 per issue, and printing fewer copies saved $10,000 in production costs. Presorting all mail in ZIP code order saved another $225,000 a year. Other measures instituted to reduce postage costs include reducing the width of newsletters, reducing the number of pages in the annual report, and using lighter-weight paper.

Source: "Vanguard Pinches Postage and Printing Costs," *In the Vanguard* (Spring 1990): 2.

To resolve this problem several alternative depreciation procedures are used. Even though these procedures may not accurately depict the decline in the value of the building, they do assign its costs, in an understandable manner, to the periods that benefit from the use of the building.

Depreciation procedures are complex, but they are not so complex as the techniques used to differentiate expired from unexpired product costs. Because manufactured products can be sold, they have a future service potential. Consequently, *the cost of raw materials and other costs incurred to transform raw materials into finished goods become part of the cost of the finished goods.* These costs are recorded as assets, since they are unexpired costs, until the finished goods are sold, when they become an expense, that is, the cost of goods sold.

Product Costs and Period Costs

In manufacturing organizations, an important distinction is made between costs assigned to products and nonproduct costs that expire during the period. **Product costs** are costs assigned to products. They are expensed when the products are sold. **Period costs** are expired nonproduct costs. They are always recorded as an expense.

For external reporting purposes, product costs include the costs of raw materials and all other factors necessary to transform raw materials into finished products. Because all manufacturing costs "attach to" or are "absorbed by" the units produced, external reports are often said to state manufacturing inventories on an *absorption cost* basis. *According to the* **absorption cost basis of external reporting,** *all manufacturing costs are product costs, and all selling and administrative costs are period costs.*

The proper treatment of several product and period costs is illustrated in Exhibit 2–2. Note in particular that depreciation, expired insurance, the cost of utilities, and so forth, are not automatically classified as period costs. When these costs are incurred in connection with manufacturing activities, they are product costs; when they are incurred in connection with other activities, they are period costs. The future service potential of factory buildings and equipment is transformed into the future service potential of manufactured products. Depreciation on manufacturing buildings and equipment is absorbed by the product; hence, this depreciation is a product cost. The future service potential of office buildings and equipment expires with the passage of time. Depreciation on office buildings and equipment is not absorbed by products; hence, this depreciation is a period cost.

Three Product Costs

The manufacture of even a simple product, such as a wooden rowboat, requires three basic ingredients: materials (such as wood), labor (such as that of a boat craftsman), and production facilities (such as a building to work in, a saw, and a hammer). Corresponding to these three basic ingredients, product costs are classified into three categories: direct materials, direct labor, and factory overhead. Just as materials, labor, and production facilities are combined to produce a finished product, the costs of direct materials, direct labor, and factory overhead

EXHIBIT 2–2   Product Costs and Period Costs

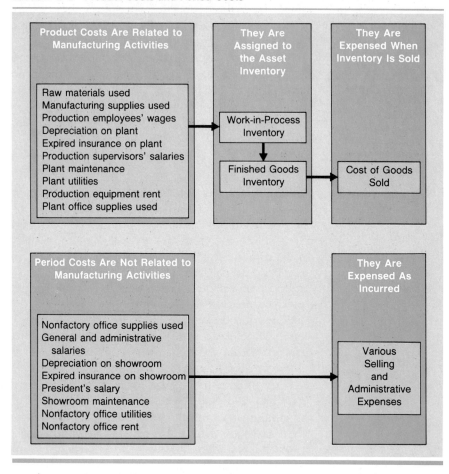

are accumulated to obtain the cost of finished goods. Exhibit 2–3 illustrates that these costs are accumulated in Work-in-Process[2] as production takes place and transferred to Finished Goods Inventory when production is completed. Product costs are finally assigned to Cost of Goods Sold when the finished goods are sold.

The costs of the primary raw materials converted into finished goods are called **direct materials.** Examples of primary raw materials include iron ore to a steel mill, coiled aluminum to a manufacturer of aluminum siding, cow's milk to a dairy, logs to a sawmill, and lumber to a builder. Note that the finished product of one firm may be the raw materials of another. Two-by-fours are the finished product of a sawmill but the raw material of a carpenter.

---

[2] Account titles are capitalized to make it easier to determine when reference is being made to a physically existing item, such as work-in-process inventory, and the account Work-in-Process, which discloses the costs assigned to work-in-process inventory.

EXHIBIT 2–3   Three Product Costs

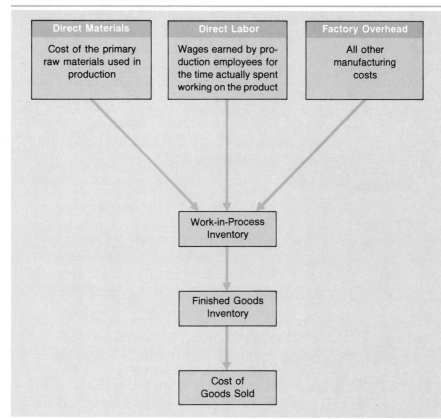

Direct Materials	Direct Labor	Factory Overhead
Cost of the primary raw materials used in production	Wages earned by production employees for the time actually spent working on the product	All other manufacturing costs

Work-in-Process Inventory

Finished Goods Inventory

Cost of Goods Sold

At the time of purchase, the costs of primary raw materials are assigned to Raw Materials Inventory. As raw materials are placed in production, their costs are removed from Raw Materials Inventory and assigned to Work-in-Process Inventory as direct materials. Direct materials costs are computed as the number of units of raw materials placed in production times their related cost per unit.

Wages earned by production employees *for the time they actually spend working on a product* are identified as direct labor. Direct labor costs are computed as the number of hours employees work on production times their hourly wage rate.

All manufacturing costs other than direct materials and direct labor are collectively identified as factory overhead.[3] Examples of factory overhead include manufacturing supplies; depreciation on manufacturing buildings and

---

[3] Factory overhead is also called "manufacturing overhead," "burden," "manufacturing burden," and "overhead." All but the last of these terms are acceptable. The word "overhead" by itself does not indicate the type of overhead. Merchandising organizations occasionally refer to administrative costs as overhead.

equipment; and the costs of plant taxes, insurance, maintenance, and utilities. Also included are production supervisors' salaries and all other manufacturing labor costs not specifically classified as direct labor. The assignment of factory overhead costs to Work-in-Process Inventory is discussed later in this chapter.

Analyzing Activity in Inventory Accounts

An understanding of account activity and account interrelationships is extremely important for product costing and for internal planning and control. During any time period, the activity in any account can be broken down into four parts:

Beginning balance + Increases − Decreases = Ending balance.

Knowing any three of these items, we can always find the fourth. Typical accounts and their activity include:

Cash	Merchandise Inventory	Accounts Payable
Beginning balance	Beginning balance	Beginning balance
+ Cash receipts	+ Purchases	+ Purchases on account
= Total cash available	= Total available	= Total payable
− Cash disbursements	− Cost of goods sold	− Payments on account
= Ending balance	= Ending balance	= Ending balance

The totals are inserted for computational ease. Assume that the management of a department store is trying to budget purchases for the coming year. The beginning merchandise inventory costs $50,000, and management desires to have an inventory of $45,000 at the end of the year. If the cost of goods sold is budgeted to be $350,000, knowledge of account activity can be used to budget purchases:

Activity	Given Information	Solution
Beginning balance	$ 50,000	$ 50,000
+ Purchases	+ ?	+345,000
= Total available	$?	$395,000
− Cost of goods sold	−350,000	−350,000
= Ending balance	$ 45,000	$ 45,000

Purchases should be budgeted at $345,000.

Activity in one account always affects at least one other account. Inventory purchased on account in a merchandising organization increases Merchandise Inventory and Accounts Payable. Payments on account reduce Cash and Accounts Payable. Inventory issued to the factory in a manufacturing organization decreases Raw Materials Inventory and increases Work-in-Process Inventory. A complete analysis of a manufacturing organization's inventory account relationships is presented in Exhibit 2–4.

EXHIBIT 2–4   Analysis of Activity in Manufacturing Inventory Accounts

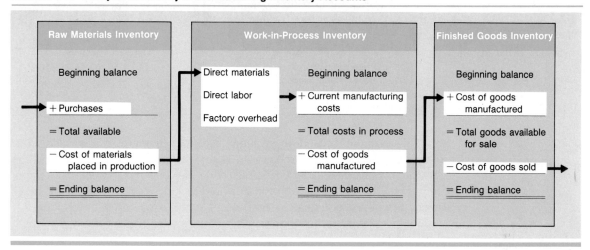

In Exhibit 2–4 the cost of raw materials placed in production reduces Raw Materials Inventory and increases Work-in-Process Inventory. The total additions to Work-in-Process Inventory are collectively identified as **current manufacturing costs,** and the total costs assigned to products completed are collectively identified as the **cost of goods manufactured.** The cost of goods manufactured is deducted from Work-in-Process Inventory and added to Finished Goods Inventory. Once the relationships between inventory accounts are known, items of interest (such as the cost of materials placed in production, the cost of goods manufactured, or the cost of goods sold) are readily determined. Consider the following example.

On September 1, 19x4, the beginning inventory balances of the Harmon Manufacturing Company were

Raw Materials Inventory	$ 5,000
Work-in-Process Inventory	8,000
Finished Goods Inventory	11,000

During the month of September, raw materials costing $12,000 were purchased. Direct labor and factory overhead costs were $20,000 and $15,000, respectively.

The September 30 inventory account balances were

Raw Materials Inventory	$ 7,000
Work-in-Process Inventory	14,000
Finished Goods Inventory	6,000

An analysis of activity in inventory accounts is presented in Exhibit 2–5. For computational ease the ending balance in each account is subtracted from the total to determine the items of interest:

Cost of materials placed in production	$10,000
Cost of goods manufactured	39,000
Cost of goods sold	44,000

This example focused on inventory account activity. Cost of goods sold is, of course, just one item on the income statement. Harmon's September income statement would also include revenues and other expenses. Harmon's September 30 statement of financial position would include inventory and many other assets, as well as liability and shareholders' equity accounts.

Because activity in one account always affects at least one other account, the analysis here is incomplete. The acquisition of raw materials and direct labor and the incurrence of factory overhead costs affect many other accounts. We

EXHIBIT 2–5   Analysis of Harmon's Inventory Accounts

Raw Materials Inventory		
Beginning balance		$ 5,000
Purchases		12,000
Total available		$17,000
Ending balance		− 7,000
Cost of materials placed in production (direct materials)		$10,000
Work-in-Process Inventory		
Beginning balance		$ 8,000
Current manufacturing costs:		
Direct materials	$10,000	
Direct labor	20,000	
Factory overhead	15,000	45,000
Total costs in process		$53,000
Ending balance		−14,000
Cost of goods manufactured		$39,000
Finished Goods Inventory		
Beginning balance		$11,000
Cost of goods manufactured		39,000
Total goods available for sale		$50,000
Ending balance		− 6,000
Cost of goods sold		$44,000

have ignored these accounts for the moment in order to emphasize the essential inventory relationships found in product costing.

Statement of Cost of Goods Manufactured

The activity in Raw Materials and Work-in-Process is formally summarized in a statement of cost of goods manufactured. Harmon Manufacturing Company's September 19x4 Statement of Cost of Goods Manufactured is presented in Exhibit 2–6. To show the relationship between this statement and the income statement, Harmon's September 19x4 Income Statement is also presented in the exhibit. For this example assume September sales of $90,000 and selling and administrative expenses of $30,000.

The activity in all major inventory accounts can be summarized in a single statement of cost of goods manufactured and sold, such as the one presented in Exhibit 2–7, along with an accompanying income statement. These statements, like all formal accounting statements, begin with a heading that

---

EXHIBIT 2–6   Statement of Cost of Goods Manufactured

Harmon Manufacturing Company
Statement of Cost of Goods Manufactured
For the month ending September 30, 19x4

Current manufacturing costs:			
Cost of materials placed in production:			
Raw materials, 9/1/x4	$ 5,000		
Purchases	12,000		
Total available	$17,000		
Raw materials, 9/30/x4	− 7,000	$10,000	
Direct labor		20,000	
Factory overhead		15,000	$45,000
Work-in-process, 9/1/x4			8,000
Total costs in process			$53,000
Work-in-process, 9/30/x4			−14,000
Cost of goods manufactured			$39,000

Harmon Manufacturing Company
Income Statement
For the month ending September 30, 19x4

Sales		$90,000
Cost of goods sold:		
Finished goods inventory, 9/1/x4	$11,000	
Cost of goods manufactured	39,000	
Total goods available for sale	$50,000	
Finished goods inventory, 9/30/x4	− 6,000	−44,000
Gross profit		$46,000
Selling and administrative expenses		−30,000
Net income		$16,000

EXHIBIT 2–7   Statement of Cost of Goods Manufactured and Sold

Harmon Manufacturing Company
Statement of Cost of Goods Manufactured and Sold
For the month ending September 30, 19x4

Current manufacturing costs:			
Cost of materials placed in production:			
Raw materials, 9/1/x4	$ 5,000		
Purchases	12,000		
Total available	$17,000		
Raw materials, 9/30/x4	– 7,000	$10,000	
Direct labor		20,000	
Factory overhead		15,000	$45,000
Work-in-process, 9/1/x4			8,000
Total costs in process			$53,000
Work-in-process, 9/30/x4			–14,000
Cost of goods manufactured			$39,000
Finished goods inventory, 9/1/x4			11,000
Total goods available for sale			$50,000
Finished goods inventory, 9/30/x4			– 6,000
Cost of goods sold			$44,000

Harmon Manufacturing Company
Income Statement
For the month ending September 30, 19x4

Sales	$90,000
Cost of goods sold	–44,000
Gross profit	$46,000
Selling and administrative expenses	–30,000
Net income	$16,000

indicates the name of the organization, the name of the statement, and the statement date or time period. Statement formats and details vary. Factory overhead may, for example, be itemized rather than be presented as a single amount.

Combined Product Costs

A clear association exists between the physical product and the direct materials and direct labor costs. Direct materials and direct labor costs are easily traced to finished goods. The number of units of raw materials that enter into each finished unit can be counted, and the time production employees work to produce a finished unit can be measured. Because of this direct association with the finished product, direct materials and direct labor costs are jointly identified as **direct product costs** or **prime product costs.**

All product costs other than direct materials and direct labor are classified as factory overhead. It is difficult to associate factory overhead costs with specific units of product. Factory overhead costs (such as depreciation on plant, insurance on plant, production supervisors' salaries, plant maintenance, and plant utilities) are incurred to facilitate the production of all products. Because it is difficult to

EXHIBIT 2–8   Product Costing Terminology

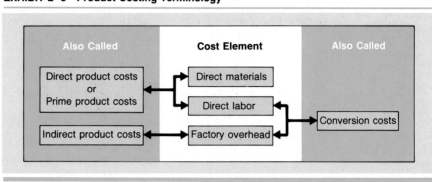

establish an explicit (direct) association between these costs and individual units of product, factory overhead costs are often identified as **indirect product costs.**

Direct labor and factory overhead costs, which are incurred to convert raw materials into finished goods, are jointly identified as **conversion costs.** The relationships between these new cost terms are illustrated in Exhibit 2–8. The September 19x4 amounts for the Harmon Manufacturing Company are as follows:

Direct product costs:		
Direct materials	$10,000	
Direct labor	20,000	$30,000
Prime product costs:		
Direct materials	$10,000	
Direct labor	20,000	$30,000
Indirect product costs		
(factory overhead)		$15,000
Conversion costs:		
Direct labor	$20,000	
Factory overhead	15,000	$35,000

Note that direct materials refers to the cost of materials placed in production rather than the cost of materials purchased.

A Closer Look at Factory Overhead

As production occurs, direct materials, direct labor, and factory overhead are assigned to Work-in-Process. Direct materials costs are transferred from Raw Materials Inventory. The number of units of raw materials transferred to the factory multiplied by the related cost per unit equals the direct materials cost. Direct labor costs are the number of direct labor hours worked times the appropriate rate per direct labor hour. But what about overhead?

Factory overhead is the most broadly defined and difficult to measure product cost. It includes all production costs other than those specifically identified as direct materials and direct labor. If there is a company-subsidized cafeteria in the plant, factory overhead will even include depreciation on the kitchen sink.

Selecting a Basis for Overhead Application. The costs and benefits of alternative measurement techniques are important considerations in the accumulation and assignment of factory overhead. As a cost reducing measure, all factory overhead costs may be grouped together into a single collection of related costs, called a **cost pool.** These costs are then assigned (applied) to Work-in-Process Inventory on the basis of some factor that has a high correlation with the incurrence of overhead, is common to all products, and is easy to measure. Frequently used bases of overhead application include direct labor dollars, direct labor hours, and machine hours.

The variety and different natures of factory overhead costs make it difficult to accurately apply them using a single application basis. Some factory overhead costs are related to people, others are related to the existence of buildings and equipment, and still others are related to the use of buildings and equipment. Accuracy could be improved by grouping overhead costs into two or more cost pools that have common characteristics and applying each on a separate basis.

MANAGERIAL PRACTICE 2.3

Caterpillar Rolls into a New Accounting Era

Many large companies are beginning to realize that their cost systems are not responding to today's changing competitive environment. Some companies are gaining a competitive advantage by modernizing their account practices. Caterpillar Tractor breaks down costs in its heavy-equipment plant into over a thousand overhead brackets. Each major piece of production machinery is treated as an individual cost center. The controller of the facility explains, "We have the ability to look at our costs all the way from the total product cost down to an individual part within that product, and then down to an individual operation within that part."

Source: Ford S. Worthy, "Accounting Bores You? Wake Up," *Fortune*, 12 October 1987, 43–51.

For example, labor related costs might be pooled and applied on the basis of labor hours, whereas equipment related costs might be placed in another cost pool and applied on the basis of machine hours. This should be done if the management accountant believes the increased accuracy is worth the added cost of operating the more complex cost measurement system.[4]

Using Predetermined Overhead Rates. The timely assignment of actual factory overhead costs is difficult because the amount of many overhead costs cannot be determined until after the period. September's electric utility and water bills, for example, may not be received until mid-October. Waiting until September's actual overhead costs are known would necessitate an undesirable delay in product costing. September's statement of cost of goods manufactured could not be prepared until mid to late October.

To overcome this timing problem, and other problems such as smoothing the work load of the bookkeepers, most firms use a predetermined rate to assign factory overhead costs. A **predetermined factory overhead rate** is determined at the start of the year by dividing the predicted overhead costs for the year by the predicted activity for the year. A predetermined overhead rate per direct labor hour is computed as

$$\frac{\text{Predetermined overhead rate}}{\text{per direct labor hour}} = \frac{\text{Predicted total overhead for the year}}{\text{Predicted total direct labor hours for the year}}.$$

Using a predetermined overhead rate based on direct labor hours, we compute the assignment of overhead to Work-in-Process Inventory as

$$\begin{array}{l}\text{Factory overhead} \\ \text{assigned to} \\ \text{Work-in-Process Inventory}\end{array} = \begin{array}{l}\text{Actual} \\ \text{direct} \\ \text{labor} \\ \text{hours}\end{array} \times \begin{array}{l}\text{Predetermined} \\ \text{overhead rate per} \\ \text{direct labor hour.}\end{array}$$

Late in 19x3 Harmon Manufacturing Company predicted a 19x4 activity level of 25,000 direct labor hours with factory overhead totaling $187,500. Using this information, their 19x4 predetermined overhead rate per direct labor hour was computed as

$$\frac{\text{Predetermined}}{\text{overhead rate}} = \frac{\$187,500}{25,000}$$

$$= \$7.50 \text{ per direct labor hour.}$$

If 2,000 direct labor hours were used in September 19x4, the applied overhead would equal $15,000:

$$2,000 \times \$7.50 = \$15,000.$$

---

[4] Cost systems that use two or more factory overhead cost pools are discussed in Chapters 11, 12, and 13.

When a predetermined overhead rate is used, monthly variations between actual and applied factory overhead are expected. In some months actual overhead is less than applied overhead; in some months it can be more. If the difference between cumulative actual and cumulative applied overhead builds up in a single direction over a period of time, it will be necessary to change the predetermined overhead rate. Underapplied and overapplied overhead costs are considered further in Chapter 11.

Materials and Labor Costs in Factory Overhead. As discussed earlier, direct materials costs include only the costs of primary raw materials clearly identified with the finished product, and direct labor costs include only the wages earned by production employees for time spent working on products. All other materials and labor costs are elements of factory overhead. Materials and labor costs normally in factory overhead include: indirect materials, indirect labor, idle time, overtime premiums, and employee fringe benefits.

Indirect materials are relatively low cost materials that are difficult to associate with specific units of final product. Wood is a primary raw material in the manufacture of wooden bookcases; its cost is a direct materials cost. Nails, screws, glue, and varnish are indirect materials whose costs are assigned to Manufacturing Supplies Inventory at the time of purchase and transferred to the factory overhead cost pool as they are used.

Indirect labor includes the salaries and wages earned by production employees for the time they spend performing all production related tasks, except physically working on the product. Production related tasks include receiving instructions, oiling machinery, and cleaning the work area. Salaries earned by production supervisors and wages earned by maintenance personnel may also be classified as indirect labor.

Idle time is time employees are not working on the product or performing other production related tasks. Included in this category are the time employees wait for instructions, materials, or repairs. Unless idle time becomes excessive, the salaries and wages paid employees for idle time are regarded as a normal operating cost and included in the factory overhead cost pool. In most organizations it is difficult to structure activities so that employees have no unassigned time. Some employers also pay idle time wages to employees who report for work when no work is available.

Overtime premiums are bonus wages in excess of the regular hourly rate that are paid to production employees for working more than the regular number of hours. Employees who regularly work 40 hours per week receive an overtime premium for working more than 40 hours. Assume an employee whose regular wage rate is $12 per hour is entitled to a 50 percent overtime premium. If the employee works 45 hours in a given week, the employee's total wages will be $570.

Regular hourly wages (45 × $12)	$540
Overtime premium (5 × $6)	30
Total wages	$570

Overtime premiums are usually treated as factory overhead even if the overtime hours are identified with particular units of product. Overtime is the result of the overall level of activity. If there were less activity, products worked on during overtime hours would be worked on during regular hours. Accordingly, overtime premiums are spread over all production as part of factory overhead. In the above example, $540 is classified as direct labor, and $30 is classified as factory overhead.

Employee fringe benefits are additional labor costs paid by the employer on behalf of the employees. Employee fringe benefits are not included in the computation of employees' salary or wage rates, nor are they disclosed on employees' pay stubs as part of gross earnings or as a deduction in arriving at net earnings. Typical employee fringe benefits include: the employer's share of social security (FICA) taxes, federal and state unemployment taxes, workmen's compensation insurance, medical insurance premiums, employer paid pension plans, and vacation pay.

In the past, employee fringe benefits were a small percentage of total labor costs. Because of their relatively small size, management accountants believed that the increased accuracy that would result from separately accounting for them was not worth the additional bookkeeping cost. Consequently, the cost of employee fringe benefits has traditionally been assigned to the factory overhead cost pool.

However, a recent U.S. Chamber of Commerce survey reported that, in many organizations, employee fringe benefits now exceed 35 percent of the total labor bill. This has led some management accountants to question the propriety of the traditional method of accounting for them. There is a concern that employee fringe benefits will dominate the factory overhead cost pool and cause an inaccurate allocation of either the employee fringe benefits or the other overhead costs. Rather than mixing the cost of fringe benefits with other overhead costs, many firms now place employee fringe benefits in a separate cost pool and assign them to products on the basis of direct labor costs.

COST CONCEPTS FOR MANAGEMENT ACTION

The product costing concepts and techniques introduced above are used to develop the historical cost information presented in general purpose financial statements. Management is interested in historical cost information primarily because it is useful in controlling current operations and planning future operations.

Historical Costs for Prediction and Control

To plan a trip you need to know your current location, your destination, and alternative ways of traveling between them. Likewise, to plan for the future a manager must understand the organization's current situation, its goals, and alternative ways of traveling between them. A manager can obtain an understanding of where the organization is (its current economic situation) by studying historical cost data and reports. A detailed analysis of historical cost data also assists in determining whether the organization has the capabilities needed to achieve its goals. If, for example, an organization's plant is old and its production costs exceed competitor's selling prices, the organization cannot currently compete in the market for its final product.

Management is often interested in how costs respond to changes in the volume of activity. Some costs increase in direct proportion to increases in activity, whereas others do not change at all. An analysis of historical cost data provides an excellent starting point in determining cost behavior. Furthermore, predictions of future costs are often based on historical cost relationships, adjusted for changes in prices and technology. Cost behavior is studied in Chapter 3, and predicted cost relationships are used for profit planning in Chapters 4 through 6.

Subsequent to planning, actual (historical) costs are accumulated and analyzed for the purpose of controlling operations. In Chapters 7 through 10, performance reports are developed that compare allowed and actual costs. Special attention is given to the problem of determining who is responsible for each cost.

M ANAGERIAL PRACTICE 2.4

Trickle-down of Basic Cost Concepts at USAA

To make the most informed operating decisions possible, United Services Automobile Association (USAA), an insurance company, decided to require *all* managers to become involved in cost control. It began the change from corporate-level accounting to control by operating managers by implementing a cost/benefit analysis program; other accounting applications followed. For the first implementation, all day-to-day cost/benefit studies became the responsibility of the operating managers, with technical assistance provided by the controller's office. The managers are now expected to know the most commonly used analytical techniques, such as cash flow versus accrual accounting. They must be able to apply the company's standard costing analyses, such as lease-versus-buy decision models, and they must know the costing factors used to quantify both costs and benefits for a given analysis. All department managers at USAA must have a basic understanding of cost concepts if they are to progress up the corporate ladder.

Source: Martha A. Fasci, Timothy J. Weiss, and Robert L. Worrall, "Everyone Can Use This Cost/Benefit Analysis System," *Management Accounting* (January 1987): 44–47.

Sunk Costs and Relevant Costs

Although an analysis of historical cost information is a useful starting point in predicting future costs, it is the predicted future costs, rather than the historical costs, that are of interest to decision makers. In and of themselves, historical costs are irrelevant to decisions about the future. In the context of decision making, historical costs are called sunk costs.

Sunk costs result from past decisions that management no longer has control over. Because sunk costs cannot be changed, they are irrelevant to decisions about the future and should be omitted from any analysis prepared to assist in decision making. Including sunk costs makes it difficult for management to focus on important decision variables; furthermore, management may be misled into making bad decisions on the basis of sunk costs that cannot be changed.

Relevant costs are future costs that differ among competing alternatives. Because relevant costs can be changed by management decisions (selecting one alternative rather than another), they should be included in any analysis prepared to assist in decision making. Assume management is evaluating the desirability of replacing a four-function calculator with a new ten-function calculator that has several memory units. The old calculator was purchased yesterday for $25 and has a used sales value of $15. The new calculator costs $90. Using the new calculator rather than the old one will save three labor hours per week at a cost of $15 per hour. For simplicity assume a planning period is 10 weeks, at the end of which both calculators will cease to operate and have a zero salvage value.

The cost of the calculator purchased yesterday is irrelevant to a decision to keep it or replace it with a new calculator. The relevant factors for this decision are the cost of the new calculator, the disposal value of the old calculator, and the cost savings derived from using the new, rather than the old, calculator. The net benefit of acquiring the new calculator is $375.

Labor cost reduction (10 wk. × 3 hr. per wk. × $15 per hr.)		$450
Additional investment:		
Cost of new calculator	$90	
Less disposal value of old calculator	−15	−75
Net benefit		$375

The $25 cost of the old calculator was not included in the analysis because it is a sunk cost.

Sunk costs are not relevant to an economic analysis of decisions about the future, but they do have behavioral implications. Even though it is economically advantageous to acquire the new calculator, a manager might be reluctant to do so, because of a concern that this new decision should reflect poorly on the decision to acquire the old calculator. Sometimes accounting procedures increase this fear when, for example, it is necessary to compute and disclose a "loss" on the disposal of an old asset. This is a situation where good decisions will be made only if managers and management accountants clearly understand the proper uses and limits of accounting data.

Opportunity Cost

An **opportunity cost** is the net cash inflow that could be obtained if the resources committed to one action were used in the most desirable other alternative. An opportunity cost results from a forgone opportunity. By selecting one opportunity, management forgoes an alternative. Other things equal, management desires to select the alternative with the smallest total cost, including any opportunity cost. Consequently, opportunity costs are relevant costs and, as such, should always be considered in decision making. Note, however, that because there are no cash receipts or cash expenditures incurred in connection with a forgone opportunity, opportunity costs are not recorded in the accounting records.

Opportunity costs are a significant part of the cost of your education. How much more could you earn this year, at your current education and skill level, if you were not enrolled in college? $10,000? If so, $10,000 is the opportunity cost of your college education this year. This opportunity cost should be added to tuition, room, board, books, and so forth in computing your total educational investment.[5]

What, then, is the opportunity cost of acquiring the new calculator? The answer depends on the best other alternative use of the $75 additional investment. If the money were to remain in a noninterest bearing checking account or earn $6 interest in a short-term savings certificate, the best other alternative action would be to invest in the savings certificate, so the opportunity cost would be $6. In this case, the $6 opportunity cost should be compared to the net benefits of the new calculator to determine the net advantage or disadvantage of purchasing the calculator. The net economic advantage of purchasing the calculator would, therefore, be $369 ($375 net benefit − $6 opportunity cost).

It is important to understand that the opportunity cost of an action is a function of the *other* alternative actions. Investing in the savings certificate has an opportunity cost of $375 because this is the net cash inflow from the most desirable other action, namely, buying the calculator. Likewise, the opportunity cost of leaving the $75 in a noninterest bearing checking account is $375.

SUMMARY

Though cost is generally defined as a monetary measure of the economic sacrifice made to obtain some product or service, different cost concepts and measurements are required for different purposes. A system for cost measurement includes a costing purpose, cost objectives, cost elements, and costing techniques. For the purpose of external reporting, products are important cost objectives in manufacturing organizations. The cost of a product contains three major cost elements: direct materials, direct labor, and factory overhead. The pooling of all product costs other than direct materials and direct labor into a

---

[5] The benefits of this investment will accrue in the future. Ways to equate monetary future benefits with current investments are considered in Chapter 15. There are, of course, many nonmonetary benefits associated with a college education.

single factory overhead cost pool and the application of factory overhead to products using a predetermined overhead rate are important product costing techniques.

In manufacturing organizations a distinction is made between product costs and period costs. Product costs are assigned to products and accounted for as assets until the product is sold. At that time they become an expense, that is, the cost of goods sold. Period costs are nonproduct costs that are accounted for as expenses in the period their service potential expires.

Product costing is emphasized in this chapter because product costing is well developed, easily generalized and understood, and required for external reporting. Many of the concepts discussed here are also applicable to service costing. The accounting system used for product costing also provides the data used for many management accounting purposes.

In and of themselves, historical costs are not relevant to an economic analysis of the future. They are sunk costs that management can no longer control. An economic analysis prepared to assist management in making decisions should focus on relevant costs, that is, on future costs that differ among competing alternatives.

SUGGESTED READINGS

Hakala, Gregory, "Measuring Costs with Machine Hours," *Management Accounting* (October 1985): 57–61.

Hunt, Rick, Linda Garrett, and Mike Merz, "Direct Labor Costs Not Always Relevant at H-P," *Management Accounting* (February 1985): 58–62.

Management Accounting Practices Committee, *Statement Number 4C: Definition and Measurement of Direct Labor Cost*, Montvale, N.J.: National Association of Accountants, 1985.

Management Accounting Practices Committee, *Statement Number 4E: Definition and Measurement of Direct Material Cost*, Montvale, N.J.: National Association of Accountants, 1986.

McRay, T. W., "Opportunity and Incremental Costs: An Attempt to Define in Systems Terms," *The Accounting Review* (April 1970): 315–321.

REVIEW PROBLEM

Cost Statements and Terminology

On January 1, 19x7, the beginning inventory balances of the Poston Manufacturing Company were as follows:

Raw Materials Inventory	$ 3,000
Work-in-Process	8,200
Finished Goods Inventory	15,000

During January, raw materials costing $6,000 were purchased. Direct labor and factory overhead costs were $8,000 and $20,000, respectively.

The January 31 inventory account balances were as follows:

Raw Materials Inventory	$ 2,500
Work-in-Process	6,000
Finished Goods Inventory	13,000

January sales of finished goods amounted to $75,000 and selling and administrative expenses totaled $25,050.

Requirements

a) Prepare a statement of cost of goods manufactured and an income statement for January 19x7.

b) Prepare a statement of cost of goods manufactured and sold and an income statement for January 19x7.

c) Determine each of the following for January:

   1. Direct product costs.   3. Indirect product costs.

   2. Prime product costs.   4. Conversion costs.

The solution to this problem is found at the end of the Chapter 2 exercises and problems.

KEY TERMS

Absorption cost basis of external
  reporting
Conversion costs
Cost
Cost element
Cost objective
Cost of goods manufactured
Cost pool
Costing purpose
Costing technique
Current manufacturing costs
Direct labor
Direct materials
Direct product costs
Employee fringe benefits
Expired cost
Factory overhead
Finished goods inventory
Idle time
Indirect labor
Indirect materials
Indirect product costs

Manufacturing organization
Merchandising organization
Opportunity cost
Overtime premium
Period cost
Predetermined factory overhead
  rate
Prime product costs
Product cost
Product costing
Raw materials inventory
Relevant cost
Service costing
Service organization
Statement of cost of goods
  manufactured
Statement of cost of goods
  manufactured and sold
Sunk cost
Unexpired cost
Work-in-process inventory

2–1   What relationships exist among costing purpose, cost objectives, cost elements, and costing techniques?

2–2   Why is management accounting information subject to more stringent cost-benefit analysis than financial accounting information?

2–3   Distinguish among service, merchandising, and manufacturing organizations on the basis of the importance and complexity of inventory cost measurement.

2–4   Distinguish among raw materials, work-in-process, and finished goods inventories.

2–5   Distinguish between product costing and service costing. Why do we emphasize product costing rather than service costing in this chapter?

2–6   In general, how do we determine whether a cost is an expired cost or an unexpired cost?

2–7   When is depreciation a product cost? When is depreciation a period cost?

2–8   What are the three major product cost elements?

2–9   How can you determine when a manufacturing cost should be classified as factory overhead?

2–10 Which product cost element is both a prime cost and a conversion cost?

2–11 What are the characteristics of a good basis of overhead application?

2–12 How are predetermined overhead rates developed? Why are they widely used?

2–13 What labor costs are often elements of factory overhead?

2–14 Of what use are historical costs in planning for the future?

2–15 Are opportunity costs relevant costs? Why or why not?

EXERCISES

2–1 Cost Terms: Matching

For each of the numbered phrases or statements, select the *most appropriate* term. Each term is used only once.

1. Has three inventory categories
2. Objects or activities costs are assigned to
3. Sold to other organizations
4. Benefit forgone
5. Performs work for others
6. Cannot be changed
7. Manufacturing costs except direct materials and labor
8. Future costs that differ
9. Total additions to Work-in-Process
10. These costs are assigned to inventories

a. Product costs
b. Service organization
c. Sunk cost
d. Relevant costs
e. Opportunity cost
f. Cost objectives
g. Manufacturing organization
h. Current manufacturing costs
i. Finished goods
j. Factory overhead

2–2 Cost Terms: Matching

For each of the numbered phrases or statements, select the *most appropriate* term. Each term is used only once.

1. Direct labor and factory overhead
2. Direct materials and direct labor
3. Used to assign cost elements to cost objectives
4. Selling and administrative expenses
5. Buys and sells goods
6. Being converted to a finished product
7. All manufacturing costs are product costs
8. A collection of related costs
9. A measure of economic sacrifice
10. Transferred to Finished Goods Inventory

a. Costing technique
b. Merchandising organization
c. Work-in-process
d. Absorption cost basis of external reporting
e. Cost of goods manufactured
f. Cost pool
g. Cost
h. Direct product costs
i. Period costs
j. Conversion costs

2–3 Classification of Product and Period Costs

Classify the following costs incurred by a furniture manufacturer as product costs or period costs. Further classify the product costs as direct or indirect product costs.

1. Rent on cars used by salespersons
2. Depreciation on factory
3. Power and water consumed in the factory
4. Advertising in national magazines
5. Broken saw blades
6. Vacation pay of production workers
7. Carpenters' wages
8. Depreciation on table saws
9. Glue used in furniture assembly
10. Supervisors' salaries
11. Materials used in packing finished goods prior to shipment
12. Participation in regional trade shows
13. Management training seminar
14. Depreciation on corporate headquarters
15. Prime lumber

2–4 Classification of Product and Period Costs

Classify the following costs incurred by an automobile manufacturer as product costs or period costs. Further classify the product costs as direct materials or conversion.

1. Salaries of legal staff
2. Automobile window glass
3. Depreciation on word processor in president's office
4. Plant fire department
5. Automobile tires
6. Automobile bumpers
7. Wages paid assembly line maintenance workers
8. Salary of corporate controller
9. Automobile engines
10. Subsidy of plant cafeteria
11. Wages paid assembly line production workers
12. National sales meeting in Detroit
13. Overtime premium paid assembly line workers
14. Advertising on national television
15. Depreciation on assembly line

2–5 Account Activity and Interrelationships

For each of the following independent cases find the required information.

1. *Cash*

Beginning balance	$ 30,000
Ending balance	25,000
Cash receipts	130,000
Find: Cash disbursements	

2. *Merchandise Inventory*

Purchases	$104,000
Cost of goods sold	80,000
Ending balance	70,000
Find: Beginning balance	

3. *Accounts Payable* (to suppliers)

Ending balance	$ 65,000
Payments on account	302,000
Beginning balance	88,000
Find: Purchases on account	

4. *Accounts Receivable*

Sales on account	$260,000
Collections on account	291,000
Beginning balance	57,000
Find: Ending balance	

5. *Merchandise Inventory*

Beginning balance	$15,000
Ending balance	45,000
Cost of goods sold	95,000

Accounts Payable (to suppliers)

Beginning balance	$ 5,000
Ending balance	6,000
Find: Payments on account when all purchases are on account	

6. *Merchandise Inventory*

Beginning balance	$ 39,000
Ending balance	29,000
Purchases	110,000

Accounts Receivable

Beginning balance	$ 23,000
Ending balance	120,000
Find: Collections on account when all sales are on account and the selling price is 150 percent of cost	

2–6 Account Activity and Interrelationships

For each of the following independent cases find the required information.

1. *Raw Materials*

Beginning balance	$ 7,000
Ending balance	14,000
Purchases	48,000

   Find: Direct materials

3. *Finished Goods Inventory*

Cost of goods manufactured	$62,000
Ending balance	20,000
Cost of goods sold	61,000

   Find: Beginning balance

5. *Raw Materials*

Beginning balance	$ 8,500
Ending balance	12,000
Direct materials	42,000

   Accounts Payable (to suppliers)

Ending balance	$11,000
Beginning balance	6,000

   Find: Payments on account when all purchases are on account

2. *Work-in-Process*

Ending balance	$22,000
Cost of goods manufactured	21,000
Beginning balance	8,000

   Find: Current manufacturing costs

4. *Merchandise Inventory*

Purchases	$210,000
Cost of goods sold	223,000
Beginning balance	41,000

   Find: Ending balance

6. *Finished Goods Inventory*

Beginning balance	$ 22,000
Cost of goods manufactured	100,000
Ending balance	30,000

   Accounts Receivable

Beginning balance	$ 16,000
Ending balance	50,000

   Find: Collections on account when all sales are on account and the selling price is 200 percent of cost

2–7 Analyzing Activity in Inventory Accounts

Selected data concerning the past fiscal year's operations of the Hull Manufacturing Company are presented below.

Raw materials used	$290,000
Total manufacturing costs charged to production during the year (includes raw materials, direct labor, and factory overhead applied at a rate of 60 percent of direct labor cost)	686,000
Cost of goods available for sale	826,000
Selling and general expenses	25,000

	Inventories	
	Beginning	Ending
Raw materials	$70,000	$ 80,000
Work-in-process	80,000	30,000
Finished goods	90,000	110,000

Required: Determine each of the following:

1. The cost of raw materials purchased.
2. The direct labor costs charged to production.
3. The cost of goods manufactured.
4. The cost of goods sold.

2–8 Statements: Cost of Goods Manufactured, Income

Information from the records of the Alexandria Manufacturing Company is given below for August 19x4.

Sales	$205,000
Selling and administrative expenses	83,000
Purchases of raw materials	20,000
Direct labor	15,000
Factory overhead	32,000

	Inventories	
	August 1	*August 31*
Raw materials	$ 7,000	$ 5,000
Work-in-process	14,000	11,000
Finished goods	15,000	19,000

Requirements

a) Prepare a statement of cost of goods manufactured and an income statement for August.

b) Determine each of the following:

Direct product costs.	Indirect product costs.
Prime product costs.	Conversion costs.

2–9 Statements: Cost of Goods Manufactured and Sold, Income

Information from the records of Grand Rapids Products is given below for January 19x7.

Sales	$350,000
Selling and administrative expenses	55,000
Purchases of raw materials	90,000
Direct labor	120,000
Overhead is applied using a predetermined overhead rate of 130 percent of direct labor.	

	Inventories	
	January 1	*January 31*
Raw materials	$12,000	$ 8,000
Work-in-process	50,000	25,000
Finished goods	30,000	40,000

Requirements

a) Prepare a statement of cost of goods manufactured and sold and an income statement for January.

b) Determine each of the following:

Direct product costs.	Indirect product costs.
Prime product costs.	Conversion costs.

2–10 Developing and Using a Predetermined Overhead Rate

The following predictions were made for 19x9:

Total factory overhead for the year	$1,375,000
Total direct labor hours for the year	125,000

Actual results for January 19x9 were as follows:

Factory overhead	$82,000
Direct labor hours	8,000

Requirements

a) Determine the 19x9 predetermined overhead rate per direct labor hour.

b) Using the 19x9 predetermined overhead rate, determine the factory overhead applied to Work-in-Process during January.

c) Determine the amount of any overapplied or underapplied overhead at the end of January.

2–11 Developing and Using a Predetermined Overhead Rate

The following predictions were made for 19x2:

Total factory overhead for the year	$380,000
Total machine hours for the year	20,000

Actual results for February 19x2 were as follows:

Factory overhead	$55,200
Machine hours	3,100

Requirements

a) Determine the 19x2 predetermined overhead rate per machine hour.

b) Using the 19x2 predetermined overhead rate per machine hour, determine the factory overhead applied to Work-in-Process during February.

c) As of February 1, actual overhead was underapplied by $4,000. Determine the cumulative amount of any overapplied or underapplied overhead at the end of February.

2–12 Assignment of Overtime Premium

Susan Dove is a telephone installer in a college-oriented community. During the last week of August she spent 25 hours installing telephones in Riverview Apartments, 23 hours installing telephones in Sam's Luxury Apartments, and 3 hours on general tasks. Mrs. Dove has a regular 40-hour workweek, with scheduled daily hours from 8 A.M. to 12 P.M. and from 1 P.M. to 5 P.M., Monday through Friday. Of the 23 hours at Sam's Luxury Apartments, 11 were after 5 P.M. Mrs. Dove's wage rate is $9 per hour with time-and-a-half for overtime.

Required: Determine the amount of Mrs. Dove's labor cost that should be assigned to each apartment complex. Explain why some of Mrs. Dove's labor costs should be assigned to overhead.

2–13 Determining and Classifying Labor Related Costs

Joan Keller works on the assembly line of the National Computer Company. She installs cathode ray picture tubes in personal computers. Because of the high demand for the company's products, Joan often works overtime hours. During a recent week her total reported time was 48 hours, with 42 hours spent working on the assembly line.

The base wage rate for assembly line workers is $12 per hour. Employee fringe benefits amount to 40 percent of the base wage rate. Employees are paid time-and-a-half for overtime. The regular workweek is 40 hours.

Requirements

a) Determine the total wages and benefits earned by Joan Keller.

b) If all earnings other than the base wages paid for working on products are classified as factory overhead, classify Keller's total earnings as direct labor and factory overhead.

c) If base wages paid for working on products and related fringe benefits are classified as direct labor, with all other earnings classified as factory overhead, classify Keller's total earnings as direct labor and factory overhead.

2–14 Determining and Classifying Labor Related Costs

Gary Dicer is a teller at the Big Bucks National Bank. During a recent week he worked a total of 52 hours, with 38 hours spent at a drive-up banking window and 14 hours spent on breaks and miscellaneous tasks.

The base wage rate for tellers is $6 per hour. Employee fringe benefits amount to 30 percent of the base wage rate. Employees are paid time-and-a-half for overtime. The regular workweek is 40 hours.

Requirements

a) Determine the total wages and benefits earned by Gary Dicer.

b) To determine the cost of bank activities, Big Bucks classifies the earnings of tellers as direct labor and operating overhead. If all earnings other than the base wages paid for working at the teller's window are classified as operating overhead, classify Dicer's total earnings as direct labor and operating overhead.

c) If base wages paid for working at the teller's window and related fringe benefits are classified as direct labor, with all other earnings classified as operating overhead, classify Dicer's total earnings as direct labor and operating overhead.

2–15 Establishing Overhead Cost Pools

A cost pool is a collection of related costs. Presented are a number of factory overhead costs. Classify these costs by number into one of three cost pools:

Pool 1: The existence of buildings and equipment.

Pool 2: The use of buildings and equipment.

Pool 3: The availability and use of direct labor.

Factory overhead costs:

1. Depreciation on buildings and machinery.
2. Power.
3. Water.
4. Fringe benefits.
5. Idle time wages.
6. Property taxes.
7. Supervisors' salaries.
8. Property insurance on buildings and equipment.
9. Overtime premiums.
10. Lubricants for machines.
11. Safety hats and shoes.
12. Night and weekend security.
13. Subsidy of employee cafeteria.

2–16 Relevant Costs

Sally Byte is a computer science major just starting her senior year. To complete her extensive programming assignments, Sally goes to the computer lab every Saturday and Sunday. Because she lives off campus and does not have a car, she takes the bus to and from campus at a round trip cost of $1.20.

A local Computer Shack store has offered to rent Sally a computer terminal and modem (a telephone connection) so that she can complete her programming assignments at home by dialing the college computer. The rental fee is $300 for the academic year, payable in advance. The academic year is 30 weeks long.

If Sally rents the modem, she will be able to work four additional hours each week at a part-time job that pays $4 per hour.

Required: Determine the net benefit of renting the computer terminal and modem for the 30-week academic year.

2–17 Relevant Costs

John Bright recently spent $5 to purchase a regular flashlight that operates on two size D batteries. While walking through a discount store, John came upon a rechargeable flashlight that was on sale for $20. The promotional literature indicated that the rechargeable flashlight could be plugged into an electric outlet and recharged for only $0.25.

Additional information:

- Size D batteries cost $0.50 each.
- John will replace batteries or recharge the flashlight an average of four times a year.
- The expected life of both flashlights is 5 years.
- A friend has offered to pay John $2.00 for the regular flashlight.

Required: Determine the net benefit (or cost) of replacing the regular flashlight with a rechargeable flashlight.

2–18 Sunk Costs Versus Relevant Costs

A medium-sized consulting firm has a number of portable computers for the use of its professional staff. The firm's bookkeeper, Mr. Eyeshade, is responsible for issuing the computers to authorized persons and seeing that they are returned in good condition.

A recently hired employee checked out a computer and was crossing the street on her way to her first assignment when she slipped and fell on the ice, breaking a leg. The computer crashed to the ground and slid under the wheels of a speeding taxicab. Bystanders called an ambulance and the sound of the ambulance siren brought Mr. Eyeshade to the window. After surveying the scene, the employee with a broken leg, the damaged computer, and the angry taxi driver, Mr. Eyeshade observed, "I'm glad the computer was fully depreciated."

Required: Comment. Be sure to distinguish between relevant and irrelevant costs. What would Mr. Eyeshade's reaction have been if the computer were not fully depreciated?

2–19 Opportunity Costs

Matrix Products paid $10,000 for a specialized machine and then discovered that the market for the product the machine was intended to produce had completely disappeared. Matrix Products has two offers for the machine:

1. A machine shop has offered to buy the machine for $4,000 with the intention of disassembling it and reselling the machine's parts.

2. A promotional firm has offered to rent the machine for one year. They would pay a rental fee of $5,000; however, Matrix Products would have to spend $1,500 modifying the machine. At the end of the year the machine would be worthless.

Required: Determine the opportunity cost associated with each alternative. Which offer should Matrix Products accept?

2–20 Opportunity Costs

Mr. Fury purchased an antique Plymouth for $4,000 and spent another $16,000 reconditioning it. Mr. Fury is currently considering three alternative uses for the car:

1. DeSoto's Auto Museum has offered Mr. Fury a lease-purchase agreement that involves leasing the car to the museum for one year with the museum purchasing the car at the end of the year. The lease payment of $3,000 and the purchase price of $20,000 are both payable at the end of the year.

2. A local car buff has offered Mr. Fury $20,000 in cash for the car. If Mr. Fury accepts this offer, he will invest the money in a one year bank certificate that pays 10 percent interest.

3. He can keep the car in a local warehouse for one year, and then sell it for $25,000. The storage costs of $1,000 are payable at the end of the year.

Required: Determine the opportunity cost of each action.

PROBLEMS

2–21 Statements:
Cost of Goods
Manufactured,
Income

Presented is information from the records of the Rocking Chair Craft Shop for June 19x2.

Purchases:	
Lumber	$ 4,500
Glue, paint, sandpaper, and small tools	100
Office supplies	210
Sales	18,000
Salaries: Selling and administrative (including	
fringe benefits of $250)	2,000
Wages: Production (including fringe benefits of $400)	3,000
Rent	2,000*
Utilities	600*
Advertising	350

	Inventories	
	June 1	June 30
Lumber	$ 2,200	$ 800
Glue, paint, etc.	250	300
Office supplies	75	90
Finished goods	12,000	8,000

* Of these costs 60 percent are assigned to manufacturing and 40 percent to selling and administration.

Production employee fringe benefits are classified as factory overhead. There is no beginning or ending inventory of work-in-process.

Requirements

a) Prepare a statement of cost of goods manufactured and an income statement. Actual overhead costs are assigned to products.

b) Determine each of the following:

Direct product costs.
Prime product costs.
Indirect product costs.
Conversion costs.

2–22 Statements: Cost of Goods Manufactured, Income

Presented below is information from the records of the Saskatchewan River Production Company for July 19x3.

Purchases:	
Raw materials	$ 70,000
Manufacturing supplies	3,500
Office supplies	1,200
Sales	425,700
Administrative salaries	12,000
Direct labor	117,500
Production employees' fringe benefits	4,000*
Sales commissions	50,000
Production supervisors' salaries	7,200
Depreciation on plant	14,000
Depreciation on office	20,000
Plant maintenance	10,000
Plant utilities	35,000
Office utilities	8,000
Office maintenance	2,000
Production equipment rent	6,000
Office equipment rent	1,300

	Inventories	
	July 1	*July 31*
Raw materials	$17,000	$15,000
Manufacturing supplies	1,500	3,000
Office supplies	600	1,000
Work-in-process	51,000	40,000
Finished goods	35,000	27,100

* Classified as factory overhead.

Requirements

a) Prepare a statement of cost of goods manufactured and an income statement. Actual overhead costs are assigned to products.

b) Determine each of the following:

Direct product costs.
Prime product costs.
Indirect product costs.
Conversion costs.

2–23 Correcting Erroneous Statements: Cost of Goods Manufactured, Income

Presented are two reports prepared by the former accountant of Misclassification Manufacturing Corporation:

Misclassification Manufacturing Corporation
Statement of Cost of Goods Manufactured and Income
For the month ended December 31, 19x5

Sales		$200,000
Less direct materials		– 40,000
Gross profit		$160,000
Less other expenses:		
Cost of goods sold (computed below)	$89,000	
Office supplies	500	
Manufacturing utilities	2,000	
Office utilities	500	– 92,000
Net income		$ 68,000

Misclassification Manufacturing Corporation
Statement of Cost of Goods Sold
For the month ending December 31, 19x5

Finished goods inventory 12/1/x5			$30,000
Work-in-process 12/1/x5			6,000
Total			$36,000
Current manufacturing costs:			
Salaries and wages:			
Direct labor	$10,000		
Other manufacturing	4,000		
Sales	8,000		
Administrative	6,000	$28,000	
Other:			
Manufacturing supplies	$ 3,000		
Manufacturing depreciation	7,000		
Insurance on showroom	2,000		
Miscellaneous factory overhead	13,000	25,000	53,000
Total work-in-process			$89,000
Work-in-process 12/31/x5			– 0
Cost of goods sold			$89,000

Additional information:

- The 12/31/x5 finished goods inventory was $4,000.
- Dividends of $10,000 were declared and paid during December.
- All amounts, except those specifically computed in the presented statements, are correct.

Requirements

a) Prepare a statement of cost of goods manufactured and an income statement in good form.

b) Determine each of the following:

Direct product costs.
Prime product costs.
Indirect product costs.
Conversion costs.

2–24 Correcting Erroneous Statements: Cost of Goods Manufactured, Income

Presented is a financial statement prepared by the former accountant of the Southern Snowshoe Company:

Southern Snowshoe Company
Statement of Inventories, Revenues, and Expenses
For the year ending December 31, 19x3

Sales		$80,000
Net of finished goods inventory change:		
Finished goods inventory, 1/1/x3	$20,000	
Finished goods inventory, 12/31/x3	−30,000	10,000
Net sales		$90,000
Materials expenses:		
Direct materials	$14,000	
Factory supplies	2,800	
Office supplies	450	
Work-in-process, 1/1/x3	2,000	−19,250
Gross profit		$70,750
Labor expenses:		
Sales salaries and wages	$ 3,000	
Administrative salaries and wages	4,000	
Indirect labor	4,000	
Office utilities	300	
Direct labor	35,000	−46,300
Labor profit		$24,450
Miscellaneous costs:		
Factory utilities	$ 3,000	
Telephone and direct mail advertising	8,000	
Packing and transportation-out	12,000	
Factory depreciation	4,000	
Miscellaneous factory overhead	6,000	−33,000
Miscellaneous profit		$ (8,550)
Dividends declared and paid expense		15,000
Dividend profit		$ 6,450

Additional information:

- The 12/31/x3 work-in-process is $1,800.
- All amounts, except those specifically computed in the presented statement, are correct.

Requirements

a) Prepare a statement of cost of goods manufactured and an income statement in good form.

b) Determine each of the following:

Direct product costs.
Prime product costs.
Indirect product costs.
Conversion costs.

2–25 Account Interrelationships: Missing Production Data

Supply the missing data in each independent case in the following table.

	Case 1	Case 2	Case 3	Case 4
Raw materials, beginning	$ 5,000	$ 3,000	$?	$ 3,000
Purchases	10,000	?	20,000	7,000
Raw materials, ending	8,000	5,000	6,000	2,000
Direct materials	?	20,000	30,000	?
Direct labor	12,000	?	40,000	?
Factory overhead	20,000	20,000	?	30,000
Current manufacturing costs	?	65,000	?	90,000
Work-in-process, beginning	15,000	?	10,000	5,000
Work-in-process, ending	16,000	35,000	20,000	?
Cost of goods manufactured	?	105,000	90,000	80,000
Finished goods, beginning	25,000	?	20,000	10,000
Finished goods, ending	10,000	10,000	50,000	?
Cost of goods sold	?	98,000	?	70,000

2–26 Account Interrelationships: Missing Data

Supply the missing data in each independent case.

	Case 1	Case 2	Case 3	Case 4
Sales	$50,000	$?	$?	$?
Raw materials, beginning	10,000	13,000	?	5,300
Purchases	?	13,000	2,500	31,400
Raw materials, ending	8,000	?	500	6,200
Direct materials	?	20,000	2,000	?
Direct labor	20,000	25,000	6,000	?
Factory overhead	10,000	8,000	?	29,200
Current manufacturing costs	55,000	?	12,000	?
Work-in-process, beginning	?	8,000	8,000	5,300
Work-in-process, ending	5,000	7,000	?	4,000
Cost of goods manufactured	55,000	?	19,000	82,000
Finished goods, beginning	?	6,000	1,500	8,000
Finished goods, ending	25,000	?	500	10,000
Cost of goods sold	?	55,000	?	?
Gross profit	10,000	9,000	?	10,500
Other expenses	8,000	?	5,000	3,500
Net income (loss)	?	(4,000)	1,000	?

2–27 Statement of Cost of Goods Manufactured and Sold from Percent Relationships

Information about the Portion Company for the year ending December 31, 19x1, is given below.

- Sales $400,000
- Direct materials   64,000
- Factory overhead is 150 percent of direct labor.
- The beginning inventory of finished goods is 20 percent of the cost of goods sold.
- The ending inventory of finished goods is twice the beginning inventory.
- The gross profit is 20 percent of sales.
- There is no beginning or ending work-in-process.

Required: Prepare a statement of cost of goods manufactured and sold for 19x1. *Hint:* Set up the statement format and start the solution from known information.

2–28 Income Statement and Statement of Cost of Goods Manufactured from Percent Relationships

Information about the Lots-O-Luck Company for the year ending December 31, 19x1, is as follows:

- Sales $350,000
- Net income   5,000
- Ending inventories:
  Raw materials   18,000
  Work-in-process   8,000
  Finished goods   67,000
- Inventory changes:
  Ending raw materials are twice beginning raw materials.
  Ending work-in-process is one-third larger than beginning work-in-process.
  Finished goods inventory increased by $15,000 during the year.
- Selling and administrative expenses are five times net income.
- Prime costs are 60 percent of manufacturing costs.
- Conversion costs are 80 percent of manufacturing costs.

Required: Prepare an income statement and a statement of cost of goods manufactured for 19x1. *Hint:* Set up the statement formats and start the solution from known information.

2–29 Statement of Cost of Goods Manufactured with Predetermined Overhead and Labor Cost Classification

Presented is information pertaining to Little Bear Productions for December 19x4.

Purchases of raw materials	$ 41,000
Sales	310,000
Supervisors' salaries (production), including fringe benefits	20,000
Depreciation on office	17,500
Depreciation on plant	35,000
Plant utilities	51,000
Plant insurance	6,000
Purchases of office supplies	350
Plant property taxes	40,000

	Inventories	
	December 1	December 31
Raw materials	$ 3,000	$ 5,000
Office supplies	250	150
Work-in-process	25,000	15,000
Finished goods	12,000	18,000

Additional information:

- Factory overhead is applied to products at the rate of 200 percent of direct labor dollars.
- Employee base wages are $10 per hour.
- Employee fringe benefits amount to 50 percent of the base wage rate. They are classified as factory overhead.
- During December, production employees worked 9,000 hours, including 8,500 spent working on products.

Requirements

a) Prepare a statement of cost of goods manufactured.

b) Determine underapplied or overapplied overhead for December.

2–30 Statements: Cost of Goods Manufactured, Income with Predetermined Overhead and Labor Cost Classification

Presented is information pertaining to Big Bear, Incorporated, for April 19x9.

Sales	$200,000
Purchases:	
Raw materials	35,000
Manufacturing supplies	800
Office supplies	500
Salaries (including fringe benefits):	
Administrative	6,000
Production supervisors	3,600
Sales	15,000
Depreciation:	
Plant and machinery	8,000
Office and office equipment	4,000
Utilities:	
Plant	5,250
Office	890

	Inventories	
	April 1	April 30
Raw materials	$5,000	$3,500
Manufacturing supplies	1,000	1,100
Office supplies	900	800
Work-in-process	2,000	2,300
Finished goods	8,000	9,000

Additional information:

- Factory overhead is applied to products at 80 percent of direct labor dollars.
- Employee base wages are $12 per hour.
- Employee fringe benefits amount to 40 percent of the base wage rate. They are classified as factory overhead.
- During April, production employees worked 5,600 hours, including 4,800 regular hours and 200 overtime hours spent working on products.
- Employees are paid a 50 percent overtime premium.

Requirements

a) Prepare a statement of cost of goods manufactured and an income statement.

b) Determine underapplied or overapplied overhead for April.

c) Recompute direct labor and actual factory overhead assuming employee fringe benefits for direct labor hours are classified as direct labor.

REVIEW PROBLEM SOLUTION

a) **Poston Manufacturing Company**
Statement of Cost of Goods Manufactured
For the month ending January 31, 19x7

Current manufacturing costs:			
Cost of materials placed in production:			
Raw materials, 1/1/x7	$3,000		
Purchases	6,000		
Total available	$9,000		
Raw materials, 1/31/x7	−2,500	$ 6,500	
Direct labor		8,000	
Factory overhead		20,000	$34,500
Work-in-process, 1/1/x7			8,200
Total costs in process			$42,700
Work-in-process, 1/31/x7			− 6,000
Cost of goods manufactured			$36,700

Poston Manufacturing Company
Income Statement
For the month ending January 31, 19x7

Sales		$75,000
Cost of goods sold:		
Finished goods inventory, 1/1/x7	$15,000	
Cost of goods manufactured	36,700	
Total goods available for sale	$51,700	
Finished goods inventory, 1/31/x7	−13,000	−38,700
Gross profit		$36,300
Selling and administrative expenses		−25,050
Net income		$11,250

b)   **Poston Manufacturing Company**
Statement of Cost of Goods Manufactured and Sold
For the month ending January 31, 19x7

Current manufacturing costs:
  Cost of materials placed in production:

Raw materials, 1/1/x7	$3,000		
Purchases	6,000		
Total available	$9,000		
Raw materials, 1/31/x7	−2,500	$ 6,500	
Direct labor		8,000	
Factory overhead		20,000	$34,500
Work-in-process, 1/1/x7			8,200
Total costs in process			$42,700
Work-in-process, 1/31/x7			− 6,000
Cost of goods manufactured			$36,700
Finished goods inventory, 1/1/x7			15,000
Total goods available for sale			$51,700
Finished goods inventory, 1/31/x7			−13,000
Cost of goods sold			$38,700

Poston Manufacturing Company
Income Statement
For the month ending January 31, 19x7

Sales	$75,000
Cost of goods sold	−38,700
Gross profit	$36,300
Selling and administrative expenses	−25,050
Net income	$11,250

c) **1.** Direct product costs:

Direct materials	$ 6,500	
Direct labor	8,000	$14,500

  2. Prime product costs:

Direct materials	$ 6,500	
Direct labor	8,000	$14,500

  3. Indirect product costs
   (factory overhead): $20,000

  4. Conversion costs:

Direct labor	$ 8,000	
Factory overhead	20,000	$28,000

C H A P T E R 3

Cost Behavior Analysis

Learning Objectives

Upon completion of this chapter you should:

- **Be able to prepare a graph showing the relationship between the amount of cost and the volume of activity for any given cost element, and determine the slope of the line representing the relationship.**

- **Understand the following important cost behavior patterns: variable, fixed, mixed, and step.**

- **Be thoroughly familiar with the total cost equation: Total costs = Fixed costs + (Variable costs per unit × Unit volume).**

- **Have a general awareness of the differences and similarities between the accounting and economic models of cost behavior.**

- **Be able to separate mixed costs into their variable and fixed components using the high-low, scatter diagram, and least-squares methods.**

- **Understand the importance of selecting an appropriate independent variable.**

- **Understand the effect of changing prices and technology on cost estimation and cost prediction.**

Activities undertaken to achieve an organization's short-range and long-range objectives result in the incurrence of various costs. Because economic resources are limited, managers must carefully control both costs and the activities that cause them. To plan and control costs, managers must know how costs respond to changes in activity. Some costs increase in direct proportion to changes in activity, whereas others do not change at all. Still others, which do not change throughout a range of activity, will then increase suddenly to a different amount. Managers need to know which costs will change, the circumstances that cause them to change, and the amount they will change.

The purpose of this chapter is to introduce **cost behavior analysis,** which is the study of how costs respond to changes in the volume of activity. We will study the major cost behavior patterns used in accounting models, mention several representative costs that display each pattern, and survey methods used to estimate cost behavior.

Managerial Practice 3.1

Cost Behavior Analysis:
A Key to Success

"The company's financial control and reporting system has become the common language of such diversified businesses as heart pumps, masking tape, laser disks, and road signs." So states the controller of Minnesota Mining and Manufacturing Company (3M). Analyzing costs is a critical part of its success. First, all reporting is broken into one of five categories: manufacturing, research, sales, marketing, or administrative. Within each category is a line item for each department. Each department, with a few exceptions, becomes a cost center where its costs are monitored. Within one plant, which may have many departments, there may be "20–25 breakdowns of types of wages. . . . 60 breakdowns of benefits, 10 splits of utilities, 20–25 splits on types of maintenance," and the list goes on. "The breakdown continues until you get to your fixed costs." Fixed costs that cannot be traced are simply aggregated at the plant or divisional level.

Source: Kathy Williams, "The Magic of 3M Management Accounting Excellence," *Management Accounting* (February 1986): 20–27.

PLOTTING COST BEHAVIOR

The relationship between the volume and the total cost of an activity is often illustrated with a graph, such as the one in Exhibit 3–1(a). Volume of activity, the independent variable that causes the incurrence of costs, is measured on the horizontal axis. Total cost, the dependent variable that responds to changes in volume, is measured on the vertical axis. Combinations of observed activity and cost are represented by dots. Total cost and total volume increase up and to the right from the origin (where the horizontal and vertical axes intersect). Each unit of activity, in Exhibit 3–1(a), results in the incurrence of an additional $1 in total costs.

EXHIBIT 3–1   Plotting Cost Behavior

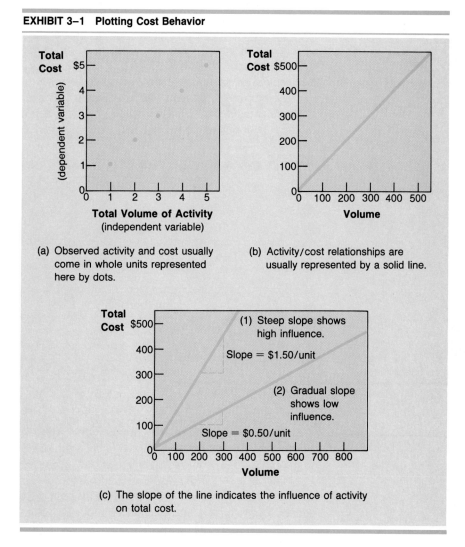

(a) Observed activity and cost usually come in whole units represented here by dots.

(b) Activity/cost relationships are usually represented by a solid line.

(c) The slope of the line indicates the influence of activity on total cost.

By compressing the measurement scale, it is possible to move the individual dots so close together that the relationship between volume and total cost appears to be a solid line. In Exhibit 3–1(b) the unit cost is still $1, but the range of activity is now 0 to 500 units rather than 0 to 5 units. For ease of presentation, lines are often used to represent cost behavior even when the scale of activity is such that dots might be better. In cost behavior analysis, the horizontal axis is, by convention, labeled "volume" rather than "total volume of activity," "total activity," or "total volume." Because there are a variety of cost concepts, care should be taken to label the vertical axis "total cost," "average cost," "unit cost," or whatever other term is appropriate.

The slope of a line measures the change in the dependent variable for each unit of change in the independent variable. In cost behavior analysis, the slope indicates the responsiveness of costs to changes in volume. The slope of the total cost line is the incremental cost of one unit. In Exhibit 3–1(c) the slope of line (1) illustrates a situation where volume has a relatively large influence on total cost, whereas the slope of line (2) illustrates a situation where volume has a relatively small influence on total cost.

The slope of a straight line is computed as the change in the total cost between two selected volumes divided by the difference between the two volumes. The slopes of the two lines in Exhibit 3–1(c) are

$$\text{Slope of line (1)} = \frac{\$450 - \$300}{300 - 200} = \$1.50 \text{ per unit,}$$

and

$$\text{Slope of line (2)} = \frac{\$150 - \$100}{300 - 200} = \$0.50 \text{ per unit.}$$

The 300 and 200 unit volumes were randomly selected. Any pair of volumes on either line would give identical results.

IMPORTANT COST BEHAVIOR PATTERNS

Four cost behavior patterns—variable, fixed, mixed (or semivariable), and step costs—are widely used in accounting models. Although the behavior of each is illustrated with a straight line drawn between zero units and an arbitrarily chosen high volume of activity, management is only interested in cost behavior within the range of *probable* activity. Illustrated cost behavior patterns are seldom valid over the entire range of *possible* activity. This limitation will be examined further immediately after the introduction of important total cost behavior patterns.

Variable Costs

A **variable cost** is a cost that is uniform for each incremental unit of volume. Total variable costs change in direct proportion to changes in volume, equaling zero dollars when activity is zero and increasing at a constant amount per unit of activity. Typical variable costs include sales commissions, direct materials, direct labor, cost of goods sold in merchandising, postage in magazine publishing, gasoline in trucking, and asphalt in road maintenance. A behavior pattern for total variable costs is illustrated in Exhibit 3–2(a) by an upward sloping straight line that starts at the origin. The slope of this line represents the variable cost per unit. The equation for total variable costs is

$$\begin{array}{ccc} \text{Total variable} \\ \text{costs} \end{array} = \begin{array}{c} \text{Variable cost} \\ \text{per unit} \end{array} \times \begin{array}{c} \text{Unit} \\ \text{volume.} \end{array}$$

A 50 percent increase in volume results in a 50 percent increase in total variable costs. If hamburger patties cost Big Burger Restaurant $0.50 each, and Big Burger serves 10,000 hamburgers during February, the cost of hamburger patties consumed is $5,000 (10,000 × $0.50). If volume increases 50 percent in March, the cost of hamburger patties consumed increases proportionally, to $7,500 (15,000 × $0.50).

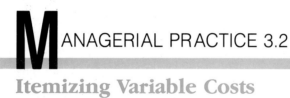

MANAGERIAL PRACTICE 3.2

Itemizing Variable Costs by Category at Reeves

In order to control costs in the hotly competitive trucking industry, Reeves Transportation Company had to carefully define every phase of transportation that incurs costs. One critical area was the cost of handling the freight. After studying the cost behavior of freight handling, the management accountants determined that all handling costs were variable. Unfortunately, they decided that this still did not provide enough control, so they decided to define handling costs by type of activity. This resulted in the traditional variable cost category of freight handling being segregated into six variable cost areas—from pickup at shipper's dock to billing and collection of the freight bill. This and similar cost controls have enabled the company to remain competitive and profitable in a deregulated industry.

Source: Frank Rader, "Keep on Trucking," *Management Accounting* (April 1989): 43–45.

EXHIBIT 3-2   Important Total Cost Behavior Patterns

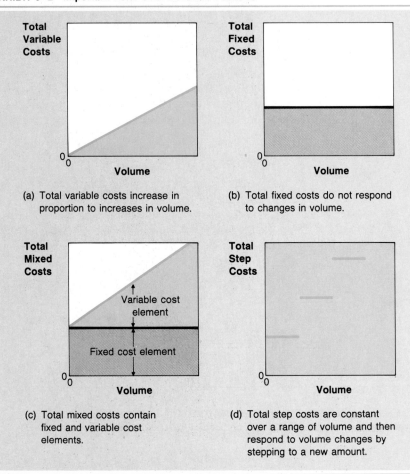

(a) Total variable costs increase in proportion to increases in volume.

(b) Total fixed costs do not respond to changes in volume.

(c) Total mixed costs contain fixed and variable cost elements.

(d) Total step costs are constant over a range of volume and then respond to volume changes by stepping to a new amount.

Fixed Costs

A **fixed cost** is a cost that does not respond to changes in the volume of activity within a given period. Total fixed costs are a constant amount per period regardless of the level of activity. Typical fixed costs include depreciation, supervisors' salaries, property taxes, rent, advertising, research and development, and charitable contributions. Total fixed costs are illustrated in Exhibit 3–2(b) by a straight line drawn parallel to the horizontal axis. Because fixed costs do not respond to changes in activity, the slope of the line is zero.

Organizations can control the relative portions of their variable and fixed costs by making long-run decisions about their methods of operation. For example, the frame of an automobile can be welded by skilled laborers or by robots. If the welding is performed by skilled labor, the direct labor cost per unit will be relatively high. If the welding is performed by a robot, fixed costs, such as depreciation, property taxes, and maintenance, will be relatively high. The trade-off between the fixed and variable costs of welding is summarized as follows:

	Relative Welding Costs	
	Skilled Labor	Robot
Variable	High	Low
Fixed	Low	High

Since the start of the industrial revolution more than 200 years ago, there has been a systematic shift toward more fixed and fewer variable costs. Though this shift has been generally beneficial, it has also reduced the flexibility of organizations, especially their ability to respond to decreases in activity. The decision to have welding operations performed automatically by a machine can provide an opportunity for great cost savings at high levels of output. However, this course of action is risky because the fixed costs of machine ownership are incurred regardless of the level of output. At low levels of output total costs might be lower if skilled labor were used.

Committed Fixed Costs Maintain Current Capacity. Fixed costs are classified as "committed" or "discretionary," depending on their immediate impact on the organization if they are changed. Committed fixed costs are required to maintain the current service or production capacity. Ordinarily, these costs can be reduced only by reducing the organization's capacity. Because they are related to capacity, committed fixed costs are frequently called capacity costs. Typical committed fixed costs include depreciation, supervisors' salaries, property taxes, and rent.

Committed fixed costs result from long-range decisions made by top management about the size and nature of the organization. For example, years ago the management of the Delaware and Hudson Railroad made a number of decisions about the railroad, including what communities the railroad would serve. Track was laid on the basis of these decisions, and the Delaware and Hudson now pays property taxes each year on the railroad's miles of track. These property taxes can be reduced by disposing of track. However, reducing the track will also reduce the railroad's capacity to serve.

Capacity is usually thought of in terms of a maximum *volume* of activity, such as the number of automobiles that can be produced in a month, the number of beds in a hospital, the number of seats in a church, and the monthly passenger seat miles in an airplane. There is also a *quality* dimension to current capacity. For example, a restaurant can retain its seating capacity while reducing its committed fixed costs by selling nonessential depreciable assets and reducing expenditures on entertainment, maintenance, heating, cooling, and so forth. The physical capacity remains, but the quality is lower; the restaurant is not what it was before the cost reductions.

Discretionary Fixed Costs Do Not Affect Current Capacity. Discretionary fixed costs, sometimes called managed fixed costs, are set at a fixed amount each year at the discretion of management. It is possible to change these costs and not change production or service capacity in the near-term. Typical discretionary fixed costs include advertising, charitable contributions, employee training programs, and research and development.

Expenditures on discretionary fixed costs are frequently regarded as investments in the future. Research and development, for example, is undertaken to produce new or improved products that can be profitably produced and sold in future periods. During periods of financial well-being, organizations may make large expenditures on discretionary cost items. Conversely, during periods of financial stress, organizations will likely reduce discretionary expenditures before reducing capacity costs. Managers should, of course, exercise care before making drastic changes in the level of funding of discretionary cost items. Fluctuations in funding reduce the effectiveness of long-range programs. A high-quality research staff may be difficult to reassemble if key personnel are laid off; even the contemplation of such layoffs may reduce the staff's effectiveness. In all periods discretionary costs are subject to debate and are likely to be changed in the give and take of the budgeting process. The alternative designation, managed fixed costs, is intended to reflect the importance of management's judgment in setting their amount.

Mixed Costs

Mixed costs, sometimes called semivariable costs, contain a fixed and a variable cost element. Total mixed costs are positive (like fixed costs) when volume is zero, and they increase in a linear fashion (like total variable costs) as volume increases. Typical mixed costs include power, maintenance, and automobile rental charges. Some power is required to light buildings and to provide the heat necessary to keep water pipes from freezing in the winter, and additional power is required to operate machinery. Some maintenance is required to prevent the deterioration of buildings and equipment, and additional maintenance is required as the use of these assets increases. Finally, automobiles are frequently rented on the basis of a fixed charge per day plus an additional charge per mile driven. Total mixed costs are illustrated in Exhibit 3–2(c) by an upward sloping straight line that starts above the origin. The equation for total mixed costs is

$$\text{Total mixed costs} = \text{Fixed costs} + \left(\text{Variable cost per unit} \times \text{Unit volume}\right).$$

Because of the presence of fixed costs, total mixed costs do not increase in proportion to volume. Assume Big Burger Restaurant pays a franchise fee of $1,000 per month plus 2 percent of sales. The franchise fee for a month when sales revenue totals $50,000 is $2,000 [$1,000 + ($50,000 × 0.02)]. If sales revenue increases by 50 percent, only the variable cost element of the franchise fee will increase, whereas the fixed element will remain $1,000.

Step Costs

Step costs are constant within a range of activity but different between ranges of activity. Total step costs increase in a steplike fashion as volume increases. The steps are caused by input indivisibilities. Typical step costs include the salaries of quality inspectors and production supervisors. In some states the maximum legal first grade student-to-teacher ratio is 25 to 1. These laws cause first grade instructional costs to follow a step pattern. The first step is fixed over the range of 1 to 25 students. The 26th student requires the addition of a second full-time teacher. The third step starts with the 51st student, and so forth.

Step costs are illustrated in Exhibit 3–2(d) by a series of lines drawn parallel to the horizontal axis. Moving to the right, each line steps up to a level higher than the preceding line. The discontinuity that occurs at each increment makes step costs difficult to analyze, to represent by an equation, or to graphically illustrate in a chart depicting the total effect of several different costs. To overcome these problems, step costs are frequently approximated by mixed or fixed costs. The selection of a proxy depends on the range of activity included in each step and the cost difference between steps.

MANAGERIAL PRACTICE 3.3

Categorizing Cost Behavior at General Hospital

After being in existence for over 80 years, General Hospital, a community hospital in Massachusetts, decided to implement a financial planning model. One major phase of the model was the operations module, which required cost centers. Each cost center had to analyze whether its costs were variable, fixed, or mixed. (For example, costs that do not change with activity [anesthesiologist's salary, regardless of number of patients] were called fixed.) Costs also had to be categorized as direct or indirect. The units of service (patient days, meals served, and so on) were multiplied by the average cost of each cost center. Direct fixed costs were added to the accumulated variable costs to provide total direct costs for each cost center for each period. Indirect costs, such as depreciation, were treated as separate cost centers and were included in hospital totals when needed for third-party reimbursements (insurance companies, Medicare, and others).

Source: Susan A. Larracey, "Hospital Planning for Cost-Effectiveness," *Management Accounting* (July 1982): 44–48.

EXHIBIT 3–3   Step Costs Approximated by Mixed and Fixed Costs

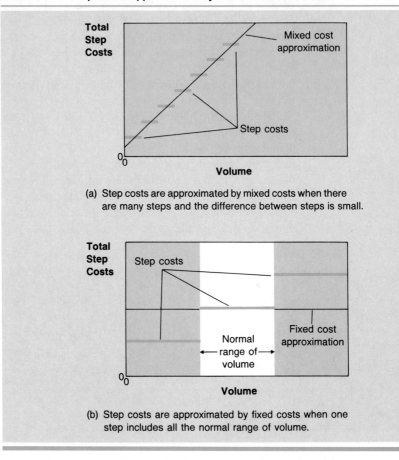

(a) Step costs are approximated by mixed costs when there are many steps and the difference between steps is small.

(b) Step costs are approximated by fixed costs when one step includes all the normal range of volume.

Step costs are approximated by mixed costs when there are many steps and the cost difference between steps is small. The illustration in Exhibit 3–3(a) shows that the mixed cost approximation passes through the midpoint of each step and intersects the vertical axis at one half the height of the first step. The mixed cost approximation is subject to a maximum error of one half the cost difference between steps. The mixed cost approximation may be used if this error is acceptable.

Step costs are approximated by fixed costs when one step includes all the organization's probable range of volume. The illustration in Exhibit 3–3(b) shows that the fixed cost approximation is drawn through the step in the expected range of volume and extended parallel to the horizontal axis. The fixed cost approximation is only valid in the activity range of a single step. Large errors can occur if this approximation is used to predict step costs outside this range. If the difference between steps is large, and one step does not include the expected range of activity, step costs must be analyzed as step costs.

EXHIBIT 3–4   Total Cost Behavior

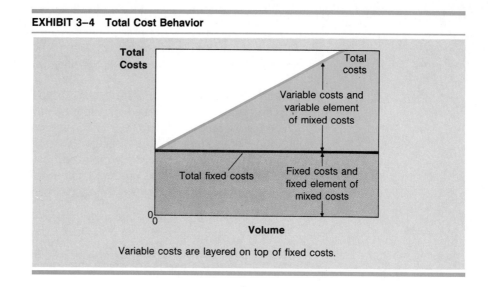

Variable costs are layered on top of fixed costs.

Total Costs for the Organization

An organization's total costs consist of the sum of its variable, fixed, mixed, and step costs. With mixed costs approximating step costs, a behavior pattern for total costs is developed by combining variable, fixed, and mixed costs, as in Exhibit 3–4.

The equation for total costs is

$$\frac{\text{Total}}{\text{costs}} = \frac{\text{Fixed}}{\text{costs}} + \left(\frac{\text{Variable costs}}{\text{per unit}} \times \frac{\text{Unit}}{\text{volume}}\right).$$

In the equation for total costs, fixed costs and the fixed element of mixed costs are both included in the "fixed costs." Likewise, variable costs and the variable cost element of mixed costs are both included in the "variable costs." The equation for total costs corresponds to the general equation for a straight line.

$$Y = a + bX,$$

where Y = the value of the dependent variable,
  a = a constant term,
  b = the slope of the line, and
  X = the value of the independent variable.

To save space we will occasionally use the general equation.

ECONOMIC COST PATTERNS AND THE RELEVANT RANGE

The use of straight lines in accounting models of cost behavior assumes a linear relationship between cost and volume, with each unit of additional volume being accompanied by a uniform increment in total costs. Accountants identify this uniform increment as the variable cost of one unit. The relationship between volume and the variable cost per unit is illustrated in Exhibit 3–5(a). Note that the vertical axis is labeled unit cost rather than total cost. Because the variable cost of each unit is identical, the slope of the unit cost line in Exhibit 3–5(a) is zero.

Economic models show a curvilinear relationship between cost and volume, with each unit of additional volume being accompanied by a varying increment in total cost. Economists identify the varying increment in total cost as the marginal cost of one unit. The relationship between volume and marginal cost is illustrated in Exhibit 3–5(b). At low volumes marginal costs are relatively high. They decline and level off as production becomes more efficient and then start to rise because of the existence of capacity constraints and increases in operating costs.

EXHIBIT 3–5   Incremental Costs in Accounting and Economic Cost Behavior Models

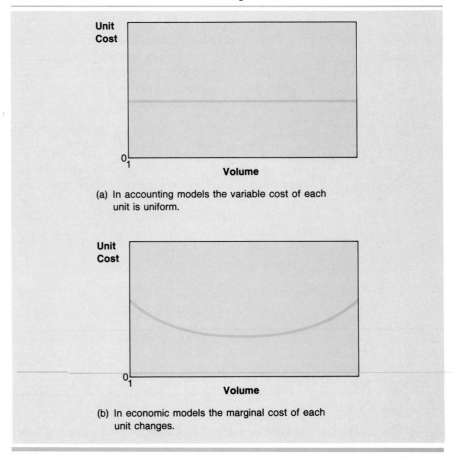

(a) In accounting models the variable cost of each unit is uniform.

(b) In economic models the marginal cost of each unit changes.

The economists' short-run total cost pattern is illustrated in Exhibit 3–6(a). The vertical axis intercept represents capacity costs. Note the influence of marginal costs. The initial slope of the total cost line is quite steep in the range where marginal costs are high. The slope becomes less steep for a while as marginal costs decline and then increases again as marginal costs increase.

The economists' cost behavior patterns certainly sound plausible. The initially high marginal costs might represent a production situation where there is much excess capacity and idle time. Employees complete their assignments at a leisurely pace; indeed, they may try to make work. Marginal costs logically decline and then level off in the optimal range of production for which the plant was designed to operate. Again, we expect marginal costs to rise as capacity limits are reached. Near capacity, older equipment is brought out of retirement, new employees with little or no experience are hired, and experienced employees are paid overtime premiums to work additional hours.

EXHIBIT 3–6   Economic Cost Patterns and the Relevant Range

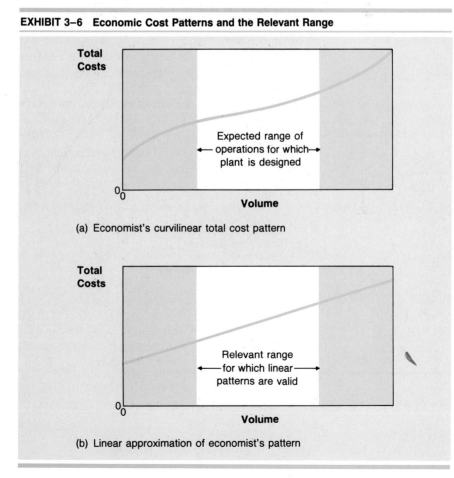

(a) Economist's curvilinear total cost pattern

(b) Linear approximation of economist's pattern

If the economists' total cost pattern is valid, how can we reasonably approximate it with a straight line? The answer to this question is in the notion of a relevant range. A linear pattern may be a poor approximation of the economists' curvilinear pattern over the entire range of possible activity, but a linear pattern is often sufficiently accurate within the range of probable operations. The range of operations within which a linear cost function is a good approximation of the economists' curvilinear cost function is called the relevant range. Linear estimates of cost behavior are only valid within the relevant range. Managers and accountants must exercise extreme care when making statements about cost behavior outside the relevant range, which is illustrated in Exhibit 3–6(b).

AVERAGE COSTS

According to the absorption cost basis of external reporting, all manufacturing costs are product costs that are assigned to the units produced each period. For a single product company, the absorption cost of each unit is an average cost, computed as the cost of goods manufactured divided by the number of units produced. In the absence of beginning or ending inventories of work-in-process, the cost of goods manufactured is the same as the current manufacturing costs, and the average cost per unit is computed as the current manufacturing costs divided by the number of units produced. The following example illustrates the computation of average costs and the effect of volume on this amount.

The Springfield Bean Company manufactures bean bag chairs. The unit variable and monthly fixed production costs are as follows:

	Variable Costs	Fixed Costs
Direct materials	$2.75	
Direct labor	1.50	
Factory overhead	0.75	$3,000
Total	$5.00	$3,000

In the absence of beginning or ending inventories of work-in-process, the equations for the total manufacturing costs per month and the average cost per unit produced during a given month are

$$\text{Total manufacturing costs} = \$3,000 + \$5X,$$

$$\text{Average cost per unit} = (\$3,000 + \$5X)/X$$
$$= \$3,000/X + \$5,$$

where X represents the unit volume.

The total and average production costs at several unit volumes are computed here and illustrated in Exhibit 3–7.

Volume	Total Fixed Costs	Total Variable Costs (Volume × $5)	Total Manufacturing Costs	Average Cost per Unit
100	$3,000	$ 500	$3,500	$35.00
200	3,000	1,000	4,000	20.00
300	3,000	1,500	4,500	15.00
400	3,000	2,000	5,000	12.50
500	3,000	2,500	5,500	11.00

The average cost declines as volume increases because fixed costs are spread over a larger number of units.

If the Springfield Bean Company regularly produced 300 bags per month, the average cost per unit would be $15. Although this cost would be used to value inventory and compute the cost of goods sold in external financial statements, it should not be used for internal planning and control. A manager may be tempted to conclude that the unit cost reported in external financial statements represents the incremental cost of producing one unit. If this cost is $15, the manager might budget production costs for 250 units as $3,750 ($15 × 250) and conclude that production was inefficient if the actual costs of producing 250 units were $4,250. A proper analysis of cost behavior reveals that $4,250 is, in fact, the expected production costs of 250 units:

$$\text{Total costs} = \$3,000 + (\$5 \times 250) = \$4,250.$$

EXHIBIT 3–7   Total and Average Costs

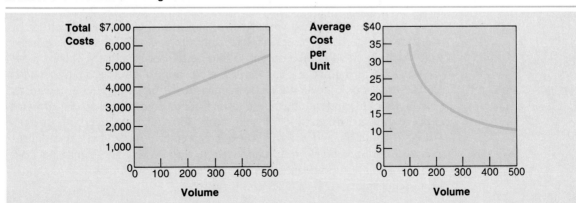

Here we see the significance of different costs for different purposes. Though average costs are widely used for external reporting, total costs should be used for internal planning and control. *Bad decisions can occur if cost information developed for one purpose is incorrectly used for another purpose.*

DETERMINING COST BEHAVIOR

Cost behavior is often determined through an analysis of historical cost data. To properly estimate the relationship between activity and cost, it is necessary (1) to be familiar with basic cost behavior patterns, (2) to understand the characteristics of the accounting data base, and (3) to be knowledgeable of cost estimating techniques. The first part of this chapter introduced important cost behavior patterns. A significant feature of the accounting data base, discussed in Chapter 2, is its orientation to information needed for external reporting. Managers must be very cautious in using these data for internal purposes. As illustrated in the preceding section, average costs presented in financial statements are of limited use in planning and control. To obtain appropriate data, it may be necessary to analyze individual cost elements rather than final cost figures.

MANAGERIAL PRACTICE 3.4

Defining Items for Cost Behavior Analysis?

As part of a development program on productivity measurement, the American Productivity Center defined what types of activities should be included in the major cost categories for most manufacturing companies. (1) All *labor* associated with obtaining the specified output should be treated separately. This includes each manufacturing process and each related support (overhead) process. (2) All *materials* should be identified by manufacturing process as either raw materials or supplies, and all other items as selling or administrative. (3) All items of *energy* (electricity, gas, fuel oil, and so on) should be separated by manufacturing, distribution, and other overhead cost centers. (4) *Capital* expenditures include interest charges, rent, depreciation, and leases. These may be both manufacturing and nonmanufacturing related. (5) *Miscellaneous* items should be all other items, such as taxes and insurance.

Source: Gary N. Brayton, "Productivity Measure Aids in Profit Analysis," *Management Accounting* (January 1985): 54–58.

Estimating Mixed Costs

Costs known to display a variable or a fixed cost pattern are readily estimated by studying the costs of a representative period. Unit variable costs are estimated by dividing total variable costs by unit volume, and fixed costs are estimated by totaling the known fixed costs of the period. It is the mixed costs that cause most cost estimation problems.

Assume the Springfield Bean Company incurred the following production costs in April 19x3 when 4,000 bean bag chairs were produced:

Direct materials		$11,000
Direct labor		6,000
Factory overhead:		
Supervisors' salaries	$1,800	
Depreciation	800	
Utilities and maintenance	3,400	6,000
Total		$23,000

Direct materials and direct labor are known to display variable cost patterns. Assuming April 19x3 is a representative month, the variable costs of direct materials and direct labor are $2.75 and $1.50, respectively:

$$\frac{\text{Variable costs}}{\text{per unit}} = \frac{\text{Total variable costs}}{\text{Unit volume}},$$

$$\frac{\text{Variable cost}}{\text{of direct materials}} = \frac{\$11,000}{4,000}$$

$$= \$2.75,$$

$$\frac{\text{Variable cost}}{\text{of direct labor}} = \frac{\$6,000}{4,000}$$

$$= \$1.50.$$

Assuming supervisors' salaries and depreciation are fixed costs, total fixed costs amount to $2,600:

Supervisors' salaries	$1,800
Depreciation	800
Total	$2,600

Utilities and maintenance are neither wholly variable nor wholly fixed; they are mixed costs that contain fixed and variable cost elements. According to a basic rule of algebra, two equations are needed to determine two unknowns. Following this rule at least two observations are needed to determine the variable and the fixed cost elements of a mixed cost.

High-Low Cost Estimation. The most straightforward approach to determining the variable and fixed elements of mixed costs is to use the **high-low method of cost estimation.** This method utilizes data from two time periods, a representative high volume period and a representative low volume period, to estimate fixed and variable costs. Assuming identical fixed costs in both periods, the difference in total costs between these two periods is due entirely to the difference in total variable costs, and the variable costs per unit are found by dividing the difference in total costs by the difference in activity. The general formula to find variable costs using the high-low method is

$$\frac{\text{Variable costs}}{\text{per unit}} = \frac{\text{Difference in total costs}}{\text{Difference in activity}}.$$

Once the variable costs per unit are determined, the fixed costs, which are identical in both periods, are computed by estimating the total variable costs of either the high or the low volume period and subtracting them from the corresponding total costs:

$$\text{Fixed costs} = \text{Total costs} - \text{Variable costs}.$$

Assume April and May 19x2 are representative high and low volume periods. The mixed costs and production volumes in these months are shown below.

	Utilities and Maintenance	Unit Production
April	$3,400	4,000
May	2,650	3,000

Equations for total mixed costs are

$$\text{April:} \quad \$3,400 = a + b(4,000),$$

$$\text{May:} \quad \$2,650 = a + b(3,000),$$

where a = fixed costs per month, and
b = variable costs per unit (the slope of the mixed cost line).

$$b = \frac{\$3,400 - \$2,650}{4,000 - 3,000}$$

$$= \frac{\$750}{1,000}$$

$$= \$0.75$$

The variable cost element is $0.75 per unit.

The fixed element of Springfield's monthly utilities and maintenance costs is found by substituting the $0.75 for b in *either* the April or May total cost equation:

$$
\begin{aligned}
\text{April:} \quad \$3,400 &= a + \$0.75(4,000) \\
a &= \$3,400 - \$0.75(4,000) \\
&= \$3,400 - \$3,000 \\
&= \$400,
\end{aligned}
$$

or

$$
\begin{aligned}
\text{May:} \quad \$2,650 &= a + \$0.75(3,000) \\
a &= \$2,650 - \$0.75(3,000) \\
&= \$2,650 - \$2,250 \\
&= \$400.
\end{aligned}
$$

The fixed cost is $400 per month. The use of the high-low method to estimate the variable and fixed elements of this mixed cost is illustrated in Exhibit 3–8.

Springfield Bean Company's cost estimating equation for total monthly production costs is determined by adding together the total cost equations for variable and fixed costs.

	Fixed Costs		Variable Costs
Direct materials			$2.75X
Direct labor			1.50X
Factory overhead:			
Supervisors' salaries	$1,800		
Depreciation	800		
Utilities and maintenance	400		0.75X
Total costs =	$3,000	+	$5.00X

This cost estimating equation can be used to predict total production costs in a subsequent period. If July 19x2 production is budgeted at 3,800 units, the budgeted production costs are $22,000:

$$\$3,000 + \$5.00(3,800) = \$22,000.$$

If detailed cost information is not available, the high-low method can be applied to total cost data. Similar results are obtained because the total costs consist of fixed and variable cost elements.

In using the high-low method, *it is very important to select high and low volumes representative of normal operating conditions.* As illustrated in Exhibit 3–9, the periods of highest and lowest activity may not be representative of normal operating conditions. Even within the usual range of activity, the results

EXHIBIT 3–8   High-Low Cost Estimation

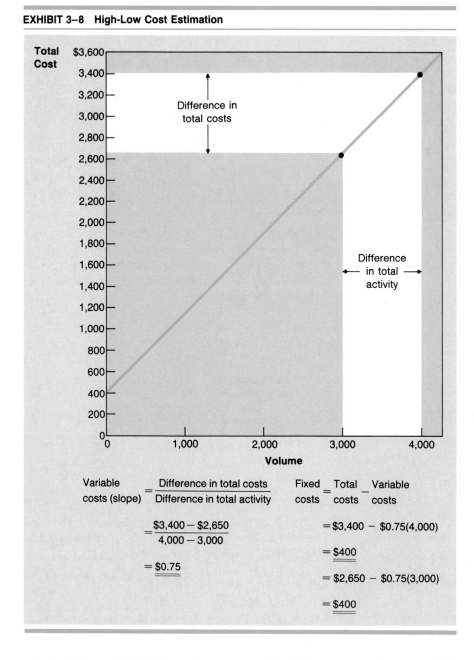

$$\frac{\text{Variable}}{\text{costs (slope)}} = \frac{\text{Difference in total costs}}{\text{Difference in total activity}} \qquad \frac{\text{Fixed}}{\text{costs}} = \frac{\text{Total}}{\text{costs}} - \frac{\text{Variable}}{\text{costs}}$$

$$= \frac{\$3,400 - \$2,650}{4,000 - 3,000} \qquad\qquad = \$3,400 - \$0.75(4,000)$$

$$\qquad\qquad\qquad\qquad = \$400$$

$$= \$0.75 \qquad\qquad\qquad = \$2,650 - \$0.75(3,000)$$

$$\qquad\qquad\qquad\qquad = \$400$$

of a particular period might not be representative if there was a strike, a materials shortage, a severe storm, or some other abnormal event. Because management is interested in predicting cost behavior under normal operating conditions, cost estimating equations should be developed from data reflecting normal

EXHIBIT 3–9   Selecting Representative High and Low Volumes

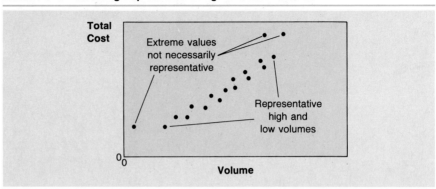

operating conditions. Professional judgment is required to select the appropriate data.

Scatter Diagrams. A scatter diagram is a graph of past volume and cost data, with individual observations represented by dots. Plotting historical volume and cost data on a scatter diagram is a useful approach to cost estimation, especially when used in conjunction with other cost estimating techniques such as the high-low method. The scatter diagram in Exhibit 3–9 would help identify representative high and low volumes. A scatter diagram is also useful in determining if costs can be reasonably approximated by a straight line.

Scatter diagrams are sometimes used alone as a basis of cost estimation. This requires the use of professional judgment to draw a representative straight line through the plot of historical data. Typically, the analyst tries to ensure that an equal number of observations are on either side of the line. Once a line is drawn, cost estimates at any representative volume are made by studying the line. Alternatively, an equation for the line may be developed by applying the high-low method to any two points on the line.

Exhibit 3–10(b) illustrates the use of the scatter diagram method to estimate the Springfield Bean Company's total production costs. The specific values of each observation are presented in Exhibit 3–10(a). Studying this line, the estimated production costs at 3,000 units are approximately $18,000.

Least-Squares Method. The least-squares method of developing a cost estimating equation is conceptually similar to the scatter diagram method. However, the least-squares method uses a mathematical criterion, rather than professional judgment, to develop a cost estimating equation. The mathematical criterion is to fit a straight line to the observed data in a manner that minimizes the sum of the squared vertical differences between the observations and the line. The least-squares criterion is illustrated in Exhibit 3–11.

EXHIBIT 3–10   Use of Scatter Diagram in Cost Estimation

Observation	Unit Volume	Total Production Costs
1	4,000	$23,000
2	3,000	18,000
3	2,400	16,000
4	4,400	24,000
5	2,000	11,000
6	3,600	23,000
7	2,200	15,000

(a) Data

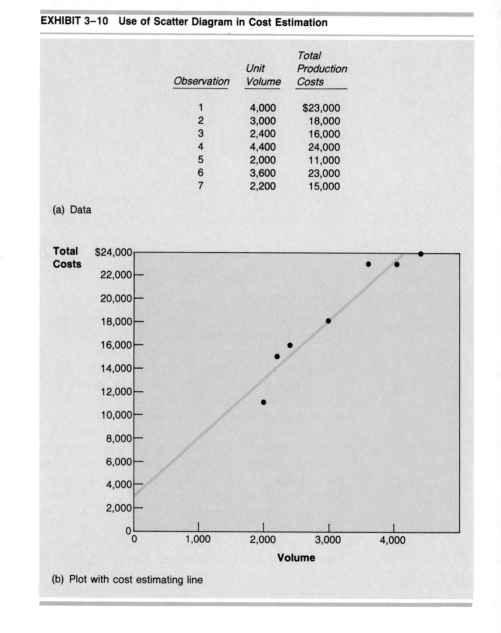

(b) Plot with cost estimating line

The observations plotted in Exhibit 3–11 are the same as in Exhibit 3–10. The line drawn through the data is based on an equation developed using the least-squares method. The deviations are measured as the differences between the estimated cost and the actual cost at each observation.

Many managers and management accountants believe the least-squares method is superior to the high-low and the scatter diagram methods of cost

EXHIBIT 3–11   Least-Squares Criterion

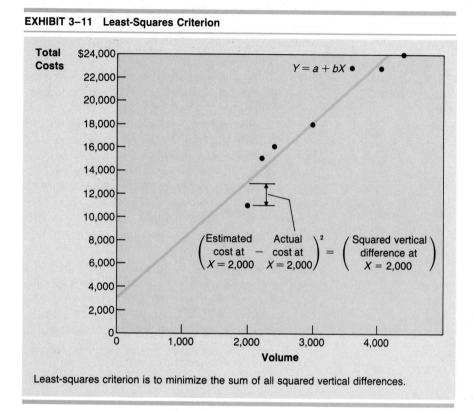

Least-squares criterion is to minimize the sum of all squared vertical differences.

estimation. The least-squares method can use all available data, rather than just two observations, as does the high-low method. Its use of a mathematical criterion provides an objective approach to cost estimation, rather than the subjective approach involved in visually fitting a line through a scatter diagram. Most significant, the least-squares method can provide information on how good the cost estimating equation fits the historical cost data and information needed to construct probability intervals for cost estimates.

The computations required to estimate fixed and variable costs using the least-squares method are illustrated in Appendix A of this chapter. Until recent years these computations were regarded as too complex for practical application. Today there is little need to perform them manually. Computers of all sizes and many hand calculators have programs available to perform least-squares calculations. Users need only provide paired observations of volume and cost.

With computational ease has come widespread application and an increased danger of inappropriate use. The analyst should not merely feed raw data into a computer and accept the output as truth. He or she must always be prepared to exercise professional judgment and evaluate the reasonableness of the least-squares approach, the solution, and the data. If the analyst's objective is to predict future costs expected under normal operating conditions, observations reflecting abnormal operating conditions should be deleted. The analyst should also verify that the cost behavior pattern is linear. Scatter diagrams assist in both of these judgmental activities.

Selecting the Independent Variable

The objective of cost behavior analysis is to determine how cost (the dependent variable) responds to changes in volume (the independent variable). The most appropriate measure of volume depends on the cost being studied. The measure of volume should have a logical relationship to the cost being studied, and it should be easy to measure. The sales volume of a department store in Miami, Florida, is logically related to the number of persons who enter the store; the store's sales are not logically related to the number of fish in a New England pond. Although the factory overhead of a furniture manufacturer may be mathematically related to the amount of sawdust swept from the factory floor, sawdust is a bad basis for estimating overhead because of measurement difficulties and because residual items do not have a causal influence on the incurrence of overhead.

Care must also be taken to ensure that the independent and dependent variables are properly matched within each observation. In merchandising organizations, goods are purchased before they are sold. Though the cost of goods sold is matched with sales within each observation, the cost of purchases is matched with sales only when goods are purchased and sold in the same period. In manufacturing organizations, raw materials are purchased before they are used in production, and finished goods are produced before they are sold. Though the cost of goods sold is matched with sales within each observation, the current manufacturing costs are matched with sales only when goods are produced and sold in the same period. If production and sales differ, production volume rather than sales volume should be used as the independent variable in an analysis of manufacturing costs. In an analogous manner, if the purchases and use of raw materials differ, the volume of purchases rather than the volume of production should be used as the independent variable in an analysis of purchasing costs.

In selecting an independent variable for cost behavior analysis, it is important to determine the activity that causes the incurrence of the cost being analyzed. Professional judgment is very important in selecting an activity measure for a particular cost. Statistical measures, such as the correlation coefficient, are often used to assist in this effort. However, an activity measure should not be selected solely on the basis of a high past correlation with cost. A high correlation between two variables does not prove that one causes the other. Changes in both variables may be caused by a third variable, or the correlation between the two variables may be a chance event that will not recur. Factory overhead and sawdust may be correlated in a furniture plant, but unless sawdust is a major product of the plant it should not be treated as an independent variable. Both factory overhead and sawdust are caused by a third variable, the production of furniture. The correlation coefficient is discussed further in Appendix B of this chapter.

THE IMPACT OF CHANGING PRICES AND TECHNOLOGY

Cost estimation is the determination of previous or current relationships between cost and activity. Historical data from the accounting data base are used in cost estimation. Cost prediction is the forecasting of future relationships between cost and activity and is a frequent purpose of cost estimation. As a starting point in the prediction of future costs, managers study cost behavior by analyzing historical cost data.

Cost estimation and cost prediction are made difficult by changes in technology and prices. If an automobile manufacturer changes from skilled labor to computer controlled assembly procedures, the past data are of little or no value in predicting future costs. Only data accumulated subsequent to the initiation of the new assembly technique are useful in predicting the cost of robot assembly.

If prices have remained stable in the past but then uniformly increase by 20 percent, cost estimating equations developed for previous periods will underpredict future costs. In this example all that is required is a 20 percent increase in the prediction.

Unfortunately, adjustments for price changes are seldom this simple. The prices of various cost elements are likely to change at different rates and at different times. Furthermore, there are apt to be several different price levels included in the past data used to develop cost estimating equations. During periods of changing prices only data reflecting a single price level should be used in cost estimation and cost prediction. The analyst should always be suspicious of old data. If data from different price levels are used, an attempt should be made to restate the data to a single price level.

One response to the cost prediction problems resulting from changing prices is to use something other than cost as the dependent variable. It is, for example, possible to substitute direct labor hours for direct labor dollars and kilowatt hours for the cost of electricity. In terms of kilowatt hours, the monthly use of electricity might be stated as

$$\text{Total kilowatt hours} = 20{,}000 + 50X,$$

where X = unit volume.

If X is budgeted at 5,000 units, the total use of electricity is predicted to be 270,000 [20,000 + (50 × 5,000)] kilowatt hours. If the current cost of electricity is 12 cents per kilowatt hour, this translates into an electric bill of $32,400 ($0.12 × 270,000).

A disadvantage of this approach is that it must be implemented on a very disaggregated basis. Data for labor costs and electric costs can be added together and analyzed in total. Because labor hours and kilowatt hours cannot be added, they must be analyzed separately before totaling the final cost predictions for each cost element.

SUMMARY

Activities undertaken to achieve an organization's objectives result in the incurrence of costs. Because economic resources are limited, the costs that result from activity also limit activity. Consequently, managers must plan and control both costs and activities. To plan and control costs, managers must know how costs respond to changes in activity.

Managers must be familiar with variable, fixed, mixed, and step costs. A variable cost is the uniform incremental cost of each additional unit. Total variable costs change in direct proportion to changes in volume. A fixed cost does not respond to changes in the volume of activity within a given period. Total fixed costs are a constant amount regardless of the level of activity. Mixed costs contain a fixed and a variable cost element, they are positive when volume is zero, and they increase in a linear fashion as volume increases. Step costs are constant within a range of activity but different between ranges of activity. Total step costs increase in a steplike fashion as volume increases.

The cost behavior of a particular activity is often determined through an analysis of historical cost data. Three techniques used to develop an equation for total cost behavior are the high-low method, the scatter diagram method, and the least-squares method. The high-low method uses data from a representative high volume period and a representative low volume period. The scatter diagram method requires the use of professional judgment to draw a representative straight line through a plot of historical data. The least-squares method fits a straight line to the observed data in a manner that minimizes the sum of the squared deviations between individual observations and the line.

Regardless of the cost estimating technique used, the development of a cost estimating equation should be guided by professional judgment. The analyst must be familiar with the characteristics of the accounting data base, the data must display a linear trend within the relevant range, and observations reflecting abnormal operating conditions should be deleted from the analysis. Particular care should be taken to ensure that the data base reflects constant technology and a single price level. Even when proper precautions are taken, cost predictions are only valid within the relevant range and for the current technology and price level.

APPENDIX A
LEAST-SQUARES COST ESTIMATION

The equation for a straight line is

$$Y = a + bX,$$

where Y = the value of the dependent variable,
a = a constant term,
b = the slope of the line, and
X = the value of the independent variable.

The objective of least-squares cost estimation is to fit this equation to obser-vations of X and Y in a manner that minimizes the sum of the squared differences between the actual and estimated values of Y. Mathematicians have proved that the appropriate values of a and b can be found by the simultaneous solution of the following equations:

$$\sum XY = a \sum X + b \sum X^2, \qquad (3\text{--}1)$$

$$\sum Y = an + b \sum X, \qquad (3\text{--}2)$$

where Σ is a capital sigma, meaning "the sum of" (i.e., ΣXY means the sum of the products of X and Y) and

n = the number of observations.

The above equations, called the **normal equations,** are used to compute the constant term and the slope that best meets the least-squares criterion.

The computations required to apply the normal equations to the data in Exhibit 3–10(a) are shown below.

Observation	Unit Volume X	Total Costs Y	XY	X²
1	4,000	$ 23,000	92,000,000	16,000,000
2	3,000	18,000	54,000,000	9,000,000
3	2,400	16,000	38,400,000	5,760,000
4	4,400	24,000	105,600,000	19,360,000
5	2,000	11,000	22,000,000	4,000,000
6	3,600	23,000	82,800,000	12,960,000
7	2,200	15,000	33,000,000	4,840,000
	21,600	$130,000	427,800,000	71,920,000

Substituting these values into the normal equations we obtain

$$427{,}800{,}000 = a21{,}600 + b71{,}920{,}000, \qquad (3\text{--}3)$$

$$130{,}000 = a7 + b21{,}600. \qquad (3\text{--}4)$$

We can solve for b by eliminating a from an equation for the difference between Eqs. (3–3) and (3–4). To do this, we must have the same coefficient for a in each equation. This can be accomplished in a number of ways. We will multiply Eq. (3–3) by 7 and Eq. (3–4) by 21,600. Doing this we obtain

$$2{,}994{,}600{,}000 = 151{,}200a + 503{,}440{,}000b \qquad (3\text{--}5)$$

$$2{,}808{,}000{,}000 = 151{,}200a + 466{,}560{,}000b \qquad (3\text{--}6)$$

$$186{,}600{,}000 = \qquad\qquad 36{,}880{,}000b \qquad (3\text{--}7)$$

Equation (3–7) is the difference between Eqs. (3–5) and (3–6). Solving Eq. (3–7) for b, we obtain

$$b = \frac{186,600,000}{36,880,000} = 5.06 \quad \text{(rounded)}.$$

We can solve for a by substituting the value of b in any equation containing a. Doing this in Eq. (3–4), we obtain

$$7a = 130,000 - (5.06)(21,600)$$
$$7a = 20,704$$
$$a = 20,704/7 = 2,958 \quad \text{(rounded)}.$$

The resulting cost estimating equation is

$$\text{Total costs} = \$2,958 + \$5.06X.$$

Computations involving large numbers are often simplified by expressing the numbers in thousands. In thousands, the unit volume and total cost of observation 1 are 4 and $23, respectively. The value of XY then becomes 92, and the value of X^2 becomes 16. Restating all seven observations into thousands and solving for a and b, we obtain $2.958 and $5.06. The slope of the line (value of b) is not affected when all data are expressed in thousands. However, the vertical axis intercept (value of a) is $2.958 thousand, that is, $2,958, not $2.958.

In addition to the constant term and the slope, the correlation coefficient, the coefficient of determination, and the standard error of the estimate are often computed when the least-squares method is used. The **correlation coefficient,** a standardized measure of the degree to which two variables move together, is discussed in Appendix B of this chapter. The **coefficient of determination** is a measure of the percent of variation in the dependent variable that is explained by the cost estimating equation; it indicates how good the equation fits the historical data. The **standard error of the estimate** is a measure of the variability of actual costs around the cost estimating equation; it is used to construct probability intervals for cost estimates. Readers interested in studying this further should consult a basic statistics or cost accounting book.

APPENDIX B
THE CORRELATION COEFFICIENT

The **correlation coefficient** is a standardized measure of the degree to which two variables move together and can take on values between -1 and $+1$. Negative correlation implies that the two variables move in opposite directions; as one increases the other decreases. Positive correlation implies that the two variables move in the same direction; as one increases the other also increases. A correlation coefficient of zero implies that the movement of the two variables is unrelated.

When two variables that are logically related have a high correlation, knowledge of a change in one variable is useful in predicting a change in the other. Management accountants use the correlation coefficient to assist in selecting the best basis for overhead application and for cost estimation. In the selection process the management accountant is usually looking for the basis of activity measurement that has the highest correlation with total costs.

Assume we are trying to determine the best basis for applying overhead to products. We selected four possible bases and calculated their past correlation with total overhead.

Basis	Correlation with Total Overhead
Direct labor hours	0.752
Direct labor dollars	0.885
Machine hours	0.630
Number of employee coffee breaks	−0.100

We would select direct labor dollars as the basis of overhead application; it has the highest correlation with total overhead. Note that the number of employee coffee breaks had a small negative correlation with total overhead. This indicates a slight tendency for total overhead to decrease as the number of employee coffee breaks increases. This may be due to such factors as reduced power consumption by machines while employees are away on breaks.

The basis selected to apply overhead must also be logical and easy to implement. Direct labor dollars has a logical relationship to overhead and, in most organizations, it is easy to relate direct labor dollars to individual products. Even if the number of employee coffee breaks had the highest positive correlation with total overhead, we would not use it as a basis for overhead application. A large positive relationship between these variables does not seem logical. And it would be difficult to relate employee coffee breaks to individual products.

Mathematicians have developed the following equation to compute the correlation coefficient:

$$r = \frac{\Sigma(X - \bar{X})(Y - \bar{Y})}{\sqrt{\Sigma(X - \bar{X})^2 \ \Sigma(Y - \bar{Y})^2}} ,$$

where

r = the correlation coefficient

$\bar{X}$ = the average value of the independent variable, computed as ΣX divided by n

$\bar{Y}$ = the average value of the dependent variable, computed as ΣY divided by n

$\Sigma(X - \bar{X})(Y - \bar{Y})$ = the sum of each difference between individual values of X and $\bar{X}$ multiplied by the corresponding difference between individual values of Y and $\bar{Y}$

$\Sigma(X - \bar{X})^2$ = the sum of the squared differences between X and $\bar{X}$ and

$\Sigma(Y - \bar{Y})^2$ = the sum of the squared differences between Y and $\bar{Y}$.

EXHIBIT 3–12 Computation of the Correlation Coefficient

Observation	X	$(X - \bar{X})$	$(X - \bar{X})^2$	Y	$(Y - \bar{Y})$	$(Y - \bar{Y})^2$	$(X - \bar{X})(Y - \bar{Y})$
1	4,000	914	835,396	$23,000	4,429	19,616,041	4,048,106
2	3,000	−86	7,396	18,000	−571	326,041	49,106
3	2,400	−686	470,596	16,000	−2,571	6,610,041	1,763,706
4	4,400	1,314	1,726,596	24,000	5,429	29,474,041	7,133,706
5	2,000	−1,086	1,179,396	11,000	−7,571	57,320,041	8,222,106
6	3,600	514	264,196	23,000	4,429	19,616,041	2,276,506
7	2,200	−886	784,996	15,000	−3,571	12,752,041	3,163,906
			5,268,572			145,714,287	26,657,142

$$r = \frac{26,657,142}{\sqrt{(5,268,572)(145,714,287)}} = 0.962$$

The average unit volume, $\bar{X}$, and the average total production cost, $\bar{Y}$, for the data in Exhibit 3–10(a) are 3,086 and $18,571, respectively.

$$\bar{X} = (4,000 + 3,000 + 2,400 + 4,400 + 2,000 + 3,600 + 2,200)/7$$
$$= 3,086 \quad \text{(rounded)}$$

$$\bar{Y} = (\$23,000 + \$18,000 + \$16,000 + \$24,000 + \$11,000 + \$23,000 + \$15,000)/7$$
$$= \$18,571 \quad \text{(rounded)}$$

The computation of the correlation coefficient between unit volume and total production costs is presented in Exhibit 3–12. The correlation coefficient of 0.962 indicates a high positive relationship between these two variables. An increase in unit volume has a high statistical correlation with an increase in total production costs. It appears that unit volume is a good basis for estimating total production costs.

REVIEW PROBLEM

Estimating Cost Behavior and Predicting Future Costs

Dan's Submarine Sandwich Shop reported the following results for April and May 19x2.

	April	May
Unit sales	2,100	2,700
Cost of food sold	$1,575	$2,025
Wages and salaries	1,525	1,675
Rent on building	1,500	1,500
Depreciation on equipment	200	200
Utilities	710	770
Supplies	225	255
Miscellaneous	113	131
Total	$5,848	$6,556

Requirements

a) Identify each cost as being variable, fixed, or mixed.

b) Develop a schedule identifying the amount of each cost that is fixed per month or variable per unit. Total the amounts in each category to develop a cost estimating equation for total monthly costs.

c) Predict total and average costs for monthly volumes of 1,000 units and 2,000 units.

d) Explain why the average costs differ at these two volumes.

The solution to this problem is found at the end of the Chapter 3 exercises and problems.

KEY TERMS

Capacity cost
Committed fixed cost
Cost behavior analysis
Cost estimation
Cost prediction
Discretionary fixed cost
Fixed cost
High-low method of cost estimation
Least-squares method of cost estimation

Managed fixed cost
Marginal cost
Mixed cost
Relevant range
Scatter diagram
Semivariable cost
Step cost
Variable cost

APPENDIX KEY TERMS

Coefficient of determination
Correlation coefficient

Normal equations
Standard error of the estimate

REVIEW QUESTIONS

3–1 In cost behavior analysis, what is the relationship between the cost and the volume of an activity?

3–2 How do you compute the slope of a straight line?

3–3 Briefly describe four widely used total cost behavior patterns.

3–4 What long-run trade-offs are there between fixed and variable costs?

3–5 Under what circumstances are step costs approximated by mixed costs? By fixed costs?

3–6 In what range of activity is a straight line often a reasonable approximation of the economist's short-run total cost pattern?

3–7 Why do average unit costs decline as volume increases?

3–8 Average inventory costs are widely used for what purpose? Give an example of a purpose they should not be used for.

3–9 What minimum number of observations of past data are necessary to estimate the fixed and variable elements of mixed costs?

3–10 Why should we use data reflecting normal operating conditions as a basis for developing cost estimating equations?

3–11 Name two reasons why scatter diagrams are used in conjunction with the high-low and least-squares methods of cost estimation.

3–12 What is the least-squares criterion?

3–13 Why might current unit sales not be a good activity measure for the cost of current purchases in a manufacturing organization?

3–14 Distinguish between cost estimation and cost prediction on the basis of their time orientation.

3–15 Name two dynamic factors which limit the usefulness of historical cost data in cost prediction.

EXERCISES

3–1 Classifying Cost Behavior

Classify the total costs of each of the following as variable, fixed, mixed, or step.

a) Pulpwood in a paper mill.

b) Salaries of two supervisors.

c) Real estate taxes.

d) Direct labor.

e) Salaries of quality inspectors.

f) Electric power in a factory.

g) Raw materials used in production.

h) Automobiles rented on the basis of a fixed charge per day plus an additional charge per mile driven.

i) Sales commissions.

j) Depreciation on office equipment.

3–2 Classifying Cost Behavior

Classify the total costs of each of the following as variable, fixed, mixed, or step.

a) Maintenance costs at a college.

b) Property taxes on a building.

c) Rent on a photocopy machine charged as a fixed amount per month plus an additional charge per copy.

d) Cost of goods sold in a bookstore.

e) Salaries paid temporary instructors in a college as the number of sections offered of a course varies.

f) Lumber used by a house construction company.

g) The costs of operating a research department.

h) The cost of hiring a dance band for three hours.

i) Typing paper used in a steno pool.

j) Electric power in a restaurant.

3–3 Classifying Cost Behavior

For each situation, select the most appropriate cost behavior pattern. Lines represent the cost behavior pattern. The vertical axis represents total costs. The horizontal axis represents total volume. Dots represent actual costs. Each pattern may be used more than once.

Pattern

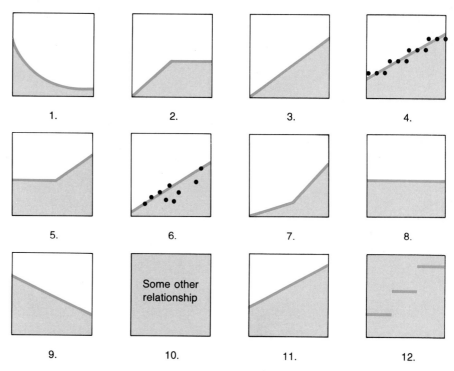

1.   2.   3.   4.

5.   6.   7.   8.

9.   10. Some other relationship   11.   12.

Situation

a) Variable costs per unit.

b) Total mixed costs.

c) Total fixed costs.

d) Average fixed costs per unit.

e) Total current manufacturing costs.

f) High-low cost estimation influenced by unusual observations.

g) Employees are paid $10 per hour for the first forty hours worked each week and $15 per each additional hour.

h) Employees are paid $10 per hour and guaranteed a minimum weekly wage of $200.

i) A consultant is paid $50 per hour with a maximum fee of $1,000.

j) Total variable costs.

k) Salaries of social workers where each social worker can handle a maximum of 20 cases.

l) A water bill where a flat fee of $800 is charged for the first 100,000 gallons and additional water costs $0.005 per gallon.

m) Variable costs properly used to estimate step costs.

n) Total direct materials costs.

o) Rent on exhibit space at a convention.

3–4 Classifying Cost Behavior

For each situation, select the most appropriate cost behavior pattern. Lines represent the cost behavior pattern. The vertical axis represents total costs. The horizontal axis represents total volume. Dots represent actual costs. Each pattern may be used more than once.

Pattern

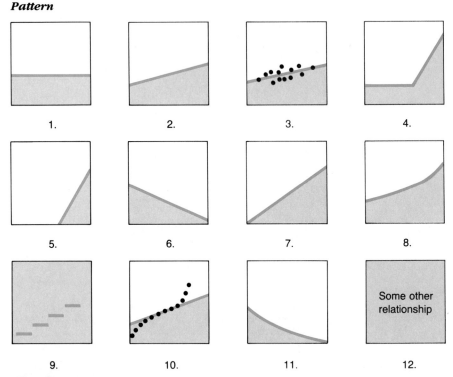

1.   2.   3.   4.

5.   6.   7.   8.

9.   10.   11.   12. Some other relationship

Situation

a) A telephone bill where a flat fee is charged for the first twenty calls per month and additional calls cost $0.25 each.

b) Total selling and administrative costs.

c) Total direct labor costs.

d) Total overtime premium paid production employees.

e) Average total cost per unit.

f) Salaries of supervisors when each can supervise a maximum of ten employees.

g) Total idle time costs when employees are paid for a minimum forty-hour week.

h) Direct materials costs per unit.

i) High-low method properly used to estimate cost behavior.

j) Electric power consumption in a restaurant.

k) Total costs when high volumes of production require the use of overtime and obsolete equipment.

l) Total sales commissions.

m) A linear cost estimation valid only within the relevant range.

n) Average variable costs per unit.

o) Once the capacity of a plant that has only fixed costs is reached, additional parts are purchased from outside vendors.

3–5 High-Low Cost Estimation

Jack's Taxi Company has the following information available about fleet miles and operating costs.

Year	Miles	Operating Costs
19x3	556,000	$115,060
19x4	684,000	132,340

Required: Use the high-low method to develop a cost estimating equation for annual operating costs.

3–6 High-Low Cost Estimation

An examination of monthly maintenance costs and direct labor hours reveals the following:

	Highest	Lowest
Maintenance	$64,000	$40,800
Direct labor hours	13,000	7,200

Required: Use the high-low method to develop a cost estimating equation for monthly maintenance costs.

3–7 High-Low Cost Estimation

Jackson, Inc., is preparing a budget for 19x1 and requires a breakdown of the cost of steam used in its factory into the fixed and variable elements. The following data on the cost of steam used and direct labor hours worked are available for the last six months of 19x0:

Month	Cost of Steam	Direct Labor Hours
July	$ 15,850	3,000
August	13,400	2,050
September	16,370	2,900
October	19,800	3,650
November	17,600	2,670
December	18,500	2,650
Total	$101,520	16,920

Required: Use the high-low method to develop an equation for the monthly cost of steam.

(CPA Adapted)

3–8 High-Low Cost Estimation and Predetermined Overhead Rates

Presented is information on 19x7 and 19x8 factory overhead and direct labor hours:

	19x7	19x8
Factory overhead	$156,000	$187,400
Direct labor hours	55,500	71,200

Management predicts that 60,000 direct labor hours will be used in 19x9.

Required: Determine the 19x9 predetermined overhead rate per direct labor hour.

3–9 High-Low Cost Estimation and Predetermined Overhead Rates

Tastee-Treat Company prepares, packages, and distributes six frozen vegetables. The different vegetables are prepared in large batches. Manufacturing overhead is assigned to batches by a predetermined rate on the basis of direct labor hours. The manufacturing overhead costs incurred by the company during two recent years are presented below.

	19x2	19x3
Direct labor hours worked	2,760,000	2,160,000
Manufacturing overhead costs incurred (adjusted for changes in current prices and wage rates)		
Indirect labor	$11,040,000	$ 8,640,000
Employee benefits	4,140,000	3,240,000
Supplies	2,760,000	2,160,000
Power	2,208,000	1,728,000
Heat and light	552,000	552,000
Supervision	2,865,000	2,625,000
Depreciation	7,930,000	7,930,000
Property taxes and insurance	3,005,000	3,005,000
Total overhead costs	$34,500,000	$29,880,000

Required: Tastee-Treat Company expects to operate at a 2,300,000 direct labor hour level of activity in 19x4. Using the data from two recent years, calculate the rate Tastee-Treat should employ to assign manufacturing overhead to its products during 19x4.

(CMA Adapted)

3–10 Scatter Diagrams and High-Low Cost Estimation

Presented are monthly production and cost data.

Month	Volume	Total Cost
1	3,000	$40,000
2	1,500	28,000
3	4,000	65,000
4	2,800	39,000
5	2,300	32,000
6	1,000	20,000
7	2,000	30,000

Requirements

a) Using information from the high and low volume months, develop a cost estimating equation for monthly production costs.

b) Plot the data on a scatter diagram. Using information from *representative* high and low volume months, develop a cost estimating equation for monthly production costs.

c) What factors might cause the difference in the equations developed in requirements (a) and (b)?

3–11 Scatter Diagrams and High-Low Cost Estimation

From April 1 through October 31 the Central County Highway Department hires temporary employees to mow and clean the right-of-way along county roads. A county road commissioner has asked you to assist her in determining the variable labor cost of mowing and cleaning a mile of road. The following information is available regarding 19x5 operations.

Month	Miles Mowed and Cleaned	Labor Cost
April	350	$7,500
May	300	7,000
June	400	8,500
July	250	5,000
August	375	8,000
September	200	4,500
October	100	4,300

Requirements

a) Using information from the high and low volume months, develop a cost estimating equation for monthly labor costs.

b) Plot the information on a scatter diagram. Using information from *representative* high and low volume months, develop a cost estimating equation for monthly labor costs.

c) What factors might cause the difference in the equations developed in requirements (a) and (b)?

d) Adjust the equation developed in requirement (b) to incorporate the effect of a 7 percent increase in wages.

3–12 Computing Average Unit Costs

The total monthly operating costs of Del Rio Chili To Go are

$$\$10,000 + \$0.30X,$$

where X = servings of chili.

Requirements

a) Determine the average cost per serving at each of the following monthly volumes: 10, 100, 200, 400, 800.

b) Determine the monthly volume at which the average cost per serving is $0.50.

3–13 Computing Average Unit Costs: Review of Relevant Costs

The local chapter of a professional organization is organizing a one-day continuing education program. Program costs are as follows:

Advertising	$1,000 per program
Instructor's fee	600 per program
Room rental and set-up	200 per program
Instructional materials	20 per participant
Lunch and coffee breaks	15 per participant

Requirements

a) Develop an equation for total program costs.

b) Determine the average cost per participant at each of the following volumes: 10, 20, 30, 50.

c) Determine the volume at which the average cost per participant is $50.

d) The program is scheduled for October 1, 19x4. The budgeted advertising expenditures are made on September 1, and a $100 nonrefundable deposit for the room rental and set-up is made on September 15. All other costs, except the instructor's fee, are payable at the start of the program. The instructor's fee is payable at the end of the program.

One week before the scheduled date of the program, the chapter's director of continuing education becomes concerned about a lack of preregistered participants and considers whether or not to cancel the program. Identify the sunk and relevant costs for this decision, and develop a cost estimating equation that contains only relevant costs.

3–14 Developing an Equation from Average Costs

The average unit cost at a volume of 4,000 units is $2.00, and the average unit cost at a volume of 10,000 units is $1.25.

Required: Develop an estimating equation for total cost.

3–15 Developing an Equation from Average Costs

The Dog House is a pet hotel located on the outskirts of town. In March, when dog (occupancy) days were at an annual low of 500, the average cost per dog day was $18.50. In July, when dog days were at a capacity level of 3,100, the average cost per dog day was $5.50.

Requirements

a) Develop an equation for *monthly* operating costs.

b) Determine the average cost per dog day at an *annual* volume of 24,000 dog days.

3–16 Mixed Cost Approximation of Step Costs

The Civic Center has asked you to develop a cost estimating equation for ticket takers. Ticket takers are on duty for a one-hour period starting 45 minutes before a performance is scheduled to begin. Ticket takers are paid $8 per hour, and each ticket taker can collect a maximum of 1,000 tickets per hour.

Requirements

a) The labor cost of ticket takers is a step function with each step being 1,000 tickets collected. Develop a mixed cost approximation of the cost of taking tickets.

b) Use the equation developed in requirement (a) to estimate the labor cost of collecting 10,000 and 10,001 tickets. What is the dollar amount of the error with this approximation?

3–17 Mixed Cost Approximation of Step Costs

Quality Aviation manufactures guidance systems for single-engine aircraft. To ensure a high level of conformance between the performance of each unit and product specifications, Quality Aviation recently instituted a program management called "Total Quality Assurance." As part of this program, all purchased parts are inspected when they are received, and additional inspections are performed at various points during manufacturing, as well as before finished goods are approved for shipment.

Given the intensive and extensive nature of the inspection program, management has determined that one inspector is needed for each 100 guidance systems produced per week. Inspectors are paid at the rate of $15 per hour for a forty-hour week. The union contract specified they will be paid for forty hours even if they work fewer than forty hours.

Requirements

a) Develop a mixed cost approximation of the weekly cost of inspecting aircraft guidance systems.

b) Use the equation developed in requirement (a) to estimate the cost of inspecting 500 and 501 guidance systems per week. What is the dollar amount of the error with this approximation?

c) Assuming inspectors are paid a 50 percent overtime premium, how should management respond when production temporarily increases from 480 to 510 units per week?

3–18 Automatic Versus Manual Processing

The Fast Photo Company operates a 60-minute film development and print service. The current service, which relies extensively on manual operations, has monthly operating costs of $5,000 plus $2 per roll of film developed and printed. Management is evaluating the desirability of acquiring a machine that will automatically develop film and make prints. If the machine is acquired, the monthly fixed costs of the service will increase to $23,000, and the variable costs of developing and printing a roll of film will decline to $1.40.

Requirements

a) Determine the total costs of developing and printing 20,000 and 50,000 rolls per month:

With the current process.
With the automatic process.

b) Determine the monthly volume at which the total operating costs of both processes are identical.

3–19 Automatic Versus Manual Processing

The Kopy Tat Photocopy Service processes 1,000,000 photocopies per month at its midtown service center. Approximately 60 percent of the photocopies, 600,000 per month, require collating. Collating is currently performed by high school and college students who are paid $4.00 per hour. Each student collates an average of 5,000 copies per hour.

Management is contemplating the lease of an automatic collating machine that has a monthly capacity of 5,000,000 photocopies with operating costs of $795 plus $0.05 per 1,000 units collated.

Requirements

a) Determine the total costs of collating 500,000 and 1,500,000 copies per month:
With the student help.
With the collating machine.

b) Determine the monthly volume of collating at which the total operating costs of both processes are equal.

c) Should Kopy Tat acquire the automatic collating machine at this time?

PROBLEMS

3-20 Cost Behavior Analysis with Changing Prices

The Wildcat Auto Insurance Company has asked you to develop an equation that will be useful in predicting the labor cost of processing insurance claims. The following information regarding the operation of their claims office is available.

Year	Claims Processed	Labor Hours	Labor Dollars
19x2	3,300	3,700	$18,500
19x3	4,200	4,300	21,500
19x4	3,200	3,500	21,000
19x5	5,000	5,300	31,800
19x6	4,000	4,400	44,000
19x7	3,600	4,000	40,000

Wage rates have increased substantially over the six-year period from 19x2 through 19x7. However, no additional increases are expected until 19x9.

Required: Develop an equation to predict the 19x8 labor cost of processing claims. Use the high-low method.

3-21 Cost Behavior Analysis with Changing Prices

Julie Schultz is trying to develop an equation to predict the cost of electricity consumed at an apartment she rents each summer. Julie believes that the primary factor affecting monthly power consumption is the amount by which the average daily high temperature exceeds 75 degrees Fahrenheit. Presented is information Julie has accumulated from her electric bill and the local newspaper:

Period	Average Daily High Temperature	Kilowatt Hours Used	Electric Bill
June 19x3	82.1	1,780	$133.50
July 19x3	93.6	3,490	261.75
August 19x3	89.4	2,800	210.00
June 19x4	81.0	1,690	160.55
July 19x4	90.1	3,100	294.50
August 19x4	86.3	2,250	213.75
June 19x5	80.4	1,510	173.65
July 19x5	90.1	2,950	339.25
August 19x5	87.6	2,550	258.75

The cost of electricity per kilowatt hour (KWH) has increased during each of the past three years and is anticipated to be 13.5 cents per KWH during 19x6.

Required: Develop an equation to predict the 19x6 monthly cost of electricity for the apartment.

3–22 Cost Behavior Analysis in a Restaurant: High-Low Method

The Pizza House Restaurant has the following information available regarding costs at various levels of monthly sales.

	5,000	8,000	10,000
Monthly sales in units			
Cost of food sold	$ 5,250	$ 8,400	$10,500
Wage and fringe benefits of restaurant employees	4,250	4,400	4,500
Fees paid delivery help	1,250	2,000	2,500
Rent on building	1,200	1,200	1,200
Depreciation on equipment	300	300	300
Utilities	500	560	600
Supplies (soap, floor wax, etc.)	150	180	200
Administrative costs	1,300	1,300	1,300
Total	$14,200	$18,340	$21,100

Requirements

a) Identify each cost as being variable, fixed, or mixed.

b) Develop a schedule identifying the amount of each cost that is fixed per month or variable per unit. Total the amounts under each category to develop an equation for total monthly costs.

c) Predict total costs for a monthly sales volume of 9,500 units.

3–23 Cost Behavior Analysis in a Store: High-Low Method

The Eleventh Avenue Convenience Store has the following information available regarding costs and revenues for two recent months.

	April	May
Sales revenue	$60,000	$100,000
Cost of goods sold	−36,000	− 60,000
Gross profit	$24,000	$ 40,000
Less other expenses:		
Advertising	$ 600	$ 600
Utilities	4,200	5,600
Salaries and commissions	3,200	4,000
Supplies (bags, cleaning supplies, etc.)	320	400
Depreciation	2,300	2,300
Administrative costs	1,900	1,900
Total	−12,520	− 14,800
Net income	$11,480	$ 25,200

Requirements

a) Identify each cost as being fixed, variable, or mixed.

b) Develop a schedule identifying the amount of each cost that is fixed per month or variable per sales dollar. Express fixed costs as an amount per month and variable costs as a portion of sales revenue. Develop a cost estimating equation for total monthly costs.

c) Predict total costs for a monthly sales volume of $70,000.

3–24 Average Costs and Internal Decisions

The production supervisor of Confusion Reigns bursts into your office declaring that accounting information is of little or no use to him:

"Back in early August I asked the accounting department for production cost information. They told me that the July production costs were $13 per unit. Well, I knew that July was a typical month in which we had good cost control, so I used the $13 amount in my production cost budgets for August and September.

In August I was scheduled to produce 12,000 units, so I budgeted my costs at $156,000 (12,000 × $13). I figured that something was wrong when actual costs turned out to be $150,000. However, when the vice president congratulated me for saving $6,000, I decided to keep my mouth shut. But last month was a disaster! In September I produced 5,000 units at a budgeted cost of $65,000 (5,000 × $13), and the V.P. is now demanding an explanation of the $15,000 difference between the budgeted costs and the actual costs of $80,000. I am totally confused because I believe I did an equally good job of controlling costs in all three months. You've got to help me!"

The first thing you did was obtain the following statements for the months in question.

Confusion Reigns
Statements of Cost of Goods Manufactured
For the months of July, August, and September, 19x2

	July	August	September
Current manufacturing costs:			
Raw materials	$ 30,000	$ 36,000	$15,000
Direct labor	50,000	60,000	25,000
Factory overhead	50,000	54,000	40,000
Total	$130,000	$150,000	$80,000
Work-in-process, beginning	0	0	0
Total costs-in-process	$130,000	$150,000	$80,000
Work-in-process, ending	− 0	− 0	− 0
Cost of goods manufactured	$130,000	$150,000	$80,000
Units manufactured	10,000	12,000	5,000

Required: Prepare a report explaining what happened. Based on your analysis, did the production supervisor do an equally good job of controlling costs in all three months?

3–25 Selecting an Independent Variable: Scatter Diagrams

Valley Production Company produces backpacks that are sold to sporting goods stores throughout the Rocky Mountains. Presented is information on production costs and inventory changes for five recent months.

	January	February	March	April	May
Finished goods inventory in units:					
Beginning	30,000	40,000	50,000	30,000	60,000
Manufactured	60,000	90,000	80,000	90,000	100,000
Available	90,000	130,000	130,000	120,000	160,000
Sold	− 50,000	− 80,000	−100,000	− 60,000	−120,000
Ending	40,000	50,000	30,000	60,000	40,000
Manufacturing costs	$300,000	$500,000	$450,000	$450,000	$550,000

Requirements

a) With the aid of scatter diagrams, determine whether units sold or units manufactured is a better predictor of manufacturing costs.

b) Prepare an explanation for your answer to requirement (a).

c) Which independent variable, units sold or units manufactured, should be a better predictor of selling costs? Why?

3–26 Selecting a Basis of Overhead Allocation: Scatter Diagrams

The Roth Company manufactures two products, A and B. In the past, factory overhead costs have been allocated equally to all products on the basis of the number of units produced. However, Mr. Roth is concerned that this method does not provide a proper cost basis for product pricing. Mr. Roth has noted that most of the company's factory overhead costs are related to the use of machinery, and that each unit of product A requires twice as many machine hours as a unit of product B. Consequently, he believes the allocation should be made on the basis of machine hours.

You have been asked to study this matter and determine the more accurate basis of allocating factory overhead costs. The following information is available.

Month	Units Produced A	Units Produced B	Units Produced Total	Machine Hours	Factory Overhead
1	50	100	150	300	$30,000
2	200	100	300	500	40,000
3	100	50	150	250	25,000
4	150	50	200	350	30,000
5	50	350	400	450	32,000
6	100	300	400	500	35,000

Requirements

a) With the aid of scatter diagrams, determine whether units produced or machine hours is the better basis of overhead application.

b) Which product is assigned too few overhead costs, and which product is assigned too many overhead costs, when the allocation is made on the basis of units produced? Explain your answer. If prices are based on cost, what may happen to the prices Roth charges for its products compared to the prices of competitors' products?

3–27 Selecting a Basis for Predicting Shipping Expenses

The Tyson Company assembles and sells computer boards in western Pennsylvania. In an effort to improve the planning and control of shipping expenses, management is trying to determine which of three variables—units shipped, weight shipped, or sales value of units shipped—has the closest relationship with shipping expenses. The following information is available.

Month	Units Shipped	Weight Shipped (lbs.)	Sales Value of Units Shipped	Shipping Expenses
May	3,000	6,200	$50,000	$2,500
June	5,000	8,000	55,000	3,500
July	4,000	8,100	40,000	3,000
August	7,000	10,000	57,000	5,000
September	6,000	7,000	70,000	4,000
October	4,500	8,000	80,000	3,800

Requirements

a) With the aid of scatter diagrams, determine whether units shipped, weight shipped, or sales value of units shipped has the closest relationship with shipping expenses.

b) Using the independent variable that appears to have the closest relationship to shipping expense, develop a high-low cost estimating equation for total monthly shipping expenses.

c) Use the equation developed in requirement (b) to predict total shipping expenses in a month when 5,000 units, weighing 7,000 lbs., with a total sales value of $57,000 are shipped.

3–28 Least-Squares Cost Estimation (Appendix A)

The Quartz Watch Repair Center is trying to determine the cost of repairing a quartz watch. The following information is available regarding the number of units repaired and labor hours.

Week	Watches Repaired	Labor Hours
1	150	45
2	50	20
3	75	25
4	200	60
5	175	40
6	250	50

Requirements

a) Determine the average and the incremental time to repair a quartz watch. Use the least-squares method to compute the incremental time. Round your answer to three decimal places.

b) Predict the total labor hours required for a week when 200 quartz watches are repaired. If the labor cost is $12 per hour, what is the predicted total labor cost for this week?

3–29 Least-Squares Cost Estimation (Appendix A)

The following information is available about shipping costs.

Month	Pounds Shipped	Total Shipping Cost
January	5,000	$12,000
February	7,000	16,000
March	6,000	15,000
April	9,000	17,000

Required: Use the least-squares method to develop an equation for total monthly shipping costs. Round answers to three decimal places. *Hint:* Perform calculations in thousands, and then adjust the constant term in your answer.

3–30 Predicting Selling Expenses (Appendix B)

The Grackly Company is trying to determine the best independent variable to use in predicting selling expenses. In the past this prediction has been made on the basis of expected unit sales. However, the increasing diversity of the company's products has led the sales manager to suggest that expected sales revenue might be a better predictor. You have gathered the following information:

Month	Units Sold	Sales Revenue	Selling Expense
1	5,000	$25,000	$2,200
2	7,000	35,000	2,400
3	6,000	20,000	1,800
4	9,000	40,000	3,200
5	8,000	30,000	2,400

Requirements

a) Use the correlation coefficient to determine the best predictor of selling expenses.

b) Use the least-squares method to develop an equation for predicting monthly selling expenses. Select the basis of prediction that has the highest correlation with actual selling expenses. If you select sales revenue as the independent variable, variable costs should be expressed as a portion of sales revenue.

3–31 Selecting a Basis of Overhead Application (Appendix B)

Presented is information on manufacturing activity and total overhead costs for five recent months.

Month	Direct Labor Hours	Machine Hours	Total Factory Overhead
April	20,000	6,000	$ 90,000
May	40,000	10,000	150,000
June	30,000	8,000	140,000
July	60,000	10,000	260,000
August	50,000	6,000	160,000

Requirements

a) Use the correlation coefficient to determine the best basis of overhead application.

b) Use the least-squares method to develop an equation to predict monthly overhead. Select the basis of prediction that has the highest correlation with actual overhead.

c) Modify the equation developed above to predict annual overhead, and then compute the predetermined overhead rate for a year when management predicts the use of 480,000 direct labor hours and 120,000 machine hours.

REVIEW PROBLEM SOLUTION

a) Fixed costs are easily identified. They are the same at each activity level. Variable and mixed costs are determined by dividing the total cost for an item by unit sales at two activity levels. The quotients of variable cost items will be the same at both activity levels. The quotients of mixed costs will differ, being lower at the higher activity level because the fixed costs are spread over a larger number of units.

Cost	Behavior
Cost of food sold	Variable
Wages and salaries	Mixed
Rent on building	Fixed
Depreciation on equipment	Fixed
Utilities	Mixed
Supplies	Mixed
Miscellaneous	Mixed

b)

	Fixed Costs	Variable Costs
Cost of food sold ($1,575/2,100)		$0.75X
Wages and salaries		
($1,675 − $1,525)/(2,700 − 2,100)		0.25X
$1,525 − $0.25(2,100)	$1,000	
Rent on building	1,500	
Depreciation on equipment	200	
Utilities ($770 − $710)/(2,700 − 2,100)		0.10X
$710 − $0.10(2,100)	500	
Supplies ($255 − $225)/(2,700 − 2,100)		0.05X
$225 − $0.05(2,100)	120	
Miscellaneous		
($131 − $113)/(2,700 − 2,100)		0.03X
$113 − $0.03(2,100)	50	
Total	$3,370	$1.18X

Total costs = $3,370 + $1.18X$

where X = unit sales.

c)

Volume	Total Cost	Average Cost
1,000	$4,550	$4.550
2,000	$5,730	$2.865

d) The average costs differ at 1,000 and 2,000 units because the fixed costs are being spread over differing numbers of units. The larger the number of units, the smaller the average fixed cost per unit.

C H A P T E R   4

Cost-Volume-Profit Analysis

Cost-volume-profit analysis is a technique used to examine the relationships between volume, total costs, total revenues, and profit. Cost-volume-profit analysis is particularly useful in the early stages of planning because it provides a framework for discussing planning issues and for organizing relevant data.

Cost-volume-profit analysis is widely used in for-profit and not-for-profit organizations, and it is equally applicable to service, merchandising, and manufacturing activities. In for-profit organizations cost-volume-profit analysis is used to answer such questions as: How many photocopies must the College Avenue Copy Service produce to earn a profit of $20,000? At what sales volume will Burger King's total costs and total revenues be equal? What profit will General Electric earn at an annual sales volume of 3 billion dollars? What will happen to the profits of Duff's Smorgasbord if there is a 20 percent increase in the cost of food and a 10 percent increase in the selling price of meals?

In not-for-profit organizations cost-volume-profit analysis is used to plan service levels, plan fund-raising activities, and determine funding requirements: How many meals can the Downtown Salvation Army serve with an annual budget of $200,000? How many tickets must be sold for the benefit concert to raise $10,000? Given current tuition rates and projected enrollments, how much money must City University obtain from other sources?

The purpose of this chapter is to introduce cost-volume-profit analysis. We begin by developing a profit formula and presenting a new type of income statement based on that formula. Next we examine cost-volume-profit relationships and illustrate their use in planning. Then we summarize the assumptions that are an inherent part of cost-volume-profit analysis. Appendices A and B consider operating leverage, which is a measure of the responsiveness of income to changes in sales, and methods of analyzing the effect on profits of changes in the portion of sales derived from different products.

A BASIC ASSUMPTION

In Chapter 2 *cost* was defined as a monetary measure of the economic sacrifice made to obtain some product or service. The cost of a product or service that has a future service or revenue generating potential is recorded as an asset, whereas the cost of a product or service that has been consumed or no longer has a revenue generating potential is recorded as an expense. An important distinction was made between product costs and period costs. *Product costs—* which include the cost of raw materials and other factors necessary to transform raw materials into finished goods—are recorded as assets until the finished goods are sold; at that time they become the expense cost of goods sold. *Period costs—*which are expired nonproduct costs, such as selling or administrative expenses—are recorded as expenses in the period they are incurred.

To simplify the discussion of cost-volume-profit relationships, inventories are assumed to be constant or at zero. All merchandise is sold and all supplies are consumed in the period they are purchased. In manufacturing organizations raw materials are converted into finished goods in the period they are purchased, and finished goods are sold in the period they are produced. With this assumption, product costs and period costs are both expenses of the period in which they are incurred. By limiting the discussion to these two types of costs, the words "cost" and "expense" have equivalent meaning and may be used interchangeably. In cost-volume-profit analysis, the word "cost(s)" refers to product costs and period costs that are expenses of the period in which they are incurred. Additional assumptions of cost-volume-profit analysis are discussed at the end of this chapter.

THE PROFIT FORMULA

An organization's profit is equal to the difference between its total revenues and its total costs:

$$\text{Profit} = \text{Total revenues} - \text{Total costs}.$$

Total revenues are a function of the unit sales volume and the unit selling price:

$$\frac{\text{Total}}{\text{revenues}} = \frac{\text{Selling}}{\text{price}} \times \frac{\text{Unit}}{\text{volume}}.$$

The computation of profit can be expanded to include the detailed elements of revenues and costs:

$$\text{Profit} = \left(\frac{\text{Selling}}{\text{price}} \times \frac{\text{Unit}}{\text{volume}} \right) - \left[\frac{\text{Fixed}}{\text{costs}} + \left(\frac{\text{Variable costs}}{\text{per unit}} \times \frac{\text{Unit}}{\text{volume}} \right) \right].$$

Given information on the selling price, the fixed costs per period, and the variable costs per unit, this formula is used to determine profit at any specified volume. Consider the following example.

The Benchmark Card Company manufactures high-quality seasonal greeting cards that are sold at $8 per box of 100 cards. Variable and fixed costs are shown below.

Variable Costs per Box			Fixed Costs per Month	
Manufacturing:			Factory overhead	$ 5,000
Direct materials	$1.00		Selling and	
Direct labor	0.50		administrative	10,000
Factory overhead	0.50	$2.00	Total	$15,000
Selling and				
administrative		1.00		
Total		$3.00		

If Benchmark produces and sells 4,000 boxes of cards in October 19x7, their profit would be $5,000.

$$\text{Profit} = (\$8 \times 4{,}000) - [\$15{,}000 + (\$3 \times 4{,}000)]$$
$$= \$5{,}000.$$

ALTERNATIVE INCOME STATEMENTS

Assuming Benchmark does not maintain beginning or ending inventories, and that monthly production equals monthly sales, the cost of goods manufactured is the cost of goods sold, and a detailed list of current manufacturing costs can be disclosed in the income statement as the cost of goods sold. There are two alternative formats for disclosing manufacturing and other costs in an income statement. Each is discussed and illustrated below.

Functional Income Statements Classify Expenses by Function

Benchmark Card Company's income statement is presented at the top of Exhibit 4–1 in the form most frequently used for external reporting. This statement is called a **functional income statement** because costs are classified according to function, such as manufacturing or selling and administrative. Variable and fixed costs are included within each functional category. The cost of goods sold includes variable and fixed manufacturing costs; likewise, the selling and administrative expenses include variable and fixed costs. For the purpose of exposition, detailed computations of cost of goods sold and selling and administrative expenses are shown in Exhibit 4–1. In reality, it is unlikely that each functional cost would be further classified by cost behavior.

One immediate problem with a functional income statement is the difficulty of relating it to the profit formula where costs are classified according to behavior rather than function. The cost and profit consequences of changes in sales

MANAGERIAL PRACTICE 4.1

Variable Costing for External Reporting

Variable costing (the basis for contribution income statements) has been available for over 50 years as an alternative to absorption costing. Although thought of as an internal reporting concept, several large corporations have begun using it for external reporting. The main change is the moving of plant and equipment depreciation from factory overhead to a period expense. Since this is the dominant fixed manufacturing item for most companies, it causes a substantial change in the structure of the income statement. Companies following this practice include USX Corporation, Republic Steel, International Paper, and Bethlehem Steel.

Source: Michael Schiff, "Variable Costing: A Closer Look," *Management Accounting* (February 1987): 36–39.

EXHIBIT 4–1   Functional and Contribution Income Statements

Benchmark Card Company
Functional Income Statement
For the month of October, 19x7

Sales (4,000 × $8)		$32,000
Cost of goods sold:		
Direct materials (4,000 × $1)	$ 4,000	
Direct labor (4,000 × $0.50)	2,000	
Variable factory overhead (4,000 × $0.50)	2,000	
Fixed factory overhead	5,000	−13,000
Gross profit		$19,000
Selling and administrative expenses:		
Variable (4,000 × $1)	$ 4,000	
Fixed	10,000	−14,000
Net income		$ 5,000

Benchmark Card Company
Contribution Income Statement
For the month of October, 19x7

Sales (4,000 × $8)			$32,000
Less variable costs:			
Cost of goods sold:			
Direct materials (4,000 × $1)	$4,000		
Direct labor (4,000 × $0.50)	2,000		
Factory overhead (4,000 × $0.50)	2,000	$ 8,000	
Selling and administrative			
(4,000 × $1)		4,000	−12,000
Contribution margin			$20,000
Less fixed costs:			
Factory overhead		$ 5,000	
Selling and administrative		10,000	−15,000
Net income			$ 5,000

---

volume are not readily apparent in a functional income statement, especially when cost information is presented at an aggregated level. *For planning and control purposes, costs should be classified by behavior.* This classification assists in determining how costs and, hence, profits respond to changes in volume.

Contribution Income Statements Classify Expenses by Cost Behavior

A contribution income statement is presented at the bottom of Exhibit 4–1. Such statements are used for internal planning and control. In a contribution income statement costs are classified according to behavior. The variable manufacturing costs and the variable selling and administrative expenses are grouped together and subtracted from revenues. The difference between revenues and variable costs, called the contribution margin, is the amount of money contributed to cover fixed costs and to provide a profit. The fixed manufacturing costs and the fixed selling and administrative expenses are also grouped together and subtracted from the contribution margin to obtain net income.

When production and sales are equal (no beginning or ending inventories), the same net income will be obtained with either type of income statement. However, the gross profit (or gross margin) in a functional income statement will seldom be the same as the contribution margin in a contribution income statement. This is because the computation of gross profit includes a deduction for fixed manufacturing costs while excluding a deduction for variable selling and administrative expenses. The mixing of fixed and variable costs in the computation of a *manufacturing* firm's gross profit makes it difficult to determine how gross profit responds to changes in sales volume. Note, however, that a *merchandising* firm's cost of goods sold includes only the variable cost of goods purchased and sold; hence, the gross profit of a merchandising firm represents a contribution or margin that is available to cover selling and administrative costs and to provide for a profit. It should change in direct proportion to changes in sales volume.

Unit Contribution Margin. For planning purposes it is useful to express sales, variable costs, and contribution margin by dollars per unit, as a percentage of the total dollar amount of sales, or both. Condensing Benchmark's October 19x7 contribution income statement, we obtain the following:

	Total	Per Unit	Percent of Sales
Sales (4,000 units)	$32,000	$8	100.0
Variable costs	−12,000	−3	−37.5
Contribution margin	$20,000	$5	62.5
Fixed costs	−15,000		
Net income	$ 5,000		

The **unit contribution margin** is the difference between the unit selling price and the unit variable costs, including the variable cost of goods sold and the variable selling and administrative costs. The unit contribution margin is also described as the dollar amount that each unit sold contributes to cover fixed costs and to provide for a profit. This relationship is often used to determine the effect on profit of changes in the unit sales volume.

The change in profit is calculated as follows:

$$\frac{\text{Change}}{\text{in profit}} = \frac{\text{Unit contribution}}{\text{margin}} \times \frac{\text{Change in}}{\text{unit volume.}}$$

Management may want to know what will happen to Benchmark's profit if sales increase by 500 units. With a unit contribution margin of $5, the impact on profit of a 500 unit increase in sales volume is quickly computed as $5 multiplied by 500:

$$\$5 \times 500 = \$2,500 \qquad \text{increase in profit.}$$

If the current profit is $5,000 at a monthly volume of 4,000 units, the new profit will be $7,500 at a monthly volume 500 units higher.

Current profit	$5,000
Increase (500 × $5)	2,500
New profit	$7,500

We could use the profit formula to compute the new profit and then subtract the current profit from this amount to determine the increase; however, this approach is more time consuming. Alternatively, we could start with the current contribution income statement and show the impact of the possible sales increase on revenues and variable costs:

	Current 4,000 Units	Increase 500 Units	New 4,500 Units
Sales ($8 per unit)	$32,000	$4,000	$36,000
Variable costs ($3 per unit)	−12,000	−1,500	−13,500
Contribution margin	$20,000	$2,500	$22,500
Fixed costs	−15,000	—	−15,000
Net income	$ 5,000	$2,500	$ 7,500

In addition to being a useful way of presenting information to management, this also illustrates one of the advantages of contribution income statements for internal planning. The effect of a volume change is much easier to illustrate with a contribution income statement than with a functional income statement.

Contribution Margin Ratio. The **contribution margin ratio,** which is the ratio of contribution margin to sales revenue, indicates the portion of each sales dollar that is available to cover fixed costs and provide for a profit. It is computed as the contribution margin divided by sales revenue:

$$\frac{\text{Contribution}}{\text{margin ratio}} = \frac{\text{Contribution}}{\text{margin}} \div \frac{\text{Sales}}{\text{revenue.}}$$

The calculation may be made on total dollars ($20,000 ÷ $32,000 = 0.625) or on dollars per unit ($5 ÷ $8 = 0.625).

Using the contribution margin ratio, the profit impact of a change in sales revenue is easily determined as the change in sales revenue multiplied by the contribution margin ratio:

$$\text{Change in profit} = \text{Change in total revenues} \times \text{Contribution margin ratio.}$$

Benchmark has a contribution margin ratio of 0.625. If Benchmark's monthly sales increase by $4,000, their monthly profit will increase by $2,500:

$$\text{Change in profit} = \$4,000 \times 0.625$$
$$= \$2,500 \text{ increase.}$$

The unit contribution margin and the contribution margin ratio are equally useful in determining the effect on profit of volume changes in single product firms. However, because sales dollars provide a common denominator that can be meaningfully added across products, *the contribution margin ratio is easier to use in firms that sell several products in a constant sales mix.* A furniture company may sell several different styles of desks, tables, and bookcases. Given the different selling prices, costs, and contribution margins of each product, calculating the change in profit for total revenues using the contribution margin ratio is much simpler than aggregating the information from each product's unit contribution margin and unit selling price.

Variable Cost Ratio. The **variable cost ratio** indicates the portion of each sales dollar that is used to cover variable costs. It provides useful information regarding an organization's cost structure. The variable cost ratio is computed as variable costs divided by sales revenue:

$$\text{Variable cost ratio} = \text{Variable costs} \div \text{Sales revenue.}$$

This calculation may be made on total dollars ($12,000 ÷ $32,000 = 0.375) or on dollars per unit ($3 ÷ $8 = 0.375). Note that the contribution margin ratio can be computed as 1.000 minus the variable cost ratio (1.000 − 0.375 = 0.625). Of each sales dollar received by Benchmark, 37.5 percent goes to cover variable costs and 62.5 percent goes to cover fixed costs and provide for a profit.

COST-VOLUME-PROFIT RELATIONSHIPS

A **cost-volume-profit graph** illustrates the relationships between volume, total revenues, total costs, and profit. Its usefulness comes from its depicting revenue and cost relationships over a range of activity, rather than only at selected volumes. Although less precise than quantitative schedules, this representation of an organization's revenues and costs allows management to view the relative

amount of important variables at any graphed volume without making computations. A comparison of graphs illlustrating the costs, revenues, and profits
of alternative products or production procedures assists management in selecting the most desirable product or method of operation.

The Benchmark Card Company's cost-volume-profit graph is presented in
Exhibit 4–2. Total revenues and total costs are measured on the vertical axis,
and volume of activity is measured in units on the horizontal axis. Separate lines
are drawn for total costs and total revenues. When total costs exceed total
revenues, losses occur, and when total revenues exceed total costs, profits occur.
The amount of profit or loss at a given volume is depicted by the vertical distance
between the total revenue and the total cost lines. The **break-even point** occurs
at the unit or dollar sales volume where total revenues equal total costs. Graphically, this happens when the total revenue and total cost lines intersect.

M ANAGERIAL PRACTICE 4.2

Another Alternative Income Statement

After working with various cost accounting systems over a period of 15 years,
Warren G. Wolf came to realize that no single system can meet the needs of
every organization. He therefore developed a new unit reporting system for a
company (name withheld), based on its needs. While keeping the contribution
margin approach as a base, the new statement added a new profit margin
concept—*prime gross profit*, as shown below.

Selling price (per unit)		$50
Prime costs:		
Direct materials	$15	
Direct labor	3	−18
Prime gross profit		$32
Variable overhead costs:		
Indirect labor and benefits	$ 3	
Utilities	2	
Supplies and other	1	−6
Contribution margin		$26

Source: Warren G. Wolf, "Developing a Cost System for Today's Decision Making," *Management Accounting* (December 1982): 19–23.

EXHIBIT 4–2   Typical Cost-Volume-Profit Graph

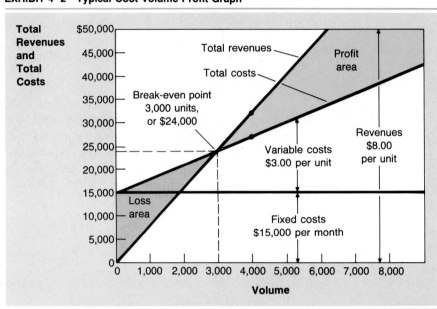

Before developing a cost-volume-profit graph, it is necessary to obtain information on the behavior of costs and revenues. The three lines graphed in Exhibit 4–2 are developed as follows:

1. A line representing monthly fixed costs of $15,000 is drawn parallel to the horizontal axis. The distance between the horizontal axis and this line depicts Benchmark's monthly fixed costs.

2. Variable costs are layered on top of fixed costs to obtain total costs. To draw this line, it is necessary to determine total costs at some selected volume. At 4,000 units Benchmark's total costs are $27,000 [$15,000 + ($3 × 4,000)]. This point is plotted on the graph, and a straight line is drawn through it and the point where the fixed cost line intersects the vertical axis. The distance between the total cost line and the fixed cost line represents Benchmark's variable costs at each level of production.

3. A straight line depicting total revenues is drawn through the origin and a point representing total revenues at some selected volume. At 4,000 units Benchmark's total revenues are $32,000 ($8 × 4,000). The distance between the total revenue line and the horizontal axis represents Benchmark's total revenues at each level of sales.

A widely used variation of the cost-volume-profit graph is presented in Exhibit 4–3. Here a line is drawn first for variable costs with fixed costs layered on top of variable costs to obtain total costs. By layering fixed costs on top of

EXHIBIT 4–3   Cost-Volume-Profit Graph Emphasizing the Contribution Margin

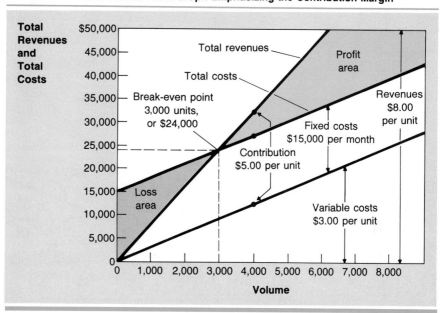

variable costs, this graph emphasizes the contribution margin available to cover fixed costs and to provide for a profit. The contribution margin is represented by the vertical distance between the total revenue and the total variable cost lines. Up to the break-even point, the entire contribution margin goes to cover fixed costs; at the break-even point, the contribution margin equals the fixed costs; and beyond the break-even point, the contribution margin is large enough to cover fixed costs and provide for a profit.

The lines in Exhibit 4–3 are developed in a manner similar to those in Exhibit 4–2. Straight lines are drawn through plotted values at a selected volume and at the appropriate vertical axis intercepts. A useful feature of this second graph is its relationship to the contribution income statement. Compare the contribution income statement in Exhibit 4–1 with the graph in Exhibit 4–3. The income statement is merely a formal presentation of the relationships graphed at 4,000 units. With the graph it is easy to determine income statement amounts at other volumes.

Another variation of the cost-volume-profit graph is shown in Exhibit 4–4. Here total revenues are shown on the horizontal axis as well as on the vertical axis. The objective is to show total costs and the profit or loss at each dollar sales volume. The graph in Exhibit 4–4 is most appropriate for multiple-product firms, where the concept of unit sales volume has less meaning. For single-product firms, or for the purpose of analyzing the cost-volume-profit relationships of an individual product, the graphs in Exhibit 4–2 or 4–3 are preferred

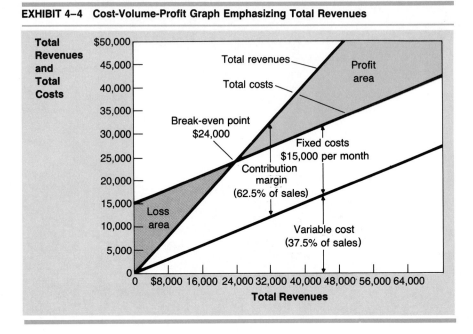

EXHIBIT 4–4   Cost-Volume-Profit Graph Emphasizing Total Revenues

because they contain more information (that is, information regarding the unit sales volume) than the graph in Exhibit 4–4.

Determining the Break-even Point

Three approaches are widely used to determine the break-even point: (1) the graphic approach, (2) the formula approach, and (3) the contribution approach. Each is used to determine the break-even point in units or sales dollars.

Graphic Approach. The graphic approach involves the graphing of cost-volume-profit relationships. The break-even point in units or sales dollars is then determined by studying the graph. In Exhibits 4–2, 4–3, and 4–4 the break-even point is 3,000 units, or 24,000 sales dollars. The break-even point always occurs where the total revenue and total cost lines intersect.

Formula Approach. The formula approach to determining the break-even point involves the use of the profit formula with profits set equal to zero.

$$\text{Profit} = \left(\begin{array}{c}\text{Selling} \\ \text{price}\end{array} \times \begin{array}{c}\text{Unit} \\ \text{volume}\end{array}\right) - \left[\begin{array}{c}\text{Fixed} \\ \text{costs}\end{array} + \left(\begin{array}{c}\text{Variable costs} \\ \text{per unit}\end{array} \times \begin{array}{c}\text{Unit} \\ \text{volume}\end{array}\right)\right] = 0.$$

With zero profits, total revenues equal total costs.

$$\underbrace{\begin{array}{c}\text{Selling} \\ \text{price}\end{array} \times \begin{array}{c}\text{Unit} \\ \text{volume}}_{\textbf{Total Revenues}} = \underbrace{\begin{array}{c}\text{Fixed} \\ \text{costs}\end{array} + \left(\begin{array}{c}\text{Variable costs} \\ \text{per unit}\end{array} \times \begin{array}{c}\text{Unit} \\ \text{volume}\end{array}\right)}_{\textbf{Total Costs}}.$$

The break-even unit volume is now computed by placing prices and costs in this equation and solving for unit volume. Let X equal the break-even *unit* volume. Then, with a selling price of $8 per box, variable costs of $3 per box, and fixed costs of $15,000 per month:

$$\$8X = \$15,000 + \$3X.$$

Solving for X:

$$\$8X - \$3X = \$15,000$$
$$\$5X = \$15,000$$
$$X = \$15,000/\$5$$
$$= 3,000 \text{ units.}$$

The break-even point in sales dollars is found by multiplying the unit selling price by the break-even unit volume:

$$\$8 \times 3,000 = \$24,000.$$

M ANAGERIAL PRACTICE 4.3

Using Break-even Charts for Comparative Analysis

There are many barriers and restrictions to consolidating standard break-even analyses. Some of the more common are (1) inflation, (2) product mix, (3) production capacity changes, (4) changing fixed costs, and (5) changing inventory levels. Mobay Chemical Corporation was concerned with how it could use break-even analyses to compare different operating periods. After much experimentation, the company's management accountants found a way to portray the company's break-even history—past and future break-even points—in one chart, using a graphic technique they labeled "profit geometry." The basic equation is

$$\text{Gross profit margin} = \text{Sales} - \left(\text{Variable costs} + \frac{\text{Fixed costs adjusted for}}{\text{capacity utilization}} \right)$$

It displays the data for each year as a percentage of sales revenue (Y axis) against percentage utilization of capacity (X axis).

Source: Howard Martin, "Breaking Through the Breakeven Barriers," *Management Accounting* (May 1985): 31–34.

Alternatively, the break-even point in terms of sales dollars can be found using the variable cost ratio:

$$\frac{\text{Total}}{\text{revenues}} = \frac{\text{Fixed}}{\text{costs}} + \left(\frac{\text{Variable}}{\text{cost ratio}} \times \frac{\text{Total}}{\text{revenue}}\right).$$

The break-even dollar sales volume can be found by placing fixed costs and the variable cost ratio in this equation and solving for total revenues. Let X equal the break-even *dollar* sales volume. Then, with fixed costs of $15,000 per month and a variable cost ratio of 37.5 percent,

$$X = \$15,000 + 0.375X.$$

Solving for X:

$$X - 0.375X = \$15,000$$
$$0.625X = \$15,000$$
$$X = \$15,000/0.625$$
$$= \$24,000.$$

Contribution Approach. Focusing on the final computation in the formula approach provides a third approach to determining the break-even unit or dollar sales volume. With fixed costs of $15,000 and a unit contribution margin of $5, the unit break-even point was computed as

$$\frac{\$15,000}{\$5} = 3,000 \text{ units.}$$

The unit break-even volume indicates the number of unit contribution margins needed to cover the fixed costs. With fixed costs of $15,000 and a $5 unit contribution margin, 3,000 unit contribution margins are required to break even. In general,

$$\frac{\text{Break-even point}}{\text{in units}} = \frac{\text{Fixed costs}}{\text{Unit contribution margin}}.$$

In sales dollars, the break-even point was found as follows:

$$\frac{\$15,000}{0.625} = \$24,000,$$

where 0.625 is the contribution margin ratio. Recall that the contribution margin ratio is one minus the variable cost ratio.

To contribute $15,000 to cover fixed costs, a total revenue of $24,000 is required. This is verified as follows:

$$\$24,000 \times 0.625 = \$15,000.$$

In general,

$$\frac{\text{Break-even point}}{\text{in sales dollars}} = \frac{\text{Fixed costs}}{\text{Contribution margin ratio}}.$$

Profit Planning

Cost-volume-profit relationships are used to determine profit or loss at any specified level of activity. The Benchmark Card Company, for example, anticipates a profit of $5,000 at a sales volume of 4,000 units, or 32,000 sales dollars. Using the graphs in Exhibits 4–2, 4–3, and 4–4, observe that a volume of 1,000 units, or 8,000 sales dollars, should result in a loss of $10,000.

Margin of Safety. The **margin of safety** is the excess of actual or budgeted sales over break-even sales. Expressed in units or sales dollars, the margin of safety indicates the amount that sales could decline before losses occur. The Benchmark Card Company's margin of safety for October 19x7 is 1,000 units, or $8,000.

	Units	Sales Dollars
Anticipated sales	4,000	$32,000
Break-even sales	−3,000	−24,000
Margin of safety	1,000	$ 8,000

MａNAGERIAL PRACTICE 4.4

Accounting Helps a Small Business Survive

How does a small ($6 million in sales), family-owned business—not so very different from Benchmark Card Company in size—stay competitive with large competitors? A small manufacturer of baking products can provide one example of how accounting can help. Faced with a financial crisis, the company set a five-year plan for improving its accounting function. Although by accident, the first area that management took on was cost behavior. They had started out to improve monthly reporting but found that some costs behaved oddly when examined on a monthly basis. This led to a thorough investigation of the behavior of all costs. Next, profitability was examined by product, using the contribution margin approach. Many other costing techniques soon followed. To conclude, the authors state, "the firm prospers in a difficult environment because of the high priority it attaches to improved cost information and upgraded technical skills. Other small manufacturing firms may find that relatively sophisticated cost and profit analysis is available to them at a reasonable cost."

Source: John H. Evans, III, and Frank C. Evans, "A Small Manufacturer's Success Story," *Management Accounting* (August 1986): 47–49.

Activity Planning. Establishing profit objectives is an important part of planning in for-profit organizations. Profit objectives are determined in many ways. They can be set at a percentage of last year's profits, at a percentage of total assets at the start of the current year, or at a percentage of average owner's equity over some past period. They might be based on a profit trend, or they might be expressed as a percent of sales. The economic outlook for the firm's products and anticipated changes in products, costs, and technology are also considered in establishing profit objectives.

Before incorporating profit plans into a detailed budget, it is useful to obtain some preliminary information on the feasibility of profit plans. Cost-volume-profit analysis is one way of doing this. By manipulating cost-volume-profit relationships, management can determine the sales volume required to obtain a desired profit. Management would then evaluate the feasibility of this sales volume. If the profit plans are feasible, a complete budget might be developed for this activity level. The required sales volume may be infeasible because of market conditions or because the required volume exceeds production capacity, in which case management might lower its profit objective or consider other ways of achieving it. Alternatively, the required sales volume might be less than management believes the firm is capable of producing and selling, in which case management would raise its profit objective.

Assume Benchmark's management desires to know the unit sales volume required to achieve a monthly profit of $12,000. Using the formula approach, the required unit sales volume is determined by setting profits equal to $12,000 and solving for X, the *unit* sales volume:

$$\text{Profit} = \text{Revenues} - \text{Costs}$$
$$\$12,000 = \$8X - (\$15,000 + \$3X)$$
$$\$8X - \$3X = \$15,000 + \$12,000$$
$$X = (\$15,000 + \$12,000)/\$5$$
$$= 5,400 \text{ units.}$$

The required dollar sales volume is found by multiplying 5,400 units times the unit selling price:

$$\$8 \times 5,400 = \$43,200.$$

Alternatively, the dollar sales volume required to achieve a monthly profit of $12,000 can be found using the profit formula with the variable cost ratio:

$$\$12,000 = X - (\$15,000 + 0.375X)$$
$$X - 0.375X = \$15,000 + \$12,000$$
$$X = (\$15,000 + \$12,000)/0.625$$
$$= \$43,200,$$

where X equals the dollar sales volume.

Once again, the final computation in the formula approach provides a contribution approach to determining the required unit or dollar sales volume. The alternative computations using the contribution approach are shown below.

	Volume required to achieve a desired profit	
	X = Units	**X = Sales dollars**
In general:		
$X =$	$\dfrac{\text{Fixed costs} + \text{Desired profit}}{\text{Unit contribution margin}}$	$\dfrac{\text{Fixed costs} + \text{Desired profit}}{\text{Contribution margin ratio}}$
For Benchmark:		
$X =$	$\dfrac{\$15{,}000 + \$12{,}000}{\$5}$	$\dfrac{\$15{,}000 + \$12{,}000}{0.625}$
$=$	5,400 units	\$43,200

In units the contribution approach indicated the number of physical units of production and sales needed to cover the fixed costs and provide the desired profit. In sales dollars the contribution approach indicated the total sales revenue required to provide a total contribution equal to the fixed costs and the desired profit.

The Impact of Income Taxes. Income taxes are imposed on individuals and for-profit organizations by units of government. The amount of an individual's or an organization's income tax is determined by laws that specify the calculation of taxable income (the income subject to tax) and the calculation of the amount of tax on taxable income. Income taxes are computed as a percentage of taxable income with increases in taxable income usually subject to progressively higher tax rates. The laws governing the computation of taxable income differ in many ways from the accounting principles and standards that guide the computation of accounting income. Consequently, taxable income and accounting income are seldom the same.

In the *early stages* of profit planning, income taxes are sometimes incorporated into an organization's cost-volume-profit model by assuming that taxable income and accounting income are equal and that the tax rate is constant. Although these assumptions are seldom true, they are useful because they assist management in developing an early prediction of the sales volume required to earn a desired after-tax profit. Once management has developed a general plan, this early prediction should be refined with the advice of tax experts.

Assuming income taxes are imposed at a constant rate per dollar of before-tax profit, income taxes are computed as before-tax profit multiplied by the tax rate. An organization's after-tax profit is equal to its before-tax profit minus income taxes:

$$\frac{\text{After-tax}}{\text{profit}} = \frac{\text{Before-tax}}{\text{profit}} - \left(\frac{\text{Before-tax}}{\text{profit}} \times \frac{\text{Tax}}{\text{rate}}\right).$$

After-tax profit can also be expressed as before-tax profit times 1 minus the tax rate.

$$\frac{\text{After-tax}}{\text{profit}} = \frac{\text{Before-tax}}{\text{profit}} \times \left(1 - \frac{\text{Tax}}{\text{rate}}\right).$$

This formula can be rearranged to isolate before-tax profit as follows:

$$\frac{\text{Before-tax}}{\text{profit}} = \frac{\text{After-tax profit}}{(1 - \text{Tax rate})}.$$

Since all costs and revenues in the profit formula are expressed on a before-tax basis, the most straightforward way of determining the volume required to earn a desired after-tax profit is to

1. Determine the required before-tax profit,
2. Substitute the required before-tax profit into the profit formula,
3. Solve for the required volume using the formula or the contribution approach.

Assume that the Benchmark Card Company is subject to a 40 percent tax rate, and that management desires to earn a November 19x7 after-tax profit of $12,000. The required before-tax profit is readily determined to be $20,000:

$$\frac{\text{Required before-}}{\text{tax profit}} = \frac{\$12,000}{1 - 0.40}$$

$$= \$20,000.$$

Using the contribution approach, a sales volume of 7,000 units or $56,000 is required to earn a before-tax profit of $20,000, shown as follows.

	Volume required to achieve a before-tax profit	
	X = Units	**X = Sales dollars**
In general:		
X =	$\dfrac{\text{Fixed costs} + \text{Before-tax profit}}{\text{Unit contribution margin}}$	$\dfrac{\text{Fixed costs} + \text{Before-tax profit}}{\text{Contribution margin ratio}}$
For Benchmark:		
X =	$\dfrac{\$15,000 + \$20,000}{\$5}$	$\dfrac{\$15,000 + \$20,000}{0.625}$
=	7,000 units	$56,000

It is apparent that *income taxes increase the sales volume required to earn a desired after-tax profit.* A 40 percent tax rate increased the sales volume required for Benchmark to earn a profit of $12,000 from 5,400 to 7,000 units, or from $43,200 to $56,000. These amounts are verified in Exhibit 4–5.

Sensitivity Analysis

Sensitivity analysis is the study of the responsiveness of a model's dependent variable(s) to changes in one or more of the model's independent variables. It is often applied to an organization's cost-volume-profit model to determine how profits or some other variable will respond to some proposed change. Managers are particularly interested in performing sensitivity analysis on those variables that are most likely to change. Knowing what will happen to profits if cost or revenue or volume changes assists management in developing contingency plans that can be implemented as soon as an event occurs.

The management of the Benchmark Card Company might, for example, anticipate a decline in sales if the U.S. Post Office announces a December 15 increase in the cost of first class postage. To determine the possible profit impact of this change and to evaluate alternative responses, management would use sensitivity analysis. Possible responses might include doing nothing, instituting an offsetting reduction in selling prices, increasing advertising to encourage potential customers to mail early, lobbying to delay the postage increase, or introducing a new holiday postcard that can be mailed at a lower rate. By analyzing each alternative in advance, management will know what action to initiate if an increase in first class postage is announced.

To offset this increase in postage, management is considering a reduction in selling price from $8 to $7 per box of cards. Management needs to know the

---

EXHIBIT 4–5   Contribution Income Statement with Income Taxes

Benchmark Card Company
Contribution Income Statement
Planned for the month of November, 19x7

Sales (7,000 × $8)		$56,000
Less variable costs:		
Cost of goods sold (7,000 × $2.00)	$14,000	
Selling and administrative (7,000 × $1.00)	7,000	−21,000
Contribution margin		$35,000
Less fixed costs:		
Factory overhead	$ 5,000	
Selling and administrative	10,000	−15,000
Income before taxes		$20,000
Income taxes ($20,000 × 0.40)		− 8,000
Net income		$12,000

number of boxes Benchmark will have to sell at the new, lower price to earn a monthly before-tax profit of $20,000.

The $1 reduction in selling price would reduce the unit contribution margin from $5 to $4 ($7 − $3). With fixed costs of $15,000 the unit sales volume required to earn a before-tax profit of $20,000 is now 8,750:

$$X = \frac{\$15,000 + \$20,000}{\$4}$$

$$= 8,750 \text{ units.}$$

This is an increase of 1,750 units:

Required sales volume at $7 selling price	8,750
Required sales volume at $8 selling price	−7,000
Increase in required sales volume	1,750

PROFIT-VOLUME GRAPHS

In cost-volume-profit graphs, profits are represented by the difference between total revenues and total costs. When management is primarily interested in the impact on profits of changes in sales volume, and less interested in the related revenues and costs, a profit-volume graph is sometimes used instead of a cost-volume-profit graph. A **profit-volume graph** illustrates the relationship between volume and profits; it does not illustrate revenues and costs. A manager primarily interested in profit-volume relationships prefers a profit-volume graph because it clearly illustrates profits. Profits are read directly from a profit-volume graph rather than being computed as the difference between total revenues and total costs.

The Benchmark Card Company's monthly profit-volume graph is presented in Exhibit 4–6. Profit or loss is measured on the vertical axis, and volume is measured in units on the horizontal axis, which intersects the vertical axis at zero profit. A single line, representing total profit, is drawn intersecting the vertical axis at a zero unit sales volume loss equal to the fixed costs. The profit line crosses the horizontal axis at the break-even unit sales volume. The profit or loss at any volume is depicted by the vertical distance between the profit line and the horizontal axis.

The profit line is drawn by determining and plotting profit or loss at two different volumes and then drawing a straight line through the plotted values. Perhaps the easiest values to select are the loss at a volume of zero (this amount is the fixed costs) and the volume at which the profit line crosses the horizontal axis (this is the break-even unit sales volume). It is also possible, using the profit formula, to determine profit or loss at any other volumes. Note that the slope

EXHIBIT 4–6   Typical Profit-Volume Graph

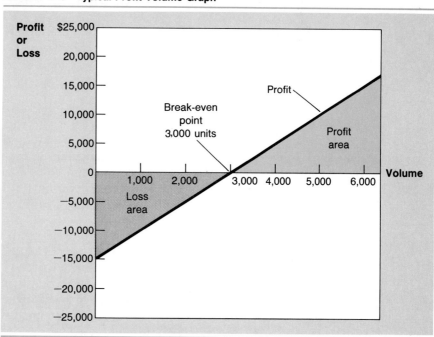

of the profit line is equal to the unit contribution margin, the amount by which profits increase, or losses decrease, as one additional unit is sold.

NOT-FOR-PROFIT APPLICATIONS

Cost-volume-profit relationships and related break-even concepts are widely used in not-for-profit organizations. To make these concepts more acceptable in such organizations, they might be renamed "cost-volume-contribution" or "cost-volume-subsidy" relationships. Although managers of not-for-profit organizations are not specifically interested in earning a profit for the organization as a whole, they often desire that some activities provide a positive contribution that can be used to subsidize other activities. Consider the following example.

Martha Montgomery is a candidate for the U.S. House of Representatives. To obtain money to finance her campaign, a fund-raising dinner with a required donation of $100 per plate is scheduled in a rented hall. The costs of renting and decorating the hall are $3,000. The variable cost of each meal served is $30. The total contribution to Martha Montgomery's campaign can be expressed as a function of the number of persons who attend the dinner. Substituting desired contribution for desired profits, campaign organizers can determine the number of tickets they must sell to net $25,000 from the dinner:

$$\text{Required number of tickets} = \frac{\text{Fixed costs} + \text{Desired contribution}}{\text{Donation per unit} - \text{Variable costs per unit}}$$

$$= \frac{\$3,000 + \$25,000}{\$100 - \$30}$$

$$= 400 \text{ tickets.}$$

The concept of the break-even point is also widely used in not-for-profit organizations. The Student Association of City University may be interested in the break-even point for such association-sponsored activities as concerts, festivals, and plays. They could also use cost-volume-profit relationships to determine the amount of any required subsidy if ticket sales fall short of the break-even point, or the amount of any contribution if ticket sales exceed the break-even point.

Many not-for-profit organizations provide goods or services for less than cost: The U.S. government subsidizes school lunches, civic orchestras stage children's concerts for a nominal fee, and the tuition charged by most colleges is inadequate to cover operating costs. Here cost-volume-profit relationships (or variations of the profit formula) are used to determine the required subsidy, or the activity level that can be supported with a given subsidy.

LIMITING ASSUMPTIONS

The models and graphs presented in this chapter are subject to a number of limiting assumptions. Although these assumptions do not negate the usefulness of these models in the early stages of planning, they do suggest the need for further analysis before plans are completed. This additional analysis is normally reflected in an organization's budget for a coming period. Among the more important assumptions are:

1. *All costs are classified as fixed or variable.* Step costs must be approximated by fixed or mixed costs, and mixed costs must be broken down into their fixed and variable cost elements.

2. *The total cost function is linear.* This assumption may be valid only within a relevant range. Over the entire range of possible volumes, changes in productivity and efficiency are likely to result in a curvilinear cost function.

3. *The total revenue function is linear.* Unit selling prices are assumed to be constant over the entire range of possible volumes. This implies a purely competitive market for final products. In some economic models (monopolistic and oligopolistic), where the demand for a product responds to price changes, the revenue function is curvilinear. In these situations the linear approximation is accurate only within a limited range of activity.

4. *The analysis is for a single product or the sales mix of multiple products is constant.* The sales mix refers to the relative portion of unit or dollar sales that is derived from each product or service. If multiple products have different unit costs or revenues, changes in the sales mix will cause changes in the slopes of total revenue or cost lines, or both. Changes in the sales mix are examined in Appendix B to this chapter.

5. *Inventories are constant.* This assumption means that all current expenditures for acquiring or producing inventories are reported as expenses on the current income statement. In the absence of this assumption, current manufacturing or inventory acquisition costs can be greater or less than the expenses reported on the income statement. This assumption, which was discussed at the beginning of this chapter, is examined further in Chapter 10.

SUMMARY

Cost-volume-profit analysis is used to examine the relationships among volume, total costs, total revenues, and profit. Because cost-volume-profit analysis provides a framework for discussing planning issues and organizing relevant data, it is widely used in the early stages of planning.

We illustrated the usefulness of this technique in determining the break-even point, the margin of safety, and the volume required to earn a desired profit with and without income taxes. In all these applications we used either the unit contribution margin or the contribution margin ratio. The unit contribution margin is the difference between the unit selling price and the unit variable costs. The contribution margin ratio is the ratio of contribution margin to sales dollars. In making short-run decisions managers should think in terms of these concepts. We will use them frequently in subsequent chapters.

APPENDIX A
OPERATING LEVERAGE

Operating leverage is a measure of the responsiveness of income to changes in sales. An organization's operating leverage at a *given sales volume* is computed as contribution margin divided by net income.

$$\text{Operating leverage} = \frac{\text{Contribution margin}}{\text{Net income}}$$

Information regarding a firm's operating leverage can be used to assist in profit planning. Multiplying a proposed percentage change in sales by a firm's operating leverage indicates the percentage effect the proposed change will have on income.

$$\frac{\text{Percentage change}}{\text{in income}} = \frac{\text{Percentage change}}{\text{in sales}} \times \frac{\text{Operating}}{\text{leverage}}$$

Recall that the Benchmark Card Company manufactures a product that has a unit selling price of $8, variable costs of $3, and monthly fixed costs of $15,000. At a monthly volume of 4,000 units, Benchmark has a contribution margin of $20,000 [($8 − $3) × 4,000] and realizes an income of $5,000 ($20,000 − $15,000). At this sales volume, Benchmark's operating leverage is 4 ($20,000 contribution margin/$5,000 income).

With an operating leverage of 4, a 37.5 percent increase in sales, from 4,000 to 5,500 units, should result in a 150 percent increase in income:

$$\text{Percentage change in income} = 37.5\% \times 4$$

$$= \underline{\underline{150\%}}$$

With an increase in income of $7,500 ($5,000 × 1.50) Benchmark's monthly profits would be $12,500 ($5,000 current + $7,500 increase), as verified below.

	Current 4,000 Units	Increase 1,500 Units	New 5,500 Units
Sales ($8 per unit)	$32,000	$12,000	$44,000
Variable costs ($3 per unit)	−12,000	− 4,500	−16,500
Contribution margin	$20,000	$ 7,500	$27,500
Fixed costs	−15,000	− 0	−15,000
Net income	$ 5,000	$ 7,500	$12,500

The difference between contribution margin and net income, fixed costs, is a constant. Because of this mathematical relationship, net income constitutes a larger portion of contribution margin as sales volume increases. This disproportionate increase in net income, as sales volume increases, produces a decrease in operating leverage, computed as the ratio of contribution margin to net income. The numerator, contribution margin, changes at a slower rate than the denominator, net income.

Because operating leverage varies with sales volume, it is important to specify both operating leverage and a corresponding sales volume. If, for example, the current sales volume was 5,000 units and management was contemplating the effect of a 10 percent increase in sales to 5,500 units, it would be inappropriate to use an operating leverage of 4 to predict the effect of the increased sales on profits. At 5,000 units the operating leverage is 2.5 ($25,000 contribution margin/$10,000 net income). If sales increase by 10 percent, profits will increase by 25 percent (10 percent increase in sales × 2.5 operating leverage), or $2,500 ($10,000 × 0.25), not by 40 percent (10 percent increase in sales × 4 operating leverage).

At the break-even point, where profits are zero, operating leverage is undefined because division by zero is undefined. Operating leverage is highest *near* the break-even point, where a percentage change in sales has the greatest percentage effect on profits. As demonstrated above for the Benchmark Card Company, the absolute value of operating leverage is lower at sales volumes farther from the break-even volume.

In addition to its use in profit planning, operating leverage is also used as an indication of an organization's cost structure. The higher the portion of an organization's fixed costs (in comparison with variable costs), the higher its operating leverage. In evaluating different firms and alternative ways of producing goods or providing services, information of operating leverage is useful in determining the sensitivity of income to changes in sales. The higher a firm's operating leverage, the more sensitive are its profits to changes in sales volume. Consider the following example.

The High Fixed Card Company manufactures a product that has a unit selling price of $8, variable costs of $1.50, and monthly fixed costs of $21,000. At a monthly volume of 4,000 units, High Fixed has a contribution of $26,000 [($8.00 − $1.50) × 4,000] and a before-tax profit of $5,000 ($26,000 − $21,000). Although High Fixed and Benchmark have identical profits at a monthly sales volume of 4,000 units, High Fixed's profits are more sensitive to changes in sales. This higher sensitivity can be determined by comparing Benchmark's and High Fixed's operating leverages:

	High Fixed	Benchmark
Contribution margin	$26,000	$20,000
Net income	÷5,000	÷5,000
Operating leverage	5.2	4.0

High Fixed's higher operating leverage results from its greater use of resources that have fixed costs (its fixed costs are $21,000, whereas Benchmark's are only $15,000).

If monthly sales increase by 12.5 percent to 4,500 units, High Fixed's profits will increase more than Benchmark's:

	High Fixed	Benchmark
Percentage change in sales	12.5%	12.5%
Operating leverage	×5.2	×4.0
Percentage change in profits	65.0%	50.0%

Conversely, if monthly sales decrease, High Fixed's profits will decrease more than Benchmark's.

In addition to helping management plan for the future, investors use information on operating leverage to predict how businesses will perform in different economic conditions. Given their cost structures, High Fixed will perform better during periods of economic growth, whereas Benchmark will perform better during periods of economic contraction. With information on operating leverage and predictions of future economic activity, investors are better able to make sound investment decisions.

APPENDIX B
SALES MIX ANALYSIS

Sales mix refers to the relative portion of unit or dollar sales that are derived from each product. One of the limiting assumptions of the basic cost-volume-profit model is that the analysis is for a single product or the sales mix is constant. When the sales mix is constant, managers of multiple-product organizations can use the average unit contribution margin, or the average contribution margin ratio, to determine the break-even point or the sales volume required to earn a desired profit. Often, however, management is interested in the effect of a change in the sales mix, rather than in the effect of a change in the sales volume at a constant mix. In this situation it is necessary to determine either the average unit contribution margin or the average contribution margin ratio for each alternative mix.

Unit Sales Analysis   Assume the Benchmark Card Company sells two kinds of greeting cards, Deluxe and Regular. At a 1:1 (one-to-one) unit sales mix, where Benchmark sells one box of Regular cards for every box of Deluxe cards, the following revenue and cost information is available:

	Deluxe Box	Regular Box	Average Box
Unit selling price	$12.00	$4.00	$8.00
Unit variable costs	− 3.00	−3.00	−3.00
Unit contribution margin	$ 9.00	$1.00	$5.00*
Fixed costs per month			$15,000

* At a 1:1 unit sales mix, 50 percent of the units are Deluxe and 50 percent of the units are Regular; hence, the average unit contribution margin is $5.00 [($9.00 × 0.50) + ($1.00 × 0.50)].

Benchmark's current monthly break-even sales volume is 3,000 units ($15,000/$5), consisting of 1,500 boxes of Deluxe cards and 1,500 boxes of Regular cards.

Product	Total Sales (Units)		Sales Mix (Units)		Product Sales (Units)
Deluxe cards	3,000	×	0.50	=	1,500
Regular cards	3,000	×	0.50	=	1,500

The current unit sales mix is represented by the top line in Exhibit 4–7.

Benchmark's management wants to know what the break-even unit sales volume would be if the unit sales mix became 1:3, that is, 25 percent Deluxe and 75 percent Regular. There are no changes in prices or costs.

At the revised mix the average unit contribution margin would be $3 per box [($9 × 0.25) + ($1 × 0.75)], and the break-even unit sales volume would be 5,000 units ($15,000/$3), consisting of 1,250 boxes of Deluxe cards and 3,750 boxes of Regular cards.

Product	Total Sales (Units)		Sales Mix (Units)		Product Sales (Units)
Deluxe cards	5,000	×	0.25	=	1,250
Regular cards	5,000	×	0.75	=	3,750

EXHIBIT 4–7   Sales Mix Analysis: Unit Sales Approach

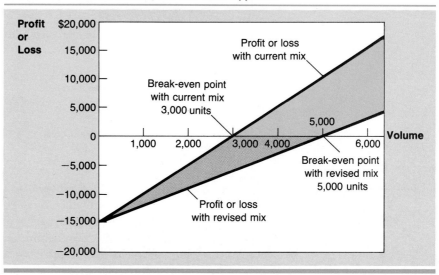

The revised mix is represented by the bottom line in Exhibit 4–7. The effect of the shift in the mix would be to increase the break-even unit sales volume. This occurs because a greater portion of the unit sales in the revised mix comes from Regular cards, which have a lower unit contribution margin.

Sales Dollar Analysis

The preceding analysis focused on unit sales and the unit contribution margin. The sales mix was expressed in terms of units. An alternative approach is to focus on dollar sales and the unit contribution margin ratio. Following this approach, the sales mix is expressed in terms of sales dollars.

Benchmark currently derives 75 percent of its sales revenue from Deluxe cards and 25 percent of its sales revenue from Regular cards. At a current monthly sales volume of $32,000, the following information is available:

	Deluxe	Regular	Total
Sales	$24,000	$8,000	$32,000
Less variable costs	− 6,000	−6,000	−12,000
Contribution margin	$18,000	$2,000	$20,000
Contribution margin ratio	0.75	0.25	0.625*

* At a sales dollar mix consisting of 75 percent Deluxe and 25 percent Regular, the overall contribution margin ratio is 0.625 [(0.75 Deluxe contribution margin ratio × 0.75 Deluxe sales dollars) + (0.25 Regular contribution margin ratio × 0.25 Regular sales dollars)].

With fixed costs of $15,000 per month, Benchmark's current monthly break-even dollar sales volume is $24,000 ($15,000/0.625), consisting of $18,000 from Deluxe card sales and $6,000 from Regular card sales.

Product	Break-even Sales (Dollars)		Sales Mix (Dollars)		Product Sales (Dollars)
Deluxe cards	$24,000	×	0.75	=	$18,000
Regular cards	$24,000	×	0.25	=	$ 6,000

The current unit sales mix is represented by the top line in Exhibit 4–8.

Benchmark's management wants to know what the break-even dollar sales volume would be if the dollar sales mix became 30 percent Deluxe and 70 percent Regular. There are no changes in prices or costs.

At the revised mix, the average contribution margin ratio would be 0.40 [(0.75 Deluxe contribution margin ratio × 0.30 Deluxe sales dollars) + (0.25

EXHIBIT 4–8   Sales Mix Analysis: Sales Dollar Approach

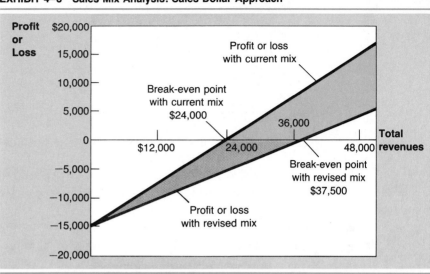

Regular contribution margin ratio × 0.70 Regular sales dollars)], and the break-even dollar sales volume would be $37,500 ($15,000/0.40), consisting of $11,250 from Deluxe cards and $26,250 from Regular cards.

Product	Total Sales (Dollars)		Sales Mix (Dollars)		Product Sales (Dollars)
Deluxe cards	$37,500	×	0.30	=	$11,250
Regular cards	$37,500	×	0.70	=	$26,250

The revised mix is represented by the bottom line in Exhibit 4–8. The effect of the shift in the mix would be to increase the break-even dollar sales volume. This occurs because a greater portion of the sales revenue in the revised mix comes from Regular cards, which have a lower contribution margin ratio.

Sales mix analysis is an interesting and important topic in multiple-product firms. Management must be just as concerned with the mix of product sales as they are with the total unit or dollar volume of sales. A shift in the sales mix can lead to unexpected results. Profits may decline with an increase in unit or dollar sales if the sales mix shifts to products with smaller contribution margins. Conversely, profits may increase even though unit or dollar sales decrease, if the sales mix shifts to products with larger contribution margins. Other things being equal, management should strive to increase sales of products that have higher contribution margins.

SUGGESTED READINGS

Givins, Horace R., "An Application of Curvilinear Break-even Analysis," *The Accounting Review* (January 1966): 141–143.

Morse, Wayne J., and Imogene A. Posey, "Taxes Do Make a Difference in Cost-Volume-Profit Analysis," *Management Accounting* (December 1979): 20–24.

Mowen, Maryanne M., *Accounting for Costs as Fixed and Variable*, Montvalle, N.J.: National Association of Accountants, 1986.

Powers, Thomas L., "Breakeven Analysis with Semifixed Costs," *Industrial Marketing Management* (February 1987): 35–41.

Srinivasan, Venkatesan, "More on Break-Even Analysis," *Journal of Commercial Bank Lending* (July 1984): 53–62.

Wichmann, Henry, "Cost-Volume-Profit Analysis for Small Business Retailers and Service Businesses," *Cost and Management* (May–June 1984): 31–35.

REVIEW PROBLEM

Income Statements and Cost-Volume-Profit Analysis

The Memorabilia Cup Company produces keepsake beverage containers for educational institutions that are sold for $40 per box of 50 containers. Variable and fixed costs are shown below:

Variable Costs per Box		Fixed Costs per Month	
Manufacturing:			
Direct materials	$15	Factory overhead	$15,000
Direct labor	3	Selling and	
Factory overhead	10	administrative	10,000
Total manufacturing	$28	Total fixed	$25,000
Selling and			
administrative	2		
Total variable	$30		

In September 19x3, Memorabilia produced and sold 3,000 boxes.

Requirements

a) Prepare a functional income statement for September.

b) Prepare a contribution income statement for September.

c) Determine Memorabilia's unit contribution margin and contribution margin ratio.

d) Determine Memorabilia's monthly break-even point in units.

e) Determine the dollar sales volume required to produce a monthly profit of $5,000. Ignore taxes.

f) Assuming Memorabilia is subject to a 40 percent income tax, determine the monthly unit sales volume required to produce a monthly after-tax profit of $4,500.

The solution to this problem is found at the end of the Chapter 4 exercises and problems.

KEY TERMS

Break-even point
Contribution income statement
Contribution margin
Contribution margin ratio
Cost-volume-profit analysis
Cost-volume-profit graph
Functional income statement

Margin of safety
Profit-volume graph
Sales mix
Sensitivity analysis
Unit contribution margin
Variable cost ratio

**APPENDIX
KEY TERM**

Operating leverage

**REVIEW
QUESTIONS**

4–1   At what stage of planning is cost-volume-profit analysis particularly useful? Why?

4–2   Present the profit equation in detail.

4–3   Why is a contribution income statement superior to a functional income statement for planning and control purposes?

4–4   What is the unit contribution margin? What does it tell us?

4–5   Distinguish between the contribution margin ratio and the variable cost ratio.

4–6   Using the contribution approach, how is the unit break-even point computed? In words, what does it tell us?

4–7   Using the contribution approach, how is the break-even dollar sales volume computed?

4–8   Using the contribution approach, how do we determine the unit sales volume required to earn a desired profit?

4–9   Using the contribution approach, how do we determine the dollar sales volume required to earn a desired profit?

4–10 What assumptions are made when income taxes are incorporated into cost-volume-profit models?

4–11 Given a desired after-tax profit and a tax rate, how do we determine the desired before-tax profit?

4–12 Why is sensitivity analysis often applied to an organization's cost-volume-profit model?

4–13 Why do some managers prefer profit-volume graphs to cost-volume-profit graphs?

4–14 Name three uses of cost-volume-profit models in not-for-profit organizations.

4–15 Name five assumptions that limit the usefulness of cost-volume-profit models.

EXERCISES

4–1 Functional and Contribution Income Statements

The Central Ohio Company produces a product that is sold for $15 per unit. Variable and fixed costs are shown below.

Variable Costs per Unit			Fixed Costs per Month	
Manufacturing:			Factory overhead	$20,000
Direct materials	$5		Selling and	
Direct labor	2		administrative	10,000
Factory overhead	2	$ 9	Total	$30,000
Selling and				
administrative		3		
Total		$12		

The company produced and sold 12,000 units during July of 19x1. There were no beginning or ending inventories.

Requirements

a) Prepare functional and contribution income statements for July.

b) Which of these income statements is more useful to management? Why?

c) Compute the unit contribution margin, and use it to determine the impact on profit of a 600 unit decrease in sales.

d) Compute the contribution margin ratio, and use it to determine the impact on profit of a $12,000 increase in sales revenue.

4–2 Functional and Contribution Income Statements

The Alberta Company produces a product that is sold for $50 per unit. Variable and fixed costs are shown below.

Variable Costs per Unit			Fixed Costs per Month	
Manufacturing:			Factory overhead	$40,000
Direct materials	$ 8		Selling and	
Direct labor	12		administrative	20,000
Factory overhead	10	$30	Total	$60,000
Selling and				
administrative		5		
Total		$35		

The company produced and sold 6,000 units during May 19x3. There were no beginning or ending inventories.

Requirements

a) Prepare functional and contribution income statements for May.

b) Explain why gross profit in the functional income statement differs from contribution margin in the contribution income statement.

c) Compute the unit contribution margin, and use it to determine the impact on profit of a 200 unit increase in sales.

d) Compute the contribution margin ratio, and use it to determine the impact on profit of a $10,000 increase in sales revenue.

4–3 Contribution Margin Concepts

At a price of $12 the estimated monthly sales of a product is 10,000 units. Variable costs include manufacturing, $6, and distribution, $1. Fixed costs are $24,000 per month.

Requirements

Determine each of the following:

a) Unit contribution margin.

b) Monthly break-even unit sales volume.

c) Monthly profit. (Ignore taxes.)

d) Monthly margin of safety in units.

4–4 Contribution Margin Concepts

At a monthly volume of $20,000 a company incurs variable costs of $8,000 and fixed costs of $9,000.

Requirements

Determine each of the following:

a) Variable cost ratio.

b) Contribution margin ratio.

c) Monthly break-even dollar sales volume.

d) Monthly margin of safety in dollars.

4–5 Contribution Margin Concepts

In 19x5 the Duke Art Shop had the following experience:

	Fixed	Variable	
Sales			$800,000
Costs:			
Goods sold		$300,000	
Labor	$160,000	60,000	
Supplies	2,000	5,000	
Utilities	12,000	3,000	
Rent	24,000	—	
Advertising	6,000	2,000	
Miscellaneous	6,000	10,000	
Total costs	$210,000	$380,000	−590,000
Net income			$210,000

Requirements

a) Determine the annual break-even dollar sales volume.

b) Determine the current margin of safety in dollars.

c) What is the annual break-even dollar sales volume if management makes a decision that increases fixed costs by $52,500?

4–6 Cost-Volume-Profit Graphs with Sensitivity Analysis

Presented is a typical cost-volume-profit graph.

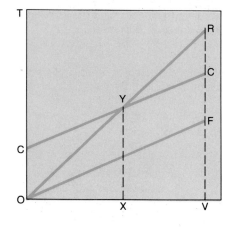

Requirements

a) Identify each of the following:

   1. Line OF.

   2. Line OR.

   3. Line CC.

   4. The difference between lines OF and OV.

   5. The difference between lines CC and OF.

   6. The difference between lines CC and OV.

   7. The difference between lines OR and OF.

   8. Point X.

   9. Area CYO.

   10. Area RCY.

b) Indicate the effect of each of the following independent events on lines CC, OR, and the break-even point:

   1. A decrease in fixed costs.

   2. An increase in the unit selling price.

   3. An increase in unit variable costs.

   4. An increase in fixed costs and a decrease in the unit selling price.

   5. A decrease in fixed costs and a decrease in the unit variable costs.

4–7 Preparing Cost-Volume-Profit Graphs

Little Nero's Pizza Shop has the following monthly revenue and cost functions.

$$\text{Total revenues} = \$6.00X,$$

$$\text{Total costs} = \$9,000 + \$1.50X.$$

Requirements

a) Prepare a graph, similar to that in Exhibit 4–2, illustrating Little Nero's cost-volume-profit relationships. The vertical axis should vary between $0 and $18,000, with increments of $3,000. The horizontal axis should vary between 0 units and 3,000 units, with increments of 500 units.

b) Prepare a graph, similar to that in Exhibit 4–3, illustrating Little Nero's cost-volume-profit relationships. Use the same scale for the graph as in requirement (a).

c) What does the graph prepared for requirement (b) emphasize?

d) Prepare a graph, similar to that in Exhibit 4–4, illustrating Little Nero's cost-volume-profit relationships. Use the same scale for the graph as in requirement (a). Be sure to label the horizontal axis in dollars.

e) What is the objective of the graph in requirement (d)? When is it most appropriate to use this type of graph?

4–8 Preparing Cost-Volume-Profit Graphs

The Mountain View Custard Shop has the following monthly revenue and cost functions:

$$\text{Total revenues} = \$1.25X,$$

$$\text{Total costs} = \$3,000 + \$0.75X.$$

Requirements

a) Prepare a graph, similar to that in Exhibit 4–2, illustrating Mountain View's cost-volume-profit relationships. The vertical axis should vary between $0 and $12,500 in increments of $2,500. The horizontal axis should vary between 0 and 10,000 units in increments of 2,000 units.

b) Prepare a graph, similar to that in Exhibit 4–3, illustrating Mountain View's cost-volume-profit relationships. Use the same scale for the graph as in requirement (a).

c) What does the graph prepared for requirement (b) emphasize?

d) Prepare a graph, similar to that in Exhibit 4–4, illustrating Mountain View's cost-volume-profit relationships. Be sure to label the horizontal axis in dollars.

e) What is the objective of the graph in requirement (d)? When is it most appropriate to use this type of graph?

4–9 Profit Planning with Taxes

In 19x5 the Fenwick Processing Company had the following income statement:

Sales		$950,000
Variable costs:		
Variable cost of goods sold	$420,000	
Variable selling and administrative expenses	150,000	−570,000
Contribution margin		$380,000
Fixed costs:		
Fixed factory overhead	$110,000	
Fixed selling and administrative expenses	80,000	−190,000
Net income before taxes		$190,000
Income taxes @ 0.36		− 68,400
Net income		$121,600

Requirements

a) Determine the 19x5 break-even point in sales dollars.

b) Determine the 19x5 margin of safety in sales dollars.

c) What is the break-even point in sales dollars if management makes a decision that increases fixed costs by $50,000?

d) What dollar sales volume is required to provide an after-tax net income of $200,000? Assume fixed costs are $190,000.

e) Prepare an abbreviated contribution income statement to verify that the solution to requirement (d) will provide the desired after-tax income.

4–10 Profit Planning with Taxes

The Brown Manufacturing Company produces a product that is sold for $35 per unit. Variable and fixed costs are shown below.

Variable Costs per Unit		Fixed Costs per Year	
Manufacturing	$18	Manufacturing	$ 80,000
Selling and administrative	7	Selling and administrative	30,000
Total	$25	Total	$110,000

Last year Brown manufactured and sold 20,000 units to obtain a net income after taxes of $49,500.

Requirements

a) Determine the tax rate Brown paid last year.

b) What unit sales volume is required to provide an after-tax net income of $88,000?

c) If Brown reduces the unit variable cost by $2.50 and increases fixed manufacturing costs by $20,000, what unit sales volume is required to provide an after-tax income of $88,000?

d) What assumptions are made about taxable income and tax rates in requirements (a) through (c)?

4–11 Profit Planning with Taxes

Pawnee Company operated at normal capacity during the current year producing 40,000 units of its single product. Sales totaled 40,000 units at an average price of $20 per unit. Variable manufacturing costs were $8 per unit, and variable marketing costs were $4 per unit sold. Fixed costs were incurred uniformly throughout the year and amounted to $188,000 for manufacturing and $64,000 for marketing. There was no year-end work-in-process inventory.

Requirements

a) Determine Pawnee's break-even point in sales dollars for the current year.

b) Pawnee is subject to an income tax rate of 30 percent. Determine the number of units required to be sold in the current year to earn an after-tax income of $126,000.

c) Pawnee's variable manufacturing costs are expected to increase 10 percent in the coming year. Determine Pawnee's break-even point in sales dollars for the coming year.

d) Assuming Pawnee's variable manufacturing costs do increase by 10 percent in the coming year, determine the selling price that will yield the current contribution margin ratio in the coming year.

(CMA Adapted)

4–12 Profit-Volume Graph: Identification and Analysis

Presented is a typical profit-volume graph.

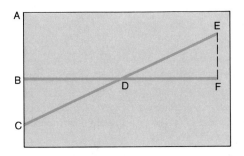

Requirements

a) Identify each of the following:

1. Area BDC.	**4.** Line AC.
2. Area DEF.	**5.** Line BC.
3. Point D.	**6.** Line EF.

b) Indicate the effect of each of the following on line CE and the break-even point.

1. An increase in the unit selling price.

2. An increase in the variable costs per unit.

3. A decrease in fixed costs.

4. An increase in fixed costs and a decrease in the unit selling price.

5. A decrease in fixed costs and an increase in the variable costs per unit.

4–13 Preparing Cost-Volume-Profit and Profit-Volume Graphs

Maritime Petro operates several self-service gas stations in the Maritime Provinces of Canada. Maritime Petro has a selling price of $0.90 per liter. Variable operating costs are $0.70 per liter, and fixed operating costs are $80,000 per month.

Requirements

a) Determine the monthly break-even point in liters.

b) Prepare a cost-volume-profit graph for Maritime Petro. Use a format that emphasizes the contribution margin. The vertical axis should vary between 0 dollars and $540,000 in increments of $90,000. The horizontal axis should vary between 0 liters and 600,000 liters in increments of 100,000 liters. Label the graph in thousands.

c) Prepare a profit-volume graph for Maritime Petro. The vertical axis should vary between $(100,000) and $60,000 in increments of $20,000. The horizontal axis should vary between 0 liters and 600,000 liters in increments of 100,000 liters. Label the graph in thousands.

d) Evaluate the profit-volume graph. In what ways is it superior and in what ways is it inferior to the traditional cost-volume-profit graph?

4–14 Preparing Cost-Volume-Profit and Profit-Volume Graphs

Happy Hawkers is a hot dog concession operator at five baseball stadiums. Happy Hawkers sells hot dogs, with all the fixings, for $1.50 each. Variable costs are $1.20 per hot dog, and fixed operating costs are $150,000 per year.

Requirements

a) Determine the annual break-even point in hot dogs.

b) Prepare a cost-volume-profit graph for Happy Hawkers. Use a form that emphasizes the contribution margin. The vertical axis should vary between 0 dollars and $1,500,000 in increments of $250,000. The horizontal axis should vary between 0 hot dogs and 1,000,000 hot dogs, in increments of 250,000 hot dogs. Label the graph in thousands.

c) Prepare a profit-volume graph for Happy Hawkers. The vertical axis should vary between $(200,000) and $200,000 in increments of $100,000. The horizontal axis should vary as described in requirement (b). Label the graph in thousands.

d) Evaluate the profit-volume graph. In what ways is it superior and in what ways is it inferior to the traditional cost-volume-profit graph?

4–15 Not-for-Profit Applications

Determine the solution to each of the following independent cases.

1. Lakeside College has annual fixed operating costs of $5,000,000 and variable operating costs of $1,000 per student. Tuition is $4,000 per student for the academic year. The projected enrollment for the coming year is 1,500 students. Expected revenues from endowments and federal and state grants are $250,000. Determine the amount Lakeside must obtain from other sources.

2. The Lakeside College Student Association is planning a fall concert. Expected costs of renting a hall, hiring a band, and so forth, are $30,000. Assuming 5,000 persons attend the concert, determine the break-even price per ticket. How much will the association lose if this price is charged and only 4,250 tickets are sold?

3. City Hospital has a contract with the city to provide indigent health care on an out-patient basis for $25 per visit. The patient will pay $5 of this amount, and the city will pay the balance of $20. Determine the amount the city will have to pay if the hospital has 10,000 patient visits.

4. A civic organization is engaged in a fund-raising program. On Civic Sunday they will sell newspapers at $1.25 each. The organization will pay $0.75 for each newspaper. Costs of the necessary permits, signs, and so forth, are $500. Determine the amount they will raise if 5,000 newspapers are sold.

5. Christmas for the Needy is a civic organization that provides Christmas presents to disadvantaged children. The annual costs of this activity are $5,000 plus $10 per present. Determine the number of presents the organization can provide with $20,000.

4–16 High-Low Cost Estimation and Profit Planning

Presented are comparative 19x8 and 19x9 income statements for Montana Products, Inc.

Montana Products, Inc.
Comparative Income Statements
For the years ending December 31, 19x8 and 19x9

	19x8	19x9
Unit sales	5,000	8,000
Sales revenue	$ 65,000	$104,000
Expenses	− 75,000	− 90,000
Net income (loss)	$(10,000)	$ 14,000

Requirements

a) Determine the break-even point in units.

b) Determine the unit sales volume required to earn a profit of $10,000.

4–17 High-Low Cost Estimation and Profit Planning

Presented are comparative 19y3 and 19y4 income statements for Nevada Products, Inc.

Nevada Products, Inc.
Comparative Income Statements
For the years ending 19y3 and 19y4

	19y3	19y4
Sales revenue	$500,000	$300,000
Expenses	−440,000	−360,000
Net income (loss)	$ 60,000	$ (60,000)

Requirements

a) Determine the break-even point in sales dollars.

b) Determine the dollar sales volume required to earn a profit of $180,000.

PROBLEMS

4–18 Cost-Volume-Profit Relationships: Missing Data

Supply the missing data in each independent case.

	Case 1	Case 2	Case 3	Case 4
Unit sales	1,000	800	?	?
Sales revenue	$20,000	?	?	$60,000
Variable cost per unit	$ 10	$ 1	$ 12	?
Contribution margin	?	$800	?	?
Fixed costs	$ 8,000	?	$80,000	?
Net income	?	$400	?	?
Unit contribution margin	?	?	?	$ 15
Break-even point (units)	?	?	4,000	2,000
Margin of safety (units)	?	?	300	1,000

4–19 Cost-Volume-Profit Relationships: Missing Data

Supply the missing data in each independent case.

	Case 1	Case 2	Case 3	Case 4
Sales revenue	$100,000	$80,000	?	?
Contribution margin	$ 60,000	?	$20,000	?
Fixed costs	$ 30,000	?	?	?
Net income	?	$15,000	$10,000	?
Variable cost ratio	?	0.25	?	0.20
Contribution margin ratio	?	?	0.40	?
Break-even point (dollars)	?	?	?	$25,000
Margin of safety (dollars)	?	?	?	$15,000

4–20 Cost Analysis

In 1979 Winnebago Industries Inc. reported a loss of $4.2 million on sales of $214.6 million. In an effort to save the company, John K. Hanson reduced the firm's employees to 1,400 from 4,000 and sold two assembly plants. This reduced Winnebago's break-even point to 100 million sales dollars. In 1981 Winnebago reported a profit of $10.1 million on sales of $146.6 million.

Required: Determine Winnebago's margin of safety, contribution margin ratio, variable cost ratio, and fixed costs during 1981. Round calculations to four decimal places.

4–21 Potpourri of Profit Planning without Taxes

1. Lindsay Company reported the following results from sales of 5,000 units of product A for June 19x1.

Sales	$200,000
Variable costs	120,000
Fixed costs	60,000
Operating income	20,000

Assume that Lindsay increases the selling price of product A by 10 percent on July 1, 19x1. How many units of product A would have to be sold in July 19x1 in order to generate an operating income of $20,000?

2. Singer, Inc., sells product R for $5 per unit. The fixed costs are $210,000, and the variable costs are 60 percent of the selling price. Determine the dollar sales volume required for Singer to realize a profit of 10 percent of sales.

3. Birney Company is planning its advertising campaign for 19x1 and has prepared the following budget data based on a zero advertising expenditure.

Normal plant capacity	200,000 units
Sales	150,000 units
Selling price	$25.00 per unit
Variable manufacturing costs	$15.00 per unit
Fixed costs:	
Manufacturing	$800,000
Selling and administrative	$700,000

An advertising agency claims that an aggressive advertising campaign would enable Birney to increase its unit sales by 20 percent. What is the maximum amount that Birney can pay for advertising and obtain an operating profit of $200,000?

4. Pitt Company is considering a proposal to replace existing machinery used for the manufacture of product A. The new machines are expected to cause increased annual fixed costs of $120,000; however, variable costs should decrease by 20 percent because of a reduction in direct labor hours and more efficient usage of direct materials. Before this change was under consideration, Pitt had budgeted product A sales and costs for 19x1 as follows:

Sales	$2,000,000
Variable costs	70 percent of sales
Fixed costs	$400,000

Assuming that Pitt implemented the above proposal by January 1, 19x1, what would be the increase in budgeted operating profit for product A for 19x1?

(CPA Adapted)

4–22 Break-even Analysis in a Not-for-Profit Organization

Melford Hospital operates a general hospital, but rents space to separately owned entities rendering specialized services, such as pediatrics and psychiatric. Melford charges each separate entity for patients' services such as meals and laundry and for administrative services such as billings and collections. Space and bed rentals are fixed charges for the year, based on bed capacity rented to each entity.

Melford charged the following costs to Pediatrics for the year ended June 30, 19x2:

	Patient Days (Variable)	Bed Capacity (Fixed)
Dietary	$ 600,000	
Janitorial		$ 70,000
Laundry	300,000	
Laboratory	450,000	
Pharmacy	350,000	
Repairs and maintenance		30,000
General and administrative		1,300,000
Rent		1,500,000
Billings and collections	300,000	
Total	$2,000,000	$2,900,000

In addition to the above charges from Melford Hospital, Pediatrics incurred the following personnel costs:

	Annual Salaries
Supervising nurses	$100,000
Nurses	200,000
Assistants	180,000
Total	$480,000

These salaries are fixed within the ranges of annual patient-days considered in this problem.

During the year ended June 30, 19x2, Pediatrics charged each patient $300 per day, had a capacity of 60 beds, and had revenues of $6,000,000 for 365 days. Pediatrics operated at 100 percent of capacity on 90 days during the year ended June 30, 19x2. It is estimated that during these 90 days the demand exceeded 80 beds (Pediatrics' capacity is 60 beds). Melford has an additional 20 beds available for rent during the year ending June 30, 19x3. Such additional rental would proportionately increase Pediatrics' annual fixed charges based on bed capacity.

Requirements

a) Calculate the minimum number of patient-days required for Pediatrics to break even for the year ending June 30, 19x3, if additional beds are not rented. Patient demand is unknown, but assume that revenue per patient-day, cost per patient-day, cost per bed, and salary rates for the year ending June 30, 19x3, remain the same as for the year ended June 30, 19x2.

b) Assume that patient demand, revenue per patient-day, cost per patient-day, cost per bed, and salary rates for the year ending June 30, 19x3, remain the same as for the year ended June 30, 19x2. Prepare a schedule of increases in revenue and increases in costs for the year ending June 30, 19x3, in order to determine the net increase or decrease in earnings from an additional 20 beds if Pediatrics rents this extra capacity from Melford.

(CPA Adapted)

4–23 Cost-Volume-Profit Analysis of Alternative Products

Siberian Ski Company recently expanded its manufacturing capacity to allow production of up to 15,000 pairs of cross-country skis of the mountaineering model or the touring model. The sales department assures management that it can sell between 9,000 and 13,000 of either product this year. Because the models are very similar, Siberian Ski will produce only one of the two models.

The following information was compiled by the accounting department.

	Model	
	Mountaineering	Touring
Selling price per unit	$88.00	$80.00
Variable costs per unit	$52.80	$52.80

Fixed costs will total $369,600 if the mountaineering model is produced, but only $316,800 if the touring model is produced. Siberian Ski Company is subject to a 40 percent income tax rate.

Requirements

a) Determine the contribution margin ratio of the touring model.

b) If Siberian Ski Company desires an after-tax net income of $24,000, how many pairs of touring model skis will the company have to sell? Round answer to nearest unit.

c) Determine the *unit* sales volume at which Siberian Ski Company would make the same before-tax profit or loss regardless of the ski model it decides to produce. Also determine the resulting before-tax profit or loss.

d) Determine the *dollar* sales volume at which Siberian Ski Company would make the same before-tax profit or loss regardless of the ski model it decides to produce. Also determine the resulting before-tax profit or loss. *Hint:* Work with contribution margin ratios.

e) What action should Siberian Ski Company take if the annual sales of either model were guaranteed to be at least 12,000 pairs? Why?

f) Determine how much the unit variable costs of the touring model would have to change before both models have the same break-even point in units. Round calculations to the nearest cent.

g) Determine the new unit break-even point of the touring skis if their variable costs per unit decrease by 10 percent and their fixed costs increase by 10 percent. Round answer to nearest unit.

(CMA Adapted)

4–24 Alternative Production Procedures and Operating Leverage (Appendix)

Candice Corporation has decided to introduce a new product. The new product can be manufactured by either a capital intensive method or a labor intensive method. The manufacturing method will not affect the quality of the product. The predicted manufacturing costs for each method are as follows:

	Capital Intensive	Labor Intensive
Direct materials	$5.00	$5.60
Direct labor		
(0.5 hours × $12)	6.00	
(0.8 hours × $9)		7.20
Variable overhead		
(0.5 labor hours × $6)	$3.00	
(0.8 labor hours × $6)		4.80
Fixed overhead per year	$2,440,000	$1,320,000

Candice's market research department has recommended an introductory unit sales price of $30. The incremental selling costs are predicted to be $500,000 per year plus $2 per unit sold.

Requirements

a) Calculate the annual break-even point in units of the new product if Candice uses the:

1. Capital intensive manufacturing method.

2. Labor intensive manufacturing method.

b) Determine the annual unit volume at which Candice would be indifferent between the two manufacturing methods. Indicate when Candice should use each of the two methods.

c) Management must decide which manufacturing method to employ. One factor it must consider is operating leverage.

1. Explain operating leverage and the relationship between operating leverage and the volatility of earnings.

2. Determine the operating leverage of each manufacturing method at an annual volume of 250,000 units. Round your answer to two decimal places.

3. Explain the difference in operating leverage.

(CMA Adapted)

4–25 Contribution Income Statements and Operating Leverage (Appendix)

The Woodchopper Company cuts and sells firewood in Vermont and New Hampshire. The wood is sold by the face cord, which is a stack 4 feet high, by 2 feet deep, by 8 feet long. The Woodchopper Company pays high school and college students to saw, split, and transport the wood using company-owned equipment. Woodchopper uses newspaper advertising extensively in the fall and maintains a toll-free "hot line" to accept customer orders. The selling price is $45 per cord, variable costs are $25 per cord, and fixed costs are $20,000 per year. In 19x6 Woodchopper sold 1,400 cords.

Requirements

a) Prepare a contribution income statement for the year ended December 31, 19x6.

b) Determine Woodchopper's operating leverage.

c) Using Woodchopper's current operating leverage, calculate the percentage change in profits if sales increase 50 percent, to 2,100 cords per year.

d) Could the operating leverage determined for requirement (b) be used to calculate the percentage change in profits if sales increased 5 percent, from 2,000 cords to 2,100 cords? Explain your answer.

e) Woodchopper's management is considering the desirability of purchasing several log-splitting machines. This will increase their annual fixed costs while reducing their variable costs. What effect will this acquisition have on Woodchopper's operating leverage? Explain your answer.

4–26 Contribution Income Statements and Operating Leverage (Appendix)

The Alabama Berry Basket harvests early season strawberries for shipment throughout the eastern United States in late March. The strawberry farm is maintained by a permanent staff of ten employees and a large number of seasonal workers who pick and pack strawberries. The strawberries are sold in crates containing 100 individually packaged one-quart containers. Affixed to each one-quart container is the distinctive Alabama Berry

Basket logo inviting buyers to enjoy "the berry best strawberries in the world" and an invitation to visit the Alabama Berry Basket, located near Interstate Highway 65. The selling price is $90 per crate, variable costs are $80 per crate, and fixed costs are $275,000 per year. In 19x8 Alabama Berry Basket sold 40,000 crates.

Requirements

a) Prepare a contribution income statement for the year ended December 31, 19x8.

b) Determine Alabama Berry Basket's operating leverage.

c) Using Alabama Berry Basket's current operating leverage, calculate the percentage change in profits if sales decreased 10 percent, to 36,000 containers per year.

d) Could the operating leverage determined for requirement (b) be used to calculate the percentage change in profits if sales increased 20 percent, from 30,000 crates to 36,000 crates? Explain your answer.

e) Management is considering the desirability of purchasing several berry-picking machines. This will increase their annual fixed costs to $375,000 while reducing their variable costs to $77.50 per crate. Calculate the effect this acquisition will have on operating leverage. Explain the change in operating leverage.

4–27 Unit Sales Analysis of Break-even Point for Multiple Products (Appendix)

Presented is information regarding the Triangle Company's three products.

	A	B	C
Unit Selling price	$5.00	$7.00	$6.00
Unit variable costs	−4.00	−5.00	−3.00
Unit contribution margin	$1.00	$2.00	$3.00

Triangle sells two units of A for each unit of B and three units of B for each unit of C. Fixed costs are $90,000 per month.

Required: Determine the unit sales of product A at the monthly break-even point.

4–28 Sales Dollars Analysis of Break-even Point for Multiple Products (Appendix)

Bob's Tax Service prepares tax returns for low to middle income taxpayers. Bob's service operates January 2 through April 15 at a counter in a local department store. All jobs are classified into one of three categories: standard, multiform, and complex. Presented is information on each category.

	Standard	Multiform	Complex
Billing rate	$50	$125	$250
Average variable cost	−30	− 75	−150
Average contribution margin	$20	$ 50	$100
Returns prepared last year	1,750	500	250

All employees are paid on a per-return basis. The fixed costs of rent, utilities, and so forth, were $30,000 last year.

Requirements

a) Determine Bob's break-even dollar sales volume.

b) Determine Bob's margin of safety in sales dollars.

c) Prepare a profit-volume graph.

4–29 Unit Sales Analysis of Break-even Point for Multiple Products (Appendix)

Tennessee Instruments manufactures and sells two types of hand calculators: student and professional. Information about selling prices and costs follows:

	Student	Professional
Unit selling price	$20.00	$50.00
Unit variable costs:		
Manufacturing	$ 7.00	$15.00
Selling	3.00	5.00
Total	−10.00	−20.00
Unit contribution margin	$10.00	$30.00
Fixed costs are $60,000 per month.		

Monthly calculator sales total 5,000 units. The current sales mix is 50 percent student calculators and 50 percent professional calculators. Management believes that a $10 reduction in the price of professional calculators will change the mix to 40 percent student calculators and 60 percent professional calculators while increasing the monthly calculator sales to 6,000 units.

Requirements

a) Determine the current unit break-even point and monthly profit.

b) Determine the revised unit break-even point and monthly profit with the reduced price for professional calculators.

c) Prepare a profit-volume graph that contains profit lines for the current mix and prices as well as for the revised mix and prices.

d) Based on your analysis, what action do you recommend?

4–30 Sales Dollars Analysis of Break-even Point for Multiple Products (Appendix)

Currently, the Corner Lunch Counter only sells Super Burgers. During a typical month, the Counter reports a profit of $9,000, with sales of $50,000 and fixed costs of $21,000. Management desires to introduce a new Super Chicken Sandwich. The new sandwich will sell for $3 and have variable costs of $1.80. The addition of Super Chickens will require the counter to hire additional personnel and purchase new equipment. These actions will increase monthly fixed costs by $7,760.

In the short run, management believes that 10,000 Super Chickens will be sold each month. However, almost all the sales will come from regular customers who will switch from Super Burgers to Super Chickens. Consequently, monthly sales of Super Burgers will decline to $20,000.

In the long run, management believes that Super Chicken sales will increase to 15,000 units per month and that Super Burger sales will increase to $75,000 per month.

Requirements

a) Determine each of the following:

   1. The current monthly break-even point in sales dollars.

   2. The short-run monthly profit and break-even point in sales dollars subsequent to the introduction of Super Chickens.

   3. The long-run monthly profit and break-even point in sales dollars subsequent to the introduction of Super Chickens. Round your answer to the nearest dollar.

b) Prepare a profit-volume graph with profit lines for the current, short-run, and long-run mixes. Label the horizontal axis in sales dollars.

**REVIEW PROBLEM
SOLUTION**

a)

Memorabilia Cup Company
Functional Income Statement
For the month of September, 19x3

Sales (3,000 × $40)		$120,000
Cost of goods sold:		
Direct materials (3,000 × $15)	$45,000	
Direct labor (3,000 × $3)	9,000	
Variable factory overhead (3,000 × $10)	30,000	
Fixed factory overhead	15,000	− 99,000
Gross profit		$ 21,000
Selling and administrative expenses:		
Variable (3,000 × $2)	$ 6,000	
Fixed	10,000	− 16,000
Net income		$ 5,000

b)

Memorabilia Cup Company
Contribution Income Statement
For the month of September, 19x3

Sales (3,000 × $40)			$120,000
Less variable costs:			
Cost of goods sold:			
Direct materials (3,000 × $15)	$45,000		
Direct labor (3,000 × $3)	9,000		
Factory overhead			
(3,000 × $10)	30,000	$84,000	
Selling and administrative			
(3,000 × $2)		6,000	− 90,000
Contribution margin			$ 30,000
Less fixed costs:			
Factory overhead	$15,000		
Selling and administrative	10,000		− 25,000
Net income			$ 5,000

c)

	Per Unit
Selling price	$40
Variable costs	−30
Contribution margin	$10

$$\text{Contribution margin ratio} = \frac{\text{Unit contribution margin}}{\text{Selling price}}$$

$$= \$10/\$40$$

$$= 0.25$$

d) Contribution approach:

$$\text{Break-even point in units} = \frac{\text{Fixed costs}}{\text{Unit contribution margin}}$$

$$= \frac{\$25,000}{\$10}$$

$$= 2,500 \text{ units}$$

Formula approach:

$$\text{Profit} = \left(\begin{matrix}\text{Selling} \\ \text{price}\end{matrix} \times \begin{matrix}\text{Unit} \\ \text{volume}\end{matrix}\right) - \left[\begin{matrix}\text{Fixed} \\ \text{costs}\end{matrix} + \left(\begin{matrix}\text{Variable costs} \\ \text{per unit}\end{matrix} \times \begin{matrix}\text{Unit} \\ \text{volume}\end{matrix}\right)\right]$$

$$\$0 = \$40X - [\$25,000 + \$30X]$$

$$X = 2,500 \text{ units}$$

e)

$$\text{Dollar sales for a monthly profit of }\$5,000 = \frac{\text{Fixed costs} + \text{Required before-tax profit}}{\text{Contribution margin ratio}}$$

$$= \frac{\$25,000 + \$5,000}{0.25}$$

$$= \$120,000$$

f)

$$\text{Required before-tax profit} = \frac{\text{Desired after-tax profit}}{1.0 - \text{Tax rate}}$$

$$= \frac{\$4,500}{1 - 0.40}$$

$$= \$7,500$$

$$\text{Unit sales for a monthly after-tax profit of }\$4,500 = \frac{\text{Fixed costs} + \text{Required before-tax profit}}{\text{Unit contribution margin}}$$

$$= \frac{\$25,000 + \$7,500}{\$10}$$

$$= 3,250 \text{ units}$$

C H A P T E R 5

Relevant Costs for Management Decisions

Learning Objectives

Upon completion of this chapter you should:

- **Understand how the concept of relevant costs is used in decision making.**

- **Be able to distinguish between relevant and nonrelevant costs for special decisions.**

- **Be able to organize relevant costs in a manner that clearly indicates how they differ under each decision alternative.**

- **Be familiar with the differential analysis approach to cost analysis.**

- **Understand the application of differential analysis to important decisions, including: evaluating multiple changes in profit plans, accepting or rejecting special orders, deciding to make or buy a part or service, determining how best to use limited resources, and deciding to sell a product at some stage of completion or to process it further.**

- **Understand the basic alternative approaches to pricing products and services, including economic and cost-based approaches.**

Cost-volume-profit analysis was presented in Chapter 4 as a useful framework for discussing planning issues and organizing relevant data. Cost-volume-profit analysis is especially useful in the early stages of planning. The overview it provides helps managers avoid getting lost in the details of individual decisions. Yet, despite the immense value of cost-volume-profit analysis, a sharper focus is often needed to make specific decisions. This need is particularly evident in multiple-product or multiple-service organizations. Here managers are frequently faced with the problem of too much rather than too little information.

When evaluating alternative actions, management should not place all information within the framework of their organization's overall cost-volume-profit model or profit formula. Instead, they should focus their attention on those costs and revenues that differ under alternative actions.

The purpose of this chapter is to examine concepts used to identify and analyze cost information for specific management decisions. While examining these concepts, a number of decision situations are discussed: whether to accept or reject a special order, whether to make or buy a part or service, how best to use limited capacity, whether to sell a product or process it further, and what price to charge for a product or service.

The decision situations presented here are not exhaustive; they are only intended to illustrate relevant cost concepts. Once these concepts are understood, they can be applied to a variety of management decisions. Because income taxes would unnecessarily complicate the discussion of relevant cost concepts, they are omitted from the examples presented in this chapter.

Although the emphasis in this chapter is on identifying and analyzing cost information, it is important to keep in mind that decisions should not be based solely on the criterion of short-run cost minimization or profit maximization. A proper analysis of cost information *assists* management in making decisions; however, management must also consider legal, ethical, social, and other non-quantitative factors. These factors may lead management to select a course of action other than that suggested by cost information alone.

RELEVANT COSTS AND DIFFERENTIAL ANALYSIS

Cost concepts for management action were introduced in Chapter 2. *Relevant costs* were defined as future costs that differ among competing alternatives, and *sunk costs* were defined as costs that result from past decisions management no longer has control over. Management must avoid being influenced by sunk costs that cannot be changed or by future costs that are not affected by the decision at hand. *The key to effective cost analysis is to (1) identify the relevant costs (and revenues), and (2) organize them in a manner that clearly indicates how they differ under each alternative.* Consider the following equipment replacement decision.

The Ace Stamping Company uses a Model I stamping machine to produce 10,000 widgets per year. Widgets sell for $15 each. Ace's variable and fixed costs are as follows:

Variable:	
Direct materials	$3 per unit
Direct labor	4 per unit
Factory overhead	1 per unit
Selling and administrative	1 per unit
Fixed:	
Factory overhead other than depreciation	$19,000 per year
Depreciation of Model I stamping machine	15,000 per year
Selling and administrative	12,000 per year

The Model I stamping machine is two years old and has a remaining useful life of four years. It cost $90,000 and has an estimated salvage value of zero dollars at the end of its useful life. Its current book value (original cost less accumulated depreciation) is $60,000, but its current disposal value is only $35,000.

Management is evaluating the desirability of replacing the Model I stamping machine with a new Model II stamping machine. The new machine costs $80,000, has a useful life of four years, and a predicted salvage value of zero dollars at the end of its useful life. Though the new machine has the same productive capacity as the old machine, its operating costs would be lower because it would require only one operator rather than the two needed by the old machine. Furthermore, it has fewer moving parts, so it would require less maintenance and use less power. The new labor and overhead costs are predicted to be as follows:

Direct labor	$2.00 per unit
Variable factory overhead	0.80 per unit
Fixed factory overhead other than depreciation	$16,000 per year

All other costs would be the same as for the old machine.

Identifying Relevant Costs

The decision at hand is either to keep the old Model I stamping machine or to replace it with a new Model II stamping machine. To assist management in making this decision, the accountant should prepare an analysis of those costs and revenues that differ under each alternative. Although the clearest presentation is one that contains only those costs and revenues that differ, the first objective of this chapter is to study the distinction between relevant and irrelevant items. To help accomplish this objective, a complete analysis of all costs and revenues under each alternative is presented in Exhibit 5–1. After evaluating the relevance of each item, a more focused differential analysis of relevant costs will be prepared.

The first thing to notice in Exhibit 5–1 is that many costs and revenues are the same under each alternative. These items are not relevant to the replacement decision. The only relevant items are those that have an entry in the difference column.

Future Revenues May Be Relevant. Revenues, which are inflows of resources from operations, are relevant if they differ between alternatives. Revenues in this example are not relevant because they are identical under each

EXHIBIT 5–1   Complete Analysis of All Costs and Revenues

	Complete Analysis of Four-Year Totals		
	(1) Keep Old Model I Machine	(2) Replace with New Model II Machine	(1) − (2) Difference (Effect of Replacement on Income)
Sales (10,000 units × $15 × 4 years)	$600,000	$600,000	
Costs:			
Direct materials			
(10,000 units × $3 × 4 years)	$120,000	$120,000	
Direct labor:			
Old (10,000 units × $4 × 4 years)	160,000		
New (10,000 units × $2 × 4 years)		80,000	$80,000
Variable overhead:			
Old (10,000 units × $1 × 4 years)	40,000		
New (10,000 units × $0.80 × 4 years)		32,000	8,000
Variable selling and administrative			
(10,000 units × $1 × 4 years)	40,000	40,000	
Fixed overhead except depreciation:			
Old ($19,000 × 4 years)	76,000		
New ($16,000 × 4 years)		64,000	12,000
Depreciation or write-off of			
old machine	60,000	60,000*	
Disposal value of old machine		(35,000)*	35,000
Cost of new machine		80,000	(80,000)
Fixed selling and			
administrative ($12,000 × 4 years)	48,000	48,000	
Total costs	−544,000	−489,000	
Net income	$ 56,000	$111,000	$55,000
Advantage of replacement		$55,000	

* A single loss on disposal of $25,000 ($60,000 − $35,000) would be shown on an income statement prepared for external users.

alternative. They would be relevant if the new machine had greater capacity that would be used, or if management intended to change the unit selling price should they acquire the new machine.

The keep or replace decision facing Ace's management might be called a **cost reduction proposal** because it is based on the assumption that the organization is committed to an activity and that management desires to minimize the cost of the activity. Here the alternatives are (1) continue operating with the old machine or (2) replace with a new machine.

Although this approach is appropriate for many activities, managers of for-profit organizations should always remember that they have another alternative; namely, discontinue operations. To simplify the analysis, managers normally do not consider the alternative to discontinue when operations appear to be profitable. However, if there is any doubt about an operation's profitability, this alternative should be considered. Because revenues will change if an operation is discontinued, revenues are relevant whenever this alternative is considered.

M ANAGERIAL PRACTICE 5.1

Remembering Managerial Accounting in a New Venture

Why do approximately 50 percent of new businesses fail during their first year of operation? Ask Gary Gaskill and his partner, Michael Hyland. When they opened their franchise takeout and delivery sandwich shop, Bubba's Breadaway, they had high expectations; both were accountants, so running a business would be easy, or so they thought. After one year of operations, their high hopes had turned to despair. The partners found themselves caught up in operating the business while ignoring sound accounting practices, like preparing estimates of revenues and expenses. They had failed to analyze the costs and cash outflows of operating the business along with other basic management accounting techniques. "We were slow to make needed management changes because we were managing with insufficient information. It cost us literally thousands of dollars simply because we did not install adequate financial reporting systems from the very beginning." Three years and many mistakes later, the partners are finally having success with their business, which now includes several sound managerial accounting applications.

Source: Gary T. Gaskill with J. Michael Hyland, "Starting and Managing a Small Business," *Management Accounting* (December 1989): 28–31.

Outlay Costs May Be Relevant. **Outlay costs** are future costs that require future expenditures of cash or other resources. Outlay costs that differ under the decision alternatives at hand are relevant; those that do not differ are irrelevant. It is a mistake to assume that variable costs are always relevant and fixed costs always irrelevant. The relevant and the irrelevant outlay costs for Ace Stamping Company's equipment replacement decision are as follows:

Relevant Outlay Costs	*Irrelevant Outlay Costs*
Direct labor	Direct materials
Variable factory overhead	Variable selling and administrative
Fixed factory overhead	Fixed selling and administrative
except depreciation	
Cost of new machine	

Variable and fixed costs are included in both categories.

MANAGERIAL PRACTICE 5.2

Computer Owners Opt Not to Buy Service Contracts

Not too long ago, most computer owners purchased service contracts (a form of outlay cost) with annual costs often equaling 10 percent of the computer's purchase price. The choice was between buying the contract and paying for every service call. Computer reliability was such that the low-cost alternative was obvious. However, times have changed. Tandy Corporation claims that its PCs are designed to run 30,000 hours without a failure. That's the same as 10 hours a day, 300 days a year, for 10 years. With this level of reliability, computer owners are more reluctant to buy service contracts. Blue Cross/Blue Shield of Ohio reduced its data processing costs $125,000 a year by eliminating computer service contracts. According to the director of telecommunications at the Bank of Boston Corporation, "It's getting to the point where they're [PCs] cheaper to chuck than repair."

Source: Gary McWilliams, "If It Ain't Broke, Why Pay to Fix It?" *Business Week*, 5 March 1990, 82, 84.

Because variable costs respond to changes in the volume of activity, they are relevant when decision alternatives have different activity levels. *Variable costs may not be relevant when decision alternatives have the same activity level.* In this case, variable costs will differ only if there is a difference in the variable cost per unit of activity.

The Model II stamping machine requires fewer operators, less maintenance, and less power. Hence, direct labor and variable overhead are relevant to the replacement decision. Because there is no change in the production and sales volume, nor any other change in selling or administrative procedures, the variable selling and administrative costs are not relevant.

Fixed costs may be relevant. A decision to increase activity may necessitate an increase in capacity and an accompanying increase in fixed costs. Conversely, a decision to reduce activity may provide an opportunity to reduce fixed costs. Alternative production or service procedures may have different fixed costs at the same activity level. This is the situation faced by the Ace Stamping Company. The Model II machine's fixed factory overhead is lower than the Model I's.

Because the fixed administrative costs are the same with both machines, they are irrelevant to the replacement decision. Indeed, fixed administrative costs, such as those incurred to pay the president's salary, have little or nothing to do with the operation of the stamping machine. These costs are not associated with the decision at hand.[1] The acquisition cost of the new machine is obviously relevant. This cost will be incurred only if the replacement alternative is selected.

Sunk Costs Are Never Relevant. Though the relevance of outlay costs is determined by the decision at hand, sunk costs (aside from possible tax consequences) are never relevant. Sunk costs result from past expenditures that cannot be changed. The cost of the Model I machine is a historical cost, not a future cost. This historical cost, and the related depreciation, result from the past decision to acquire the old machine. Even though all the outlay costs discussed above would be relevant to a decision to continue or discontinue operations, the sunk cost of the Model I machine is not relevant even to this decision.

If management elects to keep the old machine, its book value will be depreciated over its remaining useful life of four years, whereas if management elects to replace the old machine, its book value will be written off when it is replaced. Even if management elects to discontinue operations, the book value of the old machine must be disposed of.

Although the book value of the old machine has no economic significance, the accounting treatment of past costs can make it difficult for managers to

---

[1] In textbook examples and problems, and in professional examinations, it is assumed, in the absence of specific information, that fixed costs do not differ between decision alternatives. This is a simplifying assumption. In practice the manager or the management accountant would have to ask many questions to determine whether or not fixed outlay costs are relevant to a decision situation.

regard them as irrelevant. If management replaces the old machine, a loss from disposal of $25,000 will be recorded in the year of replacement:

Book value	$60,000
Disposal value	−35,000
Loss on disposal	$25,000

Managers are often reluctant to have such a loss recorded out of fear that it will lead superiors to question the wisdom of past decisions. The loss acts as an attention-getting flag. A manager might prefer using the old machine, with lower total profits over the four-year period, to replacing it and being forced to record a loss on disposal.

From an economic viewpoint, a mistake made in acquiring the old machine cannot be corrected by continuing to use the old machine. When a preferred alternative is available, continued commitment to the original decision compounds the first mistake with a second. Though there is no easy solution to this behavioral problem, managers and management accountants should be aware of its potential impact.

Disposal and Salvage Values.   Revenues are inflows of resources from operations. The Ace Stamping Company's revenues, which are from the sale of widgets, were discussed above. The sale of fixed assets is also a source of resources. Because the sale of fixed assets is a nonoperating item, cash inflows obtained from these sales are discussed separately.

The disposal value of the Model I machine is a relevant cash inflow. It is obtained only if the replacement alternative is selected. Any salvage value available at the end of the useful life of either machine would also be relevant. A loss on disposal may have a favorable tax impact if the loss can be offset against taxable gains or taxable income. In this case, though the book value of the old asset remains irrelevant, the expected tax reduction would be relevant.

Differential Analysis of Relevant Costs

Differential cost analysis is an approach to the analysis of relevant costs that focuses on the costs that differ under alternative actions. A differential analysis of relevant costs for the Ace Stamping Company's equipment replacement decision is presented in Exhibit 5–2. Replacement provides a net advantage of $55,000 over the life of both machines.[2]

---

[2] Our current objectives are (1) to distinguish between relevant and irrelevant costs and (2) to demonstrate the advantages of analyzing only relevant costs. An analysis of long-lived projects should also consider the time value of money. The time value of money is discussed in Chapter 15.

EXHIBIT 5–2   Differential Analysis of Relevant Costs

	Differential Analysis of Four-Year Totals		
	(1) Keep Old Model I Machine	(2) Replace with New Model II Machine	(1) − (2) Difference (Effect of Replacement on Income)
Costs:			
Direct labor:			
Old (10,000 units × $4 × 4 years)	$160,000		
New (10,000 units × $2 × 4 years)		$ 80,000	$80,000
Variable overhead:			
Old (10,000 units × $1 × 4 years)	40,000		
New (10,000 units × $0.80 × 4 years)		32,000	8,000
Fixed overhead except depreciation:			
Old ($19,000 × 4 years)	76,000		
New ($16,000 × 4 years)		64,000	12,000
Disposal value of old machine		(35,000)	35,000
Cost of new machine		80,000	(80,000)
Total	$276,000	$221,000	$55,000
Advantage of replacement		$55,000	

A differential analysis of relevant costs and revenues (such as the one in Exhibit 5–2) is preferred to a complete analysis of all costs and revenues (such as the one in Exhibit 5–1) for a number of reasons:

- Focusing only on those items that differ provides a clearer picture of the impact of the decision at hand. Management is less apt to be confused by a differential analysis than by an analysis that intermingles relevant and irrelevant items.

- Because a differential analysis contains fewer items, it is easier and quicker to prepare.

- In complex situations, such as those encountered by multiple-product or multiple-plant firms, it is difficult, if not impossible, to develop complete firmwide statements to analyze all decision alternatives.

Predicting Relevant Costs

Information on relevant costs is almost always given in textbook examples and problems. Here the task is to (1) distinguish between relevant and irrelevant costs and (2) properly classify the relevant costs. In practice the analyst would also have the difficult job of obtaining the relevant cost information, which is a very time-consuming process that requires questioning, observing, and analyzing. Obviously, an understanding of relevant cost concepts is a prerequisite to obtaining relevant cost information. Simply stated, the analyst must know what to look for. The knowledge of this helps guide the search for the few pieces of relevant information contained in voluminous sets of data.

Predicting relevant costs may involve an examination of past cost trends. If one of the alternatives under consideration is to continue operations as in the past, the techniques discussed in Chapter 3 can be used to estimate past costs and to develop predictions of future costs. The predicted operating costs of the Model I stamping machine would be developed in this manner.

It is more difficult to predict costs when technology changes. The substitution of the Model II for the Model I stamping machine is an example of a technological change. Because the Model II is new, the Ace Stamping Company's historical information is of little or no value in predicting its future operating costs. Cost predictions for the Model II machine must be deduced from information obtained from the manufacturer, other users, trade associations and publications, and engineers employed by Ace. Management should carefully evaluate the credibility of this information.

A **cost prediction error** is the difference between a predicted future cost and the actual amount of the cost when, or if, it is incurred. Because cost predictions may be inaccurate, management should determine how sensitive a decision is to prediction errors. This would include, for example, determining how much a prediction could change before affecting the decision.

The Ace Stamping Company's new machine has a net advantage of $55,000 over its four-year life; hence, cost predictions could increase by $55,000 before affecting the decision.[3] Given the size of the operating costs, a $55,000 prediction error seems unlikely. If the net advantage of the new machine were smaller, say $10,000, management might want to consider the likelihood of a $10,000 prediction error.

APPLICATIONS OF DIFFERENTIAL ANALYSIS

Differential analysis is used to provide information for a variety of planning and decision situations. Illustrated in this section are some of the more frequently encountered applications of differential analysis, including multiple changes in profit plans, whether to accept or reject a special order, whether to make or buy a product or service, how best to use limited resources, and whether to sell a product or process it further.

---

[3] See footnote 2.

**Multiple Changes
in Profit Plans**

Mind Trek, Ltd. manufactures an electronic game that is sold to distributors for $22 per unit. Manufacturing and other costs are as follows:

Variable Costs per Unit			Fixed Costs per Month	
Manufacturing:			Factory overhead	$30,000
Direct materials	$5.00		Selling and administrative	15,000
Direct labor	3.00		Total	$45,000
Factory overhead	2.00	$10.00		
Selling and administrative		2.00		
Total		$12.00		

The unit contribution margin is $10 ($22 selling price − $12 variable costs). Mind Trek's April 19x6 Contribution Income Statement is presented in Exhibit 5–3. The April 19x6 operations are typical. Monthly production and sales average 5,000 units, and monthly profits average $5,000.

Management wants to know the effect on monthly profits of the following three alternative actions.

1. Increasing the monthly advertising budget by $4,000, which should result in a 1,000 unit increase in monthly sales.

2. Increasing the unit selling price by $3, which should result in a 2,000 unit decrease in monthly sales.

EXHIBIT 5–3   Contribution Income Statement

Mind Trek, Ltd.
Contribution Income Statement
For the month of April 19x6

Sales (5,000 units × $22)			$110,000
Less variable costs:			
Cost of goods sold:			
Direct materials (5,000 units × $5)	$25,000		
Direct labor (5,000 units × $3)	15,000		
Factory overhead (5,000 units × $2)	10,000	$50,000	
Selling and administrative (5,000 units × $2)		10,000	− 60,000
Contribution margin			$ 50,000
Less fixed costs:			
Factory overhead		$30,000	
Selling and administrative		15,000	− 45,000
Net income			$ 5,000

3. Decreasing the unit selling price by $2, which should result in a 2,000 unit increase in monthly sales. However, because of capacity constraints, the last 1,000 units would be produced during overtime, when the direct labor costs increase by $1 per unit.

It is possible to develop contribution income statements for each alternative and then determine the profit impact of the proposed change by comparing the new net income with the current net income. A more direct approach is to use differential analysis and focus only on those items that differ under each alternative.

Alternative 1:

Profit increase from increased sales (1,000 units × $10)	$ 10,000
Profit decrease from increased advertising	(4,000)
Increase in monthly profit	$ 6,000

Alternative 2:

Profit decrease from reduced sales if there were no changes in prices or costs (2,000 units × $10)	$(20,000)
Profit increase from increased selling price [(5,000 units − 2,000 units) × $3]	9,000
Decrease in monthly profit	$(11,000)

Alternative 3:

Profit increase from increased sales if there were no changes in prices or costs (2,000 units × $10)	$ 20,000
Profit decrease from reduced selling price of all units [(5,000 units + 2,000 units) × $2]	(14,000)
Profit decrease from increased direct labor costs of the last 1,000 units (1,000 units × $1)	(1,000)
Increase in monthly profit	$ 5,000

Alternative 2 is undesirable because it would result in a decrease in monthly profit. Because Alternative 1 results in a larger increase in monthly profit, it is preferred to Alternative 3.

Special Orders

Assume a Brazilian distributor has proposed to place a special, one-time order for 1,000 units next month, at a reduced price of $12 per unit. The distributor will pay all packing and transportation costs, and there will be no incremental selling or administrative expenses associated with the order. Mind Trek has sufficient production capacity to produce the additional units without reducing sales to other customers. Management desires to know the profit impact of accepting the order. The following analysis focuses on those costs and revenues that will differ if the order is accepted.

Increase in revenues (1,000 units × $12)		$12,000
Increase in costs:		
Direct materials (1,000 units × $5)	$5,000	
Direct labor (1,000 units × $3)	3,000	
Variable factory overhead (1,000 units × $2)	2,000	−10,000
Increase in profits		$ 2,000

Accepting the order will result in a profit increase of $2,000.

If management were unaware of management accounting concepts, they might be tempted to compare the special order price to the average unit cost of goods sold used for financial accounting purposes. If management made their decision by comparing the special order price to the unit cost of goods sold found in Mind Trek's April 19x6 financial statements, they might reject the order. With all manufacturing costs assigned to the units produced, the April cost of goods sold averaged $16 per unit:

Cost of goods sold:		
Direct materials (5,000 units × $5)		$25,000
Direct labor (5,000 units × $3)		15,000
Factory overhead:		
Variable (5,000 units × $2)	$10,000	
Fixed	30,000	40,000
Total		$80,000
Unit production and sales		÷ 5,000
Average unit cost of goods sold		$ 16

Comparing the special order price of $12 per unit to the average unit cost of goods sold of $16, management might conclude the order would result in a loss of $4 per unit.

It is apparent that the $16 figure is composed of variable manufacturing costs of $10 per unit and fixed manufacturing costs of $30,000 spread over 5,000 units. But remember that management may not have detailed cost information. To obtain appropriate information for decision-making purposes, management must ask their accounting staff for the specific information needed. Different configurations of cost information are provided for different purposes. In the absence of special instructions the accounting staff will probably supply the most readily available data, namely, that used for financial reporting.

Importance of Time Span. The special order is a one-time order for 1,000 units that will use current excess capacity. Because no special setups or equipment are required to produce the order, it is appropriate to consider only variable costs in computing the order's profitability.

But what if the Brazilian distributor wanted Mind Trek to sign a multiyear contract to provide 1,000 units per month at $12 each? Under these circumstances management would be well advised to reject the order because there is a high probability that cost increases would make the order unprofitable in later years. At the very least, management should insist that a cost escalation clause be added to the purchase agreement, specifying that the selling price be increased to cover any cost increases and detailing how cost is computed.

Of more concern is the variable nature of all long-run costs. *In the long run all costs, including costs classified as fixed in a given period, are relevant.* To remain in business in the long run, Mind Trek must replace equipment, pay property taxes, pay administrative salaries, and so forth. Consequently, management should consider all costs (fixed and variable, manufacturing and nonmanufacturing) in evaluating a long-term contract.

Full costs include all (fixed and variable) product and period costs. The average full cost per unit is sometimes used to approximate long-run variable costs. If accepting a long-term contract increases the monthly production and sales volume to 11,000 units, the average full cost per unit will be $16.09:

Direct materials	$ 5.00
Direct labor	3.00
Variable factory overhead	2.00
Fixed factory overhead ($30,000 ÷ 11,000 units)	2.73
Variable selling and administrative costs	2.00
Fixed selling and administrative costs ($15,000 ÷ 11,000 units)	1.36
Average full cost per unit	$16.09

If the Brazilian distributor agrees to pay separately all variable selling and administrative expenses associated with the contract, the estimated long-run variable costs are $14.09 per unit ($16.09 − $2.00). Many managers would say this is the minimum acceptable unit selling price for the order, especially if the order extends over a long period of time.

Opportunity Costs May Also Be Relevant. Recall from Chapter 2 that an *opportunity cost* is the net cash inflow that could be obtained if the resources committed to one action were used in the most desirable other alternative. Because Mind Trek has excess productive capacity, no opportunity cost is associated with accepting the Brazilian distributor's one-time order. There is no alternative use of the productive capacity in the short run, so there is no opportunity cost.

But what if Mind Trek were operating with no excess capacity? In this case accepting the special order would require either reducing regular sales or using overtime. To simplify the illustration, assume overtime production is not possible. Because Mind Trek is operating at capacity, there is an alternative use of the productive capacity and, hence, an opportunity cost associated with its use to fill the special order. Each unit sold to the Brazilian distributor could generate a $10 contribution from regular customers. Accepting the special order would cause Mind Trek to incur an opportunity cost of $10,000, the net benefit of the most desirable other action, selling to regular customers:

Lost sales to regular customers	1,000 units
Regular unit contribution margin	×$10
Opportunity cost of accepting special order	$10,000

Because this opportunity cost exceeds the $2,000 contribution derived from the special order, management should reject the special order. Accepting the order will reduce profits by $8,000 ($2,000 − $10,000).

Nonquantitative Considerations. Although an analysis of cost and revenue information may indicate that a special order would be profitable in the near term, management might still reject the order because of nonquantitative, short-run or long-run considerations. Because of a concern for the order's impact on regular customers, management might reject an order even if they had excess capacity. If the order involves a special low price, regular customers might demand a similar price reduction and threaten to take their business elsewhere. Alternatively, management might accept the special order even though they were operating at capacity if they believed there were long-term benefits associated with penetrating a new market. Legal factors must also be considered if the special order is from a buyer who competes with regular customers. These legal factors are discussed later in this chapter.

Make or Buy Decisions

Now suppose a foreign manufacturer has offered a one-year contract to supply Mind Trek with an electronic component at a cost of $2.20 per unit. If Mind Trek accepts the offer, they will be able to reduce materials costs by 10 percent and direct labor and variable factory overhead costs by 20 percent. Fixed factory overhead can be reduced by $20,000 per year. A differential analysis of Mind Trek's make or buy decision is presented in Exhibit 5–4. Making the component has a net advantage of $22,000.

But what if the space currently used to manufacture the electronic component can be rented to a third party for $40,000 per year? In this case the productive capacity has an alternative use, and the net cash flow from this alternative use is an opportunity cost of making the component. In analyzing the make or buy decision, this opportunity cost should be treated as a cost of making. Buying now has a net advantage of $18,000:

	Cost to Make	Cost to Buy	Difference (Effect of Buying on Income)
Cost to buy		$132,000	$(132,000)
Cost to make:			
Outlay*	$110,000		110,000
Opportunity	40,000		40,000
Total	$150,000	$132,000	$ 18,000
Advantage of buying		$18,000	

* See Exhibit 5–4.

Even if buying appears financially advantageous in the short run, management should not decide to buy before considering a variety of nonquantitative factors. Is the outside supplier attempting to use some temporarily idle capacity? If so, what will happen at the end of the contract period? Will the supplier extend the contract at all, or at a higher price? What impact would a decision to buy have on the morale of Mind Trek's employees? Will Mind Trek have to rehire laid-off employees after the contract expires? Will the outside supplier meet delivery schedules? Does the supplied part meet Mind Trek's quality standards, and will it continue to meet them? Organizations often manufacture products or provide services they can obtain elsewhere in order to control quality and have an assured source of supply with on-time delivery.

MANAGERIAL PRACTICE 5.3

Beware of Make-Versus-Buy Decisions

"Suppose," says Michael E. McGrath, a director of Pittiglio, Rabin, Todd & McGrath Inc., "a certain subassembly costs $500 to make. Then the company learns it can buy the item offshore for $200, thus saving $300. The gain is illusory because the overhead burden is little changed—it is merely spread across less production. So the remaining products get hit with additional costs, making the factory appear less efficient. That probably prompts the company to buy even more items overseas."

Source: Otis Port, with Resa King and William J. Hampton, "The Productivity Paradox," *Business Week,* 6 June 1988, 108.

EXHIBIT 5–4   Differential Analysis for Make or Buy Decision

	(1) Cost to Make	(2) Cost to Buy	(1) – (2) Difference (Effect of Buying on Income)
Cost to buy ($2.20 × 60,000 units*)		$132,000	$(132,000)
Cost to make:			
Direct materials			
($5 × 0.10 × 60,000 units*)	$ 30,000		30,000
Direct labor			
($3 × 0.20 × 60,000 units*)	36,000		36,000
Variable factory overhead			
($2 × 0.20 × 60,000 units*)	24,000		24,000
Fixed factory overhead	20,000		20,000
Total	$110,000	$132,000	$ (22,000)
Advantage of making		$22,000	

* 5,000 units per month × 12 months = 60,000 units.

How Best to Use Limited Resources

No doubt you have experienced time as a limiting resource. With two exams the day after tomorrow and a paper due next week, your problem was how to allocate limited study time. The solution depended on your objectives, your current status (grades, knowledge, skill levels, and so forth), and the available time. Given this information, you devised a work plan to most nearly meet your objectives.

Managers must also decide how best to use limited resources to accomplish organizational goals. A supermarket may lose sales because limited shelf space prevents stocking all available brands of cereal. A manufacturer may lose sales because limited machine or labor hours prevents filling all orders. Managers of for-profit organizations will likely find the problems of capacity constraints less troublesome than the problems of excess capacity; nonetheless, these problems are real.

The long-run solution to these problems may be to expand capacity. However, this is usually not feasible in the short run. Economic models suggest that another solution is to reduce demand by increasing the price. Again, this may not be desirable. The supermarket, for example, may want to maintain competitive prices, and the manufacturer might want to maintain a long-run price or to avoid accusations of "price-gouging."

The allocation of limited resources should be made only after a careful consideration of many nonquantitative factors. The following rule provides a useful starting point in making short-run decisions of how best to use limited resources: *To achieve short-run profit maximization, a for-profit organization should allocate limited resources in a manner that maximizes the contribution per unit of constraining factor.* The application of this rule is illustrated in the following example.

The Delta Manufacturing Company produces three products: A, B, and C. A limitation of 100 machine-hours per week prevents Delta from meeting the sales demand for these products. Product information is as follows:

	A	B	C
Unit selling price	$100	$80	$50
Unit variable costs	− 90	−50	−25
Unit contribution margin	$ 10	$30	$25
Machine-hours per unit	2	2	1

Product A has the highest selling price, product B has the highest unit contribution margin, and product C is shown below to have the highest contribution per machine-hour.

	A	B	C
Unit contribution margin	$10	$30	$25
Machine-hours per unit	÷ 2	÷ 2	÷ 1
Contribution per machine-hour	$ 5	$15	$25

Following the rule of maximizing the contribution per unit of constraining factor, Delta should use its limited machine-hours to produce product C. As shown in the following analysis, any other plan would result in lower profits.

	A	B	C
	Highest Selling Price	Highest Contribution per Unit	Highest Contribution per Unit of Constraining Factor
Machine hours available	100	100	100
Machine hours per unit	÷ 2	÷ 2	÷ 1
Weekly production	50	50	100
Unit contribution margin	×$10	× $30	× $25
Total contribution	$500	$1,500	$2,500

Despite this analysis, management may decide to produce some units of A, or B, or both to satisfy the requests of some "good" customers, or to offer a full product line. However, such decisions sacrifice short-run profits. Each machine-hour used to produce A or B has an opportunity cost of $25, the net cash flow from using that hour to produce a unit of C, the most desirable other alternative.

Producing all A, for example, results in an opportunity cost of $2,500 (100 units of C × $25). The net disadvantage of producing all A is $2,000:

Contribution from A	$ 500
Opportunity cost of not producing C	− 2,500
Net disadvantage of producing A	$(2,000)

The opportunity cost of producing all C is $1,500. This is the net cash flow from the most desirable other alternative, producing B. However, when compared to producing B, producing C has a net advantage of $1,000:

Contribution from C	$2,500
Opportunity cost of not producing B	−1,500
Net advantage of producing C	$1,000

When an organization has alternative uses for several (rather than one) limiting resources, the optimal use of those resources cannot be determined using the rule for short-run profit maximization. In these situations techniques such as linear programming (discussed in Chapter 13) may be used to assist in determining the optimal mix of products or services.

Sell or Process Further

Single Product Decisions. When a product is saleable at various stages of completion, management must determine the product's most advantageous selling point. As each stage is completed, management must determine whether to sell it then or to process it further. Assume the Boston Rocking Company manufactures rocking chairs from precut and shaped wood. The chairs are saleable once they are assembled; however, Boston Rocking sands and paints all chairs before they are sold. Management wishes to know if this is the optimal selling point.

A complete listing of unit costs and revenues for the alternative selling points is as follows:

	Per Chair		
	Sell After Assembly	Sell After Painting	Difference (Effect of Painting on Income)
Selling price	$40	$75	$35
Assembly costs	(25)	(25)	
Sanding and painting costs		(12)	(12)
Contribution margin	$15	$38	$23
Advantage of painting		$23	

The chairs should be sold after they are painted. The sanding and painting operation has an additional contribution of $23 per unit.

Note that the assembly costs are the same under both alternatives. This illustrates that *all costs incurred prior to the decision point are irrelevant.* Given the existence of an assembled chair, the decision alternatives are to sell it now or process it further. A differential analysis for the decision to sell or process further should include only revenues and the incremental costs of further processing:

Increase in revenues:		
Sell after painting	$75	
Sell after assembly	−40	$35
Additional costs of sanding		
and painting		−12
Advantage of sanding and painting		$23

The identical solution is obtained if the selling price without further processing is treated as an opportunity cost:

Revenues after painting		$75
Additional costs of sanding		
and painting	$12	
Opportunity cost of not selling		
after assembly	40	−52
Advantage of sanding and painting		$23

By processing the chairs further, Boston Rocking has forgone the opportunity to receive $40 from its sale. Since the chair is already made, this $40 is the net cash inflow from the most desirable alternative; hence, it is the opportunity cost of painting.

Joint Product Decisions. Two or more products simultaneously produced from a common set of inputs by a single process are called **joint products.** Joint products are often found in basic industries that process natural raw materials, such as dairy products, chemicals, meat products, petroleum, and wood products. In the petroleum industry, crude oil is refined into fuel oil, gasoline, kerosene, lubricating oil, and other products.

The point in the process where the joint products become separately identifiable is called the **split-off point,** and product costs incurred prior to the split-off point are called **joint costs.** For external reporting purposes a number of techniques are used to allocate joint costs among joint products. (Some of these techniques are considered in the appendix to Chapter 12.) We are not interested in these techniques here, except to note that none of them provides information that is useful in determining what to do with a joint product once it is produced. Because joint costs are incurred prior to the decision point, they are sunk costs. Consequently, *joint costs are irrelevant to a decision to sell a joint product or process it further.*

THE PRICING DECISION

Product pricing is one of the most important and complex decisions facing management. The saleability of individual products or services is directly affected by pricing decisions, as is the profitability and even the survival of the organization. This section introduces some basic pricing concepts and indicates the important role of costs in pricing decisions.

Economic Approaches to Product Pricing

In economic models, the firm has a profit maximizing goal and known cost and revenue functions. The firm continues to produce as long as the marginal revenue derived from the sale of each additional unit exceeds the marginal cost of producing that unit. **Marginal revenue** is the varying increment in total revenue derived from the sale of an additional unit. **Marginal cost** is the varying increment in total cost required to produce and sell an additional unit. Profits are maximized by producing until marginal revenue equals marginal cost.

Economic models provide a useful framework for thinking about pricing decisions, but they are seldom used for day-to-day pricing decisions. Their primary weaknesses stem from the assumptions of profit maximization and known cost and revenue functions. Most for-profit organizations attempt to achieve a target profit rather than a maximum profit. One reason for this is an inability to determine the single set of actions out of all possible actions that will lead to profit maximization. Furthermore, managers are more apt to strive to satisfy a number of goals (such as profits for owners, job security for themselves and their employees, and being a "good" corporate citizen) than to strive for the maximization of a single profit goal. In any case, to maximize profits a company's management would have to know the cost and revenue functions of every product their firm sells. For most products this information either cannot be developed or cannot be developed at a reasonable cost.

Cost-Based Approaches to Product Pricing

Though cost is not the only consideration in product pricing, it is important. There are several reasons for this.

- *Cost data are available.* When hundreds of different prices must be set in a short time, cost may be the only feasible basis for product pricing.
- *Cost based prices are defensible.* Managers threatened by legal action or public scrutiny may feel secure using cost based pricing. They can argue that prices are set in a manner that provides a "fair" profit.
- *Revenues must exceed costs in the long run if the firm is to remain in business.* In the long run the unit selling price must exceed the full cost of each unit, including the product cost of the unit and a portion of all other costs.

In a typical pricing decision, management uses cost information to arrive at an initial selling price. Other available information about the market, competitors, and so forth, is then evaluated in arriving at a final selling price.

Price Setting in Single Product Companies.   Determining the initial cost based price in a single product company is straightforward if everything is known but the selling price. In this case all known information can be substituted into the profit formula, which is then solved for the variable price.

Assume that Bright Rug Cleaning Company has annual fixed costs of $200,000 and variable costs of $10 per rug cleaned. Management desires to achieve a target profit of $30,000. The estimated annual volume is 10,000 units. As a matter of policy, management charges the same price regardless of the type, size, or shape of the rug. Using the profit formula, the unit price required to achieve the target profit is determined to be $33:

	Total costs		
Total revenue	Fixed	Variable	Profit

$$(\text{Price} \times 10,000) - [\$200,000 + (\$10 \times 10,000)] = \$30,000.$$

Solving for the price:

$$(\text{Price} \times 10,000) - \$300,000 = \$30,000$$
$$\text{Price} = \$330,000/10,000$$
$$= \$33.$$

To achieve its target profit, Bright would charge $33 to clean a rug.

Price Setting in Multiple-Product Companies.   In multiple-product companies, desired profits are determined for the company as a whole, and standard procedures are established for determining the initial selling price of each product. These procedures typically specify the initial selling price as cost, plus a markup stated as a percentage of cost, which is determined by the cost base used in the computations. The larger the cost base for a given product the smaller the markup. Two possible cost bases that we consider are variable costs and manufacturing costs.

When the markup is based on variable costs, it must be large enough to cover all fixed costs and the target profit:

$$\frac{\text{Variable}}{\text{cost markup}} = \frac{\text{Predicted fixed costs} + \text{Target profit}}{\text{Predicted variable costs}}.$$

Once the variable cost markup is determined, it is then used to determine the initial selling price of each product:

$$\frac{\text{Initial}}{\text{selling price}} = \frac{\text{Variable costs}}{\text{per unit}} + \left(\frac{\text{Variable costs}}{\text{per unit}} \times \frac{\text{Variable}}{\text{cost markup}} \right).$$

Assume the predicted 19x9 variable and fixed costs for Magnum Enterprises are as follows:

Variable Costs		Fixed Costs	
Manufacturing	$600,000	Manufacturing	$400,000
Selling and		Selling and	
administrative	200,000	administrative	200,000
Total	$800,000	Total	$600,000

To achieve a target profit of $200,000, Magnum Enterprises needs a 100 percent markup on variable costs:

$$\text{Variable cost markup} = \frac{\$600,000 + \$200,000}{\$800,000} = 1.00.$$

M ANAGERIAL PRACTICE 5.4

Cash Crash at Piper Aircraft

Piper Aircraft Corporation set a low price on its Cadet model in an attempt to win business with corporate customers looking to replace aging training fleets. Unfortunately, the $45,000-per-unit selling price did not cover variable costs, and Piper experienced cash flow problems as sales of the Cadet rose from 282 units in 1987 to 621 units in 1989. After raising the price to $60,000, Piper is just breaking even on the Cadet. Even so, cash flow problems are so severe that Piper is "stretching out" delivery on the Cadet while concentrating on such high-priced models as the Seneca and Cheyenne.

Source: Gail DeGeorge, with Sandra D. Atchison, "Without Cash, Piper May Have Trouble Keeping Its Nose Up," *Business Week,* 5 March 1990, 32.'

Assume the following information is available about product A:

		Unit
Direct material		$ 4
Direct labor		4
Factory overhead:		
Variable	$2	
Fixed	5	7
Total manufacturing costs		$15
Variable selling and administrative costs		$ 2

Variable costs for product A are $12 per unit:

	Unit
Direct material	$ 4
Direct labor	4
Variable factory overhead	2
Variable selling and administrative	2
Total variable costs	$12

Using the variable cost markup, the initial selling price of A is $24:

$$\text{Initial selling price} = \$12 + (\$12 \times 1.00)$$
$$= \$24.$$

To make appropriate pricing decisions, management must be aware of the variable costs of a product or service and the markup required to cover fixed costs and to provide for a target profit. One way of doing this is to break the markup on variable costs into two parts: one part to cover fixed costs and another part to provide for a profit. For Magnum Enterprises this might be done as follows:

	Product A
Variable costs	$12
Markup to cover fixed costs	
[($600,000/$800,000 = 0.75) × $12]	9
Markup to achieve target profit	
[($200,000/$800,000 = 0.25) × $12]	3
Initial price	$24

With this information management can readily see that any price in excess of $12 increases short-run profits or reduces short-term losses. However, all products must have an average markup of 75 percent on variable costs if the firm is to be profitable in the long run. Using this guideline, the suggested markup for product A is at least $9. To achieve target profits, all products must have an additional average markup of 25 percent on variable costs. The suggested additional markup for product A is $3 using this guideline. Management would modify this initial price to reflect current market conditions and other factors.

When the markup percentage is based on manufacturing costs, it must be large enough both to cover selling and administrative costs and to provide for the desired profit:

$$\textbf{Manufacturing cost markup} = \frac{\text{Predicted selling and administrative costs} + \text{Desired profit}}{\text{Predicted manufacturing costs}}.$$

To compute the manufacturing cost markup, it is necessary to determine the desired profit and to predict all costs for the pricing period. The initial prices of individual products are then computed as their unit manufacturing costs plus the markup.

$$\begin{array}{l}\text{Initial} \\ \text{selling} \\ \text{price}\end{array} = \begin{array}{l}\text{Manufacturing} \\ \text{costs} \\ \text{per unit}\end{array} + \left(\begin{array}{l}\text{Manufacturing} \\ \text{costs} \\ \text{per unit}\end{array} \times \begin{array}{l}\text{Manufacturing} \\ \text{cost} \\ \text{markup}\end{array}\right).$$

Magnum Enterprises has the following cost predictions for 19x9:

Manufacturing Costs		Selling and Administrative Costs	
Variable	$ 600,000	Variable	$200,000
Fixed	400,000	Fixed	200,000
Total	$1,000,000	Total	$400,000

To achieve a target profit of $200,000, Magnum Enterprises needs a 60 percent markup on manufacturing costs:

$$\begin{array}{l}\text{Manufacturing} \\ \text{cost markup}\end{array} = \frac{\$400,000 + \$200,000}{\$1,000,000}$$
$$= 0.60.$$

Using the manufacturing cost markup, with total manufacturing costs of $15, the initial selling price of product A is $24:

$$\text{Initial selling price} = \$15 + (\$15 \times 0.60)$$
$$= \$24.$$

Because of the availability of manufacturing cost data, this approach to product pricing is widely used. However, it has several weaknesses. The manufacturing cost markup indiscriminately mixes fixed and variable costs in the base and in the markup. If the variable selling and administrative expenses can be identified with individual products, they should be included in the base rather than in the markup. Conversely, the nonvarying nature of fixed manufacturing costs and the difficulty of accurately associating them with individual products suggest that they should be included in the markup rather than in the base.

Legal Forces Increase the Role of Costs

Cost has always been an important determinant of price in regulated industries such as utilities, communications, and transportation. In recent years a number of legal forces have greatly increased the role of costs in many other industries. Large government defense contracts, for example, are often awarded on the basis of cost, which is determined in a manner specified by government regulations, plus an allowance for profit. Medicare and Medicaid reimbursements to hospitals are often based on cost as well, which again is determined in a specified manner.

The Robinson–Patman Act prohibits charging purchasers different prices when these purchasers compete with one another in the sale of their products or services. There are three exceptions to the act:

1. The discriminatory lower price is in response to changing conditions in the market for, or the marketability of, the commodities involved (such as the sale of discontinued products);

2. The discriminatory lower price is made to meet an equally low price of a competitor; and

3. The discriminatory lower price makes only due allowance for specific cost differences, such as those resulting from long production runs and bulk shipments.

Management must always take care to ensure that accepting a special order does not violate the provisions of the Robinson–Patman Act.

SUMMARY

A number of decision situations were presented in this chapter, including whether to accept or reject a special order, whether to make or buy a product or service, how best to use limited resources, and whether to sell a product or process it further. When evaluating alternative actions such as these, managers should focus their attention on the decision at hand. They should evaluate only those costs and revenues that differ under each alternative.

Relevant costs include all future costs that differ among competing alternatives, namely, outlay costs that differ under each alternative, and sometimes an opportunity cost. An outlay cost is a future cost that requires a future expenditure. An opportunity cost is the net cash flow from the most desirable other alternative. When resources are limited, the initiation of one action requires

EXHIBIT 5–5   Summary Classification of Relevant and Irrelevant Costs

Relevant Costs			Irrelevant Costs
Future costs that differ among competing alternatives			Costs that do not differ among competing alternatives
Opportunity Cost	Outlay Costs		Sunk Cost
Net cash flow from the best alternative	Future costs requiring future expenditures that differ	Future costs requiring future expenditures that do not differ	A historical cost resulting from a past decision

management to forgo competing alternative actions. The net cash flow from the most desirable other alternative is the opportunity cost of the action selected.

Irrelevant costs, which include sunk costs and certain outlay costs, do not differ among competing alternatives. Sunk costs are historical costs resulting from past decisions. There is absolutely nothing management can do to change the total amount of these costs. All outlay costs are relevant to some decisions, such as the decision to continue or discontinue operations, but not all outlay costs are relevant to all decisions. Outlay costs that do not differ under decision alternatives are not relevant to that decision. A summary classification of relevant and irrelevant costs is presented in Exhibit 5–5.

Although this chapter has focused on short-run decisions, decisions should not be based solely on short-run cost minimization or profit maximization. This is especially true in price setting and determining whether to accept or reject a special order. Any price in excess of variable cost increases current profits. In the long run, all costs are variable. Accordingly, average prices must exceed the full cost of products or services if the firm is to remain in business in the long run.

SUGGESTED READINGS

Baxter, W. T., and A. R. Oxenfeld, "Costing and Pricing: The Cost Accountant versus the Economist," *Business Horizons* (Winter 1961): 77–90.

Dillon, Ray D., and J. F. Nash, "The True Relevance of Relevant Costs," *The Accounting Review* (January 1978): 11–17.

Gordon, Lawrence, Robert Cooper, Haim Falk, and Danny Miller, *The Pricing Decision*, Montvale, N.J.: National Association of Accountants, 1981.

Govindarajan, Vijay, and John K. Shank, "Strategic Cost Analysis: The Crown Cork and Seal Case," *Journal of Cost Management* (Winter 1989): 5–16.

Lee, John Y., "Developing a Pricing System for Small Businesses," *Management Accounting* (March 1987): 50–53.

Sias, Randall, G., "Pricing Bank Services," *Management Accounting* (July 1985): 48–50.

The Carbon Copy produces cartridge ribbons for electronic typewriters. The ribbons are sold to mail-order distributors for $4.80. Manufacturing and other costs are as follows:

Variable Costs per Unit		Fixed Costs per Month	
Direct materials	$2.00	Factory overhead	$15,000
Direct labor	0.20	Selling and administration	5,000
Factory overhead	0.25	Total	$20,000
Distribution	0.05		
Total	$2.50		

The variable distribution costs are for transportation to mail-order distributors. The current monthly production and sales volume is 15,000. Monthly capacity is 20,000 units.

Requirements

Determine the effect of the following on monthly profits. Each situation is to be evaluated independent of all others.

a) A $1.50 increase in the unit selling price should result in a 1,800 unit decrease in monthly sales.

b) A $1.80 decrease in the unit selling price should result in a 6,000 unit increase in monthly sales. However, because of capacity constraints, the last 1,000 units would be produced during overtime, when the direct labor costs increase by 50 percent.

c) A New Zealand distributor has proposed to place a special one-time order for 4,000 units next month at a reduced price of $4 per unit. The distributor would pay all transportation costs. There would be additional fixed selling and administrative costs of $500.

d) An Australian distributor has proposed to place a special one-time order for 8,000 units at a special price of $4 per unit. The distributor would pay all transportation costs. There would be additional fixed selling and administrative costs of $500. Assume overtime production is not possible.

e) A Mexican manufacturer has offered a one-year contract to supply cartridges for the ribbons at a cost of $1.00 per unit. If Carbon Copy accepts the offer, they will be able to reduce variable manufacturing costs by 40 percent and rent some space currently used to manufacture cartridges for $1,000 per month.

f) The cartridge ribbons are currently unpackaged; that is, they are sold in bulk. Packaging them individually would increase costs by $0.10 per unit. However, the units could now be sold for $5.05.

g) Carbon Copy produces a variety of carbon ribbons. The given information is for an average unit. Determine the variable cost markup required to earn an annual profit of $120,000.

The solution to this problem is found at the end of the Chapter 5 exercises, problems, and cases.

KEY TERMS

Cost prediction error
Cost reduction proposal
Differential cost analysis
Full cost
Joint cost
Joint products
Manufacturing cost markup

Marginal cost
Marginal revenue
Outlay costs
Robinson–Patman Act
Split-off point
Variable cost markup

REVIEW QUESTIONS

5–1   Distinguish between relevant and irrelevant revenues.

5–2   In evaluating a cost reduction proposal, what three alternatives are available to the management of a for-profit organization?

5–3   When are outlay costs relevant? When are outlay costs irrelevant?

5–4   Are variable costs always relevant? Why or why not?

5–5   Are fixed costs always irrelevant? Why or why not?

5–6   Are sunk costs ever relevant? Why or why not?

5–7   Why is a differential analysis of relevant items preferred to a detailed listing of all costs and revenues associated with each alternative?

5–8   In evaluating a special order management might erroneously compare the special price to the average unit cost of goods sold. Mention two ways that management can avoid this error.

5–9   What costs should be considered in evaluating a special order that will extend over several years?

5–10 When are opportunity costs relevant to the evaluation of a special order?

5–11 How should limited resources be used to achieve short-run profit maximization?

5–12 In the decision to sell or process further, of what relevance are costs incurred prior to the decision point? Explain your answer.

5–13 How is the optimal production and sales volume determined in economic models?

5–14 Why are cost data widely used as a starting point in pricing decisions?

5–15 In cost-based pricing, what is the most useful way of presenting the variable cost markup to management?

EXERCISES

5–1 Relevant Cost Terms: Matching

A company that produces three products, M, N, and O, is evaluating a proposal that will result in doubling the production of N and discontinuing the production of O. The facilities that are currently used to produce O will be devoted to the production of N. Furthermore, additional machinery will be acquired to produce N. The production of M will not be affected. All products have a positive contribution margin.

Presented are a number of phrases or statements related to the proposal. For each phrase or statement, select the most appropriate cost term. Each term is used only once.

1. Increased revenues from the sale of N
2. Increased variable costs of N
3. Property taxes on the new machinery
4. Revenues from the sale of M
5. Cost of the equipment used to produce O
6. Contribution margin of O
7. Variable costs of M
8. The salary of the company president

a. Opportunity cost
b. Sunk cost
c. Irrelevant variable outlay cost
d. Irrelevant fixed outlay cost
e. Relevant variable outlay cost
f. Relevant fixed outlay cost
g. Relevant revenues
h. Irrelevant revenues

5–2 Relevant Cost Terms: Matching

A company that produces and sells 4,000 units per month, but has the capacity to produce 5,000 units per month, is evaluating a one-time special order for 2,000 units from a large chain store. Accepting the order will result in an increase in variable manufacturing costs and certain fixed selling and administrative costs. It will also require the company to forgo the sale of 1,000 units to regular customers.

Presented are a number of statements related to the proposal. For each statement, select the most appropriate cost term. Each term is used only once.

1. Cost of equipment used to produce special order
2. Lost contribution margin from forgone sales to regular customers
3. Increased revenues from special order
4. Variable cost of 4,000 units sold to regular customers
5. Increase in fixed selling and administrative expenses
6. Revenues from 4,000 units sold to regular customers
7. Salary paid to supervisor who oversees manufacture of special order
8. Increased variable costs of special order

a. Irrelevant variable outlay cost
b. Irrelevant fixed outlay cost
c. Sunk cost
d. Relevant variable outlay cost
e. Relevant fixed outlay costs
f. Opportunity cost
g. Relevant revenues
h. Irrelevant revenues

5–3 Identifying Relevant Costs and Revenues

The Ames Company manufactures two components (A and B) and assembles them into a final product. Ames is evaluating two alternative proposals.

Proposal 1 calls for buying component B. This action would free up facilities to manufacture more units of component A and assemble more units of final product. Management believes the additional production can be sold at the current market price. No new assembly equipment would be needed.

Proposal 2 calls for replacing the equipment currently used to manufacture component B. The new equipment would operate with fewer workers and less power. The salvage value of the old equipment is equal to its removal costs.

Presented are a number of cost and revenue items related to the operations of the Ames Company. Under the columns for proposals 1 and 2 indicate whether each item is relevant or irrelevant to that proposal.

Management has set a $150,000 profit goal for 19x1.

Requirements

a) Determine the markup percentage on variable costs required to earn the desired profit.

b) Use variable cost markup to determine a suggested selling price for the type A clamp.

c) For the type A clamp, break the markup on variable costs into separate parts for fixed costs and profit. Explain the significance of each part.

d) Determine the markup percentage on manufacturing costs required to earn the desired profit.

e) Use the manufacturing cost markup to determine a suggested selling price for the type A clamp.

f) Evaluate the variable and the manufacturing cost approaches to determining the markup percentage.

5–21 Multiple Product Price Setting

The Chesapeake Tackle Company produces a wide variety of commercial fishing equipment. In the past the prices of individual products have been set by product managers on the basis of professional judgment. John Marlin, the new Controller, believes this practice has led to the significant underpricing of some products (and lost profits) and the significant overpricing of other products (and lost sales volume). You have been asked to assist Mr. Marlin in developing a corporate approach to pricing. The output of your work should be a cost-based formula that can be used to develop initial selling prices for each product. Though product managers are allowed to adjust these prices to meet competition and take advantage of market opportunities, they must explain such deviations in writing.

You have obtained the following 19x4 cost information from the accounting records:

Manufacturing Costs		Selling and Administrative Costs	
Variable	$350,000	Variable	$ 50,000
Fixed	150,000	Fixed	200,000
Total	$500,000	Total	$250,000

In 19x4 Chesapeake reported earnings of $80,000. However, the Controller believes that proper pricing should produce earnings of at least $120,000 on the same sales mix and unit volume. Accordingly, you are to use the above cost information and a target profit of $120,000 in developing a pricing formula.

Selling and administrative expenses are not currently associated with individual products. However, you have obtained the following unit production cost information for the Tigershark Reel.

Variable manufacturing costs	$120 per unit
Fixed factory overhead	60 per unit
Total	$180 per unit

Requirements

a) Determine the standard markup percentage for each of the following cost bases. Round answers to three decimal places.

   1. Full cost, including fixed and variable manufacturing costs, and fixed and variable selling and administrative costs.

   2. Manufacturing costs plus variable selling and administrative costs.

   3. Manufacturing costs.

   4. Variable costs.

   5. Variable manufacturing costs.

b) Explain why the markup percentages became progressively larger between parts 1 and 5 of requirement (a).

c) Determine the initial price of a Tigershark Reel using the manufacturing cost markup and the variable manufacturing cost markup.

d) Do you believe the Controller's approach to product pricing is reasonable? Why or why not?

5–22 Relevant Costs and Differential Analysis

The Third National Bank of Outback paid $50,000 for a check-sorting machine in January 19x1. The machine had an estimated life of 10 years and annual operating costs of $40,000, excluding depreciation. Although management is pleased with the machine, recent technological advances have made it obsolete. Consequently, as of January 19x5, the machine has a book value of $30,000, a remaining operating life of 6 years, and a salvage value of $0.

The manager of operations is evaluating a proposal to acquire a new Perfect Reader II—Optical Scanning and Sorting Machine. The new machine would cost $60,000 and reduce annual operating costs to $25,000, excluding depreciation. Because of expected technological improvements, the manager believes the new machine will have an economic life of only 6 years and no salvage value at the end of that life.

Prior to signing the papers authorizing the acquisition of the new machine, the president of The Third National Bank prepared the following analysis:

Six-year savings [($40,000 − $25,000) × 6 years]	$ 90,000
Cost of new machine	(60,000)
Loss on disposal of old machine	(30,000)
Advantage (disadvantage) of replacement	$ 0

After looking at these numbers he rejected the proposal and commented that he was ". . . tired of looking at marginal projects. This bank is in business to make a profit, not to break even. If you want to break even, go work for the government."

Requirements

a) Evaluate the president's analysis.

b) Prepare a differential analysis of six-year totals for the old and the new machines.

5–23 Cost Plus Pricing and a Special Order

Thousand Islands Propulsion Company produces a variety of electric trolling motors. Management follows a pricing policy of manufacturing cost plus 60 percent. In response to a request from Northern Sporting Goods, the following price has been developed for an order of 300 Minnow Motors (this is the smallest motor Thousand Island produces):

Manufacturing costs:	
Direct materials	$10,000
Direct labor	12,000
Factory overhead	18,000
Total	$40,000
Markup (60 percent)	24,000
Selling price	$64,000

Mr. Bass, the president of Northern Sporting Goods, rejected this price as too high and offered to purchase the 300 Minnow Motors at a price of $44,000.

Additional information:

- Thousand Islands has sufficient excess capacity to produce the motors.
- Factory overhead is applied on the basis of direct labor dollars.
- Budgeted factory overhead is $400,000 for the current year. Of this amount, $100,000 is fixed.
- Selling and administrative expenses are budgeted as follows:

Fixed	$90,000 per year
Variable	$20 per unit manufactured and sold

Requirements

a) The president of Thousand Islands Propulsion wants to know if he should allow Mr. Bass to have the Minnows for $44,000. Determine the effect on profits of accepting Mr. Bass' offer.

b) Briefly explain why you omitted certain costs from your analysis in requirement (a).

c) Assume Thousand Islands is operating at capacity and that they could sell the 300 Minnows at their regular markup.

  1. Determine the opportunity cost of accepting Mr. Bass' offer.

  2. Determine the effect on profits of accepting Mr. Bass' offer.

5–24 Special Order

Every Halloween the Glacier Ice Cream Shop offers a Trick-or-Treat package of 20 coupons for $3. The coupons are redeemable, by children of 12 or under, for a single-scoop cone of Glacier ice cream, with a limit of one coupon per child per visit. Coupon sales average 500 books per year. The printing costs are $60.

A single-scoop cone of Glacier Ice Cream normally sells for $0.60. The variable costs of a single-scoop cone are $0.40.

Requirements

a) Determine the loss if all coupons are redeemed without any other effect on sales.

b) Not all coupons will be redeemed. Assuming regular sales are not affected, determine the coupon redemption rate at which Glacier will break even on the offer.

c) Assuming regular sales are not affected and that each time a coupon is redeemed one additional single-scoop cone is sold at the regular price, determine the coupon redemption rate at which Glacier will break even on the offer.

d) Determine the profit or loss incurred on the offer if the coupon redemption rate is 60 percent and:

  ■ One fourth of the redeemed coupons have no effect on sales.

  ■ One fourth of the redeemed coupons result in additional sales of 2 single-scoop cones.

  ■ One fourth of the redeemed coupons result in additional sales of 3 single-scoop cones.

  ■ One fourth of the redeemed coupons come out of regular sales of single-scoop cones.

5–25 Applications of Differential Analysis

The Bird Box produces squirrel-proof bird feeders. The bird feeders are sold to mail-order distributors for $25.00. Manufacturing and other costs are as follows:

Variable Costs per Unit		Fixed Costs per Month	
Direct materials	$ 8.00	Factory overhead	$10,000
Direct labor	7.00	Selling and administrative	5,000
Factory overhead	2.00	Total	$15,000
Distribution	3.00		
Total	$20.00		

The variable distribution costs are for transportation to mail-order distributors. The current monthly production and sales volume is 5,000 units. Monthly capacity is 6,000 units.

Requirements

Determine the effect of each of the following on monthly profits. Each situation is to be evaluated independent of all others.

a) A $2.50 increase in the unit selling price should result in a 1,000 unit decrease in monthly sales.

b) A $2.00 decrease in the unit selling price should result in a 2,000 unit increase in monthly sales. However, because of capacity constraints, the last 1,000 units would be produced during overtime, when the direct labor costs increase by 60 percent.

c) A British distributor has proposed to place a special one-time order for 1,000 units next month at a reduced price of $20 per unit. The distributor would pay all transportation costs. There would be additional fixed selling and administrative costs of $100.

d) A Dutch distributor has proposed to place a special one-time order for 2,500 units at a special price of $20 per unit. The distributor would pay all transportation costs. There would be additional fixed selling and administrative costs of $200. Assume overtime production is not possible.

e) A Canadian manufacturer has offered a one-year contract to supply a squirrel guard that attaches to the bottom of the feeder at a cost of $4 per unit. If the Bird Box accepts the offer, they will be able to reduce variable manufacturing costs by 10 percent, reduce fixed costs by $500 per month, and rent some space currently used to manufacture bird feeders for $900 per month.

f) The bird feeders are currently sold assembled and ready for mounting. Selling the feeders unassembled would reduce costs by $5.00 per unit. However, the units could now be sold for only $21.00.

g) The Bird Box produces a variety of bird feeders. The given information is for an average unit. Determine the variable cost markup required to earn a monthly profit of $20,000.

5–26 Applications of Differential Analysis

Bush-Wack Expeditions offers guided back-country hiking/camping trips in British Columbia. Bush-Wack provides a guide and all necessary food and equipment at a fee of $50 per person per day. Bush-Wack currently provides an average of 600 guide-days per month in June, July, August, and September. Based on available equipment and staff, maximum capacity is 800 guide-days per month. Monthly variable and fixed operating costs are as follows:

Variable Costs per Guide-Day		Fixed Costs per Month	
Food	$ 5.00	Equipment rental	$ 5,000
Guide salary	25.00	Administration	5,000
Supplies	2.00	Advertising	2,000
Insurance	8.00	Total	$12,000
Total	$40.00		

Requirements

Determine the effect of each of the following on monthly profits. Each situation is to be evaluated independent of all others.

a) A $12 increase in the daily fee should result in a 200 unit decrease in monthly sales.

b) A $5 decrease in the daily fee should result in a 300 unit increase in monthly sales. However, because of capacity constraints, the last 100 guide-days would be provided by subcontracting to another firm at a cost of $46 per guide-day.

c) A French tour agency has proposed to place a special one-time order for 80 guide-days next month at a reduced fee of $45 per guide-day. The agency would pay all insurance costs. There would be additional fixed administrative costs of $200.

d) An Italian tour agency has proposed to place a special one-time order for 300 guide-days next month at a special fee of $45 per guide-day. The agency would pay all insurance costs. There would be additional fixed administrative costs of $200. Assume additional capacity beyond 800 guide-days is not available.

e) An Alberta outdoor supply company has offered to supply all necessary food and camping equipment at $7.50 per guide-day. This eliminates the current food costs and reduces the monthly equipment rental costs to $1,500.

f) Clients must currently carry a backpack and assist in camp activities such as cooking. Bush-Wack is considering the addition of mules to carry all food and equipment and the hiring of college students to perform camp activities such as cooking. This will increase variable costs by $10 per guide-day and fixed costs by $1,200 per month. However, 600 full-service guide-days per month could now be sold at $75.00 each.

g) Bush-Wack provides a number of different types of wilderness experiences. The given information is for an average tour. Determine the variable cost markup required to earn a monthly profit of $6,000.

5–27 Differential Analysis of Alternative Facilities

Williams Company owns and operates a nationwide chain of movie theaters. The 500 properties in the Williams chain vary from low volume, small town, single-screen theaters to high volume, big city, multiscreen theaters.

Management is considering installing machines that will make popcorn on the premises. These machines would allow the theaters to sell freshly popped popcorn daily rather than the prepopped popcorn that is currently purchased in large bags. This proposed feature would be properly advertised and is intended to increase patronage at the company's theaters.

The machines are available from a leasing company in several different sizes. The annual rental and operating costs vary with the size of the machine. The machine capacities and costs are shown below.

	Popper Model		
	Economy	Regular	Super
Annual capacity (boxes)	50,000	120,000	300,000
Costs:			
Annual machine rental	$8,000	$11,000	$20,000
Popcorn cost per box	0.13	0.13	0.13
Other costs per box	0.22	0.14	0.05
Cost of each box	0.08	0.08	0.08

Requirements

a) Calculate the sales volume in boxes at which the Economy Popper and the Regular Popper would earn the same profit.

b) Management can estimate the number of boxes to be sold at each theater. Present a decision rule, based on sales volume in boxes, that would enable Williams' management to select the most profitable machine without having to make a separate cost calculation for each theater.

c) Could management use the average number of boxes sold per seat for the entire chain and the capacity of each theater to develop the decision rule? Explain your answer.

(CMA Adapted)

5–28 Relevant Costs for Various Decisions   The income statement for Davann Co. presented below represents the operating results for the fiscal year just ended. Davann had sales of 1,800 tons of product during the current year. The manufacturing capacity of Davann's facilities is 3,000 tons of product.

Davann Co.
Income Statement
For the year ended December 31, 19y0

Sales	$900,000
Variable costs:	
Manufacturing	$315,000
Selling	180,000
Total variable costs	−495,000
Contribution margin	$405,000
Fixed costs:	
Manufacturing	$ 90,000
Selling	112,500
Administrative	45,000
Total fixed costs	−247,500
Net income before taxes	$157,500
Income taxes (40%)	− 63,000
Net income	$ 94,500

Requirements

a) Determine the 19y0 break-even volume in tons of product.

b) Determine the expected 19y1 after-tax net income, assuming a sales volume of 2,100 tons and no changes in selling prices or cost behavior.

c) Assume demand from regular customers equals 1,800 tons in 19y1 and there are no changes in regular selling prices or cost behavior. Davann has a potential foreign customer that has offered to buy 1,500 tons at $450 per ton. What net income after taxes would Davann make in 19y1 if it took this order and rejected some business from regular customers so as not to exceed capacity?

d) Assume Davann will have additional capacity in 19y1 and there are no changes in sales to regular customers, selling prices, or cost behavior. Davann plans to market its product at the regular price in a new territory. This will require an additional promotion program costing $61,500 annually. Additionally, an extra $25 per ton sales commission, over and above the current sales commission, would be required in the new territory. How many tons would have to be sold in the new territory to maintain Davann's current after-tax income of $94,500?

e) Davann is considering replacing a highly labor intensive process with an automatic machine. This would result in an increase of $58,500 in annual fixed manufacturing costs. The variable manufacturing costs would decrease by $25 per ton. Determine the new break-even volume in tons.

f) Davann estimates the per ton selling price will decline by 10 percent next year. If variable costs increase $40 per ton and fixed costs remain unchanged, what sales volume *in dollars* would be required to earn an after-tax net income of $94,500?

(CMA Adapted)

5–29 Potpourri of Relevant Costs

1. Plainfield Company manufactures Part G for use in its production cycle. The costs per unit for 10,000 units of Part G are as follows:

Direct materials	$ 3
Direct labor	15
Variable overhead	6
Fixed overhead	8
	$32

Verona Company has offered to sell Plainfield 10,000 units of Part G for $30 per unit. If Plainfield accepts Verona's offer, the released facilities could be used to save $45,000 in relevant costs in the manufacture of Part H. In addition $5 per unit of the fixed overhead applied to Part G would be totally eliminated. What alternative is more desirable and by what amount is it more desirable?

Alternative	Amount
a) Manufacture	$10,000
b) Manufacture	$15,000
c) Buy	$35,000
d) Buy	$65,000

2. Boyer Company manufactures basketballs. The forecasted income statement for the year before any special orders is as follows:

	Amount	Per Unit
Sales	$4,000,000	$10.00
Manufacturing cost of goods sold	−3,200,000	− 8.00
Gross profit	$ 800,000	$ 2.00
Selling expenses	− 300,000	− 0.75
Operating income	$ 500,000	$ 1.25

Fixed costs included in the forecasted income statement are $1,200,000 in manufacturing cost of goods sold and $100,000 in selling expenses.

A special order offering to buy 50,000 basketballs for $7.50 each was made to Boyer. There will be no additional selling expenses if the special order is accepted. Assuming Boyer has sufficient capacity to manufacture 50,000 more basketballs, by what amount would operating income be increased or decreased as a result of accepting the special order?

a) $25,000 decrease

b) $62,500 decrease

c) $100,000 increase

d) $125,000 increase

3. Gandy Company has 5,000 obsolete desk lamps that are carried in inventory at a manufacturing cost of $50,000. If the lamps are reworked for $20,000, they could be sold for $35,000. Alternatively, the lamps could be sold for $8,000 to a jobber located in a distant city. In a decision model analyzing these alternatives, the sunk cost would be?

a) $8,000

b) $15,000

c) $20,000

d) $50,000

4. Kingston Company needs 10,000 units of a certain part to be used in its production cycle. The following information is available.

Cost to Kingston Company to make the part:	
Direct materials	$ 6
Direct labor	24
Variable overhead	12
Fixed overhead applied	15
Total	$57
Cost to buy the part from Utica Company	$53

If Kingston buys the part from Utica instead of making it, Kingston could not use the released facilities in another manufacturing activity. Sixty percent of the fixed overhead applied will continue regardless of what decision is made.

In deciding whether to make or buy the part, which of the following is the total relevant cost to make the part?

a) $342,000

b) $480,000

c) $530,000

d) $570,000

5. Yardley Corporation uses a joint process to produce products A, B, and C. Each product may be sold at its split-off point or processed further. Additional processing costs are entirely variable and are traceable to the respective products produced. Joint production costs for 19x5 were $50,000. Relevant data follow.

| | | | Sales Values and Additional Costs If Processed Further | |
Product	Units Produced	Sales Value at Split-Off	Sales Value	Additional Costs
A	20,000	$ 45,000	$60,000	$20,000
B	15,000	75,000	98,000	20,000
C	15,000	30,000	62,000	18,000
		$150,000		

To maximize profits, which products should Yardley subject to further processing?

a) A only

b) C only

c) B and C only

d) None, because of joint costs

6. Brike Company, which manufactures robes, has enough idle capacity available to accept a special order of 10,000 robes at $8 a robe. A predicted income statement for the year without this special order is as follows:

	Per Unit	Total
Sales	$12.50	$1,250,000
Manufacturing costs (variable)	$ 6.25	$ 625,000
Manufacturing costs (fixed)	1.75	175,000
Manufacturing costs (total)	− 8.00	− 800,000
Gross profit	$ 4.50	$ 450,000
Selling expenses (variable)	$ 1.80	$ 180,000
Selling expenses (fixed)	1.45	145,000
Selling expenses (total)	− 3.25	− 325,000
Operating income	$ 1.25	$ 125,000

Assuming no additional selling expenses, what would be the effect on operating income if the special order were accepted?

a) $8,000 increase

b) $17,500 increase

c) $32,500 decrease

d) $40,000 increase

(CPA Adapted)

Auer Company had received an order for a piece of special machinery from Jay Company. Just as Auer Company completed the machine, Jay Company declared bankruptcy, defaulted on the order, and forfeited the 10 percent deposit paid on the selling price of $72,500.

Auer's manufacturing manager identified the costs already incurred in the production of the special machinery for Jay as follows:

Direct materials used		$16,600
Direct labor incurred		21,400
Overhead applied:		
Manufacturing:		
Variable	$10,700	
Fixed	5,350	16,050
Fixed selling and		
administrative		5,405
Total cost		$59,455

Another company, Kaytell Corp., would be interested in buying the special machinery if it were reworked to Kaytell's specifications. Auer offered to sell the reworked special machinery to Kaytell as a special order for a net price of $68,400. Kaytell has agreed to pay the net price when it takes delivery in two months. The additional identifiable costs to rework the machinery to the specifications of Kaytell are as follows:

Direct materials	$ 6,200
Direct labor	4,200
Total	$10,400

A second alternative available to Auer is to convert the special machinery to the standard model. The standard model lists for $62,500. The additional identifiable costs to convert the special machinery to the standard model are:

Direct materials	$2,850
Direct labor	3,300
Total	$6,150

A third alternative for the Auer Company is to sell, as a special order, the machine as is (e.g., without modification) for a net price of $52,000. However, the potential buyer of the unmodified machine does not want it for 60 days. The buyer offers a $7,000 down payment with final payment upon delivery.

The following additional information is available regarding Auer's operations:

■ The sales commission rate on sales of standard models is 2 percent, whereas the sales commission rate on special orders is 3 percent. All sales commissions are calculated on net sales price (i.e., list price less cash discount, if any).

■ Normal credit terms for sales of standard models are 2/10, net/30, that is, customers who pay within 10 days receive a 2 percent cash discount; otherwise, the full sales price is due within 30 days. Ordinarily, customers take the discounts. Credit terms for special orders are negotiated with the customer.

■ The application rates for manufacturing overhead and the fixed selling and administrative costs are as follows:

Manufacturing:	
Variable	50 percent of direct labor costs
Fixed	25 percent of direct labor costs
Selling and administrative:	
Fixed	10 percent of the total of direct material, direct labor, and manufacturing overhead costs

■ Normal time required for rework is 1 month.

■ A surcharge of 5 percent of the sales price is placed on all customer requests for minor modifications of standard models.

■ Auer normally sells a sufficient number of standard models for the company to operate at a volume in excess of the break-even point.

Auer does not consider the time value of money in analyses of special orders and projects whenever the time period is less than one year because the effect is not significant.

Requirements

a) Determine the dollar contribution each of the three alternatives will make to the Auer Company's before-tax profits.

b) If Kaytell makes Auer a counteroffer, what is the lowest price Auer should accept for the reworked machinery from Kaytell? Explain your answer.

c) Discuss the influence fixed factory overhead cost should have on the sales prices quoted by Auer Company for special orders when

1. A firm is operating at or below the break-even point.

2. A firm's special orders constitute efficient utilization of unused capacity above the break-even volume.

(CMA Adapted)

5–31 Differential Analysis with Joint Costs

Helene's, a high fashion women's dress manufacturer, is planning to market a new cocktail dress for the coming season. Helene's supplies retailers in the east and mid-Atlantic states.

Four yards of material are required to lay out the dress pattern. Some material remains after cutting that can be sold as remnants.

The leftover material could also be used to manufacture a matching cape and handbag. However, if the leftover material is to be used for the cape and handbag, more care will be required in the cutting, which will increase the cutting costs.

The company expected to sell 1,250 dresses if no matching capes or handbags were available. Helene's market research reveals that dress sales will be 20 percent higher if a matching cape and handbag are available. The market research indicates that the cape or handbag will only sell well as optional accessories with the dress. The various combinations of dresses, capes, and handbags that are expected to be manufactured by Helene's and sold by retailers are as follows:

	Percent of Total
Complete sets of dress, cape, and handbag	70
Dress and cape	6
Dress and handbag	15
Dress only	9
Total	100

The material used in the dress costs $12.50 a yard or $50.00 for each dress. The cost of cutting the dress if the cape and handbag are not manufactured is estimated at $20.00 a dress, and the resulting remnants can be sold for $5.00 for each dress cut out. If the cape and handbag are to be manufactured, the cutting costs will be increased by $9.00 per dress. There will be no saleable remnants if the capes and handbags are manufactured in the quantities estimated.

The selling prices and the costs to complete the three items once they are cut are presented below.

	Selling Price Per Unit	Unit Cost to Complete (Excludes Cost of Material and Cutting Operation)
Dress	$200.00	$80.00
Cape	27.50	19.50
Handbag	9.50	6.50

Requirements

a) Calculate Helene's incremental profit or loss from manufacturing the capes and handbags in conjunction with the dresses.

b) Identify any nonquantitative factors that could influence Helene's management in its decision to manufacture the matching capes and handbags.

(CMA Adapted)

**REVIEW PROBLEM
SOLUTION**

Unit selling price	$4.80
Unit variable costs	−2.50
Unit contribution margin	$2.30

a)

Profit decrease from reduced sales if there were no changes in prices or costs (1,800 units × $2.30)	$ (4,140)
Profit increase from increase in selling price [(15,000 units − 1,800 units) × $1.50]	19,800
Increase in monthly profit	$15,660

b)

Profit increase from increased sales if there were no changes in prices or costs (6,000 units × $2.30)	$ 13,800
Profit decrease from reduced selling price of all units [(15,000 units + 6,000 units) × $1.80]	(37,800)
Profit decrease from increased direct labor costs of the last 1,000 units [1,000 units × ($0.20 × 0.50)]	(100)
Decrease in monthly profit	$(24,100)

c)

Increase in revenues (4,000 units × $4)		$16,000
Increase in costs:		
Direct materials (4,000 units × $2.00)	$8,000	
Direct labor (4,000 units × $0.20)	800	
Factory overhead (4,000 units × $0.25)	1,000	
Selling and administrative	500	−10,300
Increase in profits		$ 5,700

d)

Increase in revenues (8,000 units × $4)		$32,000
Increase in costs:		
Direct materials (8,000 units × $2.00)	$16,000	
Direct labor (8,000 units × $0.20)	1,600	
Factory overhead (8,000 units × $0.25)	2,000	
Selling and administrative	500	
Opportunity cost of lost regular sales [(15,000 units + 8,000 units − 20,000 unit capacity) × $2.30]	6,900	−27,000
Increase in profits		$ 5,000

e)

	Cost to Make	Cost to Buy	Difference (Effect of Buying on Income)
Cost to buy (15,000 units × $1)		$15,000	$(15,000)
Cost to make:			
Direct materials			
(15,000 units × $2.00 × 0.40)	$12,000		12,000
Direct labor			
(15,000 units × $0.20 × 0.40)	1,200		1,200
Factory overhead			
(15,000 units × $0.25 × 0.40)	1,500		1,500
Opportunity cost	1,000		1,000
Totals	$15,700	$15,000	$ 700
Advantage of buying		$700	

f) Increase in revenues:

Package individually (15,000 units × $5.05)	$75,750	
Sell in bulk (15,000 units × $4.80)	−72,000	$3,750
Additional packaging costs (15,000 units × $0.10)		−1,500
Advantage of individual packaging		$2,250

g)

Predicted annual fixed costs ($20,000 × 12 months)	$240,000
Predicted annual variable costs (15,000 units × $2.50 × 12)	450,000

$$\frac{\text{Variable}}{\text{cost markup}} = \frac{\$240,000 + \$120,000}{\$450,000}$$

$$= 0.80$$

P A R T 2

Planning and Control

or many managers, budgeting is the first thing that comes to mind when planning is mentioned. The managers at MCI are no different. In July the company begins an annual planning and review process for the next year, which officially begins in January. By October of each year, the financial plans and budget for the next year are finalized and readied for implementation. Several review and adjustment sessions are conducted between July and October, to allow top and middle management to negotiate and fine-tune their budget needs.

However, budgeting doesn't stop with the planning phase. In MCI's case, there are two budget review periods: monthly and quarterly. Monthly reviews are basically an evaluation of actual versus budgeted results, with related variances reported. Quarterly reviews compare actual results with anticipated results for the past quarter and adjust the budget for the next quarter if necessary. No budget at MCI is considered static; changes are made as needed during the year to reflect changing conditions and to keep the budget as realistic as possible. MCI uses, to some degree, essentially all of the budgeting and financial performance reporting techniques presented in Chapters 6 and 7. Budgeting at MCI is something to be respected, not feared. It is a valuable management tool.

Chapter 8 introduces standard costing and the related standard cost variances of materials, labor, and factory overhead. It is revealing that, because of rapid changes in technology and the wide variation in its uncontrollable costs, MCI does not compute detailed standard cost variances.

From the budgeting process, MCI moves on to the control and evaluation of divisional performance, covered here in Chapter 9. Except for approval of capital expenditures, MCI is a strongly decentralized organization, with seven domestic divisions and one international division. Each division is evaluated separately on the contribution margin that it generates for the company. In addition to the revenues and variable costs associated with its telecommunications activities, each division must be accountable for the following:

Sales expenses	Leasing
Salaries	Commissions
Wages	Advertising
Consultants	Travel
Rent	Training

Divisional income, along with budget variances, is used to evaluate the operating performance of each division and as the primary basis for executive bonuses at the divisional level. All division heads attend monthly reporting meetings in which each one must explain the key reporting variables of revenue streams, departmental expenses, and hours of telecommunication usage and related customer demands.

Chapter 10 contrasts absorption and variable costing and describes segment reporting. MCI's major segments are its divisions, and its variable costing is tied to divisional reporting rather than to valuations of manufactured inventories.

C H A P T E R 6

Operating Budgets

Learning Objectives

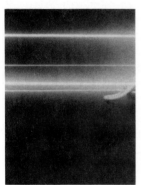

Upon completion of this chapter you should:

- **Understand the importance of budgeting.**

- **Understand the input/output, incremental, and minimum level approaches to budgeting, and when each approach is most likely to be used.**

- **Be aware of the alternative procedures used to collect budget information.**

- **Be familiar with the parts of a complete operating budget and how they are assembled within an organization.**

- **Be able to compile the following operating budgets for a small manufacturing firm: sales, production, purchases, manufacturing disbursements, selling expense, general and administrative expense, and cash.**

- **Be able to prepare a pro forma income statement and a pro forma balance sheet.**

- **Be aware of common problems encountered in budgeting.**

The planning and control cycle involves anticipating future activities before they happen and undertaking measures to ensure they occur in a way that is in the best interest of the organization. More than simply forecasting what will take place and reporting what actually did take place, this cycle is an ongoing process of guiding, monitoring, and governing the organization. In this and the next four chapters, a structure for planning and controlling is developed, along with alternative procedures for reporting activities within this structure. One purpose of this chapter is to develop a basic framework for financial planning.

The process of projecting the operations of the organization and their financial impact into the future is called operations budgeting. An **operating budget** is a set of formal financial documents that reports expected revenues and expenses as well as all other expected operating and financing transactions for a future period of time (usually one year). Another purpose of this chapter is to discuss the basic concepts and benefits of operating budgets and alternative approaches to budget preparation. An example of a complete operations budget is developed, starting with the forecasting of sales and concluding with the preparation of pro forma financial statements. Throughout the chapter consideration is given to the behavioral implications of budgeting and the difficulties and problems often encountered in operations budgeting.

JUSTIFICATIONS OF BUDGETING

Preparing budgets is an important activity in all organizations. It requires making estimates about future needs and developments that may be difficult to predict and even more difficult to control. Many future events almost defy accurate prediction (e.g., a company trying to anticipate the cost of complying with union demands or federal regulations). Despite the difficulty and the inherent uncertainty involved in budgeting, numerous benefits normally accrue to firms whose managers engage in operations budgeting. These benefits include: systematic planning, improved communications and coordination among organizational elements, and an improved basis of performance evaluation.

Systematic Planning

Budgeting is planning for a future period and, as applied to the accounting aspects of an organization, requires management to systematically examine what is anticipated in its financial environment. This look into the future invariably compels management to establish goals and objectives for the future and, maybe more important, it helps management identify major problems that may develop later if corrective action is not taken. Budgeting moves the organization from an informal reaction method of management to a formal proactive method of management. As a result, less time is spent solving unanticipated problems, and more time is spent on positive measures and preventive actions.

Improved Communication

The operating budget encompasses the entire organization; hence, its preparation requires the participation of all levels of management. The process of compiling, reviewing, and revising budget data requires managers to communicate with each other and with subordinates and superiors.

Improved Coordination

Once completed, the operating budget becomes the plan of action for the entire organization and must therefore reflect the coordinated efforts of all components of the organization. The production and sales managers cannot make their plans independent of each other. The personnel department must know the needs of all other departments before it can budget its needs for new employees and training costs. The final version of the operating budget emerges after an extensive, and often lengthy, process of communication and coordination. It represents a synthesis of the experience and knowledge of management at every level of the organization.

Performance Evaluation

Effective control requires a basis for evaluating performance. The traditional bases for measuring performance are historical, industry, and budgeted data. The first two bases have some disadvantages. If *historical data* regarding the firm's performance are used for measuring current performance, past inefficiencies may be allowed to continue as long as the organization operates at the same level. Also, changes in the organization's operating environment will not be reflected in the basis on which performance is evaluated—for example, a change in the sales volume and mix of products demanded by customers.

Using *industry data* to measure performance has the disadvantage of comparing one organization to other companies that may be substantially different from it, thus leading to erroneous conclusions. Comparisons of one organization with others in an industry may be interesting, and they may provide a general perspective of how well one firm is doing compared to similar ones, but this is usually a poor basis for evaluating management's performance for a particular operating period.

Budgeted data prepared for the period under review is a more realistic basis for evaluating performance because the benchmarks are relevant and current. Comparing actual and budgeted data produces variances that are meaningful measures of performance.

MOTIVATION ASPECTS AND HUMAN BEHAVIOR

All organizations are composed of individuals who perform a wide variety of activities in pursuit of the organization's common goals. To accomplish these goals, it is important for management to recognize the effects that budgeting and performance evaluation methods and techniques may have on the behavior of the people in the organization.

Budgeting often produces strong reactions from employees. Some managers use budgets in such a way that employees perceive the budgets as a means of squeezing the last unit of productivity out of them, or merely as a means of identifying the poor performers. Because people inherently dislike restrictions on their behavior, we often see only the negative aspects of budgeting. Budgeting can and should be used as a means of bringing out the best in people without threatening their security and self-esteem.

Properly used, the operating budget can be an effective mechanism for motivating workers to higher levels of performance and productivity. Improperly developed and administered, it can foster feelings of animosity toward both management and the budget process. Research has shown that when workers participate in the preparation of budgets and feel that the budgets represent fair standards for evaluating their performance, they receive personal satisfaction from accomplishing the goals set forth in the budgets.

Another important motivational aspect of operating budgets is related to management's recognition that the budget is not infallible. Mistakes in prediction and judgment are sometimes made, and unforeseen circumstances often develop, necessitating modification of the budget. Unless top management is willing to recognize when changes in the budget are needed, support for the

Managerial Practice 6.1

Buying into Budgets at General Dynamics

General Dynamics uses a management control system called Cost Account Directive (CAD) as a means of securing both employee adherence to budgets and schedules and cooperation across functional lines—in an organization that pulls teams together from different functional groups. It can be used as a practical method of project management and control by almost any organization.

The CAD describes the work to be completed (in a detailed task description) and helps build a project spreadsheet (the personnel, materials, expenses, computer time, and schedule necessary for the project). The four goals of each cost account directive are (1) coordinating the goals of a project's manager with the goals of project team members from different functional groups; (2) motivating employees through specific goal setting; (3) monitoring the project's progress through budgeting; and (4) providing more accurate time and cost estimates. Although such a budget control process may appear time consuming and complicated, it is a useful management tool when implemented correctly.

Source: Terence J. Plaza and Mary M. K. Fleming, "Cost Account Directive—An Effective Management Tool," *Management Accounting* (May 1987): 49–54.

budget at lower levels will quickly erode. If the organization is to receive maximum benefit from the budget process, support for the budget at the top management level, as well as at lower levels, must be maintained. Achieving this support may be the most difficult challenge facing an organization that is undertaking budgeting for the first time.

Lower level managers will not respect the budget and the related performance reports if they perceive a lack of commitment by top management. Violations of the budget by top management can quickly destroy the effectiveness of the budget throughout the organization.

In summary, managers who follow the suggestions below are more likely to be successful in using budgets as a positive tool for accomplishing organizational goals through people.

1. Emphasize the importance of budgeting as a planning device.

2. Encourage wide participation in budget preparation at all levels of management.

3. Demonstrate through appropriate communications that the budget has the complete support of top management.

4. Recognize that the budget is not unalterable, that it may require modification if conditions change.

5. Use budget performance reports not just to identify the poor performer, but also to recognize good performance.

6. Conduct programs in budget education to provide new managers with information about the purposes of budgets and to dispel erroneous misconceptions that may exist.

FORMAL PLANNING CONCEPTS

Before an organization can develop operating budgets, management must decide which approaches to budgeting will be used for various activities. Widely used planning approaches to budgeting include (1) the input/output approach, (2) the incremental approach, and (3) the minimum level approach. Exhibit 6–1 contains a summary of the typical cost characteristics found when each approach to budgeting is used.

EXHIBIT 6–1 Planning Concepts

Approach to Budgeting	Typical Cost Characteristics
Input/output	Variable and mixed costs
Incremental	Discretionary fixed costs
Minimum level	Committed fixed costs

Input/Output Approach

The **input/output approach** budgets physical inputs and costs as a function of planned activity. This approach is often used for manufacturing and distribution activities where there are clearly defined relationships between effort and accomplishment. For example, if each unit produced requires two pounds of raw materials that cost $5 each, and the planned production volume is 25 units, then the budgeted inputs and costs for raw materials are 50 (25 × 2) pounds and $250 (50 × $5). Note that the budgeted inputs are a function of the planned outputs. The input/output approach starts with the planned outputs and works backward to budget the inputs. In evaluating the proposed budget, management would focus its attention on the physical and cost relationships between the inputs and the outputs. For variable costs, the input/output approach is most appropriate. This approach is seldom used for activities that do not have clearly defined input/output relationships, such as advertising, research and development, and executive training.

Incremental Approach

The **incremental approach** budgets costs for a coming period as a dollar or percentage change from the amount budgeted for (or spent during) some previous period. This approach is often used where the relationships between inputs and outputs are weak or nonexistent, particularly where fixed costs dominate. For example, it is difficult to establish a clear relationship between sales volume and advertising expenditures. Consequently, the budgeted amount of advertising for some coming period is often based on the budgeted or actual advertising expenditures in a previous period. If budgeted advertising expenditures for 19x1 were $200,000, the budgeted expenditures for 19x2 would be some increment based on $200,000. In evaluating the proposed 19x2 budget, management would accept the $200,000 base and focus its attention on a justification for the increment.

This approach to budgeting has been more widely used in government than in business organizations (see the appendix to this chapter). In seeking an annual budget appropriation, a department operating under the incremental approach would be required to justify only proposed expenditures in excess of its previous budget appropriation.

The primary advantage of the incremental approach is that it simplifies the budget process by considering only the increments in the various budget items, which in most cases would be smaller and easier to handle than the total budgeted amount. On the other hand, a major disadvantage is that existing waste and inefficiencies may escalate year after year without ever being discovered.

Minimum Level Approach

Using the **minimum level approach,** an organization establishes a base amount for all budget items and requires explanation or justification for any budgeted amount above the minimum. Under this method an absolute minimum amount of expenditures is presumed necessary to support ongoing activity in the organization. This method is very useful where many committed costs continue from period to period. Proponents of this approach maintain that requiring extensive justifications of budget items up to the minimum amount is an ineffective use of managerial time. Like the incremental approach, the minimum level approach is often used for activities that do not have clearly defined input/output relationships. For example, the corporate director of product development would need some minimum provision in the budget to support a minimum level of activity for ongoing projects. Additional increments might also be included first to support the current level of product development and second to undertake desirable new projects.

All three approaches are often used in the same organization. A manufacturing firm might, for example, use the input/output approach to budget manufacturing and distribution expenditures; the incremental approach to budget administrative salaries, advertising, and contributions; and the minimum level approach to budget research and development, employee training, and computer operations.

BUDGET PREPARATION

There are probably no two organizations that use the same budget development procedures, but there are two approaches to budgeting that seem to characterize budget preparation in most organizations: the *imposed budget* and the *participation budget*. These are sometimes referred to as, respectively, the *top-down* approach and the *bottom-up* approach.

Under the **imposed budget,** or **top-down,** approach to budget preparation, top management decides on the goals and objectives for the whole organization and communicates these to lower management levels. This *nonparticipative approach* to budgeting can have serious motivational consequences. Personnel who do not participate in budget preparation are likely to lack a commitment in achieving their part of the budget.

The **participation budget** uses the benefits of improved communication, coordination, and motivation. The participation budget requires managers at all levels, and in some cases even nonmanagers, to become involved in budget preparation. This approach is sometimes referred to as the **bottom-up** approach. Budget proposals are made first at the lowest level of management and then are integrated into the proposals for the next level, and so on, until the proposals reach the top level of management where the budget is completed. Although the imposed budget approach was used quite frequently in the past, today most companies encourage greater participation in budget preparation.

In the participative approach to budgeting, managers who are directly responsible for a given area have the initial input into the budgeting process for that area. This builds confidence into the budgeting process at the operating levels of the organization and is likely to promote a better budgeting system. Budget predictions are likely to be more accurate and the person responsible for the budget is more likely to strive to accomplish its objectives. These *self-imposed* budgets reinforce the concept of participative management and should strengthen the overall budgeting process.

Also important to budget preparation are the types of forecasts used. Though the sales forecast is primary to most organizations, other types of forecasts vary in importance. Other forecasts or predictions often used include: estimates of uncollectibles, production output as a ratio of resources input, production days available, employee turnover and subsequent training of new employees, and cash balance needs per month. Because of the diverse sources of these predictions, the preparation process requires coordination of most of the functions in an organization. Unfortunately, with the forecasts come new and additional demands by those providing input; for example, marketing wants to change the product unit, production wants to operate only four days a week, and the treasurer wants a smaller daily cash balance.

Obviously, all requests cannot be included in the budget. Someone must be responsible for deciding which requests are most important to the organization. Most organizations have a budget committee that is responsible for supervising budget preparation and serves as a review board for evaluating requests for discretionary cost items and new projects. The final responsibility for decisions rests with the budget committee, which is usually composed of

MANAGERIAL PRACTICE 6.2

Bottom-Up Budgeting at Johnson & Johnson

Johnson & Johnson has an elaborate planning and budgeting process. "It encompasses every aspect of the business and requires managers to reassess constantly budget goals and action plans." The budget is detailed down to the expense center level for each operating division for each year. It also includes a second-year forecast in somewhat less detail.

In addition, "budget projections are prepared from the bottom up." The requirements for the budget are never issued by top management in advance of budget preparation. All initial inputs for the budget come from the operating departments. Final budgets are then developed with reference to the long-range plans of the company. After about six months of preparation and review at all levels, the budgets for the upcoming year and the second-year forecasts are presented and discussed at the corporate executive level.

Source: Robert Simons, "Planning, Control, and Uncertainty: A Process View," in *Accounting and Management Field Study Perspectives*, ed. William J. Burns, Jr., and Robert S. Kaplan (Boston: Harvard Business School Press, 1987), 339–349.

top-level managers. In addition, larger companies frequently will have a *budget office*, responsible to the controller, that performs a staff function of assisting the budget committee. The budget office is responsible for the preparation, distribution, and processing of forms used in gathering budget data and handles most of the work of actually formulating the budget schedules and reports. The budget office staff may also assist the budget committee by preparing various analyses and special reports.

Large organizations frequently have a full-time budgeting staff that works year-round on the budget. This does not mean that it takes twelve months to prepare the budget, or that once the annual budget is completed the budgeting staff has nothing else to do until the next year. Preparing a budget may take most of the year in some companies; also, the final budget is really never final—it may have to be revised several times during the course of the budget period. Furthermore, the multiyear, long-range plans of many companies are updated constantly to reflect changing conditions. Revisions and updating are part of the responsibility of the budget office.

MANAGERIAL PRACTICE 6.3

Meeting the Challenge of Increased Competition

The University of Illinois Hospital and Clinics in Chicago began an improvement program in 1983 in response to the challenge of dramatically increased competition in the health care industry. The planning process there included specific plans for both short term and long term, based on an "accurate assessment of management, operations, services, patient volume, market segment, and finances." The primary emphasis was on developing strategies for a five-year span. A secondary priority was even longer range plans. Financial planning was coordinated with other strategic plans to provide a clearer picture of all the underlying economic factors. First, a productivity improvement review zeroed in on services that could more effectively control costs. Second, reimbursements were reviewed, to prepare for the Medicare prospective payment program and improve financial management in general. And third, an information system needs analysis uncovered the need for a common database. Although changes have been gradual, there have already been increased revenues, productivity gains, and improved management decision making.

Source: James Malloy, "Mission Possible," *Management Focus* (March–April 1985): 20–23.

BUDGETING PERIODS

Up to this point the normal budget period has been assumed to be one year. Although the annual budget period is certainly the most common, many organizations budget for shorter periods (such as a month or a quarter of a year) and for longer periods (such as two years, five years, or more). In addition to fixed length budget periods, two other types of budget periods are commonly used, *cycle budgeting* and *continuous budgeting.*

For some businesses, a fixed time period is not particularly relevant to the planning of operations. A company engaged in large construction projects might find it more advantageous to prepare a budget for the entire project life, which may be more than a year in some cases and less than a year in others. In these cases the firm may use **cycle budgeting,** which is appropriate when the entire life of the cycle or project represents a more useful planning horizon than an artificial period of one year. Such cycles could be reduced to shorter planning periods by breaking the overall project into several components, such as construction phases.

Another type of budgeting that is gaining in popularity is *continuous,* or *perpetual,* budgeting. Under **continuous budgeting,** the budget is based on a moving time-frame that extends over a fixed period. For example, an organization on a continuous four-quarter budget system adds a quarter to the budget at the end of each quarter of operations, thereby always maintaining a budget four quarters into the future. Under this system, plans for a full year into the future are always available; whereas under a fixed annual budget, operating plans for a full year ahead are available only at the beginning of the budget year. Because management is constantly involved in this type of budgeting, the budget process becomes an active and integral part of the management process. Management is forced to be future-oriented throughout the year, rather than just once each year. Continuous budgeting, which is now feasible with the aid of computers, helps to elevate the level of visibility and recognition of the planning function.

TYPES OF BUDGETS

The types of budgets that must be prepared vary, depending on the nature of the business and its activities. The operating cycle of most businesses, as shown in Exhibit 6–2, involves the conversion of cash into other assets, which are intended to produce revenues in excess of their costs. The cycle generally follows a path from cash, to inventory, to receivables, and back to cash. There are, of course, intermediate phases in the cycle such as the purchase or manufacture of inventories, payment of accounts payable, and the collection of receivables. The operating budget is merely a detailed model of the firm's operating cycle.

EXHIBIT 6–2   Operating Cycle

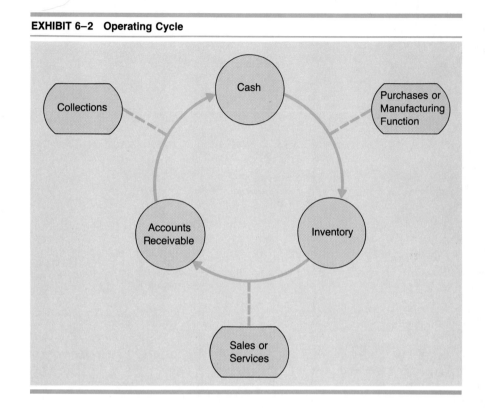

In most organizations the budgeting process begins with the development of the sales budget and concludes with the development of pro forma financial statements. Exhibit 6–3 depicts the annual budget assembly process in a manufacturing firm. Note how all the critical activities converge from sales toward cash and then toward the pro forma financial statements.

To illustrate the procedures involved in budget assembly, an operating budget will be developed for the All American Wagon Company (AAW) (a manufacturer of wooden wagons for children) for the year 19x5. The assembly sequence follows the overview illustrated in Exhibit 6–3. Each element of the budget process in Exhibit 6–3 is illustrated in a separate exhibit as given. Because of the numerous elements in the budget process illustrated for AAW, you will find it useful to refer back to Exhibit 6–3 often.

The activities of a business can be summarized under three broad categories: operating activities, financing activities, and investing activities. For our purposes, and to simplify our discussion, assume that All American Wagon Company engaged in no investing activities during the budget period and that the only financing activity is short-term borrowing. Normal profit-related activities performed in conducting the daily affairs of an organization are called **operating**

EXHIBIT 6–3   Overview of Budget Assembly in a Manufacturing Firm

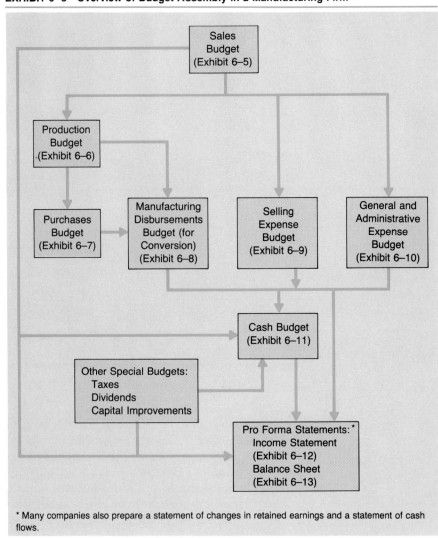

* Many companies also prepare a statement of changes in retained earnings and a statement of cash flows.

activities. These, of course, are the major concern of management in preparing operating budgets. The operating activities of the All American Wagon Company include:

1. Sales of goods or services.

2. Purchase of materials, labor, and overhead for the manufacture of saleable goods.

3. Purchase and use of goods and services classified as selling expenses.

4. Purchase and use of goods and services classified as general and administrative expenses.

In addition to preparing the budget for each operating activity, a cash budget is prepared that summarizes the projected cash receipts and disbursement for the budget period. The importance of cash planning makes the cash budget a vital part of the total budget process. Management must, for example, be aware of the need to borrow and have some idea when borrowed funds can be repaid.

The budgets for AAW provide information for each of the four quarters in 19x5 and totals for the year. The balance sheet at the end of 19x4, presented in Exhibit 6–4, contains information to use as a starting point in preparing the various budgets. The input/output approach is used to budget variable production and selling costs. The budgets for other costs are developed using either the incremental approach or the minimum level approach. Budgets to be prepared include sales, production, purchasing, manufacturing disbursements, selling expense, general and administrative expense, and cash.

EXHIBIT 6–4   Initial Balance Sheet

All American Wagon Company
Balance Sheet
December 31, 19x4

Assets

Current Assets:			
Cash		$ 15,000	
Accounts receivable (net)		19,200	
Inventory, raw materials*		5,720	
Inventory, finished goods (1,000 units)†		21,000	$ 60,920
Plant, property, and equipment:			
Land		$ 60,000	
Buildings and equipment	$260,000		
Less accumulated depreciation	−124,800	135,200	195,200
Total assets			$256,120

Liabilities and stockholders' equity

Current liabilities:			
Accounts payable			$ 17,200
Stockholders' equity:			
Capital stock		$150,000	
Retained earnings		88,920	238,920
Total liabilities and stockholders' equity			$256,120

---

* Direct materials included $3,120 of lumber (1,560 sq. ft. of lumber at $2 per sq. ft.) and $2,600 of hardware sets (520 sets at $5 per set).

† Unit costs for 19x4 averaged $21 composed of direct materials, $11; direct labor, $6; variable overhead, $2; and fixed overhead, $2.

Sales Budget

The sales budget contains a forecast of unit sales volume and sales dollars, and it may also contain a forecast of sales collections. The sales budget is a critical element in the overall operating budget process because so many of the other elements, such as production, purchases, labor needs, and other resource requirements, are based on projected sales. Management uses the best available information to forecast future market conditions accurately. These forecasts, when considered along with product development plans, promotion and advertising plans, and expected pricing policies, should lead to the most dependable sales predictions. The sales budget for 19x5 is presented in Exhibit 6–5.

Once the sales predictions are made, information on credit terms, collections policy, and past collection experience are used to develop a sales collections budget. Collections on sales normally include receipts from the current period's sales and the collections from sales of prior periods. An allowance for bad debts, which reduces each period's collections, is also predicted. Other items often included are sales discounts, allowances for volume discounts, and seasonal changes of sales prices and collections. For AAW 75 percent of the cash is collected in the quarter of sales and 24 percent in the quarter after the sales take place. Bad debts are budgeted at 1 percent of sales.

Production Budget

The production budget is based on sales predictions with adjustments for beginning inventory and desired ending inventory. It establishes the production quotas for each period necessary to cover sales and provide desired ending inventory levels. Assume AAW's experience indicates ending inventories should

---

EXHIBIT 6–5   Sales Budget

All American Wagon Company
Sales Budget
For the year ended December 31, 19x5

	First Quarter	Second Quarter	Third Quarter	Fourth Quarter	Year Total
Sales (units)	5,000	6,000	8,500	5,500	25,000
Sales ($38 each)	$190,000	$228,000	$323,000	$209,000	$950,000
Collections on sales					
For current quarter (75% of sales)	$142,500	$171,000	$242,250	$156,750	$712,500
For previous quarter (24% of sales)	19,200*	45,600	54,720	77,520	197,040
Total	$161,700	$216,600	$296,970	$234,270	$909,540
Budgeted bad debts (1% of current quarter sales)	$ 1,900	$ 2,280	$ 3,230	$ 2,090	$ 9,500

* This is the January 1, 19x5, Accounts Receivable balance.

Note: The Accounts Receivable balance on December 31, 19x5, is $50,160 ($209,000 − $156,750 − $2,090).

amount to 20 percent of the next quarter's expected sales. First we determine the total needs for sales and desired ending inventories and then subtract the expected beginning inventories from this amount. The difference is what the company needs to produce. The production budget for 19x5 is presented in Exhibit 6–6.

Purchases Budget

The **purchases budget** indicates the raw materials that must be acquired to meet production needs and ending inventory requirements. It may be referred to as a direct materials purchases budget if it contains only purchases of raw materials. However, it often contains factory supplies and may even contain office and selling supplies. For simplicity, the purchases budget developed in this chapter includes only purchases of raw materials.

This budget is critical to the overall budget process because it may contain the largest commitment of cash outflows from the organization. From this budget, cash disbursements for purchases are predicted based on the expected timing of payments on account. A firm often delays cash disbursements as long as possible within any available discount period. For AAW, payments for purchases are assumed to be made 50 percent in the quarter purchased and 50 percent in the next quarter.

AAW's purchases budget is shown in Exhibit 6–7. Supplies are assumed to be immaterial and therefore are assumed to be included in variable factory overhead and office expenses. For each wagon, the materials requirements consist of 3 square feet of lumber and one set of hardware, which includes such items as wheels, bolts and nuts, a tongue, and other assembly items. These sets come to the workstations prepackaged.

EXHIBIT 6–6   Production Budget

All American Wagon Company
Production Budget
For the year ended December 31, 19x5
(In units)

	First Quarter	Second Quarter	Third Quarter	Fourth Quarter	Year Total
Wagons					
Budgeted sales (Exhibit 6–5)	5,000	6,000	8,500	5,500	25,000
Plus required ending inventory*	1,200	1,700	1,100	1,200†	1,200
Total inventory requirements	6,200	7,700	9,600	6,700	26,200
Less beginning inventory	−1,000	−1,200	−1,700	−1,100	−1,000
Budgeted production	5,200	6,500	7,900	5,600	25,200

* Equals 20 percent of the next quarter's sales.
† Sales for 19x6 are projected to be 6,000 units each quarter.

EXHIBIT 6–7   Purchases Budget

All American Wagon Company
Purchases Budget
For the year ended December 31, 19x5

	First Quarter	Second Quarter	Third Quarter	Fourth Quarter	Year Total
Production units (from Exhibit 6–6)	5,200	6,500	7,900	5,600	25,200
Lumber (sq. ft.)					
Target ending inventory*	1,950	2,370	1,680	1,800	1,800
Production needs**	15,600	19,500	23,700	16,800	75,600
Total requirements	17,550	21,870	25,380	18,600	77,400
Less beginning inventory	− 1,560	− 1,950	− 2,370	− 1,680	− 1,560
Purchases needed	15,990	19,920	23,010	16,920	75,840
Cost ($2 per sq. ft.)	× $2	× $2	× $2	× $2	× $2
Total lumber purchases	$31,980	$39,840	$46,020	$33,840	$151,680
Hardware sets (each)					
Target ending inventory*	650	790	560	600	600
Production needs	5,200	6,500	7,900	5,600	25,200
Total requirements	5,850	7,290	8,460	6,200	25,800
Less beginning inventory	− 520	− 650	− 790	− 560	− 520
Purchases needed	5,330	6,640	7,670	5,640	25,280
Cost ($5 per set)	× $5	× $5	× $5	× $5	× $5
Total hardware set purchases	$26,650	$33,200	$38,350	$28,200	$126,400
Total Purchases					
Lumber	$31,980	$39,840	$46,020	$33,840	$151,680
Hardware sets	26,650	33,200	38,350	28,200	126,400
Total	$58,630	$73,040	$84,370	$62,040	$278,080
Disbursements for purchases					
Payments of material purchases:					
For current quarter (50 percent)	$29,315	$36,520	$42,185	$31,020	$139,040
For previous quarter (50 percent)	17,200†	29,315	36,520	42,185	125,220
Total	$46,515	$65,835	$78,705	$73,205	$264,260

* Target ending inventory equal to 10 percent of next quarter's production.

** Each wagon requires three square feet of lumber.

† Unpaid balance at December 31, 19x4, reflects prior year payment terms.

All purchases are made by a centralized purchasing department and the quarterly purchases budget is very helpful in controlling the activities of this department. By using appropriate procedures for getting bids and placing orders, the department helps the organization to minimize the cost of carrying inventory.

Manufacturing Disbursements Budget

The **manufacturing disbursements budget,** which is based on an analysis of the production budget, is used to plan the conversion cost (labor and factory overhead) requirements for the budgeted volume of production. These requirements are then used to budget the actual disbursement dollars for labor and overhead. Recall that required disbursements for purchases of direct materials are included in the purchases budget.

Direct labor and overhead costs for each wagon produced by AAW have been estimated by management to be as follows:

Direct materials (lumber and hardware sets)	$11
Direct labor, $\frac{1}{2}$ hour at $20 per hour	10
Variable factory overhead, $\frac{1}{2}$ hour of direct labor at $8 per hour	4
Fixed factory overhead, $75,600/25,200 units	3
Total cost per unit	$28

Fixed manufacturing costs are as follows:

Fixed factory overhead requiring cash expenditures	$15,000 per quarter
Fixed factory overhead not requiring cash expenditures (depreciation)	$3,900 per quarter

Direct labor and factory overhead, except for depreciation, are acquired and paid for in the quarter they are used. Information on budgeted labor hours is presented in the upper portion of Exhibit 6–8. The budgeted manufacturing

EXHIBIT 6–8   Manufacturing Disbursements Budget

All American Wagon Company
Manufacturing Disbursements Budget
For the year ended December 31, 19x5

	First Quarter	Second Quarter	Third Quarter	Fourth Quarter	Year Total
Budgeted production					
Wagons	5,200	6,500	7,900	5,600	25,200
Direct labor hours ($\frac{1}{2}$ hour per unit)	2,600	3,250	3,950	2,800	12,600
Manufacturing disbursements (for conversion)					
Direct labor					
$20 per hour	$52,000	$ 65,000	$ 79,000	$56,000	$252,000
Variable overhead					
$8 per direct labor hour	20,800	26,000	31,600	22,400	100,800
Fixed overhead	15,000	15,000	15,000	15,000	60,000
Total	$87,800	$106,000	$125,600	$93,400	$412,800

disbursements for conversion costs are presented in the lower portion of Exhibit 6–8. Depreciation is not included because cash flow is not associated with depreciation but is incurred in connection with the acquisition of fixed assets.

Selling Expense Budget

The selling expense budget presents the costs and disbursements the organization plans to incur in connection with sales and distribution. Budgeted selling expenses include variable selling expenses and fixed selling expenses other than depreciation of $4,000 per quarter. Note in the Selling Expense Budget, Exhibit 6–9, that the budgeted variable selling expenses are based on budgeted sales as a percentage of budgeted sales dollars. The budgeted fixed selling expenses are based on amounts obtained from the manager of the sales department. Budgeted selling costs for AAW are paid in the quarter they are incurred.

General and Administrative Expense Budget

The general and administrative expense budget presents the expected costs and disbursements for the overall administration of the organization, such as the accounting department, the computer center, and the president's office. Depreciation of $2,000 per quarter is omitted since it requires no cash dis-

---

EXHIBIT 6–9   Selling Expense Budget

All American Wagon Company
Selling Expense Budget
For the year ended December 31, 19x5

	First Quarter	Second Quarter	Third Quarter	Fourth Quarter	Year Total
Budgeted sales (from Exhibit 6–5)	$190,000	$228,000	$323,000	$209,000	$950,000
Selling costs and disbursements					
Variable costs:					
Delivery (1% sales)	$ 1,900	$ 2,280	$ 3,230	$ 2,090	$ 9,500
Commissions (2% sales)	3,800	4,560	6,460	4,180	19,000
Miscellaneous (1% sales)	1,900	2,280	3,230	2,090	9,500
Total	$ 7,600	$ 9,120	$12,920	$ 8,360	$38,000
Fixed costs:					
Advertising	$ 2,250	$ 2,250	$ 2,250	$ 2,250	$ 9,000
Office expenses	1,250	1,250	1,250	1,250	5,000
Miscellaneous	1,000	1,000	1,000	1,000	4,000
Total	4,500	4,500	4,500	4,500	18,000
Total selling costs and disbursements	$12,100	$13,620	$17,420	$12,860	$56,000

EXHIBIT 6–10   General and Administrative Expense Budget

All American Wagon Company
General and Administrative Expense Budget
For the year ended December 31, 19x5

	First Quarter	Second Quarter	Third Quarter	Fourth Quarter	Year Total
General and administrative costs and disbursements					
Compensation	$20,000	$20,000	$20,000	$20,000	$ 80,000
Research and development	5,000	5,000	5,000	5,000	20,000
Insurance	2,000	2,000	2,000	2,000	8,000
Property taxes	3,000	3,000	3,000	3,000	12,000
Miscellaneous	1,000	1,000	1,000	1,000	4,000
Total budgeted general and administrative costs and disbursements	$31,000	$31,000	$31,000	$31,000	$124,000

bursement. Note in Exhibit 6–10 that there are no variable general and administrative costs. This is because most expenditures categorized as general and administrative are related to top management operations that do not vary with current sales or production. For AAW all general and administrative costs except depreciation are assumed to be paid in the quarter they are incurred.

Cash Budget

The **cash budget** summarizes all cash receipts and disbursements expected to occur during the budget period. Almost all activities affect cash sooner or later. AAW's cash budget, presented in Exhibit 6–11, is affected by credit policies, sales discounts taken by customers, collection experiences, payment policies, purchase and volume discounts taken, and myriad other factors. The tax information is furnished by AAW's tax department, and the information for dividends by the Board of Directors. The cash budget shows the cash operating deficiencies and surpluses expected to occur at the end of each quarter. This information is used to predict cash borrowing, loan payment, and cash investment needs.

The cash maintenance policy for All American Wagon requires that a minimum balance of $15,000 be maintained at the end of each quarter. AAW has a line of credit with a major bank, with any interest on borrowed funds computed at the simple interest rate of 12 percent per year, or 1.0 percent per month. All necessary borrowing is assumed to occur at the start of each quarter in increments of one thousand dollars. The cash budget presented in Exhibit 6–11 indicates that AAW will need to borrow $18,000 at the beginning of the first quarter and $2,000 at the beginning of the second. At the end of the third quarter, AAW will be able to repay the loan.

EXHIBIT 6–11   Cash Budget

All American Wagon Company
Cash Budget
For the year ended December 31, 19x5

	First Quarter	Second Quarter	Third Quarter	Fourth Quarter	Year Total
Cash balance beginning	$ 15,000	$ 15,285	$ 15,430	$ 35,935	$ 15,000
Plus cash collections on sales (Exhibit 6–5)	161,700	216,600	296,970	234,270	909,540
Total available from operations	$176,700	$231,885	$312,400	$270,205	$924,540
Less budgeted disbursements:					
Purchasing (from Exhibit 6–7)	$ 46,515	$ 65,835	$ 78,705	$ 73,205	$264,260
Manufacturing (from Exhibit 6–8)	87,800	106,000	125,600	93,400	412,800
Selling (from Exhibit 6–9)	12,100	13,620	17,420	12,860	56,000
General and administrative (from Exhibit 6–10)	31,000	31,000	31,000	31,000	124,000
Other:					
Income taxes	2,000	2,000	2,000	1,200	7,200
Dividends	—	—	—	30,000	30,000
Total	−179,415	−218,455	−254,725	−241,665	−894,260
Excess (deficiency) cash available over disbursements	$ (2,715)	$ 13,430	$ 57,675	$ 28,540	$ 30,280
Short-term financing*					
New loans	$ 18,000	$ 2,000	—	—	$ 20,000
Repayments	—	—	$ (20,000)	—	(20,000)
Interest†	—	—	(1,740)	—	(1,740)
Net cash flow from financing	18,000	2,000	(21,740)	—	(1,740)
Cash balance, ending	$ 15,285	$ 15,430	$ 35,935	$ 28,540	$ 28,540

* Short-term loans are obtained in increments of $1,000 to maintain cash at a minimum balance of $15,000 at all times. Accordingly, new loans required are budgeted for the beginning of the quarter and repayments are budgeted for the end of the quarter. Loan repayments are made on a first-borrowed, first-repaid basis and interest is paid only at the time of repayment.

† Interest computation for repayment of $20,000 is ($18,000 × 9 months × 0.01 = $1,620) + ($2,000 × 6 months × 0.01 = $120) = $1,740.

PRO FORMA STATEMENTS

The preparation of operating budgets culminates in the preparation of *pro forma financial statements*. Pro forma financial statements are hypothetical statements that reflect the "as if" effects of the budgeted activities on the actual financial position of the organization. That is, the statements reflect what the results of operations will be if all the predictions in the budget are correct. The preparation of pro forma financial statements has been simplified greatly by computer programs, especially financial spreadsheets that permit the user to immediately determine the impact of any assumed changes. These statements may use either the functional or contribution format for the income statement with the balance sheet accounts reflecting the corresponding entries.

Exhibit 6–12 presents the pro forma income statement for the year ended December 31, 19x5, using the functional format. If all the predictions made in the operating budget are correct, All American will produce a net income for

---

EXHIBIT 6–12   Pro Forma Income Statement

All American Wagon Company
Pro Forma Income Statement (functional format)
For the year ended December 31, 19x5

Sales (Exhibit 6–5)				$950,000
Cost of goods sold:				
Finished goods inventory, 1/1/x5 (Exhibit 6–4)			$ 21,000	
Cost of materials placed in production:				
Raw materials, 1/1/x5 (Exhibit 6–4)	$ 5,720			
Purchases (Exhibit 6–7)	278,080			
Total available	$283,800			
Raw materials, 12/31/x5*	− 6,600	$277,200		
Direct labor (Exhibit 6–8)		252,000		
Variable factory overhead (Exhibit 6–8)		100,800		
Fixed factory overhead ($60,000 + $15,600**)		75,600	705,600	
Total goods available for sale			$726,600	
Finished goods inventory, 12/31/x5 (1,200 units × $28)†			− 33,600	−693,000
Gross profit				$257,000
Other operating expenses:				
Selling expenses (Exhibit 6–9)			$ 56,000	
Selling expenses, depreciation ($4,000 per quarter)			16,000	
General and administrative (Exhibit 6–10)			124,000	
General and administrative, depreciation				
($2,000 per quarter)			8,000	
Bad debt expense (Exhibit 6–5)			9,500	−213,500
Income from operations				$ 43,500
Interest expense (Exhibit 6–11)				− 1,740
Net income before taxes				$ 41,760
Allowance for income taxes				− 7,200
Net income				$ 34,560

* Lumber	1,800 sq. ft. × $2	$3,600
Hardware sets	600 sets × $5	3,000
Total		$6,600

** Depreciation = 4 × $3,900 = $15,600.

† AAW uses a FIFO cost flow assumption. Hence, the ending inventory includes goods manufactured during the current period at a unit cost of $28 ($705,600/25,200 units).

the year of $34,560. Note that just about every item on the pro forma income statement comes from one of the budget schedules. The only exceptions are depreciation expense and taxes. Depreciation expense is predicted by the company's chief accountant; it is based on historical asset costs. Income taxes are determined on the basis of predicted taxable income following rules established by the Internal Revenue Service.

The pro forma balance sheet, presented in Exhibit 6–13, shows the financial position of AAW at the end of 19x5, assuming all the budget predictions are correct. Sources of the pro forma balance sheet data are included as part of the exhibit.

POTENTIAL PROBLEMS OF BUDGETING

Like many other tools available to managers, budgeting offers the potential for vast benefits but also has potential pitfalls and problems. This section briefly mentions some of the more important problems that may be encountered in budgeting.

Preparation Time

Preparing a budget for a large company can be a massive task, requiring hundreds, and perhaps thousands, of hours of valuable management time. Careful coordination and planning are required to keep budget preparation from becoming too onerous for managers or from interfering with their other responsibilities. To minimize the time required by each manager, the budget preparation calendar should be carefully planned, and easy-to-use forms should be provided.

Accuracy

In some cases the prediction ability of management is very weak. The more limited management's ability to make the accurate forecasts and predictions that are necessary for the budget, the more limited the usefulness of a single budget becomes. This is particularly true for newer businesses. Rapidly changing economic conditions also make budgeting difficult. Even then, however, managers who study the budgetary impact of possible changes can learn what factors to monitor most closely and to develop contingency plans that can be implemented if needed. Many statistical and mathematical techniques, such as those discussed in the appendix to Chapter 3, are available to improve the reliability of the budget data.

Budgetary Slack

Budgetary slack, sometimes referred to as "padding the budget," occurs when managers intentionally request more funds in the budget for their departments than they need to support the anticipated level of operations. If a department consistently produces large favorable variances—or even small favorable variances with little apparent effort—this may be a symptom of slack built into the budget. The desire by managers to pad their budgets may indicate poor relations between upper and lower management, or poor administration of the budget.

EXHIBIT 6–13   Pro Forma Balance Sheet

All American Wagon Company
Pro Forma Balance Sheet
December 31, 19x5

Assets

Current assets:
Cash (Exhibit 6–11)	$ 28,540	
Accounts receivable (net) (Exhibit 6–5)	50,160	
Inventory, raw materials (Exhibit 6–12)	6,600	
Inventory, finished goods (Exhibit 6–12)	33,600	$118,900

Plant, property, and equipment:
Land		$ 60,000	
Buildings and equipment	$260,000		
Less accumulated depreciation	−164,400	95,600	155,600

Total assets $274,500

Liabilities and stockholders' equity

Current liabilities:
Accounts payable (Exhibit 6–7)	$ 31,020

Stockholders' equity:
Capital stock	$150,000	
Retained earnings	93,480	243,480

Total liabilities and stockholders' equity $274,500

Sources of data:

1. Cash balance was obtained from the cash budget.

2. Accounts receivable represents 24 percent of the fourth quarter sales that are expected to be collected in 19x6.

3. Raw material inventory represents the purchases of direct materials in the fourth quarter that will be used in manufacturing in 19x6.

4. The finished goods inventory values are at the 19x5 average unit costs of $28.

5. Land and buildings and equipment are the same as at the end of 19x4.

6. Accumulated depreciation is equal to the balance at the end of 19x4 increased by the 19x5 depreciation [$124,800 + $15,600 (building and equipment) + 16,000 (selling) + $8,000 (general and administrative)].

7. The balance in accounts payable is 50 percent of the fourth quarter purchases of direct materials ($62,040 × 0.50).

8. Capital stock is the same as at the end of 19x4.

9. Retained earnings is equal to the balance at the end of 19x4 plus pro forma net income less dividends of $30,000 reported in the cash budget.

**Economy and
Industry Relations**

Although each organization is a unique entity whose peculiar characteristics are reflected in its operations budget, most organizations are also affected by general economic or industry conditions. Any inability to obtain accurate and reliable information about these conditions can pose serious problems for managers trying to make predictions about their own companies. For example, many organizations that depend on external sources of funds have found it very difficult to predict the cost and availability of acquiring funds.

MANAGERIAL PRACTICE 6.4

Computerized Budgeting at Lord Corporation

Lord Corporation has developed a computerized budgeting system that has made the annual budget planning process faster and easier. The system has also reduced the risk of mathematical error.

Transaction screens are used to help the budget center managers prepare their budgets. Five screens are available. The *hourly personnel screen* is used to determine the number of labor hours/personnel needed to operate a department during the next year. The *salaries worksheet screen* provides the calculations for individual salaries. The *salaries and personnel screen* summarizes salaries and allows managers to calculate additional expenses, such as bonuses and salary incentives. The *spending budget screen* displays the budget information for several different expense accounts at the same time. Finally, the *hourly rate computation screen* is used to prepare the variable budgets. The system provides hard copies of the information to the budget center managers.

Upper management has access to the different managers' budgets through the use of summary codes. The system also improves communication among different departments. Many problems and questions can be resolved over the phone while all parties are looking at the same information.

Source: Keith G. Gourley and Thomas R. Blecki, "Computerized Budgeting at Lord Corporation," *Management Accounting* (August 1986): 37–40.

SUMMARY

Operating budgets are an integral part of the overall planning and control system. They represent management's expectations about the events and activities scheduled to occur during a specified future period. Budgets provide the basis for evaluating actual performance and modifying subsequent plans. Budgeting offers many potential benefits for organizations, including forcing managers to look at the future of the company, improving communication, improving coordination between various departments and functions in the organization, and motivating managers to achieve organizational objectives.

The input/output approach to budget planning is based on clearly defined relationships between effort and accomplishment. The incremental approach requires budget review of proposals in excess of the budgeted (or actual) expenditures for the previous period. The minimum level approach requires review of any budgeted amounts in excess of some minimum amount. The budgeting process is usually implemented on an annual schedule, although companies in certain industries find the cyclical approach more appropriate. Continuous budgeting consists of adding a new time unit to the end of the budget period upon completing a unit of time.

Most manufacturing organizations prepare budgets for sales, production, purchases, manufacturing disbursements, selling expenses, general and administrative expenses, and cash. Budget preparation culminates with the presentation of pro forma financial statements reflecting the "as if" effects on the company of carrying out the budget.

Feedback is an essential part of budgeting. Without interpretation of actual performance much of the benefit, including that of motivating people, would be lost. To receive maximum benefits from budgeting requires participation by all management levels, commitments by top management, and both positive and negative feedback.

Pitfalls of operations budgeting include placing excessive time demands on managers, expecting accurate and reliable predictions of all general economic and industry conditions, failure of top management to support the budget, poorly established organizational lines of authority and responsibility, and possible budgetary slack.

APPENDIX
NOT-FOR-PROFIT BUDGETING

In not-for-profit organizations, budgeting plays a vital role in planning and monitoring the effective and efficient use of scarce resources. In most not-for-profit organizations, the key element is budgeted revenue. It is often the primary determinant of all the expenditures in other parts of the budget. The budget is essentially a legal document for governmental units and a restraining document for nongovernmental units. Not-for-profit organizational agencies or units cannot exceed budgeted amounts until the proper authorities have approved budget amendments.

EXHIBIT 6–14   Control Budget

Ohio Valley Children's Foundation
Budget for 19x6

Estimated revenues:		
Contributions	$1,000,000	
Service fees	600,000	
Interest income	400,000	$2,000,000
Appropriations:		
Children's Home	$1,500,000	
Summer Camp	200,000	
Emergency Care	275,000	−1,975,000
Balance to general fund		$ 25,000

For most not-for-profit organizations the budget is the primary control element. It is through the budget process that the projected revenues and expenditures for each of the accounts are established. Two types of budgets, revenue budgets and appropriation budgets, are used by many organizations. Revenue budgets establish the amount expected to be collected from each revenue source during the upcoming period. Appropriation budgets provide the authorization for expenditures during the specified period.[1] Very seldom do agencies or units have equal revenues and expenditures. For example, many units of a municipality generate revenue, but others receive no revenue. A city-supported college receives revenue through student fees and contributions, whereas a city prison system receives no revenues. To make up for the deficits, a municipality will usually impose income taxes, sales taxes, or property taxes, which are allocated to the different agencies that do not raise enough revenue to be self-supporting.

Once the budget is approved, it is considered the authority for expenditures of funds to carry out the goals and objectives of each organizational unit. The budgetary control accounts are then created for the coming period (see Exhibit 6–14). The parent group (a state, a religious organization, a private college) establishes the general control accounts that break the budget into its major elements. For the Ohio Valley Children's Foundation the control accounts are Contributions, Service Fees, Interest Income, Children's Home, Summer Camp, and Emergency Care.

The revenue accounts represent an accounting of revenues from all sources and are used to maintain control of all revenues, much as the master budget does for a corporation. The estimated revenues are a function of the various revenue-generating activities of an organizational unit. The appropriations accounts represent an accounting of budgeted appropriations. The detailed

---

[1] An appropriation is an authorization to make expenditures and incur obligations with limitations on amount, purpose, and time period.

appropriations accounts specify the funds allocated to the different areas of the organization.

Organizations use two types of budgeting to control the different operational units. In a lump-sum budget only general areas are allocated revenues and expenditures. Appropriations for a lump-sum budget appear in Exhibit 6–14. In this budget the Children's Home was allocated $1,500,000 for the period. In the other type of budget, a line-item budget revenues and expenditures are assigned to specific categories and items of responsibility. Using this method, the $1,500,000 to the Children's Home is allocated by major categories. A line-item budget for the Children's Home might appear as in Exhibit 6–15. Using this budget, the management of the Children's Home would be required to adhere to the appropriation limits set for each category. Most organizations resist shifting funds from one line item to another without approval of the governing body. This type of budgeting places tight control over the expenditures, but it does not attempt to measure the efficiency or effectiveness of the expenditures.

Revenue and Appropriation Budgets

Because revenues in most not-for-profit organizations come from many sources, each major source of revenue should be itemized, as in Exhibit 6–16 for the City of Dothan. For comparison purposes, Exhibit 6–16 also shows the actual revenues of the prior period.

The itemization of the revenue budget allows the city to evaluate each revenue source separately. Some revenue sources are more susceptible to prediction errors than others. For example, it is much easier to predict the revenue received from property taxes than it is to predict the fees collected from exhibitors in the city park.

Appropriation budgets show how each organizational unit is authorized to spend its resources or allocations during the budget period. The format of a

---

EXHIBIT 6–15   Line-Item Budget

Children's Home
Ohio Valley Children's Foundation
Budget for 19x6

Estimated revenues:		
Contributions		$ 700,000
Appropriations:		
Building maintenance	$200,000	
Staff salaries and benefits	300,000	
Food and clothing	600,000	
Utilities	100,000	
Equipment	150,000	
Schooling	150,000	−1,500,000
Excess appropriations over revenues		$ (800,000)
Balance from general fund		800,000
Fund balance		$ 0

EXHIBIT 6–16   Revenue Budgets

City of Dothan
Budgeted Revenue
Fiscal year 19x6–x7

	Actual 19x5–x6	Budget 19x6–x7
Taxes:		
Property	$2,000,000	$2,300,000
Sales	600,000	750,000
Total taxes	$2,600,000	$3,050,000
Fees and licenses:		
Business	$ 20,000	$ 25,000
Water sales	310,000	315,000
Police	32,000	40,000
Total fees and licenses	362,000	380,000
Other revenues:		
Federal and state grants	$ 150,000	$ 150,000
Investment income	25,000	30,000
Sales of equipment	10,000	25,000
Total other revenues	185,000	205,000
Total revenues budgeted	$3,147,000	$3,635,000

given budget depends on the type of organizational unit and budget being used. The overall appropriation budget for the City of Dothan and a line-item budget for the fire department are shown in Exhibit 6–17. In this case there are only five line items.

Appropriation budgets are the primary basis for the evaluation and control of not-for-profit organizations. Nonprofit organizations generally emphasize accountability of funds rather than efficiency of operation; therefore, each operating period is measured by the funds expended (cash payments) rather than by the matching of revenues and expenses. To ensure adherence to the budgets, the manager of each operating unit is responsible for accepting the budget as the operating plan for the next period. Performance reports that compare actual results with the budgets are prepared to determine how well the plans were carried out. The City of Dothan fire department performance report for fiscal year 19x5–x6 is illustrated in Exhibit 6–18.

For most not-for-profit organizations, the performance report is the key means of evaluating a unit. Each item should be evaluated separately and both unfavorable and favorable variances should receive detailed analysis. For example, a department could have a favorable variance for salaries simply because not enough people were employed to carry out its services. In such a situation management would be able to evaluate whether or not the services were weakened because of the lack of personnel or if, in fact, the category was overbudgeted at the beginning of the period.

EXHIBIT 6–17   Budget Relationships

City of Dothan
Appropriation Budget
Fiscal year 19x6–x7

	Actual 19x5–x6	Budget 19x6–x7
Schools	$1,300,000	$1,350,000
Police	800,000	900,000
►Fire	200,000	220,000
Water	47,000	50,000
Street maintenance	500,000	600,000
Administration and courts	200,000	275,000
Parks and recreation	100,000	240,000
Totals	$3,147,000	$3,635,000

City of Dothan
Fire Protection Budget
Fiscal year 19x6–x7

	Actual 19x5–x6	Budget 19x6–x7
Salaries	$160,000	$175,000
Maintenance (equipment)	20,000	10,000
Supplies	11,000	22,000
Operating expenses	5,000	8,000
Gas and oil	4,000	5,000
►Total	$200,000	$220,000

EXHIBIT 6–18   Performance Report

City of Dothan
Fire Protection
Performance Report
Fiscal year 19x5–x6

	Actual	Budget	Variances*
Salaries	$160,000	$162,000	$2,000 F
Maintenance (equipment)	20,000	19,000	1,000 U
Supplies	11,000	18,000	7,000 F
Operating expenses	5,000	5,500	500 F
Gas and oil	4,000	4,000	—
Total	$200,000	$208,500	$8,500 F

* F = Favorable
  U = Unfavorable

Approaches to Budget Preparation

The budgets of governmental units are authorized by law. The collection of revenues and the appropriation of expenses must conform with constitutional law and must be specifically authorized through an approved budgetary process. Once the budgets of governmental units are approved, they have binding legal authority. Rather than just being a guide to action, the budget of a governmental unit is a mandate to act. Frequently used approaches to preparing budgets in governments and other not-for-profit organizations include incremental budgeting, programming budgeting, and zero base budgeting.

Incremental budgeting, discussed earlier in the chapter, is often used where the relationships between inputs and outputs are weak or nonexistent. The input/output approach, also discussed earlier, is often difficult to use in not-for-profit organizations, thereby resulting in the popularity of incremental budgeting. As an example, the cost of police protection is not necessarily a function of the measurable output of the agency (arrests) but of the inputs (size of city, previous crime rate, and level of trained personnel).

In seeking an annual appropriation, an agency is required to justify only proposed expenditures in excess of its previous budget. Because input/output relationships are difficult to determine, this method considers only the increments from an established base. The biggest advantages of incremental budgeting are simplicity and ease of preparation. However, a major disadvantage is that current inefficiencies may continue undetected for years.

Planning, programming, and budgeting systems (PPBS) emphasize outputs of an organization in programmed areas rather than inputs. A program is a specific activity or set of activities established to achieve a desired objective, such as fire protection. PPBS is based on three control ideas: (1) It is a formal planning system, (2) it uses a program budget, and (3) it emphasizes cost-benefit analysis. PPBS requires a careful specification and analysis of program objectives for each area or agency as a first step. Next, the process analyzes, insofar as possible, the output of a program in terms of its objectives. The third step is to measure the total costs of the program for several periods into the future. The fourth step is to analyze alternatives and seek those that have the greatest benefits as related to the stated objectives. The fifth and last step is the systematic implementation of the selected alternatives.

PPBS emphasizes control through responsibility accounting. The key to successful PPBS is forcing agencies to back away from their current operations and to evaluate their overall objectives. Through such evaluations each agency head accepts the responsibility of current and planned activities and must account for the results. Unfortunately, PPBS has not been well received in recent years because of implementation difficulties. All managers involved in the process must be familiar with it, and its implementation is very time consuming.

Zero-base budgeting begins with the premise that every dollar of a budgeted expenditure must be justified, including current expenditures that are to be continued. Incremental budgeting starts with the current level of expenditures and requires justification only for any proposed increases. Unlike incremental budgeting, which usually allows account increase differentiation but often requires spending cuts across the board, zero-base budgeting permits each program, subject to available resources, to receive any allocations that can be justified and supported.

Zero-base budgeting, as a planning tool, forces management to identify the activities that each agency or department engages in, to evaluate these activities, and to rank them in order of priority. The availability of funds will determine how many of the activities will be implemented.

The zero-base budgeting approach often assumes that decision makers have the capacity to eliminate programs. However, the political forces in any jurisdiction are such that few programs, if any, can be eliminated in any given year. For this reason zero-base budgeting may be better applied to selected programs than to entire organizations. Proposals for zero-base budgeting for the federal government would have program review occur only once every four or five years, with all programs of a given agency or department reviewed in the same year.[2]

The basic steps in zero-base budgeting are (1) development of decision packages consisting of departmental or agency activities, (2) evaluation of each decision package, (3) ranking of decision packages, (4) compilation of acceptable decision packages into the budget up to the limit of available resources, and (5) monitoring, control, and follow-up.

A decision package identifies each activity or department or agency. Decision packages may relate to goods, services, geographic areas, capital projects, or any other activity that relates to the organization's goals and objectives. Each decision package must be complete and able to stand alone, and it must include all direct costs and the cost of support activities. The budget of a city library could be defined as a decision package.

Decision packages should include an evaluation of what the organization is getting for each proposed expenditure and an identification of the cost and benefit relationships. The effects of different spending levels on costs and benefits should also be determined. Because cost and benefit relationships are not always linear, significant increases in total benefits may be accomplished by small increases in total costs. By comparing the incremental effect of additional expenditures on different programs, decision makers are better able to determine the optimal funding level. For the city library the cost of adding video packages would have to be evaluated against the increased service to the public and the public's acceptance of the new service.

Starting at the lowest decision level in the organization, decision packages are ranked and reranked until some upper level of management establishes a final order of priority. For example, the library director ranked the new video packages as the top priority for the coming year, the city budget review committee ranked it in the top 20 percent of the new requests, and the city council placed it in the middle of all new budgetary needs. Starting with the highest

---

[2] Joel Havemann, "Congress Tries to Break Ground Zero in Evaluating Federal Programs," *National Journal*, Volume 8, 1976, p. 708.

ranked package, the organization approves decision packages as long as uncommitted funds exist. The rankings are made on a variety of economic, social, bureaucratic, and political criteria. The funds available determines the number of decision packages accepted; generally, they are accepted in descending order. Therefore, any reduction in funds should result in dropping only the marginal decision packages.

Budgeting Problems

Like for-profit organizations, not-for-profit organizations have used budgeting for many years. The emphasis on formalized budgeting programs in government began long before that of most businesses. Although the benefit of experience has been a positive influence, there have also been some negative effects. Because many not-for-profit organizations have used budgeting for compliance rather than for coordinating and planning, many negative attitudes toward budgeting have developed.

For governments a budget is an authorization to spend that is founded in law. If an unusual occurrence causes activities to increase, the funding may be inadequate, but if the activities fall below planned levels, there will likely be an abundance of funds. For a given period the not-for-profit budget usually does not change. Another detrimental effect of the static (nonflexible) budget of not-for-profit organizations is that when a program does not spend all its budgeted funds, it may receive a smaller appropriation the following year. The fear of this occasionally sends managers into a spending frenzy at the end of the fiscal year, which usually results in wasted resources.

The inability of managers to obtain additional resources as their activities increase also has a negative effect. Because their agencies are funded for a definite period, usually one year, additional resources are usually unavailable. Managers often build slack into their budget, preparing their requests for all possible situations. These budget manipulations destroy confidence in the process and create situations where managers falsify inputs to ensure proper operations of their departments.

From these negative experiences two improvements can be suggested. First, organizations can strive to maintain flexible budgets where resources are related directly to activities. Second, organizations should commit their objectives to writing. Planning and control can be facilitated by the establishment of specific objectives, with funds appropriated on the basis of these objectives.

In not-for-profit organizations the revenue budget strongly influences the quantity and quality of services and programs. However, it should be remembered that revenue is not a goal in itself; it merely provides the means of operating the various programs and services that are desired. The appropriations budget is the organization's plan for using the resources that it has available. Revenue and appropriations budgets should be prepared in sufficient detail to provide control over the activities of not-for-profit organizations.

The budget plays a critical role in not-for-profit organizations because it represents approval for expenditures at each operating level. It is also a critical tool for management accounting. Traditional budgeting has focused on input and accountability, but recent advances in management accounting in not-for-profit organizations include the program budget and zero-base budgeting. Management is provided with a structure that establishes priorities and allows allocation of resources based on priorities. Zero-base budgeting has application in most areas of the not-for-profit sector. If possible, unit evaluations should also consider both efficiency and effective measures.

SUGGESTED READINGS

Dalrymple, Douglas J., and Hans B. Thorelli, "Sales Force Budgeting," *Business Horizons* (July–August 1984): 31–36.

Davis, James R., "Indexing Costs to Improve Budgeting," *Business and Planning Quarterly*, 2, No. 2 (1986): 27–33.

Donaldson, Gordon, "Financial Goals and Strategic Consequences," *Harvard Business Review* (May–June 1985): 56–66.

Doost, Roger K., "Public vs. Private Budgeting: A Comparative Study," *Government Accountants Journal* (Fall 1984): 47–52.

Hockenberger, William A., "How to Improve a Company's Cash Management—And Increase Its Profits," *Practical Accountant* (August 1984): 65–68, 70–76.

Jacobs, Vernon K., "Sales Forecasting and Budgeting with 1-2-3," *Computers in Accounting* (October 1988): 72–83.

Samsell, L. Patrick, "Why Proposed Changes in Government Accounting Won't Work," *Management Accounting* (December 1989): 38–40.

Schiff, Michael, and Arie Y. Lewin, "The Impact of People on Budgets," *The Accounting Review* (April 1970): 259–268.

REVIEW PROBLEM

Handy Company manufactures and sells two industrial products in a single plant. The new manager wants to have quarterly budgets and has prepared the following information for the first quarter of 19x1.

Estimated sales:

Drills	60,000 at $100 each
Saws	40,000 at $125 each

Predicted inventories:

	Beginning	Ending
Drills, finished	20,000	25,000
Saws, finished	8,000	10,000
Metal, raw materials	32,000 lbs.	36,000 lbs.
Plastic, raw materials	29,000 lbs.	32,000 lbs.
Handles, raw materials	6,000	7,000

Manufacturing requirements:

	Raw Materials	Direct Labor
Drills	Metal 5 lbs. at $8 per lb. Plastic 3 lbs. at $5 per lb. Handles 1 each at $3	2 hours at $12 per hour
Saws	Metal 4 lbs. at $8 per lb. Plastic 3 lbs. at $5 per lb.	3 hours at $16 per hour

Variable factory overhead is applied at the rate of $1.50 per direct labor hour for each product. Fixed factory overhead is $214,000 per quarter, including noncash expenditures of $156,000, and is allocated on total units completed.

Financial information:

- Beginning cash balance is $1,800,000.
- Purchases of raw materials and labor costs are paid for in quarter acquired.
- Overhead expenses are paid in the next quarter. The accounts payable for these expenses from the last quarter of 19x0 is $380,000.
- Sales are on credit and are collected 50 percent in current period and the remainder the next period. Last quarter's sales were $8,400,000. There are no bad debts.
- Selling and administrative expenses are paid quarterly and total $340,000 including $90,000 of depreciation.
- All unit costs for the first quarter of 19x1 are the same as for the last quarter of 19x0.

Requirements

For the first quarter of 19x1 prepare a:

a) Sales budget in dollars.

b) Production budget in units.

c) Purchases budget.

d) Manufacturing disbursements budget.

e) Cash budget.

f) Budgeted income statement using the functional format. *Hint:* First determine the total costs per unit.

The solution to this problem is found at the end of the Chapter 6 exercises, problems, and cases.

KEY TERMS

Bottom-up approach
Budget committee
Budgetary slack
Cash budget
Continuous budgeting
Cycle budgeting

General and administrative expense
  budget
Imposed budget
Incremental budgeting
Input/output approach
Manufacturing disbursements budget

Minimum level approach   Production budget
Operating activities   Purchases budget
Operating budget   Sales budget
Participation budget   Selling expense budget
Pro forma financial statements   Top-down approach

**APPENDIX
KEY TERMS**

Appropriations budget   Planning, programming, and
Decision package   budgeting systems
Line-item budget   Revenue budget
Lump-sum budget   Zero-base budgeting

**REVIEW
QUESTIONS**

6–1   What is the relationship between budgeting and planning and control?

6–2   Does budgeting require formal planning? Identify and briefly describe three budget planning concepts.

6–3   Identify the types of organizations or situations the incremental approach to budgeting is best suited for.

6–4   Identify the advantages and disadvantages of the incremental approach to budgeting.

6–5   Discuss the three bases used for performance evaluation.

6–6   Why should motivational. considerations be a part of budget planning and utilization?

6–7   Contrast the top-down and bottom-up approaches to budget preparation.

6–8   What is the role of the budget committee? Who should be on the budget committee?

6–9   Why are annual budgets not always desirable? What are some alternative budget periods?

6–10 Explain how continuous budgeting works.

6–11 Which budget brings together all other budgets? How is this accomplished?

6–12 What are pro forma statements?

6–13 Why is prediction ability important to budgeting?

6–14 Is budgetary slack a desirable feature? Can it be prevented?

EXERCISES

6–1 Cash Budget

Wilson's Retail Company is planning a cash budget for the next three months. Estimated sales revenue is as follows:

Month	Sales Revenue	Month	Sales Revenue
January	$300,000	March	$200,000
February	225,000	April	175,000

All sales are on credit. Forty percent of the sales are collected during the month of sale, and 60 percent are collected during the next month.

Cost of goods sold is 70 percent of sales. Payments for merchandise sold are made in the month following the month of sale. Operating expenses to be paid amount to $41,000 each month and are paid during the month incurred.

The cash balance on February 1 is estimated to be $20,000.

Required: Prepare monthly cash budgets for February, March, and April.

6–2 Cash Budget

Boston Tea Company began July with a cash balance of $142,000. A cash receipts and payment budget for each six-month period is prepared in advance. Sales have been estimated as follows:

Month	Sales Revenue	Month	Sales Revenue
May	$120,000	September	$ 80,000
June	140,000	October	100,000
July	80,000	November	100,000
August	60,000	December	120,000

All sales are on credit with 75 percent collected during the month of sale, 20 percent collected during the next month, and 5 percent collected during the second month following the month of sale.

Cost of goods sold averages 70 percent of sales revenue. Ending inventory is one half of the next month's predicted cost of sales. The other half of the merchandise is acquired during the month of sale. All purchases are paid for in the month after purchase.

Operating costs are estimated at $18,000 each month and are paid for during the month incurred.

Required: Prepare monthly cash budgets for six months from July to December.

6–3 Cash Receipts

The sales budget for Cards, Inc., is forecasted as follows:

Month	Sales Revenue	Month	Sales Revenue
May	$60,000	July	$90,000
June	80,000	August	60,000

To prepare a cash budget, the company must determine the budgeted cash collections from sales. Historically, the following trend has been established regarding cash collection of sales:

60 percent in month of sale,

20 percent in month following sale,

15 percent in second month following sale,

5 percent uncollectible.

The company gives a 2 percent cash discount for payments made by customers during the month of sale. The accounts receivable balance on April 30 is $24,000, of which $7,000 represents uncollected March sales, and $17,000 represents uncollected April sales.

Required: Prepare a schedule of budgeted cash collections from sales for May, June, and July. Include a three-month summary of estimated cash collections.

6–4 Cash Receipts

Chicago Metal Company is currently estimating cash receipts for the next six months. The accounts receivable balance is to be estimated at the end of each month also. Cash sales are estimated at 10 percent of sales for the month. The balance of sales should be collected as follows:

50 percent during the month of sale,

40 percent during the following month,

10 percent during the second month following month of sale.

The accounts receivable balance at April 1 was $93,600. Budgeted and actual sales are as follows:

Month	Sales Revenue	Month	Sales Revenue
January	$200,000	April	$150,000
February	190,000	May	180,000
March	170,000	June	200,000

Required: Prepare a schedule of budgeted cash collections for each month of the second quarter. Determine the estimated balance of accounts receivable at the end of each month.

6–5 Cash Disbursements

Oregon Timber Company is in the process of preparing its budget for next year. Cost of goods sold has been estimated at 70 percent of sales. Lumber purchases and payments are to be made during the month preceding the month of sale. Wages are estimated at 15 percent of sales and are paid during the month of sale. Other operating costs amounting to 10 percent of sales are to be paid in the month following the month of sales. Additionally, a monthly lease payment of $10,000 is paid to BMI for computer services. Sales revenue is forecast as follows:

Month	Sales Revenue	Month	Sales Revenue
February	$100,000	May	$210,000
March	160,000	June	180,000
April	180,000	July	230,000

Required: Prepare a schedule of cash disbursements for April, May, and June.

6–6 Purchases Budget in Units and Dollars

Budgeted sales of The Record Shop for the first six months of 19x3 are as follows:

Month	Unit Sales	Month	Unit Sales
January	120,000	April	210,000
February	160,000	May	180,000
March	200,000	June	240,000

Beginning inventory for 19x3 is 40,000 units. The budgeted inventory at the end of a month is 40 percent of units to be sold the following month. Purchase price per unit is $3.

Required: Prepare a purchases budget in units and dollars for each month, January through May.

6–7 Purchases Budget in Units and Dollars

Unit sales estimates for Snow King Plow Company for next year are as follows:

Month	Unit Sales	Month	Unit Sales
January	45,000	March	90,000
February	60,000	April	93,000

There were 10,000 units of finished goods in inventory at the beginning of January. Plans are to have an inventory of finished product equal to one third of the sales for the next month.

Four hundred pounds of materials are required for each unit produced. Each pound of material costs $10. Inventory levels for materials are to be equal to one fourth of the needs for the next month. Materials inventory on January 1 was 5.5 million pounds.

Requirements

a) Prepare production budgets for January, February, and March.

b) Prepare a purchases budget in pounds and dollars for January and February.

6–8 Pro Forma Income Statement

Pendleton Company, a merchandising company, is developing its master budget for 19x2. The income statement for 19x1 is as follows:

Pendleton Company
Income Statement
For the year ending December 31, 19x1

Gross sales	$750,000
Less estimated uncollectible accounts	– 7,500
Net sales	$742,500
Cost of goods sold	–430,000
Gross profit	$312,500
Operating expenses (including $25,000 depreciation)	–200,500
Net income	$112,000

The following are management's goals and forecasts for 19x2.

1. Selling prices will increase by 8 percent, and sales volume will increase by 5 percent.
2. The cost of merchandise will increase by 4 percent.
3. All operating expenses are fixed and are paid in the month incurred. Price increases for operating expenses will be 10 percent.
4. The estimated uncollectibles are 1 percent of budgeted sales.

Required: Prepare a budgeted functional income statement for 19x2.

6–9 Pro Forma Income Statement

Big Burger Drive-in is planning a budget for the next fiscal year. Sales revenue has been estimated at $1,000,000. The cost of goods sold has been estimated at 70 percent of sales revenue. Depreciation on the office building and fixtures is budgeted at $50,000. Salaries and wages should amount to 15 percent of sales revenue. Advertising has been budgeted at $75,000, and utilities should amount to $20,000. Income tax is estimated at 40 percent of operating income.

Required: Prepare a pro forma functional income statement for the next fiscal year.

6–10 Sales Budget

Jennifer's T-shirt Shop has very seasonal sales. For 19x7 she is trying to decide whether to establish a sales budget based on average sales or sales estimated by quarter. The unit sales for 19x7 are expected to be 10 percent higher than 19x6 sales. Unit sales by quarter for 19x6 were as follows:

	Children's Shirts	Women's Shirts	Men's Shirts	Total Shirts
Winter quarter	200	200	100	500
Spring quarter	200	250	200	650
Summer quarter	400	300	200	900
Fall quarter	200	250	100	550
Total sales	1,000	1,000	600	2,600

Children's T-shirts sell for $4.00 each, women's sell for $8.00, and men's sell for $7.00.

Requirements

Assuming a 10 percent increase in sales, prepare a sales budget for each quarter of 19x7 using:

a) Average quarterly sales. *Hint:* Winter quarter children's shirts are 275 [(1,000 × 1.10)/4].
b) Actual quarterly sales. *Hint:* Winter quarter children's shirts are 220 [200 × 1.10].
c) Suggest advantages of each method.

6–11 Sales Budget

Quick Mix Company sells three products. The seasonal sales pattern for 19x6 is as follows:

	Products		
Quarter	Gravel	Limestone	Sand
1	10%	25%	20%
2	20	25	30
3	30	25	40
4	40	25	10
	100%	100%	100%

The annual sales budget shows forecasts of: Gravel, 150,000 tons; Limestone, 120,000 tons; and Sand, 180,000 tons. Next year's selling prices per ton will be: Gravel, $10; Limestone, $5; and Sand, $4.

Required: Prepare a sales budget in units and dollars by quarters for the company for the coming year.

6–12 General Budget (Appendix)

The City of Taylorsville has budgeted the following general fund revenues and appropriations for the 19x3 fiscal year.

Revenue forecasts:	
Property taxes	$400,000
Sales taxes	100,000
Income taxes	220,000
Sales revenue sharing	70,000
Appropriations:	
Police protection	$300,000
Fire protection	180,000
Public works	90,000
Administration	125,000
Health and welfare	100,000

Requirements

a) Set up a revenue and appropriation budget for 19x3.

b) Is this a lump-sum or line-item budget? Explain.

6–13 General Budget (Appendix)

The Zuker Foundation has established the following revenue and appropriation budgets for 19x1.

Revenues:	
Donations	$800,000
Interest and dividends	250,000
Federal grants	620,000

Appropriations:	
Administration	$115,000
Research and development	980,000
Lab equipment	470,000

Requirements

a) Set up a revenue and appropriation budget for 19x1.

b) What happens if projected revenues do not equal appropriations?

6–14 General Budget (Appendix)

The following accounts are from the general fund of the St. Louis General Hospital for October 19x4.

Cash	$100,000	Investments	$500,000
Taxes receivable	80,000	Accounts payable	86,000
Food preparation	44,000	Maintenance	41,000
Nursing services	781,000	Cafeteria revenue	15,000
Security costs	6,000	Patient charges	837,000
Supplies	41,000	Notes payable	400,000

Required: Prepare a revenue and appropriation budget for October 19x4.

6–15 Cash Budget (Appendix)

Tulsa Water Service had the following sales of water for selected months of 19x8.

Month	Sales Revenue	Month	Sales Revenue
February	$120,000	May	$150,000
March	130,000	June	170,000
April	140,000	July	190,000

All sales are on credit. Historically, 60 percent is collected in the month of sale, 30 percent during the first month following sale, and 10 percent in the second month following sale.

Cost of water averages 70 percent of sales revenue. Desired ending inventories are sufficient for 5 percent of the next month's sales. All purchases are paid during the month following purchase.

Operating costs of $20,000 are paid each month.

The April 1 cash balance is expected to be $20,000.

Required: Prepare a cash budget for April, May, and June.

PROBLEMS

6–16 Inventory and Purchases Budgets

The Midwest Belt Company sells men's and boys' belts that are cut to order. Each foot or fraction thereof sells for $2.00. Small belts average two feet, and large belts average three feet in length. The leather is purchased from a local tannery for 90 cents per foot. The buckles are purchased at $2.00 for the small size and $2.50 for the large size. No changes are expected in any of the purchasing and selling prices.

Sales should increase 20 percent this year over last year. Last year the company sold 300 small belts and 140 large belts during January and February. The inventories are as follows:

December 31 Actual		February 28 Target	
Leather (feet)	900	Leather (feet)	800
Small buckles	200	Small buckles	200
Large buckles	300	Large buckles	250

Purchases are made to provide sufficient stock for each two-month period.

Requirements

a) Prepare a purchases budget in units for total January and February purchases of buckles and leather.

b) Compute the budgeted cost of the raw materials to be used in manufacturing small and large belts during January and February.

6–17 Purchases Budget

Crown Candy Company manufactures various products to sell to retail stores. A sales budget for pecan turtles for the next several months is as follows:

Month	Budgeted Units in Boxes
June	20,000
July	24,000
August	30,000
September	36,000
October	40,000

There is no inventory of turtles on hand at June 1. During the summer the company desires an ending finished goods inventory of 10 percent of the following month's sales. The raw materials must be purchased one month before they are needed in production. The June 1 raw materials inventory meets these requirements.

Pecan turtles require direct materials as follows:

	Pounds of Materials per Box of Product
Caramel	3
Pecans	2
Chocolate	5

Required: Prepare a purchases budget in pounds of each ingredient for June and July. *Hint:* A production budget will be helpful.

6–18 Cash Budget

Cash budgeting of Carolina Apple is done on a quarterly basis. The company is planning its cash needs for the third quarter of 19x1 and the following information is available to assist in preparing a cash budget.

Budgeted income statements for July through October 19x1 are as follows:

	July	August	September	October
Sales	$18,000	$24,000	$28,000	$36,000
Cost of goods sold	−10,000	−14,000	−16,000	−20,000
Gross profit	$ 8,000	$10,000	$12,000	$16,000
Less other expenses:				
Selling	$ 2,300	$ 3,000	$ 3,400	$ 4,200
Administrative	2,600	3,000	3,200	3,600
Total	− 4,900	− 6,000	− 6,600	− 7,800
Net income	$ 3,100	$ 4,000	$ 5,400	$ 8,200

Additional information:

1. Other expenses, which are paid monthly, include $1,000 a month of depreciation.
2. Sales are 30 percent for cash and 70 percent on credit.
3. Credit sales are collected 20 percent in the month of sale, 70 percent one month after sale, and 10 percent two months after sale.
4. May sales were $15,000, and June sales were $16,000. Merchandise is paid for 50 percent in the month of purchase. The remaining 50 percent is paid in the following month. Accounts payable for merchandise at June 30 totaled $6,000.
5. The company maintains its ending inventory levels at 25 percent of the cost of goods to be sold in the following month. The inventory at June 30 is $2,500.
6. An equipment note of $5,000 per month is being paid through August.
7. The company must maintain a cash balance of at least $5,000 at the end of each month. The cash balance on June 30 is $5,100.
8. The company can borrow from its bank as needed. Borrowings must be in multiples of $100. All borrowings take place at the beginning of a month, and all repayments are made at the end of a month. At the time the principal is repaid, interest is also paid on the portion of the principal repaid. The interest rate is 12 percent per annum.

Requirements

a) Prepare a monthly schedule of budgeted operating cash receipts for July, August, and September.

b) Prepare a monthly purchases budget and a schedule of budgeted cash payments for purchases for July, August, and September.

c) Prepare a monthly cash budget for July, August, and September. Show borrowings from the company's bank and repayments to the bank as needed to maintain the minimum cash balance.

6–19 Cash Budget

The Mobile Supply Company sells one product that is purchased for $20 and sold for $30. Budgeted sales in total dollars for next year are $720,000. The sales information needed for preparing the July budget is as follows:

Month	Sales Revenue	Month	Sales Revenue
May	$30,000	July	$48,000
June	42,000	August	60,000

Account balances at July 1 include:

Cash	$15,000
Merchandise inventory	16,000
Accounts receivable (sales)	23,000
Accounts payable (purchases)	15,000

The company pays for one half of its purchases in the month of purchase, and the remainder in the following month. End-of-month inventory must be 50 percent of the budgeted sales in units for the next month.

A 2 percent cash discount on sales is allowed if payment is made during the month of sale. Experience indicates that 50 percent of the billings will be collected during the month of sale, 40 percent in the following month, 8 percent in the next following month, and 2 percent will be uncollectible.

Total budgeted selling and administrative expenses (excluding bad debts) for the fiscal year are estimated at $186,000, of which half is fixed expense (inclusive of a $20,000 annual depreciation charge). Fixed expenses are incurred evenly during the year. The other selling and administrative expenses vary with sales. Expenses are paid during the month incurred.

Requirements

a) Prepare a schedule of estimated cash collections for July.

b) Prepare a schedule of estimated July cash payments for purchases. (Round calculations to the nearest dollar.)

c) Prepare schedules of all July selling and administrative expenses and of those requiring cash payments.

d) Prepare a cash budget in summary form for July.

6–20 Purchases Budget

Topper Toys makes plastic riding tractors that require 3 pounds of material. The company wants raw materials on hand at the beginning of each month equal to one half of the month's production needs. This requirement was met on April 1, the start of the second quarter. There are no work-in-process inventories. A sales budget in units for the next four months is given below.

Month	Unit Sales	Month	Unit Sales
April	15,000	June	24,000
May	18,000	July	26,000

Finished goods inventory at the end of each month must be equal to 40 percent of the next month's sales. On March 31 the finished goods inventory totaled 7,500 units.

Requirements

a) Prepare a production budget for April, May, and June.

b) Prepare a purchases budget for April and May.

6–21 Pro Forma Statements

Madison Butter Sales Company is preparing a budget for January and February of next year. The balance sheet as of December 31, 19x1 is given below.

Madison Butter Sales Company
Balance Sheet
December 31, 19x1

Assets		Equities	
Cash	$100,000	Accounts payable	$125,000
Accounts receivable	60,000	Operating expenses payable	10,000
Inventory	30,000	Miscellaneous payable	20,000
Equipment leasehold	60,000	Capital stock	25,000
		Retained earnings	70,000
Total assets	$250,000	Total equities	$250,000

Monthly sales data for the current year and the budgeted data for next year are as follows:

November 19x1	$180,000	February 19x2	$250,000
December 19x1	100,000	March 19x2	260,000
January 19x2	240,000	April 19x2	280,000

For 19x2 the following conditions are expected to be present:

■ Forty percent of the sales revenue is collected during the month of sale, with the balance collected during the following month.

■ Cost of goods sold is 60 percent of sales. Merchandise inventory sufficient for 20 percent of next month's sales is to be maintained at the end of each month. All butter purchased for resale is paid for in the month following the month of purchase.

■ Operating expenses for each month are estimated at 10 percent of sales revenue. All operating expenses are paid during the following month.

■ Income taxes are estimated at 40 percent of income before taxes. Income taxes are paid fifteen days after the end of the quarter. There were no taxes payable on December 31. The miscellaneous payables at December 31, 19x1 are to be paid during January 19x2.

Requirements

a) Prepare a budgeted income statement for the quarter ending March 31, 19x2 using a functional format. Do not prepare monthly statements.

b) Prepare a pro forma balance sheet as of March 31, 19x2. *Hint:* Prepare purchases and cash budgets.

6–22 Budgets and Pro Forma Statements   The Peyton Department Store prepares budgets quarterly. The following information is available for use in planning the second quarter budgets for 19x1.

Peyton Department Stores
Balance Sheet
March 31, 19x1

Assets		Equities	
Cash	$ 3,000	Accounts payable	$26,000
Accounts receivable	25,000	Dividends payable	17,000
Inventory	30,000	Rent payable	2,000
Prepaid insurance	2,000	Stockholders' equity	40,000
Fixtures	25,000		
Total assets	$85,000	Total equities	$85,000

Actual and forecasted monthly sales for selected months in 19x1 are as follows:

Month	Sales Revenue	Month	Sales Revenue
January	$60,000	May	$60,000
February	50,000	June	70,000
March	40,000	July	90,000
April	50,000	August	80,000

Monthly operating expenses are as follows:

Wages and salaries	$25,000
Depreciation	100
Utilities	1,000
Rent	2,000

Cash dividends of $17,000 are paid during the first month of each quarter and declared during the third month of each quarter for the next quarter. Operating expenses are paid as incurred, except insurance, rent, and depreciation. Rent is paid during the following month. The prepaid insurance is for five more months. Cost of goods sold is equal to one half of sales.

Beginning inventories are sufficient for 120 percent of the next month's sales. Purchases during any given month are paid in full during the following month. All sales are on account, with 50 percent collected during the month of sale, 40 percent during the next month, and 10 percent during the month thereafter.

Money can be borrowed and repaid in multiples of $1,000 at an interest rate of 12 percent per annum. The company desires a minimum cash balance of $3,000 at the first of each month. At the time the principal is repaid, interest is paid on the portion of principal that is repaid. All borrowing is at the start of the month, and all repayment is at the end of the month. Money is never repaid at the end of the month it is borrowed.

Requirements

a) Prepare a purchases budget for each month of the quarter ending June 30, 19x1.

b) Prepare a cash receipts schedule for each month of the quarter ending June 30, 19x1. Do not include borrowings.

c) Prepare a cash disbursements schedule for each month of the second quarter ending June 30, 19x1. Do not include repayments of borrowings.

d) Prepare a cash budget for each month of the quarter ending June 30, 19x1.

e) Prepare an income statement for each month of the quarter ending June 30, 19x1.

f) Prepare a pro forma balance sheet as of June 30, 19x1.

6–23 Behavioral Implications of Budgeting

Andrea Rawls, controller of Data Scientific, believes that effective budgeting greatly assists in meeting the goals and objectives of the organization. She argues that the budget serves as a blueprint for the operating activities during each reporting period and as such is an important control device. She believes that sound management evaluations can be based on the comparisons of performance and budgetary schedules and that employees respond more favorably when they participate in the budgetary process.

Jeff Cooke, treasurer of Data Scientific, agrees that budgeting is essential for overall organizational success, but argues that human resources are too valuable to spend much time planning and preparing the budgetary process. He thinks that the roles people play in budgetary preparation are not important in the final analysis of a budget's effectiveness.

Required: Contrast the participative versus imposed budgeting concepts and indicate how the ideas of Ms. Rawls and Mr. Cooke fit the two categories.

6–24 Comprehensive Budgets

Overton Products assembles and sells computer terminals in a single plant. The controller has decided to begin a new evaluation system, which includes quarterly budgets. She has prepared the following information for the first quarter of 19x1.

Estimated sales:
20,000 units at $100 each

Predicted inventories:

	Beginning	Ending
Finished units	5,000	6,000
Frames, raw materials	2,000	3,000
Tubes, raw materials	1,000	1,200

Manufacturing requirements per unit:

Raw Materials	Direct Labor
1 frame at $16 1 tube at $20	2 hours at $15 per hour

Variable factory overhead is applied at the rate of $5 per direct labor hour. Fixed factory overhead is $147,000 per quarter, including noncash expenditures of $30,000, and is allocated to total units completed.

Financial information:

- Beginning cash balance is $300,000.
- Purchases of raw materials and labor costs are paid for in the quarter acquired.
- Overhead expenses are paid in the next quarter. The accounts payable for these expenses from the last quarter of 19x0 is $320,000.
- Sales are on credit and are collected 40 percent in current period and the remainder the next period. Last quarter's sales were $1,800,000. There are no bad debts.
- Selling and administrative expenses are paid quarterly and total $240,000 including $70,000 of depreciation.
- All unit costs for the first quarter of 19x1 are the same as for the last quarter of 19x0.

Requirements

For the first quarter of 19x1 prepare a:

a) Sales budget in dollars.
b) Production budget in units.
c) Purchases budget.
d) Manufacturing disbursements budget.
e) Cash budget.
f) Budgeted functional income statement. *Hint:* First determine the total costs per unit.

6–25 Comprehensive Budgets

Tuscaloosa Tire Company manufactures plastic tires for automated cleaning machines. It is completing its financial plans for 19x8 and is in need of assistance in the budgeting phase. You are provided the following information that may be useful in preparing the necessary budgets and schedules for 19x8.

Tuscaloosa Tire Company
Balance Sheet
December 31, 19x7

Assets

Current Assets:			
Cash		$200,000	
Accounts receivable (net)		294,000	$494,000
Plant, property, and equipment:			
Land		$100,500	
Buildings and equipment	$350,000		
Less accumulated depreciation	−118,000	232,000	332,500
Total assets			$826,500

Liabilities and stockholder's equity

Current liabilities:			
Accounts payable			$132,000
Stockholder's equity:			
Capital stock		$400,000	
Retained earnings		294,500	694,500
Total liabilities and stockholder's equity			$826,500

Estimated sales:

	First Quarter	Second Quarter	Third Quarter
Sales (units)	15,000	16,000	18,000
Sales ($30 each)	$450,000	$480,000	$540,000

All sales are on credit and are collected 30 percent in month of sale and 70 percent in month following sale. The company has a history of no bad debts. The sales from the last quarter of 19x7 were $420,000.

The company will have no inventories at the beginning of the year. Management desires 5,000 pounds of unmolded plastic at the end of the first quarter and 6,000 pounds at the end of the second quarter. Each wheel takes 2 pounds of plastic, including waste trimmings. There should be 2,000 wheel rims at the end of the first quarter and 2,500 at the end of the second quarter. Finished inventory should total 1,000 wheels at the end of the first quarter and 1,500 at the end of the second quarter.

Manufacturing requirements:

	Raw Materials	Direct Labor
Plastic	2 lbs. at $3 per lb.	One half-hour
Rims	1 each at $2	

Variable factory overhead is applied at the rate of $3 per direct labor hour for each finished unit. Fixed factory overhead is $170,000 per quarter, including noncash expenditures of $54,000, and is allocated on total units completed. Direct labor averages $20 per hour.

Additional information:

- Purchases of raw materials and labor costs are paid for in the quarter acquired.
- Overhead expenses are paid in the next quarter.
- The accounts payable on the balance sheet is for these expenses from the last quarter of 19x7.
- Selling and administrative expenses are paid quarterly and total $40,000, including $10,000 of depreciation.

Requirements

For the first and second quarters of 19x8 prepare a:

a) Sales budget in dollars.

b) Production budget in units.

c) Purchases budget.

d) Manufacturing disbursements budget.

e) Cash budget.

6–26 Reporting (Appendix)

Washington County makes the following report public on July 31 for its educational program.

Washington County
Annual Report
Education Program
July 31, 19x4

	Budget	Actual
Revenues (all sources)	$4,500,000	$4,400,000
Expenditures:		
Salaries	2,250,000	2,270,000
Maintenance	600,000	700,000
Other	1,650,000	1,580,000

Notes to report:

1. Revenues were lower than expected.
2. Teachers did not get a pay raise.
3. Twelve new buses were purchased.

Requirements

a) As a commissioner of Washington County, what additional information would you want in the body of the financial report?

b) What management accounting information could be furnished?

c) How could the notes section be improved?

6–27 Financial Statement (Appendix)   The City of Naples conducts all its activities through a general fund account. At the beginning of the 19x1 fiscal year the town's assets consisted of cash, $12,000; city hall, $132,000; city park, $19,500; and equipment, $68,000.

At the beginning of the year the town council approved the following line-item budget.

Budgeted revenues:	Taxes, $75,000; other revenues, $28,600
Appropriations:	Salaries, $56,000; supplies, $2,000; equipment, $3,000; contractual services, $14,000; miscellaneous, $2,000

Actual transactions for the year were as follows:

Revenues:	Taxes, $80,000; other revenues, $25,000
Expenditures:	Salaries, $55,500; supplies, $1,400; equipment, $3,000; contractual services, $14,000; miscellaneous, $1,500

Requirements

a) Prepare a budget statement of revenues and expenditures for the fiscal year ending October 31, 19x1, for the general fund of Naples.

b) Prepare a performance report for the year ended October 31, 19x1.

c) One citizen group complained that the cut in expenditures hurt the town park; another group complained that not enough was spent on streets. In preparing the next budget, what could you do to be more responsive to citizen groups?

6–28 Budget by Function (Appendix)

The city of Flowershine prepares functional budgets based on the estimated needs of its managers. These are limited by the general budget, which is approved by the city council. For 19x5 the council approved the following line-item general budget.

Salaries and wages	$ 800,000
Supplies	100,000
Repairs and parts	212,000
Capital expenditures (buildings)	400,000
Equipment purchases	170,000
General and miscellaneous	62,000
Total	$1,744,000

This budget is then allocated to the service functions based on a program evaluation of services. For 19x5 the needs are as follows:

	Utilities	Fire Protection	Police Protection	Welfare	Administration
Salaries and wages	10%	20%	30%	15%	25%
Supplies	40	15	20	10	15
Repairs and parts	20	30	40	5	5
Capital expenditures	50	5	10	5	30
Equipment purchases	30	35	20	5	10
General and miscellaneous	15	20	20	25	20

Required: Prepare a budget for each fund.

CASES

6–29 Behavioral Considerations and Budgeting

Scott Weidner, the Controller in the Division of Social Services for the state, recognizes the importance of the budgetary process for planning, control, and motivation purposes. He believes that a properly implemented participative budgeting process for planning purposes and a management by exception reporting procedure based on the participative budget will motivate his subordinates to improve productivity within their particular departments. Based on this philosophy, Weidner has implemented the following budget procedures.

- An appropriation target figure is given to each Department Manager. This amount is the maximum funding that each department can expect to receive in the next fiscal year.

- Department Managers develop their individual budgets within the following spending constraints as directed by the controller's staff.

    1. Expenditure requests cannot exceed the appropriation target.

    2. All fixed expenditures should be included in the budget. Fixed expenditures would include such items as contracts and salaries at current levels.

    3. All government projects directed by higher authority should be included in the budget in their entirety.

- The controller's staff consolidates the departmental budget requests from the various departments into one budget that is to be submitted for the entire division.

- Upon final budget approval by the legislature, the controller's staff allocates the appropriation to the various departments on instructions from the Division Manager. However, a specified percentage of each department's appropriation is held back in anticipation of potential budget cuts and special funding needs. The amount and use of this contingency fund is left to the discretion of the Division Manager.

- Each department is allowed to adjust its budget when necessary to operate within the reduced appropriation level. However, as stated in the original directive, specific projects authorized by higher authority must remain intact.

- The final budget is used as the basis of control for a management by exception form of reporting. Excessive expenditures by account for each department are highlighted on a monthly basis. Department Managers are expected to account for all expenditures over budget. Fiscal responsibility is an important factor in the overall performance evaluation of Department Managers.

Weidner believes his policy of allowing the Department Managers to participate in the budget process and then holding them accountable for their performance is essential, especially during these times of limited resources. He further believes the Department Managers will be motivated positively to increase the efficiency and effectiveness of their departments because they have provided input into the initial budgetary process and are required to justify any unfavorable performances.

Requirements

a) Explain the operational and behavioral benefits that generally are attributed to a participative budgeting process.

b) Identify deficiencies in Scott Weidner's participative budgetary policy for planning and performance evaluation purposes. For each deficiency identified, recommend how the deficiency can be corrected.

(CMA Adapted)

6–30 Budget
Preparation
(Appendix)

The Board of Education of the Victoria School District is developing a budget for the school year ending June 30, 19x1. The budgeted expenditures follow.

Victoria School District
Budgeted Expenditures
For the year ending June 30, 19x1

Current operating expenditures:			
Instruction:			
General	$1,401,600		
Vocational training	112,000	$1,513,600	
Pupil service:			
Bus transportation	$ 36,300		
School lunches	51,700	88,000	
Attendance and health service		14,000	
Administration		46,000	
Operation and maintenance of plant		208,000	
Pensions, insurance, etc.		154,000	
Total current operating expenditures			$2,023,600
Other expenditures:			
Capital outlays from revenues		$ 75,000	
Debt service (annual installment and interest on long-term debt)		150,000	
Total other expenditures			225,000
Total budgeted expenditures			$2,248,600

The following data are available.

1. The estimated average daily school enrollment of the school district is 5,000 pupils, including 200 pupils enrolled in a vocational training program.

2. Estimated revenues include equalizing grants-in-aid from the state of $150 per pupil. The grants were established by state law under a plan intended to encourage raising the level of education.

3. The federal government matches 60 percent of state grants-in-aid for pupils enrolled in a vocational training program. In addition, the federal government contributes toward the cost of bus transportation and school lunches a maximum of $12 per pupil based on total enrollment within the school district but not to exceed $6\frac{2}{3}$ percent of the state per-pupil equalization grants-in-aid.

4. Interest on temporary investment of school tax receipts and rents of school facilities are expected to be $75,000 and are earmarked for special equipment acquisitions listed as "Capital outlays from revenues" in the budgeted expenditures. Cost of the special equipment acquisitions will be limited to the amount derived from these miscellaneous receipts.

5. The remaining funds needed to finance the budgeted expenditures of the school district are to be raised from local taxation. An allowance of 9 percent of the local tax levy is necessary for possible tax abatements and losses. The assessed valuation of the property located within the school district is $80,000,000.

Requirements

a) Prepare a schedule computing the estimated total funds to be obtained from local taxation for the ensuing school year ending June 30, 19x1, for the Victoria School District.

b) Prepare a schedule computing the estimated current operating cost per regular pupil and per vocational pupil to be met by local tax funds. Assume that costs other than instructional costs are assignable on a per capita basis to regular and vocational students.

c) Without prejudice to your solution to requirement (a), assume that the estimated total tax levy for the ensuing school year ending June 30, 19x1, is $1,092,000. Prepare a schedule computing the estimated tax rate per $100 of assessed valuation of the property within the Victoria School District required to meet the tax levy.

(CPA Adapted)

REVIEW PROBLEM SOLUTION

a) **Handy Company**
Sales Budget
First Quarter, 19x1

Sales

Product	Units	Price	Sales
Drills	60,000	$100	$ 6,000,000
Saws	40,000	125	5,000,000
Total			$11,000,000

Collections on sales

Current quarter's sales (50%)	$5,500,000
Previous quarter's sales (50%)	4,200,000
Total cash collections	$9,700,000

b) **Handy Company**
Production Budget
First Quarter, 19x1

	Drills	Saws
Budget sales	60,000	40,000
Plus required ending inventory	25,000	10,000
Total inventory requirements	85,000	50,000
Less beginning inventory	−20,000	−8,000
Budgeted production	65,000	42,000

c) **Handy Company**
Purchases Budget
First Quarter, 19x1

Metal purchases

	Drills	Saws	Total
Production units (from part b)	65,000	42,000	
Metal	× 5 lbs.	× 4 lbs.	
Production needs	325,000 lbs.	168,000 lbs.	493,000 lbs.
Target ending inventory			36,000
Total metal needs			529,000
Less beginning inventory			− 32,000
Purchases needed			497,000 lbs.
Cost per lb.			× $8
Total purchases			$3,976,000

Plastic purchases

	Drills	Saws	Total
Production units (from part b)	65,000	42,000	107,000
Plastic			× 3 lbs.
Production needs			321,000 lbs.
Target ending inventory			32,000
Total plastic needs			353,000
Less beginning inventory			− 29,000
Purchases needed			324,000 lbs.
Cost per lb.			× $5
Total purchases			$1,620,000

Handle purchases

	Drills	Total
Production units (from part b)	65,000	65,000
Handles		× 1
Production needs		65,000
Target ending inventory		7,000
Total handle needs		72,000
Less beginning inventory		− 6,000
Purchases needed		66,000
Cost per handle		× $3
Total purchases		$ 198,000

Total purchases

Metal	$3,976,000
Plastic	1,620,000
Handles	198,000
Total	$5,794,000

d) Handy Company
Manufacturing Disbursements Budget
First Quarter, 19x1

	Drills	Saws	Total
Budgeted production	65,000	42,000	
Direct labor hours per unit	× 2	× 3	
Total direct labor hours	130,000	126,000	
Labor rate	× $12	× $16	
Labor expenditures	$1,560,000	$2,016,000	$3,576,000
Direct labor hours	130,000	126,000	
Variable factory overhead rate	× $1.50	× $1.50	
Total variable overhead	$195,000	$189,000	$384,000
Fixed factory overhead			214,000
Total overhead			$598,000
Less noncash items			−156,000
Overhead expenditures to be paid next quarter			$442,000

e) Handy Company
Cash Budget
First Quarter, 19x1

Cash balance, beginning	$1,800,000	
Plus cash collections (sales budget)	9,700,000	
Cash available from operations		$11,500,000
Less budgeted disbursements:		
Materials (Purchases budget)	$5,794,000	
Labor (Manufacturing disbursements budget)	3,576,000	
Overhead (last quarter)	380,000	
Selling and administrative ($340,000 − $90,000 depreciation)	250,000	−10,000,000
Cash balance, ending		$ 1,500,000

f) Schedule of Total Unit Costs

		Drills	Saws
Metal:	5 lbs. at $8	$40.00	
	4 lbs. at $8		$32.00
Plastic:	3 lbs. at $5	15.00	15.00
Handles:	1 each at $3	3.00	
Direct labor:	2 hrs. at $12	24.00	
	3 hrs. at $16		48.00
Variable factory overhead:	2 hrs. at $1.50	3.00	
	3 hrs. at $1.50		4.50
Fixed factory overhead:	$214,000/107,000*	2.00	2.00
Total unit costs		$87.00	$101.50

* From production budget.

Handy Company
Income Statement
First Quarter, 19x1

Sales (Sales budget)			$11,000,000
Less costs of goods sold:			
Finished goods inventory, beginning			
Drills (20,000 × $87)	$1,740,000		
Saws (8,000 × $101.50)	812,000	$ 2,552,000	
Cost of materials placed in production (Purchases budget):			
Metal (493,000 lbs × $8)	$3,944,000		
Plastic (321,000 lbs × $5)	1,605,000		
Handles (65,000 × $3)	195,000		
Total	$5,744,000		
Labor (Manufacturing disbursements budget)	3,576,000		
Variable overhead (Manufacturing disbursements budget)	384,000		
Fixed overhead	214,000	9,918,000	
Total goods available for sale		$12,470,000	
Finished goods inventory, ending			
Drills (25,000 × $87)	$2,175,000		
Saws (10,000 × $101.50)	1,015,000	− 3,190,000	− 9,280,000
Gross profit			$ 1,720,000
Selling and administrative expenses			− 340,000
Net income			$ 1,380,000

C H A P T E R   7

Responsibility Accounting and Flexible Budgets

Learning Objectives

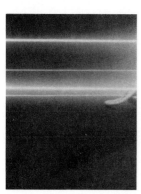

Upon completion of this chapter you should:

- **Understand the importance of feedback reports in budgeting and in performance evaluation.**

- **Understand how the concept of responsibility accounting is used to structure a performance reporting system for organizations with more than one management level.**

- **Be familiar with the four primary types of responsibility centers (investment centers, profit centers, revenue centers, and cost centers).**

- **Know the difference between a standard cost center and a discretionary cost center.**

- **Be able to compute flexible budget cost variances and prepare a flexible budget performance report for a responsibility center.**

- **Be able to analyze revenue center performance and prepare variances for sales price and sales volume. Also be able to prepare, for revenue centers that incur costs, variances for selling expenses and net sales volume.**

- **Be able to reconcile budgeted and actual income using sales variances and flexible budget cost variances.**

Feedback in the form of performance reports is essential if the benefits of budgeting are to be fully realized. Managers need to know how actual results compare with the current budget in order to control current operations and improve budgets for future periods. Consider a relatively simple situation where the unit cost of raw materials exceeds the cost allowed in the budget. A performance report addressed to the appropriate manager indicates the existence of the disparity, and the manager initiates an investigation to determine its cause. The manager may find that a new employee in the Purchasing Department is buying from unauthorized vendors or in small lots. In this case the manager will take action to bring performance into line with plans, perhaps by having the new employee work closely with a more experienced colleague. Alternatively, the investigation may reveal unanticipated price increases. In this case the budget should be revised to reflect the price increases, and the new prices should also be used in future budgets.

The importance of feedback to budgeting is illustrated in Exhibit 7–1. Here budgeting and performance evaluation are presented as a continuous cycle. Assume the cycle starts with the current budget. As the year passes, actual operating data are accumulated and compared with the current budget in the form of performance reports. The appropriate managers receive these reports and then obtain additional information to explain significant deviations from the budget. Based on this information, management attempts to improve current operations and plans for the future, which are summarized in the new budget. The new budget becomes the current budget and the cycle continues.

The purpose of this chapter is to examine the nature of financial performance reports and the concepts that underlie their development and use. The relationship between performance reports and organization structure, as well as the types of financial performance reports that are best suited to various activities, are discussed. Much of the material presented here is examined in greater detail in later chapters.

EXHIBIT 7–1   The Budgeting–Performance Evaluation Cycle

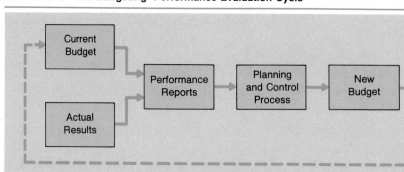

RESPONSIBILITY ACCOUNTING

By serving as a scorecard and an attention director, performance reports, which contain comparisons of actual results and plans, help managers determine and control the organization's activities. In accordance with the concept of management by exception, the absence of significant differences indicates that activities are proceeding as planned, whereas the presence of significant differences indicates a need either to take corrective action or to revise plans.

Performance reports should be prepared in accordance with the concept of responsibility accounting, which is the structuring of performance reports addressed to individual or group members of an organization in a manner that emphasizes the factors controllable by them. In responsibility accounting the focus is on specific units within the organization that are responsible for the

MANAGERIAL PRACTICE 7.1

The Iron Rule at ITT

Although the management literature is replete with statements that managers should be held accountable only for results that they can control, this is not always true in practice. A survey by Richard Vancil of 291 large companies found that their profit center managers almost never had control over all the items for which they were held responsible. The former chief executive of ITT, Harold Geneen, was adamant in how he expected his managers to control their operations and divisions. He stated that, "once you set your business plan and budget for the year, you must achieve the sales, the market share, the earnings, and whatever to which you committed yourself." He further stated that you can "choose from among a thousand good plausible explanations for a no-fault rationale of why the company failed to achieve the results. . . . However, if you believe that *management must manage*, then all those perfectly logical explanations do not count. The only thing that counts is that the desired results were . . . or . . . were not achieved." In other words, if you set a goal or target of performance, you *must* be able to manage the resources at your disposal to achieve your goals while working around those resources that you cannot control.

Source: Kenneth A. Merchant, "How and Why Firms Disregard the Controllability Principle," in *Accounting and Management Field Study Perspectives*, ed. William J. Burns, Jr., and Robert S. Kaplan (Boston: Harvard Business School Press, 1987), 316–319.

accomplishment of specific activities or objectives. Performance reports are customized to emphasize the activities of each specific organizational unit. For example, a financial performance report addressed to the head of a production department contains manufacturing costs controllable by the department head; it does not contain costs (such as advertising, sales commissions, or the president's salary) that the head of the production department cannot control. Including noncontrollable costs distracts the manager's attention from controllable costs and thereby dilutes a manager's efforts to deal with controllable items. Lower level managers may also become frustrated with the entire performance reporting system if they believe upper level managers expect them to control costs they cannot influence.

Financial Performance Reports and Corporate Structure

Before implementing a responsibility accounting system all areas of authority and responsibility within an organization must be clearly defined. Organization charts and other documents should be examined to determine an organization's authority and responsibility structure. However, when an attempt is made to implement a responsibility accounting system, management may find many instances of overlapping duties, of authority not commensurate with responsibility, and of expenditures for which no one appears responsible. These circumstances make the development of a responsibility accounting system difficult, but their resolution is a benefit of successful installation.

Though performance reports can be developed for areas of responsibility as narrow as a single worker, the basic responsibility unit in most organizations is the department. In manufacturing plants, separate responsibility centers are set up for individual production and service departments. In large universities, separate responsibility centers are set up for individual academic departments (such as accounting, psychology, and sociology) and service departments (such as admissions, cafeteria, and maintenance). When a large department performs a number of diverse and significant activities, responsibility accounting may be further refined so that a single department contains several responsibility centers with performance reports prepared for each.

An abbreviated organization chart for a manufacturing firm is presented in Exhibit 7–2. The short-run objective of the firm is to earn a profit by the production and sale of finished goods. The president and the executive vice president are responsible for overall operations and profitability. The authority to set selling prices and to incur costs in connection with the sale of goods is delegated to the vice president of sales, who in turn delegates a portion of this authority to each of two district sales managers. The authority to incur costs in connection with the manufacture of goods is delegated to the vice president of production, who in turn delegates a portion of this authority to each of two plant managers. Finally, each plant manager delegates the authority to incur costs, in connection with specific manufacturing activities, to department heads.

Commensurate with their authority, the responsibility of individual department heads is quite narrow. And, commensurate with greater authority, responsibility is broader at higher levels in the organization. A series of financial

EXHIBIT 7–2   Partial Organization Chart of a Manufacturing Firm

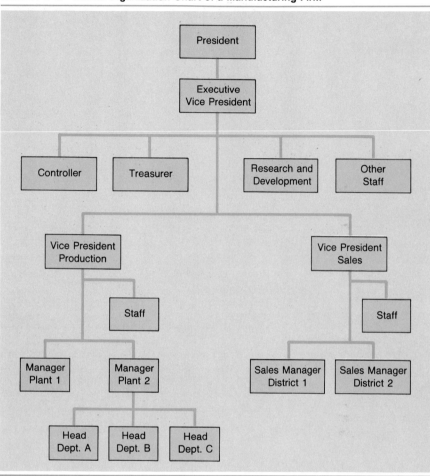

performance reports, illustrating expanding authority for manufacturing costs, is presented in Exhibit 7–3. A plant manager is responsible for more costs than is a department head, and the vice president of production is responsible for more costs than is a single plant manager. Note how the performance reports tie together. The totals for the head of Department C are included as one line in the plant manager's report, and the totals for the manager of Plant 2 are included as one line in the report for the vice president of production. This aggregation takes place because the managers closest to actual activities need detailed information to control day-to-day activities, whereas upper level managers spend less time controlling activities and more time planning them.

EXHIBIT 7–3   Responsibility Accounting Reports for Manufacturing

	Actual Cost	Allowed Cost	Variance*
Vice president: Production			
Plant 1	$ 55,000	$ 54,800	$ 200 U
Plant 2	69,600	68,400	1,200 U
Vice president's office (itemized)	10,900	12,000	1,100 F
Total	$135,500	$135,200	$ 300 U

	Actual Cost	Allowed Cost	Variance*
Manager: Plant 2			
Department A	$ 25,400	$ 24,700	$ 700 U
Department B	17,500	18,000	500 F
Department C	20,500	19,900	600 U
Plant manager's office (itemized)	6,200	5,800	400 U
Total	$ 69,600	$ 68,400	$1,200 U

	Actual Cost	Allowed Cost	Variance*
Head: Department C			
Direct materials	$ 6,000	$ 5,000	$1,000 U
Direct labor	6,500	7,000	500 F
Factory overhead (itemized)	8,000	7,900	100 U
Total	$ 20,500	$ 19,900	$ 600 U

* F = Favorable, if actual costs are less than allowed costs.
  U = Unfavorable, if actual costs are greater than allowed costs.

Nonmonetary Performance Measures

An organization's basic performance reports are almost always stated in terms of dollars, which provide a common, additive unit of measure for all activities. Once the dollar impact of each activity is determined, the dollar measures can be summarized and reported up the corporate ladder. Furthermore, both the immediate supervisor of an activity and other managers far removed from the activity can understand the impact of dollars on cash flow and income. Dollars should not, however, be used to the exclusion of nondollar performance measures. A favorable variance that resulted from an unethical or illegal action should not be rewarded. Short-sighted managers may also take actions that appear favorable in the short run but are detrimental to the organization in the long run. Excessive pressures for employee productivity may result in strikes and employee turnover, and bargain purchases of raw materials may result in excess waste. These examples illustrate the need for upper level management to inquire about the causes of favorable as well as unfavorable variances. What is more, there should be some legitimate way for concerned employees to communicate with upper management without violating the chain of command. For example, an employee in a waste treatment department should be able to legitimately express a concern to upper management about a supervisor's illegal cost cutting measures. A corporate ombudsman might be useful in this regard.

The persons responsible for the accomplishment of specific activities, especially first line supervisors, should be routinely provided with dollar and non-dollar performance measures. The nondollar measures should be stated in terms of the activities or resources for which first line supervisors are responsible. The head of a production department, for example, should receive information on materials use, labor hours, machine hours, units produced, defective units, scrap, and so forth. A district sales manager would like information on market share, number of orders, number of salespersons' visits, and customer complaints.

Frequency of Performance Reports

Performance reports must be provided with sufficient frequency for managers to take timely corrective action. Although performance reports for an entire year may assist in developing plans and evaluating managers' performance, they are of no use in adjusting operations during the year. On the other hand, daily or hourly performance reports may be of great value to some managers but a distraction to others. The solution to this dilemma is to recognize that different levels of management, and different personnel at each level, have differing needs for performance information. The head of a production department may require daily, hourly, or even continuous information about operations under his or her control, whereas a plant manager may need only weekly reports from each department head. Similarly, the vice president of production may require only monthly performance reports from each plant. The further a manager is from actual operations, the less the manager's need for frequent feedback. Higher level managers spend more time planning operations and motivating personnel to execute these plans, and lower level managers spend more time executing plans. Hence, lower level managers have greater need for frequent and fast feedback.

Types of Responsibility Centers

Under responsibility accounting, performance reports are prepared for departments, segments of departments, or groupings of departments that operate under the control and authority of a responsible manager. Each organizational unit for which performance reports are prepared is identified as a **responsibility center.** For the purpose of evaluating their financial performance, responsibility centers may be classified as investment centers, profit centers, revenue centers, or costs centers.

An **investment center** is responsible for the relationship between its profits and the total assets invested in the center. In general, the management of an investment center is expected to earn a target profit per dollar invested. Investment center managers are evaluated on the basis of how well they use the total resources entrusted to their care to earn a profit.

An investment center is the broadest and most inclusive type of responsibility center. The entire organization depicted in Exhibit 7–2 would be regarded as an investment center, with the president and the executive vice president being the investment center's management. These officials have more authority and responsibility than other managers and are primarily responsible for planning, organizing, and controlling firm activities. Their decisions regarding the size of the company determine the total assets for which they are responsible. Because of their authority regarding the size of corporate assets, they are held responsible for the relationship between profits and assets. Investment centers are discussed further in Chapter 9.

A **profit center** is responsible for the difference between revenues and costs. A profit center may refer to an entire organization but is more frequently a segment of an organization, such as a product line, marketing territory, or store. In the context of performance evaluation the word "profit" may not refer to the bottom line of an income statement; instead, it is likely to refer to the profit center's contribution to common corporate costs and profit. Profit is computed as the center's revenues less all costs identified with operating the center.

A large retail organization might evaluate each of its stores as a profit center, with the store manager being the administrative officer. The store manager, who has responsibility for the overall operation of the store, accepts the store's physical structure and the organization's investment in the store as givens. Though the store manager may request that additional investments be made for a variety of purposes, the manager seldom has the authority to make investment or financing decisions. Having limited authority regarding the size of the store's total assets, the store manager is not held responsible for the relationship between profits and assets. For making special analyses, management may, of course, evaluate the store as an investment center.

A **revenue center** is responsible for the generation of sales revenues. In Exhibit 7–2 there are three revenue centers: District 1, District 2, and the Vice President of Sales. A performance report is prepared for each district and the Vice President of Sales. Even though the basic performance report of a revenue center emphasizes sales, revenue centers are likely to be assigned responsibility for the controllable costs they incur in generating revenues. If revenues and costs are evaluated separately, the center has dual responsibility as a revenue center and as a cost center. If controllable costs are deducted from revenues to obtain some bottom-line contribution, the center is, in fact, being treated as a quasi-profit center.

A **cost center** is financially responsible only for the incurrence of costs; it does not have a revenue responsibility. A cost center may be as small as a segment of a department or large enough to include a major aspect of the organization, such as all manufacturing activities. The financial performance reports in Exhibit 7–3 illustrate an increasing responsibility for manufacturing costs. The head of a production department is responsible only for costs incurred in his or her department, but the vice president of manufacturing is responsible for all manufacturing costs. Cost centers are established for nonmanufacturing as well as for manufacturing activities. In Exhibit 7–2 each of the staff departments, such as the Controller's Department, is evaluated as a cost center. Cost centers are

MANAGERIAL PRACTICE 7.2

Deregulation Spawns New Cost System

Telephone industry accounting has been influenced by changes brought about by the AT&T divestiture and deregulation. The original Uniform System of Accounts (USOA) used by the industry was established back in 1934 by the Federal Communications Commission (FCC). The FCC allowed companies to enter into deregulated services only through totally separated subsidiaries. This required not only separate employees but also separate books.

In 1978 the FCC began working on a new financial accounting process. The new USOA was to be implemented by all telephone companies as of January 1, 1988. In addition, the FCC required all telephone companies with more than $100 million in annual revenues to file a cost manual for approval. For example, Pacific Bell uses a cost manual prototype developed by Price Waterhouse, an international accounting firm, and the United States Telephone Association. Pacific Bell uses the same accounting system and the same books for both regulated and nonregulated revenues, investment, and expenses. However, regulated and nonregulated costs are separated and recorded each month in subsidiary cost records. The purpose for this separation is to prevent cross-subsidization of nonregulated activities by the regulated business. This cost accounting system allows Pacific Bell to focus on total company costs without being concerned with where the costs are finally assigned.

Source: Raymond H. Peterson and Alyce Zahorsky, "Telephone Industry Develops New Cost Standards," *Management Accounting* (December 1988): 47–49.

also established in merchandising, service, and not-for-profit organizations. Typical examples of these cost centers include the following:

Organization	Cost Center
Retail store	Advertising department
	Maintenance department
TV station	Audio/video engineering
	Buildings and grounds
College	History department
	Power plant
City government	Public safety (police and fire)
	Welfare

In the remainder of this chapter we introduce concepts that are important to the development of financial performance reports for cost and revenue centers. We conclude by illustrating how the performance reports of cost centers and revenue centers can be combined to reconcile the difference between an organization's budgeted and actual income. We will look closer at cost center performance reports in Chapter 8, investment centers are considered in Chapter 9, and performance reports for important segments of a business (profit centers) are examined in Chapter 10.

PERFORMANCE REPORTS FOR COST CENTERS

Financial performance reports for cost centers should always include a comparison of actual and allowed costs, with the difference identified as a variance. The variance is favorable if actual costs are less than allowed costs and unfavorable if actual costs are greater than allowed costs. These comparisons are made in total and for each type of controllable cost assigned to the cost center. The allowed costs used in performance reports are based on a flexible budget for the actual level of activity.

Development of Flexible Budgets

A budget that is based on a prior prediction of expected sales and production is called a static budget. The operating budget explained in Chapter 6 is a static budget. Budgets may also be drawn up for a series of possible production and sales volumes or adjusted to a particular level of production after the fact. These budgets, based on cost-volume-profit or cost-volume relationships, are called flexible budgets; they are used to determine what costs should have been for an attained volume of activity. Before a flexible budget can be developed, management must understand how costs respond to changes in activity.

Assume the Meridian Clock Company contains three departments, Production, Sales, and Administration. In this chapter we will develop financial performance reports for each of them, starting with the Production Department. The flexible budget cost estimating equation for total monthly production costs is as follows:

	Fixed Costs		Variable Costs
Direct materials			$10X
Direct labor			6X
Factory overhead	$50,000		4X
Total cost	= $50,000	+	$20X

where X equals the number of units produced.

If management planned to produce 10,000 units in July 19x7, the budgeted manufacturing costs for July would amount to $250,000:

Meridian Clock Company
Manufacturing Budget
For the month of July, 19x7

Manufacturing costs:	
Direct materials (10,000 × $10)	$100,000
Direct labor (10,000 × $6)	60,000
Variable overhead (10,000 × $4)	40,000
Fixed overhead	50,000
Total	$250,000

Flexible Budgets Emphasize Efficiency

If actual production happened to equal 10,000 units, the performance of the Production Department in controlling costs could be based on a comparison of actual and budgeted manufacturing costs. But, if production were at some volume other than that specified in the original manufacturing budget, it would be inappropriate to compare actual manufacturing costs with the costs predicted in the original static budget. Doing so would intermix two separate Production Department responsibilities; namely, the manufacturing responsibility for production volume and the financial responsibility for cost control.

The original budget for production volume was set on the basis of predicted needs for sales and inventory requirements, taking into consideration materials, labor, and facilities constraints. In the absence of any changes in these needs, the Production Department's manufacturing responsibility for production volume is evaluated by comparing the actual and budgeted production volumes. If, however, production needs change, perhaps due to an unexpected increase or decrease in sales volume, the Production Department should attempt to make appropriate changes in its production volume. And, when the actual production volume is anything other than the originally budgeted amount, the Production Department's financial responsibility for cost control should be based on the actual level of production.

For the purpose of evaluating the financial performance of cost centers, a flexible budget is tailored, after the fact, to the actual level of activity. A **flexible budget variance** is computed for each cost as the difference between the actual cost and the flexible budget cost of producing a given quantity of product or service. Examples of performance reports for July manufacturing costs, based on static and flexible budgets, are presented in Exhibit 7–4. When the Production Department's financial performance is evaluated using the static budget, the actual cost of producing 11,000 units is compared to the budgeted cost of producing 10,000 units. The result is a series of large, unfavorable static budget variances, totaling $23,000. When the Production Department's financial performance is evaluated by comparing actual costs with costs allowed in a flexible budget that was drawn up for the actual production volume, the results are mixed. Direct materials have a $2,000 favorable flexible budget variance. Direct labor has a $4,000 unfavorable flexible budget variance. There is no variable overhead flexible budget variance. And fixed overhead has a $1,000 unfavorable variance. The net unfavorable flexible budget variance is $3,000.

MANAGERIAL PRACTICE 7.3

Flexible Budgets Work for Hospitals

At Washington Hospital Center (WHC), flexible budgeting is being used as a relatively simple way to introduce department heads to cost management. Flexible budgeting is a detail-oriented task that takes several months to implement each year. All managers must use flexible budgets to set financial targets for their departments and to track progress toward those goals. Special software provides immediate feedback on a department's performance in terms of both dollars and staffing hours. WHC's success with flexible budgeting is due in large part to department training, activity measures, and everyone's cooperation, from budget planning through final variance analysis. For WHC it has become a building block for future applications of cost management.

Source: Glenn M. Lohrmann, "Flexible Budget System a Practical Approach to Cost Management," *Healthcare Financial Management* (January 1989): 38–47.

EXHIBIT 7–4   Flexible Budgets and Performance Evaluation

Meridian Clock Company
Production Department Performance Report
For the month of July, 19x7

	Based on Static Budget			Based on Flexible Budget			
	Actual	Original Budget	Static Budget Variance*	Flexible Budget Formula	Actual	Flexible Budget	Flexible Budget Variance*
Volume	11,000	10,000			11,000	11,000	
Manufacturing costs:							
Direct materials	$108,000	$100,000	$ 8,000 U	$10/unit	$108,000	$110,000	$2,000 F
Direct labor	70,000	60,000	10,000 U	6/unit	70,000	66,000	4,000 U
Variable overhead	44,000	40,000	4,000 U	4/unit	44,000	44,000	0
Fixed overhead	51,000	50,000	1,000 U	$50,000/month	51,000	50,000	1,000 U
	$273,000	$250,000	$23,000 U		$273,000	$270,000	$3,000 U

* F = Favorable
  U = Unfavorable

Standard Costs

A standard cost, a budget for one unit of product, indicates what it should cost to produce one unit of product under efficient operating conditions. Standard costs can be developed from an engineering analysis or from an analysis of historical data adjusted for expected changes in the product, production technology, or costs. When standards are developed using historical data, management must be careful to ensure that past inefficiencies are excluded from current standards. The standard variable product costs for the Meridian Clock Company are $20 per unit, including direct materials, direct labor, and factory overhead costs of $10, $6, and $4, respectively. These standard costs were used in developing the flexible budget in Exhibit 7–4.

Standard costs are used for budgeting, performance evaluation, and product costing. In Chapter 6 standard costs for materials, labor, and overhead were used in developing the operating budget for the All American Wagon Company. In this chapter and in Chapter 8, standard costs are used for performance evaluation. In the appendix of Chapter 11, standard costs are used for product costing. When standard costs are used to value product inventories in external financial statements, the unit standard cost must also include an element for fixed overhead.[1] For purposes of internal planning and control, it is better to classify costs by their behavior. Accordingly, since fixed costs are constant in the short run without regard to the level of operations, they are treated as a lump

---

[1] External reporting requires that inventories be stated on an absorption cost basis in which all manufacturing costs, including fixed costs, are product costs.

sum in this chapter. In the Meridian Clock Company's flexible budget for manufacturing costs (see Exhibit 7–4), the budgeted fixed overhead does not vary with production volume.

To obtain the full benefit of standard costs, the standards must be based on realistic expectations. Some organizations intentionally set "tight" standards to motivate employees toward higher levels of production. The management of

MANAGERIAL PRACTICE 7.4

Changing Operations Demand Changes in Standard Costing

GenCorp Polymer Products (GPP) has successfully completed the evolution from a cost accounting system to a cost management system. This change occurred in response to changing production technologies.

In order to succeed, GPP had focused on product quality and product innovation. However, despite major changes to the production process, its cost accounting system had remained unchanged. When its plant reached capacity limits in 1985, GPP was unable to make informed decisions concerning product mix and pricing based on its current cost system. No distinction was made between variable and fixed overhead costs. The standard cost system simply attached materials, labor, and overhead to products based on each product's engineering specifications. While regular adjustments were made for material standards, labor and overhead adjustments were haphazard. Products were costed at standard labor, but all the changes in the production process had undermined that procedure.

Modification of the standard cost accounting system was necessary to recognize changes in the production process. Interviews with key users of the system and historical cost data were used to identify factors driving the cost of production decisions. With this information a new system was implemented that helped link costs to pricing. The new management information system and accounting database are now meeting the needs of the new cost management system, which in turn is able to respond to GPP's changing technology.

Source: Gary B. Frank, Steven A. Fisher, and Allen R. Wilkie, "Linking Cost to Price And Profit," *Management Accounting* (June 1989): 22–26.

the Meridian Clock Company might set their standard for direct labor at $4 per unit, rather than at the expected $6 per unit, hoping that employees will strive toward the lower cost. The use of tight standards often causes planning and behavioral problems. Management expects them to result in unfavorable variances. Accordingly, tight standards should not be used to budget input requirements and cash flows—management expects to incur more labor costs than the standards allow. The use of tight standards can have undesirable behavioral effects if lower level managers and employees find that a second set of standards are used in the "real" budget or if they are constantly subject to unfavorable performance reports. They may come to distrust the entire budgeting and performance evaluation system, or they may quit trying to achieve any of the organization's standards.

Tight standards are more likely to occur in an imposed budget and less likely to occur in a participation budget where employees are actively involved in budget preparation. In a participation budget the problems may be to avoid loose standards that are easily attained and to avoid overstating the costs required to produce a product. Loose standards may fail to properly motivate employees; what is more, they may lead the company into an uncompetitive market position with costs and prices that are higher than those of competitors.

Standard and Discretionary Cost Centers

A distinction is often made between standard and discretionary cost centers. A standard cost center is a cost center that has clearly defined relationships between effort and accomplishment. A discretionary cost center is a cost center that does not have clearly defined relationships between effort and accomplishment.

The financial performance of standard cost centers is evaluated with the aid of flexible budgets drawn up for the actual level of activity. A production department is the most obvious example of a standard cost center. However, the growth of services and service industries, and the resultant need to control service costs, has led to an expanding use of standard cost centers. Standard cost centers can be established for any segment of a business for which it is possible to develop standard costs per unit of activity. Possible applications include the costs of packaging, transportation, commissions, utilities, room cleaning, residential fire inspection, laundry, automobile repair, and processing loan applications.

Recall that discretionary costs are set at a fixed amount at the discretion of management. Changing these costs does not affect production or service capacity in the near term. Because of the absence of a relationship between effort and accomplishment, the financial performance of a discretionary cost center cannot be evaluated with the aid of a flexible budget. Indeed, it is difficult to evaluate the performance of a discretionary cost center by any means. The best monetary evaluation is based on a comparison of the actual and budgeted costs for a given period, with the results identified as over budget or under budget.

If a research and development budget for 19x9 contained authorized expenditures of $1.5 million, but the actual 19x9 expenditures amounted to $1.2 million, the $300,000 difference is not necessarily favorable. Research and development was $300,000 under budget. Whether or not this is good or bad depends on what was accomplished during the year. If the money was saved by canceling a program critical to the organization's future, the net result is hardly favorable. Again, all the variance does is inform management that actual results were not in line with plans. Management must investigate further to determine the significance of the variance.

Though it is difficult to evaluate the under-budget performance of a discretionary cost center, an over-budget performance has an undesirable implication regardless of the results achieved. If, after the budget is approved, the manager of a discretionary cost center realizes the center's budget is inadequate, the manager should immediately request additional funds, or notify his or her supervisor of the need to reduce activity. Going over budget implies that the manager is unable to operate with the budgeted resources. Obviously, a manager should not be allowed unlimited use of the organization's resources. To control such use, the organization's treasurer is often prohibited from providing financial resources in excess of an authorized limit (like the limit on a bank credit card). If this limit is exceeded, the matter should be brought immediately to the attention of the next level of management.

In for-profit organizations, an increase in demand for a product or service is usually accompanied by an increase in financial resources that more than covers the increase in variable costs. This is often not the case in not-for-profit organizations. Here the funds provided for an activity may be fixed regardless of the level of the activity. A city in upstate New York might budget $1,000,000 per year for snow removal with the money collected from property taxes. If this budget is based on an average of five snowfalls per year at an average removal cost of $200,000 per snowfall, the city department responsible for snow removal may have to operate with this amount even if there are seven snowfalls. The problem is that the department, a natural standard cost center, receives resources as if it were a discretionary cost center. Consequently, the department may not have enough resources to do its job in periods of high activity, and it may have excess resources (which it might be tempted to waste) in periods of low activity. The unique problems of planning and control in not-for-profit organizations are considered further in the appendix to Chapter 6.

As management's ability to define the relationships between effort and accomplishment becomes more refined, there is a tendency for managers to replace discretionary cost centers with standard cost centers. A computer center that was initially established as a discretionary cost center may be changed to a standard cost center, once management determines the relationships between the computer's operating costs and some measure of its activity. A management that desires to better plan and control costs will encourage the evolution from discretionary to standard cost centers wherever practicable.

PERFORMANCE REPORTS FOR
REVENUE CENTERS

The financial performance reports for revenue centers include a comparison of actual and budgeted revenues, with the difference identified as a variance. Revenue centers are sometimes assigned responsibility for controllable costs they incur in generating revenues. In this case they have a dual responsibility as a revenue center and as a cost center. Controllable costs may be deducted from revenues to obtain some bottom-line contribution. If the center is then evaluated on the basis of this contribution, it is being treated as a profit center.

Revenue Center Reports Reconcile with the Original Budget

If the organization is to meet its budgeted profit goal for a period, with its budgeted fixed and variable costs, the organization's revenue centers must meet their original revenue budgets. Consequently, the original budget (a static budget), rather than a flexible budget, is used to evaluate the financial performance of revenue centers.

Assume the Meridian Clock Company's sales budget for July 19x7 called for the sale of 10,000 units at $40 each. If Meridian actually sold 11,000 units at $39 each, the total revenue variance would be $29,000:

Actual revenues (11,000 × $39)	$429,000
Budgeted revenues (10,000 × $40)	−400,000
Revenue variance	$ 29,000 F

Because actual revenues exceeded budgeted revenues, the revenue variance is favorable. Note that two distinct events occurred to create the $29,000 favorable variance: the selling price declined from $40 to $39, and the sales volume increased from 10,000 to 11,000 units. These two causes of the total revenue variance are identified as the sales price variance and the sales volume variance.

The **sales price variance** indicates the impact on revenues of a change in selling price, given the actual sales volume. It is computed as the change in selling price times the actual sales volume:

$$\text{Sales price variance} = \left(\begin{array}{c}\text{Actual selling price} - \text{Budgeted selling price}\end{array}\right) \times \text{Actual sales volume.}$$

The **sales volume variance** indicates the impact on revenues of the change in sales volume, assuming there was no change in selling price. It is computed as the difference between the actual and the budgeted sales volume times the budgeted selling price:

$$\text{Sales volume variance} = \left(\begin{array}{c}\text{Actual sales volume} - \text{Budgeted sales volume}\end{array}\right) \times \text{Budgeted selling price.}$$

The July sales price and volume variances for the Meridian Clock Company are $11,000 U and $40,000 F, respectively:

Sales price variance	= ($39 − $40) × 11,000	= $11,000 U
Sales volume variance	= (11,000 − 10,000) × $40	= 40,000 F
Total revenue variance		$29,000 F

The interpretation of variances is subjective. In this case we might say that if the increase in sales volume had not been accompanied by a decline in selling price, revenues would have increased $40,000. The $1 per unit decline in selling price cost the company $11,000 in revenues. Alternatively, we might note that a $1 reduction in the unit selling price was more than offset by an increase in sales volume.

In any case, variances are merely signals that actual results are not proceeding according to plan. They help managers identify potential problems and opportunities. An investigation into their cause(s) may even indicate that a manager who received a favorable variance was doing a poor job, whereas a manager who received an unfavorable variance was doing an outstanding job. Consider Meridian's favorable sales volume variance. This occurred because actual sales exceeded budgeted sales by 1,000 units or 10 percent, which on the surface indicates good performance. But what if the total market for the company's products exceeded the company's forecast by 20 percent? In this case Meridian's sales volume fell below its expected percentage share of the market, and the favorable variance may have occurred, despite a poor marketing effort, because of strong customer demand that competitors could not fill.

Revenue Center Reports Sometimes Include Costs

Controllable costs should also be considered when evaluating the overall performance of revenue centers. A failure to consider costs might encourage uneconomic selling practices, such as excessive advertising and entertaining, and spending too much time on small accounts. The controllable costs of revenue centers include variable and fixed selling costs. These costs are sometimes further classified into order getting and order filling costs. **Order getting costs** are costs incurred to obtain a customer's order, for example, advertising, salespersons' salaries and commissions, travel, telephone, and entertainment. **Order filling costs** are costs incurred to place finished goods in the hands of purchasers, for example, storing, packaging, and transportation. Many of these costs are fixed (committed and discretionary); others are variable.

The performance of a revenue center in controlling costs can be evaluated with the aid of a flexible budget drawn up for the actual level of activity. Assume the Meridian Clock Company's July 19x7 budget for the Sales Department calls for fixed costs of $10,000 and variable costs of $5 per unit sold. If the actual fixed and variable selling expenses for July are $9,500 and $65,000, respectively, the total cost variances assigned to the Sales Department are $9,500 unfavorable:

Meridian Clock Company
Sales Department Performance Report for Costs
For the month of July, 19x7

	Flexible Budget Formula	Actual	Flexible Budget	Flexible Budget Variance*
Volume		11,000	11,000	
Selling expenses:				
Variable	$5/unit	$65,000	$55,000	$10,000 U
Fixed	$10,000/month	9,500	10,000	500 F
Total		$74,500	$65,000	$ 9,500 U

*F = Favorable
U = Unfavorable

In evaluating the performance of the Sales Department as both a cost center and a revenue center, management would consider these cost variances as well as the revenue variances.

Revenue Centers Are Sometimes Evaluated as Profit Centers

Even though we have computed revenue and cost variances for Meridian's Sales Department, we are still left with an incomplete picture of the performance of this revenue center. Is the Sales Department's performance best represented by the $29,000 favorable revenue variance, by the $9,500 unfavorable cost variance, or by the net favorable variance of $19,500 ($29,000 F + $9,500 U)? Actually, it is inappropriate to attempt to obtain an overall measure of the Sales Department's performance by combining these separate revenue and cost variances. The combination of revenue and cost variances is only appropriate for a profit center and, so far, we have left out one important cost that must be assigned to the Sales Department before it can be treated as a profit center. That cost is the standard variable cost of goods sold.

As a profit center, the Sales Department acquires units from the Production Department and sells them outside the firm. Its total responsibilities include revenues, the standard variable cost of goods sold, and actual selling expenses. Note that the Sales Department is assigned the standard, rather than the actual, variable cost of goods sold. Because the Sales Department does not control production activities, it should not be assigned actual production costs. Doing so would result in the Production Department's variances being passed on to the Sales Department. Fixed manufacturing costs are not assigned to the Sales Department because short-run variations in sales volume do not normally affect the total amount of these costs.

To evaluate the Sales Department as a profit center, the computation of the sales volume variance must be adjusted for the corresponding variations in allowed costs. In its current form the sales volume variance does not consider that costs as well as revenues respond to changes in sales volume. Consequently, to evaluate the performance of a profit center, this variance must be stated net of its impact on the flexible budgets for manufacturing and selling costs. The standard variable costs that respond to changes in sales volume are as follows:

Direct materials	$10
Direct labor	6
Factory overhead	4
Selling	5
Total	$25

When standard variable costs are considered, the net impact of the sales volume variance is $15,000 favorable:

Sales volume variance [(11,000 − 10,000) × $40]	$40,000 F
Less increase in standard variable costs	
[(11,000 − 10,000) × $25]	−25,000
Net sales volume variance	$15,000 F

In general, the **net sales volume variance** indicates the impact of a change in sales volume on the contribution margin, given the budgeted selling price and the standard variable costs. It is computed as the difference between the actual and the budgeted sales volume times the budgeted unit contribution margin. The budgeted unit contribution margin is the budgeted selling price minus the standard variable costs per unit:

$$\begin{matrix} \text{Net sales} \\ \text{volume} \\ \text{variance} \end{matrix} = \left(\begin{matrix} \text{Actual} \\ \text{sales} \\ \text{volume} \end{matrix} - \begin{matrix} \text{Budgeted} \\ \text{sales} \\ \text{volume} \end{matrix} \right) \times \begin{matrix} \text{Budgeted} \\ \text{unit contribution} \\ \text{margin.} \end{matrix}$$

The Meridian Clock Company's budgeted unit contribution margin is $15:

Budgeted unit selling price	$40
Standard unit variable costs	−25
Budgeted unit contribution margin	$15

Using the formula presented above, the net sales volume variance is computed as follows:

$$\text{Net sales volume variance} = [(11,000 − 10,000) \times \$15]$$
$$= \$15,000 \text{ F.}$$

In summary, as a profit center the Sales Department has responsibility for the sales price variance, the net sales volume variance, and any cost variances associated with its operations. The Meridian Clock Company's sales price variance was previously computed to be $11,000 U, the $1 reduction in selling price times the actual sales volume of 11,000 units. The net sales volume variance was determined to be $15,000 F, the 1,000 unit increase in sales volume times the budgeted unit contribution margin of $15. The cost variances assigned to the Sales Department net to $9,500 U, the difference between $74,500 in actual selling costs and $65,000 in selling costs allowed for the actual sales volume. As a profit center, the Sales Department's net variances are $5,500 unfavorable:

Sales price variance	$11,000 U
Net sales volume variance	15,000 F
Selling expense variances	9,500 U
Net Sales Department variances	$ 5,500 U

In an attempt to improve their overall performance, managers often commit themselves to unfavorable variances in some areas, believing these variances will be more than offset by other favorable variances. In the case above, it appears that the favorable net sales volume variance was not sufficient to offset the price reductions and the higher selling expenses. Also note that the more complete evaluation of the Sales Department as a profit center (with a $5,500 unfavorable variance) gives a very different impression than the evaluation of the Sales Department as a revenue center (with a $29,000 favorable variance) or as a dual revenue and cost center (with additional $9,500 unfavorable cost variances).

RECONCILING BUDGETED AND ACTUAL INCOME

It is possible to reconcile the difference between budgeted and actual net income for an entire organization. This can be done either by (1) assigning all costs and revenues to responsibility centers and summarizing the financial performance of each responsibility center or (2) developing a detailed reconciliation of actual and budgeted costs and revenues for the organization as a whole. Assume the Meridian Clock Company's budgeted and actual income statements, in a contribution format, for July 19x7 are as presented in Exhibit 7–5.

Following the first reconciliation approach, assume that the Meridian Clock Company contains three responsibility centers: a Production Department, a Sales Department, and an Administration Department. Further assume that the Production and the Administration Departments are cost centers and that the Sales Department is a profit center. The Production Department's variances, as itemized in Exhibit 7–4, net to $3,000 U. The Sales Department's variances, as summarized above, net to $5,500 U. The only variance for the Administration Department is the $200 difference between actual and budgeted fixed administrative costs ($3,800 actual − $4,000 budget). Because the Administration Department is a discretionary cost center, this variance is best identified as under budget.

EXHIBIT 7–5   Budgeted and Actual Income Statements

Meridian Clock Company
Budgeted Income Statement
For the month of July, 19x7

Sales (10,000 units × $40)			$400,000
Less variable costs:			
Variable cost of goods sold:			
Direct materials (10,000 units × $10)	$100,000		
Direct labor (10,000 units × $6)	60,000		
Factory overhead (10,000 units × $4)	40,000	$200,000	
Selling (10,000 units × $5)		50,000	−250,000
Contribution margin			$150,000
Less fixed costs:			
Factory overhead		$ 50,000	
Selling		10,000	
Administrative		4,000	− 64,000
Net income			$ 86,000

Meridian Clock Company
Actual Income Statement
For the month of July, 19x7

Sales (11,000 units × $39)			$429,000
Less variable costs:			
Variable cost of goods sold:			
Direct materials	$108,000		
Direct labor	70,000		
Factory overhead	44,000	$222,000	
Selling		65,000	−287,000
Contribution margin			$142,000
Less fixed costs:			
Factory overhead		$ 51,000	
Selling		9,500	
Administrative		3,800	− 64,300
Net income			$ 77,700

For consistency in the performance reports, however, it is labeled favorable. Assigning all previously computed variances to these three responsibility centers, the reconciliation of budgeted and actual income is as follows:

Budgeted net income		$86,000
Sales Department variances		
(a profit center)	$5,500 U	
Production Department variances		
(a standard cost center)	3,000 U	
Administration Department variances		
(a discretionary cost center)	200 F	− 8,300 U
Actual net income		$77,700

Following the second approach, a detailed reconciliation of budgeted and actual costs and revenues for the organization as a whole is presented in Exhibit 7–6. The actual results for the year are presented in column (1). The information in this column is based on the actual sales volume, the actual selling prices, and the actual costs. The original budget for the year is presented in column (7). The information in this column is based on the budgeted volume, the budgeted selling prices, and the budgeted costs. The three possible sources of variation between the original budget and the actual results (costs, selling prices, and volume) are analyzed in columns (2), (4), and (6).

The cost variances in column (2) reconcile the difference between the actual costs in column (1) and the costs allowed for the actual volume in column (3). Included in column (2) are the manufacturing cost variances (direct materials, direct labor, variable factory overhead, and fixed factory overhead, totaling $3,000 U), the selling expense variances (variable and fixed, totaling $9,500 U), and the administrative cost variances (all fixed, totaling $200 F). The sales revenues in columns (1) and (3) are based on actual volume at actual prices. Hence, no sales variances are included in column (2).

The sales price variance in column (4) reconciles the difference between the actual volume at actual selling prices in column (3) and the actual volume

EXHIBIT 7–6   Reconciliation of Budgeted and Actual Income

	(1) Actual Volume at Actual Selling Prices and Actual Costs (Actual results)	(2) Cost Variances	(3) Actual Volume at Actual Selling Prices and Standard Costs	(4) Sales Price Variance	(5) Actual Volume at Budgeted Selling Prices and Standard Costs (Flexible budget)	(6) Net Sales Volume Variance	(7) Budgeted Volume at Budgeted Selling Prices and Standard Costs (Original budget)
Volume (units)	11,000		11,000		11,000	1,000	10,000
Sales	$429,000		$429,000	$11,000 U	$440,000	$40,000	$400,000
Less variable costs:							
Direct materials	$108,000	$ 2,000 F	$110,000		$110,000	$10,000	$100,000
Direct labor	70,000	4,000 U	66,000		66,000	6,000	60,000
Factory overhead	44,000		44,000		44,000	4,000	40,000
Selling	65,000	10,000 U	55,000		55,000	5,000	50,000
Total	−287,000		−275,000		−275,000	−25,000	−250,000
Contribution margin	$142,000		$154,000		$165,000	$15,000 F	$150,000
Less fixed costs:							
Factory overhead	$ 51,000	1,000 U	$ 50,000		$ 50,000		$ 50,000
Selling	9,500	500 F	10,000		10,000		10,000
Administration	3,800	200 F	4,000		4,000		4,000
Total	− 64,300		− 64,000		− 64,000		− 64,000
Net income	$ 77,700	$12,300 U	$ 90,000	$11,000 U	$101,000	$15,000 F	$ 86,000

at budgeted selling prices in column (5). Note that the allowed costs for the actual volume, first computed in column (3), are restated in column (5). This means that column (5) is the flexible budget for both revenues and costs at the actual volume of production and sales. The differences between the actual results in column (1) and the flexible budget in column (5) are explained by the cost and price variances in columns (2) and (4).

Finally, the net sales volume variance in column (6) reconciles the difference between the flexible budget for revenues and costs based on actual volume and the original budget for revenues and costs based on budgeted sales. The differential effects of the production and sales volume on revenues and costs are disclosed in this column and totaled to determine the net sales volume variance of $15,000 F.

SUMMARY

Responsibility accounting is the structuring of performance reports addressed to individual members of an organization in a manner that emphasizes the factors controllable by them. Each administrative unit for which performance reports are prepared is identified as a responsibility center. For the purpose of evaluating their financial performance, responsibility centers are classified as investment centers, profit centers, revenue centers, or cost centers. An investment center is responsible for the relationship between its profits and the total assets invested in the center. A profit center is responsible for the difference between revenues and costs. Although a revenue center is responsible for the generation of sales revenue, it is often assigned responsibility for the controllable costs incurred in generating revenues. If this is done, the revenue center has a dual responsibility as a revenue and cost center. If controllable costs are deducted from revenues, the center is, in fact, being treated as a profit center. A cost center is financially responsible only for the incurrence of costs and is often further classified as either standard or discretionary.

A standard cost center is a cost center that has clearly defined relationships between effort and accomplishment. The performance of a standard cost center is evaluated by comparing actual costs with the costs allowed in a flexible budget drawn up for the actual level of activity. A discretionary cost center is a cost center that does not have clearly defined relationships between activity and accomplishment. Discretionary cost centers are evaluated, for accounting purposes, by comparing the actual and budgeted costs for a given period. The difference is identified as over budget or under budget.

It is possible to reconcile the difference between budgeted and actual income for an entire organization. This can be done by (1) assigning all costs and revenues to responsibility centers and then summarizing the financial performance of each responsibility center or (2) developing a detailed reconciliation of all costs and revenues for the organization as a whole.

SUGGESTED READINGS

Cornick, Michael, William D. Cooper, and Susan B. Wilson, "How Do Companies Analyze Overhead?" *Management Accounting* (June 1988): 44–19.

Doost, Roger K., and Evans Pappas, "Frozen-to-Current Cost Variance," *Management Accounting* (March 1988): 41–43.

Govindarajan, Vijay, and John K. Shank, "Profit Variance Analysis: A Strategic Focus," *Issues in Accounting Education, 4*, No. 2 (Fall 1989): 396–410.

Parra, Serigo A., and Joanne A. Collins, "Cost Control: A Key Element in Quality." *Controller's Quarterly, 2*, No. 4 (1986): 13–18.

Sprohge, Hans, and John Talbott, "How Variance Analysis Helped a Thoroughbred Farm," *Journal of Accountancy* (April 1989): 137–141.

REVIEW PROBLEM

Reconciling Budgeted and Actual Income

Presented are the budgeted and actual contribution income statements of the Well Read Publishing Company for April 19x7.

Well Read Publishing Company
Budgeted Contribution Income Statement
For the month of April, 19x7

Sales (22,000 × $8.50)		$187,000
Less variable costs:		
Variable cost of goods sold:		
Direct materials (22,000 × $0.75)	$16,500	
Direct labor (22,000 × $1.25)	27,500	
Factory overhead (22,000 × $1.50)	33,000	
Selling (22,000 × $2.50)	55,000	−132,000
Contribution margin		$ 55,000
Less fixed costs:		
Factory overhead	$20,000	
Selling	15,000	
Administration	10,000	− 45,000
Net income		$ 10,000

Well Read Publishing Company
Actual Contribution Income Statement
For the month of April, 19x7

Sales (21,000 × $9.00)		$189,000
Less variable costs:		
Variable cost of goods sold:		
Direct materials	$15,750	
Direct labor	25,000	
Factory overhead	32,500	
Selling	56,000	−129,250
Contribution margin		$ 59,750
Less fixed costs:		
Factory overhead	$17,500	
Selling	16,000	
Administration	12,000	− 45,500
Net income		$ 14,250

Well Read Publishing Company contains three responsibility centers: a Production Department, a Sales Department, and an Administration Department. The Production and Administration Departments are cost centers, and the Sales Department is a profit center.

Requirements

a) Prepare a performance report for the Production Department that compares actual and allowed costs.

b) Prepare a performance report for selling expenses that compares actual and allowed costs.

c) Determine the sales price and the net sales volume variances.

d) Prepare a report that summarizes the performance of the Sales Department.

e) Determine the amount by which the Administration Department was over or under budget.

f) Prepare a report reconciling budgeted and actual net income. Your report should focus on the performance of each responsibility center.

g) Prepare a detailed reconciliation of actual and budgeted costs, revenues, and income for the organization as a whole.

The solution to this problem is found at the end of the Chapter 7 exercises, problems, and cases.

KEY TERMS

Cost center	Responsibility accounting
Discretionary cost center	Responsibility center
Flexible budget	Revenue center
Flexible budget variance	Sales price variance
Investment center	Sales volume variance
Net sales volume variance	Standard cost
Order filling costs	Standard cost center
Order getting costs	Static budget
Profit center	

REVIEW QUESTIONS

7–1   Briefly describe the budgeting and performance evaluation cycle.

7–2   What is responsibility accounting? Why should noncontrollable costs be excluded from performance reports prepared in accordance with responsibility accounting?

7–3   Why are an organization's basic performance reports stated in terms of dollars?

7–4   Why does a production supervisor need more frequent performance measurements than the vice president of production?

7–5   Distinguish between investment and profit centers.

7–6   Why is a flexible budget rather than a static budget used to evaluate the financial performance of production departments?

7–7   Identify three alternative uses of standard costs.

7–8   What problems can result from the use of tight standards?

7–9   Distinguish between standard and discretionary cost centers.

7–10 Why are revenue center performance reports based on the original (static) budget?

7–11 How are the sales price and the sales volume variances computed?

7–12 Why are revenue centers often assigned responsibility for controllable costs?

7–13 Why is a sales department, when it is evaluated as a profit center, assigned responsibility for the standard variable cost of goods sold rather than the actual cost of goods sold?

7–14 How is the net sales volume variance computed?

7–15 Briefly describe two alternative approaches to reconciling the differences between budgeted and actual income.

EXERCISES

7–1 Developing a Flexible Budget

Complete the following flexible budget for each level of activity.

	Flexible Budget Formula	Annual Production (units)		
		10,000	15,000	20,000
Direct materials	$ 4.00/unit			
Direct labor	10.00/unit			
Variable overhead:				
Indirect materials	0.75/unit			
Equipment maintenance	0.10/unit			
Utilities	0.50/unit			
Overtime	0.05/unit			
Fringe benefits	4.00/unit			
Fixed overhead:				
Depreciation	$220,000/year			
Supervision	40,000/year			
Insurance	25,000/year			
Property taxes	28,000/year			
Building maintenance	35,000/year			
Total				

7–2 Developing a Flexible Budget

Complete the following flexible budget for each level of activity.

	Flexible Budget Formula	Monthly Pages Typed		
		20,000	30,000	40,000
Direct materials	$0.05/page			
Typist's fees	1.25/page			
Other variable costs:				
Indirect materials	0.02/page			
Pick-up & delivery	0.05/page			
Equipment maintenance	0.01/page			
Franchise fees	0.015/page			
Fixed costs:				
Supervision	$8,000/month			
Rent	5,000/month			
Advertising	3,000/month			
Insurance	1,500/month			
Telephone	800/month			
Electricity	750/month			
Total				

7–3 Flexible Budgets and Performance Evaluation

Presented is the January 19x1 performance report for the production department of the Thompson Company.

Thompson Company
Production Department Performance Report
For the month of January, 19x1

	Actual	Budget	Variance
Volume	30,000	28,000	
Manufacturing costs:			
Direct materials	$ 89,600	$ 84,000	$ 5,600 U
Direct labor	165,000	140,000	25,000 U
Variable overhead	64,000	56,000	8,000 U
Fixed overhead	27,500	28,000	500 F
Total	$346,100	$308,000	$38,100 U

Requirements

a) Evaluate the performance report.

b) Prepare a more appropriate performance report.

7–4 Flexible Budgets and Performance Reports

Presented is the March 19x3 performance report for the Finishing Department of the Maple Chair Company.

Maple Chair Company
Finishing Department Performance Report
For the month of March, 19x3

	Actual	Budget	Variance
Volume	16,000	20,000	
Manufacturing costs:			
Direct materials	$ 35,000	$ 40,000	$ 5,000 F
Direct labor	150,000	200,000	50,000 F
Variable overhead	73,000	100,000	27,000 F
Fixed overhead	13,000	12,000	1,000 U
Total	$271,000	$352,000	$81,000 F

Requirements

a) Evaluate the performance report.

b) Prepare a more appropriate performance report.

7–5 Sales Revenue Variances

The following information is available regarding a product sold by the Maxell Company.

	Actual	Budget
Unit selling price	$ 85	$ 80
Unit sales	× 5,000	× 6,000
Revenue	$425,000	$480,000

Required: Compute the sales price and the sales volume variances. Use these variances to reconcile the difference between budgeted and actual revenues.

7–6 Sales Revenue Variances

The following information is available regarding a product sold by the Jones Company.

	Actual	Budget
Unit selling price	$ 26	$ 30
Unit sales	× 11,000	× 8,000
Revenue	$286,000	$240,000

Required: Compute the sales price and the sales volume variances. Use these variances to reconcile the difference between budgeted and actual revenues.

7–7 Sales Revenue Variances

The sales revenues of the Beach Company for the years 19x7 and 19x8 were as follows:

	19x7	19x8
Sales	$500,000	$583,000

Selling prices were 6 percent higher during 19x8.

Required: Treating 19x7 as the standard, compute the sales price and the sales volume variances for 19x8. Use these variances to reconcile the difference between 19x7 and 19x8 revenues.

7–8 Sales Variances

Presented is information pertaining to an item sold by the Winding Creek General Store.

	Actual	Budget
Unit sales	150	125
Unit selling price	$ 26	$ 25
Unit standard variable costs	− 20	− 20
Unit contribution margin	$ 6	$ 5
Revenues	$3,900	$3,125
Standard variable costs	−3,000	−2,500
Contribution margin at standard costs	$ 900	$ 625

Requirements

a) Compute the sales price and the sales volume variances.

b) Use the variances computed in requirement (a) to reconcile the budgeted and the actual revenues.

c) Compute the net sales volume variance.

d) Use the sales price and the net sales volume variances to reconcile the difference between the budgeted and the actual contribution margin at standard costs.

7–9 Sales Variances

Presented is information pertaining to a product of the Blue Mountain Supply Company.

	Actual	Budget
Unit sales	550	800
Unit selling price	$ 10	$ 8
Unit standard variable costs	− 5	− 5
Unit contribution margin	$ 5	$ 3
Revenues	$5,500	$6,400
Standard variable costs	−2,750	−4,000
Contribution margin at standard costs	$2,750	$2,400

Requirements

a) Compute the sales price and the sales volume variances.

b) Use the variances computed in requirement (a) to reconcile the budgeted and the actual revenues.

c) Compute the net sales volume variance.

d) Use the sales price and the net sales volume variances to reconcile the difference between the budgeted and the actual contribution margin at standard costs.

7–10 Reconciling Budgeted and Actual Gross Profit

The Bommer Company is a merchandising firm that buys and sells a single product. Presented is information from Bommer's 19x4 and 19x3 income statements.

	19x4	19x3
Unit sales	220,000	250,000
Sales revenue	$770,000	$750,000
Cost of goods sold	−506,000	−500,000
Gross profit	$264,000	$250,000

Requirements

a) Reconcile the variation in sales revenue using appropriate sales variances. Treat 19x3 as the base or standard.

b) Reconcile the variation in gross profit using appropriate sales and cost variances. Treat 19x3 as the base or standard.

7–11 Reconciling Budgeted and Actual Gross Profit

Garfield Company is a merchandising firm that buys and sells a single product. Presented is information from Garfield's 19x8 and 19x7 income statements.

	19x8	19x7
Unit sales	150,000	180,000
Sales revenue	$750,000	$720,000
Cost of goods sold	−525,000	−576,000
Gross profit	$225,000	$144,000

Requirements

a) Reconcile the variation in sales revenue using appropriate sales variances. Treat 19x7 as the base or standard.

b) Reconcile the variation in gross profit using appropriate sales and cost variances. Treat 19x7 as the base or standard.

(CPA Adapted)

7–12 Profit Center Performance Reports

The Record Rack is a store that specializes in the sale of recordings of classical music. Due to a recent upsurge in the popularity of J. S. Bach's works, the Record Rack has established a separate room, Bach's Concert Room, dealing only in recordings of Bach's music. The albums are purchased from a wholesaler for $4.25 each. Though the standard retail price is $7.75 per album, the manager of Bach's Concert Room may undertake price reductions and other sales promotions in an attempt to increase sales volume. With the exception of the cost of albums, the operating costs of Bach's Concert Room are fixed.

Presented are the budgeted and the actual August 19x3 contribution statements of Bach's Concert Room.

Record Rack: Bach's Concert Room
Budgeted and Actual Contribution Statements
For the month of August, 19x3

	Actual	Budget
Unit sales	4,200	4,000
Unit selling price	$ 7.25	$ 7.75
Sales revenue	$30,450	$31,000
Cost of goods sold	−17,850	−17,000
Gross profit	$12,600	$14,000
Operating costs	− 5,000	− 6,000
Contribution to corporate costs and profits	$ 7,600	$ 8,000

Required: Compute variances to assist in evaluating the performance of Bach's Concert Room as a profit center. Use these variances to reconcile the budgeted and actual contribution to corporate costs and profits.

7–13 Profit Center Performance Reports

Dip-In Donuts produces donuts in a central Chicago bakery and ships them to Dip-In Donut Shops throughout the Chicago area. Each shop is evaluated as a profit center. The shops purchase the Dip-In Donuts from the bakery at $1.50 per dozen. The standard retail price is $3.00 per dozen; however, individual shop managers may issue coupons and undertake other promotions to increase sales volume. With the exception of the cost of donuts, each shop's operating costs are fixed.

Presented are the budgeted and the actual May 19x6 contribution statements of the Wicker Park Shop.

Dip-In Donuts: Wicker Park Shop
Budgeted and Actual Contribution Statements
For the month of May, 19x6

	Actual	Budget
Unit sales (dozen)	15,500	14,000
Unit selling price (dozen)	$ 2.80	$ 3.00
Sales revenue	$43,400	$42,000
Cost of food sold	−23,250	−21,000
Gross profit	$20,150	$21,000
Operating costs	−19,500	−17,000
Contribution to corporate costs and profits	$ 650	$ 4,000

Required: Compute variances to assist in evaluating the performance of the Wicker Park Shop as a profit center. Use these variances to reconcile the budgeted and actual contribution to corporate costs and profits.

7–14 Discretionary Cost Center Performance Reports

Buggywhip Products had been extremely profitable at the turn of the century, but the company had been "whipped" in recent years by tough competition and a failure to introduce new consumer products. In 19x2 Tom Bright became head of Consumer Product Research (CPR) and began a number of product development projects. Although the group had several good ideas that led to the introduction of several promising products at the start of 19x6, Mr. Bright was criticized for poor cost control. The financial performance reports for CPR under Mr. Bright's leadership were consistently unfavorable. Management was quite concerned about cost control because profits were low and the company's cash budget indicated that additional borrowing would be required throughout 19x6 to cover out-of-pocket costs.

Because of his inability to exert proper cost control, Mr. Bright was relieved of his responsibilities in 19x6 and John Tight became head of Consumer Product Research. Mr. Tight vowed to improve the performance of CPR and scaled back CPR's developmental activities to obtain favorable financial performance reports.

By the end of 19x7, Buggywhip Products had improved its market position, profitability, and cash position. At this time the Board of Directors promoted Mr. Tight to President, congratulating him for the contribution CPR made to the revitalization of the company as well as his success in improving the financial performance of CPR. Mr. Tight assured the Board that the company's financial performance would improve even more in the future as he applied the same cost reducing measures that had worked so well in CPR to the company as a whole.

Requirements

a) For the purpose of evaluating financial performance, classify the Consumer Products Research department as a responsibility center. What unique problems are associated with evaluating the financial performance of this type of responsibility center?

b) Compare the performances of Mr. Bright and Mr. Tight in their role as head of Consumer Product Research. Did Mr. Tight do a much better job, thereby making him deserving of the promotion? Why or why not?

7–15 Discretionary Cost Center Performance Reports

The budget for the Literature Department of Classic University is set by the Dean of the School of Arts in consultation with the Chairperson of the Literature Department. It is a line item budget with separate appropriations for such things as faculty salaries, secretarial support, travel, research, equipment, and instructional supplies. The budget for each year is a function of the budget for the previous year, with an adjustment for certain items that were funded at an excess or inadequate level during the previous year.

While the Chairperson of the Literature Department has done a good job in controlling most departmental costs, the Dean is concerned about the Chairperson's inability to keep instructional supplies in line with the budget. Prior to meeting with the Dean to discuss the 19x8 departmental budget, the Chairperson developed the following summary of the financial performance of the Literature Department in controlling the cost of instructional supplies.

Classic University
Literature Department Summary of Financial Performance
for Instructional Supplies
For the years 19x3–19x7

	Student Enrollment	Actual	Budget	Budget Variance
19x3	4,500	$15,500	$12,000	$3,500 U
19x4	6,000	20,000	13,750	6,250 U
19x5	5,250	17,750	16,875	875 U
19x6	6,300	20,900	16,438	4,462 U
19x7	5,500	18,500	18,669	169 F

Required: Comment on the financial performance of the Literature Department. What budgetary planning and control problem is illustrated by the above data?

PROBLEMS

7–16 Flexible Budget for Selling Expenses: Cost Estimation

Wielson Company employs flexible budgeting techniques to evaluate the performance of several of its activities. The selling expense flexible budgets for three representative monthly activity levels are shown as follows.

Wielson Company
Selling Expense Flexible Budget
For Representative Monthly Volumes

Activity measures:			
Unit sales volume	400,000	425,000	450,000
Dollar sales volume	$10,000,000	$10,625,000	$11,250,000
Number of orders	4,000	4,250	4,500
Number of sales personnel	75	75	75
Monthly expenses:			
Advertising & promotion	$1,200,000	$1,200,000	$1,200,000
Administrative salaries	57,000	57,000	57,000
Sales salaries	75,000	75,000	75,000
Sales commissions	200,000	212,500	225,000
Salesperson travel	170,000	175,000	180,000
Sales office expense	490,000	498,750	507,500
Shipping expense	675,000	712,500	750,000
Total	$2,867,000	$2,930,750	$2,994,500

The following assumptions were used to develop the budget:

■ The average size of Wielson's sales force during the year was planned to be 75 people.

■ Sales personnel are paid a monthly salary plus commission of gross dollar sales.

■ The travel costs are best characterized as step-variable costs. The fixed portion is related to the number of sales personnel, whereas the variable portion tends to fluctuate with gross dollar sales.

- Sales office expense is a mixed cost with the variable portion related to the number of orders processed.
- Shipping expense is a mixed cost with the variable portion related to the number of units sold.

A sales force of 80 persons generated a total of 4,300 orders, resulting in a sales volume of 420,000 units during November 19x9. The gross dollar sales amounted to $10.9 million. The selling expenses incurred for November were as follows.

Monthly expenses:	
Advertising & promotion	$1,350,000
Administrative salaries	57,000
Sales salaries	80,000
Sales commissions	218,000
Salesperson travel	185,000
Sales office expense	497,000
Shipping expense	730,000
Total	$3,117,000

Required: Prepare a selling expense performance report for November that Wielson Company can use to evaluate its control over selling expenses.

(CMA Adapted)

7–17 Multiple Product Flexible Budgets

Creative Products manufactures two models of cassette tape storage cases, Regular and Deluxe. Presented is standard cost information for each model:

	Regular		Deluxe	
Direct materials:				
Lumber	2 board feet × $3 =	$ 6.00	3 board feet × $3 =	$ 9.00
Assembly kit		2.00		2.00
Direct labor	1 hour × $4 =	4.00	1.25 hours × $4 =	5.00
Variable overhead	1 labor hour × $2 =	2.00	1.25 labor hours × $2 =	2.50
Total		$14.00		$18.50

Budgeted fixed factory overhead is $15,000 per month.

During July 19x1 Creative Products produced 5,000 regular and 3,000 deluxe storage cases while incurring the following manufacturing costs:

Direct materials	$ 80,000
Direct labor	34,000
Variable overhead	16,000
Fixed overhead	17,500
Total	$147,500

Required: Prepare a flexible budget performance report for July 19x1 manufacturing activities.

7–18 Multiple Product Flexible Budget

Cozy Hearth manufactures two models of glass fireplace doors, Cozy I and Cozy II. Presented is standard cost information for each model:

	Cozy I	Cozy II
Direct materials:		
Frame	$10.00	$15.00
Glass	8.00	20.00
Installation kit	5.00	7.00
Direct labor:		
Class A:		
Cozy I (0.5 hour × $5)	2.50	
Cozy II (0.75 hour × $5)		3.75
Class B:		
Cozy II (0.25 hour × $8)		2.00
Variable overhead:		
Cozy I (0.5 labor hour × $4)	2.00	
Cozy II (0.75 labor hour × $4)		3.00
Total	$27.50	$50.75

Budgeted fixed factory overhead is $30,000 per month.

During August 19x3 Cozy Hearth produced 1,000 Cozy I and 800 Cozy II glass fireplace doors while incurring the following manufacturing costs:

Direct materials	$ 60,200
Direct labor	8,100
Variable overhead	4,900
Fixed overhead	29,000
Total	$102,200

Required: Prepare a flexible budget performance report for August 19x3 manufacturing activities.

7–19 Reconciling Budgeted and Actual Income

JK Enterprises sold 550,000 units during the first quarter ended March 31, 19x1. These sales represented a 10 percent increase over the number of units budgeted for the quarter. In spite of the sales increase, profits were below budget, as is shown in the condensed income statement presented at the top of the next page.

The Accounting Department always prepares a brief analysis to explain the difference between budgeted net income and actual net income. This analysis, which has not yet been completed for the first quarter, is submitted to top management with the income statement.

JK Enterprises
Income Statement
For the first quarter ended March 31, 19x1

	Budget	Actual
Sales	$2,500,000	$2,530,000
Variable expenses:		
Cost of goods sold	$1,475,000	$1,540,000
Selling	400,000	440,000
Total variable expenses	−1,875,000	−1,980,000
Contribution margin	$ 625,000	$ 550,000
Fixed expenses:		
Selling	$ 125,000	$ 150,000
Administration	275,000	300,000
Total fixed expenses	− 400,000	− 450,000
Income before taxes	$ 225,000	$ 100,000
Income taxes (40 percent)	− 90,000	− 40,000
Net income	$ 135,000	$ 60,000

Required: Prepare an explanation of the $125,000 unfavorable variance between the first quarter budgeted and actual before-tax income for JK Enterprises by calculating a single amount for each of the following:

1. Sales price variance.

2. Variable cost variance.

3. Net sales volume variance.

4. Fixed cost variance.   (CMA Adapted)

7–20 Reconciling Budgeted and Actual Income

Presented are the budgeted and actual contribution income statements of Queen's Encyclopedia, Limited, for October 19x8.

Queen's Encyclopedia, Limited
Budgeted Contribution Income Statement
For the month of October, 19x8

Sales (900 × $300)			$270,000
Less variable costs:			
Variable cost of goods sold:			
Direct materials (900 × $50)	$45,000		
Direct labor (900 × $20)	18,000		
Factory overhead (900 × $30)	27,000	$ 90,000	
Selling (900 × $70)		63,000	−153,000
Contribution margin			$117,000
Less fixed costs:			
Factory overhead		$ 40,000	
Selling		50,000	
Administration		10,500	−100,500
Net income			$ 16,500

Queen's Encyclopedia, Limited
Actual Contribution Income Statement
For the month of October, 19x8

Sales (1,000 × $320)			$320,000
Less variable costs:			
Cost of goods sold:			
Direct materials	$50,000		
Direct labor	22,000		
Factory overhead	35,000	$107,000	
Selling		100,000	−207,000
Contribution margin			$113,000
Less fixed costs:			
Factory overhead		$ 38,000	
Selling		65,000	
Administration		12,000	−115,000
Net income (loss)			$ (2,000)

Queen's Encyclopedia contains three responsibility centers: a Production Department, a Sales Department, and an Administration Department. The Production and Administration Departments are cost centers, and the Sales Department is a profit center.

Requirements

a) Prepare a performance report for the Production Department that compares actual and allowed costs.

b) Prepare a performance report for selling expenses that compares actual and allowed costs.

c) Determine the sales price and the net sales volume variances.

d) Prepare a report that summarizes the performance of the Sales Department.

e) Determine the amount by which the Administration Department was over or under budget.

f) Prepare a report reconciling budgeted and actual net income. Your report should focus on the performance of each responsibility center.

7–21 Reconciling Budgeted and Actual Income

The budgeted and the actual income statements of Queen's Encyclopedia, Limited, for October 19x8 are presented in Problem 7–20.

Required: Prepare a detailed reconciliation of actual and budgeted costs, revenues, and income for the organization as a whole.

7–22 Reconciling Budgeted and Actual Income

Presented are the budgeted and the actual income statements of the Jones Valve Company, for the year ended December 31, 19x2.

Jones Valve Company
Budgeted and Actual Income Statements
For the year ending December 31, 19x2

	Budget	Actual
Unit sales	20,000	18,000
Unit selling price	$ 18	$ 21
Sales	$360,000	$378,000
Less variable costs:		
Direct materials ($2 per unit standard)	$ 40,000	$ 45,000
Direct labor ($3 per unit standard)	60,000	54,000
Factory overhead ($3 per unit standard)	60,000	50,400
Selling ($1 per unit standard)	20,000	20,000
Total	−180,000	−169,400
Contribution margin	$180,000	$208,600
Less fixed costs:		
Factory overhead	$ 55,000	$ 56,000
Selling	60,000	54,000
Administration	40,000	47,500
Total	−155,000	−157,500
Net income	$ 25,000	$ 51,100

The Jones Valve Company contains three responsibility centers: a Production Department, a Sales Department, and an Administration Department. The Production and Administration Departments are cost centers, and the Sales Department is a profit center.

Requirements

a) Prepare a performance report for the Production Department that compares actual and allowed costs.

b) Prepare a performance report for selling expenses that compares actual and allowed costs.

c) Determine the sales price and the net sales volume variances.

d) Prepare a report that summarizes the performance of the Sales Department.

e) Determine the amount by which the Administration Department was over or under budget.

f) Prepare a report reconciling budgeted and actual net income. Your report should focus on the performance of each responsibility center.

7–23 Reconciling Budgeted and Actual Income

The budgeted and the actual income statements of the Jones Valve Company, for the year ended December 31, 19x2, are presented in Problem 7–22.

Required: Prepare a detailed reconciliation of actual and budgeted costs, revenues, and income for the organization as a whole.

7–24 Evaluating a Sales Compensation Plan

Prior to 19x3 the Carbon Chemical Company paid its sales representatives a straight salary plus selling expenses. In an attempt to better motivate them, the company changed their basis of compensation from salary to commissions based on gross sales. The commission rate was computed as 19x2 sales salaries divided by 19x2 gross sales revenues.

Early in 19x4 Martha Childs, the company President, was reviewing Carbon Chemical's 19x3 performance, as compared to its 19x2 performance. She is concerned that the commissions are not motivating the sales representatives to work in the company's best interest, and she wants your advice.

Presented is comparative 19x2 and 19x3 information.

	19x2	19x3
Gross sales	$648,000	$934,000
Less sales returns and allowances	− 8,000	− 34,000
Net sales	$640,000	$900,000
Variable costs:		
Cost of goods sold	$388,800	$560,400
Commissions	—	74,720
Total	−388,800	−635,120
Contribution margin	$251,200	$264,880
Fixed costs:		
Sales salaries	$ 51,840	$ —
Other selling	20,000	55,000
Administration	80,000	90,000
Total	−151,840	−145,000
Net income	$ 99,360	$119,880

Required: Evaluate the sales compensation plan, and suggest some alternative plans that might better motivate the sales representatives to work in the company's interest.

7–25 Evaluating a Companywide Performance Report

Mr. Micawber, the production supervisor, bursts into your office carrying the Crupp Company's 19x2 performance report:

> *There is villainy here, sir! And I shall get to the bottom of it. I will not stop searching until I have found the answer! Why is Mr. Heep so down on my department? I thought we did a good job last year. But Heep claims I and my production people cost the company $31,500! I plead with you, sir, explain this performance report to me.*

Trying to calm Mr. Micawber, you take the report from him and ask to be left alone for 15 minutes. The report is presented at the top of the next page.

Crupp Company, Limited
Performance Report
For the year 19x2

	Actual	Budget	Variance
Unit sales	7,500	5,000	
Sales	$262,500	$225,000	$37,500 F
Less manufacturing costs:			
Direct materials	$ 55,500	$ 47,500	$ 8,000 U
Direct labor	48,000	32,500	15,500 U
Factory overhead	40,000	32,000*	8,000 U
Total	−143,500	−112,000	−31,500 U
Gross profit	$119,000	$113,000	$ 6,000 F
Less selling and administrative expenses:			
Selling (all fixed)	$ 60,000	$ 40,000	$20,000 U
Administrative (all fixed)	55,000	50,000	5,000 U
Total	−115,000	− 90,000	−25,000 U
Net income	$ 4,000	$ 23,000	$19,000 U
Performance summary:			
Budgeted net income			$23,000
Sales department variances:			
Sales revenue	$ 37,500 F		
Selling expenses	20,000 U	$ 17,500 F	
Administration department variances		5,000 U	
Production department variances		31,500 U	19,000 U
Actual net income			$ 4,000

* Includes fixed factory overhead of $22,000.

Requirements

a) Evaluate the performance report. Is Mr. Heep correct? Or, is there "villainy here"?

b) Assume that the Sales Department is a profit center and that the Production and Administration Departments are cost centers. Determine the responsibility of each for cost, revenue, and income variances, and prepare a report reconciling budgeted and actual net income. Your report should focus on the performance of each responsibility center.

7–26 Evaluating Companywide Performance: The Case of Multiple Profit Centers

Computeraid produces a variety of computer accessories. To improve financial incentives, the Production Department and the Sales Department are both treated as profit centers, with all goods produced in the Production Department being "sold" to the Sales Department at 150 percent of variable cost. The costs of the Administrative Department are allocated equally to the Production and Sales Departments. Presented at the top of the next page are performance reports prepared for the Production and Sales Departments for the year 19x8.

Computeraid
Production Department Performance Report
For the year 19x8

	Actual	Budget	Variance
Unit sales	10,000	7,000	
Sales revenue	$241,500	$147,000	
Less variable manufacturing costs:			
Direct materials	$ 69,000	$ 35,000	
Direct labor	32,000	21,000	
Factory overhead	60,000	42,000	
Total	−161,000	− 98,000	
Contribution margin	$ 80,500	$ 49,000	
Less fixed costs:			
Factory overhead	$ 24,000	$ 25,000	
Administration	15,000	10,000	
Total	− 39,000	− 35,000	
Manufacturing profit	$ 41,500	$ 14,000	$27,500 F

Computeraid
Sales Department Performance Report
For the year 19x8

	Actual	Budget	Variance
Unit sales	10,000	7,000	
Sales revenue	$310,000	$217,000	
Less variable costs:			
Cost of goods sold	$241,500	$147,000	
Selling & distribution	50,000	35,000	
Total	−291,500	−182,000	
Contribution margin	$ 18,500	$ 35,000	
Less fixed costs:			
Selling & distribution	$ 8,000	$ 8,000	
Administration	15,000	10,000	
Total	− 23,000	− 18,000	
Selling profit (loss)	$ (4,500)	$ 17,000	$21,500 U

Management congratulated the Production Department supervisor for another outstanding performance and offered him a raise. The manager of the Sales Department, on the other hand, was called to a special meeting of the Board of Directors and told that unless she provided an adequate explanation of her department's performance, she would be terminated.

Required: Extremely concerned about her future with the organization, the manager of the Sales Department has asked you to (1) evaluate the 19x8 performance reports and (2) assist in preparing revised 19x8 performance reports for each department and Computeraid as a whole.

CASES

7–27 Evaluating Cost Center Performance Reports

Berwin Inc. is a manufacturer of small industrial tools with an annual sales volume of approximately $3.5 million. Sales growth has been steady during the year, and there is no evidence of cyclical demand. Production has increased gradually during the year and has been distributed evenly throughout each month. The company employs a sequential processing system with all production activities located in the same building. Fixed manufacturing overhead is applied to all products using a single rate.

Berwin has always been able to compete with other manufacturers of small industrial tools. However, its market has expanded only in response to product innovations. Thus, research and development is very important and has helped Berwin to expand as well as maintain demand.

Carl Viller, Controller, has designed and implemented a new budget system in response to concerns voiced by George Berwin, President. An annual budget that has been divided into 12 equal segments has been prepared to assist in the timely evaluation of monthly performance. Berwin was visibly upset upon receiving the May performance report for the Machining Department (reproduced below). Berwin exclaimed, "How can they be efficient enough to produce nine extra units every working day and still miss the budget by $300 a day?" Gene Jordan, Machining Department supervisor, could not understand "all the red ink" when he knew the department had operated more efficiently in May than it had in the preceding months. Jordan stated, "I was expecting a pat on the back and instead the boss tore me apart. What's more, I don't even know why!"

Berwin Inc.
Machining Department Performance Report
For the month ended May 31, 19x4

	Budget	Actual	(Over) Under Budget
Volume in units	3,000	3,180	(180)
Variable manufacturing costs:			
Direct materials	$24,000	$ 24,843	$ (843)
Direct labor	27,750	29,302	(1,552)
Factory overhead	33,300	35,035	(1,735)
Total	$85,050	$ 89,180	$(4,130)
Fixed manufacturing overhead:			
Indirect labor	$ 3,300	$ 3,334	$ (34)
Depreciation	1,500	1,500	
Taxes	300	300	
Insurance	240	240	
Other	930	1,027	(97)
Total	$ 6,270	$ 6,401	$ (131)
Corporate overhead:			
Research & development	$ 2,400	$ 3,728	$(1,328)
Selling & administration	3,600	4,075	(475)
Total	$ 6,000	$ 7,803	$(1,803)
Total costs assigned to department	$97,320	$103,384	$(6,064)

Requirements

a) Review the May performance report for the Machining Department. Based on the information presented in the report:

   1. Discuss the strengths of the new budget system in general.

   2. Identify the weaknesses of the performance report and explain how the report should be revised to eliminate each weakness.

b) Prepare a revised May performance report for the Machining Department.

(CMA Adapted)

7–28 Evaluating Cost Center Performance Reports with Behavioral Implications

Denny Daniels is Production Manager of the Alumalloy Division of WRT Inc. Alumalloy has limited contact with outside customers and has no sales staff. Most of its customers are other divisions of WRT. All sales and purchases with outside customers are handled by other corporate divisions. Therefore, Alumalloy is treated as a cost center for reporting and evaluation purposes rather than as a revenue or profit center.

Daniels perceives accounting as an historical number generating process that provides little useful information for conducting his job. Consequently, the entire accounting process is regarded as a negative motivational device that does not reflect how hard or how effectively he works as a production manager. Daniels tried to discuss these perceptions and concerns with John Scott, the Controller for the Alumalloy Division. Daniels told Scott, "I think the cost report is misleading. I know I've had better production over a number of operating periods, but the cost report still says I have excessive costs. Look, I'm not an accountant, I'm a production manager. I know how to get a good quality product out. Over a number of years, I've even cut the raw materials used to do it. But the cost report doesn't show any of this. Basically, it's always negative, no matter what I do. There's no way you can win with accounting or the people at corporate headquarters who use those reports."

Scott gave Daniels little consolation. The accounting system and the cost reports generated by headquarters, Scott stated, are just part of the corporate game and almost impossible for an individual to change. "Although these accounting reports are pretty much the basis for evaluating the efficiency of your division and the means corporate management uses to determine whether you have done the job they want, you shouldn't worry too much. You haven't been fired yet! Besides, these cost reports have been used by WRT for the last twenty-five years."

Daniels perceived from talking to the production manager of the Zinc Division that most of what Scott said was probably true. However, some minor cost reporting changes for Zinc had been agreed to by corporate headquarters. He also knew from the trade grapevine that the turnover of production managers was considered high at WRT, even though relatively few were fired. Most seemed to end up quitting, usually in disgust, because of beliefs that they were not being evaluated fairly. Typical comments of production managers who have left WRT are:

■ "Corporate headquarters doesn't really listen to us. All they consider are those misleading cost reports. They don't want them changed, and they don't want any supplemental information."

■ "The accountants may be quick with numbers, but they don't know anything about production. As it was, I either had to ignore the cost reports entirely or pretend they are important even though they didn't tell how good a job I had done. No matter what they say about not firing people, negative reports mean negative evaluations. I'm better off working for another company."

A recent copy of the cost report prepared by corporate headquarters for the Alumalloy Division is shown below. Daniels does not like this report because he believes it fails to reflect the division's operations properly, thereby resulting in an unfair evaluation of performance.

**Alumalloy Division
Cost Report
For the month of April, 19x0**

	Original Budget	Actual Cost	Excess Cost
Aluminum	$ 400,000	$ 437,000	$37,000
Labor	560,000	540,000	
Overhead	100,000	134,000	34,000
Total	$1,060,000	$1,111,000	

Requirements

a) Comment on Denny Daniels' perceptions of John Scott, the Controller; corporate headquarters; the cost report; and himself as a Production Manager. Discuss how his perceptions affect his behavior and probable performance as a production manager and employee of WRT.

b) Identify and explain three changes that could be made in the cost information presented to the production managers that would make the information more meaningful and less threatening to them.

(CMA Adapted)

7–29 Evaluating a Sales Compensation Plan

Betterbuilt Corporation manufactures a full line of windows and doors, including casement windows, bow windows, and patio doors. The bow windows and patio doors have a significantly higher gross profit per unit than casement windows, as is shown in the following schedule.

	Unit Price and Cost Data		
	Casement Windows	Bow Windows	Patio Doors
Sales price	$130	$250	$260
Manufacturing costs:			
Direct materials	$ 25	$ 40	$ 50
Direct labor	20	35	30
Variable overhead*	16	28	24
Fixed overhead†	24	42	36
Total manufacturing costs	− 85	−145	−140
Gross profit	$ 45	$105	$120

* Variable manufacturing overhead is applied at the rate of 80 percent of direct labor cost.

† Fixed manufacturing overhead is applied at the rate of 120 percent of direct labor cost.

The company sells almost entirely to general contractors of residential housing. Most of these contractors complete and sell fifteen to fifty houses per year. Each contractor builds tract houses that are similar, with some variations in exteriors and rooflines.

When contractors contact Betterbuilt, they are likely to seek bids for all the windows in the houses they plan to build in the next year. At this point, the Betterbuilt salespeople have an opportunity to influence the window configuration of these houses by suggesting patio doors or bow windows as variations for one or more casement windows for each of the several exteriors and rooflines built by the contractor.

The bow windows and patio doors are approximately twice as wide as the casement windows. A bow window or a patio door usually is substituted for two casement windows. Casement windows are usually ordered in pairs and placed side-by-side in those houses that could be modified to accept bow windows and patio doors.

Joseph Hite, President of Betterbuilt Corporation, is perplexed with the company's profit performance. In a conversation with his sales manager he declared, "Our total dollars sales volume is growing, but our net income has not increased as it should. Our unit sales of casement windows have increased proportionately more than the sale of bow windows or patio doors. Why aren't our salespeople pushing our more profitable products?" The sales manager responded with a sense of frustration, "I don't know what else can be done. The salespeople have been told which type of windows we want sold because of the greater profit margin. Furthermore, they have the best compensation plan in the industry, with $500 monthly draw against their commissions of 10 percent on sales dollars."

Requirements

a) Explain why Betterbuilt's present compensation program for its salespeople does not support the President's objectives to sell the more profitable units.

b) Identify and explain alternative compensation program(s) that may be more appropriate for motivating Betterbuilt Corporation's salespeople to sell the more profitable units.

(CMA Adapted)

7–30 Evaluating Alternative Sales Compensation Plans

Pre-Fab Corporation, a relatively large company in the manufactured housing industry, is known for its aggressive sales promotion campaigns. Pre-Fab's innovative advertising and sales strategies have resulted in generally satisfactory performance in the last few years.

One of Pre-Fab's objectives is to increase sales revenue by at least 10 percent annually. This objective has been attained. Return on investment is considered good and had increased annually until last year when net income decreased for the first time in nine years. The latest economic recession could be the cause of the change, but other factors, such as sales growth, discount this reason.

A significant portion of Pre-Fab's administrative expenses are fixed, but the majority of the manufacturing expenses are variable in nature. The increases in selling prices have been consistent with the 12 percent increase in manufacturing expenses. Pre-Fab has consistently been able to maintain a companywide contribution margin of approximately 30 percent. However, the contribution margin on individual product lines varies from 15 to 45 percent.

Sales commission expenses increased 30 percent over the past year. The prefabricated housing industry has always been sales oriented and Pre-Fab's management has believed in generously rewarding the efforts of its sales personnel. The sales force compensation plan consists of three segments:

- A guaranteed annual salary, which is increased annually at about a 6 percent rate. The salary is below industry average.

- A sales commission of 9 percent of total sales dollars. This is higher than the industry average.

- A year-end bonus of 5 percent of total sales dollars to each salesperson when their total sales dollars exceed the prior year by at least 12 percent.

The current compensation plan has resulted in an average annual income of $42,500 per sales employee, compared with an industry annual average of $30,000. However, the compensation plan has been effective in generating increased sales. Further, the sales department employees are satisfied with the plan. Management, however, is concerned about the financial implications of the current plan. They believe the plan has caused higher selling expenses and a lower net income relative to the sales revenue increase.

At the last staff meeting, the Controller suggested that the sales compensation plan be modified so that sales employees could earn an annual average income of $37,500. The Controller believed that such a plan still would be attractive to its sales personnel and, at the same time, allow the company to earn a more satisfactory profit.

The Vice President for sales voiced strong objection to altering the current compensation plan because employee morale and incentive would drop significantly if there were any change. Nevertheless, most of the staff believed that the area of sales compensation merited a review. The President stated that all phases of a company operation can benefit from a periodic review, no matter how successful they have been in the past.

Several compensation plans known to be used by other companies in the manufactured housing industry are:

- Straight commission as a percentage of sales.
- Straight salary.
- Salary plus compensation based on sales to new customers.
- Salary plus compensation based on contribution margin.
- Salary plus compensation based on unit sales volume.

Requirements

a) Discuss the advantages and disadvantages of Pre-Fab Corporation's current sales compensation plan with respect to (1) the financial aspects of the company and (2) the behavioral aspects of the sales personnel.

b) For each of the alternative compensation plans known to be used by other companies in the manufactured housing industry, discuss whether the plan would be an improvement over the current plan in terms of (1) the financial performance of the company and (2) the behavioral implications for the sales personnel.

(CMA Adapted)

REVIEW PROBLEM
SOLUTION

a) **Well Read Publishing Company**
    Production Department Performance Report
    For the month of April, 19x7

	Flexible Budget Formula	Actual	Flexible Budget	Flexible Budget Variance
Volume		21,000	21,000	
Manufacturing costs:				
Direct materials	$0.75/unit	$15,750	$15,750	$ -0-
Direct labor	1.25/unit	25,000	26,250	1,250 F
Variable overhead	1.50/unit	32,500	31,500	1,000 U
Fixed overhead	$20,000/month	17,500	20,000	2,500 F
Total		$90,750	$93,500	$2,750 F

b) **Well Read Publishing Company**
    Selling Expenses Performance Report for Costs
    For the month of April, 19x7

	Flexible Budget Formula	Actual	Flexible Budget	Flexible Budget Variance
Volume		21,000	21,000	
Selling expenses:				
Variable	$2.50/unit	$56,000	$52,500	$3,500 U
Fixed	$15,000/month	16,000	15,000	1,000 U
Total		$72,000	$67,500	$4,500 U

c)
Budgeted selling price		$8.50
Standard variable costs:		
Direct materials	$0.75	
Direct labor	1.25	
Factory overhead	1.50	
Selling	2.50	−6.00
Budgeted unit contribution margin		$2.50

Sales price variance = ($9.00 − $8.50) × 21,000 = $10,500 F

Net sales volume variance = (21,000 − 22,000) × $2.50 = $2,500 U

d) **Well Read Publishing Company**
    Sales Department Performance Report
    For the month of April, 19x7

Sales price variance	$10,500 F
Net sales volume variance	2,500 U
Selling expense variances	4,500 U
Net sales department variances	$ 3,500 F

e) Administrative department variance:

$12,000 actual − $10,000 budget = $2,000 U (over budget)

---

f) **Well Read Publishing Company**
Reconciliation of Budgeted and Actual Net Income
For the month of April, 19x7

Budgeted net income		$10,000
Sales department variances	$3,500 F	
Production department variances	2,750 F	
Administrative department variances	2,000 U	4,250 F
Actual net income		$14,250

---

g)

Well Read Publishing Company
Reconciliation of Budgeted and Actual Income
For the month of April, 19x7

	(1) Actual Volume at Actual Selling Prices and Actual Costs (Actual results)	(2) Cost Variances	(3) Actual Volume at Actual Selling Prices and Standard Costs	(4) Sales Price Variance	(5) Actual Volume at Budgeted Selling Prices and Standard Costs (Flexible budget)	(6) Net Sales Volume Variance	(7) Budgeted Volume at Budgeted Selling Prices and Standard Costs (Original budget)
Volume (units)	21,000		21,000		21,000	1,000	22,000
Sales	$189,000		$189,000	$10,500 F	$178,500	$8,500	$187,000
Less variable costs:							
Direct materials	$ 15,750	$ 0	$ 15,750		$ 15,750	$ 750	$ 16,500
Direct labor	25,000	1,250 F	26,250		26,250	1,250	27,500
Factory overhead	32,500	1,000 U	31,500		31,500	1,500	33,000
Selling	56,000	3,500 U	52,500		52,500	2,500	55,000
Total	−129,250		−126,000		−126,000	−6,000	−132,000
Contribution margin	$ 59,750		$ 63,000		$ 52,500	$2,500 U	$ 55,000
Less fixed costs:							
Factory overhead	$ 17,500	2,500 F	$ 20,000		$ 20,000		$ 20,000
Selling	16,000	1,000 U	15,000		15,000		15,000
Administration	12,000	2,000 U	10,000		10,000		10,000
Total	− 45,500		− 45,000		− 45,000		− 45,000
Net income	$ 14,250	$3,750 U	$ 18,000	$10,500 F	$ 7,500	$2,500 U	$ 10,000

C H A P T E R 8

Performance Evaluation of Standard Cost Centers

Learning Objectives

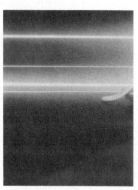

Upon completion of this chapter you should:

- Be familiar with the relationship between flexible budgeting and standard cost variance analysis.

- Understand the general model for analyzing variances between actual and flexible budget costs.

- Be able to apply the general variance analysis model to compute the following variable cost variances: materials price, materials quantity, labor rate, labor efficiency, variable overhead spending, and variable overhead efficiency.

- Know possible causes of favorable and unfavorable variances for each of the variances identified above.

- Understand why the total flexible budget variance for fixed overhead is usually not broken down into price and quantity variances for financial control purposes.

- Be able to identify major benefits and applications of standard cost variance analysis.

In Chapter 7 two types of cost centers were introduced, standard cost centers and discretionary cost centers. This chapter discusses standard cost centers in greater depth. You recall that standard cost centers are cost centers that have clearly defined relationships between effort (inputs) and accomplishment (outputs) that can be expressed in terms of standard costs per unit produced. These unit standards provide the basis for the budget formula used to prepare each period's flexible budget for the firm's actual production output. Manager performance, then, is evaluated by comparing actual costs incurred with flexible budget costs. Because of their role in determining flexible budget costs, standard costs are the basis for evaluating managers in standard cost centers.

The purpose of this chapter is to discuss how standard costs are established for direct materials, direct labor, and variable factory overhead,[1] and to show how they are used in evaluating standard cost centers. To use and interpret standard cost variances properly, it is essential for managers to understand both the standard-setting process and the framework for computing and analyzing standard cost variances. In this chapter we focus on these aspects of standard cost planning and control systems.

BASIC VARIANCE ANALYSIS CONCEPTS

Standard cost variance analysis provides a system for examining the flexible budget variance, which is the difference between the *actual cost* and *flexible budget cost* of producing a given quantity of product or service. Flexible budget cost is computed as actual output times standard unit cost. Recall from Chapter 7 that standard unit cost represents what it should cost to produce a completed unit of product or service under efficient operating conditions. To determine standard unit cost, management establishes separate quantity and price (or rate) standards for each production component (materials, labor, and overhead). For example, the standard direct materials cost of manufacturing neckties might be $5 per necktie, consisting of $\frac{1}{3}$ yard standard quantity of fabric at a standard price of $15 per yard.

For the following general discussion of standard cost variance analysis, assume Wonderful Widgets, Inc., set its total standard cost of manufacturing widgets at $10 each. The company produced 250 widgets in July at an actual cost of $2,805; therefore, the total flexible budget variance was $305:

Actual cost to produce 250 widgets	$2,805
Less: Flexible budget cost for 250 widgets at $10 each	−2,500
Total flexible budget variance	$ 305 U

---

[1] Standard unit costs ordinarily are not calculated for fixed factory overhead costs for performance evaluation purposes because these costs are incurred based on production capacity provided, not production capacity used. Accordingly, they are not controlled on a per unit of production basis.

Since actual cost exceeded flexible budget cost, the variance was unfavorable (U).

Actual cost is based on actual *inputs*, and flexible budget cost is based on completed *outputs*. Actual cost is determined by multiplying actual quantities of materials, labor, and overhead inputs used in producing goods and services times the actual prices paid for the inputs. Flexible budget cost is determined by multiplying standard input quantities allowed for materials, labor, and overhead times the standard price per input unit. Standard cost variance analysis identifies the general causes for the total flexible budget variance by breaking it down into separate price and quantity variances for each production component. Two possible reasons why actual cost may differ from flexible budget cost for a given amount of output produced are: (1) there was a difference between the actual quantity and the standard quantity allowed for the production components and (2) there was a difference between actual and standard prices paid for the production components.

To simplify the Wonderful Widgets illustration, assume that widgets are manufactured from a single production component, called MLO, which contains

MANAGERIAL PRACTICE 8.1

Up-Front Standard Cost
Variance Analysis at IBM

In recent years, IBM has begun moving toward a standard cost system. Although not a total standard cost system, as might be found in an accounting text, it is a simple system that computes standard-to-actual variances up front to simplify the accounting process. These changes were made because the accounting department was always late with the actual costs. Sometimes products were shipped out before vendors had submitted their invoices, so accounting was not solely to blame. In a just-in-time (JIT) inventory environment with high-volume purchases, a vendor might be billing monthly but delivering daily, and you in turn might be shipping finished goods daily. Therefore, up-front costs are necessary in order to price finished goods as they are shipped. With standard costing, you don't have to wait until after the end of the production process to determine the cost and price of products. If the production process is in control, the standard costs will yield approximately the same results as actual costs.

Source: Robert H. Kelder, "Era of Cost Accounting Changes," in *Cost Accounting, Robotics, and the New Manufacturing Environment*, ed. Robert Capettini and Donald K. Clancy (Sarasota, Fla.: American Accounting Association, 1987): 3.24.

all the normal elements of production—Materials, Labor, and Overhead. The actual cost of $2,805 (for the 250 widgets produced) consisted of 510 input units of MLO purchased at a price of $5.50 each. Also, assume the standards allow the use of two units of MLO, purchased at a standard price of $5, for each widget manufactured.

The following model shows the calculation of the total flexible budget variance using detailed quantity and price information for actual and flexible budget costs:

Flexible budget variance analysis		

Input component: MLO		Output: 250 widgets	
Actual cost		**Flexible budget cost**	
Actual quantity	510	Standard quantity allowed	500*
Actual price	× $5.50	Standard price	× $5
Total	$2,805.00	Total	$2,500

Total flexible budget variance $305 U

*250 widgets × 2 units of MLO

Careful comparisons of actual quantity with standard quantity allowed and of actual price with standard price indicate that Wonderful Widgets had two variances in July that contributed to the total $305 unfavorable variance. They had a "quantity" variance that resulted from actually using 510 units of MLO instead of the standard quantity allowed of 500 units (two per widget). Also, they had a "price" variance that resulted from actually paying $5.50 for each unit of MLO, when the standard price was only $5. Therefore, the $305 unfavorable total flexible budget variance is explained by (1) the excess use of ten units of MLO and (2) the excess payment of 50 cents for each unit of MLO used during the period.

The graphs in Exhibit 8–1 show how quantity and price factors interrelate to produce total cost. Exhibit 8–1(a) shows the area representing total actual cost of MLO used in making 250 widgets, calculated by multiplying the actual quantity of MLO used (510 units) times the actual price paid for MLO ($5.50). Exhibit 8–1(b) shows the area representing total flexible budget cost for 250 widgets, calculated by multiplying the standard quantity allowed for MLO (500 units) times the standard price for MLO ($5). When both *actual* cost and *flexible budget* cost are shown on the same graph (see Exhibit 8–1(c)), the $305 total variance between the actual cost and flexible budget cost of producing 250 widgets can be observed as being related to the difference between actual quantity and standard quantity allowed for MLO (510 units versus 500 units) and the difference between actual price and standard price paid for MLO ($5.50 versus $5).

EXHIBIT 8–1   Graphic Illustrations of Actual Costs, Standard Costs, and Basic Variances

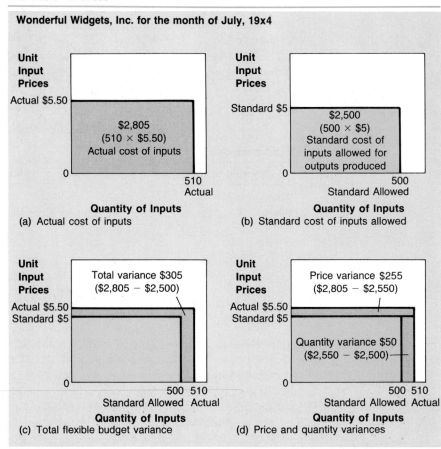

Wonderful Widgets, Inc. for the month of July, 19x4

(a) Actual cost of inputs

$2,805
(510 × $5.50)
Actual cost of inputs

(b) Standard cost of inputs allowed

$2,500
(500 × $5)
Standard cost of inputs allowed for outputs produced

(c) Total flexible budget variance

Total variance $305
($2,805 − $2,500)

(d) Price and quantity variances

Price variance $255
($2,805 − $2,550)

Quantity variance $50
($2,550 − $2,500)

To separate the $305 total flexible budget variance into detailed variances for price and quantity factors, a third value for production costs must be introduced; the standard cost of inputs, calculated as the actual quantity of inputs times the standard price per unit of input. We now have the following three possible production costs:

1. Actual cost
2. Standard cost of actual inputs
3. Flexible budget cost

Information about the standard cost of actual inputs enables the company to separately evaluate management's effectiveness in controlling both the prices paid for production inputs and the quantities of production inputs used. In our example, the standard cost of actual MLO inputs is $2,550, or 510 units times $5. The three costs calculated for Wonderful Widgets' production of 250 widgets, and the resulting standard cost variances, are summarized as follows:

	Quantity		Price		Total	
Actual cost	510 (actual)	×	$5.50 (actual)	=	$2,805	} $255 difference equals price variance
Standard cost of actual inputs	510 (actual)	×	$5.00 (standard)	=	$2,550	
Flexible budget cost	500* (standard)	×	$5.00 (standard)	=	$2,500	} $50 difference equals quantity variance

* (250 widgets × 2 units of MLO allowed per widget)

Note that in calculating the costs for determining the price variance, the quantity amounts are the same (actual/actual), but the prices are different (actual/standard); whereas, in calculating the costs for determining the quantity variance, the prices are the same (standard/standard), but the quantity amounts are different (actual/standard).

Wonderful Widgets actually paid $2,805 (or $5.50 per unit) for the 510 units of MLO used during the period; however, if management had paid the standard price of $5 for each unit of MLO used, the total amount spent for MLO would have been $2,550. Consequently, the $255 difference between actual cost and the standard cost of actual inputs represents the **price variance.** The price variance may also be calculated as the actual quantity used (AQ) times the difference between the actual price (AP) and standard price (SP):

$$\text{Price variance} = AQ(AP - SP)$$
$$= 510(\$5.50 - \$5)$$
$$= \$255 \text{ U.}$$

In Exhibit 8–1(d), the price variance is the horizontal portion of the total flexible budget variance area.

Using the standard cost of actual inputs, we can also determine the portion of the total flexible budget variance attributable to the quantity factor. Based on its standards, Wonderful Widgets allowed 2 units of MLO per widget completed, or 500 units of MLO, to complete 250 widgets. Instead, 510 units of MLO were used, representing 10 more units of MLO than the standards allowed. Even if the standard price of $5 had been paid for the actual units of MLO used, total actual cost would have exceeded total flexible budget cost by $50, or by the 10 excess units used times the $5 standard unit cost. This $50 difference between the standard cost of actual inputs ($2,550) and the flexible budget cost ($2,500) represents the **quantity variance.** The quantity variance may also be calculated as the standard price (SP) times the difference between the actual quantity (AQ) and standard quantity allowed (SQ):

$$\begin{aligned} \text{Quantity variance} &= \text{SP(AQ} - \text{SQ)} \\ &= \$5(510 - 500) \\ &= \$50 \text{ U.} \end{aligned}$$

In Exhibit 8–1(d), the quantity variance is represented by the vertical portion of the variance area of the total flexible budget variance. Another version of the model for calculating the price and quantity variances for Wonderful Widgets is presented at the top of page 335. This general model is used for standard cost variance analysis throughout the remainder of this chapter.

M ANAGERIAL PRACTICE 8.2

Alternative to Standard Cost Measures

"An effective productivity measurement requires the development of an index that identifies the contribution of each factor of production and then tracks and combines them." A multifactor index provides managers with a means of evaluating performance using something other than labor, the traditional measurement base. It focuses on the overall capabilities of the production facilities. It establishes a relationship between physical inputs and output. The basic equation is

$$\text{Productivity} = \frac{\text{Units of output}}{\text{Units of inputs}}$$

Northern Telecom implemented a multifactor productivity measurement system to improve its cost reporting system. To obtain this goal, workers and managers were included in the design of the department-specific indices. The indices were used to measure, in an understandable way, the progress of each department toward established goals. Northern Telecom limited the department-generated performance ratios to no fewer than three and no more than seven. Although the limited number of ratios was arbitrary, the purpose was to develop a system that promised the greatest effect. "The central mission of a productivity index is to illuminate how a business can get more units of output per labor hour, per machine or per pound of materials than its competitors."

Source: W. Bruce Chew, "No-Nonsense Guide to Measuring Productivity," *Harvard Business Review* (January–February 1988): 110–118.

Standard cost variance analysis

Input component: MLO   **Output: 250 widgets**

Actual cost		Standard cost of actual inputs		Flexible budget cost	
Actual quantity (AQ)	510	Actual quantity (AQ)	510	Standard quantity allowed (SQ)	500*
Actual price (AP)	×$5.50	Standard price (SP)	× $5	Standard price (SP)	× $5
	$2,805		$2,550		$2,500

Price variance $255 U   Quantity variance $50 U

Total flexible budget variance $305 U

* 250 output units × 2 input units each

Before moving on to a more detailed standard cost variance analysis example, it should be emphasized that standard cost variance analysis involves comparison of three different input cost values for a given amount of output. By comparing these values, we are able to isolate the total effect on actual costs of paying a price other than the standard price for actual inputs, and of using amounts other than the standard allowed quantity of inputs. Do not confuse the number of inputs with the number of outputs. In the Wonderful Widgets example, the actual inputs were 510 units of MLO, the actual outputs were 250 widgets, and the standard inputs allowed were 500 units of MLO (or two units of MLO per widget produced).

VARIANCE ANALYSIS FOR VARIABLE COSTS

In the Wonderful Widgets example, we assumed that each input unit contained some amount of materials, labor, and overhead. In an actual manufacturing situation, these three production components are acquired, used, and controlled separately—which is why these cost components are discussed separately in the following sections of this chapter. For each of these cost components, price and quantity variances are computed; however, these variances are ordinarily referred to by different names for direct labor and variable factory overhead. The commonly used names of the price and quantity variances for materials, labor, and variable overhead are as follows:

Cost Component	Price Variance Name	Quantity Variance Name
Direct materials	Materials price variance	Materials quantity variance
Direct labor	Labor rate variance	Labor efficiency variance
Variable overhead	Variable overhead spending variance	Variable overhead efficiency variance

To facilitate our discussion of materials, labor, and variable overhead variance analysis, we use the March 19x6 standard and actual cost information for Execupens, Inc., presented in Exhibit 8–2. Execupens manufactures gold casings for high-priced writing pens. Except for minor design differences, the casings are identical. Completed casings are sold to other manufacturers, who add their own writing element and a spring. Each casing has a standard cost of $68.

Note in Exhibit 8–2 that the $68 standard cost per unit includes only direct materials, direct labor, and variable overhead. These costs vary in total with the volume of production. As production increases, the flexible budget for the direct materials, direct labor, and variable overhead also increases. Fixed overhead is excluded from the unit standard cost because, within the relevant range of normal activity, it does not vary with the volume of production. For the purpose of internal planning and control, fixed costs are budgeted and evaluated for total capacity rather than on a per unit basis. Our focus in the body of this chapter is on internal planning and control. For external reporting, fixed overhead costs are normally assigned to products on a per unit basis. Also, to facilitate product costing, many organizations develop a standard fixed overhead cost per unit. Standard cost variances that arise under these circumstances are discussed in the appendix to this chapter.

The performance report showing the flexible budget variances for Execupens, Inc., is presented in Exhibit 8–3. In the following sections we analyze the

---

EXHIBIT 8–2   Cost and Production Data

Execupens, Inc.
Cost and Production Data
For the month of March, 19x6

	Standard Quantity Allowed	Standard Price		Standard Cost (Flexible Budget Formula)
Standard cost per unit manufactured:				
Direct materials	6 grams	×	$ 8 =	$48
Direct labor	1 hour	×	$14 =	14
Variable overhead (based on direct labor)	1 hour	×	$ 6 =	6
Total standard cost per unit				$68
Budgeted fixed overhead per month				$198,000
Number of units manufactured during March, 19x6				20,000
Actual production costs:				
Direct materials	124,000 grams at $7.96			$ 987,040
Direct labor	19,200 hours at $14.84			284,928
Variable overhead				126,000
Fixed overhead				200,000
Total actual costs				$1,597,968

EXHIBIT 8–3   Performance Report

Execupens, Inc.
Production Department Performance Report
For the month of March, 19x6

	Flexible Budget Formula	Actual Costs	Flexible Budget Costs	Flexible Budget Variances
Volume		20,000	20,000	
Manufacturing costs:				
Direct materials	$48/unit	$ 987,040	$ 960,000	$27,040 U
Direct labor	$14/unit	284,928	280,000	4,928 U
Variable overhead	$6/unit	126,000	120,000	6,000 U
Fixed overhead	$198,000/month	200,000	198,000	2,000 U
Totals		$1,597,968	$1,558,000	$39,968 U

---

flexible budget cost variances for each of the variable cost components and compute the appropriate price and quantity variances. Control of the fixed factory overhead flexible budget variance is also discussed.

MATERIALS STANDARDS AND VARIANCES

There are two basic elements contained in the standards for direct materials—the *standard price* and the *standard quantity*. Materials standards indicate (1) how much should be paid for each unit of direct materials used and (2) the quantity of direct materials allowed to produce one unit of output. The standard price per unit of direct materials should include all reasonable costs necessary to acquire the materials. These costs include the invoice price of materials, less planned discounts, plus freight, insurance, special handling, and any other costs related to the acquisition of the materials.

The standard quantity represents the number of units of raw materials *allowed* for the production of one unit of finished product. The standard quantity of raw materials allowed to produce a unit of finished product should include the amount dictated by the physical characteristics of the process and the product, plus a reasonable allowance for normal spoilage, waste, and other inefficiencies. The quantity standard may be determined by engineering analysis, professional judgment, or by averaging the actual amount used for several periods. An average of actual past materials usage may not be a good standard because it includes excessive wastes and inefficiencies in the standard quantity. Execupens, Inc., has a direct materials quantity standard of 6 grams per finished unit produced. In fact, each unit may physically contain only 5 grams of raw materials, with the additional gram representing the amount allowed by the standards for normal spoilage, waste, and other inefficiencies.

Materials Variances Illustrated

Using the general variance analysis model introduced earlier, we can compute the materials price and quantity variances. The materials price variance is the difference between the actual materials cost and the standard cost of actual materials inputs. The materials quantity variance is the difference between the standard cost of actual materials inputs and the flexible budget cost for materials.

Standard cost variance analysis

Input component: direct materials					Output: 20,000 casings	
Actual cost			**Standard cost of actual inputs**		**Flexible budget cost**	
Actual quantity (AQ)	124,000		Actual quantity (AQ)	124,000	Standard quantity allowed (SQ)	120,000*
Actual price (AP)	× $7.96		Standard price (SP)	× $8.00	Standard price (SP)	× $8.00
	$987,040			$992,000		$960,000

Materials price variance $4,960 F   Materials quantity variance $32,000 U

Total flexible budget materials variance $27,040 U

* 20,000 units × 6 grams per unit

Execupens, Inc., had a favorable materials price variance of $4,960 because the actual cost of materials used ($987,040) was less than the standard cost of actual materials used ($992,000). Stated another way, for the materials actually used, the total price paid was $4,960 less than the price allowed by the standards. The price variance can also be viewed as the actual quantity used times the difference between the actual price and the standard price. Execupens, Inc., paid 4 cents below the standard price for 124,000 grams of gold used, for a total savings of $4,960:

$$\text{Materials price variance} = AQ(AP - SP)$$
$$= 124,000 \, (\$7.96 - \$8.00)$$
$$= 124,000 \times \$0.04$$
$$= \$4,960 \, F$$

The unfavorable quantity variance of $32,000 occurred because the standard cost of actual materials used ($992,000) was greater than the flexible budget cost of materials ($960,000). A total of 120,000 grams of raw materials is allowed to produce 20,000 units of finished outputs. This is computed as 20,000 finished units times 6 grams of raw materials per unit. The materials quantity variance may also be computed as the standard price per gram times the difference between the number of grams actually used and the number of grams allowed. The use of 4,000 grams of gold more than the standard quantity allowed at a standard price of $8 per gram resulted in an additional cost of $32,000:

$$\begin{aligned}
\text{Materials quantity variance} &= \text{SP(AQ} - \text{SQ)} \\
&= \$8.00\,(124{,}000 - 120{,}000) \\
&= \$8.00 \times 4{,}000 \\
&= \$32{,}000 \text{ U.}
\end{aligned}$$

In the Execupens example, computation of the price variance was based on *materials actually used* during the period. However, since materials prices are ordinarily controlled at the point of purchase, rather than at the point of usage, many managers prefer to compute the materials price variance on the basis of *materials purchased* instead of materials used. If 125,000 grams of materials had been purchased at $7.96 but only 124,000 had been used, the materials variances would be computed as shown in the following illustration.

Standard cost variance analysis

Input component: direct materials   **Output: 20,000 casings**

Actual cost	Standard cost of actual inputs	Flexible budget cost
Actual quantity purchased (AQ)　125,000	Actual quantity purchased (AQ)　　125,000	
Actual price (AP)　×　$7.96	Standard price (SP)　×　　$8.00	
$995,000	Standard cost of materials purchased　　$1,000,000	

Materials purchased price variance $5,000 F

	Actual quantity used (AQ)　124,000	Standard quantity allowed (SQ)　120,000*
	Standard price (SP)　×　$8.00	Standard price (SP)　×　$8.00
	Standard cost of materials used　$ 992,000	$960,000

Materials quantity variance $32,000 U

Total flexible budget materials variance $32,000 U

* 20,000 units × 6 grams per unit

Note that now there are two actual quantities for materials. First, the actual quantity *purchased* is used to compute the materials price variance. The materials purchased price variance is the actual cost of materials purchased minus the standard cost of actual materials purchased. Second, the actual quantity *used* is utilized in computing the materials quantity variance. When the materials price variance is computed at the point of purchasing, all units of materials are charged to production at the standard price. Therefore, the materials price variance is not charged to production, and the flexible budget variance for materials consists entirely of the quantity variance.

Measuring the price variance at the point of materials purchases is desirable in situations where raw materials purchases vary substantially from the amount used during a given period. The purchasing manager needs to receive price variance information as soon as possible after the actual purchase of materials. If the price variance is measured when materials are used (which may be weeks or months after materials are purchased), the price variance information may be received too late to be useful in controlling materials prices. Also, timely reporting of price variance information is necessary for making pricing decisions, as it is for making other decisions based on current replacement costs.[2]

Interpreting Materials Variances

Accountants often overemphasize the computation of variances and forget that the main objectives of variance analysis are reporting and interpreting the variances. It is necessary to understand how variances are computed, but it is even more important to know what to do with the variances after they are computed.

A *favorable materials price variance* indicates that the manager responsible for materials purchases paid less per unit than the price allowed by the standards. This may result from receiving discounts for purchasing larger than normal quantities, effective bargaining by the manager, purchasing substandard quality materials, purchasing from a distress seller, or other factors. Ordinarily when a favorable price variance is reported, the manager's performance will be interpreted as favorable. However, if the favorable price variance resulted from the purchase of materials of lower than standard quality, or purchasing in larger than desirable quantities, the manager's performance would be questionable.

An *unfavorable materials price variance* means that the purchasing manager paid more per unit for materials than the price allowed by the standards. This may be caused by failure to buy in sufficient quantities to get normal discounts, failure to place materials orders on a timely basis thereby requiring a more expensive shipping alternative, uncontrollable price changes in the market for raw materials, failure to bargain for the best available prices, or other factors. It should be emphasized that the type of evaluation the purchasing manager receives depends on the reasons for the variance. An unfavorable variance does not always mean that the manager performed unfavorably, and a favorable variance does not always indicate favorable performance.

---

[2] In working the exercises and problems in this chapter, assume (unless otherwise stated) that the production manager is responsible for raw materials purchases and that the quantity used equals the quantity purchased.

A *favorable materials quantity variance* means that the actual quantity of raw materials used was less than the quantity allowed for the units produced. This may result from factors such as less materials waste than allowed by the standards, better than expected machine efficiency, raw materials of higher quality than required by the standards, and more efficient use of raw materials by employees.

An *unfavorable materials quantity variance* occurs when the quantity of raw materials used exceeds the quantity allowed for the units produced. This may result from incurring more waste than provided for in the standards, poorly maintained machinery requiring larger amounts of raw materials, raw materials of lower quality than required by the standards, or poorly trained employees who were unable to use the materials at the level of efficiency required by the standards.

One possible cause for any standard cost variance (materials, labor, or overhead) is that the standard quantity or price used in computing the variance was too high or too low. A necessary consideration in evaluating any variance is that an inappropriate standard value may have been used in its computation. Thus, when investigating the causes for a given variance, always consider this possibility. If the standards are determined to be incorrect, they should be revised to reflect current efficient operating conditions. Higher level managers should always be eager to revise the standards to reflect changes in the environment not controllable by their subordinate managers. This attitude encourages responsibility center managers to have greater respect for both the reported variances and the entire performance evaluation system.

LABOR STANDARDS AND VARIANCES

Direct labor standards, like direct materials standards, consist of two components, *quantity* and *price*. The direct labor quantity standard is usually referred to as the labor efficiency, or usage, standard; the price standard is referred to as the labor rate standard. To evaluate management performance in controlling labor costs by using a standard cost system, it is necessary to determine the *standard labor time allowed* to produce a unit and the *standard labor rate* for each hour of labor allowed.

The standard labor time per unit can be determined by an engineering approach or an empirical observation approach. When using an engineering approach, industrial engineers ascertain the amount of labor required to produce a unit of finished product by applying time and motion methods or other available techniques. Normal operating conditions are assumed in arriving at the labor efficiency standard; therefore, allowances must be made for normal machine downtime, employee personal breaks, and so forth. Under the empirical approach, the long-run average time required in the past to produce a unit under normal operating conditions is used as a basis for the standard. By using normal operating conditions, inefficiencies such as machine downtime and employee breaks are automatically factored into the standard. The tightness of the standard can be adjusted by increasing or decreasing the observed average.

Setting labor rate standards may be quite simple or extremely complex, depending on the particular circumstances. If only one class of employees is used to make each product, and all employees have the same wage rate, determination of the standard cost is relatively easy: simply adopt the normal wage rate as the standard labor rate. If several different classes of employees are used in making each unit of product, separate efficiency and rate standards must be established for each class. For example, the standard direct labor cost per unit for making heavy machine components may be stated as follows:

Millwright labor (3 hrs at $15 per hr)	$ 45
Machinist labor (5 hrs at $12 per hr)	60
Standard labor cost per unit produced	$105

If wage rates vary for a given class of employees because of seniority or other differences, an average wage rate is ordinarily used for the labor rate standard.

Managerial Practice 8.3

New Measures of Labor Efficiency Are Catching on

Michael A. Wright, controller for the Hybrid Components division of Tektronix, Inc., learned that, when a JIT system is in operation, traditional measures of worker efficiency no longer apply. "In a Just-in-Time manufacturing line, once the excess inventory has been flushed out, it is essentially impossible for any person on that line to work faster or slower than the line moves." The old cost methods reported that the efficiency of the workers was declining. However, costs were actually decreasing while production was increasing. Tektronix was faced with the task of developing a new accounting system to support their JIT and quality programs. The new, state-of-the-art cost management system provides less data but gives greater control than the old system, which generated large amounts of useless data. By simplifying the process, Tektronix was able to see the big picture of the relationship between costs and actions.

Source: J. William Semich, "Accounting for Quality," *Purchasing* (19 January 1989): 74–79.

In these cases any variance caused by using an average rate should be negligible, unless there are large variations in wage rates within a particular employee class. To simplify our examples, we assume there is only one class of employees with all employees earning the same wage rate. As stated in Chapter 2, labor related fringe benefit costs are usually considered to be factory overhead and, therefore, are not included in the actual or standard labor rate.

Labor Variances Illustrated

Using the general variance model, we can compute the labor rate and efficiency variances. The **labor rate variance** is the difference between the actual labor cost and the standard cost of actual labor inputs. The **labor efficiency variance** is the difference between the standard cost of actual labor inputs and the flexible budget cost for labor.

Execupens' direct labor standards and labor usage data for March 19x6 are presented in Exhibit 8–2 on page 336. Note that the standards provide for 1 hour of direct labor time per unit at a cost of $14 per hour. During March 19x6, 19,200 hours were used at a cost of $14.84 per hour. Using these data, the labor rate (price) variance and labor efficiency (quantity) variance can be computed as shown in the following illustration.

Standard cost variance analysis

Input component: direct labor   **Output: 20,000 casings**

Actual cost		Standard cost of actual inputs		Flexible budget cost	
Actual hours (AH)	19,200	Actual hours (AH)	19,200	Standard hours allowed (SH)	20,000*
Actual rate (AR)	× $14.84	Standard rate (SR)	× $14.00	Standard rate (SR)	× $14.00
	$284,928		$268,800		$280,000

Labor rate variance $16,128 U

Labor efficiency variance $11,200 F

Total flexible budget labor variance $4,928 U

* 20,000 units × 1 hour per unit

The labor rate variance can also be computed as the actual hours used times the difference between the actual labor rate and the standard labor rate:

$$\text{Labor rate variance} = \text{AH}(\text{AR} - \text{SR})$$
$$= 19,200(\$14.84 - \$14.00)$$
$$= 19,200 \times \$0.84$$
$$= \$16,128 \text{ U}.$$

This computation of the labor rate variance shows that the company paid 84 cents above the standard rate for each of the 19,200 hours worked.

Since 20,000 units of product were finished during the period, and 1 hour of labor was allowed for each unit, the total standard hours allowed was 20,000. The labor efficiency variance can also be computed as the standard rate times the difference between the actual direct labor hours and the standard hours allowed for the output achieved:

$$
\begin{aligned}
\text{Labor efficiency variance} &= SR(AH - SH) \\
&= \$14(19,200 - 20,000) \\
&= \$14 \times 800 \\
&= \$11,200 \text{ F.}
\end{aligned}
$$

This computation of the labor efficiency variance indicates that the company used 800 fewer direct labor hours than the budget permitted and that each of these hours saved $14, or a total of $11,200.

Interpreting Labor Variances

The possible explanations for labor rate variances are rather limited. An *unfavorable labor rate variance* may be caused by the use of higher skilled (and thus higher paid) laborers than provided for by the standards. Also, a new labor union contract increasing wages may have been implemented after the standards were set. In this case the standards should have been revised to account for the wage rate change. In a nonunion situation, where wages are not controlled by negotiated contract, there is the possibility that a manager may arbitrarily increase employee wages above the standard rate. This will also give rise to an unfavorable labor rate variance.

A *favorable labor rate variance* occurs if lower skilled (and thus lower paid) workers were used or if actual wage rates were below standard labor rates. As an example of falling wage rates, in the mid 1980s economic problems in the airline industry forced some union negotiators to relinquish previously awarded employee benefits. Such adjustments, however, should be reflected in the standards before the variances are reported.

Unfavorable labor efficiency variances occur whenever workers require more than the number of hours allowed by the standards to produce a given amount of product. This may be caused by a management decision to use poorly trained workers or poorly maintained machinery or by downtime resulting from the use of low-quality materials. Low employee morale, and generally bad working conditions, may also adversely affect the efficiency of workers, resulting in an unfavorable labor efficiency variance.

A *favorable labor efficiency variance* occurs when fewer labor hours are used than are allowed by the standards. This above normal efficiency may be caused by the company's use of higher skilled (and higher paid) workers, better machinery, or raw materials of higher quality than provided for by the standards. High employee morale, improved job satisfaction, or generally improved working conditions may also account for the above normal efficiency of the workers.

It is important to understand the potential interactive effect of the use of raw materials, direct labor, and machinery on the overall efficiency of the production process. These three factors must be combined efficiently to produce a unit of finished product of optimal quality. The quality of one factor usually affects the efficiency in using the other two components. For example, low-quality materials ordinarily reduces the efficiency of workers and machinery. Likewise, poorly maintained machinery reduces the efficiency of the workers and causes excessive waste of raw materials. And use of poorly trained workers often results in lower than normal output from the use of materials and machinery. Because of these interactive relationships, the interpretation of one variance is often interrelated with the interpretation of other variances. Seldom are there clear-cut and isolated explanations for each variance reported. Because of complexities of this sort, *using* variances is far more challenging than *computing* them.

VARIABLE OVERHEAD STANDARDS AND VARIANCES

Factory overhead costs are usually separated into fixed and variable elements for control purposes. Such a division is necessary because the variance between actual costs and expected costs is caused by different factors for fixed and variable costs. In this section we discuss the standards and variances related to variable overhead costs. Fixed overhead costs will be discussed in the next section.

MANAGERIAL PRACTICE 8.4

Planned Variances for Overhead

American Transtech, a telemarketing company, needed a costing system that would permit variable rates for its services. Its existing system used a full-cost approach in pricing its services, which caused certain types of services to be priced too high, therefore discouraging customers. To achieve the desired results, the services were divided into peak and off-peak categories. The original system reported spending and volume cost variances from the budgeted amounts, but no adjustments were made for activities during off-peak times. After realizing that the activities could be isolated, the company devised a new system that allowed for acceptable variances if they occurred during off-peak periods. The company, in effect, created a system that allowed for planned variances from budget. This permitted variances for off-peak services, thereby resulting in reduced prices and increased business.

Source: Thomas L. Barton and Robert J. Fox, "Evolution at American Transtech," *Management Accounting* (April 1988): 49–52.

In Chapter 2, factory overhead was defined as all manufacturing costs other than direct materials and direct labor. Variable factory overhead includes all variable manufacturing costs other than direct materials and direct labor. Examples of variable factory overhead are indirect materials and supplies, certain indirect labor, overtime costs, employee fringe benefits, utilities, and so forth.

Unlike direct materials and direct labor costs, which represent specific cost components, factory overhead represents a *group* of different costs. Consequently, setting standards is often more difficult for overhead costs than for materials or labor costs. Because of the difficulty of tracing overhead costs to the finished product, the engineering approach to setting overhead standards is seldom used. For mixed factory overhead costs (those that have variable and fixed components), an estimation technique, such as the high-low, least-squares, or scatter diagram method, is often used to separate the fixed and variable overhead components. These techniques were discussed in Chapter 3. If management believes the observations used in estimating variable costs reflect normal operating conditions, the estimate will probably be adopted as the standard variable cost.

Because it includes many heterogeneous costs, variable factory overhead poses a unique problem in measuring standard quantity and standard price. Direct materials have a natural physical measure of quantity such as tons, barrels, pounds, and meters. Similarly, direct labor is measurable in hours. However, no natural quantity measure is common to all variable overhead items. Variable overhead is a cost group that may include, at the same time, costs measurable in hours, pounds, grams, kilowatts, and gallons.

To deal with the problem of multiple quantity measures in variable factory overhead, most companies use an artificial, or substitute, measure of quantity for all items in the group. Typical substitute measures are *direct labor hours* and *machine hours*. The variable overhead standard then is stated in terms of this *common activity base,* and the amount of variable overhead budgeted is based on this artificial activity measure. To illustrate, assume that Execupens' standard variable overhead rate of $6 per direct labor hour consists of the following:

Variable Overhead Cost Item	Quantity Consumed per Direct Labor Hour	Standard Cost per Direct Labor Hour
Indirect materials:		
Silicon coating	2 fluid ounces	$0.25
Machine lubricants	3 centimeters	0.20
Cleaning supplies	3 grams	0.15
Indirect labor:		
Inspection	5 minutes	0.40
Fringe benefits	1 direct labor hour	3.50
Electricity	1 kilowatt hour	0.05
Machine depreciation	1 hour of machine time	1.45
Total variable factory overhead cost per direct labor hour		$6.00

Execupens, Inc., chose to measure variable factory overhead in terms of direct labor hours because a large portion of these costs is related to direct labor activity. Thus *direct labor hours worked* is better than *units of product finished* as a measure of how much variable overhead cost should be incurred because these costs tend to vary in relation to direct labor hours worked whether or not the workers are producing the standard one finished unit per direct labor hour. Also, if common facilities are used to produce two or more products that use unequal amounts of overhead, the same hourly overhead rate can be used to budget and charge different amounts of overhead for production of the products. For example, if one product required $\frac{1}{2}$ standard hour of direct labor and another required 1 hour, at a rate of $6 per direct labor hour, $3 of variable overhead would be allowed for making the first product, and $6 would be allowed for the second. The use of activity bases for allocating common costs, such as variable overhead, is discussed in greater depth in Chapter 13.

Variable Overhead Variances Illustrated

The general model for computing standard cost variances for materials and labor can also be used in computing variable overhead variances. However, the actual costs of inputs, such as indirect materials, indirect labor, and utilities, are ordinarily obtained directly from the accounting records rather than being computed as quantity times price.

The **variable overhead spending variance** is the difference between the actual variable overhead cost and the standard variable overhead cost for the actual activity base inputs (direct labor hours in this example). The **variable overhead efficiency variance** is the difference between the standard variable overhead cost for the actual activity base inputs and the flexible budget cost for variable overhead.

For Execupens, Inc., the actual variable overhead is given at $126,000. This represents the actual cost of indirect materials, variable indirect labor, utilities, and machine depreciation recorded during the period. Since actual variable overhead is expected to vary with labor hours, the standard cost of actual activity base inputs is calculated as 19,200 actual direct labor hours times the standard variable overhead rate of $6, or $115,200. The flexible budget cost for variable overhead allowed for the actual outputs is based on the 20,000 direct labor hours allowed for the units produced during the period (20,000 units × 1 hour). Consequently, the variable overhead flexible budget cost is 20,000 labor hours times the variable overhead rate of $6, or $120,000. Using these data, the variable overhead spending (price) variance and the variable overhead efficiency (quantity) variance are shown in the illustration at the top of page 348.

Note that the spaces for actual hours and actual rate are left blank in the actual cost calculation. Since variable overhead is assumed to be incurred as direct labor hours are incurred, we could say that the actual quantity of inputs of variable overhead was 19,200 direct labor hours. Using 19,200 as the quantity of overhead inputs, the actual average variable overhead per labor hour can be determined as the actual variable overhead cost of $126,000 divided by 19,200 hours, or $6.56 per hour. Because variable overhead costs are not actually purchased in units of direct labor hours, it is probably less confusing to omit

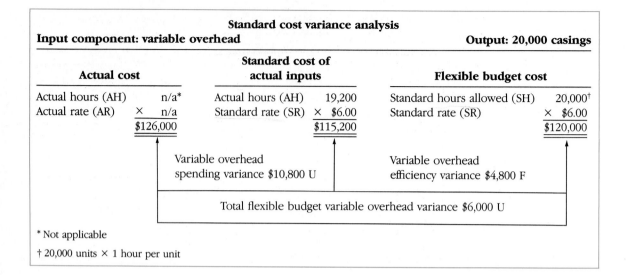

Standard cost variance analysis

Input component: variable overhead   Output: 20,000 casings

	Actual cost		Standard cost of actual inputs		Flexible budget cost	
Actual hours (AH)	n/a*		Actual hours (AH)	19,200	Standard hours allowed (SH)	20,000†
Actual rate (AR)	×	n/a	Standard rate (SR)	× $6.00	Standard rate (SR)	× $6.00
		$126,000		$115,200		$120,000

Variable overhead
spending variance $10,800 U

Variable overhead
efficiency variance $4,800 F

Total flexible budget variable overhead variance $6,000 U

* Not applicable

† 20,000 units × 1 hour per unit

this computation. A more compelling reason for not making the computation is that it provides no benefit to management in controlling variable overhead costs.

An alternative to the computation of the variable overhead efficiency variance is as follows:

$$\text{Variable overhead efficiency variance} = SR(AH - SH)$$
$$= \$6.00(19,200 - 20,000)$$
$$= \$6.00 \times 800$$
$$= \$4,800 \text{ F.}$$

This approach emphasizes that the 800 labor hours saved should have produced a variable overhead savings of $4,800, at the standard rate of $6 per direct labor hour.

Interpreting Variable Overhead Variances

The variable overhead spending variance measures the difference between actual variable overhead and the amount of overhead cost expected for the actual use of the activity base. Operating at 19,200 actual hours, with a standard rate of $6 per hour, management expected $115,200 (19,200 × $6) to be spent on variable overhead. Since actual costs were $126,000, management overspent, and a $10,800 unfavorable spending variance resulted.

Why did Execupens spend $10,800 too much? Was it caused by increasing prices for indirect materials, by higher than expected wage rates for indirect labor, or by higher than expected kilowatt rates for electricity? Or was it caused by workers' use of excessive quantities of indirect materials, indirect labor, and electricity for the actual direct labor hours worked? The answer is that the unfavorable spending variance could have resulted *both* from increasing prices for variable overhead goods and services used *and* from excessive consumption of these goods and services. Thus the term *spending* variance is used instead of the term *price* variance.

For variable overhead the *unfavorable spending variance* encompasses all factors that cause actual expenditures to exceed the amount expected for the actual labor hours, including consuming excessive quantities of variable overhead items, as well as paying too much for the variable overhead items consumed. Conversely, a *favorable spending variance* results when the actual expenditures are less than expected for the actual labor hours. This is caused by consuming fewer overhead items than expected, or by paying less than the expected amount for overhead items consumed, or by both of these.

The key to understanding the variable overhead spending variance is recognizing that the amount of variable overhead cost that can be incurred without exceeding the variable overhead spending budget is based on the actual level of the activity base chosen for budgeting variable overhead cost. For Execupens, actual direct labor hours determine the spending budget for variable overhead. Any deviation from this spending budget—due to mismanagement of variable overhead price or quantity variables—causes a spending variance to occur.

The variable overhead efficiency variance measures the difference between the standard variable overhead cost for the actual use of the activity base and the standard variable overhead cost for the allowed use of the activity base. This variance measures the amount of variable overhead that should have been incurred or saved because of the efficient or inefficient use of the activity base. It provides no information about the degree of efficiency in using variable overhead items such as indirect materials and indirect labor. This information is reflected in the spending variance. When overhead is being measured and budgeted on the basis of labor hours, it is logical to expect overhead costs to be affected by the degree of labor efficiency. This effect is measured by the variable overhead efficiency variance. Because of the connection of this variance to labor efficiency, it will always move in the *same direction* as the labor efficiency variance; when the labor efficiency variance is favorable, the variable overhead efficiency variance will be favorable, and vice versa.

In the Execupens illustration of variable overhead variances, the activity base selected for budgeting variable overhead cost was direct labor hours. Observations similar to those made for direct labor hours could also be made for other activity bases such as machine hours.

FIXED OVERHEAD STANDARDS AND VARIANCES

Because of the nature of fixed costs, the quantity of goods and services purchased by fixed expenditures does not change in proportion to changes in the level of production. For example, in the short run the production level does not affect the amount of depreciation on buildings, the number of fixed salaried employees, or the amount of real property subject to property taxes. Whether 20,000 or 30,000 units are produced, the same amount of fixed overhead is expected to be incurred so long as the production level is within the relevant range of activity provided by the current fixed overhead items. Therefore, a quantity or efficiency variance is ordinarily not computed for fixed overhead costs.

Even though the components of fixed overhead are not affected by the production activity level in the short run, the actual amount spent for fixed overhead items can differ from the amount budgeted by management. For example, higher than budgeted supervisors' salaries can be paid, extreme temperatures can cause heating or cooling costs to exceed budget, and price increases can cause the amounts paid for fixed property maintenance costs to be higher than expected. Fixed overhead costs in excess of the amount budgeted are reflected in the fixed overhead budget variance. The **fixed overhead budget variance** is the difference between budgeted and actual fixed overhead:

$$\text{Fixed overhead budget variance} = \text{Actual fixed overhead} - \text{Budgeted fixed overhead.}$$

Using the fixed overhead data in Exhibit 8–2 for Execupens, Inc., the fixed overhead budget variance is computed as $2,000 unfavorable, or $200,000 of actual fixed overhead costs minus $198,000 of budgeted fixed overhead costs. The fixed overhead budget variance is always the *same* as the total fixed overhead flexible budget variance. Because budgeted fixed overhead is the same for all outputs within the relevant range, the budget variance accounts for the total flexible budget variance between actual and allowed fixed overhead.

REPORTING STANDARD COST VARIANCES

Two critical factors in the operation of a responsibility accounting system are (1) the reporting of variances to the appropriate managers and (2) management's responding with explanations and control decisions. The method and format used to report variances to managers should be tailored to the specific needs of each situation. Exhibit 8–4 illustrates, for Execupens, one approach that is available for reporting performance results and standard cost variances for a standard cost center. This report is an expanded version of the flexible budget performance report presented in Exhibit 8–3. In this example, Execupen's production manager is assumed to be responsible for all raw materials purchases and the quantity used equals the quantity purchased. If purchases had been the responsibility of someone else, the materials price variance would not have been included in the production manager's performance report.

Managers receiving performance reports are usually required to respond to their immediate superiors within a designated period of time with explanations for variances that are significant in amount. Ordinarily, it is not economically feasible to investigate all variances. Each company must determine what constitutes a significant variance warranting managerial attention. All significant variances, both *unfavorable* and *favorable*, should be investigated. As stated before, a favorable variance does not necessarily indicate favorable managerial performance.

EXHIBIT 8–4   Standard Cost Performance Report

Execupens, Inc.
Production Department Standard Cost Performance Report
For the month of March, 19x6

	Actual Costs	Flexible Budget Cost	Flexible Budget Variances	Variance Analysis	
Direct materials	$ 987,040	$ 960,000	$27,040 U	$ 4,960 F	Materials price variance
				32,000 U	Materials quantity variance
Direct labor	284,928	280,000	4,928 U	16,128 U	Labor rate variance
				11,200 F	Labor efficiency variance
Variable factory overhead	126,000	120,000	6,000 U	10,800 U	Variable overhead spending variance
				4,800 F	Variable overhead efficiency variance
Fixed factory overhead	200,000	198,000	2,000 U	2,000 U	Fixed overhead budget variance
Totals	$1,597,968	$1,558,000	$39,968 U	$39,968 U	

APPLICATIONS AND BENEFITS OF VARIANCE ANALYSIS

Standard costs are used primarily for performance evaluation, budgeting, and product costing. Throughout this chapter we have emphasized the performance evaluation aspect of standard costing. Closely related to the objective of performance evaluation is the objective of cost control, which is an important part of management responsibility that must be routinely evaluated. Although cost control is not a manager's only important responsibility, in a cost center it is a high priority with upper management. Standard costs provide a logical basis for evaluating a manager's performance. Standard cost reports are an important part of a responsibility reporting system for standard cost centers, and, as such, help to identify good and bad performers.

Standard cost reports can assist in formulating performance evaluations of managers by providing a beginning point, but serious consequences can result if standard cost reports are used exclusively to evaluate managers. Managers may learn quickly how to manipulate the system in order to generate favorable variances. For example, purchasing managers may buy substandard raw materials, and production managers may sacrifice quality for quantity, or sacrifice employee morale for higher productivity. Though these ploys may produce favorable variances in the short run, often they have negative effects on the organization in the long run. To avoid these types of manipulations, standard cost performance reports should be used as only *a part of an overall performance evaluation system* that considers all areas of manager performance.

Another use of standard costs discussed in Chapter 6 is to provide information useful in budgeting. If cost standards exist and are current, they can be used to budget manufacturing costs after sales and inventory requirements are budgeted. Having standard costs readily available significantly reduces the time and effort required to determine the budgeted costs for the planned production.

Standard costs are also useful in product costing. In a standard product costing system, manufactured inventory is always costed at standard allowed cost. Consequently, the cost of the finished inventory can be readily determined as the number of units in inventory times the standard cost per unit. This eliminates the product costing delays often associated with using actual costs for product costing. Product costing is considered in Chapters 11 and 12, and standard product cost systems are explained in an appendix to Chapter 11.

SUMMARY

Cost centers that have a predictable relationship between production inputs and outputs often use standard costs for controlling costs and evaluating manager performance. Standard cost systems require that cost standards be developed for each type of product produced (or service provided) and that they include standard unit costs for materials, labor, and overhead. Periodically, actual costs are compared with standard costs, and cost variances are reported to managers for possible corrective action.

Variance analysis involves breaking down flexible budget variances into specific variances caused by price and quantity departures from standards. Both price and quantity variances are reported for materials, labor, and overhead. Most companies measure the quantity of variable overhead consumed in terms of a substitute activity base, such as direct labor hours, rather than in terms of the quantity of overhead goods and services consumed. Therefore, the variable overhead efficiency variance measures the impact on overhead cost of the efficiency with which the activity base is used. The variable overhead spending variance measures the combined impact of price and quantity deviations from standards for variable overhead goods and services used.

For internal planning and control, fixed overhead is budgeted and reported in a lump sum and, therefore, is not affected by the level of activity achieved during the period. The fixed overhead budget variance is the difference between actual fixed overhead and budgeted fixed overhead. An additional fixed overhead variance is often computed when fixed overhead is applied to products on a unit basis for external reporting purposes. This variance is discussed in the following appendix.

APPENDIX
A CLOSER LOOK AT FIXED
OVERHEAD VARIANCES

The absorption cost method of external reporting treats all manufacturing costs as product costs. In Chapter 2 we indicated that most firms use a predetermined rate to assign factory overhead to products. This predetermined factory overhead rate is established at the start of the year by dividing the predicted overhead costs for the year by the predicted activity for the year. Many firms prefer to use separate overhead rates for fixed and variable overhead. When this is done, often variable overhead is assigned using the standard variable overhead rate, and fixed overhead is assigned using a separate *standard fixed overhead rate*.

The development of the variable overhead rate and its subsequent use in computing standard cost variances was considered in the body of this chapter. In this appendix we consider the development of a standard fixed overhead rate and its subsequent use in computing standard cost variances.

The motivation for using a standard fixed overhead rate is the same as the motivation for using a predetermined overhead rate, namely, more rapid product costing and smoothing the bookkeeping work load. Furthermore, the use of a standard fixed overhead rate results in identical fixed costs being assigned to identical products regardless of when they are produced during the year.

When a standard fixed overhead rate is used, *total fixed overhead* costs assigned to production behave as *variable* costs. As production increases, the total fixed overhead assigned to production increases. Because total budgeted fixed overhead does not vary, differences arise between budgeted and assigned fixed overhead, and managers often inquire about the cause of the differences.

The standard fixed overhead rate is computed as the *budgeted fixed costs* divided by some *budgeted standard level of activity.* Since budgeted fixed overhead is the same for all levels of output (within the relevant production range), the standard fixed overhead rate varies depending on the budgeted level of activity. In our example of Execupens, Inc. (see Exhibit 8–2), budgeted monthly fixed overhead is $198,000. To simplify the illustration, assume that Execupens develops their standard fixed overhead rate monthly, instead of annually, and that Execupens bases the rate on a budgeted activity level of 22,000 labor hours per month. The standard fixed overhead rate per direct labor hour is $9:

$$\text{Standard fixed overhead rate} = \frac{\text{Budgeted total fixed overhead}}{\text{Budgeted activity level}}$$

$$= \frac{\$198,000}{22,000 \text{ hours}}$$

$$= \$9.$$

The total fixed overhead assigned to production is computed as the standard rate of $9 multiplied by the standard hours allowed for the units produced.

Therefore, the assigned fixed overhead equals the budgeted monthly fixed overhead only if the allowed activity is 22,000 hours. This is illustrated in Exhibit 8–5(a). If the company operates below the 22,000 budgeted hours, the fixed overhead assigned to production is less than the $198,000 budgeted; if it operates above the 22,000 budgeted hours, the fixed overhead assigned to production is more than the amount budgeted.

Even though total fixed overhead is not affected by producing below or above the standard activity level, the fixed overhead assigned to production increases at the rate of $9 per allowed labor hour. The difference between total budgeted fixed overhead and total standard fixed overhead assigned to production is called the fixed overhead volume variance. This variance is sometimes referred to as the denominator variance, a term that emphasizes the accounting origin of the variance. The fixed overhead volume variance indicates neither good nor bad performance by the production personnel. Instead, it merely indicates a difference between the activity allowed for the actual output and the activity level used as the denominator in computing the standard fixed overhead rate.

To explain the difference between actual fixed overhead and standard fixed overhead assigned to production, two fixed overhead variances are computed, the budget variance and the volume variance. These variances are illustrated in graphic form in Exhibit 8–5(b). They are computed below for Execupens, Inc., assuming the following data:

Budgeted fixed overhead	$198,000
Actual fixed overhead	$200,000
Budgeted activity level	22,000 units (or 22,000 hours)
Actual activity level	20,000 units (or 20,000 standard hours allowed)

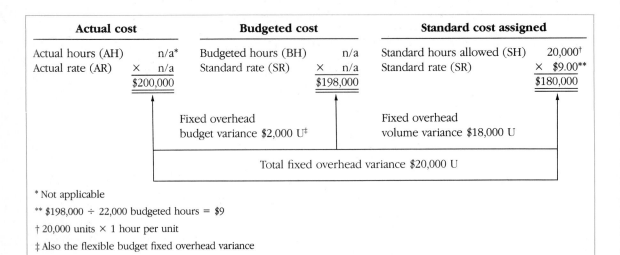

* Not applicable

** $198,000 ÷ 22,000 budgeted hours = $9

† 20,000 units × 1 hour per unit

‡ Also the flexible budget fixed overhead variance

EXHIBIT 8–5   Graphic Analysis of Fixed Overhead Costs and Variances

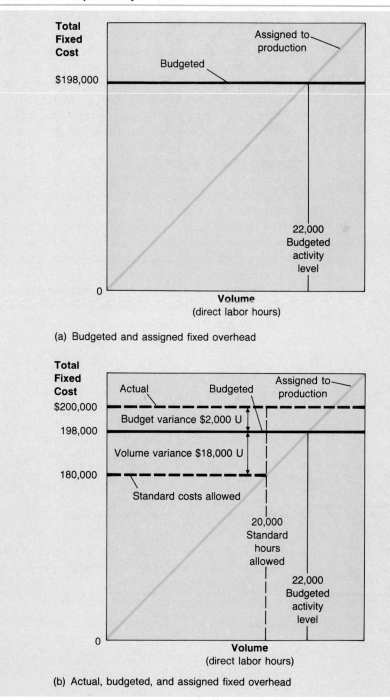

(a) Budgeted and assigned fixed overhead

(b) Actual, budgeted, and assigned fixed overhead

Because actual and budgeted fixed overhead do not vary for activity within the relevant range, their amounts are stated in total rather than computed as a function of some volume activity. The amount of fixed overhead assigned to production does vary with activity and is computed as the standard hours allowed for the actual outputs times the standard fixed overhead rate per hour. The fixed overhead budget variance represents the difference between actual fixed overhead and budgeted fixed overhead. The budget variance is caused by a combination of price and quantity factors related to the use of fixed overhead goods and services (e.g., heating or cooling costs, indirect labor, etc.). The $2,000 unfavorable budget variance for Execupens was caused either by using excessive quantities of fixed overhead goods and services, or by paying higher prices than expected for those items, or both.

The volume variance represents the difference between budgeted and assigned fixed overhead and is caused by a difference between the activity level allowed for the actual output and the budgeted activity used in computing the fixed overhead rate. The $18,000 unfavorable volume variance for Execupens means that the activity level allowed for the actual output was less than the budgeted activity level. As stated above, this variance ordinarily cannot be used to control costs. If the budgeted activity level is based on production capacity, this variance can be used only to alert management that facilities are under-utilized, or utilized above management's expectations.

SUGGESTED READINGS

Barnes, John L., "How to Tell if Standard Costs are Really Standard," *Management Accounting* (June 1983): 50–54.

Barnes, Keith, and Peter Targett, "Standard Costing in Distribution—A Neglected Technique?" *Management Accounting* (May 1984): 26–27.

Bennett, James P., "Standard Cost Systems Lead to Efficiency and Profitability," *Healthcare Financial Management* (September 1985): 46–54.

Chandler, Warren L., "Integrating Standard Cost Information into Operating Budgets," *Healthcare Financial Management* (September 1986): 127–128.

Stromberg, Dan, and Brian H. Kleiner, "Implementing a Participative Cost Management Program," *Journal of Cost Management* 6, No. 3, (Fall 1989): 17–21.

REVIEW PROBLEM

Standard Cost Variance Analysis

The flexible budget performance report for Teltek, Inc., for March 19x5 is presented below. Teltek manufactures PGX, its only product.

	Flexible Budget Formula	Actual Costs	Flexible Budget Costs	Flexible Budget Variances
Output volume		5,000	5,000	
Manufacturing costs:				
Direct materials	$20/unit	$104,125	$100,000	$4,125 U
Direct labor	$15/unit	82,400	75,000	7,400 U
Variable overhead	$12/unit	56,000	60,000	4,000 F
Fixed overhead	$30,000/month	32,000	30,000	2,000 U
Totals		$274,525	$265,000	$9,525 U

The standard unit cost for PGX is as follows:

Direct materials	4 pounds at $5 per pound	$20
Direct labor	1.5 hours at $10 per hour	15
Variable overhead	$8 per direct labor hour	12
Total standard cost per unit		$47

Actual cost of materials is based on 21,250 pounds of direct materials purchased and used, and actual cost of direct labor is based on 8,000 direct labor hours. Variable overhead is applied based on direct labor hours. The production supervisor is responsible for the purchase of all materials.

Requirements

a) Calculate all standard cost variances for direct materials, direct labor, and variable factory overhead.

b) Prepare a March 19x5 standard cost performance report for the Production Department.

The solution to this problem is found at the end of the Chapter 8 exercises, problems, and cases.

KEY TERMS

Fixed overhead budget variance
Labor efficiency variance
Labor rate variance
Materials price variance
Materials purchased price variance
Materials quantity variance
Price variance

Quantity variance
Standard cost variance analysis
Variable overhead efficiency variance
Variable overhead spending variance

APPENDIX
KEY TERMS

Denominator variance   Fixed overhead volume variance

REVIEW
QUESTIONS

8–1   What is a standard cost variance, and what is the objective of variance analysis?

8–2   How do production inputs affect the cost of production outputs?

8–3   Standard cost variances can usually be broken down into two basic types of variances. Identify and describe these two types of variances.

8–4   What costs should be included in the determination of the standard materials price?

8–5   Identify two ways that materials standards can be determined. Which method is more precise?

8–6   Should the materials price variance be determined on the basis of materials purchased or materials used? Explain.

8–7   Identify possible causes for (1) a materials price variance and (2) a materials quantity variance.

8–8   Show two ways of computing the labor rate variance.

8–9   Explain how an unfavorable labor efficiency variance may be related to a favorable materials price variance.

8–10   What is the appropriate treatment in the standard cost system of a change in wage rates in the contract with the labor union?

8–11   How is the variable overhead spending variance computed, and what factors may cause it to occur?

8–12   If prices of indirect materials exceed the prices used in budgeting variable overhead, which variance is likely to be affected? Explain.

8–13   If the basic monthly rate for telephone service (not including long distance calls) increases beyond the amount budgeted, which variance will be affected?

8–14   Explain why only one variance is computed for fixed overhead for companies that use the contribution approach to internal reporting.

EXERCISES
8–1 Input/Output
Analysis

Como Company manufactures a product called Powerpack. The standard input allowed for each unit of output is 8 units. Each unit of input has a standard cost of $5.00. During a recent period 9,000 units of input, acquired at a cost of $5.25 per unit, were used to manufacture 1,100 actual units of output.

Requirements

a) Determine the price variance.

b) Determine the quantity variance.

8–2 Graphical
Representations

Prepare a graph depicting the variances computed in Exercise 8–1.

**8–3 Materials
Variances**

Fisher Company uses standard costs to control materials costs. The standards call for 2 pounds of materials for each finished unit produced. The standard cost per pound of materials is $1.50. During May 4,800 finished units were manufactured and 8,800 pounds of materials were used. The price paid for the materials was $1.52 per pound. There were no beginning or ending materials inventories.

Requirements

a) Determine the flexible budget cost for the manufacture of 4,800 finished units.

b) Determine the actual materials cost incurred for the manufacture of 4,800 finished units, and compute the total materials variance.

c) How much of the difference between the answers to requirements (a) and (b) was related to the price paid for the purchase of materials?

d) How much of the difference between the answers to requirements (a) and (b) was related to the quantity of materials used?

**8–4 Materials Price
Variance Based on
Purchases and on
Usage**

The Charleston Company manufactures decorative weather vanes that have a standard cost of $1.50 per pound for direct materials used in the manufacturing process. During September 11,000 pounds of materials were purchased for $1.55 per pound, and 10,000 pounds were actually used in making weather vanes. There were no beginning inventories.

Requirements

a) Determine the materials price variance assuming that materials costs are the responsibility of the materials purchasing manager.

b) Determine the materials price variance assuming that materials costs are the responsibility of the production manager.

c) Discuss the issues involved in determining the price variance at the point of purchase versus the point of consumption.

**8–5 Direct Labor
Variances**

Dolex Company manufactures specialty electronic circuitry through a unique photo-electronic process. One of the primary products, Model ZX40, has a standard labor time of $\frac{1}{2}$ hour, and a standard labor rate of $13.50 per hour. During February the following activities pertaining to direct labor for ZX40 were recorded.

Direct labor hours used	2,200
Direct labor cost	$34,000
Units of ZX40 manufactured	4,600

Requirements

a) Determine the total flexible budget labor cost variance.

b) Determine the labor rate variance.

c) Determine the labor efficiency variance.

8–6 Variable Overhead Variances

Tea Bone Pickens Company bases standard variable overhead cost on direct labor hours. Standard variable overhead cost has been set at $15 per unit of output, based on $5 of variable overhead per direct labor hour for three hours allowed to produce one finished unit. Last month 4,300 direct labor hours were used and 1,400 units of output were manufactured. The following actual variable overhead costs were incurred.

Indirect materials	$ 4,500
Indirect labor	8,200
Utilities	5,800
Miscellaneous	3,500
Total variable overhead	$22,000

Requirements

a) Determine the variable overhead spending variance.

b) Determine the variable overhead efficiency variance.

c) How is the variable overhead efficiency variance related to labor efficiency?

d) If the company were to use smaller quantities of indirect materials than reflected in the standards, in which variance would the resulting cost savings be reflected? Explain.

8–7 Fixed Overhead Budget Variance

The Gainesville Company uses standard costs for cost control and internal reporting. Fixed costs are budgeted at $7,500 per month at a normal operating level of 10,000 units of production output. During October, actual fixed costs were $7,900, and actual production output was 9,500 units.

Requirements

a) Determine the fixed overhead budget variance.

b) Was the fixed overhead budget variance affected because the company operated below the normal activity level of 10,000 units? Explain.

8–8 Fixed Overhead Volume Variance (Appendix)

Assume that the Gainesville Company in Exercise 8–7 applied fixed overhead to inventory on a per unit basis.

Requirements

a) Determine the fixed overhead volume variance.

b) Explain the possible causes for the volume variance. How is reporting of the volume variance useful to management?

8–9 Causes for Variances

During January the May Company reported the following variances in the production of flagpoles, its only product.

1. Materials price variance

2. Materials quantity variance

3. Labor rate variance

4. Labor efficiency variance

5. Variable overhead spending variance
6. Variable overhead efficiency variance
7. Fixed overhead budget variance

Requirements

a) Identify the variances that are caused primarily by price factors.

b) Identify the variances that are caused primarily by quantity usage factors.

c) Identify the variances that are caused by both price and quantity factors.

8–10 Standard Costs of Services

The President of Guinnett Dekalb Bank has decided that his bank should be using a standard cost system to evaluate management's efficiency in controlling costs of various services that the bank performs for its customers.

Requirements

a) Identify five typical services that banks perform for their retail customers for which it would be practical to use standards costs.

b) What major obstacles is the bank likely to encounter in developing standard costs for its services and using them in performance evaluation and variance analysis?

8–11 Standard Costs and the Flexible Budget

The following performance report was prepared for a cost center in the Hoosier Company for March 19x2. The production volume was 1,800 units.

	Actual Costs	Flexible Budget Costs	Flexible Budget Variances
Direct materials	$ 8,200	$ 9,000	$800 F
Direct labor	5,550	5,400	150 U
Variable overhead:			
Supplies	680	630	50 U
Inspection	700	810	110 F
Indirect labor	900	990	90 F
Utilities	1,335	1,170	165 U
Fixed overhead:			
Depreciation	400	400	—
Supervision	950	900	50 U
Other	485	550	65 F
Totals	$19,200	$19,850	$650 F

Requirements

a) Determine the flexible budget formula for this cost center.

b) Determine the total variable standard cost per unit.

c) Assuming a production volume of 2,500 units, determine the flexible budget cost separately for direct materials, direct labor, and variable overhead.

PROBLEMS

8–12 Computation of Variable Cost Variances

Information pertaining to the standard costs and actual activity for the Tyler Company for September is presented below.

Standard cost per unit	
Direct materials	4 units of material A at $2 per unit
	1 unit of material B at $3 per unit
Direct labor	3 hours at $8 per hour
Variable overhead	$1.50 per direct labor hour
Activity for September	
Materials purchased:	
Material A	4,500 units at $2.05 per unit
Material B	1,100 units at $3.10 per unit
Materials used:	
Material A	4,150 units
Material B	1,005 units

There were no beginning raw materials inventories.

Direct labor used	2,950 hours at $8.20 per hour
Variable overhead costs incurred	$3,800
Production output	1,000 units

Requirements

a) Determine the materials price and quantity variances assuming materials purchases are the responsibility of the purchasing manager.

b) Determine the labor rate and efficiency variances.

c) Determine the variable overhead spending and efficiency variances.

8–13 Materials and Labor Variances; Alternative Computations; Interpretation of Variances

The Laxalt Company manufactures bookcases that have the following unit standard costs for direct materials and direct labor.

Direct materials—lumber (36 feet at $0.70 per foot)	$25.20
Direct labor (1 hour at $10 per hour)	10.00
Total standard direct cost per bookcase	$35.20

The following activities were recorded for March:

- 1,400 bookcases were manufactured.
- 51,200 feet of lumber costing $36,864 was purchased and used.
- $14,700 was paid for 1,500 hours of direct labor.

There were no beginning or ending work-in-process inventories.

Requirements

a) Compute the direct materials variances using two different computational techniques.

b) Compute the direct labor variances using two different computational techniques.

c) Give the possible reasons for the occurrence of each of the above variances.

8–14 Variance Computations: Performance Report

The Outdoor Company is a new firm that manufactures camping tents from a lightweight synthetic fabric. Each tent has a standard materials cost of $20, consisting of 4 yards of fabric at $5 per yard. The standards call for 2 hours of direct labor at $12 per hour and variable overhead at the rate of $2.50 per direct labor hour. Fixed costs are budgeted at $10,000 per month.

The following data were recorded for October 19x5, the first month of operations.

Fabric purchased	9,000 yards at $4.90 per yard
Fabric used in production of 1,700 tents	7,000 yards
Direct labor used	3,600 hours at $12.50 per hour
Variable overhead costs incurred	$8,900
Fixed overhead costs incurred	$13,000

Requirements

a) Compute all standard cost variances for variable costs (materials, labor, and overhead).

b) Determine the fixed overhead budget variance.

c) Determine the standard variable cost of the 1,700 tents produced, broken down into direct materials, direct labor, and variable overhead.

d) Prepare a standard cost performance report using the format illustrated in Exhibit 8–4. The production manager is not responsible for the materials price variance.

e) Give one possible reason for each of the variances computed above.

8–15 Determining Unit Costs: Variance Analysis and Interpretation

The Harmon Company, a manufacturer of dog food, produces its product in 1,000 bag batches. The standard cost of each batch consists of 8,000 pounds of direct materials at $0.30 per pound, 48 direct labor hours at $8.50 per hour, and variable overhead cost (based on machine hours) at the rate of $10 per hour for 16 machine hours per batch. The following variable costs were incurred for the last 1,000 bag batch produced.

Direct materials	8,200 pounds costing $2,378 were purchased and used
Direct labor	45 hours costing $450
Variable overhead	$200
Machine hours used	18

Requirements

a) Determine the actual and standard variable costs per bag of dog food produced, broken down into direct materials, direct labor, and variable overhead.

b) For the last 1,000 bag batch, determine the standard cost variances for direct materials, direct labor, and variable overhead.

c) Explain the possible causes for each of the variances determined in requirement (b).

8–16 Computation of Variances and Other Missing Data

The following data for the O'Keefe Company pertain to the production of 300 units of product X during December. Selected data items are omitted.

Direct materials (All materials purchased were used in current production.)
Standard cost per unit: ___(a)___ pounds at $3.20 per pound
Total actual cost: ___(b)___ pounds costing $5,673
Standard cost allowed for units produced: $5,760
Materials price variance: ___(c)___
Materials quantity variance: $96 U

Direct labor
Standard cost: 2 hours at $7.00
Actual cost per hour: $7.25
Total actual cost: ___(d)___
Labor rate variance: ___(e)___
Labor efficiency variance: $140 U

Variable overhead
Standard costs: ___(f)___ hours at $4 per direct labor hour
Actual cost: $2,250
Variable overhead spending variance: ___(g)___
Variable overhead efficiency variance: ___(h)___

Total units produced were 300.

Required: Fill in the missing amounts in the blanks lettered (a) through (h).

8–17 Computation of Missing Variances and Other Data

The following data pertaining to the production of the Dalko Company's primary product are for a recent month, with selected items omitted. Two thousand units of product were produced during the month, and the total flexible budget cost allowed was $100,000.

Direct materials
Standard cost per unit: 4 gallons at $7.90 per gallon
Total actual cost of materials used: ___(a)___ gallons at $8.00 per gallon
Total standard cost allowed: ___(b)___
Total flexible budget variance: ___(c)___
Materials price variance: ___(d)___
Materials quantity variance: $553 U

Direct labor
Standard cost per unit: 0.4 hour at $15 per hour
Total actual cost of labor: ___(e)___ hours at ___(f)___ per hour
Total standard cost allowed: ___(g)___
Total flexible budget variance: $485 F
Labor rate variance: $235 U
Labor efficiency variance: ___(h)___

Variable overhead

    Standard cost per unit: ___(i)___ labor hours at $4 per hour

    Actual cost: $4,200

    Total standard cost allowed: ___(j)___

    Total flexible budget variance: ___(k)___

    Variable overhead spending variance: ___(l)___

    Variable overhead efficiency variance: ___(m)___

Fixed overhead

    Actual cost: ___(n)___

    Budgeted cost: ___(o)___

    Budget variance: $1,000 F

Required: Fill in the missing amounts in the blanks lettered (a) through (o).

8–18 Overhead Variances

The Grogan Coach Company controls variable overhead costs based on direct labor hours, and controls fixed costs on the basis of total budgeted costs. Each unit of output is allowed 10 standard direct labor hours. The standard variable overhead cost per unit of output, broken down by cost components, is presented below.

Indirect materials	$125
Indirect labor	90
Plant and facilities cost	60
Miscellaneous variable overhead	50
Standard variable overhead	
cost per unit of output	$325

Budgeted fixed costs per month are as follows:

Indirect labor	$ 8,000
Plant and facilities cost	3,000
Depreciation	2,500
Miscellaneous fixed costs	1,200
Total budgeted fixed costs	$14,700

During July 2, 100 actual direct labor hours were worked, and the production output was 200 units. Actual costs incurred were as follows:

	Variable	Fixed
Indirect materials	$23,500	—
Indirect labor	19,000	$ 8,800
Plant and facilities	12,200	3,750
Depreciation	—	2,500
Miscellaneous	10,400	1,100
Total actual overhead costs	$65,100	$16,150

Required: Prepare a performance report that shows variable and fixed overhead variances broken down by cost items. Use the following column headings for your report.

				Variance Analysis	
Cost Item	Actual Costs	Standard Costs (Flexible Budget)	Total Variance	Spending or Budget	Efficiency
	$	$	$	$	$

8–19 Causes of Standard Cost Variances

Below are ten unrelated situations that would ordinarily be expected to affect one or more standard cost variances.

1. A salaried production foreman is given a raise, and no adjustment is made in the labor cost standards.

2. The materials purchasing manager gets a special reduced price on raw materials by purchasing a train carload. A warehouse had to be rented to accommodate the unusually large amount of raw materials. The rental fee was charged to rent expense, a fixed overhead item.

3. An unusually hot August caused the company to use 25,000 kilowatts more electricity than provided for in the variable overhead standards.

4. The local electric utility company raised the charge per kilowatt hour. No adjustment was made in the variable overhead standards.

5. The plant manager traded in his leased company car for a new Cadillac in July, increasing the monthly lease payment by $150.

6. A machine malfunction on the assembly line caused by using cheap and inferior raw materials resulted in decreased output by the machine operator and higher than normal machine repair costs. Repairs are treated as variable overhead costs.

7. The production maintenance supervisor decreased routine maintenance checks, resulting in lower maintenance cost and lower machine production output per hour. Maintenance costs are treated as fixed costs.

8. An announcement that vacation benefits had been increased resulted in improved employee morale. Consequently, raw materials pilferage and waste declined, and production efficiency increased.

9. The plant manager reclassified her secretary to administrative assistant and gave him an increase in salary.

10. A union contract agreement was signed calling for an immediate 5 percent increase in production worker wages. No changes were made in the standards.

Required: For each of the above situations indicate by letter which of the following standard cost variances would be affected. More than one variance will be affected in some cases.

a) Materials price variance

b) Materials quantity variance

c) Labor rate variance

d) Labor efficiency variance

e) Variable overhead spending variance

f) Variable overhead efficiency variance

g) Fixed overhead budget variance

8–20 Measuring the Effects of Decisions on Standard Cost Variances

Below are five unrelated situations that affect one or more standard cost variances for materials, labor, and overhead.

1. Lois Jones, a production worker, announced her intentions to resign in order to accept another job paying $1.20 per hour more. To keep from losing her, the production manager agreed to raise her salary from $7.00 to $8.50 per hour. Lois works an average of 175 hours per month.

2. At the beginning of the month a supplier of a component used in our product notified us that, because of a minor design improvement, the price will be increased by 15 percent above the current standard price of $100 per unit. As a result of the improved design, we expect the number of defective components to decrease by 80 units per month. On the average 1,200 units of the component are purchased each month. Defective units are identified prior to use and are not returnable.

3. In an effort to meet a deadline on a rush order in Department A, the plant manager reassigned several higher skilled workers from Department B, for a total of 300 labor hours. The average salary of the Department B workers was $1.85 more than the standard $7.00 per hour rate of the Department A workers. Since they were not accustomed to the work, the average Department B worker was able to produce only 36 units per hour instead of the standard 48 units per hour. (Consider only the effect on Department A labor variances.)

4. Rob Celiba is an inspector who earns a flat salary of $700 per month plus a piece rate of 20 cents per bundle inspected. His company accounts for inspection costs as factory overhead. Because of a payroll department error in June, Rob was paid $500 plus a piece rate of 30 cents per bundle. He received gross wages totaling $1,100.

5. The materials purchasing manager purchased 5,000 units of component K2X from a new source at a price $12 below the standard unit price of $200. These components turned out to be of extremely poor quality with defects occurring at three times the standard rate of 5 percent. The higher rate of defects reduced the output of workers (who earn $8 per hour) from 20 units per hour to 15 units per hour on the units containing the discount components. Each finished unit contains one K2X component. To appease the workers, who were irate at having to work with inferior components, the production manager agreed to pay the workers an additional 25 cents for each of the components (good and bad) in the discount batch. Variable factory overhead is applied at the rate of $4 per direct labor hour. The defective units also caused a 20 hour increase in total machine hours. The actual cost of electricity to run the machines is $2 per hour.

Required: For each of the above situations determine which standard cost variance(s) will be affected, and compute the amount of the effect for one month on each variance. Indicate whether the effect is favorable or unfavorable. Assume the standards are not changed in response to these situations. (Round calculations to two decimal places.)

8–21 Developing Cost Standards for Materials and Labor

After several years of operating without a formal system of cost control, the Carlsen Company, a tools manufacturer, has decided to implement a standard cost system. The system will be established first for the department that makes lug wrenches for automobile mechanics. The standard production batch size is 100 wrenches. The actual materials and labor required for eight batches selected randomly from last year's production are as follows:

Batch	Materials Used (in pounds)	Labor Used (in hours)
1	504	10
2	508	9
3	506	9
4	521	5
5	516	8
6	518	7
7	520	6
8	515	8
Average	513.5	7.75

Management has obtained the following recommendations concerning what the materials and labor quantity standards should be.

- The manufacturer of the equipment used in making the wrenches advertises in the toolmakers' trade journal that the machine Carlsen uses can produce 100 wrenches with 500 pounds of raw materials and 5 labor hours. Carlsen's engineers believe the standards should be based on these data.

- The accounting department believes a more realistic standard would be 504 pounds and 5 hours.

- The production supervisor believes the standard should be 513.5 pounds and 7.75 hours.

- The production workers argue for standards of 515 pounds and 8 hours.

Requirements

a) State the arguments for and against each of the recommendations and the probable effects of each recommendation on the quantity variances for materials and labor.

b) Which recommendation provides the best combination of cost control and motivation to the production workers? Explain.

8–22 Variance Analysis for Services Costs

Atlantic Manufacturers Bank uses standard costs in its commercial loan department. The standard cost to process a loan has been determined as follows:

Direct materials (20 pages of forms at 10 cents per page)	$ 2
Direct labor (2 hrs at $8)	16
Variable overhead cost (2 hrs at $1 per labor hr)	2
Total standard variable cost per loan application	$20

Fixed costs in the commercial loan department are budgeted at $1,500 per month.

Last month 160 loan applications were processed, and the following costs were incurred.

Direct materials	3,500 pages of forms totaling $420
Direct labor	345 hrs at $8.20 per hr
Variable overhead	$400
Fixed overhead	$1,650

Requirements

a) Determine all standard variable cost variances discussed in this chapter for direct materials, direct labor, and variable overhead.

b) Determine the fixed overhead budget variance.

c) Identify some of the problems of using standard costing in a service oriented business.

8–23 Data Computations from Variance Information

On May 1, 19x5, Bovar Company began the manufacture of a new mechanical device known as "Dandy." The company installed a standard cost system in accounting for manufacturing costs. The standard costs for a unit of "Dandy" are as follows:

Raw materials (6 lbs at $1 per lb)	$ 6
Direct labor (1 hr at $4 per hr)	4
Overhead (75% of direct labor costs)	3
	$13

The following data were obtained from Bovar's records for May.

Actual production of "Dandy"	4,000 units
Unsold units of "Dandy"	2,500 units
Sales	$50,000
Purchases	$27,300
Materials purchased price variance	$ 1,300 U
Materials quantity variance	$ 1,000 U
Direct labor rate variance	$ 760 U
Direct labor efficiency variance	$ 800 F
Total overhead flexible budget variance	$ 500 U

Required: Compute each of the following items for Bovar for May.

1. Total standard quantity of raw materials allowed (in pounds)

2. Total actual quantity of raw materials used (in pounds)

3. Total standard labor hours allowed

4. Total actual hours worked

5. Actual direct labor rate per hour

6. Actual total overhead costs

(CPA Adapted)

8–24 Variance Analysis: Factory Overhead Based on Labor Cost

Armando Corporation manufactures a product with the following standard costs.

Direct materials (20 yds at $1.35 per yd)	$ 27
Direct labor (4 hrs at $9 per hr)	36
Variable factory overhead costs (based on $5 per labor hour)	20
Total variable standard cost per unit of output	$ 83
Total budgeted fixed factory overhead per month	$6,000

The following information pertains to July 19x1.

Direct materials purchased (18,000 yds at $1.38)	$24,840
Direct materials used (9,500 yds)	n/a
Direct labor (2,100 hrs at $9.15)	19,215
Total factory overhead ($6,800 fixed)	16,650
Total actual costs	$60,705

500 units of product were actually produced in July 19x1.

Requirements

a) Determine the standard variable overhead rate per direct labor hour.

b) Compute the following variances:

Materials purchased price variance
Materials quantity variance
Labor rate variance
Labor efficiency variance
Variable overhead spending variance
Variable overhead efficiency variance
Fixed overhead budget variance

c) Prepare a Production Department performance report showing actual costs, flexible budget costs, total flexible budget variances, and standard cost variances for July. The production manager is not responsible for the materials price variance.

(CPA Adapted)

8–25 Fixed Overhead Budget and Volume Variances (Appendix)

The Starling Company assigns fixed overhead costs to inventory for external reporting purposes by using a predetermined standard overhead rate based on direct labor hours. The standard rate is based on a normal (or denominator) activity level of 10,000 standard allowed direct labor hours per year. There are 5 standard allowed hours for each unit of output. Budgeted fixed overhead costs are $200,000 per year. During 19x8 the Starling Company produced 2,100 units of output, and actual fixed costs were $205,000.

Requirements

a) Determine the standard fixed overhead rate used to assign fixed costs to inventory.

b) Determine the amount of fixed overhead assigned to inventory in 19x8.

c) Determine the fixed overhead budget variance.

d) Determine the fixed overhead volume variance.

e) Even though the cost of security guards is controlled as a fixed cost, the number of hours worked by the guards may fluctuate somewhat. If the number of hours worked by the guards in 19x8 had been smaller, which fixed overhead variance would have been affected? Explain. If the wage rate for security guards had increased during the year (with no revision of the standard), which variance would have been affected? Explain.

f) What information does the fixed overhead volume variance computed above convey to management?

8–26 Variance Computations with Fixed Cost Assigned on a Unit Basis (Appendix)

The Terry Company manufactures a commercial solvent that is used for industrial maintenance. This solvent is sold by the drum and generally has a stable selling price. Because of a decrease in demand for this product, Terry produced and sold 60,000 drums in December 19x6, which is 50 percent of normal capacity. The following information is available regarding Terry's operations for December 19x6.

Standard costs per drum of product manufactured were as follows:

Materials:	
10 gallons of raw materials at $2 per gallon	$20
1 empty drum	1
Total materials cost	$21
Direct labor: 1 hour	$ 7
Variable factory overhead: per labor hour	$ 6
Fixed factory overhead: per labor hour	$ 6
(Fixed overhead is assigned to production	
based on a normal production volume of	
120,000 allowed direct labor hours.)	

Costs incurred during December 19x6 were as follows:

Raw materials:	
600,000 gallons were purchased at a cost of $1,150,000.	
700,000 gallons were used.	
Empty drums:	
85,000 drums were purchased at a cost of $85,000.	
60,000 drums were used, and 60,000 drums	
of product were produced.	
Direct labor: 65,000 hours for a total of $470,000.	
Factory overhead:	
Variable factory overhead	$ 76,500
Supervision and indirect labor (contains $320,000 variable and	
$140,000 fixed)	460,000
Depreciation (fixed)	330,000
Total factory overhead	$866,500

Required: Compute the following variances.

1. Materials purchased price variance
2. Materials quantity variance
3. Labor rate variance
4. Labor efficiency variance
5. Variable overhead spending variance
6. Variable overhead efficiency variance
7. Fixed overhead budget variance
8. Fixed overhead volume variance

(CPA Adapted)

8–27 Sales, Flexible Budget, and Standard Cost Variances: Reconcilation of Actual and Budgeted Net Income

The Robson Company's Macon plant produces alloy ingots for industrial use. Andrew O'Brian, who was recently appointed general manager, just received the following income statement for his plant for May 19x6, his first month as manager.

	Actual	Budgeted	Variance
Units	5,500	6,000	500 U
Sales	$132,000	$120,000	$12,000 F
Less variable costs:			
Direct materials	$ 22,275	$ 23,400	$ 1,125 F
Direct labor	20,805	21,000	195 F
Factory overhead	15,860	16,500	640 F
Total variable costs	− 58,940	− 60,900	1,960 F
Contribution margin	$ 73,060	$ 59,100	$13,960 F
Less fixed manufacturing costs	− 26,500	− 25,000	− 1,500 U
Plant net income	$ 46,560	$ 34,100	$12,460 F

There were no beginning or ending inventories. The variable standard costs per unit are as follows:

Direct materials: $1\frac{1}{2}$ kilograms at $2.60 per kilogram
Direct labor: $\frac{1}{2}$ hour at $7.00 per hour
Variable overhead: $\frac{1}{2}$ direct labor hour at $5.50 per hour

The following actual data were collected.

Direct materials used: 8,250 kilograms
Direct labor hours used: 2,850 hours

Requirements

(*Note:* Parts (a) through (d) provide a review of material discussed in Chapter 7.)

a) Determine the amount of the plant net income variance traceable to the decision to raise the selling price. *Hint:* Compute the sales price variance.

b) Determine the amount of the plant net income variance traceable to selling 500 units below the budget. *Hint:* Compute the net sales volume variance.

c) Determine the amount of the plant net income variance traceable to manufacturing cost control factors. *Hint:* Compute the flexible budget variance for total manufacturing costs, including variable and fixed.

d) What does the sum of the answers to requirements (a) through (c) represent?

e) Determine the total flexible budget variance for direct materials and the appropriate standard cost variances.

f) Repeat requirement (e) for direct labor.

g) Repeat requirement (e) for variable factory overhead.

h) Determine the fixed factory overhead budget variance.

i) O'Brian feels very good about exceeding the original budgeted net income in spite of selling 500 fewer units of product than budgeted. From a cost control standpoint, does he have any reason to be pleased about his performance? Explain.

CASES

8–28 Compiling and Reporting Standard Cost Variances

The Carberg Corporation manufactures and sells a single product. The cost system used by the company is a standard cost system. The variable standard cost per unit of product is shown below:

Material (1 lb of plastic at $2)	$ 2.00
Direct labor (1.6 hrs at $4)	6.40
Variable overhead cost	3.00
	$11.40

The overhead cost per unit was calculated from the following annual overhead cost budget for a 60,000 unit volume.

Variable overhead cost:		
Indirect labor (30,000 hrs at $4)	$120,000	
Supplies—oil (60,000 gals at $0.50)	30,000	
Utilities	30,000	$180,000
Fixed overhead costs:		
Supervision	$ 27,000	
Depreciation	45,000	
Other fixed costs	15,000	87,000
Total budgeted overhead costs for 60,000 units		$267,000

The charges to the manufacturing department for November, when 5,000 units were produced, are given as follows.

Materials (5,300 lbs at $2)	$10,600
Direct labor (8,200 hrs at $4.10)	33,620
Indirect labor (2,400 hrs at $4.10)	9,840
Supplies—oil (6,000 gals at $0.55)	3,300
Utilities	3,200
Supervision	2,475
Depreciation	3,750
Other fixed costs	1,250
Total	$68,035

The purchasing department normally buys about the same quantity as is used in production during a month. In November 5,200 pounds were purchased at a price of $2.10 per pound.

Requirements

a) Calculate the following variances from standard costs for the data given above.

   1. Materials purchased price variance

   2. Materials quantity variance

   3. Direct labor rate variance

   4. Direct labor efficiency variance

   5. Total flexible budget variance for each overhead item

b) The company has divided its responsibilities so that the purchasing department is responsible for the price at which materials and supplies are purchased, and the manufacturing department is responsible for the quantities of materials used. Does this division of responsibilities solve the conflict between price and quantity variances? Explain.

c) Prepare a report that details the flexible overhead budget variances. The report, which will be given to the manufacturing department manager, should display only that part of each variance that is the obvious responsibility of the manager. It should highlight the information in ways that would be useful to that manager in evaluating departmental performance and when considering corrective action. *Hint:* This part requires considerable thought, rather than technical analysis.

d) Assume that the department manager performs the timekeeping function for this manufacturing department. From time to time an analysis of overhead and direct labor variances has shown that the department manager has deliberately misclassified labor hours (e.g., listed direct labor hours as indirect labor hours, and vice versa) so that only one of the two labor variances is unfavorable. It is not feasible economically to hire a separate timekeeper. What should the company do, if anything, to resolve this problem?

(CMA Adapted)

**8–29 Evaluating
Standard Costs**

Comtech, Inc., which uses a simplified standard cost system, manufactures a lap-top computer that has a standard cost of $640 per unit broken down as follows:

Direct materials components (1 materials kit per unit)	$525
Direct labor (6¼ hours at $12)	75
Overhead ($6.40 per direct labor hour)	40
Total	$640

Direct materials consist of a kit of 5 component modules used in assembling the computers. All the modules are manufactured by either outside contractors or by other divisions of Comtech. Management is free to buy the components from any available source so long as the components meet the company engineering and quality standards. During October 19x9, the following report was prepared for the production department.

	Actual Costs	Flexible Budget Costs	Standard Cost Variances
Direct materials	$286,125	$262,500	$23,625 U
Direct labor	45,000	37,500	7,500 U
Overhead	20,875	20,000	875 U
Totals	$352,000	$320,000	$32,000 U

When asked to explain the flexible budget variances, the production manager argued that the report was not an accurate indication of his performance. He provided the following information to defend his claim that the standards were not appropriate.

1. Standard direct materials costs are based on the lowest prices available for the various components during the preceding period. Market prices during the current period are 2 percent higher than those of the previous period. Also, the standards did not allow for any defective parts that had to be scrapped or for any pilferage or other materials losses.

2. The standard direct labor cost of $12 per hour is a weighted average of all workers' wages on the production line during the preceding period. The manager maintains that, due to transfers of workers into the production department from other departments, there are more high-paid workers in the production department currently than when the standards were established. He also stated that skilled workers who normally earn $15 per hour are being averaged with unskilled workers who earn $8 per hour.

3. The standard overhead cost includes a variable overhead cost of $5 per labor hour as well as a fixed overhead cost based on a budgeted capacity of 1,000 computers per month.

Requirements

a) Evaluate Comtech's standard cost system. Is the production manager's lack of confidence in the performance report justified? Explain.

b) Given the information provided, can quantity and price standard cost variances be determined for materials, labor, and overhead? If not, what additional information is needed for you to compute these variances?

c) Make recommendations for improving Comtech's standard cost variance analysis and reporting system. Create hypothetical data as necessary to illustrate your recommendations.

8–30 Behavioral Effects of Standard Costs

The Deleware Corp. has used a standard cost system for evaluating the performance of its responsibility center managers for three years. Top management feels that standard costing has not produced the cost savings or increases in productivity and profits promised by the accounting department. Large unfavorable variances are consistently reported for most cost categories and employee morale has fallen since the system was installed. To help pinpoint the problem with the system, top management asked for separate evaluations of the system by the plant department manager, the accounting department manager, and the personnel department manager. Their responses are summarized below:

Plant Manager: The standards are unrealistic. They assume an ideal working environment that does not allow materials defects or errors by the workers or machines. Consequently, morale has gone down and productivity has declined. Standards should be based on expected actual prices and recent past averages for efficiency. Thus, if we improve over the past, we receive a favorable variance.

Accounting Manager: The goal of accounting reports is to measure performance against an absolute standard and the best approximation of that standard is ideal conditions. Cost standards should be comparable to "par" on a golf course. Just as the game of golf uses a handicap system to allow for differences in individual players' skills and scores, it may be necessary for management to interpret variances based on the circumstances that produced the variances. Accordingly, in one case, a given unfavorable variance may represent poor performance; whereas, in another case, it may represent good performance. The managers are just going to have to recognize these subtleties in standard cost systems and depend on upper management to be fair.

Personnel Manager: The key to employee productivity is employee satisfaction and a sense of accomplishment. A set of standards that can never be met denies managers of this vital motivator. The current standards would be appropriate in a laboratory with a controlled environment, but not in the factory with its many variables. If we are to recapture our old "team spirit," we must give the managers a goal that they can achieve through hard work.

Required: Discuss the behavioral issues involved in the Deleware Corp.'s standard cost dilemma. Evaluate each of the three responses (pros and cons) and recommend a course of action.

**REVIEW PROBLEM
SOLUTION**

a)

Standard cost variance analysis

Input component: direct materials   **Output: 5,000 units**

Actual cost		**Standard cost of actual inputs**		**Flexible budget cost**	
Actual quantity	21,250	Actual quantity	21,250	Standard quantity allowed	20,000*
Actual price	× $4.90	Standard price	× $5.00	Standard price	× $5.00
	$104,125		$106,250		$100,000

Materials price
variance $2,125 F

Materials quantity
variance $6,250 U

Total flexible budget materials variance $4,125 U

* Standard quantity of direct materials equals 5,000 units of PGX produced times 4 direct
materials units allowed per PGX unit produced.

Standard cost variance analysis

Input component: direct labor   **Output: 5,000 units**

Actual cost		**Standard cost of actual inputs**		**Flexible budget cost**	
Actual hours	8,000	Actual hours	8,000	Standard hours allowed	7,500*
Actual rate	×$10.30	Standard rate	×$10.00	Standard rate	×$10.00
	$ 82,400		$ 80,000		$ 75,000

Labor rate
variance $2,400 U

Labor efficiency
variance $5,000 U

Total flexible budget labor variance $7,400 U

* Standard quantity of labor hours equals 5,000 units of PGX produced times 1.5 direct
labor hours allowed per PGX unit produced.

Standard cost variance analysis

Input component: variable overhead   Output: 5,000 units

Actual cost		Standard cost of actual inputs		Flexible budget cost	
Actual hours	n/a	Actual hours	8,000	Standard hours allowed	7,500*
Actual rate	n/a	Standard rate	× $8.00	Standard rate	× $8.00
	$56,000		$64,000		$60,000

Variable overhead
spending
variance $8,000 F

Variable overhead efficiency
variance $4,000 U

Total flexible budget variable overhead variance $4,000 F

* Standard quantity of variable overhead in terms of direct labor hours equals 5,000 units of PGX produced times 1.5 direct labor hours allowed per PGX unit produced. Note that the standard hours allowed of variable overhead will always be the same as the standard direct labor hours when variable overhead has direct labor hours as an activity base.

b)

Toytek, Inc.
Production Department
Standard Cost Performance Report
For the month of March, 19x5

	Actual Costs	Flexible Budget Costs	Flexible Budget Variances	Variance Analysis
Direct materials	$104,125	$100,000	$4,125 U	$2,125 F Price Variance
				6,250 U Quantity Variance
Direct labor	82,400	75,000	7,400 U	2,400 U Rate Variance
				5,000 U Efficiency Variance
Variable overhead	56,000	60,000	4,000 F	8,000 F Spending Variance
				4,000 U Efficiency Variance
Fixed overhead	32,000	30,000	2,000 U	2,000 U Budget Variance
Totals	$274,525	$265,000	$9,525 U	$9,525 U

C H A P T E R 9

Control of Decentralized Operations

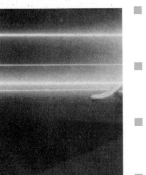

Learning Objectives

Upon completion of this chapter you should:

■ Have a general understanding of the organizational theories of centralization and decentralization and be familiar with the advantages and disadvantages of each.

■ Be able to compute the following ratios for a decentralized organizational unit: return on investment, investment turnover, and return on sales.

■ Understand the problems in decentralized organizations related to defining the investment base and the investment center income.

■ Be able to compute residual income for a decentralized organizational unit.

■ Be familiar with the relative advantages of the residual income and return on investment methods for evaluating performance in decentralized units.

■ Understand the concept of transfer pricing and be familiar with the major transfer pricing bases: market prices, variable costs, variable costs plus opportunity cost, absorption cost plus markup, negotiated prices, and dual prices.

■ Understand when and how the use of transfer prices can lead to suboptimization for the organization as a whole.

Organizations that operate in several different industries, or widely dispersed geographic areas, are often segregated into quasi-independent parts. Although a centralized organizational structure is appropriate for many organizations, it has several limitations and is often replaced by a decentralized structure in diverse and complex organizations.

The purpose of this chapter is to present techniques used to measure and evaluate the performance of segments of decentralized organizations. The various ways in which such operations can be evaluated, how they interact with each other, and the problems large organizations encounter when they have decentralized operations are all discussed.

The decentralized units normally become quasi-independent, often having their own controller function, computer system, and administrative and marketing staffs. When this occurs, the corporate office faces several problems in keeping the units properly functioning for the benefit of the entire organization. These problem areas are discussed in this chapter.

MANAGEMENT PHILOSOPHIES OF DECENTRALIZED OPERATIONS

To establish a proper framework for *decentralization,* it is necessary to examine some of the issues surrounding *centralization.* Centralization exists when the major functions of an organization (such as manufacturing, sales, accounting, computer operations, marketing, research and development, and management control) are controlled by top management. Reasons for centralization include the following:

- Economies of scale—Centralized resources can be more fully utilized than the same resources divided into smaller groupings.

- Sophistication of applications—By combining the firm's resources, greater efficiency may be achieved and more complex tasks performed.

- Improved control—Direct lines of authority provide better control of resources. Improved control permits the organization to rapidly shift resources to achieve changing corporate goals. Centralization also permits a greater perspective by top managers because they are in contact with a larger proportion of activities than if decentralized.

However, centralization does have its limitations, the most significant of which are given below:

- Span of control—After the size of a given function increases to a certain level, it becomes difficult to control from the top of an organization.

- Complexity—Combining activities into large centralized functions may create organizations of such complexity that they become unmanageable.

- Diseconomies of scale—When functions become too large, problems of control and efficiency begin to occur. Almost every organizational function has a point of diminishing returns where adding another employee, work task, or manager does little toward reaching the overall organizational objectives.

Decentralization is the delegation of decision-making authority to successively lower management levels in an organization. The lower in the organization the authority is delegated, the greater the decentralization. This approach offers several advantages that tend to counter the problems of centralization. The most compelling arguments for decentralization are based on the need for management to be more responsive to the various operating units and segments of the organization. The advantages of decentralization include the following:

- First-hand decision making—Personnel closely associated with problems and situations are allowed to make decisions. What's more, experience in decision making at low management levels results in trained managers when higher level positions become available.

- Faster decisions—Decisions are made locally without having to feed information up the chain of command and then wait for a response.

MANAGERIAL PRACTICE 9.1

IBM Decentralizes

After two years of falling profits, IBM chairman John Akers announced a major reorganization aimed at improving efficiency of decision making at the top levels of the organization. The reorganization created six new product and marketing groups reporting to a group president. Mr. Akers stated that "this is a major delegation of authority," which in reality creates six different IBM companies. Stating that "our development and manufacturing teams will frankly spend less time at corporate headquarters," he expects this reorganization to improve the process and speed with which new products are developed and brought to the market.

Source: Michael W. Miller and Paul B. Carroll, "IBM Unveils a Sweeping Restructuring in Bid to Decentralize Decision-Making," *Wall Street Journal* (29 January 1988): 3.

- Specialization—Corporate management can concentrate on strategic planning and policy, and divisional management can concentrate on operating decisions.
- Motivation—Managers who actively participate in decision making are more committed to the success of their programs and are more willing to accept responsibility for the consequences of their actions.

Before accepting decentralization as the answer to organizational problems, its disadvantages must be considered. The primary problems associated with this type of organizational structure are given below:

- Competent personnel—Division management may not be able to carry out and control its operations in accordance with company policy because of a lack of competent personnel.
- Performance measurement—It is difficult to keep all operating units on the same measurement system in a large organization. This includes reporting periods, methods of reporting, and consistency of data collection.
- Suboptimization—It is difficult to keep each unit operating for the benefit of the entire organization rather than for its own selfish benefit.

As organizations expand in size and complexity, centralized control becomes more difficult. Planning, organizing, and controlling may overwhelm top management in a large centralized organization. The solution to this problem is the decentralization of the organization into smaller operating units. With proper planning and staffing of each unit or division, the organization can often overcome the disadvantages of decentralization and improve overall organizational performance.

In most large decentralized organizations, the primary operating units are called divisions. Each division is largely autonomous, with the division manager being responsible for sales, production, and administration of the unit. Division managers frequently have control over all activities, although capital budgeting and long-range planning activities are often limited. These two activities are often centralized within corporate headquarters, with the various division managers given control over the investments once they are made. As generally organized, divisions are the most common example of investment centers.

A decentralized organizational structure is illustrated in Exhibit 9–1. The theory behind this structure is to delegate most responsibilities to each division and let each division operate as a quasi-independent business. You might want to contrast this with the centralized organizational chart in Exhibit 7–2.

The division management group usually includes managers from the computer center, personnel, marketing, controller's office, production, and other necessary functions. One potential problem of such a structure is the conflict of two superiors. The dashed lines in Exhibit 9–1 represent each staff's responsibility to corporate headquarters, whereas the solid lines connect each staff to the division vice president who has day-to-day authority. For example, the controller has a dual responsibility: (1) to the divisional vice president who exercises

EXHIBIT 9–1   Decentralized Organizational Chart

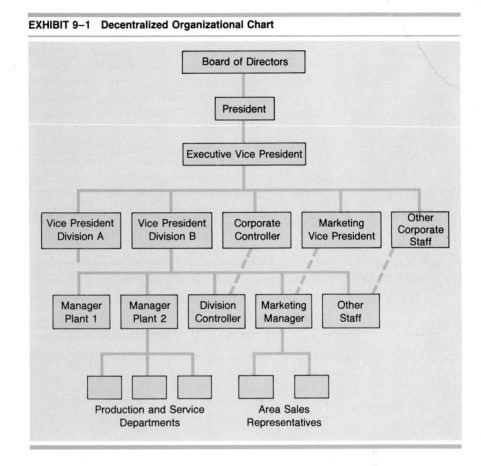

line authority and (2) to the corporate controller who exercises functional authority. The divisional controller performs at the division level most of the controllership tasks outlined in Chapter 1. The divisional controller must follow certain firmwide accounting procedures specified by the corporate controller. Sometimes the divisional controller is regarded as an extension of the corporate controller or as a "front-office employee." In this case the divisional controller has a direct-line relationship with the corporate controller and a staff-line relationship with the division manager.

EVALUATION METHODS

Recall from Chapter 7 that responsibility accounting is the structuring of performance reports addressed to individual members of an organization in a manner that emphasizes the factors controllable by them. Responsibility accounting reports may be prepared for cost centers, revenue centers, profit centers, or investment centers. Cost centers are evaluated by comparing actual with allowed costs, and revenue centers are evaluated by comparing actual with budgeted revenues. Because divisions operate as quasi-independent businesses with significant authority over their activities and the size of their investments, they are evaluated as investment centers. When the investment center concept is implemented, the use of net income as a performance measure is not sufficient because different centers may have substantially different asset bases. In these situations net income does not properly reflect the efficient use of the assets employed. Today, most organizations use the *return on investment* ratio as the primary basis for evaluating investment centers. This concept is more relevant than traditional net income because investment center performance reports need to emphasize the relationship between each investment center's income and the size of its asset base. A closely related concept, *residual income,* is also frequently used and is discussed in a later section.

Return on Investment (ROI)

Return on investment is a measure of the earnings per dollar of investment.[1] The return on investment of an investment center is computed by dividing the income of the center by its asset base (usually total assets):

$$ROI = \frac{\text{Investment center income}}{\text{Investment center asset base}}.$$

It can also be computed as investment turnover times the return-on-sales ratio (also called margin, income percentage of revenue, and income-sales ratio):

$$ROI = \text{Investment turnover} \times \text{Return-on-sales ratio},$$

where,

$$\text{Investment turnover} = \frac{\text{Sales}}{\text{Investment center asset base}}, \text{ and}$$

$$\text{Return-on-sales ratio} = \frac{\text{Investment center income}}{\text{Sales}}$$

When investment turnover is multiplied by the return-on-sales ratio, the product is the same as investment center income divided by investment center asset base:

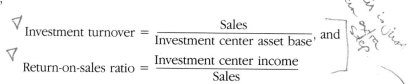

$$ROI = \frac{\text{Sales}}{\text{Investment center asset base}} \times \frac{\text{Investment center income}}{\text{Sales}}$$

$$= \frac{\text{Investment center income}}{\text{Investment center asset base}}.$$

Once ROI is computed, it is compared to some previously identified performance criteria, such as the investment center's previous ROI, overall company ROI, the ROI of similar divisions, or the ROI of nonaffiliated companies that

---

[1] Other similar concepts that are often used to supplement or replace ROI, but are not discussed here, include return on assets, return on net assets, and return on production assets.

operate in similar markets, produce similar products, or provide similar services. The breakdown of ROI into investment turnover and return-on-sales ratio is useful in determining the source of variance in overall performance.

To illustrate the computation and use of ROI, the following information is available concerning the 19x3 operations of the Maine Division of North American Steel:

Sales	$1,200,000
Income	144,000
Asset base	800,000

From these facts ROI can be computed as

$$ROI = \frac{\text{Investment center income}}{\text{Investment center asset base}}$$

$$= \frac{\$144,000}{\$800,000}$$

$$= 0.18, \text{ or } 18 \text{ percent,}$$

or as

$$ROI = \frac{\text{Sales}}{\text{Investment center asset base}} \times \frac{\text{Investment center income}}{\text{Sales}}$$

$$= \frac{\$1,200,000}{\$800,000} \times \frac{\$144,000}{\$1,200,000}$$

$$= 1.5 \times 0.12$$

$$= 0.18, \text{ or } 18 \text{ percent.}$$

During 19x3, Maine Division earned a return on its investment base of 18 percent, consisting of an investment turnover of 1.5 times and a return-on-sales ratio of 0.12. Using such an analysis, the company has three measurement criteria with which to evaluate the performance of Maine Division: (1) ROI, (2) investment turnover, and (3) return-on-sales ratio.

For 19x3, North American chose to evaluate its divisions based on company ROI and its interrelated components of investment turnover and income-sales ratio. The information for each division is shown in Exhibit 9–2. Because each division is different in size, the company evaluation standard is not a simple average of the divisions but is based on desired levels of company sales, assets, and income.

Based on ROI, the Tijuana Division had the best performance, Alberta excelled in investment turnover, and Utah had the highest return-on-sales ratio. From Exhibit 9–2 it is obvious that Tijuana had the best year because it was the only division that exceeded each of the company's performance criteria. For 19x3, each division equaled or exceeded the minimum ROI established by the company, even though the component criteria of ROI were not always achieved. For example, Maine Division achieved the minimum ROI even though its return-

EXHIBIT 9–2   Division Evaluation Data

North American Steel
Performance Measures
For the year ended June 30, 19x3

| | | Performance Measures | |
	ROI	Investment Turnover	Return-on-Sales Ratio
Operating unit:			
Maine division	0.18	1.5	0.12
Alberta division	0.24	3.0	0.08
Utah division	0.22	1.1	0.20
Tijuana division	0.27	1.5	0.18
Average (company)	0.21	1.4	0.15
Company performance criteria:			
Projected minimums	0.18	1.2	0.15

on-sales ratio was below 0.15. It accomplished this by having an investment turnover that exceeded the minimum by 0.3 (1.5 less 1.2).

To properly evaluate each division the company should study the underlying components of ROI. For the Maine Division, management would want to know why the minimum investment turnover was exceeded while the return-on-sales ratio minimum was not. The Maine Division may have incurred unfavorable cost variances by producing inefficiently. As a result of inefficient production, the return-on-sales ratio declined to a point below the minimum desired level. It is difficult to evaluate a large operating division based on one financial figure. Management should select several key indicators of performance when conducting periodic reviews of its operating segments.

A similar analysis of ROI and its components can be made when planning for future periods. In developing plans for 19x4, management wants to know the possible effect of changes in the major elements of ROI for Maine Division. Sensitivity analysis can be used to predict the impact of changes in sales, the investment center asset base, or investment center income.

Assuming the investment base is unchanged, a projected ROI can be determined for Maine Division for a sales goal of $1,600,000 and an income goal of $160,000:

$$\text{ROI} = \frac{\text{Sales}}{\text{Investment center asset base}} \times \frac{\text{Investment center income}}{\text{Sales}}$$

$$= \frac{\$1,600,000}{\$800,000} \times \frac{\$160,000}{\$1,600,000}$$

$$= 2.0 \times 0.10$$

$$= 0.20, \text{ or } 20 \text{ percent.}$$

Note that ROI increased from 18 to 20 percent, even though the return-on-sales ratio decreased from 12 to 10 percent. The change in turnover from 1.5 to 2.0 more than offset the reduced return-on-sales ratio.

Starting from Maine's 19x3 performance, now assume that projected operating efficiencies reduce expenses by $12,000, and that sales remain constant, thereby increasing income to $156,000. The ROI increases from 18 percent to 19.5 percent:

$$\text{ROI} = \frac{\text{Sales}}{\text{Investment center asset base}} \times \frac{\text{Investment center income}}{\text{Sales}}$$

$$= \frac{\$1,200,000}{\$800,000} \times \frac{\$156,000}{\$1,200,000}$$

$$= 1.5 \times 0.13$$

$$= 0.195, \text{ or } 19.5 \text{ percent.}$$

Sensitivity analysis may involve changing only one factor in the ROI model or a combination of factors. When more than one factor is changed, the user must be careful to properly analyze exactly how much change is caused by each factor.

Management may desire a minimum ROI. In this case the major elements of the ROI model can be manipulated to determine the best way to meet this minimum. If, for example, ROI is set at 24 percent, it may be obtained by changing only the investment base (from $800,000 to $600,000):

$$\text{ROI} = \frac{\text{Sales}}{\text{Investment center asset base}} \times \frac{\text{Investment center income}}{\text{Sales}}$$

$$= \frac{\$1,200,000}{\$600,000} \times \frac{\$144,000}{\$1,200,000}$$

$$= 2.0 \times 0.12$$

$$= 0.24, \text{ or } 24 \text{ percent.}$$

Or it may be obtained by changing a combination of the investment base (from $800,000 to $900,000) and income (from $144,000 to $216,000):

$$\text{ROI} = \frac{\text{Sales}}{\text{Investment center asset base}} \times \frac{\text{Investment center income}}{\text{Sales}}$$

$$= \frac{\$1,200,000}{\$900,000} \times \frac{\$216,000}{\$1,200,000}$$

$$= 1.333 \times 0.18$$

$$= 0.24, \text{ or } 24 \text{ percent.}$$

It may also be obtained by changing any combination of the three factors, together or separately.

Statistics such as ROI, investment turnover, and return-on-sales ratio mean little by themselves. They take on meaning only when compared with an objective, a trend, another division, a competitor, or an industry average. Many businesses establish minimum ROIs for each of their divisions, which are expected to attain or exceed this minimum return. The salaries, bonuses, and promotions of division managers may be tied directly to the ROI of their divisions. Without other evaluation techniques, managers often strive for ROI maximization, sometimes to the long-run detriment of the entire organization.

Investment Base. Despite the relevance and conceptual simplicity of ROI, a division's ROI cannot be computed until management determines how divisional investment and income are to be measured. Because the primary purpose for computing ROI is to evaluate the effectiveness of a division's operating management in using the assets entrusted to them, most organizations define investment as the average total assets of a division during the evaluation period.

For most companies the investment base is limited to each division's operating assets. These normally include those assets held for productive use as well as cash, accounts receivable, inventory, and plant and equipment. Nonproductive assets, such as land for a future plant site, would not be included in the investment base of a division, only for the company.

Corporate cash and receivables are sometimes held by corporate headquarters, which permits more efficiency in billings and collections. This enables the corporation to hold a smaller total amount of cash than would be required if each division had its own bank account. Although it is relatively easy to assign receivables held by corporate headquarters to divisions (on the basis of their origin) for ROI computations, the assignment of cash presents some problems. Because of operating economies, the total cash requirements of the entire organization are less than the cash requirements of all divisions acting as independent units. However, assigning cash on the basis of the division's independent cash needs is likely to raise objections. The best approach seems to be to allocate cash based on the amount of incremental cash needed to support each division as compared to the company as a whole; nevertheless, cash allocations are most frequently based on relative sales or cash expenditures.

The next problem relates to general corporate assets. It is not advisable to allocate the cost of physical assets utilized by corporate headquarters to the operating divisions. Though the divisions might need additional administrative facilities if they were truly independent, they have no control over the headquarter's facilities. Additionally, the joint nature and use of these facilities make any allocation arbitrary.

One of the problems with the comparisons of ROI among divisions is the difference in the historical cost of each division's assets. It is somewhat difficult to compare a division whose asset base is measured in 1991 dollars with one that has most of its asset base measured in 1974 dollars. To overcome this problem, many companies require all divisions to use some common dollar base.

Investment Center Income. Divisional income is equal to divisional revenues less divisional operating expenses. Except for service expenses that can be clearly identified with the activities of individual divisions (such as the variable costs of processing accounts receivable), the expenses of operating corporate headquarters should not be allocated to the division for ROI purposes. Some managers advocate not allocating even if the absence of corporate headquarters would cause divisions to incur additional expenses. In many decentralized operations, corporate general and administrative expenses are often allocated to divisions for internal reporting purposes, but they are excluded when computing divisional ROI.

Some companies allocate all expenses in determining ROI based on management's belief that these expenses represent the value of services rendered by the home office. Other managers believe that allocated expenses should not be included because division management has no control over the incurrence or allocation of headquarters' expenses. Also, the allocations are often for items of questionable value to the division, such as the corporation's legal costs.

Generally, such allocations are not included in the computation of divisional ROI. Only expenses directly associated with the division should be included in ROI computations. An example of a directly associated cost is the advertising expense of products only produced by the division. The amount of expenses allocated should be approximately the same as it would be if the division had incurred the services on its own. If allocated corporate costs are substantially greater than a division's independently incurred costs would be, costs are allocated in excess of benefits received, a very undesirable situation.

Asset Measurement. Once divisional investment and income have been operationally defined and ROI computations have been made, the significance of the resulting ratios may still be questioned. Return on investment may be overstated in terms of constant dollars because inflation and arbitrary depreciation procedures cause an undervaluation of the inventory and fixed assets included in the investment center asset base. Asset measurement is particularly troublesome if inventories are valued at last-in, first-out (LIFO) cost and fixed assets were acquired many years ago. A division manager may hesitate to replace an old inefficient asset with a new efficient one because the replacement may lower income and ROI through an increased investment base and increased depreciation.

To improve the comparability between divisions' old and new assets, some firms value assets at original cost rather than at net book value (cost less accumulated depreciation) in ROI computations. This procedure does not reflect inflation, however. An old asset that cost $120,000 ten years ago is still being compared with an asset that costs $200,000 today. A better solution might be to value old assets at their replacement cost, although obtaining replacement cost data can be a problem. This raises issues about the cost and value of information and about whether or not the old asset would be replaced in kind at today's prices.

Residual Income

Residual income is an often-mentioned alternative for measuring investment center performance. **Residual income** is the excess of investment center income over the minimum return set by the corporation. The minimum return is computed as a percentage of the investment center's asset base. When residual income is the primary basis of evaluation, the management of each investment center is encouraged to maximize residual income rather than ROI.

To illustrate the computation, assume a company requires a minimum return of 12 percent on each division's investment base. The residual income of a division of the company that has an annual net operating income of $200,000 and an investment base of $1,500,000 is $20,000:

Division income	$200,000
Minimum return ($1,500,000 × 0.12)	−180,000
Residual income	$ 20,000

Many executives view residual income as a better measure of performance than ROI. They believe that residual income encourages managers to make profitable investments that would otherwise be rejected by managers who are being measured by ROI. To illustrate, assume that two divisions of Color Company have an opportunity to make an investment of $100,000 that will generate a return of 20 percent. The manager of Green Division is evaluated using ROI, and the manager of Orange Division is evaluated using residual income. The current ROI of each division is 24 percent, and each division has a current income of $120,000 and a minimum rate of 18 percent on invested capital. If each division has a current investment base of $500,000, the effect of the proposed investment on each division's performance is as follows:

	Current	+	Proposed	=	Total
Green division:					
Investment center income	$120,000		$ 20,000		$140,000
Asset base	$500,000		$100,000		$600,000
ROI	0.24		0.20		0.233
	or 24 percent		or 20 percent		or 23.3 percent
Orange division:					
Asset base	$500,000		$100,000		$600,000
Investment center income	$120,000		$ 20,000		$140,000
Minimum return (0.18 × base)	− 90,000		− 18,000		−108,000
Residual income	$ 30,000		$ 2,000		$ 32,000

Since the performance of the Green Division is being measured according to the best rate of return that can be generated, the manager will not want to make the new investment because it reduces the current ROI of 24 percent to 23.3 percent. This is true, even though the company's minimum return is only 18 percent. Not wanting to explain a decline in the division's ROI, the manager will probably reject the opportunity even though it may have benefited the company as a whole.

The Orange Division manager will probably be happy to accept the new project because it increases residual income by $2,000. Any investment that provides a return greater than the required minimum of 18 percent will be acceptable to the Orange Division manager. Given a profit maximization goal for the organization, the residual income method is preferred because it encourages division managers to accept all projects with returns above the 18 percent cutoff.

The primary disadvantage of the residual income method is that it measures performance in dollars. It cannot be used to compare the performance of divisions of different sizes; for example, the residual income of a multimillion dollar sales division would be expected to be larger than that of a half-million dollar sales division.

TRANSFER PRICING

Transfer pricing is used when products or services are exchanged between quasi-independent units of an organization. A **transfer price** is the internal value assigned a product or service that one division provides to another. Transfer-pricing transactions normally occur between profit or investment centers rather than between cost centers of an organization.

The objective of transfer pricing is to transmit financial data between departments or divisions of a company as they use each other's goods and services. Transfer-pricing systems are normally used in decentralized operations to determine whether organizational objectives are being achieved in each division. For division managers to be accountable for all transactions, both external and internal, transfer prices must be determined for the internal transfers of goods and services.

Management Considerations

The desire of the selling and buying divisions of the same company to maximize their individual performance measures often creates transfer-pricing problems. Acting as independent units, the divisions may take actions that are not in the best interest of the organization as a whole. The three examples that follow illustrate the need for the organization to maintain a corporate profit-maximizing viewpoint while attempting to allow divisional autonomy and responsibility.

Rex Manufacturing has five divisions that interchange products and product components with each other. Assume that Division 6 manufactures two products, Alpha and Beta. Alpha is sold externally for $50 per unit and Beta is transferred

Read this!!

to Division 13 for $60 per unit. The costs associated with the two products are shown below:

	Product	
	Alpha	Beta
Direct materials	$15	$14
Direct labor	5	10
Variable manufacturing overhead	5	16
Fixed manufacturing overhead	6	15
Variable selling	4	—
Total	$35	$55

A proposal has just been received from another company to supply Division 13 with a substitute product similar to Beta at a price of $52. From the company's viewpoint, this is merely a make-or-buy decision. The relevant costs are the differential outlay costs of the alternative actions. If the fixed manufacturing costs of Division 6 cannot be reduced, the relevant costs are as follows:

Buy		$52
Make:		
Direct materials	$14	
Direct labor	10	
Variable manufacturing overhead	16	−40
Difference favors making		$12

The decision for Division 13's management is basically one of cost minimization—buy from the source that charges the lowest price. If Division 6 cannot transfer at a price of $52 or less, the management of Division 13 may go to the external supplier so that the division's profits can be maximized. Although Division 13's managers are concerned about the cost of Beta, they are also concerned about the quality of the goods. If the $52 product is inferior in quality, Division 13's management may decide to buy from Division 6 at the higher price.

Prior to Division 13's receipt of the external offer to buy Beta for $52 per unit, Division 6 had been transferring Beta for $60. For Division 6 this is a decision to reduce the contribution margin of Beta and therefore lower divisional profits or find an alternative use of its resources. Of course, corporate management may intervene and require the internal transfer.

For the second example, assume that Division 6 can either transfer Beta to Division 13 or sell an equivalent amount externally for $60 per unit. Now the decision for Division 6's management is simple—sell to the buyer willing to pay the most.

To examine a slightly different transfer-pricing conflict, assume that Division 6 can sell all the Alpha that it can produce (it is operating at capacity). While there is no external market for Beta, there is a one-to-one trade-off between the production of Alpha and Beta. They both use equal amounts of the limited capacity of Division 6.

The corporation still regards this as a make-or-buy decision, but the costs of producing Beta have changed. Beta now includes an outlay cost and an opportunity cost. The outlay cost is the variable cost of $40 ($14 + $10 + $16) computed above. The opportunity cost is the net benefit forgone if the limited capacity of Division 6 is used to produce Beta rather than Alpha:

Selling price of Alpha		$50
Outlay costs of Alpha:		
Direct materials	$15	
Direct labor	5	
Variable manufacturing overhead	5	
Variable selling	4	−29
Opportunity cost of making Beta		$21

Accordingly, the relevant costs in the make-or-buy decision are as shown below:

Make:		
Outlay cost of Beta	$40	
Opportunity cost of Beta	21	$61
Buy		$52

Product Beta should be purchased from the outside supplier. If there were no outside suppliers, the relevant cost of manufacturing Beta would still be $61—which is another way of saying that Beta should not be produced and processed further in Division 13 unless the resultant revenues cover all outlay costs (including the $40 in Division 6) and provide a contribution of at least $21 ($61 − $40). *From the viewpoint of the corporation, the relevant costs in a make-or-buy decision are the external price, the outlay costs of manufacture, and the opportunity cost to manufacture.* The opportunity cost is zero if there is excess capacity.

Determining Transfer Prices

As illustrated above, the transfer price of goods or services may be subject to much controversy. Although a price must be agreed upon for each item or service transferred between divisions, the selection of the pricing method is dependent upon many factors. The conditions surrounding the transfer determines which of the alternative methods discussed below is selected.

In considering each method, observe that each transfer results in a revenue entry on the books of the supplier and a cost entry on the books of the receiver. Transfers may be considered as sales by the supplier and as purchases by the receiver. Although no method is likely to be ideal, one must be selected if the profit or investment center concept is used.

Market Price. When there is an existing market with established prices for an intermediate product and the transfer actions of the company will not affect prices, market prices are ideal transfer prices. If divisions are free to buy and sell outside the firm, the use of market prices preserves divisional autonomy and leads divisions to act in a manner that maximizes corporate goal congruence. Unfortunately, not all product transfers have equivalent external markets. Furthermore, the divisions should carefully evaluate whether the market price is competitive or controlled by one or two large companies.

When there are substantial selling expenses associated with outside sales, many firms specify the transfer price as market price less selling expenses. The internal sale may not require the incurrence of costs to get and fill the order.

MANAGERIAL PRACTICE 9.2

Transfer Pricing at American Transtech

The pricing of internal service transfers is a major element of the management control system at American Transtech, an AT&T spinoff service company. Originally, transfer prices were derived through a complex set of mathematical formulas which attempted to measure full cost of internal service transfers. Overhead allocations were based on budgeted costs and budgeted capacity. "Management felt this costing approach did not optimize the organization's use of resources." To minimize the impact of fixed costs on internal service transfer decisions, American Transtech changed its calculation to include fixed cost at practical full capacity. Flexibility has been introduced by a new willingness to compromise further to offer transfer prices below full cost if the provider was operating below full capacity and the lower price made the service attractive to the user. The net effect of this flexibility was to spread the fixed costs over a larger base, thereby lowering the costs of services to the normal users.

Bob Fox, controller of American Transtech, commented that "the organization had 'settled down' and there didn't seem to be much impetus for large-scale changes." Of course, he knew that changes in American Transtech's operations or business philosophy would necessitate system modifications but then that was true of any ongoing, dynamic company.

Source: Thomas L. Barton and Robert J. Fox, "Evolution at American Transtech," *Management Accounting* (April 1988): 49–52.

To illustrate, assume that product Alpha of Division 6 can be sold competitively at $50 per unit or transferred to Division 24 for additional processing. Under most situations, Division 6 will never sell Alpha for less than $50, and Division 24 will likewise never pay more than $50 for it. However, if any variable expenses related to marketing and shipping can be eliminated by divisional transfers, these costs are generally subtracted from the competitive market price. In our illustration, where variable selling expenses are $4 for Alpha, the transfer price could be reduced to $46 ($50 − $4). A price between $46 and $50 would probably be better than either extreme price. To the extent that these transfer prices represent a near competitive situation, the profitability of each division can then be evaluated fairly.

Variable Costs. If there is excess capacity in the supplying division, establishing a transfer price equal to variable costs leads the purchasing division to act in a manner that is optimal from the corporation's viewpoint. The buying division has the corporation's variable cost as its own variable cost as it enters the external market. Unfortunately, establishing the transfer price at variable cost causes the supplying division to report zero profits or a loss equal to any fixed costs. If excess capacity does not exist, establishing a transfer price at variable cost may not lead to optimal action because the supplying division may have to forgo sales that include a markup for fixed costs and profits. If Beta could be sold externally for $60, Division 6 would not want to transfer Beta to Division 13 for a $40 transfer price based on the following variable costs:

Direct materials	$14
Direct labor	10
Variable manufacturing overhead	16
Total variable costs	$40

Division 6 would much rather sell outside the company for $60, which covers variable costs and provides for a profit contribution margin of $20:

Selling price of Beta	$60
Variable costs	−40
Contribution margin	$20

Variable Costs Plus Opportunity Costs. From the viewpoint of the corporation this is the optimal transfer price. Because all relevant costs are included in the transfer price, the purchasing division is led to act in an optimal manner regardless of whether or not excess capacity exists.

With excess capacity in the supplying division, the transfer price is the variable cost per unit. Without excess capacity the transfer price is the sum of the variable and opportunity costs. Following this rule in the above example, if

Division 6 had excess capacity, the transfer price of Beta would be set at Beta's variable costs of $40 per unit. At this transfer price, Division 13 would buy Beta internally rather than externally at $52 per unit. If Division 6 cannot sell Beta externally, but can sell all the Alpha it can produce and is operating at capacity, the transfer price per unit would be set at $61, the sum of Beta's variable and opportunity costs ($40 + $21) computed previously. At this transfer price, Division 13 would buy Betas externally for $52. In both situations, the management of Division 13 has acted in accordance with the profit-maximizing goal of the organization.

However, there are two problems with this method. First, when the supplying division has excess capacity, establishing the transfer price at variable cost causes the supplying division to report zero profits or a loss equal to any fixed costs. Second, it is difficult to determine opportunity costs when the supplying division produces several products. If the problems with the previously mentioned transfer-pricing methods are too great, three other methods are available: absorption cost plus markup, negotiated prices, and dual prices.

Absorption Costs Plus Markup. According to absorption costing, all variable and fixed manufacturing costs are product costs. Pricing internal transfers at *absorption cost* eliminates the supplying division's reported loss on each product

MANAGERIAL PRACTICE 9.3

"Accounting for Management" at Philips

One of the world's largest industrial companies, the Philips Company, headquartered in The Netherlands with worldwide subsidiaries, is widely known for its innovations in both external and internal financial reporting. It uses a uniform system of accounting for all subsidiaries, which supports decision making and evaluation of management. Unlike most American-based companies, Philips recognizes profits only when a sales transaction with outsiders takes place. Sales between internal units of the company are recorded at standard cost plus a modest markup. All manufacturing units are treated as cost centers, with only marketing departments treated as profit centers. Investment centers are evaluated based on the relationship of profits to assets employed, with both measures based on current costs.

Source: Elwood L. Miller, *Responsibility Accounting and Performance Evaluations* (New York: Van Nostrand Reinhold, 1982), 130–134.

that may occur using a variable cost transfer price. *Absorption cost plus markup* provides the supplying division with a contribution toward unallocated costs. In "cost plus" transfer pricing, "cost" should be defined as standard cost rather than actual cost. This prevents the supplying division from passing on the cost of inefficient operations to other divisions, and it allows the buying division to know its cost in advance of purchase. Even though cost plus transfer prices may not maximize company profits, they are widely used. Their popularity stems from several factors including ease of implementation, justifiability, and perceived fairness. Once everyone agrees on "absorption cost plus markup" pricing rules, internal disputes are minimized.

Negotiated Prices. Negotiated transfer prices are used when the supplying and buying divisions independently agree on a price. Like market-based transfer prices, negotiated transfer prices are believed to preserve divisional autonomy. Negotiated transfer prices may lead to some suboptimal decisions, but this is regarded as a small price to pay for other benefits of decentralization. When negotiated transfer prices are used, some corporations establish arbitration procedures to help settle disputes between divisions. However, the existence of an arbitrator with any real or perceived authority reduces divisional autonomy.

Negotiated prices should have market prices as their ceiling and variable costs as their floor. Although frequently used where there is an external market for the product or component, the most common use of negotiated prices is where no identical-product external market exists. Negotiations may start with a floor price plus add-ons such as overhead and profit markups, or it may start with a ceiling price less adjustments for selling and administrative expenses and allowances for quantity discounts. Where no identical-product external market exists, the market price for a similar completed product may be used less the estimated cost of completing the product from the transfer stage to the completed stage.

Assume that service EDProcessing is transferred from Consulting Division to Auditing Division. There is no comparable external market, but Consulting Division provides a similar service, DPConsult, which is billed externally for $132 an hour. The cost to Consulting Division for service EDProcessing is as follows:

Direct labor	$35
Direct materials	10
Variable overhead	30
Direct costs	$75
Fixed overhead (estimated)	20
Total	$95

The managers of the Consulting and Auditing divisions decide to negotiate a fee for the service using a ceiling of $132. Consulting's management recognizes that the additional direct labor of service DPConsult is $12 per hour more than for service EDProcessing and thereby offers service EDProcessing for $120 per hour to Auditing. Auditing argues that the fixed overhead needs to be adjusted or maybe even eliminated. Consulting finally agrees to reduce the fixed overhead by 20 percent. The final transfer price (fee) of service EDProcessing to Auditing is $109 based on the following analysis:

Direct labor	$ 35
Direct materials	10
Variable overhead	30
Fixed overhead	16
Total costs	$ 91
Profit margin (20%)	18
Transfer price	$109

The transfer price of $109 is between the variable cost to produce, $75, and the adjusted external fee of $120. Auditing accepts the fee because it appears fair, and Consulting accepts the price because it exceeds variable costs and provides an adequate contribution margin. If the Consulting Division has idle capacity, Auditing should also argue that the fixed items be eliminated because they will not change if the service is provided.

Dual Prices. Dual prices exist when a company allows a difference in the supplier's transfer price and the receiver's transfer price for the same product. This method allegedly minimizes internal squabbles of division managers and problems of conflicting divisional goals. The supplier's price normally approximates market price, which allows the selling division to show a "normal" profit on items that it transfers internally. The receiver's price is usually variable cost or absorption cost. Dual prices eliminate the receiver's need for covering internally transferred profits when the final external price is established. The receiver is also allowed to make a profit from the final product that was transferred in.

Applying Transfer Pricing

Once transfer prices have been determined, they can be used to record interdivisional sales. Although most divisional income statements are very complex, the following illustrations concentrate only on the elements related to the transfer of goods and services. Leigh Ann's Fashions, a dress manufacturer, has two divisions, Sewing and Sales. The Sewing Division sells to the Sales Division and to other distributors. Sales buys from no one but Sewing. During the first quarter of 19x7 the Sewing Division incurred the following unit costs:

Direct materials	$ 8
Direct labor	5
Variable manufacturing overhead	3
Variable selling	1
Total	$17

Total production for the quarter was 30,000 dresses, of which 20,000 were sold to the Sales Division for $20 each. External sales were $25 for each dress. There were no beginning or ending inventories. Fixed manufacturing overhead for the quarter totaled $60,000.

After the Sales Division receives the dresses, they affix private labels where necessary and then package and ship to retail customers. The variable unit costs are $4, and the Sales Division incurs $40,000 in fixed costs each quarter. The Sales Division sold all dresses received during the first quarter for $30 each.

Exhibit 9–3 provides a simple illustration of how transfer pricing affects each division's income statement and the company as a whole. The 20,000 units transferred from Sewing to Sales shows up as $400,000 of internal sales for Sewing and as $400,000 of transferred-in cost to Sales. Note that both amounts are ignored for the overall company income statement. The reason for this elimination at the company level is the desire to provide external users of financial statements information related to economic activities with outside parties and not internal transfers.

Now assume Sales is allowed to buy from outside suppliers. An outside supplier has offered to sell the Sales Division dresses of similar style and quality for $18. The Sewing Division's management is offered the option of reducing its transfer price to $18, but it refuses even though Sewing has no other use for

---

EXHIBIT 9–3   Divisional and Company Income Statements, Internal Transfer

Leigh Ann's Fashions
Divisional and Company Income Statements
First Quarter, 19x7

	Sewing Division	Sales Division	Company
Sales:			
External*	$250,000	$600,000	$850,000
Internal**	400,000	—	—
Total	$650,000	$600,000	$850,000
Variable costs:			
Incurred†	$510,000	$ 80,000	$590,000
Transferred-in‡	—	400,000	—
Total	−510,000	−480,000	−590,000
Contribution margin	$140,000	$120,000	$260,000
Fixed costs	− 60,000	− 40,000	−100,000
Net income	$ 80,000	$ 80,000	$160,000

* 10,000 units × $25 = $250,000, and 20,000 units × $30 = $600,000.

** 20,000 units × $20 = $400,000.

† 30,000 units × $17 = $510,000, and 20,000 units × $4 = $80,000.

‡ Transferred-in costs is the same as internal sales.

the production capacity. The Sales Division's management contends that Sewing will have a markup of $2 on each dress because its variable selling cost is not necessary for internal sales, but Sewing's management disagrees. Note in Exhibit 9–4 that the company and the Sewing Division had a lower net income when the Sales Division purchased outside, but the Sales Division increased its income by $40,000 when it bought internally from the Sewing Division.

Finally, assume that Sewing is willing to negotiate a transfer price with Sales for $18. The resulting income statements for each division and the company as a whole are illustrated in Exhibit 9–5. Comparing Exhibits 9–3 and 9–5, the income to the company remains the same when there are internal transfers even though the transfer price changes from $20 to $18. However, the divisional incomes change by increasing one and reducing the other. No doubt the management of Sales is pleased to have the outside competition because its income increases under each alternative.

These examples illustrate that transfer prices affect the profitability of divisions and the evaluations of the division managers. By simply adjusting the transfer price, the Sewing Division's income is reduced from $80,000 to $40,000, a substantial difference for evaluation purposes.

It is often necessary to determine the impact of transfer prices on a company to fully assess the results of decisions involving transfer pricing. Depending on how these types of decision are resolved, divisional managers are often very pleased or displeased with the reporting system and responsibility accounting.

EXHIBIT 9–4   Divisional and Company Income Statements, External Supplier

Leigh Ann's Fashions
Divisional and Company Income Statements
First Quarter, 19x7

	Sewing Division	Sales Division	Company
Sales:			
External*	$250,000	$600,000	$850,000
Internal	—	—	—
Total	$250,000	$600,000	$850,000
Variable costs:			
Incurred**	$170,000	$ 80,000	$250,000
External purchases†	—	360,000	360,000
Total	−170,000	−440,000	−610,000
Contribution margin	$ 80,000	$160,000	$240,000
Fixed costs	− 60,000	− 40,000	−100,000
Net income	$ 20,000	$120,000	$140,000

* 10,000 units × $25 = $250,000, and 20,000 units × $30 = $600,000.
** 10,000 units × $17 = $170,000, and 20,000 units × $4 = $80,000.
† 20,000 units × $18 = $360,000.

EXHIBIT 9–5   Divisional and Company Income Statements

Leigh Ann's Fashions
Divisional and Company Income Statements
First Quarter, 19x7

	Sewing Division	Sales Division	Company
Sales:			
External*	$250,000	$600,000	$850,000
Internal**	360,000	—	—
Total	$610,000	$600,000	$850,000
Variable costs:			
Incurred†	$510,000	$ 80,000	$590,000
Transferred-in‡	—	360,000	—
Total	−510,000	−440,000	−590,000
Contribution margin	$100,000	$160,000	$260,000
Fixed costs	− 60,000	− 40,000	−100,000
Net income	$ 40,000	$120,000	$160,000

* 10,000 units × $25 = $250,000, and 20,000 units × $30 = $600,000.
** 20,000 units × $18 = $360,000.
† 30,000 units × $17 = $510,000, and 20,000 units × $4 = $80,000.
‡ Transferred-in costs is the same as internal sales.

SUBOPTIMIZATION

A transfer-pricing problem exists when divisions, acting in their own best interest, set transfer prices or make decisions based on transfer prices that are not in the best interest of the organization as a whole. The seriousness of the transfer-pricing problem depends on the extent to which the affairs of divisions are intertwined. When intermediate products have established markets and divisions are free to buy and sell outside the firm, the use of market prices avoids the transfer-pricing problem.

A potential transfer-pricing problem exists when divisions exchange goods or services for which there is not an established market. If the actual or potential amount of such transfers is relatively small, the use of cost-plus or negotiated prices seems most appropriate. The benefits of decentralization are believed to more than offset any loss of profit on individual products.

Though suboptimization may be tolerated on some products to obtain the benefits of decentralization, the transfer-pricing problem sometimes becomes so severe that cost and revenue centers should be used in place of investment or profit centers. Consider a single-product firm that attempts to operate its manufacturing and marketing activities as separate profit or investment centers. The affairs of these two divisions cannot be disentangled, and any attempt to do so will reduce the profits of the entire business.

The ideal solutions for the supplying division and for the buying division generally conflict. From the organization's perspective, the desired transfers may not occur because the division managers, pursuing their own best interests, could decide against a transfer. These conflicts sometimes are overcome by having a higher ranking manager impose a transfer price and insist that a transfer be made. But the managers of divisions in an organization that has a policy of decentralization often regard these orders as undermining their autonomy. So the imposition of a price may solve the goal congruence and incentive problem but exacerbate the autonomy problem. Transfer pricing thus becomes a problem with no ideal solutions.

MANAGERIAL PRACTICE 9.4

Simple Adjustments Can Make a Big Difference

Bellcore (Bell Communications Research) designed a state-of-the-art transfer pricing system in 1983. However, with the passing of time, defects in the system began to appear. Engineering was spending time performing word processing, graphics, technical publications, and secretarial duties because they couldn't afford the high prices those in-house departments were charging. The word processing, graphics, technical publications, and secretarial departments were unable to contain their costs even with a large work volume and were losing corporate customers because of their high prices. This situation highlighted a problem with the transfer pricing system and the method used to allocate overhead and rent. After a careful review, it was determined that part of the reason for the high costs was because these departments were paying more than their share for overhead and rent. Nonusage-based services (travel planning, libraries, purchasing, and so on) were charged on a headcount basis. These in-house departments accounted for 12 percent of the company's employment and were charged for 12 percent of the nonusage-based services. However, their actual usage was considerably less. A change in allocation methods reduced the service centers' total costs by 19 percent. Bellcore is committed to its transfer pricing system and feels that by making necessary adjustments the system will continually improve.

Source: Edward J. Kovac and Henry P. Troy, "Getting Transfer Prices Right: What Bellcore Did," *Harvard Business Review* (September–October 1989): 148–154.

It has been pointed out that there is seldom a single transfer price that will meet all the criteria for inducing top management's desired decisions. The best transfer price depends on the circumstances at hand. Furthermore, the optimal price for either division may differ from that employed for external needs, including tax requirements.

SUMMARY

When an organization expands in size, management must decide whether to adopt a centralized or decentralized structure. As individual units within an organization become large enough to be separately evaluated as quasi-independent businesses, management generally decides to decentralize its operations into investment centers. During such a change, sound practices of responsibility accounting must be developed.

The selection of the evaluation method to be used for each responsibility center is generally determined by what the center can realistically be responsible for in its operations. Centers that receive no revenues can hardly be labeled profit centers, but centers that have unique product lines sold externally can be considered profit or investment centers.

To properly evaluate each responsibility center, management must select some type of measurement system. The two most popular methods of evaluating investment center performance are return on investment (ROI) and residual income. In most situations, it is recommended that both methods be used if feasible.

Organizations that have internal transfers between profit or investment centers are faced with using transfer pricing and its related problems of goal congruence. Although there are no easy solutions to transfer-pricing problems, several workable alternatives were discussed in this chapter.

SUGGESTED READINGS

Benke, Ralph L., Jr., and Ashton C. Bishop, "Transfer Pricing in an Oligopolistic Market," *The Journal of Cost Analysis 4*, No. 2 (Fall 1986): 69–82.

Corr, Paul J., and Donald D. Bourque, "Managing in a Reorganization," *Management Accounting* (January 1988): 33–37.

Dearden, John, "Measuring Profit Center Managers," *Harvard Business Review* (September–October 1987): 84–88.

Edwards, James B., *Uses of Performance Measures*, Montvale, N.J.: National Association of Accountants, 1986.

Hall, George E., "Reflections on Running a Diversified Company," *Harvard Business Review* (January–February 1987): 84–92.

Lesser, Fredic E., "Does Your Transfer Pricing Make Cents?" *Management Accounting* (December 1987): 43–47.

McGee, Robert W., "Measuring Divisional Performance. . . Three Companies. . . Three Approaches," *Controller's Quarterly 2*, No. 1 (1986): 23–26.

REVIEW
PROBLEM
ROI and
Residual Income

Parent Company, a decentralized organization, has three divisions, X, Y, and Z. Corporate management desires a minimum return of 15 percent on its investments.

The divisions' 19x8 results were as follows:

Division	Income	Investment
X	$30,000	$200,000
Y	50,000	250,000
Z	22,000	100,000

The company is planning an expansion project that will cost $50,000 and return $9,000 per year.

Requirements

a) Compute the ROI for each division for 19x8.

b) Compute the residual income for each division for 19x8.

c) Rank the divisions according to their ROI and residual income.

d) Assume other income and investments will remain unchanged. Determine the effect of adding the new project on each division's ROI and residual income.

The solution to this problem is found at the end of the Chapter 9 exercises, problems, and cases.

KEY TERMS

Centralization
Decentralization
Residual income

Return on investment
Transfer price

REVIEW
QUESTIONS

9–1   What are the primary advantages of having a centralized organizational structure?

9–2   What are the primary advantages of having a decentralized organizational structure?

9–3   What criteria should management use when changing from one organizational structure to the other?

9–4   How can the problems of decentralization be minimized?

9–5   For what purpose do organizations use return on investment? Why is this measure preferred to net income?

9–6   How does residual income assist in the evaluation process?

9–7   List the elements in the ROI equation and tell how they are related.

9–8   How is an investment center's asset based determined?

9–9   How is overhead allocated to divisions using ROI? Why?

9–10 What information does residual income provide that ROI does not?

9–11 Should rates of return for each division using residual income be the same? Why? How are they determined?

9–12 In what types of organizations and for what purpose are transfer prices used?

9-13 What problems arise when transfer pricing is used?

9-14 From the viewpoint of the corporation, what is the best method of transfer pricing? What problems may limit the use of this method?

9-15 When do transfer prices lead to suboptimization? How can suboptimization be minimized? Can it be eliminated? Why or why not?

EXERCISES

9-1 ROI: Basic Computations

Salmon Company uses return on investment as one of the evaluation tools for division managers.

Selected operating data for three divisions of the company are given below.

	East Division	West Division	Central Division
Sales	$600,000	$750,000	$900,000
Operating assets	300,000	250,000	350,000
Net operating income	51,000	56,000	59,000

Requirements

a) Compute the return on investment for each division. (Round answers to three decimal places.)

b) Which divisional manager is doing the best job based on ROI? Why?

9-2 ROI: Basic Computations

Flexy Corporation allows its divisions to operate as autonomous units. The operating data for 19x4 are presented below:

	Lex Division	Rex Division	Tex Division
Sales	$4,500,000	$1,000,000	$9,600,000
Operating assets	2,000,000	800,000	3,500,000
Net operating income	440,000	120,000	980,000

Requirements

a) Compute each division's return on investment.

b) Which division has the best performance based on ROI?

c) What other factors should be considered in making an overall evaluation of the most effective division manager?

9-3 ROI and Residual Income: Basic Computations

The three divisions of the Atta Moore Company had the following results for 19x6:

	Division A	Division B	Division C
Sales	$60,000	$80,000	$100,000
Operating income	9,000	9,500	10,000
Investment base	60,000	61,000	62,000

The company has a minimum desired rate of return on investment of 15 percent.

Requirements

a) Compute each division's return on investment. (Round answers to three decimal places.)

b) Compute each division's residual income.

9-4 ROI and Residual Income: Basic Computations

The Firebird Division of Central Motors had an operating income of $90,000 and net assets of $400,000. Central Motors has a target rate of return of 16 percent.

Requirements

a) Compute the return on investment.

b) Compute the residual income.

9-5 ROI and Residual Income: Impact of a New Investment

From Exercise 9-4, Firebird has an opportunity to increase operating income by $20,000 with an investment in assets of $85,000.

Requirements

a) Compute the Firebird Division's return on investment if the project is undertaken. (Round your answer to three decimal places.)

b) Compute the Firebird Division's residual income if the project is undertaken.

9-6 ROI and Residual Income: Impact of a New Investment

The Aspirin Division of International Drugs reported an operating income of $2,100,000 for 19x3 with an investment of $9,000,000. The division manager desires to know the effect on the division's performance of an incremental investment of $6,000,000, which will increase annual operating income by $900,000 per year.

Required: Determine the impact of the new investment on ROI and residual income. Assume that an 18 percent return on investment is considered acceptable. (Round calculations to three decimal places.)

9-7 ROI: Fill in the Blanks

Provide the missing data in the following situations:

	Division K	Division L	Division M
Sales	$?	$5,000,000	$?
Net operating income	$100,000	$ 200,000	$144,000
Operating assets	$?	$?	$800,000
Return on investment	16%	10%	?
Return-on-sales ratio	0.04	?	0.12
Investment turnover	?	?	1.5

9-8 ROI: Fill in the Blanks

Provide the missing data in the following situations:

	Sun Division	Star Division	Moon Division
Sales	$4,000,000	$?	$900,000
Operating assets	$1,000,000	$?	$?
Net operating income	$?	$500,000	$180,000
Return-on-sales ratio	0.10	0.05	?
Investment turnover	?	2.0	?
Return on investment	?	?	0.20

9–9 ROI and Residual Income with Different Bases

Basic Company requires a return on capital of 12 percent. The following financial information is available for 19x8:

	Division 200 Value Base		Division 300 Value Base		Division 400 Value Base	
	Book	Current	Book	Current	Book	Current
Sales	$100,000	$100,000	$200,000	$200,000	$800,000	$800,000
Income	12,000	10,000	16,000	17,000	50,000	52,000
Assets	60,000	80,000	90,000	100,000	600,000	580,000

Requirements

a) Compute return on investment using both book and current values for each division. (Round answers to three decimal places.)

b) Compute residual income for both book and current values for each division.

c) Does book value or current value provide the better basis for performance evaluation? Which division do you consider the most successful?

9–10 ROI and Residual Income with Different Bases

Forward Trinket Company is considering evaluating its divisions on both a historical and replacement cost basis. The following information is available for 19x1:

	Assets		Income	
Division	Book Value	Replacement Value	Book Value	Replacement Value
Trinket	$ 600,000	$ 900,000	$120,000	$110,000
Gadget	700,000	700,000	120,000	120,000
Widget	1,000,000	1,400,000	200,000	180,000

The company has a minimum desired rate of 15 percent.

Requirements

a) Compute return on investment using book value and replacement value amounts for each division. (Round your answer to two decimal places.)

b) Compute residual income using book value and replacement value amounts for each division.

c) Does book value or replacement value provide the better basis for performance evaluation? Which division do you consider the most successful?

9–11 Transfer Pricing and Divisional Gross Profit

Leitch Consulting Company has two divisions, Tax Consultants and Financial Consultants. In addition to their external sales, each division performs work for the other division. The external fees earned by each division in 19x0 were $400,000 for Tax Consultants and $700,000 for Financial Consultants. Tax Consultants worked 3,000 hours for Financial Consultants and Financial Consultants worked 1,200 hours for Tax Consultants. The costs of services performed were $220,000 for Tax Consultants and $480,000 for Financial Consultants.

Requirements

a) Determine the gross profit for each division and for the company as a whole if the transfer price from Tax to Financial is $30 per hour and the transfer price from Financial to Tax is $25 per hour.

b) Determine the gross profit for each division and for the company as a whole if the transfer price from each division is $30 per hour.

c) What are the gross profit results for the divisions and the company as a whole if the two divisions net their hours and charge a transfer fee of $25 per excess hour? Which division manager would favor this arrangement?

9–12 Transfer Pricing and Divisional Gross Profit

Greenwood Paper Company has two divisions. The Pulp Division prepares the wood for processing. The Paper Division processes the pulp into paper. No inventories exist in either division at the beginning of 19x3. During the year, the Pulp Division prepared 40,000 cords of wood at a cost of $240,000. All the pulp was transferred to the Paper Division where additional operating costs of $5 per cord were incurred. The 400,000 pounds of finished paper were sold for $1,000,000.

Requirements

a) Determine the gross profit for each division and for the company as a whole if the transfer price from Pulp to Paper is, at cost, $6 per cord.

b) Determine the gross profit for each division and for the company as a whole if the transfer price is $5 per cord.

c) Determine the gross profit for each division and for the company as a whole if the transfer price is $7 per cord.

9–13 Internal or External Acquisition: No Opportunity Costs

The Van Division of the CP Corporation has offered to purchase 180,000 wheels from the Wheel Division for $52 per wheel. At a normal volume of 500,000 wheels per year, production costs per wheel for the Wheel Division are as follows:

Direct materials	$20
Direct labor	10
Variable overhead	6
Fixed overhead	20
Total	$56

The Wheel Division has been selling 500,000 wheels per year to outside buyers at $68 each. Capacity is 700,000 wheels per year. The Van Division has been buying wheels from outside suppliers at $65 per wheel.

Requirements

a) Should the Wheel Division manager accept the offer? Show computations.

b) From the standpoint of the company, will the internal sale be beneficial?

9–14 Appropriate Transfer Prices: Opportunity Costs

The Plains Peanut Butter Company recently acquired a peanut processing company that has a normal annual capacity of 4,000,000 pounds and that sold 2,800,000 pounds last year at a price of $2 per pound. The purpose of the acquisition is to furnish peanuts for the peanut butter plant. The peanut butter plant needs 1,600,000 pounds of peanuts per year. It has been purchasing peanuts from suppliers at the market price.

Production costs of the peanut processing company per pound are as follows:

Direct materials	$0.50
Direct labor	0.25
Variable overhead	0.12
Fixed overhead at normal capacity	0.20
Total	$1.07

Management is trying to decide what transfer price to use for sales from the newly acquired Peanut Division to the Peanut Butter Division. The manager of the Peanut Division argues that $2, the market price, is appropriate. The manager of the Peanut Butter Division argues that the cost price of $1.07 should be used—or perhaps even less, since fixed overhead costs should be recomputed.

Any output of the Peanut Division, up to 2,800,000 pounds, not sold to the Peanut Butter Division could be sold to regular customers at $2 per pound.

Requirements

a) Compute the annual gross profit for the Peanut Division using a transfer price of $2.00.

b) Compute the annual gross profit for the Peanut Division using a transfer price of $1.07.

c) What transfer price(s) will lead the manager of the Peanut Butter Division to act in a manner that will maximize company profits?

9–15 Negotiating a Transfer Price with Excess Capacity

The Weaving Division of Carolina Textiles, Inc., produces cloth that is sold to the Company's Dyeing Division and to outside customers. Operating data for the Weaving Division for 19x3 are as follows:

	To the Dyeing Division	To Outside Customers
Sales:		
300,000 yards at $5	$1,500,000	
200,000 yards at $6		$1,200,000
Variable expenses at $2	− 600,000	− 400,000
Contribution margin	$ 900,000	$ 800,000
Fixed expenses*	− 750,000	− 500,000
Net income	$ 150,000	$ 300,000

* Allocated on the basis of unit sales

The Dyeing Division has just received an offer from an outside supplier to supply cloth at $4.30 per yard. The manager of the Weaving Division is not willing to meet the $4.30 price. She argues that it costs her $4.50 per yard to produce and sell to the Dyeing Division, so she would show no profit on the Dyeing Division sales. Sales to outside customers are at a maximum, 200,000 yards.

Requirements

a) Verify the Weaving Division's $4.50 unit cost figure.

b) Should the Weaving Division meet the outside price of $4.30 for Dyeing Division sales? Explain.

c) Could the $4.30 be met and still show a profit for the Weaving Division sales to the Dyeing Division? Show computations.

9–16 Dual Transfer Pricing

The Greek Company has two divisions, Beta and Gamma. Gamma Division produces a product at a variable cost of $6 per unit and sells 150,000 units to outside customers at $10 per unit and 40,000 units to Beta Division at variable cost plus 40 percent. Under the dual transfer price system, Beta Division pays only the variable cost per unit. The fixed costs of Gamma Division are $250,000 per year.

Beta Division sells its finished product to outside customers at $23 per unit. Beta has variable costs of $5 per unit in addition to the costs from Gamma Division. The annual fixed costs of Beta Division are $170,000. There are no beginning or ending inventories.

Required: Prepare the income statements for the two divisions and the company as a whole. Why is the income for the company less than the sum of the profit figures shown on the income statements for the two divisions? Explain.

9–17 Transfer Pricing and Divisional Gross Profit

Century Company has two divisions. Division Jeff manufactures chocks and Division Sam finishes them. The unfinished chocks can be sold for $2.50 each or finished and sold for $3.00 each. After Jeff manufactures the chocks, some are sold to outsiders and some are transferred to Division Sam, which finishes them. The following information pertains to 19x7:

Manufacturing cost of Division Jeff to produce 2,000,000 units	$3,000,000
Sales revenue from 800,000 units sold by Jeff to outside market	2,000,000
Market value of 1,200,000 units when transferred to Sam	3,000,000
Sales revenue from 1,200,000 units processed by Sam and sold	3,600,000
Total additional processing cost of Sam	750,000

Required: Compute the gross profit for the company and for each division. Use market value as the transfer price.

9–18 Transfer Prices at Full Cost with Excess Capacity: Divisional Viewpoint

The Dairy Company has a Cheese Division that produces cheese that sells for $12 per unit in the open market. The cost of the product is $8 (variable manufacturing of $5 plus fixed manufacturing of $3). Total fixed manufacturing costs are $210,000 at the normal annual production volume of 70,000 units.

The Overseas Division has offered to buy 15,000 units at the full cost of $8. The Producing Division has excess capacity, and the 15,000 units can be produced without interfering with the current outside sales of 70,000 units. The total fixed cost of the Cheese Division will not change.

Required: Explain whether the Cheese Division should accept or reject the offer. Show calculations.

9–19 Transfer Pricing with Excess Capacity: Divisional and Corporate Viewpoints

The Boyett Art Company has a Print Division that is currently producing 100,000 prints per year but has a capacity of 150,000 prints. The variable costs of each print are $30, and the annual fixed costs are $900,000. The prints sell for $40 in the open market.

The Retail Division of the company wants to buy 50,000 prints at $28 each. The Print Division manager refuses the order because the price is below variable cost. The Retail Division manager argues that the order should be accepted because it will lower the fixed cost per print from $9 to $6.

Requirements

a) Should the order from Retail Division be accepted? Why or why not?

b) From the viewpoints of the Print Division and the company, should the order be accepted if the manager of the Retail Division intends to sell each print in the outside market for $42 after incurring additional costs of $10 per print?

c) What action should the company take assuming it believes in divisional autonomy?

PROBLEMS

9–20 Transfer Pricing

The International Building Company owns its own clay mine, which supplies clay for the Brick Division. The clay is charged to the Brick Division at market price. Income statements for 19x5 were as follows:

International Building Company
Divisional Income Statements
For the year ended December 31, 19x5

	Clay Mine	Brick Division
Sales	$800,000	$2,000,000
Production costs:		
Materials	$ —	$ 800,000
Labor	380,000	500,000
Overhead	160,000	300,000
Total	−540,000	−1,600,000
Gross profit	$260,000	$ 400,000
Selling and administrative costs	−120,000	− 300,000
Income of division	$140,000	$ 100,000

In 19x5 and 19x6 the clay mine sold 20,000 tons of clay. In 19x6 the market prices of clay increased 50 percent and conversion costs increased 10 percent, whereas the

Brick Division increased its price by 10 percent. Income statements for 19x6 were as follows:

International Building Company
Divisional Income Statements
For the year ended December 31, 19x6

	Clay Mine	Brick Division
Sales	$1,200,000	$2,200,000
Production costs:		
Materials	$ —	$1,200,000
Labor	418,000	550,000
Overhead	176,000	330,000
Total	− 594,000	−2,080,000
Gross profit	$ 606,000	$ 120,000
Selling and administrative costs	− 120,000	− 330,000
Income (loss) of division	$ 486,000	$ (210,000)

Corporate management is concerned about the Brick Division's 19x6 loss.

Requirements

a) Prepare income statements for the company in 19x5 and 19x6.

b) Evaluate the company's performance in 19x6.

c) What should be the transfer price for clay? Discuss.

9–21 ROI and Residual Income: Impact of a New Investment

Office Equipment, Inc., is a decentralized organization with four autonomous divisions. The divisions are evaluated on the basis of the change in their return on invested assets. Operating results in the Modern Division for 19x1 are given below:

Office Equipment, Inc.
Modern Division Income Statement
For the year ended December 31, 19x1

Sales	$2,500,000
Less variable expenses	−1,250,000
Contribution margin	$1,250,000
Less fixed expenses	− 900,000
Net operating income	$ 350,000

Operating assets for Modern Division currently average $1,800,000. The Modern Division can add a new product line for an investment of $300,000. Relevant data for the new product line are as follows:

Sales	$800,000
Variable expenses	0.60 of sales
Fixed expenses	$300,000

Requirements

a) Determine the effect on ROI of accepting the new product line. (Round calculations to three decimal places.)

b) If a return of 6 percent is the minimum that should be earned by any division, and residual income is used to evaluate managers, would this encourage the division to accept the new product line? Explain and show computations.

9–22 Transfer Pricing at Absorption Cost

Division 23 of Numbers Company produces large metal numbers that are sold to Division 86. This division uses numbers in constructing signs that are sold to highway departments of local governments.

Division 23 contains two operations, stamping and finishing. The unit variable cost of materials and labor used in the stamping operation is $100. The fixed stamping overhead is $800,000 per year. Current production of 20,000 units is at full capacity.

The variable cost of labor used in the finishing operation is $12 per number. The fixed overhead in this operation is $340,000 per year.

The company uses an absorption-cost transfer price. The price data for each operation presented to Division 86 by Division 23 are shown below:

Stamping:		
Variable cost per unit	$100	
Fixed overhead cost per unit ($800,000/20,000 units)	40	$140
Finishing:		
Labor cost per unit	$ 12	
Fixed overhead cost per unit ($340,000/20,000 units)	17	29
Total cost per unit		$169

An outside company has offered to lease Division 86 machinery that would perform the finishing part of the number manufacturing. The lease is $200,000 per year. With the new machinery, the labor cost per frame would remain at $12. If Division 23 transfers the units for $140, the following analysis can be made:

Current process:		
Finishing process costs (20,000 × $29)		$580,000
New process:		
Machine rental cost per year	$200,000	
Labor cost ($12 × 20,000 units)	240,000	−440,000
Savings		$140,000

The manager of Division 86 wants approval to acquire the new machinery.

Requirements

a) How would you advise the company concerning the proposed lease?

b) How could the transfer-pricing system be modified or the transfer-pricing problem eliminated?

9–23 Transfer Pricing with and without Capacity Constraints

The National Carpet Company has just acquired a new Backing Division. The Backing Division produces a rubber backing, which it sells for $2.00 per square yard. Sales are about 1,200,000 square yards a year. Since the Division has a capacity of 2,000,000 yards a year, top management is thinking that it might be wise for the company's Assembly Division to start purchasing from the newly acquired Backing Division.

The Assembly Division now purchases 600,000 square yards a year from an outside supplier at a price of $1.80 per square yard. That the current price is lower than the competitive $2.00 price is a result of the large quantity discounts.

The Backing Division's cost per square yard is shown below:

Direct materials	$1.00
Direct labor	0.20
Variable overhead	0.25
Fixed overhead (1,200,000 level)	0.10
Total cost	$1.55

Requirements

a) If both divisions are to be treated as investment centers, and their performance evaluated by the ROI formula, what transfer price would you recommend? Why?

b) What will be the effect on the profits of the company using your transfer price?

c) Based on your transfer price, would you expect the ROI in the Backing Division to increase, decrease, or remain unchanged? Explain.

d) What would be the effect on the ROI of the Assembly Division using your transfer price? Explain.

e) Assume that the Backing Division is now selling 2,000,000 square yards a year to retail outlets. What transfer price would you recommend? Explain what will happen between Backing and Assembly.

f) If the Backing Division is at capacity and decides to sell to the Assembly Division for $1.80 per square yard, what will be the effect on the profits of the company?

9–24 Transfer Pricing with and without Capacity Constraints

The Northern Clock Company is a decentralized organization containing three divisions. The Windup Division has asked the Dial Division, which is operating at capacity, to supply it with a large quantity of dials. The Dial Division sells dials outside for $2.50 each. The Windup Division, which is operating at 50 percent of capacity, wants to pay $2.00 each for the dials.

The Dial Division has a variable cost of production of $1.80. The current costs of the clock being built by the Windup Division are shown below:

Materials (except dials)	$30.00
Dials	2.00
Other variable costs	18.00
Fixed overhead	10.00
Total cost per clock	$60.00

The manager of the Windup Division believes that the $2.00 price from the Dial Division is necessary if the division is to compete with its competitor, Clockex.

Requirements

a) As division controller of the Dial Division, would you recommend that your division supply Windup Division as requested? Why?

b) If the Dial Division has excess capacity, would it be desirable for the Dial Division to supply the Windup Division with the fittings at $2.00 each? Explain.

c) Assuming the Dial Division has excess capacity, as the corporate controller, what would you advise?

9–25 Transfer Pricing and Special Orders Atlantic Telephone Company has several manufacturing divisions. The Pacific Division produces a component part that is used in the manufacture of electronic equipment. The cost per part for July is as follows:

Variable cost	$ 90
Fixed cost (at 2,000 units per month capacity)	60
Total cost per part	$150

Some of Pacific Division's output is sold to outside manufacturers, and some is sold internally to the Electronics Division. The price per part is $175.

The Electronics Division's cost and revenue structure is shown below:

Selling price per unit		$1,000
Less variable costs per unit:		
Cost of parts from the Pacific Division	$175	
Other variable costs	400	
Total variable costs		− 575
Contribution margin per unit		$ 425
Less fixed costs per unit (at 200 units per month)		− 100
Net income per unit		$ 325

The Electronics Division received an order for 10 units. The buyer wants to pay only $500 per unit.

Requirements

a) From the perspective of the Electronics Division, should the $500 price be accepted? Explain.

b) If both divisions have excess capacity, would the Electronics Division's action benefit the company as a whole? Explain.

c) If the Electronics Division has excess capacity, but the Pacific Division does not, and can sell all its parts to outside manufacturers, what would be the advantage or disadvantage to the Electronics Division of accepting the 10 unit order at the $500 price?

d) To make a decision that is in the best interest of Atlantic Telephone, what transfer-pricing information is needed by the Electronics Division?

9-26 Transfer Pricing with an Outside Market

French Vision has four divisions, Frame, Glass, Plastic, and Assembly, that collectively produce protective industrial eyeglasses. The Frame, Glass, and Plastic Divisions supply parts to the Assembly Division, which produces the final product.

The monthly fixed outlay costs of all divisions, except the Plastic Division, are identical at $150,000 each. Plastic's monthly fixed outlay costs are $300,000. In addition, fixed costs that do not require the use of cash amount to $50,000 per month per division, except for Plastic, where these costs are $100,000. Average production is 50,000 eyeglasses per month.

The full costs of each component are shown below:

Division	Part	Variable Cost per Unit	+	Fixed Cost per Unit	=	Full Cost per Unit
Frame	Frame	$15		$4		$19
Glass	Glass	20		4		24
Plastic	Ear pieces	5		4		9
Plastic	Nose pieces	2		4		6

Full absorption-cost transfer prices are used. In the Assembly Division, the manager has authority to buy inside the company or to buy from an outside supplier. The outside prices vary somewhat throughout the year. For next month the outside prices are as follows:

Part	Outside Price
Frame	$20
Glass	26
Ear pieces	7
Nose pieces	6

The Assembly Division manager notices that the outside purchase price of ear pieces is $2 lower than the transfer price and places an order with an outside supplier. Consequently, the Plastic Division stops producing ear pieces, reallocates all its fixed cost to the remaining units of nose pieces, and adjusts the full cost transfer price.

Requirements

a) Reallocate the fixed cost in the Plastic Division, and determine the adjusted transfer prices for nose pieces. What action might the manager of the Assembly Division take? What are the likely consequences of this action?

b) What action might French Vision take in establishing transfer prices and organizing its operations to avoid similar problems in the future?

9-27 Evaluating ROI

The Independent Consulting Company has several decentralized divisions. Each division manager is responsible for service revenue, cost of operations, acquisition and financing of divisional assets, and working capital management.

The vice president of general operations is considering changing from annual to multiyear evaluations of division managers. Currently, a review of the performance, attitudes, and skills of management is undertaken annually. As a trial run, two managers will be selected for the new evaluation procedure. The selection has been narrowed to the managers of Divisions 11 and 14.

Both managers became division managers in 19x1. Their divisions have the following operating results for the last three years:

(in thousands)	Division 11			Division 14		
	19x1	19x2	19x3	19x1	19x2	19x3
Estimated industry sales	$1,000,000	$1,200,000	$1,300,000	$500,000	$600,000	$650,000
Division sales	$ 100,000	$ 110,000	$ 121,000	$ 45,000	$ 60,000	$ 75,000
Variable costs	$ 30,000	$ 32,000	$ 34,500	$ 13,500	$ 17,500	$ 21,000
Fixed operating costs	40,000	40,500	42,000	17,000	20,000	23,000
Fixed administrative costs	27,500	32,500	32,500	14,000	20,000	25,000
Total costs	− 97,500	− 105,000	− 109,000	− 44,500	− 57,500	− 69,000
Net income	$ 2,500	$ 5,000	$ 12,000	$ 500	$ 2,500	$ 6,000
Net assets	$ 22,700	$ 23,500	$ 24,500	$ 12,300	$ 14,000	$ 17,000
Return on investment	?	?	?	?	?	?

Requirements

a) Determine ROI for each year for each manager.

b) Is ROI an appropriate measurement for manager evaluation? Why?

c) What additional measures might be used?

d) Per year, which manager performed the best?

e) Over three years, which manager performed the best?

(CMA Adapted)

9–28 An Evaluation of Market Based Transfer Prices

A large, diversified corporation operates its divisions on a decentralized basis. Division A makes Product X, which can be sold either to Division B or to outside customers.

At current levels of production, the variable cost of making Product X is $1.40 per unit, the fixed cost is 30 cents, and the market price is $2.75 per unit.

Division B processes Product X into Product Y. The additional variable cost of producing Product Y is $1.00 per unit.

Top management is developing a corporate transfer pricing policy. The bases for setting transfer prices being reviewed are full absorption cost, total variable costs, and market price.

Requirements

a) In order to avoid waste and maximize efficiency up to the transfer point, which of the transfer price bases being reviewed should be used and why?

b) Which of the transfer price bases in the short run would tend to encourage the best use of the corporation's productive capacity? Why would this not be true in the long run?

c) Identify *two* possible advantages that Division B might expect if it purchased Product X from Division A at the current market price.

d) What possible disadvantage might accrue to Division A if it was committed to sell all its production of X to Division B at the current market price?

(CIA Adapted)

CASES

9–29 Decentralization and Autonomy

Edwin Hall, Chairman of the Board and President of Arrow Works Products Company, founded the company in the mid-1960s. He is a talented and creative engineer. Arrow Works was started with one of his inventions, an intricate die-cast item that required a minimum of finish work. The item was manufactured for Arrow Works by a Gary, Indiana, foundry. The product sold well in a wide market.

The company issued common stock in 1972 to finance the purchase of the Gary foundry. Additional shares were issued in 1975 when Arrow purchased a fabricating plant in Cleveland to meet the capacity requirement of a defense contract.

The company now consists of five divisions. Each division is headed by a manager who reports to Hall. The Chicago Division contains the product development and engineering department and the finishing (assembly) operation for the basic products. The Gary Plant and Cleveland Plant are the other two divisions engaged in manufacturing operations. All products manufactured are sold through two selling divisions. The Eastern Sales Division is located in Pittsburgh and covers the country from Chicago to the east coast. The Western Sales Division, which covers the rest of the country, is located in Denver. The Western Sales Division is the newest operation and was established just eight months ago.

Hall, who still owns 53 percent of the outstanding stock, actively participates in the management of the company. He travels frequently and regularly to all the company's plants and offices. He says, "Having a business with locations in five different cities spread over half the country requires all of my time." Despite his regular and frequent visits, he believes the company is decentralized with the managers having complete autonomy. "They make all the decisions and run their own shops. Of course they don't understand the total business as I do, so I have to straighten them out once in a while. My managers are all good men, but they can't be expected to handle everything alone. I try to help all I can."

The last two months have been a period of considerable stress for Mr. Hall. During this period, John Staple, manager of the fabricating plant, was advised by his physician to request a six-month sick leave to relieve the work pressures that had made him nervous and tense. This request had followed by three days a phone call in which Hall had directly and bluntly blamed Staple for the lagging production output and increased rework and scrap of the fabricating plant. Hall made no allowances for the pressures created by the operation of the plant at volumes in excess of normal and close to its maximum rated capacity for the previous nine months.

Hall thought Staple and he had had a long and good relationship before this event. Hall attributed his loss of temper in this case to his frustration with several other management problems that had arisen in the past two months. The sales manager of the Denver office had resigned shortly after a visit from Hall. The letter of resignation stated he was seeking a position with greater responsibility. The sales manager in Pittsburgh asked to be reassigned to a sales position in the field; he did not feel he could cope with the pressure of management.

Requirements

a) Explain the difference between centralized and decentralized management.

b) Is Arrow Works Products Company decentralized, as Edwin Hall believes? Explain your answer.

c) Could the events that have occurred over the past two months in Arrow Works Products Company have been expected? Explain your answer.

(CMA Adapted)

9–30 A Transfer Pricing Dispute

MBR Inc. consists of three divisions that formerly were three independent manufacturing companies. Bader Corporation and Roper Company merged in 19x5, and the merged corporation acquired Mitchell Company in 19x6. The name of the corporation was subsequently changed to MBR Inc., and each company became a separate division retaining the name of its former company.

The three divisions have operated as if they were still independent companies. Each division has its own sales force and production facilities. Each division management is responsible for sales, cost of operations, acquisition and financing of divisional assets, and working capital management. The corporate management of MBR evaluates the performance of the divisions and division managements on the basis of return on investment.

Mitchell Division has just been awarded a contract for a product that uses a component manufactured by the Roper Division as well as by outside suppliers. Mitchell used a cost figure of $3.80 for the component manufactured by Roper in preparing its bid for the new product. This cost figure was supplied by Roper in response to Mitchell's request for the average variable cost of the component and represents the standard variable manufacturing cost and variable selling and distribution expense.

Roper has an active sales force that is continually soliciting new prospects. Roper's regular selling price for the component Mitchell needs for the new product is $6.50. Sales of this component are expected to increase. However, the Roper management has indicated that it could supply Mitchell with the required quantities of the component at the regular selling price less variable selling and distribution expenses. Mitchell's management has responded by offering to pay standard variable manufacturing cost plus 20 percent.

The two divisions have been unable to agree on a transfer price. Corporate management has never established a transfer price policy because interdivisional transactions have never occurred. As a compromise, the corporate vice president of finance has suggested a price equal to the standard full manufacturing cost (i.e., no selling and distribution expenses) plus a 15 percent markup. This price has also been rejected by the two division managers because each considered it grossly unfair.

The unit cost structure for the Roper component and the three suggested prices are shown below:

Standard variable manufacturing cost	$3.20
Standard fixed manufacturing cost	1.20
Variable selling and distribution expenses	0.60
	$5.00
Regular selling price less variable selling and distribution expenses ($6.50 − $0.60)	$5.90
Standard full manufacturing cost plus 15% ($4.40 × 1.15)	$5.06
Variable manufacturing plus 20% ($3.20 × 1.20)	$3.84

Requirements

a) What should be the attitude of the Roper Division's management toward the three proposed prices?

b) Is the negotiation of a price between the Mitchell and Roper Divisions a satisfactory method of solving the transfer price problem? Explain your answer.

c) Should the corporate management of MBR Inc. become involved in this transfer price controversy? Explain your answer.

(CMA Adapted)

REVIEW PROBLEM SOLUTION

a) Return on investment = $\dfrac{\text{Investment center income}}{\text{Investment center asset base}}$

Division X = $30,000/$200,000
= 0.15 or 15 percent

Division Y = $50,000/$250,000
= 0.20 or 20 percent

Division Z = $22,000/$100,000
= 0.22 or 22 percent

b) Residual income = Investment center income − (Minimum return × Investment center asset base)

Division X = $30,000 − (0.15 × $200,000)
= $0.00

Division Y = $50,000 − (0.15 × $250,000)
= $12,500

Division Z = $22,000 − (0.15 × $100,000)
= $7,000

c)

ROI ranks: Division Z First
Division Y Second
Division X Third

Residual income ranks: Division Y First
Division Z Second
Division X Third

Because the investments for each division are different, it is difficult to rank the divisions by residual income. Division Y had the largest residual income, but it also had the largest investment. Division Z's residual income was 56 percent of Division Y's income, but only 40 percent of the investment of Division Y. This fact, along with the best ROI ranking probably justifies Division Z being the best division of Parent Company.

d) Return on investment

$$\text{Investment} = \$9,000/\$50,000$$
$$= 0.18 \text{ or } 18 \text{ percent}$$
$$\text{Division X} = (\$30,000 + \$9,000)/(\$200,000 + \$50,000)$$
$$= 0.156 \text{ or } 15.6 \text{ percent}$$
$$\text{Division Y} = (\$50,000 + \$9,000)/(\$250,000 + \$50,000)$$
$$= 0.1967 \text{ or } 19.67 \text{ percent}$$
$$\text{Division Z} = (\$22,000 + \$9,000)/(\$100,000 + \$50,000)$$
$$= 0.2067 \text{ or } 20.67 \text{ percent}$$

ROI will increase for Division X, but decrease for Divisions Y and Z even though the project's ROI of 18 percent exceeds the company's minimum return of 15 percent.

Residual income

$$\text{Division X} = (\$30,000 + \$9,000) - [0.15 \times (\$200,000 + \$50,000)]$$
$$= \$1,500$$
$$\text{Division Y} = (\$50,000 + \$9,000) - [0.15 \times (\$250,000 + \$50,000)]$$
$$= \$14,000$$
$$\text{Division Z} = (\$22,000 + \$9,000) - [0.15 \times (\$100,000 + \$50,000)]$$
$$= \$8,500$$

Because the project's ROI exceeds the company's minimum return, the residual income of all divisions will increase.

C H A P T E R   10

Inventory Valuation Approaches and Segment Reporting

Learning Objectives

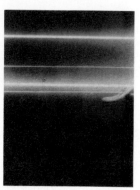

Upon completion of this chapter you should:

■ **Understand the basic difference between absorption costing and variable costing.**

■ **Be able to compute ending inventory under absorption and variable costing and be able to reconcile the difference between the two.**

■ **Be able to reconcile the difference between absorption costing net income and variable costing net income.**

■ **Be familiar with the primary arguments for and against variable costing.**

■ **Be able to describe segment reporting and know the primary purposes of segment reporting.**

■ **Be familiar with the segment reporting format that provides contribution margin and segment margin for each segment, and net income for the company as a whole.**

■ **Understand the difference between single-level and multilevel segment reporting.**

A fundamental internal reporting decision that every manufacturing company makes is how to account for fixed factory overhead. The outcome of this decision affects inventory valuation and, thus, income measurement. Though the absorption costing procedures used for external reporting purposes treat fixed factory overhead as a product cost, an alternative concept, called variable costing, is often used for internal reporting. Variable costing procedures assign only variable manufacturing costs to products. All other costs, including fixed manufacturing overhead, are treated as period costs.[1]

One of the purposes of this chapter is to present an analysis of absorption and variable costing. Each method is defined and its effects on inventory valuation and income measurement are illustrated. The advantages and limitations of each procedure are also discussed.

Organizations with multiple products, multiple plants, or multiple markets for their products often find it desirable to report the profits of each segment of the organization separately. Segment reporting allows a company's internal profitability reports to be prepared by divisions, products, territories, or on some other basis. Basic issues in segment reporting include the definition of business segments and the assignment of costs and revenues to each segment.

Another purpose of this chapter is to illustrate the development of segment reports and to discuss their usefulness in internal decision making, especially the decision to continue or discontinue a segment. In our discussion, special attention is given to problems caused by costs that are common to several segments of a business.

ABSORPTION COSTING AND VARIABLE COSTING

Under absorption costing, also called full costing, all manufacturing costs are assigned to products. Direct materials, direct labor, variable factory overhead, and fixed factory overhead costs are assigned to inventory, whereas selling and administrative costs, both fixed and variable, are immediately expensed as period costs.

Under variable costing, also called direct costing, only variable manufacturing costs are assigned to products. Direct materials, direct labor, and variable factory overhead costs are assigned to inventory, whereas fixed factory overhead and both fixed and variable selling and administrative costs are immediately expensed as period costs. A summary of product and period costs under absorption costing and variable costing is presented in Exhibit 10–1.

The difference between absorption costing and variable costing is the inclusion or exclusion of fixed factory overhead as a product cost. Under absorption

---

[1] Recall from Chapter 2 that *product costs* are costs assigned to products. They are expensed when the products are sold. *Period costs* are expired nonproduct costs. They are treated as an expense in the period they are incurred.

EXHIBIT 10–1   A Comparison of Absorption and Variable Costing

Absorption Costing	Variable Costing
Product costs	
Direct materials	Direct materials
Direct labor	Direct labor
Variable factory overhead	Variable factory overhead
Fixed factory overhead	
Period costs	
Variable selling and administrative	Variable selling and administrative
Fixed selling and administrative	Fixed selling and administrative
	Fixed factory overhead

MANAGERIAL PRACTICE 10.1

Absorption or Variable Costing?

Schrader Bellows, an international manufacturer of pneumatic products, continually has conflicts between variable and absorption costing. The company advocates and uses absorption costing, while many of its managers prefer some modified system approaching variable costing. The managers believe that certain products do not "earn their keep" because they are very difficult to produce, yet the cost system shows them as some of the company's most profitable. For other products, the managers are concerned that small competitors understate their prices even though Schrader Bellows's production lines are just as efficient. Management suspects the cost system is responsible for these discrepancies of opinion over a product's value to the company. Schrader Bellows has worked to eliminate these problems by improving the way fixed costs are allocated to products. Many arbitrary allocations have been eliminated, and others have been refined, resulting in new costing values for many of its products. While variable costing has not yet gained overall acceptance, it has forced a rethinking of how absorption costing should be implemented and has in fact eliminated some fixed cost allocations.

Source: Robin Cooper and Robert S. Kaplan, "How Cost Accounting Systematically Distorts Product Costs," in *Accounting and Management Field Study Perspectives*, ed. William J. Burns, Jr., and Robert S. Kaplan (Boston: Harvard Business School Press, 1987), 204–205, 212.

costing, fixed factory overhead is assigned to products and expensed as part of the cost of goods sold when inventories are sold. Under variable costing, fixed factory overhead is immediately expensed as a period cost.

Inventory Valuations

The differing treatments of fixed factory overhead under absorption and variable costing result in different inventory valuations. To illustrate these differences, consider the following predicted cost data for the Morehart Company at a monthly volume of 4,000 units.

Direct materials	$7 per unit
Direct labor	$5 per unit
Variable factory overhead	$4 per unit
Total fixed factory overhead	$8,000 per month

To determine the unit cost of inventory using absorption costing, it is necessary to compute the average fixed overhead cost per unit by dividing the predicted monthly fixed overhead of $8,000 by the predicted monthly activity level of 4,000 units ($2 per unit). This per unit fixed overhead figure is essentially a predetermined factory overhead rate. Even though fixed factory overhead is not a variable cost, under absorption costing it is applied to inventory on a per unit basis the same as variable costs.

At a monthly volume of 4,000 units, Morehart's inventory costs per unit under variable and absorption costing are as shown below:

	Cost per Unit	
Cost Category	Variable Costing	Absorption Costing
Direct materials	$ 7	$ 7
Direct labor	5	5
Variable factory overhead	4	4
Fixed factory overhead ($8,000/4,000 units)	—	2
Total unit costs	$16	$18

The $2 difference in unit cost results from assigning fixed costs to the product by the absorption method, but not by the variable method.

Assume that Morehart had no beginning inventory in March 19x4 but produced 4,000 units and sold 3,500 units. The March 31 ending inventories under absorption costing and variable costing are $9,000 and $8,000, respectively (see Exhibit 10–2).

The $1,000 difference in ending inventory between the two costing methods is due entirely to the treatment of fixed manufacturing costs. Under the variable

EXHIBIT 10–2   Absorption and Variable Costing Inventory Valuation

March 19x4	Absorption Costing			Variable Costing		
	Units	Costs	Dollars	Units	Costs	Dollars
Beginning inventory	—		$ —	—		$ —
Production costs	4,000	$18	72,000	4,000	$16	64,000
Goods available for sale	4,000		$72,000	4,000		$64,000
Cost of goods sold	−3,500	$18	−63,000	−3,500	$16	−56,000
Ending inventory	500	$18	$ 9,000	500	$16	$ 8,000

costing method, all fixed manufacturing costs are treated as period costs and expensed. The difference can be explained as follows:

$$\text{Inventory difference} = \text{Change in inventory units} \times \text{Fixed costs per unit}$$
$$= 500 \text{ units} \times \$2$$
$$= \$1,000.$$

Reconciliations of absorption costing and variable costing inventory valuations may be more complex where product costs vary from period to period, or if production volume differs from period to period. Variations in cost behavior or production volume require explicit considerations of the treatment of over- or underabsorbed overhead and inventory cost flow assumptions, such as LIFO, FIFO, or weighted average.

Income Determination

The different treatments of fixed factory overhead under absorption costing and variable costing require different income statement formats and often result in different net income amounts. Under absorption costing, variable and fixed manufacturing costs are mixed together in the cost of goods sold. Under variable costing, the cost of goods sold includes only variable manufacturing costs.

Income statements presented in a functional format are used in connection with absorption costing. In functional income statements, costs are classified according to business *function*, such as manufacturing, selling, or administration. Both variable and fixed costs are included within each category. Manufacturing costs (cost of goods sold) are subtracted from sales to determine gross profit, and selling and administration costs are subtracted from gross profit to obtain net income.

Income statements presented in the contribution format are ordinarily used in connection with variable costing. In contribution income statements, costs are classified according to *behavior*. The difference between revenues and variable costs is identified as the contribution margin—the amount contributed to cover fixed costs and provide for a profit. Accordingly, contribution margin minus fixed costs equals net income.

To compare functional and contribution income statements for variable and absorption costing, assume the following additional information is available for the Morehart Company.

Selling price	$30 per unit
Variable selling and administrative expenses	$3 per unit
Fixed selling and administrative expenses	$10,000 per month

Sales Varying and Production Constant. Assume production remains constant at 4,000 units per month during June, July, and August while sales are 4,000 units, 2,500 units, and 5,500 units, respectively. Previously, the unit cost at this production level was computed to be $18 under absorption costing and $16 under variable costing. Absorption costing and variable costing income statements for June, July, and August 19x4 are presented in Exhibit 10–3. A summary of unit inventory changes is presented at the bottom of the exhibit.

The first set of statements is prepared in a functional format using absorption costing. The second set of statements is prepared in a contribution format using variable costing.

In June, production and sales were equal, resulting in no deferral of costs in inventory. All current costs were deducted under both methods, as either product or period costs, resulting in the same net income under both methods.

In July, production exceeded sales (4,000 produced; 2,500 sold). Absorption costing results in deferring part of the current fixed overhead costs in the ending inventory of finished goods as product costs, whereas direct costing expenses all current fixed overhead costs as period costs. Consequently, absorption costing net income for July exceeded variable costing net income by $3,000, the increase in inventory (1,500 units) times the fixed overhead per unit ($2).

In August, sales exceeded production (4,000 produced; 5,500 sold). All production and all beginning inventory were sold. Consequently, under absorption costing, all the current period's fixed factory overhead and fixed factory overhead previously deferred in Finished Goods Inventory are expensed through cost of goods sold. Under variable costing, the prior period's ending inventory sold during August included only variable cost. The only fixed costs deducted on the August variable costing income statement are those incurred in August. As a result, expenses are greater and net income is smaller under absorption costing than under variable costing. The difference in net income of $3,000 is equal to the change in inventory (1,500 units) times the fixed overhead per unit ($2).

Sales Constant and Production Varying. Assume the sales remain constant at 4,000 units for the Morehart Company during October, November, and December 19x4. Production units were 4,000 for October, 5,000 for November, and 3,200 for December. Unlike the previous illustration where production was

EXHIBIT 10–3   Absorption and Variable Costing Income (Production Constant)

Morehart Company
Absorption Costing Income Statements
For June, July, and August, 19x4

	Sales Equal Production	Production Exceeds Sales	Sales Exceed Production
	June	July	August
Unit sales	4,000	2,500	5,500
Sales (at $30 per unit)	$120,000	$75,000	$165,000
Cost of goods sold (at $18 per unit)	− 72,000	−45,000	− 99,000
Gross profit	$ 48,000	$30,000	$ 66,000
Selling and administrative expenses:			
Variable (at $3 per unit)	$ 12,000	$ 7,500	$ 16,500
Fixed	10,000	10,000	10,000
Total	− 22,000	−17,500	− 26,500
Net income	$ 26,000	$12,500	$ 39,500

Morehart Company
Variable Costing Income Statements
For June, July, and August, 19x4

	June	July	August
Unit sales	4,000	2,500	5,500
Sales (at $30 per unit)	$120,000	$75,000	$165,000
Variable expenses:			
Cost of goods sold (at $16 per unit)	$ 64,000	$40,000	$ 88,000
Selling and administrative (at $3 per unit)	12,000	7,500	16,500
Total	− 76,000	−47,500	−104,500
Contribution margin	$ 44,000	$27,500	$ 60,500
Fixed expenses:			
Factory overhead	$ 8,000	$ 8,000	$ 8,000
Selling and administrative	10,000	10,000	10,000
Total	− 18,000	−18,000	− 18,000
Net income	$ 26,000	$ 9,500	$ 42,500

Summary of Unit Inventory Changes

	June	July	August
Beginning inventory	—	—	1,500
Production	4,000	4,000	4,000
Total available	4,000	4,000	5,500
Sales	− 4,000	− 2,500	− 5,500
Ending inventory	—	1,500	—

constant and fixed factory overhead costs were $2 per unit, this illustration (assuming an actual overhead rate is used) has the following fixed factory overhead costs per unit.

	October	November	December
Fixed factory overhead	$8,000	$8,000	$8,000
Units produced	÷4,000	÷5,000	÷3,200
Fixed costs per unit	$ 2.00	$ 1.60	$ 2.50

As a result of this situation, the unit cost of inventory and, subsequently, the cost of goods sold, will vary each period. Given the variable unit costs of $16 from the previous illustration, the total unit manufacturing costs for these months are as follows:

	October	November	December
Variable costs per unit	$16.00	$16.00	$16.00
Fixed costs per unit	2.00	1.60	2.50
Total manufacturing costs per unit	$18.00	$17.60	$18.50

If sales remain the same over several periods, it is expected that income should be the same, especially if cost behavior is constant. However, as Exhibit 10–4 shows, absorption income varies even though sales and cost behavior remained constant. Under the variable costing method income remains constant when both sales and cost behavior are the same for different periods.

When sales equal production, the income under both methods is the same (see June in Exhibit 10–3, and October in Exhibit 10–4). All other things being equal, absorption income increases when production goes up and declines when production goes down.

Reconciliation of Income Differences

An examination of the previous illustrations reveals several important differences between absorption costing and variable costing.

- When production equals sales, absorption costing net income equals variable costing net income.

- When production exceeds sales, absorption costing net income exceeds variable costing net income.

- When production is less than sales, absorption costing net income is less than variable costing net income.

EXHIBIT 10–4   Absorption and Variable Costing Income (Sales Constant)

Morehart Company
Absorption Costing Income Statements
For October, November, and December, 19x4

	Sales Equal Production	Production Exceeds Sales	Sales Exceed Production
	October	November	December
Unit sales	4,000	4,000	4,000
Sales (at $30 per unit)	$120,000	$120,000	$120,000
Cost of goods sold:			
Beginning inventory	$ —	$ —	$ 17,600
Variable manufacturing costs	64,000	80,000	51,200
Fixed factory overhead	8,000	8,000	8,000
Cost of goods available	$ 72,000	$ 88,000	$ 76,800
Less: Ending inventory	— —	– 17,600	– 3,700
Cost of goods sold	– 72,000	– 70,400	– 73,100
Gross profit	$ 48,000	$ 49,600	$ 46,900
Selling and administrative expenses:			
Variable (at $3 per unit)	$ 12,000	$ 12,000	$ 12,000
Fixed	10,000	10,000	10,000
Total	– 22,000	– 22,000	– 22,000
Net income	$ 26,000	$ 27,600	$ 24,900

For each period, the income differences between absorption and direct costing can be explained by analyzing the change in inventoried fixed factory overhead under absorption costing net income. In general,

Variable costing net income	+	Increase (or minus decrease) in inventoried fixed factory overhead	=	Absorption costing net income.

This equation may be reversed to reconcile absorption costing net income to variable costing net income:

Absorption costing net income	+	Decrease (or minus increase) in inventoried fixed factory overhead	=	Variable costing net income.

EXHIBIT 10–4   (Continued)

Morehart Company
Variable Costing Income Statements
For October, November, and December, 19x4

	Sales Equal Production	Production Exceeds Sales	Sales Exceed Production
	October	November	December
Unit sales	4,000	4,000	4,000
Sales (at $30 per unit)	$120,000	$120,000	$120,000
Variable expenses:			
Cost of goods sold (at $16 per unit)	$ 64,000	$ 64,000	$ 64,000
Selling and administrative			
(at $3 per unit)	12,000	12,000	12,000
Total	− 76,000	− 76,000	− 76,000
Contribution margin	$ 44,000	$ 44,000	$ 44,000
Fixed expenses:			
Factory overhead	$ 8,000	$ 8,000	$ 8,000
Selling and administrative	10,000	10,000	10,000
Total	− 18,000	− 18,000	− 18,000
Net income	$ 26,000	$ 26,000	$ 26,000

Summary of Unit Inventory Changes

	October	November	December
Beginning inventory	—	—	1,000
Production	4,000	5,000	3,200
Total available	4,000	5,000	4,200
Sales	− 4,000	− 4,000	− 4,000
Ending inventory	—	1,000	200

Exhibit 10–5 presents a set of reconciliations for June, July, and August, which reconciles from variable income to absorption income, as well as a set for October, November, and December, which reconciles in the reverse order.

Note in the following totals for the three-month period (June to August) that total production equals total sales and total absorption costing net income equals total variable costing net income.

Month	Production	Sales	Absorption Costing Income	Variable Costing Income
June	4,000	4,000	$26,000	$26,000
July	4,000	2,500	12,500	9,500
August	4,000	5,500	39,500	42,500
Total	12,000	12,000	$78,000	$78,000

EXHIBIT 10–5   Reconciliation of Absorption and Variable Costing Net Income

	June	July	August
Variable costing net income	$26,000	$ 9,500	$42,500
Change in inventoried fixed costs:			
Fixed overhead in ending inventory units	$ —	$ 3,000*	$ —
Less fixed overhead in beginning inventory	– —	– —	– 3,000†
Increase (decrease) in inventoried fixed costs	—	3,000	(3,000)
Absorption costing net income	$26,000	$12,500	$39,500

	October	November	December
Absorption costing net income	$26,000	$27,600	$24,900
Change in inventoried fixed costs:			
Fixed overhead in beginning inventory units	$ —	$ —	$ 1,600†
Less fixed overhead in ending inventory	– —	– 1,600**	– 500‡
Increase (decrease) in inventoried fixed costs	—	(1,600)	1,100
Variable costing net income	$26,000	$26,000	$26,000

* 1,500 units × $2.00 of fixed factory costs per unit.
** 1,000 units × $1.60 of fixed factory costs per unit.
† Ending of July is beginning of August and ending of November is beginning of December.
‡ 200 units × $2.50 of fixed factory costs per unit.

For any given time period, regardless of length, if total units produced equals total units sold, net income will be the same for absorption costing and variable costing, all other things being equal. Under absorption costing, all fixed factory overhead is released as a product cost through cost of goods sold when inventory is sold. Under variable costing, all fixed factory overhead is reported as a period cost and expensed in the period incurred. Consequently, over the life of a product the income differences within periods are offset since they are caused only by the timing of the release of fixed factory overhead to the income statement.

An Evaluation of Variable Costing

Few accounting topics have generated as much controversy as variable costing. The central theoretical issue in this controversy is whether or not the incurrence of fixed manufacturing costs adds value to products. Proponents of variable costing argue that the incurrence of these costs does not add value to a product. Fixed costs are incurred to provide the capacity to produce during a given period, and these costs expire with the passage of time regardless of whether the related capacity was used. Variable manufacturing costs, on the other hand, are incurred only if production takes place. Consequently, these costs are properly assignable to the units produced.

Proponents of variable costing also argue that inventories have value only to the extent that they avoid the necessity for incurring costs in the future. Having inventory available for sale does avoid the necessity of incurring some future variable costs, but the availability of finished goods inventory does not avoid the incurrence of future fixed manufacturing costs. They conclude that inventories should be valued at their variable manufacturing cost, and fixed manufacturing costs should be expensed as incurred.

When considering the accounting principle of matching, variable costing has an advantage over absorption costing because it matches revenues with the direct cost of producing the revenues. This results in net income varying only with sales and not with both sales and production, as is often found in absorption costing. In absorption costing, overproduction especially distorts net income during a period because the excess inventory is assigned fixed costs that would otherwise be assigned to the units produced and sold. Using absorption costing, a company may increase net operating income by simply producing more than it sells.

Opponents of variable costing argue that fixed manufacturing costs are incurred for only one purpose, namely, to manufacture the product. Because they are incurred to manufacture the product, they should be assigned to the product. It is also argued that in the long run all costs are variable. Consequently, by omitting fixed costs, variable costing understates long-run variable costs and misleads decision makers into underestimating true production costs.

On a pragmatic level, the central arguments for variable costing center around the fact that the use of variable costing facilitates the development of contribution income statements and cost-volume-profit analysis when production and sales are not equal. If all costs are accumulated on an absorption costing

M ANAGERIAL PRACTICE 10.2

Strong Opinions on Aborption Costing

According to the vice president for administration of Stanadyne Automotive Products Group, "We had a cost system that concentrated on full absorption costing. There's been a lot of opinions . . . on . . . the value of the . . . system, and I'll just say . . . it didn't meet what we were trying to accomplish. In other companies it might have an application, but not for us. Our prices are set by the market. We don't sell based on fully absorbed costs, so having a full absorption costing system did not meet our objective."

Source: William G. Holbrook, "Accounting Experiences in a JIT Environment," in *Cost Accounting, Robotics, and the New Manufacturing Environment*, ed. Robert Capettini and Donald K. Clancy (Sarasota, Fla.: American Accounting Association, 1987), 4.8.

basis, contribution income statements are difficult to develop, and cost-volume-profit analysis becomes very complicated unless production and sales are equal.

Variable costing is now widely used for internal reporting. However, it is not acceptable for external reporting in published financial statements or for income tax determination. Consequently, accountants should routinely use variable costing for internal reports and absorption costing for external reports. The simultaneous use of variable and absorption costing is a prime example of the use of different costs for different purposes.

SEGMENT REPORTING

Most top-level managers must have more than cost reports to aid them in evaluating large operating units. Income statements are often a vital part of the evaluation process. In this section of the chapter, emphasis is on cost classifications and the evaluation of individual segments.

Segment reports are income statements that show operating results for portions or segments of a business. When the reporting of operating activities is presented for product lines, it is often labeled product reporting. Segment reporting is used primarily for internal purposes, although generally accepted accounting principles also require disclosure of segment information for some public corporations.

Segment reporting is very common in organizations where there are distinct divisions of product lines, geographic territories, or organizational units. The segments or products of the organization for which reports are prepared depend on the information needs of management. The four most common types of segment reports are as follows:

1. Income statements for each plant or division.
2. Income statements for each product line.
3. Income statements for each sales territory.
4. Cost reports for cost centers (segments without sales or revenue).

Segment reports usually include the costs of both manufacturing and nonmanufacturing activities. Divisional income statements and product reports include product costs and appropriate selling and administrative costs. A given report may often include operating data for several products or territories, which may require further segmentation.

The format and frequency of segment reports is limited only by the decision needs and willingness of management to pay for preparing the reports. Although there are many different types of segment reports, three functions basic to the preparation of every report are:

1. Identification of the reporting objective.
2. Assignment of direct costs to the reporting objective.
3. Allocation of indirect costs to the reporting objective.

Segment reporting requires careful control over data collection and storage because of the different reporting formats. To properly compute the income for each segment or product, all costs, fixed and variable, must be considered. To effectively report the activities of a business segment, management should use the contribution approach, which focuses on the contribution made by each segment to cover common costs and to provide for a profit. The contribution approach discussed in the first section of this chapter (and in Chapter 4) is used for detailed segment statements.

Reporting Objective   A company with a single product or a homogeneous activity has little difficulty defining the activities to be included in its operating report, but the reporting structure of a multisegment business is not so easily defined. For example, if management wants to know the profit contributed by a certain product in a

MANAGERIAL PRACTICE 10.3

The Relative Performance Evaluation Concept

Honeywell Corporation has almost one hundred divisions that must be evaluated. Rather than comparing them to each other at the corporate level, the corporation assigns each to one of four product areas: Aerospace and Defense, Control Products, Control Systems, and Information Systems. At this level, each one is evaluated on its profit margin, return on assets, and revenue growth, using the relative performance evaluation (RPE) concept. When the RPE method is used, the divisions are compared to each other rather than with divisions outside the product area. Evaluation criteria include how well a division implements top management orders, meets production schedules, and achieves cost and efficiency standards. Historically at Honeywell the emphasis has not been on financial performance but on growth, customer satisfaction, and new product development. Only recently has the company started to shift its attention to financial measures of performance—the most important of which is return on investment.

Source: Michael W. Maher, "The Use of Relative Performance Evaluation in Organizations," in *Accounting and Management Field Study Perspectives*, ed. William J. Burns, Jr., and Robert S. Kaplan (Boston: Harvard Business School Press, 1987), 308–309.

particular sales region, cost determination may be complicated in that certain marketing efforts promote several products within the sales region, whereas others overlap different sales regions. Each reporting objective must be identified and described as precisely as possible to ensure that only relevant revenues and costs are assigned to each reporting segment.

Contribution Margin

In preparing segment income statements, management must decide whether to use the functional (absorption) approach or the contribution (variable) approach. Segment reports are more useful if they emphasize the segment's contribution to profit. To compute the contribution margin by segments, sales and variable expenses must be assigned to each reporting segment. Since records are generally kept by segments, the accumulation of these data is relatively easy.

Segment reporting is an excellent example of how the contribution margin approach can be used for evaluation purposes. It can be used for determining the effect on profit of certain types of short-run changes when other types are held constant. Examples include changes in sales volume, product mix, temporary changes in capacity, special orders, and product promotions. As sales volume changes in a particular segment, the impact on net income can be determined by multiplying the segment contribution margin per unit by the change in units sold, or by multiplying the contribution margin ratio by the changes in sales dollars. Many decisions relating to the short run involve only variable costs and sales.

Segment Report Configurations

The nature and extent of segmentation of operating reports depends on the organizational structure of the company. A highly decentralized multilevel organization with different levels of operation may use a reporting structure similar to that presented in Exhibit 10–6 for the Offshore Refining Company for 19x4. The benefits accruing to management from such a series of segment reports are many. Segment reporting can aid in identifying trends, percentage relationships, and other income information that management uses to evaluate the performance of the various activities of the organization.

For the reports in Exhibit 10–6, the reporting objective was defined by territories. Sales and expense data are presented for the two reporting territories of Offshore Refining. The direct manufacturing costs (variable costs) are deducted from territory sales to determine the manufacturing margin. The variable expenses of nonmanufacturing activities are then deducted to obtain the contribution margin. All direct fixed expenses identifiable with each territory are subtracted from the contribution margin to arrive at the territory margin, which is the amount that each territory contributes toward covering common corporate expenses and generating corporate profits. Common corporate expenses include the general administrative expenses of operating the corporate offices and conducting corporate activities. These expenses are necessary in the operations of the company, but they are not identifiable with specific territories or divisions.

EXHIBIT 10–6   Segment Report Configuration by Territory

Offshore Refining Company
Territory and Company Income Statements
For the year ended December 31, 19x4
(in thousands)

	Atlantic	Gulf	Company Totals
	Segments		*Company Totals*
Sales	$150,000	$150,000	$300,000
Less: Variable manufacturing expenses	− 30,000	− 40,000	− 70,000
Manufacturing margin	$120,000	$110,000	$230,000
Less: Variable selling expenses	$ 14,000	$ 11,000	$ 25,000
Variable administrative expenses	25,000	30,000	55,000
Total	− 39,000	− 41,000	− 80,000
Contribution margin	$ 81,000	$ 69,000	$150,000
Less direct fixed expenses:			
Manufacturing	$ 30,000	$ 32,000	$ 62,000
Selling	9,000	11,000	20,000
Administrative	18,000	12,000	30,000
Total	− 57,000	− 55,000	−112,000
Territory margin	$ 24,000	$ 14,000	$ 38,000
Less common expenses:			
Manufacturing			$ 9,000
Selling			4,000
Administrative			2,000
Total			− 15,000
Net income			$ 23,000

Multilevel Segment Report Configurations

The needs of large organizations are usually not met with just one segment report, whether segmented by territory, product, division, or other reporting objective. Exhibit 10–7 illustrates a set of multilevel reports for the Offshore Refining Company. Exhibit 10–7(a) segments the totals for the company in terms of divisions, Exhibit 10–7(b) further segments one of these divisions in terms of the product lines sold within the division, and Exhibit 10–7(c) divides one of these product lines into the areas where it is sold. As each segment is further divided, the report shows more detailed aspects of the company.

The *first-level statements* for Offshore Refining show the company totals and a set of income statements segmented by its major reporting objective, operating divisions. Sales and cost data are presented for Offshore's two divisions in Exhibit 10–7(a). The company totals column includes the same total sales and expenses as the company totals column in Exhibit 10–6, except that the fixed costs are allocated differently below the contribution margin level. All direct fixed expenses identifiable with each division are subtracted from the contribution margin to arrive at the which is the amount each division contributes toward covering common corporate expenses and generating corporate profits.

EXHIBIT 10–7   Report Configurations Segmented by Division, Products of Division, and Territories of Product

(a) Segment margins by divisions of
Offshore Refining Company
(first level)
(in thousands)

| | Segments | | Company |
	Division A	Division B	Totals
Sales	$100,000	$200,000	$300,000
Less: Variable manufacturing expenses	− 20,000	− 50,000	− 70,000
Manufacturing margin	$ 80,000	$150,000	$230,000
Less: Variable selling expenses	$ 10,000	$ 15,000	$ 25,000
Variable administrative expenses	25,000	30,000	55,000
Total	− 35,000	− 45,000	− 80,000
Contribution margin	$ 45,000	$105,000	$150,000
Less direct fixed expenses:			
Manufacturing	$ 15,000	$ 50,000	$ 65,000
Selling	5,000	17,000	22,000
Administrative	10,000	18,000	28,000
Total	− 30,000	− 85,000	−115,000
Divisional margin	$ 15,000	$ 20,000	$ 35,000
Less common expenses:			
Manufacturing			$ 6,000
Selling			2,000
Administrative			4,000
Total			− 12,000
Net income			$ 23,000

Second-level statements may be presented for each first-level reporting objective. In our illustration, a product line contribution statement is presented for each product of Division A. These reports, in Exhibit 10–7(b), are useful to management in making decisions related to product pricing, sales strategy, inventory levels, break-even analysis, and production scheduling. The decision to continue or discontinue a product may also be based, in part, on information provided by these statements.

In Exhibit 10–7(b), the computations of the manufacturing margin and the contribution margin follow the same format as the divisional contribution statement. However, the computation of the product margin (product sales less direct segment costs) is somewhat different from the computation of the divisional contribution. This difference occurs because some of the fixed expenses regarded as direct at the divisional segment level are not direct at the product level. These fixed expenses include such items as divisional office salaries and plant security, which pertain to the general operation of the division rather than to the products. Therefore, only part of the fixed expenses of the division is assigned to products, with the balance of $6,000,000 reported as common costs.

EXHIBIT 10–7   (Continued)

(b) Segment margins by products within Division A of Offshore Refining Company (second level) (in thousands)

	Segments		Division A
	Oil Products	Gas Products	Totals
Sales	$ 40,000	$ 60,000	$100,000
Less: Variable manufacturing expenses	− 5,000	− 15,000	− 20,000
Manufacturing margin	$ 35,000	$ 45,000	$ 80,000
Less: Variable selling expenses	$ 5,000	$ 5,000	$ 10,000
Variable administrative expenses	12,000	13,000	25,000
Total	− 17,000	− 18,000	− 35,000
Contribution margin	$ 18,000	$ 27,000	$ 45,000
Less direct fixed expenses:			
Manufacturing	$ 4,000	$ 8,000	$ 12,000
Selling	1,000	3,000	4,000
Administrative	4,000	4,000	8,000
Total	− 9,000	− 15,000	− 24,000
Product margin	$ 9,000	$ 12,000	$ 21,000
Less common expenses:			
Manufacturing			$ 3,000
Selling			1,000
Administrative			2,000
Total			− 6,000
Divisional margin			$ 15,000

(continued)

These divisional expenses are similar to the common fixed expenses of the company in the divisional contribution statement.

The next set of reports, *third-level statements,* is a breakdown of a second-level reporting objective. Exhibit 10–7(c) shows the amount of contribution margin of Oil Products in Division A generated by each sales region. The territory margin is the contribution margin less direct fixed expenses associated with a given market area. The margins for the same product often vary because of different environments. For example, the company office that serves the Atlantic area may experience significantly higher marketing and distribution costs than the office serving the Gulf area. Though the Atlantic area is more populated, it is farther from the refineries. Additionally, the company may have a better reputation in the Gulf area, thereby making sales easier.

Note from Exhibit 10–7 that fewer fixed expenses are allocated to segments as the reporting process is separated into specific segments within segments of the business. Because the allocation would be very subjective, none of the fixed manufacturing expense is assignable to the sales territories in Exhibit 10–7(c),

EXHIBIT 10–7   (Continued)

(c) Segment margins by territories of Oil Products within Division A of Offshore Refining Company (third level)

| | Segments | | Oil Products |
	Atlantic	Gulf	Totals
Sales	$ 12,000	$ 28,000	$ 40,000
Less: Variable manufacturing expenses	– 1,500	– 3,500	– 5,000
Manufacturing margin	$ 10,500	$ 24,500	$ 35,000
Less: Variable selling expenses	$ 2,000	$ 3,000	$ 5,000
Variable administrative expenses	4,000	8,000	12,000
Totals	– 6,000	– 11,000	– 17,000
Contribution margin	$ 4,500	$ 13,500	$ 18,000
Less direct fixed expenses:			
Selling	$ 100	$ 400	$ 500
Administrative	1,000	2,000	3,000
Total	– 1,100	– 2,400	– 3,500
Territory margin	$ 3,400	$ 11,100	$ 14,500
Less common expenses:			
Manufacturing			$ 4,000
Selling			500
Administrative			1,000
Total			– 5,500
Product margin			$ 9,000

and smaller amounts of the selling and administrative expenses are allocated at this level. Each level has certain costs that can be defined as direct or indirect, and at each subsequent level the total expenses are smaller because the indirect expenses are not carried forward from the previous level. This reduction is evident for the Atlantic and Gulf areas where the territorial margins totaled $14,500,000, whereas the total product margin was only $9,000,000.

Other Configurations

In addition to, or instead of, the segments shown in Exhibits 10–6 and 10–7, management may desire first-level statements for other reporting objectives. For example, Exhibit 10–8 illustrates how the company can be segmented into first-level reporting by products. The product segment report, when used as a first-level statement, includes the products of both Divisions A and B.

In Exhibits 10–6, 10–7(a), and 10–8, the same total costs and revenues are allocated and assigned through the contribution margin level. Because of differences in allocating fixed costs, the company's total fixed costs of $127,000,000 (direct plus common) are treated differently in each of the various first-level statements.

In Exhibit 10–6, $112,000,000 of fixed costs is assigned to segments with $15,000,000 treated as common costs to both territories. For the division segment reports (Exhibit 10–7a), $115,000,000 of fixed costs is assigned and $12,000,000

EXHIBIT 10–8   Alternative Reporting Examples

**Segment margins by products
of Offshore Refining Company
(first level)**

	Segments				
	Oil Products	Gas Products	Chemical Products	Saline Products	Company Totals
Sales	$40,000	$60,000	$120,000	$80,000	$300,000
Less: Variable manufacturing expenses	− 5,000	−15,000	− 35,000	−15,000	− 70,000
Manufacturing margin	$35,000	$45,000	$ 85,000	$65,000	$230,000
Less: Variable selling expenses	$ 5,000	$ 5,000	$ 14,000	$ 1,000	$ 25,000
Variable administrative expenses	12,000	13,000	22,000	8,000	55,000
Total	−17,000	−18,000	− 36,000	− 9,000	− 80,000
Contribution margin	$18,000	$27,000	$ 49,000	$56,000	$150,000
Less direct fixed expenses:					
Manufacturing	$ 4,000	$ 8,000	$ 24,000	$28,000	$ 64,000
Selling	1,000	3,000	5,000	6,000	15,000
Administrative	4,000	4,000	4,000	4,000	16,000
Total	− 9,000	−15,000	− 33,000	−38,000	− 95,000
Product margin	$ 9,000	$12,000	$ 16,000	$18,000	$ 55,000
Less common expenses:					
Manufacturing					$ 7,000
Selling					9,000
Administrative					16,000
Total					− 32,000
Net income					$ 23,000

is common. And for the product reports (Exhibit 10–8), $95,000,000 is assigned and $32,000,000 is common.

It is typical for the common costs to be different for each type of first-level segment report because cost traceability for each reporting objective is different. Because manufacturing expenses are assumed to occur at the divisional level, they should all be assigned to the division incurring them. Even though manufacturing expenses are incurred to produce the products, it is often difficult to assign every expense to a specific product. In Exhibit 10–6, only $62,000,000 is assigned to products, with $9,000,000 treated as common expenses; and in Exhibit 10–8, $64,000,000 is assigned to the territories, with $7,000,000 treated as common expenses.

Other segment configurations are used by organizations to meet different management needs. Although reports segmented by division, product line, and territory are the most common, segment reports can also be based on plants, single products, industries (for conglomerates), and domestic and foreign operations. Because segment reporting allows a company to examine itself from various perspectives, management will select the types of segment reports that are most beneficial for decision making.

Segment Margin

The segment margin represents the amount that a segment contributes toward the common (indirect) costs of the organization and toward profits.[2] It is generally considered one of the best gauges of profitability for a given segment of a company.

At the operating management level, segment margins are helpful in making decisions related to production, such as those pertaining to capacity changes and long-range pricing policies. The contribution margin is most useful in those situations involving short-run operating decisions, such as pricing of special orders, and accepting or rejecting special projects.

Direct Versus Common Segment Costs

It may be difficult to distinguish between direct and common costs. Direct segment costs are often defined as costs that would not be incurred if the segment being evaluated were to be discontinued. They are specifically identifiable with a particular segment. For example, if the Gas Products segment in Exhibit 10–8 were discontinued, Gas Product advertising would probably be discontinued; therefore, it should be classified as a direct cost of Gas Products. Other examples include equipment depreciation and segment management salaries. On the other hand, the Division A vice president would probably not be terminated even if Gas Products was discontinued. Therefore the vice president's salary is common to both product lines.

Common segment costs, also called indirect segment costs, are related to more than one segment and not directly traceable to a particular segment. These costs are referred to as common costs because they are incurred at one level for the benefit of two or more segments at a lower level. Nonmanufacturing activities often have numerous indirect costs. A large organization, for example, may provide a centralized computer operation to serve all its production and marketing activities. Other examples of common costs include salaries of corporate management, companywide sales promotion, and expenses of the corporate accounting department.

Note from Exhibit 10–7(a) that when segments are defined as divisions, Division A has $30,000,000 in direct fixed costs. In Exhibit 10–7(b), only $24,000,000 of this amount remains direct when the definition of a segment is narrowed from divisions to that of product lines in a division. The other $6,000,000 becomes a common cost of Division A product lines.

There are several possible reasons that the $6,000,000 of direct fixed costs is a common cost when the division is broken down into product line segments; for example, the amount could include the monthly salary of the division manager. The division manager's salary is a direct cost when considering the division as a whole, but it is common to the separate product lines within the divisions. Other items that might be treated the same way include plant depreciation, security costs, computer costs, or office equipment.

---

[2] Segment margin can also be used to assist in measuring the segment return on investment, a very popular evaluation tool in decentralized organizations. See Chapter 9 for a detailed discussion.

The $24,000,000 of fixed costs that remain direct ($9,000,000 for Oil and $15,000,000 for Gas) after the division is separated into product line segments consists of items that can be assigned to the products. These might include product research, equipment rental, and product advertising.

Common segment costs should not be allocated; they should simply be deducted from the segment margin in total to arrive at the net income for the company or the segment income for the next higher level segment. Nothing is added to the usefulness of segment reports by allocating common costs to the various segments; in fact, allocations of this sort may significantly reduce the usefulness of the information. These arbitrary allocations will draw attention away from direct segment costs toward those items that are not directly traceable to a given segment.

MANAGERIAL PRACTICE 10.4

Better Cost Assignments Help Weyerhaeuser Chop "Common" Costs

In measuring the profit performance of its three primary business groups, Weyerhaeuser Company has ignored the conventional wisdom that corporate overhead costs should normally not be allocated to business segments. Their approach is not a traditional allocation of so-called common costs based on a volume measure, such as sales. Instead, they charge each business group based on actual services received from corporate service departments. Weyerhaeuser attributes costs to the "use of resources by carefully analyzing the activities that drive the consumption of corporate resources. . . . And they prompt profit oriented responses because users and suppliers are now free to acquire or sell these corporate services outside the company in the market."

The major advantages of the system at Weyerhaeuser are that end users of corporate services now recognize and accept the costs of activities they require; corporate and business group managers understand each other better; and corporate service units are encouraged to provide services at a competitive "price." Corporate service units failing to charge all their costs to business groups are apt to be disbanded—often at significant cost savings.

Source: H. Thomas Johnson and Dennis A. Loewe, "How Weyerhaeuser Manages Corporate Overhead Costs," *Management Accounting* (August 1987): 20–26.

Segment Decisions   Decisions to continue or drop a segment are frequently based on segment reports. A problem (similar to that previously discussed in comparing direct and common segment costs) arises when determining whether a cost is relevant to a segment or product being considered for continuation or noncontinuation. When a company is able to identify relatively small segments, accountants generally find that the smaller the segments used for reporting, the more the costs tend to be common and, therefore, irrelevant to most short-term decisions.

The isolation of direct costs is complicated in that accounting reports often show allocations of common costs among various segments as expenses in the segment reports. To illustrate, if common facilities are used by a dairy processor in the manufacture of various milk products, the income statement for each product would probably include a portion of the depreciation on these facilities. In Exhibit 10–9(a), Yogurt appears unprofitable, and management might be tempted to discontinue it. If the depreciation is $100,000 per year and a total of 1,000,000 liters of all products are made, each liter of product could be charged with $0.10. Suppose that Yogurt, with current sales of 200,000 liters, is dropped. The $20,000 depreciation expense now allocated to Yogurt will not be avoided, but the remaining 800,000 liters of the other products must be charged with $0.125 per liter. As a result, the apparent profitability of the remaining products would be reduced, and company profits would decline, as shown in Exhibit 10–9(b). In fact, the profit decline is due to the decision to drop

---

EXHIBIT 10–9   Continuing or Discontinuing a Product

(a) Current period product income statements (partial)

	Cream	Ice Cream	Yogurt	Company Totals
		Segments		
Sales (liters)	500,000	300,000	200,000	
	× $0.22	× $0.30	× $0.40	
	$110,000	$ 90,000	$ 80,000	$280,000
Variable costs	− 40,000	− 30,000	− 65,000	−135,000
Contribution margin	$ 70,000	$ 60,000	$ 15,000	$145,000
Depreciation expense	− 50,000	− 30,000	− 20,000	−100,000
Segment and company income	$ 20,000	$ 30,000	$ (5,000)	$ 45,000

(b) Pro forma product income statements (partial)

	Cream	Ice Cream	Company Totals
	Segments		
Sales	$110,000	$90,000	$200,000
Variable costs	− 40,000	−30,000	− 70,000
Contribution margin	$ 70,000	$60,000	$130,000
Depreciation expense	− 62,500	−37,500	−100,000
Segment and company income	$ 7,500	$22,500	$ 30,000

Yogurt. When a segment is dropped, there may be no short-run reduction in common costs. For this reason allocated common costs are generally irrelevant to a decision about whether a particular segment should be dropped. In making these decisions, managers must be wary of any sunk costs. Even if they are direct costs of a segment, they should be ignored in the decision analysis.

SUMMARY

Absorption costing and variable (sometimes called direct) costing are two alternative approaches to inventory valuation. The essential difference between absorption and variable costing is the inclusion, or exclusion, of fixed factory overhead as a product cost. Under absorption costing, fixed factory overhead is assigned to products and expensed as part of the cost of goods sold when inventories are sold. Under variable costing, fixed factory overhead is immediately expensed as a period cost.

Although absorption costing is generally accepted for external and income tax reporting, variable costing provides better information for use internally by management in evaluating the consequences of short-run decisions and in planning operations in the near term. Variable costing is superior primarily because it permits the development of contribution income statements, where costs are classified by behavior to assist management in understanding cost-volume-profit relationships.

Segment reports are income statements that show operating results for portions or segments of a business. The format and frequency of segment reports is limited only by management's needs and willingness to incur the cost for these reports.

The distinction between direct segment costs and indirect, or common, segment costs is very important in segment reporting. Direct segment costs are costs specifically identifiable with a particular segment of a business. By subtracting a segment's direct costs from its revenues, segment margin is obtained. Indirect, or common, segment costs are costs that are not directly traceable to a particular segment but are necessary to support the activities of two or more segments. Indirect segment costs may be allocated to segments for a variety of reporting purposes, but unavoidable indirect segment costs should not be allocated in internal reports that are to be used for management decisions such as whether to continue or discontinue a segment.

SUGGESTED READINGS

Ajinkya, Bipan, Rowland Atiase, and Linda Smith Bamber, "Absorption versus Direct Costing: Income Reconciliation and Cost-Volume-Profit Analysis." *Issues in Accounting Education* (Fall 1986): 268–281.

Chalos, Peter, "A Spreadsheet Analysis of Different Costing Systems," *Journal of Accounting Education* (Fall 1988): 345–353.

Fremgen, J. M., "The Direct Costing Controversy—An Identification of Issues," *The Accounting Review* (January 1964): 43–51.

Schill, Michael, "Variable Costing: A Closer Look," *Management Accounting* (February 1987): 36–39.

Sorter, George H., and Charles T. Horngren, "Asset Recognition and Economic Attributes—The Relevant Costing Approach," *The Accounting Review* (July 1962): 391–399.

REVIEW PROBLEM

Absorption and Variable Costing

Colorado Ski Company has just completed its first year of operation on December 31, 19x3. The President says she needs financial statements for both managerial review and external reporting purposes. The Controller informs the President that two sets of statements will be needed: one based on absorption costing and other based on variable costing. Although concerned about the cost of preparing two reports, the President agrees to let the Controller try it.

The following data are from the first year of operations:

Direct labor	$200,000
Direct materials	250,000
Variable manufacturing overhead	100,000
Fixed manufacturing overhead	130,000
Variable selling expenses	75,000
Fixed administrative expenses	112,000
50,000 pairs of skis were manufactured and 40,000 pairs sold at a price of $40.	

Requirements

a) Compute the cost of the inventory at the end of the year using (1) absorption costing and (2) variable costing.

b) Prepare income statements for 19x3 using both absorption and variable costing methods.

c) Reconcile the difference in the net incomes in part (b).

d) Explain to the President why both sets of statements are needed.

The solution to this problem is found at the end of the Chapter 10 exercises, problems, and cases.

KEY TERMS

Absorption costing
Common segment costs
Direct costing
Direct segment costs
Divisional segment margin
Full costing
Indirect segment costs

Manufacturing margin
Product margin
Product reporting
Segment margin
Segment reports
Territory margin
Variable costing

REVIEW QUESTIONS

 10–1 Explain the difference between product costs and period costs.

10–2 Can period costs exist under the absorption method? If so, give some examples.

10–3   How can full costing be a synonym for absorption costing?

10–4   Explain the basic difference between variable and absorption costing?

10–5   Is inventory more consistently valued using variable or absorption costing? Why?

10–6   What is the relationship between variable costing and the contribution income method?

10–7   How do you reconcile the differences in net income between the variable costing and absorption costing methods of inventory valuation?

10–8   What is the relationship between segment reports and product reports?

10–9   How are contribution margins and segment margins similar? How are they different?

10–10   What is a reporting objective? How is it determined?

10–11   How do you distinguish between direct and indirect segment costs?

10–12   Can a company have more than one type of first-level statements in segment reporting?

10–13   Explain the relationships between any two levels of statements in segment reporting.

10–14   What types of information are needed before management should decide on dropping a product?

EXERCISES

10–1 Absorption and Variable Costing Inventory Valuations

Piedmont Paper Company had the following information available for 19x8.

Direct labor	$750,000
Variable manufacturing overhead	400,000
Direct materials	600,000
Variable selling and administrative expenses	400,000
Fixed selling and administrative expenses	400,000
Fixed manufacturing overhead	800,000

For the period sales were 75,000 units, and production totaled 100,000 units.

Requirements

a) Compute the ending finished goods inventory under both absorption costing and variable costing.

b) Compute the cost of goods sold under both absorption and variable costing.

10–2 Absorption and Variable Costing Inventory Valuation

Automotive Electric Company projects the following costs for 19x1.

	Per Unit
Direct materials	$6
Direct labor	$8
Variable overhead	$2
Fixed overhead ($40,000 for 20,000 units)	$2

During May, 20,000 units were produced, but only 10,000 were sold. During June, 20,000 units were produced and sold. During July, 20,000 units were produced, and 24,000 units were sold. There was no inventory on May 1.

Required: Compute the amount of ending inventory and cost of goods sold under variable costing and absorption costing for each month.

10–3 Absorption and Variable Costing Income Statements

The Franklin Company sells its product at a unit price of $11.00. Unit manufacturing costs are direct materials, $2.00; direct labor, $3.00; and variable factory overhead, $1.50. Total fixed manufacturing costs are $30,000 per year. Selling and administrative expenses are $1.00 per unit variable and $10,000 per year fixed. Though 25,000 units were produced during 19x1, only 20,000 units were sold. There was no beginning inventory.

Requirements

a) Prepare an income statement using absorption costing.

b) Prepare an income statement using variable costing.

10–4 Absorption and Variable Costing Income Statements

Sky Company began the year 19x1 with great optimism. During 19x1 it had no sales, but there were $60,000 in variable manufacturing costs and $20,000 in fixed manufacturing costs. In 19x2 it sold half of the finished goods inventory from 19x1 for $50,000, but it had no manufacturing costs. In 19x3 it sold the remainder of the inventory for $60,000, did no manufacturing, and went out of business December 31. Selling and administrative expenses were all fixed at $10,000 each year.

Requirements

a) Prepare an income statement for each year using absorption costing.

b) Prepare an income statement for each year using variable costing.

10–5 Absorption and Variable Costing Income Statements

The Uncontrolled Profit Corporation was disappointed to find that increased sales volume in 19x2 did not result in increased profits. Both variable unit and total fixed manufacturing costs for 19x1 and 19x2 remained constant at $10 and $1,000,000, respectively.

In 19x1 the company produced 100,000 units and sold 80,000 units at a price of $25 per unit. There was no inventory at the beginning of 19x1. In 19x2 the company made 70,000 units and sold 90,000 units at a price of $25 per unit. Selling and administrative expenses, all fixed, were $50,000 each year.

Requirements

a) Prepare income statements for 19x1 and 19x2 using the absorption costing method.

b) Prepare income statements for 19x1 and 19x2 using the variable costing method.

c) Explain why the profit was different each year using the two methods. Show computations.

10–6 Absorption and Variable Costing Comparisons: Production Equals Sales

Hammond Catsup Company manufactures and sells 15,000 cases of catsup each quarter. The following data are available for the third quarter of 19x3.

Sales price per case	$ 25
Direct materials per case	$ 12
Direct labor per case	$ 4
Variable manufacturing overhead per case	$ 3
Total fixed manufacturing overhead	30,000
Fixed selling and administrative expenses	10,000

Requirements

a) Compute the cost per case under both absorption costing and variable costing.

b) Compute net income under both absorption costing and variable costing.

c) Reconcile the income differences, if any. Explain.

10–7 Absorption and Variable Costing Comparisons: Production Exceeds Sales

Daniel Derma Company produces hand lotion which it sells in bulk to distributors who in turn bottle the product under private labels. The sales price per five-gallon container is $10. The production information for July 19x9 is as follows:

Fixed selling and administrative expenses	$20,000
Fixed manufacturing overhead	66,000
Variable manufacturing overhead per container	2
Direct labor costs per hour	12
Direct material costs per container	1

The average direct labor per container is 15 minutes. During July the company produced 30,000 containers of hand lotion, but sold only 28,000 containers. There was no beginning inventory on July 1, 19x9.

Requirements

a) Compute the cost per container under both absorption and variable costing.

b) Compute net income under both absorption and variable costing.

c) Compute the ending inventories under both absorption and variable costing.

10–8 Absorption and Variable Costing Comparisons: Sales Exceed Production

Goldberg Development sells commercial building lots. During 19x8 the company bought 1,000 acres of land for $5,000,000 and divided it into 200 sites of equal size. As the lots are sold, they are cleared at an average cost of $2,500. Storm drains and driveways are then installed at an average cost of $4,000 per site. Selling costs are 10 percent of sales price. Administrative costs are $425,000 per year. The average selling price per site was $80,000 during 19x8 when 50 sites were sold.

During 19x9 the company purchased and developed an identical 1,000 acres with all costs remaining constant. Sales totaled 300 sites in 19x9 at an average price of $80,000.

Required: Compute net income under both absorption costing and variable costing for 19x8 and 19x9.

10–9 Conversion from Absorption to Variable Costing Statements

The Greenville Company began operation on January 1, 19x1. The 19x1 income statement on an absorption costing basis is as follows:

Greenville Company
Absorption Costing Income Statement
For the year ended December 31, 19x1

Sales (15,000 units)		$450,000
Less cost of goods sold:		
Beginning inventory	$ —	
Cost of goods manufactured (20,000 units)	280,000	
Ending inventory (5,000 units)	− 70,000	−210,000
Gross profit		$240,000
Selling and administrative expenses		− 40,000
Net income		$200,000

All the selling and administrative expenses are fixed. Manufacturing costs include the following unit costs:

Direct materials	$ 4
Direct labor	5
Variable manufacturing overhead	2
Fixed manufacturing overhead	3
Total	$14

Required: Prepare a variable costing income statement for 19x1.

10–10 Conversion from Absorption to Variable Costing Statements

Blacksburg Company's absorption costing income statement for 19x6 was as follows:

Blacksburg Company
Absorption Costing Income Statement
For the year ended June 30, 19x6

Sales (8,000 units)		$900,000
Cost of goods sold:		
Beginning inventory	$ —	
Cost of goods manufactured (10,000 units)	400,000	
Less ending inventory	− 80,000	−320,000
Gross profit		$580,000
Selling expenses, 10% of sales	$ 90,000	
Administrative expenses	50,000	−140,000
Net income		$440,000

During 19x6 the direct labor totaled $100,000 and direct materials were $50,000. Variable overhead costs were $2 per direct labor hour and 20,000 hours were worked. Administrative expenses were fixed.

Required: Prepare a variable costing income statement for 19x6.

10–11 Conversion from Variable to Absorption Costing Statements

The variable costing income statement for Sahota Company is as follows:

Sahota Company
Variable Costing Income Statement
For the year ended June 30, 19x7

Sales (9,000 units at $50)		$450,000
Variable expenses:		
Cost of goods sold (9,000 units at $24)	$216,000	
Selling (10% of sales)	45,000	−261,000
Contribution margin		$189,000
Fixed expenses:		
Manufacturing overhead	$100,000	
Administrative	45,000	−145,000
Net income		$ 44,000

Selected data for 19x7 concerning the operations of the company are as follows:

Beginning inventory	0 units
Units produced	10,000 units
Manufacturing costs:	
Direct labor	$12 per unit
Direct materials	9 per unit
Variable overhead	3 per unit

Required: Prepare an absorption costing income statement for 19x7.

10–12 Conversion from Variable to Absorption Costing Statements

The variable costing income statement for Friedberg Ltd. is as follows:

Friedberg Ltd.
Variable Costing Income Statement
For the year ended June 30, 19x4

Sales (4,000 units at $100)		$400,000
Variable expenses:		
Cost of goods sold (4,000 units at $30)	$120,000	
Selling (12% of sales)	48,000	−168,000
Contribution margin		$232,000
Fixed expenses:		
Manufacturing overhead	$100,000	
Administrative	60,000	−160,000
Net income		$ 72,000

Selected data for 19x4 concerning the operations of the company are as follows:

Beginning inventory	0 units
Units produced	5,000 units
Manufacturing costs:	
Direct labor	$16 per unit
Direct materials	10 per unit
Variable overhead	4 per unit

Required: Prepare an absorption costing income statement for 19x4.

10–13 Profit Planning with Absorption and Variable Costing

The Profit Control Corporation wants to ensure that its profits do not decline in proportion to sales declines. To prevent profits from decreasing, Profit Control plans to increase production above normal capacity. For 19x1 and 19x2 the following budget information is available:

	19x1	19x2
Sales volume estimates	500,000 units	400,000 units
Normal production capacity	500,000 units	500,000 units
Planned production	500,000 units	700,000 units
Fixed manufacturing overhead	$1,000,000	$1,000,000
Fixed selling and administrative expenses	$ 100,000	$ 100,000
Total variable manufacturing costs	$10 per unit	$10 per unit
Sales	$20 per unit	$20 per unit

Requirements

a) Prepare pro forma income statements using absorption costing for 19x1 and 19x2. (Round computations to the nearest dollar.)

b) Prepare pro forma income statements using variable costing for 19x1 and 19x2.

c) Can the company actually control profits? Explain.

10–14 Profit Planning with Absorption and Variable Costing

The Profit Planning Corporation wants to plan its production so that sales and production have a close relationship with each other. To accomplish this objective, the company depends on sales forecasts to alter the amount of its production during each year. For 19x5 and 19x6 the following budget information is available:

	19x5	19x6
Sales volume estimates	500,000 units	400,000 units
Normal production capacity	500,000 units	500,000 units
Planned production	500,000 units	400,000 units
Fixed manufacturing overhead	$1,000,000	$1,000,000
Fixed selling and administrative expenses	$ 100,000	$ 100,000
Total variable manufacturing costs	$10 per unit	$10 per unit
Sales	$20 per unit	$20 per unit

Requirements

a) Prepare pro forma income statements using absorption costing for 19x5 and 19x6.

b) Prepare pro forma income statements using variable costing for 19x5 and 19x6.

c) Was the company's objective reflected in the income statements? Which statement is the best indicator? Why?

10–15 Income Statements Segmented by Territory

The Dual Manufacturing Company has two product lines. The 19x1 income statements of each product line and the company are as follows:

Dual Manufacturing Company
Product Line and Company Income Statements
For the year ended December 31, 19x1

| | Product Lines | | |
	Pens	Pencils	Total
Sales	$20,000	$30,000	$50,000
Less variable expenses	− 8,000	−12,000	−20,000
Contribution margin	$12,000	$18,000	$30,000
Less direct fixed expenses	− 8,000	− 7,000	−15,000
Product margin	$ 4,000	$11,000	$15,000
Less common fixed expenses			− 6,000
Net income			$ 9,000

The pens and pencils are sold in two territories, Alaska and Alabama, as follows:

	Alaska	Alabama
Pen sales	$12,000	$ 8,000
Pencil sales	9,000	21,000
Total sales	$21,000	$29,000

The common fixed expenses above are traceable to each territory as follows:

Alaska fixed expenses	$2,000
Alabama fixed expenses	3,000
Home office administration fixed expenses	1,000
Total common fixed expenses	$6,000

The direct fixed expenses of pens, $8,000, and of pencils, $7,000, cannot be identified with either territory.

Requirements

a) Prepare income statements segmented by territory for 19x1, and include a column for the entire firm.

b) Why are direct expenses of one type of segment reports not necessarily direct expenses of another type of segment reports?

10–16 Income Statements Segmented by Products

Clayton Consulting Firm provides three types of client services. The income statement for 19x2 is as follows:

Clayton Consulting Firm
Income Statement
For the year ended December 31, 19x2

Sales		$800,000
Less variable costs		−535,000
Contribution margin		$265,000
Less fixed expenses:		
Service	$70,000	
Selling and administrative	65,000	−135,000
Net income		$130,000

The sales, contribution margin ratios, and direct fixed expenses for the three types of services are as follows:

	Service 14	Service 28	Service 33
Sales	$250,000	$250,000	$300,000
Contribution margin ratio	30%	40%	30%
Direct fixed expenses of services	$ 20,000	$ 18,000	$ 16,000

Required: Prepare income statements segmented by products, and include a column for the entire firm in the statement.

PROBLEMS

10–17 Variable Costing Income Statement

For the first three quarters of 19x4, Mustang Motor Company has had wide fluctuations in production and sales. Sales volume and the variable cost of production have increased with no increase in the selling price. Variable manufacturing costs per unit were as follows:

		Quarter	
	First	Second	Third
Direct materials	$1,500	$2,000	$2,500
Direct labor	2,000	2,000	3,000
Variable factory overhead	500	1,000	2,000

The motors sell for $10,000 each. The fixed manufacturing costs are $250,000,000 each quarter. The variable selling and administrative expenses are $600 for each unit sold, and the fixed selling and administrative expenses are $80,000,000 a quarter. Beginning motor inventory at the start of the first quarter, 20,000 units, was recorded at $110,000,000, including $30,000,000 of fixed costs. The company uses the FIFO inventory method. Production and sales data are as follows:

Quarter	Produced	Sold
First	150,000	140,000
Second	160,000	150,000
Third	160,000	170,000

Requirements

a) Prepare income statements for each quarter using variable costing.

b) Prepare income statements for each quarter using absorption costing.

c) Reconcile the incomes for each quarter between the two methods.

10–18 Absorption and Variable Costing Income Statements with Income Taxes

The operating data for the Silver Spoon Company are given below.

	19x1	19x2	19x3
Units manufactured	80,000	100,000	80,000
Units sold	70,000	90,000	100,000
Unit selling price	$10	$10	$10
Variable manufacturing costs per unit	$4	$4	$4
Fixed manufacturing cost	$200,000	$250,000	$300,000

There was no inventory on hand on January 1, 19x1. The company uses the FIFO method to maintain its inventories. Variable selling expenses are $1.20 per unit, and fixed selling and administrative expenses for each year are $60,000. Income tax is estimated at 30 percent of before-tax income.

Requirements

a) Prepare income statements for each year using absorption costing.

b) Prepare income statements for each year using variable costing.

c) Reconcile the income differences for each year between the two methods.

10–19 Variable Costing Income Statements with Income Taxes

The manager of a newly organized division of Brown Manufacturing does not understand why income went down when sales went up.

Information for the first and second quarters of 19x1 is given as follows for Arizona Division.

Brown Manufacturing Company
Absorption Costing Income Statements
For the first two quarters of 19x1

	First Quarter	Second Quarter
Units produced	20,000	15,000
Units sold	15,000	20,000
Sales	$300,000	$400,000
Cost of goods sold:		
Inventory, beginning of quarter	$ —	$ 75,000
Current production cost	300,000	275,000
Cost of merchandise available for sale	$300,000	$350,000
Less inventory, end of quarter	− 75,000	− —
Cost of goods sold	−225,000	−350,000
Gross profit	$ 75,000	$ 50,000
Selling and administrative expenses	− 25,000	− 25,000
Income before income taxes	$ 50,000	$ 25,000
Income tax (30%)	− 15,000	− 7,500
Net income	$ 35,000	$ 17,500

The company operated at normal capacity during the first quarter. Variable manufacturing cost per unit was $5, and the fixed cost was $200,000. Selling and administrative expenses are all fixed.

Requirements

a) Revise the statement for each of the two quarters on the variable costing basis. *Hint:* Variable costing is not acceptable for tax purposes.

b) Explain the profit differences. How would variable costing help the manager avoid confusion?

10–20 Absorption Costing and Variable Costing Income Statements: All Fixed Costs

The Fixed Rock Company has only fixed costs. It built its building over a pile of rocks and simply sells them when customers visit the plant.

All employees of the plant are paid a fixed annual wage. There are no material costs and no variable overhead because the rocks came with the land and they do not need processing. They are washed in a creek that flows through the property. Costs are estimated as follows for 19x5 and 19x6.

Labor	$200,000
Depreciation	50,000
Insurance	20,000
Administration	40,000

Production capacity is 2,000 tons per year. Rocks sell for $200 per ton. Results for two years are as follows:

	19x5	19x6
Tons produced	1,600	2,000
Tons sold	1,500	2,100

Required: Prepare income statements for each year under both absorption costing and variable costing. Which method is better? Why?

10–21 Absorption and Variable Costing Comparisons

The March Manufacturing Company had two identical divisions, Left and Right. Their sales, production volume, and fixed manufacturing costs have been the same for both divisions for the last five years. These amounts for each division are as follows:

	19x1	19x2	19x3	19x4	19x5
Units produced	100,000	110,000	110,000	88,000	88,000
Units sold	90,000	90,000	100,000	100,000	100,000
Fixed manufacturing costs	$110,000	$110,000	$110,000	$110,000	$110,000

Left uses absorption costing, and Right uses variable costing. Both use FIFO inventory methods. Variable manufacturing costs are $5 per unit. Both have identical selling prices and selling and administrative expenses. There were no 1/1/x1 inventories.

Required: Which division reports the higher income in each year? Explain.

10–22 Absorption and Variable Costing Comparisons

Never Quit Shoe Company is concerned with changing to the variable costing method of inventory valuation for making internal decisions. The absorption statements of income for January and February are shown below.

Never Quit Shoe Company
Absorption Costing Income Statements
For January and February, 19x9

	January	February
Sales (8,000 units)	$160,000	$160,000
Cost of goods sold	− 99,200	−108,800
Gross profit	$ 60,800	$ 51,200
Selling and administrative expenses	− 30,000	− 30,000
Net income	$ 30,800	$ 21,200

Production data are as shown below.

	January	February
Production units	10,000	6,000
Variable costs per unit	$10	$10
Fixed overhead costs	$24,000	$24,000

Selling and administrative expenses above include variable costs of $1 per unit sold.

Requirements

a) Compute the absorption cost per unit manufactured in January and February.

b) Explain why the net income for January was higher than the net income for February when the same number of units was sold in each month.

c) Prepare income statements for both months using variable costing.

d) Reconcile the absorption costing and variable costing net income figures for each month. Start with variable costing net income.

10–23 Absorption and Variable Costing Comparisons

The Sweet Company manufactures peach jam. Because of bad weather, the crop was small. The following data have been gathered for the summer quarter of 19x3:

Beginning inventory, cases	—
Cases produced	10,000
Cases sold	9,600
Sales price per case	$50
Direct materials per case	$7
Direct labor per case	$6
Variable manufacturing overhead per case	$3
Total fixed manufacturing overhead	$400,000
Variable selling and administrative cost per case	$2
Fixed selling and administrative cost	$48,000

Requirements

a) Prepare an income statement for the quarter using absorption costing.

b) Prepare an income statement for the quarter using variable costing.

c) What is the value of ending inventory under absorption costing?

d) What is the value of ending inventory under variable costing?

e) Explain the difference in ending inventory under absorption costing and variable costing.

10–24 Conversion from Absorption to Variable Costing Statements

The income statement for Mug and Cup Company has been prepared on an absorption costing basis.

Mug and Cup Company
Absorption Costing Income Statement
For the month ended December 31, 19x1

Sales (5,000 units)		$25,000
Cost of goods sold:		
Inventory, beginning	$ 5,000	
Cost of goods manufactured	10,000	
Cost of products available for sale	$15,000	
Less inventory ending	− 2,500	12,500
Gross profit		$12,500
Selling and administrative expenses		− 3,000
Net income		$ 9,500

Variable unit costs have remained unchanged during the year. In 19x1 the monthly fixed factory overhead was $2,000. During December 4,000 units were manufactured.

Requirements

a) Recast the income statement for December to place it on a variable costing basis.

b) Reconcile the two statements.

10–25 Segment Reporting

Protection Company has provided you with the following information about its operations.

1. There are two products, umbrellas and hats.

2. There are two sales territories, Southeast and Northwest.

3. Monthly traceable direct fixed costs are $15,000 in the Southeast territory and $14,000 in the Northwest territory.

4. During January of 19x3, Southeast sold $40,000 of umbrellas and $20,000 of hats and Northwest sold $10,000 of umbrellas and $30,000 of hats.

5. Variable cost of sales and selling expenses total 40 percent for umbrellas and 70 percent for hats.

6. Of Northwest's direct fixed costs, $5,000 is traceable to umbrellas and $5,000 to hats.

7. Of Southeast's direct fixed costs, $4,000 is traceable to umbrellas and $2,000 to hats.

8. Total fixed costs of the Protection Company were $40,000 during January.

9. Total variable costs of the Protection Company were $55,000 during January.

Requirements

a) Prepare January 19x3 segment income statements for both territories, and include a column for the entire firm.

b) Prepare income statements segmented by product within each territory, and include a column for the entire firm.

10–26 Multiple Segment Reports

Ottawa Snow Company has two divisions: Snow and Ice. Because of increasing costs, the president wants to review overall operations by means of segment reporting. For 19x7 total revenue was $40,000,000: $14,000,000 for Snow and $26,000,000 for Ice. For Ice, $20,000,000 was generated by retail customers and $6,000,000 by manufacturing customers.

Total variable costs were $8,000,000 for Snow and $14,000,000 for Ice. For Ice, $11,500,000 was for retail customers and $2,500,000 for manufacturing customers. Total direct fixed costs were $2,000,000 for Snow and $10,000,000 for Ice. For Ice, $7,000,000 was for retail customers and $3,000,000 was for manufacturing customers.

In addition to the above, there were common corporate fixed costs of $4,000,000 for selling and administrative facilities. Common corporate fixed costs of $1,000,000 were also incurred for administrative personnel and supplies. These costs are not allocated to divisions.

Requirements

a) Prepare segment income statements for the divisions, and include a column for the entire firm.

b) Prepare segment income statements for the separate parts of the Ice Division, and include a column for the entire division.

10–27 Multiple Segment Reports

Earth Products, Incorporated, sells throughout the world in three sales territories: Europe, the East, and the West. For July 19x3 all $50,000 of administrative expense are allocated, except $10,000, which is common to all units and cannot be traced to the sales territories. The percentage of product line sales made in each of the sales territories and the allocations of traceable fixed expenses are shown below.

	Sales Territory			
	Europe	East	West	Total
Cookware sales	40%	50%	10%	100%
China sales	40	40	20	100
Vases sales	20	20	60	100
Fixed administrative expense	$15,000	$15,000	$10,000	$ 40,000
Fixed selling expense	30,000	60,000	60,000	150,000

The manufacturing takes place in one large facility with three distinct manufacturing operations. Selected cost data are shown below.

	Product Line			
	Cookware	China	Vases	Total
Variable costs	$ 9	$ 9	$ 5	
Depreciation and supervision	15,000	15,000	12,000	$ 45,000*
Other factory overhead (common)				10,000
Fixed administrative expense (common)				50,000
Fixed selling expense (common)				150,000

* Includes common costs of $3,000.

The unit sales and selling price for each product are shown below.

	Unit Sales	Selling Price
Cookware	10,000	$10
China	20,000	15
Vases	15,000	20

Requirements

a) Prepare an income statement for July 19x3 segmented by product line, and include a column for the entire firm.

b) Prepare an income statement for July 19x3 segmented by sales territories and include a column for the entire firm.

10–28 Segment Reporting and Analysis

Neighborhood Bakery, Incorporated, bakes three products: donuts, pies, and cakes. It sells them in the cities of Irmo and Jackson. For March 19x4 the following absorption costing income statement was prepared.

Neighborhood Bakery, Inc.
Territory and Company Income Statements
For the month of March, 19x1

	Irmo	Jackson	Total
Sales	$2,100	$500	$2,600
Cost of goods sold	−1,500	−300	−1,800
Gross profit	$ 600	$200	$ 800
Selling and administrative expenses	− 400	−100	− 500
Net income	$ 200	$100	$ 300

Sales and selected variable expense data are as follows:

	Products		
	Donuts	Pies	Cakes
Fixed baking expenses	$200	$140	$100
Variable baking expenses as a percentage of sales	50%	50%	60%
Variable selling expenses as a percentage of sales	4%	4%	5%
City of Irmo, sales	$800	$900	$400
City of Jackson, sales	$200	$100	$200

The fixed selling expenses were $260 for March, of which $210 was a direct expense of the Irmo market and $50 a direct expense of the Jackson market. Fixed administrative expenses were $130, which management has decided not to allocate when using the contribution approach.

Requirements

a) Prepare a segment income statement for each sales territory for March, and include a column for the entire firm.

b) Prepare segment income statements for each product, and include a column for the entire firm.

c) Should any products or territories be dropped?

10–29 Segment Reporting and Analysis

The Hardback Book Company has prepared income statements segmented by divisions, but management is still uncertain about actual performance. Financial information for 19x8 is given as follows:

	Segments		Total Company
	Textbook Division	Professional Division	
Sales	$180,000	$410,000	$590,000
Less variable expenses:			
Manufacturing	$ 32,000	$205,000	$237,000
Selling and administration	4,000	20,500	24,500
Total	− 36,000	−225,500	−261,500
Contribution margin	$144,000	$184,500	$328,500
Less direct fixed expenses	− 15,000	−220,000	−235,000
Net income	$129,000	$ (35,500)	$ 93,500

The Professional Division is of concern to management and needs additional analysis. Additional information regarding the 19x8 operations of the Professional Division is as follows:

	Accounting	Executive	Management
Sales	$140,000	$140,000	$130,000
Variable manufacturing expenses as a percentage of sales	60%	40%	50%
Other variable expenses as a percentage of sales	5%	5%	5%
Direct fixed expenses	$ 50,000	$ 75,000	$ 50,000

The professional accounting books are sold to auditors and controllers. The current information on these markets is as follows:

	Sales Market	
	Auditors	Controllers
Sales	$30,000	$110,000
Variable manufacturing expenses as a percentage of sales	60%	60%
Other variable expenses as a percentage of sales	16%	2%
Direct fixed expenses	$20,000	$ 25,000

Requirements

a) Prepare an income statement segmented by products of the Professional Division, and include a column for the division as a whole.

b) Prepare an income statement segmented by markets of the accounting books of the Professional Division.

c) Evaluate which accounting books the Professional Division should keep or discontinue.

10–30 Segment Reports

The Justa Corporation produces and sells three products. The three products, A, B, and C, are sold in a local market and in a regional market. After the end of the first quarter of 19x2, the following income statement was prepared.

Justa Corporation
Territory and Company Income Statements
For the first quarter of 19x2

	Local	Regional	Total
Sales	$1,000,000	$300,000	$1,300,000
Cost of goods sold	− 775,000	−235,000	−1,010,000
Gross profit	$ 225,000	$ 65,000	$ 290,000
Selling expenses	$ 60,000	$ 45,000	$ 105,000
Administrative expenses	40,000	12,000	52,000
Total	− 100,000	− 57,000	− 157,000
Net income	$ 125,000	$ 8,000	$ 133,000

Management has expressed special concern with the regional market because of the extremely poor return on sales. This market was entered a year ago because of excess capacity. It was originally believed that the return on sales would improve with time, but after a year no noticeable improvement can be seen from the results as reported in the above quarterly statement.

In attempting to decide whether to eliminate the regional market, the following information has been gathered.

	Products		
	A	B	C
Sales	$500,000	$400,000	$400,000
Variable manufacturing expenses as a percentage of sales	60%	70%	60%
Variable selling expenses as a percentage of sales	3%	2%	2%

Sales by Markets		
Product	Local	Regional
A	$400,000	$100,000
B	300,000	100,000
C	300,000	100,000

All administrative expenses and fixed manufacturing expenses are common to the three products and the two markets and are fixed for the period. The remaining selling expenses are fixed for the period and separable by market. All fixed expenses are based on a prorated yearly amount.

Requirements

a) Prepare the quarterly income statement showing contribution margins by markets (territories), and include a column for the company as a whole.

b) Assuming there are no alternative uses for the Justa Corporation's present capacity, would you recommend dropping the regional market? Why or why not?

c) Prepare the quarterly income statement showing contribution margins by products and include a column for the company as a whole.

d) It is believed that a new product can be ready for sale next year if the Justa Corporation decides to go ahead with continued research. The new product can be produced by simply converting equipment now used in producing Product C. This conversion will increase fixed costs by $10,000 per quarter. What must be the minimum contribution margin per quarter for the new product to make the change-over financially feasible?

(CMA Adapted)

CASES

10–31 Segmented Reports by Revenue Center

Music Teachers, Inc., is an educational association for music teachers that had 20,000 members during 19x5. The association operates from a central headquarters but has local membership chapters throughout the United States and Canada. Monthly meetings are held by the local chapters to discuss recent developments on topics of interest to music teachers. The association's journal, *Teachers' Forum,* is issued monthly with features about recent developments in the field. The association publishes books and reports and sponsors professional courses that qualify for continuing professional education credit. The statement of revenues and expenses is presented below:

Music Teachers, Inc.
Statement of Revenues and Expenses
For the year ended November 30, 19x5

Revenues		$3,275,000
Expenses:		
Salaries	$920,000	
Personnel costs	230,000	
Occupancy costs	280,000	
Reimbursement to local chapters	600,000	
Other membership services	500,000	
Printing and paper	320,000	
Postage and shipping	176,000	
Instructors' fees	80,000	
General and administrative	38,000	−3,144,000
Excess of revenues over expenses		$ 131,000

The board of directors has requested that a segmented statement of operations be prepared showing the contribution of each revenue center (i.e., Membership, Magazine Subscriptions, Books and Reports, and Continuing Education). Mickie Doyle, who has been assigned this responsibility, has gathered the following data prior to statement preparation:

- Membership dues are $100 per year, of which $20 is considered to cover a one-year subscription to the association's journal. Other benefits include membership in the association and chapter affiliation. The portion of the dues covering the magazine subscription ($20) should be assigned to the Magazine Subscriptions revenue center.

- One-year subscriptions to *Teacher's Forum* were sold to nonmembers and libraries at $30 each. A total of 2,500 of these subscriptions were sold. In addition to subscriptions, the magazine generated $100,000 in advertising revenue. The costs per magazine subscription were $7 for printing and paper and $4 for postage and shipping.

- A total of 28,000 technical reports and professional texts were sold by the Books and Reports Department at an average unit selling price of $25. Average costs per publication were as follows:

  Printing and paper $4
  Postage and shipping $2

- The association offers a variety of continuing education courses to both members and nonmembers. During 19x5, the one-day course, which cost participants $75 each, was attended by 2,400 people. A total of 1,760 people took two-day courses at a cost of $125 per person. Outside instructors were paid to teach some courses.

- Salary and occupancy data were as follows:

	Salaries	Square Footage
Membership	$210,000	2,000
Magazine Subscriptions	150,000	2,000
Books and Reports	300,000	3,000
Continuing Education	180,000	2,000
Corporate Staff	80,000	1,000
Totals	$920,000	10,000

The Books and Reports Department also rents warehouse space at an annual cost of $50,000. Personnel costs are 25 percent of salaries.

- Printing and paper costs other than for magazine subscriptions, books, and reports relate to the Continuing Education Department.

- General and administrative expenses include all other costs incurred by the corporate staff to operate the association.

Doyle has decided she will assign all revenues and expenses to the revenue centers that can be: (1) traced directly to a revenue center, and (2) allocated on a reasonable and logical basis to a revenue center. The expenses that can be traced or assigned to corporate staff, as well as any other expenses that cannot be assigned to revenue centers, will be grouped with the general and administrative expenses and not allocated to the revenue centers. She believes that allocations often tend to be arbitrary and are not useful for management reporting and analysis. She believes that any further allocation of the general and administrative expenses associated with the operation and administration of the association would be arbitrary.

Requirements

a) Prepare a segmented statement of revenues and expenses that presents the contribution of each revenue center and includes the common costs of the organization that are not allocated to the revenue centers.

b) If segmented reporting is adopted by the association for continuing usage, discuss the ways the information provided by the report can be utilized by the association.

c) Mickie Doyle decided not to allocate some indirect or nontraceable expenses to revenue centers because she believed that allocations tend to be arbitrary.

1. Besides the arbitary argument, what reasons are often presented for not allocating indirect or nontraceable expenses to revenue centers?

2. Under what circumstances might the allocation of indirect or nontraceable expenses to revenue centers be acceptable?

(CMA Adapted)

10–32 Segment Reports and Cost Allocations

Clive Mathews and Sons has three sales divisions. One of the key evaluation inputs for each division manager is the performance of his/her division based upon divisional income. The divisional statements for 19x4 are as follows:

| | Division | | | |
	Kiwi	Queensland	Hawaiian	Total
Sales	$400,000	$500,000	$450,000	$1,350,000
Cost of sales	$200,000	$240,000	$230,000	$ 670,000
Division overhead	100,000	110,000	110,000	320,000
Divisional expenses	−300,000	−350,000	−340,000	− 990,000
Division contribution	$100,000	$150,000	$110,000	$ 360,000
Corporate overhead	− 70,000	− 90,000	− 80,000	− 240,000
Division income	$ 30,000	$ 60,000	$ 30,000	$ 120,000

The Hawaiian manager is unhappy that his profitability is the same as that of the Kiwi Division and half that of the Queensland Division when his sales are half way between these two divisions. The manager knows that his division must carry more product lines because of customer demands, and many of these additional product lines are not very profitable. He has not dropped these marginal product lines because of idle capacity; all of them cover their own variable costs.

After analyzing the product lines with the lowest profit margins, the divisional controller for Hawaiian provided the manager with the following:

Sales of marginal products		$90,000
Cost of sales	$50,000	
Avoidable fixed costs	20,000	−70,000
Product margin		$20,000
Proportion of corporate overhead		−16,000
Product income		$ 4,000

Although these products were 20 percent of Hawaiian's total sales, they contributed only about 13 percent of the division's profits. The controller also noted that the corporate overhead allocation was based on a formula of sales and divisional contribution margin.

Requirements

a) Prepare a set of segment statements for 19x5 assuming all facts remain the same except that the weak product lines of Hawaiian are dropped and corporate overhead is allocated as follows: Kiwi, $80,000; Queensland, $95,000; and Hawaiian, $65,000. Does the Hawaiian Division appear better after this action? What will be the responses of the two other division managers?

b) Suggest improvements to Mathews and Sons' reporting process that will better reflect the actual operations of the divisions. Keep in mind the utilization of the reporting process to assist in the evaluation of the managers. What other changes might be made to improve the manager evaluation process?

REVIEW PROBLEM SOLUTION

a)

	Cost per Unit	
	Absorption Costing	*Variable Costing*
Direct labor ($200,000/50,000)	$ 4.00	$ 4.00
Direct materials ($250,000/50,000)	5.00	5.00
Variable manufacturing overhead		
($100,000/50,000)	2.00	2.00
Fixed manufacturing overhead		
($130,000/50,000)	2.60	—
Total unit costs	$13.60	$11.00
Ending inventory units	10,000	10,000
Unit cost	× $13.60	× $11.00
Ending inventory value	$136,000	$110,000

b) **Colorado Ski Company**
    Absorption Costing Income Statement
    For the year ended December 31, 19x3

Sales (40,000 units × $40)		$1,600,000
Cost of goods sold (40,000 units × $13.60)		− 544,000
Gross profit		$1,056,000
Selling and administrative expenses:		
Selling expenses	$ 75,000	
Administrative expenses	112,000	− 187,000
Net income		$ 869,000

Colorado Ski Company
Variable Costing Income Statement
For the year ended December 31, 19x3

Sales (40,000 units × $40)		$1,600,000
Variable expenses:		
Cost of goods sold (40,000 units × $11.00)	$440,000	
Variable selling	75,000	− 515,000
Contribution margin		$1,085,000
Fixed expenses:		
Manufacturing overhead	$130,000	
Administrative	112,000	− 242,000
Net income		$ 843,000

c) Reconciliation of absorption and variable costing net income

Absorption costing net income		$869,000
Change in inventoried fixed costs:		
Fixed overhead in beginning inventory units	$ —	
Less fixed overhead in ending inventory	−26,000	− 26,000
Variable costing net income		$843,000
Variable costing net income		$843,000
Change in inventoried fixed costs:		
Fixed overhead in ending inventory	$26,000	
Less fixed overhead in beginning inventory	− —	26,000
Absorption costing net income		$869,000

d) Generally accepted accounting principles require that absorption cost financial statements be used for external reporting. This includes all reports to creditors, stockholders, and governments. Absorption costing financial statements treat all
manufacturing costs (fixed and variable) as product costs and assign them to the
products produced, the premise being that all products should bear their share of
all manufacturing costs. Although many companies use these statements for internal

reporting, the analysis of operating results using absorption costing can be misleading because the various cost elements are not separated by fixed and variable behavior.

For variable costing financial statements, the analysis of cost behavior is required, which in itself provides an additional component in the overall analysis of the operating results. The fixed manufacturing costs are treated as period costs and not assigned to inventories. Therefore variable costing provides a decision base for analysis, which includes a contribution margin (sales less variable costs) that permits an evaluation of costs that are directly related to the revenues.

P A R T 3

Product Costing and Cost Reassignment

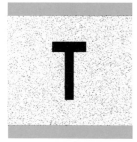

he chapters in Part 3 have largely to do with accounting for manufacturing organizations, with an emphasis on standard costing and cost allocation.

Chapter 11 deals with job costing and presents the basic record-keeping process behind maintaining a proper job costing system. A detailed discussion of accounting for factory overhead is presented. State-of-the-art topics relating to the computerization of the manufacturing process are also considered. These topics include automatic identification systems, computer-aided design and computer-aided manufacturing (CAD/CAM), flexible manufacturing systems, and computer integrated manufacturing (CIM). Although a service company, MCI makes frequent use of job costing. When it builds network control and data center facilities, for example, the costs of each facility are accumulated and assigned to that cost objective (that is, to the particular facility). This form of cost control facilitates allocation of these buildings' costs when the buildings are shared with local telephone companies—a frequent occurrence.

Chapter 12 is devoted entirely to process costing. It explains the types of operations that are best suited to process costing and provides a detailed example of how the process costing application works. Both weighted average and FIFO inventory situations are illustrated with complete cost of production reports. As a service company, MCI does not use process costing.

Reassignment of indirect costs and activity-based costing are the key topics considered in Chapter 13. The chapter begins by explaining the nature of indirect costs and the uses and limitations of cost reassignment. The three most common methods of indirect cost reassignment—direct, step, and linear algebra—are presented and illustrated. Next, activity-based costing is explained, with several illustrations. Last, a discussion of the reassignment of home office expenses is presented, with expanded discussions of the peculiarities of not-for-profit organizations. MCI makes limited use of cost reassignment—about its only application at MCI is the reassignment of sales literature costs to the appropriate divisions and territories.

C H A P T E R   11

Job Costing and the Manufacturing Environment

Learning Objectives

Upon completion of this chapter you should:

- **Be familiar with the manufacturing environment and production planning activities.**

- **Be aware of the impact of computers, flexible manufacturing systems, and inventory reduction techniques on the manufacturing environment and product costs.**

- **Be able to prepare journal entries recording the flow of costs for a manufacturing organization.**

- **Be familiar with the costing procedures used to record data in a job cost system.**

- **Understand the uses of predetermined factory overhead rates and how to dispose of underapplied or overapplied factory overhead.**

- **Be familiar with the potential problem of systematically assigning costs to the wrong product (cross-subsidization) when unlike (heterogeneous) products are produced.**

- **Understand how product costing concepts can be applied to service organizations.**

Product cost information is used for a variety of purposes, including inventory valuation in financial statements, special decisions related to continuing or discontinuing a product, make or buy decisions, and pricing. In the past, when competition was primarily on a local or regional basis, many companies were able to sell all products with large markups, and the primary purpose of product costing was financial reporting. Three recent trends have increased the importance of product costs for management decisions, such as pricing, and have reduced the importance of product costing for financial reporting.

First, the emergence of global competition has placed downward pressure on prices. What's more, world class manufacturers are constantly striving to improve their production processes and compete with firms around the world on the basis of quality and services such as timely delivery, as well as on the basis of price. Second, there is a trend toward more diverse product lines. When a factory produces only one product, all costs are easily associated with that single product. When a factory produces a variety of products, it becomes increasingly difficult to determine the cost of each product. The more diverse, or heterogeneous, the range of products, the more difficult it is to determine product costs correctly. Yet if product costs are not accurately determined, misassigned costs will lead to uncompetitively high prices on some products and unprofitably low prices on others. Finally, there is a third trend toward lower inventory levels due to the implementation of modern manufacturing and management techniques. As inventory levels decline the financial reporting implications of cost assignments decrease. With lower inventories most product costs become part of the cost of goods sold during the period incurred, reducing the importance of product costs for inventory valuation in external financial statements.

The purpose of this chapter is to examine the manufacturing environment and job costing, one of the basic methods of determining product costs. We introduce job costing in the context of an organization that produces a homogeneous product line. We then expand our discussion to consider complications arising when heterogeneous products are produced. Finally, we consider how product costing concepts are equally applicable to project management and the delivery of services.

THE MANUFACTURING ENVIRONMENT

In Chapter 6, Operating Budgets, quarterly production budgets are developed for an entire year. Although quarterly production budgets are important in planning overall operations, they are not detailed enough to run a factory. Manufacturing personnel need to know what specific products to produce on specific machines on a daily or even hourly basis. The detailed scheduling of products on machines is performed by production scheduling personnel. Exactly how production is scheduled depends on whether process or job production is used and whether job production is in response to a specific customer sales order or for speculative inventory.

In process production, a single product is produced on a continuous basis. Here, a production facility may be devoted exclusively to one product or to a closely related set of products. Typical products produced on a continuous basis include beverages, electrical wire, cotton yarn, and newsprint. When continuous production involves only a single product, the costing issues are relatively straightforward. Costs accumulated for each period are assigned to ending inventories and goods sold. Process costing is considered in Chapter 12.

In **job production**, also called **job-order production**, products are produced in single units or in batches of identical units. The products included in different jobs may vary considerably. Single unit jobs might include constructing a house, a ship, or a satellite. Typical batch jobs include machine parts, clothing, and furniture. The job may be produced in response to a customer's order for intermediate materials (parts) that are to go into a final product. A large automobile manufacturer, for example, may purchase steering assemblies from another manufacturer. When a job results from a customer's order, marketing personnel forward the order to production scheduling personnel, who determine when and how the products specified in the order are to be produced. Important scheduling considerations include the overall workload, raw materials availability, specific equipment or labor requirements, and the delivery date or dates of the finished product.

The need for accurate production scheduling has increased in recent years as customers, attempting to reduce raw material inventories and related inventory holding costs, often require delivery in many small batches at specific times rather than in a single large batch. In extreme cases, customers now specify daily or even hourly delivery directly to the production floor. An automobile manufacturer, for example, might specify that tires be delivered twice a day directly to the assembly line. Hence, a single customer order may generate a series of suborders, each with its own production schedule and delivery date.

The job may also be produced in response to a need to build speculative inventories intended for future sale. Speculative production is especially common in consumer products, such as furniture and home appliances. Here, production requirements are based on existing inventory levels and predicted sales. Because of inventory holding costs and a need to produce a variety of products, production of each product is likely to take place throughout the year in a series of small batches. A furniture company that anticipates total annual production of 2,000 units for a particular style of chair will not produce all 2,000 units in a single job. Rather, the required annual production is broken into a series of small jobs to be produced as needed throughout the year. Procedures used to determine the number of units included in each job are considered in Chapter 14, Relevant Costs for Quantitative Models and JIT Inventory Management.

Production Planning and Control

Important staff groups involved in production planning and control include engineering, scheduling, expediting, quality control, and accounting. Engineering is primarily concerned with determining how a product should be produced. On the basis of an engineering analysis, aided by cost data, engineering develops manufacturing specifications for each product. These manufacturing specifications are often summarized in two important documents, a bill of materials and an operations list. Each product's bill of materials specifies the kinds and quantities of raw materials required to produce one unit of product. Each product's operations list specifies the manufacturing operations and related times required to produce one unit or batch of product. The operations list should also include information on any machine set-up time required before production of the product can begin.

Production scheduling prepares a production order for each job. The production order assigns a unique identification number to a job, specifies the quantity to be produced in the job, the total raw materials requirements of the job, the manufacturing operations to be performed on the job, and perhaps even the time when each manufacturing operation should be performed. In preparing a production order, scheduling uses the product's bill of materials and operations list to determine the materials and the manufacturing times required to complete the job. They also use information concerning production deadlines and available manufacturing capabilities. When a job consists of several units, the materials and time requirements are determined by making appropriate computations. The production order serves as authorization for manufacturing personnel to requisition raw materials and utilize manufacturing facilities.

A job-cost sheet is prepared as production begins. The job-cost sheet serves as the basic record for recording actual progress on the job. As production takes place actual materials, labor, and machine resources utilized are recorded on the job-cost sheet along with the related job costs.

Manufacturing activities should be controlled on three dimensions: time, quality, and cost. In a manufacturing plant, with high fixed costs and limited resources, time is money. Hence there is a need to ensure that operations proceed according to schedule. Actual production times, including start and stop times for each operation, should be monitored and compared to scheduled start and stop times, as specified on the job's production order. If a job falls behind schedule or progresses significantly ahead of schedule, production scheduling should act immediately to determine the cause and make necessary adjustments in plant operations. In large plants these adjustments are often handled by personnel known as expediters.

Because high quality provides an important competitive advantage, product quality is carefully monitored in a well managed factory. Historically, the job of monitoring quality was often left to quality inspectors who typically performed their task after all units in each job were completed. Today, quality inspection is likely to take place throughout production with the goal of not wasting effort working on defective units. Equally important is the goal of identifying and correcting the cause of defects before additional units are damaged. Many companies are currently implementing procedures that call for production employees to inspect constantly the quality of intermediate goods entering and leaving their work area. Defective goods are immediately removed from production. In some companies production employees are even given the authority to halt production until the cause of a defective unit has been identified and corrected.

Cost is the third dimension used for production control. Financial performance reports, such as those considered in Chapters 7 and 8, should be prepared at least once a week. In a well run job-cost system, it is also possible to prepare financial performance reports for each job. Being aware of specific materials, facility, and manufacturing time requirements, standard costs may be budgeted for individual jobs by multiplying resource requirements by standard cost information per unit of resource. Cost performance on the job is evaluated comparing actual job costs to the standard costs of the job.

It is important to note that financial performance reports are typically distributed to plant and product managers rather than to individual production employees. Financial performance reports are intended to provide an overview of operations and to identify problem areas. Managers must investigate further to determine the cause of financial variances. Time and quality performance measures, on the other hand, are intended to provide rapid feedback to operating personnel, who take immediate corrective action. If time, quality, and other operating performance measures are effective, there should be few unfavorable financial performance measures.

Production Files and Records

Important files in any product cost system include inventory files for raw materials and finished goods as well as files for bills of materials and operations lists. A   is a collection of related records. A   is a related set of alphabetic and/or numeric data items. The relationship between a file and the records it contains is illustrated as follows:

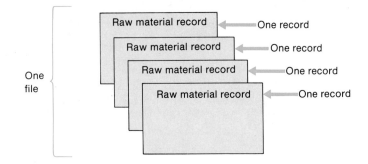

Sample raw materials, finished goods, bill of material, and operation lists records are illustrated in Exhibit 11–1.

Each type of raw materials is accounted for in a separate record, indicating increases, decreases, and the available balance in terms of units and costs. The total of the cost balances of all raw materials inventory records should equal the balance in the general ledger account Raw Materials.[2]

---

[2] As in Chapter 2, account titles are capitalized to make it easier to distinguish between the physically existing item, such as raw materials, and the account Raw Materials, which discloses the costs assigned to raw materials inventory.

EXHIBIT 11–1　Basic Production Records

Raw Materials Inventory Record

Part No. ....   Description ....

	Purchased			Issued			Balance		
Date	Units	Unit Cost	Total Cost	Units	Unit Cost	Total Cost	Units	Unit Cost	Total Cost

Finished Goods Inventory Record

Product No. ....   Description ....

	Received From Factory			Sold			Balance		
Date	Units	Unit Cost	Total Cost	Units	Unit Cost	Total Cost	Units	Unit Cost	Total Cost

Bill of Materials
Raw Materials Requirements Per Unit of Product

Product No. ....   Description ....

Part Number	Description	Quantity Per Unit

Operations List
Production Operations and Times Per Unit of Product

Product No. ....   Description ....

Department Number	Operation Description	Machine/Labor Requirements	Set-up Time	Operating Time

A general ledger account, supported by a related set of records, whose total amount should equal the balance in the general ledger account, is identified as a control account. A file that contains a related set of records whose total amount should equal the balance in a general ledger account is identified as a subsidiary ledger. Hence the general ledger account Raw Materials is a control account and the file of raw materials inventory records is a subsidiary ledger.

Each type of finished goods is accounted for in a separate record, indicating increases, decreases, and the available balance in terms of units and costs. The file of finished goods inventory records is also a subsidiary ledger, and the total of the cost balances of all finished goods inventory records should equal the balance in the general ledger control account, Finished Goods Inventory.

Each product produced has a record in the bill of materials and the operations list files indicating the resources required to produce one unit of the product. These files do not have related general ledger accounts. Hence they are not subsidiary ledgers.

Other records required to operate a job-cost system include production orders, job-cost sheets, materials requisition forms, and work tickets. These records are illustrated in Exhibit 11–2.

Production orders and job-cost sheets were discussed previously. The job number assigned in the production order is also recorded on a job-cost sheet. The production order serves as authorization for production supervisors to obtain materials from the storeroom and issue work orders to production employees. A materials requisition form indicates the type and quantity of each raw material issued to the factory. This form is used to record the transfer of responsibility for materials and to make appropriate notations on raw materials and job-cost sheet records. The materials requisition form has a field to record the job number, and the job-cost sheet has a field to record the requisition number. If a question arises regarding the issuance of materials, the requisition number and job number provide a trail for tracing the destination and the source of the materials. The materials requisition form also identifies the stores employee who issued the materials and the production employee who received them.

A work ticket is used to record the time a job spends in a specific manufacturing operation. Each manufacturing operation performed on a job is documented by a work ticket. The work tickets completed for a job should correspond to the operations specified on the job's production order. Time information on the work tickets is used by production scheduling or expediting personnel to determine whether the job is on schedule. When production times are multiplied by appropriate rates in the lower portion, the work ticket is used to assign costs to the job.

A manufacturing operation may involve a single direct labor employee, a group of direct labor employees, a machine, or even a heating, cooling, or aging process. When the operation involves a single employee, the rate recorded on the work ticket is simply the employee's wage rate. When it involves a group of employees, the rate is composed of the wage rates of all employees in the

EXHIBIT 11–2 Job Cost System Records

Production Order

Job No._____ Start Date_____

Product No._____ Description_____ Quantity_____

Raw Materials

Part Number	Description	Total Quantity

Operation

Department Number	Operation Description	Labor/Machine Requirements	Start Time	Stop Time	Total Time

Authorized by_____ Date_____

Job Cost Sheet

Job No._____

Product No._____ Description_____ Quantity_____

Raw Materials Costs

Date	Department Number	Requisition Number	Description	Total Cost

Conversion Costs: Direct Labor or Machine

Date	Department Number	Work Ticket Number	Description	Total Time	Total Cost

Applied Overhead

Date	Department Number	Basis of Application	Total Cost

Total Cost of Job	
Unit Cost	

EXHIBIT 11–2 (Continued)

EXHIBIT 11–2   (Continued)

Materials Requisition Form

Requisition No._____   Job No._____   Date_____

Department_____

Part Number	Description	Total Quantity	Unit Cost	Total Cost

Issued by _____   Received by_____

Work Ticket

Work Ticket No._____   Date_____

Department_____   Job No._____

Time Started_____   Time Completed_____

Employee/Machine Operator_____

Office Use
Total Time _____   Rate_____   Total Cost _____

---

group. When the work involves a machine operation, the rate includes a charge for machine time as well as the time of any machine operators. Other operations, such as heating, cooling, or aging will also have a rate for each unit of time.

In labor based operations, costs other than raw materials and direct labor are usually grouped into a factory overhead cost pool. In nonlabor based operations, all costs except materials are often placed into a single pool of conversion costs. When this is done there is no separation of the operation's labor and overhead costs. Any additional overhead costs not associated with specific operations are assigned to jobs using a basis common to all jobs passing through an operation or a group of operations. Practice varies widely in overhead cost assignment.

Impact of Computers on Manufacturing

Significant changes are taking place in production planning and control procedures. Perhaps the most significant changes involve the increasing use of computers for scheduling, monitoring, and costing. Just a few years ago the files and records illustrated in Exhibits 11–1 and 11–2 were maintained manually, making data collection and analysis costly and time consuming. With centralized data processing, the original transactions were still manually recorded on materials requisitions or work tickets and then entered into the computer. Today, computer terminals are often spread throughout the factory. As each operation on a job is started and completed, the job's status is entered into a computer terminal.

Leading firms are in the process of implementing bar coding and automatic identification systems (AIS) that allow inventory and production information to be entered into a computer without writing or keying. In an AIS, laser scanners connected to a computer database "read" bar codes attached to production orders, materials, machines, or employee badges. The bar codes may be read as materials pass by a fixed laser scanner, or they may be read by a hand-held laser scanner. In this environment managers can keep information at almost any level of detail they wish. And production supervisors have the capability of continuously monitoring inventory levels, the status of all personnel and machines, the location of each job in the plant, the on-time status of each job, and the costs assigned to each job. Exception reports are easily developed to alert appropriate personnel when operations are not proceeding according to schedule. Computer programs are even used to adjust production schedules when necessary.

MANAGERIAL PRACTICE 11.1

Automatic Identification Systems Are Here

Stanadyne Automotive Products Group uses an event-activated system that attempts to have the accounting event do as much of transaction recording as possible. One of the company's defined events, for example, is receipt of an inventory item. By passing a wand across a bar code, a great deal of information can be captured by a single act. Inventory is updated, the on-order purchase file is closed for that item, spending variances are calculated, and the vendor file is updated.

Source: William G. Holbrook, "Accounting Experiences in a JIT Environment" in *Cost Accounting, Robotics, and the New Manufacturing Environment,* ed. Robert Capettini and Donald K. Clancy (Sarasota, Fla.: American Accounting Association, 1987), 4.1–4.7.

In addition to being used to monitor production and rapidly process data, computers aid in designing new products, controlling machine operations, and even automating machine set-ups. **Computer-aided design (CAD)** involves the use of computers to design products. Using high-resolution computer monitors with graphics software, custom products can be rapidly designed. Engineering drawings for the product, as well as a bill of materials and an operations list, can be developed when needed.

Computer-aided manufacturing (CAM) involves the use of computers to control the operation of machines. Although few firms have operations that are completely controlled by computers, many have "islands of automation" for some operations existing alongside more traditional labor- and machine-intensive manufacturing techniques. **Flexible manufacturing systems (FMS)** are an extension of computer-aided manufacturing techniques through a series of manufacturing operations, including the automatic movement of units between operations and the automatic and rapid set-up of machines to produce each product. A FMS virtually eliminates all direct labor in the manufacturing process.

Computer integrated manufacturing (CIM) is the ultimate extension of the CAD, CAM, and FMS concepts to a completely automated and computer controlled factory where production is automatic once a product is designed and the decision to produce is made. In their advanced stages, factories utilizing flexible manufacturing systems and computer integrated manufacturing are sometimes referred to as "lights out factories" because they can be operated in the dark, without people. Obviously, CIM represents a seldom encountered extreme point on a continuum that begins with paper, pencil, and hand tools.

The attractions of these computer-based monitoring, design, and production techniques are lower production times, higher-quality products, and lower product cost. With lower production times, a firm obtains a competitive advantage by being able to fill customers' orders quickly, thereby providing better service. Lower production times also reduce the need for speculative inventories that provide for variability in the demand for products or components. Again, there is less need for speculative inventories when an unexpected demand can be filled quickly. Lower inventories result in lower inventory holding costs such as spoilage, theft, warehousing, and obsolescence. High quality arises from better design, rapid identification of defects, and correction of the cause of defects before large numbers of defective units are produced. Higher quality production, with fewer defects, reduces the cost of goods units. Hence, both speed and quality improvements make it possible to reduce costs. Lower costs mean greater profits at a given price or an increased ability to compete on the basis of price.

Just-in-Time Inventory Management

Using the just-in-time philosophy of inventory management, many managers have found it possible to reduce manufacturing times, lower work-in-process inventories, and improve product quality without making significant investments in the most current technological innovations. **Just-in-time (JIT)** inventory management stresses having available only the inventory required to meet immediate production or sales requirements. Doing this requires the reduction and eventually the elimination of wasted activities (such as excessive inventory move-ment and placing work-in-process inventories into temporary storage between work stations) and the production of defective units. Emphasis is placed on doing the job right the first time and engaging in only "value added" manufac-turing activities. The increasingly successful proponents of JIT argue that auto-mation and computerization should not be the initial response to production time, inventory quantity, or production quality problems. Managers should first engage in numerous lower cost activities, such as:

- Rearranging the factory floor from groupings of similar machines to group-ing machines around types of products, thereby reducing excessive materials movement.
- Reducing the batch size as much as possible to avoid the temporary storage of in-process inventories.
- Simplifying and improving the efficiency of manufacturing activities.
- Working to improve product quality.

M ANAGERIAL PRACTICE 11.2

Hewlett-Packard's Accounting System Produces Numbers It Can Trust

Over the past five years, Hewlett-Packard's Roseville Networks Division (RND) has developed an accounting system that provides accurate and timely cost information that is essential in their highly competitive market. The roots of the new official accounting system lie in a private system developed by manufac-turing to provide the information they use to estimate product cost. The cost manager at RND was instrumental in developing a system that would meet the needs of multiple users—not just accounting. The new system began with a very simple model, but has become more sophisticated with time, and is con-tinually being improved in response to the people who use it. Initially, it was decided to continue to use the original categories: direct labor, direct materials, and overhead. Direct labor was eliminated and combined with overhead in 1986. This unprecedented change was in response to the fact that direct labor had shrunk to 2 percent of the manufacturing cost. The system is constantly reviewed and updated in response to changing needs.

Source: Debbie Berlant, Reese Browning, and George Foster, "How Hewlett-Packard Gets Numbers It Can Trust," *Harvard Business Review* (January–February 1990): 178–182.

Automation and computerization should take place only after all excessive inventory and wasted steps are eliminated. Otherwise, management may mistakenly invest in the automation of unnecessary activities. JIT inventory management is discussed further in Chapter 14.

JOB COSTING FOR HOMOGENEOUS PRODUCTS

Manufacturing Cost Flows

Inventory costs in a manufacturing organization flow in a logical pattern through the accounting system. The costs of purchased raw materials are recorded in the Raw Materials account, and the cost of other incidental supplies are recorded as Manufacturing Supplies. The offsetting credits are usually to Accounts Payable. As primary raw materials are requisitioned to the factory, direct materials costs are transferred from Raw Materials to Work-in-Process. In labor based operations, direct labor costs are added to Work-in-Process on the basis of the time devoted to processing raw materials. As incurred, all other costs are accumulated in Factory Overhead. Factory overhead costs are periodically assigned to Work-in-Process.

When products are completed, their accumulated product costs are transferred from Work-in-Process to Finished Goods Inventory. When finished goods are sold, their costs are transferred from Finished Goods Inventory to Cost of Goods Sold. The general pattern of cost flows for a factory that contains only labor intensive manufacturing operations is shown in Exhibit 11–3.

The numbered journal entries posted to the accounts in Exhibit 11–3 are presented, in journal entry form, in Exhibit 11–4. Before the journal entries can be recorded, the supporting data (materials requisition slips, work tickets, and so forth) must be completed, collected, and summarized. Although data can be processed using either a manual or a computerized accounting system, accounting procedures are best illustrated within the context of a paper-based manual accounting system.

A possible pattern of cost flows for a factory containing only machine-intensive manufacturing operations is shown in Exhibit 11–5. The major difference between Exhibits 11–3 and 11–5 is the combining of direct labor and factory overhead into a single conversion cost pool. Note especially journal entry number 3. Although factory overhead in a labor intensive operation is most often applied on the basis of direct labor hours or dollars, it is more appropriate to apply conversion costs in a machine-intensive operation on the basis of machine hours.

Job Costing Illustrated

Fox Brothers, Inc., manufactures a line of men's wool sports jackets. All production is in response to orders from wholesale customers. Goods are shipped shortly after completion. The product line is homogeneous, and manufacturing operations are identical for all products. The only difference between products

EXHIBIT 11–3   Basic Manufacturing Cost Flows for Labor Intensive Operations

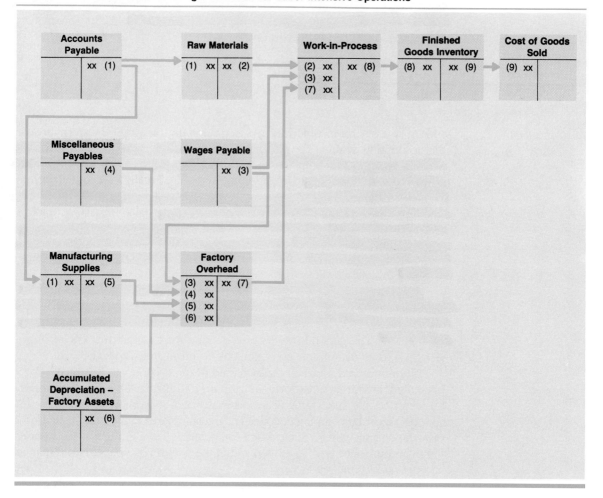

is in the quality of the wool and the pattern on the wool. Each product has a bill of materials and an operations list. These records are designed for lots of 100 units, and all production is in multiples of 100-unit lots. What's more, the 100-unit lots consist of specified quantities of a variety of jacket sizes, for example, 10 size 36 regular jackets, 10 size 36 long jackets, and so forth. Production orders, job-cost sheets, materials requisitions, and work tickets are used in planning and controlling operations.

Because of its small size, Fox Brothers' cost system is manual and very simple. Even though there are three distinct manufacturing operations—cutting, sewing, and finishing—all manufacturing times and costs are accounted for as

EXHIBIT 11–4   Basic Manufacturing Journal Entries for Labor Intensive Operations

(1)	Raw Materials	xx	
	Manufacturing Supplies	xx	
	Accounts Payable		xx
	To record purchase of raw materials and manufacturing supplies on account.		
(2)	Work-in-Process	xx	
	Raw Materials		xx
	To record requisition and transfer of raw materials to the factory from materials stores.		
(3)	Work-in-Process	xx	
	Factory Overhead	xx	
	Wages Payable		xx
	To assign direct labor cost incurred to Work-in-Process and indirect labor cost to Factory Overhead.		
(4)	Factory Overhead	xx	
	Miscellaneous Payables*		xx
	To record incurrence of various factory overhead costs, such as repairs and maintenance, and property taxes.		
(5)	Factory Overhead	xx	
	Manufacturing Supplies		xx
	To record supplies used in manufacturing.		
(6)	Factory Overhead	xx	
	Accumulated Depreciation—Factory Assets		xx
	To recognize depreciation on factory assets.		
(7)	Work-in-Process	xx	
	Factory Overhead		xx
	To assign factory overhead costs to Work-in-Process.		
(8)	Finished Goods Inventory	xx	
	Work-in-Process		xx
	To record transfer of finished goods from work-in-process inventory to finished goods inventory.		
(9)	Cost of Goods Sold	xx	
	Finished Goods Inventory		xx
	To record the cost of finished goods sold.		

* The account Miscellaneous Payables is used for convenience in this example to record any liability other than for wages and inventory purchases. Miscellaneous payables include utilities payable, taxes payable, and rent payable.

EXHIBIT 11–5   Basic Manufacturing Cost Flows for Machine Intensive Operations

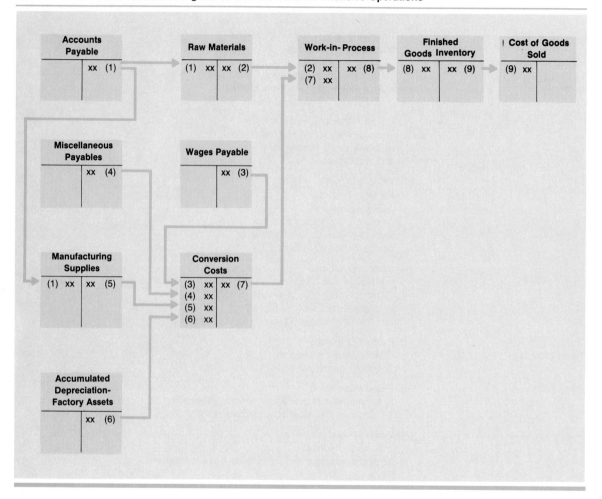

if they were incurred in a single department. Because all products are produced in an identical manner, management believes this treatment of conversion costs produces accurate information. With significant differences in materials costs and the need to control inventories carefully, detailed records are kept of the raw materials assigned to specific jobs. Raw materials consist of wool fabric, interfacing fabric, liner fabric, and button sets.

Total inventories at the beginning of August, 19x4, included raw materials, $36,100; work-in-process, $109,900; and finished goods, $75,000. In addition there were manufacturing supplies, consisting of such items as thread, needles, shears, and lubricant, in the amount of $1,600.

Raw Materials

Description	Quantity	Unit Cost	Total Cost
Wool fabric W09	3,000 yards	$ 7	$21,000
Wool fabric W12	500 yards	12	6,000
Interfacing	1,500 yards	1	1,500
Liner	2,000 yards	3	6,000
Buttons	400 sets	4	1,600
Total			$36,100

Work-in-Process		Finished Goods Inventory	
Job	Total Cost	Job	Total Cost
425	$58,600	424	$75,000
426	51,300		
Total	$109,900		

To illustrate manufacturing cost flows in a job-cost system, summary manufacturing-cost journal entries recorded by Fox Brothers, Inc., during August, 19x4, are presented. In reality, there would be a number of journal entries of each type. Included are the entries recorded in the general journal and the procedures performed in the cost system records. Cost system procedures consist of supporting documentation recorded in subsidiary records and other records related to recognizing changes in Raw Materials, Work-in-Process, and Finished Goods Inventory.

1. Purchased raw materials on account.

Journal entry	Raw Materials	30,000	
	Accounts Payable		30,000

Cost system procedures

Recorded purchases on raw material inventory records:

Wool fabric W12	1,000 yards @ $12 = $12,000
Liner	2,000 yards @ $3 = 6,000
Buttons	3,000 sets @ $4 = 12,000

2. Requisitioned materials needed to complete jobs 425 and 426. Started two new jobs, 427 and 428, and requisitioned direct materials for them.

Journal entry	Work-in-Process	54,300	
	Raw Materials		54,300

Cost system procedures

a) Prepare production orders and job-cost sheets.

b) Prepare materials requisition forms.

c) Record issuances on raw materials inventory records and assign costs to jobs.

	Job 425	Job 426	Job 427	Job 428	Total
Buttons:					
1,200 sets @ $4	$4,800				$ 4,800
900 sets @ $4		$3,600			3,600
500 sets @ $4			$ 2,000		2,000
Wool fabric W12:					
1,500 yds. @ $12			18,000		18,000
Wool fabric W09:					
2,400 yds. @ $7				$16,800	16,800
Interfacing:					
500 yds. @ $1			500		500
800 yds. @ $1				800	800
Liner:					
1,000 yds. @ $3			3,000		3,000
1,600 yds. @ $3				4,800	4,800
Total	$4,800	$3,600	$23,500	$22,400	$54,300

3. Recorded August payroll liability for direct labor of $34,450 and indirect labor of $7,200.

Journal entry

Work-in-Process	34,450	
Factory Overhead	7,200	
Wages Payable		41,650

Cost system procedures

a) Prepare work tickets.

b) Assign costs to jobs.

	Job 425	Job 426	Job 427	Job 428	Total
Labor hours	600	900	1,000	945	
Labor rate	× $10	× $10	× $10	× $10	
Total	$6,000	$9,000	$10,000	$9,450	$34,450

4. Recorded additional factory overhead costs.

Journal entry

Factory Overhead	7,090	
Manufacturing Supplies Inventory		950
Accumulated Depreciation: Factory		1,500
Utilities Payable		2,400
Property Taxes Payable		1,200
Miscellaneous Payables		1,040

Cost system procedures	Factory Overhead is a control account with a subsidiary ledger (file) containing a record for each type of overhead cost. Each factory overhead cost is recorded on the appropriate record.	
	Manufacturing supplies used	$ 950
	Factory depreciation	1,500
	Utilities	2,400
	Property taxes	1,200
	Miscellaneous	1,040
	Total	$7,090

5. Applied factory overhead of $13,780 to jobs using a predetermined rate of $4 per direct labor hour.

Journal entry	Work-in-Process	13,780	
	Factory Overhead		13,780

Cost system procedures

Record overhead on job-cost sheets.

	Job 425	Job 426	Job 427	Job 428	Total
Labor hours	600	900	1,000	945	
Overhead	× $4	× $4	× $4	× $4	
Total	$2,400	$3,600	$4,000	$3,780	$13,780

6. Completed Jobs 425, 426, and 427.

Journal entry	Finished Goods Inventory	176,800	
	Work-in-Process		176,800

Cost system procedures

a) Complete job-cost sheets to determine total cost of completed jobs.

	Job 425	Job 426	Job 427	Total
Beginning balance	$58,600	$51,300	$ 0	$109,900
Current costs:				
Direct materials	4,800	3,600	23,500	31,900
Direct labor	6,000	9,000	10,000	25,000
Applied overhead	2,400	3,600	4,000	10,000
Total cost of jobs	$71,800	$67,500	$37,500	$176,800

b) Transfer job-cost sheets for completed jobs to finished goods subsidiary file.

c) Perform any additional analysis desired for completed jobs, such as unit costs.

	Job 425	Job 426	Job 427
Total cost of jobs	$71,800	$67,500	$37,500
Units in job	÷ 1,200	÷ 900	÷ 500
Unit cost	$ 59.83	$ 75.00	$ 75.00

7. Delivered Jobs 424, 425, and 426 to customers.

Journal entry

Cost of Goods Sold	214,300	
Finished Goods Inventory		214,300

Cost system procedures

Transferred job-cost sheets for jobs 424, 425, and 426 from finished goods subsidiary file to a file for jobs completed and shipped.

Job 424	$ 75,000
Job 425	71,800
Job 426	67,500
Total	$214,300

Exhibit 11–6 shows the various manufacturing inventory accounts, Cost of Goods Sold, and the cost system records reflecting the above transactions. Note how the cost system records provide supporting documentation for the ending balances in the inventory accounts.

Fox Brothers' product costing system is adequate for determining the cost for each job. Although there are significant differences in materials costs, the system accounts carefully track each type of material as a separate cost pool. Because all direct labor employees are paid the same rate, it is necessary to maintain only one labor cost pool. Although there are three distinct operations (cutting, sewing, and finishing), the products are homogeneous, with the same proportionate time spent in each operation. Hence, with only one factory overhead cost pool applied on the basis of direct labor hours, individual product costs are accurately recorded.

Even though the system is adequate for product costing, it does not provide information for decisions concerning individual operations. Although the system does track total labor hours for the plant, it does not, for example, allow a comparison of budgeted and planned cutting hours. This information may be useful in evaluating the cutting operation. Nor does the system provide the detailed information required to make special decisions, such as a decision to subcontract cutting operations rather than performing them internally. To answer these questions, Fox Brothers' accountants would have to perform a special cost study. In spite of these deficiencies, management might continue to operate the current system if the costs of improving the cost system exceed the perceived benefits.

If management elected to refine the cost system, they would most likely replace the single work-in-process account with three work-in-process accounts, one each for cutting, sewing, and finishing. As jobs progressed through the factory, the accumulated cost of a job would be transferred from one work-in-process account to another. Additional labor and overhead costs would be assigned to the appropriate work-in-process account. Representative journal entries for transactions using multiple work-in-process accounts are illustrated in Exhibit 11–7.

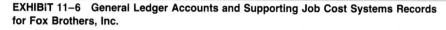

EXHIBIT 11–6   General Ledger Accounts and Supporting Job Cost Systems Records for Fox Brothers, Inc.

Raw Materials		
Beginning balance	36,100	54,300 (2)
(1)*	30,000	
Ending balance	11,800	

Work-in Process		
Beginning balance	109,900	176,800 (6)
(2)	54,300	
(3)	34,450	
(5)	13,780	
Ending balance	35,630	

Finished Goods Inventory		
Beginning balance	75,000	214,300 (7)
(6)	176,800	
Ending balance	37,500	

Cost of Goods Sold	
(7) 214,300	

Raw materials at August 30
(inventory records balance)

Wool fabric W09	$ 4,200
Wool fabric W12	0
Interfacing	200
Liner	4,200
Buttons	3,200
Total	$11,800

Work in process at August 30
(cost sheet balances)

Job 428	$35,630

Finished goods at August 30
(cost sheet balances)

Job 427	$37,500

Orders shipped:
(cost sheet balances)

Job 424	$ 75,000
Job 425	71,800
Job 426	67,500
Total	$214,300

Wool fabric W09:

Beginning balance	$ 21,000
Issued (2)	(16,800)
Ending balance	$ 4,200

Wool fabric W12:

Beginning balance	$ 6,000
Purchased (1)	12,000
Issued (2)	(18,000)
Ending balance	$ 0

Interfacing:

Beginning balance	$ 1,500
Issued (2)	(1,300)
Ending balance	$ 200

Liner:

Beginning balance	$ 6,000
Purchased (1)	6,000
Issued (2)	(7,800)
Ending balance	$ 4,200

Buttons:

Beginning balance	$ 1,600
Purchases (1)	12,000
Issued (2)	(10,400)
Ending balance	$ 3,200

Job 428:

Beginning balance	$ 0
Current costs:	
Materials (2)	22,400
Labor (3)	9,450
Overhead (5)	3,780
Ending balance	$ 35,630

Job 427:

Beginning balance	$ 0
Current costs:	
Materials (2)	23,500
Labor (3)	10,000
Overhead (5)	4,000
Total	$37,500

Job 424** | $75,000

Job 425:

Beginning balance	$58,600
Current costs:	
Materials (2)	4,800
Labor (3)	6,000
Overhead (5)	2,400
Total	$71,800

Job 426:

Beginning balance	$51,300
Current costs:	
Materials (2)	3,600
Labor (3)	9,000
Overhead (5)	3,600
Total	$67,500

*Numbers in parentheses ( ) refer to transaction numbers.
**In Finished Goods at beginning of period.

EXHIBIT 11–7   Possible Fox Brothers Flow of Costs with Three Work-in-Process Accounts

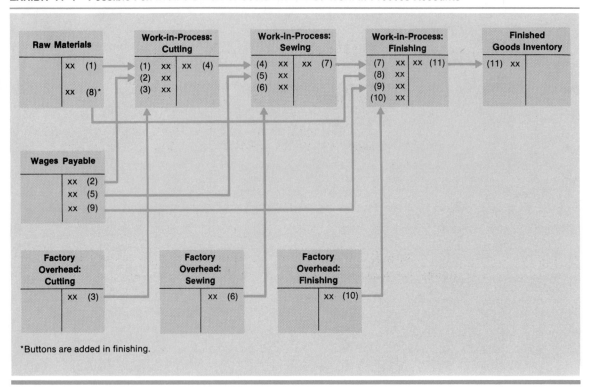

*Buttons are added in finishing.

In Exhibit 11–7, a single job is traced through the cutting, sewing, and finishing operations. Note that each operation has its own work-in-process and factory overhead accounts. The cost of all fabric requisitioned for a job is assigned to the job-cost sheet and the cutting operation. After the completion of the cutting operation, and the assignment of cutting labor and factory overhead costs, the job and the costs assigned to the job are transferred to the sewing operation. The process continues through the finishing operation, where buttons are added, and when the job is completed, all costs are transferred to Finished Goods Inventory.

There is yet another variation in multiple-operation cost systems. Some companies maintain separate work-in-process accounts but only a single factory overhead account. In this case factory overhead would be assigned to all jobs using a single plantwide overhead rate. Although this may simplify accounting procedures and still provide labor cost information by operation, it may not provide satisfactory cost control if operations have significantly different overhead costs.

ACCOUNTING FOR FACTORY OVERHEAD

In the illustration of Fox Brothers, Inc., factory overhead was assigned to Work-in-Process and to specific jobs at the predetermined rate of $4 per direct labor hour. When a predetermined overhead rate is used, the total cost of a particular job can be determined as soon as the job is completed and the number of labor hours is tabulated. If actual overhead was assigned to jobs, total cost could not be determined until after the end of the period, when total factory overhead is known.

What's more, assigning actual overhead to jobs is likely to result in identical jobs being assigned different overhead costs, depending on when they are produced. Assigned actual overhead costs will be higher during periods of low production because fixed overhead costs are spread over fewer products. Assigned actual overhead costs will also be higher during winter, if heating costs are significant, or summer, if cooling costs are significant. The use of predetermined rates smooths these sources of variation in the cost of identical jobs.

The predetermined factory overhead rate is computed by dividing predicted total overhead for the year by the predicted activity for the year. Assuming Fox Brothers, Inc., estimates total factory overhead for the year to be $100,000 and total production activity (measured in terms of direct labor hours) to be 25,000 direct labor hours, the predetermined factory overhead rate is $4 per direct labor hour.

$$\frac{\text{Predetermined}}{\text{factory overhead rate}} = \frac{\text{Predicted total overhead for the year}}{\text{Predicted total activity level for the year}}$$

$$= \frac{\$100,000}{25,000 \text{ hours}}$$

$$= \$4.$$

Two important questions must be addressed whenever predetermined factory overhead rates are used: (1) What is the appropriate basis for overhead allocation, and (2) what disposition should be made of any underapplied or overapplied balance in factory overhead at the end of the period?

Basis for Overhead Allocation

In addition to direct labor hours, other common bases for overhead allocation include machine hours, direct labor dollars, and number of units produced. A company, such as a clothing manufacturer, that has a labor-intensive manufacturing process would probably select a labor-related activity base, such as direct labor hours or direct labor dollars. Labor intensive companies usually find a close correlation between the amount of factory overhead incurred and the volume of labor-related activities. On the other hand, a company whose production is machine intensive, such as a chemical company, would probably use an activity base reflecting machine activity, such as machine hours. Companies that have more than one production department may use a different base for each department.

The primary goal in selecting an allocation base is to make sure that a logical association exists between the base and the significant factory overhead cost components. Also, the quantity of the base for each period, and for each job or department, should be fairly easy to measure.

Overapplied and Underapplied Overhead

Using the Fox Brothers example (where predicted factory overhead for the year was $100,000, and direct labor hours were 25,000), assume that the company actually incurred $100,000 in factory overhead and that actual direct labor hours for the year were 25,000. Summary entries for actual and applied overhead are as follows:

Journal entry

Factory Overhead	100,000	
Various balance sheet accounts		100,000
Work-in-Process	100,000	
Factory Overhead		100,000

M ANAGERIAL PRACTICE 11.3

Changing Cost Flows and Manufacturing Overhead

Although the vast majority of traditional cost accounting systems in place today still apply manufacturing overhead cost to products based on direct labor hours and dollars charged to a specific product, many companies are changing their cost assignment methods. Many large companies have very small labor hours and dollars per product. For example, in 1985 IBM's labor was less than 3 percent of total product cost. Vendor purchases were in the range of 50 percent, with the balance being manufacturing engineering and manufacturing expense. With this cost breakdown, IBM was looking at two basic elements of cost: materials and conversion. For such a situation it was unrealistic to assign any costs on the basis of labor. Cost systems need to identify the cause of costs—the cost drivers—in addition to capturing the resultant costs. Once this is accomplished, an improved costing system results.

Sources: Robert H. Kelder, "Era of Cost Accounting Changes," in *Cost Accounting, Robotics, and the New Manufacturing Environment,* ed. Robert Capettini and Donald K. Clancy (Sarasota, Fla.: American Accounting Association, 1987), 3.23; and Robert D. McIlhattan, "How Cost Management Systems Can Support the JIT Philosophy," *Management Accounting* (September 1987): 21–23.

Because the actual cost recorded equals the applied cost, there is no balance in Factory Overhead at the end of the year. However, if either the actual overhead cost or the actual level of the production activity base differed from its predicted value, there would be a balance in Factory Overhead, representing overapplied or underapplied overhead.

Now assume that the prediction of 25,000 direct labor hours was correct but that actual overhead cost was $105,000. In this case, Factory Overhead shows a $5,000 debit balance representing underapplied factory overhead:

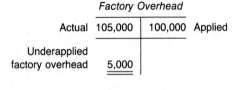

Factory Overhead

Actual 105,000	100,000 Applied
Underapplied factory overhead 5,000	

If actual factory overhead were only $98,000, Factory Overhead would be overapplied and show a $2,000 credit balance:

Factory Overhead

Actual 98,000	100,000 Applied
	2,000 Overapplied factory overhead

It is apparent that if the *prediction* of total factory overhead cost is not accurate, there will be an underapplied or overapplied balance in Factory Overhead at the end of the year. A similar result occurs when the actual production activity level is different from the predicted activity level used in computing the predetermined rate. Any balances in Factory Overhead during the year representing overapplied or underapplied overhead are usually allowed to accumulate from month to month. In the absence of evidence to the contrary, it is assumed that differences during the year result from variations in production or seasonal cost differences or both. Any balance in Factory Overhead at the end of the year is usually disposed of by one of the two methods discussed in the following section.

Disposition of Factory Overhead Balances

To illustrate the disposition of a Factory Overhead balance at the end of the accounting period, assume the following year-end account balances (all debits) for a manufacturing company:

Work-in-Process	$300,000
Finished Goods Inventory	200,000
Cost of Goods Sold	500,000
Factory Overhead (underapplied)	8,000

A common method for disposing of the $8,000 debit balance in Factory Overhead at the end of the period is merely to write it off to Cost of Goods Sold by the following journal entry:

Journal entry

Cost of Goods Sold	8,000	
Factory Overhead		8,000

The effect of this entry is to close out the Factory Overhead account and to charge the underapplied balance to Cost of Goods Sold, thus increasing total expenses on the income statement and reducing net income. If Factory Overhead has a credit balance, representing overapplied overhead, Factory Overhead would be debited, and Cost of Goods Sold would be credited, reducing total expenses and increasing net income.

Another method of disposing of an end-of-period balance in Factory Overhead is to allocate it among Work-in-Process, Finished Goods Inventory, and Cost of Goods Sold. This allocation is frequently made on the basis of the relative total cost in each account at the end of the period. The following computations show how the $8,000 would be disposed of under the allocation method.

	Account Balance	Relative Portion of Total		Underapplied Factory Overhead		Allocation
Work-in-Process	$ 300,000	0.30	×	$8,000	=	$2,400
Finished Goods Inventory	200,000	0.20	×	8,000	=	1,600
Cost of Goods Sold	500,000	0.50	×	8,000	=	4,000
Total	$1,000,000	1.00				$8,000

The entry to record the assignment of the Factory Overhead balance to Work-in-Process, Finished Goods Inventory, and Cost of Goods Sold is shown in the following journal entry.

Journal entry

Work-in-Process	2,400	
Finished Goods Inventory	1,600	
Cost of Goods Sold	4,000	
Factory Overhead		8,000

The rationale for writing over- or underapplied overhead off against Cost of Goods Sold is that it is convenient and simple. If the predicted amounts used in calculating the predetermined rate are relatively accurate, the underapplied or overapplied amount should be relatively small, thereby justifying the use of the most convenient method.

The allocation method, however, is more desirable if the Factory Overhead balance is relatively large. An overapplied or underapplied balance in Factory Overhead is always caused by the use of a predetermined overhead rate that differs from the actual overhead rate. If we waited until the end of the period to apply overhead, an accurate overhead rate based on actual cost could be used. Therefore it is logical to allocate the ending balance in Factory Overhead to the accounts affected by the inaccurate predetermined rate, that is, to Work-in-Process, Finished Goods Inventory, and Cost of Goods Sold. After the allocation, the balance in each account should be approximately the same as it would have been had an actual rate been used.

JOB COSTING FOR HETEROGENEOUS PRODUCTS

A cost driver is an activity, such as meals served, packages mailed, pages typed, or units manufactured, that causes costs to be incurred. For purposes of planning and controlling costs, it is important to identify an organization's cost drivers. Production is the ultimate cost driver in a manufacturing facility. When all units produced in a plant are identical, a simple division of total production costs by total units produced provides accurate unit costs. When the products produced in a plant differ significantly, it is necessary to use a multitude of cost drivers to recognize the extent to which different products use different resources with different costs. Hence, as products become more heterogeneous, it is necessary to perform an increasingly detailed analysis of cost drivers.

Even the Fox Brothers example, which concerned a homogeneous product line of sports jackets, used seven cost pools and related cost drivers:

Cost Pool	Cost Driver
Direct materials:	
Wool fabric W09	Yards
Wool fabric W12	Yards
Interfacing	Yards
Liner	Yards
Buttons	Sets
Direct labor	Direct labor hours
Factory overhead	Direct labor hours

Fox Brothers has separate cost pools for materials because of differing materials costs and handling characteristics. With a single labor rate of $10 per hour, only one direct labor cost pool is required. Assuming factory overhead is caused by and highly correlated with the use of direct labor, direct labor hours is an acceptable basis of overhead allocation.

The Problem of Cross-Subsidization

If, in addition to continuing to manufacture jackets, Fox Brothers installed a fully automated flexible manufacturing system used exclusively to manufacture designer jeans, the cost accounting system could be operated by simply adding cost pools for the new raw materials items and adding all costs of operating the new equipment to factory overhead. (In a flexible manufacturing system virtually all labor costs are classified as indirect labor.) With factory overhead assigned on the basis of direct labor hours, the predetermined overhead rate per direct labor hour would increase significantly. Although the system would account for all costs in a systematic manner, sports jackets would receive all overhead costs because they receive all the direct labor hours and the designer jeans receive no direct labor hours.

With this cost system, sports jackets would cross-subsidize designer jeans because a portion of the cost of manufacturing designer jeans would be assigned to sports jackets. Fox Brothers' management may be mislead, believing designer jeans are very profitable and sports jackets are unprofitable. Clearly, this could be a serious error. Its cause is a bad cost accounting system. Even if overhead costs are allocated on some other basis, such as the number of units produced, in order to assign some overhead costs to jeans, the resulting costs are unlikely

MANAGERIAL PRACTICE 11.4

More Suggestions for Job Shop Improvement

Robert H. Goldsmith, president and chief operating officer of Rohr Industries, Inc., wrote in response to the article "Time to Reform Job Shop Manufacturing." He noted the following additional measures that were necessary when Rohr made changes to their job shop manufacturing approach: organizational, product and process, customer, technology, bottlenecks, and people. His suggestions included downsizing the production department, reducing complexity, and improving quality. Customers and employees need to be included in the problem solution process. As Goldsmith explains, changing the "old job shop culture is difficult, but nothing worth doing is every easy." Job shop improvement is necessary if American industry hopes to regain its position of world manufacturing leadership.

Source: Robert H. Goldsmith, letter to the editor, *Harvard Business Review* (September–October 1989): 180–181.

to be sufficiently accurate for such decisions as pricing or evaluating Fox Brothers' ability to compete.

When jobs are heterogeneous and require varying degrees of attention in operations that have different cost drivers, significant cost assignment errors may result from the use of a single, plantwide overhead rate. With sports jackets produced in a labor intensive operation and designer jeans produced using a fully automated flexible manufacturing system, Fox Brothers' cost system should contain at least nine cost pools and should recognize machine hours as an additional cost driver:

Cost Pool	Cost Driver
Direct materials:	
Wool fabric W09	Yards
Wool fabric W12	Yards
Interfacing	Yards
Liner	Yards
Buttons	Sets
Denim	Yards
Labor intensive operations:	
Direct labor	Direct labor hours
Factory overhead	Direct labor hours
FMS operations:	
Conversion	Machine hours

This is an extreme example, but many companies that started with focused factories producing a single product have failed to modernize their accounting system when new products and production procedures were added. The resulting cross-subsidization of costs hinders the organization's ability to compete as competition intensifies and becomes more global. *The more varied the production alternatives and the product mix, the greater the need for a cost system that recognizes a diverse set of detailed cost drivers.* It is no longer adequate to perform detailed costing of direct materials and direct labor while lumping overhead into an amorphous blob. Overhead must be analyzed in detail and divided into a number of homogeneous cost pools. Cost drivers must be identified for each cost pool. And the costs in each cost pool must be assigned to products using the most appropriate cost driver. Although such detailed analysis would not have been possible a few years ago, the rapid changes in the manufacturing environment related to the increasing use of computers makes the detailed tracing of costs possible as a by-product of ongoing planning and control operations required for other purposes. Overhead cost pools are given additional consideration in Chapter 13.

NONPRODUCT COSTS

Our focus has been on the accurate assignment of product costs to jobs. Product costs must be assigned to products for inventory valuation and cost determination in general purpose financial statements. Nonproduct, period, costs, on the other hand, are not assigned to jobs for financial reporting purposes. Instead, they are treated as an expense when they are incurred.

The distinction between product and period costs is necessary for external financial reporting, but it is not always useful for internal decision making. When feasible, such traditional period costs as marketing, research and development, and administration should be associated with specific jobs to assist in management decision making. The interested reader is referred to Chapters 4 and 5.

OTHER APPLICATIONS OF JOB COSTING

The previous examples focused on the use of job costing for batch production. Job costing procedures are extremely versatile and widely used for other purposes as well, such as project costing and service costing.

Project Costing

Job costing concepts are used for projects, such as constructing a building or a ship. In this case a simple job-cost sheet, such as the one illustrated in Exhibit 11–2, is inadequate. Instead, the project is broken into a series of jobs, which may be further divided into subjobs. The construction of a building, for example, may be divided into jobs for excavation, foundation, framing, plumbing, wiring, roofing, and so forth. A production order, or perhaps a subcontract, will be issued for each of the jobs at the most detailed level. Each production order will specify what is to be done, when it is to be done, who is to do it, the materials required, and the estimated cost. As work on the job progresses, actual material, time, and cost data are accumulated on job-cost sheets at the most detailed job level.

Although the detailed job-cost sheets for each subjob may specify costs for materials, labor, and overhead, all of these costs will be recorded in a single category at the project level. Hence materials, labor, and overhead costs incurred to install electrical wire in a building are recorded in the summary category of electrical wiring at the project level. When completed, all the costs of the building will be summarized in a single asset account. The costs of materials, labor, and overhead incurred in constructing the building are aggregated into the cost of the building.

Control of the project is exercised on the dimensions of time, quality, and cost. Time for the entire project is planned and controlled using project management tools such as Gantt Charts, the critical path method (CPM), and the program evaluation and review technique (PERT). Using these tools, detailed plans are developed indicating when work on each subjob should begin and end. If a subjob falls behind schedule, it is imperative that management immediately determine the cause and take corrective action. Failure to do so may result in the incurrence of significant cost overruns as later work falls behind schedule as a result of delays in earlier work. Gantt charts, the critical path method, and the program evaluation and review technique are typically considered in production or operations research courses.

Quality control is also critical in major construction projects. All work must meet quality standards at the scheduled completion time. If the electrical wiring, for example, is determined unacceptable after all interior walls and ceilings are finished, correction of the problem will likely cause major time and cost overruns.

Finally, financial performance reports comparing actual and allowed costs for the work completed to date should be prepared periodically. These reports are intended to provide an overview of operations and identify problem areas. Time and quality performance measures, on the other hand, are intended to provide immediate feedback to operating personnel, who take immediate corrective action. If time, quality, and other operating performance measures are effective, there should be few unfavorable financial performance measures.

Service Costing

Service costing, the assignment of costs to services, makes extensive use of job-costing concepts to determine the cost of filling customer service orders in organizations such as automobile repair shops, charter airlines, CPA firms, hospitals, and law firms. Many of these organizations bill clients on the basis of resources consumed. Consequently, they maintain detailed job records for billing purposes. On the invoice sent to the client, the organization will itemize any materials consumed on the job at a selling price per unit, the labor hours worked on the job at a billing rate per hour, and the time special facilities were used at a billing rate per unit of time. Employees with different capabilities and experience often have different billing rates. In a CPA firm, for example, a partner or a senior manager has a higher billing rate than a staff accountant.

The prices and rates must be high enough to cover costs not assigned to specific jobs and, in for-profit organizations, to provide for a profit. To evaluate the contribution to common costs and profit from a job, a comparison must be made between the price charged the customer and the actual cost of the job. This is easily done when the actual cost of resources itemized on the customer's invoice is presented on a job-cost sheet. A CPA firm, for example, should accumulate the actual hardware and software costs of an accounting system installed for a client along with the actual wages earned by employees while working on the job and any related travel costs. Comparing the total of these costs with the price charged the client indicates the total contribution of the job to common costs and profit.

Although service organizations may identify costs with individual jobs for management accounting purposes, there is considerable variation in the way job cost information is presented in financial statements. Some organizations report the cost of jobs completed in their income statement using an account such as Cost of Services Provided. Accomplishing this requires accounting procedures similar to those outlined in Exhibits 11–3 and 11–4. The only major change involves replacing Cost of Goods Sold with Cost of Services Provided.

More often, however, service organizations do not formally establish detailed financial accounting procedures to trace the flow of service costs. Instead, service job costs are left in their original cost categories, such as materials expense, salaries and wages expense, travel expense, and so forth.

Because all service costs are typically regarded as period rather than product costs, either procedure is acceptable. Regardless of the formal treatment of service costs in financial accounting records and statements, the managers of a well run service organization should have information regarding job cost and contribution.

The above examples of service costing all dealt with examples in which the order was filled in response to a specific customer request. Job order costing can also be used to determine the cost of making services available even when the names of specific customers are not known in advance and the service is being provided on a speculative basis. A regularly scheduled airline flight, for example, could be regarded as a job. Management is interested in knowing the cost of the job in order to determine its profitability. This is but another example of the versatility of job order costing.

SUMMARY

Management control should be exercised on the dimensions of time, quality, and cost. This chapter has considered job costing, an extremely versatile approach to determining the cost of products or services provided in batches or single units. The basic approach involves accumulating the costs associated with a job in three categories: materials, labor, and overhead. When operations have little or no direct labor content, job costs may be accumulated in two categories: materials and conversion.

Important job-cost records in a manufacturing organization include materials requisition forms, work tickets, and job-cost sheets. As work on a job progresses, job costs are recorded on a job-cost sheet and assigned to Work-in-Process. When the job is complete, the assigned costs are transferred from Work-in-Process to Finished Goods Inventory. Very often the formal job-cost records in a manufacturing organization capture only manufacturing costs.

In service organizations, where costs are typically treated as period costs for financial reporting purposes, job cost information is not always recorded in the financial accounting records or separately identified in financial statements. Nevertheless, management is likely to use job cost information for internal planning and control.

APPENDIX
PRODUCT COSTING USING STANDARD COSTS

In Chapter 8[3] we discussed the concept of standard cost and developed a model for computing standard cost variances. The main focus of that discussion was cost control and management performance evaluation. In addition, standard costs are often integrated into the product costing system in which they are used for inventory valuation. When this is done, the manufacturing accounts are charged with standard costs instead of actual costs, and the differences between standard costs and actual costs are recorded as standard cost variances. These variances are then disposed of in a manner similar to the disposition of under-applied and overapplied factory overhead, which was discussed in this chapter.

To illustrate, assume that Execupens, Inc. (discussed in Chapter 8) uses standard costs in costing its only product, gold casings for writing pens. For product costing purposes, standard costs usually include both variable costs and fixed costs. The standard product cost of one casing is $77, consisting of $68 of variable costs and $9 of assigned fixed costs:

Materials (6 gms at $8)	$48
Direct labor (1 hr at $14)	14
Variable overhead (1 hr at $6)	6
Total variable cost	$68
Fixed overhead (1 hr at $9)	9
Standard cost per unit	$77

The fixed overhead rate of $9 is computed by dividing budgeted fixed overhead of $198,000 by 22,000 standard direct labor hours allowed for a normal level of 22,000 units of output. Execupens' transactions for March 19x6, summarized from Chapter 8, were as follows:

- There were no beginning or ending units in process.
- 124,000 grams of materials were purchased by the production manager at $7.96 per gram for a total of $987,040.
- All 124,000 grams of materials were issued to processing.
- The direct labor payroll was $284,928 for 19,200 hours, an average of $14.84 per hour.
- Actual overhead costs were $126,000 variable and $200,000 fixed.
- 20,000 units were produced during the period.
- 16,000 units were sold.

---

[3] Note to the instructor: Although Chapter 11 may be assigned anytime after Chapter 3, this appendix should not be assigned until after Chapter 8.

Standard Cost Variances

The standard cost variances for Execupens, Inc., are summarized below. These variances were computed and discussed in Chapter 8.

Materials purchased price variance	$ 4,960 F
Materials quantity variance	32,000 U
Labor rate variance	16,128 U
Labor efficiency variance	11,200 F
Variable overhead spending variance	10,800 U
Variable overhead efficiency variance	4,800 F
Fixed overhead budget variance	2,000 U
Fixed overhead volume variance	18,000 U

Journal Entries

The cost of materials purchases are usually recorded at standard cost with any price variance recognized at the time of purchase. The entry to record Execupens' materials acquisitions at the time of purchase is as follows:

Journal entry

Raw Materials	992,000	
Materials Purchased Price Variance		4,960
Accounts Payable		987,040
To record at standard cost, $8, the purchase of 124,000 grams of gold.		

As units are transferred out of processing to finished goods inventory, the following entry is made.

Journal entry

Finished Goods Inventory	1,540,000	
Work-in-Process		1,540,000
To record completion of 20,000 units at the standard cost of $77.		

As units are sold, the following entry is made to record the cost of goods sold.

Journal entry

Cost of Goods Sold	1,232,000	
Finished Goods Inventory		1,232,000
To record the Cost of Goods Sold and decrease in Finished Goods Inventory at the standard cost of $77 for 16,000 units sold.		

At the end of the period when actual costs are known and standard cost variances are determined, the following entries are made to assign costs to Work-in-Process, to recognize actual costs, and to record standard cost variances. Work-in-Process is debited for the standard cost per unit for the 20,000 units produced in the following entries for materials, labor, variable overhead, and fixed overhead.

Journal entries

Work-in-Process (20,000 × $48)	960,000	
Materials Quantity Variance	32,000	
Raw Materials		992,000
To record raw materials cost assigned to		
Work-in-Process at standard cost.		
Work-in-Process (20,000 × $14)	280,000	
Labor Rate Variance	16,128	
Labor Efficiency Variance		11,200
Wages Payable		284,928
To record direct labor assigned to		
Work-in-Process at standard cost.		
Work-in-Process (20,000 × $6)	120,000	
Variable Overhead Spending Variance	10,800	
Variable Overhead Efficiency Variance		4,800
Factory Overhead		126,000
To record variable factory overhead assigned to		
Work-in-Process at standard cost.		
Work-in-Process (20,000 × $9)	180,000	
Fixed Overhead Budget Variance	2,000	
Fixed Overhead Volume Variance	18,000	
Factory Overhead		200,000
To record fixed factory overhead assigned to		
Work-in-Process at standard cost.		

Note in the journal entries that *unfavorable variances* are recorded as *debits* and *favorable variances* are recorded as *credits*. Unfavorable variances are viewed as current manufacturing costs incurred but not charged to processing, whereas favorable variances are viewed as excess charges of manufacturing costs to processing. At the end of the period after standard manufacturing costs and the cost variances have been recorded, it is necessary to dispose of the balances in the variance accounts. Probably the most common procedure for disposing of standard cost variances is to close them out with the net variance debited or credited to Cost of Goods Sold. Another method sometimes used is to allocate them pro rata among Work-in-Process, Finished Goods, and Cost of Goods Sold. This is the same procedure that was discussed earlier for allocating overapplied and underapplied factory overhead.

SUGGESTED READINGS

Bennett, Robert E., James A. Hendricks, David E. Keys, and Edward J. Rudnicki, *Cost Accounting for Factory Automation* Montvalle, N.J.: National Association of Accountants, 1987.

Cleverly, William O., "Product Costing for Health Care Firms," *Health Care Management Review* (Fall 1987): 39–49.

Cooper, Robin, and Robert S. Kaplan, "How Cost Accounting Distorts Product Cost," *Management Accounting* (April 1988): 20–27.

_____ , "Measure Costs Right: Make the Right Decisions," *Harvard Business Review* (September–October 1988): 96–103.

Kaplan, Robert S., "The Four Stage Model of Cost Systems Design," *Management Accounting* (February 1990): 22–26.

Krause, Paul, and Donald E. Keller, "Bringing World-Class Manufacturing and Accounting to a Small Company," *Management Accounting* (November 1988): 28–33.

Lere, John C., "Explaining Alternative Standard Cost Journal Entries," *Journal of Accounting Education* (Fall 1985): 187–193.

Sandretto, Michael J., "What Kind of Cost System Do You Need?" *Harvard Business Review* (January–February 1985): 110–118.

Stokes, Carolyn, and Kay W. Lawrimore, "Selling a New Cost Accounting System," *Journal of Cost Management, 6,* No. 3, (Fall 1989): 29–34.

Vollum, Robert B., "Cost Accounting: The Key to Capturing Cost Information on the Factory Floor," *Journal of Accounting and EDP* (Summer 1985): 44–51.

REVIEW PROBLEM

Job Costing Journal Entries

Quad-Star Publishing Company prints sales fliers for retail and mail-order companies. Production costs are accounted for using a job cost system. At the beginning of June 19x5 raw materials inventories totaled $7,000, manufacturing supplies amounted to $800, two jobs were in process—Job 225 with assigned costs of $13,750 and Job 226 with assigned costs of $1,800—and there were no finished goods inventories. The following information summarizes June manufacturing activities.

- Raw materials costing $40,000 were purchased on account.
- Manufacturing supplies costing $9,000 were purchased on account.
- Requisitioned materials needed to complete Job 226. Started two new jobs, 227 and 228, and requisitioned direct materials for them.

Direct materials:	
Job 226	$ 2,600
Job 227	18,000
Job 228	14,400
Total	$35,000

■ June salaries and wages were as follows:

Direct labor:		
Job 225	500 hours × $10/hour	$ 5,000
Job 226	1,500 hours × $10/hour	15,000
Job 227	2,050 hours × $10/hour	20,500
Job 228	800 hours × $10/hour	8,000
Total direct labor		$48,500
Indirect labor		5,000
Total		$53,500

■ Used manufacturing supplies costing $5,500.

■ Depreciation on factory fixed assets totaled $5,000.

■ Miscellaneous factory overhead costs of $8,750 were incurred on account.

■ Factory overhead was applied at the rate of $5 per direct labor hour.

■ Jobs 225, 226, and 227 were completed.

■ Jobs 225 and 226 were delivered to customers.

Requirements

a) Prepare summary journal entries to record June 19x5 manufacturing activities. Number all journal entries. (*Hint:* Prepare cost sheets for completed jobs.)

b) Prepare T-accounts for all inventory accounts and the Cost of Goods Sold. Record all beginning balances, post June transactions, and determine ending balances in these accounts.

c) Show the job-cost details to support the June 30, 19x5 balance in Work-in-Process.

The solution to this problem is found at the end of the Chapter 11 exercises, problems, and cases.

KEY TERMS

Automatic identification system
   (AIS)
Bill of materials
Computer integrated manufacturing
   (CIM)
Computer-aided design (CAD)
Computer-aided manufacturing
   (CAM)
Control account
Cost driver
File
Flexible manufacturing systems
   (FMS)

Job-cost sheet
Job production
Job-order production
Just-in-time (JIT)
Materials requisition form
Operations list
Production order
Record
Service costing
Subsidiary ledger
World class manufacturer
Work ticket

REVIEW QUESTIONS

11–1   Identify three trends that have increased the importance of product costs for management decisions, such as pricing, and that have reduced the importance of product costing for financial reporting.

11–2   Briefly distinguish between process and job production. Provide examples of products typically produced under each.

11–3   Briefly describe the role of engineering and production scheduling personnel in the production planning process.

11–4   On what three dimensions should manufacturing activities be controlled?

11–5   Identify the primary records involved in the operation of a job-cost system.

11–6   Why are managers interested in computer-based monitoring, design, and production techniques?

11–7   Describe the flow of inventory costs through the accounting system of a labor intensive manufacturing organization.

11–8   Assuming products pass through multiple production operations, when will maintaining only one factory overhead cost pool not distort individual product costs?

11–9   Present the general equation for computing a predetermined factory overhead rate.

11–10   What are the primary reasons for using a predetermined overhead rate?

11–11   Briefly describe two methods for disposing of underapplied or overapplied factory overhead.

11–12   When is it necessary to use multiple cost drivers for product costing?

11–13   When is the problem of cost cross-subsidization most likely to occur?

11–14   Identify two reasons why a service organization should maintain detailed job information.

11–15   Mention two alternative procedures service organizations may use to account for job costs in financial statements.

EXERCISES

11–1 Manufacturing Cost Flows with Machine Hours Allocation: Journal Entries

Fork Manufacturing Company's November 1, 19x6, Work-in-Process balance was $5,000. During November, Fork Manufacturing completed the following manufacturing transactions:

- Purchased raw materials costing $60,000 and manufacturing supplies costing $3,000 on account.
- Requisitioned raw materials costing $40,000 to the factory.
- Incurred direct labor costs of $27,000 and indirect labor costs of $4,800.
- Used manufacturing supplies costing $3,000.
- Recorded factory depreciation of $15,000.
- Miscellaneous payables for factory overhead totaled $3,600.
- Applied factory overhead at a predetermined rate of $10 per machine hour, with 2,250 machine hours.
- Completed jobs costing $85,000.
- Finished goods costing $96,000 were sold.

Requirements

a)   Prepare summary journal entries to record November 19x6 manufacturing activities. Number all journal entries.

b)   Prepare a T-account for Work-in-Process, record the beginning balance, post all transactions, and determine the ending balance.

11–2 Manufacturing Cost Flows with Labor Hours Allocation: Journal Entries

Malone Manufacturing Company's June 1, 19x2, Work-in-Process balance was $4,000. During November Malone Manufacturing completed the following manufacturing transactions:

- Purchased raw materials costing $24,000 and manufacturing supplies costing $2,000 on account.
- Requisitioned raw materials costing $28,000 to the factory.
- Manufacturing payroll for the month consists of 2,200 hours of direct labor and 400 hours of indirect labor, both at $11 per hour.
- Used manufacturing supplies costing $800.
- Recorded factory depreciation of $12,000.
- Miscellaneous payables for factory overhead totaled $2,800.
- Applied factory overhead at a predetermined rate of $8 per direct labor hour.
- Completed jobs costing $72,000.
- Finished goods costing $81,500 were sold.

Requirements

a) Prepare summary journal entries to record June 19x2 manufacturing activities. Number all journal entries.

b) Prepare a T-account for Work-in-Process, record the beginning balance, post all transactions, and determine the ending balance.

11–3 Service Cost Flows: Journal Entries

Video Marketing Ltd. produces television advertisements for businesses marketing products in the western provinces of Canada. To achieve cost control, Video Marketing uses a job cost system, similar to that found in a manufacturing organization. Some different account titles are used:

Account	Replaces
Videos-in-Process	Work-in-Process
Production Supplies Inventory	Manufacturing Supplies Inventory
Cost of Videos Completed	Cost of Goods Sold
Studio Overhead	Factory Overhead

Video Marketing does not maintain raw materials or finished goods inventory accounts. Materials, such as props, needed for videos are purchased as needed from outside sources and charged directly to Videos-in-Process and the appropriate job when received. Videos are delivered directly to clients upon completion. The October 1, 19x2, Videos-in-Process balance was $1,000. During October, Video Marketing completed the following production transactions:

- Purchased production supplies costing $1,500 on account.
- Purchased materials chargeable to specific jobs costing $27,000 on account.
- Incurred direct labor costs of $65,000 and indirect labor costs of $32,000.
- Used production supplies costing $850.
- Recorded studio depreciation of $3,000.
- Miscellaneous payables for studio overhead totaled $1,800.

- Applied studio overhead at a predetermined rate of $9.50 per studio hour, with 480 studio hours.
- Completed jobs costing $97,000 and delivered them directly to clients.

Requirements

a) Prepare summary journal entries to record November 19x6 production activities. Number all journal entries.

b) Prepare a T-account for Videos-in-Process, record the beginning balance, post all transactions, and determine the ending balance.

11–4 Manufacturing T-Accounts: Missing Data

Presented are partially completed manufacturing T-accounts:

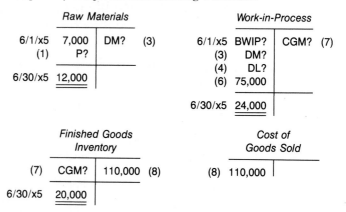

Additional information:

- Ending Work-in-Process is three times as large as the beginning Work-in-Process.
- Factory overhead is applied at 150 percent of direct materials.

Required: Determine each of the following amounts:

1. Purchases (P).
2. Direct materials (DM).
3. Beginning Work-in-Process (BWIP).
4. Direct labor (DL).
5. Cost of goods manufactured (CGM).

11–5 Construction T-Accounts: Missing Data

Presented are partially completed T-accounts of a construction company:

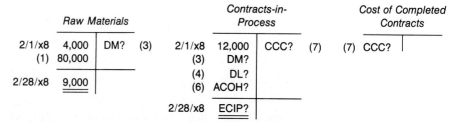

Additional information:

- Ending Contracts-in-Process is half as large as the beginning Contracts-in-Process.
- Conversion costs amount to two-thirds of the total current construction costs.
- Construction overhead is applied at 50 percent of direct labor dollars.

Required: Determine each of the following amounts:

1. Direct materials (DM).
2. Direct labor (DL).
3. Applied construction overhead (ACOH).
4. Ending contracts-in-process (ECIP).
5. Cost of completed contracts (CCC).

11–6 Analyzing a Job-Cost Sheet of a Service Company

Accounting Software Solutions assigns all direct costs to jobs. When jobs are complete their costs are transferred from Work-in-Process to Cost of Completed Service Contracts. The following information pertains to Job 385, completed on December 31, 19x1.

Job Number 385
Description: *Install accounting software package*

Raw Materials Costs

Date	Description	Units	Cost
11/20/x1	Oak Tree Accounting Complete	1	$1,200

Direct Labor Costs

Date	Description	Units	Cost
11/15/x1	Needs assessment (manager)	16 hours	800
11/30/x1	Installation (staff)	24 hours	840
12/15/x1	Training (staff)	16 hours	560
12/31/x1	Review and acceptance (partner)	4 hours	400

Other Direct Costs

Date	Description	Units	Cost
11/12/x1	Travel expense reimbursement #x1-1107		126
11/27/x1	Travel expense reimbursement #x1-1123		250
12/13/x1	Travel expense reimbursement #x1-1213		130
12/29/x1	Travel expense reimbursement #x1-1227		65
Total cost of job			$4,371

Additional information:

- The company maintains an inventory of accounting software and assigns software to jobs at cost.
- Travel expense reimbursements, for such items as mileage, food, and lodging, are paid directly to employees upon receipt of a completed expense form.

- Employees are paid twice a month.
- Transactions are journalized on the date indicated on the related job-cost sheet.

Requirements

a) Prepare chronological journal entries, with a date column, to record the costs assigned to Job 385. Also prepare the journal entry to record the completion of the job.

b) Prepare chronological journal entries, with a date column, for Job 385 assuming management elected to expense job costs as incurred rather than assign them to specific jobs.

c) Why might a service company assign costs to jobs for internal purposes even if they immediately expense job costs for financial reporting?

11–7 Analyzing the Job-Cost Sheet of a Machine Intensive Manufacturing Company

The following information is taken from the records of the Flexible Machine Shop for Job 1432, completed on February 27, 19x9.

Job Number 1432
Description: *Complete 100 motor housings*

Raw Materials Costs

Date	Description	Units	Cost
2/25/x9	Medium gage sheet metal	200 sq. ft.	$420

Conversion Costs

Date	Description	Units	Cost
2/26/x9	Cutting	0.5 hours	200
2/26/x9	Welding	2.0 hours	600
2/27/x9	Tempering	3.0 hours	450

Applied Overhead

Date	Description	Units	Cost
2/26/x9	Plantwide overhead, cutting	0.5 hours	25
2/26/x9	Plantwide overhead, welding	2.0 hours	100
2/27/x9	Plantwide overhead, tempering	3.0 hours	150
Total cost of job			$1,945

Additional information:

- All materials are added in the cutting operation.
- The company maintains separate Work-in-Process and Conversion Cost accounts for each operation.

- Common, plantwide overhead costs are accumulated in a separate Plant Factory Overhead account and assigned on the basis of work hours as jobs are worked on in each operation.
- Transactions are journalized on the date indicated on the related job-cost sheet.

Requirements

a) Prepare chronological journal entries, with a date column, to record the costs assigned to Job 1432, the transfer of Job 1432 between operations, and the completion of the job.

b) Prepare a set of chronological journal entries, with a date column, for Job 1432 and the completion of the job assuming the company does not maintain separate Work-in-Process and Conversion Cost accounts for each operation.

c) Why might a company producing a homogeneous product line desire to accumulate conversion costs for each major operation rather than simply accumulating and assigning them on a plantwide basis?

11–8 Underapplied and Overapplied Factory Overhead

The December 31, 19x4, Factory Overhead account for Columbia Manufacturing Company is as follows:

Factory Overhead

265,000	275,000
	10,000

Requirements

a) How much was actual factory overhead?

b) How much factory overhead was applied to work-in-process?

c) What does the $10,000 balance represent?

d) Describe two alternatives available for disposing of the $10,000 balance.

e) Which of the alternatives in requirement (d) will result in the largest net income for the year? Explain.

11–9 Underapplied and Overapplied Factory Overhead

Presented are selected account balances of the Mouser Company at the end of 19x4:

Work-in-Process	$ 55,000 debit
Finished Goods Inventory	75,000 debit
Cost of Goods Sold	370,000 debit
Factory Overhead	32,000 credit

Requirements

a) Does Mouser Company use a predetermined overhead rate or does it assign actual overhead to Work-in-Process? Explain.

b) Were factory overhead costs underapplied or overapplied in 19x4? Explain.

c) Prepare the journal entry to dispose of the Factory Overhead balance assuming it is written off to Cost of Goods Sold.

d) Prepare the journal entry to dispose of the Factory Overhead balance assuming it is allocated to Work-in-Process, Finished Goods Inventory, and Cost of Goods Sold.

e) Which method of disposing of underapplied or overapplied factory overhead is more accurate? Explain.

11–10 Underapplied and Overapplied Factory Overhead

The management of the Norcross Company decided to use a predetermined rate to assign factory overhead. The following predictions were made for 19x4.

Factory overhead costs	$270,000
Direct labor hours	30,000 hours
Direct labor costs	$300,000
Machine hours	45,000 hours

Requirements

a) Compute the predetermined factory overhead rate under three different bases: (1) direct labor hours, (2) direct labor dollars, and (3) machine hours.

b) Assume actual factory overhead was $268,000 and that management elected to apply factory overhead to Work-in-Process based on direct labor hours. If 32,000 direct labor hours were used in 19x4, determine the amount factory overhead was underapplied or overapplied.

c) The Norcross Company follows a policy of writing off any underapplied or overapplied Factory Overhead to Cost of Goods Sold at the end of the year. Make the entry necessary at the end of 19x4 to dispose of the balance determined in requirement (b).

d) Describe an alternative procedure that might be used to dispose of underapplied or overapplied Factory Overhead.

PROBLEMS

11–11 Job Costing Journal Entries: Predetermined Overhead Rate

Top Drawer Office Equipment manufactures desks, chairs, file cabinets, and similar office products in batches for speculative inventories. Production costs are accounted for using a job cost system. At the beginning of April 19x3 raw materials inventories totaled $8,500, manufacturing supplies amounted to $1,200, and two jobs were in process: Job 522 with assigned costs of $5,640 and Job 523 with assigned costs of $2,400. Finished goods inventories totaled $6,000. The following information summarizes April manufacturing activities.

■ Raw materials costing $25,000 were purchased on account.

■ Manufacturing supplies costing $3,000 were purchased on account.

■ Requisitioned materials needed to complete Job 523. Started two new jobs, 524 and 525, and requisitioned direct materials for them.

Direct materials:	
Job 523	$ 3,400
Job 524	12,500
Job 525	9,600
Total	$25,500

■ April salaries and wages were as follows:

Direct labor:		
Job 522	300 hours × $12/hour	$ 3,600
Job 523	800 hours × $12/hour	9,600
Job 524	1,200 hours × $12/hour	14,400
Job 525	1,000 hours × $12/hour	12,000
Total direct labor		$39,600
Indirect labor		6,400
Total		$46,000

■ Used manufacturing supplies costing $2,250.

■ Depreciation on factory fixed assets totaled $4,000.

■ Miscellaneous factory overhead costs of $5,500 were incurred on account.

■ Factory overhead was applied at the rate of $6 per direct labor hour.

■ Jobs 522, 523, and 524 were completed.

Requirements

a) Prepare summary journal entries to record April 19x3 manufacturing activities. Number all journal entries. (*Hint*: Prepare cost sheets for completed jobs.)

b) Prepare T-accounts for raw materials and work-in-process. Record beginning balances, post April transactions, and determine ending balances in these accounts.

c) Show the job-cost details to support the April 30, 19x3, balance in Work-in-Process.

11–12
A Comprehensive
Financial Accounting
Extension to Problem
11–11

This is a continuation of Problem 11–11. Completion of this problem may require you to review material contained in your financial accounting text and in Chapter 2 of this book.

Presented is a condensed version of Top Drawer Office Equipment's April 1, 19x3, Balance Sheet as well as information regarding administrative, marketing, and financial transactions for the month of April.

Top Drawer Office Equipment
Balance Sheet
As of April 1, 19x3

Cash	$ 12,880
Accounts receivable	125,000
Raw materials	8,500
Manufacturing supplies	1,200
Work-in-process	8,040
Finished goods	6,000
Factory overhead (overapplied)	(500)
Office supplies	1,700
Prepaid office rent	3,600
Net plant equipment	340,000
Total	$506,420
Accounts payable	$ 20,000
Wages payable	21,000
Miscellaneous payables	3,000
Capital stock	400,000
Retained earnings	62,420
Total	$506,420

- Sold finished goods costing $69,000 on account for $120,000.
- Purchased office supplies costing $280 on account.
- Used office supplies costing $350.
- Wages earned by administrative and marketing employees were as follows:

Administrative	$3,800
Selling	8,400

- Miscellaneous expenses were as follows:

Administrative	$ 3,500
Selling	12,390

- Expired prepaid office rent for April amounted to $1,200.
- Paid accounts payable totaling $26,000.
- Paid wages payable of $61,000.
- Paid miscellaneous payables totaling $21,500.
- Collected $130,000 on account.
- Recorded profit or loss for the month in Expense and Revenue Summary and closed account to Retained Earnings.

Requirements

a) Prepare summary journal entries for all additional transactions.

b) Prepare the following financial statements:

  Cost of goods manufactured for the month of April 19x3.

  Income statement for the month of April 19x3.

  Balance sheet as of April 30, 19x3.

(*Hint:* Use previously determined balances for inventory accounts. Determine the effect of posting other journal entries to permanent accounts. Post net effect of all transactions affecting temporary accounts to Retained Earnings.)

11–13 Job Costing Journal Entries: Predetermined Overhead Rate

Neatlawn Mower Company manufactures a variety of gasoline-powered mowers for discount hardware and department stores. Neatlawn uses a job-cost system and treats each customer's order as a separate job.

The primary mower components (motors, chassis, and wheels) are purchased from three different suppliers under long-term contracts that call for the delivery of raw materials as needed directly to the production floor. When a customer's order is received, a raw materials purchase order is electronically placed with suppliers. The purchase order specifies the scheduled date production is to begin on the customer's order as the delivery date for motors and chassis, and the scheduled date production is to be completed as the delivery date for the wheels. As a consequence, there are no raw materials inventories, and raw materials are charged directly to Work-in-Process upon receipt.

Upon completion goods are shipped directly to customers rather than being transferred to finished goods inventory.

At the beginning of July, 19x8, Neatlawn had the following work-in-process inventories.

Job 365	$20,000
Job 366	16,500
Job 367	15,000
Job 368	9,000
Total	$60,500

During July the following activities took place:

- Started Jobs 369, 370, and 371.
- Ordered and received the following raw materials for specified jobs:

Job	Motors	Chassis	Wheels	Total
366	$ 0	$ 0	$ 800	$ 800
367			1,200	1,200
368			1,600	1,600
369	12,000	4,000	1,000	17,000
370	9,000	3,500	900	13,400
371	8,500	3,800		12,300
Total	$29,500	$11,300	$5,500	$46,300

■ July manufacturing payroll is summarized below:

Direct labor:	
Job 365	$ 500
Job 366	3,200
Job 367	3,400
Job 368	4,160
Job 369	1,300
Job 370	2,620
Job 371	2,000
Total	$17,180
Indirect labor	3,436
Total	$20,616

■ Additional July factory overhead costs were:

Manufacturing supplies purchased on account and used	$ 2,800
Depreciation on factory fixed assets	6,000
Miscellaneous payables	5,100
Total	$13,900

■ Factory overhead was applied using a predetermined rate based on predicted annual overhead of $180,000 and predicted annual direct labor of $200,000.

■ Jobs 365 through 370 were completed and shipped.

Requirements

a) Prepare summary journal entries to record July 19x8 manufacturing activities. Number all journal entries. (*Hint:* Prepare cost sheets for completed jobs.)

b) Prepare a T-account for work-in-process. Record the beginning balance, post July transactions, and determine ending balance in this account.

c) Show the job-cost details to support the July 31, 19x8, balance in Work-in-Process.

11–14
A Comprehensive
Financial Accounting
Extension to Problem
11–13

This is a continuation of Problem 11–13. Completion of this problem may require you to review material contained in your financial accounting text and in Chapter 2 of this book.

Presented is a condensed version of Neatlawn Mower Company's July 1, 19x8, Balance Sheet as well as information regarding administrative, marketing, and financial transactions for the month of April.

■ Sold finished goods on account for $175,000.

■ Purchased office supplies costing $300 on account.

■ Used office supplies costing $290.

Neatlawn Mower Company
Balance Sheet
As of July 1, 19x8

Cash	$ 21,900
Accounts receivable	80,000
Work-in-process	60,500
Factory overhead (underapplied)	1,200
Office supplies	950
Net plant and equipment	280,000
Net office and equipment	190,000
Total	$634,550
Accounts payable	$ 47,000
Wages payable	14,000
Miscellaneous payables	6,500
Capital stock	350,000
Retained earnings	217,050
Total	$634,550

- Wages earned by administrative and marketing employees were as follows:

  Administrative $4,900

  Selling   2,500

- Recorded depreciation of $4,000 on office and equipment.
- Miscellaneous expenses were as follows:

  Administrative $2,750

  Selling   5,800

- Paid accounts payable totaling $51,000.
- Paid wages payable of $41,000.
- Paid miscellaneous payables totaling $8,000.
- Collected $190,000 on account.
- Recorded profit or loss for the month in Expense and Revenue Summary and closed account to Retained Earnings.

Requirements

a) Prepare summary journal entries for all additional transactions.

b) Prepare the following financial statements:

  Cost of goods manufactured for the month of July 19x8.

  Income statement for the month of July 19x8.

  Balance sheet as of July 31, 19x8.

(*Hint:* Use previously determined balances for inventory accounts. Determine the effect of posting other journal entries to permanent accounts. Post net effect of all transactions affecting temporary accounts to Retained Earnings.)

11–15 Production Planning and Job Costing with Multiple Cost Centers

Adirondack Cedar Products manufactures wooden furniture in three production operations: sawing/beveling, drilling, and assembling/sanding. Each operation is treated as a cost center with a combined predetermined conversion rate for direct labor and overhead. Presented are bills of materials and operations lists for two styles of wooden bookcases, standard and deluxe, produced by the firm:

Bill of Materials

Product: Standard bookcase
Product number: 201

Part	Quantity
1-inch cedar	26 board feet
$1\frac{1}{2}$-inch screw	24

Bill of Materials

Product: Deluxe bookcase
Product number: 202

Part	Quantity
1-inch cedar	55 board feet
$\frac{1}{4}$-inch cedar	20 board feet
brackets	2 sets
handle	2
$1\frac{1}{2}$-inch screw	40

Operations List

Product: Standard bookcase
Product number: 201

Operation	Operating Time
Saw	5 minutes
Drill	5 minutes
Assemble/sand	20 minutes

Operations List

Product: Deluxe bookcase
Product number: 202

Operation	Operating Time
Saw/bevel	20 minutes
Drill	10 minutes
Assemble/sand	30 minutes

Cost information is as folows:

1-inch cedar	$ 0.50 per board foot
$\frac{1}{4}$-inch cedar	0.20 per board foot
$1\frac{1}{2}$-inch screws	0.015 each
Brackets	0.75 per set
Handles	0.25 each
Sawing/beveling conversion rate	24.00 per hour
Drilling conversion rate	15.00 per hour
Assembling/sanding conversion rate	10.00 per hour

Requirements

a) Prepare a production order, including start and stop times, for the manufacture of 20 deluxe bookcases. Production is to begin at 10:00 AM on Tuesday, April 4, 19x4, and continue during normal business hours until completed. Units are not to be passed from saw/bevel until 75 percent of the units are completed. At that time units will be passed directly from one operation to the next as they are completed. Normal business hours are 8:00 AM to 12:00 PM and 1:00 PM to 5:00 PM. Identify the production order as Job 387.

b) Prepare materials requisitions for Job 387. All wood is added at the start of operations in sawing/beveling, and all other parts are added during assembly/sanding. The next materials requisition is number 1,093.

c) Prepare work tickets for Job 387 assuming operations proceed exactly according to plan. The next work ticket is number 2,413.

d) Prepare a cost sheet for Job 387.

e) Prepare all journal entries to assign costs to Job 387 as it passes from one operation to the next and as it is completed.

f) Using T-accounts for inventory and conversion cost accounts, prepare a diagram illustrating the flow of costs through the cost system.

g) Evaluate Adirondack Cedar Products' cost system. Is it appropriate for the firm's product mix and production operations? Suggest any specific changes that might result in more accurate product costs. Suggest any simplifications that might be implemented without reducing the accuracy of cost information.

11–16 Actual and Predetermined Overhead Rates

Note: Predetermined overhead rates are used throughout the chapter. An alternative is to accumulate actual overhead costs for the period in Factory Overhead Control and apply actual costs at the close of the period to all jobs in process during the period.

Al's Job Shop started operations on January 1, 19x2. During the month the following events occurred:

- Materials costing $8,000 were purchased on account.

- Direct materials costing $3,000 were placed in process.

- A total of 400 direct labor hours were charged to individual jobs at a rate of $6 per hour.

- Overhead costs for the month of January were as follows:

Depreciation on plant and equipment	$ 500
Indirect labor	1,500
Utilities	600
Property taxes on plant	650
Insurance on plant	550

- Only one job, B42, with materials costs of $600, direct labor charges of $300 for 50 direct labor hours, and applied overhead, was in process on January 31.

The plant and equipment were purchased before operations began. The insurance was prepaid. All other costs will be paid during the following month.

Requirements

a) Assuming Al's Job Shop assigned actual monthly overhead costs to jobs on the basis of actual monthly direct labor hours, prepare summary journal entries for the month of January.

b) Assuming Al's Job Shop uses a predetermined overhead rate of $10 per direct labor hour, prepare summary journal entries for the month of January. Describe the appropriate treatment of any overapplied or underapplied overhead for the month of January.

c) Review the overhead items and classify each as fixed or variable in relation to direct labor hours. Next, predict the actual overhead rates for months when 200 and 1,000 direct labor hours are used. Assuming jobs similar to B42 were in process at the end of each month, determine the costs assigned to these jobs. (*Hint:* Determine a variable overhead rate.)

d) Why do you suppose predetermined overhead rates are preferred to actual overhead rates?

11–17 Plantwide and Departmental Overhead Rates: Cross-Subsidization

Gauche Company manufactures two products, A and B, and incurs overhead costs in two production departments, I and II. The equations for annual overhead costs in each production department are as follows:

Department I overhead = $400,000 + $20 per machine hour
Department II overhead = $400,000 + $50 per machine hour

Each unit of product A requires 2 machine hours in Department I and 3 hours in Department II. Each unit of product B requires 7.5 hours in Department I and 1.25 hours in Department II. During 19x8, 50,000 units of A and 40,000 units of B were produced.

Requirements

a) Use the information on resource consumption for each product and the equations for total overhead to determine the total 19x8 overhead costs in each production department.

b) Assuming departmental overhead rates based on machine hours are used, determine the total overhead costs assigned to each product and to each unit of products A and B.

c) Assuming a plantwide overhead rate based on machine hours is used, determine the total overhead costs assigned to each product and to each unit of products A and B.

d) Determine the cross-subsidization involved in using a plantwide rate for each product and each unit of products A and B.

e) Mention several erroneous decisions management may make if costs are assigned using the plantwide rate.

11–18 Plantwide and Departmental Overhead Rates: Cross-Subsidization

Droit Company manufactures two products, Alpha and Beta, and incurs overhead costs in two departments, purchasing and manufacturing. The equations for annual overhead costs in each department are as follows:

Purchasing overhead = $72,000 + $0.10 per dollar of raw materials issued
Manufacturing overhead = $500,000 + $4 per labor hour

Each unit of Alpha requires raw materials costing $20 and four labor hours. Each unit of Beta requires raw materials costing $80 and two labor hours. During 19x9, 10,000 units of Alpha and 20,000 units of Beta were produced.

Requirements

a) Use the information on resource consumption for each product and the equations for total overhead to determine the total 19x9 overhead costs in the purchasing and manufacturing departments.

b) Assume that purchasing used a departmental overhead rate based on the dollar value of raw materials issued and that manufacturing uses an overhead rate based on labor hours, determine the total overhead costs assigned to each product and to each unit of products Alpha and Beta.

c) Assuming a plantwide overhead rate based on labor hours is used, determine the total overhead costs assigned to each product and to each unit of products Alpha and Beta.

d) Determine the cross-subsidization involved in using a plantwide rate for each product and each unit of products Alpha and Beta.

e) Mention several erroneous decisions management may make if costs are assigned using the plantwide rate.

11–19 Standard Cost Journal Entries (Appendix)

Konrad Company uses a standard cost system in accounting for the production of its only product, a gadget called "de-slicer" that attaches to golf clubs to help golfers hit the ball straighter. The standard cost of producing one de-slicer is $7.65. During a recent month the following activities occurred:

- Raw materials with a standard cost of $73,000 were purchased for $75,000.
- Twenty thousand units were completed.
- Eighteen thousand-five hundred units were sold.

At the end of the month, actual manufacturing activities were summarized as follows:

- Actual raw materials issued to processing had a standard cost of $71,000. There was an unfavorable materials quantity variance of $2,000.
- The direct labor flexible budget for the units produced during the period was $50,000, whereas actual direct labor was $47,500. The difference is explained by an unfavorable labor rate variance of $800 and a favorable labor efficiency variance of $3,300.
- Actual factory overhead was $38,000, and the flexible budget factory overhead for the units produced was $35,000. The difference is explained by the following factory overhead standard cost variances:

Variable overhead spending variance	$1,200 U
Variable overhead efficiency variance	1,100 F
Fixed overhead budget variance	1,400 F
Fixed overhead volume variance	4,300 U

Required: Prepare standard cost journal entries to record (1) the purchase of raw materials; (2) the completion of finished goods; (3) the sale of finished goods; and (4) actual and standard costs for direct materials used, direct labor, and factory overhead.

11–20 Standard Cost Journal Entries (Appendix)

The Greenwich Clock Company manufactures clocks with movements purchased from a Swiss company and housings purchased from a British company. The standard cost per finished unit of model AJ9 is $40:

Movement	$15
Housing	10
Labor (0.5 hours × $16 per labor hour)	8
Applied variable overhead	
(per completed unit)	4
Applied fixed overhead	
(per completed unit)	3
Total	$40

During a recent month the following activities related to the production of model AJ9 occurred:

- Purchased 2,200 movements for $31,200 and 3,000 housings for $32,500.
- Three thousand units were completed.
- Twenty-nine hundred units were sold.

At the end of the month, actual manufacturing activities were summarized as follows:

- Actual raw materials issued to production consisted of 3,000 movements and 3,050 housings.
- Actual direct labor costs consisted of 1,450 hours at $16 per hour.
- Actual variable overhead was $14,000.
- Budgeted fixed overhead was $8,500 and actual fixed overhead was $10,000.

Required: Prepare standard cost journal entries to record (1) the purchase of raw materials; (2) the completion of finished goods; (3) the sale of finished goods; and (4) actual and standard costs for direct materials used, direct labor, variable factory overhead, and fixed factory overhead. (*Hint:* Because overhead is applied on the basis of units produced there is no variable overhead efficiency variance.)

CASES

11–21 Alternative Treatment of Set-up Costs with Set Market Prices

Good Buddy Electronics is the producer of the popular "Good Buddy" citizens band (CB) radio. Although Good Buddy Electronics was one of the early producers of CB radios, in recent years the profitability of CB radios has declined because of market saturation and foreign price competition. To utilize its production capacity fully, Good Buddy has started producing a variety of consumer electronic appliances to order. This additional business necessitated a change in the firm's accounting system.

When a single product was produced on a continuous basis, product costs were computed as current manufacturing costs divided by the number of units produced. With the expansion of activities to include products made to customer specifications, Good Buddy instituted a job cost system. The system assigns actual direct materials costs to jobs. Because production operations make extensive use of machine assembly operations, direct labor and overhead costs are combined into a single conversion rate per machine operating hour.

Last year Good Buddy produced 100,000 Good Buddy CB radios and 250 other jobs to customer order. These additional jobs averaged 200 units each. Presented is unit selling price and cost information for last year:

	Good Buddy CB Radio	Other Products
Selling price	$90.00	$125.00
Manufacturing costs:		
Direct materials	$60.00	$ 60.00
Conversion	25.20	50.40
Total	−85.20	−110.40
Gross profit	$ 4.80	$ 14.60
Selling and distribution costs	− 2.00	− 2.00
Profit	$ 2.80	$ 12.60

Godfrey (Good Buddy) Beckles, the president, is concerned about the declining profitability of CB radios in comparison with specialty products and is considering a proposal to discontinue the production of CB radios to specialize on other products. Even though other products have a relatively low volume and require additional selling and manufacturing effort, they are more profitable due to the premium prices they command.

Prior to finalizing his recommendation, Mr. Beckles has asked his bright young assistant, you, to take a final look at the situation and prepare a written report by noon tomorrow. You eagerly talk with personnel in sales, accounting, and production, where you acquire the following aditional information.

Additional information:

- CB radios require 0.1 machine operating hours each, and the custom products require an average of 0.2 machine operating hours each.
- All products are produced using similar types of equipment that have similar original costs and hourly operating costs.
- To avoid excess finished goods inventory levels, CB radios are produced in ten equal size batches throughout the year rather than in one batch of 100,000 units.
- Regardless of the product or the length of the production run, machine set-up time is approximately 20 machine hours per batch.
- Variable operating costs are the same per unit of time regardless of whether machines are operating or being set up.
- Conversion costs are assigned to jobs on the basis of machine operating hours.
- Last year's selling and distribution costs for CB radios included a fixed element of $50,000 and a variable element of $0.50 per unit.
- Selling and distribution costs for other products average $800 per order.

Required: Determine the actual unit profitability of CB radios and other products, and prepare a report recommending whether or not the production of CB radios should be discontinued.

11–22 Plantwide versus Departmental Overhead Rates

When Cornell Products started operation five years ago their only product was a radar detector known as the Bear Detector. The production system was simple, with Bear Detectors manually assembled from purchased components. With no ending work-in-process inventories, unit costs were calculated once a month, dividing current manufacturing costs by units produced.

Last year Cornell Products began to manufacture a second product, named the Lion Tamer. The production of Lion Tamers involved both machine intensive fabrication and assembly.

The introduction of the second product necessitated a change in the firm's simple accounting system. Cornell Products now separately assigns direct materials and direct labor costs to each product using information contained on materials requisitions and work tickets. Factory overhead is accumulated in a single cost pool and assigned on the basis of direct labor hours, which is common to both products.

Presented are last year's financial results by product:

	Bear Detector	Lion Tamer
Sales:		
Units	5,000	2,000
Dollars	$500,000	$300,000
Cost of goods sold:		
Direct materials	$100,000	$ 60,000
Direct labor	150,000	45,000
Applied overhead	270,000	81,000
Total	−520,000	−186,000
Gross profit	$ (20,000)	$114,000

Management is concerned about the mixed nature of last year's financial performance. It appears that the Lion Tamer is a roaring success. The only competition, the Nittney Company, which has been selling a competing product for considerably more than Cornell's Lion Tamer, is in financial difficulty and likely to file for bankruptcy. The management of Cornell Products attributes the Lion Tamer's success to excellent production management.

Management is concerned, however, about the future of the Bear Detector and is likely to discontinue that product unless its profitability can be improved.

Required: You have been asked to evaluate the profitability of Cornell's two products and make any recommendations you feel appropriate. You obtain the following information.

- The labor rate is $15 per hour.
- Cornell has two separate production operations, fabrication and assembly. Bear Detectors undergo only assembly operations. Lion Tamers undergo both fabrication and assembly. Bear Detectors require two assembly hours per unit. Lion Tamers require one fabrication hour and one-half assembly hour per unit.

■ The annual fabricating department overhead cost function is:

$$\$200,000 + \$5 \text{ (labor hours)}.$$

■ The annual assembly department overhead cost function is:

$$\$20,000 + \$11 \text{ (labor hours)}.$$

11–23 Designing a Job Costing System for Heterogeneous Products

The Montana Machine Shop is organized by function: that is, each type of machine or activity is grouped together. The plant layout is presented below:

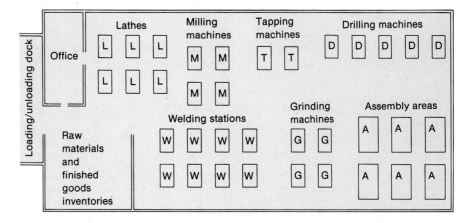

Each rectangle represents a machine or work area. The six lathes operate with little operator assistance once they are set up and a unit of product is loaded. Consequently, there is one operator for every two machines. Each of the four milling, two tapping, five drilling, and four grinding machines has one operator. Each welding station has two operators, and each assembly area has two employees. The welding and assembly operations are labor intensive; all other operations are machine paced. The original cost and the operating costs of each type of machine differ significantly.

The shop produces a variety of metal products for speculative inventory. The products are quite heterogeneous, requiring varying amounts of raw materials and attention in each production operation. Jobs follow a jumbled path from start to finish. Parts of a job, for example, might require work on the lathes and milling machines, followed by welding, drilling, assembly, and then more welding.

Requirements

a) Identify the basic records required to plan and initiate production and to accumulate information for product costing purposes.

b) Describe a cost system that will provide accurate job-cost information for the Montana Machine Shop. Your answer should consider the number and names of cost centers and how materials, labor, and overhead costs are to be assigned to jobs worked on in each cost center. Do not be overly concerned about developing information to evaluate individual machines and their operators. Do be concerned about the cost and complexity of the cost system.

11–24 Designing a Job Costing System for Heterogeneous Products

This is a continuation of Problem 11–23. In an effort to reduce the cycle time between starting and completing a product and work-in-process inventories, the management of the Montana Machine Shop performed a detailed analysis of the firm's products and production procedures. They found that although there was considerable diversity in finished products, all products underwent one of two standard production sequences. At the end of these sequences some products went directly to finished goods inventory, and others underwent some additional welding, grinding, or assembly operations. Basically, the company produced two products, with some units of each undergoing additional manufacturing operations to meet particular product specifications.

Management believed that this information would help them look at their products in a new way. Organizing the factory to produce two primary products would greatly simplify bills of materials, operations lists, and production orders. Other products based on these two products could then have product specifications starting with the appropriate intermediate product. On the factory floor, most operations could be rearranged around the two primary products, rather than by function. What's more, with proper line balancing there would be no need to change machine settings for the machines dedicated to the production of the two primary products. The proposed plant layout is as follows:

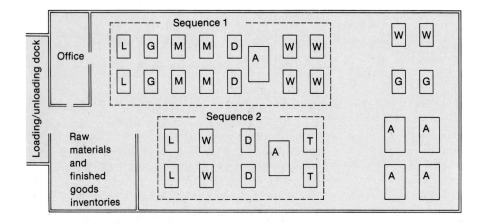

Sequences 1 and 2 refer to the homogeneous set of activities required to produce products 1 and 2. The other operations on the right are used only for products that undergo additional manufacturing activities. Because of increased productivity due to the reduction in the number of machine setups, management was able to eliminate two lathes and one drill press.

Required: Describe how the cost system proposed for Problem 11–23 should be modified. The primary purpose of the system is to provide accurate job cost information. Your answer should consider the number and names of cost centers and how materials, labor, and overhead costs are to be assigned to jobs worked on in each cost center. Do not be overly concerned about developing information to evaluate individual machines and their operators. Do be concerned about the cost and complexity of the cost system.

11–25 Designing a
Job Costing System
for Heterogeneous
Products[3]

Rantoul Tool, Inc., is a medium size producer of custom machine tools. The company's single production facility is located just west of Pittsburgh, Pennsylvania. Last year's sales totaled $93 million. Rantoul's 115 employees include 7 sales representatives, 4 industrial and mechanical engineers, 16 office employees (order entry, accounting, scheduling, secretarial services, and health), 5 corporate officers, and 83 plant employees (supervisors, expediters, machine operators, materials handling, and maintenance).

Rantoul's products are used as manufacturing supplies by large manufacturers. Products vary considerably in their raw materials and manufacturing requirements. Because of competitive pressures, accurate product cost information is required for pricing and cost control.

Until about five years ago, Rantoul's factory contained a total of 35 machines of eight different types, distributed as follows

Type	Number	Type	Number
A	5	E	8
B	6	X	1
C	4	Y	1
D	9	Z	1

The machines differed significantly in their original cost, operating life, power consumption, and maintenance requirements.

Production Flows—Plant Layout: Rantoul's machines were laid out and organized into departments by machine type, with a supervisor in charge of each department. Although each was unique, the three specialty machines (X, Y, and Z) were placed in one department. Hence there was a total of six departments. The layout of the 35 machines is diagramed in Exhibit 11–8. Each department's work area is enclosed in dashed lines.

The firm's products, produced in batches of identical units referred to as a job, were quite heterogeneous. Some required work on only three machines, but others required work on as many as seven machines. Nor was there a consistent flow of work among machines. Some jobs, for example, went from B to D to Z while others went from A to Z to D to C, and so forth.

A work team of one or more employees was asssigned to each machine center. In general, each operator worked on only the machine to which he or she was assigned and only one job at a time. A worker would occasionally help another operator who was having difficulty.

At the start of each morning and afternoon, each department supervisor received information on job assignments for the next four hours. Employees obtained materials for jobs from either the raw materials storage area or the in-process storage area, located as shown in Exhibit 11–8. After performing the required operation, employees placed the job in either the in-process storage area or the inspection/packing/shipping area.

---

[3] Adapted with permission from "Instructional Case: Rantoul Tool, Inc." by Wayne J. Morse, *Issues in Accounting Education 5,* no. 1 (Spring 1990): pp. 78–87. Copyrighted by the American Accounting Association.

EXHIBIT 11–8   Rantoul Tool, Inc.: Original Plant Layout

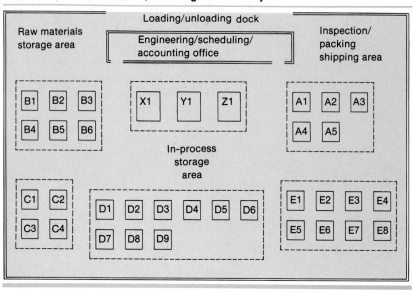

Systems Redesign—Dedicated Production Lines: The production system described above served management well for many years. But beginning in the early 1980s, as competitive pressures increased, management became concerned about the high storage cost of in-process inventories and the amount of time production employees spent on activities that did not add value to the final product.

About seven years ago management instituted a special study of work flows with the goal of reducing in-process inventories and nonvalue added activities. Only activities that physically changed materials were classified as value added. All other activities, including receiving instructions, moving inventories, looking for jobs in the in process storage area, and setting up machines to work on jobs, were classified as nonvalue added.

The study revealed that although the products were quite heterogeneous, approximately 50 percent of the company's products could be placed in one of two homogeneous categories. Products in each of these categories required work on the same types of machines, in the same sequence, and with the same proportion of work time on each machine in the sequence. What's more, the machine settings for products in each category were similar, so virtually no additional set-up time was required in the changeover from one job to another within the same product category.

Management believed that significant improvements in productivity and reductions in inventory could be obtained by changing the plant layout so the jobs in these two homogeneous categories would never enter the in-process storage area. Instead, employees would move the units in each job directly from one machine to the next.

Management anticipated that shorter production times and reduced selling prices, made possible by increased productivity, would result in an increase in sales. Consequently, management elected to maintain the current number of machines. Management also anticipated a reduction in the complexity of machine set-ups and the need to expedite orders. This made possible a reduction in the number of departments and production supervisors from six to five. The new departments were Category 1 products, Category 2 products, Machine Groups B, E, and C, Machine Group D, and Machine Groups X, Z, and A.

The number of machines placed in the first two departments was selected to achieve balanced flows within the departments, given the varying speeds of individual machines. The redesigned plant layout is presented in Exhibit 11–9. Each department's work area is enclosed in dashed lines.

The Flexible Manufacturing System: Rantoul's management was delighted with the results obtained from the plant reorganization. As a result of reduced materials movement and less in-process inventory in storage, manufacturing and storage costs fell and production times decreased. Even more welcome was a decline in the percentage of Category 1 and Category 2 products identified as defective. The increase in quality appeared to result from (1) an increased ability to spot quality problems when there is less inventory to deal with, and (2) the immediate identification of quality problems by subsequent machine operators. The immediate identification of problems facilitated corrective action before many units were spoiled.

Management has now turned its attention to correcting the problem of high set-up costs and in-process inventories of products not in Category 1 or 2. These products are now called Category 3 products. In an attempt to reduce the cost of Category 3 products, management has decided to replace all machines used to manufacture them, installing in their place a flexible manufacturing system (FMS). The lines for Category 1 and Category 2 products will not be changed. As before, each Category 3 product will follow its own production path; each will require its own combination of operations.

EXHIBIT 11–9   Rantoul Tool, Inc.: Redesigned Plant Layout

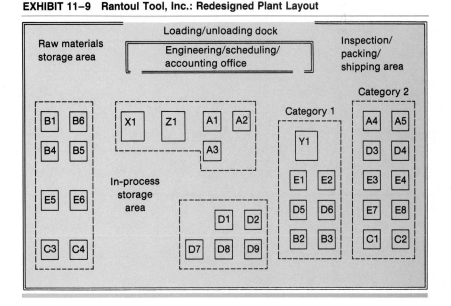

In the new FMS line for Category 3 products, jobs will be subdivided into individual units. Employees will place all materials for each unit on a portable platform. Subsequent movements to appropriate machines and all machine work will be automatic and computer controlled. Because each of the new machines will be highly flexible, labor set-up time will be virtually nil. The work platforms will be of identical size. Each platform will contain coded information about the operations to be performed at each work station and the materials or partially completed units required for those operations. As the platform arrives at a machine, the coded information will be used to verify the job and the specified work will be performed. If materials are misplaced or the coding is incorrect, a call for manual assistance will be sent automatically.

Computers will monitor all operations and keep detailed records on job status and the amount of time each unit spends on each machine. Maintenance employees will continually inspect machines and make needed adjustments. As units are completed, employees will remove the units from the portable platforms, inspect the units, assemble the units by job, and pack the jobs for shipment. The in-process storage area will be eliminated.

The redesigned plant layout, with the FMS line, is presented in Exhibit 11–10. The computer controlled machines in Category 3 are identified as H1 through L1. There is only one machine of each type, and the operating costs of each machine differ significantly. The broad lines around and to the machines represent the computer controlled movement system.

The redesigned factory will have only three production departments for Category 1, 2, and 3 products. The number of direct labor employees will be significantly reduced, but there will be an increase in their responsibilities. Support activities will expand to include two new service departments, computer control and maintenance.

EXHIBIT 11–10   Rantoul Tool, Inc.: Redesigned Plant Layout with a Flexible Manufacturing System

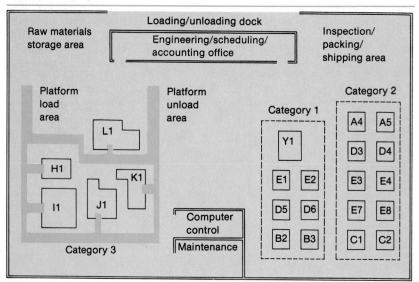

Requirements

1. For a job cost system, identify the basic records required to plan and initiate production and to accumulate information for product costing purposes.

2. Describe a cost system that would have provided accurate job cost information for Rantoul's management when the original plant layout was used. Do not be overly concerned about developing information to evaluate individual machines and their operators. Do be concerned about the cost and complexity of the cost system.

3. Describe a cost system that would have provided accurate cost information for Rantoul's management when it changed its plant layout to accommodate products in Categories 1 and 2.

4. Describe a cost system that will provide accurate product cost information for the new flexible manufacturing system.

REVIEW PROBLEM SOLUTION

a) Journal entries:

1. Raw Materials	40,000	
Accounts Payable		40,000
2. Manufacturing Supplies Inventory	9,000	
Accounts Payable		9,000
3. Work-in-Process	35,000	
Raw Materials		35,000
4. Work-in-Process	48,500	
Factory Overhead	5,000	
Wages Payable		53,500
5. Factory Overhead	19,250	
Manufacturing Supplies Inventory		5,500
Accumulated Depreciation-Factory		5,000
Miscellaneous Payables		8,750
6. Work-in-Process	24,250	
Factory Overhead (4,850 hours × $5)		24,250
7. Finished Goods Inventory	96,900	
Work-in-Process		96,900

	Job 225	Job 226	Job 227	Total
Beginning balance	$13,750	$ 1,800	$ 0	
Current costs:				
Direct Materials	0	2,600	18,000	
Direct Labor	5,000	15,000	20,500	
Factory Overhead	2,500	7,500	10,250	
Total cost	$21,250	$26,900	$48,750	$96,900

8. Cost of Goods Sold	48,150	
Finished Goods Inventory ($21,250 + $26,900)		48,150

b) Accounts:

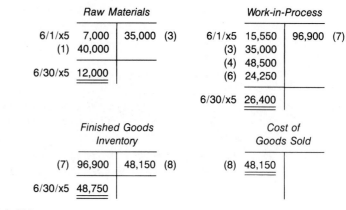

Raw Materials				Work-in-Process			
6/1/x5	7,000	35,000	(3)	6/1/x5	15,550	96,900	(7)
(1)	40,000			(3)	35,000		
				(4)	48,500		
6/30/x5	12,000			(6)	24,250		
				6/30/x5	26,400		

Finished Goods Inventory				Cost of Goods Sold			
(7)	96,900	48,150	(8)	(8)	48,150		
6/30/x5	48,750						

c) Job 228:

Direct materials	$14,400
Direct labor	8,000
Applied overhead (800 × $5)	4,000
Total	$26,400

C H A P T E R   12

Process Costing

Learning Objectives

Upon completion of this chapter you should:

- **Understand the differences between job order and process costing and be able to determine which is most appropriate for a particular costing situation.**

- **Be familiar with the basic procedures used in recording cost data in process costing systems.**

- **Understand how to develop and maintain records and reports using both the weighted average and FIFO methods of process costing.**

- **Be able to prepare journal entries for recording the flow of costs in a process costing system.**

- **Understand the concept of backflush costing as used with process costing applications.**

- **Understand the nature of joint products and by-products and be able to identify related accounting issues (appendix).**

The type of manufacturing process a company uses, combined with the needs of managers, determines the type of costing procedures that should be used. Chapter 11 introduced the manufacturing environment and the important issues currently affecting manufacturing organizations. These issues include the emergence of global competition, the trend toward more diverse product lines, and the trend toward lower inventory levels. Basic product costing records and procedures were also introduced in Chapter 11. This chapter continues with a discussion of manufacturing situations that require costing methods other than job-order.

Recall from Chapter 11 that jobs were defined as products that were produced as single units or in batches of identical units. A coat manufacturer, for instance, may produce gray winter coats in batches. In this case job costing is used to determine the cost of each batch. A chemical manufacturer, on the other hand, may produce a product on a continuous basis rather than in batches. Often the complexity of the chemical process makes it difficult and costly to stop. These types of operations require something other than job costing.

The purpose of this chapter is to examine the environment of continuous manufacturing and processing systems and introduce process costing, the second basic method of determining product costing. Process costing involves the determination of product costs of a homogenous product as units pass continuously from one production operation to another and finally into finished goods. Process costing also involves the allocation of costs between finished and unfinished units of production.

DISTINCTIONS BETWEEN JOB AND PROCESS COSTING

Although the procedures of assigning costs to units are different, both job and process costing are methods of identifying raw materials and conversion costs with products. Job costing, introduced in Chapter 11, is used when unique products are produced, or when products are produced in batches. In job costing, the job is the primary cost objective for which manufacturing costs are accumulated. The job might be a single space satellite or a batch of identical pieces of furniture or clothing. Accordingly, the job is the primary cost objective, and the cost of a particular job is determined from the cost records maintained for that job. If the job consists of a batch of units, the cost of each unit is determined by dividing the total cost of the job by the number of units in the batch. For example, if 20 bookcases are manufactured in a batch at a total cost of $2,000, the cost per bookcase is $100.

Process costing is used when large quantities of a homogeneous product are manufactured through a continuous process. The process might include the production of chemicals, newsprint, or cotton yarn. In process costing systems the manufacturing department is the primary cost objective for which costs are accumulated, and the cost of a single unit is equal to the total accumulated product cost for the department divided by the number of units produced. For example, if a process manufacturing department produces 4,000 gallons of paint during the month at a total cost of $16,000, the cost per gallon is $4.

In process costing, conversion costs (composed of direct labor and factory overhead) are often grouped together. This is because the amount of direct labor and overhead incurred usually parallels the completion of a process.

Time Period

Another important distinction between job and process costing is related to the time period used in accounting for manufacturing costs. In a job cost system, job costs are accumulated on the job cost records and remain in Work-in-Process inventory until the job is completed. Each job is discrete and is not considered completed until all units in the job are finished. The cost of the completed job (and the units in the job) is determined when the job is finished, which will not necessarily coincide with the end of an accounting period. The costs of unfinished jobs are reflected in ending work-in-process inventories.

In a process costing system, the manufacturing process consists of a continuous stream of homogeneous goods entering and leaving the production process. During each accounting period the goods worked on usually consist of three groups: (1) goods started in the previous period and completed in the current period, (2) goods both started and completed in the current period, and (3) goods started but not completed in the current period. In a process cost system, costs are accumulated for each accounting period (for example, week, month, or year) and assigned to the units produced during the period. Since some goods are only partially processed during the period, it is necessary to determine the total production for the period in terms of the equivalent number of completed units. For example, if 200 units were started and completed through 50 percent of the process during the period, then the equivalent of 100 fully completed units was produced. The total number of equivalent units is divided into the total costs for the period to determine the average cost per unit.

To summarize, in a job cost system, costs are accumulated separately for each job, and unit production cost is determined when each job is completed. In process costing, manufacturing costs are accumulated for each cost center, and average unit costs are determined each accounting period.

Manufacturing Environment

As companies change their inventory and production control systems through the use of modern management techniques, costing procedures should be evaluated and changed if they are no longer appropriate. Materials requirements planning (MRP), a very popular approach for manufacturing management, is a system that ties inventories to production scheduling on the basis of planned outputs. An MRP system establishes needs in reverse, going from output needs to production needs to raw materials (also subassembly) inventory needs to purchasing needs. It also determines the time and place that everything is needed.

As these new systems are implemented, managers realize the need to improve the timeliness of inventory movements, including movements both to the company and within the company. From these needs various applications of just-in-time (JIT) inventory systems are implemented. Just-in-time inventory management stresses the minimization of inventories by scheduling the arrival of the inventories (or subassemblies) at the warehouse or work station just as they are needed. JIT goes beyond MRP. Although MRP tries to ensure materials will be available when needed, JIT (recognizing the costs of holding

MANAGERIAL PRACTICE 12.1

Increasing Efficiency with MRP

The AccuRate Division of Moksnes Manufacturing Co. has successfully implemented a materials requirement planning (MRP) system to reduce inventory shortages and increase the efficiency of production. AccuRate produces dry-product processing feeders. Dry feeders are used to feed pills into bottles, chocolate chips into cookie mix, or chemicals into municipal water systems. To meet the increasing demand for their product, AccuRate had to increase its number of employees 94 percent and quadruple its parts requirements in the three-year period between 1983 and 1986. This rapid growth resulted in the need for a new system for inventory planning and control and for production scheduling.

The MRP system at AccuRate breaks down the master schedule into what components are needed to meet production and when those components will be needed to meet the production schedule. "Traditional inventory systems, such as order point, answer such questions as what and how much. MRP adds a time-phasing dimension to purchase ordering." MRP also facilitates improved vendor quality and delivery performance. Long-term vendor agreements can be established, and then the MRP system can be used to issue weekly updates on projected production requirements. MRP has resulted in a 10 percent decrease in inventory for AccuRate, while sales have increased 45 percent. Although MRP cannot be used by all industries, it has played a key role in the success of AccuRate.

Source: Joseph R. Biggs and Ellen J. Long, "Gaining the Competitive Edge with MRP/MRP II," *Management Accounting* (May 1988): 27–32.

excess inventory) attempts to prevent inventory from becoming available before it is needed. Particularly for internal transfers, it requires the movement of items in very small batches, or possibly in a continuous flow from one work station to another. Chapter 14 contains a detailed discussion of JIT inventory management.

Efforts to control work-in-process inventories have led to a reorganization of manufacturing operation away from making batches and the movement of products in batches toward the organization of machines around products and the continuous production of homogeneous products. This creates costing characteristics more similar to process costing than to job costing. Converting to process costing saves accounting costs through the reduction in paperwork as job cards and records are eliminated. Because most process costing systems are easier and less expensive to operate than job costing systems, management should convert from job-order to process costing whenever production changes from batch to continuous processing.

MANAGERIAL PRACTICE 12.2

Counting on Suppliers for Just-in-Time Inventory Management

To obtain suppliers for just-in-time (JIT) inventory management systems, a company must have confidence not only in the suppliers' ability to deliver, but also in their long-term viability. Many times, a company wants to see a supplier's financial statements and make its own analysis about the financial condition of the supplier.

General Motors' evaluation of a supplier begins with the supplier's completing a self-assessment form that asks about operating philosophy, business systems, and research and development and overhead costs, to list just a few items. An evaluation team from GM then visits the supplier and examines its organizational effectiveness, planning systems, cost awareness, scheduling and delivery systems, and technology capabilities. An additional purpose of this review is to improve communication between the companies once GM accepts a given supplier.

Source: Marybeth Pallas, "GM's Evaluation Procedure," *Harvard Business Review* (July–August 1989): 130.

PROCESS COSTING WITHOUT
BEGINNING INVENTORIES

In a process cost system, costs are typically accumulated at the department level. If, however, two or more processes are performed within a department, it may be desirable to have two or more cost centers. The costs accumulated for each center should relate to a single process.

Recall from Chapter 11 how the cost sheets are used to collect cost information in a job costing system. Cost collection is much simpler in a process costing system because each department's production is treated as if it were the one job worked on during the period. In a department that has only one manufacturing process, process costing is particularly simple because the Work-in-Process account is, in fact, the departmental cost record. Where a department has more than one manufacturing process, separate records should be maintained for each process.

To illustrate process costing, let us assume Micro Systems Co. began business on June 1, 19x3, to manufacture memory chips for microcomputers. Sophisticated machinery was purchased for manufacturing the chips in a one-step process. Each finished unit requires that one unit of raw materials be added at the beginning of the manufacturing process. The production and cost data for the first month of operations for Micro Systems are as follows:

June Production Data	Units
Units in process, beginning of period	0
Units started	20,000
Completed and transferred to finished goods	16,000
Units in process, end of period (75% converted)	4,000

June Cost Data		Dollars
Purchases of raw materials (21,000 units × $4)		$ 84,000
Raw materials transferred to processing		$ 80,000
Conversion costs:		
Direct labor for June	$38,000	
Factory overhead applied	19,000	57,000
Current manufacturing costs		$137,000

The key to mastering process costing is understanding the cost of production report, which summarizes unit and cost data for each department. It consists of the following sections:

- Summary of units in process.
- Equivalent units.
- Total cost to be accounted for and cost per equivalent unit.
- Accounting for total cost.

EXHIBIT 12–1   Process Costing without Beginning Inventories

Micro Systems Co.
Cost of Production Report
For the month ended June 30, 19x3

Summary of units in process

Beginning	0
Units started	20,000
In process	20,000
Completed	−16,000
Ending	4,000

Equivalent units in process	*Materials*	*Conversion*
Units completed	16,000	16,000
Plus: equivalent units in ending inventory	4,000	3,000*
Equivalent units in process	20,000	19,000

Total cost to be accounted for and *cost per equivalent unit in process*	*Materials*	*Conversion*	*Total*
Work-in-Process, beginning	$ 0	$ 0	$ 0
Current cost	80,000	57,000**	137,000
Total cost in process	$80,000	$57,000	$137,000
Equivalent units in process	÷20,000	÷19,000	
Cost per equivalent unit in process	$ 4	$ 3	$ 7

Accounting for total cost

Transferred out (16,000 × $7)		$112,000
Work-in-Process, ending:		
Materials (4,000 × $4)	$16,000	
Conversion (3,000 × $3)	9,000	25,000
Total cost accounted for		$137,000

---

* 4,000 units 75% converted.

** Includes direct labor of $38,000 and applied factory overhead of $19,000.

The cost of production report for Micro Systems Co. is shown in Exhibit 12–1 and its four sections are discussed below.

Summary of Units in Process

This section of the report provides a summary of all units in the department during the period. Units in process at the beginning of the period plus units started equals the total units in process during the period. Units in process during the period were either completed or still on hand at the end of the period.[1]

---

[1] In some processes units may be lost through spoilage or pilferage. These special situations are introduced in a subsequent example and covered in detail in advanced courses in cost accounting.

All units are treated the same in this section regardless of the amount of processing that took place on them during the period. The objective is to account for all the discrete units of product in process during the period. Note in Exhibit 12–1 that 20,000 individual units were in process during the period, 16,000 units were completed, and 4,000 units were still in process at the end of the period.

Equivalent Units

In this section of the cost of production report, the objective is to translate the number of units in process during the period into equivalent completed units. Equivalent completed units represents the number of completed units that is equal, in terms of production inputs, to a given number of partially completed units. For example, 80 units 50 percent completed in terms of processing costs are the equivalent of 40 completed units (80 × 0.50). Micro Systems Co. adds all materials at the beginning of the process, and all conversion costs—direct labor and factory overhead—are added evenly throughout the manufacturing process. Therefore, separate computations must be made for equivalent units of *materials* and equivalent units of *conversion*. Although the department worked on 20,000 units during the period, the total number of equivalent units completed with respect to conversion was only 19,000 units, 16,000 finished units plus 3,000 equivalent units (4,000 units 75 percent converted). All 20,000 units (16,000 finished and 4,000 in process) were completed with respect to materials.

It is often helpful to examine the physical flow of the units in equation form, especially when beginning and ending inventories exist. To ensure that all units have been accounted for, the following physical-flow equation can be used when there are no beginning inventories:

$$\text{EU in process} = \text{Units completed} + \text{EU in ending inventory},$$

where EU is equivalent units.

For materials of Micro Systems the equation would be

$$\text{EU materials in process} = 16,000 + 4,000$$
$$= 20,000,$$

and for conversion the equation would be

$$\text{EU conversion in process} = 16,000 + 3,000$$
$$= 19,000.$$

Total Cost to be Accounted for and Cost per Equivalent Unit

This section of the report summarizes the total cost assigned to the department during the period. The disposition of total cost is summarized in the next section of the report. Since there were no units in process at the beginning of the period, the only production cost that Micro Systems Co. had to account for during June was the current period's cost. Therefore, to compute the average cost per equivalent unit, the total cost charged to the department is divided by the equivalent units worked on during the period. Because the number of equivalent units in process differs for materials and conversion, separate computations of units cost are made for these cost components. The total cost per equivalent unit in process during the period is determined by adding together the unit materials and conversion costs.

Accounting for Total Cost

This section shows the disposition of the total cost charged to the department during the period. The general rule in assigning cost to units of production is that product costs follow the units worked on. Therefore the total cost to be accounted for is assigned to two groups of units: (1) the units completed during the period and (2) the units in process at the end of the period. The 16,000 units finished during the period are completed with respect to materials and conversion; hence, their total cost is $7 per unit—the unit materials cost of $4 plus the unit conversion cost of $3. The 4,000 units in ending work-in-process are assigned a full equivalent unit of cost for materials, or $4 per unit. However, for conversion costs only 3,000 equivalent units are assigned to ending Work-in-Process because the 4,000 units in process have gone through only 75 percent of the conversion (or manufacturing) process. Processing will be completed on these units in a subsequent period. As suggested by the arrow in Exhibit 12–1, the total costs accounted for should equal the total costs in process.

Like equivalent units, it is also important to understand the cost flows of the production cycle. The first illustration of Micro Systems is relatively simple because it does not include beginning inventories. However, as inventories are added, the cost flows can become difficult to follow. The basic equation is

$$\text{Total cost to be accounted for} = \text{Total cost accounted for,}$$

or

$$\begin{array}{c}\text{Beginning work-} \\ \text{in-process}\end{array} + \begin{array}{c}\text{Current manu-} \\ \text{facturing cost}\end{array} = \begin{array}{c}\text{Cost of goods} \\ \text{manufactured} \\ \text{(or transferred)}\end{array} + \begin{array}{c}\text{Ending work-} \\ \text{in-process.}\end{array}$$

For Micro Systems the equation would be

$$\$0 + \$137,000 = \$112,000 + \$25,000$$
$$\$137,000 = \$137,000.$$

Journal Entries

The cost of production report summarizes the manufacturing costs assigned to Work-in-Process during the period and provides information for preparing the journal entry to record the cost of goods completed and transferred to finished goods inventory (or to another department) during the period. The journal entries and the supporting documents to record the assignment of costs to Work-in-Process are essentially the same as those discussed for job costing. Summary June 19x3 journal entries for Micro Systems Co. are as follows:

Journal entries	(1) Raw Materials	84,000	
	Accounts Payable		84,000
	To record cost of raw material purchases.		
	(2) Work-in-Process	80,000	
	Raw Materials		80,000
	To record materials requisitioned to factory.		
	(3) Work-in-Process	38,000	
	Wages Payable		38,000
	To record wages for the period.		
	(4) Work-in-Process	19,000	
	Factory Overhead		19,000
	To apply factory overhead.		
	(5) Finished Goods Inventory	112,000	
	Work-in-Process		112,000
	To record transfer of completed units to finished goods.		

After the above entries have been made the Work-in-Process account appears as follows:

Work-in-Process

(2) Direct materials	80,000	112,000	(5)	To Finished Goods Inventory
(3) Direct labor	38,000			
(4) Factory overhead	19,000			
Ending Balance	25,000			

Note in Exhibit 12–1 that the $112,000 assigned to 16,000 units transferred out is equal to the amount credited to Work-in-Process for costs transferred to Finished Goods Inventory. Also, the $25,000 balance in Work-in-Process is equal to the amount assigned to ending work-in-process on the cost of production report.

Process Costing With Backflush Journal Entries

Many manufacturing firms have all but eliminated work-in-process inventories by using the just-in-time approach to inventory management, thereby making the assignment of costs to ending Work-in-Process of little concern. This has allowed firms to simplify their accounting systems by implementing backflush costing systems that use production outputs as the starting point and assign costs throughout the system after the process is completed. The initialization of the backflush entries begins either at the completion of the finished goods or at the point of sale, with several variations as to how the entries are made.

Another difference between backflush costing and the traditional journal entry methods is the combining of Raw Materials and the Work-in-Process inventory accounts into a single account, "Raw Materials-in-Process." This eliminates the need to make an entry transferring costs from Raw Materials to Work-in-Process. And instead of transferring labor and overhead costs to the Work-in-Process account, these costs are entered into a new account labeled "Conversion Costs." Therefore, the Work-in-Process account, now merged into the new account, Raw Materials-in-Process, contains only materials.

Backflush costing entries can be illustrated using items from Micro Systems' June 19x3 production data and the related Cost of Production Report, Exhibit 12–1. Although this example is for the first month of operation for Micro Systems, it could be a typical illustration for a company that has extensive use of JIT inventory systems and ends many of its accounting periods with little or no inventory except finished goods. The journal entries using backflush costing for June 19x3 are as follows:

**Journal
entries**

(1)	Raw Materials-in-Process	84,000	
	Accounts Payable		84,000
	To record cost of raw material purchases.		
(2)	Conversion Costs	38,000	
	Wages Payable		38,000
	To record wages for the period.		
(3)	Conversion Costs	19,000	
	Factory Overhead		19,000
	To apply factory overhead.		
(4)	Finished Goods Inventory	121,000	
	Raw Materials-in-Process (16,000 × $4)		64,000
	Conversion Costs ($38,000 + $19,000)		57,000
	To record transfer of completed units to finished goods.		

MANAGERIAL PRACTICE 12.3

In Support of Backflush Accounting

Paul Danesi of Texas Instruments wrote a letter in defense of backflush accounting in response to an article entitled "Beware the New Accounting Myths" (*Management Accounting*, December 1989). A backflush costing system begins with the outputs of a firm and then works in reverse to allocate costs between cost of goods sold and inventory. Danesi proposes, "Backflush accounting is one attempt by [accounting] to gain relevance with the manufacturing organization. There is no question that it is breaking new ground and has discontinuity with past practice, but I am convinced that it allows the JIT productivity gain to be realized in the control/MIS organizations and therefore provides a competitive edge in indirect productivity and asset management."

Source: Paul Danesi, letter to the editor, *Management Accounting* (February 1990): 8.

After the preceding entries have been made, the Raw Materials-in-Process account appears as follows:

Raw Materials-in-Process

(1) Direct materials	84,000	64,000	(4) To Finished Goods Inventory
Ending balance*	20,000		

---

* The $20,000 includes $16,000 of materials in production (4,000 units × $4) and $4,000 of materials that are unused (1,000 units × $4).

The $64,000 credit to Raw Materials-in-Process can be computed either by multiplying the output by the cost per unit shown on the Cost of Production Report (16,000 units × $4) or by subtracting the ending inventory from the total amount of materials available ($84,000 − (5,000 units × $4)).

Note the difference between the cost of the finished goods with this method and that previously presented. The above journal entry debited Finished Goods Inventory with $121,000; the traditional methods debited only $112,000. The $9,000 difference is the amount shown in Exhibit 12–1 as the conversion cost of the ending Work-in-Process inventory. Backflush costing normally charges all conversion costs to the finished goods, entry (4) above.

Although backflush costing concepts reduce paperwork and eliminate many details of product costing, it has limitations. The most critical limitation is the length of the processing time from raw materials to finished goods. This costing technique is appropriate only for very short processing times, preferably one day or less, with a week usually being the outside limit. For manufacturing processes that take several days or weeks, the backflushing techniques may significantly understate Raw Materials-in-Process inventories, and users must be careful to analyze possible differences. This is because the conversion costs are considered to be consumed in their entirety, and only raw materials in process are carried forward to the next reporting period. In this particular example for Micro Systems, the ending in-process inventory represents about six days. This is near the outside acceptable limit, so the differences between the traditional and backflush costing should be evaluated. Backflush costing assigned $20,000 rather than $25,000 to the ending in-process inventories. Although 20 percent [($25,000 − $20,000)/$25,000] is a significant amount of the ending in-process inventories, the $5,000 amounts to less than 4 percent ($5,000/$137,000) of the total manufacturing costs shown in Exhibit 12-1. If management considers this difference to be typical for most months, and the procedure cost effective, Micro Systems may choose to use backflush costing on a permanent basis.

Another limitation to backflush costing is its possible use for external reporting. Total in-process inventories for external reporting must include appropriate direct materials, direct labor, and overhead. Backflush costing does not include the direct labor and overhead items. However, if these items are immaterial in relation to total production costs and other inventory amounts, they may be excluded from the ending in-process inventories, making it possible to use backflush costing for external reporting purposes.

PROCESS COSTING WITH BEGINNING INVENTORIES

Because the previous examples considered Micro Systems' first month of operation, there were no beginning inventories. Let us continue the example into July of 19x3, the second month of operations, to illustrate costing procedures for both beginning and ending inventories. The pertinent information for July 19x3 is summarized below.

July Production Data	Units
Units in process, beginning of period (75% converted)	4,000
Units started	36,000
Completed and transferred to finished goods	35,000
Units in process, end of period (20% converted)	5,000

July Cost Data		Dollars
Beginning costs:		
Materials		$ 16,000
Conversion		9,000
Total		$ 25,000
Purchases of raw materials (36,250 × $4)		$145,000
Raw materials transferred to processing (36,900 × $4)*		$147,600
Conversion costs:		
Direct labor for July	$62,200	
Factory overhead applied	46,700	108,900
Current manufacturing costs		$256,500

*All materials are added at the start of the production process. Hence, during July, when 36,000 units were started, it is reasonable to expect that 36,000 units of raw materials would be issued to the factory. However, the identification of defective raw materials and quality control problems required the issuance of an additional 900 units.

Whenever partially completed units in beginning Work-in-Process inventory are carried forward from the previous period, the cost of these equivalent units is likely to be different from the cost of equivalent units processed in the current period. For costing purposes using traditional methods, it is necessary to either (1) average the total costs of beginning inventory and current production over the total equivalent units in process, or (2) make a cost flow assumption, such as FIFO (first-in, first-out), about the beginning inventory equivalent units and current production units. However, if backflush costing is used, it is assumed that beginning and ending work-in-process inventories are negligible. Hence all conversion costs are assigned to units completed during the current period, and the cost flow assumptions pertain only to raw materials.

**Weighted Average
Process Costing**

In the weighted average inventory method, the costs of partially completed units in beginning work-in-process are combined with current manufacturing costs, and the total is assigned on an average basis to all equivalent units in process during the period. In this context, "in process" means being physically located in the production department at some time during the period. The weighted average method, is shown in Exhibit 12–2. Note that the equivalent units of 40,000 for materials and 36,000 for conversion are called *equivalent units in process*. These amounts include the number of equivalent units in process during the period—partially completed units in beginning inventory plus equivalent units of work performed during the current period. Similarly, the cost computations of $163,600 and $117,900 are called *total costs in process* and include beginning Work-in-Process plus current manufacturing costs.

Micro Systems' cost of production report for July, prepared under the weighted average method, is shown in Exhibit 12–2. Note that the equivalent units of 40,000 for materials and 36,000 for conversion are called equivalent units in process. These amounts include the number of equivalent units in process during the period—partially completed units in beginning inventory plus equivalent units of work performed during the current period. Similarly, the cost computations of $163,600 and $117,900 are called *total costs in process* and include beginning Work-in-Process plus current manufacturing costs.

Consequently, the unit cost figures represent the costs per equivalent unit in process. Note that although all materials were purchased for $4.00 per unit, the cost per equivalent unit in process is $4.09. This happened because the existence of defective raw materials and other quality problems during the production process required the issuance of additional raw materials. The total unit cost of $7.365 ($4.09 + $3.275) is assigned to all units transferred out during the period, whether they were started in the previous period or in the current period.

Equations like those of the previous section are also used to account for the unit and cost flows when beginning inventories exist. For the physical flows, the equation is

$$\text{EU in process} = \text{Units completed} + \text{EU in ending inventory.}$$

The materials equation for Exhibit 12–2 is

$$\text{EU materials in process} = 35,000 + 5,000$$
$$= 40,000.$$

The equation for the equivalent units of conversion for Exhibit 12–2 is

$$\text{EU for conversion} = 35,000 + 1,000$$
$$= 36,000.$$

The equation for *total costs to be accounted for* and *total cost accounted for* is

$$\text{Beginning work-in-process} + \text{Current manufacturing cost} = \text{Cost of goods manufactured} + \text{Ending work-in-process.}$$

EXHIBIT 12–2   Weighted Average Process Costing with Beginning Inventories

Micro Systems Co.
Cost of Production Report
For the month ended July 31, 19x3

Summary of units in process

Beginning	4,000
Units started	36,000
In process	40,000
Completed	−35,000
Ending	5,000

Equivalent units in process	*Materials*	*Conversion*	
Units completed	35,000	35,000	
Plus: equivalent units in ending inventory	5,000	1,000*	
Equivalent units in process	40,000	36,000	

Total cost to be accounted for and cost per equivalent unit in process	*Materials*	*Conversion*	*Total*
Work-in-Process, beginning	$ 16,000	$ 9,000	$ 25,000
Current cost	147,600	108,900†	256,500
Total cost in process	$163,600	$117,900	$281,500
Equivalent units in process	÷ 40,000	÷ 36,000	
Cost per equivalent unit in process	$ 4.09	$ 3.275	$ 7.365

Accounting for total cost			
Transferred out (35,000 × $7.365)			$257,775
Work-in-Process, ending:			
Materials (5,000 × $4.09)		$ 20,450	
Conversion (1,000 × $3.275)		3,275	23,725
Total cost accounted for			$281,500

---

* 5,000 units 20% converted.
† Includes direct labor of $62,200 and applied factory overhead of $46,700.

The cost equation for the illustration in Exhibit 12–2 for Micro Systems is

$$\$25,000 + \$256,500 = \$257,775 + \$23,725$$
$$\$281,500 = \$281,500.$$

FIFO Process Costing

Under the FIFO inventory method of process costing, partially completed units held at the beginning of the period are not combined with currently produced units for costing purposes. Instead, the units in beginning inventory are costed as a separate group consisting of two components—the portion processed in the previous period is assigned the unit costs for that period, and the portion processed in the current period is assigned the current period's unit costs. For example, assume a company using the FIFO method had unit conversion costs of $5 in June and $6 in July and had one unit of inventory 60 percent converted at the end of June. In July when the unit is completed, the conversion cost assigned to that unit would be $5.40:

Portion processed in June:	0.60 × $5.00 = $3.00
Portion processed in July:	0.40 × $6.00 = 2.40
Total unit cost	$5.40

This method of computing costs for units partially processed in two different periods is the distinguishing characteristic of the FIFO method of process costing.

A July FIFO cost of production report for the Micro Systems example developed earlier in this chapter is shown in Exhibit 12–3. Note in the computation of equivalent units that the FIFO method identifies the number of *equivalent units manufactured* during the current period by subtracting the partially completed equivalent units contained in beginning inventory from the equivalent units in process. In the weighted average method, the computation of equivalent units was based on total *equivalent units in process*.

In the FIFO method, the cost per equivalent unit manufactured consists of only *current manufacturing costs,* computed by dividing current costs (not total costs) by the equivalent units manufactured in the current period. This unit cost is then used to determine the cost of (1) currently completed units in beginning inventory, (2) units started and completed during the period, and (3) units started but not completed. Note in the last section of Exhibit 12–3 that the FIFO method assumes the units completed first are the units started in the previous period and completed in the current period. These units are assigned a cost based partially on the previous period's unit costs and partially on current unit costs. The next units completed are those that were both started and completed in the current period (computed as the units completed minus the units in process in the beginning inventory). These units are valued using only the current period's unit costs. The remaining units—those started but not completed— are assigned a full unit of current materials cost and a partial unit of current conversion cost based on their percentage of completion.

By using only the current period's cost and equivalent units manufactured, the cost per equivalent units is different from that of the weighted average method. Material costs under FIFO are $4.10 instead of $4.09, and conversion costs are $3.30 instead of $3.275. The total equivalent unit cost is therefore $7.40 ($4.10 + $3.30).

The equations used to account for the unit and cost flows under FIFO process costing are different from those previously used in this chapter because of the need to account for the units, or dollars, already placed into beginning work-in-process inventories. For the physical flows, the equation is

$$\text{EU manufactured} = \frac{\text{Units}}{\text{completed}} + \frac{\text{EU in ending}}{\text{inventory}} - \frac{\text{EU in beginning}}{\text{inventory.}}$$

EXHIBIT 12–3   FIFO Process Costing with Beginning Inventories

Micro Systems Co.
Cost of Production Report
For the month ended July 31, 19x3

Summary of units in process

Beginning	4,000
Units started	36,000
In process	40,000
Completed	−35,000
Ending	5,000

Equivalent units manufactured	*Materials*	*Conversion*
Units completed	35,000	35,000
Plus: Equivalent units in ending inventory	5,000	1,000*
Equivalent units in process	40,000	36,000
Less: Equivalent units in beginning inventory	− 4,000	− 3,000**
Equivalent units manufactured	36,000	33,000

Total cost to be accounted for and cost per equivalent unit manufactured	*Materials*	*Conversion*	*Total*
Work-in-Process, beginning	omit †	omit †	$ 25,000
Current cost	$147,600	$108,900§	256,500
Total cost in process	omit †	omit †	$281,500
Equivalent units manufactured	÷ 36,000	÷ 33,000	
Cost per equivalent unit manufactured	$ 4.10	$ 3.30	$ 7.40

Accounting for total cost

Transferred out:			
Work-in-Process, beginning	$ 25,000		
Cost to complete (1,000†† × $3.30)	3,300	$ 28,300	
Started and completed this period			
(31,000§§ × $7.40)		229,400	$257,700
Work-in-Process, ending:			
Materials (5,000 × $4.10)		$ 20,500	
Conversion (1,000 × $3.30)		3,300	23,800
Total cost accounted for			$281,500

* 5,000 units 20% converted.

** 4,000 units 75% converted.

† Cost per equivalent unit manufactured is based on current costs only.

†† 4,000 units were 75% complete. Hence they required an additional 1,000 equivalent units of conversion this period (4,000 × 0.25).

§ Includes direct labor of $62,200 and applied factory overhead of $46,700.

§§ 35,000 units completed minus 4,000 units in beginning in process inventory, or 36,000 units started minus 5,000 units in ending in process inventory.

The equation for the equivalent units of materials manufactured (Exhibit 12–3) is

$$\text{EU materials manufactured} = 35{,}000 + 5{,}000 - 4{,}000$$
$$= 36{,}000.$$

The equation for the equivalent units of conversion manufactured (Exhibit 12–3) is

$$\text{EU conversion manufactured} = 35{,}000 + 1{,}000 - 3{,}000$$
$$= 33{,}000.$$

For *total costs to be accounted for* and *total cost accounted for* the equation is

Beginning work-in-process	+	Current manufacturing cost	=	Beginning work-in-process	+	Cost to complete beginning work-in-process
				+ Cost of units started and completed	+	Ending work-in-process.

The cost equation for the illustration in Exhibit 12–3 for Micro Systems is

$$\$25{,}000 + \$256{,}500 = \$25{,}000 + \$3{,}300 + \$229{,}400 + \$23{,}800.$$
$$\$281{,}500 = \$281{,}500$$

In the case of Micro Systems Co., the difference in the cost valuations between the weighted average and FIFO methods was only $75 ($23,725 − $23,800) for ending work-in-process and ($257,775 − $257,700) for goods completed and transferred to finished goods. *Differences* in inventory cost valuations between weighted average and FIFO costing tend to be small if the change in unit manufacturing costs (materials, labor, and overhead) from one period to the next is small or if the equivalent units in beginning work-in-process represent a small percentage of the total equivalent units worked on during the year.

Under the weighted average method, the cost of goods completed was larger and the cost of ending work-in-process was smaller than under the FIFO method. These relationships between FIFO and weighted average will previal as long as prices are rising from period to period. In times of falling prices, FIFO will produce a higher valuation for completed units and a lower valuation for units in process.

Journal Entries for Various Process Costing Methods

The cost of production reports, Exhibits 12–2 and 12–3, summarize the manufacturing costs assigned to Finished Goods and Work-in-Process during the period and provide information necessary for preparing journal entries. The traditional July 19x3 journal entries for weighted average and FIFO process costing are as follows:

Traditional journal entries		Weighted Average		FIFO	
(1)	Raw Materials	145,000		145,000	
	Accounts Payable		145,000		145,000
	To record cost of raw material purchases.				
(2)	Work-in-Process	147,600		147,600	
	Raw Materials		147,600		147,600
	To record materials requisitioned to factory.				
(3)	Work-in-Process	62,200		62,200	
	Wages Payable		62,200		62,200
	To record wages for the period.				
(4)	Work-in-Process	46,700		46,700	
	Factory Overhead		46,700		46,700
	To apply factory overhead.				
(5)	Finished Goods Inventory	257,775		257,700	
	Work-in-Process		257,775		257,700
	To record transfer of completed units to finished goods.				

Although all the entries for weighted average and FIFO are the same except for number (5), entry (2) will differ when raw materials have multiple purchases at different unit costs. During June and July 19x3 Micro Systems bought all raw materials for $4 per unit, resulting in the same amounts for entry (2). Entry (5) amounts are the costs transferred out in Exhibits 12–2 and 12–3, respectively.

Regardless of the process method used, backflush costing techniques can be applied if the manufacturing system has the appropriate characteristics previously discussed. Journal entries with backflush costing for both weighted average and FIFO costing methods are as follows:

Backflush journal entries		Weighted Average		FIFO	
(1)	Raw Materials-in-Process	145,000		145,000	
	Accounts Payable		145,000		145,000
	To record cost of raw material purchases.				
(2)	Conversion Costs	62,200		62,200	
	Wages Payable		62,200		62,200
	To record wages for the period.				
(3)	Conversion Costs	46,700		46,700	
	Factory Overhead		46,700		46,700
	To apply factory overhead.				
(4)	Finished Goods Inventory	252,050		252,000	
	Raw Materials-in-Process		143,150		143,100
	Conversion Costs		108,900		108,900
	To record transfer of completed units to finished goods.				

Unlike the traditional method of journalizing process costing, the backflush method has only one different entry, number (4). The credit to Raw Materials-in-Process for the weighted average method is found by multiplying the cost per equivalent unit for materials by the units transferred out ($4.09 × 35,000 units); refer to Exhibit 12–2. Raw Materials-in-Process for the FIFO method is found by adding the materials costs of beginning inventory to the materials costs of the units started and completed this period [($4.00 × 4,000 units) + ($4.10 × 31,000)]; refer to Exhibit 12–3.

PROCESS COSTING WITH MULTIPLE DEPARTMENTS

In the previous section the product was converted from raw materials into finished goods in a single department. It is common in many manufacturing organizations for products to be processed in more than one department before they are completed. For example, a company that manufactures appliances may have separate departments for sheet metal stamping, assembly, painting, and inspection. A textile mill has several departments, including spinning, weaving, and bleaching.

To illustrate process costing for a multiple-department manufacturing organization, assume that at the beginning of August, because of quality control problems, Micro Systems Co. is forced to add another department to its manufacturing process to test and inspect its products before they are shipped to customers. It now has two departments, the Molding Department where the memory chips are molded from raw materials and the Testing Department where the chips are tested for defects. When units are completed in the Molding Department, they are transferred to the Testing Department for further processing. Separate departmental cost records are maintained for Molding and Testing, including separate Work-in-Process accounts. When goods are completed in the Molding Department, their accumulated costs are transferred to the Testing Department by the following entry, which may also be visualized as the entry between Departments A and B in Exhibit 12–4.

Journal entry	Work-in-Process, Testing Department	xx
	Work-in-Process, Molding Department	xx

Assume that all materials are added at the beginning of the Molding Department process and that only additional conversion costs—direct labor and factory

EXHIBIT 12–4   Flows of Costs in a Process Cost System with Multiple Departments

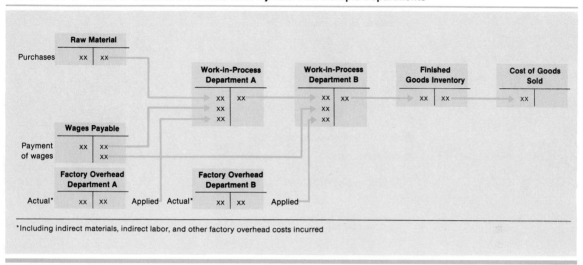

*Including indirect materials, indirect labor, and other factory overhead costs incurred

overhead—are added in the Testing Department. When a unit of product is completed through both departments, its total cost consists of the following components:

- Direct materials, Molding Department.
- Conversion costs, Molding Department.
- Conversion costs, Testing Department.

To illustrate the August 19x3 costing procedures for Micro Systems Co., assume the following data:

August Production Data	*Units*	
	Molding	*Testing*
Units in process, beginning of period		
(20% converted in Molding)	5,000	0
Units started	35,000	N/A
Units transferred to Testing	33,000	N/A
Units received from Molding	N/A*	33,000
Units transferred to finished goods	N/A	28,000
Units in process, end of period		
(50% converted in Molding and 40% in Testing)	7,000	5,000

*N/A is for "not applicable."

August Cost Data	Dollars	
Purchases of raw materials	$162,000	
	Molding	Testing
Beginning costs:		
(based on weighted average)		
Materials	$ 20,450	$ 0
Conversion	3,275	0
Total	$ 23,725	$ 0
Raw materials issued to Molding	$155,550	N/A*
Conversion costs:		
Direct labor for August	$ 83,200	$16,800
Factory overhead applied	44,925	8,100
Total	$128,125	$24,900

* N/A is for "not applicable."

Exhibit 12–5 presents the combined August Cost of Production Reports for the Molding and Testing Departments using the weighted average method. A few differences should be noted in comparing Exhibit 12–5 with the cost of production reports prepared for Micro Systems Co. in June and July, when it was a single department company. First, there are two cost components (materials and conversion) added to units processed by the Molding Department. However, when units are transferred to the Testing Department, these costs are combined and called **transferred-in costs,** with no further separation into materials and conversion costs. Additional conversion costs are added to transferred-in costs in the Testing Department.

The total cost per unit transferred out of the Testing Department into finished goods in August is computed by adding the Testing Department conversion cost of $0.83 per unit to the transferred-in costs of $8 per unit for a total unit cost of $8.83. Another way to compute the total unit cost of $8.83 is to add the Molding Department materials cost of $4.40 and conversion cost of $3.60 with the conversion cost of $0.83 in the Testing Department. Exhibit 12–5 presents the cost of production reports for Molding and Testing in a combined format to make it easier to see the transfer of costs from Molding to Testing. Most companies, however, ordinarily prepare separate reports for each department.

PROCESS COSTING IN SERVICE ORGANIZATIONS

There are many applications of process costing in service organizations. Process costing in service organizations is similar to that of manufacturing organizations. The primary purpose is to assign costs to cost objectives. Many service activities parallel the operations of the manufacturing situation of Micro Systems Co.

EXHIBIT 12–5 Weighted Average Process Costing with Beginning Inventories and Two Departments

Micro Systems Co.
Cost of Production Report
For the month ended August 31, 19x3

Flow of Units in Process

	Molding	Testing
Beginning	5,000	—
Units started	35,000	33,000
In process	40,000	33,000
Completed	−33,000	−28,000
Ending	7,000	5,000

Equivalent Units in Process	Molding Department		Testing Department	
	Materials	Conversion	Transferred-in	Conversion
Units completed	33,000	33,000	28,000	28,000
Plus: Equivalent units in ending inventory	7,000	3,500*	5,000	2,000†
Equivalent units in process	40,000	36,500	33,000	30,000

Total Costs to Be Accounted for and Cost per Equivalent Unit in Process	Molding Department		Testing Department	
	Materials	Conversion	Transferred-in	Conversion
Work-in-Process, beginning	$ 20,450	$ 3,275	$ 0	$ 0
Current costs	155,550	128,125‡	264,000	24,900§
Total costs in process	$176,000	$131,400	$264,000	$ 24,900
Total department costs		$307,400		$288,900
Equivalent units in process	÷ 40,000	÷ 36,500	÷ 33,000	÷ 30,000
Cost per equivalent unit in process	$ 4.40	$ 3.60	$ 8.00	$ 0.83
Total department unit cost		$8.00		$8.83

Accounting for Total Costs

	Molding Materials	Molding Conversion	Testing Transferred-in	Testing Conversion
Molding department:				
Transferred out (33,000 × $8.00)		$264,000		
Work-in-Process, ending				
Materials (7,000 × $4.40)	$ 30,800			
Conversion (3,500 × $3.60)	12,600	43,400		
Total molding department costs accounted for		$307,400		
Testing department:				
Transferred out (28,000 × $8.83)				$247,240
Work-in-Process, ending:				
Transferred-in cost (5,000 × $8.00)			$ 40,000	
Conversion (2,000 × $0.83)			1,660	41,660
Total testing department costs accounted for				

---

* 7,000 units 50% converted.
† 5,000 units 40% converted.
‡ Includes direct labor of $83,200 and applied factory overhead of $44,925.
§ Includes direct labor of $16,800 and applied factory overhead of $8,100.

Generally the use of process costing techniques for service organizations is easier than for manufacturing organizations because the materials element is not necessary. The applications for the labor and overhead costs would be similar, if not identical, to those of the manufacturing firm.

However, there are several important aspects to consider before using process costing in the service organization. The difficulty in many service situations is defining the cost objective. For manufacturing applications the normal cost objective is inventory, or units thereof. Inventory does not exist in most service applications, so the selection of the cost objective becomes a major management decision. Is the cost objective a general activity (check processing in a bank), a specific activity (sorting only letters, as opposed to letters and packages), or a mission activity (patient care in a hospital as opposed to individual patients)?

General activities should be used when the service process is identical for all processing even though some of the items processed are different. The bank processes many types of checks—personal, business, cashiers', and travelers'—but they all go through the same chain of activities. Specific activity cost objectives should be used when the items processed take different activity paths. Although the mail center processes all mail via the same steps—receiving, sorting, bundling, etc.—the handling operations are different. For example, the letters can be sorted and bundled by machine, but the packages must be sorted and grouped by hand.

Using mission activity as the cost objective is the latest approach to applying process costing to service situations. Rather than tracking the cost of every service rendered per unit or batch (a job processing approach), a company can assign costs over a longer period of time to another reasonable objective—for example, patient care. At the end of a set period, all costs assigned to patient care are divided by the total number of patient days during the period to obtain the evaluation data, cost per patient day. This approach assumes that all processed units (patients in this example) receive approximately the same activity (patient care) and therefore the average cost per unit (patient day) is sufficient for evaluation purposes.

After it is determined that process costing would be appropriate for a service activity, the actual decision to use it is generally contingent on two important factors about the items being evaluated. First, is average cost per unit acceptable as an input item to the decision process? For some activities the answer is obvious—tracking the actual cost of processing each check through a bank would probably not be as useful as determining the average cost of processing checks for a given period; therefore, average cost is acceptable. For other activities the answer is more difficult to determine. Should the decision model include average cost per patient day or actual cost per individual patient?

The second item to be considered relates to the benefits versus the costs of the resulting information. Normally it is easier to track and record the cost of an activity or process than it is to track and record the cost of each individual item in the activity. Often actual cost tracking is impossible for practical reasons (the actual cost of processing a check through a banking system, for example).

With appropriate planning, every service organization can establish a means of proper reporting through cost assignment. Although process costing will not work in every situation, it has many applications in service organizations. And as illustrated in this text, there are many possibilities for applying either job or process costing to activities in service organizations.

SUMMARY

Product costing involves the determination of the cumulative cost of inventories as they flow through the manufacturing process using either individual jobs or manufacturing processes as the assignment base. Process costing involves the determination of the cost per unit of a homogeneous product as the units pass continuously from one production operation to another. This chapter has examined the process costing technique, methods of determining equivalent units, the cost of production report, and related journal entries. When units worked on are not completely processed in one period, process costing utilizes the concept of equivalent unit to determine the unit costs.

Many manufacturing processes involve more than one department and require multiple cost computations. The determination of equivalent units, ending work-in-process, and unit costs for each department or process are required. The costs of the intermediate processes are carried forward to the next process and are referred to as transferred-in costs. These costs are accounted for as separate components in the receiving departments, and any additional raw materials and conversion costs that might be incurred in the new department are added to them.

Process costing has many applications in service organizations. Service organizations can use process costing techniques for activity evaluations and cost reports. Although in this chapter we presented process costing in a manufacturing setting, the only major change required to apply process costing to a service setting is likely to be the elimination of the materials flow. Labor and overhead surely exist in all service organizations.

APPENDIX
JOINT PRODUCTS AND BY-PRODUCTS

Joint products are two or more products produced simultaneously by a common manufacturing process. The costs of producing joint products are called **joint costs.** An example of joint products is crude oil products (such as gasoline, diesel, and kerosene) that are produced by a common refining process. Similarly, various chemical products are often produced by a single process. A **by-product** is a product with insignificant value that is produced jointly with one or more other products.

Joint Product Cost Allocation

For product costing purposes, it is necessary to allocate joint product costs to the respective joint products. Joint cost allocation occurs at the split-off point in the production process. The **split-off point** is the point in the process where the joint products emerge as separate identifiable products. Any costs incurred in further processing of a joint product after split-off are specific product costs, *not joint costs.*

To illustrate joint cost allocation, assume Aem Enterprises manufactures two automotive fuel additives, Speedo and Econo, from a common manufacturing process. In August 19x3, Aem incurred joint costs of $24,000 in producing 8,000 pints of Speedo and 12,000 pints of Econo, as illustrated below.

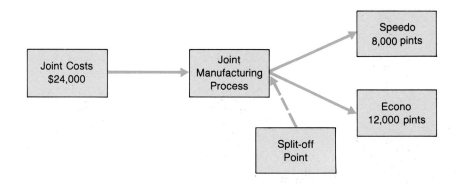

Two methods available for allocating joint costs are the physical quantity method and the sales value method. Under the **physical quantity allocation method,** joint costs are allocated on the basis of relative quantities of a common physical characteristic possessed by the joint products. Physical characteristics used for joint cost allocation include the number of units of product, weight measures, and volume measures. For Aem Enterprises the unit measure (pint) is also a volume measure because 1 physical unit of product consists of 1 pint of volume measure. Under the physical quantity method, using pints of production as the allocation base, the allocated costs, $9,600 for Speedo and $14,000 for Econo, are computed as follows:

Product	Quantity (pints)	Relative Quantity		Joint Cost		Allocation
Speedo	8,000	0.40	×	$24,000	=	$ 9,600
Econo	12,000	0.60	×	$24,000	=	14,400
	20,000	1.00				$24,000

Each product has a cost of $1.20 per pint ($9,600 ÷ 8,000 and $14,400 ÷ 12,000).

If Speedo sells for $3 per pint and Econo sells for $1 per pint, the gross profit for Speedo is $14,400, whereas Econo has a negative $2,400 gross profit.

	Speedo	Econo	Total
Unit sales (pints)	8,000	12,000	20,000
Sales price per unit	$3	$1	
Sales	$24,000	$12,000	$36,000
Cost of goods sold	− 9,600	−14,400	−24,000
Gross profit	$14,400	$ (2,400)	$12,000

MANAGERIAL PRACTICE 12.4

Joint Costs for Computer Chips

Although joint costing has long been used in the agricultural, chemical, extractive, and other industries, it also provides sensible cost allocations when applied to the costs of making computer chips. In the computer chip manufacturing process, common inputs of silicon wafers produce memory chips that have different speeds, temperature tolerances, life expectancies, and so on. Market value–based joint costing provides the most accurate cost allocations in manufacturing computer chips, because the cost inputs (silicon wafers) can be varied to produce a different mix of outputs (memory chips). Hence, if established market values are available for the joint products at the split-off point, they should be used in making the joint cost allocations. Otherwise, net realizable values following further processing can be used.

"It seems reasonable that the preferred method of joint cost allocation should be the one which is most sensitive to improvements in the production process. Because market price differences reflect all of the differences in relevant quality dimensions, a strong argument in favor of using a [market value–based] approach to joint cost allocation [in the semiconductor industry] can be made."

Source: William L. Cats-Baril, James F. Gatti, and D. Jacque Grinnell, "Joint Product Costing in the Semiconductor Industry," *Management Accounting* (February 1986): 28–35.

Allocating joint costs on the basis of physical quantities produces a distortion in the gross profit computations any time the selling price per unit of quantity is not the same for all joint products. The reason for this distortion is that the physical quantity method assigns an *equal amount of cost* to each *unit of physical measure*—in this case to each pint—regardless of its selling price. If allocated on the basis of physical quantity, the cost per pint is $1.20 for both Speedo and Econo, but the selling price of Speedo is three times as much as Econo's selling price. Since together the products generate a total gross profit of $12,000, and one product cannot be produced without the other, it is unreasonable to assume that one is produced at a profit and the other is produced at a loss.

If selling prices vary significantly between the joint products, sales value is a more realistic basis for allocating joint costs. Under the **sales value allocation method** each dollar of sales value for all products is assigned an equal amount of cost. The sales value method allocations for Speedo and Econo are as follows:

Product	Sales Value Computation	Amount	Relative Sales Value		Joint Cost		Allocation
Speedo	8,000 × $3 =	$24,000	0.667	×	$24,000	=	$16,000
Econo	12,000 × $1 =	12,000	0.333	×	$24,000	=	8,000
		$36,000	1.000				$24,000

Speedo has a cost of $2 per pint ($16,000 ÷ 8,000), and Econo has a cost of $0.667 per pint ($8,000 ÷ 12,000).

Using the costs for Speedo and Econo determined by the sales value allocation method, the respective gross profits are $8,000 and $4,000, as shown in the partial income statements below.

	Speedo	Econo	Total
Units sales (pints)	8,000	12,000	20,000
Sales price per unit	$3	$1	
Sales	$24,000	$12,000	$36,000
Cost of goods sold	−16,000	− 8,000	−24,000
Gross profit	$ 8,000	$ 4,000	$12,000

Under the sales value method, the gross margin ratio is the same (one third of selling price) for both products.

Additional processing may be required after split-off on some joint products. In this case the sales value method must be modified to allocate joint costs on the basis of net realizable value at the point of split-off rather than on the basis of sales value for completed units. Net realizable value is computed as ultimate sales value less additional processing costs incurred beyond the split-off point.

For example, if $4,000 of additional processing costs were required after split-off before the 8,000 pints of Speedo could be sold for $24,000, the joint cost allocation would be made on the basis of relative net realizable values of $20,000 ($24,000 − $4,000) for Speedo and $12,000 for Econo.

The decision of whether to continue with additional processing after split-off is unrelated to the cost allocation procedure. Sometimes additional processing is necessary before the product can be sold, in which case further processing ordinarily must be done. In other cases, the product may be sold either at split-off or after additional processing. The decision of whether to continue processing is based entirely on relevant cost analysis. If the additional revenue from processing exceeds the additional cost of processing, the product should be processed further; otherwise, the product should be sold at split-off. These relevant cost issues are discussed and illustrated in Chapter 5.

Accounting for By-products

A by-product is not treated as a joint product and therefore is not allocated costs in the joint cost allocation procedure. Production of by-products is not a major objective of the manufacturing process; it is a result of production of the main products. For example, a furniture factory primarily manufactures furniture, but it produces sawdust (which is saleable) as an inevitable and natural result.

If by-products do not generate revenues, which is the case for many waste by-products, there is no special accounting required other than recording any disposition costs as additional manufacturing expense. If by-products can be sold, and the selling price is insignificant, revenues from the sale of by-products are usually recorded either as other income or as a reduction of joint manufacturing costs. The remaining joint processing costs are then allocated to the joint products by either the physical quantity or sales value method. By costing by-products at selling price, no profit or loss is recognized when they are sold.

Products initially considered to be by-products may later become main products as new uses and applications for them are discovered. When this occurs, the accounting treatment should be revised to reflect a change in assumptions and to begin allocating costs to the products as joint products.

SUGGESTED READINGS

Biggs, Joseph R., and Ellen J. Long, "Gaining the Competitive Edge with MRP/MRPII," *Management Accountant* (May 1988): 27–32.

Calvasina, Richard V., Eugene J. Calvasina, and Gerald E. Calvasina, "Beware the New Accounting Myths," *Management Accounting* (December 1989): 41–45.

Dinius, Sara H., "A Matrix Solution to Process Costing Problems," *Issues in Accounting Education* 2 No. 1, (Spring 1987): 44–56.

Foster, George, and Charles T. Horngren, "Cost Accounting and Cost Management in a JIT Environment," *The Journal of Cost Management* (Winter 1988): 34–39.

Howell, Robert A. and Stephen R. Soucy, "The New Manufacturing Environment: Major Trends for Management Accountants," *Management Accounting* (July 1987): 21–27.

_____, "Cost Accounting in the New Manufacturing Environment," *Management Accounting* (August 1987): 42–48.

Patell, James M., "Cost Accounting, Process Control, and Product Design: A Case Study of the Hewlett-Packard Personal Office Computer Division," *The Accounting Review* (October 1987): 808–839.

Wilner, Neil A., "A Simple Teaching Approach for Process Costing Using Logic and Pictures," *Issues in Accounting Education* (Fall 1987): 388–396.

REVIEW PROBLEM

Weighted Average Process Costing: Journal Entries

Magnetic Media, Inc., manufactures magnetic data disks which are used in the computer industry. Since there is very little product differentiation between Magnetic's products, it uses a process costing system to determine inventory costs. Production and manufacturing cost data for 19x7 are as follows:

Production Data:	Units
Units in process, beginning of period (60% converted)	3,000,000
Units started	27,000,000
Completed and transferred to finished goods	25,000,000
Units in process, end of period (30% converted)	5,000,000
Manufacturing Costs:	Dollars
Work-in-Process, beginning of period	
(materials – $468,000; conversion – $252,000)	$ 720,000
Current manufacturing costs:	
Raw materials transferred to processing	6,132,000
Direct labor for the period	1,550,000
Factory overhead for the period	3,498,000

All materials are added at the start of the production process.

Requirements

a) Prepare a cost of production report for Magnetic Media, Inc., for 19x7 using the weighted average approach to process costing.

b) Prepare journal entries to record current manufacturing costs and inventory completed and transferred to finished goods during the period.

The solution to this problem is found at the end of Chapter 12 exercises, problems, and cases.

KEY TERMS

Backflush costing system
Cost of production report
Equivalent completed units
FIFO inventory method
Just-in-time inventory management

Materials requirements planning
  (MRP)
Process costing
Transferred-in costs
Weighted average inventory method

APPENDIX KEY TERMS	By-product Joint costs Joint products	Physical quantity allocation method Sales value allocation method Split-off point

REVIEW QUESTIONS

12–1   Describe the difference between job-order and process costing in terms of the primary cost objective and time period for which costs are accumulated.

12–2   What are the three groups of goods normally worked on during a given processing period?

12–3   Explain how environmental influences have caused some production processes to shift from job-order costing to process costing.

12–4   What major changes in inventory control and levels are caused by using a just-in-time approach to inventory management?

12–5   Which record in a process cost system provides cost data used to record the transfer of completed goods from Work-in-Process to Finished Goods?

12–6   Present the equation for comparing the incoming costs of production with the outgoing costs of the manufactured goods.

12–7   Identify the main differences between traditional process costing journal entries and backflush costing journal entries.

12–8   Why are the costs assigned to finished goods under backflush costing different from those assigned under traditional process costing?

12–9   In backflush costing, what is the purpose of the account Raw Materials-in-Process?

12–10   Under what conditions will equivalent units in process be different for materials and conversion costs?

12–11   Describe the treatment of beginning work-in-process inventory under the weighted average method of process costing.

12–12   Present the general equation for computing cost per equivalent unit for the weighted average method.

12–13   Describe the calculation of the cost of units completed and transferred to finished goods under the weighted average method.

12–14   Describe the typical cost flows for materials in a multiple manufacturing process.

12–15   In a multi-processing environment, what cost category is found in all departments or processes except the first?

EXERCISES

12–1 Job-Order Costing and Process Costing Applications

For each of the following manufacturing situations indicate whether job-order or process costing is more appropriate and why:

a)   A manufacturer of peanut butter.

b)   A chemical plant that produces household cleaners.

c)   A shoe manufacturer.

d)   A modular home builder.

e)   A company that makes only original equipment front windshields for automobile manufacturers.

12–2 Job-Order Costing and Process Costing Applications

For each of the following situations indicate whether job-order or process costing is more appropriate and why.

a) A building contractor for residential dwellings.

b) A manufacturer of nylon yarn that sells to textile companies that make fabric.

c) A clothing manufacturer that makes suits in several different fabrics, colors, styles, and sizes.

d) A hosiery mill that manufactures one product that fits all sizes.

e) A vehicle battery manufacturer that has just received an order for 500,000 identical batteries to be delivered as manufactured over the next twelve months.

12–3 Costing Work-in-Process and Finished Goods

King Manufacturing Company makes one product that is produced on a continuous basis in one department. All materials are added at the beginning of production. The total cost per equivalent unit in process in March 19x4 was $4.60, consisting of $3 for materials and $1.60 for conversion. During the month, 8,000 units of product were transferred to finished goods inventory, and on March 31, 4,000 units were in process, 10 percent converted. King uses weighted average costing.

Requirements

a) Determine the cost of goods transferred to finished goods inventory.

b) Determine the cost of the ending work-in-process inventory.

c) What was the total cost of the beginning work-in-process inventory, plus the current manufacturing costs?

12–4 Costing Work-in-Process and Finished Goods without Beginning Inventories

Kiwi Manufacturing makes glue in a continuous process in one department. All materials are added at the beginning of the process, and labor and overhead is incurred evenly throughout the process. The unit cost for 19x3 was $35 per drum, consisting of $21 for materials and $14 for conversion. During the year 4,800 drums of glue were produced, and on December 31, 19x3, 12 drums were in process, 40 percent completed as to conversion. There was no beginning inventory.

Requirements

a) Determine the cost of goods transferred to finished goods inventory.

b) Determine the cost of the ending work-in-process inventory.

c) What was the total cost of the beginning work-in-process plus the current manufacturing costs?

12–5 Equivalent Units Computations

During April 19x6, Four Corners Manufacturing placed 220,000 kilograms of horse feed in its mixing department. At the end of the month, 10,000 kilograms were still in process, 30 percent complete as to conversion. All raw materials are placed in mixing at the beginning of the process. Four Corners uses weighted average costing.

Requirements

a) Determine the equivalent units in process for materials and conversion costs assuming there was no beginning inventory.

b) Determine the equivalent units in process for materials and conversion costs assuming that 12,000 kilograms of feed, 40 percent complete, were in process prior to the addition of the 220,000 kilograms.

12–6 Equivalent Units Computations

During February 19x5, Apex Co. had 15,000 units of product in process in its Mixing Department, of which 3,000 were still in process (25 percent converted) at the end of the period.

Requirements

a) Determine the equivalent units in process for conversion costs assuming there was no beginning inventory.

b) Determine the equivalent units in process for conversion costs assuming that 2,800 of the 15,000 units were in beginning work-in-process, 30 percent converted, and that Apex uses weighted average costing.

c) Determine the equivalent units in process for conversion costs assuming that 2,800 of the 15,000 units were in beginning work-in-process, 30 percent converted, that 5,000 units were in ending inventory, 50 percent complete, and that Apex uses weighted average costing.

12–7 Journal Entries: Traditional Method

Tight Fit manufactures ladies belts. The company produces the belts in a continuous process, mixing sizes and colors at random. The following cost data have been gathered for October 19x8.

	Dollars
Current manufacturing costs:	
Raw materials purchased	$125,000
Raw materials issued in production	110,000
Conversion costs:	
Direct labor	32,000
Factory overhead	16,000
Cost of goods manufactured	142,000
Ending work-in-process inventory:	
Materials	10,667
Conversion costs	5,333

Required: Prepare traditional journal entries to record the production activities for the period. Include a journal entry for purchases of raw materials. There were no beginning inventories.

12–8 Journal Entries: Backflush Costing Method

Using the data from Exercise 12–7 for Tight Fit, prepare journal entries using backflush costing. If Exercise 12–7 was worked, explain any differences in the ending account balances between the traditional and backflush costing methods. Assume zero beginning inventories.

12–9 Journal Entries: Traditional Method

Perfect Match produces and sells microcomputer software. The disk department creates the disks that are necessary for each software package. July 19x0 disk department cost and production data are as follows:

	Dollars
Current manufacturing costs:	
Raw materials purchased	$55,000
Raw materials issued in production	50,000
Conversion costs:	
Direct labor	18,000
Factory overhead	14,000
Cost of goods manufactured	70,000
Ending work-in-process inventory:	
Materials	6,800
Conversion costs	5,200

Required: Prepare traditional journal entries to record the production activities for the period. Include a journal entry for raw material purchases. There were no beginning inventories.

12–10 Journal Entries: Backflush Costing Method

Using the data from Exercise 12–9 for Perfect Match, prepare backflush costing journal entries. If Exercise 12–9 was worked, compare answers and explain the differences. There were no beginning inventories.

12–11 Cost of Production Report: No Beginning Inventories

Fisk Manufacturing Company is a new company that produces newsprint paper through a special recycling process which uses scrap paper products. Production and cost data for October 19x7, the first month of operations for the company, are presented below.

Units of product started in process during October	90,000
Units completed and transferred to finished goods	75,000
Machine hours operated	10,000
Direct materials cost incurred	$243,000
Direct labor cost incurred	$95,265

Raw materials are added at the beginning of the process for each unit of product produced, and labor and factory overhead are added evenly throughout the manufacturing process. Factory overhead is applied to Work-in-Process at the rate of $12 per machine hour. Units in process at the end of the period were 65 percent converted.

Required: Prepare a cost of production report for Fisk Manufacturing Company for October 19x7.

12–12 Cost of Production Report: No Beginning Inventories

Rodeway Paving Products Company manufactures asphalt paving materials for highway construction through a single-step process in which all materials are added at the beginning of the process. During October 19x4, Rodeway accumulated the following data in its process costing system.

Production data:	
Work-in-process, October 1	0 tons
Raw materials transferred to processing	25,000 tons
Work-in-process, October 31 (75% converted)	5,000 tons
Cost data:	
Raw materials transferred to processing	$300,000
Conversion costs:	
Direct labor cost incurred	19,000
Factory overhead applied	?

Factory overhead is applied at the rate of $1 per equivalent unit (ton) processed.

Required: Prepare a cost of production report for Octo ber 19x4.

12–13 Equivalent Units: Weighted Average and FIFO Methods

Gerdons Refinery began December 19x4 with 5,000 barrels of inventory in process, 30 percent completed. During the period, 24,000 barrels were completed and transferred to the finished goods warehouse. Ending inventory consisted of 4,500 barrels, 85 percent completed.

Requirements

a) Calculate the equivalent units in process for conversion cost under the weighted average process cost method.

b) Calculate the equivalent units manufactured for conversion cost under the FIFO process cost method.

12–14 Accounting for Total Cost: FIFO Method

Arnoud Company had a cost per equivalent unit manufactured for January 19x7 of $4.56 for materials and $2.75 for conversion cost. During the period, 10,250 units were completed and transferred to finished goods. At the end of the month, 3,200 units were in work-in-process, 100 percent completed with regard to materials costs and 60 percent completed with regard to conversion costs. At the beginning of January, there were 1,500 units in process, 100 percent completed with regard to materials cost and 50 percent completed with regard to conversion cost. The beginning balance in Work-in-Process was $8,775. Arnoud uses FIFO process costing.

Requirements

a) Calculate the cost of the units completed and transferred to finished goods during January 19x7.

b) Calculate the cost of the units in work-in-process at the end of January 19x7.

12–15 Process Costing in a Service Organization

Dr. W. J. Alson is an optometrist who has been in business for two years. Dr. Alson recalled from a survey course in accounting that it was important to track operating costs if one wanted to know the true cost per performance unit. During the first few months of practice the job cost system that was implemented was easy to operate. Only 12 to 15 patients were seen on an average day, and no patient's visit overlapped any other visit. Therefore the amount of time the doctor and nurse met with any patient was easily monitored. Equipment usage and medical supplies were also tracked and charged per patient. At the end of each month all other costs were considered as overhead and allocated on a per patient basis. The cost data included on a typical job sheet were as follows:

	Minutes	Dollars
Doctor's time @ $2 per minute	20	$40
Nurse's time @ $1 per minute	15	15
Equipment utilization @ $5 per minute	4	20
Overhead (assigned at end of month)		22
Total costs		$97

During the past few months the practice has grown rapidly, and the office administrator has encountered much difficulty in tracking and recording the cost for every patient. The doctor now sees an average of four patients an hour and frequently moves between the patient rooms without recording the time in and out. It is not unusual for the nurse to make several visits with each patient, and it is impractical to track the nurse's time per patient. Equipment usage, however, must be recorded on the patient's chart, and the administrator is confident that these charges per patient are correct.

Required: How can the costing system be changed to reflect the demands now placed upon the existing system?

12–16 Joint Cost Allocation: Physical Quantity Method (Appendix)

Chemco, Inc., processes two products, Bugoff and Weedout, used in the control of weeds and pests in lawn care. These products begin from a unique joint refining process in batches of 10,000 liters of mixture. At split-off, one fourth of the mixture emerges as Bugoff and three fourths as Weedout. Both products require further processing after split-off. The following cost and production data for August 19x1 were determined.

Total joint costs per batch	$15,000
Cost of further processing of Bugoff	5,000
Cost of further processing of Weedout	10,000
Beginning inventories	none

Requirements

a) Determine the joint cost allocation per batch for each product using the physical quantity method.

b) Determine the total cost per liter for each product. (Round answer to the nearest cent.)

12–17 Joint Cost Allocation: Physical Quantity and Relative Sales Value Methods (Appendix)

Hills and Dales Farms is a large poultry producer that processes and sells various grades of packaged chicken to grocery chains. Chickens are grown and accounted for in groups of 50,000. At the end of the standard growing period, the chickens are separated and sold by grades. Grades A and B are sold to grocery chains, and grades C and D are sold for other uses. For costing purposes, Hills and Dales treats each batch of newly hatched chicks as a joint product. The following data pertain to the last batch of 50,000 chicks.

Grade	Number of Chickens	Average Pounds per Chicken	Selling Price per Pound
A	25,000	4	$0.50
B	15,000	3	0.40
C	6,000	$2\frac{1}{2}$	0.30
D	4,000	$1\frac{1}{4}$	0.20

Total joint costs for this batch were $40,000.

Requirements

a) Compute the cost allocations for each product using the physical quantity number of chickens.

b) Compute the cost allocations for each product using physical quantity if measured in pounds per chicken.

c) Compute the cost allocations for each product using the relative sales value method.

PROBLEMS

12–18 Manufacturing Cost Flows: Journal Entries

Frankfort Manufacturing Co. completed the following transactions with respect to its manufacturing operations during November 19x5.

- Raw materials costing $60,000 and manufacturing supplies costing $9,000 were purchased on account.

- A total of $30,000 of raw materials were requisitioned to the factory for manufacturing operations conducted during November.

- Manufacturing payroll for the month consisted of 2,250 hours of direct labor and 400 hours of indirect labor, both at $12 per hour.

- Manufacturing supplies costing $3,000 were used.

- Depreciation on the factory building and equipment was $15,000.

- Miscellaneous factory overhead expenses totaled $3,600 for November.

- Factory overhead cost was applied to Work-in-Process at the rate of $10 per direct labor hour.

- Units of product with a total manufacturing cost of $45,000 were completed and transferred to the finished goods warehouse.

- Finished goods costing $36,000 were sold during November.

- Ending Work-in-Process included $4,000 of raw materials.

Requirements

a) Prepare journal entries for each of the transactions that occurred during November 19x5.

b) Prepare T-accounts for the ledger accounts used in recording the transactions in requirement (a), and post all entries to the appropriate accounts.

12–19 Manufacturing Cost Flows: Backflush Method Journal Entries

Using the information in Problem 12–18 for Frankfort Manufacturing Co., prepare journal entries using a backflush costing system. What accounts will be different under this system versus the traditional journal entry system? How much will they differ?

12–20 Cost of Production Report: No Beginning Inventories with Backflush Journal Entries

Hendersonville Apple, Inc., produces apple juice in a single process that runs 24 hours a day, five days a week. The company adds all materials (apples) at the beginning of the process, and because of possible spoilage, completes all units started during the week by week-end. However, when an accounting period ends during a workweek, ending work-in-process must be computed. The third quarter of 19x9 ended on a Wednesday and thus required the computation of work-in-process inventories. The following information for the third quarter was provided by the cost information system.

Production data:	
Beginning work-in-process	0 barrels
Apples placed in process	880 bushels
Ending work-in-process (output equivalents)	20 barrels
Cost data:	
Apples placed in process	$5 per bushel
Conversion costs:	
Direct labor	2,000 hours at $7.00/hr.
Factory overhead	$1.64 per direct labor hour

The processing of apples requires two bushels of input for each barrel of output. At midnight on September 30, 19x9, the work-in-process was 60 percent complete.

Requirements

a) Prepare a cost of production report for the third quarter of 19x9.

b) Using backflush costing, prepare all journal entries to record costs incurred during the third quarter of 19x9.

12–21 Weighted Average Process Costing with Beginning Inventories: Production Report and Journal Entries

Chamblee Processing Company manufactures a product on a continuous basis in two departments, Processing and Finishing. All materials are added at the beginning of work on the product in the Processing Department. During December 19x5, the following events occurred in the Processing Department.

■ Units started .... 16,000 units

■ Units completed and transferred to Finishing .... 15,000 units

■ Costs assigned to Processing:

Raw materials (one unit of raw materials for each unit of product started)	$142,000
Manufacturing supplies used	18,000
Direct labor costs incurred	51,000
Supervisors' salaries	12,000
Other production labor costs	14,000
Depreciation on equipment	6,000
Other production costs	18,000

Additional information:

■ Chamblee uses weighted average costing and applies factory overhead to Work-in-Process at the rate of 100 percent of direct labor cost.

■ Ending inventory in the Processing Department consists of 3,000 units that are one-third converted.

■ Beginning inventory contained 2,000 units one-half converted, with a cost of $27,300 ($17,300 for materials and $10,000 for conversion).

Requirements

a) Prepare a cost of production report for the Processing Department for December.

b) Prepare all journal entries to record costs incurred by the Processing Department in December and to record the transfer of units to the Finishing Department. Over-applied or underapplied factory overhead is written off to Cost of Goods Sold at the end of each month.

12–22 Weighted Average Process Costing with Beginning Inventories: Production Report and Journal Entries

Hillsborough, Inc., processes its only product in a single process and uses weighted average process costing to account for inventory costs. The following inventory, production, and cost data are provided for June 19x8:

Production data:		
Beginning inventory (25 percent converted)	210,000 units	
Units started	650,000 units	
Ending inventory (50 percent converted)	180,000 units	
Manufacturing costs:		
Beginning inventory in process:		
Materials cost	$146,000	
Conversion cost	88,000	$234,000
Raw materials cost added at beginning of process		739,800
Direct labor cost incurred		410,000
Factory overhead applied		333,600

Requirements

a) Prepare a cost of production report for Hillsborough for June.

b) Prepare journal entries to record costs incurred during the month for raw materials and direct labor, and to record factory overhead applied. Also prepare the entry to record the cost of goods completed and transferred to finished goods inventory.

c) Prepare a cost of goods manufactured report for Hillsborough for June. *Hint:* Review Chapter 2, if necessary, to complete this requirement.

12–23 Process Costing: Work-in-Process Analysis: Weighted Average Costing

Karkare Products, Inc. manufactures automobile polish through a process involving two departments (Mixing and Bottling). All materials are added at the beginning of the Mixing Department process. Factory overhead is applied at the rate of 125 percent of direct labor costs. The Work-in-Process account for the Mixing Department for May 19x5 is presented below.

Work-in-Process: Mixing

May 1 balance (100,000 units, 40% converted) 260,200	(c) ?	Finished and transferred to Bottling Department (a) ? units
May costs assigned:		
Raw materials (400,000 units) 460,000		
Direct labor (b) ?		
Factory overhead 100,000		
May 31 balance (60,000 units, 45% converted) (d) ?		

The beginning Work-in-Process balance consists of materials, $140,000, and conversion cost, $100,200.

Required: Determine the values for the missing items lettered (a) through (d) in the Mixing Department Work-in-Process account. Assume the company uses weighted average costing. (*Hint:* You may want to prepare a cost of production report.)

12–24 Cost of Production Report: FIFO and Beginning Inventories

Agrikill Chemical Co. manufactures a patented chemical product called WPK that is used by farmers to kill weeds and pests. WPK is produced through a continuous process, entirely in one department, with all materials added at the beginning of processing. Production and cost data for the company for February 19x8 are as follows:

Production data:	
In process, beginning of month (40% converted)	15,000 units
Started during February	95,000 units
Completed and transferred to finished goods	100,000 units
In process, end of month (50% converted)	10,000 units

Manufacturing costs:	
Work-in-process, beginning	$ 55,000
Raw materials transferred to processing	275,500
Conversion costs:	
Direct labor cost for February	82,170
Factory overhead (applied at the rate of $1 per equivalent unit for conversion cost)	?

Required: Prepare a cost of production report for February 19x8. Use FIFO process costing.

12–25 Joint Cost Allocation: Physical Quantity and Sales Value Methods (Appendix)

Vreeland, Inc., manufactures products X, Y, and Z from a joint process. Joint product costs were $120,000 during September. Additional information is as follows:

Product	Units Produced	Sales Value at Split-Off	Sales Value and Additional Costs if Processed Further	
			Sales Value	Additional Costs
X	6,000	$40,000	$55,000	$9,000
Y	4,000	35,000	45,000	7,000
Z	2,000	25,000	30,000	5,000

Requirements

a) Determine the amount of joint product costs to be allocated to each of the products during September assuming the company uses the physical quantity method of joint cost allocation.

b) Determine the amount of joint product costs to be allocated to each of the products during September assuming the company uses the sales value method of joint cost allocation. (Round calculations to four decimal places.)

c) Should any of the products be processed further? Explain.

(CPA Adapted)

12–26 Process Costing Production Reports for Two-Department Process: A Challenge Problem

The Dexter Production Company manufactures a single product. Its operations are a continuing process carried on in two departments—Machining and Finishing. In the production process, materials are added to the product in each department without increasing the number of units produced. For June 19x5, the company records indicated the following production statistics for each department.

	Machining	Finishing
Units in process, June 1	—	—
Units transferred from previous department	—	60,000
Units started in production	80,000	—
Units completed and transferred out	60,000	50,000
Units in process, June 30	20,000	10,000
Percent of completion of units in process at June 30:		
Materials	100%	100%
Conversion	50%	70%
Cost records showed the following charges for June:		
Materials	$240,000	$ 88,500
Labor	140,000	141,500
Overhead	65,000	25,700

Required: Prepare separate cost of production reports for the Machining and Finishing Departments for June 19x5. In preparing the report for the Finishing Department, the cost of the units transferred in from the Machining Department are treated the same as raw materials added at the beginning of the process. (Round calculations to three decimal places.)

(CPA Adapted)

12–27 Process Costing: Two-Department Cost of Production Report

Atlantic Paper Company manufactures paper used in printing newspapers. The process involves two departments, Processing and Bleaching. Raw materials are added at the beginning of the Processing Department. Goods are transferred from the Processing Department to the Bleaching Department and from Bleaching to finished goods inventory. Production and cost data for Atlantic Paper Company are presented below for the month of January, 19x5.

	Processing	Bleaching
Production data (units):		
In process, January 1 (33⅓% converted in Processing, 25% converted in Bleaching)	150,000	80,000
Raw materials transferred to Processing	450,000	
Transferred to Bleaching from Processing	500,000	500,000
Transferred to Finished Goods		520,000
Cost data:		
Raw materials transferred to Processing	$3,600,000	
Conversion costs:		
Direct labor cost	2,000,000	$3,000,000
Factory overhead applied (210% of direct labor cost for Processing and 120% of direct labor cost for Bleaching)	4,200,000	3,600,000

Additional information:

■ Assume that 1 unit of raw materials is required to produce 1 unit of product.

■ Ending work-in-process inventory was 50 percent converted in the Processing Department and 20 percent converted in the Bleaching Department.

■ The company uses weighted average costing.

■ Beginning work-in-process consisted of the following:

	Processing	Bleaching
Raw materials	$1,125,000	
Transferred-in costs		$1,520,000
Conversion costs	575,000	242,400
Total	$1,700,000	$1,762,400

Requirements

a) Prepare a combined cost of production report for the Processing and Bleaching Departments using the format illustrated in Exhibit 12–5. (Round calculations to three decimal places.)

b) Prepare the journal entries to record (1) transfer of units from the Processing Department to the Bleaching Department and (2) the transfer of units from the Bleaching Department to finished goods inventory.

12–28 Joint Cost Allocation: Net Realizable Sales Value Method (Appendix)

Doe Corporation grows, processes, cans, and sells three main pineapple products—sliced pineapple, crushed pineapple, and pineapple juice. The outside skin is cut off in the Cutting Department and processed as animal feed. The skin is treated as a by-product. Doe's production process is as follows:

■ Pineapples are first processed in the Cutting Department. The pineapples are washed, and the outside skin is cut away. Then the pineapples are cored and trimmed for slicing. The three main products (sliced, crushed, and juice) and the by-product (animal feed) are recognized after processing in the Cutting Department. Each product is then transferred to a separate department for final processing.

■ The trimmed pineapples are forwarded to the Slicing Department, where the pineapples are sliced and canned. Any juice generated during the slicing operation is packed in the cans with the slices.

■ The pieces of pineapple trimmed from the fruit are diced and canned in the Crushing Department. Again, the juice generated during this operation is packed in the can with the crushed pineapple.

■ The core and surplus pineapple generated from the Cutting Department are pulverized into a liquid in the Juicing Department.

■ The outside skin is chopped into animal feed in the Feed Department.

The Doe Corporation uses the relative sales value method (based on net realizable value) to assign costs of the joint process to its main products. The by-product is inventoried at its market value. A total of 270,000 pounds were entered into the Cutting Department during May. The schedule below shows the costs incurred in each department, the proportion by weight transferred to the four final processing departments, and the selling price of each product.

Department	Costs Incurred	Percent of Product by Weight Transferred to Departments	Selling Price per Pound of Final Product
Cutting	$60,000	—	None
Slicing	4,700	35	$0.60
Crushing	10,580	28	0.55
Juicing	3,250	27	0.30
Animal feed	700	10	0.10
Total	$79,230	100	

Requirements

a) Calculate the number of pounds of pineapple that result as output for pineapple slices, crushed pineapple, pineapple juice, and animal feed.

b) Calculate the net realizable value at the split-off point of the three main products.

c) Calculate the amount of the cost of the Cutting Department assigned to each of the three main products and to the by-product in accordance with corporate policy. (Round calculations to four decimal places.)

d) Calculate the gross profits for each of the three main products.

(CMA Adapted)

CASES

12–29 Changing Environments

Massey Lawn Products has been in business for four years. The company initially implemented a job-cost system for its production operations. Separate job-cost systems were implemented for the production of lawn mowers, garden tillers, and leaf mulchers. The company had one assembly line, and each batch operation produced only 30 to 45 units. The amount of time, labor, materials and parts, and equipment usage were easily monitored. Factory supplies were also tracked and charged per batch. Other factory overhead items were charged using a predetermined overhead rate that was set each quarter. The job-cost data for a typical job is as follows:

Product Name 8 HP Tiller		Job Number 613	
Product # 11		Date 12-11-x7	
		Hours	*Dollars*
Direct labor @ $16 per hour		200	$3,200
Assembly line time @ $42 per hour		16	672
Components and parts:			
Motors, 32 @ $100 each			3,200
Component sets, 32 @ $70 each			2,240
Overhead, $24 per assembly line hour		16	384
Total costs			$9,696
Units completed			32
Cost per unit, ($9,696/32)			$303

During the past year the demand for each of the products has grown rapidly, and the job costing accountant has encountered much difficulty in tracking and recording the cost for every batch. The plant now has three assembly lines, one for each product line. Within each product line there are three models, the only major difference between them being the horsepower size of the motors. The assembly line workers are trained for all three lines, and many of the component parts, such as handles and wheels, are interchangeable between products.

Requirements

a) What arguments can be made for maintaining the job-cost system?

b) What arguments can be made for changing to process costing?

c) Make a recommendation as to which system you prefer, and explain how your system will meet the demands now placed upon the production system.

12–30 Selection of Costing Method in a Service Environment

Successful Services prepares tax returns only for successful individuals, that is, those with incomes over $100,000 annually. The company employs 25 experienced tax preparers. When clients come for service, they are randomly assigned to one of the preparers. Clients can ask for, but seldom get, the preparer from last year because the company has a very high turnover. Therefore, almost every return is prepared by someone unfamiliar with the client's tax history. Of course, if the company prepared an individual's tax return the prior year, a copy is on file in the computerized data bank.

At the end of each tax season, the company president knows how well the company performed overall, but she does not have any idea of the performance of the individual tax preparers. Some of the data available to help her make performance evaluations include:

- Actual hours spent on each return.
- Number of forms prepared for each return.
- Number of years a given individual's return has been prepared.
- Salary of each preparer per month.
- Minutes of computer time used per return.
- Minutes of computer time available for return preparation per day.
- Total overhead cost of the company per month.
- On a scale of 1 to 10, each preparer evaluates the difficulty of each return; this is one of the factors used in setting a fee for each client.
- Fee factors include difficulty rating, number of forms, and time to prepare.

Required: Selecting from either a job or process costing method, what do you recommend be used to accumulate and report the cost of the production operation of Successful Services? Justify your answer.

12–31 Selection of Costing System

Sydney Newspapers publishes two daily newspapers, the *Morning Star* and the afternoon *Bulletin*. Because each paper has a large circulation, the printing presses run almost constantly. As soon as the last edition of the morning paper is completed the first edition of the afternoon is ready for running. About the only downtime for the presses is on Sunday, when only the morning paper is published.

In the 1960s the company published the papers on alternating days with a combined edition on Sunday. During this period the first cost accounting system was installed. Because each paper had distinct starting and stopping points and a different set of workers, a job-costing system was designed to account for each paper by day. This resulted in seven cost reports a week, three for each paper and one for the combined Sunday edition. These reports assisted management in determining which paper was the most efficient and which one was the most profitable. Comparisons were made between papers, between days, and by size (number of pages).

As the city grew, so did the circulation of newspapers. About six years ago the company began daily operations of both papers. The job-costing system was adapted for these changes and at the same time placed in a computerized database to assist the management accountants in preparing the increased number of reports, 13 a week.

Requirements

a) What do you consider to be the most important cost reporting needs of Sydney Newspapers?

b) Describe the type of product costing system that you think would be best for Sydney Newspapers. Include journal entry method.

12–32 Traditional Process Costing versus Backflush Process Costing

Pendleton Oil Mill is a manufacturer of lawn and garden fertilizers. In recent years the company's president has been dissatisfied with the results of operations; he believes that accounting for finished goods is one of the problems. He prefers the company to expense items faster rather than slower; and following this philosophy, he insists that a better method be used to account for finished goods and cost of goods sold. Also, he believes that the operations managers worry too much about building inventories rather than keeping production costs low. He knows that costs for a given period can be kept artificially low by overproducing. (He has studied Chapter 10 of this text.)

Due to extreme cold weather, the mill closes for the month of January each year. When the mill resumes operation in February no work-in-process inventories exist and there are few raw materials. During February 19x7 the company purchased 200 tons of raw materials at $150 per ton; this is also the standard cost per ton for the new year. February's production used 180 tons of input, 10 of which were in process on February 28, 40 percent complete. The standard cost of labor is $20 per input ton processed in each department, and factory overhead is applied at $14 per ton of output in each department. All variances from standard are charged to cost of goods sold each month.

The mixing department completed all 180 tons received in February. The processing department also finished all 180 tons it received, but the screening department finished only 170 tons, with 10 left in process on February 28. Sales during February totalled 168 tons.

The assignments of conversion costs are by department, and each department manager is responsible for keeping costs under control to the extent possible. Unfortunately, the managers have trouble separating some of the direct labor costs because the employees are cross-trained and are frequently moved from one area to another to help handle equipment failures and other problems. Most of the managers never agree with the results presented by the product reports for their departments, although the production reports for the company tend to show efficient operations. The president is aware of these problems and would like to avoid them if possible by eliminating the departmental reports. The standard cost system implemented three years ago has helped, but there are still problems.

Requirements

a) Make journal entries for February 19x7 assuming traditional process costing.

b) Make journal entries for February 19x7 assuming backflush process costing.

c) Which method best satisfies the president's concerns about production reporting and why?

12–33 Designing a Product Costing System

Carolina Wood Products manufactures a single product, bookcases, in a series of five manufacturing operations: sawing, drilling, sanding, assembly, and varnishing. All units are identical in all respects. The plant layout is as follows:

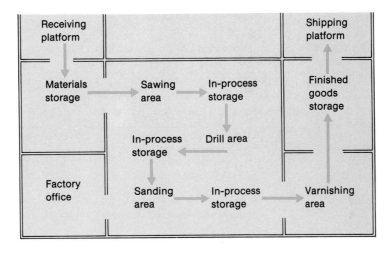

The flow of work is indicated by the arrows. All operations are either labor intensive or labor paced.

Bookcases are produced for speculative inventory, rather than in response to specific customer orders, in batches of 30 units. A job-cost sheet is maintained for each batch. All work on a batch is completed at each operation before the batch is placed in either in-process or finished goods storage. All units in a batch are then taken to the next operation for further manufacturing.

Requirements

a) Identify the basic records required to plan and initiate production and accumulate information for product costing purposes.

b) For the purpose of obtaining accurate product costs only, identify the number of cost centers that should be established, indicate why this number of cost centers is required, and describe how labor and overhead costs should be assigned to each job.

c) To reduce in-process inventories, management has decided to change from batch to continuous production. Under continuous production, units will move continuously from one operation to the next without being placed in in-process storage.

1. Is it possible to continue to utilize a job-cost system with batches of 30 units?

2. Briefly describe a more efficient approach to product costing under the new manufacturing environment.

3. What are the minimum number of cost centers required for accurate product costing under the cost system that you described above?

4. Identify one major subjective judgment that would likely be made each period under the cost system that you described above.

**REVIEW PROBLEM
SOLUTION**

a)   **Magnetic Media, Inc.
Cost of Production Report
For the year ended December 31, 19x7**

Summary of units in process

Beginning	3,000,000
Units started	27,000,000
In process	30,000,000
Completed	−25,000,000
Ending	5,000,000

Equivalent units in process	*Materials*	*Conversion*
Units completed	25,000,000	25,000,000
Plus: Equivalent units in ending inventory	5,000,000	1,500,000*
Equivalent units in process	30,000,000	26,500,000

Total cost to be accounted for and cost per equivalent unit in process	*Materials*	*Conversion*	*Total*
Work-in-Process, beginning	$ 468,000	$ 252,000	$ 720,000
Current cost	6,132,000	5,048,000**	11,180,000
Total cost in process	$ 6,600,000	$ 5,300,000	$11,900,000
Equivalent units in process	÷30,000,000	÷26,500,000	
Cost per equivalent unit in process	$0.22	$0.20	$0.42

Accounting for total cost

Transferred out		
(25,000,000 × $0.42)		$10,500,000
Work-in-Process, ending:		
Materials (5,000,000 × $0.22)	$ 1,100,000	
Conversion (1,500,000 × $0.20)	300,000	1,400,000
Total cost accounted for		$11,900,000

---

* 5,000,000 units 30% converted.

** Includes direct labor of $1,550,000 and applied factory overhead of $3,498,000.

b)	Work-in-Process	6,132,000	
	Raw Materials		6,132,000
	To record requisition of raw materials to factory.		

Work-in-Process 1,550,000
Factory Overhead 210,000
  Wages Payable 1,760,000
To record wages for the month and assign direct labor cost to Work-in-Process and indirect labor cost to Factory Overhead.

Factory Overhead 3,343,000
  Manufacturing Supplies 860,000
  Accumulated Depreciation 1,400,000
  Miscellaneous Payables 1,083,000
To record actual factory overhead expenses incurred for the period.

Work-in-Process 3,498,000
  Factory Overhead 3,498,000
To apply factory overhead to Work-in-Process at the rate of $12 per machine hour.

Finished Goods Inventory 10,500,000
  Work-in-Process 10,500,000
Cost of Goods Sold 55,000
  Factory Overhead 55,000
To close underapplied factory overhead to Cost of Goods Sold.

C H A P T E R 13

The Reassignment of Indirect Costs and Activity-Based Costing

Learning Objectives

Upon completion of this chapter you should:

■ **Understand the nature of indirect costs.**

■ **Understand the uses and limitations of the reassignment of indirect costs.**

■ **Understand the relationship between cost pools and cost objectives.**

■ **Be familiar with the alternative bases for cost reassignment.**

■ **Be able to determine cost reassignments using the direct, step, and linear algebra methods.**

■ **Be familiar with the activity-based costing approach to indirect cost reassignment.**

■ **Have a general understanding of the problems related to the reassignment of nonmanufacturing costs, including home office costs and indirect costs in not-for-profit organizations.**

In Chapter 2, cost objectives were defined as the objects or activities to which costs are assigned. All cost measurement involves assigning and/or reassigning costs to cost objectives. Although all costs can be directly associated with at least one cost objective, it is not always possible to directly associate costs with a specific cost objective.

Assume the cost objective is the personnel department and that management desires information on the total costs of operating this department. In determining the total costs of the personnel department, the salary of the personnel manager is directly related to the department. On the other hand, the cost of electricity used by the personnel department (which occupies half a floor in the administrative office building) cannot be measured directly unless there is an electric meter for the department. With one electric meter for the entire building, electricity is a direct cost of the building but an indirect cost of each department in the building. It is necessary to make an indirect, estimated, measure of the cost of electricity consumed by the personnel department. This is accomplished by reassigning a portion of the total electricity cost of the building to each department occupying the building.

The cost of electricity may be reassigned to individual departments based on their relative quantities of such items as floor space, electric lights, electric outlets, or employees using electricity. Regardless of the basis used for reassigning the cost of electricity, there will be inherent weaknesses in the measurement of department costs because the reassignments are only indirect estimates of departmental electricity costs. To measure the actual cost directly for each department in the building, the building would have to be rewired with separate electric meters installed for each department.

Like the personnel department, most cost objectives have both direct and indirect costs associated with them. The purpose of this chapter is to explore the nature of indirect costs, consider the uses and limitations of reassigned costs, and examine some of the alternative methods of reassigning indirect costs. Newer approaches to cost reassignment, such as activity-based costing, are also considered. Finally, there are brief discussions of cost reassignment issues related to corporate home offices and not-for-profit organizations.

THE NATURE OF INDIRECT COSTS

All costs are direct costs of at least one cost objective within an organization. When costs are reassigned to another objective they become indirect costs. With respect to products, direct materials and direct labor were identified in Chapter 2 as **direct product costs** because of their immediate association with products. All other product costs, which are placed in cost pools before being assigned to products, were identified as **indirect product costs.**

A similar analysis can be made of costs with respect to departments or cost centers. Assume that manufacturing costs in a company are incurred at the following levels: (1) plant administration, (2) plant services, and (3) production departments. If all manufacturing related costs are to be assigned to products, procedures must be established to reassign plant administration and plant services costs to products or to the production departments prior to their being reassigned to products. The traditional approach to cost assignment specifies the reassignment of plant administration and service costs to production departments prior to the assignment of these costs to products. Although the costs of plant administration and services may be direct costs of their respective departments, they are regarded as indirect costs of production departments. They are also indirect product costs.

To summarize, a **direct department cost** is a cost assigned to a department upon its incurrence, and an **indirect department cost** is a cost reassigned to a department from another cost objective. Various relationships between direct and indirect costs are illustrated in Exhibit 13–1, which shows a typical pattern of cost assignments and reassignments for the purpose of product costing in a job-cost system. Here plant administrative costs are reassigned to service and production departments. Service department costs, including costs reassigned from plant administration, are reassigned to production departments. Finally, all production department costs, including reassigned plant administration and service department costs, are reassigned to products. In job costing, direct materials and direct labor are also direct costs of the production departments; hence they are assigned to products without being placed in a cost pool. In process costing all product costs are placed in one or more production department cost pools before being assigned to products.

The terminology used in connection with indirect costs varies widely and is often inconsistent. In general, we restrict the use of the phrase "cost assignment" for use in reference to the initial assignment of direct costs to a cost objective. We use the phrase "cost reassignment" in reference to indirect costs that were initially assigned to another cost objective. The term "cost allocation" is often used in place of, or interchangeably with, the term "cost reassignment." Because we believe it is more descriptive, we favor the term "cost reassignment."

The notion of common costs is closely related to indirect department costs. **Common costs** are incurred within a department or cost center for the benefit of two or more cost objectives. Hence common costs are direct costs of the department or cost center to which they were initially assigned and indirect costs of the department, cost center, or product to which they are reassigned. Synonyms for *common* include *joint, habitual, widespread, base, normal,* and *ordinary.* All of these terms suggest a difficulty in controlling common costs or identifying them with the activities that cause them.

Accountants often lump indirect costs into broad cost pools and dismiss them as common. The dramatic growth taking place in indirect product costs, in relationship to direct product costs, makes this treatment unacceptable. Many costs that were thought to be joint and placed in broad-based pools of common costs have, upon closer inspection, turned out to be driven by specific activities in cost centers other than the one where the so-called common costs were initially recorded. Hence a desirable goal when developing or revising an

EXHIBIT 13–1   Relationships between Direct and Indirect Costs in a Job Cost System (Arrows Represent Cost Reassignments)

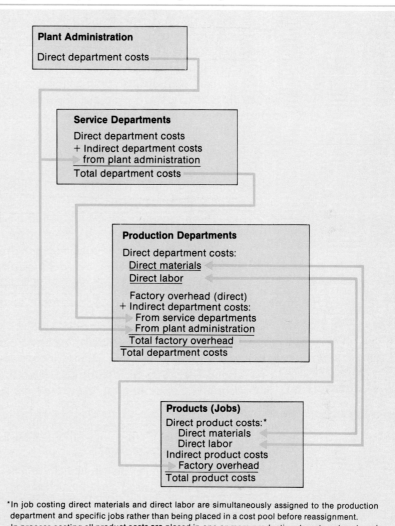

*In job costing direct materials and direct labor are simultaneously assigned to the production department and specific jobs rather than being placed in a cost pool before reassignment.
In process costing all product costs are placed in one or more production department cost pools before being assigned to products.

accounting system is to break pools of common costs further into segments that can be more accurately identified with specific cost objectives. To avoid implying that indirect costs cannot be affected by activities in other departments, we will make only limited use of the phrase *common costs*.

USES AND LIMITATIONS OF INDIRECT COST REASSIGNMENTS

For financial reporting and tax purposes, when there are significant beginning or ending inventories, all manufacturing costs are normally assigned or reassigned to products. This requires the reassignment of many manufacturing costs that are not directly identified with specific products or production departments. However, just because costs are reassigned to a product for financial reporting or tax purposes does not mean that reassigned costs can be used effectively for other purposes, such as cost control and performance evaluation. There are two reasons for this:

1. Cost reassignments for financial reporting and tax purposes often rely on a limited number of broadly defined cost pools and volume-based cost assignment schemes that are relatively simple to implement but not necessarily reflective of the many activities that cause the incurrence of indirect costs. These broad cost pools and volume-based measures merely ensure that all manufacturing costs are accounted for in a systematic manner. Inventory and the cost of goods sold may be correctly valued in total, but the costs of individual products are often inaccurate.

2. Even though much effort may be expended, there will likely be some indirect costs that cannot be accurately reassigned to specific departments and products. These are the residual common costs.

Where care is taken to ensure that costs are reassigned on the basis of the activities that cause (drive) their incurrence, the resulting numbers can be useful for a variety of decisions, including those related to product pricing, cost control, and performance evaluation. In other cases, the reassigned costs might best be ignored by managers.

Managers will resist having their performance evaluated on the basis of reassigned costs they cannot control. When reassignments can be justified for purposes of performance evaluation (because activities in consuming departments cause, or drive, the incurrence of costs in other departments), the reassignments should be based on a predetermined or standard cost of services provided, not on the basis of actual costs incurred. Using predetermined or standard costs prevents actual cost inefficiencies from being passed on to the users of the services.

Indirect cost data should be used with discretion when evaluating the overall profitability of a business segment. Each cost reassigned to a segment should be painstakingly evaluated to determine whether it will change depending on the activities of the business segment. Reassigned costs that are unavoidable (and thus continue to be incurred whether or not a segment is continued) should be disregarded in measuring the segment's contribution to total company profits.

The key to using reassigned costs effectively is recognizing their uses and limitations, and recognizing that these attributes are often a function of the care taken in developing accurate systems of cost reassignment. Reassigned costs are fundamentally different from direct costs. With effort, many indirect costs can be associated with the activities, business segments, or products that caused them. Other indirect costs are truly common to a variety of activities and cannot be accurately reassigned to other departments or products.

REASSIGNMENT OF INDIRECT COSTS

A major difference between direct cost assignment and indirect cost reassignment is related to measurement precision. Initial cost assignment is a direct measurement of costs incurred for the benefit of a specific cost objective, whereas subsequent cost reassignments are often estimates of the costs incurred to provide services to cost objectives. Occasionally subsequent reassignments are unrelated to the incurrence of indirect costs.

MANAGERIAL PRACTICE 13.1

Choosing New Cost Reassignment Methods

"The high degree of automation in new production processes changes the way products are produced and therefore changes the cost structure of products," says Nancy Brunton, cost accounting manager of the Engine Systems Division of Simmonds Precision. At Simmonds Precision, new cost structures are developed formally, with specified procedures. The first step is analysis of indirect factory cost allocations. This step begins with an evaluation of current reassignment methods used in each production process. Next, managers determine whether a more appropriate method of reassignment can be used. They also review the base used for each type of reassignment, to determine its appropriateness given the new technologies being implemented. The selection of the appropriate reassignment method is made after the advantages and disadvantages of each method have been evaluated. The final decision depends on several factors, the most important being what type of information will prove most useful in management decision making.

Source: Nancy M. Brunton, "Evaluation of Overhead Allocations," *Management Accounting* (July 1988): 22–26.

The accuracy of a reassigned cost is a function of the activity being measured and the quality of an organization's cost system. What's more, reassigned costs are often combined with direct costs (as in the case of product costing); therefore, any error in the reassignment of indirect costs affects not only the reassigned cost component but also the total cost for the cost objective (such as a product). To understand the factors that affect the accuracy of indirect cost reassignment, it is necessary to examine the basic components of cost reassignment systems:

- Cost objectives.
- Cost pools.
- Reassignment bases.

Cost Objectives

As noted previously, a cost objective is an object or activity to which costs are assigned. Although the most traditional cost objectives are departments, products, and services, managements' needs for cost information are quite varied. In serving management it is important for accountants to think beyond these traditional cost objectives. Likewise, it is important for managers to seek the advice of their management accountant when they need nontraditional cost information. A cost objective can be anything for which management desires cost information.

For example, management might desire to accumulate information concerning the firmwide cost of overnight package delivery. In this case relevant cost information could be gathered from all organizational units that use this type of service and totaled for the cost objective "Cost of Overnight Package Delivery." This information might be useful in negotiating with an express carrier for a firmwide discount.

As another example, management might desire information on the total costs associated with the failure to produce products that conform to quality specifications. In this case information concerning such costs as rework, spoiled or defective units, and warranty claims could be gathered from throughout the organization for each product and totaled for the cost objective "Cost of Quality Failure." This information might be useful in justifying expenditures for better product design, simplified manufacturing procedures, training, or new equipment.

Other examples of useful cost objectives include: (1) the cost of moving materials between work stations (used in evaluating the desirability of rearranging equipment), (2) the cost of inspecting incoming raw materials and returning raw materials that do not meet quality specifications (used to rate and negotiate with vendors), and (3) the firmwide cost of long distance telephone service (used to evaluate the desirability of switching carriers and/or subscribing to wide-area telephone service). It may not be possible to accurately associate all indirect costs with these cost objectives, but the resulting cost information should assist management in determining (1) if immediate action is warranted;

(2) if no action is warranted; or (3) if the situation, although not in need of immediate action, is worth further study.

Cost Pools

A **cost pool** is a collection of related costs, such as factory overhead, that is reassigned to other cost objectives. As a practical matter it is not feasible in many situations to reassign each item of cost (such as the plant manager's salary) separately. Instead, several similar costs are combined into a cost pool, and the entire pool is reassigned as a single item. Indirect costs are often pooled along departmental lines, such as payroll department costs, computer center costs, or maintenance department costs. Pooling all building-related costs, or the costs for any other natural function, is also frequently done. Sometimes these functional cost pools are referred to as departments even though they may not exist as such on the organization chart. For example, all building-related costs (depreciation, insurance, repairs, etc.) are often pooled together to form building department costs, which are then reassigned to the departments that use the building.

The key consideration in establishing cost pools is that the items pooled together should be relatively homogeneous and have a logical *cause-and-effect* relation to the allocation base. For instance, a building cost pool would include all costs related to the maintenance and operation of the building and might be reassigned on the basis of square footage occupied. The costs in this pool, such as insurance, property taxes, and depreciation, have a logical cause-and-effect relation to the amount of square footage provided. As the square footage increases, these costs are naturally expected to increase.

Within functional cost pools it may be useful to provide separate pools for fixed costs and variable costs. This will result in cost reassignments that more accurately reflect the factors that drive costs. Fixed costs are often driven by capacity, whereas variable costs are driven by actual activity.

To illustrate the reassignment of fixed and variable costs, assume that Alco Manufacturing Company has one factory with three producing departments: Stamping, Assembly, and Inspection. There is also a Maintenance Department that provides services to the producing departments. Costs incurred by the Maintenance Department are placed in separate fixed and variable cost pools and reassigned to the producing departments. Fixed costs consist of maintenance staff salaries, depreciation, insurance, and utilities on the maintenance shop facilities. Variable costs consist of supplies and parts used in performing maintenance services for the producing departments. Maintenance Department costs for 19x8 were as follows:

Fixed costs	$60,000
Variable costs	37,500
Total Maintenance Department costs	$97,500

Five hundred hours of service were performed for the three producing departments as follows:

Stamping Department	250
Assembly Department	200
Inspection Department	50
Total standard service hours	500

In setting up the Maintenance Department, Alco's management decided on a maintenance service *capacity* of 800 standard service hours per year. This capacity was based on a maximum need of 400 hours for the Stamping Department, and 200 hours each for the Assembly and Inspection Departments. It was also determined that *fixed costs* should be reassigned on the basis of *capacity provided* each production department, and that *variable costs* should be reassigned on the basis of *actual usage* of Maintenance Department services. Exhibit 13–2 shows the reassignment computations for fixed and variable Maintenance Department costs. The fixed cost percentages (50%, 25%, and 25%) reflect the cost of the capacity provided for each department, whereas the variable cost percentages (50%, 40%, and 10%) are intended to reflect the variable costs actually incurred on behalf of each department during the period.

Reassignment Bases The reassignment base is the connecting link between cost objectives and cost pools. The cost reassignment base is the factor, or characteristic, common to the cost objectives that determines how much of the cost pool is reassigned to each cost objective. The reassignment base selected varies depending on the nature of the indirect costs and the nature of the cost objectives. For example, labor-related costs may be reassigned according to some measure (or estimate) of the labor time devoted to the various cost objectives. Depreciation and other building-related costs are often reassigned on the basis of square footage occupied. Other examples of indirect costs and frequently used reassignment bases include the following:

Cost Category	Reassignment Base
Employee health services	Number of employees or calls
Personnel	Number of employees or new hires
Plant and grounds	Square footage occupied
Maintenance repairs	Number of repair orders or service hours
Purchasing	Number of orders placed
Warehouse	Square footage used or value of materials stored

EXHIBIT 13–2   Reassignment of Fixed and Variable Costs

Fixed cost reassignment

Department	Capacity Provided			Total Fixed Cost		Fixed Cost Reassignment
	Service Hours	*Percent*				
Stamping	400	50	×	$60,000	=	$30,000
Assembly	200	25	×	60,000	=	15,000
Inspection	200	25	×	60,000	=	15,000
Total	800	100				$60,000

Variable cost reassignment

Department	Actual Service Hours		Variable Cost per Hour*		Variable Cost Reassignment	Percent of Reassignment
Stamping	250	×	$75	=	$18,750	50
Assembly	200	×	75	=	15,000	40
Inspection	50	×	75	=	3,750	10
Total	500				$37,500	100

Total maintenance department cost reassignment

Department	Fixed Cost	Variable Cost	Total Reassignment
Stamping	$30,000	$18,750	$48,750
Assembly	15,000	15,000	30,000
Inspection	15,000	3,750	18,750
Total	$60,000	$37,500	$97,500

* Variable cost per service hour:

Total variable cost		Total hours		Variable cost per hour
$37,500	÷	500	=	$75.

The most important consideration in selecting an allocation base is making sure there is a logical cause-and-effect association between the base selected and the costs incurred. For instance, it is logical to reassign personnel department costs according to the number of employees because the function of the personnel department is to provide employee-related services to the various departments. Thus personnel costs are incurred as these services are provided. It follows that departments with a large number of employees should ordinarily receive a larger allocation of personnel department costs than departments with few employees.

Another consideration in selecting an allocation base is whether to reflect the service capacity provided or only the actual services used. Refer to Exhibit 13–2, where we use different bases for reassigning fixed and variable costs.

Fixed costs are allocated based on the capacity provided, and variable costs are allocated according to the actual services used. Basing fixed costs on capacity provided eliminates the possibility that the amount of the cost allocation to one department is affected by the level of services utilized by other departments. In Exhibit 13–2, the Assembly Department used 200 service hours during the year, equaling the capacity provided for it. The 200 hours represent 25 percent (200 hours ÷ 800 hours) of the total capacity of the service department, but they represent 40 percent (200 hours ÷ 500 total actual hours) of the total actual services rendered. If fixed costs had been allocated based on actual services used rather than on capacity provided, $24,000 (40 percent of the fixed costs), instead of $15,000, would have been reassigned to the Assembly Department. This additional charge of $9,000 would have resulted from other producing departments failing to use the capacity provided for them. When fixed service department costs are allocated according to capacity provided, managers of producing departments are charged for the capacity provided whether they use it or not, and their use of services has no effect on the amount of costs reassigned to other departments. A benefit of this allocation system is that it reduces the temptation for managers to avoid or delay services in order to minimize fixed cost allocations to their departments.

SERVICE DEPARTMENT COST REASSIGNMENT

A service department is a department that provides support functions primarily for one or more production departments. Examples of service departments are maintenance, personnel, payroll, security, grounds, data processing, food services, and health services. These departments, which are considered essential elements in the overall manufacturing process, do not work directly on the "product," but they do provide auxiliary support to the producing departments. In addition to providing support for the various producing departments, some service departments also provide services to other service departments. For example, the payroll and personnel departments may provide services for all departments, both production and service, and maintenance may provide services for the producing departments as well as limited services for food and health services. Services provided by one service department to other service departments are called interdepartmental services.

Three methods are discussed in this section for reassigning service department costs: the *direct method,* the *step method,* and the *linear algebra method.* To illustrate each method we will reassign service department costs for the Kona Kola Company for 19x8, which has two producing departments, Mixing and Bottling, and three service departments. The service departments and their respective service functions and cost allocation bases are as follows:

Department	Service Functions	Reassignment Base
Administrative Services	Accounting, audit, payroll, and inventory control	Total department capital investment
Human Resources	Personnel, training, and health services	Number of employees
Plant and Facilities	Maintenance, security, depreciation, and insurance	Square footage occupied

Difficulty in choosing a reassignment base for service department costs is not uncommon. Kona Kola readily determined the appropriate allocation bases for the Human Resources Department and the Plant and Facilities Department; however, for Administrative Services the choice was much less clear. After conducting correlation studies it was determined that the most equitable base for reassigning Administrative Services costs was total capital investment in each department.

The data used to illustrate Kona Kola's 19x8 service department cost reassignments are summarized as follows.

	Direct Department Costs	Number of Employees	Square Footage Occupied	Department Capital Investment
Service departments:				
Administrative Services	$ 27,000	15	4,000	$ 75,000
Human Resources	20,000	10	2,000	45,000
Plant and Facilities	10,000	5	3,000	50,000
Producing departments:				
Mixing	40,000*	24	11,000	180,000
Bottling	90,000*	56	33,000	270,000
Total	$187,000	110	53,000	$620,000

* Direct department overhead

Direct Method

The direct method reassigns all service department costs directly to the producing departments without any recognition of interdepartmental services. Exhibit 13–3 shows the flow of costs using the direct method. Note that all arrows depicting the cost flows extend only from service departments to producing departments; there are no cost reassignments between the service departments.

Exhibit 13–4 shows the service department cost allocations for the direct method. To explain the basic approach of the direct method, note the base used to reassign Human Resources Department costs. Only the employees in the

EXHIBIT 13–3   Flow of Costs—Direct Method

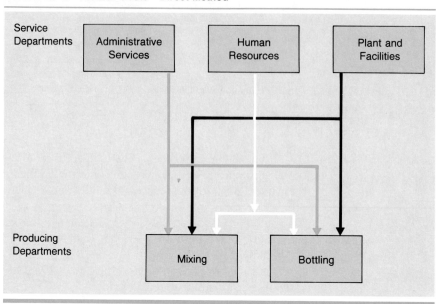

producing departments are considered in computing the allocation percentages—24 in the Mixing Department and 56 in the Bottling Department, for a total of 80 employees in the allocation base. Thirty percent (24 ÷ 80) of the producing department employees work in the Mixing Department; therefore, 30 percent of the Human Resources Department costs are reassigned to the Mixing Department. Applying the same reasoning, 70 percent of the Human Resources Department costs are reassigned to the Bottling Department. Similar logic is followed in computing the cost allocations for the Plant and Facilities Department and the Administrative Services Department.

The cost reassignment summary at the bottom of Exhibit 13–4 shows that all service department costs have been reassigned, increasing the producing department balances by the amounts of the respective allocations. Also note that total costs are not affected by the allocations—the total of $187,000 was merely redistributed so that all costs are assigned to the producing departments.

The total overhead costs of the producing departments after reassignment of service costs are $59,300 for the Mixing Department and $127,700 for the Bottling Department. If Kona Kola applies actual factory overhead costs to production, these amounts will be reassigned to products. If the company uses predetermined overhead rates, any difference between applied and actual overhead (after service department cost reassignments) is identified as underapplied or overapplied factory overhead.

EXHIBIT 13–4   Service Department Cost Reassignments—Direct Method

	Total	Mixing	Bottling
Administrative Services Department:			
Reassignment base (capital investment)	$450,000	$180,000	$270,000
Percent of total base	100%	40%	60%
Cost reassignments	$ 27,000	$ 10,800	$ 16,200
Human Resources Department:			
Reassignment base (number of employees)	80	24	56
Percent of total base	100%	30%	70%
Cost reassignments	$ 20,000	$ 6,000	$ 14,000
Plant and Facilities Department:			
Reassignment base (square footage occupied)	44,000	11,000	33,000
Percent of total base	100%	25%	75%
Cost reassignments	$ 10,000	$ 2,500	$ 7,500

Cost Reassignment Summary:

	Administrative Services	Human Resources	Plant and Facilities	Mixing	Bottling	Total
Departmental costs before reassignments	$27,000	$20,000	$10,000	$40,000	$ 90,000	$187,000
Cost reassignments:						
Administrative Services	(27,000)			10,800	16,200	—
Human Resources		(20,000)		6,000	14,000	—
Plant and Facilities			(10,000)	2,500	7,500	—
Departmental costs after reassignments	$ —	$ —	$ —	$59,300	$127,700	$187,000

Step Method

Unlike the direct method, which gives no recognition to interdepartmental services, the step method of reassigning service department costs gives at least partial recognition to interdepartmental services. Under the step method, management first determines the service department that provides the most interdepartmental services. That department's total costs are then reassigned to the other service departments and the producing departments. The service department whose costs are reassigned first receives no allocations from other service departments even though it may receive services from them. The service department reassigned second (including costs received from the first department) has its total costs reassigned to the remaining service departments and to the producing departments. The last service department to have its costs reassigned (including all costs received from other service departments) has its total costs allocated only to the producing departments.

Exhibit 13–5 shows the flow of service department costs for Kona Kola Company under the step method. Note that Human Resources costs are reassigned to all other departments. Administrative Services costs are reassigned to Plant and Facilities and to the producing departments. Plant and Facilities costs are reassigned only to the producing departments.

Although there is no generally accepted rule for determining the order for reassigning service department costs under the step method, as explained above, the department that provides the most services to other service departments usually has its costs reassigned first. Reassignments of other service department costs follow in order based on their relative levels of *interdepartmental services*.

Exhibit 13–6 shows the computations for determining the sequence of cost reassignments for Kona Kola's service departments. The measure of services provided by the service departments is stated in terms of the *reassignment base*. For example, the services provided by the Administrative Services Department are measured in terms of total investment. The total investment in all departments other than Administrative Services is $545,000, and the total investment in other *service* departments is $95,000. Therefore, in terms of its reassignment base, Administrative Services provided 17.4 percent ($95,000 ÷ $545,000) of its

EXHIBIT 13–5   Flow of Costs—Step Method

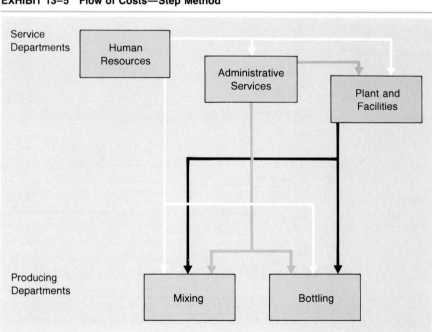

EXHIBIT 13–6 Reassignment Sequence for Step Method

	Administrative Services	Human Resources	Plant and Facilities
Reassignment base	Capital investment	Number of employees	Square footage
(a) Total base for other service and producing departments	$545,000	100	50,000
(b) Total base for other service departments	$ 95,000	20	6,000
Percent of total services provided to other service departments			
[(b) ÷ (a)]	17.4%	20%	12%
Reassignment sequence	Second	First	Third

total services to other service departments. The total investment in all departments of $545,000 excludes the investment in Administrative Services, since only services to other departments are considered. Since interdepartmental services amounted to 20.0 percent for Human Resources and 12.0 percent for Plant and Facilities, the sequence of reassignment of service department costs under the step method is Human Resources first, followed by Administrative Services and then Plant and Facilities.

Reassignment of service department costs using the step method is shown in Exhibit 13–7. The mathematical procedures are essentially the same as in the direct method. Note, however, that under the step method the reassignment base includes the appropriate base measure for the producing and service departments to which costs are reassigned. For example, the Human Resources cost reassignment base includes the number of employees in the producing departments and the other service departments. For Administrative Services, the base includes the total capital investment for the producing departments and the Plant and Facilities Department. For Plant and Facilities, the base includes only the square footage for the producing departments since its costs are reassigned to only these departments.

Note in Exhibit 13–7 that the total cost reassigned from each service department includes the department's direct costs plus any costs reassigned from other service departments. Since Human Resources costs are reassigned first, they include only direct department costs. However, Administrative Services costs include $27,000 of direct department costs plus $3,000 of costs reassigned from Human Resources. Plant and Facilities costs include $10,000 of direct department costs plus reassignments of $1,000 from Human Resources and $3,000 from Administrative Services. These interdepartmental cost reassignments are summarized at the bottom of Exhibit 13–7. Once again, for product costing purposes, the total overhead costs of Mixing and Bottling would be reassigned to products.

EXHIBIT 13-7   Service Department Cost Reassignments—Step Method

	Total	Administrative Services	Plant and Facilities	Mixing	Bottling
Human Resources Department:					
Reassignment base (number of employees)	100	15	5	24	56
Percent of total base	100%	15%	5%	24%	56%
Cost reassignments	$ 20,000	$3,000	$ 1,000	$ 4,800	$ 11,200
Administrative Services Department:					
Reassignment base (capital investment)	$500,000		$50,000	$180,000	$270,000
Percent of total base	100%		10%	36%	54%
Cost reassignments	$ 30,000*		$ 3,000	$ 10,800	$ 16,200
Plant and Facilities Department:					
Reassignment base (square footage occupied)	44,000			11,000	33,000
Percent of total base	100%			25%	75%
Cost reassignments	$ 14,000*			$ 3,500	$ 10,500

Cost Reassignment Summary:

	Human Resources	Administrative Services	Plant and Facilities	Mixing	Bottling	Total
Departmental costs before reassignments	$20,000	$27,000	$10,000	$40,000	$ 90,000	$187,000
Cost reassignments:						
Human Resources	(20,000)	3,000	1,000	4,800	11,200	—
Administrative Services		(30,000)	3,000	10,800	16,200	—
Plant and Facilities			(14,000)	3,500	10,500	—
Departmental costs after reassignments	$ —	$ —	$ —	$59,100	$127,900	$187,000

*From cost reassignment summary.

Linear Algebra Method

The *direct method* provides an easy way of reassigning the service department costs to producing departments. Its primary weakness is that it does not recognize *any* interdepartmental services among service departments. This weakness is not crucial so long as all service departments are providing approximately the same level of services to all producing departments. When the quantity of services provided to the producing departments is significantly disproportionate, the service department cost reassignments may be distorted using the direct method. This distortion may, in turn, cause some products to be assigned costs that are related to the production of other products.

The *step method* recognizes interdepartmental services *only partially* because a service department cannot receive a reassignment from other departments once its costs have been reassigned. Although the step method overcomes much of the distortion inherent in direct reassignments, significant distortions may remain under some circumstances. The only sure way of eliminating all distortions of this type is to recognize all interdepartmental services simultaneously.

The linear algebra method reassigns all service department costs simultaneously to service departments and to producing departments. To use this method, a linear algebraic equation is developed for each service and production department. Each equation represents total departmental costs, that is, direct department costs plus a percentage of service department costs. To illustrate the equations, assume a company has two service departments (S1 and S2) and two producing departments (P1 and P2). The percentage distribution of services is shown below for each department.

Services Provided from	Services Provided to				
	S1	S2	P1	P2	Total
S1	—	5%	40%	55%	100%
S2	10%	—	30%	60%	100%

Total direct department costs for the service and producing departments are as follows:

S1	$ 20,000
S2	$ 35,000
P1	$150,000
P2	$ 90,000

The algebraic equations expressing the total costs (direct and reassigned) for each department are as follows:

$$S1 = 20,000 + 0.10\ S2$$
$$S2 = 35,000 + 0.05\ S1$$
$$P1 = 150,000 + 0.40\ S1 + 0.30\ S2$$
$$P2 = 90,000 + 0.55\ S1 + 0.60\ S2.$$

Using the substitution method, these equations are solved as shown below.

Substituting S2 into S1:

$$S1 = 20,000 + 0.10(35,000 + 0.05\ S1)$$
$$S1 = 20,000 + 3,500 + 0.005\ S1$$
$$0.995\ S1 = 23,500$$
$$S1 = 23,618.$$

Substituting the solution of S1 into S2:

$$S2 = 35,000 + 0.05(23,618)$$
$$S2 = 35,000 + 1,181$$
$$S2 = 36,181.$$

Substituting the solutions of S1 and S2 into P1:

$$P1 = 150,000 + 0.40(23,618) + 0.30(36,181)$$
$$P1 = 150,000 + 9,447 + 10,854$$
$$P1 = 170,301.$$

Substituting the solutions of S1 and S2 into P2:

$$P2 = 90,000 + 0.55(23,618) + 0.60(36,181)$$
$$P2 = 90,000 + 12,990 + 21,709$$
$$P2 = 124,699.$$

How do we interpret these solutions? First, note that the solutions to S1 and S2 consist of two components, their respective direct department costs plus the cost reassigned from the other service department. For example, since the solved value for S1 is $23,618, the reassigned costs from S2 are $3,618, or the difference between the final value assigned to S1 and the S1 direct department costs. In a similar fashion, the solutions to P1 and P2 consist of three components. P1 consists of $150,000 plus $9,447 plus $10,854, and P2 consists of $90,000 plus $12,990 plus $21,709. For each of these producing department variables, the first component represents the *direct costs* of the department. The second component represents the reassignment of S1 costs to the producing department, and the third component represents the reassignment of S2 costs to the producing departments.

A summary of all cost reassignments among service departments and producing departments is shown below, and a diagram of these reassignments is provided in Exhibit 13–8.

	S1	S2	P1	P2	Total
Departmental costs before reassignments	$20,000	$35,000	$150,000	$ 90,000	$295,000
S1 reassignment	(23,618)	1,181	9,447	12,990	—
S2 reassignment	3,618	(36,181)	10,854	21,709	—
Departmental costs after reassignments	$ —	$ —	$170,301	$124,699	$295,000

The substitution method of simultaneously solving linear equations is inefficient except in the simplest of situations (such as our example). Where there are more than two service departments providing interdepartmental services,

EXHIBIT 13–8   Flow of Costs—Linear Algebra Method

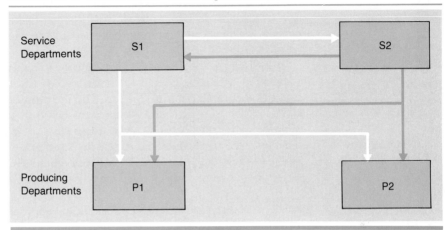

it is necessary to use matrix algebra for solving equations simultaneously. Using matrix algebra would also be very laborious were it not for the aid of computers. With a computer and appropriate software, solving matrix algebra problems is relatively easy. Several spreadsheet software programs contain easy-to-use matrix algebra routines. (A detailed discussion of matrix algebra is beyond the scope of this text.)

ACTIVITY-BASED COSTING

The overhead cost pool has sometimes been referred to as a "blob" of common costs. The constant growth of costs classified as overhead has forced accountants to search for increasingly detailed methods to analyze overhead costs. When overhead costs were low in comparison with other costs, when factories produced few products in long production runs, and when there was little global competition, the use of a single plantwide overhead rate may have been adequate. However, as overhead costs grew, manufacturing facilities began to produce a wider variety of products; and as competition intensified, the inadequacies of a single plantwide overhead rate became noticeable. These conditions caused attention to shift to departmental overhead rates and the reassignment of service department costs.

As the trends toward product diversity, proportionately higher overhead costs, and global competition continues, management's need for accurate cost information becomes increasingly acute. Managers must know the costs of their products or services to compete successfully by means of intelligent decisions regarding pricing, product mix, product design, making or buying, and continuing or discontinuing. Fortunately, advances in information technology and the declining costs of computerized information systems have facilitated the development and maintenance of increasingly detailed databases. These and other factors, such as declining inventory levels that make product costing less significant for financial reporting, have led to the emergence of activity-based costing.

Activity-based costing (ABC) involves, to the extent practicable, the assignment and reassignment of costs to cost objectives on the basis of the activities that cause costs. ABC is based on the premise that activities cause costs and that the cost of activities should be assigned to cost objectives on the basis of the activities they consume. ABC traces costs to products on the basis of the activities used to produce them. Activity-based costing is not conceptually different from service department cost reassignment when the reassignment of service department costs is based on a cost causing activity (cost driver).

Activity and Traditional Costing

Activity-based costing differs from traditional approaches to cost reassignment in terms of the number of cost pools, the frequent assignment of costs to inventories rather than to overhead cost pools, the rejection of volume-based reassignment, the need to understand the production process, and the frequent use of judgment. Four examples will help illustrate the differences between activity-based costing and traditional methods of cost reassignment (direct, step, and linear algebra).

1. Using a traditional reassignment system, maintenance department costs might be reassigned to production departments on the basis of the number of repair orders *or* the number of service hours. Using an activity-based cost system, an attempt would be made to determine the extent that each

MANAGERIAL PRACTICE 13.2

Success of Activity-Based Costing

When activity-based costing was tried at an auto-stamping plant, management found that previous calculations of production costs for individual products were off by as much as 60 percent. As a result of using traditional cost systems, the plant had let other manufacturers make some parts it should have kept in house, and vice versa.

Source: Otis Port, Resa King, and William J. Hampton, "How the New Math of Productivity Adds Up," *Business Week*, 6 June 1988, 103–114.

of these (and perhaps other) activities cause the incurrence of maintenance department costs. If more than one important cost driver were identified, two (or more) maintenance department cost pools would be established with separate reassignment bases for each.

2. Using a traditional reassignment system, purchasing department costs might be reassigned to production departments on the basis of the dollar value of raw materials issued to each department. Using an activity-based cost system an attempt would be made to determine the activities causing the incurrence of purchasing department costs. Perhaps purchasing costs would be a function of the number of orders *and* the dollar value of orders. In this case separate cost pools would be established for each cost driver. Relying on computer-based computational capacity, these costs could be reassigned to individual units of raw materials in an activity-based cost system, rather than being reassigned to production departments.

3. Using a traditional cost system, a portion of the electricity costs of a building might be reassigned to each department in the building on the basis of floor space,[1] or a portion of central administrative costs might be reassigned to each plant and ultimately to each product on the basis of sales revenue. Activity-based costing would not be used to reassign these costs unless they could be associated with cost drivers.

4. Using a traditional cost system, all of the direct and indirect overhead costs of a production department are reassigned to products on the basis of a single factor such as direct labor hours or machine hours. Using an activity cost system, an attempt would be made to develop a more detailed list of cost drivers. If machine set-up time, machine operating hours, and the number of components joined in final assembly were identified as cost drivers, activity-based costing would use three cost pools and reassignment bases.

Several characteristics of activity-based costing emerge from these examples:

1. *Activity-based costing uses a greater number of cost pools* than traditional cost reassignment methods. Traditional costing tends to equate one department with one cost pool, but activity-based costing often uses multiple cost pools within a single department. This is true of service and production departments.

2. *Activity-based costing does not always involve the reassignment of service department costs to production departments.* If a more direct cost assignment is possible, such as to units of raw materials or product, the more direct assignment will be used.

3. Although traditional costing procedures attempt to find causal bases for cost reassignment, *activity-based costing is even more insistent on the uses of causal factors*. This is emphasized through the use of the term "cost driver."

---

[1] This is the example used in the introduction to the chapter.

4. When a causal basis cannot be found for cost reassignment, traditional costing procedures often rely on some measure of volume, such as sales dollars, implying a belief that this is "fair" because it reflects an "ability to bear" the costs. *Activity-based costing cannot be used to reassign costs when a cost driver cannot be identified.* Instead, if a reassignment must be made, it is identified as being made on the basis of "volume" rather than on the basis of "activity."

5. *The implementation of an activity-based cost system requires an understanding of the production process and cost drivers.* Hence a team approach that involves accountants, engineers, production personnel, and information systems specialists is often required to implement an activity-based cost system. At a minimum the accountant designing the system must leave his or her air-conditioned office, don a hard hat, and seek assistance from operating personnel.

6. *The implementation and operation of an activity-based cost system is more likely to involve the use of judgment* than the operation of a traditional cost system. Many decisions pertaining to the establishment of activity cost pools are based on observation and interviews.

To contrast the traditional and activity-based approaches to cost reassignment, consider the treatment of purchasing department costs in a manufacturing plant. These are indirect product costs that should ultimately be reassigned to products. Assume the following information is available concerning monthly purchasing department activities and costs:

Purchases:	
Number of purchase orders	200
Dollar amount of purchases	$800,000
Raw materials issued to production:	
Department 1	$300,000
Department 2	200,000
Department 3	100,000
Total	$600,000
Purchasing Department Costs	
Salaries and wages	$33,000
Other	12,000
Total	$45,000

Using the traditional approach to service department cost reassignment, purchasing department costs would be accumulated in a single cost pool and reassigned to production departments on the basis of a single factor, such as the purchase price of raw materials issued to production. Purchasing department costs would then be accumulated in each production department's factory overhead cost pool and reassigned to products. The reassignment to the production departments might be as follows:

	Total	Dept. 1	Dept. 2	Dept. 3
Reassignment base (raw materials issued)	$600,000	$300,000	$200,000	$100,000
Percent of total base	100%	50%	33.33%	16.67%
Cost reassignment	$45,000	$22,500	$15,000	$7,500

Reassignment on the basis of raw materials issued could result in cross-subsidization if the firm produced a variety of final products requiring the heterogeneous use of raw materials and the characteristics of different raw materials or the way they were purchased caused differences in their acquisition costs. Some materials might be purchased in small lots, causing disproportionate purchase order processing costs. Others might be fragile or heavy, requiring disproportionate handling costs. Still others might have a high incidence of defects, requiring disproportionate costs for inspection and returns.

Every case is different and has a different set of cost drivers. Professional judgment must be applied to determine the activities that drive costs in a particular organization and to establish the related cost pools. Interviews and observation are required. Assume that a series of personal interviews produced the following information:

- The major activities driving Purchasing Department costs are the number of purchase orders and the dollar value of purchases.

- Three purchasing agents are involved in contacting suppliers and processing purchase orders. Each purchase order receives identical attention regardless of its dollar value. Purchasing agents are paid $4,000 per month.

- Five receiving room employees are involved in unloading, unpacking, and inspecting incoming goods. They spend approximately 20 percent of their time verifying the specific requirements of each order and 80 percent of their time on factors related to the dollar amount of each order. Receiving room employees are paid $3,000 per month.

- The time of the departmental supervisor, a ninth employee, is equally divided among the eight employees. The supervisor is paid $6,000 per month.

- Other costs are related to space. The purchase order processing activity contains approximately 15 percent of the department's space; the unloading/unpacking/inspecting area contains the remainder.

On the basis of this information, the accountant may establish two Purchasing Department cost pools for: (1) the number of purchase orders and (2) the dollar amount of purchases. The accountant would next develop a cost per unit of each activity. This cost per unit of activity is the essence of activity-based costing. Costs are associated with activities, as shown at the top of the next page, and then assigned to cost objectives, such as units of raw materials, on the basis of their consumption of activities.

	Number of Purchase Orders	Dollar Amount of Purchase Orders
Purchasing agents' salaries ($4,000 × 3)	$12,000	
Receiving room employees ($3,000 × 5 × 0.20) ($3,000 × 5 × 0.80)	3,000	$12,000
Supervisor ($6,000 × 3/8) ($6,000 × 5/8 × 0.20) ($6,000 × 5/8 × 0.80)	2,250 750	3,000
Other costs ($12,000 × 0.15) ($12,000 × 0.85)	1,800	10,200
Total	$19,800	$25,200
Activity base: Orders Dollar purchases	÷200	÷$800,000
Charge per unit of activity	$ 99	$0.03150

Purchasing costs are now reassigned to inventory rather than to production departments. Assume a purchase order was for 30 units at an invoice price of $500 each for a total of $15,000. The Purchase Department costs charged to this order would total $571.50 ($99 + ($15,000 × 0.03150)). The final inventory cost of each unit would be $519.05 (($15,000 + $571.50)/30 units). When raw materials are issued to production, the related raw materials costs assigned to the production department now include the purchase price and reassigned purchasing department costs.

Implementation Issues

For accountants familiar with only straightforward product costing procedures, the complexity of activity-based costing may be troublesome. It is important to keep in mind that the primary reason for implementing an ABC system is to provide better information for management decision making, not to obtain product costs for external reporting. To minimize auditing complexities, an organization may use a less complex costing approach for external reporting. The objectives of the costing approach used for external reporting are likely to be simplicity, low cost, objectivity, and verifiability. The objective of the ABC system used for internal purposes is to provide relevant[2] information for decision making purposes.

---

[2] Relevance in accounting information means that the information is an important factor in the decision under consideration. Relevant costs differ with the decision at hand.

Increased computational power makes the operation of two or more costing systems feasible. What's more, with inventory levels approaching zero in many organizations, product costing for external reporting is becoming less important. With zero inventories, all product costs may be immediately assigned to Cost of Goods Sold, rather than having costs flow through inventory accounts to the Cost of Goods Sold.

Proponents of ABC argue that management must reassert its authority to control what are often dismissed as "common" and "fixed" costs. Activity costing attacks the shapeless mass of common costs, decomposing them into smaller, more homogeneous, cost pools related to specific activities. Activity costing also takes a long-run viewpoint of fixed costs, and in the long run all costs are variable. Management must manage fixed costs and take action to bring them down when activity levels decline.

One of the primary benefits of implementing an activity-based cost system stems from the detailed analysis of the manufacturing process required to identify cost drivers. This analysis is likely to identify activities, such as the unnecessary movement of materials or an extra inspection operation, that do not add value to the product. The elimination of these costly activities will reduce final product costs and improve the organization's profitability. The availability of activity cost

MANAGERIAL PRACTICE 13.3

GM Tries Activity-Based Costing

According to Roger B. Smith, former chairman and CEO of General Motors, "traditional methods of cost allocation aren't giving us accurate information about value generated as resources are consumed (and costs incurred). They may also be distorting the costs of individual products because overhead is allocated to products on bases that change proportionally with volume. The result is a less-than-optimal product mix. So back in 1986, we began piloting activity-based costing. It's a system of developing product-cost on the basis of resources-consuming activities that are required to design, engineer, manufacture, sell, deliver, and service specific products."

Source: Roger B. Smith, "Competitiveness in the '90s," *Management Accounting* (September 1989): 24–29.

information also assists in designing competitively priced products by making design engineers aware of the probable costs of alternative product designs and manufacturing procedures.

Once a detailed list of activities and the related cost per unit of activity is developed, the activity costs of a current or proposed product can be determined. This is done by identifying the activities required to produce the product and assigning costs to each activity. Management can evaluate each activity and its related cost to determine if changing activities or eliminating unnecessary activities can reduce costs. Once the best method of producing a product is determined, activity cost information can be used to develop detailed standard costs for elements included in the product's operations list.

Although an activity-based cost system may seem complex, the system merely mirrors the complexity of an organization's design, manufacturing, and delivery systems. If a firm's products are diverse and its production and delivery procedures complex, the activity-based costing system will, of necessity, be complex. If the firm's products are homogeneous and its production and delivery procedures relatively simple, its activity-based cost system should also be relatively simple.

THE REASSIGNMENT OF NONMANUFACTURING COSTS

Many of the reassignment concepts discussed in this chapter are often applied to nonmanufacturing costs in manufacturing organizations and to operating costs in service organizations, both for-profit and not-for-profit. Some of these applications are discussed below.

Home Office Expenses

Many top-level managers feel that all costs, including home office expenses, should be reassigned for internal reporting purposes to the operating divisions of companies. Home office expenses consist of central corporate expenses, including the salaries of the president and other executive officers, public relations expenses (such as corporate advertising and corporate contributions), expenses of the legal and tax department, and corporate planning and development costs. The functions provided by these costs are vitally important to the operation of the organization, but some of these functions (such as the president's activities) are often not considered to directly benefit the operating divisions and profit centers. Because there is no direct association between profit producing functions and central home office functions, it is often difficult, if not impossible, to find a widely supported basis for reassigning these costs to the divisions.

One of the most frequently used bases for allocating home office expenses is total revenues of the divisions. Using this basis, a division producing 30 percent of the company's total revenues is allocated 30 percent of all home office expenses, whereas another producing only 5 percent of total revenues is allocated just 5 percent. This allocation basis is often denounced by managers as a "soak the rich" approach that does not reflect an appropriate matching of effort and accomplishment. Managers of successful divisions argue that a disproportionate share of home office efforts is often devoted to struggling divisions and product lines, and to new or potential endeavors of the company, and not to the most successful divisions and product lines, which nevertheless carry the burden of cost allocation.

Despite the problems in making an equitable allocation of home office expenses, many top managers feel that such allocations are important because they draw attention to the total cost of operating the business. Moreover, it is felt that home office cost allocation encourages managers to think in terms of total corporate profitability, not just of the profitability of their own areas. Allocation proponents emphasize that the company as a whole has not earned a profit until all costs, including home office costs, have been covered by revenues. Notwithstanding these alleged benefits, allocation of central corporate expenses is not the best means of achieving them unless division management perceives the allocation system to be fair and equitable. These favorable perceptions probably will not exist if top management uses broad, arbitrary allocation bases,

MANAGERIAL PRACTICE 13.4

Weyerhaeuser Reassigns Virtually All Organizational Costs

Almost all organizational activities, not just manufacturing and marketing, exist to support the production of goods and services. Weyerhaeuser Company's corporate office has introduced a system to trace corporate overhead charges. For example, Weyerhaeuser originally applied the cost of accounts receivable as a flat percentage of a division's sales. This did not take into account the fact that a division with a few high-volume customers had different needs than a division with many low-volume customers. Weyerhaeuser now allocates the costs based on the amount of usage. By breaking down the activities performed in a department, the company is able to trace the factors creating a demand for the activities. It is now able to allocate the costs to the department (division, product line) that creates them.

Source: Robin Cooper and Robert S. Kaplan, "Measure Costs Right: Make the Right Decisions," *Harvard Business Review* (September–October 1988): 96–103.

such as total revenues or total profits. As in allocating manufacturing costs, the best results can be achieved only by relating the costs to the cost objectives on a logical cause-and-effect basis. For some home office costs, these bases may not exist.

Even if accurate and equitable allocations can be determined for home office costs, *imposed services* may still present a problem. Frequently, managers feel that the services received from corporate headquarters are not beneficial to their divisions but are imposed by top management, and given the opportunity, they would elect not to buy them at any price. Even if managers believe the services are needed, some would prefer to control the acquisition of the services by purchasing them from sources outside the company. When attitudes like these prevail among a company's managers, probably little is gained from home office cost allocation. Ordinarily, these kinds of negative attitudes are prevalent only in companies where home office costs are allocated to division managers for performance evaluation purposes.

In recent years some companies have implemented activity-based costing procedures to reassign home office expenses to other organization units. Rather than treating home office expenses as a single cost pool, home office expenses are accumulated in a number of more homogeneous cost pools (such as those for processing an invoice or preparing a paycheck) that can be more readily identified with specific activities consumed by other organization units. The costs are then reassigned using a predetermined rate per unit of activity. The desirability of developing such refined cost pools is highly dependent on relative costs and benefits. If the dollar volume of home office costs is high and data processing costs are low, the implementation of an activity-based cost system may be economically justifiable.

Not-for-Profit Applications

So far we have discussed cost assignment and reassignment only in for-profit organizations. Many of the concepts and procedures introduced, however, can be generalized for use in not-for-profit organizations. Historically, not-for-profit accounting has been based on the concept of stewardship (or fund) accounting, which emphasizes the reporting of funds received and their disposition. The use of accounting data to determine the cost of services and to evaluate manager performance has not been widely practiced in not-for-profit organizations.

As we have seen in our discussions of for-profit organizations, the reassignment of costs to various cost objectives may be useful in certain circumstances. In not-for-profit organizations, cost reassignments may play an even more significant role than in for-profit organizations. Cost reassignments may actually reduce the funds available to an agency or operating unit to carry on its programs. For example, the fire department of a small local municipality may have an annual budget of $300,000; however, the cost allocations for general city services to the department may use up $20,000 of the budget, leaving disposable funds of only $280,000. An academic department in a university may have no choice but to obtain computer services from the university's central computer system at a cost substantially higher than comparable services received from outside sources. Charges for these internal services ordinarily are made against the operating funds of the departments.

Because the procedures for allocating costs in not-for-profit organizations are essentially the same as those discussed in for-profit organizations, we will not present a detailed discussion. The following is a summary of frequently reassigned costs and reassignment bases of selected not-for-profit organizations.

Organization	Cost Category	Reassignment Base
Hospital	Administration	Patient days
	Cafeteria	Meals served
	Operating room	Actual time used
City government	Municipal building	Space occupied
	Tax assessment and collection	Amount of budget appropriation
	Accounting	Number of transactions processed
University	Classroom costs	Class hours used
	Computer services	Actual or CPU time used
	Academic administration	Student credit hours
Church	Buildings and grounds	Space occupied
	Printing and publicity	Actual services received
	Office and administration	Amount of budget appropriation

SUMMARY

All cost measurement involves assigning or reassigning costs to cost objectives. The cost objective may be a department, activity, service, product, or any other item of interest to management. Although some costs can be directly identified with a specific cost objective, many other costs can be only indirectly associated with a specific cost objective. In general, direct costs are initially assigned to the cost objective whereas indirect costs are initially assigned to another cost objective. The determination of a cost objective's total costs often requires the reassignment of indirect costs. The reassignment of indirect costs is relatively imprecise; the accuracy of indirect cost reassignment is a function of the quality of an organization's cost system.

Prior to being reassigned to cost objectives, indirect costs are often placed into homogeneous groupings of related costs identified as cost pools. The pooled costs are then reassigned to cost objectives using a reassignment basis that is common to all cost objectives. A good cost reassignment basis has a causal relationship between the costs to be reassigned and the activities consumed by cost objectives. Fixed costs are often reassigned on the basis of capacity provided, whereas variable costs are reassigned according to actual activity.

Manufacturing organizations ordinarily contain production departments (where products are made) and service departments (that provide support to production departments). Service departments are an essential part of the manufacturing process, so their costs must be reassigned to products to determine the total cost of each product. This is typically accomplished by reassigning service department costs to production departments and including these reassigned costs as part of the indirect product costs (factory overhead). Specific approaches to the reassignment of service department costs include the direct, step, and linear algebra methods. In recent years activity-based costing has gained acceptance as a more accurate but detailed approach to determining the cost of a product, service, or activity.

Most of the cost reassignment procedures discussed for manufacturing departments can also be applied to nonmanufacturing departments and to service and not-for-profit organizations. The key to the development of any cost system (and the distinction between direct and indirect costs) is the determination of appropriate cost objectives, which can be virtually any product, service, business segment, or activity of interest to management. Although it may not be possible to accurately reassign all relevant indirect costs to the cost objectives of interest, the cost information developed with the careful application of concepts presented in this chapter should assist management in decision making.

SUGGESTED READINGS

Berlant, Debbie, Reese Browning, and George Foster, "How Hewlett-Packard Gets Numbers It Can Trust," *Harvard Business Review* (January–February 1990): 178–183.

Cooper, Robin, "The Rise of Activity-Based Costing—Part One: What Is an Activity-Based Cost System?" *The Journal of Cost Management 2,* No. 2 (Summer 1988): 45–53.

_____ , "The Rise of Activity-Based Costing—Part Two: When Do I Need an Activity-Based Cost System?" *The Journal of Cost Management 2,* No. 3 (Fall 1988): 41–48.

_____ , "The Rise of Activity-Based Costing—Part Three: How Many Cost Drivers Do You Need and How Do You Select Them?" *The Journal of Cost Management 2,* No. 4 (Winter 1989): 34–35.

_____ , "The Rise of Activity-Based Costing—Part Four: What Do Activity-Based Cost Systems Look Like?" *The Journal of Cost Management 3,* No. 1 (Spring 1989): 38–49.

Dhavale, Dileep G., "Product Costing in Flexible Manufacturing Systems," *Journal of Management Accounting Research* (Fall 1989): 66–88.

Fremgen, James M., and Shu S. Liao, *The Allocation of Corporate Indirect Costs,* Montvalle, N.J.: National Association of Accountants, 1981.

Johnson, H. Thomas, "Activity Measurement: Reviewing the Past and Future of Cost Management," *The Journal of Cost Management 3,* No. 4 (Winter 1990): 4–7.

Ostrenga, Michael R., "Activities, the Focal Point of Total Cost Management," *Management Accounting* (February 1990): 42–49.

Roth, Harold P., and A. Faye Borthick, "Getting Closer to *Real* Product Costs," *Management Accounting* (May 1989): 28–33.

Turney, Peter B. B., "What Is the Scope of Activity-Based Costing?" *The Journal of Cost Management 3,* No. 4 (Winter 1990): 40–42.

REVIEW PROBLEM

Indirect Cost Reassignment: Direct, Step, and Linear Algebra Methods

Cotswald's Clothiers, Inc., is organized into four departments: Women's Apparel, Men's Apparel, Administrative Services, and Facilities Services. The former two departments are the primary producing departments, and the latter two departments exist to provide services to the producing departments. Top management has decided that, for internal reporting purposes, the cost of service department operations should be reassigned to the producing departments.

Administrative Services costs are reassigned on the basis of the number of employees, and Facilities Services costs are reassigned based on the number of floor square footage occupied. The service departments provide services to both producing departments as well as to each other. Data pertaining to the reassignments for February 19x7 are as follows:

Department	Direct Department Cost	Number of Employees	Square Footage Occupied
Women's Apparel	$ 60,000	15	15,000
Men's Apparel	50,000	9	7,500
Administrative Services	18,000	3	2,500
Facilities	12,000	2	1,000
Total	$140,000	29	26,000

Required: Determine the amount of service department cost to be reassigned to the producing departments under each of the following cost reassignment methods:

1. Direct method.

2. Step method.

3. Linear algebra method.

The solution to this problem is found at the end of the Chapter 13 exercises, problems, and cases.

KEY TERMS

Activity-based costing (ABC)
Common costs
Cost objective
Cost pool
Cost reassignment base
Direct department cost
Direct method (of cost reassignment)
Direct product costs

Home office expenses
Indirect department cost
Indirect product costs
Interdepartmental services
Linear algebra method (of cost reassignment)
Service department
Step method (of cost reassignment)

REVIEW
QUESTIONS

13–1   Distinguish between the following terms:

- Direct product costs and indirect product costs.
- Direct department costs and indirect department costs.

13–2   Can any generalized distinctions be made about direct and indirect costs?

13–3   Explain the difference between cost assignment and cost reassignment. What alternative term is often used when referring to cost reassignment?

13–4   Can a cost item be both a direct cost and an indirect cost?

13–5   Why might cost reassignments developed for financial reporting or tax purposes not be adequate for other purposes that require the accurate determination of individual product costs?

13–6   What is a cost objective? Give several examples of cost objectives that may be of interest to management.

13–7   Why are cost pools used in reassigning indirect costs?

13–8   What key consideration should be used in establishing cost pools?

13–9   What is the primary advantage of reassigning fixed and variable indirect costs separately?

13–10   To what extent are interdepartmental services recognized under the direct, step, and linear algebra methods of service department cost reassignment?

13–11   Until recent years, what has been the major limitation of the linear algebra method?

13–12   What is the premise of activity-based costing?

13–13   In what ways does activity costing differ from traditional cost reassignment?

13–14   Reassigning home office expenses to divisions on the basis of sales revenue is often characterized as a soak-the-rich tactic. Explain.

13–15   Name three indirect costs that might require reassignment if your college or university decides to compute the total cost of offering a section of management accounting.

EXERCISES

13–1 Selecting Cost Reassignment Bases

Below is a list of service departments typically found in manufacturing and nonmanufacturing organizations.

Payroll	Personnel
Cafeteria	Building
Electricity	Maintenance
Computer Services	Security
Health Services	General Administration

Required: For each of the above service departments indicate the bases likely to be used to reassign costs to the producing departments.

13–2 Indirect Cost Reassignment Computations

Sunset Strip Sign Company manufactures hotel signs through a process involving three departments—Molding, Fabrication, and Wiring. The following data were accumulated for 19x9 for these three departments.

	Molding	Fabrication	Wiring
Direct labor hours	10,000	38,000	2,000
Direct labor cost	$70,000	$400,000	$30,000
Number of employees	5	18	2
Square feet occupied	3,000	5,000	2,000

Total indirect costs incurred for all three departments in 19x9 were $150,000.

Required: Determine the costs reassigned to each department on the basis of the following:

1. Direct labor hours.
2. Direct labor cost.
3. Number of employees.
4. Square feet occupied.

13–3 Reassigning Service Department Costs: Allocation Basis Alternatives

Clayton Glassworks has two producing departments, P1 and P2, and one service department, S1. Estimated direct overhead costs per month are as follows:

P1	$100,000
P2	200,000
S1	60,000

Other data:

	P1	P2
Number of employees	75	25
Production capacity (units)	50,000	30,000
Space occupied (sq ft)	2,500	7,500
Five-year average percent of S1's service output used	65%	35%

Required: For each of the following allocation bases, determine the total estimated overhead cost for P1 and P2 after reassigning S1 cost to the producing departments.

1. Number of employees.
2. Production capacity in units.
3. Space occupied.
4. Five-year average percentage of S1 services used.
5. Estimated direct overhead costs. (Round your answer to the nearest dollar.)

13–4 Indirect Cost Reassignment: Direct Method

The School of Business Administration of Alpha University consists of three academic departments and three service departments. The Dean of the School has asked you, his assistant, to compute the cost per student credit hour for each of the academic departments. Although the Dean gave no specific instructions on how to make the computations, you have decided that the service department costs should be reassigned to the academic departments. You have accumulated the following data for the last school term to be used in the cost computations.

Department	Direct Cost	Reassignment Base		
Service:				
Administration	$150,000	Number of faculty		
Student services	75,000	Number of students		
Faculty services	60,000	Number of credit hours		
		Number of Faculty	Number of Students	Number of Credit Hours
Academic:				
Accounting / Finance	$380,000	20	350	4,500
Management / Marketing	440,000	25	250	3,000
Economics / Quantitative methods	350,000	15	150	1,500

Requirements

a) Prepare a schedule showing the reassignment of service department direct costs to the academic departments.

b) Compute the total cost per student credit hour for each academic department.

c) Could the step method have been used with the information provided? Explain.

13–5 Indirect Cost Reassignment: Direct Method

Springfield Manufacturing Company has two production departments, Melting and Molding. Direct General Plant Management and Plant Security costs benefit both production departments. Springfield reassigns General Plant Management costs on the basis of the number of production employees, and Plant Security costs on the basis of space occupied by the production departments.

In November 19x5, the following costs were recorded.

Melting Department direct overhead	$125,000
Molding Department direct overhead	300,000
General plant management	90,000
Plant security	25,000

Other pertinent data are provided below:

	Melting	Molding
Number of employees	20	40
Space occupied (sq ft)	10,000	40,000
Machine hours	10,000	2,000
Direct labor hours	4,000	20,000

Requirements

a) Prepare a schedule reassigning general plant management costs and plant security costs to the Melting and Molding Departments.

b) Determine the total departmental overhead costs for the Melting and Molding Departments.

c) Assuming the Melting Department uses machine hours and the Molding Department uses direct labor hours to apply overhead to production, calculate the overhead rate for each production department.

13–6
Interdepartmental
Services: Step Method

O'Brian's Department Stores reassigns the costs of the Personnel and Payroll Departments to three retail sales departments, Housewares, Clothing, and Furniture. In addition to providing services to the operating departments, Personnel and Payroll provide services to each other. O'Brian's allocates Personnel Department costs on the basis of the number of employees, and allocates Payroll Department costs on the basis of gross payroll. Cost and allocation information for June is as follows:

	Personnel	Payroll	Housewares	Clothing	Furniture
Direct department cost	$6,900	$3,200	$12,200	$20,000	$15,750
Number of employees	5	3	8	15	4
Gross payroll	$6,000	$3,300	$11,200	$17,400	$ 8,100

Requirements

a) Determine the percentage of total Personnel Department services that was provided to the Payroll Department.

b) Determine the percentage of total Payroll Department services that was provided to the Personnel Department.

c) Prepare a schedule showing Personnel Department and Payroll Department cost reassignments to the operating departments assuming O'Brian's uses the step method. (Round calculations to the nearest dollar.)

13–7
Interdepartmental
Services: Direct
Method

Portland Manufacturing Company has five operating departments, two of which are producing departments (P1 and P2), and three of which are service departments (S1, S2, and S3). All costs of the service departments are reassigned to the producing departments. The table below shows the distribution of services from the service departments.

Services Provided from	Services Provided to				
	S1	S2	S3	P1	P2
S1	—	5%	25%	50%	20%
S2	10%	—	5%	45%	40%
S3	15%	5%	—	20%	60%

The direct operating costs of the service departments are as follows:

S1	$42,000
S2	80,000
S3	19,000

Required: Using the direct method, prepare a schedule reassigning the service department costs to the producing departments.

13–8
Interdepartmental
Services: Step Method

Refer to the data in Exercise 13–7. Using the step method, prepare a schedule reassigning the service department costs to the producing departments. (Round calculations to the nearest dollar.)

13–9 Indirect Cost
Reassignment: Direct
and Linear Algebra
Methods

Fargo Company's filament plant has two service departments (Administration and Maintenance) and two producing departments (Cutting and Assembling). Service and cost data for these departments are presented below:

Services Provided from	Services Provided to			
	Administration	Maintenance	Cutting	Assembling
Administration	—	30%	35%	35%
Maintenance	5%	—	60%	35%
Direct department costs:	$235,000	$126,500	$540,000	$360,000

Requirements

a) Prepare a schedule reassigning the service department costs to the producing departments using the direct method.

b) Prepare a schedule reassigning the service department costs to the producing departments using the linear algebra method.

c) Explain why the reassignments to the producing departments are different under the direct and linear algebra methods.

13–10 Indirect Cost Reassignment: Linear Algebra Method

Hannibal, Inc., has two service departments (S1 and S2) and two producing departments (P1 and P2). The distribution of services provided by the service departments is as follows:

Services Provided from	Services Provided to			
	S1	S2	P1	P2
S1	—	10%	40%	50%
S2	20%	—	55%	25%

Total direct department costs for each department are as follows:

S1	$ 45,000
S2	30,000
P1	180,000
P2	260,000
Total	$515,000

Requirements

a) Set up algebraic equations expressing the total cost for each department reflecting simultaneous reassignment of service department costs to all departments receiving services.

b) Solve the equations in requirement (a) using the substitution method or any other method that you may have learned for simultaneously solving linear equations, including use of a computer. (Round calculations to the nearest dollar if the substitution method is used.)

c) How much cost is reassigned between S1 and S2? How much S1 and S2 cost is reassigned to P1 and P2?

PROBLEMS

**13–11 Using Activity
Cost Data: Productive
and Nonproductive
Activities**

Morvis, Inc., has developed the following activity cost data for its purchasing and manufacturing activities:

Purchase order and receiving report	$20.00/order
Unpack and inspect incoming goods	$ 0.50/unit purchased
Raw materials inventory carrying cost	1% of invoice cost
Issue raw materials	$14.00/type of item/job
Move to a work or inspection station in-process or to finished goods	$ 1.50/unit in job
In-process inventory carrying cost*	$ 0.50/unit in job/day
Labor activities	$25.00/hour
Quality inspection	$ 0.50/inspection

Machine activities:

	A	B	C
Set-up	$50.00/job	$60.00/job	$55.00/job
Operation	40.00/hour	42.00/hour	30.00/hour

*Applicable to all units, regardless of whether they are being worked on or are awaiting work.

Management is contemplating the production of a new product, number G57, and desires to know the average annual unit cost at an annual production volume of 10,000 units.

Purchasing, engineering, and production scheduling have developed the following information for an annual volume of 10,000 units:

Raw material	Annual requirements	Order quantity	Orders per year	Unit price
D34	20,000	5,000	4	$ 5.00
G77	30,000	10,000	3	0.50
H65	10,000	1,000	10	20.00

Production requirements per batch of 1,000 units:

Raw materials:	
D34	2,000 units
G77	3,000 units
H65	1,000 units
Machine activities:	
A	100 hours
B	50 hours
C	50 hours
Labor	60 hours
Two quality inspections per unit	

All raw materials required for the batch will be issued at the start of production. All machines will be set up before production on the batch begins, and units will be moved directly from one operation to the next as each is ready. This will reduce work-in-process inventories to the extent possible. The average cycle time for a unit from start to finish is estimated to be three days.

Requirements

a) Use activity cost data to determine the total annual and average unit cost of product G57. Round computations to the nearest cent.

b) At a recent seminar a discussion leader told management that all materials movement, inspection, and carrying activities are unproductive. What's more, conversion costs related to materials movement, inspection, and carrying inventory are wasted; and management should strive to eliminate the activities that cause them. Management has asked you to break total conversion costs into the categories of productive and nonproductive, as defined by the discussion leader.

13–12 Using Activity Cost Data and Quality Costs

Borroth Manufacturing has developed the following activity cost data for its purchasing and manufacturing activities:

Purchase order and receipt of order	$36.00/order
Unpack and inspect incoming goods	0.50/unit purchased
Move in-process goods	2.50/unit in job
In-process holding costs (no work being performed)	0.50/unit in job/day
Machine setup	60.00/machine/job
Machine operation A	80.00/hour
Machine operation B	60.00/hour
Rework	150.00/hour
Inspect work-in-process or finished goods	1.50/unit
Pack and ship finished goods	5% previous costs + $25.00/job

Borroth produces only to fill customer orders. Because suppliers deliver on 24 hours notice, Borroth does not maintain raw materials inventories. Materials are purchased as needed in the quantities needed and, after being unpacked and inspected, are sent immediately to the shop floor. Finished goods are inspected, packed, and immediately shipped to customers.

The information at the top of the next page is available for Job 91-Z24, which consisted of 20 units of a special machine part.

Requirements

a) Use activity cost data to determine the total cost of Job 91-Z24. Round computations to the nearest cent.

b) Quality costs are defined as costs incurred because products of poor quality can or do exist. Included in this category are such costs as inspection and rework. Determine the quality costs associated with Job 91-Z24. Assume 40 percent of the costs of unpacking and inspecting incoming goods are attributable to inspection.

Purchase order 91-B34:		
Material M1	100 units	$1,200
Material J2	300 units	300
Purchase order 91-B35:		
Material N6	50 units	800
Move materials for job to machine A		
Store at machine A	1 day	
Setup machine A		
Run time on machine A	4 hours	
Setup machine B		
Move job to machine B		
Run time on machine B	12 hours	
Move job to inspection		
Inspect goods	20 units	
Move job to rework station		
Store at rework station	2 days	
Rework	2.5 hours	
Move job to inspection		
Inspect reworked goods	6 units	
Move to packing and shipping		
Pack and ship finished goods		

13–13 Predetermined Overhead Rates with Reassignment of Budgeted Service Department Costs

The Albany Company applies factory overhead in its two producing departments using a predetermined rate based on budgeted machine hours in the Stamping Department and based on budgeted labor hours in the Fabricating Department. The following data concerning next year's operations have been developed.

	Service Departments		Producing Departments	
Budgeted costs	Human Resources	Maintenance and Repairs	Stamping	Fabricating
Variable costs:				
Indirect materials	—	$16,000	$200,000	$ 80,000
Indirect labor	$60,000	50,000	140,000	200,000
Miscellaneous	—	—	28,000	30,000
Fixed costs:				
Miscellaneous	20,000	42,000	80,000	120,000
Other data:				
Direct labor hours (capacity)			20,000	30,000
Direct labor hours (budgeted)			14,000	20,000
Machine hours (capacity)			16,000	8,000
Machine hours (budgeted)			12,000	6,000
Number of employees (capacity)			20	30
Number of employees (budgeted)			12	18

Fixed Human Resources costs are reassigned to the producing departments based on employee capacity, and variable costs are reassigned based on the budgeted number of employees. Fixed Maintenance and Repairs costs are reassigned based on machine hour capacity, and variable costs are reassigned based on the budgeted number of machine hours.

Requirements

a) Prepare a schedule showing the direct reassignment of budgeted service department costs to the producing departments.

b) Determine the predetermined overhead rates for the producing departments.

13–14 Predetermined Overhead Rates with Reassignment of Budgeted Service Department Costs

The Gervais Company has one plant with two producing departments, Assembly and Testing. All manufacturing overhead costs not directly traceable to these departments are accumulated in one cost pool called General Service Department costs. General Service costs are, then, reassigned to the producing departments based on direct labor hours. In the process of establishing predetermined overhead rates for 19x5, the chief cost accountant obtained the following data:

	General Service	Assembly	Testing
Budgeted variable overhead costs per direct labor hour	—	$4	$8
Budgeted fixed department overhead	$30,000	$15,000	$30,000

Gervais's operations for 19x5 are budgeted at 6,000 direct labor hours in Assembly and 1,500 direct labor hours in Testing.

Requirements

a) Prepare a budget of total overhead costs for 19x5 for the producing departments showing both direct department costs and reassigned indirect department costs.

b) Determine the predetermined overhead rates for 19x5 for the Assembly and Testing Departments. (Round to the nearest cent.)

c) Assuming that Job 146 processed in 19x5 required 75 direct labor hours in Assembly and 5 direct labor hours in Testing, determine the amount of factory overhead that should be applied to the job.

13–15 Actual Overhead Rates with Reassignment of Actual Service Department Costs

The Fresno Company, a commercial printer, uses a job-order cost system to compute product costs. All costs other than direct job costs are accounted for as department overhead in either the producing departments (Office Products and Advertising) or the service departments (Administration and Facilities). Administration and Facilities costs are reassigned to the producing departments on the basis of the number of employees and the space occupied, respectively. Actual overhead is applied to specific jobs on the basis of direct labor hours. The following data were collected for September 19x8:

	Administration	Facilities	Office Products	Advertising
Direct department costs	$2,500	$1,000	$3,200	$4,800
Number of employees	2	1	4	6
Space occupied (sq ft)	750	—	3,000	2,000
Direct labor hours	—	—	480	640

Requirements

a) Prepare a schedule reassigning the service department costs to the producing departments using the direct method.

b) Determine the overhead rate per direct labor hour for each of the producing departments. (Round answer to the nearest cent.)

c) Job 168 required 12 direct labor hours during the month in the Office Products Department. If the direct job cost was $850, how much was the total job cost?

13–16 Selecting Cost Reassignment Bases   The Minot Company, a new company, has three producing departments, P1, P2, and P3, for which direct department costs are accumulated. In January, the following indirect costs of operation were incurred.

Plant manager's salary and office expense	$ 4,800
Plant security	1,200
Plant nurse's salary and office expense	1,500
Plant depreciation	2,000
Machine maintenance	2,400
Plant cafeteria cost subsidy	1,200
	$13,100

The following additional data have been collected for the three producing departments:

	P1	P2	P3
Number of employees	10	15	5
Space occupied (sq ft)	2,000	5,000	3,000
Direct labor hours	1,600	4,000	750
Machine hours	4,800	8,000	3,200
Number of nurse office visits	20	45	10

Requirements

a) Group the indirect cost items into cost pools based on the nature of the costs and their common basis for reassignment. Identify the most appropriate reassignment basis for each pool and determine the total January costs in the pool. *Hint:* A cost pool may consist of one or more cost items.

b) Reassign the cost pools directly to the three producing departments using the reassignment bases selected in requirement (a).

13–17 Evaluating Reassignment Bases and Computations

The Cheyenne Company has two service departments, Maintenance and Cafeteria, that serve two producing departments, Mixing and Packaging. The following data have been collected for these departments for the current year.

	Cafeteria	Maintenance	Mixing	Packaging
Direct department costs	$176,000	$112,000	$465,000	$295,000
Number of employees			50	30
Number of meals served			9,000	7,000
Number of maintenance hours used			800	600
Number of maintenance orders			180	170

Requirements

a) Using the direct method, reassign the service department costs under the following independent assumptions:

 1. Cafeteria costs are reassigned based on the number of employees, and Maintenance costs are reassigned based on the number of maintenance hours.

 2. Cafeteria costs are reassigned based on the number of meals served, and Maintenance costs are reassigned based on the number of maintenance orders.

b) Comment on the reasonableness of the bases used in the calculations in requirement (a). What considerations should determine which bases to use for reassigning Cafeteria and Maintenance costs?

13–18 Cost Reimbursement and Step Method

Community Clinic is a not-for-profit outpatient facility that provides medical services to both fee paying and low-income government supported patients. Reimbursement from the government is based on total actual costs of services provided, including both direct cost of patient services and indirect operating costs. Patient services are provided through two producing departments, Medical Services and Ancillary Services (includes X-ray, therapy, etc.). In addition to the direct costs of these departments, the clinic incurs indirect costs in two service departments, Administration and Facilities. Administration costs are reassigned based on the number of full-time employees, and Facilities costs are reassigned on the basis of space occupied. Costs, and related data, for the current month are as follows:

	Administration	Facilities	Medical Services	Ancillary Services
Direct costs	$9,000	$2,000	$60,700	$24,800
Number of employees	5	4	12	8
Space occupied (sq ft)	1,500	—	8,000	2,000
Number of patient visits	—	—	4,000	1,500

Requirements

a) Using the step method, prepare a schedule reassigning the common service department costs to the producing departments.

b) Determine the amount to be reimbursed from the government for each low-income patient visit.

13–19 Common Cost Reassignment in a Not-for-Profit Organization

Dunwoody Community Church is organized into four operating divisions: Education, Benevolence, Community Services, and Recreation. Direct costs for each division for the year are as follows:

Education	$ 85,000
Benevolence	230,000
Community Services	125,000
Recreation	50,000
Total	$490,000

Other data pertaining to church operations are as follows:

	Building Space Occupied	Participants Served during Year	Number of Employees
Education	15,000	10,000	8
Benevolence	1,000	2,500	5
Community Services	4,000	7,500	3
Recreation	5,000	5,000	4
Totals	25,000	25,000	20

The common costs of operating the church and the reassignment bases are as follows:

	Cost	Reassignment Base
Building and utilities	$ 60,000	Space occupied
General administration	45,000	Number of employees
Miscellaneous supplies and costs	25,000	Participants served
Total common costs	$130,000	

Requirements

a) Using the direct method, prepare a schedule reassigning each common cost to the operating divisions.

b) Determine the total cost of each operating division broken down into direct and indirect costs.

13–20 Budgeted Service Department Cost Reassignment: Pricing a New Product

Trimco Products Company is adding a new diet food concentrate called Body Trim to its line of body building and exercise products. A plant is being built for manufacturing the new product. Management has decided to price the new product based on a 100 percent markup on total manufacturing costs. A direct cost budget for the new plant projects that direct department costs of $2,100,000 will be incurred in producing an expected normal output of 700,000 pounds of finished product. In addition, indirect costs for Human Resources and Computer Services will be shared by the Body Trim Division with the two exercise products divisions, Commercial Products and Retail Products. Budgeted annual data to be used in making the reassignments are summarized below.

	Human Resources	Computer Services	Commercial Products	Retail Products	Body Trim
Number of employees	5	5	50	30	20
Computer time (hrs)	500	—	1,500	1,250	750

Direct costs are budgeted at $90,000 for the Human Resources Department and $160,000 for the Computer Services Department.

Requirements

a) Using the step method determine the total direct and indirect costs of Body Trim.

b) Determine the selling price per pound of Body Trim. (Round calculations to the nearest cent.)

13–21 Reassignment of Home Office Costs

Megacorp, Inc., is a large conglomerate holding company with five major divisions. Home office costs are substantial, and top management insists on reassigning these costs to the five operating divisions. As corporate controller you are considering alternative reassignment bases including sales revenue, number of employees, and total assets of the subsidiaries. Your assistant has collected the following data for you to use in making the reassignments:

Total Home Office Costs	$ 20 million
Sales Revenue:	
Division A	$100 million
Division B	100 million
Division C	400 million
Division D	500 million
Division E	900 million
Number of Employees:	
Division A	1,500
Division B	1,200
Division C	2,000
Division D	2,500
Division E	2,800
Total Assets:	
Division A	$ 20 million
Division B	30 million
Division C	30 million
Division D	50 million
Division E	170 million

Requirements

a) Discuss the reasons why top management of Megacorp would want to reassign home office costs to the operating divisions. Are any of these reasons valid? Explain.

b) Calculate the home office cost reassignment to each of the operating divisions for each of the bases under consideration.

c) What are some of the primary criticisms the division managers are likely to have of top management's decision to reassign home office costs to the divisions?

13–22 Cost Reassignment and Responsibility Accounting

The Austin Company uses a responsibility accounting system for evaluating its managers. Abbreviated performance reports for the company's three divisions for the month of March are presented below.

	Total	East	Central	West
Income before reassigned costs	$165,000	$60,000	$75,000	$30,000
Less reassigned costs:				
Computer Services	(66,000)	(22,000)	(22,000)	(22,000)
Personnel	(72,000)	(28,000)	(32,000)	(12,000)
Division income	$ 27,000	$10,000	$21,000	$ (4,000)

The manager of the West Division is very disturbed over his performance report and recent rumors that his division may be abolished because of its failure to report a profit in recent periods. He feels that the reported profit figures do not fairly present operating results because his division is being unfairly burdened with service department costs. He is particularly concerned over the amount of Computer Services costs charged to his division. He feels that it is inequitable for his division to be charged with one third of the total cost when it is using only 20 percent of the services. He feels that the Personnel Department's use of the Computer Services Department should also be considered in the cost reassignments.

Cost reassignments were based on the following distributions of services provided.

Services Provided from	Personnel	Computer Services	East	Central	West
Computer Services	40%	—	20%	20%	20%
Personnel	—	10%	35%	40%	15%

Requirements

a) What method is the company using to reassign Personnel and Computer Service costs?

b) Recompute the cost reassignments using the step method. (Round calculations to the nearest dollar.)

c) Revise the performance reports to reflect the cost reassignments computed in requirement (b).

d) Comment on the complaint of the manager of the West Division.

13–23 Reassigning Service Department Costs: Direct, Step, and Linear Algebra Methods

Brook Windshields, Inc., reassigns Human Resources Department costs to the producing departments (Cutting and Welding) based on direct labor hours and reassigns Facilities Department costs based on square footage occupied. Direct department costs, labor hours, and square footage data for the four departments for October 19x9 are as follows:

	Human Resources	Facilities	Cutting	Welding
Direct costs	$63,000	$90,000	$450,000	$600,000
Labor hours	2,000	2,000	8,000	10,000
Square footage	3,000	3,000	30,000	15,000

Requirements

a) Prepare a schedule showing the percentage of services provided from each service department to each of the service and producing departments.

b) Prepare a schedule showing the service department cost reassignments using the direct method.

c) Prepare a schedule showing the service department cost reassignments using the step method. Reassign in the order of greatest interdepartmental services.

d) Prepare a schedule showing the service department cost reassignments using the linear algebra method. (Round allocations to nearest dollar.)

e) Discuss the relative advantages and disadvantages of the direct, step, and linear algebra methods of reassigning service department costs.

13–24 Developing Activity Cost Data

The Gothom National Bank has ten automatic teller machines spread throughout the city. The machines are maintained by the Automatic Teller department. You have been assigned the task of determining the cost of operating each machine. Management will use the information you develop, along with other information pertaining to the volume and type of transactions at each machine, to evaluate the desirability of continuing to operate each machine and/or changing security arrangements for a particular machine.

The Automatic Teller department consists of a total of six employees: a supervisor, a head cashier, two associate cashiers, and two maintenance personnel. The associate cashiers make between two and four routine trips each day to each machine for the purpose of replenishing and collecting cash, supplies, deposit tickets, and so forth. Each machine contains a small computer that automatically summarizes and reports transactions to the head cashier. The activities of the two associate cashiers are reconciled to the computerized reports by the head cashier and reviewed by the supervisor, who does not handle cash.

When a problem is reported by an automatic teller's computer, a customer, or a cashier, the two maintenance employees and a cashier are dispatched immediately. The cashier removes all cash and transaction records while the maintenance employees repair the machine. Maintenance employees spend all of their time on maintenance related activities, and the associate cashiers spend approximately 50 percent of their time on maintenance related activities. The associate cashiers spend the other 50 percent of their time on routine trips.

Seventy-five percent of the time of the head cashier is directly related to routine trips to each machine, and 25 percent is related to supervising cashiers on maintenance calls. Twenty percent of the time of the supervisor is related to routine trips to each machine, and 80 percent is related to the equal supervision of each employee. Cost information for a recent month is as follows:

Supervisor's salary	$ 3,000
Head cashier's salary	2,000
Other salaries ($1,800 each)	7,200
Lease and operating costs:	
Cashiers' service vehicle	1,200
Maintenance service vehicle	1,400
Office rent and utilities	2,300
Machine lease, space rent, and	
utilities ($1,500) each	15,000
Total	$32,100

Related monthly activity information is as follows:

Machine	Routine Trips	Maintenance Hours
1	30	5
2	90	17
3	60	15
4	60	30
5	120	15
6	30	10
7	90	25
8	120	5
9	60	20
10	60	18
Total	720	160

Additional information:

▪ The office is centrally located, with approximately equal travel time to each machine.

▪ Maintenance hours include travel time.

▪ The cashiers' service vehicle is used exclusively for routine visits.

▪ The office space is divided equally between that assigned to the supervisor and that assigned to the head cashier.

Requirements

a) Determine the monthly operating costs of machines 7 and 8 when cost assignments are based on the number of machines.

b) Determine the activity cost of a routine trip and a maintenance hour for the month given. Round answers to the nearest cent.

c) Determine the operating costs assigned and reassigned to machines 7 and 8 when activity-based costing is used.

13–25 Traditional and Activity-Based Cost Reassignments

Mobar, Inc., produces three products in a single production department. For years Mobar produced a single type of electric motor, the Standard A. Last year Mobar added two new specialty products: Deluxe B and Special C. Although these new products have relatively low annual sales and are produced in relatively short production runs, product B and especially product C have proven to be so profitable that management is contemplating becoming a specialty producer of short-run products. The marketing manager observed that it made sense to move into areas where there is little foreign competition and where Mobar's ability to respond quickly to customer needs can be exploited.

The production supervisor is opposed to this action, arguing that the profits of B and C are illusionary. You have been called to perform a special study of the profitability of each product. You quickly obtain the following information:

	Unit Data	
Product	Selling Price	Direct Costs
A	$35	$20
B	50	30
C	65	40

After discussions with the production supervisor you determine that Mobar uses highly automated equipment that has fast unit cycle times but relatively slow set-up times. What's more, set-ups are expensive because they require the work of a supervisor and several highly-trained production employees. Once set up, however, the machines operate with little attention. This information has led you to question Mobar's procedure of reassigning production costs on the basis of units produced.

Further discussions with production personnel and a statistical analysis of historical data revealed the following information pertaining to the actual production last year and the actual behavior of Mobar's factory overhead costs:

Product	Total Units	Job (batch) Size (units)	Set-up Time/Job	Production Time/Unit
A	40,000	5,000	5 hours	0.10 hours
B	10,000	500	10 hours	0.20 hours
C	5,000	100	5 hours	0.10 hours

Factory overhead costs:

Setup	$200 per hour
Operations	100 per hour

Requirements

a) Determine the gross profit per unit of each product when overhead is applied on the basis of (1) units produced and (2) operating time. (Round calculations to nearest cent.)

b) On the basis of this analysis, what conclusions are management likely to reach about relative profitability?

c) Determine the gross profit per unit when overhead is applied on the basis of the activities that drive overhead costs. (Round calculations to nearest cent.)

d) Based on the analysis in part (c) what conclusions are management likely to reach about relative profitability?

13–26 Service Department Cost Reassignment: Direct and Step Methods

The Parker Manufacturing Company has two production departments (Fabrication and Assembly) and three service departments (General Factory Administration, Factory Maintenance, and Factory Cafeteria). The costs of the General Factory Administration Department, Factory Maintenance Department, and Factory Cafeteria are reassigned to the production departments on the basis of direct labor hours, square footage occupied, and number of employees, respectively. A summary of costs and other data for each department prior to reassignment of service department costs for the year ended June 30, 19x3, appears below.

	Fabrication	Assembly	General Factory Administration	Factory Maintenance	Factory Cafeteria
Direct labor costs	$1,950,000	$2,050,000	$90,000	$82,100	$87,000
Direct materials costs	$3,130,000	$950,000	—	$65,000	$91,000
Manufacturing overhead costs	$1,650,000	$1,850,000	$70,000	$56,100	$62,000
Direct labor hours	562,500	437,500	31,000	27,000	42,000
Number of employees	280	200	12	8	20
Square footage occupied	88,000	72,000	1,750	2,000	4,800

Requirements

a) Assuming that Parker elects to distribute service department costs directly to production departments without recognizing interdepartmental services, how much Factory Maintenance Department costs would be reassigned to the Fabrication Department?

b) Assuming the same method of allocation as in requirement (a), how much General Factory Administration Department costs would be reassigned to the Assembly Department?

c) Assuming that Parker elects to distribute service department costs to other service departments (starting with the service department with the greatest total costs) as well as to the production departments, how much Factory Cafeteria Department costs would be reassigned to the Factory Maintenance Department?

d) Assuming the same method of reassignment as in requirement (c), how much Factory Maintenance Department costs would be reassigned to the General Factory Administration Department?

(CPA Adapted)

CASES

13–27 Reassignment of Home Office Costs: Aggregate Versus Detail

Partial income statements for the three divisions of International Computer Company are presented as follows (in thousands).

	Microcomputer Division	Software Division	Mainframe Division	Total
Income before home office costs	$25,000	$5,000	$45,000	$75,000
Home office costs	−10,000	−2,000	−18,000	−30,000
Net income	$15,000	$3,000	$27,000	$45,000

Home office costs are reassigned based on income before the home office cost deduction. The manager of the microcomputer division is distressed over her division's net income, and she feels that a major reason for the poor showing is the arbitrary and inequitable method by which home office costs are being reassigned. She believes that much of the company's home office efforts in the past year have been directed at getting the new Software Division started and that the reassignments do not reflect the relative benefits received by the divisions from home office activities.

She further suggests that home office costs should not be reassigned in total but should be broken down into cost components with each component reassigned on the basis that best reflects the services received by the three divisions. Corporate accounting reports show that home office costs consist of the following cost categories:

Administration	$ 6 million
Planning and Development	10 million
Legal and regulatory	12 million
Personnel relations and communications	2 million
	$30 million

The following data have been prepared for possible use in reassigning home office costs:

Cost	Reassignment Base	Microcomputer Division	Software Division	Mainframe Division
Administration	Total sales (millions)	$100	$25	$275
Planning and Development	New products in development	20	75	5
Legal and regulatory	Legal department hours used	1,000	4,000	1,000
Personnel relations	Number of employees	500	100	400

Requirements

a) Assuming all of the home office costs are controlled at the home office level and that the performance of services by the home office is determined solely by the home office staff, is it reasonable to include home office costs in performance evaluation reports for the division managers? Explain.

b) Discuss the pros and cons of reassigning home office costs in total versus reassigning them by individual cost components. Are division managers likely to be more receptive of home office cost reassignment if costs are reassigned by components instead of in the aggregate?

c) Revise the division income statements to reflect home office cost reassignments by individual cost components. Is this revised statement a reasonable basis for evaluating performance by the division managers? Discuss.

13–28 Whether or Not to Reassign: Selecting Bases for Reassignment

Bonn Company recently reorganized its computer and data processing activities. The small installations located within the accounting departments at its plants and subsidiaries have been replaced with a centralized data processing department at corporate headquarters responsible for the operations of a newly acquired large-scale computer system. The new department has been in operation for two years and has been regularly producing reliable and timely data for the past twelve months. Because the department has focused its activities on converting applications to the new system and producing reports for the plant and subsidiary managements, little attention has been devoted to the costs of the department. Now that the department's activities are operating relatively smoothly, company management has requested that the departmental manager recommend a cost accumulation system to facilitate cost control and the development of suitable rates to charge users for service. For the past two years, the departmental costs have been recorded in one account. The costs have been reassigned to user departments on the basis of computer time used. The schedule at the top of the next page reports the costs and charging rate for 19x5.

The department manager recommends that the department costs be accumulated by five activity centers within the department: Systems Analysis, Programming, Data Processing, Computer Operations (processing), and Administration. He then suggests that the costs of the Administration activity should be reassigned to the other four activity centers before a separate rate for charging users is developed for each of the first four activities. After reviewing the details of the accounts, the manager made the following observations regarding the charges to the several subsidiary accounts within the department.

1. Salaries and benefits—records the salary and benefit costs of all employees in the department.

2. Supplies—records punch card costs, paper costs for printers, and a small amount for miscellaneous other costs.

3. Equipment maintenance contracts—records charges for maintenance contracts; all equipment is covered by maintenance contracts.

4. Insurance—records cost of insurance covering the equipment and furniture.

5. Heat and air conditioning—records a charge from the corporate Heating and Air Conditioning Department estimated to be the incremental costs to meet the special needs of the computer department.

(1) Salaries and benefits	$ 622,600
(2) Supplies	40,000
(3) Equipment maintenance contract	15,000
(4) Insurance	25,000
(5) Heat and air conditioning	36,000
(6) Electricity	50,000
(7) Equipment and furniture depreciation	285,400
(8) Building improvements depreciation	10,000
(9) Building occupancy and security	39,300
(10) Corporate administrative charges	52,700
Total costs	$1,176,000
Computer hours for user processing	2,750
Hourly rate ($1,176,000/2,750)	$ 428 (rounded)
Use of available computer hours:	
Testing and debugging programs	250
Setup of jobs	500
Processing jobs	2,750
Downtime for maintenance	750
Idle time	742
Total	4,992

6. Electricity—records the charge for electricity based on a separate meter within the department.

7. Equipment and furniture depreciation—records the depreciation for all owned equipment and furniture within the department.

8. Building improvements depreciation—records amortization of the depreciation of all building improvements required to provide proper environmental control and electrical service for the computer equipment.

9. Building occupancy and security—records the Computer Department's share of the depreciation, maintenance, heat, and security costs of the building; these costs are allocated on the basis of square feet occupied.

10. Corporate administrative charges—records the Computer Department's share of the corporate administrative costs; they are allocated on the basis of the number of employees.

Requirements

a) For each of the ten cost items, state whether or not it should be reassigned to the five activity centers, and for each cost item that should be reassigned, recommend the basis upon which it should be allocated. Justify your conclusion in each case.

b) Assume that the costs of the Computer Operations (processing) activity will be charged to the user departments on the basis of computer hours. Using the analysis of computer utilization shown above, determine the total number of hours that should be employed to determine the charging rate for Computer Operations (processing). Justify your answer.

(CMA Adapted)

13–29 Cost
Reassignment and
Performance
Evaluation

The Village Branch of Citizens and Northern Bank is managed by Ron Short who has full responsibility for the bank's operations. The Village Branch is treated as a profit center within the company's responsibility accounting system and, according to rumors throughout the company, if the Village Branch does not become more profitable it is likely to be closed. Ron is upset with the corporate accounting department because of the number of different indirect costs which are reassigned to his branch each period. He feels that many of these costs provide no direct benefits to his branch and that they are not relevant to an evaluation of his performance or that of the Village Branch. An income statement for the Village Branch is presented below for February 19x4.

Branch revenues		$145,000
Direct branch costs		− 90,000
Branch margin		$ 55,000
Reassigned costs:		
Computer Operations Department	$ 4,500	
Personnel Department	5,000	
Payroll Department	3,800	
Maintenance Department	6,000	
Accounting Department	5,200	
Legal and Audit Department	4,200	
Transportation Department	9,000	
Administrative Overhead	12,000	− 49,700
Branch Net Income		$ 5,300

An investigation of Mr. Short's complaint by the controller's office provided the following additional information:

▪ Computer operations costs are billed based on actual CPU and computer connect time used by the branch.

▪ Personnel and payroll costs are primarily fixed and are reassigned to the various operating departments based on the number of employees in each division.

▪ Maintenance costs are charged to the operating departments based on the standard hours actually worked in each department plus the actual cost of materials and supplies used.

▪ Accounting costs are reassigned based on the number of transactions processed by the computer for each branch.

▪ Legal and audit costs are reassigned based on total revenues of the operating departments. The Village Branch has been involved in only one lawsuit which was about five years ago. Mr. Short gets a copy of the company audit report each year but seldom reads it.

▪ Transportation costs consist primarily of the costs of operating the company helicopter and the company airplane. The helicopter is used to deliver checks to the local clearing center and for local executive transportation and the airplane is used primarily for executive travel out of town. Transportation costs are reassigned to the operating departments based on revenues. Mr. Short has never flown in the corporate airplane.

■ Administrative overhead consists of all other administrative costs including home office salaries and office expenses. These costs are reassigned to the operating departments based on revenues. Mr. Short seldom ever sees anyone from the home office.

Requirements

a) Evaluate each of the cost reassignments to determine whether it seems appropriate to reassign it to the operating divisions. Also evaluate the basis upon which each cost is reassigned to the operating departments.

b) Prepare a revised income statement for the Village Branch based on your evaluations in requirement (a).

c) Do you agree with Mr. Short's complaint? How do the cost reassignments affect the decision to continue or discontinue the Village Branch?

REVIEW PROBLEM SOLUTION

1. Direct Method

	Total	Women's	Men's
Administrative Services Department:			
Reassignment base (number of employees)	24	15	9
Percent of total base	100%	62.5%	37.5%
Cost reassignment	$18,000	$11,250	$6,750
Facilities Services Department:			
Reassignment base (square footage)	22,500	15,000	7,500
Percent of total base	100%	66.7%	33.3%
Cost reassignment	$12,000	$8,000	$4,000

Cost reassignment summary:

	Administrative	Facilities	Women's	Men's	Total
Departmental costs before reassignments	$18,000	$12,000	$60,000	$50,000	$140,000
Cost reassignments:					
Administrative	(18,000)	—	11,250	6,750	-0-
Facilities	—	(12,000)	8,000	4,000	-0-
Departmental costs after reassignments	$ -0-	$ -0-	$79,250	$60,750	$140,000

2. Step Method

Reassignment sequence:

	Administrative	Facilities
	Number of Employees	Square Footage
Reassignment Base		
Total base for other service and producing departments (a)	26	25,000
Total base for other service departments (b)	2	2,500
Percent of total services provided to other service departments (b)/(a)	7.7%	10.0%
Order of reassignment	Second	First

Step reassignments:

	Total	Administrative	Women's	Men's
Facilities Services Department:				
Reassignment base (square footage)	25,000	2,500	15,000	7,500
Percent of total base	100%	10%	60%	30%
Cost reassignment	$12,000	$1,200	$7,200	$3,600
Administrative Services Department:				
Reassignment base (number of employees)	24	—	15	9
Percent of total base	100%	—	62.5%	37.5%
Cost reassignments	$19,200	—	$12,000	$7,200

Cost reassignment summary:

	Facilities	Administrative	Women's	Men's	Total
Departmental costs before reassignments	$12,000	$18,000	$60,000	$50,000	$140,000
Cost reassignments:					
Facilities	(12,000)	1,200	7,200	3,600	-0-
Administrative	—	(19,200)	12,000	7,200	-0-
Departmental costs after reassignments	$ -0-	$ -0-	$79,200	$60,800	$140,000

3. Linear Algebra Method

Legend:

A = Administrative Services Department
F = Facilities Services Department
W = Women's Apparel Department
M = Men's Apparel Department

Summary of services:

Services Provided from	Services Provided to			
	A	F	W	M
A	—	2/26 = 7.7%	15/26 = 57.7% 15,000/25,000 =	9/26 = 34.6%
F	2,500/25,000 = 10%	—	60%	7,500/25,000 = 30%

Total cost equations:

$$A = 18,000 + 0.10F$$
$$F = 12,000 + 0.077A$$
$$W = 60,000 + 0.577A + 0.60F$$
$$M = 50,000 + 0.346A + 0.30F$$

Solutions to equations using substitution method:

$$A = 18,000 + 0.10(12,000 + 0.077A)$$
$$A = 18,000 + 1,200 + 0.0077A$$
$$0.9923A = 19,200$$
$$A = 19,349 \text{ (or \$18,000 direct cost plus \$1,349 reassigned from F)}$$

$$F = 12,000 + 0.077(19,349)$$
$$F = 12,000 + 1,490$$
$$F = 13,490 \text{ (or \$12,000 direct cost plus \$1,490 reassigned from A)}$$

$$W = 60,000 + 0.577(19,349) + 0.60(13,490)$$
$$W = 60,000 + 11,164 + 8,094$$
$$W = 79,258 \text{ (or \$60,000 direct cost plus \$11,164 reassigned from A}$$
$$\text{and \$8,094 reassigned from F)}$$
$$M = 50,000 + 0.346(19,349) + 0.30(13,490)$$
$$M = 50,000 + 6,695 + 4,047$$
$$M = 60,742 \text{ (or \$50,000 direct cost plus \$6,695 reassigned}$$
$$\text{from A and \$4,047 reassigned from F)}$$

Cost reassignment summary:

	Administrative	Facilities	Women's	Men's	Total
Departmental costs before reassignments	$18,000	$12,000	$60,000	$50,000	$140,000
Cost reassignments:					
Administrative	(19,349)	1,490	11,164	6,695	-0-
Facilities	1,349	(13,490)	8,094	4,047	-0-
Departmental costs after reassignments	$ -0-	$ -0-	$79,258	$60,742	$140,000

P A R T 4

Selected Topics for Further Study

Part 4 contains a variety of topics which your instructor may assign to meet particular course objectives. Chapter 14 presents decision alternatives—many having to do with inventories—that are used frequently in management accounting. Economic order quantity and economic lot size, as related to inventories, are presented in detail, along with the critical elements of ordering costs, carrying costs, and demand. The support areas of safety stocks and the reorder point are integrated into the discussion. Just-in-time inventory management is discussed in detail here, with explanations of how this inventory management technique helps reduce raw materials, work-in-process, and finished goods inventories. The linear programming technique is presented as a decision tool for situations with resource constraints. Although used by MCI, linear programming has only general applications at MCI, with no frequently recurring situations. Other topics covered in the chapter include payoff models, risk analysis, and an appendix on quality costs.

Chapter 15 covers long-range planning and capital budgeting techniques. MCI incorporates several of the chapter's capital budgeting models in its capital budgeting decision process, which is controlled out of the home office. Although these models provide much relevant information for each capital budgeting opportunity, MCI's management also considers other factors in making capital budgeting decisions. Some of the most critical factors include sources and methods of financing, general economic conditions, competition, and owning versus leasing possibilities.

As in all for-profit businesses, taxes are a factor in MCI's decision making. Chapter 16 provides an overview of taxes and their impact on the decision process. Included are discussions of tax effects on income, property, sales, and capital budgeting. Detailed illustrations, using various inventory methods and capital budgeting techniques, are presented, extending the discussions of capital budgeting from the previous chapter.

Chapter 17 presents the most frequently used tools of financial statement analysis. Separate sections on measures of solvency and measures of performance are provided, each with its own group of ratios and evaluation techniques. To monitor company activities, MCI uses a total of 18 financial ratios, each of which is tracked over time and evaluated from period to period. However, MCI believes that the most critical measure of its success is earnings per share (EPS). EPS is so important because the company pays only a nominal dividend, and its stockholders are very concerned about their earnings increasing through company growth. The most closely monitored operating area is accounts receivable.

MCI was one of the first companies to adopt the new statement of cash flows when it became a requirement for external reporting. In accordance with Financial Accounting Standards, the new reporting requirement outlines the format and content of the statement and includes definitions of its various terms and concepts. Chapter 18 provides a detailed discussion of the statement of cash flows as currently required by the Financial Accounting Standards Board (FASB) and explains the benefits of using such a statement for evaluation purposes.

Relevant Costs for Quantitative Models and Inventory Management

Learning Objectives

Upon completion of this chapter you should:

- Understand the nature of quantitative models and their use in aiding decision making.

- Understand the issues involved in developing relevant cost data for use in quantitative models.

- Understand the uses and limitations of the economic order quantity and lot size models.

- Understand why many organizations are emphasizing just-in-time purchases and production.

- Be able to apply the safety stock assumptions to determine the minimum amount of safety stock required to prevent stockouts.

- Be aware of the effect of just-in-time inventory management on performance evaluation and product costing procedures.

- Have a general understanding of the basic elements of the linear programming model and be able to solve a simple linear programming model using the graphical approach.

- Be able to prepare payoff tables as an aid in evaluating decision alternatives that have different risk levels.

- Understand what is meant by the value of perfect information and why a decision maker might find this concept useful.

A model is a simplified representation of some real-world phenomenon. Models are used to learn about the related phenomenon and to quickly and inexpensively determine the effect of some proposed action. Children learn by playing with model houses, boats, cars, and horses. Museums and libraries contain educational models of buildings, drilling platforms, spaceships, prehistoric animals, and ecosystems. Airframe manufacturers study the aerodynamics of model planes in wind tunnels. Captains of supertankers learn how to pilot their craft using models in small lakes. These are all examples of physical models, scaled down versions or replicas of physical reality.

Managers and other decision makers also use quantitative models that are simply a series of algebraic relationships. Quantitative models can be further classified into descriptive models that merely specify the relationships between a series of independent and dependent variables and optimizing models that suggest a specific choice between decision alternatives. Cost-volume-profit relationships, contribution income statements, and operating budgets are all descriptive models.

The purposes of this chapter are to discuss the proper use of accounting data in optimizing models and to consider how changes in inventory management are affecting optimizing models and accounting. Attention is focused on four models that are widely used by managers and accountants: the economic order quantity, the economic lot size, linear programming, and payoff tables. The models introduced in this chapter are not accounting models per se, but they often use accounting data. Consequently, the accuracy and relevance of accounting data are critical to their proper use. Special attention is given to the effect of just-in-time inventory management on the economic order quantity and economic lot size.

QUANTITATIVE MODELS ARE DECISION AIDS

Quantitative, especially optimizing, models are often criticized as being over-simplistic, unrealistic, and prone to "make" incorrect decisions. It is true that models are a simplified representation of reality, but this is also one of their strengths. The use of a model helps management focus on the few variables that are most critical to a decision. Furthermore, the assumptions that underlie a model can be specified and evaluated.

All quantitative models, descriptive and optimizing, are intended to *assist* managers in decision making. Managers cannot relinquish their decision-making responsibility to models that are merely intended to be decision support systems. In the final analysis, *managers, not models, make decisions.* Managers must carefully evaluate the data used in the model, the assumptions underlying the model, and the output of the model. If everything appears satisfactory, a manager may implement the action suggested by an optimizing model. If a manager suspects faulty data, an oversimplistic assumption, or changed circumstances that invalidate the model, the suggested action should not be implemented. Instead, the manager should undertake further analysis or make a decision based on professional judgment.

Optimizing models, like many other aspects of a business, should be managed using the principle of exception. When everything is going according to plan, management implements the action suggested by the model. If any invalidating circumstances are suspected, management should intervene. Properly used as decision aids, models increase the speed and quality of management's decisions.

ECONOMIC ORDER QUANTITY FOR PURCHASES

The operating budget (discussed in Chapter 6) specifies the number of units to be purchased or manufactured during a period of time. In merchandising organizations, for example, the number of units to be purchased is computed, for each inventory item, as the total needs for current sales, plus the desired ending inventory, less the expected beginning inventory. The operating budget does not specify the order quantity or the reorder point. The **order quantity** is the quantity of inventory ordered *at one time,* and the **reorder point** is the inventory level at which an order for additional units is placed.

Consider the order quantity. If budgeted 19x4 purchases of inventory item B-25 are 2,400 units, management might place one order for 2,400 units, three orders for 800 units, 2,400 orders for 1 unit, or some other combination of number of orders and order size.

Assume that the demand for item B-25 is constant throughout the year and that new orders are timed to arrive just as the previous order is exhausted. In this case, an order quantity of 800 units might produce the variations in inventory level illustrated in Exhibit 14–1. The maximum inventory level is reached just as a new order is received. Subsequent to the receipt of an order, the inventory level falls at a constant rate per unit of time, and another order is received just as the inventory level falls to zero. With a maximum inventory of 800 units, a minimum inventory of 0 units, and a constant rate of decline per unit of time, the average inventory of item B-25 is 400 units [(800 + 0)/2].

Inventory Costs

A variety of costs are associated with inventory, including the costs of the units purchased, of ordering inventory, of carrying inventory, and of insufficient inventory. Several costs in each of these categories are listed in Exhibit 14–2. Management's objective is to determine the **economic order quantity** (EOQ), the order quantity that results in the minimum total annual inventory costs. Because only costs that vary with the order quantity are relevant to this decision, each of the cost categories in Exhibit 14–2 is examined to identify the relevant and the irrelevant costs.

EXHIBIT 14–1   Variation in Inventory Level over Time

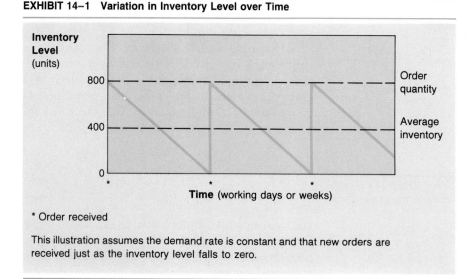

* Order received

This illustration assumes the demand rate is constant and that new orders are received just as the inventory level falls to zero.

In the absence of quantity discounts, the total annual costs of the units purchased vary only with total units purchased, not with the order quantity or the number of orders. Consequently, the total annual costs of the units purchased are irrelevant to determining the order quantity and are excluded from order quantity models.

EXHIBIT 14–2   Inventory Costs for Purchased Goods Intended for Resale*

Costs of units purchased	*Costs of ordering inventory*
Unit price	Processing the order
Transportation-in	Receiving and inspecting the order
	Processing payment for the order
Costs of carrying inventory	
	Costs of insufficient inventory
Insurance	
Personal property taxes	Lost contribution from missed sales
Storage space costs	Lost customer goodwill
Deterioration and obsolescence	Cost of special orders
Handling costs	Cost of processing backorders
Opportunity cost of money invested in inventory	

* In the case of manufactured goods, variable manufacturing costs are substituted for the unit price and the cost of ordering inventory includes machine set-up costs. If goods are to be processed further in a subsequent department, the costs of insufficient inventory include the costs of excessive idle time and the costs of expediting production once the goods are available.

The total annual costs of ordering inventory are computed as follows:

$$\begin{array}{c} \text{Total annual} \\ \text{ordering costs} \end{array} = \begin{array}{c} \text{Cost of placing} \\ \text{an order} \end{array} \times \begin{array}{c} \text{Number of orders} \\ \text{per year.} \end{array}$$

Because the number of orders per year is computed as the annual demand divided by the order size, the total annual costs of ordering inventory vary with the order size. As the order size increases, the number of orders per year decreases, and the total annual ordering costs decrease. Conversely, as the order size decreases, the number of orders per year increases, and the total annual ordering costs increase.

Assume that the cost of placing an order for part B-25 is $25. If the order quantity is 800 units, the total annual ordering costs are $75 [$25 × (2,400/800)]. A decrease in the order size to 600 units would increase the total available ordering costs to $100 [$25 × (2,400/600)].

MANAGERIAL PRACTICE 14.1

How to Reduce Materials Costs with Inventory Management

In 1980, most Japanese companies were selling copiers for what it cost Xerox to manufacture them. Manufacturing costs of similar machines often exceeded some Japanese manufacturers' costs by as much as 50 percent, and new product development time often took twice as long as for their closest competitors. Because of these factors, Xerox was losing market share.

To survive, Xerox responded. Suppliers of parts and components were reduced from over 5,000 vendors to about 400. Xerox helped suppliers improve their quality control over shipments, implemented a just-in-time inventory management system, and included suppliers' engineers in the designing phase of new products. This latter activity led to improvements in productivity for both parties. By 1985 the outlook for the company was much improved, and product costs had been reduced by nearly 40 percent—primarily through improved relations with suppliers and the ability of the suppliers to reduce the costs of materials and parts that were shipped to Xerox.

Source: Daivd N. Burt, "Managing Suppliers Up to Speed," *Harvard Business Review* (July–August 1989): 127–135.

As might be suspected, the costs of carrying inventory also vary with the order size. Increasing the order size increases the average inventory and the total annual costs of carrying inventory. Conversely, decreasing the order size reduces the average inventory and the total annual carrying costs.

Note that the cost of carrying inventory includes an opportunity cost for the money invested in inventory. The interest rate on borrowed money is frequently used to estimate this opportunity cost. However, the rate of return management desires to earn on inventory investments is a better choice. The issues involved in determining this rate are discussed in financial management textbooks; one possible rate is the organization's cost of capital (discussed in Chapter 15).

Carrying costs are often expressed as a percentage of the unit purchase price. Assume the carrying costs for part B-25 are 25 percent of the unit purchase price. If the unit purchase price is $12 and the order size is 800 units, the cost of carrying 1 unit in inventory for 1 year is $3 ($12 × 0.25), and the total annual carrying costs are $1,200 [$3 × (800/2)].

Operations research textbooks sometimes contain sophisticated models that allow stockouts and backorders to occur. These models then include stockout costs in the determination of the economic order quantity. We shall assume that management does not intentionally allow stockouts to occur. Consequently, the costs of insufficient inventory are irrelevant to the determination of our economic order quantity.

In summary, only the costs of ordering and carrying inventory are relevant to determining the economic order quantity, and these costs vary inversely with each other. As the order size increases, total annual ordering costs decrease and total annual carrying costs increase. As the order size decreases, total annual ordering costs increase and total annual carrying costs decrease. The total relevant costs for determining the economic order quantity are computed as follows:

$$
\begin{aligned}
\text{Total annual ordering} \atop \text{and carrying costs} &= \left({\text{Cost of placing} \atop \text{an order}} \times \frac{\text{Annual demand}}{\text{Order quantity}} \right) \\
&+ \left({\text{Unit carrying} \atop \text{costs per year}} \times \frac{\text{Order quantity}}{2} \right).
\end{aligned}
$$

Determining the Economic Order Quantity

There are two basic approaches to determining the economic order quantity (EOQ): (1) a trial and error tabular approach and (2) a formula approach. Both approaches are based on the following assumptions.

1. The demand rate is known and uniform.

2. There are no quantity discounts.

3. Ordering costs are a known function of the number of orders.

4. Carrying costs are a known function of average inventory.

5. Stockouts are not intentionally permitted.

Though these assumptions are seldom completely valid, the EOQ model is useful because it often produces lower total annual inventory costs than order quantities based on professional judgment.

Trial and Error Approach. Recall that the annual demand for inventory part B-25 is 2,400 units, the cost of placing an order is $25, and the cost of carrying 1 unit in inventory for 1 year is $3. If management orders 800 units at a time, the total annual ordering and carrying costs are $1,275 (see Exhibit 14–3).

Also tabulated in Exhibit 14–3 are the total annual ordering and carrying costs for several additional order sizes. The information tabulated in Exhibit 14–3 is graphed in Exhibit 14–4. Both exhibits illustrate that *the minimum annual costs occur at the order size where the annual ordering costs equal the annual carrying costs,* 200 units in this example. The essence of the trial and error approach is to find the order size where these two costs are equal by repeated trial and error.

Even though the EOQ model suggests that an order size of exactly 200 units is most economical, management might order in other lot sizes because of quantity discounts, warehouse capacity constraints, limited shelf life of an inventory item, or a variety of other factors. An examination of Exhibit 14–4 reveals that small deviations from the economic order quantity are not very costly. The total cost curve is high at both ends but relatively low between 100 and 300 units. The existence of this wide low-cost area near the EOQ, with high costs at order quantities far from the EOQ, is what makes this model so valuable despite its restrictive assumptions. Even if the model is not completely accurate, it helps management get into the low-cost area.

EXHIBIT 14–3   Relevant Annual Costs for Determining the Economic Order Quantity

Order quantity (units)	20	50	150	200	300	800	1,200	2,400
Number of orders (annual demand ÷ order quantity)	120	48	16	12	8	3	2	1
Average inventory (order quantity divided by two)*	10	25	75	100	150	400	600	1,200
Relevant annual costs:								
Ordering (number of orders × $25)	$3,000	$1,200	$400	$300	$200	$ 75	$ 50	$ 25
Carrying (average inventory × $3)	30	75	225	300	450	1,200	1,800	3,600
Total	$3,030	$1,275	$625	$600**	$650	$1,275	$1,850	$3,625

* This assumes that the demand rate is constant and that the inventory level is zero when the new order is received.

** Minimum annual ordering and holding costs.

EXHIBIT 14–4   Behavior of Inventory Ordering and Carrying Costs

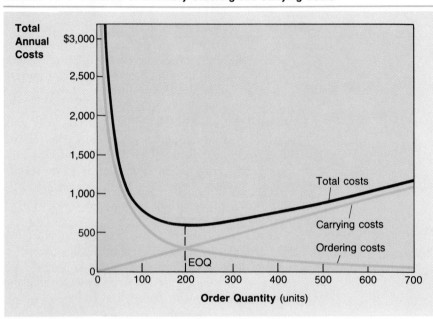

Formula Approach. By setting annual ordering costs equal to annual carrying costs, and solving for the order quantity, the economic order quantity formula is derived.

$$\underline{\textbf{Annual Ordering Costs}} = \underline{\textbf{Annual Carrying Costs}}$$

$$\frac{\text{Cost of placing}}{\text{an order}} \times \frac{\text{Annual demand}}{\text{Order quantity}} = \frac{\text{Unit carrying}}{\text{costs per year}} \times \frac{\text{Order quantity}}{2}$$

$$\begin{array}{c}\text{Economic} \\ \text{order} \\ \text{quantity}\end{array} = \sqrt{\frac{2 \times \begin{array}{c}\text{Annual} \\ \text{demand}\end{array} \times \begin{array}{c}\text{Cost of placing} \\ \text{an order}\end{array}}{\begin{array}{c}\text{Unit carrying} \\ \text{cost per year}\end{array}}}$$

For part B-25, the economic order quantity is once again determined to be 200 units:

$$EOQ = \sqrt{\frac{2 \times 2{,}400 \times \$25}{\$3}}$$

$$= 200 \text{ units.}$$

Reorder Point

The reorder point is the inventory level at which an order for additional units is placed. The reorder point must allow sufficient inventory to cover demand during the lead time, the time between the placement and the receipt of an order. Assuming demand takes place evenly throughout a year containing n work days, the equation for daily demand is

$$\text{Daily demand} = \text{Annual demand}/n.$$

If the lead time required to fill an order is known and certain, the reorder point that results in a new order arriving just as the previous order is exhausted is computed as

$$\frac{\text{Reorder}}{\text{point}} = \frac{\text{Daily}}{\text{demand}} \times \frac{\text{Lead}}{\text{time}}.$$

Assume the organization using part B-25 operates 240 days per year and that the lead time for this item is 5 days. Under these circumstances the reorder point for B-25 is 50 units:

$$\begin{aligned}\text{Daily demand} &= \text{2,400 units}/\text{240 days} \\ &= \text{10 units per day.}\end{aligned}$$

$$\begin{aligned}\text{Reorder point} &= \text{10 units per day} \times \text{5 days} \\ &= \text{50 units.}\end{aligned}$$

Management places an order whenever the inventory level falls to 50 units.

Safety Stocks

Safety stocks are extra units of inventory carried to prevent stockouts due to variations in the demand for units during the lead time. Stockouts can occur because of delays in the receipt of an order or increases in the daily demand for an inventory item. If management desires to avoid stockouts, and daily demand or lead time or both are uncertain, they must carry safety stocks.

Safety stocks can be computed as the difference between the maximum lead time demand and the reorder point without safety stocks. Safety stocks do not increase the economic order quantity; they do, however, increase the reorder point and total carrying costs. Assume the maximum daily demand for part B-25 is 12 units, and the maximum lead time is 8 days. Under these circumstances, the safety stock for this item would be set at 46 units:

Maximum demand per day	12 units
Maximum lead time	× 8 days
Maximum lead time demand	96 units
Reorder point without safety stocks	−50 units
Safety stock	46 units

Safety stocks can be viewed as a base inventory. If the safety stocks for part B-25 are never used, they will have an annual carrying cost of $138, computed as the $3 carrying costs per unit per year times 46 units of safety stock.

The economic order quantity for part B-25 will remain at 200 units, but the reorder point will increase to 96 units, the reorder point plus the safety stock. Possible patterns for part B-25's inventory level with safety stocks and variations in demand are illustrated in Exhibit 14–5. Note that the presence of the base inventory layer increases the maximum inventory to 246 units. Also, when some of the safety stock is used, the new order will not bring the total inventory level to 246 units but to an amount equal to 246 less the amount of safety stocks used.

ECONOMIC LOT SIZE FOR PRODUCTION

Production may take place in response to a specific customer order or to manufacture speculative inventories in anticipation of future sales. The manufacturing process may involve the continuous production of identical units or the production of batches of different products. Job costing, discussed in Chapter 11, is appropriate for batch production; process costing, discussed in Chapter 12, is appropriate for continuous production.

EXHIBIT 14–5   Variations in Inventory Level with Safety Stock

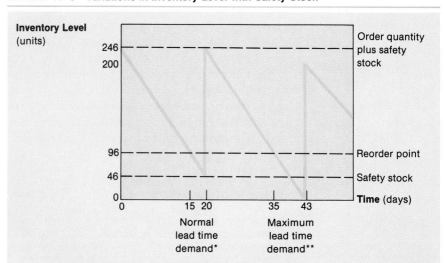

*The first reorder is placed on day 15. It takes 5 days to arrive with normal daily demand.
**The second reorder is placed on day 35 and takes 8 days to arrive with maximum daily demand during the lead time. Hence the safety stock is completely used, and replenishment brings the inventory level to 200 units.

The economic order quantity model is applicable to the batch production of speculative inventory. In this case, variable unit manufacturing costs are substituted for the unit price, and the cost of ordering inventory includes machine set-up and scheduling costs. With these modifications, the model is used to compute an economic lot (batch) size (ELS) that results in the minimum ordering and carrying costs.

Assume the annual use of subcomponent PK45 totals 2,500 units, spread evenly throughout the year. Variable manufacturing costs of subcomponent PK45 are $50 per unit; machine set-up, scheduling, and other ordering costs total $125 per batch; and annual carrying costs are 20 percent of unit variable costs. In this case the cost of carrying one unit in inventory for one year is $10 ($50 × 0.20) and the economic lot size is 250 units:

$$\text{Economic lot size} = \sqrt{\frac{2 \times 2,500 \times \$125}{\$10}}$$

$$= 250 \text{ units.}$$

The ELS size model should not be applied to situations in which continuous production is more appropriate than batch production. This would lead to excessive set-up, scheduling, and other ordering costs as the production process is artificially segmented. When a job must pass through several operations in sequence, proper scheduling to minimize carrying costs normally calls for production in subsequent operations to begin before all units pass through preceding operations. When a job calls for the manufacture and subsequent assembly of several components, careful scheduling is required to avoid the buildup of excessive inventories between work stations. These and other issues, such as the proper timing of raw materials purchases and assembly of subcomponents for large jobs (materials requirement planning), are considered in operations management textbooks.

JUST-IN-TIME INVENTORY MANAGEMENT

Just-in-time (JIT) inventory management stresses having available only the inventory required to meet current production or sales requirements. JIT is a philosophy rather than a quantitative model; it is considered here because JIT, while worthy of study by itself, also illustrates the limitations of blindly following quantitative models, such as those for the economic order quantity or lot size.

Proponents of JIT argue that inventory is an enemy because it causes the incurrence of carrying and handling costs, increases production times, and hides quality problems. To achieve the goal of reducing inventories, proponents of JIT believe high levels of employee involvement in decision making are required. Key elements of the JIT philosophy include: inventory reduction, reduced production times, increased product quality, and employee involvement.

In manufacturing organizations there are three types of inventory to be reduced: raw materials, work-in-process, and finished goods. Approaches to reducing each are considered below.

Reducing Raw Materials Inventories

The JIT approach to reducing raw materials includes: (1) developing long term relationships with a limited number of vendors; (2) selecting vendors on the basis of service and material quality as well as price; (3) establishing procedures for production employees to order raw materials for current production needs directly from approved vendors; and (4) accepting vendor deliveries directly to the shop floor. Fully implemented, these steps would minimize or eliminate raw materials inventories. There would be sufficient raw materials on hand to meet only near term needs, and the raw materials inventories would be located on the shop floor.

To achieve this reduction, it is apparent that vendors and buyers must work as a team and that production employees must be involved in decision making. The goal of the JIT approach to purchasing is not merely to shift raw materials carrying costs to vendors. A close and long-term working relationship between purchasers and vendors should be beneficial to both. Purchaser's scheduling information is provided to vendors so that vendors can also reduce inventories and minimize costs. Vendors are therefore able to manufacture small batches frequently, rather than to manufacture large batches infrequently. What's more, vendors are more confident of future sales.

MANAGERIAL PRACTICE 14.2

Counting the Blessings of JIT

Following the implementation of JIT at Brunswick's Mercury Marine Division, floor space was cut in half, inventory turnover increased by 300 percent, and labor costs went down by 25 percent. At Harley-Davidson, inventory was reduced by 50 percent, and setup times were cut 75 percent. JIT was considered one of the changes in the production system that saved Harley-Davidson from bankruptcy in the face of stiff competition in the motorcycle industry.

Source: Joseph D. Blackburn, "Trends in Manufacturing," in *Cost Accounting, Robotics, and the New Manufacturing Environment,* ed. Robert Capettini and Donald K. Clancy (Sarasota, Fla.: American Accounting Association, 1987), 1.11.

Reducing Work-in-Process Inventories

Reducing cycle time, the total time required to produce a unit or batch, is the key to reducing work-in-process inventories. Cycle time is composed of set-up time, processing time, movement time, waiting time, and inspection time. Set-up time is the time required to prepare equipment to produce a specific product. Processing time is the time spent working on units. Movement time is the time units spend moving between work or inspection stations. Waiting time is the time units spend in temporary storage waiting to be processed, moved, or inspected. Inspection time is the amount of time it takes units to be inspected. Of the five elements of cycle time, only processing time adds value to the product. Efforts to reduce cycle time are appropriate for both continuous and batch production.

Devising means of reducing set-up times will directly reduce the cycle time for batch production and also, to the extent that setup costs are reduced, lower the economic lot size. Set-up times can also be reduced by shifting from batch to continuous production whenever practical. Rearranging the shop floor to eliminate unnecessary materials movements can help reduce movement time for continuous and batch production. Giving employees more authority and responsibility for quality, including the right to stop production whenever quality problems are noted, can reduce the need for separate inspection time.

In the case of batch production, waiting time can be reduced by better job scheduling. In the case of continuous production, waiting time can be reduced by moving from a materials push to a materials pull approach to production.

Under a traditional materials push system, employees work to reduce the pile of inventory building up at their work stations. Workers at each station remove materials from an in-process storage area, complete their operation, and place the output in another in-process storage area. Hence they push the work to the next work station. The emphasis is on production efficiency at each station. In a push system, one of the functions of work-in-process inventory is to help make work stations independent of each other. Inventories are large enough to allow for variations in processing speeds, discarding defective units without interrupting production, and machine downtime.

Under a materials pull (often called a Kanban) system, employees at each station work to replenish the inventory used by employees at subsequent stations. The building of excess inventories is strictly prohibited. When the number of units in inventory reaches a specified limit, work at the station stops until workers at a subsequent station pull a unit from the in-process storage area. Hence, the pull of inventory by a subsequent station authorizes production to continue. A pull, or Kanban, system's low inventory levels require a team effort. To avoid idle time, processing speeds must be balanced and equipment must be kept in good repair. Quality problems are identified immediately, and the low inventory levels require immediate correction of quality problems.

To make a pull system work, management must accept the notion that it is better to have employees idle than to have them building excess inventory. A pull system also requires careful planning by management, active participation in decision making by employees, and a shift from an emphasis on performance at each work station to an emphasis on performance for the entire operation.

Reducing Finished Goods Inventory

Finished goods inventory can be reduced by decreasing the batch size and the size of safety stocks. Lowering cycle times is the key to reducing the need for speculative inventories. If finished goods can be replenished faster, there is less need for large inventory levels to satisfy customer needs and to provide for unanticipated fluctuations in customer orders or production lead times.

EOQ and ELS with JIT

The economic order quantity model is intended to assist managers in making purchasing decisions. The economic lot size model is intended to assist managers in making decisions concerning the number of units in batches produced for speculative inventory. The JIT philosophy is applicable to all inventories and all production situations, batch and continuous. Hence the JIT philosophy is more generalizable than the EOQ and ELS models.

In recent years the EOQ and ELS models have been criticized by proponents of just-in-time production, who argue that management should try to minimize inventories rather than optimize the batch size. The root of these criticisms appears to be a tendency of many managers to optimize production for the current cost structure. Often these managers attempt to manage by the numbers rather than becoming familiar enough with operations to try and change the numbers.

Meanwhile, managers in firms that do not rely solely on inventory quantity models have achieved significant reductions in inventories and cycle times while improving product quality. The by-product of their efforts has been a significant reduction in their organizations' cost structures. It appears that the blind application of quantitative models to a set of numbers is less profitable than becoming familiar with operations and engaging in actions that reduce cost structures.

Managers cannot shift the blame for bad decisions to a model. Managers, not models, make decisions. The economic lot size model is intended for batch production. It should not be used for situations in which continuous production is more appropriate. The model assumes the demand rate is known and uniform. If the demand rate is uncertain or variable, use of the model may result in excess inventory or inventory stockouts. The model is intended to optimize for a given cost structure. If managers fail to make competitive reductions in ordering and set-up costs (which will reduce the economic quantity), their firms will be less competitive, even if they properly use the model.

It is the authors' opinion that even better results can be obtained by adopting the JIT philosophy *and* using inventory models where appropriate. The results will be unsatisfactory if managers inappropriately apply EOQ or ELS models to situations in which the assumptions of these models are not valid, attempt to manage a business exclusively with the use of models, fail to develop a detailed understanding of the business, or fail to encourage employee involvement in improving operations. Managers of competitive firms must strive to reduce their firms' cost structures and make appropriate use of quantitative models as decision aids.

ACCOUNTING IN A JUST-IN-TIME ENVIRONMENT

When organizations make significant changes in their operating procedures, they should reevaluate their accounting system for any needed changes. Movement toward a JIT inventory philosophy requires changes in performance evaluation procedures and offers opportunities for significant reductions in bookkeeping costs. These changes are considered below.

Performance Evaluation

JIT regards inventory as something to be eliminated. Hence, in a manufacturing organization, inventories are kept as small as possible, and under the JIT ideal, they do not exist. Raw materials are delivered in small batches directly to the shop floor. JIT also strives to eliminate work-in-process inventory, to reduce cycle time to processing time, and to have processing time as short as possible. Ideally, set-up, waiting, movement, and inspection times are to be eliminated.

Dysfunctional Effects of Financial Performance Measures. There is a potential conflict between the goals of JIT and those of traditional financial performance measures applied at the level of the department or cost center. Although JIT emphasizes overall efficiency, many traditional financial performance measures emphasize local (departmental) cost savings and local (departmental) efficiency. Consider traditional performance measures for a purchasing agent and a departmental production supervisor:

- To achieve quantity discounts and favorable materials price variances, a purchasing agent may order excess inventory, thereby increasing subsequent storage, obsolescence, and handling costs.
- To obtain a low price, a purchasing agent may order from a supplier whose goods have not been certified as meeting quality specifications, thereby causing subsequent inspection, rework, and spoilage costs, and, perhaps, dissatisfied customers.
- To avoid unfavorable labor efficiency and variable overhead efficiency variances, a departmental production supervisor may refuse to halt production to determine the cause of a quality problem, thereby increasing inspection, rework, and spoilage costs.
- To obtain favorable fixed overhead variances, a departmental production supervisor may produce in excess of current needs (preferably in long production runs), thereby causing subsequent increases in storage, obsolescence, and handling costs.

Use of Nonfinancial Performance Measures. To avoid the problems associated with traditional financial performance measures that stress local efficiency and cost savings, nonfinancial performance measures should be emphasized for first-level control in a JIT environment. Financial performance measures are reserved for overall evaluation rather than for detailed or daily evaluation. In accordance with the goal of eliminating inventory and reducing cycle time to processing time, JIT performance measures emphasize inventory turnover, cycle time, and cycle efficiency (the ratio of value-added to nonvalue-added manufacturing activities).

When applied to a specific item of raw materials or finished goods, inventory turnover is computed as the annual demand in units divided by the average inventory in units:

$$\text{Inventory turnover} = \frac{\text{Annual demand in units}}{\text{Average inventory in units}}.$$

Progress toward the goal of reducing inventory is measured by comparing successive inventory turnover ratios. The higher the inventory turnover, the better.

When stated in dollars, inventory turnover can be used as a measure of the overall success of the organization in reducing inventory:

$$\text{Inventory turnover} = \frac{\text{Cost of goods sold}}{\text{Average inventory (in dollars)}}.$$

This financial measure can be derived directly from a firm's financial statements.

Cycle time is a measure of the total time required to produce one unit of a product:

$$\frac{\text{Cycle}}{\text{time}} = \frac{\text{Setup}}{\text{time}} + \frac{\text{Process}}{\text{time}} + \frac{\text{Move}}{\text{time}} + \frac{\text{Wait}}{\text{time}} + \frac{\text{Inspection}}{\text{time}}.$$

MANAGERIAL PRACTICE 14.3

JIT—Not for Everyone

Just-in-time inventory management is out of fashion, or so Apple Computer would have us believe. Apple is deliberately increasing stocks of almost-finished computers. The reason, says Apple, "is that our warehousing is more efficient than any Japanese electronics producer's. . . . By centrally locating inventory, we have increased our ability to respond flexibly to differing demands in different countries." Because of Apple's diverse product mix—27 different configurations just for PCs—and the ever-changing market for its products, it was easy to stock the wrong finished products. Therefore, by stocking its products in near-completion stages, it could respond quickly to changes in the marketplace.

Source: "Apple Flouts Just-in-Time," *The Dominion* (Wellington, New Zealand), 22 May 1989, 24.

The lower the cycle time, the better. Under ideal circumstances, cycle time would consist of only processing time, and processing time would be as low as possible. Only processing time adds value to the product, and the time required for all other activities should be driven toward zero. If flexible manufacturing systems are used, jobs properly sequenced, and tools properly placed, there is little set-up time. If the shop floor is optimally arranged, workers pass products directly from one work station to the next. If production is optimally scheduled, inventory will not wait in temporary storage between work stations. If raw materials are of high quality and products are manufactured so that they always conform to specifications, there is no need for separate inspection activities.

Manufacturing efficiency is computed as the ratio of processing time to total cycle time:

$$\text{Cycle efficiency} = \frac{\text{Processing time}}{\text{Cycle time}}.$$

The higher the cycle efficiency, the better. If all nonvalue-added activities are eliminated this ratio equals one.

Simplified Accounting Procedures for External Reporting

Just-in-time inventory allows significant reductions in the number of accounting transactions required for purchasing and production activities. This can result in cost savings for bookkeeping activities and shifting accounting resources from the detailed bookkeeping required for external reporting to the development of more useful activity cost data.

Purchasing

In a traditional accounting system, every purchase results in the generation of several documents and two journal entries. Additional documents and journal entries record the issuance of raw materials to the factory. These items are discussed in detail in accounting information systems textbooks, but it is useful to consider them briefly here. The documents include:

- A *purchase requisition* completed by a computerized inventory control system or an inventory clerk who notes the need to place an order.
- A *purchase order* prepared in the purchasing department.
- A *receiving report* prepared by receiving room personnel.
- An *invoice* sent by the vendor indicating the amount due.
- A *payment voucher* prepared by accounts payable authorizing the preparation of a check.
- A *check* prepared by the cashier.

After the goods and the vendor's invoice are received, a journal entry debiting Raw Materials or Merchandise Inventory and crediting Accounts Payable is made. The preparation of a check results in a journal entry debiting Accounts Payable and crediting Cash.

Tracking of inventory takes place as raw materials are issued to production. A *materials requisition* is used to document the transfer of inventory from the storeroom to the shop floor. This transaction is accompanied by a journal entry debiting Work-in-Process and crediting Raw Materials. In batch processing, appropriate notations are also made on *job-cost sheets.*

The above documents are required to ensure that purchases and issuances are authorized in accordance with company policy. Detailed documentation is especially important with high inventory levels and when purchases are made from a large number of vendors who compete on the basis of price.

JIT, on the other hand, attempts to minimize inventory levels and stresses long-term relationships with a limited number of vendors who have demonstrated their ability to provide quality raw materials on a timely basis, as well as at a competitive price. Hence, with JIT, there is a significant reduction in inventory levels and the number of vendors. What's more, vendors are just as interested in future sales as they are in current sales. The reductions in inventory and the number of vendors, and the development of vendor expectations for future business, reduce the need for much of the documentation previously used to ensure that purchases and issuances are authorized.

Under a JIT inventory system, a company often has standing purchase orders for specified materials from specified vendors at specified prices. Production personnel are authorized to requisition materials directly from authorized vendors, who deliver limited quantities of materials as needed directly to the shop floor. Production personnel verify receipt of the raw materials. Periodically, each vendor sends an invoice for several shipments, which the company acknowledges and pays. The accompanying journal entries include a debit to Raw Materials-in-Process (discussed below) with an offsetting credit to Accounts Payable.

Electronic data interchange (EDI), the electronic communication of data between organizations, is also affecting JIT inventory systems and accounting procedures. Using EDI, production personnel enter a materials requisition into a computer terminal and transmit the order by electronic mail to an authorized vendor. This procedure reduces the lead time required to order goods. When the vendor's EDI system is integrated in such a manner that data reentry is eliminated, order-processing costs and errors are reduced. Vendor invoices may also be sent using EDI. It is even possible to pay the invoice using EDI rather than by check.

Note how standing purchase orders and EDI reduce the number of documents and the amount of data entry involved in purchase transactions. In a traditional system each purchase order might require a separate materials requisition, purchase order, receiving report, invoice, payment voucher, and check. Multiple copies are often required. The existence of all the documents and booking procedures associated with traditional accounting systems causes high order-processing costs. With the EOQ model, high order-processing costs result in correspondingly high order quantities. Standing orders with direct delivery to the shop floor and the electronic transmission of purchase orders, invoices, and payments significantly reduce order-processing costs. With the EOQ model, low order-processing costs result in correspondingly low order quantities.

Product Costing

Because JIT stresses low inventory levels and high inventory turnover, there is little need for inventory costing for external financial reporting. Ending inventories are nonexistent or so small that the costs assigned to them are insignificant in comparison with the costs assigned to goods sold.

Under these circumstances, when virtually all product costs are properly assignable to Cost of Goods Sold at the end of the period, it makes little sense to track product costs through inventory accounts. For financial reporting purposes, detailed product costing is not required when JIT inventory management is fully implemented. Instead, a simple set of journal entries, such as those developed for backflush costing in Chapter 12, are used.

Under backflush costing, Raw Materials and Work-in-Process are combined into a single account called "Raw Materials-in-Process." The costs of purchases are immediately assigned to Raw Materials-in-Process rather than to Raw Materials. (Note how this parallels the direct delivery of raw materials to the shop floor.) At the end of the period, the raw materials costs associated with completed units are transferred to Finished Goods Inventory or Costs of Goods Sold. Conversion costs for direct labor and factory overhead are accumulated in an account such as Conversion Costs. These costs are assigned to Finished Goods Inventory or Cost of Goods Sold at the end of the period, rather than to an in-process inventory account. The only end-of-period costs in Raw Materials-in-Process are those for unused or partially completed raw materials. Although backflush costing may result in an understatement of ending in-process inventory (to the extent that goods are partially completed), if inventories are very small the understatement is acceptable.

Another inventory costing approach under JIT is to assign all raw materials purchases and conversion costs directly to Cost of Goods Sold. At the end of the period an adjusting entry is used to assign some costs to Raw Materials-in-Process and Finished Goods Inventory. The costs assigned to inventories may be based on the standard or budgeted cost of the units in inventory multiplied by their percentage of completion. At the start of the next period a reversing entry reassigns all costs to Cost of Goods Sold.

There are a number of variations in accounting procedures for JIT inventory systems. All emphasize a reduction in the number of accounting transactions and journal entries in an attempt to save bookkeeping costs. Given low JIT inventory levels, virtually all provide acceptable numbers for external reporting.

Management Still Needs Accurate Cost Data

Although JIT inventory management reduces the importance of product costing for external reporting, it does not reduce management's need for accurate product cost information for internal purposes. Indeed, the same competitive pressures that lead managers to adopt the JIT philosophy of inventory management also increase the need for detailed and accurate cost data. With simplified external reporting requirements, management has an opportunity to shift resources to the development of activity cost data, discussed in Chapter 13.

LINEAR PROGRAMMING

Linear programming is an optimizing model used to assist managers in making decisions under constrained conditions when linear relationships exist between all variables. This model may be applied to a variety of business decisions, including product mix, raw materials mix, production scheduling, transportation scheduling, and cash management. The objective in linear programming is to determine the action that will maximize profits or minimize costs. The constraints can represent limited resources (such as labor hours, machine hours, raw materials, or money), limited consumer demand, or required physical characteristics of the final product (such as a minimum percentage of protein or a maximum percentage of fat).

Although the concepts underlying linear programming are straightforward, the actual solution to linear programming problems can be extremely complex. Fortunately, the availability of computers and modeling specialists has resulted in situations where the manager need not be concerned about the detailed operation of the solution technique. The manager should, of course, have a general understanding of how the solution is determined (the model's assumptions) and be able to evaluate both the data used and the suggested solution.

Assumptions and Uses of Accounting Data

As its name implies, the most critical linear programming assumption is that linear relationships exist between all variables. The total contribution from the sale of products X and Y, for example, must be of the form $aX + bY$, where a is the unit contribution of product X, and b is the unit contribution of product Y. Curvilinear relationships, such as $aX - 0.05X^2 + bY - 0.0002bY^3$ are not allowed. Another assumption of linear programming is that fractional solutions are permitted. The suggested solution to a linear programming problem might, for example, specify the production and sale of 25.2 units of X and 32.7 units of Y.

When these assumptions are not valid, the manager might elect to use other models. Alternatively, if it seems appropriate, the manager might use professional judgment to adjust the suggested linear programming solution; for example, the production of X might be rounded to 25 units, and the production of Y might be rounded to 32 units.

Every linear programming model includes an **objective function,** or goal to be maximized or minimized. Accounting data are often used in the objective function. *If the objective is to maximize profits, the coefficients of the variables in the objective function should be unit contribution margins*. If the objective is to minimize costs, the coefficients should be unit variable costs. The total contribution margin or variable costs of each product will vary in proportion to changes in volume. Profit and cost measures that include an allocation of fixed costs should not be used in the objective function. They do not vary in direct proportion to changes in production; hence their use violates the linearity assumption.

Graphic Analysis of Product Mix Decisions

We use graphic analysis to illustrate the solution of linear programming problems. Though graphic analysis can be used to solve problems containing only two variables, it provides the general understanding necessary to evaluate more complex problems containing three or more variables. The following steps are involved in graphic analysis.

1. *Develop an equation for the objective function* indicating how each variable affects the profit maximization or cost minimization goal.

2. *Develop an equation for each constraint* indicating how each variable affects the total use of the constraint.

3. *Graph the constraints.*

4. *Identify the feasible solutions* that are bounded by the constraints.

5. *Determine the optimal solution* that maximizes or minimizes the value of the objective function.

Assume the Martin Company produces two products, A and B, in two departments, Assembly and Finishing. Product A has a unit contribution margin of $50, and product B has a unit contribution margin of $40. The demand for each product exceeds Martin's capacity to produce. Production information is as follows:

	Labor Hours per Unit		Total Labor Hours Available per Week
	A	B	
Assembly Department	20	20	600
Finishing Department	20	10	400

Martin can only obtain raw materials sufficient to produce 25 units of B each week. Management desires the product mix that will maximize the weekly contribution of products A and B toward fixed costs and profits. Using the five steps, the problem is solved as follows:

1. *Objective function.* The objective is to maximize the total weekly contribution of products A and B. Given information on the unit contribution margin, Martin's objective function is

$$\text{Maximize } \$50A + \$40B.$$

2. *Constraints.* There are constraints for maximum assembly hours, maximum finishing hours, and maximum production of product B. Because each constraint indicates an upper limit on the use of some resource, the less than or equal to symbol is used in each:

$$20A + 20B \leq 600 \text{ Assembly Department hours,}$$
$$20A + 10B \leq 400 \text{ Finishing Department hours,}$$
$$B \leq 25 \text{ units.}$$

The assembly hours constraint indicates that any combination of A and B can be produced, providing it does not require more than 600 assembly hours. The finishing hours constraint indicates that any combination of A and B can be produced, providing it does not require more than 400 finishing hours. Finally, because of raw materials limitations, no more than 25 units of B can be produced.

To be technically precise, two more constraints are added to indicate that negative production is prohibited:

$$A \geq 0,$$
$$B \geq 0.$$

Hence the production of A and the production of B must be greater than or equal to zero.

3. *Graph.* One axis must be designated to represent each variable. In Exhibit 14–6, the horizontal axis is labeled product A, and the vertical axis is labeled product B. The opposite could also have been done.

The set of all feasible A and B values is determined by solving each constraint for its maximum A and B values, assuming all production was devoted to that product, and drawing lines on graph paper connecting, for each constraint, the maximum value of each product. The maximum values of A and B, for each constraint, are computed as follows:

	Maximum Values	
	Product A	*Product B*
Assembly hours	600/20 = 30	600/20 = 30
Finishing hours	400/20 = 20	400/10 = 40
Raw materials		25

The lines connecting these maximum values are illustrated in Exhibit 14–6. Because the raw materials constraint affects only product B, it does not intersect the horizontal axis for product A. Instead, it is drawn parallel to the horizontal axis. The nonnegativity constraints are represented by the horizontal and vertical axes.

4. *Feasible solutions.* After the lines representing each constraint are drawn, the **feasible region,** representing all possible production volumes and mixes, is depicted by the area between the vertical and horizontal axes and the first set of enclosing lines that represent constraints (this is the area enclosed by the solid lines from points 1–2–3–4–5 in Exhibit 14–6). The firm can produce anywhere within the feasible region; however, it is likely that one product mix will provide a higher total contribution than any other mix.

5. *Optimal solution.* In linear programming, the **optimal solution** is the feasible solution that maximizes or minimizes the value of the objective function, depending on management's goal. An important characteristic of linear pro-

EXHIBIT 14–6 Graphic Approach to Linear Programming

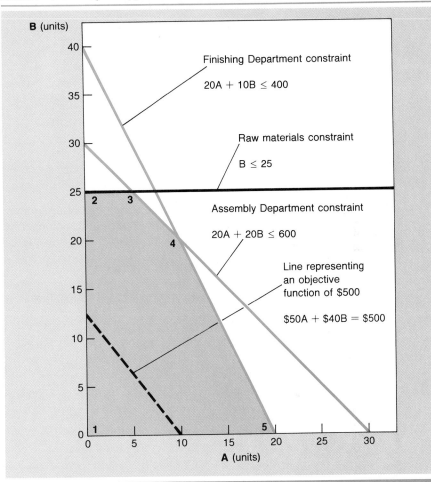

gramming is that *if there is a single optimal solution, it is found at a corner point where the lines representing two or more constraints intersect.* Knowing this, it is only necessary to evaluate the solutions represented by corner points. In Exhibit 14–6, there are five corner points, which, for convenience, are numbered 1 through 5. The value of the objective function at each corner point is computed in Exhibit 14–7. The maximum optimal solution, represented by corner 4, calls for a weekly production of 10 units of product A and 20 units of product B. This solution will provide a weekly contribution of $1,300. Fixed costs, of course, would be deducted from this amount to determine the weekly profit.

EXHIBIT 14–7   Evaluation of Alternative Corner Solutions

Corner	Value of A	Value of B	Value of Objective Function $50A + $40B =
1	0	0	$ —
2	0	25	1,000
3	5	25	1,250
4	10*	20*	1,300
5	20	0	1,000

* Optimal solution

The Corner Solution

The reason that the unique solution is always found at a corner point can be illustrated by drawing a line representing some arbitrary value for the objective function. In the case of the Martin Company, the end points for an objective function with a value of $500 are 10 units of product A and 12.5 units of product B. In general,

$$\text{Desired contribution} \div \text{Unit contribution} = \text{End point}.$$

For A,

$$\$500 \div \$50 = 10 \text{ units}.$$

For B,

$$\$500 \div \$40 = 12.5 \text{ units}.$$

Drawing this line in Exhibit 14–6, observe that 10 units of A or 12.5 units of B or any combination along this line will provide a weekly contribution of $500. An objective function having a higher value would be drawn farther from the origin, parallel to the first line. To maximize the value of the objective function, additional lines are drawn parallel to the first line, but farther from the origin, until only one point on a line touches the feasible solution. This one unique point will be a corner point; corner 4 in this case. You may draw these additional lines as an exercise.

Simplex Method

Though it is possible to solve two variable problems with the aid of graphic analysis, linear programming problems containing three or more variables must be solved by a mathematical solution technique known as the **simplex method.** The mechanics of the simplex method are far from simple, even though the method arrives at a solution by comparing objective function values at multi-dimensional corner points, just as was done earlier with the graphic approach. To solve the Martin Company's product mix problem, the same set of equations would be used as in the previous illustration. Software packages are available to solve linear programming problems on most computers.

PAYOFF TABLES

Certainty means the probability of an event's occurring is 100 percent, whereas uncertainty means the probability of an event's occurring is less than 100 percent. When the outcome of a decision alternative is uncertain, managers often desire information on the expected value of that alternative. A decision alternative's expected value is simply the weighted average of the possible cash flows associated with that alternative. Identifying each possible cash flow as an outcome, the expected value of a decision alternative is computed as follows:

$$\text{Expected value} = \Sigma\ (\text{Outcome} \times \text{Probability of outcome}),$$

where Σ is a summation sign indicating that the product of each cash flow multiplied by its related probability is to be summed.

Assume a particular investment has the following possible outcomes.

Outcome	Net Cash Flow	Probability
1	$2,000	0.50
2	5,000	0.20
3	8,000	0.30
		1.00

This investment has three possible outcomes, and, because one of them will occur, the associated probabilities sum to 1.00, or 100 percent. The expected value of this investment is $4,400:

$$\text{Expected value} = (\$2,000)(0.50) + (\$5,000)(0.20) + (\$8,000)(0.30)$$
$$= \$4,400.$$

The expected cash flow of $4,400 is the weighted average of the possible cash flows of $2,000, $5,000, and $8,000. A cash flow of exactly $4,400 will not occur, but this weighted amount is a better *summary measure* of the project's cash flows than any one of the three possible outcomes. The advantages of expected value as a summary measure increase with the number of possible outcomes. With only three possible outcomes the situation is fairly simple, but imagine a situation where there are ten or fifteen possible outcomes; here a summary measure of possible outcomes would be welcome.

Constructing Payoff Tables

Expected value is frequently employed as a decision criterion when a manager must select one of several alternative actions, with the outcomes of each subject to uncertainty. A payoff table is often used to enumerate the alternative actions management may take and the possible monetary outcomes of each action. Each monetary outcome results from the joint effect of management's action and an event that can occur. Once the payoff table is constructed, the outcome and probability information in it are used to compute each action's expected value.

The following example illustrates the relationship between actions, events, and outcomes, as well as the construction and use of payoff tables.

On Saturdays during July and August, Janet Gaines sells hotdogs at a Long Island beach. She acquires the precooked and prepackaged hotdogs for $0.60 each and sells them for $1.00. She must order her hotdogs in lots of 100 on Thursdays. Past daily demand has varied between 200 and 500 units with the following probability distribution.

Event	Probability Distribution
200 units demanded	0.20
300 units demanded	0.30
400 units demanded	0.40
500 units demanded	0.10

Janet wants to know how many hotdogs to order each Thursday to maximize the expected value of hotdog sales. Unsold hotdogs are donated to a local orphanage.

The payoff table for this particular decision is presented in Exhibit 14–8. The decision alternatives are the order sizes listed in the left column. The possible events are the levels of demand listed across the top (along with the related probability of each event). The outcomes, resulting from the joint effect of the order size and the demand, are presented in the center of the table. These outcomes range from a loss of $100 if 500 units are ordered but only 200 are sold to a profit of $200 if 500 units are ordered and sold. Sample computations for other outcomes are presented below the table.

The expected values, shown in the right column, are computed for each action as the sum of each outcome times the related probability. The probability of an outcome is the same as the probability of the event that results in that

EXHIBIT 14–8   Payoff Table Illustrated

Action	Event Demand (probability)				Expected Value of Action
Order Size	200 (0.20)	300 (0.30)	400 (0.40)	500 (0.10)	
200	$ 80*	$ 80	$ 80	$ 80	$ 80
300	20	120	120	120	100 maximum
400	(40)**	60	160	160	90†
500	(100)	—	100	200	40

* Example of computation: ($1 × 200) − ($0.60 × 200) = $80.

** Example of computation: ($1 × 200) − ($0.60 × 400) = $(40).

† Example of computation: ($−40)(0.20) + ($60)(0.30) + ($160)(0.40) + ($160)(0.10) = $90.

outcome, given an action. In this example, an order size of 300 units has the highest expected value; therefore, using expected value as the decision criterion, Janet Gaines should order 300 hotdogs each Thursday.

Value of Perfect Information

A manager sometimes has an opportunity to acquire additional information before making a decision, but because information is seldom free, the manager should evaluate the potential benefits of the additional information and the cost of obtaining it. The potential benefits are derived from the ability to make decisions that result in increased cost savings, increased revenues or net cash inflows. The cost of information includes the cost of resources used in obtaining it and the cost of delaying a decision. The *value of perfect information* is the maximum amount a manager would be willing to pay for additional information. It is computed as the difference between the expected profits with perfect information and the current expected profits. Though perfect information is seldom available, a manager might still desire to know its value because the value of perfect information serves as an upper limit on the amount he or she would pay for additional information.

If Janet Gaines had perfect information, she would always order the number of hotdogs she could sell. Ordering less would result in lost sales, and ordering more would result in excess costs. A payoff table with perfect information is shown in Exhibit 14–9. The expected value *with* perfect information is $136. This value is computed for the entire set of actions, rather than for each action, because the order size varies with demand. She will order 200 units 20 percent of the time, 300 units 30 percent of the time, and so forth. The expected value *of* perfect information is $36:

Expected profits with perfect information	$136
Current expected profits	−100
Expected value of perfect information	$ 36

EXHIBIT 14–9 Payoff Table for Perfect Information

Action	Event				Weighted
	Demand (probability)				
Order Size	200 (0.20)	300 (0.30)	400 (0.40)	500 (0.10)	Value
200	$80				$ 16*
300		$120			36
400			$160		64
500				$200	20
Expected value with perfect information					$136

* Example of computation: ($80 × 0.20) = $16.

Knowing the expected value of perfect information, Janet is in a better position to bargain with someone who offers her any additional information, perfect or imperfect.

Attitudes Toward Risk

The previous discussion assumed that management is completely indifferent toward risk and makes decisions solely on the basis of expected value. Obviously, this is not true. Few managers would be indifferent to the following investment alternatives.

Investment	Outcome	Probability
A	$ (10,000)	0.90
	240,000	0.10
B	$ 5,000	0.50
	25,000	0.50

Both investments have an expected value of $15,000.

$$\text{Expected value (A)} = (\$-10{,}000 \times 0.90) + (\$240{,}000 \times 0.10)$$
$$= \$15{,}000.$$
$$\text{Expected value (B)} = (\$5{,}000 \times 0.50) + (\$25{,}000 \times 0.50)$$
$$= \$15{,}000.$$

MANAGERIAL PRACTICE 14.4

Tonka Learns to Manage Risk

Risk is a measurement of uncertainty about the outcome of a certain activity. Managers are responsible for decisions based on tradeoffs between the return on investment and the risks they feel are warranted. Tonka Corporation purchased Kenner Parker Toys in October 1987. This purchase resulted in a debt of 86 percent of capital and a loss of nearly $6 million in 1988. Steve Shank, chairman and chief executive officer of Tonka Corporation, is in the process of rebuilding Tonka's line of stable toys. The purchase of Kenner increased Tonka's toy line, increased their ability to compete for shelf space, and expanded their market abroad. Shank feels Tonka is a solidly competitive company despite its heavy debt. Tonka experienced a profitable second quarter in 1989 and expects to remain consistently profitable in the future.

Source: Steve Weiner, "Keep on Truckin'," *Forbes,* 16 October 1989, 220–221.

Yet investment A has a 90 percent probability of a $10,000 loss, whereas investment B has all positive outcomes. Most decision makers would prefer investment B.

In addition to information on each action's expected value, management should obtain information on the variability of an action's outcome. This information might be the range of possible outcomes, the probability of negative outcomes, or statistical measures such as the standard deviation or the coefficient of variation. Statistical measures are discussed in introductory statistics textbooks. With information on expected values and variability, managers can make whatever trade-offs between return and risk they believe are appropriate.

SUMMARY

A model is a simplified representation of some real-world phenomenon. Managers and other decision makers often use optimizing models, such as the economic order quantity, economic lot size, linear programming, and payoff tables that suggest a specific choice among decision alternatives. These models are decision aids; they do not make decisions.

Before implementing a decision suggested by a model, a manager should carefully evaluate the data used in the model, the assumptions underlying the model, and the output of the model. If the manager suspects any problems, the suggested action should not be implemented. Instead, the manager should undertake further analysis or make a decision based on professional judgment.

Models, such as those for the economic order quantity and economic lot size, develop optimal solutions for a given cost structure. If managers fail to understand their products and production process, continually improve their products and procedures, or reduce their cost structure, their firm will be less competitive. This is true even if they properly use optimizing models. When the outcome of an action is subject to uncertainty, the manager should not act only on the basis of expected value but should obtain information on the outcome's variability and make whatever trade-offs between return and risk he or she believes are appropriate.

APPENDIX
QUALITY COSTS

Quality as a Competitive Factor

Quality, defined as conformance to customer expectations, is an important competitive factor.[1] Consistent product quality is a component in the success of such companies as United Parcel Service, International Business Machines, McDonald's, Toyota, and Xerox.

---

[1] Much of the material in this appendix is based on *Measuring, Planning, and Controlling Quality Costs,* by Wayne J. Morse, Harold P. Roth, and Kay M. Poston, 1987, Montvalle, N.J.: National Association of Accountants.

Sophisticated buyers now look beyond acquisition cost to life cycle costs in making decisions. Life cycle costs include the total costs associated with a cost objective, such as a refrigerator, furnace, or product, over its entire life. An automobile's life cycle costs include the purchase price, operating costs such as fuel, maintenance costs such as tires and oil, and repair costs such as replacing the transmission. The preferred automobile is the one with the lowest life cycle costs.

Applying life cycle cost concepts, the total cost of raw materials includes much more than the purchase price. They also include costs caused by raw materials quality problems such as extra materials purchased because some may be defective, the need to inspect incoming materials, and rework and production downtime necessitated by raw materials of poor quality. When life cycle costs are considered, purchasing agents are less likely to make purchasing decisions solely on the basis of price in an effort to obtain a favorable price variance.

MANAGERIAL PRACTICE 14.5

Quality at Velcro

In August 1985, Velcro was notified that General Motors was dropping it from GM's highest supplier quality rating to a rating of four on a scale of one to five. Velcro was given 90 days to initiate a total quality control program in its Manchester, New Hampshire, plant. Although Velcro's products were acceptable and it was meeting delivery schedules, General Motors found its process inadequate. Velcro was *inspecting* quality rather than *manufacturing* quality.

In response to GM's challenge, Velcro's upper management launched a campaign to introduce a quality ethic throughout the organization. The program included quality courses for employees, a comprehensive quality manual, an improved statistical process control program, and the help of outside consultants. Velcro discovered that quality is everyone's responsibility, not just manufacturing's. It is a process of continuing improvement. Velcro reduced waste by 50 percent in the first year of the program and by 45 percent in the second year. It is now back in the good graces of General Motors. However, Velcro realizes that, in order to maintain this position, it will have to continue to improve to meet GM's rising standards.

Source: K. Theodor Krantz, "How Velcro Got Hooked on Quality," *Harvard Business Review* (September–October 1989): 34–40.

When the effect of quality on subsequent costs is considered, raw materials quality becomes just as important as price.

Companies such as Xerox have found that an emphasis on quality leads to lower manufacturing costs, lower inventory levels, higher productivity, and increased profits. Purchasing high-quality raw materials reduces the need to inspect incoming raw materials, reduces the need for extra inventory, and facilitates delivery of raw materials directly to the shop floor. Throughout the manufacturing process an emphasis on "doing it right the first time" reduces the need for inspection, production of extra units, and rework. By eliminating the effort devoted to defective units, many organizations have been able to increase their productivity and profitability.

Productivity is the relationship between outputs and inputs:

$$\text{Productivity} = \frac{\text{Outputs}}{\text{Inputs}}.$$

Measurement of productivity requires a measure of output and a measure of input. Partial measures of productivity are based on the relationship of units produced to a single input, such as the number of employees, direct labor hours, or machine hours. Total measures of productivity convert all inputs into dollars (a common denominator) and restate outputs in terms of sales dollars.

Improvements in quality increase productivity by reducing the inputs required to obtain a given level of output. These improvements in productivity increase profits by lowering costs for a given level of output. If some of the cost savings are passed on to customers in the form of lower selling prices, an increase in sales volume may generate increased profits. What's more, if the organization achieves a reputation for quality it may be able to charge premium prices.

An emphasis on quality is a critical element of just-in-time inventory management. As inventories are reduced the presence of defective units becomes increasingly disruptive. Indeed, because there are no buffer stocks, JIT manufacturers may have to stop operations as soon as a defective unit is detected. Although costly in the short run, these disruptions call attention to quality problems and encourage changes that prevent their recurrence. Product quality and productivity improve as employees work to smooth production.

Quality of Design and Quality of Conformance

A key to improving quality is recognizing that quality is everyone's responsibility. Quality, or conformance to customer expectations, starts in marketing, where efforts are made to learn customers' needs and expectations. The next step in delivering a quality product is for marketing and engineering personnel to jointly develop functional specifications for a product. These are explicit statements regarding product capabilities, expressed in quantitative terms whenever possible. Working with marketing and manufacturing personnel, engineering then develops design specifications for the product. These are detailed statements regarding the physical characteristics of the product and engineering drawings illustrating those physical characteristics.

Many efforts to deliver quality products succeed or fail during the design stage. In the past, design specifications were often developed without explicitly considering the subsequent efforts required to manufacture or service products. Quality problems and manufacturing costs increase when a complex design makes manufacture difficult. Warranty costs and buyers' life cycle costs increase when a design does not consider ease of service. Today marketing, engineering, and manufacturing personnel must work together in product development and emphasize design for manufacture, that is, designing products so that they are easy to manufacture and service. Examples of design for manufacture include reducing the total number of parts to be assembled, substituting parts that snap together for parts that are welded or screwed, and designing components so that it is difficult to assemble them incorrectly.

Subsequent to the development of design specifications, manufacturing specifications are prepared, detailing how the product is to be produced and its physical characteristics at each stage of the production process. The bill of materials and operations list, discussed in Chapter 11, are important parts of these design specifications.

To develop standards for evaluating product quality, it is necessary to distinguish between quality of design and quality of conformance. Quality of design refers to the degree of conformance between customer expectations for a product or service and the design specifications of the product or service. Quality of conformance refers to the degree of conformance between a product and its design specifications.

A failure to develop design specifications that conform to customer expectations results in poor quality of design. Because design specifications serve as the benchmark for evaluating the quality of finished products, the implications of poor quality of design are similar to the implications of poor standard costs. They reduce the usefulness of performance measures based on them.

The quality of finished products is evaluated using design specifications. Products that fail to conform to design specifications have poor quality of conformance and are classified as defective or spoiled.

Measuring and Reporting Quality Costs

Many managers find financial information related to quality useful for determining the financial significance of quality problems, developing an overall strategy for improving quality, evaluating proposals to invest in quality improvement activities, and evaluating the performance of quality-improvement activities. Quality costs concepts serve as the basis for these special-purpose management accounting reports.

Quality costs are costs incurred because poor quality of conformance does exist or because poor quality of conformance may exist. There are two basic types of quality costs: (1) those incurred because of poor conformance between actual products or services and their design standards and (2) those incurred because of the possibility of poor conformance.

Costs incurred because of poor quality of conformance are further categorized into internal failure costs and external failure costs. Internal failure costs occur when materials, components, products, or services are identified as defective before delivery to customers. External failure costs occur when nonconforming products or services are delivered to customers.

Costs incurred because poor quality of conformance may exist are further classified into appraisal costs and prevention costs. Appraisal costs are incurred to identify nonconforming products or services before they are delivered to customers. Prevention costs are incurred to prevent nonconforming products from being produced or nonconforming services from being performed.

Examples of costs in each category are presented in Exhibit 14–10. Note how quality cost information cuts across organizational boundaries. The traditional distinction between product and period costs is discarded in accumulating quality costs.

Quality cost information is periodically summarized in a quality cost report, such as the one in Exhibit 14–10. Quality cost information may be prepared for any time period and cost objective of interest. Possible cost objectives include a machine, a department, a plant, a division, a company, a product, or a product line. Depending on management's information needs, quality cost reports may include fewer than four cost categories. They may even include subjective information, such as an estimate of lost sales resulting from quality problems (an external failure cost). To provide a benchmark for comparison between periods with different production volumes, quality cost information is often restated as a percent of sales or total manufacturing costs.

Notice in Exhibit 14–10 that external failure costs are very high in comparison with other quality costs. This indicates that quality problems are not being identified and corrected before goods are delivered to customers, a situation frequently encountered before the initiation of a quality improvement program. In today's highly competitive environment, passing quality problems on to customers is intolerable.

The most immediate action management can take to prevent the delivery of poor quality products is to implement a rigorous inspection program and identify defective goods before they are delivered. If the inspection program is successful, there should be a shift in quality costs, with external failure declining and appraisal and internal failure increasing. At this stage in a quality improvement program, total known quality costs are likely to increase, especially if the cost of lost sales is excluded from quality cost reports. The ultimate solution to quality problems is to increase efforts to prevent the occurrence of defects. A successful prevention program will not only result in the reduction of external and internal failure costs, but it will also make it possible to reduce appraisal costs. Inspection may be reduced when management is confident the job is done right the first time.

A trend analysis illustrating the effect on quality costs of successfully implementing a quality program is presented in Exhibit 14–11. The implementation of a quality improvement program may have a significant effect on the total amount and distribution of quality costs, but it is unlikely that quality costs can be reduced to zero. Management must continue to invest in prevention as new

EXHIBIT 14–10   Quality Cost Report

Sample Company
Quality Cost Report
For the year ending December 31, 19x1

	Amount	Percent of Sales*
Prevention		
Design for manufacture	$ 0	
Quality planning	2,000	
Quality training	3,000	
Supplier verification	0	
Total	$ 5,000	0.3%
Appraisal		
Accuracy review of sales orders	$ 0	
Depreciation on test equipment	1,000	
Field inspection and testing	0	
In-process inspection and testing	8,000	
Raw materials inspection	0	
Total	$ 9,000	0.5%
Internal failure		
Downtime (quality related)	$ 0	
Reinspection	400	
Retest	0	
Rework labor and overhead	10,000	
Scrap	1,600	
Total	$ 12,000	0.7%
External failure		
Complaint adjustments	$ 30,000	
Product recalls	60,000	
Returns and allowances	10,000	
Warranty repairs	50,000	
Warranty replacement	100,000	
Total	$250,000	13.9%
Total quality costs	$276,000	15.4%

* Sales amount to $1,792,208, or 100%.

products are introduced and production procedures are changed. Even if the goal of zero defects is reached, some prevention will be required to maintain this ideal state. Appraisal costs and internal failure costs are better than external failure costs, and prevention costs are preferred to appraisal costs or failure costs. Quality is not free, but it is less expensive than the alternative.

EXHIBIT 14–11   Quality Cost Trend Analysis

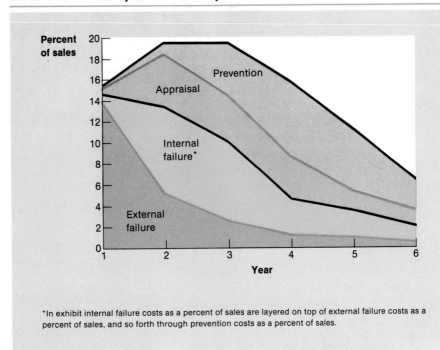

*In exhibit internal failure costs as a percent of sales are layered on top of external failure costs as a percent of sales, and so forth through prevention costs as a percent of sales.

Report Development Alternatives

There are two possible approaches to developing quality cost reports: (1) a formal, institutionalized, quality cost reporting system; and (2) periodic special studies. A few years ago there was considerable interest in developing formal quality cost reporting systems. A formal system would include specially designed forms, data gathering procedures, information processing procedures, reports, and report distribution procedures. Information gathering, processing, and reporting would take place on a regular basis as part of the ongoing accounting process. Concerns about information processing costs, the inherent subjectivity of quality cost data, the relative infrequency of use of quality cost information, and a desire to avoid stagnation in the development of quality cost concepts has led to a decreased interest in formal systems. Although more companies than ever are using quality cost information, most have quality cost information developed on an as-needed basis using special studies. Typically, a management accountant or quality control employee accumulates quality cost information from the accounting data base and by conducting interviews. The employee then analyzes the data using spreadsheet software and develops reports using graphics software.

SUGGESTED READINGS

Blackburn, Joseph D., "The New Manufacturing Environment," *The Journal of Cost Management, 2,* No. 2 (Summer 1988): 4–10.

Colberg, Thomas P., "The Compelling Case for EDI," *The Financial Manager* (January/February 1990): 20–26.

Foster, George, and Charles T. Horngren, "Cost Accounting and Cost Management in a JIT Environment," *The Journal of Cost Management* (Winter 1988): 4–19.

Gaither, Norman, Donald R. Fraser, and William G. Mister, "Accounting for Inventory Carrying Costs," *Journal of Cost Analysis,* 1987: 1–6.

"How the New Math of Productivity Adds Up," *Business Week* (June 6, 1988): 103–113.

Lessner, John, "Performance Measurement in a Just-in-Time Environment: Can Traditional Performance Measures Still be Used?" *Journal of Cost Management, 6,* No. 3, (Fall 1989): 22–28.

McIlhattan, Robert D., "How Cost Management Systems Can Support the JIT Philosophy," *Management Accounting* (September 1987): 20–26.

McNair, C. J., William Mosconi, and Thomas Norris, *Meeting the Technology Challenge: Cost Accounting in a JIT Environment,* Montvalle, N.J.: National Association of Accountants, 1988.

Mecimore, Charles D., and James K. Weeks, *Techniques in Inventory Management and Control,* Montvalle, N.J.: National Association of Accountants, 1987.

Morse, Wayne J., Harold P. Roth, and Kay M. Poston, *Measuring, Planning, and Controlling Quality Costs,* Montvalle, N.J.: National Association of Accountants, 1987.

Turk, William T., "Management Accounting Revitalized: The Harley-Davidson Experience," *The Journal of Cost Management, 3,* No. 4 (Winter 1990): 28–39.

REVIEW PROBLEM

Economic Order Quantity by Trial and Error and Formula

Presented is information pertaining to an imported plant sold by a florist shop in a major city:

Annual demand	900 units
Unit cost	$20.00
Cost of placing an order	$200.00
Carrying cost as a percent of unit cost	20%

Requirements

a) Prepare a table, similar to that in Exhibit 14–3, of the relevant annual costs for determining the economic order quantity. Complete the table for lot sizes of 100, 200, 300, 400, 600, and 900 units.

b) Prepare a graph, similar to that in Exhibit 14–4, for the behavior of inventory ordering and carrying costs.

c) Based on requirements (a) and (b), what can be said about ordering and carrying costs at the economic order quantity?

d) Use the economic order quantity formula to determine the optimal order size.

The solution to this problem is found at the end of the Chapter 14 exercises, problems, and cases.

KEY TERMS

Certainty
Cycle time
Descriptive model
Economic lot size (ELS)
Economic order quantity (EOQ)
Electronic data interchange (EDI)
Expected value
Feasible region
Just-in-time (JIT) inventory
    management
Lead time
Linear programming
Model

Objective function
Optimal solution
Optimizing model
Order quantity
Payoff table
Physical model
Quantitative model
Reorder point
Safety stocks
Simplex method
Uncertainty
Value of perfect information

APPENDIX KEY TERMS

Appraisal costs
Design for manufacture
External failure costs
Internal failure costs
Life cycle costs
Prevention costs

Productivity
Quality
Quality costs
Quality of conformance
Quality of design

REVIEW QUESTIONS

14–1   Distinguish between descriptive and optimizing models and give three examples of each.

14–2   Do optimizing models make decisions? Discuss.

14–3   Once management has decided on the number of units to order during a period of time, what inventory ordering decisions remain?

14–4   What is the relationship between order size, total annual ordering costs, and total annual carrying costs?

14–5   Present a formula to compute total annual ordering and carrying costs of inventory.

14–6   Identify five assumptions that underlie the economic order quantity model presented in this text.

14–7   What adjustments are necessary before the economic order quantity model can be applied to manufacturing firms?

14–8   Why do proponents of just-in-time inventory management believe inventory is an enemy?

14–9   Identify key elements of the just-in-time philosphy.

14–10   What elements of the JIT approach contribute to reducing raw materials inventories?

14–11   Define and identify the elements of cycle time. Which of these elements adds value to the product?

14–12   What is the objective of linear programming?

14–13   What is the most critical assumption underlying linear programming? What are the implications of this assumption for accounting data used in linear programming?

14–14   Identify the steps involved in solving a linear programming problem with graphic analysis.

14–15   How is the value of perfect information computed? Why might a manager desire to know the value of perfect information, even though it is seldom possible to obtain perfect information?

EXERCISES

14–1 Determining Order Quantity, Reorder Point, and Safety Stock

The annual demand for inventory item T-20 is 1,000 units, the cost of placing an order is $100, and the cost of carrying one unit in inventory for one year is $5.

Requirements

a) Use the economic order quantity formula to determine the optimal order size.

b) Assuming a lead time of 10 days and a work year of 250 days, determine the reorder point.

c) Assuming the maximum lead time is 15 days and the maximum daily demand is 6 units, determine the safety stock required to prevent stockouts.

14–2 Determining Order Quantity, Reorder Point, and Safety Stock

The annual demand for inventory item Q-7 is 5,000 units, the cost of placing an order is $160, and the cost of carrying one unit in inventory for one year is $10.

Requirements

a) Use the economic order quantity formula to determine the optimal order size.

b) Assuming a lead time of 15 days and a work year of 250 days, determine the reorder point.

c) Assuming the maximum lead time is 20 days and the maximum daily demand is 25 units, determine the safety stock required to prevent stockouts.

14–3 Impact of Deviations from EOQ

Faced with a cash surplus, the Loveday Department Store *increased* the size of several inventory order quantities that had previously been determined using the EOQ model. Use the words "increase," "decrease," or "no change" to indicate the impact of management's decision on each of the following:

1. Average inventory.

2. Number of orders per year.

3. Total annual carrying costs.

4. Total annual ordering costs.

5. Total annual carrying and ordering costs.

6. Cost of goods sold.

14–4 Impact of Deviations from EOQ

Faced with a cash shortage, the Arnold Discount Store *reduced* the size of several inventory order quantities that had previously been determined using the EOQ model. Use the words "increase," "decrease," or "no change" to indicate the impact of management's decision on each of the following:

1. Average inventory.
2. Number of orders per year.
3. Total annual carrying costs.
4. Total annual ordering costs.
5. Total annual carrying and ordering costs.
6. Cost of goods sold.

14–5 Cost Savings with Economic Order Quantity: Shelf Life

The Pleasant View Hospital places orders for a particular inventory item in lot sizes of 25 units. Additional information about this inventory item is as follows:

Annual demand	720 units
Ordering costs	$25 per order
Purchase price	$100 per unit

Annual inventory carrying costs are estimated to be 40 percent of the unit cost.

Requirements

a) Determine the economic order quantity.

b) Determine the annual cost savings if Pleasant View changes from an order size of 10 units to the economic order quantity.

c) The shelf life of this item is limited. Assuming that shelf life is based on the number of days it may be used after it is placed in inventory, determine the optimal lot size under each of the following circumstances. Assume a 360-day year.

  1. Shelf life = 20 days.
  2. Shelf life = 10 days.

Hint: Determine how many days an order will last.

14–6 Cost Savings with Economic Order Quantity: Quantity Discounts

The Mason Company currently purchases a particular item in sizes of 1,250 units. Mason's annual use of this item is 6,250 units. Ordering costs are $200 per order, and carrying costs are $10 per unit per year.

Requirements

a) Determine the economic order quantity.

b) Determine the amount of the annual cost savings if Mason changes from an order size of 1,250 units to the economic order quantity.

c) The supplier offers a discount of $2 per unit off of the purchase price of orders in lots of 625 units or more. What action do you recommend? *Hint:* Compare the annual cost savings from the discount to the increased total annual ordering and carrying costs required to qualify for the discount.

14–7 Materials Push and Materials Pull: Kanban

Media Storage, Inc., produces three models of hard disk drives for personal computers. Each model is produced on a separate assembly line. The production operation consists of several operations in separate work centers. Because of a high demand for Media's products, management is most interested in high production volume and operating efficiency. Each work center is evaluated on the basis of its operating efficiency. To avoid idle time caused by defective units, variations in machine times, and machine breakdowns, significant inventories are maintained between each work station.

At a recent administrative committee meeting, the director of research announced that the firm's engineers have made a dramatic breakthrough in designing a low-cost read/write optical storage device. The president of Media Storage is very enthusiastic, and the vice president of marketing wishes to add an assembly line for optical storage devices as soon as possible. The equipment necessary to manufacture the new product can be purchased and installed in less than sixty days. Unfortunately, all available plant space is currently devoted to the production of hard disk drives, and expansion is not possible at the current plant location. It appears that adding the new product will require dropping a current product, relocating the entire operation, or manufacturing the optical storage devices at a separate location.

The vice president of marketing is opposed to dropping a current product. The vice president of finance is opposed to relocating the entire operation because of financing requirements and the associated financial risks. The vice president of production is opposed to splitting up production activities because of the loss of control and the added costs for various types of overhead.

Required: Explain how switching to a materials pull (Kanban) system can help solve Media Storage's space problems while improving quality and cycle time. In your answer be sure to describe how a materials pull system works and the changes required in management's attitude toward inventory and efficiency to make it work.

14–8 Moving Toward JIT: Effect of Cost Changes on EOQ

Robertson Communications produces designer telephones. Because business has been excellent in recent years, management wishes to increase production and add several new products. This will require additional space for production. Unfortunately, the firm is in an old building located in an inner-city redevelopment region where expansion space is not readily available. Moving to a new location is contrary to a major element of the firm's strategic plan—to provide employment opportunities to residents of the inner-city community.

The only space that is readily available, amounting to 16,000 cubic feet, is currently used for storing raw materials. A junior accountant with Robertson's accounting firm has suggested that Robertson might be able to use this space for production activities if it adopted a just-in-time approach to raw materials management.

Requirements

a) Explain the elements of the JIT approach to reducing raw materials.

b) Presented is cost information pertaining to a particular raw material:

Annual demand	6,250 units
Ordering costs	$100 order
Carrying costs	$5 unit/year

Using Exhibit 14–3 as a guide, prepare a four-column table. In the first column determine the total annual ordering and carrying costs and the economic order quantity for this item. Round computations to two decimal places.

c) Firms implementing a JIT approach to inventory management following the steps outlined in requirement (a) often achieve significant reductions in ordering costs. At the same time space previously used for storage may be assigned to other value added activities. The reduction in storage space may actually increase the storage cost per unit.

Complete columns two, three, and four of the table prepared for requirement (b) when ordering and carrying costs are as follows:

	Two	Three	Four
Ordering costs per unit	$81.00	$49.00	$49.00
Carrying costs unit/year	5.00	5.00	9.80

Round computations to two decimal places.

14–9 Graphic Analysis

The graph presents a series of maximum production constraints.

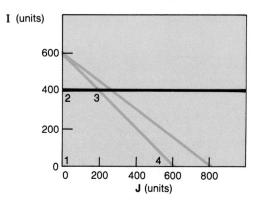

The objective function is:

$$\text{Maximize } \$40J + 50I$$

Required: Determine the optimal solution and the corresponding value of the objective function with the aid of graphic analysis.

14–10 Graphic Analysis

Presented are the objective function and the constraints for a linear programming problem:

$$\text{Maximize } \$6A + \$8B$$

Constraints:
$$1A + 2B \leq 12$$
$$1A + 1B \leq 8$$
$$A \geq 0$$
$$B \geq 0$$

Required: Determine the optimal solution and the corresponding value of the objective function with the aid of graphic analysis.

14–11 Linear Programming with Graphic Analysis

The Menz Company produces two products, X and Y, in one department. Product X has a unit contribution margin of $40, and product Y has a unit contribution margin of $70. The demand for product X exceeds Menz's production capacity, which is limited by available labor and machine hours. The maximum demand for product Y is 8 units per week. Product information follows:

	Hours per Unit		Total Hours Available per Week
	X	Y	
Labor	12	18	180
Machine	6	4	60

Management desires the product mix that will maximize the weekly contribution toward fixed costs and profits.

Requirements

a) Formulate the objective function and constraints necessary to determine the optimal product mix.

b) Determine the optimal solution and the corresponding value of the objective function with the aid of graphic analysis.

14–12 Linear Programming with Graphic Analysis

The Old Salt Desk Company produces two styles of desks, Captain's and Mate's, in two departments, Assembly and Finishing. The Captain's desks have a unit contribution margin of $200, and Mate's desks have a unit contribution margin of $150. The demand for Captain's desks exceeds Old Salt's production capacity, which is limited by the available hours in each department. The demand for Mate's desks is 80 units per month. Production information follows:

	Hours per Unit		Total Hours Available per Month
	Captain	Mate	
Assembly Department	10	10	1,500
Finishing Department	40	20	4,000

Management desires the product mix that will maximize the monthly contribution toward fixed costs and profits.

Requirements

a) Formulate the objective function and constraints necessary to determine the optimal product mix.

b) Determine the optimal solution and the corresponding value of the objective function with the aid of graphic analysis.

14–13 Payoff Tables and the Value of Perfect Information

The Wild Kat Oil Company prospects for oil in the mountains of Pennsylvania. Currently, the cost of drilling an oil well is $40,000. If oil is found, the well is sold for $800,000. If oil is not found, the well is worthless. At each drilling site, Wild Kat has two possible actions: (1) drill, or (2) do not drill. At each drilling site there are two possible states or events: (1) oil is present, or (2) oil is not present. In a particular area of the mountains, the probability of finding oil is 8 percent, and the probability of not finding oil is 92 percent.

Requirements

a) With the aid of a payoff table, determine the expected value of each action for each site.

b) A new testing service can determine in advance whether or not oil will be found at a drilling site. Determine the value of perfect information for each site.

14–14 Payoff Tables and the Value of Perfect Information

The operator of a Chalmette newsstand must determine the number of copies of the *Bourbon Street Journal* to stock each day. The operator buys the *Journal* for $0.50 per copy and sells it for $0.75 per copy. Unsold papers are worthless at the end of the day. Past daily demand has varied between 200 and 400 copies with the following probabilities.

Event	Probability
200 copies demanded	0.25
300 copies demanded	0.50
400 copies demanded	0.25

Requirements

a) With the aid of a payoff table determine whether the operator should order 200, 300, or 400 copies.

b) Determine the value of perfect information.

14–15 JIT Product Costing

Presented is information pertaining to the standard or budgeted unit cost of a product manufactured in a JIT environment:

Direct materials	$15
Conversion	10
Total	$25

All materials are added at the start of the production process. All raw materials purchases and conversion costs are directly assigned to Cost of Goods Sold. At the end of the period an adjusting entry is used to assign some costs to Raw Materials-in-Process and Finished Goods Inventory. The materials costs assigned to inventories are based on the standard or budgeted cost of materials multiplied by the number of units in inventory. The conversion costs assigned to inventories are based on the standard or budgeted cost of conversion multiplied by the percentage of completion of units in inventory. At the start of the next period a reversing entry reassigns all costs to Cost of Goods Sold.

There were no beginning inventories on August 1, 19x7. During the month the company incurred the following manufacturing related costs:

Purchase of raw materials on account	$300,000
Factory wages	125,000
Factory supervision salaries	30,000
Utilities bill for month	17,000
Factory supplies purchased	1,500
Depreciation	9,500

End of month inventories included raw materials-in-process of 600 units and finished goods inventories of 400 units. One hundred units of raw materials were 0 percent converted and the other 500 units averaged 60 percent converted.

Requirements

a) Following the company's accounting procedures, prepare summary August journal entries related to manufacturing activities. Also prepare any appropriate September 1 reversing entry.

b) Assuming August is a typical month, is it likely that the use of the company's shortcut accounting procedures will produce misleading financial statements?

14–16 JIT Product Costing with Backflush Costing Journal Entries

Speedo Cable manufactures drawn wire products in a JIT environment. Presented is information pertaining to September activities:

Purchase of raw materials on account	$200,000
Factory wages	80,000
Factory supervision salaries	15,000
Utilities bill for month	7,000
Factory supplies purchased	500
Depreciation	6,000

Raw materials costs associated with completed units amount to $180,000. Five percent of the units completed during the month are in the ending finished goods inventory.

Requirements

a) Prepare backflush costing journal entries for September.

b) Assuming September is a typical month, is it likely that the use of the company's shortcut accounting procedures will produce misleading financial statements?

14–17 JIT Performance Evaluation

To control operations Justa Company makes extensive and exclusive use of financial performance reports for each department. Although all departments have been reporting favorable cost variances in most periods, management is perplexed by the firm's low overall return on investment. You have been asked to look into the matter.

Believing the purchasing department is typical of Justa's operations, you obtained the following information concerning the purchases of parts for a product Justa started producing in 19x1:

Year	Purchase Price Variance	Quantity Used (units)	Average Inventory (units)
19x1	$ 1,000 F	20,000	4,000
19x2	10,000 F	30,000	7,500
19x3	12,000 F	30,000	10,000
19x4	20,000 U	25,000	6,250
19x5	8,000 F	27,000	9,000
19x6	9,500 F	29,000	11,600

Requirements

a) Compute the inventory turnover for each year. Can any conclusions be drawn for a yearly comparison of the purchase price variance and the inventory turnover?

b) Identify problems likely to be caused by evaluating purchasing only on the basis of the purchase price variance.

c) Offer whatever recommendations you believe appropriate.

14–18 JIT Performance Evaluation

The vice president of manufacturing is perplexed. When the new Southside Plant began operations three years ago it appeared to live up to the expectations of top management. The plant was modern, well lighted, and spacious. Cost variances were favorable, customers were highly satisfied with quality and service, and the plant reported large segment contributions to common costs and profits despite high start-up costs and early period depreciation.

Just three years later the Southside Plant seems to be declining into crisis management. Although most cost variances, especially those dealing with cost center efficiency, remain favorable, the plant's segment contribution is declining and customers are complaining about poor quality and slow delivery. Several customers have suggested that if the firm cannot correct its quality and delivery problems they will take their business elsewhere. The shop floor is a mess with in-process inventory piled everywhere. Production employees complain of difficulty in locating jobs to be worked on, and scheduling personnel have recently requested a larger computer to help keep track of work-in-process.

The vice president said she does not even know where to begin to try and figure out how to solve the plant's problems. She commented, "What is really weird is that we all work so hard. Our facilities are the best in the business, and I know our employees are dedicated, well trained, and hard working. They do exactly what we ask, and we have never had any labor problems. It just seems like the harder we work the worse our problems become."

Required: Suggest the nature of the Southside Plant's problems and recommend how the vice president might begin to try and figure out how to solve the plant's problems.

14–19 Classifying Quality Costs (Appendix)

Classify each of the following quality costs as prevention, appraisal, internal failure, or external failure:

1. Disposal of spoiled work-in-process.
2. Downtime due to quality problems.
3. Expediting work to meet delivery schedule.
4. Field testing.
5. Internal audits of inventory.
6. Maintaining complaint department.
7. Opportunity cost of lost sales because of bad quality reputation.
8. Product liability.
9. Quality circles.
10. Quality training.
11. Reinspection.
12. Revision of computer programs due to software errors.
13. Rework labor and overhead.
14. Scrap.
15. Supplier verification.
16. Technical support provided to vendors.
17. Test and inspection of equipment.
18. Test and inspection of purchased raw materials.
19. Utilities in inspection area.
20. Warranty repairs.

14–20 Developing Quality Cost Categories for a Service Company (Appendix)

The management of Good Morning Inns, a national hotel chain, is interested in implementing a total quality control program. Although management is not interested in developing a quality cost reporting system at this time, the controller believes the identification of activities and types of costs the hotel may incur in each of the four quality cost categories would be useful as a starting point in initiating the program.

Required: Based on your knowledge of quality costs and the hotel industry, identify activities and costs in each of the four basic quality cost categories.

PROBLEMS

14–21 Economic Order Quantity by Trial and Error and Formula

The Mountain Shop sells 240 Mt. Washington sleeping bags each year. Mt. Washington sleeping bags retail for $175 and wholesale for $100. The Mountain Shop's ordering and carrying costs are as follows:

Cost of placing each order	$50
Annual carrying costs as a percentage of unit cost	15%

Requirements

a) Prepare a table, similar to that in Exhibit 13–3, of the relevant annual costs for determining the economic order quantity. Complete the table for lot sizes of 10, 20, 30, 40, 50, and 60 units. Identify the economic order quantity.

b) Prepare a graph, similar to that in Exhibit 13–4, for the behavior of inventory ordering and carrying costs.

c) Based on requirements (a) and (b), what can be said about ordering and carrying costs at the economic order quantity?

d) Use the economic order quantity formula to determine the optimal order size.

14–22 Economic Lot Size by Trial and Error and Formula

The Designer Phone Company manufactures telephones, in a variety of styles, for residential use. Presented is information about the Classic Touch, one of Designer's models.

Annual sales	500 units
Variable manufacturing costs per unit	$80
Set-up and ordering costs per batch	$50

Carrying costs per year as a percentage of variable manufacturing costs are:

Insurance	2.0%
Personal property taxes	0.5
Storage space	3.0
Deterioration and obsolescence	4.5
Opportunity cost of money invested in inventory	15.0
Total	25.0%

Requirements

a) Prepare a table, similar to that in Exhibit 13–3, of the relevant annual costs for determining the economic lot size. Complete the table for lot sizes of 10, 20, 40, 50, 80, and 100 units. Identify the economic lot size.

b) Prepare a graph, similar to that in Exhibit 13–4, for the behavior of inventory ordering and carrying costs.

c) Based on requirements (a) and (b), what can be said about ordering and carrying costs at the economic lot size?

d) Use the economic order quantity formula to determine the optimal lot size.

14–23 Plotting Variations in Inventory Levels with Safety Stocks

An inventory item with an average daily demand of 5 units and a maximum daily demand of 10 units has an economic order quantity of 100 units. In the absence of safety stocks, the item's reorder point is 25 units. Safety stocks are set at 75 units.

Requirements

a) Determine each of the following:

   1. Reorder point with safety stocks.

   2. Maximum inventory level.

   3. Average lead time.

   4. Maximum lead time.

b) Graph the variations in inventory levels over a period of 60 days. Start at the beginning of day 1 (time 0) with maximum inventory. Assume that daily demand is normal during the first inventory cycle and that inventory is replenished at the end of the first cycle without the use of safety stocks. Assume that daily demand is normal during the second cycle until inventory is reordered. Assume maximum daily demand and lead time until the second order is received. Continue the graph through the end of 60 days with normal daily demand and lead times.

14–24 Economic Order Quantity and Reorder Point: Missing Data

Supply the missing data in each case. Assume that all costs and quantities are optimal, according to the EOQ formula.

	Case 1	Case 2	Case 3	Case 4
Annual demand	250	?	200	?
Economic order quantity	?	?	?	200
Average inventory	?	50	?	?
Orders per year	?	30	5	?
Working days per year	250	?	?	?
Average daily demand	?	12	0.8	?
Lead time in days	10	?	5	8
Reorder point	?	60	?	80
Annual ordering costs	$?	$?	$?	$?
Annual carrying costs	?	1,500	?	?
Total	$?	$?	$?	$?
Cost of placing an order	$100	$?	$ 20	$ 80
Annual unit carrying costs	$ 20	$?	$?	$ 10

Hint: For cases 2 and 3, costs are equal at the EOQ; for case 4, work backward from the EOQ.

14–25 Accounting Inputs to Linear Programming: Graphic Analysis

The Smile Camera Company manufactures two popular cameras, Little Smile and Big Smile. Recent increases in demand have pushed Smile Camera to the limits of their production capacity. The president is a former engineer who knows that linear programming can be used to determine the optimal product mix. However, he needs your assistance in formulating the objective function coefficients and in determining the profit implications of the optimal solution.

The following information is available from the accounting records.

	Little Smile	Big Smile
Unit selling price	$150	$220
Unit manufacturing costs:		
Direct materials	$ 38	$ 54
Direct labor	30	30
Factory overhead	48	80
Total	$116	$164

Production employees are paid $10 per direct labor hour. A total of 450 direct labor hours is available each month. Factory overhead is applied at the rate of $16 per machine hour. Seventy-five percent of the overhead rate is for variable costs, and 25 percent is for fixed costs. A total of 750 machine hours is available each month. The factory overhead rate is based on the full utilization of 750 machine hours each month.

Additional information:

- Because of insufficient raw materials, only 100 Big Smile Cameras can be produced each month.

- Variable selling and administrative expenses are $6 per unit of either product.

- Fixed selling and administrative expenses are $2,300 per month.

Requirements

a) Formulate the objective function and constraints necessary to determine the optimal monthly production mix.

b) Determine the optimal solution and the corresponding value of the objective function with the aid of graphic analysis.

c) Determine the Smile Camera Company's expected monthly profit.

14–26 Accounting Inputs to Linear Programming: Graphic Analysis

Kyoto Electric produces two video cassette recorders, a manual model that does not contain an automatic timer, and an automatic model that does. Though demand for the automatic model is only 75 units per month, Kyoto has been unable to satisfy the demand for the lower priced manual model. The following information is available from the accounting records.

	Manual	Automatic
Unit selling price	$200	$329
Unit manufacturing costs:		
Direct materials	$105	$190
Conversion:		
Department 1	24	24
Department 2	45	90
Total	$174	$304

The conversion costs include direct labor, variable overhead, and fixed overhead. In Department 1, conversion costs are assigned at the rate of $20 per hour. Fifty percent is for variable costs, and 50 percent is for fixed costs. A total of 180 hours is available each month in Department 1. In Department 2, conversion costs are assigned at the rate of $30 per hour. Eighty percent is for variable costs, and 20 percent is for fixed costs. A total of 300 hours is available each month in Department 2. The fixed overhead rates, as a portion of total conversion costs, are based on the full utilization of production capacity.

Additional information:

- Variable selling and administrative expenses are $10 per unit of either product.
- Fixed selling and administrative expenses are $1,200 per month.

Requirements

a) Formulate the objective function and the constraints necessary to determine the optimal monthly production mix.

b) Determine the optimal solution and the corresponding value of the objective function with the aid of graphic analysis.

c) Determine Kyoto Electric's expected monthly profit.

14–27 Formulating Objective Function and Constraints

Presented is unit information about three products manufactured and sold by Camden Products, Inc.

	Product		
	X	Y	Z
Selling price	$110	$130	$200
Direct materials	35	40	50
Direct labor	32	24	48
Variable factory overhead	25	30	40
Fixed factory overhead	20	24	32
Variable selling and administrative expenses	8	6	10

Additional information:

- Fixed selling and administrative expenses are $60,000 per year.
- The direct labor rate is $16 per hour.
- Variable factory overhead is applied at the rate of $10 per machine hour, and fixed factory overhead is applied at the rate of $8 per machine hour.
- A total of 120,000 direct labor hours and 125,000 machine hours are available each year.
- The fixed overhead rate is based on total available machine hours.
- Management desires to produce a minimum of 10,000 units of product X and a maximum of 20,000 units of product Z each year.
- The demand for products X and Y exceeds production capacity.

Requirements

a) Formulate the objective function and the constraints necessary to determine the optimal yearly production mix.

b) Determine the expected annual profit if Camden produces 10,000 units of X, 4,000 units of Y, and 20,000 units of Z.

14–28 Formulating Objective Function

A processing department of the East Orange Chemical Company can vary the production mix of two products, Compound B1 and Compound B2. Because of the high demand for these products, a chemical engineer has been requested to determine the optimal monthly volumes of each product. The engineer has formulated all the constraints needed to determine the optimal mix with the aid of linear programming and has asked you to assist in developing the objective function coefficients. The engineer has provided you with the following production information.

	Per Two-Liter Bottle*	
	Compound B1	*Compound B2*
Raw materials:		
C25	1 liter	2 liters
D80	3 liters	1 liter
MA5	—	1 liter
Bottle	1	1
Direct labor	0.4 hours	0.6 hours

* The difference between total inputs and outputs is due to shrinkage, waste, and evaporation.

You obtain the following information from an analysis of the accounting records.

Selling prices:	
Compound B1	$12.20/bottle
Compound B2	18.00/bottle
Raw materials costs:	
C25	$ 0.80/liter
D80	0.40/liter
MA5	0.65/liter
Bottles	0.50/each
Direct labor rate	$ 9.00/hour
Monthly factory overhead = $20,000 + 0.40 direct labor dollars	
Monthly selling and administrative costs = $15,000 + 0.25 sales revenue	

Required: Formulate the objective function necessary to determine the optimal monthly production in bottles.

14–29 Evaluating and Formulating Objective Function and Constraints

The Elon Co. manufactures two industrial products, X-10, which sells for $90 a unit, and Y-12, which sells for $85 a unit. Each product is processed through both of the company's manufacturing departments. The limited availability of labor, material, and equipment capacity has restricted the ability of the firm to meet the demand for its products. The plant manager believes that linear programming can be used to routinize the production schedule for the two products.

The following data are available to the plant manager.

	Amount Required per Unit	
	X-10	Y-12
Direct materials:		
Weekly supply limited to 1,800 pounds at $12 per pound	4 pounds	2 pounds
Direct labor:		
Department 1—weekly supply limited to 10 people at 40 hours each at an hourly rate of $6	$\frac{2}{3}$ hour	1 hour
Department 2—weekly supply limited to 15 people at 40 hours each at an hourly rate of $8	$1\frac{1}{4}$ hour	1 hour
Machine time:		
Department 1—weekly capacity limited to 250 hours	$\frac{1}{2}$ hour	$\frac{1}{2}$ hour
Department 2—weekly capacity limited to 300 hours	0 hours	1 hour

The overhead costs for Elon are accumulated on a plantwide basis. The overhead is assigned to products on the basis of the number of direct labor hours required to manufacture the product. This base is appropriate for overhead assignment because most of the variable overhead costs vary as a function of labor time. The estimated overhead cost per direct labor hour is as follows:

Variable overhead cost	$ 6
Fixed overhead cost	6
Total overhead cost per direct labor hour	$12

The plant manager formulated the following equations for the linear programming statement of the problem.

A = number of units of X-10 to be produced.
B = number of units of Y-12 to be produced.

Objective function to minimize costs:

Minimize 85A + 62B

Constraints:

Material
$$4A + 2B \leq 1{,}800 \text{ pounds}$$
Department 1 labor
$$\tfrac{2}{3}A + 1B \leq 400 \text{ hours}$$
Department 2 labor
$$1\tfrac{1}{4}A + 1B \leq 600 \text{ hours}$$
Nonnegativity
$$A \geq 0, \qquad B \geq 0.$$

Requirements

a) The formulation of the linear programming equations as prepared by the plant manager of Elon Co. is incorrect. Explain what errors have been made in the formulation prepared by the plant manager.

b) Formulate and label the proper equations for the linear programming statement of Elon's production problem.

(CMA Adapted)

14–30 Preparing and Analyzing Quality Cost Reports (Appendix)

Concerned about competitive pressures, in 19x4 the Hitec Company implemented a program to reduce inventory levels, improve productivity, improve on-time delivery of products to customers, and reduce customer complaints about quality. To help evaluate the success of these efforts, management requested you to prepare a quality cost report for the year ended December 31, 19x4.

After a detailed review of the accounting records and a number of interviews you have developed the following 19x4 data:

Inspection of purchased raw materials	$ 50,000
Inspection of finished goods	110,000
Rework	80,000
Disposal cost of spoiled goods	30,000
Reinspection of finished goods	10,000
Planning a design for manufacture program	5,000
Customer out-of-warrants adjustment	50,000
Warranty adjustments	60,000
Returns and allowances (net)	8,000
Indirect costs of inspection department	25,000
Developing quality control training programs	8,000
Downtime due to quality problems	210,000

Sales totaled $5,100,000 in 19x4.

Requirements

a) Prepare a quality cost report similar to the one in Exhibit 14–10.

b) Management is concerned about the success of the recently implemented program. The vice president of finance observed, "Although sales were essentially unchanged from 19x3, profits declined. What's more, the decline in profits appears entirely due to increases in inspection, downtime, rework, and similar costs. Increases in these costs far exceeded the cost savings from lower customer complaints." Prepare a response to the concerns expressed by the vice president of finance.

14–31 Quality Cost Trend Analysis (Appendix)

Presented is information pertaining to quality costs and total sales for Ray Company for the years 19x1 through 19x5:

	19x1	19x2	19x3	19x4	19x5
Prevention	$ 20,000	$ 40,000	$ 25,000	$ 10,000	$ 5,000
Appraisal	10,000	10,000	10,000	5,000	5,000
Internal failure	50,000	55,000	40,000	20,000	10,000
External failure	50,000	25,000	15,000	55,000	65,000
Sales	1,000,000	1,500,000	1,600,000	1,200,000	1,000,000

Requirements

a) Prepare a quality cost trend analysis based on total dollars of quality costs in each category.

b) Prepare a quality cost trend analysis based on quality costs as a percent of total sales.

c) Compare the graphs prepared for requirements (a) and (b). Which is more meaningful? Why?

d) Based on the graphs, can any conclusions be made about the Ray Company's quality control program?

CASES

14–32 Estimating Inventory Ordering and Carrying Costs

Evans, Inc., is a large wholesale distributor that deals exclusively in baby shoes. Because of the substantial costs related to ordering and storing the shoes, the company has decided to employ the economic order quantity (EOQ) model to help determine the optimum quantities of shoes to order from the different manufacturers.

Before Evans, Inc., can employ the EOQ model, it needs to develop values for two of the cost parameters—ordering costs and carrying costs. As a starting point, management has decided to develop the values for the two cost parameters by using cost data from the most recent fiscal year, 19x5.

The company placed 4,000 purchase orders during 19x5. The largest number of orders placed during any one month was 400 orders in June, and the smallest number of orders placed was 250 in December. Selected cost data for these two months and the year for the Purchasing, Accounts Payable, and Warehouse Departments appear below.

The Purchasing Department is responsible for placing all orders. The costs listed for the Accounts Payable Department relate only to the processing of purchase orders for payment. The Warehouse Department's costs reflect two operations—receiving and shipping. The receiving clerks inspect all incoming shipments and place the orders in storage. The shipping clerks are responsible for processing all sales orders to retailers.

The company leases space in a public warehouse. The rental fee is priced according to the square feet occupied during the month. The annual charges during 19x5 totaled $34,500. Annual insurance and property taxes on the shoes vary with the value of the average monthly inventory. In 19x5 they amounted to $5,700 and $7,300, respectively. The company's opportunity cost of inventory investments is 20 percent.

	Costs for High Activity Month (June: 400 Orders)	Costs for Low Activity Month (December: 250 Orders)	Annual Costs
Purchasing Department:			
Purchasing manager	$ 1,750	$ 1,750	$ 21,000
Buyers	2,500	1,900	28,500
Clerks	2,000	1,100	20,600
Supplies	275	150	2,500
Accounts Payable Department:			
Clerks	2,000	1,500	21,500
Supplies	125	75	1,100
Data processing	2,600	2,300	30,000
Warehouse Department:			
Supervisor	1,250	1,250	15,000
Receiving clerks	2,300	1,800	23,300
Receiving supplies	50	25	500
Shipping clerks	3,800	3,500	44,000
Shipping supplies	1,350	1,200	15,200
Freight-out	1,600	1,300	16,800
	$21,600	$17,850	$240,000

The inventory balances tend to fluctuate during the year depending on the demand for baby shoes. The average monthly inventory during 19x5 was $190,000.

The boxes in which the baby shoes are stored are all approximately the same size. Consequently, the shoes all occupy about the same amount of storage space in the warehouse.

Required: Using the 19x5 data, determine estimated values appropriate for (1) the cost of placing an order and (2) the annual carrying costs per dollar of inventory investment.

(CMA Adapted)

14–33 Inventory Costs, EOQ, JIT, and Systems Design

West Window and East Window were formed in 19x1 when the Glass brothers, who had been jointly operating the Unity Glass Company, broke up their partnership. William Glass, the former general manager for business and finance of Unity Glass, became president of West Window; Edwin Glass, the former chief engineer and production supervisor of Unity Glass, became president of East Window.

When they began operations in 19x1 both had similar products (aluminum storm windows and doors), similar cost structures, and similar facilities. However, William Glass made extensive use of optimizing models in an attempt to manage by the numbers, while Edwin Glass emphasized analyzing activities, breaking costs into small pieces for each activity, and then eliminating or cutting the cost of each activity. This difference in philosophy led to differences in each firm's approach to inventory management.

Presented is 19x1 and 19x5 information pertaining to the manufacture of aluminum storm windows for each company:

	19x1 and 19x5, West	19x1, East	19x5, East
Annual demand (each firm/units)	20,000	20,000	30,000
Costs:			
Production order, etc. (batch)	$ 60.00	$ 60.00	$21.25
Set-up (batch)	100.00	100.00	40.00
Materials (unit)	20.00	20.00	20.00
Processing (unit)	40.00	40.00	40.00
Handling (unit)	8.00	8.00	2.00
Rework costs (average per unit)	3.00	3.00	0.00
Inspection (unit)	5.00	5.00	0.00
Carrying (unit/year)	10.00	10.00	30.00
Lot size (units)	800	100	50

West Window's production facilities and procedures are essentially unchanged over the period. William Glass is concerned about his firm's ability to compete against lower priced foreign and crosstown competitors in the mass market for aluminum storm windows. West Window has been forced to lower prices significantly during the past four years due to competitive pressure. William Glass is quoted as saying that at this point profit margins are so fragile on aluminum storm windows that the sun may be setting on West Window's ability to compete in this market. He plans to change the firm's production and market strategy to produce specialty products for the government.

Edwin Glass, who says he saw the light of a new day dawning on East Window, implemented a just-in-time approach to inventory management in 19x2. The result has been a significant change in production procedures with an emphasis on reducing cycle time, lot size, and inventory levels. As a result, East Window has experienced significant reductions in production order and set-up costs. The early identification of quality problems and constant work to prevent their recurrence has resulted in the virtual elimination of inspection and rework costs. The space previously devoted to inventory has been used to increase production facilities for a variety of products, thereby increasing the value of the remaining space and carrying costs.

Requirements

a) Determine the total annual and average unit costs associated with producing aluminum storm windows for each company in 19x1 and 19x5. Round answers to the nearest cent. (*Hint:* Ultimately all of the costs discussed in this problem are product costs.)

b) Determine the economic lot size for both companies in 19x1 and 19x5.

c) Comment on the approaches to inventory management followed by William and Edwin Glass. Might they have done better if they had not broken up the Unity Glass Company? Why or why not? Use numbers to illustrate as appropriate.

d) Can you recommend any additional changes in production procedures that might further enhance either company's competitive position?

e) Describe an accounting system that seems most appropriate for the recommendation in requirement (d).

REVIEW PROBLEM SOLUTION

a)

Order quantity (units)	100	200	300	400	600	900
Number of orders (Annual demand / order quantity)	9	4.5	3	2.25	1.5	1
Average inventory (Order quantity/2)	50	100	150	200	300	450
Relevant annual costs:						
Ordering	$1,800	$ 900	$ 600	$ 450	$ 300	$ 200
Carrying	200	400	600	800	1,200	1,800
Total	$2,000	$1,300	$1,200	$1,250	$1,500	$2,000

b) **Total Annual Costs**

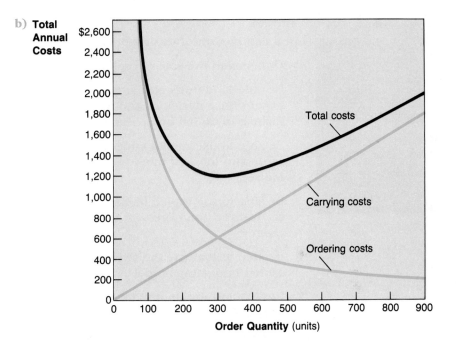

c) Annual ordering and carrying costs are equal at the economic order quantity.

d) Economic order quantity $= \sqrt{\dfrac{2 \times 900 \times \$200}{\$20 \times 0.20}}$

$= \underline{\underline{300}}$ units.

Capital Budgeting

Learning Objectives

Upon completion of this chapter you should:

- **Understand the role of capital budgeting in long-range planning.**

- **Be able to identify cost and revenue data relevant to capital expenditure decisions and be able to properly organize the data for use in capital budgeting models.**

- **Be able to use capital budgeting models, such as net present value and internal rate of return, that consider the time value of money.**

- **Be able to use capital budgeting models, such as payback and accounting rate of return, that do not consider the time value of money.**

- **Be able to evaluate the strengths and weaknesses of alternative capital budgeting models.**

- **Understand the importance of management's judgment and attitude toward risk in finalizing capital expenditure decisions.**

- **Understand the differences between a total cost approach and a differential analysis approach to organizing project cash flows.**

The emphasis in most of this text is on short-range planning and control, where we assume the organization's basic facilities and products or services do not change. In this chapter we relax this assumption and turn our attention to a portion of long-range planning that deals with the identification and evaluation of major investment proposals to expand or change the organization's activities or facilities.

Capital expenditures involve investment of significant financial resources in projects to develop or introduce new products or services, to expand current production or service capacity, or to change current production or service facilities. Changes in current facilities might, for example, be intended to achieve lower operating costs, lower levels of environmental pollution, or make operating conditions safer. Investments in the financial securities of another entity are not capital expenditures.

Capital budgeting is a process that involves the identification of potentially desirable projects for capital expenditure, the subsequent evaluation of capital expenditure proposals, and the selection of proposals that meet certain criteria. A number of quantitative models have been developed to assist managers in evaluating capital expenditure proposals. The purpose of this chapter is to introduce important capital budgeting concepts and models and to discuss the proper use of accounting data in these models.

The best capital budgeting models are similar in many respects to the short-range planning models used in Chapters 5 and 6. They all emphasize cash flows and focus on future costs (and revenues) that differ between competing alternatives. The major difference is that capital budgeting models involve cash flows over several years, whereas short-range models involve only single-year cash flows. When the cash flows associated with a proposed activity extend over several years, an adjustment should be made to make the future cash flows comparable.

The time value of money concept explains why monies received or paid at different points in time must be adjusted to make them comparable. The time value of money is introduced in the appendix to this chapter. If you have not previously studied the time value of money, or feel you would benefit from a review of time value concepts, read the appendix before continuing this chapter.

LONG-RANGE PLANNING AND CAPITAL BUDGETING PROCEDURES

Most organizations plan not only for operations in the current period, but also for the longer term, perhaps five to ten or even twenty years in the future. Most planning beyond the next budget year is called *long-range planning*.

Increased uncertainty and an increased number of alternatives makes planning more difficult as the planning horizon increases. Nevertheless, the fact that long-range planning is difficult and involves uncertainties does not relieve management of long-range planning and capital expenditure decisions. Capital expenditure decisions will be made; the question is how will they be made? Will they be made on the basis of the best information available? Will care be taken to ensure that capital expenditure decisions are in line with the organization's long-range goals? Will the potential consequences, both good and bad, of capital expenditures be considered? Will important alternative uses of the organization's limited financial resources be considered in a systematic manner? Will managers be held accountable for the results of major capital expenditure programs they initiate? The alternative to a systematic approach to capital budgeting is the haphazard expenditure of significant resources on the basis of hunch, immediate need, and persuasion—without accountability by the person(s) making the capital expenditure decisions.

A basic requirement for a systematic approach to capital budgeting is a well-formulated set of long-range goals the organization hopes to achieve over a multiyear period. These goals serve as a guideline, thereby reducing the types of capital expenditure decisions considered by management. If, for example, Swift Clippers' primary goal is to become the largest chain of hair stylists in the nation, its management should not consider a proposal to construct and operate a meat packing plant.

Procedures should also be developed for the review, evaluation, approval, and post-audit of capital expenditure proposals. Central to these procedures in a large organization is a capital budgeting committee that provides guidance to managers in the formulation of capital expenditure proposals. This committee also reviews, analyzes, and approves or rejects major capital expenditure proposals. Very significant projects may also require the approval of top management and even the board of directors. The capital budgeting committee should include persons knowledgeable of capital budgeting models, financing alternatives and

MANAGERIAL PRACTICE 15.1

Changes in Capital Budgeting Strategy

According to a recent article in *Business Week,* managers in a number of companies have changed their thinking about making capital expenditure decisions. "Instead of automating to cut costs, these executives invest to keep customers—and win new ones. Instead of buying a new machine to save on labor, they buy it to cut lead times, boost quality, reduce inventory, and add flexibility."

Source: Karen Pennar, "The Productivity Paradox," *Business Week,* 6 June 1988, 101.

costs, production techniques, cost estimation and prediction methods, research and development efforts, overall organization strategy, and the expectations of the organization's stockholders or owners. A management accountant—who is generally expert in data collection, retrieval, and analysis—is normally part of the capital budgeting committee.

Not all capital expenditure proposals will require committee approval. With the approval of top management, the committee may provide guidelines to line managers at each level of the organization, indicating the type and dollar amount of capital expenditures they can make without committee approval. Typically, managers at higher levels have greater discretion in making capital expenditures. In a college or university, for example, a department chairman may have authority to purchase office and instructional equipment with a maximum limit of $3,000 per year; a dean may have authority to renovate offices or classrooms with a maximum limit of $20,000 per year; but the formal review of a capital budgeting committee and final approval of the board of trustees may be required to convert the power plant from fuel oil to wood chips at a cost of $225,000.

The post-auditing of approved capital expenditure proposals is an important part of a well-formulated approach to capital budgeting. Such a post-audit involves the development of project performance reports comparing planned and actual results. Project performance reports should be provided to the manager who initiated the capital expenditure proposal, to the manager assigned responsibility for the project (if a different person), to the project manager's supervisor, and to the capital budgeting committee. These reports help keep the project on target, help identify the need to reevaluate the project if the initial analysis was in error or significant environmental changes occur, and help improve the quality of investment proposals. When managers know they will be held accountable for the results of projects they initiate, they are likely to put more care into the development of capital expenditure proposals and take a greater interest in approved projects.

A post-audit review of approved projects also helps the capital budgeting committee do a better job in evaluating new proposals. The committee may learn how to adjust proposals for the biases of individual managers; learn of new factors that should be considered in evaluating proposals; and avoid the routine approval of projects that appear desirable by themselves, but are related to larger projects that are not meeting management's expectations.

CAPITAL BUDGETING MODELS THAT CONSIDER THE TIME VALUE OF MONEY

The capital budgeting models presented in this chapter have gained wide acceptance by for-profit and not-for-profit organizations. All managers should have at least a rudimentary knowledge of the operation of these models and their strengths and weaknesses. Our primary focus is on the net present value and internal rate of return models, which are superior because they consider the time value of money. Later discussions in the chapter consider more traditional capital budgeting models, such as payback and the accounting rate of return, which, although useful under certain circumstances, do not consider the time value of money. Also, the cost of financing capital expenditures is briefly considered; however, a detailed treatment of this topic, as well as a detailed examination of the sources of funds for financing investments, is left to books on financial management.

Organizing Expected Cash Flows

The focus of capital budgeting models that consider the time value of money is on future cash receipts and future cash disbursements that differ under decision alternatives. It is often convenient to distinguish between three phases of a project's cash flows:

- Initial investment
- Operation
- Disinvestment

All cash expenditures necessary to begin operations are classified as part of the project's initial investment. Expenditures to acquire property, plant, and equipment are clearly part of the initial investment. Less obvious, but equally important, are expenditures to acquire working capital such as inventories and to recruit and train employees. Although the initial investment phase often

MANAGERIAL PRACTICE 15.2

Quantifying the Nonlabor Benefits of Investing in Automation

Herman M. Reininga proposed the purchase of an $80,000 laser to etch contract numbers on communications systems sold to the Pentagon in 1982. He was turned down because the small amount saved on direct labor each year would result in a 20-year payback period. Three years later, Reininga resubmitted his proposal. This time, he included information that indicated the laser would expedite shipments and save $200,000 a year in inventory holding costs. Since then, Reininga, who is now vice president for Rockwell's defense communications division in Cedar Rapids, Iowa, has been responsible for the installation of shop-floor personal computers and robots, which have increased production 79 percent and on-time deliveries 95 percent.

Source: Gregory L. Miles, "Selling Rockwell on Automation," *Business Week,* 6 June 1988, 104.

extends over many years, in most textbook examples and problems we assume that the initial investment takes place at a single point in time.

Cash receipts from sales of goods or services, as well as normal cash expenditures for materials, labor, and other operating expenses, occur during the operation phase. The operation phase is typically broken down into one-year periods. For each period, operating cash expenditures are subtracted from operating cash receipts to determine the net operating cash inflow or outflow for the period.

The disinvestment phase occurs at the end of the project's life when assets are disposed of and any initial investment of working capital is recovered. Although this phase may also extend over many years, in textbook examples and problems we assume disinvestment takes place at a single point in time. Cash received from the sale of a fixed asset at the end of its useful life is often referred to as salvage value.

To illustrate the analysis of a project's cash flows, assume the management of Mobile Yogurt Shoppes is considering a capital expenditure proposal to operate a new Mobile Yogurt Shoppe in a resort community in the Ozark Mountains. Each Mobile Yogurt Shoppe is located in a specially constructed motor vehicle that moves on a regular schedule, such as that of a bus, throughout the community it serves. The predicted cash flows associated with the project, which has an expected life of five years, are presented in Exhibit 15–1.

Net Present Value

A project's net present value, usually computed as of the time of the initial investment, is the present value of the project's net cash inflows from operations and disinvestment less the amount of the initial investment. In computing a

---

EXHIBIT 15–1   Analysis of a Project's Predicted Cash Flows

Initial investment:		
Vehicle and equipment		$ 90,554
Inventories and other working capital		4,000
Total		$ 94,554
Operation (per year for five years):		
Sales		$175,000
Cash expenditures:		
Food	$47,000	
Labor	65,000	
Supplies	9,000	
Fuel and utilities	8,000	
Advertising	4,000	
Miscellaneous	12,000	−145,000
Net annual cash inflow		$ 30,000
Disinvestment (at the end of five years):		
Sale of vehicle and equipment		$ 8,000
Recovery of investment in inventories and other working capital		4,000
Total		$ 12,000

project's net present value, the cash flows occurring at different points in time are adjusted for the time value of money using a discount rate that is the minimum rate of return required for the project to be acceptable. Projects whose net present values are positive, or at least equal to zero, are acceptable, and projects whose net present values are negative are unacceptable. Assuming management uses a 12 percent discount rate, the net present value of the proposed investment in a Mobile Yogurt Shoppe is shown in Exhibit 15–2 to be $20,400. Since the net present value is greater than zero, the investment in the Mobile Yogurt Shoppe is expected to be profitable, even when adjusted for the time value of money.

As an exercise, you should verify the amounts and computations in Exhibit 15–2. Start by tracing the cash flows back to Exhibit 15–1. Next verify the 12 percent present values factors in Tables 15–1 and 15–2 found at the end of the appendix to this chapter, p. 735. Note that the initial investment is assumed to occur at a single point in time, identified as time zero, the start of the project. In net present value computations, all cash flows are restated in terms of their value at time zero. Hence, time zero cash flows have a present value factor of one. To simplify computations, all other cash flows are assumed to occur at the end of years one through five, even if they occurred during the year. Although further refinements could be made to adjust for the fact that cash flows occur throughout each year rather than at the end of the year, such adjustments are seldom necessary. Observe that the net operating cash inflows are treated as an annuity, whereas the cash flows for the initial investment and the disinvestment are treated as lump-sum amounts. If the net operating cash flows varied from year to year, we would have to treat each year's cash flow as separate amounts.

Internal Rate of Return

The internal rate of return (IRR), often called the time adjusted rate of return, is the discount rate that equates the present value of a project's cash inflows with the present value of the project's cash outflows. It may also be stated as:

1. The minimum rate that could be paid for the money invested in a project without losing money, or

EXHIBIT 15–2   Net Present Value Analysis of a Project's Predicted Cash Flows

	Predicted Cash Inflows (Outflows) (A)	Year(s) of Cash Flows (B)	12% Present Value Factor (C)	Present Value of Cash Flows (A) × (C)
Initial investment	$(94,554)	0	1.000	$ (94,554)
Operation	30,000	1–5	3.605	108,150
Disinvestment	12,000	5	0.567	6,804
Net present value of all cash flows				$ 20,400

2. The discount rate that results in a project's net present value equaling zero.

Computing IRR with Equal Cash Inflows. An investment proposal's internal rate of return is relatively easy to compute in simple situations involving a single investment and a series of equal annual net cash inflows. In general, the relationship between the initial investment and the equal annual cash inflows can be expressed as follows:

$$\frac{\text{Initial}}{\text{investment}} = \frac{\text{Present value factor}}{\text{for an annuity of \$1}} \times \frac{\text{Annual net}}{\text{cash inflow.}}$$

We can solve for the appropriate present value factor as follows:

$$\frac{\text{Present value factor}}{\text{for an annuity of \$1}} = \frac{\text{Initial investment}}{\text{Annual net cash inflows}}.$$

Once the present value factor is calculated, we enter Table 15.2 and go across the row corresponding to the expected life of the project until we find a table factor equal to the present value factor computed for the project. The corresponding percentage for the present value factor is the proposal's internal rate of return. If a table factor does not exactly equal the proposal's present value factor, a more accurate answer can be obtained by interpolation.

To illustrate, assume the Mobile Yogurt Shoppes' proposed investment has a zero disinvestment value. Using all information in Exhibit 15–1, except that for disinvestment, the proposal's present value factor is 3.152:

$$\frac{\text{Present value factor}}{\text{for an annuity of \$1}} = \frac{\text{Initial investment}}{\text{Annual net cash inflows}}$$

$$= \frac{\$94,554}{\$30,000}$$

$$= 3.152.$$

Entering Table 15.2, and going across the row for five periods, the closest table factor is 3.127, which corresponds to an internal rate of return of 18 percent. Because the proposal's present value factor is slightly larger than 3.127, a more accurate answer can be obtained by interpolation:

	Present Value Factors	
16 percent	3.274	3.274
Internal rate of return	−3.152	
18 percent		−3.127
Difference	0.122	0.147

$$\frac{\text{True internal}}{\text{rate of return}} = 0.16 + \left(\frac{0.122}{0.147} \times (0.18 - 0.16)\right)$$

$$= 0.1766.$$

Hence, the proposal's internal rate of return, ignoring any disinvestment value, is 17.66 percent.

The calculated internal rate of return should be compared to the discount rate established by management to evaluate investment proposals. If the proposal's IRR is greater than or equal to the discount rate, the project is acceptable; if the proposal's IRR is less than the discount rate, the project is unacceptable. Because Mobile Yogurt Shoppes' has a 12 percent discount rate, the project is acceptable using the IRR model.

Computing IRR with Unequal Cash Inflows. If periodic cash flows subsequent to the initial investment are unequal, the simple procedure of determining a present value factor and looking up the closest corresponding factor in Table 15.2 cannot be used. Instead, a trial-and-error approach is used to determine the internal rate of return.

The first step is to select a discount rate estimated to be close to the proposal's IRR and compute the proposal's net present value. If the resulting net present value is zero, the selected discount rate is the actual rate of return. However, it is unlikely that the first rate selected will be the proposal's IRR. If the resulting net present value is positive, this indicates that the actual IRR is greater than the initially selected rate. In this case, the next step is to compute the proposal's net present value using a higher rate. If the second computation produces a negative net present value, the actual IRR is less than the selected rate. Therefore, the actual IRR is between the first and the second rates. This trial-and-error approach continues until a discount rate is found that equates the proposal's cash inflows and outflows. For the Mobile Yogurt Shoppes' investment proposal outlined in Exhibit 15–1, the details of the trial-and-error approach are presented in Exhibit 15–3.

Note in Exhibit 15–3 that the first rate produced a negative net present value, indicating that the proposal's IRR is less than 24 percent. To produce a positive net present value, a smaller rate was selected for the second trial. Since the second rate produced a positive net present value, the proposal's true IRR must be between 16 and 24 percent. The 20 percent rate selected for the third trial produced a net present value of zero, indicating that this is the proposal's IRR.

Although manual calculation of an investment proposal's IRR can be tedious, accurate results are easily obtained with the aid of a computer and appropriate software. Furthermore, many hand calculators contain IRR calculation functions. All the user must do is enter the predicted cash flows for each period. This computational ease does, however, increase the opportunity for inappropriate use. Being able to plug numbers into a computer or calculator and obtain a number labeled IRR may mislead the unwary user into believing it is easy to use this capital budgeting model. This simply is not true. Training and professional judgment are required to identify relevant costs, implement procedures to obtain relevant cost information, and make a good decision on the basis of IRR information.

EXHIBIT 15–3   Computations of Internal Rate of Return with Unequal Cash Flows

First trial with a 24 percent discount rate:

	Predicted Cash Inflows (Outflows) (A)	Year(s) of Cash Flows (B)	24% Present Value Factor (C)	Present Value of Cash Flows (A) × (C)
Initial investment	$(94,554)	0	1.000	$(94,554)
Operation	30,000	1–5	2.745	82,350
Disinvestment	12,000	5	0.341	4,092
Net present value of all cash flows				$ (8,112)

Second trial with a 16 percent discount rate:

	Predicted Cash Inflows (Outflows) (A)	Year(s) of Cash Flows (B)	16% Present Value Factor (C)	Present Value of Cash Flows (A) × (C)
Initial investment	$(94,554)	0	1.000	$(94,554)
Operation	30,000	1–5	3.274	98,220
Disinvestment	12,000	5	0.476	5,712
Net present value of all cash flows				$ 9,378

Third trial with a 20 percent discount rate:

	Predicted Cash Inflows (Outflows) (A)	Year(s) of Cash Flows (B)	20% Present Value Factor (C)	Present Value of Cash Flows (A) × (C)
Initial investment	$(94,554)	0	1.000	$(94,554)
Operation	30,000	1–5	2.991	89,730
Disinvestment	12,000	5	0.402	4,824
Net present value of all cash flows				$ 0

Cost of Capital

When discounting models are used to evaluate capital expenditure proposals, management must determine the discount rate (1) used to compute a proposal's net present value or (2) used as the standard for evaluating a proposal's IRR. An organization's cost of capital is often used as this discount rate.

The cost of capital is the average cost of obtaining the resources necessary to make investments. The cost of capital is the average rate an organization must pay for invested funds. This average rate takes into account such items as interest paid on notes or bonds, the effective dividend rate on preferred stock, and the discount rate that equates the present value of all dividends expected on common stock over the life of the organization to the current market value of the organization's common stock. Investing in a project that has an internal rate of return equal to the cost of capital should not affect the market value of the firm's securities. Investing in a project that has a return greater than the cost of capital should increase the market value of a firm's securities. If, however, a firm invests in a project that has a return of less than the cost of capital, the market value of the firm's securities should fall.

The cost of capital is the minimum return that is acceptable for investment purposes. Any investment proposal not expected to yield this minimum rate should normally be rejected. Because of difficulties encountered in determining the cost of capital, many organizations adopt a discount rate or target rate of return without complicated mathematical analysis.

CAPITAL BUDGETING MODELS THAT DO NOT CONSIDER THE TIME VALUE OF MONEY

Until recent years, capital budgeting models that did not consider the time value of money were more widely used than discounting models. Although their popularity has declined, nondiscounting models are sometimes used as an initial screening device. Two nondiscounting models, payback and accounting rate of return, are considered.

Payback Period

The payback period is the time required to recover the initial investment in a project from its operations. The payback method decision rule states that acceptable capital expenditure proposals must have less than some maximum payback period designated by management. The payback method emphasizes management's concern with liquidity and the need to minimize risk through a rapid recovery of the initial investment.

When a proposal is expected to have equal annual operating cash inflows, its payback period is computed as follows:

$$\frac{\text{Payback}}{\text{period}} = \frac{\text{Initial investment}}{\text{Annual operating cash inflows}}.$$

For the Mobile Yogurt Shoppes' investment proposal, outlined in Exhibit 15–1, the payback period is 3.15 years:

$$\frac{\text{Payback}}{\text{period}} = \frac{\$94,554}{\$30,000}$$

$$= \underline{\underline{3.15}}.$$

Determining the payback period for an investment proposal that has unequal cash flows is slightly more complicated. Assume the Alderman Company is evaluating a capital expenditure proposal that requires an initial investment of $50,000 and has the following expected cash inflows:

Year	Cash Inflow
1	$15,000
2	25,000
3	40,000
4	20,000
5	10,000

To compute the payback period, the net unrecovered amount must be deter-mined as of the end of each year. In the year of full recovery, the cash inflows are assumed to occur evenly and are prorated based on the unrecovered invest-ment at the start of the year. Full recovery of the Alderman Company's investment proposal is expected to occur in year 3:

Year	Cash Inflow	Unrecovered Investment
0	$ 0	$50,000
1	15,000	35,000
2	25,000	10,000
3	40,000	

Therefore, $10,000 of $40,000 is needed in year 3 to complete the recovery of the initial investment. This provides a proration of 0.25 ($10,000/$40,000) and a payback period of 2.25 years (2 years plus 0.25 of year 3). If management specified a maximum payback period of 3 years, this proposal would be accept-able. Note that the cash inflows of years 4 and 5 are ignored.

The bail-out period is an often used variation of the payback period. The bail-out period is the time required to recover the initial investment in a project from any source of funds. Unlike the payback method, which recognizes only operating cash inflows, the bail-out method recognizes cash inflows from either operations or early disposal.

Assume that the Baker Company is considering a capital expenditure pro-posal requiring an initial investment of $50,000. The net cash inflows from operations are estimated to be $10,000 per year for eight years. The disposal value of the investment is $30,000 during the first year, and it declines by $5,000 during the second year and each subsequent year. As shown in the table at the top of the next page, the bail-out period of the investment proposal is three years, and the payback period is five years.

The bail-out period indicates how soon an organization can get out of a project and recover all its initial investment. It provides additional information to assist management in making investment decisions.

Year	(1) Disposal Value	(2) Cumulative Operating Inflows	(1) + (2) Total Recovery
1	$30,000	$10,000	$40,000
2	25,000	20,000	45,000
3 Bail-out	20,000	30,000	**50,000**
4	15,000	40,000	55,000
5 Payback	10,000	**50,000**	60,000
6	5,000	60,000	65,000

Accounting Rate of Return

The accounting rate of return, sometimes called the **simple rate of return,** is a less popular nondiscounting model. It is computed as the average annual increase in net income that results from acceptance of a capital expenditure proposal divided by either the initial investment or the average investment in the project. This method differs from all other capital budgeting models discussed in this chapter in that it focuses on accounting income rather than cash flow. In most capital budgeting applications, accounting net income is computed as net cash inflow from operations minus expenses not requiring the use of cash, such as depreciation.

Consider the Mobile Yogurt Shoppes' capital expenditure proposal, whose cash flows are outlined in Exhibit 15–1. The vehicle and equipment cost $90,554 and have a disposal value of $8,000 at the end of five years, resulting in an average annual increase in net income of $13,489.20:

Annual net cash inflow from operations	$30,000.00
Less average annual depreciation [($90,554 − $8,000)/5]	−16,510.80
Average annual increase in net income	$13,489.20

Taking the investment in inventories and other working capital into account, the initial investment is $94,554 ($90,554 + $4,000), and the accounting rate of return on initial investment is 14.27 percent:

$$\text{Accounting rate of return} = \frac{\$13,489.20}{\$94,554.00}$$

$$= 0.1427.$$

The average investment, computed as the initial investment plus the expected value of any disinvestment, all divided by two, is $53,277 [($94,554 + $12,000)/2]. The accounting rate of return on average investment is 25.32 percent:

$$\text{Accounting rate of return} = \frac{\$13,489.20}{\$53,277}$$

$$= 0.2532.$$

When using the accounting rate of return, management specifies some minimum acceptable rate of return. Capital expenditure proposals with a lower accounting rate of return are rejected, whereas acceptable proposals have an accounting rate of return greater than or equal to the minimum.

EVALUATION OF CAPITAL BUDGETING MODELS

As a single criterion for evaluating capital expenditure proposals, capital budgeting models that consider the time value of money are superior to capital budgeting models that do not consider the time value of money. The payback model is merely concerned with how long it takes to recover the initial investment from a project. Yet, investments are not made with the objective of merely getting the investment back. Indeed, not investing has a payback period of zero. Investments are made to earn a profit. Hence, what happens after the payback period is just as important as the payback period itself. The payback model, when used as the sole investment criterion, has a fatal flaw in that it fails to consider cash flows after the payback period.

For total life evaluations, the accounting rate of return is superior to the payback period in that it does consider the profitability of a capital expenditure proposal. Using the accounting rate of return, a project that merely returns the initial investment will have an average annual increase in net income of zero and an accounting rate of return of zero. The problem with the accounting rate of return is that it fails to consider the timing of cash flows. All cash flows within the life of an investment proposal are treated equally, despite the fact that cash flows early in a project's life are more valuable than cash flows late in a project's life. Early period cash flows can earn additional profits by being reinvested elsewhere. Consider the two investment proposals summarized in Exhibit

EXHIBIT 15–4   The Accounting Rate of Return Illustrated with Differences in the Timing of Cash Flows

	Project A	Project B
Predicted net cash inflow from operations:		
Year 1	$ 50,000	$ 10,000
Year 2	50,000	10,000
Year 3	10,000	50,000
Year 4	10,000	50,000
Total	$120,000	$120,000
Total depreciation	−100,000	−100,000
Total net income	$ 20,000	$ 20,000
Project life	÷4 years	÷4 years
Average annual increase in net income	$ 5,000	$ 5,000
Initial investment	÷100,000	÷100,000
Accounting rate of return on initial investment	0.05	0.05

15–4, both of which have the same net cash flows and an accounting rate of return of 5 percent. Yet, Proposal A is superior to Proposal B because most of its cash flows occur in the first two years.

The net present value and internal rate of return models both consider the time value of money and project profitability. They almost always provide the same evaluation of individual projects whose acceptance or rejection will not affect other projects.[1] There are, however, two basic differences between the net present value and the internal rate of return models that often lead to differences in the evaluation of competing investment proposals:

1. The net present value model gives explicit consideration to investment size. The internal rate of return model does not.

2. The net present value model assumes that all net cash inflows are reinvested at the discount rate, whereas the internal rate of return model assumes that all net cash inflows are reinvested at the project's internal rate of return.

These differences are considered later when we discuss mutually exclusive investments.

ADDITIONAL ASPECTS OF CAPITAL BUDGETING

Screening and Selection

The capital budgeting models discussed above do not make investment decisions. Rather, they help managers separate capital expenditure proposals that meet certain criteria from those that do not. Managers then focus additional attention on those proposals that pass the initial screening performed using the capital budgeting models. In performing this initial screening, management may use a single capital budgeting model, or they may use multiple models, including some we have not discussed. Management might specify that proposals must be in line with the organization's long-range goals, have a maximum payback period of three years, have a positive net present value when discounted at 14 percent, and have an initial investment of less than $500,000. The maximum payback period might be intended to reduce risk, the present value criterion might be to ensure an adequate return to investors, and the maximum investment size might reflect the resources available for investment.

Nonquantitative factors are apt to play a decisive role in management's final decision to accept or reject a capital expenditure proposal that has passed the initial screening. Very important at this point are management's attitudes toward risk and financing alternatives, their confidence in the professional judgment of managers making investment proposals, their beliefs about the future direction

---

[1] An exception often occurs when periods of net cash outflows are mixed with periods of net cash inflows. Under these circumstances, an investment proposal may have multiple internal rates of return. For a further discussion of this point, consult a financial management textbook.

of the economy, and their evaluation of alternative investments. In the following sections, we focus on the evaluation of risk, an approach to the differential analysis of project cash flows, predicting differential costs and revenues for high-tech investments, and evaluating mutually exclusive investments.

Evaluating Risk   All capital expenditure proposals involve many sources of risk, including risk related to:

- The cost of the initial investment.
- The time required to complete the initial investment and begin operations.
- Whether or not the new facilities will operate as planned.
- The life of the facilities.
- The customers' demand for the product or service.
- The final selling price.
- Operating costs.
- Disposal values.

MANAGERIAL PRACTICE 15.3

Making Unconventional Capital Decisions

Cone Drive Operations, Inc., was faced with the reality that, in order to survive, they would need to overhaul operations from top to bottom. Profits were falling, costs were rising, deliveries were behind schedule, and customers were unhappy. The problem arose when Cone could not justify renovation through conventional methods: via labor savings. General Manager Arthur D. Swanson explained, "You can put a figure on losing customers but you can't put one on holding them." Most capital decisions are based on return on investment. It is difficult to quantify such intangibles as improved quality, faster order processing, shortened delivery times, and customer satisfaction. Cone (correctly) decided to fund the overhaul. "The project paid for itself with new business and nonlabor savings in just one year."

Source: Otis Port, Resa King, and William J. Hampton, "How the New Math of Productivity Adds Up," *Business Week,* 6 June 1988, 103–114.

Projected cash flows, such as those summarized for the Mobile Yogurt Shoppes' proposal in Exhibit 15–1, are based on management's best prediction as to what will happen. Although these predictions are likely to reflect the professional judgment of economists, marketing personnel, engineers, and accountants, they are far from certain.

Many techniques have been developed to assist in the analysis of the risks inherent in capital budgeting. Suggested approaches include the following:

- The discount rate for individual projects may be adjusted based on management's perception of the risks associated with a project. A project perceived as being almost risk free may be evaluated using a discount rate of 12 percent; a project perceived as having moderate risk may be evaluated using a discount rate of 16 percent; and a project perceived as having high risk may be evaluated using a discount rate of 20 percent.

- Several internal rates of return and/or net present values may be computed for a project. For example, a project's net present value might be computed three times: first, assuming the most optimistic projections of cash flows; second, assuming the most likely projections of cash flows; and third, assuming the most pessimistic projections of cash flows. The final decision then is based on management's attitudes toward risk.

- A capital expenditure proposal may be subject to sensitivity analysis, which was defined in Chapter 4 as a study of the responsiveness of a model's dependent variable(s) to changes in one or more of its independent variables. Management might want to know, for example, the minimum annual net cash inflows that will provide an internal rate of return of 12 percent, other cost and revenue projections being as expected.

Consider the situation presented in Exhibit 15–1 and analyzed using net present value and internal rate of return models in Exhibits 15–2 and 15–3. This proposal has a positive net present value when its cash flows are discounted at 12 percent and it has an expected IRR of 20 percent. Assuming Mobile Yogurt Shoppes has a 12 percent discount rate, management might wish to know the minimum annual net cash inflow that will meet this criterion.

In Exhibit 15–2, disinvestment cash inflows have a net present value of $6,804. When this amount is subtracted from the initial investment, $87,750 ($94,554 − $6,804) of the initial investment must be recovered from operations. If this amount is to be recovered over a five-year period, with equal annual net cash inflows, and a 12 percent discount rate, the factor 3.605 (see Table 15.2) must equate the annual net cash inflows with the portion of the initial investment to be recovered from operations. Hence, the minimum annual net cash inflows must be $24,341.19:

$$\text{Minimum annual} \atop \text{net cash inflow} = \frac{\$87,750}{3.605}$$

$$= \underline{\$24,341.19.}$$

If management could then predict the probability of annual net cash inflows being greater than or equal to $24,341.19, they would have the probability of this project meeting a 12 percent discount rate. Again, the ultimate decision to accept or reject the proposal rests with management and their attitudes toward risk.

It is interesting to note the similarity of the analysis here, determining the minimum annual net cash inflows, and the determination of the break-even point in Chapter 4. In effect, $24,341.19 in annual net cash inflows is a time-adjusted break-even point.

Total and Differential Analysis of Cash Flows

All the examples presented so far assume that the capital expenditure proposal will produce additional net cash inflows. This is not always the case. Units of government and not-for-profit organizations may provide services that do not produce any cash inflows. For-profit organizations may be required to make capital expenditures to maintain product quality or bring facilities up to environmental or safety standards. In these situations, it is impossible to compute a project's payback period, accounting rate of return, or internal rate of return. It is possible, however, to compute the present value of all costs associated with alternative ways of providing the service or meeting the environmental or safety standard. Here, the alternative with the smallest negative net present value is preferred.

Capital expenditure proposals to reduce operating costs by upgrading facilities may not have any incremental cash inflows associated with them. Again, we may use a total cost approach and calculate the present value of the costs associated with each alternative, with the low-cost alternative being preferred. Alternatively, we may perform a differential analysis of cash flows and, treating any reduced operating costs as if they were cash inflows, compute the net present value or the internal rate of return of the cost reduction proposal. Basically, a differential analysis focuses on the differences between the cash flows of the current operating conditions and the future alternative management is considering. Once the amounts are netted out, the differences can be adjusted for the time value of money. To illustrate the differential approach, we will consider an example first introduced in Chapter 5.

The Ace Stamping Company uses a Model I stamping machine to produce 10,000 widgets per year. Widgets sell for $15 each. Ace's variable and fixed costs are as follows:

Variable:	
Direct materials	$3 per unit
Direct labor	4 per unit
Factory overhead	1 per unit
Selling and administrative	1 per unit
Fixed:	
Factory overhead other than depreciation	$19,000 per year
Depreciation on Model I stamping machine	15,000 per year
Selling and administrative	12,000 per year

The Model I stamping machine is two years old and has a remaining useful life of four years. It cost $90,000 and has an estimated salvage value of zero dollars at the end of its useful life. Its current book value (original cost less accumulated depreciation) is $60,000, but its current disposal value is only $35,000.

Management is evaluating the desirability of replacing the Model I stamping machine with a new Model II stamping machine. The new machine costs $80,000, has a useful life of four years, and a predicted salvage value of zero dollars at the end of its useful life. Although the new machine would have the same productive capacity as the old machine, its operating costs would be lower because it would require only one operator rather than the two needed by the old machine. Furthermore, it has fewer moving parts, so it would require less maintenance and use less power. The new labor and overhead costs would be as follows:

Direct labor	$2.00 per unit
Variable factory overhead	0.80 per unit
Fixed overhead other than depreciation	$16,000 per year

A differential analysis of the cash flows associated with this cost reduction proposal, broken down into the three phases of the project's life, are presented in Exhibit 15–5. Because the proposal does not have a disposal value, the last portion of the analysis could have been omitted. Readers interested in a detailed explanation of the relevant costs included in this analysis are referred to Exhibit 5–1 and the accompanying Chapter 5 discussion of relevant costs. Assuming Ace Stamping has a discount rate of 16 percent, the proposal's net present value, computed in Exhibit 15–6, is $24,950. The proposal is acceptable.

Predicting Differential Costs and Revenues for High-Tech Investments

Special care must be taken when evaluating proposals for investments in the most current technological innovations, such as flexible manufacturing systems (FMS) and computer integrated manufacturing (CIM). There are three types of errors to consider: (1) investing in unnecessary or overly complex equipment, (2) overestimating cost savings, and (3) underestimating incremental sales.

Investing in Unnecessary or Overly Complex Equipment. A basic error is simply to compare the costs associated with the current inefficient way of doing things with the predicted cost of performing the identical operations with more modern equipment. Although capital budgeting models may suggest that such investments are justifiable, the result could be the costly and rapid performance of tasks that are a waste of time and money. Consider the following examples:

- A company invests in an automated system to speed the movement of goods between work stations on the shop floor without first evaluating the plant layout. The firm is still unable to compete with other companies having

EXHIBIT 15–5   Differential Analysis of Predicted Cash Flows

	Differential Analysis of Predicted Cash Flows		
	Keep Old Model I Machine	Replace with New Model II Machine	Difference (Effect of Replacement on Cash Flows)
	(A)	(B)	(A) − (B)
Initial investment:			
Cost of new machine		$80,000	$80,000
Disposal value of old machine		(35,000)	(35,000)
Net initial investment			$45,000
Annual operating cash savings:			
Direct labor:			
Old (10,000 × $4)	$40,000		
New (10,000 × $2)		20,000	$20,000
Variable overhead:			
Old (10,000 × $1)	10,000		
New (10,000 × $0.80)		8,000	2,000
Fixed overhead:			
Old	19,000		
New		16,000	3,000
Net annual cash savings			$25,000
Disinvestment at end of life:			
Old	$ 0		
New		$ 0	$ 0

better organized plants that allow lower cycle times, lower work-in-process inventories, and lower manufacturing costs. Management should have evaluated the plant layout before investing in new equipment. They may have found that rearranging the factory floor eliminated the need for the investment.

EXHIBIT 15–6   Net Present Value Analysis of Differential Cash Flows

	Predicted Cash Inflows (Outflows)	Year(s) of Cash Flows	16% Present Value Factor	Present Value of Cash Flows
	(A)	(B)	(C)	(A) × (C)
Initial investment	$(45,000)	0	1.000	$(45,000)
Operation	25,000	1–5	2.798	69,950
Disinvestment	0	5	0.552	0
Net present value of all cash flows				$ 24,950

- A company invests in a large automated warehouse to permit the rapid storage and retrieval of goods, while competitors work to eliminate excess inventory. The firm is left with large inventories and a large investment in the automated warehouse, while competitors, not having to earn a return on similar investments, are able to charge lower prices. Management should have evaluated the need for current inventory levels and perhaps shifted to a just-in-time approach to inventory management before considering the investment in an automated warehouse.

- A company invests in equipment to perform quality inspections, while competitors work to eliminate the need for quality inspections. Although defective products are now detected before shipment to customers, they are still being produced. What's more, the company has a higher capital investment than competitors. The result is, again, a less competitive cost structure. There may not have been a need for the inspection equipment if management shifted from inspecting all the finished goods for conformance to an emphasis on "doing it right the first time."

- A company invests in automated welding equipment to produce printer casings more efficiently, while competitors simplify the product design and shift from welded to molded plastic casings. Although the cost of producing the welded casings may be lower, the company's cost structure is still not competitive.

All of these examples illustrate the limitations of capital budgeting models and the need for professional judgment. In the final analysis people, not models, make decisions. Management must carefully evaluate the situations and determine if the proper alternatives and all important cash flows are considered.

Overestimating Cost Savings. When overhead rates are high and overhead is applied on the basis of direct labor, there is a significant danger of overestimating the cost savings of proposed investments in labor saving equipment. This is especially true if machine-intensive operations are cross-subsidized by labor-intensive operations. This occurs when most overhead costs are associated with machine-intensive operations while all overhead costs are assigned on the basis of direct labor. Here the predicted cost savings may be computed as the sum of predicted reductions in direct labor plus predicted reductions in overhead, computed as the overhead rate multiplied by the predicted reduction in direct labor dollars or hours. Because most of the overhead is not driven by direct labor, reducing direct labor will not provide the predicted savings. Although capital budgeting models may suggest that the investment is acceptable, the models are based on inaccurate cost data.

Management should beware of overly simplistic computations of cost savings. This is an area where management needs the assistance of well trained management accountants and engineers.

Underestimating Incremental Sales. In evaluating proposals for investments in new equipment, management often assumes that the base line for comparison is the current sales level. This may not be the case. If competitors are investing in equipment to improve their efficiency and reduce their costs, a failure to make similar investments may result in uncompetitive prices and declining, rather than steady, sales. Hence the baseline for sales without the investment is overstated, and the incremental sales aspect of the investment is understated. Not considering the likely decline in sales understates the incremental sales associated with the investment and biases the results against the proposed investment.

Investments in the most advanced manufacturing technologies, such as flexible manufacturing systems and computer integrated manufacturing, do more than simply allow the efficient production of current products. Such investments also make possible a rapid, low cost switch to new products. The result is expanded sales opportunities. Unfortunately, because such opportunities are difficult to quantify, they are often ignored in the evaluation of capital expenditure proposals. The result is a bias against investments in FMS and CIM. The solution

MANAGERIAL PRACTICE 15.4

Beyond the Numbers

Shareholder value analysis is the process of analyzing how business decisions affect the organization's economic value and its subsequent impact on shareholder worth. It applies the concept of discounted cash flow analysis to a wide range of business decisions. Managers often end the decision process with the accounting numbers and financial ratios, as was about to happen to Cone Drive Operations, a manufacturer of heavy-duty gears. Faced with losing customers because of slow deliveries, the company needed a new computer-integrated manufacturing system at a cost of $2 million. With only $26 million in sales, the $2 million investment could not be justified financially, even using discounted cash flow techniques. However, when management considered such items as better quality, faster production times, quicker order processing, and higher customer satisfaction, the decision was easier, because these were long-run considerations that would increase shareholder wealth through more profitable products and increased sales.

Source: George S. Day and Liam Fahey, "Putting Strategy into Shareholder Value Analysis," *Harvard Business Review* (March–April 1990): 156–162.

to this dilemma involves the application of management's professional judgment, a willingness to take risks based on professional judgement, and recognition that certain investments transcend capital budgeting models in that they involve strategic as well as long-range planning. At this level of planning, qualitative decisions concerning the nature of the organization are at least as important as quantified factors.

Mutually Exclusive Investments

Two or more capital expenditure proposals are mutually exclusive investments if the acceptance of one automatically causes the rejection of the other(s). When faced with mutually exclusive investments, management must determine which one to accept. The decision is relatively easy if only one of the proposals meets the organization's investment criteria. If, however, two or more proposals pass the initial screening performed by the investment criterion, management is faced with the task of selecting the best of the acceptable proposals. To help determine the best investment proposal, management may request that the proposals be ranked on the basis of some criterion, such as net present value or internal rate of return. Unfortunately, although these models almost always lead to identical decisions when used to evaluate individual investment proposals, they frequently produce different rankings of acceptable proposals. Consider the three investment proposals summarized in Exhibit 15–7.

Assuming the organization has a 12 percent cost of capital, all projects have positive net present values and all projects have an internal rate of return in excess of 12 percent. Therefore, all are acceptable. The problem is to determine which of these acceptable proposals is most desirable. Ranking the proposals by their net present values indicates that Proposal B is best, whereas ranking by IRR indicates that Proposal C is best.

EXHIBIT 15–7   Ranking Capital Budgeting Proposals

	Proposal A	Proposal B	Proposal C
Predicted cash flows:			
Initial investment	$(26,900)	$(55,960)	$(30,560)
Operation:			
Year 1	10,000	20,000	20,000
Year 2	10,000	20,000	20,000
Year 3	10,000	20,000	0
Year 4	10,000	20,000	0
Disinvestment	0	0	0
Investment criterion:			
Net present value at 12%	$ 3,470	$ 4,780	$ 3,240
Internal rate of return	18%	16%	20%
Present value index	1.129	1.085	1.106
Ranking by investment criterion:			
Net present value	2	1	3
Internal rate of return	2	3	1
Present value index	1	3	2

An often-stated criticism of net present value, when used to rank investment proposals, is that it fails to adjust for the size of the proposed investment. To overcome this difficulty, managers may rank projects on the basis of each project's present value index, which is computed as the present value of the project's subsequent cash flows divided by the initial investment:

$$\frac{\text{Present value}}{\text{index}} = \frac{\text{Present value of subsequent cash flows}}{\text{Initial investment}}.$$

For Proposal A, the present value of the subsequent cash flows, discounted at 12 percent, is $30,370 ($10,000 × 3.037), and the present value index is 1.129:

$$\frac{\text{Present value}}{\text{index}} = \frac{\$30,370}{\$26,900}$$

$$= \underline{\underline{1.129}}.$$

Using this criterion, projects that have a present value index of 1.0 or greater are acceptable, and the project with the highest present value index is preferred. Ranking the proposals in Exhibit 15–7 on the basis of their present value index results in Proposal A being ranked number 1.

We now have three acceptable proposals, three criteria, three different rankings, and the task of selecting only one of the three proposals. Many managers would select Proposal C because it has the highest IRR or Proposal A because it has the highest present value index. Either selection provides a satisfactory, but not an optimal, solution to the dilemma. If the true cost of capital is 12 percent and other investment opportunities only return 12 percent, the net present value criterion provides the proper choice. This is illustrated in Exhibit 15–8 by evaluating the additional return earned on the difference between Proposals B and A, and Proposals B and C.

The difference in the net present value and internal rate of return rankings results from differences in their reinvestment assumptions. The net present value model assumes that all net cash inflows from a project are reinvested at the discount rate, whereas the internal rate of return model assumes that all net cash inflows from a project are reinvested at the project's internal rate of return. If unlimited funds are available at the discount rate, marginal investments are made at this rate and the assumption underlying the net present value model is the correct one. Returning to Exhibit 15–8, if all funds not invested in the chosen project and all funds recovered from the chosen project can only earn the discount rate, the firm is $1,540 better off selecting Proposal B rather than Proposal C.

The present value index eliminates the impact of size from net present value computations. However, size is an important consideration in evaluating investment proposals, especially if all funds not invested in a project can only earn the discount rate. In Exhibit 15–8, we can see that if all funds not invested in the chosen project can only be invested at the discount rate, the firm is $1,310 better off by selecting Proposal B rather than Proposal A.

EXHIBIT 15–8   Analysis of Incremental Investments

	Proposal B	Proposal A	Difference B − A
Predicted cash flows:			
Initial investment	$(55,960)	$(26,900)	$(29,060)
Operation:			
Year 1	20,000	10,000	10,000
Year 2	20,000	10,000	10,000
Year 3	20,000	10,000	10,000
Year 4	20,000	10,000	10,000
Disinvestment	0	0	0
Net present value of difference			1,310

	Proposal B	Proposal C	Difference B − C
Predicted cash flows:			
Initial investment	$(55,960)	$(30,560)	$(25,400)
Operation:			
Year 1	20,000	20,000	0
Year 2	20,000	20,000	0
Year 3	20,000	0	20,000
Year 4	20,000	0	20,000
Disinvestment	0	0	0
Net present value of difference			1,540

SUMMARY

Capital budgeting involves the identification of potentially desirable projects for capital expenditures, the subsequent evaluation of capital expenditure proposals, and the selection of proposals that meet certain criteria. In this chapter we have studied a number of capital budgeting models that are used to assist managers in evaluating capital expenditure proposals. We concluded that capital budgeting models that consider the time value of money, such as net present value and internal rate of return, are superior to capital budgeting models that do not consider the time value of money, such as the payback period and the accounting rate of return.

It is important to remember that capital budgeting models do not make investment decisions. Rather, they help managers separate capital expenditure proposals that meet certain criteria from those that do not. In making the final decision to accept or reject a capital expenditure proposal that has passed the initial screening, nonquantitative factors, such as management's attitude toward risk, are apt to play a decisive role.

In the latter portion of this chapter, we outlined some suggested approaches to analyzing risk, saw how differential analysis can aid in evaluating capital expenditure proposals that do not produce additional cash inflows, and studied the problems involved in predicting differential costs and revenues for high-tech investments and selecting from among mutually exclusive investments. The impact of taxes on capital budgeting is considered in Chapter 16.

APPENDIX
TIME VALUE OF MONEY

The concept of time value of money explains why an amount of money received today is worth more than the same amount received at some future date. Because money can be invested to earn interest, a given amount of money today will accumulate to a greater amount in the future. Stated another way, for a given value one must have more money in the future than today to maintain the same value. Conversely, a sum of money to be received in the future is worth less in the present.

Future and Present Value

Future value is the amount a current sum of money earning a stated rate of interest will accumulate to at the end of a future period. Suppose you deposit $500 in a savings account at a financial institution that pays interest at the rate of 10 percent per year. At the end of the first year the original deposit of $500 will have grown to $550 ($500 × 1.10). If you leave the $550 for another year, the amount will grow to $605 ($550 × 1.10). It can be stated that $500 today has a future value in one year of $550, or conversely, that $550 one year from today has a present value of $500. Note that interest of $55 ($605 − $550) was earned in the second year, whereas interest of only $50 was earned in the first year. The reason for the increased amount is that interest during the second year has been earned on the principal plus interest from the first year ($550). When periodic interest is computed on principal plus prior period's accumulated interest, the interest is said to be compounded.

To determine future values at the end of each period, multiply the beginning amount by 1 plus the interest rate. Where multiple periods are involved, the future value is determined by repeatedly multiplying the beginning amount times 1 plus the interest rate for each period. When $500 is invested for two years at an interest rate of 10 percent per year, its future value is computed as $500 × 1.10 × 1.10. In general,

$$fv = pv(1 + r)^n,$$

where fv = future value amount,
pv = present value amount,
r = interest rate per period,
n = number of periods.

For the above situation the equation becomes

$$fv \text{ of } \$500 = pv (1 + r)^n$$
$$= \$500 (1 + 0.10)^2$$
$$= \$605.$$

From the general future value equation the compound amount, or future value, of $1.00 can be derived any time the interest rate and number of periods is known. Once the future value for $1.00 is determined, this amount may be multiplied by any present value amount to determine its future value.

Present value is the current worth of a specified amount of money to be received at some future date at some interest rate. Present value, then, is the inverse of future value. Solving for *pv* in the future value equation, the new *pv* equation can be determined as

$$fv = pv \, (1 + r)^n$$

$$pv = \frac{fv}{(1 + r)^n}$$

The present value equation is often expressed as the future value amount times the present value of $1.00:

$$pv = fv \times \frac{\$1}{(1 + r)^n}$$

Using the first equation, the present value of $8,800 to be received in one year, discounted at 10 percent, is computed as follows:

$$
\begin{aligned}
pv \text{ of } \$8,800 &= \frac{\$8,800}{(1 + 0.10)^1} \\
&= \frac{\$8,800}{1.10} \\
&= \$8,000.
\end{aligned}
$$

This amount can also be computed by multiplying $8,800 times the present value of $1.00:

$$
\begin{aligned}
pv \text{ of } \$8,800 = \$8,800 &\times \frac{\$1}{(1 + 0.10)^1} \\
&= \$8,800 \times 0.909 \\
&= \$8,000.
\end{aligned}
$$

Thus when the time value of money is 10 percent, the present value of $8,800 to be received one period from now is $8,000.

The present value of $8,800 two periods from now is $7,273 [$8,800/(1.10)²]. The computation can also be expressed as $8,800 × $1/(1.10)². Although these factors can be computed by hand, this approach is quite time-consuming for multiperiod problems. Tables providing the present value of $1.00 have been prepared for various interest rates and time periods to facilitate computations. Table 15–1 can be used to determine the present values of future amounts. Using the factors in Table 15–1 (see p. 735) for the present value of $1.00, the present values of any future amount can be determined. For example, with an interest rate of 10 percent, the present value of the following future amounts to be received in one period are as shown below.

Future Value Amount		Present Value Factor of $1.00		Present Value
$ 100	×	0.909	=	$ 90.90
628	×	0.909	=	570.85
4,285	×	0.909	=	3,895.07
9,900	×	0.909	=	8,999.10

To further illustrate the use of Table 15–1, consider the following application. Alert Company wants to invest its surplus cash at 12 percent in order to have $10,000 to pay off a long-term note due at the end of five years. Table 15–1 shows that the present value factor for $1.00, discounted at 12 percent per year for five years, is 0.567. Multiplying $10,000 by 0.567, the present value is determined to be $5,670:

$$pv \text{ of } \$10,000 = fv \times pv \text{ of } \$1 \text{ factor}$$
$$= \$10,000 \times 0.567$$
$$= \$5,670.$$

Therefore, if Alert invests $5,670 today, it will have $10,000 available to pay off its note in five years.

Present value tables are also used to make investment decisions. Assume that the Monroe Company can make an investment that will provide a cash flow of $12,000 at the end of eight years. If the company demands a rate of return of 14 percent per year, what is the most it will be willing to pay for this investment? From Table 15–1 we find that the present value factor for $1.00, discounted at 14 percent per year for eight years, is 0.351:

$$pv \text{ of } \$12,000 = fv \times pv \text{ of } \$1 \text{ factor}$$
$$= \$12,000 \times 0.351$$
$$= \$4,212.$$

If the company demands an annual 14 percent return, the most it would be willing to invest today is $4,212.

ANNUITIES

Not all investments provide a single sum of money. Many investments provide periodic cash flows called annuities. An annuity is a series of equal cash flows received or paid over equal intervals of time. Suppose that $100 will be received at the end of each of the next three years. If the time value of money is 10 percent, the present value of this annuity can be determined by summing the present value of each receipt:

Year 1	$100 ×	$\dfrac{\$1}{(1 + 0.10)^1}$ =	$ 90.90
Year 2	$100 ×	$\dfrac{\$1}{(1 + 0.10)^2}$ =	82.65
Year 3	$100 ×	$\dfrac{\$1}{(1 + 0.10)^3}$ =	75.13
Total			$248.68

Alternatively, the following equation can be used to compute the present value:

$$pva = \frac{a}{r}\left(1 - \frac{1}{(1 + r)^n}\right)$$

where pva = present value of an annuity of $1.00 (also called the annuity factor),
r = prevailing rate per period,
n = number of periods,
a = annuity amount.

This equation is used to compute the factors presented in Table 15–2. The present value of an annuity of $1.00 per period for three periods, discounted at 10 percent per period, is as follows:

$$pva \text{ of } \$1 = \frac{\$1}{0.10}\left(1 - \frac{1}{(1 + 0.10)^3}\right)$$
$$= 2.4868.$$

Using this factor, the present value of a $100 annuity can be computed by multiplying $100 × 2.4868, which yields $248.68. To determine the present value of an annuity of any amount, the annuity factor of $1.00 can be multiplied by the annuity amount:

$$pva = a \times (pva \text{ of } \$1).$$

As an additional illustration of the use of Table 15–2, assume that the Red Kite Company is considering an investment in a piece of equipment that will produce net cash inflows of $2,000 at the end of each year for five years. If the company's desired rate of return is 12 percent, an investment of $7,210 will provide such a return:

$$pva \text{ of } \$2,000 = \$2,000 \times (pva \text{ of } \$1)$$
$$= \$2,000 \times 3.605$$
$$= \$7,210.$$

Here the $2,000 annuity is multiplied by 3.605, the factor for an annuity of $1.00 for five periods, discounted at 12 percent per period. This factor is found in Table 15–2.

Another use of Table 15–2 is to determine the amount that must be received annually to provide a desired rate of return on an investment. Assume the Burnsville Company invests $33,550 and desires a return of the investment plus interest of 8 percent in equal payments at the end of each year for ten years. The minimum amount that must be received each year is determined by solving the equation for the present value of an annuity:

$$pva = a \times (pva \text{ of } \$1)$$
$$a = pva/(pva \text{ of } \$1).$$

From Table 15–2 we see that the 8 percent factor for ten periods is 6.710. When the investment of $33,550 is divided by 6.710, the required annuity is computed to be $5,000:

$$a = \$33,550/6.710$$
$$= \$5,000.$$

UNEQUAL FLOWS

Many investment situations do not produce equal periodic cash flows. When this occurs, the present value for each cash flow has to be determined independently because the annuity table can be used only for equal periodic cash flows. Table 15–1 is used to determine the present value of each future amount separately. To illustrate, assume the Atlantic Sabers wishes to acquire the contract of a popular baseball player who is known to attract large crowds. Management believes this player will return incremental cash flows to the team at the end of each of the next three years in the amounts of $25,000, $40,000, and $15,000. After three years, the player anticipates retiring. If the team's owners require a minimum return on their investment of 14 percent, how much would they be willing to pay for the player's contract?

To solve this problem, it is necessary to determine the present value of the expected future cash flows. Here we use Table 15–1 to find the $1.00 present value factors at 14 percent for periods 1, 2, and 3. The cash flows are then multiplied by these factors:

Year	Present Value at 14 Percent		Annual Cash Flow		Present Value Amount
1	0.877	×	$25,000	=	$21,925
2	0.769	×	40,000	=	30,760
3	0.675	×	15,000	=	10,125
Total					$62,810

The total present value of the cash flows for the three years, $62,810, represents the maximum amount the team would be willing to pay for the player's contract.

DEFERRED RETURNS

Many times organizations make investments for which no cash is received until several periods have passed. The present value of an investment discounted at 12 percent per year, which has a $2,000 return only at the end of years 4, 5, and 6, can be determined as follows:

Year	Amount		Present Value at 12 Percent		Present Value Amount
1	$ —	×	0.893	=	$ —
2	—	×	0.797	=	—
3	—	×	0.712	=	—
4	2,000	×	0.636	=	1,272
5	2,000	×	0.567	=	1,134
6	2,000	×	0.507	=	1,014
Total					$3,420

Computation of the present value of the deferred annuity can also be performed using the annuity tables if the cash flow amounts are equal for each period. The present value of an annuity for six years, minus the present value of an annuity for three years, yields the present value of an annuity for years 4 through 6:

Present value of an annuity for six years at 12 percent:	$2,000 × 4.111 =	$8,222
Present value of an annuity for three years at 12 percent:	$2,000 × 2.402 =	−4,804
Present value of the deferred annuity		$3,418*

*The difference between the $3,420 above and the $3,418 is caused by rounding error.

SUGGESTED READINGS

Clark, John J., Thomas J. Hindclang, and Robert E. Pritchard, *Capital Budgeting: Planning and Control of Capital Expenditures,* 2nd ed., Englewood Cliffs, N.J.: Prentice-Hall, 1984.

Corr, A. V., *The Capital Expenditure Decision,* Montvale, N.J.: National Association of Accountants, 1983.

Engwall, Richard, "CIM/JIT Investment Justification," *Journal of Cost Management, 6,* No. 3 (Fall 1989): 35–39.

Farragher, Edward J., "Capital Budgeting Practices of Non-Industrial Firms," *Engineering Economist* (Summer 1986): 293–302.

Hart, David Randolph, "Capital Budgeting—A Portfolio Approach," *Controller's Quarterly, 3,* No. 1 (1987): 21–25.

Howell, Robert A., and Stephen R. Soucy, "Capital Investment Analysis in the New Manufacturing Environment," *Management Accountant* (November 1987): 26–32.

Kaplan, Robert S., "Must CIM Be Justified by Faith Alone?" *Harvard Business Review* (March–April 1986): 87–95.

Management Accounting Practices Committee, *Statement Number 4A: Cost of Capital,* Montvale, N.J.: National Association of Accountants, 1984.

Pennar, Karen, "The Productivity Paradox," *Business Week,* 6 June 1988: 100–113.

Truitt, Jack, "The Financial Theory of the Firm: Capital Budgeting and Divisional Evaluation," *Journal of Cost Analysis* (Spring 1986): 25–31.

TABLE 15–1   Present Value of $1.00

Present value of $1.00 $= \dfrac{1}{(1 + r)^n}$.

Periods	6%	8%	10%	12%	14%	16%	18%	20%	22%	24%	26%	28%	30%
1	0.943	0.926	0.909	0.893	0.877	0.862	0.847	0.833	0.820	0.806	0.794	0.781	0.769
2	0.890	0.857	0.826	0.797	0.769	0.743	0.718	0.694	0.672	0.650	0.630	0.610	0.592
3	0.840	0.794	0.751	0.712	0.675	0.641	0.609	0.579	0.551	0.524	0.500	0.477	0.455
4	0.792	0.735	0.683	0.636	0.592	0.552	0.516	0.482	0.451	0.423	0.397	0.373	0.350
5	0.747	0.681	0.621	0.567	0.519	0.476	0.437	0.402	0.370	0.341	0.315	0.291	0.269
6	0.705	0.630	0.564	0.507	0.456	0.410	0.370	0.335	0.303	0.275	0.250	0.227	0.207
7	0.665	0.583	0.513	0.452	0.400	0.354	0.314	0.279	0.249	0.222	0.198	0.178	0.159
8	0.627	0.540	0.467	0.404	0.351	0.305	0.266	0.233	0.204	0.179	0.157	0.139	0.123
9	0.592	0.500	0.424	0.361	0.308	0.263	0.225	0.194	0.167	0.144	0.125	0.108	0.094
10	0.558	0.463	0.386	0.322	0.270	0.227	0.191	0.162	0.137	0.116	0.099	0.085	0.073
11	0.527	0.429	0.350	0.287	0.237	0.195	0.162	0.135	0.112	0.094	0.079	0.066	0.056
12	0.497	0.397	0.319	0.257	0.208	0.168	0.137	0.112	0.092	0.076	0.062	0.052	0.043
13	0.469	0.368	0.290	0.229	0.182	0.145	0.116	0.093	0.075	0.061	0.050	0.040	0.033
14	0.442	0.340	0.263	0.205	0.160	0.125	0.099	0.078	0.062	0.049	0.039	0.032	0.025
15	0.417	0.315	0.239	0.183	0.140	0.108	0.084	0.065	0.051	0.040	0.031	0.025	0.020
16	0.394	0.292	0.218	0.163	0.123	0.093	0.071	0.054	0.042	0.032	0.025	0.019	0.015
17	0.371	0.270	0.198	0.146	0.108	0.080	0.060	0.045	0.034	0.026	0.020	0.015	0.012
18	0.350	0.250	0.180	0.130	0.095	0.069	0.051	0.038	0.028	0.021	0.016	0.012	0.009
19	0.331	0.232	0.164	0.116	0.083	0.060	0.043	0.031	0.023	0.017	0.012	0.009	0.007
20	0.312	0.215	0.149	0.104	0.073	0.051	0.037	0.026	0.019	0.014	0.010	0.007	0.005

TABLE 15–2   Present Value of an Annuity of $1.00

Present value of an annuity of $1.00 $= \dfrac{1}{r}\left(1 - \dfrac{1}{(1 + r)^n}\right)$.

Periods	6%	8%	10%	12%	14%	16%	18%	20%	22%	24%	25%	26%	28%	30%
1	0.943	0.926	0.909	0.893	0.877	0.862	0.847	0.833	0.820	0.806	0.800	0.794	0.781	0.769
2	1.833	1.783	1.736	1.690	1.647	1.605	1.566	1.528	1.492	1.457	1.440	1.424	1.392	1.361
3	2.673	2.577	2.487	2.402	2.322	2.246	2.174	2.106	2.042	1.981	1.952	1.923	1.868	1.816
4	3.465	3.312	3.170	3.037	2.914	2.798	2.690	2.589	2.494	2.404	2.362	2.320	2.241	2.166
5	4.212	3.993	3.791	3.605	3.433	3.274	3.127	2.991	2.864	2.745	2.689	2.635	2.532	2.436
6	4.917	4.623	4.355	4.111	3.889	3.685	3.498	3.326	3.167	3.020	2.951	2.885	2.759	2.643
7	5.582	5.206	4.868	4.564	4.288	4.039	3.812	3.605	3.416	3.242	3.161	3.083	2.937	2.802
8	6.210	5.747	5.335	4.968	4.639	4.344	4.078	3.837	3.619	3.421	3.329	3.241	3.076	2.925
9	6.802	6.247	5.759	5.328	4.946	4.607	4.303	4.031	3.786	3.566	3.463	3.366	3.184	3.019
10	7.360	6.710	6.145	5.650	5.216	4.833	4.494	4.192	3.923	3.682	3.571	3.465	3.269	3.092
11	7.887	7.139	6.495	5.938	5.453	5.029	4.656	4.327	4.035	3.776	3.656	3.544	3.335	3.147
12	8.384	7.536	6.814	6.194	5.660	5.197	4.793	4.439	4.127	3.851	3.725	3.606	3.387	3.190
13	8.853	7.904	7.103	6.424	5.842	5.342	4.910	4.533	4.203	3.912	3.780	3.656	3.427	3.223
14	9.295	8.244	7.367	6.628	6.002	5.468	5.008	4.611	4.265	3.962	3.824	3.695	3.459	3.249
15	9.712	8.559	7.606	6.811	6.142	5.575	5.092	4.675	4.315	4.001	3.859	3.726	3.483	3.268
16	10.106	8.851	7.824	6.974	6.265	5.669	5.162	4.730	4.357	4.033	3.887	3.751	3.503	3.283
17	10.477	9.122	8.022	7.120	6.373	5.749	5.222	4.775	4.391	4.059	3.910	3.771	3.518	3.295
18	10.828	9.372	8.201	7.250	6.467	5.818	5.273	4.812	4.419	4.080	3.928	3.786	3.529	3.304
19	11.158	9.604	8.365	7.366	6.550	5.877	5.361	4.844	4.442	4.097	3.942	3.799	3.539	3.311
20	11.470	9.818	8.514	7.469	6.623	5.929	5.353	4.870	4.460	4.110	3.954	3.808	3.546	3.316

REVIEW PROBLEM

Survey of Capital Budgeting Models

Consider the following investment proposal:

Initial investment:	
Depreciable assets	$27,740
Working capital	3,000
Operation (per year for four years):	
Cash receipts	$25,000
Cash expenditures	15,000
Disinvestment:	
Salvage value of plant and equipment	$ 2,000
Recovery of working capital	3,000

Required: Determine each of the following:

1. Net present value at a 10 percent discount rate.
2. Internal rate of return.
3. Payback period.
4. Accounting rate of return on initial investment and on average investment.

Round calculations to four decimal places.

The solution to this problem is found at the end of the Chapter 15 exercises, problems, and cases.

KEY TERMS

Accounting rate of return
Bail-out period
Capital budgeting
Capital expenditures
Cost of capital
Differential analysis
Discount rate
Internal rate of return
Mutually exclusive investments

Net present value
Payback period
Present value index
Salvage value
Simple rate of return
Time adjusted rate of return
Total cost approach (to capital budgeting)

APPENDIX KEY TERMS

Annuity
Future value

Present value

REVIEW QUESTIONS

15–1   What is the relationship between long-range planning and capital budgeting?

15–2   What tasks are often assigned to the capital budgeting committee?

15–3   What purposes are served by a post-audit of approved capital expenditure proposals?

15–4   Into what three phases are a project's cash flows organized?

15–5   State three alternative definitions or descriptions of the internal rate of return.

15–6   Why is the cost of capital an important concept when discounting models are used for capital budgeting?

15–7   Distinguish between the payback period and the bail-out period.

15–8   In what way does the accounting rate of return differ from all other capital budgeting models discussed in this chapter?

15–9   What weakness is inherent in the payback period when it is used as the sole investment criterion?

15–10 What weakness is inherent in the accounting rate of return when it is used as an investment criterion?

15–11 Why are the net present value and the internal rate of return models superior to the payback and accounting rate of return models?

15–12 State two basic differences between the net present value and internal rate of return models that often lead to differences in the evaluation of competing investment proposals.

15–13 Identify several nonquantitative factors that are apt to play a decisive role in the final selection of projects for capital expenditures.

EXERCISES

15–1 Time Value of Money: Basics (Appendix)

Remember that money is of the prolific, generating nature. Money can beget money and its offspring can beget more, and so on. Five shillings turned is six; turned again it is seven and threepence, and so on until it is a hundred pounds. The more there is of it the more it produces every turning, so that the profits rise quicker and quicker.

Benjamin Franklin

Required: Using the equations and tables in the appendix, determine the answers to each of the following independent situations.

1. The future value in two years of $1,000 deposited in a savings account with interest compounded annually at 8 percent.

2. The present value of $9,000 to be received in five years, discounted at 12 percent.

3. The present value of an annuity of $2,000 per year for five years discounted at 16 percent.

4. An initial investment of $32,010 is to be returned in eight equal, annual payments. Determine the amount of each payment if the interest rate is 10 percent.

5. A proposed investment will provide cash flows of $20,000; $8,000; and $6,000; at the end of years 1, 2, and 3, respectively. Using a discount rate of 20 percent, determine the present value of these cash flows.

6. Find the present value of an investment that will pay $5,000 at the end of years 10, 11, and 12. Use a discount rate of 14 percent.

15–2 Time Value of Money: Basics (Appendix)

Required: Using the equations and tables in the appendix, determine the answers to each of the following independent situations:

1. The future value in two years of $3,000 deposited in a certificate of deposit with interest compounded annually at 10 percent.

2. The present value of $8,000 to be received in five years, discounted at 8 percent.

3. The present value of an annuity of $10,000 per year for four years discounted at 12 percent.

4. An initial investment of $14,740 is to be returned in six equal, annual payments. Determine the amount of each payment if the interest rate is 16 percent.

5. A proposed investment will provide cash flows of $6,000; $8,000; and $20,000; at the end of years 1, 2, and 3, respectively. Using a discount rate of 18 percent, determine the present value of these cash flows.

6. Find the present value of an investment that will pay $6,000 at the end of years 8, 9, and 10. Use a discount rate of 14 percent.

15–3 NPV, IRR: Equal Annual Net Cash Inflows

The Sharp Company is evaluating a capital expenditure proposal that requires an initial investment of $8,002 and has predicted cash inflows of $2,000 per year for 15 years, with no salvage value.

Requirements

a) Using a discount rate of 14 percent, determine the net present value of the investment proposal.

b) Determine the proposal's internal rate of return.

15–4 NPV, IRR: Equal Annual Net Cash Inflows

The Tack Company is evaluating a capital expenditure proposal that requires an initial investment of $28,590 and has predicted cash inflows of $7,500 per year for seven years, with no salvage value.

Requirements

a) Using a discount rate of 16 percent, determine the net present value of the investment proposal.

b) Determine the proposal's internal rate of return.

15–5 IRR, Equal Cash Flows: Interpolation

The Midway Company is evaluating a capital expenditure proposal that requires an initial investment of $26,400 and has predicted cash inflows of $10,000 per year for four years, with no salvage value.

Required: Determine the proposal's internal rate of return. Interpolate if necessary. Round all calculations to four decimal places.

15–6 IRR, Equal Cash Flows: Interpolation

The Inn Between Company is evaluating a capital expenditure proposal that requires an initial investment of $142,925 and has predicted cash inflows of $25,000 per year for 13 years, with no salvage value.

Required: Determine the proposal's internal rate of return. Interpolate, if necessary. Round all calculations to four decimal places.

15–7 NPV, IRR:
Unequal Annual
Net Cash Inflows

The Lake Ski Company is evaluating a capital expenditure proposal that has the following predicted cash flows:

Initial investment	$(42,580)
Operation:	
Year 1	18,000
Year 2	25,000
Year 3	20,000
Salvage	0

Requirements

a) Using a discount rate of 12 percent, determine the net present value of the investment proposal.

b) Determine the proposal's internal rate of return.

15–8 NPV, IRR:
Unequal Annual
Net Cash Inflows

The Alpine Ski Company is evaluating a capital expenditure proposal that has the following predicted cash flows:

Initial investment	$(40,860)
Operation:	
Year 1	20,000
Year 2	30,000
Year 3	10,000
Salvage	0

Requirements

a) Using a discount rate of 14 percent, determine the net present value of the investment proposal.

b) Determine the proposal's internal rate of return.

15–9 Payback,
Accounting Rate
of Return

Presented is information pertaining to three capital expenditure proposals:

	Proposal A	Proposal B	Proposal C
Initial investment:			
Depreciable assets	$50,000	$100,000	$70,000
Working capital	0	0	10,000
Net cash inflow from operations			
(per year for four years)	20,000	35,000	25,000
Disinvestment:			
Depreciable assets	0	20,000	10,000
Working capital	0	0	10,000

Requirements

a) Determine each proposal's payback period.

b) Determine each proposal's accounting rate of return on:

1. Initial investment.

2. Average investment.

Round calculations to three decimal places.

15–10 Payback, Accounting Rate of Return

Presented is information pertaining to three capital expenditure proposals:

	Proposal X	Proposal Y	Proposal Z
Initial investment:			
Depreciable assets	$90,000	$60,000	$95,000
Working capital	0	0	5,000
Net cash inflow from operations			
(per year for four years)	37,500	20,000	40,000
Disinvestment:			
Depreciable assets	0	10,000	15,000
Working capital	0	0	5,000

Requirements

a) Determine each proposal's payback period.

b) Determine each proposal's accounting rate of return on:

1. Initial investment.

2. Average investment.

Round calculations to three decimal places.

15–11 Survey of Capital Budgeting Models

Consider the following investment proposal:

Initial investment:	
Depreciable assets	$18,293
Working capital	2,000
Operation (per year for five years):	
Cash receipts	$ 8,000
Cash expenditures	3,000
Disinvestment:	
Salvage value of plant and equipment	$ 2,000
Recovery of working capital	2,000

Required: Determine each of the following:

1. Net present value at a 14 percent discount rate.

2. Internal rate of return.

3. Payback period.

4. Accounting rate of return on initial investment and on average investment.

Round calculations to four decimal places.

15–12 Survey of Capital Budgeting Models

Consider the following investment proposal:

Initial investment:	
Depreciable assets	$36,000
Working capital	4,000
Operation (per year for seven years):	
Cash receipts	$15,500
Cash expenditures	7,000
Disinvestment:	
Salvage value of plant and equipment	$ 4,880
Recovery of working capital	4,000

Required: Determine each of the following:

1. Net present value at a 12 percent discount rate.

2. Internal rate of return.

3. Payback period.

4. Accounting rate of return on initial investment and on average investment.

Round calculations to four decimal places.

15–13 Bail-Out, Payback, IRR, Minimum Cash Flows

The management of Low Risk, Limited, is currently evaluating the following investment proposal:

	Time 0	Year 1	Year 2	Year 3	Year 4
Initial investment	$120,000				
Disposal value during year		$60,000	$40,000	$20,000	$ 0
Net operating cash inflows		50,000	50,000	50,000	50,000

Requirements

a) Determine the proposal's bail-out period.

b) Determine the proposal's payback period.

c) Determine the proposal's internal rate of return. Do not interpolate.

d) Given the amount of the initial investment, determine the minimum annual net cash inflow required to obtain an internal rate of return of 18 percent. Round the answer to the nearest dollar.

15–14 Bail-Out, Payback, IRR, Minimum Cash Flows

The management of Limited Risk, Inc., is currently evaluating the following investment proposal:

	Time 0	Year 1	Year 2	Year 3	Year 4
Initial investment	$270,000				
Disposal value during year		$150,000	$100,000	$ 50,000	$ 0
Net operating cash inflows		100,000	100,000	100,000	100,000

Requirements

a) Determine the proposal's bail-out period.

b) Determine the proposal's payback period.

c) Determine the proposal's internal rate of return. Do not interpolate.

d) Given the amount of the initial investment, determine the minimum annual net cash inflow required to obtain an internal rate of return of 14 percent. Round the answer to the nearest dollar.

15–15 Ranking Investment Proposals with Payback, Accounting Rate of Return, and Net Present Value

Presented is information pertaining to the cash flows of three mutually exclusive investment proposals:

	Proposal A	Proposal B	Proposal C
Initial investment	$60,000	$60,000	$60,000
Operation:			
Year 1	30,000	20,000	50,000
Year 2	30,000	20,000	5,000
Year 3		20,000	5,000
Year 4		20,000	20,000
Disinvestment	0	0	0
Life	2 years	4 years	4 years

Requirements

a) Rank these investment proposals using the payback, the accounting rate of return on initial investment, and the net present value criteria. Assume that the organization's cost of capital is 10 percent. Round calculations to four decimal places.

b) Explain the difference in rankings. Which investment would you recommend?

15–16 Ranking Investment Proposals with Payback, Accounting Rate of Return, and Net Present Value

Presented is information pertaining to the cash flows of three mutually exclusive investment proposals:

	Proposal X	Proposal Y	Proposal Z
Initial investment	$45,000	$45,000	$45,000
Operation:			
Year 1	40,000	22,500	45,000
Year 2	5,000	22,500	
Year 3	22,500	22,500	
Disinvestment	0	0	0
Life	3 years	3 years	1 year

Requirements

a) Rank these investment proposals using the payback, the accounting rate of return on initial investment, and the net present value criteria. Assume that the organization's cost of capital is 14 percent. Round calculations to four decimal places.

b) Explain the difference in rankings. Which investment would you recommend?

15–17 Ranking Investment Proposals Using NPV and Present Value Index

The Megabite Dog Food Company is considering the replacement of its traditional canned dog food with dog food packaged in either resealable plastic containers or in disposable foil-lined pouches. Although either alternative will produce significant cost savings and marketing benefits, limitations on available shelf space in stores requires management to select only one alternative. Cash flow information on each alternative is presented below:

	Plastic Containers	Lined Pouches
Initial investment in necessary equipment	$50,000	$150,000
Increase in annual net cash flows	$20,000	$56,000
Life of equipment	5 years	5 years
Disposal value of equipment	$10,000	$12,000

Megabite has a 10 percent cost of capital.

Requirements

a) Evaluate the investment alternatives using the net present value and the present value index criteria.

b) Explain the difference in rankings. Which investment would you recommend?

15–18 Ranking Investment Proposals Using NPV and Present Value Index

The Sea Breeze Cat Sand Company is considering the replacement of its traditional bag packaging of "cat sand" with either reuseable plastic pails or reuseable aluminum pails. Customers would make a refundable deposit on the container each time they purchased "cat sand." Because the pails would be reuseable, the net cost of "cat sand" to customers who returned the pail for a refund would be lower than the cost of "cat sand" sold in bags. Cash flow information on each alternative is presented below:

	Plastic	Aluminum
Initial investment	$80,000	$68,000
Increase in annual net cash flows	$35,000	$30,000
Life of equipment	4 years	4 years
Disposal value of equipment	$8,000	$9,000

Sea Breeze has a 16 percent cost of capital.

Requirements

a) Evaluate the investment alternatives using the net present value and the present value index criteria.

b) Explain the difference in rankings. Which investment would you recommend?

PROBLEMS

15–19 Payback, IRR: Computational Relationships

Supply the missing data for each of the following investment proposals:

	Proposal A	Proposal B	Proposal C
Initial investment	(a)	$31,475	$113,000
Annual net cash inflow	$30,000	(c)	(e)
Economic life in years	10	6	10
Salvage value	$0	$5,000	$0
Payback period in years	(b)	(d)	5.650
Internal rate of return	12%	24%	(f)

Assume that the annual net cash inflows are equal. Round computations to four decimal places.

15–20 Accounting Rate of Return, NPV: Computational Relationships

Supply the missing data for each of the following investment proposals:

	Proposal D	Proposal E	Proposal F
Initial investment	$40,000	(c)	$80,000
Annual net cash inflow	(a)	$20,000	$30,000
Economic life in years	4	5	6
Salvage value	$0	$14,000	(e)
Accounting rate of return on initial investment	(b)	10%	(f)
Cost of capital	18%	12%	14%
Net present value	$13,800	(d)	$45,790

Assume that the annual net cash inflows are equal. Round computations to four decimal places.

15–21 NPV Analysis of Equipment Replacement Decision

DuBose Manufacturing is planning on purchasing a new machine that costs $45,000. If the new machine is purchased, an old machine will be sold for $5,000. Management is convinced that the new machine can produce the following annual cost savings:

Materials and supplies	$7,500
Maintenance	4,500

The new machine will require about $2,200 more labor annually to operate than the old machine. It will also require an overhaul, predicted to cost $6,000, at the end of six years' use. The new machine has an estimated life of eight years and a predicted salvage value of $3,000. The old machine will not have a disposal value in eight years. DuBose's cost of capital is 14 percent.

Required: Determine the net present value of purchasing the new machine. Is the replacement an acceptable investment using the net present value criterion?

15–22 NPV Analysis of Equipment Replacement Decision

The Gamma Company is interested in replacing a stamping machine with a new, improved model. The old machine has a salvage value of $10,000 now and a predicted salvage value of $2,000 in six years. If the old machine is kept, it must be rebuilt in one year at a predicted cost of $20,000.

The new machine costs $80,000 and has a predicted salvage value of $12,000 at the end of six years. If purchased, the new machine will allow cash savings of $20,000 for each of the first three years and $10,000 for each year of its remaining six-year life.

The Gamma Company's cost of capital is 14 percent.

Required: Determine the net present value of purchasing the new machine. Is the new machine an acceptable investment using the net present value criterion?

15–23 NPV Total and Differential Analysis of Replacement Decision

Gusher Petro is evaluating a proposal to purchase a new processor that would cost $120,000 and have a salvage value of $12,000 in five years. It would provide annual operating cash savings of $15,000, as detailed below:

	Old Processor	New Processor
Salaries	$34,000	$44,000
Supplies	6,000	5,000
Utilities	13,000	6,000
Cleaning and maintenance	22,000	5,000
Total cash expenditures	$75,000	$60,000

If the new processor is purchased, the old processor will be sold for its current salvage value of $30,000. If the new processor is not purchased, the old processor will be disposed of in five years at a predicted scrap value of $2,000. The old processor's present book value is $50,000. If kept, in one year the old processor will require repairs predicted to cost $40,000.

Gusher's cost of capital is 16 percent.

Requirements

a) Use the total cost approach to evaluate the alternatives of keeping the old processor and purchasing the new processor. Indicate which alternative is preferred.

b) Use the differential cost approach to evaluate the desirability of purchasing the new processor.

15–24 NPV Total and Differential Analysis of Replacement Decision

The White Snow Automatic Laundry must either have a complete overhaul of its current dry cleaning system or purchase a new one. White Snow's accountant has developed the following cost projections:

	Present System	New System
Purchase cost new	$40,000	$50,000
Remaining book value	15,000	
Overhaul needed now	20,000	
Annual cash operating costs	35,000	20,000
Current salvage value	10,000	
Salvage value in five years	2,500	10,000

If White Snow keeps the old system, the system will have to be overhauled immediately. With the overhaul, the old system will have a useful life of five more years. White Snow has a cost of capital of 20 percent.

Requirements

a) Use the total cost approach to evaluate the alternatives of keeping the old system and purchasing the new system. Indicate which alternative is preferred.

b) Use the differential cost approach to evaluate the desirability of purchasing the new system.

15–25 NPV Differential Analysis of Replacement Decision

The management of Essen Manufacturing Company is currently evaluating a proposal to purchase a new and innovative drill press as a replacement for a less efficient piece of similar equipment, which would then be sold. The cost of the equipment including delivery and installation is $175,000. If the equipment is purchased, Essen will incur costs of $5,000 in removing the present equipment and revamping service facilities. The present equipment has a book value of $100,000 and a remaining useful life of ten years. Because of new technical improvements that have made the present equipment obsolete, it now has a disposal value of only $40,000.

Management has provided you with the following tabulation of comparative manufacturing costs:

	Present Equipment	New Equipment
Annual production (units)	400,000	400,000
Annual costs:		
Direct labor	$0.075/unit	$0.05/unit
Overhead:		
Depreciation (10% of asset book value)	$20,000	$17,500
Other	$48,000	$20,000

Additional information:

- Management believes that if the current equipment is not replaced now, it will have to wait ten years before replacement is justifiable.
- Both pieces of equipment are expected to have a negligible salvage value at the end of ten years.
- Management expects to sell the entire annual production of 400,000 units.
- Essen's cost of capital is 14 percent.

Required: Evaluate the desirability of purchasing the new equipment.

15–26 Potpourri of Capital Budgeting

Select the letter corresponding to the best answer in each of the following independent cases.

1. The discount rate (hurdle rate) must be determined in advance for the:

   a) Payback period method.

   b) Time adjusted rate of return method.

   c) Internal rate of return method.

   d) Net present value method.

2. Which of the following capital budgeting techniques consider(s) cash flow over the entire life of the project?

	Internal rate of return	Payback
a)	Yes	Yes
b)	Yes	No
c)	No	Yes
d)	No	No

3. It is assumed that cash flows are reinvested at the rate earned by the investment in which of the following techniques?

	Internal rate of return	Net present value
a)	Yes	Yes
b)	Yes	No
c)	No	No
d)	No	Yes

4. On May 1, 19x5, a company purchased a new machine, which it did not have to pay for until May 1, 19x7. The total payment on May 1, 19x7, includes both principal and interest. Assuming interest at a 10 percent rate, the cost of the machine would be the total payment multiplied by what time value of money concept?

   a) Future amount of an annuity of $1.

   b) Future amount of $1.

   c) Present value of an annuity of $1.

   d) Present value of $1.

5. At December 31, 19x4, Zar Co. had a machine with an original cost of $84,000, accumulated depreciation of $60,000, and an estimated salvage value of zero. On December 31, 19x4, Zar was considering the purchase of a new machine having a five-year life, costing $120,000, and having an estimated salvage value of $20,000 at the end of five years. In its decision concerning the possible purchase of the new machine, how much should Zar consider as sunk cost at December 31, 19x4?

a) $120,000.

b) $100,000.

c) $24,000.

d) $4,000.

6. Womark Company purchased a new machine on January 1, 19x1, for $90,000 with an estimated useful life of five years and a salvage value of $10,000. The machine will be depreciated using the straight-line method. The machine is expected to produce cash inflows from operations, net of income taxes, of $36,000 a year in each of the next five years. The payback period would be:

a) 2.2 years.

b) 2.5 years.

c) 4.0 years.

d) 4.5 years.

7. Hamilton Company invested in a two-year project having an internal rate of return of 12 percent. The project is expected to produce cash flow from operations, net of income taxes, of $60,000 in the first year and $70,000 in the second year. How much will the project cost?

a) $103,610.

b) $109,370.

c) $116,090.

d) $122,510.

8. Axel Corp. is planning to buy a new machine with the expectation that this investment should earn a discounted rate of return of at least 15 percent. This machine, which costs $150,000, would yield an estimated net cash flow of $30,000 a year for ten years, after income taxes. In order to determine the net present value of buying the new machine, Axel should first multiply the $30,000 by which of the following factors?

a) 20.304 (Future amount of an ordinary annuity of $1).

b) 5.019 (Present value of an ordinary annuity of $1).

c) 4.046 (Future amount of $1).

d) 0.247 (Present value of $1).

Items 9 and 10 are based on the following data:

Amaro Hospital, a nonprofit institution not subject to income taxes, is considering the purchase of new equipment costing $20,000 in order to achieve cash savings of $5,000 per year in operating costs. The equipment's estimated useful life is ten years, with no net residual value. Amaro's cost of capital is 14 percent.

9. What factor contained in or developed from the above information should be used in computing the internal rate of return for Amaro's investment in the new equipment?

a) 5.216.

b) 4.000.

c) 1.400.

d) 0.270.

10. How much is the accounting rate of return based on Amaro's initial investment in the new equipment?

   a) 27 percent.

   b) 25 percent.

   c) 15 percent.

   d) 14 percent.

(CPA Adapted)

CASES

15–27 NPV Analysis of Labor Saving Investment: Cross-Subsidization

The Heavy Loading Company's plant has three production departments. Presented are the actual cost functions for each department:

D1: total annual overhead = $150,000 + $5DLH + $12MH.

D2: total annual overhead = $200,000 + $2DLH + $10MH.

D3: total annual overhead = $50,000 + $10DLH.

The direct labor rate is $12 per hour in all departments. Departments 1 and 2 are machine intensive, and department 3 is labor intensive. The fixed overhead in departments 1 and 2 is related to building occupancy, machine depreciation, and machine maintenance. The fixed overhead in department 3 is related to building occupancy.

The following requirements are interrelated and concern a decision to introduce labor saving equipment into department 3.

Requirements

a) Management is not aware of the actual overhead cost functions. A plantwide overhead rate, based on the historic relationship between total annual overhead for the plant and total direct labor hours for the plant, is used to assign overhead to departments and products.

   Presented are the actual number of direct labor hours (DLH) and machine hours (MH) for a typical year:

	Department 1	Department 2	Department 3
Direct labor hours	2,000	5,000	10,000
Machine hours	5,000	20,000	

   Determine the plantwide overhead rate per direct labor hour. Also determine the annual overhead assigned to department 3.

b) Management, concerned about the high cost of products subject to department 3 manufacturing operations, is evaluating a proposal to invest in a machine that would substantially reduce the labor content of department 3 operations. The machine would require an initial investment of $500,000. In addition to fixed maintenance costs of $35,000 per year, the machine would have operating costs of $15 per machine hour. It is predicted that during a typical year the machine would operate 4,000 hours. Direct labor savings would amount to 7,000 hours per year. The machine is estimated to have a life of five years with no salvage value.

Heavy Loading's cost of capital is 16 percent. In evaluating the investment proposal, management included overhead cost savings at the plantwide rate per direct labor hour determined in requirement (a). Following management's procedures, determine the investment proposal's net present value. Based on this analysis, indicate whether or not management would accept the proposal.

c) Assuming no change in costs, except in department 3, determine the plantwide overhead rate per direct labor hour if the proposal is accepted. Why does the rate change from that computed in requirement (a)? Also determine the annual overhead now assigned to department 3.

d) Evaluate the decision to invest in the new machine. Was this the correct decision? Why or why not? Provide additional analysis as appropriate.

e) Assume Heavy Loading did invest in the machine. Because the machine is special purpose, it does not have any resale value and its scrap value is exactly equal to removal costs. Based on your analysis in requirement (d), what should management do now?

15–28 NPV Analysis of Replacement and Expansion: Relevant Costs

Illinois Products Company manufactures several different products. One of the firm's principal products sells for $20 per unit. The sales manager of Illinois Products has stated repeatedly that he could sell more units of this product if they were available. In an attempt to substantiate his claim, the sales manager conducted a market research study last year at a cost of $44,000 to determine potential demand for this product. The study indicated that Illinois Products could sell 18,000 units of this product annually for the next five years.

The equipment currently in use has the capacity to produce 11,000 units annually. The variable production costs are $9 per unit. The equipment has a book value of $60,000 and a remaining useful life of five years. The salvage value is negligible now and will be zero in five years.

A maximum of 20,000 units could be produced annually on a new machine, which could be purchased for $300,000. The new machine has an estimated life of five years and no salvage value. Illinois Products' production manager has estimated that the new equipment would produce production efficiencies that would reduce the variable production costs to $7 per unit.

The sales manager felt so strongly about the need for additional capacity that he attempted to prepare an economic justification for the equipment even though this was not part of his responsibilities. His analysis, presented at the top of the next page, disappointed him because it did not justify acquiring the equipment.

Illinois Products Company has a 20 percent cost of capital.

Requirements

a) The controller of Illinois Products Company plans to prepare a discounted cash flow analysis of this investment proposal and has asked you to prepare correct calculations of:

1. The required investment in the new equipment.

2. The recurring annual cash flows.

Explain the treatment of each item you treat differently from the original analysis prepared by the sales manager.

Required investment:

Purchase price of new equipment	$300,000
Loss on disposal of old equipment	60,000
Cost of market research study	44,000
Total investment	$404,000

Annual returns:

Contribution from product:	
Using new equipment [20,000($20 − $7)]	$260,000
Using existing equipment [11,000($20 − $9)]	−121,000
Increase in contribution	$139,000
Less depreciation ($300,000/5 years)	− 60,000
Increase in income	$ 79,000
Less 20% cost of capital on additional required investment	
(0.20 × $404,000)	− 80,800
Net annual return of proposed investment in new equipment	$ (1,800)

b) Calculate the net present value of the proposed investment in the new equipment and indicate whether the investment proposal is acceptable.

(CMA Adapted)

**15–29 Project
Screening and
Evaluation
with Risk:
Multiple Criteria**

Transhemisphere uses a capital budgeting committee to evaluate and approve capital expenditure proposals. Because the committee is composed of busy executives, a staff has been assigned to assist the committee in the mechanical aspects of proposal evaluation. As a member of this staff you have been requested to evaluate five mutually exclusive capital expenditure proposals.

Transhemisphere uses multiple criteria in the evaluation of capital expenditure proposals. The criteria are designed to consider the time period monies invested in a project are unavailable for other purposes, the maximum possible time-adjusted loss on a project, and the time-adjusted relative profitability of a project. To assist in monitoring accepted proposals, the committee also requests information regarding the minimum annual cash flows required for time-adjusted break-even. The criteria are applied on a sequential basis, with only proposals that meet the earlier criteria receiving further evaluation.

Specific procedures you are to follow are as follows:

1. Determine the expected payback and bail-out period of each proposal. Only proposals having an expected bail-out and/or payback period of three years or less are subject to further evaluation.

2. Evaluate the net present value of the pessimistic cash flows associated with each project using Transhemisphere's cost of capital of 16 percent. Projects whose pessimistic cash flows have a net negative present value of $50,000 or more are eliminated from further consideration.

3. Rank the remaining projects on the basis of the internal rate of return of their expected cash flows.

4. For the highest ranked project, determine the minimum annual net cash inflows needed to obtain an internal rate of return equal to the company's cost of capital.

Information pertaining to the five capital expenditure proposals you have been asked to evaluate is presented as follows in thousands of dollars (000):

| Proposal | Initial Investment | Disposal Value at End of Year | | | Pessimistic | | Expected | |
		One	Two	Three	Annual Cash Flow	Life	Annual Cash Flow	Life
A	$196	$150	$100	$-0-	$ 40	7 years	$ 50	10 years
B	500	400	350	-0-	75	10 years	110	12 years
C	400	300	100	-0-	40	8 years	50	10 years
D	420	250	200	150	100	7 years	100	10 years
E	250	150	75	-0-	15	9 years	75	12 years

The nature of the investments is such that none of them has a disposal value after the end of their third year.

Requirements

a) Following Transhemisphere's capital budgeting procedures, evaluate the five proposals.

b) Regardless of Transhemisphere's procedures, which proposal do you recommend and why?

Round calculations to the nearest dollar. Do not interpolate.

15–30 Post-Audit and Reevaluation of Investment Proposal: NPV

The Anthony Company's capital budgeting committee is evaluating a capital expenditure proposal for the production of a stereo tuner to be sold as an add-on feature for television sets not equipped for stereophonic sound. The proposal calls for an independent contractor to construct the necessary facilities by 12/31/x0 at a total cost of $250,000. Payment for all construction costs will be made on that date and an additional $50,000 in cash will be made available on 12/31/x0 for working capital to support sales and production activities.

Management anticipates that the stereo tuner has a limited market life because of the high probability that by 19x7 all quality television sets will have built-in stereo tuners. Accordingly, the proposal specifies that production will cease on 12/31/x6. The investment in working capital will be recovered on that date, and the production facilities will be sold for $30,000. Predicted net cash inflows from operations for 19x1 through 19x6 are as follows:

19x1	$100,000
19x2	100,000
19x3	100,000
19x4	40,000
19x5	40,000
19x6	40,000

The Anthony Company has a time value of money of 16 percent. For capital budgeting purposes all cash flows are assumed to occur at the end of each year.

Requirements

a) Evaluate the capital expenditure proposal using the net present value method. Should Anthony accept the proposal?

b) Assume the capital expenditure proposal is accepted, but that construction delays caused by labor unrest and difficulties in obtaining the necessary construction permits delay the completion of the project. Payments totaling $200,000 were made to the construction company on 12/31/x0 for 19x0 construction. However, completion is now scheduled for 12/31/x1, and an additional $100,000 will be required to complete construction. If the project is continued, the additional $100,000 will be paid on 12/31/x1 and the plant will begin operations on 1/1/x2.

Because of the cost overruns, the capital budgeting committee requests a reevaluation of the project in early 19x1, before agreeing to any additional expenditures. After much effort, the following revised predictions of net operating cash inflows are developed:

19x2	$120,000
19x3	100,000
19x4	40,000
19x5	40,000
19x6	40,000

The working capital investment and disinvestment and the plant salvage values are not changed, except that the cash for working capital would now be made available on 12/31/x1.

Use the net present value method to reevaluate the initial decision to accept the proposal. Given the currently available information about the project, should it have been accepted in 19x0? *Hint:* Determine the net present value as of 12/31/x0, assuming management has not committed Anthony to the proposal.

c) Given the situation that exists in early 19x1, should management continue or cancel the project? Assume the facilities have a current salvage value of $50,000. *Hint:* Assume the decision is being made on 1/1/x1.

15–31 Post-Audit and Reevaluation of Investment Proposal: IRR

Throughout his four years in college, Ronald King worked at the local Beef Burger Restaurant in College City. Although the working conditions were good and the pay was not bad, Ron believed he could do a much better job of managing the restaurant than the current owner-manager. In particular, Ron felt that the proper use of marketing campaigns and sales incentives, such as selling a second burger for a 25 percent discount, could increase annual sales by 50 percent.

Just before graduation in 19x2, when Ron inherited $500,000 from his great-uncle, he decided to give serious consideration to buying the restaurant. It seemed like a good idea because he liked the town and its college atmosphere, knew the business, and always wanted to work for himself. He also knew that the current owner wanted to sell the restaurant and retire to Florida.

As part of a small business management course, Ron developed the following income statement for the restaurant's 19x1 operations:

Beef Burger Restaurant: College City
Income Statement
For the year ended December 31, 19x1

Sales:		$450,000
Expenses:		
Cost of food	$150,000	
Supplies	20,000	
Employee expenses	140,000	
Utilities	28,000	
Property taxes	20,000	
Insurance	10,000	
Advertising	8,000	
Depreciation	60,000	−436,000
Net income		$ 14,000

Ron believed the cost of food and supplies were all variable, the employee expenses and utilities were half variable and half fixed in 19x1, and all other expenses were fixed.

If Ron purchased the restaurant and followed through on his plans, he believed there would be a 50 percent increase in unit sales volume and all variable costs. Of the fixed costs, only advertising would increase, by $12,000. The use of discounts and special promotions would, however, limit the increase in sales revenue to only 40 percent even though sales volume increased 50 percent.

Requirements

a) Determine:

1. The current annual net cash inflow.

2. The predicted annual net cash inflow if Ron executes his plans and his assumptions are correct.

b) Ron believes his plan would produce equal net cash inflows during each of the next 15 years, the period remaining on a long-term lease for the land the restaurant is built on. At the end of that time, the restaurant would have to be demolished at a predicted net cost of $80,000. Assuming Ron would otherwise invest the money in bonds expected to yield 12 percent, determine the maximum amount he could pay for the restaurant.

c) Assume Ron accepts an offer from the current owner to buy the restaurant for $400,000. Unfortunately, although the expected increase in sales volume does occur, customers make much more extensive use of the promotions than Ron had anticipated. As a result, total sales revenues are 8 percent below projections. Furthermore, to improve employee attitudes, Ron gave a 10 percent raise immediately after purchasing the restaurant.

Reevaluate the initial decision using the actual sales revenue and the increase in labor costs, assuming conditions will remain unchanged over the remaining life of the project. Was the investment decision a wise one? Round calculations to the nearest dollar.

d) Ron can sell the restaurant to a large franchise operator for $300,000. Alternatively, he believes that additional annual marketing expenditures and changes in promotions costing $20,000 per year can bring the sales revenues up to their original projections. Should Ron sell the restaurant, or keep it and make the additional expenditures? Round calculations to the nearest dollar. *Hint:* Ron has just bought the restaurant.

REVIEW PROBLEM SOLUTION

Basic computations:

Initial investment:

Depreciable assets	$27,740
Working capital	3,000
Total	$30,740

Operation:

Cash receipts	$25,000
Cash expenditures	−15,000
Net cash inflow	$10,000

Disinvestment:

Sale of depreciable assets	$ 2,000
Recovery of working capital	3,000
Total	$ 5,000

a) Net present value at a 10 percent discount rate:

	Predicted Cash Inflows (Outflows)	Year(s) of Cash Flows	10% Present Value Factor	Present Value of Cash Flows
Initial investment	$(30,740)	0	1.000	$(30,740)
Operation	10,000	1–4	3.170	31,700
Disinvestment	5,000	4	0.683	3,415
Net present value of all cash flows				$ 4,375

b) Internal rate of return:

Because the proposal has a positive net present value when discounted at 10 percent, its internal rate of return must be greater than 10 percent. Through a trial-and-error approach, the internal rate of return is determined to be 16 percent.

	Predicted Cash Inflows (Outflows)	Year(s) of Cash Flows	16% Present Value Factor	Present Value of Cash Flows
Initial investment	$(30,740)	0	1.000	$(30,740)
Operation	10,000	1–4	2.798	27,980
Disinvestment	5,000	4	0.552	2,760
Net present value of all cash flows				$ 0

c) Payback period $= \dfrac{\$30,740}{\$10,000}$

$= \underline{3.074}$ years

d) Accounting rate of return on initial and average investments:

Annual net cash inflow from operations	$10,000
Less average annual depreciation [($27,740 − $2,000)/4]	− 6,435
Average annual increase in net income	$ 3,565

Average investment $= \dfrac{\$30,740 + \$5,000}{2}$

$= \underline{\$17,870}$

Accounting rate of return on initial investment $= \dfrac{\$3,565}{\$30,740}$

$= \underline{0.1160}$ or $\underline{11.60\%}$

Accounting rate of return on average investment $= \dfrac{\$3,565}{\$17,870}$

$= \underline{0.1995}$ or $\underline{19.95\%}$

Impact of Taxes on Capital Budgeting and Other Management Decisions

Learning Objectives

Upon completion of this chapter you should:

- **Be able to describe the four primary types of taxes.**

- **Be familiar with the general tax computation model for a corporation.**

- **Understand the major effects of taxes on capital budgeting decisions.**

- **Be able to determine the net present value of capital expenditure proposals taking tax effects into consideration.**

- **Be able to identify the four major types of organizational forms and describe generally the tax treatment of each.**

- **Be aware of the tax considerations affecting the selection of an organizational form and tax entity.**

- **Be familiar with several major areas in which alternative tax treatments are available.**

It is important for managers to be able to determine the economic impact of *taxes* on business decisions. Because cash outlays for all expenses adversely affect profitability and liquidity, planning and control measures should apply to all costs, including taxes. A primary consideration of the manager in tax planning is tax avoidance. Unlike *tax evasion* (which is the illegal nonpayment of taxes), **tax avoidance** is the reduction of taxes through legitimate means. For example, failure to report a gain on the sale of assets constitutes tax evasion, whereas planning the disposition of assets through a nontaxable exchange for other assets is a legitimate means of tax avoidance.

MANAGERIAL PRACTICE 16.1

Computers Simplify Tax Drudgery

BNA Software offers two software packages that simplify fixed asset and corporate tax calculations: Fixed Asset Management System and Corporate Tax Spreadsheet. Fixed Asset Management handles 20,000 records and offers 32 depreciation methods and 29 standard reports. It integrates with Corporate Tax Spreadsheet, which produces Lotus 1-2-3–readable files, thereby allowing the operator to perform "what-if" analyses and determine the tax consequences of various situations. The Spreadsheet package is quite thorough, including calculations for federal, state, and alternative minimum tax as well as tracking carryovers and carrybacks of net operating losses, capital losses, and tax credits.

EZTax-Prep 1040 and EZTax-Plan are template packages designed by EZWare Corp. for use with Microsoft Excel on a Macintosh. EZTax-Prep enables the user to enter revenue and deduction data into the program and generate finished tax returns. EZTax-Plan is a tax planning package that allows the user to plan tax consequences of business decisions up to 40 years into the future. It uses price indexes to take into account inflation and price changes. A clever feature of EZTax-Prep is that it includes Audit Alert, which automatically warns the user if deductions in a tax return are significantly outside the norms for taxpayers in a similar income category.

Source: Claire Barth, "Computers & Accounting," *Management Accounting* (December 1989): 14–15.

In situations where tax avoidance is not an available or feasible option, the manager should consider deferring the payment of taxes. **Tax deferral** refers to the planning and timing of transactions so that the taxpayer qualifies for delays in the payment of taxes. Because of the time value of money, delaying tax payments into the future reduces their present value. Therefore, the objective in tax deferral is to plan transactions within the provisions of the tax law so that the present value of present and future tax payments is minimized.

The purpose of this chapter is to provide an overview of the major types of taxes that affect management decisions. The specific effects of taxes on capital budgeting and other management decisions are also discussed. Because of the complexity of this subject, our objective is to expose the reader only to the general significance of taxes in business decision making. For specific applications of tax laws, managers should ordinarily consult the advice of experts in the field of taxation.

TYPES OF TAXES

The types of taxes that affect business enterprises may be classified into four categories: income taxes, property taxes, excise taxes, and foreign taxes.

Income Taxes

An **income tax** is any tax that is based on income. Some examples of income that is taxed are the incomes of individuals, corporations, estates, and trusts. The income of proprietorships or partnerships is not taxed directly; instead, it is passed through to the owners who must pay taxes on the business income based on their individual tax status. The federal government and most states and several large cities collect income taxes from individuals and corporations.

Property Taxes

A **property tax** is a tax based on the ownership of property and is usually determined by multiplying a statutory tax rate (often referred to as the tax millage) times the assessed value of the property. The assessed value is usually a specified percentage of estimated fair market value. Tangible property taxes are levied on real property (land and buildings) and tangible personal property (such as equipment and inventories). Intangible personal property taxes are levied on property such as investment securities and receivables. There is no federal property tax, tangible or intangible; however, state and local governments rely heavily on property taxes.

Excise Taxes

An **excise tax** is a tax on an activity performed by, or a privilege granted to, the taxed party. Excise taxes are the broadest form of taxes and include many different types of taxes, such as sales taxes, licenses to do business, cigarette and alcohol taxes, gasoline and other fuel taxes, telephone taxes, import duties, and gift taxes. Excise taxes are levied by government authorities at federal, state, and local levels.

Foreign Taxes

Businesses that operate in foreign countries or conduct transactions with foreign enterprises may be affected by taxes imposed by foreign governments. Most of the types of taxes discussed above can also be found in various foreign countries. In addition, several European countries have adopted a value added tax.

Under a **value added tax,** manufacturers pay taxes based on the value added to goods that they produce during the period. For example, if a manufacturer of electric motors purchases component parts for $25 and sells assembled motors for $45, the value added is $20. The value added tax would be $20 times the tax rate. An appliance manufacturer purchasing the motors for $45, and adding other parts and supplies costing $105, pays value added tax only on the excess of its selling price over $150 ($45 plus $105). Under a value added system, the total value of the final consumable product is taxed as the product moves through the manufacturing and distribution process, but without any duplication of taxes. Several members in the U.S. Congress have advocated the adoption of a value added tax as a partial or total substitute for business income taxes. Many foreign countries, however, have both value added and income taxes.

MEASURING TAXES

For all types of taxes two basic variables determine the amount of taxes owed—the tax base and the tax rate. A **tax base** is a monetary measurement of the conditions or activities subject to taxes. Examples of tax bases are taxable income for income taxes, assessed value of property for property taxes, and total sales for sales taxes. A **tax rate** is a percentage that is multiplied times the tax base to determine total taxes.

For most taxes, the tax base is either provided directly by the taxing authority or is easily determined; however, computing the tax base for income taxes is usually somewhat difficult. Federal and other income taxes are administered under a self-assessment system where the party being taxed has the responsibility of measuring the tax base and computing the taxes due. The general procedure for computing the tax base for corporate income taxes is as follows:

Total revenues earned	$xx	
Less: Nontaxable revenues	xx	
Gross income		$xx
Total expenses and deductions	$xx	
Less: Nondeductible expenses	xx	
Allowable deductions		−xx
Taxable income		$xx

Income tax rates are normally *graduated*; that is, the tax rate increases as taxable income increases. For example, federal income taxes on corporations are computed as follows:

- 15 percent on the first $50,000 of taxable income,
- 25 percent on the next $25,000 of taxable income, and
- 34 percent on all taxable income in excess of $75,000.[1]

Higher tax rates are applied only to *marginal,* or additional, taxable income; therefore, a corporation that has $100,000 of taxable income pays taxes at the 34 percent rate on only the last $25,000 of taxable income. On taxable income of $100,000, total federal income taxes are $22,250, computed as follows:

15% of $50,000	$ 7,500
25% of 25,000	6,250
34% of 25,000	8,500
Total taxes	$22,250

TAXES IN CAPITAL BUDGETING DECISIONS

Capital budgeting was discussed in Chapter 15 as a process for evaluating the desirability of alternative capital expenditure proposals. Using present value techniques, alternative capital investment projects can be reduced to a common basis for making relative comparisons. All future cash outflows and inflows are converted to present value equivalents using a predetermined discount rate. Cash flows from capital expenditures usually affect cash outflows for income taxes.

Cash flows related to capital expenditures may affect taxes in several different ways:

- Operating income[2] generated by capital expenditures increases income taxes.
- Reduced operating costs resulting from capital expenditures increase income taxes.
- Depreciation of capital assets reduces income taxes.
- A gain on the sale of capital assets increases income taxes, whereas a loss on the sale of capital assets decreases income taxes.

---

[1] An additional 5 percent tax is imposed on income between $100,000 and $335,000, which in effect creates a flat tax of 34 percent for corporations with taxable income of $335,000 or more.

[2] Operating income equals revenues less the expenses generated by a capital expenditure.

Increased Revenues

A capital expenditure that is expected to generate annual cash flows of $10,000 before taxes will not produce net annual cash flows of $10,000 unless the revenue from the project is nontaxable. Ordinarily, taxes must be paid on a capital project's net revenue, thus reducing the net cash inflow. Assuming a 34 percent tax rate,[3] the annual after-tax cash flow is $6,600:

$$\text{After-tax cash flow} = \text{Pretax cash flow} - (\text{Pretax cash flow} \times \text{Tax rate}),$$
$$\text{After-tax cash flow} = \$10,000 - (\$10,000 \times 0.34)$$
$$= \$6,600.$$

Most managers prefer to use the following variation of the above equation:

$$\text{After-tax cash flow} = \text{Pretax cash flow} \times (1 - \text{Tax rate}),$$
$$\text{After-tax cash flow} = \$10,000 \times (1 - 0.34)$$
$$= \$6,600.$$

The after-tax cash flow amount is multiplied times the appropriate discount factor to determine the present value of after-tax cash flows.

Decreased Costs

Many capital outlays have the objective of reducing costs rather than increasing revenues. Cost reduction measures decrease the amount of tax deductible expenses, increase taxable income, and increase income taxes. The after-tax effect of cost reductions can be computed using the equation discussed previously. For example, if a capital project is expected to save $8,000 per year in costs, the after-tax cost savings, assuming a 34 percent tax rate, are $5,280 [$8,000 × (1 − 0.34)].

Depreciation

Depreciation is a systematic procedure for allocating the acquisition cost of a capital asset over its useful life. The annual depreciation allocation is not accompanied by a cash outlay; however, it is an expense deduction in computing taxable income. Therefore, depreciation does provide an indirect inflow of cash from the reduction of taxes that it produces. This reduction of income taxes is often referred to as the **depreciation tax shield.** Since the income tax law does not allow capital expenditures to be fully deducted from income when they are made, it is only logical that depreciation deductions should be allowed.

---

[3] Throughout this chapter, unless otherwise stated, the maximum corporate federal tax rate of 34 percent is used to illustrate the impact of taxes on management decisions. All state and local taxes are ignored for purposes of illustration.

The current tax rules governing the depreciation deduction represent a combination of rules under two previous tax laws—the 1969 Act and the 1981 Act. The 1969 Act established the **Asset Depreciation Range (ADR)** guidelines for determining the appropriate useful life for depreciable assets. The ADR guidelines provide estimated useful lives for many different types of assets,

MANAGERIAL PRACTICE 16.2

Is It Equipment or Is It a Building?

Since tangible personal property used in a business is normally depreciated over 7 years and nonresidential real estate (and related components), over 31.5 years, taxpayers may realize substantial savings by classifying certain building-related assets as personal property rather than as structural components. Further, tangible personal property is depreciated using double declining balance depreciation, whereas buildings and their structural components are depreciated by the straight-line method.

Certain walls, partitions, ceilings, windows, and doors are clearly part of a building, and their costs should be depreciated as part of building costs. In other cases, it isn't so clear. In the case of *Minot Federal Savings & Loan Association* v. *U.S.,* the court held that movable office partitions were tangible personal property and not structural components. In the case of *Morrison* v. *U.S.,* the Tax Court held that an electrical distribution system was not a structural component of the building, because it existed to supply electricity to kitchen equipment. Further, the court held that plumbing installed below the concrete floors to provide water for specific kitchen equipment was also tangible personal property, even though it was permanently attached to the building. The IRS has held that stadium seats and flagpoles attached to the concrete stadium structure are tangible personal property, whereas the stadium structure itself is a building.

Determining the proper classification of building-related assets may not be easy, but it may well be worth the cost of the potential conflict with the IRS or of litigation if it results in substantially reducing asset life for depreciation purposes. The tax savings can be substantial.

Source: Gregory T. Bryant and Elliott Kahn, "Proper Classification of Depreciable Property Produces Large Tax Savings," *Taxation for Accountants* (November 1989): 332–337.

including assets related to specialized industries. The 1981 Act created the Accelerated Cost Recovery System (ACRS) and assigned all depreciable assets to one of four broad asset classifications, which were subject to highly accelerated rates of cost recovery. As originally designed, ACRS depreciation periods recovered cost over a period much shorter than an asset's estimated useful life.

Current depreciation rules, which are based on the Modified Accelerated Cost Recovery System (MACRS) created by the Tax Reform Act of 1986, require two steps in determining the depreciation deduction. First, the ADR guidelines are used to determine the estimated useful lives of depreciable assets. Second, based on their ADR lives, assets are assigned to MACRS classes, which determine the allowable depreciation period and depreciation method. Typically, the MACRS depreciation life is shorter than the ADR estimated useful life. For example, if an asset has an ADR estimated useful life of four years, it is classified into a three-year MACRS classification and is depreciated using the 200 percent declining balance method. The result is that most assets are depreciated over a shorter period for tax purposes than for accounting purposes.

There are eight different MACRS classes, six for personal property and two for real property. Exhibit 16–1 presents a summary of these eight classes, their related ADRs and depreciation methods, and examples of assets in each class. Note that personal property may be depreciated over periods ranging from three years to twenty years using the 200 percent or 150 percent declining balance depreciation methods, whereas real property may be depreciated over 27.5 or 31.5 years using only the straight-line depreciation method. Assets for which an ADR has not been provided are depreciated in the seven-year MACRS class. For personal property, the depreciation method may be switched to straight-line at the point where it provides higher depreciation deductions than the declining balance method. This will always occur in the year in which the straight-line rate, based on the remaining life, is greater than the original declining balance depreciation rate.

To avoid having to recognize various short periods of depreciation in the years of acquisition and retirement, most depreciation calculations for tax purposes must assume a midyear convention, which treats property as if it were placed in service at midyear in the year of acquisition and retired at midyear in the last year of its depreciable life. The midyear convention in effect causes the depreciation deductions for an asset to be spread over one year more than the number of years represented by its MACRS classification. For example, an asset in the three-year MACRS classification would be attributed one-half year's depreciation in years 1 and 4, and a full year's depreciation in years 2 and 3, resulting in the equivalent of three full years of depreciation spread over four years. The tax laws also provide for a mid-quarter convention in some situations, but throughout this chapter we will assume the use only of the midyear convention.

An alternative to the MACRS method of depreciation is also available. It allows taxpayers to depreciate assets over their ADR estimated lives using the

EXHIBIT 16–1   Tax Depreciation Asset Lives and Calculation Methods

ADR Asset Lives	MACRS Life	Depreciation Method	Examples
Personal property:			
4 years or less	3 years	200% declining balance	Specialized tools, certain breeding stock
More than 4 but less than 10 years	5 years	200% declining balance	Automobiles, computers, office machines
10 or more but less than 16 years	7 years	200% declining balance	Single-purpose agricultural or horticultural structures, office furniture and fixtures, and most machinery and equipment
16 or more but less than 20 years	10 years	200% declining balance	Railroad cars, barges, tugs
20 or more but less than 25 years	15 years	150% declining balance	Telecommunication distribution-plant equipment
25 years or more	20 years	150% declining balance	Municipal sewers, farm buildings
Real property:			
All residential	27.5 years	Straight-line	Apartments and other rental housing
All nonresidential	31.5 years	Straight-line	Offices, warehouses

straight-line method. For this alternative calculation, assets for which there is no ADR life are depreciated over 12 years and real property is depreciated over 40 years, except for low-income housing, which is depreciated over 27.5 years.

To illustrate the present value of the depreciation tax shield, assume that machinery purchased in 19x1 has an ADR estimated useful life of four years and a depreciable cost of $15,000. The amount of the annual depreciation tax shield will vary depending on whether the taxpayer elects to use the MACRS class life of three years with 200 percent double declining depreciation or the alternative straight-line depreciation for the four-year ADR useful life. Under both options, one-half year's depreciation would be recognized in the first and last years of the depreciation period.

The annual MACRS depreciation deductions calculated using the 200 percent declining balance method, and the related tax savings are as follows:

Year	Depreciation Method*	(1) Depreciation Base**	(2) Depreciation Rate***	(3) (1) × (2) Annual Depreciation	(4) Tax Rate	(5) (3) × (4) Tax Shield
1	DB	$15,000	$\frac{1}{2} \times \frac{2}{3}$	$ 5,000	0.34	$1,700
2	DB	10,000	$\frac{2}{3}$	6,667	0.34	2,267
3	SL	3,333	$1 \div 1\frac{1}{2}$	2,222	0.34	755
4	SL	3,333	$\frac{1}{2} \div 1\frac{1}{2}$	1,111	0.34	378
				$15,000		$5,100

* DB represents declining balance method, and SL represents straight-line method.

** Under declining balance depreciation, the depreciation base is the book value (cost − accumulated depreciation) of the asset at the beginning of the year. When a company switches to the straight-line method (as this company did in year 3), the depreciation base for the remaining life of the asset is the book value of the asset at the beginning of the year in which the switch occurred.

*** The depreciation rate is 200 percent times the straight-line rate of $\frac{1}{3}$, or $\frac{2}{3}$. Applying the midyear convention, the depreciation in the first year is one-half the normal first year depreciation. In year 3, the depreciation method is switched to straight-line, which results in writing off the undepreciated base of $3,333 over the remaining $1\frac{1}{2}$ years.

The annual straight-line depreciation deductions using the ADR asset life of four years and the related tax savings are as follows:

Year	(1) Cost	(2) Depreciation Rate	(3) (1) × (2) Annual Depreciation*	(4) Tax Rate	(5) (3) × (4) Tax Shield
1	$15,000	$\frac{1}{2} \times \frac{1}{4}$	$ 1,875	0.34	$ 637.50
2	15,000	$\frac{1}{4}$	3,750	0.34	1,275.00
3	15,000	$\frac{1}{4}$	3,750	0.34	1,275.00
4	15,000	$\frac{1}{4}$	3,750	0.34	1,275.00
5	15,000	$\frac{1}{2} \times \frac{1}{4}$	1,875	0.34	637.50
			$15,000		$5,100.00

* Applying the midyear convention, the depreciation amounts for years 1 and 5 are equal to one-half the normal full-year straight-line amount. Consequently, even though the MACRS life is four years, it takes five years to recognize four full years of depreciation.

Using a 12 percent discount rate, the present values of the depreciation tax shields for MACRS and straight-line depreciation are summarized below.

		MACRS Rates		Straight-Line Rates	
	(1)	*(2)*	*(3)*	*(4)*	*(5)*
	12 Percent		*(1) × (2)*		*(1) × (4)*
	Present Value	*Tax*	*Present Value*	*Tax*	*Present Value*
Year	*Factor*	*Shield*	*of Tax Shield*	*Shield*	*of Tax Shield*
1	0.893	$1,700	$1,518	$ 637.50	$ 569
2	0.797	2,267	1,807	1,275.00	1,016
3	0.712	755	538	1,275.00	908
4	0.636	378	240	1,275.00	811
5	0.567	—	—	637.50	361
		$5,100	$4,103	$5,100.00	$3,665

Note that both depreciation methods produce $5,100 of tax shield over the life of the capital project. However, because of the differences in the timing of these reductions, the present value of the depreciation tax savings is greater using the MACRS 200 percent declining balance method than using the alternative straight-line method. As long as there is taxable income to be absorbed by depreciation, the method that provides the most accelerated recovery of capital asset cost will also provide the highest present value of the tax shield.

Gain or Loss on Sale of Capital Assets

To determine the total net present value of a capital expenditure, it is necessary to include as cash inflow any expected proceeds from the sale of the asset at the end of its useful life. If a taxable gain is realized on the sale of an asset, the gain increases income taxes, which reduces the net cash generated by the sale. On the other hand, a loss on the sale of an asset is deducted in computing taxable income and, therefore, reduces income taxes. In this case the tax reduction represents additional cash inflow generated by the asset. This cash savings is added to the selling price of the asset to determine the net cash generated by the sale.

To illustrate, assume an asset has a book value (cost less accumulated depreciation) of $5,000 and is sold before the end of its useful life for $7,000. The sale results in a taxable gain of $2,000 ($7,000 − $5,000). Cash generated directly by the sale is $7,000, but the $2,000 gain increases taxes by $680 ($2,000 × 0.34); therefore, the net cash generated by the sale of the asset is $6,320 ($7,000 − $680). If the asset sells for only $3,000, there is a tax deductible loss of $2,000 ($3,000 − $5,000) that reduces taxes by $680 ($2,000 × 0.34). In this case the net cash generated is $3,680, the selling price of $3,000 plus the tax savings of $680.[4]

---

[4] In certain circumstances, part of the gain or loss may qualify for special treatment under the capital gains and losses provisions.

The tax effects of gains and losses related to asset dispositions must also be taken into consideration in a capital budgeting decision that involves replacing an asset currently in use. The gain or loss on the sale of the old asset increases or decreases both taxes and the net cash generated by the sale.

Capital Budgeting with Taxes Illustrated

To illustrate how the various effects of income taxes enter into the capital budgeting analysis, assume that Willoughby's Courier Service is considering purchasing a small delivery truck that costs $12,000 and is predicted to generate cash revenues of $6,000 per year net of operating costs. Willoughby's predicts that it can be sold for $2,500 after six years of use. Willoughby's has a $500 offer from one of its customers for the old truck, which is fully depreciated. The new truck qualifies for MACRS five-year 200 percent declining balance depreciation. Willoughby's capital investment policy requires new capital expenditures to produce a positive net present value using a 12 percent discount rate. The analysis of the proposal, including tax effects, is presented in Exhibit 16–2.

Exhibit 16–2 shows that Willoughby's can expect a positive net present value of $8,458 on the investment after considering all cash flows, including those related to income taxes. Although this alternative might appear to be a desirable investment, Willoughby's should consider all other feasible alternatives before making a decision, including purchasing other trucks, leasing possibilities, and even the alternative of keeping the old truck. In each case, the analysis of cash flows should include the cash flow effects of taxes.

FORMS OF ORGANIZATION AND TAXES

The income tax consequences of management decisions are often affected by the legal form under which a business is organized. The basic forms of business organization are *proprietorships, partnerships,* and *corporations.* As discussed earlier, the general model for computing taxes includes a tax base and the appropriate tax rates. To evaluate the differences in taxes for the three alternative business forms, it is necessary to analyze differences in their respective income tax bases and tax rates. The following discussion is limited to federal income tax considerations.

Sole Proprietorships

A **sole proprietorship** is an unincorporated business owned by one individual. Legally, a proprietorship is not a separate entity; therefore, business transactions of a proprietorship are taxed as transactions of the individual taxpayer. All business revenues increase and all business expenses reduce the proprietor's individual income tax base. A proprietor combines business net income with all other types of income (such as salaries, interest, and dividends) in determining total taxable income.

Tax rates for individuals generally range from 15 percent to 28 percent. Under the Tax Reform Act of 1986, single individuals, for years after 1987, pay taxes at the 28 percent rate on all taxable income exceeding $17,850. Married

EXHIBIT 16–2   Analysis of Capital Expenditure Including Tax Effects

	(1)	(2)	(3)	(4) (1) × (3)
Cash Flow Item*	Actual Cash Inflows (Outflows)	Year(s) of Cash Flows	12% Present Value Factor	Present Value of Cash Flows
Purchase of new truck	$(12,000)	0	1.000	$(12,000)
Sale of old truck	500	0	1.000	500
Taxes on gain on sale of old truck ($500 × 0.34)	(170)	0	1.000	(170)
Annual operating income generated by truck	6,000	1–6	4.111	24,666
Taxes on annual operating income ($6,000 × 0.34)	(2,040)	1–6	4.111	(8,386)
Tax savings on depreciation**				
Year 1	816	1	0.893	729
Year 2	1,306	2	0.797	1,041
Year 3	783	3	0.712	557
Year 4	470	4	0.636	299
Year 5	470	5	0.567	266
Year 6	235	6	0.507	119
Sale of new truck	2,500	6	0.507	1,268
Taxes on gain on sale of new truck† ($2,500 × 0.34)	(850)	6	0.507	(431)
Net present value of all cash flows				$ 8,458

* All cash flows occur at the end of the year.

** Depreciation cash flow computations:

Year	Depreciation Method	Depreciation Base		Depreciation Rate††		Annual Depreciation		Tax Rate		Cash Savings
1	DB	$12,000	×	$\frac{1}{2} \times \frac{2}{5}$	=	$2,400	×	0.34	=	$ 816
2	DB	9,600	×	$\frac{2}{5}$	=	3,840	×	0.34	=	1,306
3	DB	5,760	×	$\frac{2}{5}$	=	2,304	×	0.34	=	783
4	SL	3,456	×	$1 \div 2\frac{1}{2}$	=	1,382	×	0.34	=	470
5	SL	3,456	×	$1 \div 2\frac{1}{2}$	=	1,382	×	0.34	=	470
6	SL	3,456	×	$\frac{1}{2} \div 2\frac{1}{2}$	=	692	×	0.34	=	235

†† Depreciation based on five-year MACRS class and the 200 percent declining balance method. Switched to the straight-line method after year three and depreciated the remaining book value of $3,456 over the remaining $2\frac{1}{2}$ years.

† The gain on the sale of the truck is equal to the selling price since the truck is fully depreciated on the date of its expected sale.

individuals filing joint tax returns reach the 28 percent tax bracket at taxable income of $29,750. In addition, a limited 33 percent tax rate applies to taxable income between $44,900 and $93,130 for single individuals and between $74,850 and $155,320 for married taxpayers filing jointly. The effect of this limited tax rate increase is that it phases out the 15 percent rate for these higher-income taxpayers.

Partnerships

A **partnership** is an unincorporated business owned by two or more individuals.[5] These businesses are required to report taxable income to the Internal Revenue Service (IRS); however, they do not pay taxes on their income. Instead, *the income of partnerships is allocated to the individual partners* who include their pro rata share of partnership income in their individual taxable income. All income of the partnership is allocated to the partners whether or not an equal amount of cash or other assets is distributed to the partners. Consequently, partners may be required to pay taxes on income that they actually have not received during the period. Partnership income is taxed to the individual partners at rates applicable to the partners' income, that is, at a maximum rate of 28 percent for individuals and 34 percent for corporations.

Corporations

A **corporation** is a legally recognized entity created by an act of the state and empowered to conduct business activities within the provisions of a corporate charter issued by the government of the state of incorporation. As a separate legal entity, a corporation is not dependent on its owners for legal recognition. It can conduct in its own name almost any transaction that an individual can conduct.

Unlike proprietorships and partnerships, a corporation is a separate taxable entity that must pay taxes on its taxable income. In addition, any dividends distributed by a corporation to its owners (shareholders) must be included in the income tax base of the individual owners. Consequently, *dividend income received by corporate stockholders is subject to double taxation*—corporate taxes and individual taxes. To illustrate the potential impact of double taxation, assume that a corporation distributes a $66,000 dividend, representing the amount remaining after subtracting corporate taxes at 34 percent on $100,000 of earnings. Assuming the stockholders receiving the dividends are in the 28 percent tax bracket, they pay $18,480 taxes on the dividends received. The income available to the stockholders after taxes is only $47,520 (or $66,000 less $18,480). As shown at the top of the next page, of the $100,000 in corporate taxable income, corporate taxes of $34,000 and individual taxes of $18,480 are paid for a total of $52,480, leaving only $47,520 to the stockholders after the payment of corporate and individual income taxes.

---

[5] Although partners are ordinarily individuals, other entities may also form a partnership. For example, the partners of a partnership may consist of a combination of individuals, corporations, trusts, and even other partnerships.

Corporate income providing dividends	$100,000
Less: Corporate income taxes (34%)	– 34,000
Total dividend distributed	$ 66,000
Less: Individual income taxes (28%)	– 18,480
Income to stockholders after corporate and individual income taxes	$ 47,520

Salaries paid to corporate employees who are also stockholders are deductible business expenses of the corporation in computing taxable income. The income used to pay salaries to stockholders, therefore, avoids corporate taxes and is taxed only to the stockholders. In the example above, if the $100,000 of corporate income that provided the dividends had been distributed as salaries, no corporate income taxes would have been paid. The employee-stockholders would have received the full $100,000 as salaries and would have paid $28,000 ($100,000 × 0.28) in individual taxes, leaving them $72,000 after taxes. By paying salaries instead of dividends, total taxes decrease from $52,480 to $28,000, and total after-tax income available to the employee-shareholders increases from $47,520 to $72,000. Distributions to shareholders cannot be arbitrarily designated as salaries to avoid double taxation. According to the federal tax law, salary payments must be commensurate with services provided by the stockholders to the corporation. Otherwise, the Internal Revenue Service will disallow the salary deduction to the corporation and treat the distribution as a dividend.

Subchapter S Corporations

A **subchapter S corporation** is a business that is legally organized as a corporation, but has opted under a special provision of the tax law to be taxed as a partnership. A subchapter S corporation enjoys the legal advantages of incorporation (such as limited liability and unlimited life), without the disadvantages of corporate taxation. Like a partnership, the income of a subchapter S corporation is allocated to the owners and included in their taxable income whether or not it is actually distributed to them. The corporate income is allocated in proportion to the ownership percentages of the stockholders.

To qualify for subchapter S tax treatment, a corporation must (1) have no more than 35 stockholders; (2) have only one class of stock; (3) have no stockholders other than individuals, estates, and trusts; (4) have no shareholders who are nonresident aliens; and (5) have the approval of all stockholders for the tax option treatment.

SELECTING A TAX ENTITY

Selection of an organizational form and tax entity is an easy decision for most large business enterprises. Clearly, the majority of all large organizations find it advantageous and necessary to operate and be taxed as *corporations*. The advantages of incorporation for large businesses are related to the following:

- The ease with which capital funds can be generated through the issuance of publicly traded securities.
- The ease with which ownership can be readily transferred through the sale of shares of stock.
- The limitation of liability for owners of corporate stock to the amounts of their investments.
- The unlimited life of corporate organizations.

Although examples are not as numerous, some very large businesses operate as partnerships. For example, most public accounting firms are organized as partnerships; several of them have more than 2,000 partners and generate more than $4 billion in revenues annually. The relatively small number of owners and the low turnover of ownership make the partnership alternative feasible for these organizations. Most large corporations, however, have thousands (in many cases millions) of different owners, and changes in ownership occur daily as shares of capital stock are purchased and sold. The corporate form is the only feasible alternative for these organizations.

Organizations that are not constrained by their large size to operate as corporations may base the organizational decision to a large extent on tax considerations. Although there are no clear-cut rules for determining which organizational form and tax entity should be adopted, there are several tax-related variables discussed below that should be considered.

Utilization of Income

Business income can be either distributed to the owners or reinvested into the business for operating or expansion purposes. If the owners anticipate distribution of profits, incorporation poses the potential problem of double taxation. Even if earnings are not distributed, incorporation probably produces the highest taxes since the maximum corporate rate is higher than the maximum individual rate (34 percent versus 28 percent).

Utilization of Operating Losses

If a business has a negative taxable income (that is, expenses exceed revenues), the result is an operating loss. Obviously, in this situation no income taxes are due on current business operations; however, in some cases the taxpayer may be able to offset current business losses against profits or gains from other sources, or even against the organization's profits from other years. From the standpoint of operating losses, it is generally desirable to use the losses to offset profits from other sources. For example, if an individual has two businesses and one has taxable income of $10,000, whereas the other has an operating loss of $10,000, the taxpayer would prefer not to pay any taxes since the combined net income is zero. Operating losses of one business can be offset against profits of another business owned by the taxpayer only if the businesses are organized as proprietorships, partnerships, or subchapter S corporations. The income or loss of a regular corporation ordinarily cannot be combined with that of another corporation, except for corporations that qualify for consolidated tax reporting.

All types of tax entities are permitted to apply operating losses to reduce taxable income for the previous three years and the following fifteen years. When losses are used to reduce taxable income of previous years, the taxes that were paid in those years are refunded. Losses applied to future periods merely reduce taxable income and taxes due for those years. When applying current operating losses to other years, the losses must first be carried back to the third preceding year. If all the loss is not absorbed by the income of that year, the remainder is applied to the second preceding year, then to the first preceding year, and then to the fifteen years following the current period. With the carryback and carryover provisions, most operating losses are usually eventually used, but it may take many years to realize the total tax benefits from the current period's losses.

Employee Benefits

As explained earlier, a stockholder of a corporation may be an employee of the company and receive salary payments that are deductible as expenses by the corporation in computing its taxable income. The concept of owner-employee does not apply to proprietorships and partnerships because these businesses are inseparable from their owners. If a proprietorship or partnership deducts payments to its owners as salaries, these deductions are offset by the salaries received, which are included in the owners' taxable incomes.

All businesses are allowed under the tax law to deduct the cost of qualified fringe benefits provided for their employees, including medical insurance, certain death benefits, certain meals and lodging, recreation, and deferred compensation benefits. These expense deductions are available even for benefits paid to employees who are also stockholders of the corporations. Because proprietors and partners cannot be employees of their own companies, these tax deductible employee benefits are not available to proprietorships or partnerships. However, the tax laws allow individuals who are proprietors or partners to take a personal deduction for certain contributions to qualified retirement plans. There is no provision for individuals to deduct costs associated with the other employee benefits named above.

Dividends Received Deduction

A *dividends received deduction* is a deduction from gross income granted to *corporations* based on a percentage of dividends received from investments in other corporations. Corporations are permitted to deduct 80 percent of the dividends received from other domestic corporations, thus paying taxes on only 20 percent of the dividends. If the corporation receiving the dividend owns less than 20 percent of the stock of the corporation paying the dividend, the deduction is reduced to 70 percent. If the paying and receiving corporations are both members of an affiliated group, the deduction is 100 percent. Proprietorships, partnerships, and subchapter S corporations are not allowed this deduction.

If a business receives dividends that are expected to be reinvested in the business, the corporate dividends deduction may be a significant advantage related to the corporate form. However, if the dividends received are distributed, the owner-stockholders are required to include them in their taxable incomes.

Capital Gains and Losses

A capital asset is generally defined for tax purposes as an asset held for investment gain; it, therefore, excludes assets such as inventory, accounts receivables, and assets used in the business such as land, buildings, and equipment. A gain or loss on the sale of a capital asset is called a capital gain or loss. The excess of capital gains over capital losses is a net capital gain. Conversely, the excess of capital losses over capital gains is a net capital loss.

Corporations and individuals are required to include net capital gains in taxable income subject to taxes at ordinary income rates. *Corporations* are not permitted to deduct net capital losses from other taxable income. Net capital losses by corporations can be carried back three years and forward five years and used to reduce capital gains for those years. *Individuals* are permitted to deduct capital losses in the current year from other taxable income up to an annual limit of $3,000 with any excess carried forward indefinitely to reduce future capital gains or to be deducted against future taxable income.

From the above discussion it is obvious that there is no clear answer to the question of which organizational form provides the greatest tax advantage. On certain points incorporation is preferred, whereas on other points a noncorporate form (proprietorship or partnership) is more desirable. Each business situation must be evaluated based on its particular circumstances to determine the most desirable organizational structure from the standpoint of taxes.

OTHER TAX CONSIDERATIONS FOR MANAGEMENT

In tax accounting, just as in financial accounting, there are several areas where alternative methods and treatments are available for measuring taxable revenues and deductible expenses. In most cases the alternative selected for financial accounting purposes does not necessarily have to be the same method chosen for tax purposes. The alternative chosen for *financial accounting purposes* should be dictated by the company's particular circumstances and management's desire to present fairly the company's financial picture. For *tax purposes* the choice among alternative treatments is a management decision that should be aimed at minimizing taxes and maximizing the net present value of future cash flows. Economically, the tax alternative decision is similar to a product pricing decision or a capital budgeting decision. Several tax-related areas where management decisions are often required are discussed below.

Depreciation Alternatives

Before 1981, the costs of assets used in a trade or business were recoverable, for tax purposes, through depreciation using straight-line, sum-of-years'-digits, or declining balance depreciation. The laws restricted the applicability of these methods based on the types of assets in use and their expected useful lives.

The Economic Recovery Tax Act of 1981 replaced traditional depreciation methods (sum-of-the-years'-digits and declining balance) with the *Accelerated Cost Recovery System*. Initially, the ACRS provided for the recovery of asset costs over shortened time periods using statutory depreciation rates that approximate declining balance depreciation during the earlier years and sum-of-the-years'-digits depreciation during the remainder of the recovery period. The Tax Reform Act of 1986 generally lengthened the depreciation period and replaced the ACRS statutory rates with MACRS rates, which provided for 200 percent or 150 percent declining balance depreciation for personal property and straight-line depreciation for real property. The alternative of using straight-line depreciation and longer asset lives is also available under the 1986 law for all depreciable assets.

All depreciation methods provide an absolute tax shield equal to the cost of the depreciable asset times the tax rate. However, as observed in the capital budgeting discussion, *because of variations in the timing of the tax shield, accelerated depreciation rates produce the greatest present value of the future tax benefits from depreciation.*

Inventory Costing Alternatives

Whenever a company has inventory on hand at the end of the year, the total cost of goods available for sale during the year must be allocated between goods that were sold during the year and goods that are on hand at the end of the year. In some cases, it is appropriate to determine by specific identification the costs of units sold and units still on hand. In many cases it is necessary for organizations to use an arbitrary cost flow method in making the allocation. Even if specific costs can be determined, it may be advantageous to use a cost flow method to gain maximum benefit from the provisions in the tax law. For tax purposes, a company may use either a specific cost or a cost flow method based on a first-in, first-out (FIFO), last-in, first-out (LIFO), or average cost assumption. FIFO assigns the cost of the earliest acquired units to cost of goods sold, and the cost of the latest acquired units to ending inventory. LIFO assigns the cost of the latest acquired units to cost of goods sold, and the cost of the earliest acquired units to ending inventory. The average method assigns the average cost of all units available during the period to both units sold and units in ending inventory.

During *inflationary periods* FIFO produces the lowest cost of goods sold, the highest taxable income, and the highest taxes, whereas LIFO results in the highest cost of goods sold, the lowest taxable income, and the lowest taxes. The average cost method results in amounts for cost of goods sold, taxable income, and taxes between the two extremes of FIFO and LIFO. The net economic difference between FIFO and LIFO during an inflationary period is illustrated in Exhibit 16–3. For each of the three years, there are 200 units in both beginning and ending inventory, and 800 units are both purchased and sold. At the beginning of the first year, inventory is valued at $1 per unit, and the purchase price of inventory is $2 in the first year, $3 in the second year, and $4 in the third year. Goods are sold at twice the current purchase price.

Note in Exhibit 16–3 that under FIFO, ending inventory is $200 greater than beginning inventory for each of the three years, whereas under LIFO, beginning and ending inventory are the same. The number of units in beginning and ending inventory is the same for each period; therefore, LIFO is charging all costs of purchases to cost of goods sold. Since the purchase price of units increased by $1 per unit each year, FIFO charges $200 ($1 times 200 units) more to ending inventory each period than for the previous period. Consequently, cost of goods sold is $200 less each year for FIFO than for LIFO, FIFO taxable income for each period is $200 more than LIFO taxable income, and taxes are $68 ($200 × 0.34) more for FIFO than LIFO each year. The obvious conclusion is that *as long as prices are increasing, LIFO costing minimizes taxable income and taxes.* Ordinarily, a company that uses the LIFO method for tax purposes is also required by the tax laws to use LIFO for financial reporting purposes.

MANAGERIAL PRACTICE 16.3

New Inventory Tax Rules Alter Business Strategies

Firms with substantial inventories were faced with difficult strategic decisions in light of Tax Reform Act of 1986 rules that require capitalization of certain inventory-related costs that, previously, the tax laws permitted companies to deduct currently. Shamrock Chemicals Corp. was such a company. The result for such companies was lower expenses, higher pre-tax profits, and higher taxes. "We can't be lean and mean in our inventory policy because we can't afford to not have the stuff to ship," said William B. Neuberg, president and owner. Maintaining that the new tax rules were "a straight-up penalty for us," he said that Shamrock was unable to pass the increased cost of the taxes on to the customer because foreign competitors were not affected by the new tax rules.

Other firms, such as Hudson Valley Paper Co. in Albany, New York, complained that the new inventory rules created inordinate regulatory compliance costs for inventory-producing firms. These added requirements, which entail extensive cost allocation analyses, put increased burdens on accounting personnel in such firms. So the cost is not just the additional tax, but also the additional cost of personnel to comply with the tax rules—complicated by the fact that some costs are now required to be capitalized for tax purposes that are deducted currently for financial accounting purposes. This puts an extra burden on the outside accountants to reconcile these two items.

Source: Steven P. Galante and Sanford L. Jacobs, "New Inventory-Expense Rules Increase Costs at Many Firms," *Wall Street Journal,* 29 June 1987, 29.

EXHIBIT 16–3   Comparison of Tax Effects of FIFO and LIFO Inventory Costing Methods

FIFO inventory method	Year 1 Units	Cost	Year 2 Units	Cost	Year 3 Units	Cost
Beginning inventory	200 at $1	$ 200	200 at $2	$ 400	200 at $3	$ 600
Purchases	800 at $2	1,600	800 at $3	2,400	800 at $4	3,200
Goods available for sale	1,000	$1,800	1,000	$2,800	1,000	$3,800
Ending inventory	− 200 at $2	− 400	− 200 at $3	− 600	− 200 at $4	− 800
Goods sold	800	$1,400	800	$2,200	800	$3,000
Sales	800 at $4	$3,200	800 at $6	$4,800	800 at $8	$6,400
Cost of goods sold		−1,400		−2,200		−3,000
Taxable income		$1,800		$2,600		$3,400
Taxes (at 34%)		$ 612		$ 884		$1,156
LIFO inventory method	**Units**	**Cost**	**Units**	**Cost**	**Units**	**Cost**
Beginning inventory	200 at $1	$ 200	200 at $1	$ 200	200 at $1	$ 200
Purchases	800 at $2	1,600	800 at $3	2,400	800 at $4	3,200
Goods available for sale	1,000	$1,800	1,000	$2,600	1,000	$3,400
Ending inventory	− 200 at $1	− 200	− 200 at $1	− 200	− 200 at $1	− 200
Goods sold	800	$1,600	800	$2,400	800	$3,200
Sales	800 at $4	$3,200	800 at $6	$4,800	800 at $8	$6,400
Cost of goods sold		−1,600		−2,400		−3,200
Taxable income		$1,600		$2,400		$3,200
Taxes (at 34%)		$ 544		$ 816		$1,088
LIFO tax savings						
Excess of taxes under FIFO over taxes under LIFO		$ 68		$ 68		$ 68

As illustrated above, FIFO and LIFO are methods of assigning cost values to inventory when units of a particular inventory item held during the year were acquired at different prices. The costs of inventories manufactured by the taxpayer, rather than purchased ready to sell, must be calculated using a product costing method. Methods for measuring product costs were discussed in Chapters 10 through 14.

The federal tax laws require manufacturers to use the full absorption costing method in measuring the cost of manufactured inventories; therefore, the cost must include direct materials, direct labor, and manufacturing overhead. The variable (or direct) costing method, which was discussed in Chapter 10, is not permissible for tax purposes. The tax laws spell out clearly which manufacturing costs may be deducted as expenses in the current period and which costs must be added to the cost of inventory. The Tax Reform Act of 1986 now requires many costs to be inventoried that previously could be expensed, including costs of administrative support, engineering and design, purchasing, production officers' salaries, and storage and warehousing. Virtually all costs directly or indirectly connected with the manufacturing process must now be included in product cost.

An alternative to using one of the cost methods discussed above for valuing inventory is the **Lower of cost or market (LCM)** method. Whether cost or LCM is used to value inventories, it is still necessary for the taxpayer to determine the cost of inventory (using a method such as FIFO or LIFO) because under the LCM method the cost of each inventory item is compared with its market value (current replacement cost) to determine which value is lower. For tax purposes, the LCM method must be applied to each item of inventory rather than to total inventory. Note the following simple example of the calculation of cost, market, and LCM for a company that had one unit of three different items in its ending inventory.

	Cost	Market	LCM
Item # 101	$ 9	$10	$ 9
Item # 102	6	4	4
Item # 103	7	7	7
Total	$22	$21	$20

If LCM is applied on a total inventory basis, the value of the inventory is $21, because the total market value of $21 is lower than the total cost of $22; however, by applying LCM to each product in the inventory, the total LCM value of the inventory is $20. As shown earlier, the lower the value of ending inventory, the higher the cost of goods sold and the lower the taxable income and income taxes.

To summarize, the amount of taxes incurred by a company will be affected by how it values its inventory (cost or LCM) and by how it assigns cost to units of inventory (FIFO or LIFO). In times of rising prices, LIFO will produce the lowest inventory cost value, the highest cost of sales, and the lowest income and tax expense. Also, LCM will normally result in lower inventory values, higher cost of sales, and lower income and taxes than will the cost methods. In many companies where inventories represent a large percent of total assets, management's decisions concerning the method of costing inventory (FIFO or LIFO) and the basis for valuing inventory (cost or lower of cost or market) can affect a company's profitability and thus its tax payments by millions of dollars per year.

Revenue Recognition Alternatives

For financial reporting purposes, revenues generally may be reported either as cash is collected (*cash basis*) or as the right to receive the cash is realized (*accrual basis*). Ordinarily, a company must report income for tax purposes on the same basis used for financial reporting purposes. If inventory transactions represent a significant part of a company's operations, sales and cost of goods sold are required for tax and financial accounting purposes to be reported on the accrual basis. Although most sales made on installment are fully recognized as revenues in the financial statements at the time the sales are made, in some cases, for tax purposes, revenue recognition may be deferred until the cash payments are collected. The cases are now limited to the sale of real and personal property not held for resale to customers in the ordinary course of business.

To illustrate the *installment sales method,* assume that in 19x4 a company sells $100,000 of land that was purchased for $65,000. The $100,000 is to be collected in five equal annual payments of $20,000. The total gross profit on the sale is $35,000, or 35 percent of sales. Under the accrual basis the full $35,000 of gross profit is recognized in 19x4; however, under the installment method only the gross profit on the portion of the revenues collected, that is, $7,000 ($20,000 × 0.35), is included in taxable income in 19x4. The taxable income and taxes due in 19x4 under the accrual and installment methods are summarized as follows:

Accrual Method		Installment Method	
Selling Price	$100,000	Installment collections	$20,000
Cost of land	− 65,000	Gross profit on collections	
Gross profit (35%)	$ 35,000	($20,000 × 35%)	$ 7,000
Taxes ($35,000 × 0.34)	$ 11,900	Taxes ($7,000 × 0.34)	$ 2,380

The current tax savings from electing the installment method was $9,520 ($11,900 − $2,380). In reality this is not a tax savings but rather a tax deferral. The company still has $28,000 of unreported gross profit ($35,000 − $7,000). As the $80,000 balance in unpaid installments is collected, $28,000 ($80,000 × 0.35) of additional gross profit will be reported as taxable income resulting in taxes of $9,520 ($28,000 × 0.34).

The primary benefit in adopting the installment method is related to the time value of the deferred tax payment. By investing the $9,520 tax deferral, additional income can be earned. This income is the economic benefit resulting from the tax deferral. Another potential benefit for smaller companies, whose marginal tax rates are near or below the maximum tax rate, is that by spreading gross profit over several years the marginal tax rate may be lowered resulting in a direct tax savings. This benefit is in addition to the time value benefit realized on the deferral of the tax payment.

Capital Funding Alternatives

As previously stated, corporations are not permitted to deduct dividends paid on equity capital in computing taxable income. Interest expense on borrowed capital, however, is a deductible expense. *Because of the interest expense deduction, debt capital may be less expensive to a company than equity capital.* To illustrate, assume that a company plans to acquire a new building costing $1,000,000 and that the funds can be obtained either by selling 12 percent long-term bonds (debt capital) or by selling 12 percent preferred stock (equity capital). In both cases the annual outlay to service the capital funds is $120,000 ($1,000,000 × 0.12). However, since interest payments are deductible, the annual

MANAGERIAL PRACTICE 16.4

Is It Debt or Equity?

Because interest expense is deductible and dividends payments not deductible, a question often arises between companies and the IRS concerning the nature of certain hybrid securities, which have some debt characteristics and some equity characteristics. In the 1986 case of *Federal Express* v. *U.S.,* Federal Express contested the IRS's disallowance of interest deductions on the issuance of subordinated notes.

The primary features of the notes were as follows: the absolute promise to repay the principal; the transferability of the notes for stock; a stated interest rate (but no interest was to be earned in the first year, and the rate could be reduced based on the actual cash flow of Federal Express); optional and mandatory prepayment provisions; and the subordination of all indebtedness on a parity with trade creditors.

Although the respective risks of the investors and of Federal Express may have appeared somewhat similar to those found in an equity relationship, the Tax Court in deciding in favor of Federal Express emphasized that the securities had a definite maturity date and certainty of payment and had an adequate interest rate. The presence of a provision for participation in the success of the venture with the investors did not alter the basic character of the securities, nor did the subordination provisions, since the note holders were subordinate to shareholders.

This case illustrates that, just because a security may be called a note, a bond, or a name normally associated with an interest-bearing instrument, the IRS may not accept such characterization and may attempt to treat the security as a share of stock, thereby treating the interest payments as nondeductible dividends. Companies issuing such hybrid securities may be required to defend the right to the interest deduction before the IRS or in the courts.

Source: Federal Express v. *U.S.,* 86-2 USTC ¶9793, 645 F. Supp. 1281 W.D. Tenn.

after-tax cost of the bonds is only $79,200 [$120,000 × (1 − 0.34)], and the annual cost of the bonds after taxes as a percent of the funds obtained is 7.92 percent ($79,200 ÷ $1,000,000), compared to 12 percent for the preferred stock.

Investment Alternatives

When evaluating alternatives for investing excess funds, an important tax consideration is the taxability of the income received on the investment. The tax treatment of periodic income is not the same for all investments. Corporations are normally allowed an 80 percent special deduction on dividends received from investments in other corporations. Another tax break on investment income available to all taxpayers (corporate and noncorporate) involves interest received on *municipal bonds* issued by government agencies other than the federal government. The federal constitution prohibits the IRS from taxing income on municipal bonds; therefore, the after-tax return for these bonds is the same as the stated interest rate. Taxpayers in the 34 percent tax bracket investing in 10 percent municipal bonds pay no taxes on the interest received, and their after-tax yield on the investment is 10 percent. In contrast, if these taxpayers invest in 12 percent corporate bonds, the interest is taxable and the after-tax yield is only 7.92 percent [0.12 × (1 − 0.34)]. In this case, taking taxes into consideration, the municipal bonds offer a higher return to the investor. Ordinarily, the interest rate on municipal bonds is considerably lower than that on comparable corporate bonds; however, for a taxpayer in a high tax bracket the return on municipal bonds is often higher than the after-tax return on corporate bonds.

SUMMARY

The effects of taxes on business enterprises represent one of the most important considerations in management decision making. Effective management of resources generally requires that efforts be undertaken to avoid or defer taxes through legally available means. Probably the most important category of taxes is income taxes; however, most businesses must also contend with property and excise taxes. Taxes are exacted against businesses by the federal government as well as by state, local, and even foreign governments.

Understanding taxes is particularly important in capital budgeting. Taxes affect capital budgeting decisions through (1) the reduction of operating profits, (2) the depreciation tax shield, and (3) the tax on the sale of assets. Income taxes also play an important role in the selection of the organizational form for a business. Sole proprietorships and partnerships merely serve as conduits through which profits flow into the tax returns of the business owners. Corporations, however, are separate taxable entities whose profits are taxed directly. Corporate profits that provide dividends suffer a double tax burden; they are taxed first to the corporation and then to the stockholders.

The income tax laws provide numerous choices in reporting various types of revenues and expenses for tax purposes. Through careful planning and the effective utilization of alternative tax treatments, management can minimize the adverse effect of taxes on the firm.

SUGGESTED
READINGS

Bernstein, Peter W., Editor, *Ernst & Young's Arthur Young Tax Guide 1990,* Revised Edition, New York: Ballentine Books, 1990.

Fleischer, Gerald A., and Donald R. Smith, "The Reform Act of 1986: Potential Effects of New Plant and Equipment Investment." *Industrial Engineering* (March 1987): 22–27.

McGowan, John, and Burt Nissing, "Coping with Another Tax Year," *Management Accounting* (December 1989): 23–26.

Minter, Frank C., "Tax Reform 1990?" *Management Accounting* (December 1989): 27.

Roth, Harold, "New Rules for Inventory Costing," *Management Accounting* (March 1987): 32–36, 45.

Summerfeld, Ray M., *Federal Taxes and Management Decisions,* 1989–1990 Edition, Homewood, Ill.: Richard D. Irwin, 1989.

Waggnor, Murray, "How to Select a Tax Planning Software Package for Your Firm," *Computers in Accounting* (June 1989): 33–44.

Weber, Joseph V., John J. Mahoney, and Steven W. Hackett, "Inventory Costing Under TRA 86—Part I," *CPA Journal* (May 1988): 66–71.

_____, "Inventory Costing Under TRA 86—Part II," *CPA Journal* (June 1988): 26–33.

REVIEW
PROBLEM

Capital Budgeting
with Tax
Considerations

Roberds Supply Company is considering replacing its computer system with a more up-to-date system. The new system would cost $60,000 and would have an ADR estimated life of six years even though Roberds would expect to use the computer for at least seven years. The old computer, which is fully depreciated, can be sold for $5,000. Roberds estimates that the annual benefit in cost savings of having the new computer would be approximately $15,000 for seven years, after which it would be sold for approximately $5,000. The company's marginal income tax rate is 34 percent, and its required minimum return on new capital investments is 14 percent.

Requirements

a) Compute the present value of the depreciation tax shield for the new computer assuming Roberds uses MACRS 200 percent declining balance depreciation, with a switch to straight-line depreciation at the most advantageous time. *Hint:* Refer to Exhibit 16–1 to find the computer's MACRS life.

b) Compute the present value of the depreciation tax shield for the new computer assuming Roberds uses the alternative straight-line depreciation method.

c) Compute the net present value of the investment assuming Roberds uses the MACRS accelerated depreciation method.

d) Compute the net present value of the investment assuming Roberds uses the alternative straight-line depreciation method.

e) Which of the answers computed in requirements (c) and (d) represents the appropriate net present value of the investment for capital budgeting purposes? Explain.

The solution to this problem is found at the end of the Chapter 16 exercises and problems.

KEY TERMS

Accelerated Cost Recovery System
  (ACRS)
Asset Depreciation Range (ADR)
Capital asset
Capital gain
Capital loss
Corporation
Depreciation tax shield
Excise tax
Income tax
Lower of cost or market (LCM)
Modified Accelerated Cost Recovery
  System (MACRS)

Operating loss
Partnership
Property tax
Sole proprietorship
Subchapter S corporation
Tax avoidance
Tax base
Tax deferral
Tax rate
Value added tax

**REVIEW
QUESTIONS**

16–1 Define and differentiate the following three types of taxes: income taxes, property taxes, and excise taxes.

16–2 Many European countries have a value added tax. Explain how a value added tax works.

16–3 What are the two basic components in determining the amount of any tax?

16–4 Assuming the entire pretax cash flow is subject to taxes, complete the following equation:

$$\text{After-tax cash flow} = \underline{?} \times (1 - \underline{?}).$$

16–5 Explain the concept of depreciation as an income tax shield.

16–6 What is the absolute amount of the depreciation income tax shield provided by an asset costing $10,000 if the tax rate is 34 percent? Explain.

16–7 Why does MACRS declining balance depreciation usually provide a greater tax shield in real terms than straight-line depreciation?

16–8 Why is it desirable to switch from the declining balance method to the straight-line method before the end of an asset's life?

16–9 Describe generally how the following tax entities are treated for income tax purposes under the federal income tax law: proprietorships, partnerships, and corporations.

16–10 One of the major disadvantages of corporations is the problem of double taxation of dividends paid to shareholders. Explain.

16–11 What is an operating loss? How are operating losses treated for tax purposes?

16–12 Compare the tax treatment of net capital losses between corporations and individuals.

16–13 During a period of rising prices, which inventory method minimizes the present value of present and future taxes? Explain.

16–14 Which manufacturing costs generally are required by the tax laws to be included in inventory costs for tax purposes?

16–15 How can lower interest municipal bonds sometimes produce a higher after-tax return to the investor than higher interest corporate bonds?

EXERCISES

16–1 Corporate Tax Computation: Marginal Tax Rate

Ajax Corporation reported taxable income of $82,000 in 19x5.

Requirements

a) Using the federal corporate tax rates given in the chapter, compute the total tax liability for Ajax Company for 19x5.

b) What was Ajax's marginal tax rate?

16–2 Computation of After-Tax Cash Flows

Rustin Company has an opportunity to purchase a machine that will generate annual pretax cash inflows and additional taxable income of $50,000 before depreciation. Rustin has a marginal tax rate of 34 percent.

Required: Compute Rustin's predicted after-tax net cash flows from the purchase of the machine. Ignore depreciation.

16–3 Depreciation Tax Shield

The Statesboro Company purchased a new machine costing $20,000 at the beginning of 19x1. For tax purposes, the machine can be depreciated over its ADR life of six years on a straight-line basis, or it can be depreciated under MACRS for five years using the 200 percent declining balance method. Statesboro's marginal tax rate is 34 percent.

Requirements

a) Compute the absolute amount of the total tax shield over the life of the machine under both depreciation alternatives.

b) Compute the real amount of the total tax shield under both depreciation alternatives using a present value rate of 12 percent. (Round calculations to the nearest dollar.)

16–4 Depreciation Tax Shield

Lakeland Refinery Company is evaluating a possible investment in a new storage facility that would cost $250,000. For tax purposes, assume the capital investment has an ADR expected useful life of 10 years and qualifies for seven-year MACRS depreciation. The company is in the maximum corporate tax bracket of 34 percent.

Requirements

a) Compute the absolute amount of the total tax shield over the life of the machine assuming the company elects to use MACRS accelerated depreciation.

b) Compute the absolute amount of the total tax shield over the life of the machine assuming the company elects to use the alternative straight-line method.

c) Compute the real amount of the total tax shield under both depreciation alternatives using a present value rate of 12 percent. (Round calculations to the nearest dollar.)

d) For capital budgeting purposes, which depreciation method should the company assume will be used?

16–5 After-Tax Investment Costs

Jim Grant is considering purchasing a new machine for his business which would cost $10,000 and qualify for five-year MACRS accelerated depreciation.

Requirements

a) Compute the after-tax cost of the investment in present dollars, assuming a 12 percent discount rate and taking into account the depreciation tax shield. Assume Jim operates his business as a proprietorship and is in the 15 percent tax bracket.

b) Repeat requirement (a) assuming now that Jim is in the 28 percent tax bracket.

c) Repeat requirement (a) assuming now that Jim operates his business as a corporation and has a tax rate of 34 percent.

d) What conclusions can be drawn from this exercise?

16–6 Capital Budgeting with Tax Effects

Toco Hills Shoe Repair Shop recently purchased a new electric shoe repair machine at a cost of $5,000. Depreciation has been recorded on the machine for one year using seven-year MACRS accelerated depreciation. The owner of the shop has just returned from an equipment trade show where a new computerized shoe repair machine was introduced. This new model, which can be purchased for $7,500, has an expected useful life of ten years, and qualifies for seven-year MACRS depreciation. The manufacturer predicts that it will increase revenues by 20 percent per year without any significant increase in operating costs.

Requirements

a) Since the old repair machine is only one year old, should the owner even consider replacing it with the new computerized model? Explain.

b) What are the relevant items to be considered from a capital budgeting standpoint in replacing the old machine with the new model?

c) Which of the relevant items have related tax effects?

16–7 Capital Budgeting with Tax Effects

Colombia Coffee Cafe is considering the purchase of a new cash register to replace the wooden drawer that has been in use since the cafe opened a few months ago. The cash register is likely to have little if any direct effect on operating revenues and expenses. It would be acquired primarily for the convenience of the manager. The cash register, which can be purchased for $1,200, qualifies for five-year MACRS accelerated depreciation. A friend of the owner of the cafe told him that, because of tax considerations, the real cost of the cash register was not really $1,200 but something less.

Requirements

a) Since the purchase of the cash register could not produce a profit, should it even be evaluated as a capital budgeting expenditure? Explain.

b) Explain why the real cost of the cash register is less than $1,200.

c) Assuming the company is in the 34 percent tax bracket, compute the real cost of the cash register.

16–8 Alternative Capital Budgeting Methods with Tax Effects

Systek Corporation has a capital investment opportunity that would cost $100,000. It would generate estimated net cash inflows before taxes and depreciation of $30,000 per year for six years and would qualify for five-year MACRS accelerated depreciation. The investment would have no recoverable value at the end of six years. The company has a 34 percent tax rate.

Requirements

a) Calculate the net cash inflows after depreciation and taxes from the investment for each of the six years.

b) Compute the payback period for the investment.

c) Compute the accounting rate of return for the investment.

d) Assuming a cost of capital of 12 percent, compute the net present value of the investment.

16–9 Capital Budgeting Cash Flows

Douglas Company is considering purchasing a new machine that has a cost of $35,000. The machine qualifies for seven-year MACRS depreciation. Management predicts that the new machine would increase revenues by $5,000 per year for fifteen years and would reduce operating costs by $2,500 per year. At the end of its useful life it can be sold for $2,500.

Required: Prepare a list of the cash flow items that are relevant to Douglas Company's capital budgeting decision concerning the purchase of the machine. Do not attempt to compute the amount of each cash flow item.

16–10 Capital Funding Alternatives

Jordan Company, a soft drink producer, is engaged in negotiations for the acquisition of a company that manufactures aluminum cans. Jordan's management believes that the company can be purchased for $10 million and paid for by issuing either 15 percent long-term bonds or 15 percent preferred stock. Jordan Company has a marginal tax rate of 34 percent.

Requirements

a) Compute the annual after-tax cost of the funds used to acquire the can company assuming long-term bonds are issued.

b) Compute the annual after-tax cost of the funds used to acquire the can company assuming preferred stock is issued.

16–11 Taxability of Investment Income

To help finance future expansion, the Baldwin Company is investing a substantial portion of its excess cash resources in an expansion fund consisting of low-risk securities. At the end of 19x5 the corporate treasurer was instructed to purchase another $100,000 of securities for the fund. The following securities are being considered.

- Acme Corporation common stock, expected to pay annual dividends of $10,000 with no significant market appreciation over the next five years.

- Bilkko Corporation bonds, bearing interest at the rate of 10 percent per year, maturing in five years.

- Central County municipal bonds, bearing interest at the rate of 7 percent per year, maturing in five years.

Requirements

a) Compute the annual after-tax income from each of the securities under consideration assuming the full $100,000 is invested in the same security and the company is in a 34 percent tax bracket.

b) Repeat requirement (a) assuming the company is in a 25 percent tax bracket.

16–12 Carryback and Carryover of Operating Losses

Because of poor weather conditions, Bob Moore's Ski Shop had a 19x5 operating loss of $30,000. The company earned an operating profit of $5,000 in 19x4, $15,000 in 19x3, and $6,000 in 19x2.

Requirements

a) Explain specifically how Bob Moore may use the 19x5 operating loss to reduce taxes in other years if his store is operated as a proprietorship.

b) How may Bob Moore use the 19x5 operating loss if his business is incorporated?

16–13 Organization Form and Taxation of Income

John Devoe owns a hardware store which he has operated as a proprietorship since it opened several years ago. Now that it is profitable, he is considering whether he should incorporate the business. He expects profits to be about $75,000 per year for the foreseeable future. If incorporated, a reasonable salary for himself would be about $50,000 per year. Without regard to his business income, he is already in a 28 percent tax bracket. For purposes of this problem, assume a flat corporate tax rate of 34 percent.

Requirements

a) Compute the annual income taxes on the income from the store assuming John does not incorporate the business.

b) Compute the annual income taxes on the income from the store (both corporate and individual) assuming John does incorporate the business and pays all business net income out to himself as a dividend.

c) Compute the annual income taxes on the income from the store (both corporate and individual) assuming John does incorporate the business and retains all net income in the business for future expansion and pays no dividends to himself.

16–14 Taxation of Capital Gains and Losses

Robert Rowe has a nondepreciable capital asset which cost $15,000 but now is worth only $10,000. His net taxable income for the current year from other sources is $40,000.

Requirements

a) Compute the amount of the capital loss that will be realized if Robert sells the capital asset.

b) How much of the capital loss can be deducted from other taxable income assuming Robert is taxed as an individual? What disposition would be made of the remainder of the capital loss?

c) How much of the capital loss can be deducted from other taxable income assuming Robert is taxed as a corporation? What disposition would be made of the remainder of the capital loss?

16–15 Inventory Costing Methods and Taxes

Brunswik Wire Company is a new company that distributes a newly developed coaxial cable for use by the cable television industry. Because of increasing demand for the product, the prices have increased several times during the year. Purchases of cable by Brunswik during its first year of operations were as follows:

100 rolls at $200 per roll
250 rolls at $225 per roll
300 rolls at $240 per roll
400 rolls at $250 per roll

Brunswik has sales of $450,000 during the year (950 rolls) and other operating expenses of $75,000. Assume a flat income tax rate of 34 percent.

Requirements

a) Compute the income taxes for Brunswik for the year assuming it uses the FIFO inventory method.

b) Compute the income taxes for Brunswik for the year assuming it uses the LIFO inventory method.

c) How would the relative taxes under the FIFO and LIFO methods differ if the price of cable had been declining during the year? Explain.

16–16 Inventory Valuation Methods

Jason's Inc., a three-product company, had 19x8 ending inventories valued at $157,500 using the FIFO cost method, consisting of the following:

Product 101: 200 units acquired @ $250	$50,000
Product 102: 100 units acquired @ $525	52,500
Product 103: 50 units acquired @ $1,100	55,000
Total	$157,500

Requirements

a) Compute the total market (replacement cost) value of the ending inventory assuming the current replacement costs were $265 for product 101, $505 for product 102, and $1,150 for product 103.

b) Compute the lower of cost or market value of the inventory.

c) Can the total cost of inventory ever be less than the lower of cost or market value of inventory? Explain.

16–17 Selecting an Organizational Form

Sharon and Janice plan to open a new gifts and antiques shop in a mountain resort location. They have sought your advice on whether they should organize their business as a partnership or as a corporation. Sharon's other taxable income places her in the maximum tax bracket already, but Janice has no other income. Sharon will be working half time in the shop, and Janice will be working full time refinishing furniture and managing the shop. The anticipated profits of $50,000 per year will be divided as follows:

	Sharon	Janice	Total
Remuneration for services	$10,000	$20,000	$30,000
Division of remaining profits	10,000	10,000	20,000
Totals	$20,000	$30,000	$50,000

Requirements

a) Identify and explain the issues involved in the selection of a tax entity for this new business.

b) Which alternative tax entity do you recommend for this business based on the limited information available to you? Explain the reasons for your recommendation.

16–18 Tax Considerations in Capital Budgeting

Johnstown Company is evaluating a potential capital investment in a machine that would generate an increase in annual operating revenues of $10,000. The machine would cost $40,000 and last six years and would have no expected salvage value at the end of that period. It would qualify for five-year MACRS accelerated depreciation.

Requirements

a) Ignoring all income tax effects, compute the payback period, the accounting rate of return, and the net present value of the investment. Assume a 14 percent discount rate.

b) Considering all relevant income tax effects and assuming a 34 percent corporate tax rate, calculate the payback period, the accounting rate of return, and the net present value of the investment. Assume a 14 percent discount rate.

PROBLEMS

16–19 Capital Budgeting Decisions with Tax Considerations

J.R.'s Painting Company, a residential and commercial paint contractor, is considering expanding into industrial painting and related services, including sandblasting. This expansion would require purchasing sandblasting equipment costing about $50,000. The equipment has an ADR life of nine years; therefore, it could be depreciated under MACRS over five years. After nine years, J.R.'s expects to be able to sell the equipment for about $1,200. Predicted income and expenses related to sandblasting services are as follows:

	Year 1	Year 2	Year 3	Years 4–9 (per year)
Revenues	$20,000	$30,000	$40,000	$50,000
Expenses:				
Labor	$18,000	$18,000	$18,000	$18,000
Sand	5,000	7,500	10,000	12,500
Repairs	500	1,000	1,500	2,000
Total	−23,500	−26,500	−29,500	−32,500
Income before depreciation	$ (3,500)	$ 3,500	$10,500	$17,500

J.R.'s tax rate is 34 percent, and the required return on new investments is 16 percent.

Required: Compute the net present value of the investment in the sandblasting equipment. Should J.R.'s purchase the equipment? (Round calculations to the nearest dollar.)

16–20 Capital Budgeting with Tax Considerations

Jones, Jones, and Jones, a medium-sized law firm, currently has five secretaries employed in its secretarial pool. An office equipment salesperson recently told the Joneses that a word processing system would improve the efficiency and effectiveness of their clerical department and should save the cost of one secretary's salary each year. The proposed system would cost $15,000 and has an estimated useful life of seven years, after which it can be sold for an estimated $1,000. By adding word processing, the attorneys believe that only four secretaries will be needed—three doing conventional typing and one operating the word processor. The total cost of employing a secretary is $15,000 per year; however, word processing secretaries usually earn about 20 percent more than conventional secretaries. The annual maintenance contract on the word processing equipment would be $1,000. The equipment qualifies for five-year MACRS depreciation, and the company has a 34 percent marginal tax rate.

Requirements

a) Compute the net present value of the investment in the word processing equipment assuming a present value rate of 14 percent. (Round calculations to the nearest dollar.)

b) Was the salesperson correct in claiming that the word processing system would save the cost of one secretary?

16–21 Net Present Value Method

Delk Printing Company is considering the purchase of a coin-operated photocopy machine that will cost $3,000 and will generate estimated gross income of $1,200, $1,600, and $2,500 over a three-year period. Maintenance costs are estimated to be $150, $250, and $500 for the three years, respectively. Even though Delk will keep the machine only three years, after which it will be sold for an estimated $900, the tax code requires the machine to be depreciated on the basis of its five-year MACRS classification. Consequently, it will not be fully depreciated at the time it is sold. Delk pays income taxes at the 34 percent corporate rate and requires a return of 30 percent on machinery of this type.

Requirements

a) Compute the net present value of the investment. Should Delk proceed with the purchase of the photocopier? Explain.

b) Compute the net present value of the investment, assuming Delk is an individual paying taxes at a 28 percent rate. Should Delk proceed with the purchase of the photocopier? Explain.

16–22 Purchase versus Lease Costs

Paran Productions is considering whether to purchase or lease a high-quality teleproduction camera that can be purchased for $250,000 or leased for six years for $50,000 per year. The company estimates that the camera would have a useful life of six years and could be sold at the end of the six-year period for $50,000. Assume that lease payments are deductible when incurred for tax purposes and that, if purchased, the camera could be depreciated under five-year MACRS depreciation. Also, assume that Paran's income tax rate is 34 percent and its cost of capital rate is 12 percent.

Requirements

a) Compute the present value of the cost of leasing the camera reflecting tax considerations.

b) Compute the present value of the cost of purchasing the camera reflecting tax considerations.

16–23 Selection of Organizational Form

Bob Allen and Joyce Baker, two college professors specializing in environmental science, own a consulting firm to which they devote time during their evenings, weekends, and vacations. The firm also employs four other full-time professionals. Currently, Allen and Baker are each in a 28 percent marginal tax bracket, not including their consulting business income. In 19x6, the business had net income before owners' salaries and income taxes of $80,000. Allen and Baker believe that the time they put into their firm would justify an annual salary of $25,000 each if the business were operated as a corporation.

Requirements

a) How would the $80,000 of business income be taxed if the business operated as a partnership? How much total taxes would be paid by the partners on the business income?

b) How would the $80,000 of business income be taxed if the business operated as a regular corporation and only normal salaries were distributed to the owners? How much total taxes would be paid on the business income by the corporation and the owners?

c) Repeat requirement (b) assuming the remainder of the business income after taxes is distributed to the owners as dividends.

d) How would the $80,000 of business income be taxed if the business operated as a subchapter S corporation? How much total taxes would be paid by the corporation and the owners on the business income?

16–24 Impact of Inventory Costing Methods on Taxes

Marco Company, a regional distributor of a new microcomputer called Comp-10, has just completed its third year of operations. Purchases and sales data for each of the first three years are given as follows.

	Year 1	Year 2	Year 3
Purchases (units)	1,500	2,750	4,000
Cost per unit	$120	$100	$ 90
Sales (units)	1,450	2,720	3,980
Selling price per unit	$300	$250	$225
Tax rate	34%	34%	34%
Operating expenses (as a percent of gross profit)	50%	50%	50%

Requirements

a) Compute total income taxes for each year assuming FIFO inventory costing is used.

b) Repeat requirement (a) assuming LIFO inventory costing is used.

c) Comment on the tax effects of inventory costing methods (FIFO versus LIFO) in times of (1) falling prices and (2) rising prices.

16–25 Inventory Valuation Bases: Cost versus Lower of Cost or Market

Peachtree Computer Exchange began business in 19x0 and in its first year of business had taxable income of $225,000. Cindy Burton, owner of the business, is trying to determine the effects of inventory valuation on the amount of income taxes for the first year of operations. The $100,000 value of ending inventory, used in calculating taxable income, was based on the specifically identified actual costs of the inventory items. You have determined that the FIFO cost value of the inventory was $25,000 more and the LIFO cost value of the inventory was $25,000 less than the specifically identified costs of ending inventory items. You have also determined that the replacement value of all inventory items was higher than the FIFO and LIFO cost values, except for five units of one computer in inventory that had been recently discontinued by the vendor. Due to major price reductions, these units could now be purchased new for $10,000 less than their FIFO cost and $8,000 less than their LIFO cost. For purposes of this problem, assume an incremental income tax rate of 34 percent.

Requirements

a) Compute the amount of taxable income under the following inventory valuation alternatives:

- Inventory is valued at FIFO cost.
- Inventory is valued at LIFO cost.
- Inventory is valued at lower of FIFO cost or market.
- Inventory is valued at lower of LIFO cost or market.

b) Compute the amount of income tax expense for 19x0 for each of the above alternatives.

c) Which inventory valuation alternative will produce the highest net income after taxes?

d) Which inventory valuation alternative will produce the highest income taxes?

e) Which inventory valuation alternative will produce the lowest net income after taxes?

f) Which inventory valuation alternative will produce the lowest income taxes?

16–26 Timing the Payment of Taxes

The Burdock Company's transactions are summarized below for 19x5, its first year of operations. Recognizing the company's critical shortage of cash, the president instructed the controller (who is also the tax manager) to consider all options in the tax law that might reduce tax payments for the current year.

1. Purchased equipment in September at a cost of $20,000. The equipment qualifies for five-year cost recovery under MACRS.

2. A total of 400 units of product were sold during the year. The following purchases of inventory were made during the year.

   50 units at $40
   200 units at $45
   200 units at $50
   50 units at $55

3. Operating expenses paid during the year totaled $9,000. An additional $4,000 of expenses was accrued but unpaid at the end of the year. The only other expense was depreciation on the equipment.

Requirements

a) For each of the items listed above, indicate the alternative tax treatments that are available to the Burdock Company.

b) Assuming there were no other transactions during the year, compute the minimum tax liability for the company for 19x5. Burdock Company is organized as a regular (not subchapter S) corporation.

16–27 Effect of Inventory Alternatives on Taxes

The management of Stark Products Company has asked its accounting department to describe the effect on income taxes of accounting for inventories on the LIFO rather than the FIFO basis during 19x4 and 19x5. The accounting department is to assume that the change to LIFO would have been effective on January 1, 19x4, and that the initial LIFO inventory was the ending 19x3 FIFO inventory.

Presented below are selected data for the years 19x4 and 19x5 during which the FIFO method was employed.

	19x3	19x4	19x5
Inventory (December 31)	$69,000	$ 75,000	$ 84,000
Sales		$540,000	$617,500
Less: Cost of goods sold		$294,000	$355,000
Other expenses		135,000	154,000
Total		−429,000	−509,000
Net income before income taxes		$111,000	$108,500
Less: Income taxes (34%)		− 37,740	− 36,890
Net income		$ 73,260	$ 71,610

Additional information:

- Inventory on hand at 12/31/x3 consisted of 30,000 units valued at $2.30 each.
- Sales (all units sold at the same price throughout the year):

  19x4—120,000 units at $4.50 each
  19x5—130,000 units at $4.75 each

- Purchases (all units purchased at the same price throughout the year):

  19x4—120,000 units at $2.50 each
  19x5—130,000 units at $2.80 each

- Income taxes at the effective rate of 34 percent are paid on December 31 each year.

Required: If inventories had been valued using LIFO, determine the values for 19x4 and 19x5 for ending inventories, net income before income taxes, income taxes, and net income.

(CMA Adapted)

16–28 Capital Budgeting and Funding Alternatives

LeToy Company produces a wide variety of children's toys, most of which are manufactured from stamped parts. The Production Department recommended that a new stamping machine be acquired. The Production Department further recommended that the company consider using the new stamping machine for only six years. Top management concurs with the recommendation and has assigned Ann Mitchum of the Budget and Planning Department to supervise the acquisition and analyze the alternative financing available. After careful analysis and review, Mitchum has narrowed the financing of the project to the two following alternatives.

1. The first alternative is a lease agreement with the manufacturer of the stamping machine. The manufacturer is willing to lease the equipment to LeToy for six years even though it has an economically useful life of ten years. The lease agreement calls for LeToy to make annual payments of $62,000 at the beginning of each year.

The manufacturer (lessor) retains the title to the machine, and there is no purchase option at the end of six years. The lease payments would be deductible as operating expense for tax purposes.

2. The second alternative would be for LeToy to purchase the equipment outright from the manufacturer for $240,000. LeToy can recover the cost under MACRS over five years. The asset would be sold for $45,000 at the end of six years.

All maintenance, taxes, and insurance are the same under both alternatives and are paid by LeToy. LeToy has an average cost of capital of 12 percent and is in a 34 percent tax bracket.

Requirements

a) Calculate the net-of-tax present value cost of acquiring the stamping machine through the leasing alternative. (Round computations to the nearest dollar.)

b) Calculate the net-of-tax present value cost of acquiring the stamping machine through the purchase alternative.

(CMA Adapted)

16–29 Tax Considerations in Using Payback, Accounting Rate of Return, and Net Present Value

The Baxter Company manufactures toys and other short-lived faddish items. The Research and Development Department came up with an item that would make a good promotional gift for office equipment dealers. Aggressive and effective effort by Baxter's sales personnel has resulted in almost firm commitments for this product for the next five years. It is expected that the product's appeal will be exhausted by that time. In order to produce the quantity demanded, Baxter will need to buy additional machinery and rent some additional space. It appears that about 25,000 square feet will be needed; 12,500 square feet of presently unused, but leased, space is available now. (Baxter's present lease with ten years to run costs $3 a square foot.) There is another 12,500 square feet adjoining the Baxter facility, which Baxter will rent for five years at $4 per square foot per year if it decides to make this product. The equipment will be purchased for $720,000. It will require $30,000 in modifications, $60,000 for installation, and $90,000 for testing; all these activities will be done by a firm of engineers hired by Baxter. All the expenditures will be paid for on January 1, 19x3. The equipment will be depreciated over five years under MACRS using the 200 percent declining balance method. At the end of the five years, the asset is expected to be sold for $180,000. The following estimates of revenues and expenses (other than depreciation and taxes) for this product for the five years have been developed. The company pays income taxes at the 34 percent corporate rate.

	19x3	19x4 & 19x5	19x6 & 19x7
Sales	$1,000,000	$1,600,000	$800,000
Materials, labor, and overhead outlays	400,000	750,000	350,000
Allocated general overhead	40,000	75,000	35,000
Rent	87,500	87,500	87,500

Requirements

a) Prepare a schedule that shows the incremental after-tax cash flows for this project.

b) If the company requires a three-year payback period for its investment, would this project be undertaken?

c) Calculate the after-tax accounting rate of return on initial investment for the project. (Round answer to three decimal places.)

d) A newly hired business school graduate recommends that the company consider the use of the net present value method to study this project. If the company sets a required rate of return of 24 percent after taxes, will this project be accepted? (Round calculations to the nearest dollar.)

(CMA Adapted)

16–30 Selecting Tax Alternatives to Minimize Taxes

The Janeski Service Corporation has just completed its first year of operations. The income statement (on an accrual basis) for the year prepared by the bookkeeping department is as follows:

Sales	$325,000
Gain on sale of land	32,000
Interest income	1,000
Total revenues	$358,000
Materials and supplies	$128,000
Wages and benefits	43,000
Depreciation (straight-line)	7,000
Bad debts	500
Interest	5,500
Administrative services	11,000
Other expenses	5,000
Total expenses	−200,000
Net income	$158,000

Mr. Janeski has made the following preliminary calculation of the corporation's tax liability.

Tax on first $50,000 at 15%	$ 7,500
Tax on next $25,000 at 25%	6,250
Tax on next $83,000 at 34%	28,220
	$41,970

You have just been hired by Janeski as an accountant, and he indicates that the company is in a "cash-squeeze" position. As your first task, he asks you to review the tax computation to determine if this year's tax liability might be reduced. In reviewing the firm's records, you assemble the following information.

1. There are no ending inventories.
2. Accounts receivable at year end amount to $18,000, and accounts payable and other current payables are $4,000.
3. New equipment costing $60,000 was purchased early in the year. In the bookkeeper's depreciation calculation, salvage value was estimated to be $4,000, and the useful life of the equipment was estimated at eight years. You determined that the equipment qualified for five-year MACRS depreciation.
4. A tract of land, acquired in January as a building site at a cost of $12,000, was sold in November when a new shopping plaza was constructed on adjoining land. The land was sold for $44,000, of which $33,000 will be received in future years.

Required: Present a revised determination of taxable income and total taxes that takes advantage of all available means (discussed in this chapter) to reduce this year's taxes. Explain any items where your presentation differs from the income statement given above.

(CMA Adapted)

REVIEW PROBLEM SOLUTION

a) Using MACRS 200 percent declining balance depreciation, the computer would be written off over the five-year period from the midpoint of year 1 to the midpoint of year 6. The depreciation method would be switched to straight-line at the beginning of year 4 to maximize the present value of the depreciation tax shield.

		(1)	(2)	(3) (1) × (2)	(4)	(5) (3) × (4)	(6)	(7) (5) × (6)
Year	*Depreciation Method**	*Depreciation Base*	*Depreciation Rate*	*Annual Depreciation*	*Tax Rate*	*Tax Shield*	*14% Present Value Factor*	*Present Value of Tax Shield*
1	DB	$60,000	$\frac{1}{2} \times \frac{2}{5}$	$12,000	0.34	$ 4,080	0.877	$ 3,578
2	DB	48,000	$\frac{2}{5}$	19,200	0.34	6,528	0.769	5,020
3	DB	28,800	$\frac{2}{5}$	11,520	0.34	3,917	0.675	2,644
4	SL	17,280**	$1 \div 2\frac{1}{2}$	6,912	0.34	2,350	0.592	1,391
5	SL	17,280	$1 \div 2\frac{1}{2}$	6,912	0.34	2,350	0.519	1,220
6	SL	17,280	$\frac{1}{2} \div 2\frac{1}{2}$	3,456	0.34	1,175	0.456	536
				$60,000		$20,400		$14,389

* DB represents declining balance method, and SL represents straight-line method.

** Represents asset book value at the point where the depreciation method is switched to straight-line. The $17,280 balance is depreciated over the $2\frac{1}{2}$ year remaining asset life.

b) Using the alternative straight-line depreciation, the computer would be written off over six years (the ADR class life) from the midpoint of year 1 to the midpoint of year 7.

Year	Depreciation Method	(1) Depreciation Base	(2) Depreciation Rate	(3) (1) × (2) Annual Depreciation	(4) Tax Rate	(5) (3) × (4) Tax Shield	(6) 14% Present Value Factor	(7) (5) × (6) Present Value of Tax Shield
1	SL	$60,000	$\frac{1}{2} \times \frac{1}{6}$	$ 5,000	0.34	$ 1,700	0.877	$ 1,491
2	SL	60,000	$\frac{1}{6}$	10,000	0.34	3,400	0.769	2,615
3	SL	60,000	$\frac{1}{6}$	10,000	0.34	3,400	0.675	2,295
4	SL	60,000	$\frac{1}{6}$	10,000	0.34	3,400	0.592	2,013
5	SL	60,000	$\frac{1}{6}$	10,000	0.34	3,400	0.519	1,765
6	SL	60,000	$\frac{1}{6}$	10,000	0.34	3,400	0.456	1,550
7	SL	60,000	$\frac{1}{2} \times \frac{1}{6}$	5,000	0.34	1,700	0.400	680
				$60,000		$20,400		$12,409

c)

Cash Flow Items	(1) Actual Cash Inflows (Outflows)	(2) Year(s) of Cash Flows	(3) 14% Present Value Factor	(4) (1) × (3) Present Value of Cash Flows
Purchase of new computer	$(60,000)	0	1.000	$(60,000)
Sale of old computer	5,000	0	1.000	5,000
Taxes on gain on sale of old computer ($5,000 × 0.34)	(1,700)	0	1.000	(1,700)
Annual operating income from new computer	15,000	1–7	4.288	64,320
Taxes on annual operating income ($15,000 × 0.34)	(5,100)	1–7	4.288	(21,869)
Plus present value of depreciation tax shield (see requirement a)				14,389
Sale of new computer	5,000	7	0.400	2,000
Taxes on gain on sale of new computer ($5,000 × 0.34)	(1,700)	7	0.400	(680)
Net present value of all cash flows				$ 1,460

d)

Cash Flow Items	(1) Actual Cash Inflows (Outflows)	(2) Year(s) of Cash Flows	(3) 14% Present Value Factor	(4) (1) × (3) Present Value of Cash Flows
Purchase of new computer	$(60,000)	0	1.000	$(60,000)
Sale of old computer	5,000	0	1.000	5,000
Taxes on gain on sale of old computer ($5,000 × 0.34)	(1,700)	0	1.000	(1,700)
Annual operating income from new computer	15,000	1–7	4.288	64,320
Taxes on annual operating income ($15,000 × 0.34)	(5,100)	1–7	4.288	(21,869)
Plus present value of depreciation tax shield (see requirement a)				12,409
Sale of new computer	5,000	7	0.400	2,000
Taxes on gain on sale of new computer ($5,000 × 0.34)	(1,700)	7	0.400	(680)
Net present value of all cash flows				$ (520)

e) For capital budgeting purposes, the depreciation alternative that produces the most favorable net present value of the investment should normally be used in evaluating the investment. Hence, in evaluating the computer investment, Roberds should use the net present value calculated using MACRS depreciation (requirement c) which indicates that the investment meets the required 14 percent minimum return.

Financial Statement Analysis

Learning Objectives

Upon completion of this chapter you should:

- **Understand why it is important for managers to analyze their firm's financial statements.**

- **Be aware of factors that influence financial statements.**

- **Be familiar with alternative standards that may be used in financial statement analysis.**

- **Understand the difference between vertical and horizontal analysis.**

- **Be able to evaluate a firm's solvency.**

- **Be able to evaluate a firm's overall performance.**

General purpose financial statements are designed to provide information to a large and diverse group of users, including stockholders, creditors, and managers. Because of the broad objectives of financial statements, they do not include certain financial measures often needed by specific user groups. Through financial statement analysis, however, individual users are able to generate a considerable amount of additional useful information from the statements.

Financial statement analysis is the process of interpreting and evaluating financial statements by using data contained in them to produce additional financial measures. Financial statement analysis involves comparing financial statements for the current period with those of previous periods, studying the internal composition of the financial statements, and studying relationships within and between the financial statements.

The purpose of this chapter is to examine the basic measures of financial statement analysis and to consider how managers and others use these measures. A large amount of useful information is tapped through financial statement analysis that otherwise is not immediately obvious. For example, creditors can evaluate the likelihood that the company will make its interest and principal payments on time, stockholders can evaluate the profitability of the firm's assets and the return on investment to various equity holders, and managers can evaluate their overall effectiveness in using the resources entrusted to them by creditors and stockholders. Two measures often used in financial statement analysis are also common to internal reporting evaluations. These are return on investment (ROI) and residual income; both were discussed in Chapter 9.

FINANCIAL STATEMENT ANALYSIS BY MANAGERS

One of the most important reasons for managers to analyze their firm's financial statements is to evaluate the overall performance of the firm. Managers should be aware of total company performance, not just the performance of their particular areas of responsibility. By analyzing the financial statements for the company as a whole, managers gain a perspective on how the organization is performing.

General purpose financial statements provide the only overall measure of the firm's performance available to some managers. The internal reporting system is often limited to reporting component performances, with no report of overall performance provided to managers below the top levels.

By evaluating the overall performance of the organization, managers are able to compare their firm with similar firms and identify potential weaknesses that may be worthy of management attention. For example, if a firm has a return on equity of 8 percent while the industry norm is 15 percent, this comparison might signal a problem requiring management attention. In fact, there may be good reasons for the below-average return; without financial analysis, however, management may not even be aware of the deficiency, or the conditions causing it. Since internal reports of other companies are not available, the only basis for making comparisons with those companies is through their external financial statements and other published materials.

Financial analysis is also necessary for managers whose firms have lending agreements that impose financial restrictions on the organization. Analysis of the financial statements is often necessary to determine if restrictions are being met. For example, an agreement may require the debt-to-equity ratio to be maintained below a specified level. Failure to comply could result in a call for immediate liquidation of the debt and could damage the firm's credit rating and its ability to obtain borrowed capital in the future.

A more subtle, but no less important, reason for managers to analyze financial statements is to see their firm as outsiders see it. The financial statements are, in effect, the only window through which many outsiders view the firm. By evaluating the firm's financial statements, managers can better understand the behavior and attitudes of outsiders toward the firm and thereby develop a more realistic view of the firm.

MANAGERIAL PRACTICE 17.1

Key Evaluation Indicators

In preparing write-ups for *Barron's,* a weekly business periodical, staff writers use five key ratios to evaluate a company's performance. These ratios—profit margin, return on common equity, return on total assets, debt-to-equity, and current ratio—help to provide evidence on stability and current status of the companies being evaluated. These ratios are combined with several years' longitudinal data, which include earnings per share, revenues, net income, and book value per share, to make an overall evaluation of a company. After careful evaluation, each company write-up is presented in either positive, negative, or neutral terms. *Barron's* provides numerous company write-ups each week as a service to its readers.

Source: "General Binding Corporation," *Barron's* 8 January 1990, 34—35.

CONSIDERATIONS FOR FINANCIAL STATEMENT ANALYSIS

Before studying the procedures for financial statement analysis, it is important to consider several factors that influence the financial statements and the evaluation methods. First, no single financial statement analysis measure can summarize the performance of an organization. This is because each analysis measure is developed to evaluate an operating procedure or a specific area of the organization's performance. For example, sales ratios are used to measure various characteristics or conditions of sales. Although sales ratios help to evaluate sales, they do not contribute to the analysis of operating expenses. Before drawing conclusions about the financial condition of an organization, the manager should select several evaluation measures that are germane to the organization being evaluated.

Second, the manager must know which alternative accounting procedures are used by the firm. And if comparing the results with other companies or industry standards, the manager must also know the accounting procedures used by each. Alternative accounting procedures critical for financial statement analysis include methods of depreciation, inventory valuation (cost or lower of cost or market), and inventory cost flow method (FIFO, LIFO, average, etc.). Each of these will have an impact on various income statement and balance sheet accounts.

Third, inflation can distort the comparisons of financial statements between periods because the statements are based on historical dollars and not dollars of the same value. Allowances must be made for these effects or the analysis will be distorted. To illustrate, assume that Etson Company had sales in 19x4 of $100,000 and cost of sales totaling $40,000. During 19x5, when inflation was 5 percent, the company's selling prices also increased by 5 percent, while its costs increased only 3 percent due to having some inventory on hand at 19x4 prices. In 19x6 both selling prices and costs went up by 5 percent. Therefore the company had an increase in gross profits in 19x5, due primarily to inflation, of $3,800, and an increase in 19x6 of $3,190 due solely to inflation.

	19x4	19x5	19x6
Sales	$100,000	$105,000	$110,250
Cost of sales	−40,000	−41,200	−43,260
Gross profits	$ 60,000	$ 63,800	$ 66,990

The manager must be very careful to avoid stating that the company had increased operating efficiency when all it did was keep pace with inflation. As a general rule, ignoring inflation produces favorable results when other things remain equal. Inflation can even produce favorable results when actual, constant dollar results are unfavorable. *Remember, external financial statements are presented in historical dollars that have not been adjusted for inflation.*

Fourth, changes in the product mix can distort a comparison of financial statements because most products have unique profit margins and their mix influences the profit margin of the firm. Assume Wilson Company sells two products, CVT and GHK. During 19x0 Wilson sold 100 units of each product, and in 19x1 it sold 85 units of CVT and 125 units of GHK. The gross profit for CVT is $10 per unit, and for GHK it is $7. Total gross profits for 19x0 and 19x1 are as follows:

	19x0			19x1		
	CVT	GHK	Company	CVT	GHK	Company
Gross profit	$1,000	$700	$1,700	$850	$875	$1,725

Without looking past the total numbers on the financial statements, the analysts might conclude that the company had better performance in 19x1 than 19x0. Total sales units went up from 200 to 210, and profit increased by $25. When the individual products are analyzed, however, another opinion might emerge. Although GHK had increased unit sales of 25 percent, CVT, the product with the higher profit per unit, declined 15 percent. This could signal problems if CVT unit sales continue to decline. For companies with large numbers of products the changing product mix generally does not have strong impacts. However, companies with only a few products, or with products that have large profit margins, can have financial results that are difficult to interpret unless the underlying facts are analyzed.

Fifth, changes in the organizational structure should be reviewed as part of the financial analysis. Today's business environment of mergers, acquisitions, and other changes creates many variations in the financial statements. As organizations are restructured their accounting procedures change, new information systems are implemented, and myriad other changes take place that complicate financial analysis.

THE NEED FOR EVALUATIVE STANDARDS

Information obtained directly from financial statements, and analytical measures derived from statements, have little usefulness standing alone. To be interpreted effectively, this information must be evaluated against some *standard*. Depending on managers' objectives, several different standards may be used. The most common financial analysis standards are (1) **vertical analysis,** the restatement of amounts in the current financial statements as a percentage of some base measure, such as sales; (2) **horizontal analysis,** the comparison of a firm's current financial measures to those of previous periods; (3) the comparison of a firm's financial measures to similar measures for other firms in the industry or to industry averages; and (4) the comparison of a firm's financial measures to its budgeted measures.

Financial statement analysis often begins with an examination of the relationships between various accounts. This is normally performed through vertical analysis, where one account, the base account, is set at 100 percent, and all other accounts are presented as a percentage of the base account. In an income statement, sales is typically the base account. After all accounts of a given financial statement have been converted into percentages, the statement is known as a common size statement. The analysis of common size statements is very useful for detecting items that are out of line, that deviate from some preset amount, or that may be indications of other problems. Vertical analysis can be improved by combining it with horizontal analysis and reviewing the common size statements of more than one year. Vertical and horizontal analyses are limited in that they involve comparisons of financial measures only for a single firm. If the firm's performance has been poor or mediocre in the past, these standards do not alert management or the analyst to the need for improvements.

Evaluating financial measures against comparable measures for other firms in the same industry is also beneficial to managers, especially in heavily competitive industries. Several financial information organizations (including Dun and Bradstreet, Standard and Poors, Moody's, and Compustat Tapes) publish averages for commonly used financial measures for all major industries. Failure to perform close to industry norms could signal difficulties in competing with other firms in the future.

When comparing a firm's financial measures with those of other firms, it is necessary to consider any significant differences that might exist between the firms. For example, if one firm is located farther from major suppliers than other firms in the industry, higher freight costs and possibly lower profits may occur. Differences in accounting practices must also be taken into account in comparing firms; for example, allowances must be made in comparing two firms that use different methods of inventory valuation. Although there are limitations in making intercompany comparisons, looking at other firms' performances is a useful indicator of relative performance.

From management's perspective, probably the most realistic standard of performance is the firm's budgeted performance. Chapter 6 discussed operating budgets and pro forma financial statements, which represent management's most realistic expectations for the period. Analytical measures taken from these statements should be compared with the same measures derived from the actual financial statements for the period. For performance evaluation purposes, this comparison is likely to provide managers the most useful evaluation of current financial statements.

PROCEDURES FOR FINANCIAL STATEMENT ANALYSIS

In addition to the computation of common size statements for vertical and horizontal analysis, financial statement analysis measures include computations that measure *solvency* and *performance* of the firm. For a comprehensive analysis of a firm, these measures should be compared to industry norms if available. All of these concepts are illustrated using the 19x2, 19x3, and 19x4 balance sheets and income statements for Dunfield's, Inc., which are provided in Exhibit 17–1. The only major economic change in Dunfield's operations during this period occurred in 19x4, when a new product line was added. Financial statements for three successive periods are presented because several of the measures require multiple periods or averages. To obtain average information for a period, the beginning and ending balances are summed and divided by 2. Normally, averages computed from values for only two points during the year (beginning and ending) should be used only if monthly or quarterly data are not available. In the following discussions, each analytical measure is presented in general form, along with an example of the measure for Dunfield's. All examples use Dunfield's 19x4 data unless otherwise noted.

Common Size Statements

Converting balance sheets and income statements to common size statements is one of the simplest and most direct ways to analyze changes over time. Before the various ratios and account analyses are performed, the manager generally evaluates the income statement and balance sheet using common size statement measures such as sales and total assets. The percentages can also be related to some base period, a month or year, for example. The evaluation of trends in terms of financial statement percentages over time allows for analysis of the underlying movements and shifts in the firm's financial composition.

The percent columns of Exhibit 17–1 provide the data needed for this initial evaluation for Dunfield's, Inc., for 19x4. The computation of common size statements for three to five years allows the manager to evaluate the activities of the company based on trends of prior periods.

Vertical Analysis. The vertical analysis of the common size statements for Dunfield's uses sales from the income statement and total assets from the balance sheet as the bases; these are set at 100 percent. The analysis helps to identify significant changes that have taken place during the period and to determine whether the changes have favorable or unfavorable impacts on solvency and performance. For example, in evaluating the cash needs of Dunfield's, the manager might not be as concerned with the amount of cash as with the percentage of cash to total assets. For Dunfield's, the relationship of cash to total assets was approximately 17 percent in 19x2 and 19x3. The decline to 15.2 percent in 19x4 may indicate a need to examine the status of cash flows. Before becoming alarmed at the situation, the manager would want to compare the status of the 19x4 account balances with the company's guidelines or standards and available industry norms. Just because these items deviate from expectations does not indicate a problem. It might indicate improved cash management or changes in credit sales or credit collection policies. It should not be ignored, however, because it might indicate an undesirable trend leading to future difficulties.

Another useful application of common size balance sheet statements is the evaluation of where shifts occur within major categories. In current assets, for example, the decline in the percentage of cash was offset by increases in accounts

EXHIBIT 17–1 Comparative Financial Statements

Dunfield's, Inc.
Comparative Balance Sheets with Common Size Statements
December 31, 19x4, 19x3, and 19x2 (*in thousands*)

Assets	19x4		19x3		19x2	
Current assets:						
Cash	$1,335	15.2%	$1,341	17.7%	$1,295	17.0%
Marketable securities	250	2.9	200	2.6	228	2.9
Accounts receivable	1,678	19.2	1,386	18.3	1,371	18.0
Inventories	1,703	19.5	1,439	19.1	1,437	18.9
Other current assets	280	3.2	156	2.1	150	2.0
Total current assets	$5,246	60.0%	$4,522	59.8%	$4,481	58.8%
Property, plant and equipment	$6,861	78.4%	$6,041	80.0%	$6,011	78.9%
Less: Accumulated depreciation	−3,426	−39.2	−3,080	−40.8	−2,955	−38.8
Net	3,435	39.2	2,961	39.2	3,056	40.1
Other assets	73	0.8	72	1.0	79	1.1
Total	$8,754	100.0%	$7,555	100.0%	$7,616	100.0%

Liabilities and stockholders' equity	19x4		19x3		19x2	
Current liabilities:						
Accounts payable	$1,564	17.9%	$1,228	16.3%	$1,243	16.3%
Taxes payable	482	5.5	336	4.4	380	5.0
Other current liabilities	202	2.3	178	2.4	152	2.0
Total current liabilities	$2,248	25.7%	$1,742	23.1%	$1,775	23.3%
Long-term debt	1,208	13.8	1,192	15.8	1,748	23.0
Deferred taxes payable	271	3.1	230	3.0	228	3.0
Total liabilities	$3,727	42.6%	$3,164	41.9%	$3,751	49.3%
Stockholders' equity:						
Common stock ($1 par)	$ 404	4.6%	$ 404	5.3%	$ 404	5.3%
Additional paid-in capital	270	3.1	270	3.6	270	3.5
Retained earnings	4,353	49.7	3,717	49.2	3,191	41.9
Total stockholders' equity	$5,027	57.4%	$4,391	58.1%	$3,865	50.7%
Total liabilities and stockholders' equity	$8,754	100.0%	$7,555	100.0%	$7,616	100.0%

Dunfield's, Inc.
Comparative Income Statements with Common Size Statements
For the years ended December 31, 19x4, 19x3, and 19x2 (*in thousands*)

	19x4		19x3		19x2	
Sales	$9,734	100.0%	$8,028	100.0%	$7,841	100.0%
Cost of goods sold	−6,085	−62.5	−4,843	−60.3	−4,648	−59.3
Gross profit	$3,649	37.5	$3,185	39.7	$3,193	40.7
Operating expenses:						
Selling	$1,030	10.6%	$ 891	11.1%	$ 868	11.0%
General and administrative	602	6.2	527	6.6	500	6.4
Total	−1,632	−16.8	−1,418	−17.7	−1,368	−17.4
Operating income	$2,017	20.7%	$1,767	22.0%	$1,825	23.3%
Other revenues and expenses:						
Interest revenue	$ 90	0.9%	$ 84	1.0%	$ 86	1.1%
Interest expense	− 345	− 3.5	− 314	− 3.9	− 342	− 4.4
Total	− 255	− 2.6	− 230	− 2.9	− 256	− 3.3
Income before income taxes	$1,762	18.1%	$1,537	19.1%	$1,569	20.0%
Provision for income taxes	− 599	− 6.2	− 523	− 6.5	− 533	− 6.8
Net income	$1,163	11.9%	$1,014	12.6%	$1,036	13.2%
Earnings per share	$2.88		$2.51		$2.56	

receivable and inventories as a percent of total assets. Since the company experienced an increase in sales, it is logical for accounts receivable and inventories to increase. However, if these two accounts had gone up and cash had gone down with no increases in sales, management should be very concerned. The latter situation suggests excessive inventory investments and problems collecting accounts receivable.

Vertical analysis is also used with common size income statements. For evaluating the income statement, common size measurements allow the manager to determine quickly whether the operating goals of the company have been met. If Dunfield's target gross profit margin is 40 percent, attained in 19x3, the manager can readily see that 19x4 fell short of the goal by 2.5 percentage points. This suggests that lower prices or items within cost of goods sold were not kept in control. Although the income statement alone cannot provide the answer, it has helped identify the problem and given management a starting point in looking for the cause. Comparable evaluations can be performed on any of the income statement items and as such, provide a different perspective of evaluation rather than simply relying on dollar amounts.

Horizontal Analysis. Horizontal analysis should be used to evaluate trends in the financial condition of an organization. This analysis allows current year common size statements to be compared to those of prior years and to the goals and objectives of the organization. For companies that have few organizational changes and little growth, dollar amounts may be of use for horizontal analysis. However, for companies experiencing major economic changes during the period under evaluation (for example, new product lines, dropping product lines, new sales territories, mergers, acquisitions), comparisons of dollar amounts are not very meaningful. This is true for Dunfield's when comparing dollar amounts for 19x3 and 19x4. Because sales increased substantially when Dunfield added a new product line, it is difficult to evaluate what the dollar amounts should be for most of the other income statement items. Percentages in this case are a much better means for comparison.

Using inventories as an item for analysis, let's examine how horizontal analysis can help in the evaluation process. From 19x2 to 19x3, inventories increased by $2,000 ($1,439,000 − $1,437,000), an acceptable change for such a large dollar amount and given that sales increased also. From 19x3 to 19x4, inventories increased $264,000 ($1,703,000 − $1,439,000), an amount 18 percent over 19x3, quite alarming. However, because the company added a new product line, some increase was expected—but how much? The dollar amount seems large. But wait—are the percentages of the common size statements just as large? From Exhibit 17–1, notice that the percentages for inventory are 18.9, 19.1, and 19.5, respectively, for 19x2, 19x3, and 19x4. Although inventory as a percent of assets has increased, it does not appear unreasonable given the new product line and the overall increase in assets.

For another example, let us examine accounts payable. During 19x2 and 19x3, accounts payable remained relatively constant, but during 19x4 it increased by $336,000 ($1,564,000 − $1,228,000) and 1.6 percent (17.9 percent − 16.3

percent). In this case both measures, dollars and percentages, support each other in presenting a cause for concern. Additional analyses must be made to evaluate properly whether this account is under control and if such increases can be justified given the new product line.

After the vertical and horizontal analyses have been completed for the common size statements, the manager then begins to make computations concerning other relationships found within the financial reporting system of the company. The most common financial analysis procedures used for financial statement evaluation are considered in the remainder of this chapter.

Measures of Solvency

Solvency refers to the ability of a firm to pay its debts as they become due. The primary measures of *short-term solvency* are the current ratio, acid test ratio, inventory turnover, and the number of days receivables outstanding. The debt-to-equity ratio and the times-interest-earned measures are useful in assessing *long-term solvency*.

MANAGERIAL PRACTICE 17.2

Where to Find Measures of Solvency in an Annual Report

Many annual reports contain sufficient data to make numerous financial analyses without having to seek other financial sources. Using only the 1989 annual report of Phillips Petroleum, the following measures of solvency were computed. Except for working capital, these figures were provided in the annual report.

	1989	1988
Current ratio	1.06	1.24
Working capital	$170,000,000	$594,000,000
Acid test ratio	0.76	0.76
Inventory turnover	18.50	N/A
Days receivable outstanding	39.90	40.60
Debt-to-equity ratio	4.28	4.66
Times interest earned	1.83	2.62

Source: Phillips Petroleum Company Annual Report, 1989, 1, 31, 32.

Current Ratio.   The **current ratio** measures the relationship between current assets and current liabilities. The general equation for the current ratio and the computation for Dunfield's, as of December 31, 19x4, are as follows:

$$\textit{General equation:} \quad \text{Current ratio} = \frac{\text{Current assets}}{\text{Current liabilities}}$$

$$\textit{Example:} \qquad\qquad\qquad = \frac{\$5{,}246}{\$2{,}248}$$

$$= 2.33$$

Current assets represent cash and other assets that will be converted into cash (either directly or indirectly) through operations within a reasonably short period of time. Under normal operating conditions, cash is generated by sales of inventory and collection of accounts receivable. Current liabilities are financial obligations that will become due within a relatively short period of time and will be paid from cash currently on hand and from the pool of cash generated from current assets. Therefore, comparing current assets to current liabilities indicates the extent to which current assets are available to cover current liabilities. Dunfield's current ratio of 2.33 implies that the company has $2.33 of current assets for each $1 of current liabilities.

There is no universal guideline for evaluating the current ratio. Although a current ratio of 2.0 is often considered to be the norm, using an artificial guideline like this may lead to erroneous conclusions. For example, a current ratio of 2.0 is inadequate for a firm that has 90 percent of its total current assets tied up in obsolete or slow-moving inventory, while most of its current liabilities are due in the near term. The adequacy of a particular current ratio depends on (1) the composition of the current assets and how quickly they will convert to cash and (2) how soon current liabilities must be paid.

The current asset and current liability accounts are often referred to as *current operating,* or *current working,* accounts because assets and liabilities related to operating revenues and expenses normally flow in and out of the balance sheet through these accounts. The difference between current assets and current liabilities may be viewed as the net amount of working funds available in the short run. This fund is referred to as **working capital.** Dunfield's December 31, 19x4 working capital is computed as follows:

$$\text{Current assets} - \text{Current liabilities} = \text{Working capital,}$$
$$\$5{,}246{,}000 \quad - \quad \$2{,}248{,}000 \quad = \quad \$2{,}998{,}000.$$

This means that Dunfield's has $2,998,000 that can be used as operating funds in the near future. This working capital may be needed if accounts payable continues to increase as a result of the new product line started in 19x4. For a basic illustration as to how working capital can be used, consider the following transaction. Assume that during January 19x5 Dunfield's needs to purchase a piece of equipment for $50,000 but does not want to incur a liability. The impact of this transaction could be shown as follows:

$$\text{Current assets} - \text{Current liabilities} = \text{Working capital,}$$
$$-\$50,000 \quad - \quad \$0 \quad = \quad -\$50,000,$$

leaving a net result of

$$\text{Current assets} - \text{Current liabilities} = \text{Working capital,}$$
$$\$5,196,000 \quad - \quad \$2,248,000 \quad = \quad \$2,948,000.$$

Some transactions affect only current liabilities; others affect both current assets and current liabilities, but by different amounts; others affect both by the same amounts, resulting in no change in working capital; and some transactions have no effect on either.

In analyzing financial statements it is not unusual to find footnotes to the statements explaining major economic events that have taken place since the preparation of the statements or events that are going to take place in the near future. Applying the working capital concepts to the additional information can help assess the current operating condition of the company. Companies have been known to postpone certain transactions a few days past financial statement dates so that operating conditions would appear favorable on the date of the statements.

All economic transactions of an organization affect some aspect of the working capital equation except those that deal solely with the long-term accounts, that is, fixed assets, long-term liabilities, and equities. The next chapter considers how changes in working capital affect cash flows over an entire accounting period and examines the importance of the statement of cash flows in evaluating the changing economic conditions of an enterprise.

Acid Test Ratio. Current liabilities are usually paid with cash, not with other current assets. The acid test ratio is more specific than the current ratio as a test of short-term solvency. It measures the availability of cash, and other current monetary assets that can be quickly converted into cash, to pay current liabilities. *Current monetary assets* include cash, marketable securities, and current receivables. The general equation for the acid test ratio and the computation for Dunfield's, as of December 31, 19x4, are as follows:

General equation: $\text{Acid test ratio} = \dfrac{\text{Cash} + \text{Marketable securities} + \text{Current receivables}}{\text{Current liabilities}}$

Example: $= \dfrac{\$1,335 + \$250 + \$1,678}{\$2,248}$

$= 1.45$

Dunfield's acid test ratio indicates that it has $1.45 of current monetary assets for each $1 of current liabilities. This ratio is also referred to as the quick ratio because it shows the amount of cash that can be obtained relatively quickly for each $1 of current liabilities outstanding. Many analysts consider an acid test ratio of 1.0 to be adequate for most businesses; however, as stated earlier in discussing the current ratio, the composition of the ratio components must be considered before deciding what is an adequate ratio. When evaluating the current and acid test ratios, the manager must consider other factors, such as seasonal characteristics of the business, the availability of short-term credit lines, the collection terms for accounts receivables, and the payment terms of accounts payable.

As a follow-up to the current ratio and the acid test ratio, most analysts evaluate the liquidity of the primary assets in the cash flow stream—namely, inventory and accounts receivable. The inventory turnover and days receivables outstanding are the measures ordinarily used for this purpose.

Inventory Turnover. **Inventory turnover** indicates the approximate number of times the average stock of inventory was sold and replenished during the year. Inventory turnover is often regarded as both a measure of solvency and a measure of performance. As a solvency measure it tells how long it takes to convert inventory into current monetary assets. As a performance measure it tells how well the firm is managing investments in inventory. Inventory turnover is computed as the total cost of the inventory sold during the year divided by the average inventory on hand during the year.

$$\textit{General equation:} \quad \text{Inventory turnover} = \frac{\text{Cost of goods sold}}{\text{Average inventory}}$$

$$\textit{Example:} \quad \quad \quad \quad \quad \quad = \frac{\$6,085}{(\$1,703 + \$1,439)/2}$$

$$= 3.87 \text{ times}$$

During 19x4, Dunfield's sold inventory costing $6,085, and the average inventory for the year was $1,571 [($1,703 + $1,439)/2]; therefore, the average stock of inventory was sold and replenished 3.87 times during the year. Assuming a 365-day year, the average number of days required for each turnover of inventory was 94.3 days (365 days ÷ 3.87). That is, during the year the average inventory on hand was sufficient to meet the average sales needs for 94.3 days. Since ending inventory is somewhat higher than the average inventory for the year, inventory at year-end is sufficient to supply somewhat more than 94.3 days' average sales.

What constitutes an appropriate inventory turnover ratio varies from industry to industry and over time. Obviously, a fast food restaurant should have a high inventory turnover, whereas a jewelry store ordinarily has a low inventory turn-over. Firms adopting just-in-time approaches to inventory management should have an increase in their inventory turnovers. If a firm's competitors' inventory turnovers are increasing, this could indicate they have changed their approach to inventory management. The nature of the firm's supply sources, the use of inventory display in selling merchandise, the quickness with which inventory must be delivered to customers, and information on the industry should all be considered in interpreting the inventory turnover ratio.

Days Receivables Outstanding. Next to cash and marketable securities, receivables are the most liquid assets. They are converted directly into cash in the normal course of business. The **days receivables outstanding** ratio mea-sures the number of days, on average, it took to generate the sales uncollected at the year end. Days receivables outstanding is a measure of both solvency and performance. As a measure of solvency it tells how long it takes to convert accounts receivable into cash. As a performance measure it tells how well the firm is managing the credit extended to customers. Days receivables outstanding is computed as ending receivables divided by average daily sales.

$$\text{General equation:} \quad \text{Days receivables outstanding} = \frac{\text{Ending receivables}}{\text{Average daily sales}}$$

$$\text{Example:} \quad = \frac{\$1,678}{\$9,734/365}$$

$$= 62.9 \text{ days}$$

At the end of 19x4, Dunfield's had receivables on hand equal to the average sales for 62.9 days. In evaluating this measure, management should consider the terms under which credit sales are made. For example, if Dunfield's sells goods and services on 30-day credit terms, a ratio of 62.9 days probably indicates serious receivables collection problems. This ratio, which is a broad average, is a reliable indicator only if the amount of daily sales was fairly even throughout the year. For more precise information, management should conduct a detailed analysis of year-end receivables to determine their ages and probable collection periods.

Long-term solvency is a separate matter from that of short-term solvency. Obviously, all long-term debts must eventually be paid in some future current period; however, solvency is a matter that should be monitored both for the near term and the extended future. The debt-to-equity ratio and the times-interest-earned measure are useful in analyzing long-term solvency.

Debt-to-Equity Ratio. Most business enterprises have two basic sources of capital—*debt* and *equity*. The balance between the amounts of capital provided by creditors and owners is important in evaluating the long-term solvency of a business. Creditors regard equity as a cushion against future operating losses and bankruptcy. The larger the percentage of total assets financed by equity capital, the more secure are the creditors. Aggressive, growth-oriented organizations tend to rely more heavily on debt than equity, whereas stable, conservative organizations tend to have a larger proportion of equity. The **debt-to-equity ratio** is computed as total liabilities divided by total stockholders' equity.

$$\text{General equation:} \quad \text{Debt-to-equity ratio} = \frac{\text{Total liabilities}}{\text{Total stockholders' equity}}$$

$$\text{Example:} \quad = \frac{\$3,727}{\$5,027}$$

$$= 0.74$$

Dunfield's December 31, 19x4 debt-to-equity ratio of 0.74 indicates that the creditors have provided $0.74 of capital for each $1 provided by the stockholders. Stated another way, for each $1.74 of asset book values, the company could suffer a $1 loss and still have total assets on the books equal to total liabilities. In evaluating the debt-to-equity ratio, it is necessary to recognize the possible understatement or overstatement of assets and owners' equity. For example, if a company purchased land for $1 million that has a fair market value of $10 million, the company in effect has $9 million of unrecorded assets and owners' equity. Although the debt-to-equity ratio is useful as a general indicator of the adequacy of long-term solvency, the amount of long-term debt that a company can justify is primarily related to its ability to repay the funds plus interest.

Times Interest Earned. Because a financially sound business normally pays interest obligations out of current earnings, creditors are interested in the adequacy of earnings to provide payment of interest charges. **Times interest earned,** a measure of interest paying ability, shows the relationship between earnings available to pay interest and total interest expense.

$$\text{General equation:} \quad \text{Times interest earned} = \frac{\overset{\text{Net}}{\text{income}} + \overset{\text{Interest}}{\text{expense}} + \overset{\text{Income}}{\text{taxes}}}{\text{Interest expense}}$$

$$\text{Example:} \quad = \frac{\$1,163 + \$345 + \$599}{\$345}$$

$$= 6.11 \text{ times}$$

In the numerator, interest expense and income taxes are added to net income to determine the pool of earnings from which interest expense is paid. Since interest expense is deducted in computing taxable income, the earnings pool from which interest is paid is income before deductions for interest and taxes. For Dunfield's this pool of earnings for 19x4 is 6.11 times the amount of the current year's interest charge on debt.

Measures of Performance

Operating performance is related to the broad objective of profitability. The basic activities that characterize a typical for-profit organization are as follows:

- Generating capital (equity and debt).
- Acquiring assets with capital.
- Using assets to generate sales and profits.
- Using profits to pay the cost of capital.

The primary measures of performance are asset turnover, return on assets, return on equity, and earnings per share. Several of the measures of solvency discussed previously are also used to assist in the evaluation of these activities. It is quite common to find inventory turnover and days receivables outstanding as part of the measures of performance. The other common measures of performance are discussed in this section.

MANAGERIAL PRACTICE 17.3

Beware of Limited Analysis

The following measures of performance were computed from the 1989 annual report of Bristol-Myers Squibb Company. With the exception of asset turnover, it appears that the company had a substantial decline in performance from 1988 to 1989. However, it is very obvious when reading the annual report that 1989 was the year of merger between Bristol-Myers and Squibb. During 1989, over $855 million in expenses were attributed to the merger. If these expenses are ignored in the financial analysis, misleading conclusions could be drawn about the current operating status of the company. The astute financial analyst would probably recompute the 1989 ratios to allow for the merger.

	1989	1988
Asset turnover	1.100	1.080
Return on sales	.085	.152
Return on assets	.093	.165
Return on equity	.149	.258
Earnings per share	$1.43	$2.39

Source: Bristol-Myers Squibb Company Annual Report, 1989, 2, 88–93.

Asset Turnover. The **asset turnover** ratio measures the ability of the firm to use its assets to generate sales. It is computed as sales divided by average total assets.

$$\textit{General equation:} \qquad \text{Asset turnover} = \frac{\text{Sales}}{\text{Average total assets}}$$

$$\textit{Example:} \qquad\qquad\qquad\qquad = \frac{\$9,734}{(\$8,754 + \$7,555)/2}$$

$$= 1.19 \text{ times}$$

For Dunfield's, the asset turnover of 1.19 times indicates that on the average each \$1 of assets generated \$1.19 of sales during 19x4. The interpretation of this measure depends largely on the nature of the business. Organizations that are capital intensive, such as utilities or heavily automated manufacturers, typically have a lower asset turnover than organizations that are primarily dependent on labor, such as a garment manufacturer. Also, firms that generate a small amount of sales with each dollar of assets usually must earn a higher percentage of profit on each sales dollar than firms that produce a high amount of sales with each invested asset dollar.

Return on Sales. The ability of a firm to generate sales with available assets is important; to be profitable, however, these sales must exceed the cost of generating them. **Return on sales** is a measure of the ability of the firm to generate profits from sales produced by the firm's assets; it is computed by dividing the sum of net income and net-of-tax interest expense by sales.

$$\textit{General equation:} \qquad \text{Return on sales} = \frac{\text{Net income} + \text{Net-of-tax interest expense}}{\text{Sales}}$$

$$\textit{Example:} \qquad\qquad\qquad = \frac{\$1,163 + \$345(1 - 0.34)}{\$9,734}$$

$$= 0.143, \text{ or } 14.3\%$$

Interest expense is added to net income because it is not considered an expense of using assets, but rather a cost of providing the capital invested in assets. Since interest expense reduces taxes, it is adjusted for taxes at the current tax rate of 34 percent. On the average, 14.3 percent of each \$1 of Dunfield's 19x4 sales remained as profit after covering all expenses other than interest.

Return on Assets. The **return on assets** ratio combines the asset turnover and return on sales ratios to measure directly the ability of the firm to use its assets to generate profits. The return on assets computation is derived from the asset turnover and return on sales ratios as follows:

$$\text{Return on assets} = \text{Asset turnover} \times \text{Return on sales}$$

$$= \frac{\cancel{\text{Sales}}}{\begin{array}{c}\text{Average total}\\ \text{assets}\end{array}} \times \frac{\begin{array}{c}\text{Net}\\ \text{income}\end{array} + \begin{array}{c}\text{Net-of-tax}\\ \text{interest expense}\end{array}}{\cancel{\text{Sales}}}$$

General equation:
$$= \frac{\begin{array}{c}\text{Net}\\ \text{income}\end{array} + \begin{array}{c}\text{Net-of-tax}\\ \text{interest expense}\end{array}}{\text{Average total assets}}$$

Example:
$$= \frac{\$1{,}163 + \$345(1 - 0.34)}{(\$8{,}754 + \$7{,}555)/2}$$

$$= 0.171, \text{ or } 17.1\%$$

The 19x4 return on assets for Dunfield's may also be approximated by multiplying the asset turnover of 1.19 times the return on sales of 14.3 percent. From the previous analyses it can be concluded that on the average each dollar of assets generated $1.19 of sales and $0.171 of income, and each dollar of sales resulted in $0.143 of income. Return on assets is an important indicator of the overall performance of management because it measures management's effectiveness in using the total capital entrusted to them by both the creditors and the stockholders. A variation of this ratio (return on investment), discussed in Chapter 9, is commonly used for evaluating the performance of divisions in decentralized organizations.

The return on assets ratio measures profitability before deducting capital costs (interest and dividends); therefore, the adequacy of the profitability indicated by this ratio depends on the cost of debt and the return expected by the stockholders on their investments.

Return on Equity. **Return on equity** measures the profits attributable to the shareholders as a percentage of their equity in the firm. This measure is more specific than the return on assets ratio in measuring performance because it focuses only on *stockholders'* profits and investment. The profits available to stockholders consist of net income after deducting all costs and expenses, including interest expense. Return on equity is computed as net income divided by average stockholders' equity.[1]

---

[1] If there is more than one class of capital stock outstanding, the return on equity is computed as the return on common equity. In computing return on equity, net income must be reduced by the amount of annual dividends on preferred stock, and stockholders' equity must be reduced by the book value of preferred stock.

$$
\textit{General equation:} \quad \text{Return on equity} = \frac{\text{Net income}}{\text{Average stockholders' equity}}
$$

$$
\textit{Example:} \qquad\qquad = \frac{\$1,163}{(\$5,027 + \$4,391)/2}
$$

$$
= 0.247, \text{ or } 24.7\%
$$

The 19x4 return attributable to Dunfield's shareholders was 24.7 percent, compared to a return on assets of 17.1 percent. The return to the shareholders is higher than the return on assets as a result of financial leverage. **Financial leverage** refers to the use of capital that has a fixed interest or dividend rate. Any time capital can be acquired at a fixed rate,[2] and the return on assets is higher than that fixed rate, the return to the common shareholders is increased through *favorable financial leverage.* Conversely, if the fixed cost of capital is greater than the return it generates, the shareholders are subsidizing the cost of debt or other fixed rate capital, and there is *unfavorable financial leverage.* Dunfield's favorable financial leverage occurred because the return on assets was 17.1 percent, whereas the interest rate as a percent of average total liabilities was only 10 percent, computed as follows:

$$
\text{Average interest rate} = \frac{\text{Interest expense}}{\text{Average total liabilities}}
$$

$$
= \frac{\$345}{(\$3,727 + \$3,164)/2}
$$

$$
= 0.10, \text{ or } 10.0\%.
$$

The total debt required a return of only $345 (or 10 percent); therefore the return above 10 percent on the assets acquired with debt increased the return to the shareholders to 24.7 percent.

Earnings per Share. For external reporting purposes, earnings per share amounts are disclosed on the face of the income statement. If a company has gains or losses from extraordinary sources such as a natural disaster, or from other unusual and infrequent events, income and earnings per share figures must be presented separately for income before extraordinary items and for net income. Note on Dunfield's income statement in Exhibit 17–1 that reported earnings per share are $2.88 in 19x4 and $2.51 in 19x3. Since there were no extraordinary items, earnings per share amounts were presented only for net income.

---

[2] In an unstable money market the actual interest rate on a loan may change from period to period as the prime rate changes. These are called *variable rate loans.* Even in these situations the interest rate is fixed for a short period of time, and management's ability to generate favorable leverage varies inversely with changes in the applicable interest rate.

$$
\begin{aligned}
\textit{General equation:} \quad \text{Earnings per share} &= \frac{\text{Net income}}{\text{Average number of common shares outstanding}} \\
\textit{Example:} \quad &= \frac{\$1,163}{404} \\
&= \$2.88
\end{aligned}
$$

Earnings per share for companies with simple capital structures is computed as net income divided by the average number of shares outstanding for the period. A simple capital structure is one consisting only of common stock. The computations are more difficult for companies with more complex capital structures that include preferred stock, convertible bonds, or other types of equity securities. Since financial statements already include earnings per share figures, the manager does not have to compute these figures.

MANAGERIAL PRACTICE 17.4

An Alternative Investment Evaluation Tool

The sales-to-price ratio has been used for a number of years to indicate how much the stock market values a given company's dollar's worth of sales. Using the 1989 figures for IBM, the sales-to-price ratio is computed as follows: Multiply its 581 million outstanding shares by its March 1990 market price of $105 to get a $61 billion market value. Divide this by the latest 12-month sales figure of $62.7 billion to get a ratio of 0.97. Therefore, an investor would be paying 97 cents for every dollar's worth of IBM's sales. However, this ratio has a major shortcoming in that it ignores large debts, a critical amount for many companies.

To overcome this problem, Evan Sturza offers the total price-to-sales ratio. This ratio adds debt to the total market value. For IBM, this would change the ratio to 1.15, or ($61 billion + $10.8 billion) ÷ $62.7 billion. Therefore, including debt, the investor is paying $1.15 for each dollar's worth of IBM's sales.

Sources: Evan Sturza, "New, Improved Version," *Forbes,* 6 March 1989, 162–163, and *IBM Annual Report,* 1989, 1.

Earnings per share measures are used extensively by investors as a basis for evaluating the overall profitability of the firm. The advantage of the earnings per share measure is that it is reported on the same basis as capital stock prices— that is, on an individual share basis. Investors often use the price earnings ratio, which compares the current market price with earnings per share of the stock, to arrive at a multiple of earnings represented by the selling price.

Managers also may use earnings per share as a broad measure of overall performance; however, it should not be relied on too heavily, nor should it be substituted for other more detailed profitability ratios. Changes in the capital structure during the year make it more difficult to compare earnings per share from year to year. The other profitability measures discussed above are likely to be more beneficial to managers in evaluating overall management performance. Another reason why managers should monitor earnings per share figures is to be familiar with the measure used extensively by investors in making decisions about the company's capital stock.

Horizontal Analysis of Solvency and Performance Measures

Horizontal analysis, as already illustrated, is one of the best general measures of performance over time. This analysis can be readily extended to the financial ratios of solvency and performance measures. The annual reports of most companies include several years' data for key items such as gross sales, operating profit margin, net income, earnings per share, dividends paid, and net changes to retained earnings. However, the annual reports usually do not include the financial ratios that are important for evaluation purposes.

Horizontal analysis does not require very much in the way of additional computations because many of the items that provide input for other financial analysis techniques are already computed. A typical analysis might include the current ratio. Although a measure of solvency in the short run, the current ratio can be a measure of performance when compared over a period of years. For example, if the information for Dunfield's is extended back to 19x0 (19x0 and 19x1 supplied), a horizontal analysis of the current ratio reveals the following:

	19x4	19x3	19x2	19x1	19x0
Current ratio	2.33	2.40	2.52	2.56	2.61

From this trend, it appears that the ratio of current assets to current liabilities has been slowly declining. Such an analysis might alert the manager to take investigative action before the current ratio becomes undesirable. If creditors are using similar analysis, it might alert them to be cautious in extending credit to Dunfield's.

Horizontal analysis can be performed using both dollars and common size units. However, caution should be used when horizontal analysis is based only on dollar amounts. If we refer to Exhibit 17–1 and use dollars, horizontal analysis of the income statement reveals that cost of goods sold in 19x4 increased substantially over 19x3, whereas 19x3 and 19x2 were about the same. Is this good or bad, considering 19x4 sales also increased substantially? Additional horizontal analysis with common size units reveals another picture—the increase is only 2.2 percent (62.5 percent − 60.3 percent).

Some types of analysis combine both dollars and common size units with two or more sets of data to make performance evaluations using horizontal analysis. Suppose the income statements for Dunfield's, Inc., provided the following:

	19x4	19x3	19x2	19x1	19x0
Sales	$9,734	$8,028	$7,841	$7,260	$7,000*
Operating income	$2,017	$1,767	$1,825	$1,670	$1,610
Operating income as percent of sales	20.7%	22.0%	23.3%	23.0%	23.0%

* $ in thousands.

If only the dollars are considered, the trend for Dunfield's appears favorable, with sales increasing each year, including substantial growth in 19x4. Dollars of operating income are also increasing, except for 19x3, with 19x4 again showing a substantial increase. However, after adding the common size data to the analysis, the company's performance appears less favorable. After several years of operating with a 23 percent margin, performance slipped to 20.7 percent, even with the large 19x4 sales increase.

Another type of horizontal analysis is frequently used when a given point in time has been established as the base year or benchmark for comparison. Using the data above with 19x0 as the base year, a horizontal analysis using common size units would be as follows:

	19x4	19x3	19x2	19x1	19x0
Sales	139%	115%	112%	104%	100%
Operating income	125%	110%	113%	104%	100%

When we add this information to the previous analysis, it appears that the first sign of declining profits was really in 19x3, when operating income increased much slower than sales; in fact, it was less than 19x2 by 3 percentage points.

This application is frequently taken a step further by converting an entire financial statement to a base period and computing the change in each account for several financial statements. This allows the manager to examine the movement of all items in relation to a single starting point. Exhibit 17–2 reveals the

EXHIBIT 17–2   Base Year Common Size Statements

Dunfield's, Inc.
Common Size Comparative Income Statements
For the years ended December 31, 19x4, 19x3, and 19x2
19x2 being base year

	19x4	19x3	19x2
Sales	124.1%	102.4%	100.0%
Cost of goods sold	130.9	104.2	100.0
Gross profit	114.3	99.7	100.0
Operating expenses:			
Selling	118.7	102.5	100.0
General and administrative	120.4	105.4	100.0
Total	119.3	103.7	100.0
Operating income	110.5	96.8	100.0
Other revenues and expenses:			
Interest revenue	104.7	97.7	100.0
Interest expense	100.9	91.8	100.0
Total	99.6	89.8	100.0
Income before income taxes	112.3	98.0	100.0
Provision for income taxes	112.4	98.1	100.0
Net income	112.2	97.9	100.0

results of holding 19x2 as the base year for Dunfield's and adjusting all subsequent income statement accounts against 19x2. To illustrate this application, cost of goods sold shows an increase of 30.9 percent, whereas sales went up only 24.1 percent over the two-year period. Although gross profit increased 14.3 percent over the 19x2 base, it did not improve at the same level as sales. Therefore the manager might conclude that the increased sales attributable to the new product do not provide the same profit margin as the other products, or maybe the new production hindered the efficiency of production of the existing products. This type of analysis can also be applied to base year comparisons of balance sheets.

Industry Measures   The evaluation of the financial condition and performance of the firm is incomplete without comparisons to its industry during the same operating period(s). Industry comparisons provide insights into the relative financial condition and performance of the firm and show whether the firm is keeping pace, moving ahead, or lagging behind within its industry. As stated earlier in the chapter, there are several sources, such as Moody's, that provide industry averages on the key financial analysis ratios and indices.

These comparison evaluations should be made cautiously. First, avoid generalizations, such as every company should have a current ratio of 2.0 to 1; this caution was expressed in the section on current ratios. Second, avoid using industry averages as absolute guidelines for performance measurement. Although industry averages are probably better than generalizations, they may not apply equally to all firms within an industry. The industry average may be comprised of data from large firms, new firms, growing firms, diversified firms, and numerous other situations that do not match the situation of the firm being evaluated. It is very helpful if a distribution of the data statistics is provided within industry (this is provided for many industries in the aforementioned publications). For example, if the firm being evaluated has a current ratio of 1.6 and the industry average is 2.2, there may be cause for concern. But if it is known that the firm fits into a category of other similar firms within the industry that have an average current ratio of 1.7, cause for concern is lessened.

A third caution relates to the overall performance of the industry. A firm that is slightly below average in a financially strong industry may be better than one at the top of a financially weak industry. Again, there are business publications that give periodic ratings by industry, for example, the *Wall Street Journal.*

Fourth, a firm must be analyzed as to its diversity or homogeneity. A firm with diversified product lines may not exactly fit into any group or industry. Various reporting requirements (via government agencies) force companies to classify themselves under some predefined industry classification whether they are diversified or not. Diversified firms tend to distort the industry averages of firms that have homogeneous product lines and that fit nicely into the particular industry category.

Fifth, size influences how a firm should compare to the industry averages. The larger firms within an industry should probably be compared to the industry averages in a different way than smaller firms. This is not to imply that the large firms are better—in many industries the large firms are the weakest performers.

All of these cautions should be considered as appropriate when analyzing the financial condition of a firm and comparing that analysis to the industry averages. Comparing incompatible sets of data can result in managers making incorrect decisions, causing future performance to deteriorate.

SUMMARY

Financial statement analysis is the process of using financial statement data to generate additional financial information. Investors and creditors, as well as managers, can benefit from financial analysis. In addition to dollar statements, common size statements can be used in the analysis. Common size statements are very helpful during vertical and horizontal analyses of the financial statements. Measures for analyzing financial statements can be classified into solvency and performance measures. For evaluating short-term solvency, the current ratio and acid test ratio are used to determine the sufficiency of current assets to satisfy current liabilities. Other short-term solvency measures aimed at evaluating the liquidity of current assets are inventory turnover and the number of days receivables outstanding. Long-term solvency can be evaluated by computing the debt-to-equity ratio and the times-interest-earned multiple. These measures indicate the overall riskiness of the creditors' investment in the firm and the ability of the firm to meet its continuing interest requirements.

To evaluate current performance, several measures are available that focus both on the ability of the assets to generate sales and profits and on the profit returns attributable to creditors and stockholders. The productivity of the firm's assets is measured by asset turnover, the return-on-sales ratio, inventory turnover, days receivables outstanding, and the return-on-assets ratio. The profitability of the shareholders' investment is measured by the return-on-equity ratio. The favorable or unfavorable use of financial leverage can be determined by comparing return on assets with return on equity. Favorable leverage exists when the return on equity exceeds the return on assets; unfavorable leverage exists when the return on equity is less than the return on assets. Earnings per share may be helpful in assessing overall company performance, although it should be used with caution.

For the financial statement analysis to be complete, a comparison of industry averages should be made if the data are available. Care should be taken when making such comparisons, especially as related to generalizations, the use of industry averages without adjustments for size and diversity, and the overall condition of the industry used in the evaluation. With all of these items properly considered, along with other evaluation measures discussed in this chapter, a sound evaluation of a firm's financial condition and performance can be made.

SUGGESTED READINGS

Amernic, Joel E., "A Framework for Analyzing Financial Reporting Cases," *Journal of Accounting Education* (Spring 1986): 81–94.

Boer, Germain, "What Gross Margins Do Not Tell You," *Management Accounting* (October 1984): 50–53.

Clark, Ronald L., "Evaluating Continued Existence," *CPA Journal* (August 1986): 22–31.

Fetkyo, David F., and Michael Patterson, "How an Oil Company Analyzes Credit," *Management Accounting* (August 1983): 35–39.

Foster, George, *Financial Statement Analysis,* Englewood Cliffs, N.J.: Prentice-Hall, 1978.

Frishkoff, Paul, Patricia A. Frishkoff, and Marinus J. Bouwman, "Use of Accounting Data in Screening by Financial Analysts," *Journal of Accounting, Auditing and Finance, 1* (1984): 44–53.

Management Accounting Practices Committee, *Statement Number 4D: Measuring Entity Performance,* Montvale, N.J.: National Association of Accountants: 1986.

O'Keefe, Terrence B., "Financial Statement Analysis in Introductory Financial Accounting for MBAs," *Journal of Accounting Education* (Spring 1986): 195–201.

"Will Money Managers Wreck the Economy?" *Business Week* (13 August 1984): 86–89.

REVIEW PROBLEM

Common Size Statements and Ratio Analysis

Comparative 19x7 and 19x8 financial statements for O'Keefe's, Inc., are presented below.

O'Keefe's, Inc.
Comparative Income Statements
For the years ended December 31, 19x8 and 19x7
(*in thousands*)

	19x8	19x7
Sales	$3,000	$2,500
Cost of goods sold	−2,600	−2,300
Gross profit	$ 400	$ 200
Operating expenses:		
Selling	$ 125	$ 105
General and administrative	70	60
Total	− 195	− 165
Operating income	$ 205	$ 35
Other revenues and expenses:		
Interest income	$ 10	$ 5
Interest expense	(40)	(20)
Total	− 30	− 15
Income before income taxes	$ 175	$ 20
Provision for income taxes (34%)	− 60	− 7
Net income	$ 115	$ 13
Earnings per share	$ 1.28	$ 0.19

O'Keefe's, Inc.
Comparative Balance Sheets
December 31, 19x8 and 19x7
(*in thousands*)

Assets	19x8	19x7
Current assets:		
Cash	$ 300	$ 270
Marketable securities	75	45
Accounts receivable	325	280
Inventories	400	350
Interest receivable	60	55
Total current assets	$1,160	$1,000
Property, plant, and equipment	$1,500	$1,300
Less: Accumulated depreciation	− 800	− 750
Net	700	550
Other assets	15	12
Total assets	$1,875	$1,562

Liabilities and stockholders' equity

Current liabilities:		
Accounts payable	$ 435	$ 330
Income taxes payable	45	5
Interest payable	50	45
Total current liabilities	$ 530	$ 380
Long-term debt	300	250
Total liabilities	$ 830	$ 630
Stockholders' equity:		
Common stock ($1 par)	$ 90	$ 70
Premium on common stock	15	10
Retained earnings	940	852
Total stockholders' equity	1,045	932
Total liabilities and stockholders' equity	$1,875	$1,562

Additional information:

- During 19x8, Operating Expenses included a total of $50,000 in depreciation expense.
- Dividends of $27,000 were declared and paid during 19x8.
- Common stock of $15,000 was issued at par for cash in 19x8.
- Equipment costing $200,000 was acquired during 19x8 by paying cash of $190,000 and issuing 5,000 shares of common stock worth $10,000.
- During 19x8, long-term debt of $20,000 was paid off in cash and new long-term debt of $70,000 was issued for cash.
- The company extended a loan of $3,000 to the president during 19x8.

Requirements

a) Prepare common size statements for 19x7 and 19x8. Use sales as the base for income statements and total assets as the base for balance sheets.

b) What major changes are noted from 19x7 to 19x8 when horizontal analysis is performed?

c) Prepare a complete ratio analysis for 19x8 including measures of solvency and performance.

The solution to this problem is found at the end of the Chapter 17 exercises, problems, and cases.

KEY TERMS

Acid test ratio	Inventory turnover
Asset turnover	Price earnings ratio
Common size statement	Quick ratio
Current ratio	Return on assets
Days receivables outstanding	Return on equity
Debt-to-equity ratio	Return on sales
Earnings per share	Solvency
Financial leverage	Times interest earned
Financial statement analysis	Vertical analysis
Horizontal analysis	Working capital

17–1 What is the general purpose for conducting ratio analysis of financial statements?

17–2 Name three reasons why managers should analyze their firm's financial statements.

17–3 What is the purpose of evaluation standards in financial analysis?

17–4 What types of standards are probably most relevant for financial analysis by managers?

17–5 Explain how managers use vertical and horizontal analysis when evaluating financial statements. What changes are usually made in the statements before these techniques are used?

17–6 Explain and differentiate the terms *solvency evaluation* and *performance evaluation*.

17–7 Explain the difference between the current ratio and the acid test ratio.

17–8 Why is it useful to compute the inventory turnover and the days receivables outstanding? How is each of these measures computed?

17–9 What are the primary measures of long-term solvency? How are they computed?

17–10 Which financial statement analysis measure provides information concerning the sales output produced by a firm's assets?

17–11 Why is interest expense added in the numerator in computing return on assets?

17–12 Explain the concept of financial leverage. What causes financial leverage to be favorable? Unfavorable?

17–13 Explain why comparisons to industry norms or averages are important when analyzing financial statements.

17–14 What cautions should the manager take when using industry norms or averages for comparison?

EXERCISES

17–1 Short-Term Solvency Ratios

Windover, Inc., had the following current assets and current liabilities in its end-of-year financial statements for 19x1 and 19x0.

Current assets	19x1	19x0
Cash	$ 1,700	$ 1,500
Accounts receivable	16,200	6,900
Marketable securities	2,000	2,500
Inventory	8,300	7,400
Total	$28,200	$18,300

Current liabilities		
Accounts payable	$ 5,600	$ 3,700
Notes payable	1,000	1,000
Accrued expenses payable	5,400	4,300
Total	$12,000	$ 9,000

Additional data:

	19x1	19x0
Sales	$195,000	$220,000
Cost of goods sold	132,000	158,000
Inventory, beginning of 19x0		6,800

Required: Compute the following ratios for 19x1 and 19x0. (Round calculations to two decimal places.)

1. Current ratio.

2. Acid test ratio.

3. Inventory turnover.

4. Days receivables outstanding.

17–2 Short-Term Solvency Ratios

The following items (listed alphabetically) were taken from the 19x7 year-end financial statements of Monteray Corporation.

Accounts payable	$ 27,500
Accounts receivable	32,000
Cash	4,800
Cost of goods sold	195,000
Inventory, beginning	80,000
Inventory, ending	65,000
Marketable securities	15,750
Other current payables	8,200
Sales	325,000

Required: Compute the following ratios. (Round calculations to two decimal places.)

1. Current ratio.

2. Acid test ratio.

3. Inventory turnover.

4. Days receivables outstanding.

17–3 Short-Term Solvency Ratios

The financial data given below were obtained from the end-of-year financial statements of York Company for 19x2, 19x1, and 19x0.

	19x2	19x1	19x0
Accounts receivable	$ 153,000	$ 165,000	$ 150,000
Cost of goods sold	1,680,000	1,450,000	1,600,000
Current assets	750,000	600,000	675,000
Current liabilities	525,000	450,000	500,000
Inventory	375,000	275,000	325,000
Sales	1,850,000	2,000,000	1,750,000

Requirements

a) Compute the following financial ratios for 19x2 and 19x1. (Round calculations to two decimal places.)

   1. Current ratio.

   2. Acid test ratio.

   3. Inventory turnover.

   4. Days receivables outstanding.

b) Comment on the short-term solvency of York Company for 19x1 and 19x2. Did the company's short-term solvency improve or deteriorate during 19x2? Explain.

17–4 Long-Term Solvency Ratios

Selected financial statement data for 19x5 are given below for Vail Construction Company.

Income taxes	$ 36,018
Interest expense	4,000
Net income	48,178
Total assets	399,363
Total liabilities	133,121

Requirements (Round calculations to two decimal places.)

a) Compute the debt-to-equity ratio.

b) Compute the ratio of times interest earned.

17–5 Long-Term Solvency Ratios

Summaries of the end-of-year financial statements of Palo Alto Company for 19x6 are given as follows.

Income statement:		
Sales		$8,000,000
Less: Cost of goods sold	$3,425,000	
Selling expenses	625,000	
Administrative expenses	525,000	
Interest expense	1,475,300	
Income tax expense	50,250	−6,100,550
Net income		$1,899,450
Balance sheet:		
Total assets	$850,000	
	Total liabilities	$600,000
	Stockholders' equity	250,000
	Total	$850,000

Requirements

a) Compute the ratio of times interest earned. (Round computations to two decimal places.)

b) Compute the debt-to-equity ratio.

17–6 Ratio Analysis: Measures of Performance

Laurens Country Surveyors had sales for 19x3 of $600,000 and net income of $30,000 after taxes. The interest on the notes payable for 19x3 amounted to $3,000, and the tax rate was 30 percent. The balance sheets as of June 30, 19x3 and 19x2 were as follows:

	19x3	19x2
Assets:		
Cash	$14,000	$13,600
Accounts receivable	20,000	18,000
Equipment, net of depreciation	62,500	60,000
Total	$96,500	$91,600
Liabilities and equities:		
Accounts payable	$26,000	$29,200
Notes payable	32,500	30,400
Owner's equity (10,000 shares outstanding)	38,000	32,000
Total	$96,500	$91,600

Required: Compute the following performance measures: asset turnover, return on sales, return on assets, return on equity, and earnings per share.

17–7 Measures of Performance and Financial Leverage

The following selected data were obtained from the end-of-year financial statements of Nelox Corporation for 19x9 and 19x8.

	19x9	19x8
Total assets	$7,349,000	$6,553,000
Interest expense	115,000	102,000
Long-term liabilities	1,220,000	1,239,000
Net income	619,000	563,000
Sales	8,196,000	6,996,000
Stockholders' equity	3,624,000	3,221,000

Requirements

a) Compute the following performance measurement ratios for 19x9. (Round computations to three decimal places. Ignore income taxes.)

1. Asset turnover.

2. Return on sales.

3. Return on assets.

4. Return on equity.

b) Is Nelox Company using financial leverage? If so, is the leverage favorable or unfavorable? Explain.

17–8 Financial Leverage

The following data have been determined for McClellan Company and McDonough Company for 19x5.

	McClellan	McDonough
Net income	$ 270,000	$ 405,000
Interest expense	120,000	112,500
Total assets, beginning of 19x5	3,750,000	6,375,000
Total assets, end of 19x5	4,042,500	6,847,500
Stockholders' equity, beginning of 19x5	1,594,500	3,703,500
Stockholders' equity, end of 19x5	1,689,000	3,832,500

Requirements

a) Compute the following ratios for McClellan and McDonough Companies at the end of 19x5. (Ignore taxes and round calculations to three decimal places.)

1. Return on assets.

2. Return on equity.

b) Comment on the use of financial leverage by these two companies. Which company is the most highly leveraged? Which company's stockholders are benefiting the most from the use of leverage?

17–9 Effects of Financing Decisions

Provo, Inc., has total assets of $2,500,000 and total liabilities of $2,000,000. Provo is considering two alternatives for acquiring additional warehouse space. Under the first alternative the building would be purchased for $300,000 and financed by issuing long-term bonds. Under the other alternative the building would be rented on an annual lease of $30,000 per year.

Requirements

a) Compute the current debt-to-equity ratio.

b) What effect will the addition of the warehouse space have on the debt-to-equity ratio (1) assuming the building is purchased by issuing bonds and (2) assuming the building is rented on an annual lease?

17–10 Common Size Statements

Comparative balance sheets for Albany Products, Inc., are presented below for the years ended 19x7 and 19x6. The president is concerned about the decline in total assets and wants to know where most of the decline took place.

	19x7	19x6
Cash	$ 220,000	$ 230,000
Accounts receivable	350,000	300,000
Inventory	300,000	450,000
Property, plant, and equipment	1,200,000	1,200,000
Less: Accumulated depreciation	− 525,000	− 475,000
Total assets	$1,545,000	$1,705,000
Accounts payable	$ 260,000	$ 255,000
Long-term note payable	280,000	350,000
Common stock	500,000	500,000
Retained earnings	505,000	600,000
Total equities	$1,545,000	$1,705,000

Required: Convert these balance sheets to common size statements and explain to the president where the largest changes took place.

17–11 Common Size Statements

Comparative financial statements for Dublin Clover Company for the years ended 19x9 and 19x8 are presented below.

	19x9	19x8
Sales	$5,500,000	$4,800,000
Cost of goods sold	−3,500,000	−3,200,000
Gross profit	$2,000,000	$1,600,000
Operating expenses:		
Selling	$ 350,000	$ 200,000
General and administrative	100,000	100,000
Total	− 450,000	− 300,000
Operating income	$1,550,000	$1,300,000
Other revenues and expenses:		
Interest income	$ 20,000	$ 20,000
Interest expense	− 80,000	− 60,000
Total	− 60,000	− 40,000
Income before income taxes	$1,490,000	$1,260,000
Provision for income taxes	− 740,000	− 590,000
Net income	$ 750,000	$ 670,000

Requirements

a) Prepare common size statements for each year using sales as base.

b) What major changes are shown with the common size statements?

17–12 Changes in Working Capital

Below is a list of typical financial, investing, and operating transactions.

a) Sold capital stock for cash.

b) Purchased a building for cash.

c) Paid current liabilities.

d) Issued long-term bonds payable.

e) Purchased inventory on account.

f) Purchased a building site by issuing long-term bonds.

g) Sold equipment for an amount equal to book value.

h) Sold treasury stock for cash.

i) Long-term note matures and will be a current payable later this year.

Required: For each of the above transactions indicate whether current assets, current liabilities, or working capital increased, decreased, or remained unchanged. Use the following column headings:

Current assets − Current liabilities = Working capital.

17–13 Changes in Working Capital

Auckland Industries had a July 31 current asset balance of $31,200 and a current liability balance of $20,800. The following transactions took place in August:

- Sold land for $45,000.
- Collected $80,000 from a long-term note receivable.
- Paid $47,000 on outstanding payables.
- Purchased inventory for $65,000 on account.
- Paid long-term bond payable of $10,000 two years ahead of schedule.

Required: Determine the effects on working capital for each of the items and compute the ending working capital. Use the following format:

	Current assets	−	Current liabilities	=	Working capital
Beginning balance:	$31,200		$20,800		$10,400

17–14 Horizontal Analysis

Selected data for the Lexington Filter Company, a manufacturing firm, are given for the last five years.

	19x4	19x5	19x6	19x7	19x8
Average cash balance	$12,500	$18,400	$25,600	$62,300	$88,600
Sales	$432,000	$487,000	$539,000	$591,000	$642,000
Operating income	$3,500	$7,850	$11,600	$94,400	$129,000
Current ratio	0.23	0.31	0.56	0.77	0.81
Asset turnover	0.80	0.90	1.00	1.09	1.19

Required: What assessments can be made about the performance and operating characteristics of the company for the five year period?

17–15 Horizontal Analysis

El Paso Investment Brokers are considering purchasing Rio Valley Produce for some of its clients. The following data have been collected from recent financial statements of Rio Valley Produce.

	19x2	19x3	19x4	19x5	19x6
Sales (in thousands)	$4,000	$4,300	$4,900	$4,800	$5,100
Operating income (in thousands)	$1,100	$1,150	$1,300	$1,285	$1,425
Net income (in thousands)	$495	$520	$505	$490	$513
Current ratio	2.33	2.11	2.78	1.96	2.45
Asset turnover	1.01	1.34	1.68	1.73	2.07

Required: Determine the strengths and weaknesses evident from the above information. Select some type of common size application for the dollar numbers for your analysis. What would you recommend regarding the purchase of Rio Valley Produce?

17–16 Inflation Considerations

The president of Greenville Office Products was very pleased with the progress her company had made in recent years, but she could not understand why the company was always having to borrow funds when sales continually increased. Her office staff was small, and the largest costs outside of merchandise inventory were sales commissions, which were 20 percent of sales. As the cost of merchandise changed she continually changed the retail prices, therefore she thought the profit margin should remain near the same percentage level. However, even with her best efforts, the company still had cash problems.

After gathering additional financial data, you have prepared the following set of information for the last four years.

	19x6	19x7	19x8	19x9
Sales	$240,000	$252,000	$264,600	$277,830
Cost of goods sold	$150,000	$159,000	$168,540	$178,652
Current ratio	1.46	1.34	1.23	1.14
Inventory turnover	4.66	4.65	4.67	4.66
General inflation rate	6.00%	6.00%	6.00%	6.00%

Required: What conclusions can be drawn about the operating condition of Greenville Office Products?

17–17 Inflation Considerations

The Nova Products Company wants to start a new product to replace a current product, which is technologically obsolete. Because it is a replacement product, the first year's sales are expected to be 100,000 units at a selling price of $4.00. The initial cost of the product will be $3.00 per unit variable and $100,000 fixed. The expected sales growth is 1,000 units per year, and the expected inflation rate is in a range of 4 to 5 percent for sales and variable costs.

Requirements

a) Determine the anticipated profit margin for the new product for the first four years assuming:

1. No inflation.

2. Inflation at 4 percent.

b) Compute the profit margin difference between no inflation and 4 percent inflation. Would this make a difference in your opinion of the new product?

PROBLEMS

17–18
Comprehensive Ratio Analysis

Rocky Mountain Company's financial statements are presented below.

Rocky Mountain Company
Comparative Balance Sheets
December 31, 19x4 and 19x3

Assets	19x4	19x3
Cash	$ 243,000	$ 270,000
Accounts receivable	1,147,000	1,120,000
Inventory	637,000	556,000
Total current assets	$2,027,000	$ 1,946,000
Property, plant, and equipment (net)	7,587,000	6,952,000
Total assets	$9,614,000	$ 8,898,000

Liabilities and stockholders' equity		
Accounts payable	$ 297,000	$ 256,000
Accrued expenses payable	607,000	594,000
Total current liabilities	$ 904,000	$ 850,000
Long-term debt	1,350,000	1,282,000
Total liabilities	$2,254,000	$ 2,132,000
Common stock	$5,200,000	$ 5,200,000
Retained earnings	2,160,000	1,566,000
Total stockholders' equity	7,360,000	6,766,000
Total liabilities and stockholders' equity	$9,614,000	$ 8,898,000

Rocky Mountain Company
Income Statement
For the year ended December 31, 19x4

Sales		$11,677,000
Cost of goods sold		− 6,513,000
Gross profit		$ 5,164,000
Less operating expenses:		
Depreciation	$ 567,000	
Other expenses	2,882,000	− 3,449,000
Income from operations		$ 1,715,000
Less interest expense		− 94,000
Income before income taxes		$ 1,621,000
Less income taxes		− 486,000
Net income		$ 1,135,000

Requirements (Round all calculations to three decimal places.)

a) Prepare a short-term solvency ratio analysis for Rocky Mountain Company for 19x4.

b) Prepare a long-term solvency ratio analysis for 19x4.

c) Prepare a performance ratio analysis for 19x4.

17–19
Comprehensive
Financial Analysis

Comparative income statements and balance sheets for Seneca Company are presented below for 19x9 and 19x8.

Seneca Company
Comparative Income Statements
For the years ended December 31, 19x9 and 19x8

	19x9	19x8
Sales	$11,778,070	$11,241,498
Cost of goods sold	− 6,615,148	− 6,395,466
Gross profit	$ 5,162,922	$ 4,846,032
Less selling and administrative expenses	− 3,565,750	− 3,363,722
Operating income	$ 1,597,172	$ 1,482,310
Other revenues and expenses:		
Interest revenue	141,264	80,198
Interest expense	(76,698)	(70,204)
Other expenses	(47,230)	(18,850)
Income before income taxes	$ 1,614,508	$ 1,473,454
Income taxes	− 720,368	− 660,818
Net income	$ 894,140	$ 812,636

Seneca Company
Comparative Balance Sheets
December 31, 19x9 and 19x8

Assets	19x9	19x8
Cash	$ 241,816	$ 259,370
Marketable securities	437,268	202,802
Accounts receivable	966,982	1,046,246
Inventory	1,501,438	1,620,470
Prepaid expenses	124,988	115,618
Total current assets	$ 3,272,492	$ 3,244,506
Investments and other assets	774,836	604,368
Property, plant, and equipment (net)	2,818,912	2,681,680
Trademarks and other intangibles	263,322	281,362
Total assets	$ 7,129,562	$ 6,811,916

Liabilities and stockholders' equity	19x9	19x8
Notes payable	$ 179,294	$ 175,174
Current maturities of long-term debt	10,030	15,056
Accounts payable and accrued expenses	1,822,326	1,932,930
Total current liabilities	$ 2,011,650	$ 2,123,160
Long-term debt	556,368	539,280
Total liabilities	$ 2,568,018	$ 2,662,440
Common stock	$ 124,778	$ 124,744
Additional paid-in capital	228,388	226,344
Retained earnings	4,208,378	3,798,388
Total stockholders' equity	4,561,544	4,149,476
Total liabilities and stockholders' equity	$ 7,129,562	$ 6,811,916

Requirements

a) Prepare a comprehensive financial analysis of Seneca, Inc., for 19x9, including (1) short-term solvency ratios, (2) long-term solvency ratios, and (3) performance measurement ratios. (Round all calculations to three decimal places.)

b) Comment on the financial condition of Seneca, Inc., with respect to short-term solvency, long-term solvency, and performance.

**17–20
Comprehensive
Common Size
Statements**

After reviewing the traditional financial analyses, the managers of Seneca Company (see Problem 17–19) are still uncertain about the performance of the company during 19x9. They believe that common size statements might provide additional insights as to the company's performance.

Requirements

a) Using the data pertaining to the Seneca Company in Problem 17–19, prepare common size statements and evaluate the performance of the company in 19x9 as compared to 19x8. For the balance sheets, use total assets as the base. For the income statements, make one set using sales of each year as the base for that year and another set using the year 19x8 as the base.

b) Comment on the condition of the company now that these new statements have been prepared.

17–21 Ratio Analysis

Presented below are the 19x1 balance sheet and income statement for MND Corporation.

**MND Corporation
Balance Sheet
As of December 31, 19x1**

Assets

Cash		$ 7,500,000
Accounts receivable		12,000,000
Inventory		9,000,000
Property, plant, and equipment	$48,400,000	
Less: Accumulated depreciation	−11,900,000	36,500,000
Total assets		$65,000,000

Liabilities and stockholders' equity

Accounts payable	$10,700,000
Notes payable (short term)	5,300,000
Mortgage bonds (due in 19x4)	9,500,000
Common stock ($10 par value, 4,500,000 shares authorized, 2,500,000 shares issued and outstanding)	25,000,000
Paid in capital in excess of par value	5,000,000
Retained earnings	9,500,000
Total liabilities and stockholders' equity	$65,000,000

MND Corporation
Income Statement
For the year ended December 31, 19x1

Cash sales		$10,000,000
Credit sales		60,000,000
Total sales		$70,000,000
Cost of goods sold:		
Beginning inventory of finished goods	$ 4,000,000	
Cost of goods manufactured	50,000,000	
Goods available	$54,000,000	
Ending inventory of finished goods	− 5,000,000	−49,000,000
Gross profit		$21,000,000
Operating expenses:		
Selling	$ 3,000,000	
General	10,800,000	−13,800,000
Operating income		$ 7,200,000
Interest expense		− 1,000,000
Income before income taxes		$ 6,200,000
Income taxes (34%)		− 2,108,000
Net income		$ 4,092,000

Requirements

a) Compute the following solvency ratios for MND Corporation for the fiscal year 19x1. (Round calculations to three decimal places.)

   1. Current ratio.

   2. Acid test ratio.

   3. Days receivables outstanding (based on credit sales).

   4. Finished goods inventory turnover.

   5. Debt-to-equity.

   6. Times interest earned.

b) Compute the following performance ratios. (Round calculations to three decimal places.)

   1. Asset turnover.

   2. Return on sales.

   3. Return on assets.

   4. Return on equity.

(CMA Adapted)

17–22 Interpreting Financial Analysis Ratios

Thorpe Company is a wholesale distributor of professional equipment and supplies. The company's sales have averaged about $900,000 annually for the three-year period 19x3–19x5. The firm's total assets at the end of 19x5 amounted to $850,000. The president of Thorpe Company has asked the controller to prepare a report that summarizes the financial aspects of the company's operations for the past three years. This report will be presented to the Board of Directors at their next meeting. In addition to comparative financial statements, the controller has decided to present a number of relevant financial ratios to assist in the identification and interpretation of trends. At the request of the controller, the accounting staff has calculated the following ratios for the three-year period 19x3–19x5.

	19x5	19x4	19x3
Current ratio	2.18	2.13	2.00
Acid test ratio	0.97	1.10	1.20
Days receivables outstanding	51.20	42.60	37.60
Inventory turnover	3.80	4.80	5.25
Debt-to-equity ratio	0.61	0.69	0.79
Asset turnover	1.99	1.88	1.75
Sales as a percentage of 19x3 sales	1.06	1.03	1.00
Gross profit percent	38.50	38.60	40.00
Return on sales	8.0%	7.8%	7.8%
Return on assets	8.7%	8.6%	8.5%
Return on equity	14.1%	14.6%	15.1%

In the preparation of his report, the controller has decided first to examine the financial ratios independently of any other data to determine if the ratios themselves reveal any significant trends over the three-year period.

Requirements

Answer the following questions. Indicate in each case which ratio(s) you used in arriving at your conclusion.

a) The current ratio is increasing, whereas the acid test ratio is decreasing. Using the ratios provided, identify and explain the contributing factor(s) for this apparently divergent trend.

b) In terms of the ratios provided, what conclusion(s) can be drawn regarding the company's use of financial leverage during the 19x3–19x5 period?

c) Using the ratios provided, what conclusion(s) can be drawn regarding the company's ability to generate sales and profits from the assets available to management?

(CMA Adapted)

17–23 Comprehensive Financial Statement Analysis

You have been assigned by the acquisitions committee of Buyers, Inc., to examine a potential acquisition, Drygoods, Inc. This company is a merchandising firm that is available for acquisition. Selected financial statements from the last two years are given as follows.

Drygoods, Inc.
Comparative Balance Sheets
December 31, 19x2 and 19x1

	19x2	19x1
Cash	$ 130,000	$ 120,000
Accounts receivable	430,000	370,000
Inventory	400,000	400,000
Property, plant, and equipment	900,000	800,000
Less: Accumulated depreciation	− 325,000	− 250,000
Total assets	$1,535,000	$1,440,000
Accounts payable	$ 300,000	$ 260,000
Long-term note payable	280,000	280,000
Common stock	690,000	690,000
Retained earnings	265,000	210,000
Total equities	$1,535,000	$1,440,000

Drygoods, Inc.
Income Statement
For the year ended December 31, 19x2

Sales		$2,943,000
Less expenses:		
Cost of goods sold	$2,200,000	
Wages expense	350,000	
Supplies expense	42,600	
Depreciation expense	100,000	
Interest expense	22,400	
Loss on sale of fixed assets	75,000	−2,790,000
Net income before taxes		$ 153,000
Income taxes		− 52,020
Net income		$ 100,980

Requirements

a) Calculate the following ratios for 19x2 (round calculations to three decimal places).

  1. Current ratio.

  2. Acid test.

  3. Inventory turnover.

  4. Days receivables outstanding.

  5. Debt-to-equity ratio.

  6. Times interest earned.

  7. Asset turnover.

  8. Return on sales.

  9. Return on assets.

  10. Return on equity.

b) Prepare common size statements for all statements presented.

c) What is your recommendation regarding the acquisition of Drygoods, Inc.?

Select a recent annual report (or use one provided by your instructor) of a publicly held company and perform all of the financial analysis measures discussed in this chapter. Be sure to include vertical and horizontal analyses with common size statements. List any of the measures discussed in this chapter that you were unable to perform, and state the reasons. Give your opinion as to the financial performance trend of the company, citing financial analysis measures to support your reasons.

If industry data are available, make a comparison of the company used for analysis and its industry norms and averages. Evaluate the position it holds within its industry.

Below are excerpts from the 1989 annual report of American Greetings Corporation. Perform all of the financial statement analysis measures discussed in the chapter that are possible with the information provided. Be sure to include vertical and horizontal analyses with common size statements. List any of the measures that you could not perform, and state reasons. Give your opinion as to the financial performance trend of the company, citing financial analysis measures to support your reasons.

American Greetings Corporation
Consolidated Statement of Income
For the years ended February 28, 1989, and February 29, 1988
(*in thousands of dollars except for per share amounts*)

	1989	1988
Net sales	$1,252,793	$1,174,817
Other income	22,566	24,155
Total revenue	$1,275,359	$1,198,972
Costs and expenses:		
Material, labor, and other production costs	$ 546,214	$ 540,143
Selling, distribution, and marketing	415,597	400,033
Administrative and general	148,095	135,224
Depreciation and amortization	39,527	34,191
Interest	33,479	32,787
Restructuring charge	23,591	–
Total costs and expenses	−1,206,503	−1,142,378
Income before income taxes	$ 68,856	$ 56,594
Provision for income taxes	− 24,582	− 23,203
Net income	$ 44,274	$ 33,391
Earnings per share	$1.38	$1.04

American Greetings Corporation
Consolidated Statement of Financial Position
February 28, 1989, and February 29, 1988
(*in thousands of dollars*)

Assets	1989	1988
Current assets:		
Cash and equivalents	$ 94,292	$ 36,534
Trade accounts receivable less allowances	242,582	278,559

Inventories:		
Raw material	$ 48,478	$ 56,122
Work-in-process	51,625	61,406
Finished products	197,618	245,801
	$ 297,721	$ 363,329
Less LIFO reserve	− 83,017	− 77,274
	$ 214,704	$ 286,055
Display materials and factory supplies	25,192	30,299
Total inventories	239,896	316,354
Deferred income taxes	49,542	39,935
Prepaid expenses and other	11,020	8,672
Total current assets	$ 637,332	$ 680,054
Other assets	92,285	95,752
Property, plant, and equipment:		
Land	$ 6,471	$ 7,548
Buildings	216,545	223,491
Equipment and fixtures	340,233	319,353
	$ 563,249	$ 550,392
Less accumulated depreciation and amortization	− 205,246	− 175,917
Net property, plant, and equipment	358,003	374,475
Total assets	$1,087,620	$1,150,281

Liabilities and shareholders' equity

Current liabilities:		
Notes payable to banks	$ 17,201	$ 13,956
Accounts payable	79,591	98,270
Payrolls and payroll taxes	38,839	33,759
Retirement plans	8,573	4,148
Dividends payable	5,311	5,338
Income taxes payable	6,693	13,782
Sales returns	24,543	28,273
Current maturities of long-term debt	3,740	54,150
Total current liabilities	$ 184,491	$ 251,676
Long-term debt	246,732	273,492
Deferred income taxes	91,409	86,426

Stockholders' equity:		
Class A common stock	$ 29,692	$ 29,628
Class B common stock	2,497	2,528
Capital in excess of par value	105,245	104,209
Treasury stock	(14,767)	(14,199)
Cumulative translation adjustment	(4,790)	(7,564)
Retained earnings	447,111	424,085
Total shareholders' equity	564,988	538,687
Total liabilities and shareholders' equity	$1,087,620	$1,150,281

American Greeting Corporation
Consolidated Statement of Retained Earnings
Years ended February 28, 1989, and February 29, 1988

	1989	1988
Beginning balance	$424,085	$416,598
Net income	44,274	33,391
Cash dividends ($.66 per share)	(21,188)	(21,163)
Sale of treasury stock	(60)	(4,741)
Ending balance	$447,111	$424,085

17–26 Comparative Financial Statement Analysis with Actual Annual Reports

Below are excerpts from the 1988 annual reports of Chevron and Mobil Corporations. Perform all of the financial statement analysis measures discussed in the chapter that are possible with the information that is provided. Be sure to include vertical and horizontal analyses with common size statements. List any of the measures that you could not perform, and state reasons. Give your opinion as to the financial performance trend of each company, citing financial analysis measures to support your reasons. Which company do you think had the best performance during the period under review? Why?

Chevron Corporation
Consolidated Statement of Income
For the years ended December 31, 1988 and 1987
(*in millions of dollars except per share amounts*)

	1988	1987
Revenues:		
Sales and other operating revenues	$27,722	$28,106
Equity in net income of affiliated companies	422	376
Other income	713	638
Total revenues	$28,857	$29,120
Costs and other deductions:		
Purchased crude oil and products	$12,010	$13,627
Operating expenses	5,220	4,713
Exploration expenses	651	466
Selling, general, and administrative expenses	1,758	1,416
Depreciation, depletion, and amortization	2,436	2,514
Taxes other than income	3,255	2,913
Interest and debt expenses	628	699
Total costs and other deductions	−25,958	−26,348
Income before income tax expense	$ 2,899	$ 2,772
Income tax expense	− 1,131	− 1,522
Net income	$ 1,768	$ 1,250
Net income per share	$5.17	$3.65

Chevron Corporation
Consolidated Statement of Retained Earnings
For the years ended December 31, 1988 and 1987
(*in millions of dollars*)

	1988	1987
Balance at beginning of year	$11,884	$11,452
Net income (loss) for year	1,768	1,250
Cash dividends ($2.55 per share in 1988 and $2.40 in 1987)	(869)	(818)
Balance at end of year	$12,783	$11,884

Chevron Corporation
Consolidated Balance Sheets
December 31, 1988 and 1987
(*in millions of dollars*)

Assets	1988	1987
Current assets:		
Cash and cash equivalents	$ 1,297	$ 3,124
Marketable securities, at cost (approximates market)	518	524
Accounts and notes receivable	3,310	2,945
Inventories	2,485	2,634
Prepaid expenses and other current assets	331	288
Total current assets	$ 7,941	$ 9,515
Long-term receivables	325	333
Investments and advances	1,761	2,298
Properties, plant, and equipment:		
Properties, plant, and equipment, at cost	$42,670	$38,772
Less: accumulated depreciation, depletion, and amortization	−18,872	−17,036
Net properties, plant, and equipment	23,798	21,736
Deferred charges and other assets	143	219
Total assets	$33,968	$34,101
Liabilities and stockholders' equity		
Current liabilities:		
Accounts payable	$ 2,681	$ 2,835
Accrued liabilities	2,332	2,669
Short-term debt	469	915
Federal and other taxes on income	978	1,394
Other taxes payable	544	619
Total current liabilities	$ 7,003	$ 8,432
Other liabilities:		
Long-term debt	6,527	5,885
Capital lease obligations	306	370
Deferred income taxes	3,894	3,990
Deferred credits and other noncurrent obligations	1,450	1,527
Total liabilities	$19,180	$20,204

Stockholders' equity:

Common stock	$ 1,026	$ 1,026
Capital in excess of par value	874	874
Currency translation adjustment	105	113
Retained earnings	12,783	11,884
Total stockholders' equity	14,788	13,897
Total liabilities and stockholders' equity	$33,968	$34,101

Mobil Corporation
Consolidated Statement of Income
For the years ended December 31, 1988 and 1987
(*in millions except for per share amounts*)

	1988	1987
Revenues:		
Sales and services	$53,322	$50,721
Interest, dividends, and other revenue	1,039	666
Total revenues	$54,361	$51,387
Costs and expenses:		
Crude oil, products, operating supplies, and expenses	$30,503	$30,464
Exploration expenses	721	511
Selling and general expenses	3,706	3,368
Depreciation, depletion, and amortization	2,683	2,457
Taxes other than income	12,380	10,713
Interest and debt discount expense	907	1,059
Income taxes	1,430	1,597
Total costs and expenses	−52,330	−50,169
Income from continuing operations	$ 2,031	$ 1,218
Discontinued operations (Montgomery Ward)	56	130
Net income	$ 2,087	$ 1,348
Net income per share:		
Continuing operations	$4.93	$2.96
Discontinued operations	.14	.32
Net income per share	$5.07	$3.28

Mobil Corporation
Consolidated Statement of Retained Earnings
For the years ended December 31, 1988 and 1987
(*in millions of dollars*)

	1988	1987
Balance at beginning of year	$13,732	$13,287
Net income (loss) for year	2,087	1,348
Cash dividends paid	(968)	(903)
Balance at end of year	$14,851	$13,732

Mobil Corporation
Consolidated Balance Sheets
December 31, 1988 and 1987
(*in millions of dollars*)

Assets	1988	1987
Current assets:		
Cash	$ 191	$ 372
Marketable securities, at cost (approximates market)	846	773
Accounts and notes receivable	5,113	4,910
Inventories	4,481	4,620
Prepaid expenses and other current assets	547	422
Total current assets	$11,178	$11,097
Investments and long-term receivables	2,939	2,692
Montgomery Ward net assets held for sale	—	1,539
Net properties, plant and equipment	23,848	24,071
Deferred charges and other assets	855	873
Total assets	$38,820	$40,272

Liabilities and stockholders' equity		
Current liabilities:		
Notes and loans payable	$ 810	$ 1,613
Accounts payable and accrued liabilities	6,043	5,927
Long-term debt lease maturing within one year	92	224
Income, excise, state, and other taxes payable	2,379	2,391
Deferred income taxes	931	575
Total current liabilities	$10,255	$10,730
Long-term debt	6,402	6,998
Capital lease obligations	96	145
Deferred income taxes	3,848	4,706
Reserves for employee benefits	514	539
Deferred credits and other noncurrent obligations	1,448	1,604
Accrued restoration and removal costs	526	516
Total liabilities	23,089	25,238
Stockholders' equity:		
Minority interest in subsidiary companies	$ 45	$ 34
Common stock	869	866
Capital surplus	1,038	998
Currency translation adjustment	(466)	(86)
Treasury stock	(606)	(510)
Retained earnings	14,851	13,732
Total stockholders' equity	15,731	15,034
Total liabilities and stockholders' equity	$38,820	$40,272

**REVIEW PROBLEM
SOLUTION**

a)   **O'Keefe's, Inc.
Common Size Balance Sheets
December 31, 19x8 and 19x7**

Assets	19x8	19x7
Current assets:		
Cash	16.0%	17.3%
Marketable securities	4.0	2.9
Accounts receivable	17.3	17.9
Inventories	21.3	22.4
Other current assets	3.2	3.5
Total current assets	61.8%	64.0%
Property, plant, and equipment	80.0%	83.2%
Less: Accumulated depreciation	−42.6	−48.0
Net	37.4	35.2
Other assets	0.8	0.8
Total assets	100.0%	100.0%

Liabilities and stockholders' equity	19x8	19x7
Current liabilities:		
Accounts payable	23.2%	21.1%
Taxes payable	2.4	0.3
Other current liabilities	2.7	2.9
Total current liabilities	28.3%	24.3%
Long-term debt	16.0	16.0
Total liabilities	44.3%	40.3%
Stockholders' equity:		
Common stock ($1 par)	4.8%	4.5%
Premium on common stock	0.8	0.6
Retained earnings	50.1	54.6
Total stockholders' equity	55.7	59.7
Total liabilities and stockholders' equity	100.0%	100.0%

**O'Keefe's, Inc.
Common Size Income Statements
For the years ended December 31, 19x8 and 19x7**

	19x8	19x7
Sales	100.0%	100.0%
Cost of goods sold	−86.7	−92.0
Gross profit	13.3%	8.0%
Operating expenses:		
Selling	4.2%	4.2%
General and administrative	2.3	2.4
Total	− 6.5	− 6.6
Operating income	6.8%	1.4%
Other revenues and expenses:		
Interest income	0.3%	0.2%
Interest expense	− 1.3	− 0.8
Total	− 1.0%	− 0.6%
Income before income taxes	5.8%	0.8%
Provision for income taxes	− 2.0	− 0.3
Net income	3.8%	0.5%

b) From the common size statements, it is noted that the current assets declined as a percentage of total assets, with the largest decline being cash (1.3 percent). Although cash increased in dollar value, it did not increase at the same level as total assets. The largest change took place with net property, plant, and equipment, which went up 2.4 percent.

Total liabilities as a group increased by 4.0 percent; taxes payable were the primary contributor. The primary change in stockholders' equity was retained earnings, which decreased by 4.5 percent.

The substantial increase in dollars of net income can be easily explained via the common size statements; cost of goods sold led the way with a 5.3 percent decline. The only items that increased were interest expense and provisions for taxes.

Any time that a company experiences a major change in sales—a 20 percent increase for O'Keefe's (($3,000,000 − $2,500,000)/$2,500,000)—it is very difficult to examine the dollar amounts and tell if every item maintained its proper perspective. Common size statements permit this analysis and provide evidence as to the degree of change of each item.

c) Solvency measures:

$$\text{Current ratio} = \frac{\text{Current assets}}{\text{Current liabilities}}$$

$$= \frac{\$1,160}{\$530}$$

$$= \underline{\underline{2.19}}$$

$$\text{Acid test ratio} = \frac{\text{Cash} + \text{Marketable securities} + \text{Current receivables}}{\text{Current liabilities}}$$

$$= \frac{\$300 + \$75 + \$325}{\$530}$$

$$= \underline{\underline{1.32}}$$

$$\text{Inventory turnover} = \frac{\text{Cost of goods sold}}{\text{Average inventory}}$$

$$= \frac{\$2,600}{\dfrac{\$350 + \$400}{2}}$$

$$= \underline{\underline{6.93}} \text{ times}$$

$$\text{Days receivable outstanding} = \frac{\text{Ending receivables}}{\text{Average daily sales}}$$

$$= \frac{\$325}{\dfrac{\$3,000}{365}}$$

$$= \underline{\underline{39.54}} \text{ days}$$

$$\text{Debt-to-equity} = \frac{\text{Total liabilities}}{\text{Total stockholders' equity}}$$

$$= \frac{\$830}{\$1,045}$$

$$= \underline{\underline{0.79}}$$

$$\text{Times interest earned} = \frac{\text{Net income} + \text{Interest expense} + \text{Income taxes}}{\text{Interest expense}}$$

$$= \frac{\$115 + \$40 + \$60}{\$40}$$

$$= \underline{\underline{5.38}} \text{ times}$$

Performance measures:

$$\text{Asset turnover} = \frac{\text{Sales}}{\text{Average total assets}}$$

$$= \frac{\$3,000}{\dfrac{\$1,562 + \$1,875}{2}}$$

$$= \underline{\underline{1.75}} \text{ times}$$

$$\text{Return on sales} = \frac{\text{Net income} + \text{Net-of-tax interest expense}}{\text{Sales}}$$

$$= \frac{\$115 + \$40(1 - 0.34)}{\$3,000}$$

$$= \underline{\underline{0.047}} \quad \text{or} \quad \underline{\underline{4.7\%}}$$

$$\text{Return on assets} = \frac{\text{Net income} + \text{Net-of-tax interest expense}}{\text{Average total assets}}$$

$$= \frac{\$115 + \$40(1 - 0.34)}{\dfrac{\$1,562 + \$1,875}{2}}$$

$$= \underline{\underline{0.082}} \quad \text{or} \quad \underline{\underline{8.2\%}}$$

$$\text{Return on equity} = \frac{\text{Net income}}{\text{Average stockholders' equity}}$$

$$= \frac{\$115}{\dfrac{\$932 + \$1,045}{2}}$$

$$= \underline{\underline{0.116}} \quad \text{or} \quad \underline{\underline{11.6\%}}$$

Statement of Cash Flows

Learning Objectives

Upon completion of this chapter you should:

- **Understand the purpose of the statement of cash flows.**

- **Understand the relationship between the statement of cash flows and the balance sheet and income statement.**

- **Be able to distinguish between operating, investing, and financing activities.**

- **Be able to determine cash flows from operating, investing, and financing activities.**

- **Be able to prepare a statement of cash flows in good form.**

- **Be able to evaluate the significance of the information contained in a statement of cash flows.**

In Chapter 17 the balance sheet and income statement were used to evaluate a firm's solvency and performance. These are the financial statements investors and creditors have traditionally used more than any others—the balance sheet to determine year-end financial position and the income statement to identify activities of the period that led to the year-end financial position. However, the income statement does not tell the whole story of the year's activities that produced the year-end balance sheet. It summarizes operating activities, but only on an accrual basis, and it does not specify the cash flows from operating activities. Furthermore, nonoperating investing and financing activities for the period are not summarized specifically, on an accrual or cash basis, on either the income statement or the balance sheet. The statement of cash flows fills these critical information gaps.

The **statement of cash flows** reports the major sources and uses of cash from operating, investing, and financing activities and indicates the net increase or decrease in cash. The statement also includes a schedule of significant *non-cash* investing and financing activities that occurred during the period.

Because the statement of cash flows provides important information about the overall activities of the firm, the Financial Accounting Standards Board (FASB) requires most large, public corporations to include it in their annual financial reports. Moreover, for external reporting purposes, the format and content of the statement are governed by standards issued by the FASB. The definitions, statement content, and statement format presented in this chapter are consistent with FASB requirements.

The primary purpose of this chapter is to discuss and illustrate operating, investing, and financing transactions, and to explain the format, preparation, and usefulness (to both managers and investors) of the statement of cash flows.

OPERATING, INVESTING, AND FINANCING ACTIVITIES

In general, **operating activities** include transactions that are related to a company's normal income earning activity and that enter into the calculation of net income on the income statement. Examples include purchases of inventory and supplies, sales of merchandise or finished goods, and payments of salaries and wages. **Investing activities** include transactions related to the acquisition and disposition of marketable securities, other long-term investments, and property, plant, and equipment, as well as making and collecting loans unrelated to the sale of goods or services. **Financing activities** include resource transfers between the enterprise and its owners, and obtaining loans from and repaying creditors.

According to the FASB, interest and dividend revenue and interest expense represent operating transactions, even though (in a strict theoretical sense) many accountants consider them to be more closely related to financing or investing activities. Also, certain items that often appear on the income statement—for example, gains and losses from the acquisition or disposition of noncurrent assets and liabilities—represent financing and investing activities, not operating activities. Detailed illustrations of operating, investing, and financing activities are provided later in the chapter.

MANAGERIAL PRACTICE 18.1

Shareholders Focus on Cash Flows—Shouldn't Managers?

Although investment analysts are increasingly focusing attention on cash flows instead of accounting earnings, there has been less willingness by managers to deviate from traditional measures for internal performance analysis. Investment analysts now recognize that shareholder value is more reflective of economic value than accounting book values; hence the focus on cash flows. Since the role of management is to enhance shareholder value, it only makes sense for managers also to consider economic value, or the present value of future cash flows. Just because some part of a business is making an accounting profit doesn't mean that part of the business is enhancing the company's economic value, or its shareholder value. Despite widespread devotion to traditional accounting measures for measuring internal performance, companies like PepsiCo and Westinghouse have made shareholder value analysis an integral part of their management processes.

Performance evaluations based on accounting reports are favorable if profits are favorable; however, in real economic terms, a company or business unit reporting an accounting profit may be worse off than before. Using shareholder value analysis, which is based on discounting cash flows at a risk-adjusted interest rate, some managers who might have been very successful by traditional measures would be considered a colossal failure.

According to Wenner and LeBer, both consultants at the respected international consulting firm of McKinsey & Company, "Shareholder value is now widely accepted as an appropriate standard for performance in U.S. business. The stock market sends a clear message that earnings per share is not the most important measure. Nor is growth for growth's sake. What matters is long-term cash generation. That's what drives long-term stock performance, and that's how we should manage."

Source: David L. Wenner and Richard W. LeBer, "Managing for Shareholder Value—From Top to Bottom," *Harvard Business Review* (November–December 1989): 52–65.

CONTENT AND FORM OF THE STATEMENT OF CASH FLOWS

The FASB has determined that the statement of cash flows shall report cash inflows, cash outflows, and net cash provided or used, and that these items shall be reported separately for operating, investing, and financing activities. It should also show the net effect of all cash flows, explaining the difference between beginning and ending cash balances. Other factors involved in preparing the statement of cash flows include (1) selecting the method of reporting operating activities, (2) defining cash and cash equivalents, (3) reporting related transactions, and (4) disclosing significant noncash activities. These factors are discussed below.

Reporting Operating Activities

Because the typical accounting system does not capture net income on a cash basis, it is usually necessary to calculate operating cash flows using information provided on the income statement and balance sheet. Two methods of measuring operating cash flows are the direct and the indirect methods.

MANAGERIAL PRACTICE 18.2

Follow the Money

Increasingly, investors are looking at cash flows in addition to earnings analysis in picking investment stocks. Staggering major expenditures over several years through depreciation deductions gives a truer picture of profits, but it may obscure other developments. In fact, a company may be stronger than its earnings suggest because of stronger cash flows. Norman Weinger, an analyst with Oppenheimer & Co., states that "companies with heavy depreciation can shelter earnings" and that he is "attracted to the shares of . . . companies . . . with earnings that have been held down by capital spending."

On the other hand, a company may look stronger on an earnings basis than it really is, if its equipment is getting old and new capital additions have not been made recently. "Focusing on cash flow makes the investor confront an important question: whether the assets being depreciated really do wear out as rapidly as they are being depreciated." Professional investors maintain that looking at cash flows "can lead investors to consider stocks they might otherwise overlook."

Source: John R. Dorfman, "Stock Analysts Increase Focus on Cash Flow," *Wall Street Journal,* 17 February 1987, 35.

Under the direct method, the income statement is essentially reconstructed on a cash basis so that the primary categories of cash inflows and outflows from operating activities are presented. To reconstruct the income statement on a cash basis, it is necessary to convert each revenue and expense item on the income statement from an accrual basis to a cash basis. Although not commonly done, a company may maintain in its accounting system detailed records of major categories of operating cash flows necessary for reporting them on the direct basis.

Under the indirect method, net cash flow from operations is calculated by adjusting net income to the cash basis. The specific categories of operating cash flows are not reported under the indirect method. Both the direct and indirect methods are illustrated in detail later in this chapter.

Defining Cash and Cash Equivalents

Because companies try to keep all assets as productive as possible, they normally keep only part of their cash funds on hand or in checking accounts. Amounts of cash that are not needed immediately, but which management wishes to be able to use on short notice, are invested in cash equivalents. These are short-term, highly liquid investments that are both readily convertible into known amounts of cash and so near their maturity date that they present insignificant risk of change in value from interest or money market rate changes. Generally, only investments with original maturities of three months or less are considered to be cash equivalents. Examples of cash equivalents are treasury bills, commercial paper, and money market funds.

For purposes of the statement of cash flows, cash is defined to include both cash and cash equivalents. Because cash and cash equivalents are the same for cash flow reporting purposes, transactions involving the exchange of cash for a cash equivalent or vice versa, such as the purchase or redemption of a treasury bill, are not reported on the statement of cash flows as a cash flow transaction.

Reporting Related Transactions

The statement of cash flows should report significant cash inflows and outflows for related transactions in gross amounts, instead of netting cash inflows and outflows. For example, the purchase of equipment for $100,000 and the sale of equipment for $25,000 should be reported separately as a $25,000 cash inflow from the sale of equipment and a $100,000 cash outflow for the purchase of equipment, rather than as a $75,000 net outflow of cash for the purchase of equipment. This requirement does not apply to the reporting of operating activities under the indirect method of reporting cash flows from operations, which essentially provides only a net calculation of cash from operating activities.

Disclosure of Significant Noncash Activities

In addition to operating, investing, and financing activities that involve cash flows, companies may engage in significant investing and financing activities that have no direct or immediate effect on cash. Examples of these activities are the exchange of a long-term liability for property, plant, or equipment, and the issuance of shares of stock in settlement of a long-term liability or to acquire shares of stock in another company. Although these transactions do not represent direct cash flows, they may constitute significant (and substantive) investing and financing activities. Often the direct exchange of noncash assets and liabilities is merely a matter of convenience, and the goal is to emphasize the substance rather than the form of the transaction, thereby improving disclosure and comparability. "Form" versus "substance" issues are, however, areas of controversy in financial accounting circles. Since the purpose of the statement of cash flows is to disclose all significant operating, investing, and financing activities, not just those directly involving cash, the statement of cash flows should include (in addition to cash flows from operating, investing, and financing activities) a supplemental schedule disclosing all significant noncash *investing* and *financing* transactions. Significant noncash *operating* activities (such as revenue and expense accruals) are not disclosed in the statement of cash flows because all operating activities (both cash and noncash) are summarized on the income statement.

The format of the statement of cash flows using the direct method, with examples of typical operating, investing, and financial transactions, is presented in Exhibit 18–1. Amounts in parentheses represent cash outflows. Note the apparent inconsistency between the way dividend payments and interest payments are treated on the statement of cash flows. Dividend payments are reported as a financing activity, but interest payments are reported as an operating activity. From a theoretical standpoint, one could argue that both dividend and interest payments should be classified as financing activities because both represent the cost of using capital invested in the company. However, the FASB has taken the position that because interest payments are deductible on the income statement, it is appropriate to treat them as any other operating expense payment. A further (but less convincing) justification for this treatment is that it minimizes the difference between accrual net income and net cash flow from operations.

RELATIONSHIP BETWEEN THE BALANCE SHEET AND THE STATEMENT OF CASH FLOWS

To prepare a statement of cash flows, it is necessary to identify the various sources and uses of cash and to determine whether they were related to operating, investing, or financing activities. A careful review of the primary elements of a statement of cash flows (see Exhibit 18–1) reveals that the statement of cash flows is closely related to the balance sheet. One of the most basic accounting concepts—the balancing nature of the balance sheet—requires that every accountable business activity (or transaction) be recorded in the accounts by equal amounts of debit and credit entries. Because of this fundamental rule, any transaction that produces a net change in cash must be offset on the balance sheet by either a change in one or more other assets or by a change in one or more liability or stockholders' equity accounts. Hence the transactions that caused cash inflows and outflows can be determined by analyzing changes in the noncash accounts.

EXHIBIT 18–1   Format of Statement of Cash Flows

(Company Name)
Statement of Cash Flows
(Statement Period)

Cash flows from operating activities (direct method)

Cash received from customers	$ XX	
Cash paid to employees	(XX)	
Cash paid to suppliers for inventory	(XX)	
Cash paid to others for expenses	(XX)	
Dividends and interest received	XX	
Interest paid	(XX)	
Income taxes paid	(XX)	
Net cash provided (or used) by operating activities		$ XX

Cash flows from investing activities

Proceeds from sale of long-term and short-term marketable securities	$ XX	
Payments for purchase of long-term and short-term marketable securities	(XX)	
Collections received on long-term notes receivable	XX	
Cash loaned on long-term notes receivable	(XX)	
Proceeds from sale of property, plant, and equipment	XX	
Payments for acquisition of property, plant, and equipment	(XX)	
Net cash provided (or used) by investing activities		XX

Cash flows from financing activities

Proceeds from sale of preferred and common stock	$ XX	
Proceeds from issuance of debt	XX	
Payments to reduce or retire debt	(XX)	
Payments to reacquire preferred and common stock	(XX)	
Dividends paid	(XX)	
Net cash provided (or used) by financing activities		XX
Net increase (decrease) in cash and cash equivalents		$ XX

Schedule of noncash investing and financing activities

Noncash assets exchanged for debt	$ XX
Noncash assets exchanged for equity securities	$ XX
Equity securities exchanged for debt	$ XX

Most noncash balance sheet accounts summarize transactions related to either operating, investing, or financing activities. Only a few accounts are affected by more than one type of business activity; for example, property, plant, and equipment accounts are increased by purchases of equipment (an investing activity) and decreased by depreciation (an operating activity), and Retained Earnings is increased by net income (an operating activity) and decreased by dividend declarations (a financing activity). Exhibit 18–2 indicates the type(s) of business activity (operating, investing, or financing) that typically affect(s) each noncash balance sheet account.

Cash Flows from Operating Activities

If all revenues represented cash receipts and all expenses represented cash payments, the effect of operating activities on the balance sheet would be represented by a change in Cash and an offsetting change in Retained Earnings. Under the accrual method of income measurement, revenues are recognized when earned (not when collected) and expenses are recognized when incurred (not when paid). To account for the timing differences between revenue and expense recognition and related cash flows, several current asset and current liability accounts in the balance sheet (see Exhibit 18–2) are used to recognize cash flows that precede or follow the recognition of revenues and expenses.

MANAGERIAL PRACTICE 18.3

Developing a Cash Flow Attitude at BellSouth

"With more and more investors taking a greater interest in the company's cash flow, BellSouth is studying what modifications are appropriate to its financial planning to address such shareholder expectations," says Mike Cassity, director of financial management for BellSouth. BellSouth recognizes that the methods of evaluating shareholder value are changing, even for companies such as utilities that traditionally have been regarded as safe, conservative investments.

If investors are going to look beyond the earnings at cash flows, then it is important for company decision makers also to think cash flows as well as earnings. This requires some modification of attitudes. For example, whereas holding unnecessary inventories has little impact on earnings, it creates a drain on cash flows. The bottom line is no longer just earnings at BellSouth; it is also shareholder value, which is increasingly affected by cash flows.

Source: Susan Scott, "Cash Flow: A Key Driver in Creating Shareholder Value," *BellSouth Magazine* (Winter 1989): 5–9.

EXHIBIT 18–2   Noncash Balance Sheet Accounts and Cash Flows from Operating, Investing, and Financing Activities

	Business Activities Affecting Account
Current Assets	
Accounts and notes receivable (from sale of goods/services)	Operating
Inventories	Operating
Prepaid expenses	Operating
Marketable securities	Investing
Short-term notes receivable	Investing
Noncurrent Assets	
Long-term investments (stocks, bonds, etc.)	Investing
Long-term notes receivable	Investing
Property, plant, and equipment	Operating and Investing
Current Liabilities	
Accounts and notes payable (from purchases of inventories and other operating goods/services)	Operating
Accrued liabilities	Operating
Taxes payable	Operating
Short-term loans payable	Financing
Long-Term Liabilities	
Notes, bonds, and mortgages payable	Financing
Stockholders' Equity	
Capital stock	Financing
Paid-in capital in excess of par	Financing
Retained earnings	Operating and Financing

For example, if a company has sales revenue of $100,000 but collects only $90,000 during the year, Accounts Receivable will increase by $10,000; conversely, if it collects $100,000 but has sales revenue of $90,000 during the year, Accounts Receivable will decrease by $10,000. The change in the Accounts Receivable account during the year is equal to the amount of the difference between sales revenue recognized under the accrual accounting method and the amount of cash collected from customers. Similarly, changes in the Inventory, Prepaid Expense, Accounts Payable, and Accrued Expenses Payable accounts reflect the differences between expenses recognized under the accrual method and the amount of cash payments for operating costs and expenses.

A further word of explanation is necessary for one particular operating activity, the use of depreciating assets, which reduces net income (and retained earnings) but does not affect cash. The entry to record depreciation expense includes a debit to Depreciation Expense and a credit to Accumulated Depreciation but no entry to cash. Therefore, the use and depreciation of productive assets, which is an operating activity, reduces the book value of property, plant, and equipment, but has no effect on cash. The acquisition and sale of depreciable assets (investment activities) may use or generate cash, but the depreciation of assets (an operating activity) never has a direct effect on cash.

Cash Flows from Investing Activities

Exhibit 18–2 indicates that the balance sheet accounts potentially affected by investing activities include all noncurrent assets plus the current assets Marketable Securities and Short-Term Loans Receivable. Increases in these accounts are often accompanied by decreases in cash (for example, from loaning money or purchasing investments or equipment), and decreases in these accounts are often accompanied by increases in cash (for example, from collecting money from borrowers or from selling investments or equipment).

Cash Flows from Financing Activities

Financing activities always result in changes in either liability or stockholders' equity accounts. The liability accounts affected by financing activities are Short-Term Loans Payable and all long-term liability accounts. Increases in cash typically accompany increases in these accounts (for example, from borrowing money on short- or long-term debt), and decreases in cash typically accompany decreases in these accounts (for example, for repaying borrowed money). Similarly, increases in paid-in-capital accounts (Capital Stock and Paid in Capital in Excess of Par Value) are typically accompanied by increases in cash (for example, from the sale of capital stock), and decreases in these accounts are typically accompanied by decreases in cash (for example, the retirement of capital stock). As stated earlier, the Retained Earnings account reflects both operating activity (net income or loss) and financing activity (dividends). If a dividend is paid when it is declared, it also decreases cash; otherwise, the dividend declaration is a noncash financing activity, and the subsequent payment of the dividend liability is a cash outflow from a financing activity at the time of the payment.

PREPARATION OF THE STATEMENT OF CASH FLOWS

In the previous section we discussed how operating, investing, and financing activities produce cash inflows and outflows and how those activities affect the balance sheet. In this section we will go through the steps of preparing a statement of cash flows for Omega Corporation for 19x2, using comparative balance sheet and income statement data presented in Exhibits 18–3 and 18–4.

EXHIBIT 18–3 Comparative Balance Sheets and Account Changes for Omega Corporation for 19x1 and 19x2

Omega Corporation
Comparative Balance Sheets
December 31, 19x2 and 19x1

Assets	19x2	19x1	Increase (Decrease)
Current assets:			
Cash	$ 7,000	$ 8,000	$ (1,000)
Accounts receivable (net)	50,055	20,100	29,955
Inventory	60,800	70,500	(9,700)
Prepaid expenses	1,050	4,500	(3,450)
Total current assets	$118,905	$103,100	$15,805
Investments	250,000	200,000	50,000
Property, plant, and equipment	$630,000	$580,000	$50,000
Less: accumulated depreciation	(160,700)	(140,500)	20,200
Total property, plant, and equipment	469,300	439,500	29,800
Total assets	$838,205	$742,600	$95,605
Liabilities and stockholders' equity			
Current liabilities:			
Accounts payable	$ 30,400	$ 37,650	$ (7,250)
Accrued expenses payable	8,000	6,050	1,950
Income taxes payable	3,050	3,000	50
Total current liabilities	$ 41,450	$ 46,700	$ (5,250)
Long-term debt	437,755	400,600	37,155
Total liabilities	$479,205	$447,300	$31,905
Stockholders' equity:			
Common stock ($1 par value)	$110,000	$100,000	$10,000
Paid-in capital in excess of par value	180,200	150,000	30,200
Retained earnings	68,800	45,300	23,500
Total stockholders' equity	359,000	295,300	63,700
Total liabilities and stockholders' equity	$838,205	$742,600	$95,605

The four steps in preparing a statement of cash flows are:

1. Analyze the income statement and relevant balance sheet accounts to determine cash flows from *operating activities.*

2. Analyze relevant balance sheet accounts to determine cash flows and significant noncash effects from *investing activities.*

3. Analyze relevant balance sheet accounts to determine cash flows and significant noncash effects from *financing activities.*

4. With the information gathered in the first three steps, format the statement of cash flows, using either the direct or indirect method for reporting cash flows from operating activities.

EXHIBIT 18–4   Income Statement for Omega Corporation for 19x2

Omega Corporation
Income Statement
For the year ended December 31, 19x2

Sales		$675,000
Cost of goods sold		(310,000)
Gross Margin		$365,000
Operating expenses (excluding depreciation)		(212,500)
Depreciation expense		(35,000)
Operating income		$117,500
Other income and expense:		
Interest and dividend income	$17,300	
Interest expense	(40,000)	
Gain on sale of investments	5,500	
Loss on sale of property, plant, and equipment	(10,000)	(27,200)
Income before taxes		$ 90,300
Income taxes		(41,800)
Net income		$ 48,500

Step 1: Analyze the Income Statement and Related Balance Sheet Accounts to Determine Cash Flows from Operating Activities

The balance sheet accounts that are affected by operating activities are indicated on Exhibit 18–2. These include most current asset and current liability accounts; Property, Plant, and Equipment; and Retained Earnings. As stated earlier, the purpose of most current asset and current liability accounts is to recognize differences between current operating cash flows and current revenues and expenses recognized by the accrual method of accounting. Any changes during the year in the balances in these accounts is an indication that net income is not equal to cash flows from operating activities. To determine cash flows from operating activities, it is necessary to analyze the components of the income statement and their related balance sheet accounts to determine any differences between revenues and expenses reported on the income statement and cash flows from operating activities. This analysis is illustrated in detail for the Omega Corporation on the next several pages.

Sales and Accounts Receivable. Sales revenue is typically the first item on the income statement. If a company has uncollected sales at the end of the year, it will have an Accounts Receivable balance in its year-end balance sheet. If the balance at the end of the year differs from the balance at the beginning of the year, sales did not equal collections during the year. For Omega Corporation, Accounts Receivable increased by $29,955, indicating that 19x2 sales exceeded cash collections from customers. That is, the total sales of $675,000 reported on the 19x2 income statement exceeded cash collections by $29,955 (the amount of the Accounts Receivable increase). Therefore the total amount of cash received from customers was $645,045:

Sales (from income statement)	$675,000
Less Accounts Receivable increase (from balance sheet)	(29,955)
Cash received from customers	$645,045

We can verify that actual cash collections were $645,045 by tracing the transactions through the general ledger "T" accounts below:

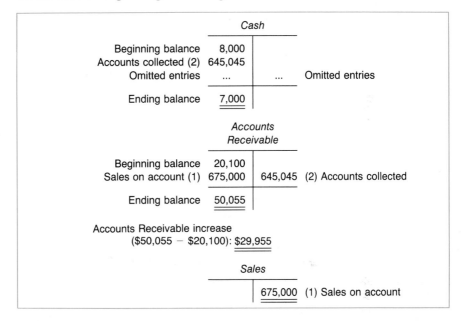

Notice that the amount of accounts receivable collected ($645,045), along with total sales, reconciles the beginning and ending Accounts Receivable balances. As shown above, accounts receivable collected can be derived by subtracting the Accounts Receivable increase of $29,955 from total sales of $675,000. Conversely, if Accounts Receivable had decreased during the period, cash collections would have been greater than total sales, and the decrease in Accounts Receivable would have been added to sales to determine the amount of cash collected from customers. To summarize, the adjustments to calculate cash receipts from sales are:

$$\text{Sales} \begin{cases} + & \text{Accounts Receivable decrease} \\ & \quad \text{(or)} \\ - & \text{Accounts Receivable increase} \end{cases} = \text{Cash receipts from sales.}$$

Cost of Goods Sold, Inventory, and Accounts Payable. The next item on the income statement is Cost of Goods Sold, and the related balance sheet accounts are Inventory and Accounts Payable. Assume that Accounts Payable is used only to record obligations related to the purchase of inventory. There are two reasons why Cost of Goods Sold is not equal to cash payments for inventory purchases made during the year: (1) not all inventory purchased is sold during the year, and (2) not all inventory purchased is paid for during the year. To determine the cash payments for inventory, a two step procedure is used: First adjust Cost of Goods Sold to derive the amount of inventory purchased, and then adjust that amount to determine the cash paid for inventory purchases during the year.

The Inventory account increases during the period if the cost of inventory purchased exceeds the cost of inventory sold. Conversely, if the cost of inventory sold exceeds purchases, the Inventory balance decreases. Therefore, to determine the cost of inventory purchased, an increase in Inventory for the year is added to Cost of Goods Sold, or a decrease in Inventory is subtracted from Cost of Goods Sold. For Omega Corporation, Cost of Goods Sold was $310,000 and Inventory decreased by $9,700; therefore the amount of inventory purchased during 19x2 was $300,300, calculated as follows:

Cost of Goods Sold (from income statement)	$310,000
Less decrease in Inventory (from balance sheet)	(9,700)
Inventory purchased	$300,300

If the amount of cash payments to vendors is not equal to inventory purchases, the difference will either increase or decrease Accounts Payable. If inventory purchases exceed cash payments to vendors, Accounts Payable will increase; and if payments to vendors exceed inventory purchases, Accounts Payable will decrease. Therefore, to determine the amount of cash payments to suppliers, an increase in Accounts Payable is subtracted from total inventory purchases, and a decrease in Accounts Payable is added to total inventory purchases. For Omega Corporation, Accounts Payable decreased by $7,250; therefore the amount paid to vendors was $307,550:

Inventory purchased (from above)	$300,300
Plus decrease in Accounts Payable (from balance sheet)	7,250
Cash paid for inventory for resale	$307,550

By tracing inventory purchases and sales transactions for Omega Corporation through the general ledger "T" accounts, we can verify that payments for inventory purchases were $307,550:

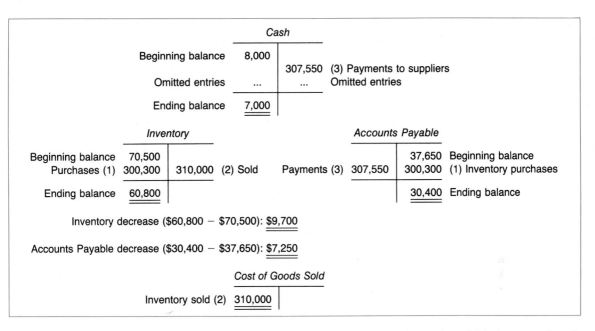

The difference between Omega's Cost of Goods Sold balance and cash payments to vendors is reconciled as follows:

Cost of Goods Sold (from income statement)	$310,000
Less decrease in Inventory (from balance sheet)	(9,700)
Plus decrease in Accounts Payable (from balance sheet)	7,250
Cash payments for inventory purchases	$307,550

To summarize, the adjustments to calculate cash payments for inventory purchases are:

$$\text{Cost of Goods Sold} \begin{Bmatrix} + & \text{Inventory increase} \\ & \text{(or)} \\ - & \text{Inventory decrease} \end{Bmatrix} \text{ and } \begin{Bmatrix} + & \text{Accounts Payable decrease} \\ & \text{(or)} \\ - & \text{Accounts Payable increase} \end{Bmatrix} = \text{Cash payments for inventory purchases.}$$

Operating Expenses, Prepaid Expenses, and Accrued Expenses Payable. The difference between cash payments for operating expenses and the amount of operating expenses reported on the income statement is explained by changes in the balance sheet accounts Prepaid Expenses and Accrued Expenses Payable. An increase in Prepaid Expenses indicates that a cash payment was recorded as an asset instead of as an expense, and a decrease in Prepaid Expenses indicates that an expense was recorded without an accompanying decrease in Cash. Similarly, an increase in Accrued Expenses Payable indicates that an expense was recorded without an accompanying decrease in Cash, and a decrease in Accrued Expenses Payable indicates that a cash payment occurred which was not simultaneously recognized as an expense.

Notice that for Omega Corporation, Prepaid Expenses decreased by $3,450 and Accrued Expenses Payable increased by $1,950. This means that Operating Expenses recorded during the year were related partially to the decrease in Prepaid Expenses and partially to the increase in Accrued Expenses Payable, with only the remainder representing a cash outlay. Thus, total payments for operating expenses were $207,100:

Operating expenses (from income statement)	$212,500
Less decrease in Prepaid Expenses (from balance sheet)	(3,450)
Less increase in Accrued Expenses Payable (from balance sheet)	(1,950)
Cash paid for Operating Expenses	$207,100

Conversely, an increase in Prepaid Expenses and a decrease in Accrued Expenses Payable would be added to Operating Expenses to determine cash payments for operating costs.

The operating transactions that affected Prepaid Expenses and Accrued Expenses Payable can be traced through the general ledger accounts, but first it is necessary for us to make some assumptions. Assume that, of the $212,500 of operating expense reported on the income statement, $15,000 was recorded as a reduction of prepayments, $35,000 was recorded in connection with operating expense accruals, and the remainder, $162,500, represented expenses paid at the time they were incurred.

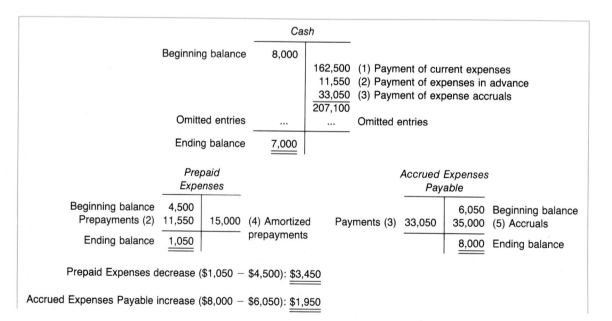

```
                                 Operating Expenses
     Incurred and paid (1)   162,500
 Amortized prepayments (4)    15,000
     Expense accruals (5)     35,000
                             ─────────
                             $212,500
                             ═════════
```

The "T" accounts above illustrate that changes in the Prepaid Expense and Accrued Expenses Payable accounts explain the difference between total operating expenses and the amount of cash payments for operating costs. It is not necessary to know the breakdown of the expenses into direct payments, accruals, and prepayments amortized to be able to determine the cash payments for operating expenses. It is necessary only to know the change in the Prepaid Expenses and Accrued Expenses Payable accounts (which can be determined from the comparative balance sheets) and the total Operating Expenses (which can be determined from the income statement). To summarize, the adjustments to calculate cash payments for operating expenses are:

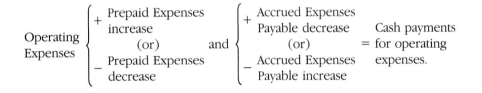

$$\text{Operating Expenses} \begin{cases} + \text{ Prepaid Expenses increase} \\ \quad\quad\text{(or)} \\ - \text{ Prepaid Expenses decrease} \end{cases} \text{and} \begin{cases} + \text{ Accrued Expenses Payable decrease} \\ \quad\quad\text{(or)} \\ - \text{ Accrued Expenses Payable increase} \end{cases} = \begin{array}{l} \text{Cash payments} \\ \text{for operating} \\ \text{expenses.} \end{array}$$

Income Taxes Expense and Income Taxes Payable. The balance sheet account Income Taxes Payable increases if the amount of Income Taxes Expense on the income statement is more than the amount of cash paid for income taxes in the current year. Conversely, it decreases if the amount paid for taxes is more than current Income Taxes Expense. Therefore, the amount of cash payments for income taxes is equal to current Income Taxes Expense plus the decrease in Income Taxes Payable, or less the increase in Income Taxes Payable. For example, Omega Corporation's Income Taxes Payable account increased by $50; so the amount paid for income taxes during the current year was $41,750:

Income Taxes Expense (from income statement)	$41,800
Less the increase in Income Taxes Payable (from balance sheet)	(50)
Cash payments for income taxes	$41,750

This relationship can also be observed in the Income Tax Expense and Income Taxes Payable ledger accounts:

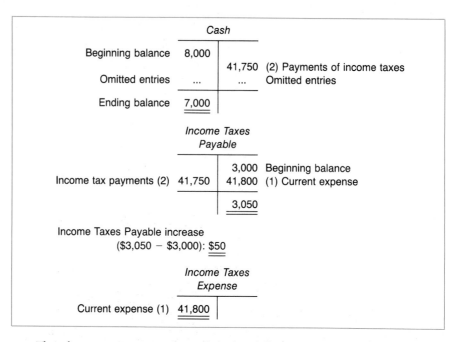

The above transactions show that the difference between the amount of cash paid for income taxes and the amount of Income Taxes Expense on the income statement is accounted for by the increase in the Income Taxes Payable account. To summarize, the adjustments to calculate cash payments for income taxes are:

$$\text{Income Taxes Expense} \begin{cases} + & \text{Income Taxes Payable decrease} \\ & \text{(or)} \\ - & \text{Income Taxes Payable increase} \end{cases} = \text{Cash payments for income taxes.}$$

Depreciation Expense and Accumulated Depreciation. Exhibit 18–2 indicates that operating activities may affect property, plant, and equipment accounts on the balance sheet. The specific account actually affected is Accumulated Depreciation, the contra account to property, plant, and equipment. As you know from studying financial accounting, the journal entry to record depreciation expense is a debit to Depreciation Expense and a credit to Accumulated Depreciation. The Omega income statement indicates that depreciation expense was $35,000 for 19x2; therefore the journal entry to record depreciation expense was:

Depreciation Expense	35,000	
Accumulated Depreciation		35,000

This transaction does not include an entry to Cash; hence recording depreciation expense has no effect on cash and, for purposes of calculating operating cash flows, Depreciation Expense should be eliminated or reduced to zero. In summary, we have:

Depreciation expense (from income statement)	$35,000
Less offsetting increase in accumulated depreciation	−35,000
Cash payments for depreciation (always zero)	$ 0

Other Income and Expenses. Notice that in the Omega income statement there are four other items under the subheading "Other income and expense." The first two items are for interest and dividend income and for interest expense, and the last two items are for a gain and a loss from the sale of noncurrent assets. The Omega balance sheet includes no beginning or ending balances related to interest or dividends. That is, there is no Interest Receivable account and no Interest or Dividends Payable account. Therefore, it must be concluded that all dividend and interest revenue earned, and all interest expense incurred during the current year, were received or paid in cash. The statement of cash flows, therefore, will include the following items, which equal the amounts reported on the income statement:

Dividends and interest received	$17,300
Interest paid	$40,000

If the balance sheet had included an Interest Receivable account or an Interest Payable account, changes in the receivable account would be adjusted to the revenue account in the same way that changes in Accounts Receivable were adjusted to Sales, and changes in the Interest Payable account would be adjusted to Interest Expense in the same way that changes in Accounts Payable were adjusted to Cost of Goods Sold.

The Gain on Sale of Investments of $5,000 and the Loss on the Sale of Property, Plant, and Equipment of $10,000, although reported on the income statement (see Exhibit 18–4), are not operating items. These items resulted from transactions defined as investing activities; therefore any cash flows related to these transactions will be determined through analysis of investing activities and will be reported in the "Cash Flows from Investing Activities" section of the cash flow statement.

Cash Flows from Operating Activities: The Direct Method. Under the direct method of presenting cash flows from operating activities, we simply summarize the cash flows for each of the major operating activities. The previous analyses calculated the cash inflows from sales and the cash outflows from inventory purchases, operating costs, and income taxes. It was also shown that depreciation involves no increase or decrease in cash, and that the amounts reported on the income statement for interest and dividend income and interest expense represented actual cash flows. Using the data from these analyses, the "Cash Flows from Operating Activities" section of the cash flow statement prepared by the direct method is as follows:

Cash received from customers	$645,045
Cash paid for inventory for resale	(307,550)
Cash paid for operating expenses	(207,100)
Cash paid for income taxes	(41,750)
Dividends and interest received	17,300
Interest paid	(40,000)
Net cash provided by operating activities	$ 65,945

All of the adjustments discussed above that are necessary to convert the accrual income statement to a cash basis are summarized in Exhibit 18–5.

Cash Flows from Operating Activities: The Indirect Method. Under the indirect method, total cash flows from operating activities are determined by adjusting net income as reported on the accrual income statement for any

EXHIBIT 18–5   Conversion of Income Statement to Operating Cash Flows for Omega Corporation

Income Statement		Adjustments to Convert from Accrual Net Income to Operating Cash Flows*	Operating Cash Flows	
Sales	$675,000	− 29,955 (increase in Accounts Receivable)	=	$645,045
Cost of goods sold	(310,000)	− 9,700 (decrease in Inventory)		
		+ 7,250 (decrease in Accounts Payable)	=	(307,550)
Gross margin	$365,000			$337,495
Operating expenses	(247,500)	− 35,000 (Depreciation Expense)		
		− 3,450 (decrease in Prepaid Expenses)		
		− 1,950 (increase in Accrued Expenses Payable)	=	(207,100)
Operating income	$117,500			$130,395
Other income and expense:				
Interest and dividend income	17,300			17,300
Interest expense	(40,000)			(40,000)
Gain on sale of investments	5,500	− 5,500 (eliminate gain—investment activity)	=	-0-
Loss on sale of property,				
plant, and equipment	(10,000)	− 10,000 (eliminate loss—investment activity)	=	-0-
Income before taxes	$ 90,300			$107,695
Income taxes	(41,800)	− 50 (increase in Taxes Payable)	=	(41,750)
Net income	$ 48,500			
Net cash flow from operating activities				$ 65,945

*These adjustments represent absolute increases (+) or decreases (−) to the income statement balances.

nonoperating items included in net income and for any noncash elements in reported revenues and expenses. The difference between the direct and indirect methods, therefore, is that the direct method adjusts the individual components of the income statement to a cash basis and the indirect method recalculates only net income on a cash basis.

The amount of net income reported on the 19x2 income statement for Omega Corporation was $48,500. In the following paragraphs we will illustrate the recalculation of this accrual net income amount to a cash basis.

Net income of $48,500 included two nonoperating items that resulted from investing activities: a Gain on Sale of Investments of $5,000, which increased net income, and a Loss on Sale of Property, Plant, and Equipment of $10,000, which decreased net income. Hence, to eliminate these two items from net income, the gain is subtracted from, and the loss is added to, net income. The income statement also included depreciation expense of $35,000, which reduced net income but involved no cash flows; therefore this amount is added back to net income in arriving at cash flows from operating activities:

Net income	$48,500
Plus (minus) adjustments to reconcile net income to net cash provided by operating activities:	
Gain on sale of investments	(5,500)
Loss on sale of property, plant, and equipment	10,000
Depreciation	35,000

Next, each of the other noncash adjustments to revenues and expenses discussed earlier is presented in terms of the adjustment required to convert net income to a cash basis. Keep in mind that net income is being adjusted to a cash basis, as opposed to adjusting individual revenues and expenses to a cash basis. Therefore, in the case of revenues, the adjustment made to convert net income to a cash basis is the same as the adjustment to convert individual revenue accounts to a cash basis, because a change in revenue produces a similar change in net income. For example, if an adjustment increases Sales by $100, net income will increase by $100; and if Sales is decreased by $100, net income will decrease by $100. Conversely, in the case of expenses, the adjustment made to convert net income to a cash basis is the opposite of the adjustment to convert expense balances to a cash basis. For example, an adjustment increasing an expense by $100 results in a $100 decrease in net income, and a $100 decrease in expense results in a $100 increase in net income.

In the analysis of Accounts Receivable and Sales by the direct method, the $29,955 increase in Accounts Receivable was subtracted from Sales to determine the amount of cash received from customers. Therefore, under the indirect method the adjustment to net income is also a decrease:

Increase in Accounts Receivable	(29,955)

To adjust Cost of Goods Sold to a cash basis under the direct method, the $9,700 decrease in Inventory was subtracted from Cost of Goods Sold, and the $7,250 decrease in Accounts Payable was added to Cost of Goods Sold. Any change in Cost of Goods Sold has the opposite effect on net income; therefore under the indirect method the adjustments to net income for the decreases in Inventory and Accounts Payable are as follows:

Decrease in Inventory	9,700
Decrease in Accounts Payable	(7,250)

In the analysis of Operating Expenses, adjustments were made to decrease the reported expense amount by $3,450 for the decrease in Prepaid Expenses and by $1,950 for the increase in Accrued Expenses Payable. Under the indirect method, net income would be increased by these amounts. Similarly, the adjustment under the direct method to decrease Income Taxes Expense by $50 for the increase in Income Taxes Payable is an increase in net income under the indirect method. These adjustments are as follows:

Decrease in Prepaid Expenses	3,450
Increase in Accrued Expenses Payable	1,950
Increase in Taxes Payable	50

The "Cash Flows from Operating Activities" section of the cash flow statement under the indirect method, including all adjustments, is as follows:

Net income	$48,500
Plus (minus) adjustments to reconcile net income to net cash provided by operating activities:	
Gain on sale of investments	(5,500)
Loss on sale of property, plant, and equipment	10,000
Depreciation	35,000
Increase in Accounts Receivable	(29,955)
Decrease in Inventory	9,700
Decrease in Accounts Payable	(7,250)
Decrease in Prepaid Expenses	3,450
Increase in Accrued Expenses Payable	1,950
Increase in Taxes Payable	50
Net cash flows from operating activities	$65,945

Note that the direct method and the indirect method yield the same net cash flow from operating activities of $65,945; however, they provide substantially different information. The direct method shows the amount of cash generated by, or used for, each major category of revenues and expenses. The indirect method shows only the net amount of cash provided by operations.

From an analytical standpoint, the direct method clearly provides a greater amount of useful information to the reader in evaluating where cash came from and where it was spent. Hence it is appropriate for a management accounting text to emphasize the direct method. A summary of the adjustments required under the direct and indirect methods to convert income statement items from an accrual basis to a cash basis are presented in Exhibit 18–6.

Step 2: Analyze Relevant Balance Sheet Accounts to Determine Cash Flows and Significant Noncash Effects from Investing Activities

Exhibit 18–2 indicates that investing activities affect the current asset accounts Marketable Securities and Short-Term Loans Receivable and the noncurrent asset accounts Investments, Long-Term Notes Receivable, and Property, Plant, and Equipment. To determine the cash flows related to transactions involving these accounts, we will identify the transactions that increased or decreased these accounts and determine if any of these transactions increased or decreased cash.

To illustrate this procedure, refer to the Omega Company's financial statements in Exhibits 18–3 and 18–4. Omega had no current asset accounts and only two noncurrent asset accounts (Investments and Property, Plant, and Equipment) that were affected by investing activities. To facilitate the analysis of investing and financing activities, each of the noncurrent accounts is reconstructed in Exhibit 18–7 for 19x2, along with detailed journal entries for each transaction that increased or decreased the account.

EXHIBIT 18–6   Adjustments to Income Statement Items to Determine Cash Flows from Operating Activities under the Direct and Indirect Methods

	Direct Method	Indirect Method
	Adjustment to Revenue or Expense	Adjustment to Net Income
Adjustments for Current Assets:		
Increase in Accounts Receivable	− Sales	− Net Income
Decrease in Accounts Receivable	+ Sales	+ Net Income
Increase in Inventory	+ Cost of Goods Sold	− Net Income
Decrease in Inventory	− Cost of Goods Sold	+ Net Income
Increase in Prepaid Expenses	+ Operating Expenses	− Net Income
Decrease in Prepaid Expenses	− Operating Expenses	+ Net Income
Adjustments for Current Liabilities:		
Increase in Accounts Payable	− Cost of Goods Sold	+ Net Income
Decrease in Accounts Payable	+ Cost of Goods Sold	− Net Income
Increase in Accrued Expenses Payable	− Operating Expenses	+ Net Income
Decrease in Accrued Expenses Payable	+ Operating Expenses	− Net Income
Increase in Taxes Payable	− Income Tax Expense	+ Net Income
Decrease in Taxes Payable	+ Income Tax Expense	− Net Income
Adjustment for Noncash Expense:		
Depreciation	− Depreciation Expense	+ Net Income
Adjustments for Nonoperating Revenue and Expense:		
Nonoperating Gains	− Gain account	− Net income
Nonoperating Losses	− Loss account	+ Net Income

EXHIBIT 18–7   Analysis of Transactions in Noncurrent Balance Sheet Accounts for Omega Corporation for 19x2

Ledger Accounts	Transactions and Related Journal Entries

	Investments		
Beginning	200,000		
(a)	75,000	25,000	(b)
Ending	250,000		

(a) Purchase of investments:

Investments	75,000	
Cash		75,000

(b) Sale of investments:

Cash	30,500	
Investments		25,000
Gain on Sale of Investments		5,500

	Property, Plant, and Equipment (PPE)		
Beginning	580,000		
(a)	70,000	50,000	(c)
(b)	30,000		
Ending	630,000		

(a) Purchase of PPE:

PPE	70,000	
Cash		70,000

(b) Exchange of long-term note for PPE:

PPE	30,000	
Long-Term Notes Payable		30,000

	Accumulated Depreciation		
		140,500	Beginning
(c)	14,800	35,000	(d)
		160,700	Ending

(c) Sale of PPE:

Cash	25,200	
Accumulated Depreciation	14,800	
Loss on Sale of PPE	10,000	
PPE		50,000

(d) Current depreciation expense:

Depreciation Expense	35,000	
Accumulated Depreciation		35,000

	Long-Term Notes Payable		
		400,600	Beginning
(a)	12,845	20,000	(b)
		30,000	(c)
		437,755	Ending

(a) Conversion of note payable to common
       stock:

Long-Term Note Payable	12,845	
Common Stock		5,000
Paid-in Capital in Excess of Par Value		7,845

(b) Money borrowed on a long-term note:

Cash	20,000	
Long-Term Note Payable		20,000

(c) Long-term note issued in exchange for PPE: See transaction
       (b) under PPE account above.

	Common Stock		
		100,000	Beginning
		5,000	(a)
		5,000	(b)
		110,000	Ending

(a) Issuance of common stock to retire long-term note: See
       transaction (a) under Long-Term Notes Payable above.

(b) Issuance of common stock for cash:

Cash	27,355	
Common Stock		5,000
Paid-in Capital in Excess of Par Value		22,355

	Retained Earnings		
		45,300	Beginning
(a)	25,000	48,500	(b)
		68,800	Ending

(a) Declared and Paid cash dividend:

Retained Earnings	25,000	
Cash		25,000

(b) Close Revenue and Expense Summary
        to Retained Earnings:

Revenue and Expense Summary	48,500	
Retained Earnings		48,500

Investments. The Investments account reflects two investing activities in 19x2, a purchase of investments and a sale of investments. The purchase transaction, which involved an increase in Investments and a decrease in Cash of $75,000, is reported on the statement of cash flows as a use of cash of $75,000. The other transaction recorded in the Investments account involved the sale of investments that originally cost $25,000 for a cash price of $30,500. This transaction resulted in a $25,000 decrease in Investments and a $30,500 increase in Cash. Even though the difference of $5,500 was reported on the income statement as a gain, you will recall that we did not include that gain in cash flows from operating activities since it was related to an investing activity. Hence this transaction should be reported on the statement of cash flows as an investment activity that increased cash by $30,500.

To summarize, the cash flows from investing transactions related to the Investments account were:

Proceeds from sale of investments	$30,500
Payments for purchase of investments	(75,000)

Property, Plant, and Equipment (PPE). Notice that in Exhibit 18–7 four 19x2 transactions affected PPE and its related contra account, Accumulated Depreciation: (a) a purchase of PPE, (b) exchange of PPE for a long-term note, (c) sale of PPE, and (d) recognition of current depreciation.

The purchase of PPE involved an increase in PPE and an offsetting decrease in Cash of $70,000 [see transaction (a)]. This was an investment activity that used $70,000 of cash.

Transaction (b) involved the acquisition of PPE for $30,000, offset by the issuance of a long-term note of equal amount. This transaction is an example of an investing activity that had no effect on cash in the current period. However, because it represented a significant investing activity, it should be reported on the statement of cash flows in the supplemental schedule of noncash investing and financing activities.

Transaction (c) in the PPE account involved the sale for $25,200 cash of PPE that originally cost $50,000, and on which $14,800 of depreciation expense had been previously recorded. This transaction resulted in a decrease in the PPE account of $50,000 and a loss of $10,000, which was reported on the income statement; however, the effect on cash of this transaction was an increase of $25,200. Therefore this sale of PPE will be reported on the statement of cash flows as an increase in cash of $25,200.

Transaction (d) represented current depreciation expense that increased the balance in Accumulated Depreciation (thereby reducing the book value of PPE) and increased Depreciation Expense (thereby decreasing net income). This transaction was discussed earlier in connection with operating activities. The current charge for depreciation is not an investing activity; therefore it is not considered in determining cash flows from investing activities.

To summarize, cash flows from investing transactions related to the PPE account were:

Proceeds from sale of PPE	$25,200
Payments for purchase of PPE	(70,000)

Noncash investing activities related to the PPE account were:

Issuance of long-term note payable in exchange for PPE	$30,000

Using the cash flow information obtained from analyzing the Investments and PPE accounts above, we present the "Cash Flows from Investing Activities" section of the statement of cash flows as follows:

Cash flows from investing activities:	
Proceeds from sale of investments	$ 30,500
Payments for purchase of investments	(75,000)
Proceeds from sale of PPE	25,200
Payments for purchase of PPE	(70,000)
Net cash used in investing activities	$(89,300)

Step 3: Analyze Relevant Balance Sheet Accounts to Determine Cash Flows and Significant Noncash Effects from Financing Activities

As explained earlier, financing activities are those nonoperating activities that involve bringing new capital into the enterprise, either from creditors or owners, and taking capital out of the firm for distribution to creditors or owners. Financing activities, therefore, result in changes in liability and owners' equity accounts in the balance sheet. Although changes in liability accounts are usually attributable to financing activities, recall from our earlier discussion that operating activities often cause changes in current liability accounts such as Accounts Payable.

Borrowing and repaying funds, which constitute financing activities, affect the Short-Term Loans Payable and Long-Term Notes, Bonds, and Mortgages Payable accounts (see Exhibit 18–2). Selling and repurchasing shares of capital stock are financing activities that affect the paid-in capital accounts Capital Stock and Paid in Capital in Excess of Par Value. Changes in the Retained Earnings account, other than for recognizing operating income or loss, are also normally caused by financing activities. The most common financing activity that affects Retained Earnings is the declaration of a dividend, which represents a distribution of earned capital to shareholders.

A review of the balance sheet for the Omega Company indicates that it has one liability account (Long-Term Debt) and three owners' equity accounts (Common Stock, Paid in Capital in Excess of Par Value, and Retained Earnings), all of which reflect financing activities that occurred during the year. Each of these is discussed below.

Long-Term Debt. Exhibit 18–7 indicates that three transactions occurred during the year that either increased or decreased the Long-Term Notes Payable account: (a) common stock was issued in payment of a $12,845 long-term note, (b) $20,000 of cash was borrowed on a long-term note, and (c) a $30,000 long-term note was issued in exchange for PPE. The journal entires for these three transactions indicate that only the second transaction had any affect on cash; the other two transactions were significant noncash financing activities that should be reported in the schedule of noncash investing and financing activities. The first transaction actually represented two financing events, the issuance of capital stock and the payment of a long-term note; the second transaction involved a $20,000 cash receipt from borrowing money; and the third transaction, which contained investing and financing elements, represented the purchase of PPE (an investing activity) by issuing a long-term note (a financing activity).

To summarize, cash flows from financing activities related to the Long-Term Debt accounts were:

Proceeds from borrowings on Long-Term Notes	$20,000

Noncash financing activities related to the Long-Term Debt account were:

Issued common stock shares in payment of long-term note payable	$12,845
Issued long-term note payable in exchange for PPE	$30,000

Capital Stock and Paid in Capital in Excess of Par Value. Exhibit 18–2 indicates that changes in the Capital Stock and Paid in Capital in Excess of Par Value accounts are related to financing activities. These transactions typically involve the sale of new shares of capital stock or the repurchase and retirement of existing shares of capital stock. Normally, a change in Paid in Capital in Excess of Par Value will not occur unless there is a transaction affecting the number of shares of stock outstanding and, thus, unless there is a change in the Capital Stock account. Hence, these two accounts are normally analyzed together.

Notice in Exhibit 18–7 that Omega Corporation had two transactions that affected the paid-in capital accounts during 19x2, one involving the issuance of new shares of capital stock to retire long-term debt and the other involving the issuance of new shares of capital stock for cash. The first transaction, which was discussed above in connection with long-term debt transactions, involved no change in cash but was a noncash financing transaction that should be disclosed on the statement of cash flows in the schedule of noncash investing and financing activities. The second transaction represented a financing transaction that provided cash inflows of $27,355.

To summarize, cash flows from financing activities related to the paid-in capital accounts were:

Proceeds from the sale of common stock	$27,355

Noncash financing activities related to the Long-Term Debt account were:

Issued common stock shares in payment of long-term note payable	$12,845

Retained Earnings. The final account in the balance sheet affected by financing activities is the Retained Earnings account. In addition to changes in Retained Earnings caused by operating activities (for a net income or net loss), the Retained Earnings account is decreased by the declaration of a dividend, a financing activity. A dividend declaration is a financing activity because it represents management's decision to return capital to the shareholders, which could have been retained for expansion or other purposes. Omega Corporation declared and paid a cash dividend of $25,000 during 19x2, representing a cash outflow from financing activities. If the dividend had been declared but not paid, the transaction would have had no immediate effect on cash and would have been disclosed only in the schedule of noncash investing and financing activities.

To summarize, the cash effect of financing activities related to the Retained Earnings account was:

Payment of cash dividend	$(25,000)

Using the cash flow information from analyzing the accounts affected by financing activities, the "Cash Flows from Financing Activities" section of the statement of cash flows is presented as follows:

Cash flows from financing activities	
Proceeds from borrowings on Long-Term Notes	$20,000
Proceeds from the sale of common stock	27,355
Payment of cash dividend	(25,000)
Net cash provided by financing activities	$22,355

Step 4: With the
Information
Gathered in the
First Three Steps,
Format the
Statement of Cash
Flows, Using Either
the Direct or
Indirect Method for
Reporting Cash
Flows from
Operating Activities

The information needed to prepare a statement of cash flows in good form is provided in the three steps discussed above. As discussed in Step 1, the operating activities section of the statement varies depending on whether the direct or indirect method is used. In either case, the investing and financing activities sections of the statement are identical. The statement of cash flows for Omega Corporation using the direct method is presented in Exhibit 18–8, and the statement using the indirect method is presented in Exhibit 18–9.

Notice in Exhibits 18–8 and 18–9 that the schedule of noncash investing and financing activities is presented below the cash flows from operating, investing, and financing activities. For Omega Corporation there were two noncash investing and financing activities, one that involved both investing and financing elements (the issuance of a note to acquire PPE), and another that involved only

---

EXHIBIT 18–8   Statement of Cash Flows for Omega Corporation (Direct Method)

Omega Corporation
Statement of Cash Flows
For the year ended December 31, 19x2

Cash flows from operating activities

Cash received from customers	$645,045	
Cash paid for inventory for resale	(307,550)	
Cash paid for operating expenses	(207,100)	
Dividends and interest received	17,300	
Interest paid	(40,000)	
Taxes paid	(41,750)	
Net cash provided by operating activities		$65,945

Cash flows from investing activities

Proceeds from sale of investments	$ 30,500	
Payments for purchase of investments	(75,000)	
Proceeds from sale of property, plant, and equipment	25,200	
Payments for purchase of property, plant, and equipment	(70,000)	
Net cash used in investing activities		(89,300)

Cash flows from financing activities

Net borrowings on long-term notes	$ 20,000	
Proceeds from sale of common stock	27,355	
Payment of cash dividend	(25,000)	
Net cash provided by financing activities		22,355
Net decrease in cash (see Exhibit 18–3)		$(1,000)

Schedule of noncash investing and financing activities

Issued long-term note payable in exchange for property, plant, and equipment	$30,000
Issued common stock shares in payment of long-term note payable	$12,845

EXHIBIT 18–9   Statement of Cash Flows for Omega Corporation (Indirect Method)

Omega Corporation
Statement of Cash Flows
For the year ended December 31, 19x2

Cash flows from operating activities

Net income		$48,500
Adjustments to reconcile net income to net cash provided by operating activities:		
Gain on sale of investments	(5,500)	
Loss on sale of property, plant, and equipment	10,000	
Depreciation	35,000	
Increase in Accounts Receivable	(29,955)	
Decrease in Inventory	9,700	
Decrease in Accounts Payable	(7,250)	
Decrease in Prepaid Expenses	3,450	
Increase in Accrued Expenses	1,950	
Increase in Taxes Payable	50	
Net cash provided by operating activities		$65,945

Cash flows from investing activities

Proceeds from sale of investments	$ 30,500	
Payments for purchase of investments	(75,000)	
Proceeds from sale of property, plant, and equipment	25,200	
Payments for purchase of property, plant, and equipment	(70,000)	
Net cash used in investing activities		(89,300)

Cash flows from financing activities

Net borrowings on long-term notes	$ 20,000	
Proceeds from sale of common stock	27,355	
Payment of cash dividend	(25,000)	
Net cash provided by financing activities		22,355
Net decrease in cash (see Exhibit 18–3)		$(1,000)

Schedule of noncash investing and financing activities

Issued long-term note payable in exchange for property, plant, and equipment	$30,000
Issued common stock shares in payment of long-term note payable	$12,845

financing elements (the issuance of capital stock to retire a note). Whether a noncash transaction involves only one element or both, it will be listed in the schedule only once. The purpose of the schedule is to disclose significant noncash transactions, not to delineate the investing and financing elements of such transactions.

USING THE STATEMENT OF CASH FLOWS

The statement of cash flows probably provides the greatest amount of information of any financial statement on how well management performed during the period. It provides a straightforward summary of where cash came from and where it was used during the period for operating, investing, and financing activities. It also indicates how noncash capital was generated and used for investing and financing activities during the period.

MANAGERIAL PRACTICE 18.4

Are Cash Flows Better Indicators of Corporate Value?

Highly leveraged companies that have been created by the recent merger mania are betting that investors will value their common stocks based on predepreciation and pre-interest cash flows in lieu of focusing on earnings, which are likely to be depressed or nonexistent for several years to come. Time president, N. J. Nicholas, Jr., expressed relief that the new emphasis on cash flows had relieved him of the burden to produce quarterly earnings. "Paramount, Time, and Warner, all traditional earnings-oriented companies, are now saying earnings aren't nearly as important as combining and building on assets that will generate cash in the future."

The switch in strategy from emphasizing earnings to emphasizing cash flows is causing some firms to seek expansion that will be financed with debt, thereby creating interest expense that will absorb earnings, and thus income taxes. Comcast is a cable TV company that has managed to increase its stock price by 150 percent while accumulating accounting losses over the past few years. The cash flow method of analyzing cable companies began more than a decade ago when Tele-Communications, Inc., found that it could add value to the firm by borrowing to acquire new cable systems instead of generating earnings and paying taxes.

Although other companies, such as Columbia Pictures Entertainment, have been unsuccessful in convincing analysts that their stocks should be based on multiples of cash flow rather than on earnings, it was predicted that "in the Time case, the cash-flow method may be an easier sell."

Source: Laura Landro, "Time's Warner Bid Reflects Emphasis on Value of Cash Flow, Not Earnings," *Wall Street Journal,* 27 June 1989, 2.

Many of the important questions that managers, investors, and creditors have about a company can be answered with information found on the statement of cash flows, including:

- Was the company's cash position strengthened or weakened by current operations?

- Was the amount of dividends declared and paid consistent with the amount of cash generated by operating activities?

- Were capital investments compatible with the sources of capital? For example, did management use short-term capital to finance long-term investments?

- Were increases in cash financed primarily by operations, reduced investments, or new capital from loans or stock issues?

- What did the company invest in property, plant, and equipment during the year?

- How were mergers and acquisitions completed during the year financed?

- What happened to the funds generated by new loans, stock issues, and disposition of corporate assets?

The sophisticated analyst may be able to piece together some or all of the answers to these questions using information from the income statement or balance sheet; however, the statement of cash flows provides clear answers to such questions so that even a casual reader of the financial statements can find the answers to them.

Notice in Exhibit 18–8 in the Omega Corporation's statement of cash flows that Omega generated $65,945 in cash from operating activities during the year, even though its net income (see Exhibit 18–4) was only $48,500. It paid cash dividends of $25,000, which represented 52 percent of net income but only 38 percent of operating cash flows. After paying dividends, $40,945 of cash provided by operations was retained in the business. Other sources of cash were $30,500 from sale of investments; $25,200 from sale of property, plant, and equipment; $20,000 from new long-term loans; and $27,355 from the sale of Omega common stock. All of these funds represent capital available for long-term or permanent use in the business. Hence $75,000 was spent on new investments and $70,000 was paid to acquire new property, plant, and equipment.

Information from the statement of cash flows can also be used to analyze the change in the productive capability of a company during the financial statement period. Overall, the company had a net cash investment in productive assets of $89,300. However, an additional investment in property, plant, and equipment of $30,000 was made without an immediate cash impact by exchanging a long-term note for the assets (see the schedule of noncash investing and financing activities in Exhibit 18–8). Thus the total investment in productive assets during the year was $119,300.

Overall, the Omega Corporation's statement of cash flows shows that Omega has expanded its productive capability during the year. This expansion was financed by a combination of funds from operations, the issuance of new common equity, and the issuance of new long-term debt.

SUMMARY

The statement of cash flows provides a summary of the major sources and uses of cash from operating, investing, and financing activities. Operating activities consist of the company's normal income-earning transactions. Investing activities are transactions related to the acquisition and disposition of productive and income-producing assets. Financing activities include all resource transfers between the company and its owners, as well as obtaining and repaying loans.

Operating activities may be presented on the statement of cash flows using either the direct method or the indirect method. Under the direct method, the primary categories of cash receipts and cash disbursements for operating activities are presented; under the indirect method, net cash flow from operations is determined by adjusting net income for noncash revenues and expenses.

One of the most effective ways of identifying cash transactions is to analyze the noncash balance sheet accounts. The type of activities (operating, investing, or financing) that produced or used cash can normally be determined by referring to the noncash accounts. For example, most transactions that affect property, plant, and equipment accounts are investing transactions; and all transactions recorded in the long-term debt and equity accounts are financing transactions.

To ensure that the statement of cash flows presents a comprehensive summary of all significant cash and noncash investing and financing activities, the statement of cash flows should also include a schedule summarizing all significant noncash transactions, such as property, plant, and equipment acquired by issuing a long-term note and the issuance of common stock to pay a long-term note.

The statement of cash flows provides a wealth of information that either is difficult to distill from the balance sheet and income statement or is not available on either of these statements. Unlike the income statement, which focuses primarily on operating performance, the statement of cash flows also provides an excellent summary of management's decisions regarding investing and financing activities.

SUGGESTED READINGS

Braken, Robert M., and Ara G. Volkan, "Cash Flows: A New Reporting Format for Turbulent Times," *Management Accounting* (January 1988): 38–41.

Financial Accounting Standards Board, *Statement of Cash Flows, Statement of Financial Accounting Standards No. 95,* Stamford, Conn.: Financial Accounting Standards Board, 1987.

Kalkbrenner, Karen W., Chuck Kremer, and Dennis D. Smith, "Why Managers Need Three Bottom Lines," *Management Accounting* (July 1989): 21–25.

Mazhin, Rezu, "Use 1-2-3 to Produce the Statement of Cash Flows," *Computers in Accounting* (October 1989): 70–78.

Seed, Allen H., III, "Improving Cost Management," *Management Accounting* (February 1990): 27–30.

Zega, Cheryl Ann, "The New Statement of Cash Flows," *Management Accounting* (September 1988): 54–59.

REVIEW PROBLEM

Statement of Cash Flows

Comparative 19x7 and 19x8 financial statements for O'Keefe's, Inc., are presented below.

O'Keefe's, Inc.
Comparative Income Statements
For the years ended December 31, 19x8 and 19x7
(*in thousands*)

	19x8	*19x7*
Sales	$3,000	$2,500
Cost of goods sold	−2,600	−2,300
Gross profit	$ 400	$ 200
Operating expenses:		
Selling	$ 125	$ 105
General and administrative	70	60
Total	− 195	− 165
Operating income	$ 205	$ 35
Other revenues and expenses:		
Interest income	$ 10	$ 5
Interest expense	(40)	(20)
Total	− 30	− 15
Income before income taxes	$ 175	$ 20
Provision for income taxes (34%)	− 60	− 7
Net income	$ 115	$ 13
Earnings per share	$ 1.28	$ 0.19

O'Keefe's, Inc.
Comparative Balance Sheets
December 31, 19x8 and 19x7
(*in thousands*)

Assets	*19x8*	*19x7*
Current assets:		
Cash	$ 300	$ 270
Marketable securities	75	45
Accounts receivable	325	280
Inventories	400	350
Interest receivable	60	55
Total current assets	$1,160	$1,000
Property, plant, and equipment	$1,500	$1,300
Less: Accumulated depreciation	− 800	− 750
Net	700	550
Other assets	15	12
Total assets	$1,875	$1,562

Liabilities and stockholders' equity

Current liabilities:		
Accounts payable	$ 435	$ 330
Income taxes payable	45	5
Interest payable	50	45
Total current liabilities	$ 530	$ 380
Long-term debt	300	250
Total liabilities	$ 830	$ 630
Stockholders' equity:		
Common stock ($1 par)	$ 90	$ 70
Premium on common stock	15	10
Retained earnings	940	852
Total stockholders' equity	1,045	932
Total liabilities and stockholders' equity	$1,875	$1,562

Additional information:

- During 19x8, Operating Expenses included a total of $50,000 in depreciation expense.

- Dividends of $27,000 were declared and paid during 19x8.

- Common stock of $15,000 was issued at par for cash in 19x8.

- Equipment costing $200,000 was acquired during 19x8 by paying cash of $190,000 and issuing 5,000 shares of common stock worth $10,000.

- During 19x8, long-term debt of $20,000 was paid off in cash and new long-term debt of $70,000 was issued for cash.

- The company extended a loan of $3,000 to the president during 19x8.

Requirements

a) Prepare a statement of cash flows for O'Keefe's, Inc., for 19x8 using the indirect method of reporting cash flows for operating activities.

b) Repeat part (a) using the direct method of reporting cash flows for operating activities.

c) What specific conclusions about O'Keefe's management of cash flows can be drawn from analyzing its statement of cash flows?

The solution to this problem is found at the end of the Chapter 18 exercises, problems, and cases.

KEY TERMS

Cash equivalents
Direct method
Financing activities
Indirect method

Investing activities
Operating activities
Statement of cash flows

18–1   What is the general purpose of the Statement of Cash Flows? Explain its relationship to the income statement and balance sheet.

18–2   Define the term "operating activities" and give a couple of examples of transactions that fall into this category.

18–3   Define the term "investing activities" and give a couple of examples of transactions that fall into this category.

18–4   Define the term "financing activities" and give a couple of examples of transactions that fall into this category.

18–5   Explain the difference between the direct method and the indirect method of reporting cash flows from operating activities.

18–6   If a company has a short-term certificate of deposit that qualifies as a cash equivalent, how should it be reported on the statement of cash flows when it matures and is converted into cash?

18–7   If a company borrows $100,000 from First National Bank during the year but also pays off a previous loan of $25,000 from the same bank, how should these transactions be reported on the statement of cash flows?

18–8   How should noncash investing and financing transactions be reported on the statement of cash flows?

18–9   Name two balance sheet accounts that are affected by operating activities. Explain.

18–10 Name three balance sheet accounts that are affected by investing activities. Explain.

18–11 Name three balance sheet accounts that are affected by financing activities. Explain.

18–12 Identify the adjustments necessary to convert the cost of goods sold to cash payments for inventory purposes.

18–13 Why is depreciation expense added back to net income to determine cash flows from operating activities?

18–14 Why are gains and losses eliminated from net income in determining cash flows from operating activities?

EXERCISES

18–1 Operating, Investing, and Financing Activities

The following is a list of noncash balance sheet accounts that may be affected by cash transactions from operating, investing, or financing activities:

a) Accounts payable.

b) Accounts receivable.

c) Accrued expenses payable.

d) Accumulated depreciation.

e) Bonds payable.

f) Common stock.

g) Inventories.

h) Long-term investments.

i) Paid-in capital in excess of par value.

j) Prepaid expenses.

k) Property, plant, and equipment.

l) Retained earnings.

m) Short-term notes payable.

n) Short-term notes receivable.

Required: Indicate for each of the accounts above whether it is normally affected by cash transactions from (1) operating activities, (2) investing activities, or (3) financing activities.

18–2 Investing Activities

Consider the following selected transactions for the Itap Corporation for 19x2:

1. Purchased new equipment for $10,000 cash.

2. Purchased new equipment by trading in old equipment and paying an additional $10,000 in cash.

3. Purchased new equipment by trading in old equipment and giving a two-year note for the $10,000 balance.

4. Acquired new equipment worth $10,000 by giving a small piece of land in an even exchange.

Requirements

a) For each of the transactions above, indicate how it will be reported on Itap's Statement of Cash Flows for 19x2.

b) What effect did each of the transactions above have on Itap's 19x2 year-end cash balance?

18–3 Identifying Operating, Investing, and Financing Activities

Listed below are ten typical business transactions:

1. Purchased inventory on 30 days credit terms.

2. Paid employees' wages.

3. Sold common stock.

4. Issued common stock in exchange for land.

5. Purchased equipment by paying cash down payment and giving a three-year note for the balance.

6. Traded in a used piece of equipment for a new machine, giving a long-term note for the balance.

7. Paid invoices for inventory purchases.

8. Purchased treasury stock.

9. Converted long-term bonds payable into common stock.

10. Split common stock.

Requirements

a) For each of the transactions above, indicate whether it is an operating, investing, or financing transaction.

b) For each of the transactions above, indicate whether it increases, decreases, or has no effect on cash.

c) For each of the transactions above, indicate whether it increases, decreases, or has no effect on net income.

18–4 Identifying Operating, Investing, and Financing Activities

Listed below are ten typical business transactions:

1. Recorded annual depreciation on plant and equipment.
2. Amortized goodwill related to acquisition of subsidiary.
3. Amortized discount on bonds payable.
4. Declared and paid a 10% stock dividend.
5. Retired preferred stock at market price.
6. Accrued year-end operating expenses.
7. Declared a cash dividend to be paid in the following year.
8. Accrued expense at year-end on long-term debt.
9. Refinanced short-term debt by issuing long-term notes.
10. Retired treasury stock acquired six months ago.

Requirements

a) For each of the transactions above, indicate whether it is an operating, investing, or financing transaction.

b) For each of the transactions above, indicate whether it increases cash, decreases cash, or has no effect on cash.

c) For each of the transactions above, indicate whether it increases net income, decreases income, or has no effect on income.

d) Which of the ten transactions will be shown only as a noncash investing or financing transaction on the statement of cash flows for the current year? Explain.

18–5 Operating, Investing, and Financing Transactions

Below is a list of ten typical business transactions:

1. Sold capital stock for cash.
2. Purchased a building for cash.
3. Declared a cash dividend.
4. Issued long-term bonds payable for cash.
5. Recorded a net loss for the period.
6. Purchased a building site by issuing long-term bonds.
7. Sold equipment with a five-year remaining life for an amount equal to book value.
8. Sold treasury stock for cash.
9. Borrowed cash on a long-term note.
10. Sold a fully depreciated piece of equipment for cash.

Requirements

a) For each of the transactions above, indicate whether it represents an operating, investing, or financing transaction.

b) Which of the transactions above are cash transactions and which ones are noncash transactions?

18–6 Cash Flow from Operations: Direct and Indirect Methods

Roswell Company's current assets and current liabilities at the end of 19x6 and 19x5 are as follows:

Current assets	19x6	19x5
Cash	$ 8,500	$ 6,400
Accounts receivable	17,000	20,200
Inventory	41,000	44,000
Prepaid expenses	800	950
Totals	$67,300	$71,550
Current liabilities		
Accounts payable	$15,500	$17,200
Accrued expenses payable	10,000	7,500
Taxes payable	1,500	1,250
Totals	$27,000	$25,950

Roswell's income statement for 19x6 is as follows:

Roswell Company
Income Statement
For the year ending December 31, 19x6

Sales	$150,000
Less cost of goods sold	(80,000)
Gross margin	$ 70,000
Operating expenses	(35,000)
Depreciation expense	(15,000)
Income before taxes	$ 20,000
Income taxes (34%)	(6,800)
Net income	$ 13,200

Requirements

a) Using the indirect method, prepare the cash flows from operating activities section of the statement of cash flows for Roswell Company for 19x6.

b) Repeat part (a) using the direct method of presenting cash flows from operating activities.

18–7 Cash Flows from Operating Activities

Conn Publishing Company had the following current assets and current liabilities for the years ending December 31, 19x7 and 19x6:

Current assets	19x7	19x6
Cash	$ 5,000	$ 2,500
Accounts receivable	42,000	53,000
Inventory	92,000	81,000
Prepaid expenses	8,500	6,000
Due from officers	10,000	10,000
Current liabilities		
Accounts payable	$28,000	$32,000
Salaries payable	10,000	16,000
Interest payable	4,500	–
Taxes payable	15,000	11,500
Notes payable (for bank loan)	25,000	12,500

Additional information:

During 19x7, Conn Publishing Company recorded depreciation expense of $22,000 and had net income of $67,500.

Requirements

a) Which current asset and current liability accounts are related to operating activities?

b) Compute the net amount of cash provided by or used for operating activities.

18–8 Cash Flows from Operating Activities

The following information about changes in selected accounts for Warren Company has been provided to you for the year ended December 31, 19x3:

Accounts Payable	$35,000 increase
Accounts Receivable	20,000 increase
Accumulated Depreciation	16,500 increase
Accrued Expenses Payable	14,800 decrease
Cash	27,000 increase
Depreciation Expense	16,500 increase
Inventory	22,000 decrease
Notes Payable—Bank	15,000 increase
Retained Earnings	32,000 increase
Supplies	3,400 decrease
Wages Payable	8,000 decrease

Dividends of $20,000 were declared and paid during 19x3.

Requirements

a) Based only on the information provided above, compute the amount of net income reported for 19x3.

b) Based only on the information provided above, compute the amount of cash provided by operating activities in 19x3.

18-9 Cash Flows from Operating Activities   The current assets and current liabilities for Macon Company are summarized below for 19x1 and 19x0.

Current assets	19x1	19x0
Cash	$ 230,000	$ 147,000
Accounts receivable	523,000	435,000
Inventory	810,000	670,000
Prepaid expenses	58,000	52,000
Total	$1,621,000	$1,304,000
Current liabilities		
Accounts payable	$ 733,000	$ 577,000
Notes payable	88,000	104,000
Accrued expenses	164,000	199,000
Current portion of long-term debt	8,000	4,000
Total	$ 993,000	$ 884,000

Additional information:

- Net income for 19x1 was $444,000.
- Depreciation expense for 19x1 was $134,000.
- Amortization expense on intangible assets for 19x1 was $38,000.
- Notes payable represents short-term cash loans.

Requirements

a) Compute the amount of cash provided by operations in 19x1 by the indirect method.

b) Explain why the amount of cash provided by operations is different from net income. Which measure is more useful to managers? To investors?

18-10 Analyzing Cash Transactions   Murphy Company had the following transactions in its Long-Term Notes Payable general ledger account for 19x7:

Beginning balance	$235,000 credit
Debit entries	
Principal payments	$ 90,000
Converted long-term debt into common stock	50,000
Refinanced unpaid balance on an outstanding loan	25,000
Credit entries	
Obtained new cash loans	$125,000
New loan obtained to refinance existing loan	25,000

Requirements

a) Compute the amount of the change in the Long-Term Notes Payable accont for 19x7.

b) Compute the effect on Cash of the transactions recorded in the Long-Term Notes Payable account.

c) Show how the transactions in the Long-Term Notes Payable account will be reflected in Murphy's Statement of Cash Flows for 19x7.

18–11 Financing Transactions

The following financing transactions have been identified for the Westcom Company for 19x9:

1. Paid $450,000 on long-term notes payable, of which $50,000 was interest.

2. A $75,000 short-term note payable was taken out with the local bank until long-term financing could be arranged on the purchase of land for construction of a new warehouse.

3. Dividends of $25,000 declared at the end of 19x8 were paid in January 19x9. Dividends of $27,500 were declared at the end of 19x9.

4. Common stock shares with $1 par value were issued for $100,000 cash.

5. Long-term bonds payable totaling $250,000 were converted into common stock.

Requirements

a) Compute the amount of cash provided by, or used for, financing activities by the Westcom Company in 19x9.

b) Show how the noncash transactions will be presented on the statement of cash flows.

c) Compute the effect of Westcom's financing activities on net income in 19x9.

18–12 Investing Activities

Fiberopt Cable Company had the following investing activities in 19x6:

1. Purchased a new cable winding machine for $150,000 cash.

2. Purchased a new computerized control panel for $240,000 by paying $50,000 in cash and giving a long-term note for $190,000.

3. Sold an old cable winding machine for $20,000 that originally cost $85,000, and for which $60,000 depreciation had been recorded.

4. Traded a vacant piece of land for another piece of land with a 10,000 square foot warehouse and gave $100,000 difference, $10,000 in cash and a three-year note for the balance.

5. Signed a letter of intent to purchase a vacant cable manufacturing plant located in Mexico at a price of $5 million.

Requirements

a) Compute the amount of cash provided by, or used for, investing activities by the Fiberopt Company in 19x6.

b) Show how the noncash transactions will be presented on the statement of cash flows.

c) Compute the effect of Fiberopt's financing activities on net income in 19x6.

18–13 Multiple Choice Questions: Statement of Cash Flows

1. A loss on the sale of machinery in the ordinary course of business should be presented in a statement of cash flows as

   a) A deduction from net income in computing cash flows from operating activities under the indirect method.

   b) An addition to net income in computing cash flows from operating activities under the indirect method.

   c) A noncash investing and/or financing activity.

   d) A decrease in cash.

2. The declaration of a 10 percent stock dividend has to be presented in a statement of cash flows as

	An Increase in Cash	A Decrease in Cash
a)	No	No
b)	No	Yes
c)	Yes	No
d)	Yes	Yes

3. A gain on the sale of a plant asset should be presented in a statement of cash flows as

   a) An increase in cash.

   b) A decrease in cash.

   c) An addition to net income in computing cash flows from operating activities under the indirect method.

   d) A deduction from net income in computing cash flows from operating activities under the indirect method.

4. Which of the following should be presented as cash flows from operating, investing, or financing activities?

	Conversion of Long-Term Debt to Common Stock	Conversion of Preferred Stock to Common Stock
a)	No	No
b)	No	Yes
c)	Yes	Yes
d)	Yes	No

5. The retirement of long-term debt by the issuance of common stock should be presented in a statement of cash flows as

	An Increase in Cash	A Decrease in Cash
a)	No	No
b)	No	Yes
c)	Yes	No
d)	Yes	Yes

(CPA Adapted)

1. The following information is available from Sand Corporation's accounting records for the year ended December 31, 19x7:

Cash received from customers	$870,000
Rent received	10,000
Cash paid to suppliers and employees	510,000
Taxes paid	110,000
Cash dividends paid	30,000

Net cash flows provided by operations for 19x7 were:

a) $220,000.   **b)** $230,000.   **c)** $250,000.   **d)** $260,000.

Parts 2 and 3 are based on the following information:
Roe Company is preparing a statement of cash flows for the year ended December 31, 19x7. It has the following year-end account balances:

	19x7	19x6
Machinery	$320,000	$250,000
Accumulated depreciation	120,000	102,000
Loss on sale of machinery	4,000	—

During 19x7, Roe sold for $26,000 a machine that cost $40,000, and purchased several items of machinery.

2. Depreciation on machinery for 19x7 was

a) $18,000.   **b)** $24,000.   **c)** $28,000.   **d)** $32,000.

3. Machinery purchases for 19x7 amounted to

a) $34,000.   **b)** $70,000.   **c)** $96,000.   **d)** $110,000.

Parts 4 through 6 are based on the following information:
Rice Corporation's balance sheet accounts as of December 31, 19x7 and 19x6, and data relating to activities during 19x7, are presented below (credit balances are in parentheses):

	19x7	19x6
Cash	$230,000	$100,000
Short-term investments	300,000	–
Accounts receivable	510,000	510,000
Inventory	680,000	600,000
Long-term investments	200,000	300,000
Plant assets	1,700,000	1,000,000
Accumulated depreciation	(450,000)	(450,000)
Goodwill	90,000	100,000
Accounts payable	(825,000)	(720,000)
Short-term debt	(325,000)	–
Common stock ($10 par)	(800,000)	(700,000)
Paid-in capital in excess of par value	(370,000)	(250,000)
Retained earnings	(940,000)	(490,000)

Other information:

- Net income for 19x7 was $690,000.
- Cash dividends of $240,000 were declared and paid in 19x7.
- Equipment costing $400,000 on which $250,000 depreciation had been recorded was sold for $150,000 in 19x7.
- A long-term investment was sold in 1987 for $135,000. There were no other transactions affecting long-term investments during 19x7.
- In 19x7, 10,000 shares of common stock were issued for $22 a share.

4. Cash flows from operating activities for 19x7 were
   a) $915,000.   **b)** $940,000.   **c)** $950,000.   **d)** $975,000.

5. Cash flows from investing activities for 19x7 were
   a) $1,640,000.   **b)** $1,400,000.   **c)** $1,115,000.   **d)** $165,000.

6. Cash flows from financing activities for 19x7 were
   a) $305,000.   **b)** $545,000.   **c)** $590,000.   **d)** $830,000.

(CPA Adapted)

PROBLEMS

18–15 Cash Flows from Operating Activities and Reconciliation of Income Statement and Cash Flows

Alpha Corporation's income statement for 19x5 is presented below:

Alpha Corporation
Income Statement
For the year ended December 31, 19x5

Sales	$450,000
Cost of goods sold	(290,000)
Gross margin	$160,000
Operating expenses	(110,000)
Depreciation expense	(35,000)
Operating income	$ 15,000
Other income and expenses:	
Interest income	7,500
Interest expense	(10,000)
Loss on sale of investments	(12,000)
Income before taxes	$ 500
Income taxes (34%)	(170)
Net income	$ 330

The beginning and ending balances in the noncash current asset and current liability accounts are as follows:

	Beginning	Ending
Accounts payable	6,500	4,250
Accounts receivable	15,000	13,000
Accrued expenses payable	3,300	2,900
Inventories	51,000	63,000
Prepaid expenses	10,000	10,000
Dividends payable	2,500	-0-
Income taxes payable	6,000	170

Requirements

a) Using the direct method, prepare the cash flows from operating activities section of the statement of cash flows for Alpha Corporation for 19x5.

b) Prepare a schedule reconciling Alpha Corporation's 19x5 net income with its cash flows from operating activities. (*Hint:* Use the format of Exhibit 18–5.)

18–16 Cash Flows from Operating Activities and Reconciliation of Income Statement and Cash Flows

The 19x0 income statement for Patterson's, Inc., is presented below:

Patterson's, Inc.
Income Statement
For the year ended December 31, 19x0

Sales	$805,200
Cost of goods sold	(490,000)
Gross margin	$315,200
Operating expenses	(190,000)
Depreciation expense	(50,000)
Operating income	$ 75,200
Other income and expenses:	
Interest income	5,200
Interest expense	(17,000)
Gain on sale of investments	14,000
Income before taxes	$ 77,400
Income taxes (34%)	(26,316)
Net income	$ 51,084

The beginning and ending balances in the noncash current asset and current liability accounts are as follows:

	Beginning	Ending
Accounts payable	26,500	24,250
Accounts receivable	35,000	33,000
Accrued expenses payable	13,300	12,900
Inventories	91,000	83,000
Prepaid expenses	15,000	20,000
Dividends payable	22,500	22,500
Income taxes payable	6,500	8,000

Requirements

a) Using the direct method, prepare the cash flows from operating activities section of the statement of cash flows for Patterson's, Inc., for 19x0.

b) Prepare a schedule reconciling Patterson's, Inc.'s 19x0 income statement with its cash flows from operating activities. (*Hint:* Use the format of Exhibit 18–5.)

18–17 Effects of Transactions on Cash and Net Income

Below is a list of selected transactions for Ammco, Inc., that occurred in 19x1.

1. On January 1, Ammco entered into an agreement to purchase $10 million of raw materials for its primary product over the next three years.

2. In March, Ammco completed negotiations to acquire all the assets and assume the outstanding liabilities of Cobb Products Company. The deal, which was completed in July, called for Cobb's shareholders to receive a combination of cash, common stock, and preferred stock.

3. In September, Ammco accepted an offer of $5 million for one of its plants located in Brazil, which had been barely profitable in recent years. Ammco's board decided the plant should be sold, even though the book value of the plant was substantially more than $5 million. The deal was completed in December.

4. Ammco exercised the call provision in a $10 million bonds issue that matures in the year 2000. Because the conversion provision for the bonds allowed the bond-holders to convert the bonds to common stock, and the conversion value of the bonds was greater than the redemption value, all of the bonds were converted into common stock.

5. Ammco has been amortizing the goodwill acquired as part of the acquisition of a small packaging company five years ago. In the current year, $75,000 of goodwill was amortized.

Required: Explain the effects of each of the above transactions on Ammco's statement of cash flows and income statement for 19x1.

18–18 Analyzing Cash Transactions

Laneer Company had the following transactions in its Common Stock and Paid-in Capital in Excess of Par Value accounts for 19x9:

Common Stock	
Beginning balance	$450,000 credit
Debit entries:	
(no entries)	
Credit entries:	
Sold additional shares of stock	$ 100,000
Converted long-term debt into shares of common stock	50,000
Issued shares of stock in exchange for land	10,000

Paid-in Capital in Excess of Par Value	
Beginning balance	$2,350,000 debit
Debit entries:	
(no entries)	
Credit entries:	
Sold additional shares of stock	$ 700,000
Converted long-term debt into shares of common stock	250,000
Issued shares of stock in exchange for land	90,000

Requirements

a) Compute the amount of the changes in the Common Stock and Paid-in Capital in Excess of Par Value accounts for 19x9.

b) Compute the effect on Cash of the transactions recorded in the Common Stock and Paid-in Capital in Excess of Par Value accounts.

c) Show how the transactions in the Common Stock and Paid-in Capital in Excess of Par Value accounts will be reflected in Laneer's Statement of Cash Flows for 19x9.

18–19 Cash Flows from Operating Activities

Heard's Manufacturing Company reported the following income statement for 19x1:

Income Statement
Heard's Manufacturing Company
For the year ended December 31, 19x1

Sales	$6,505,000
Cost of goods sold	(3,290,000)
Gross margin	$3,215,000
Operating expenses	(2,160,000)
Operating income	$1,055,000
Other income and expenses:	
Interest income	50,000
Interest expense	(210,000)
Loss on sale of investments	(125,000)
Income before taxes	$ 770,000
Income taxes (34%)	(261,800)
Net income	$ 508,200

Current Asset and Current Liability Account Balances for the beginning and end of 19x1 are as follows:

	Beginning	Ending
Accounts receivable	$275,000	$290,000
Inventories	810,000	755,000
Prepaid expenses	60,000	50,000
Acccounts payable	210,000	255,000
Income taxes payable	190,000	261,800
Accrued expenses payable	235,000	330,000
Dividends payable	95,000	125,000

Other information:
Operating expenses included $350,000 of Depreciation Expense.

Requirements

a) Using the direct method, prepare the cash flows from operating activities section of the statement of cash flows for Heard's Manufacturing Company for 19x1.

b) Repeat part (a) using the indirect method.

c) What are the relative advantages and disadvantages of using the direct method versus the indirect method?

18–20 Statement of Cash Flows: A Challenge Problem

The following information was gathered from the records of Butler Butcher Shop for 19x4:

1. Current assets were $47,000 at the beginning of the year and $39,000 at the end of the year. Current assets included Cash of $10,000 at the beginning of the year and $12,500 at the end of the year. Other current assets included Accounts Receivable, Inventory, and Prepaid Expenses. Current liabilities consisted of Accounts Payable and Accrued Expenses Payable.

2. Current liabilities were $26,000 at the beginning of the year and $31,000 at the end of the year.

3. Common stock with a par value of $25,000 was sold for cash during the year for $75,000.

4. Long-term notes payable of $60,000 were paid off during the year.

5. Purchased land for $50,000, paying 25 percent down payment and financing the balance on a five-year note payable.

6. Depreciation expense for the year was $15,000.

7. Purchased treasury stock for cash at a cost of $10,000.

8. Acquired equipment by issuing a $35,000 note to be paid in 18 months.

Requirements

a) Compute the amount of net income for 19x4.

b) Prepare a statement of cash flows for 19x4.

18–21 Statement of Cash Flows: Direct and Indirect Methods

Rocky Mountain Company's financial statements are presented below.

Rocky Mountain Company
Comparative Balance Sheets
December 31, 19x4 and 19x3

Assets	19x4	19x3
Cash	$ 243,000	$ 270,000
Accounts receivable	1,147,000	1,120,000
Inventory	637,000	556,000
Total current assets	$2,027,000	$ 1,946,000
Property, plant, and equipment (net)	7,587,000	6,952,000
Total assets	$9,614,000	$ 8,898,000

Liabilities and stockholders' equity	19x4	19x3
Accounts payable	$ 297,000	$ 256,000
Accrued expenses payable	607,000	594,000
Total current liabilities	$ 904,000	$ 850,000
Long-term debt	1,350,000	1,282,000
Total liabilities	$2,254,000	$ 2,132,000
Common stock	$5,200,000	$ 5,200,000
Retained earnings	2,160,000	1,566,000
Total stockholders' equity	7,360,000	6,766,000
Total liabilities and stockholders' equity	$9,614,000	$ 8,898,000

Rocky Mountain Company
Income Statement
For the year ended December 31, 19x4

Sales		$11,677,000
Cost of goods sold		− 6,513,000
Gross profit		$ 5,164,000
Less operating expenses:		
Depreciation	$ 567,000	
Other expenses	2,882,000	− 3,449,000
Income from operations		$ 1,715,000
Less interest expense		− 94,000
Income before income taxes		$ 1,621,000
Less income taxes		− 486,000
Net income		$ 1,135,000

Additional information:

- During the year, a new plant was purchased for $2 million cash, and an old plant was sold for cash at a price equal to book value.
- Dividends were declared and paid during the year.
- There was no accrued expense payable at the beginning or end of the year.
- Long-term debts of $50,000 were paid during the year, and a new loan was taken out during the year to help pay for the new plant.

Requirements

a) Prepare a statement of cash flows using the direct method of presenting cash flows from operating activities.

b) Prepare the cash flows from operating activities section of the statement of cash flows using the indirect method.

c) What interpretive conclusions can you draw from Rocky Mountain's statement of cash flows?

18–22 Cash Flows from Operating Activities

Ferguson Company has the following changes in selected current asset, current liability, and other accounts during 19x4.

1. Decrease in Accounts Receivable—$15,000
2. Increase in Accumulated Depreciation—$12,000
3. Increase in Accumulated Amortization on Intangible Assets—$3,000
4. Decrease in Wages Payable—$3,500
5. Decrease in Prepaid Expenses—$1,250
6. Increase in Inventory—$4,500
7. Decrease in Accounts Payable—$75
8. Increase in accrual expenses payable—$400
9. Decrease in Interest Payable—$350
10. Increase in Cash—$5,250

Additional information:

- Net income for 19x4 was $43,250.
- There were no acquisitions or dispositions of investments or fixed or intangible assets during the year.
- Long-term debt was not issued or retired during the year.

Requirements

a) Prepare a schedule showing the adjustment to net income (increase or decrease) for each of the ten items above in computing the amount of cash provided by operations.

b) Prepare the cash flows from operating activities section of the statement of cash flows for Ferguson Company for 19x4.

18–23 Statement of Cash Flows: Indirect Method

Comparative balance sheets for Arnold's Computer Repair, Inc., for 19x7 and 19x6 are given below.

Arnold's Computer Repair, Inc.
Comparative Balance Sheets
December 31, 19x7 and 19x6

Assets	19x7	19x6
Cash	$ 1,200	$1,550
Supplies	850	600
Prepaid insurance	450	375
Total current assets	$ 2,500	$2,525
Land	$15,000	$ —
Tools and testing equipment	8,750	8,750
Less accumulated depreciation	(4,375)	(3,500)
Total fixed assets	19,375	5,250
Total assets	$21,875	$7,775

Liabilities and stockholders' equity		
Accounts payable	$ 650	$ 488
Interest payable	563	—
Total current liabilities	$ 1,213	$ 488
Notes payable (equipment)	$ 4,000	$5,000
Notes payable (land)	15,000	—
Total long-term liabilities	$19,000	$5,000
Common stock	$ 1,000	$1,000
Retained earnings	662	1,287
Total stockholders' equity	1,662	2,287
Total liabilities and stockholders' equity	$21,875	$7,775

Additional information:

- Net income was $21,850.
- Land was acquired by issuing a ten-year note payable.
- Dividends were paid during the year to Arnold, the company's only stockholder.

Requirements

a) Prepare a statement of cash flows for Arnold's Computer Repair, Inc., for 19x7. Use the indirect method.

b) What general conclusions can you draw from Arnold's statement of cash flows for 19x7?

18–24 Statement of Cash Flows: Direct and Indirect Methods

Financial statements for Instaprint Corporation are given below.

Instaprint Corporation
Comparative Balance Sheets
December 31, 19x9 and 19x8

Assets	19x9	19x8
Cash	$ 530,000	$ 192,000
Accounts receivable	606,000	578,000
Inventories	792,000	822,000
Prepaid expenses	108,000	152,000
Total current assets	$2,036,000	$1,744,000
Land, buildings, and equipment	$1,606,000	$1,500,000
Less accumulated depreciation	(852,000)	(756,000)
Total fixed assets	754,000	744,000
Patents	100,000	—
Total assets	$2,890,000	$2,488,000

Liabilities and stockholders' equity		
Accounts payable	$ 342,000	$ 382,000
Accrued expenses payable	112,000	70,000
Short-term notes payable	146,000	200,000
Total current liabilities	$ 600,000	$ 652,000
Long-term debt	248,000	—
Total liabilities	$ 848,000	$ 652,000
Common stock and paid-in capital	$ 410,000	$ 310,000
Retained earnings	1,632,000	1,526,000
Total stockholders' equity	2,042,000	1,836,000
Total liabilities and stockholders' equity	$2,890,000	$2,488,000

Instaprint Corporation
Income Statement
For the year ended December 31,19x9

Sales	$2,902,000
Cost of goods sold	−1,662,000
Gross profit	$1,240,000
Less operating expenses	− 968,000
Operating income	$ 272,000
Other income (interest and gain on sale of land)	50,000
Other expense (interest)	(34,000)
Income before taxes	$ 288,000
Income taxes	− 118,000
Net income	$ 170,000

Additional information:

■ Depreciation expense for the year was $96,000.

■ Cash dividends of $64,000 were declared and paid during the year.

- Land acquired for $20,000 ten years ago was sold during the year for $50,000.
- Equipment costing $126,000 was acquired during the year.
- A patent was acquired in 19x9 in exchange for common stock.

Requirements

a) Prepare a statement of cash flows for Instaprint Corporation for 19x9, using the indirect method of presenting cash flows from operations.

b) Prepare the cash flows from operating activities section of the statement of cash flows using the direct method. Show your calculations.

18–25 Cash Provided by Operations and Cash Basis Income Statement

Parks Company's income statement for 19x5 is given below.

Parks Company
Income Statement
For the year ended December 31, 19x5

Sales		$98,000
Cost of goods sold:		
Beginning inventory	$18,000	
Plus purchases	62,000	
Less ending inventory	(23,500)	−56,500
Gross profit		$41,500
Operating expenses:		
Salaries	$14,000	
Insurance	500	
Depreciation	1,250	
Interest	900	
Supplies	450	
Other	2,500	−19,600
Net income		$21,900

Current assets and current liabilities for Parks Company at the end of 19x5 and 19x4 were as follows:

Current assets	*19x5*	*19x4*
Cash	$ 1,200	$ 800
Accounts receivable	4,900	6,000
Inventory	23,500	18,000
Prepaid insurance	525	500
Supplies	750	1,100
Total current assets	$30,875	$26,400
Current liabilities		
Accounts payable	$ 8,200	$ 8,500
Wages payable	1,150	950
Interest payable	325	400
Total current liabilities	$ 9,675	$ 9,850

Requirements

a) Compute the amount of cash provided by operations using the indirect method.

b) Compute the amount of cash provided by operations using the direct method.

c) Prepare a schedule converting Parks Company's income statement from the accrual basis to the cash basis. (*Hint:* Use format in Exhibit 18–5.)

CASES

18–26 Statement of Cash Flows

John Copeland, President of Nytex Corporation, has been attempting to explain to his board of directors that the company had an excellent year in 19x5 despite the board's decision to sell one of its less profitable plants at a substantial loss. Copeland maintains that the $1 million net loss on the income statement is less relevant than its effect on the company's cash flow statement. You have been requested to assist Copeland in preparing cash flow information to assist in his presentation to the board and have obtained the following information for the Nytex Corporation pertaining to its operations for 19x5:

Nytex Corporation
Income statement
For the year ending December 31, 19x5

Sales	$21,000,000
Less cost of goods sold	−10,000,000
Gross margin	$11,000,000
Less operating expenses	−8,000,000
Income from operations	$ 3,000,000
Less other expenses:	
Loss on sale of plant	−4,000,000
Net income (loss)	$(1,000,000)

Non-operating cash receipts

From new long-term loan	$ 500,000
From sale of old plant	2,000,000

Non-operating cash payments

Dividends paid	$ 800,000
Payments on long-term loans	250,000
Equipment purchased	500,000
Purchase of treasury stock	1,000,000

Nytex's Current Asset and Current Liability account balances for the beginning and end of 19x5 are as follows:

	Beginning	Ending
Accounts receivable	$ 75,000	$ 90,000
Inventories	310,000	255,000
Prepaid expenses	50,000	60,000
Accounts payable	110,000	125,000
Income taxes payable	90,000	80,000
Accrued expenses payable	35,000	30,000
Dividends payable	25,000	25,000

Other information:
Operating expenses included $125,000 of Depreciation Expense.

Requirements

a) Prepare a statement of cash flows for Nytex for 19x5 (use the indirect method of presenting cash flows from operating activities).

b) Prepare a brief statement explaining the effects of the sale of the plant on the income statement and the statement of cash flows.

c) Are there any items in the cash flow statement that may raise questions by the board of directors that you should alert the president to be prepared to address? Explain.

18–27 Statement of Cash Flows

The schedule shown below presents the net changes in the balance sheet accounts as of December 31, 19x2, as compared to December 31, 19x1, for the Lock Company. Lock's statement of cash flows has not yet been prepared for the year ended December 31, 19x2. Additional information regarding Lock's operations during 19x2 follows the schedule.

Debit balance accounts	Net Change Increase (Decrease)
Cash	$ (340,000)
Accounts Receivable	1,040,000
Inventories	580,000
Property, Plant, and Equipment	1,800,000
Total	$3,080,000

Credit balance accounts	
Allowance for Bad Debts	$ 600,000
Accumulated Depreciation	950,000
Accounts Payable	1,250,000
Notes Payable (current)	(150,000)
Bonds Payable	(2,000,000)
Common Stock, $10 par value	9,000,000
Paid in Capital in Excess of Par Value	1,300,000
Retained Earnings	(7,870,000)
Total	$3,080,000

Additional information:

1. Lock Company incurred a net after-tax loss from regular operations of $500,000 for the year. In addition, Lock had an extraordinary gain from the sale of condemned land of $1,400,000 net of $600,000 taxes. The condemned land had a book value of $2,500,000.

2. Accounts receivable of $650,000 were written off during 19x2 by debiting Allowance for Bad Debts. The provision for bad debts expense for the year was $1,250,000.

3. Machinery acquired five years earlier at a cost of $2,000,000 was sold for $550,000 during 19x2. The machinery had a book value of $350,000 at the date of sale.

4. A new parcel of land with a market value of $6,300,000 was purchased in April, 19x2, and was paid for with cash of $1,500,000 plus 400,000 shares of Lock's common stock.

5. Two million dollars of bonds issued at par value ten years ago were retired during 19x2.

6. A 5 percent stock dividend was declared on January 15, 19x2, on 10,000,000 shares of Lock common stock. The market value of the stock on that date was $11 per share.

7. A cash dividend of $0.30 per share of common stock was declared on December 31, 19x2, payable on January 15, 19x3.

Requirements

a) Prepare a statement of cash flows for Lock Company for the year ended December 31, 19x2 including a schedule of significant noncash resource flows.

b) Prepare a brief report evaluating the management of cash flows by Lock Company's managers in 19x2.

(CMA Adapted)

18–28 Statement of Cash Flows

You have been assigned by the acquisitions committee of Control Group, Inc., to examine a potential acquisition, Retailers, Inc. This company is a merchandising firm that appears to be available because of the death of its founder and principal shareholder. Recent financial statements of Retailers, Inc., are shown below.

Retailers, Inc.
Comparative Balance Sheets
December 31, 19x2 and 19x1

	19x2	19x1
Cash	$ 130,000	$ 120,000
Accounts receivable	430,000	370,000
Inventory	400,000	400,000
Property, plant, and equipment	900,000	800,000
Less: Accumulated depreciation	(325,000)	(250,000)
Total assets	$1,535,000	$1,440,000
Accounts payable	$ 300,000	$ 260,000
Long-term note payable	280,000	280,000
Common stock	690,000	690,000
Retained earnings	265,000	210,000
Total equities	$1,535,000	$1,440,000

Retailers, Inc.
Income Statement
For the year ended December 31, 19x2

Sales		$2,943,000
Less expenses:		
Cost of goods sold	$2,200,000	
Wages expense	350,000	
Supplies expense	42,600	
Depreciation expense	100,000	
Interest expense	22,400	
Loss on sale of fixed assets	75,000	
Total		−2,790,000
Net income before taxes		$ 153,000
Income taxes (34%)		− 52,020
Net income		$ 100,980

Other information:

- Equipment was purchased for $250,000 cash.
- Cash dividends were declared and paid.

Requirements

a) Prepare a statement of cash flows for 19x2 using the indirect method of presenting cash flows from operating activities.

b) Prepare a brief report evaluating Retailers, Inc.'s management of cash flows during 19x2.

(CMA Adapted)

18–29 Interpreting the Statement of Cash Flows

John Barfield, who owns and operates a small chain of restaurants, does not understand why his accountant keeps telling him that the business is doing well even though he never seems to have enough cash to meet obligations. In 19x0 the company reported a profit of $220,000, and yet Barfield is concerned that the company will have to fold if the situation does not improve soon. To help him better understand the cash problem, he asked the accountant to prepare a cash flow statement, which follows.

Barfield's, Inc.
Statement of Cash Flows
For the year ending December 31, 19x0

Cash flows from operating activities (direct method)

Cash received from customers	$2,650,000	
Cash paid to employees	(850,000)	
Cash paid to suppliers	(1,250,000)	
Cash paid to others for expenses	(625,000)	
Interest paid	(110,000)	
Income taxes paid	(65,000)	
Net cash used by operating activities		$(250,000)

Cash flows from investing activities

Proceeds from sale of unprofitable restaurant facility	$ 900,000	
Payments for purchase of new restaurant buildings and equipment	(2,100,000)	
Net cash used for investing activities		(1,200,000)
Proceeds from long-term loans	$ 750,000	
Proceeds from short-term loans	950,000	
Payment of dividends	(150,000)	
Payments on long-term loans	(180,000)	
Payments on short-term loans	(25,000)	
Net cash provided by financing activities		1,345,000
Net decrease in cash		$ (105,000)

Requirements

a) Explain why net income was $220,000 at the same time operating activities used $250,000 of cash. Does this mean that net income is not a reliable indicator of operating performance?

b) Critique the statement of cash flows for Barfield's, Inc., and prepare a memorandum to explain his company's cash flow problems.

18–30 Preparation and Analysis of Statement of Cash Flows

Presented below are the balance sheets of Farrell Corporation as of the end of 19x4 and 19x3 and the income statement for the year of 19x4:

Farrell Corporation
Balance Sheets
December 31, 19x4 and 19x3

Assets	19x4	19x3
Cash	$ 275,000	$ 180,000
Accounts receivable	295,000	305,000
Inventories	549,000	431,000
Long-term investments	73,000	60,000
Land	350,000	200,000
Plant and equipment	624,000	606,000
Less: accumulated depreciation	(139,000)	(107,000)
Goodwill	16,000	20,000
Totals	$2,043,000	$1,695,000

Liabilities and stockholders' equity	19x4	19x3
Accounts payable	$ 504,000	$ 453,000
Accrued expenses payable	100,000	110,000
Income taxes payable	41,000	30,000
Long-term note payable	150,000	—
Bonds payable	160,000	210,000
Common stock, par value $10	430,000	400,000
Paid-in capital in excess of par value	226,000	175,000
Retained earnings	432,000	334,000
Treasury stock	—	(17,000)
Totals	$2,043,000	$1,695,000

Farrell Corporation
Income Statement
For the year ended December 31, 19x4

Net sales	$1,950,000
Less cost of goods sold	(1,150,000)
Gross margin	$ 800,000
Less operating expenses:	
Selling and administrative	(501,000)
Depreciation	(53,000)
Amortization of goodwill	(4,000)
Operating income	$ 242,000
Other income and expense:	
Interest expense	(15,000)
Investment income	9,000
Loss on sale of equipment	(5,000)
Income before income taxes	$ 231,000
Income taxes	(90,000)
Net income	$ 141,000

Additional information:

- Dividends declared during the year were $43,000.

- In January, Farrell sold for $19,000 equipment that originally cost $45,000 and on which $21,000 of depreciation had been recorded.

- In April, Farrell issued 1,000 shares of common stock for $23,000 cash.

- In May, Farrell sold all of its treasury stock for $25,000 cash.

- In June, individuals holding $50,000 face value of Farrrell bonds exercised the conversion privilege. Each of the 50 bonds was converted into 40 shares of Farrell's common stock.

- In July, Farrell purchased equipment for $63,000 cash.

- In December, land with a fair market value of $150,000 was purchased through the issuance of a long-term note in the amount of $150,000. The note bears interest at the rate of 10 percent and is due in five years.

- Long-term investments were purchased during the year for $13,000, and cash received on investments was $9,000.

Requirements

a) Prepare a statement of cash flows for Farrell Corporation for 19x4 using the direct method for presenting cash flows from operating activities, including a schedule of noncash investing and financing activities.

b) Prepare a brief discussion of Farrell Corporation's management of operating, investing, and financing activities for the year. What information about Farrell Corporation does the statement of cash flows provide that is not readily available by reading the balance sheet and income statement? Explain.

c) Revise the cash flows from operating activities section of the statement of cash flows using the indirect method.

d) Compare and contrast the direct and indirect methods of presenting cash flows from operating activities. Which method provides the most useful information to investors and managers? Explain.

(CPA Adapted)

REVIEW PROBLEM SOLUTION

a) **O'Keefe's, Inc.**
Statement of Cash Flows
For the year ended December 31, 19x8
(*in thousands*)

Cash flows from operating activities (indirect method)

Net income	$115	
Adjustments to reconcile net income to net cash provided by operating activities:		
Depreciation expense	50	
Increase in accounts receivable	(45)	
Increase in inventory	(50)	
Increase in interest receivable	(5)	
Increase in accounts payable	105	
Increase in taxes payable	40	
Increase in interest payable	5	
Net cash provided by operating activities		$215

Cash flows from investing activities

Payments for purchase of equipment	$(190)	
Net cash used by investing activities		(190)

Cash flows from financing activities

Proceeds from issuance of common stock	$ 15	
Proceeds from issuance of long-term debt	70	
Payments on long-term debt	(20)	
Payment for loan to president	(3)	
Payment of cash dividends	(27)	
Net cash provided by financing activities		35

Net increase in cash and cash equivalents (marketable securities)		$ 60

Schedule of noncash investing and financing activities

Issued common stock in exchange for equipment		$ 10

b) *Cash flows from operating activities (direct method)*

Cash received from customers	(1)	$2,955
Cash payments for inventory for resale	(2)	(2,545)
Cash payments for operating expenses	(3)	(145)
Interest received	(4)	5
Cash payments for interest	(5)	(35)
Cash payments for taxes	(6)	(20)
Net cash provided by operating activities		$ 215

Calculations:

1. Cash received from customers:

Sales	$3,000	
Increase in accounts receivable	(45)	$2,955

2. Cash payments for inventory for resale:

Cost of goods sold	$2,600	
Increase in inventory	50	
Increase in accounts payable	(105)	$2,545

3. Cash payments for operating expenses:

Operating expenses	$ 195	
Depreciation expense	(50)	$ 145

4. Interest received:

Interest income	$ 10	
Increase in interest receivable	(5)	$ 5

5. Cash payments for interest:

Interest expense	$ 40	
Increase in interest payable	(5)	$ 35

6. Cash payments for taxes:

Provision for income taxes	$ 60	
Increase in taxes payable	(40)	$ 20

c)

- Although net income was $115,000, cash provided by operations was $215,000.

- Cash dividends of $27,000 represented 23 percent of net income but only 13 percent of cash generated by operations. Therefore, 87 percent of cash provided by operations was retained in the business.

- O'Keefe's, Inc., invested $190,000 in productive assets during the period, of which only $35,000 was financed by cash generated by financing activities. The remainder was financed by cash provided by operating activities.

- O'Keefe's, Inc., applied conservative management policies during the period that reflected a policy of modest dividends and substantial reinvestment of cash provided by operations. New financing generated during the period was compatible with new investments made during the period.

A P P E N D I X

A Career in Management Accounting

Carl Stevens, Vice President of Finance, Papyrus Newton Falls

A management accountant deals with the financial affairs of a business—from small companies to giant corporations. My experience centers around the corporate world. Starting as a staff accountant and then plant controller of an industrial chemical producer, I progressed to my current position as vice president of finance of a paper manufacturer. Management accountants also work in noncorporate entities (partnerships and sole proprietorships), in nonprofit organizations (hospitals, schools, government agencies, and private foundations), and in service operations (banks and stock brokerages). Any organization with financial affairs to manage needs a management accountant. The range of jobs and responsibilities is broad—from the inexperienced staff accountant performing routine work to the chief financial officer of a multinational giant—with many rewarding and challenging possibilities in between.

Public Versus Management Accounting

Public accounting is the special domain of the CPA. Public accountants perform audits, provide tax advice, prepare tax returns, complete or review reports filed with the Securities and Exchange Commission (SEC), and provide consulting services in various financial matters. Aided in large part by the certification process, the CPA is viewed as a financial professional.

Management accountants perform accounting and other financial functions within the context of a manufacturing or service enterprise. An accountant who works exclusively for one company becomes deeply involved in many aspects of that company. In contrast, the CPA's main focus is auditing financial reports for several clients. Despite this difference in focus, the educational track for either the public or the management accountant is similar, and for good reason. The management accountant must conduct the financial affairs of the company in compliance with and with a complete knowledge of generally accepted accounting principles (GAAP). An example: Our company signed a consent order with an environmental regulatory agency to close and cap a solid waste landfill over the next three years at an estimated cost of $1.3 million. Is this a capital project, an expense item, or a contingent liability requiring only footnote disclosure? Must it be accrued during the current year, or as incurred? How is it presented on the financial statements? Is it a material amount? (In our case, yes!)

The cost accounting system is an integral part of the company's financial structure. It provides information for both the income statement (operating expenses) and the balance sheet (inventory valuation). Tax issues face the management accountant as an ongoing part of business, not just as April 15 approaches. The day-to-day work of a company's financial operations must routinely pass audit muster.

Particularly important are the internal control procedures for handling liquid assets, such as cash and securities. So is the overall integrity of company information systems. Solid internal control procedures are essential for a firm to operate profitably and to get an unqualified audit opinion. Finally, in large firms an internal audit group monitors company operations by using auditing techniques similar to those employed by independent auditors.

Large Versus Small Company

The size of an organization affects available professional opportunities. Large, multilocation, even multinational organizations with thousands of employees differ from small, single-location companies. In large companies, disciplines may contain specialists. It is possible to focus an entire career in one specific area such as credit, risk management, internal audit, or financial analysis. This is done by moving through the ranks from the plant, to the division, to the corporate level, and perhaps even overseas, as responsibilities increase. This specialization carries with it the downside risk of "dead-ending," spending much of a career stalled in a specialty that you do not enjoy or that may not lead to higher levels of management.

Viewed another way, because of its sheer size the large company offers a large choice of potential career paths. With good management, this broad selection can provide an antidote to "dead-ending." The wise company is eager to see its up-and-coming employees take in the view from various perspectives within its ranks. A senior manager who has spent time in several departments or disciplines develops a broader, less parochial vision. Such a manager is more likely to make decisions for the good of the entire company. What's more, the many options provide alternatives for an employee who gets bored or whose current career path is unsatisfying.

The small company contrasts with the large one in several ways. The breadth of experience and involvement for a management accountant in a small company can be significant. Instead of choosing credit or cost accounting or tax work, the management accountant in a small company can replace the "or" with "and." Probably no single function within the small company has a sufficient volume of work to demand full-time attention. A management accountant in a small company will wear several hats. What's more, the management accountant in a small company is more likely to have a direct impact on operations. A cost-saving idea is more easily communicated and implemented in a small, single-location company.

Small companies, of course, have their limitations. These companies are often single-location operations, removing the possibility of travel and relocation. There is little opportunity for specialization, which some find attractive. The chief financial officer (CFO) of a company with $10 million in assets carries less financial clout than the CFO of a Fortune 500 company, making it tougher to get the attention of potential lenders. Ironically, because of the scope of issues to be addressed, life within a small company can, at times, leave you feeling like the smallest of fish in a very large pond. Yet, there is also the opportunity to be creative, to find a good solution to a tough problem, to implement it right away, and to be recognized for your contribution. The choice of large or small company, specialist or generalist, and so on is personal; no choice is inherently good or bad.

What Does a Management Accountant Do?

Let us move from the general overview of career options to job responsibilities of management accountants. These responsibilities are divided among many people in large- and medium-sized organizations. In a very small company they may rest with one or two people.

General Accounting

Let's start with the basic debits and credits. Recording the financial activities of a business is the basis for measuring its performance. The general accounting function maintains the books of record, the core of which is the general ledger. Transactions recorded in the general ledger include the acquisition and disposal of fixed assets, the issuance and payment of long-term debt, and the issuance and repurchase of stock. Detailed records for operating activities, such as purchases on account, sales on account, payment of cash on account, and receipt of cash on account, are recorded elsewhere and summarized in the general ledger. The heart of this operation is the account structure, also known as the chart of accounts. From this seemingly simple function flows the most widely used measure of a company's performance: the financial statements.

From the general ledger come the answers to many diverse questions: How much did we spend for legal and professional services last year? What were the total repair and maintenance charges for the No. 3 paper machine? What was the cost of overtime in the finishing department in the first quarter? Did we receive our state tax refund?

The construction of the chart of accounts and the integrity of the information contained within it are key ingredients in providing the answers to many of the questions posed by company management. The management accountant plays a vital role, setting up the system, ensuring the accuracy and timeliness of information, seeking answers to financial questions, posing questions, and expressing concerns to higher management. On the surface, the general accounting function appears to be a humdrum affair. It is, however, the "central nervous system" of business. Without it, employees and creditors could not be paid, customers would not be invoiced, and receipts from customers would not be recorded. In fact, without a solid general accounting function, the most basic question of all—"Did we make any money?"—is unanswerable.

<table>
<tr><td>

Cost Accounting and Inventory Management

</td><td>

Cost accounting is vital for financial planning and control, especially in a manufacturing organization. Cost accounting works with production to set up the "bill of materials," the list of materials needed to create a finished product. The bill of materials also contains the standards or yardstick against which the production department's performance is judged. Standards are the basic building blocks for the budget. Cost accounting compares actual performance (daily, weekly, or monthly) with the standards and calculates variances (the amount actual performance differs from the standard), and advises management so that actions can be taken to correct problems. Operations are expressed in terms of the final measure of success: dollars and cents. This provides the link between day-to-day operation and financial reality.

</td></tr>
</table>

Performance evaluation issues are often complex. What about paper that passes inspection at the paper machine but proves to be defective during a subsequent operation? A machine is down for an emergency repair. Maintenance people, convinced they have fixed the problem, return the machine to production to resume paper manufacture. After two hours, the machine has not run satisfactorily and maintenance is called once more. After fifteen minutes, they find a second problem unrelated to the first. The second problem is righted quickly and the machine begins papermaking without further incident. This happens three times in one week. Who is responsible for the two hours downtime between repairs, when the machine was "on-line" but no product was made? Was maintenance at fault for not finding the problem the first time? Did production adequately describe the problem the first time? These statistics are important, as senior management uses them to determine the performance of departmental managers.

Focus for a moment on inventory management, valuation, and control. Parts kept to repair equipment such as specially fabricated components, pumps, motors, and so forth may cost hundreds of thousands of dollars. Determining what is in inventory, where it is, how much is on hand, when to reorder, and how to reduce inventory investment is often the job of the management accountant.

These issues also apply to raw materials, work-in-process, and finished goods inventories. Control of these inventories, which may represent 20 to 30 percent of a manufacturing company's total assets, is essential. The inventory manager must ensure reasonable turnover of stock, identifying and eliminating obsolete or unsalable items to preserve precious capital. Even with just-in-time inventory management for raw materials and work-in-process, the value placed on inventory may have a significant impact on reported profits. Furthermore, the management accountant must ensure that the method of valuation (FIFO, LIFO, etc.) is applied consistently, as described in the financial statements.

Budgeting and Financial Analysis	The budget is the "road map" a company creates for operations in the coming fiscal year. The budget is also used for performance evaluation. Since the budget is often developed months before the actual year begins, the realities of markets, the economy, and world events can make a budget obsolete before the new year begins. Most companies rely on updated forecasts to provide a fresh guide and measurement tool. In effect, the forecast is the budget adjusted for reality. What are these realities? Is a machine running at the expected efficiency and productivity? Has an unexpected liability, such as a $1.3 million landfill closure cost, popped up? Did energy prices soar unexpectedly? Are we working additional shifts to meet unusually high demand? Did we expect a 33 percent rise in our group insurance premiums? The budget must be adjusted for major changes in business reality.

Financial analysis often focuses on the future. Would a new grade of paper be profitable? Would a new piece of equipment yield additional profits? Are some of our products consistent losers? Financial analysis represents one of the broadest areas of accounting effort within a business. A list of topics that it can focus on might fill volumes.

Computer Systems	The use of computers has brought more change to accounting than any other single event. Today the computer is an integral part of the management accountant's life. The commercial introduction of personal computers in the early 1980s is a milestone whose impact is yet to be fully felt. Hours of clerical "number-crunching" have been eliminated while accuracy has increased. A pleasant result is more time spent analyzing and understanding information, with less time spent gathering and organizing it. The power and utility of spreadsheet programs and graphics packages are transforming businesses of all sizes. There is a new freedom from the tyranny of the omnipotent corporate MIS department, as data processing power has migrated from the centralized mainframe to the individual desktop.

On the other hand, "To err is human; to really foul things up requires a computer." A good manual accounting system is the key to a good computerized accounting system. Before data are entered into a computer, it is important to understand the physical flow of information, the controls needed to manage information, and the desired outputs. For example, if you are directing a computer system installation, most of your time will be spent performing "up front" work. Until you develop a chart of accounts, you cannot implement a general ledger system. Until you understand the flow of information and the approval process for vendor invoices, a payables system will not work. You had better know your company's union contract inside-out or your payroll system will create more headaches than accurate paychecks. A good stores inventory system will fail unless users know how to fill out withdrawal requisitions correctly and inventory clerks put items on the proper shelves in the warehouse. The ability to follow information flow through a system—the audit trail—coupled with well-documented internal controls is the hallmark of a good computer system.

Fixed Assets

For many businesses, the machinery and equipment used to generate the company's product or service is the largest single balance sheet item. Accounting for, and control of, fixed assets is the job of the management accountant.

Control of new investments is a big part of the task. A multimillion dollar expansion project requires tight control of outlays to ensure that the project is completed on time and within budget. Management must be immediately informed of any significant delays or cost overruns. Even before project approval, the management accountant helps in the feasibility study for the project. What is the possible return on investment? Does it provide adequate cash flow to cover principal and interest payments?

Existing assets are equally important. The management accountant maintains the company's asset directory. This is an itemized list of the company's fixed assets, that documents the fixed assets figure on the balance sheet. Accuracy is vital to avoid misstatement and to determine the book value of assets sold, scrapped, or written-off. Asset sales may generate profits or losses, depending upon the book value of the asset, and may also affect cash flow. There are obvious tax ramifications in such transactions.

The management accountant is responsible for the preparation of depreciation schedules. For internal and financial reporting purposes, the management accountant determines the best depreciation method to distribute the cost of an asset over its useful life. The choice of useful life of an asset can affect profits for many years. A $30 million project, spread over ten years, is expensed at $3 million per year. The same project over twenty years costs only $1.5 million per year. In a year when profits are slim, one may come to regret the selection of a shorter depreciable life made years earlier.

Internal Control and Internal Audit

A sound business uses internal controls to police itself. Internal controls are the "pressure points" the management accountant checks to ensure consistent and accurate movement of information, documents, and funds throughout the company. Important pressure points include the following: (1) requiring two signatures on checks over $5000; (2) comparing computer-generated control totals from the accounts receivable system to bank deposit tickets; (3) studying system totals from the general ledger; (4) requiring strict approval procedures before capital expenditures are begun; (5) comparing periodic physical counts of inventories to perpetual records; and (6) requiring purchase orders for all purchases.

In large companies an internal audit staff checks that effective internal control routines are in place and properly used. While focused primarily on financial matters, the internal audit team may also include specialists in energy use or engineering to perform a review of the entire facility. The internal audit team travels to the company's operating sites to conduct periodic audits, with an eye toward compliance with specific company directives and policies. Is cash handled securely? Is excess cash invested as authorized by company policies? Are there adequate internal controls on payroll, payables, and receivables? Are inventories properly managed? Are reusable drums and pallets returned for credit or cash? Does the facility uniformly adhere to depreciable lives as set by corporate policy? The internal audit team performs a thorough review and reports their findings to facility managers. They also help correct any internal control deficiencies.

Many of the items reviewed by the internal audit staff are identical to those checked by the independent audit team (CPAs). The internal audit group in a sense prepares the company for the annual independent audit, and often works in concert with the independent auditors. A good set of internal controls and an internal audit staff will significantly reduce the cost of an independent audit.

Independent Audit

Companies with publicly traded stock must be audited by an independent CPA firm on a regular basis. The management accountant acts as the interface between the company and the independent auditor and prepares many of the schedules and analyses used during the audit.

The financial statements belong to the company, not the auditor. There are specific guidelines followed by auditors in order to issue an unqualified opinion on the statements, but management has the final say on the content of the statements. The management accountant must keep in mind the final users of the statements and their possible reaction to the statements, particularly if the numbers presented are not favorable. There is a lot of negotiation between the auditors and the company, especially in the choice and wording of footnotes to the statements. If there is a gray area, the management accountant argues a case for the position most favorable to the company. These negotiations require a thorough knowledge of generally accepted accounting principles and solid negotiating skills.

Taxes

Taxes are an inevitable result of doing business. The management accountant is the company's liaison with the tax authorities. Companies face several types of taxes. First, and most prevalent, are income or franchise taxes. The most obvious is the federal income tax, though states, counties, cities, and other authorities may impose taxes on profits or assets.

Sales and use taxes are imposed on a state-by-state basis, with vast differences in state laws. A multilocation operation must devote time and effort to understanding and complying with various state laws and regulations. In large corporations, annual sales and use taxes amount to millions of dollars. An in-depth understanding of the sales and use tax laws can significantly increase the bottom line and preserve cash through legal tax avoidance.

Federal and state laws require the withholding of taxes from employees. Social security taxes (FICA) must be withheld and a matching contribution made by employers. Federal and state agencies require payment of unemployment taxes on a periodic basis. Companies with employees in several states must follow each state's filing requirements.

Filing of most of these taxes requires completion of various forms. Payments of taxes must be made in periods ranging from quarterly to every few days.

Penalties for noncompliance, in both payment and filing, have grown in recent years, especially regarding federal and FICA taxes. High penalties for the underpayment of estimated taxes has put added emphasis on this aspect of tax law compliance. Electronic transfer of payments and filing of forms has become commonplace, replacing the traditional paper forms.

Companies with large real property holdings (primarily land and buildings) pay substantial amounts of property taxes. Accurate accounting of property owned and negotiation with tax authorities about property values and tax rates are effective means of controlling this expense.

The subject of taxation is a broad and often complex one. Consequently, I have had to ignore some areas, including international tax issues facing companies with worldwide operations.

Accounting for Employee Benefits

The employee relations department administers benefits programs. The management accountant must translate the complexity of premiums, retrospective adjustments, prospective rate reductions, cash flow plans, and the like onto the company's financial records. Benefit plans covering medical, life, disability, workers' compensation, and other insurances may cover annual periods that do not coincide with the company's fiscal year. Some plans, such as medical and workers' compensation, are retrospective, meaning premiums are adjusted following semiannual reviews of losses compared to paid premiums. A single policy year may remain open for many years until all claims are settled. The management accountant must supervise the analysis, recording, and payment of employee related liabilities.

Almost every company has a pension plan of some type. Some have multiple plans covering various employee groups. These plans must meet strict IRS requirements to qualify as valid plans. An actuary, using the company's plan as a base, calculates the appropriate level of funding to meet future obligations. Most plans are subject to independent audit. Many plans are placed in trust and the funds invested by an investment advisor. The management accountant often evaluates the strategy and performance of the plan's investment advisors, provides the assumptions for use by the actuary, and assists in completing the pension audit. The management accountant works with the independent auditor and the actuary to determine the correct financial statement presentation of retirement plan liabilities.

Labor issues are money issues. The management accountant is an important member of the company's union negotiation team. Contract issues go beyond simple remuneration questions. The cost of union demands for additional benefits, reduced workdays, job security, and other similar requests may be difficult to compute. The management accountant quantifies the cost of such requests.

Treasury and Cash Management

Cash management is an inherent part of much of the management accountant's job. Collections of open receivables, measured by the traditional days receivables outstanding, is the largest cash source for a company. Relationships with banks and other lenders are maintained for both day-to-day needs and long-term plans. Cash availability must be planned and monitored. Will a new capital investment program require additional credit lines? Will there be enough cash to fund operations during a buildup of inventory as the company's busy season approaches? Has poor profitability depleted cash to the point where short-term lines of credit are needed? How should a company meet its future cash needs? Is the balance sheet strong enough to handle additional debt, or is equity funding necessary to maintain financial strength? If the company is large and diverse, are there funds available from other company units? If profits decline during capital expansion, will the debt-to-equity relationship remain acceptable? Should a company lease new capital equipment or is purchase more desirable? What kinds of investments are acceptable? Should excess funds be in low-risk short-term investments? How about bonds, stocks, money funds, etc.? These are typical questions that face treasury professionals.

Foreign exchange and foreign currency issues—a subject multinational companies have dealt with for years—have gained importance in recent years. The reality of a "global marketplace" now places emphasis on this issue even for relatively small companies. The astute financier can earn a lot of money using the tools of foreign exchange. A U.S. dollar strengthening its position in relation to major foreign currencies can make overseas purchases an even better investment if the company is positioned carefully in the currency markets. This is a complex and risky area of finance, but it can be highly profitable if done well.

Risk Management

Risk management is an activity often directed by the management accountant. The risk manager assesses the risks faced by the company and develops a plan to reduce the negative effect of their occurrence. In property damage insurance, for example, the risk manager must be sure that insurance coverage, obtained at a reasonable price, is adequate to replace any assets destroyed. The cost of insurance, and the payment plan selected, must be included in the company's budget. If there is an actual loss, the accountant may develop the claim filed with the insurer.

Strategic Planning

Where is the company headed? What products make sense for future investment and growth? The management accountant assists senior management and the board of directors to evaluate potential strategies, a process quite removed from the day-to-day operation of a business.

One possible strategy for future growth is acquiring other companies or new business lines. The management accountant performs much of the "number crunching" necessary to complete such a review. The information available is often sketchy and incomplete. It is a test of the accountant's knowledge of financial systems, detective ability (in reading between the lines), and understanding of the pertinent industry to complete a meaningful analysis.

Success in management accounting obviously requires technical skills. There are other areas that, during my fifteen year career, have proven significant as well. They cannot all be obtained solely through classroom study, but an awareness of them should prove helpful to the prospective management accountant.

I mentioned this earlier, and I cannot overemphasize it: Accounting and the computer are inextricably linked. Affordable computing power is available for the smallest business. Big companies run sophisticated accounting systems on huge mainframes. The personal computer–based spreadsheet is today what the adding machine used to be for the finance professional. The more you know about hardware, software, and systems as an overall discipline, the better your chances for success in accounting.

Communication skills, both written and oral, are valuable in any type of management function. Much of this communication is internal. Information gathering requires contacts with people throughout the company, asking the right questions and listening to the answers. Managing a department involves explaining assignments and responsibilities to subordinates. Financial reports to senior management, directors, or shareholders require clear explanations and interpretations.

External communication also involves a broad population. Recipients of communication from a company include customers, vendors, regulatory agencies, lenders, insurers, investors, and consultants. With sound communication skills, you make your points forcefully, negotiate skillfully, and provide others with a lasting and favorable impression of your professionalism.

Much of management accounting involves people. The management accountant cannot operate in a remote office counting the company's money. The job functions described here require dealing with people. It is a challenge to think of aspects of a management accounting career that do not require dealing with people. Interpersonal skills adopted and cultivated throughout a career will have a significant bearing on the level of success achieved.

A knowledge of international business issues can become crucial for the management accountant—as it did for me in 1984, when our mill was purchased by a Swedish company. Within weeks we were purchasing equipment in Germany and Sweden (with contracts written in marks and krona), reporting sales and production in metric tons, and learning the intricacies of Swedish accounting practices. We had to learn a new language jokingly called "Swenglish," a sometimes mysterious and confusing mixture of Swedish and English. On one occasion, we were asked to report our annual "turnover." "Inventory or receivables?" we asked. After a few more questions we determined that "turnover" in Swenglish is "sales" to the uninformed American businessperson.

Technology has been the driving force behind this globalization. The telephone, computer, and most recently the fax machine have made doing business thousands of miles and several time zones removed as simple as dealing with the next city. Major events are televised worldwide as they happen. The management accountant must be in tune with world events and recognize the possible impact of events such as a fluctuation in currency, unstable political conditions, or a competitor's move into Eastern Europe.

Conclusion

Management accounting is a broad field, encompassing a wide range of career opportunities. It offers a chance to be creative, to specialize, and to be a member of a team that builds and runs a successful company. There are many opportunities and rewards for good performance, and the opportunity for accreditation is also available. The certified management accountant (CMA) is fast becoming a respected symbol of professional stature within the business community. Management accounting is a dynamic career choice that deserves serious consideration by anyone seeking a career in business and finance.

Glossary

The number enclosed in parentheses after each term refers to the chapter where the term is first defined.

Absorption Cost Basis of External Reporting (2) A method of external reporting under which all manufacturing costs are product costs and all selling and administrative costs are period costs.

Absorption Costing (10) A product costing procedure where all manufacturing costs (fixed and variable) are assigned to products and inventoried (also called **Full Costing**).

Accelerated Cost Recovery System (ACRS) (16) An asset depreciation method created by the Economic Recovery Tax Act of 1981 that allows personal property to be depreciated for tax purposes over a period much shorter than an asset's estimated useful life.

Accounting Rate of Return (15) A method used to evaluate capital expenditures that ignores the time value of money. It is computed as the average annual net income associated with an investment divided by the average investment amount.

Acid Test Ratio (17) A measure of the availability of cash and other current monetary assets to pay current liabilities. It is computed as the sum of cash, current receivables, and marketable securities divided by current liabilities.

Activity-Based Costing (ABC) (13) This involves, to the extent possible, the assignment and reassignment of costs to cost objectives on the basis of the activities that cause costs.

Allocation Base (12) The factor or characteristic common to cost objectives that is used to determine how much of a cost (or cost pool) is assigned to each objective.

Annuity (15) A series of equal cash flows received or paid over equal intervals of time.

Appraisal Costs (14) The costs incurred to identify nonconforming products or sevices before they are delivered to customers.

Appropriation Budgets (6) Budgets used in not-for-profit organizations to provide the authorization for expenditures during a specified period.

Asset Depreciation Range (ADR) (16) Guidelines for determining the appropriate useful life for depreciable assets as set by the 1969 Tax Act.

Asset Turnover (17) A ratio that measures the ability of an organization to use its assets to generate sales. It is computed as sales divided by average total assets.

Automatic Identification System (11) The use of bar coding of products and production processes that allows inventory and production information to be entered into a computer without writing or keying.

Backflush Costing System (12) A costing system that uses outputs as the starting point and assigns costs throughout the system after the process is completed.

Bail-Out Period (15) The time required to recover the initial investment in a capital project from any source of funds.

Bill of Materials (11) A document that specifies the kinds and quantities of raw materials required to produce one unit of product.

Bottom-Up Approach to Budgeting (6) See **Participation Budget.**

Break-Even Point (4) The unit or dollar sales volume where total revenues equal total costs.

Budget (1) A formal plan of action expressed in monetary terms.

Budget Committee (6) A group responsible for supervising budget preparation that also serves as a review board for evaluating requests for discretionary funds and new projects.

Budgetary Slack (6) Occurs when managers intentionally request more funds in the budgets for their departments than they need to support the anticipated level of operations.

By-Product (12) A product with relatively insignificant value produced jointly with one or more other products.

Capacity Costs (3) Fixed costs that are related to capacity.

Capital Asset (16) Generally defined for tax purposes as an asset held for investment gain.

Capital Budgeting (15) A process that involves the identification of potentially desirable projects for capital expenditure, the subsequent evaluation of capital expenditure proposals, and the selection of proposals that meet certain criteria.

Capital Expenditures (15) Investments of significant financial resources in projects to develop or introduce new products or services, to expand current operations, or to change current production or service facilities.

Capital Gain (16) A gain on the sale of a capital asset.

Capital Loss (16) A loss on the sale of a capital asset.

Cash Budget (6) A summary of all cash receipts and disbursements expected to occur during the budget period.

Cash Equivalents (18) Short-term, highly liquid investments that are both readily convertible into known amounts of cash and are so near their maturity date that they present insignificant risk of change in value from interest or money market rate changes.

Centralization (9) The retention of decision-making authority by top management.

Certainty (14) A condition that exists when the probability of an event's occurrence is 100 percent.

Certified Management Accountant (CMA) (1) A designation intended to recognize professional competence and educational attainment in the field of management accounting.

Certified Public Accountant (CPA) (1) A designation intended to recognize professional competence and educational attainment in the field of public accounting.

Chartered Accountant (CA) (1) A designation similar to the CPA. It is used in Canada and several other countries for people who perform independent evaluations of public organizations and the other activities normally associated with being a CPA in the United States.

Chief Financial Executive (1) A position that often combines the duties of the controller and the treasurer.

Coefficient of Determination (3) A measure of the percent of variation in the independent variable that is explained by the cost estimating equation; it indicates how good the equation fits the historical data.

Committed Fixed Costs (3) Costs required to maintain the current service or production capacity.

Common Costs (13) Costs incurred at a given level for the benefit of two or more cost objectives.

Common Segment Costs (10) Costs related to more than one segment of an organization and not directly traceable to any particular segment (also called **Indirect Segment Costs**).

Common Size Statements (17) Financial statements that are expressed in percentages instead of dollars, with one account selected to be 100 percent.

Computer-Aided Design (CAD) (11) A concept that involves the use of computers to design products.

Computer-Aided Manufacturing (CAM) (11) A concept that involves the use of computers to control the operation of machines.

Computer Integrated Manufacturing (CIM) (11) The ultimate extension of CAD, CAM, and FMS to a completely automated and computer controlled factory where production is automatic once a product is designed and the decision to produce is made.

Continuous Budgeting (6) A budget based on a moving fixed time frame that constantly extends over the same fixed period.

Contribution Income Statement (4) A type of income statement in which costs are classified according to behavior. All variable expenses are grouped together and subtracted from revenues to produce contribution margin. All fixed costs are subtracted from contribution margin to produce net income.

Contribution Margin (4) The difference between revenues and variable costs.

Contribution Margin Ratio (4) The ratio of contribution margin to sales revenue. It indicates the portion of each sales dollar available for fixed costs and profits.

Control Account (11) A general ledger account that is supported by a related set of records whose total amount should equal the balance in the general ledger account.

Controller (1) The chief accountant of an organization.

Controlling (1) The process of ensuring that results agree with plans.

Conversion Costs (2) Direct labor and factory overhead costs incurred to convert raw materials into finished goods.

Corporation (16) A legal entity recognized by an act of the state and empowered to conduct business activities.

Correlation Coefficient (3) A standardized measure of the degree to which two variables move together.

Cost (2) A monetary measure of the economic sacrifice made to obtain some product or service.

Cost Behavior Analysis (3) The study of how costs respond to changes in the volume of an activity.

Cost Center (7) A responsibility center held accountable only for the incurrence of costs. It does not have a revenue responsibility.

Cost Driver (11) An activity that causes costs to be incurred.

Cost Elements (2) The detailed categories of costs assignable to a cost objective.

Cost Estimation (3) The determination of previous or current relationships between cost and activity.

Costing Purpose (2) The basic reason a cost concept is used and a cost measurement is made.

Costing Techniques (2) The procedures used to assign cost elements to cost objectives.

Cost Objectives (2, 13) Objects or activities to which costs are assigned.

Cost of Capital (15) The average cost, expressed as a percentage, of obtaining the resources necessary to make investments.

Cost of Goods Manufactured (2) Total costs assigned to products completed during a period of time.

Cost of Production Report (12) A summary of the unit and cost data of each department in a process cost system. It includes the summary of units in process, equivalent units, the computation of unit costs, the total costs to be accounted for, and the total costs accounted for.

Cost Pool (2, 13) A group of related costs, such as factory overhead and service department costs, that are allocated together to other cost objectives.

Cost Prediction (3) The process of forecasting the future relationships between cost and activity.

Cost Prediction Error (5) The difference between a predicted future cost and the actual amount of the cost when, and if, it is incurred.

Cost Reassignment Base (13) The factor or characteristic common to the cost objectives that determines how much of the cost pool is reassigned to each cost objective.

Cost Reduction Proposal (5) A proposed action or investment intended to reduce the cost of an activity that the organization is committed to keeping.

Cost-Volume-Profit Analysis (4) A technique used to examine the relationships between volume, total costs, total revenues, and profit.

Cost-Volume-Profit Graph (4) Illustrates the relationship between volume, total revenues, total costs, and profit.

Current Manufacturing Costs (2) Total additions to Work-in-Process inventory during a given period.

Current Ratio (17) A measure of short-term solvency. It is computed as current assets divided by current liabilities.

Cycle Budgeting (6) A budget method based on the life cycle of a project.

Cycle Time (14) The total time required to produce a unit or batch.

Days Receivables Outstanding (17) The number of days, on the average, required to generate the sales uncollected at year end.

Debt-to-Equity Ratio (17) A measure of long-term solvency. It is computed as total liabilities divided by total stockholders' equity.

Decentralization (9) The delegation of decision-making authority to successively lower management levels in an organization.

Decision Package (6) Identifies activities, departments, or agencies in budget planning. They may be related to goods, services, geographic areas, capital projects, or any other activity as related to an organization's goals and objectives.

Denominator Variance (8) See **Fixed Overhead Volume Variance.**

Depreciation Tax Shield (16) The reduction in taxes due to the deductibility of depreciation from taxable revenues.

Descriptive Model (12) A type of quantitative model that specifies the relationships between a series of independent and dependent variables.

Design for Manufacture (14) Designing products so that they are easy to manufacture and service.

Differential (Cost) Analysis (5, 15) The determination of the difference between the cash flows of competing alternative actions that management is considering.

Direct Method (of Cost Allocation) (13) A procedure whereby all service department costs are allocated directly to the producing departments without any recognition of interdepartmental activities.

Direct Costing (10) See **Variable Costing.**

Direct Department Costs (13) The department to which costs are assigned at the time of their incurrence.

Direct Labor (2) Wages earned by production employees for the time they actually spend working on a product or process.

Direct Materials (2) The cost of primary raw materials that are converted into finished goods.

Direct Method (18) A method of reporting operating activities where the income statement is essentially reconstructed on a cash basis so that the major sources of cash inflows and outflows from operating activities are presented.

Direct Product Costs (2, 13) Direct materials costs plus direct labor costs.

Direct Segment Costs (10) Costs that are directly identifiable with a segment and avoidable if the segment is discontinued.

Discount Rate (15) The minimum rate of return required for a project to be acceptable.

Discretionary Cost Center (7) A cost center that does not have clearly defined relationships between effort and accomplishment.

Discretionary Fixed Costs (3) Costs that are set at a fixed amount each year at the discretion of management (also called **Managed Fixed Costs**).

Divisional Segment Margin (10) The difference between a division's contribution margin and all direct fixed expenses identifiable with the division.

Earnings per Share (EPS) (17) A measure of profitability. It is computed as net income divided by the average number of shares of stock outstanding during a given period.

Economic Lot Size (ELS) (14) Used for batch manufacturing. The economic order quantity model is modified by substituting variable unit manufacturing costs for the unit price and adding machine set-up and scheduling costs to the cost of ordering.

Economic Order Quantity (EOQ) (14) The order quantity that results in the minimum annual costs of ordering and carrying inventory.

Electronic Data Interchange (EDI) (14) The electronic communication of data between organizations.

Electronic Data Processing (EDP) (1) The storage, manipulation, retrieval, and communication of data by electronic means.

Employee Fringe Benefits (2) The additional labor costs paid by the employer on behalf of employees.

Equivalent Completed Units (12) The number of completed units that is equal (in terms of manufacturing effort) to a given number of partially completed units.

Excise Tax (16) A tax on an activity performed by, or a privilege granted to, a taxed party.

Expected Value (14) The weighted average of the possible cash flows associated with a decision alternative.

Expired Costs (2) Expenses that are deducted from revenues on the income statement.

External Failure Costs (14) The costs incurred when non-conforming products or services are delivered to customers.

Factory Overhead (2) Manufacturing costs other than direct materials and direct labor (also called **Indirect Product Costs**).

Favorable Variance (1) The resulting difference when actual costs are less than allowed costs.

Feasible Region (14) In a linear programming problem, the area that represents all possible production volumes and mixes. It is depicted by the area between the vertical axis and horizontal axis, and the first set of enclosing lines in a graphic analysis of product mix.

FIFO (First-in, First-out) Inventory Method (12) An approach to process costing in which beginning inventory units each period are costed as a separate group consisting of the portion processed during the previous period plus the additional processing required to complete them during the current period.

Financial Accounting (1) A segment of accounting concerned with providing financial information to persons outside the firm, especially investors, labor unions, creditors, and the general public.

Financial Leverage (17) The use of the capital funds from debt or equity that have a fixed interest or dividend rate.

Financial Statement Analysis (17) The process of interpreting and evaluating financial statements by using data contained in them to produce additional ratios and statistics.

Financing Activities (18) Activities such as resource transfers between the enterprise and its owners and obtaining loans from, and repaying, creditors.

Finished Goods Inventory (2) The manufactured products held for sale outside the organization.

Finished Goods Inventory Record (11) A document maintained for each completed product indicating the number of units produced, sold, and on hand, as well as the related product costs.

Fixed Cost (3) A cost that does not respond to changes in the volume of activity within a given period.

Fixed Overhead Budget (8) The difference between budgeted and actual fixed overhead cost.

Fixed Overhead Volume Variance (8) The difference between total budgeted fixed overhead and total standard fixed overhead assigned to production.

Flexible Budgets (7) Based on cost-volume-profit or cost-volume relationships, they are used to determine what costs should be at the actual level of production.

Flexible Budget Variance (7, 8) The difference between the actual cost and the flexible budget cost of producing a given quantity of product or service.

Flexible Manufacturing Systems (FMS) (11) An extension of computer-aided manufacturing techniques through a series of manufacturing operations, including the automatic movement of units between operations and the automatic and rapid set-up of machines to produce each product.

For-Profit Organizations (1) Organizations that have profit as a primary goal.

Full Costing (10) See **Absorption Costing.**

Full Costs (5) Costs that include all fixed and variable product costs and all period costs.

Functional Income Statement (4) A type of income statement in which costs are classified according to function, such as manufacturing, selling, and administrative.

Future Value (15) The amount a current sum of money earning a stated rate of interest will accumulate to at a future period.

General and Administrative Expense Budget (6) A schedule that presents the expected costs and disbursements for the overall administration of the organization.

High-Low Method of Cost Estimation (3) An approach that uses two observations to estimate the variable and fixed elements of a mixed cost.

Home Office Expenses (13) Central corporate expenses, including the salaries of the president and other executive employees, public relation expenses, legal and tax department expenses, and corporate planning and development costs.

Horizontal Analysis (17) The use of common size statements to compare the current period to different periods and to the goals and objectives of the organization.

Idle Time (2) The time employees are not working on the product or performing other production-related tasks.

Imposed Budget (6) An approach to budgeting whereby top management decides on the goals and objectives of the organization and communicates these to lower management levels (also called **Top-Down Approach**).

Income Tax (16) A tax based on the income of individuals, corporations, estates, or trusts.

Incremental Approach to Budgeting (6) A method that budgets cost for a coming period as a dollar or percentage change from the amount budgeted for (or spent during) a prior period.

Indirect Department Cost (13) A cost reassigned to a department from another cost objective to which it was directly assigned.

Indirect Labor (2) The salaries and wages earned by production employees for the time they spend performing tasks not directly related to production.

Indirect Materials (2) Low-cost materials that are difficult to associate with specific units of a final product.

Indirect Method (18) A method of reporting operating activities where the net cash flow from operations is calculated by adjusting net income to a cash basis. Individual sources of operating cash flows are not reported under this method.

Indirect Product Costs (2, 13) See **Factory Overhead.**

Indirect Segment Costs (10) See **Common Segment Costs.**

Input-Output Approach to Budgeting (6) A method of budgeting physical inputs and costs based on a planned activity level.

Interdepartmental Services (13) Support activities that one service department provides to another service department within the same organization.

Internal Auditing (1) An accounting function intended to ensure that the records are adequate and accurate, that management's operating policies are being followed and that the organization's assets are properly safeguarded from fraud or theft.

Internal Failure Costs (14) The costs incurred when materials, components, products, or services are identified as defective before delivery to customers.

Internal Rate of Return (IRR) (15) The discount rate that equates the net present value of a project's cash inflows with the initial investment in the project (also called the **Time-Adjusted Rate of Return**).

Inventory Turnover   (17) A measure of the number of times the average stock of inventory was sold and replenished during the period. It is computed as cost of goods sold divided by average inventory amount.

Investing Activities   (18) Activities such as transactions related to the acquisition and disposition of marketable securities, other long-term investments, and property, plant, and equipment, as well as making and collecting loans unrelated to the sale of goods or services.

Investment Center   (7) A responsibility center held accountable for the relationship between its profits and total assets.

Job Cost Sheets   (11) A record used to accumulate the costs for specific jobs in a job cost system.

Job-Order Production   (11) See **Job Production.**

Job Production   (11) A production environment where products are produced in single units or in batches of identical units.

Joint Costs   (5, 12) The costs of producing joint products that are incurred prior to the split-off point for joint products.

Joint Products   (5, 12) Two or more products simultaneously produced from common inputs by a single process or common manufacturing activity.

Just-in-Time Inventory Management   (11, 12, 14) An inventory control system that stresses having available only the inventory required to meet immediate production or sales requirements.

Labor Efficiency Variance   (8) The difference between the standard cost of actual labor inputs and the flexible budget cost for labor.

Labor Rate Variance   (8) The difference between the actual labor cost and the standard cost of actual labor inputs.

Lead Time   (14) The amount of time between the placement and the receipt of an order.

Least-Squares Method of Cost Estimation   (3) An approach that uses the mathematical criteria of least-squares to estimate the variable and fixed elements of a mixed cost.

Life Cycle Costs   (14) The total costs associated with a cost objective over its entire life.

Linear Algebra Allocation Method   (13) A procedure whereby all service department costs are allocated simultaneously both interdepartmentally and to producing departments.

Linear Programming   (14) An optimizing model used to assist managers in making decisions under constrained conditions when linear relationships can be assumed.

Line-Item Budget   (6) A type of budget in which revenues and expenditures are assigned to specific categories and items of responsibility, often used in not-for-profit organizations.

Lower of Cost or Market   (16) A method of valuing inventory which uses the lower of the item's cost or market value.

Lump-Sum Budget   (6) A type of budget that is very popular with not-for-profit organizations in which only general areas are allocated revenue and expenditures.

Managed Fixed Costs   (3) See **Discretionary Fixed Costs.**

Management Accounting   (1) A segment of accounting concerned with providing financial information to managers and other persons inside specific organizations.

Management by Exception   (1) A concept where managers focus their attention on those aspects of operations that are not operating as planned, rather than constantly monitoring all activities.

Management by Objectives   (1) A concept where the head of an agency or department and the immediate superior agree to a set of short-run nonmonetary objectives, which are subsequently used as a basis of performance evaluation for the agency or department head.

Managers   (1) The employees who direct the affairs of the organization.

Manufacturing Cost Markup   (5) Used for pricing, it is computed as the total predicted selling and administrative costs plus the desired profit divided by the predicted manufacturing costs.

Manufacturing Disbursements Budget   (6) A budget used to plan materials, labor and factory overhead requirements, and costs for a future period.

Manufacturing Margin   (10) Segment sales minus direct manufacturing costs.

Manufacturing Organizations   (2) Organizations that process raw materials into finished products for sale to others.

Marginal Cost   (3, 5) The varying increment in total costs required to produce and sell an additional unit.

Marginal Revenue   (5) The varying increment in total revenue derived from the sale of an additional unit.

Margin of Safety   (4) The excess of actual or budgeted sales over break-even sales. It indicates the amount that sales could decline before the organization would show a loss.

Materials Price Variance   (8) The difference between the actual materials cost and the standard cost of actual materials inputs (also see **Materials Purchased Price Variance**).

Materials Purchased Price Variance   (8) The actual cost of materials purchased minus the standard cost of materials purchased (also see **Materials Price Variance**).

Materials Quantity Variance   (8) The difference between the standard cost of actual materials inputs and the flexible budget cost for materials.

Materials Requirements Planning (MRP)   (12) An approach for manufacturing management that ties inventories to production scheduling based on planned outputs.

Materials Requisition Form   (11) A record used to record transfers of direct materials from raw materials to work-in-process.

Merchandising Organizations   (2) Organizations that buy and sell goods; included in this category are most retail organizations.

Minimum Level Approach to Budgeting   (6) An approach to budgeting in which a base amount for all budget items is established and an explanation or justification is required for all amounts in excess of the base.

Mixed Costs   (3) Costs that contain both a fixed and a variable cost element (also called **Semivariable Costs**).

Model   (1, 14) A simplified representation of some real-world phenomenon.

Modified Accelerated Cost Recovery System (MACRS) (16) An asset depreciation method defined by the Tax Reform Act of 1986 that requires two steps. First, ADR guidelines must be used to determine the useful life; and second, based on the ADR life, the asset is assigned to an ACRS class that determines the depreciation period and depreciation method.

Mutually Exclusive Investments (15) Where acceptance of an investment causes the automatic rejection of all other alternative investments under consideration.

Net Present Value Method (15) A method used to evaluate capital expenditures that compares the initial investment to the present value of all future cash flows using a predetermined discount rate.

Net Sales Volume Variance (7) Indicates the impact of a change in sales volume on the contribution margin, given the budgeted selling price and the budgeted variable costs.

Normal Equations (3) Equations used to compute the constant term and the slope that best meets the least-squares criteria.

Not-for-Profit Organizations (1) Organizations that do not have profit as a goal.

Objective Function (14) In linear programming, this is the goal to be maximized or minimized.

Operating Activities (6, 18) Normal profit-related activities performed in conducting the daily affairs of an organization. They include such things as purchasing, production, sales, and other things related to income earning activities that enter into the computation of net income.

Operating Budget (6) A formal financial document that indicates planned revenues and expenses and other activities for a future period.

Operating Leverage (4) A measure of the responsiveness of income to changes in sales.

Operating Loss (16) For tax purposes, the excess of operating expenses over operating revenues that ordinarily may be carried back three years and carried forward fifteen years.

Operations List (11) A document that lists the specific manufacturing operations and related times required to produce one unit or batch of product.

Opportunity Cost (2) The net cash inflow that could be obtained if the resources committed to one action were used in the most desirable other alternative action.

Optimal Solution (14) In linear programming, this is the feasible solution that maximizes or minimizes the value of the objective function.

Optimizing Models (14) A type of quantitative model that suggests a specific choice between decision alternatives.

Order Filling Costs (7) Costs incurred to place finished goods in the hands of the purchasers.

Order Getting Costs (7) Costs incurred to obtain a customer's order.

Order Quantity (14) The amount of inventory ordered at a particular time.

Organization (1) A group of people united to achieve a common goal.

Organization Chart (1) An illustration of the formal relationships that exist among the elements of an organization.

Organizing (1) The process of making the organization into a well-ordered whole.

Outlay Costs (5) Future costs that require future expenditures of cash or other resources.

Overtime Premiums (2) Bonus wages in excess of the regular hourly rate paid to production employees who are working more than the regular number of hours.

Participation Budget (6) An approach to budgeting in which managers at all levels, and in some cases even nonmanagers, become involved in budget preparation. Because this budget approach often starts at the lowest levels of management, it is sometimes called **Bottom-Up Budgeting.**

Partnership (16) An unincorporated business ordinarily owned by two or more individuals.

Payback Period (15) The length of time necessary for the cumulative operating cash inflows from a project to equal the initial cash investment for the project.

Payoff Table (14) A table used to enumerate the alternative actions management may take and the possible monetary outcomes of each.

Performance Reports (1) Reports provided to management during and after the budget period that compare actual results with plans.

Period Costs (2) Expired nonproduct costs; they are always an expense.

Physical Models (14) Scaled-down versions or replicas of physical reality.

Physical Quantity Method (12) A method of allocating joint costs on the basis of relative quantities of specific common physical characteristics possessed by the various joint products.

Planning (1) The formulation of a scheme or program for the accomplishment of a specific purpose or goal.

Planning, Programming, and Budgeting Systems (PPBS) (6) A concept that emphasizes outputs, rather than inputs, of an organization in programmed areas.

Predetermined Factory Overhead Rate (2) An overhead rate determined at the start of the year by dividing the predicted overhead costs for the year by the predicted activity level.

Present Value (15) The current worth of a specified amount of money to be received at some future date at some discount rate.

Present Value Index (15) The number of present value dollars generated per dollar of initial investment (also called the **Profitability Index**).

Prevention Costs (14) The costs incurred to prevent nonconforming products from being produced or nonconforming services from being performed.

Price Earnings Ratio (17) The current market price of a firm's stock divided by its earnings per share of stock.

Price Variance (8) The actual costs of actual inputs minus the standard cost of actual inputs.

Prime Product Costs (2) Direct materials costs plus direct labor costs.

Process Costing (12) A method of product costing that involves the determination of product costs of a homogeneous product as units pass continuously from one production operation to another and finally into finished goods.

Product Costing (2) The process of assigning costs to inventories as they are converted from raw materials to finished goods.

Product Costs (2) Costs assigned to products as they are produced that are expensed when the products are sold.

Production Budget (6) A budget indicating the number of units of product an organization plans to produce in a coming period. It is based on predicted sales, adjusted for beginning inventory and desired ending inventory.

Productivity (14) The relationship between outputs and inputs.

Product Margin (10) Product sales revenue less direct product costs.

Product Reporting (10) A type of reporting in which revenues and expenses are presented for product lines of an organization.

Profitability Index (PI) (14) See **Present Value Index.**

Profit Center (7) A responsibility center held accountable for both revenues and costs and evaluated on their differences.

Profit-Volume-Graph (4) A graph used to illustrate the relationship between volume and profits.

Pro Forma Financial Statements (6) Hypothetical financial statements that reflect the "as if" effects of budgeted activity on the financial position of a firm.

Property Tax (16) A tax based on the ownership of property. It is usually determined by multiplying a statutory tax rate (referred to as a tax millage) times the assessed value of the property.

Purchases Budget (6) A schedule of raw materials and supplies that must be acquired to meet production needs and inventory requirements.

Quality (14) Product or service conforming to customer expectations.

Quality of Conformance (14) The degree to which a given product or service conforms to its design specifications.

Quality Costs (14) The costs incurred because poor quality of conformance does exist or because poor quality of conformance may exist.

Quality of Design (14) The degree of conformance between customer expectations for a product or service and the design specifications of the product or service.

Quantitative Models (14) A series of algebraic relationships intended to represent some real-world relationships.

Quantity Variance (8) The standard cost of actual inputs minus the standard cost of inputs allowed for the outputs produced.

Quick Ratio (17) See **Acid Test Ratio.**

Raw Materials Inventories (2) The physically existing items that are to be converted into a finished product.

Raw Materials Inventory Record (11) A record used to record increases and decreases in the available balance for each type of raw material.

Relevant Costs (2) Future costs that differ among competing alternatives.

Relevant Range (3) The area of operation, within which a linear cost function is a good approximation of the economists' curvilinear cost function.

Reorder Point (14) The inventory level at which an order for additional units is placed.

Residual Income (9) The excess of investment center income over the minimum return set by the company.

Responsibility Accounting (7) The structuring of performance reports addressed to individual or group members of an organziation in a manner that emphasizes factors controllable by them.

Responsibility Center (7) A person or organizational unit that has been assigned certain responsibilities. Examples are investment centers, profit centers, revenue centers, and cost centers.

Return on Assets (17) A measure of the ability of the firm to profitably use its assets. It is computed as net income plus net-of-tax interest expense divided by average total assets.

Return on Equity (17) A measure of the profits attributable to the shareholders as a percentage of their equity in the firm. It is computed as net income divided by average stockholder's equity.

Return on Investment (9) A measure of the earnings per dollar of investment. It is computed by dividing the income of the investment center by its asset base.

Return on Sales (17) A measure of the ability of the firm to generate profits from sales. It is computed as net income plus net-of-tax interest expense divided by sales.

Revenue Budgets (6) Budgets that establish the amount expected to be collected from each revenue source during the upcoming period.

Revenue Center (7) A responsibility center held accountable for generating sales revenue.

Robinson–Patman Act (5) A law of the United States that prohibits firms from charging purchasers different prices when the purchasers compete with each other in the sale of their products.

Safety Stocks (14) The actual units of inventory carried to prevent stockouts due to variations in the demand for units during the lead time.

Sales Budget (6) A forecast of unit and dollar sales volume. It may also contain a forecast of sales collections.

Sales Mix (4) The relative portion of unit or dollar sales that is derived from each product or service.

Sales Price Variance (7) The total difference in revenues for the actual sales volume resulting from a change in the selling price from the budgeted price.

Sales Value Allocation Method (12) A method of allocating joint costs based on the relative sales values of the joint products.

Sales Volume Variance (7) The impact on revenues of a change in sales volume, assuming no change in selling price.

Salvage Value (14) The cash, or cash value equivalent, received for the sale of a fixed asset at the end of its useful life.

Scatter Diagram (3) A graph of volume and cost data.

Segment Margin (10) The amount that a segment contributes toward the common (indirect) costs of an organization and toward profit of the organization.

Segment Reports (10) Income statements that show operating results for some portion or segment of a business.

Selling Expense Budget (6) A schedule of the costs and disbursements the organization plans to incur in connection with budgeted sales and distribution.

Semivariable Costs (3) See **Mixed Costs.**

Sensitivity Analysis (4) The study of the responsiveness of a model's dependent variable(s) to changes in one or more of the model's independent variables.

Service Costing (2) The process of assigning costs to services.

Service Department (13) A department that provides support functions for one or more production departments.

Service Organizations (2) Nonmanufacturing firms that perform work for others. Included in this category are banks, hospitals, and real estate agencies.

Simple Rate of Return (15) See **Accounting Rate of Return.**

Simplex Method (14) A mathematical technique used to solve linear programming problems.

Sole Proprietorship (16) An unincorporated business owned by one individual.

Solvency (17) The ability of a firm to pay its debts as they come due.

Split-Off Point (5, 12) The point in a process where the joint products emerge as separately identifiable products or units.

Standard Cost (7) A budget for one unit of product. It indicates what it should cost to produce one unit of product under efficient operating conditions.

Standard Cost Center (7) A cost center that has clearly defined relationships between effort and accomplishment and uses a standard cost system.

Standard Cost Variance Analysis (8) The process of analyzing flexible budget variances.

Standard Error of the Estimate (3) A measure of the variability of actual costs around the cost estimating equation. It is used to construct probability intervals for cost estimates.

Statement of Cash Flows (18) A summary of resource inflows and outflows stated in terms of cash.

Statement of Cash Flows Worksheet (18) A worksheet that shows the individual cash flows from operating, investing, and financing activities.

Statement of Cost of Goods Manufactured (2) A financial summary of the activity in the Work-in-Process inventory accounts. It may also summarize activity in the Raw Materials inventory account.

Statement of Cost of Goods Manufactured and Sold (2) A financial summary of the activity in all major inventory accounts.

Static Budget (7) A budget based on a prior prediction of expected sales and production.

Step Allocation Method (13) A procedure whereby service department costs are allocated in a manner that gives partial recognition to interdepartmental services among the service departments.

Step Costs (3) Costs that are constant within a range of activity, but different between ranges of activity.

Subchapter S Corporation (16) A business legally organized as a corporation, that has opted under a special provision of the tax law to be taxed as a partnership with income flowing directly to the individuals holding the shares of stock.

Subsidiary Ledger (11) A file that contains a related set of records whose total amount should equal the balance in a general ledger account.

Sunk Costs (2) Historical costs that result from past decisions that management no longer has control over.

Tax Avoidance (16) The reduction of taxes by legitimate means.

Tax Base (16) A monetary measurement of the conditions or activities subject to taxes, such as taxable income and assessed value.

Tax Deferral (16) The planning and timing of transactions to cause legal delays in the payment of taxes.

Tax Rate (16) A percentage that is multiplied times the tax base to determine total taxes.

Time-Adjusted Rate of Return (15) See **Internal Rate of Return.**

Times Interest Earned (17) A measure of interest paying ability, computed as the earnings available to pay interest divided by the total interest expense.

Top-Down Approach to Budgeting (6) See **Imposed Budget.**

Total Cost Approach (to capital budgeting) (15) The calculation of the present value of the cost associated with each alternative, with the low-cost alternative being preferred.

Transfer Price (9) The internal value assigned a product or service that one division provides to another.

Transferred-in Costs (12) The combined title for material, labor, and overhead as they are transferred from one department to another while accompanying in-process products as they are transferred from one department to another.

Treasurer (1) The officer responsible for money management in an organization.

Uncertainty (14) A condition that exists when the probability of an event's occurring is less than 100 percent.

Unexpired Costs (2) Incurred costs recorded as assets on the statement of financial position.

Unfavorable Variances (1) Variances that result when actual costs exceed allowed costs.

Unit Contribution Margin (4) The difference between unit selling price and unit variable costs.

Value Added Tax (16) A tax based on the value added to the goods produced during a period.

Value of Perfect Information (14) The maximum amount a manager would be willing to pay for additional information.

Variable Cost (3) The uniform incremental cost of each additional unit.

Variable Costing (10) A product costing procedure whereby only variable manufacturing costs are assigned to products (also called **Direct Costing**).

Variable Cost Markup (5) Used for product pricing, it is computed as the total of the predicted fixed costs plus targeted profit divided by the predicted variable costs.

Variable Cost Ratio (4) The ratio of variable costs to sales revenue. It indicates the portion of each sales dollar that is used to cover variable costs.

Variable Overhead Efficiency Variance (8) The difference between the standard variable overhead cost for the actual activity base inputs and the flexible budget variable overhead costs for the actual outputs.

Variable Overhead Spending Variance (8) The difference between the actual variable overhead cost incurred and the standard variable overhead cost for the actual activity base inputs.

Variance (1) The difference between actual and allowed costs.

Variance Analysis (8) The process of analyzing the difference between the actual cost and the standard cost allowed by the flexible budget for manufacturing a product or providing a service.

Vertical Analysis (17) Used with common size statements to identify significant changes that have taken place during a period to determine if they are favorable or unfavorable.

Volume Variance (8) See **Fixed Overhead Volume Variance.**

Weighted Average Method (12) In process costing, an inventory valuation procedure where all equivalent units in process are assigned the same average cost.

Working Capital (17) The difference between current assets and current liabilities.

Work-in-Process Inventories (2) The raw materials that are in the process of being converted into a finished product.

Work Ticket (11) A document used to record the time a job spends in a specific manufacturing operation.

World Class Manufacturer (11) An organization that strives to improve its production processes and compete with firms around the world on the basis of quality and services, such as timely delivery and competitive prices.

Zero-Base Budgeting (6) An approach to budgeting based on the premise that every dollar of a budget expenditure must be justified.

Index